The National Library of Poetry

11419-10 Cronridge Drive • Post Office Box 704 • Owings Mills, Maryland 21117 • (410) 356-2000

Viola Zumault
4432 N Grand
Kansas City MO 64116

Dear Viola,

Thank you for your entry in our recent contest. Your poem was recognized by the judges as being among the best 3% of all entries judged. We are therefore pleased to award you our Editor's Choice Award for your contest entry as published in <u>Outstanding Poets of 1994</u>. Congratulations on your significant achievement.

Sincerely,

The National Library of Poetry

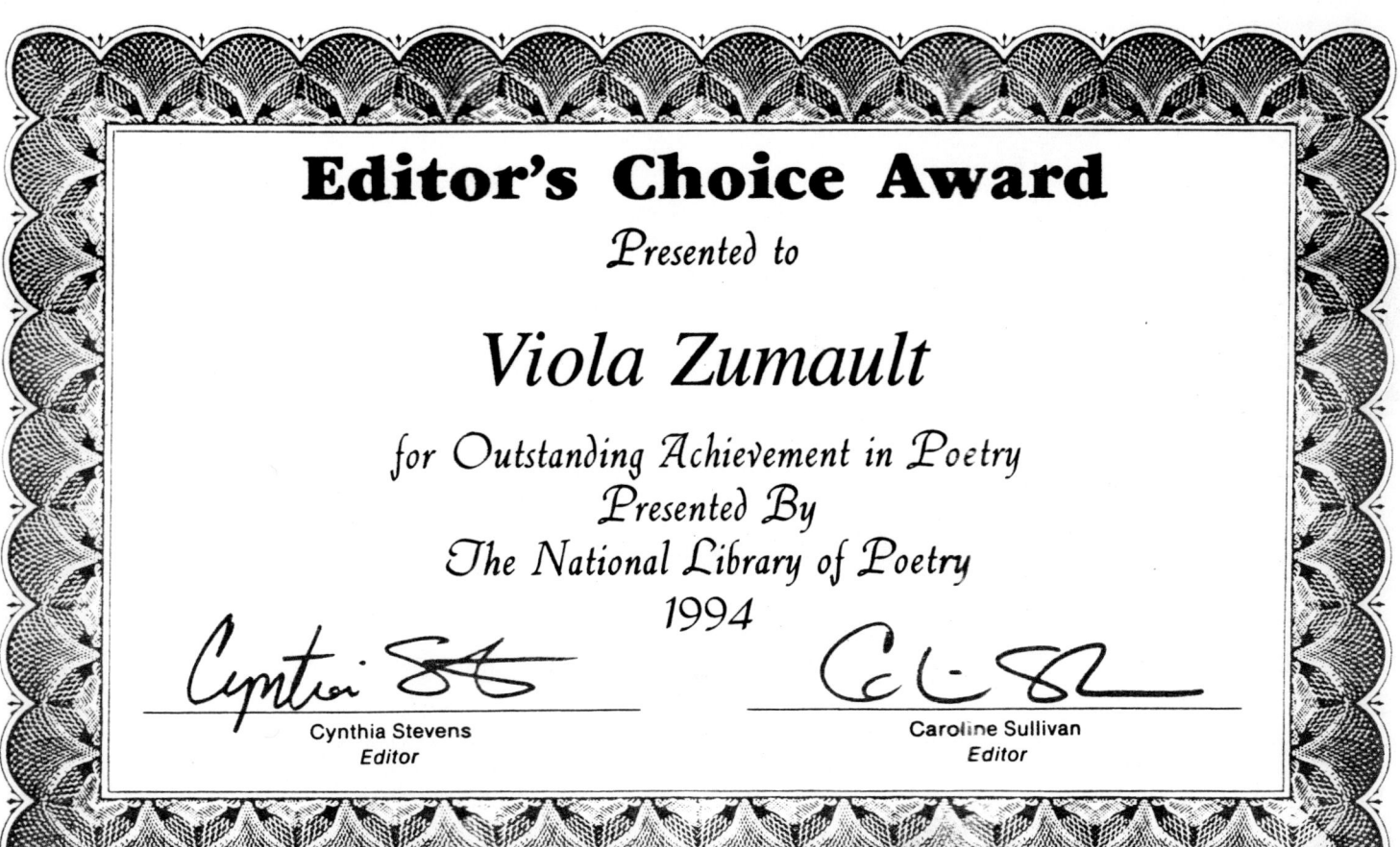

WALKING IN THE FOOTSTEPS OF SOCRATES

On a blistering hot summer day,
after a climb to the fabled Acropolis,
we entered the Agora in Athens, the "city of classics".
Dust clouds rose like thick gray fog to grip the throat
and blur the vision, where fragments of ancient walls
scarred the market place. The streets were over run
with tourists, and foreign archaeologists dedicated to
unearthing rare artifacts from tombs of ancient history.
Peddlers, in temporary stalls, hawked their wares,
from exotic perfumes to tangy red pomegranates and
pungent pickled fish.
Twenty five hundred years ago Socrates, model of an
exemplary life, symbol of strict moral ethics,
with his companions, frequented this place,
mixing philosophy with good humor and spicy gossip.
In this ancient place where, daily, wars were fought and won,
and ideas widely explored, Democracy was born.
In a building in a corner of the square, Socrates,
the Great Philosopher, was convicted and sentenced to die
for refusing to compromise his principles.
Calmly he drank the lethal hemlock cup and
"lay down to die in peace."
His philosophy has survived the centuries;
his final act a lasting symbol of his courage.

Viola Zumault

Viola Zumault's national award winning poem,
WALKING IN THE FOOTSTEPS OF SOCRATES,
has been selected by the National Library of Poetry
for inclusion in the National Anthology,
Outstanding Poets of 1994.

OUTSTANDING POETS
OF
1994

John J. Purcell, III, Editor

THE NATIONAL LIBRARY OF POETRY

Outstanding Poets of 1994

Copyright © 1994 by The National Library of Poetry
as a compilation.

Rights to individual poems reside with the artists themselves.

All rights reserved under International and Pan-American copyright conventions. No part of this book may be reproduced, stored in a retrieval system or transmitted in any form, electronic, mechanical, or by other means, without written permission of the publisher. Address all inquiries to Jeffrey Franz, Publisher, P.O. Box 704, Owings Mills, MD 21117.

Library of Congress
Cataloging in Publication Data

ISBN 1-56167-048-0

Proudly manufactured in the United States of America by
Watermark Press
11419 Cronridge Dr., Suite 10
Owings Mills, MD 21117

Editor's Note

It has been my pleasure to serve as editor of Outstanding Poets of 1994. This anthology contains some of the best poetry I have seen in my tenure at National Library of Poetry, and I have enjoyed the opportunity to read this work, some of which, as I have said, is very good.

Much of this anthology reflects the remarkable insight some of our poets possess, whether addressing social ills or more simple fare. Following are several pieces which I believe deserve special mention.

Our grand prize winner, "In Marrakech," penned by Marian Gagne, is a wonderfully crafted poem celebrating the centuries-old physical steadfastness of Marrakech with descriptions which take the reader there on a carpet ride. In the fabric of this carpet, Marian contrasts the past and present physical restlessness, beauty, seaminess and mystery of Marrakech to set up a moral reflection on its past of slavery and persecution, which can be found in the not so distant past and present of many nations and cultures. Truly a masterful, tightly woven piece.

Cecilia Haupt refreshes an oft-used subject in "Every Tent A Stage." Cecilia, too, uses her descriptions and juxtapositions to create a sense of action in the mind of the reader, much like the sense of action at a circus--where for the casual observer, lulls in acitivity are few and far between. Cecilia opens with the solid image of a clown removing his livelihood--his happy face--and progresses through the aforementioned action images, closing again with the clown, whose life is his performance, "dying" with its end. Haupt, as well as Gagne, exemplify the strength of a poet who has the discipline to adhere to one thread, and use his/her skill to create a wonderfully interesting and reflective fabric around it.

Another excellent poem comes from the pen and heart of Magda Herzberger, a person with a great amount of courage and resolve. Every time I read her work, I get an indescribable feeling. She has an uncanny ability to create an incredible amount of emotion while employing an economy of language so desperately lacking in much of the work which pours through the weir at the National Library of Poetry.

All of our poets are winners, because they have the courage to subject their work to the scrutiny of others, a truly nerve-wracking experience. I commend and admire all of you.

John J. Purcell III

Acknowledgements

The publication Oustanding Poets of 1994 is a culmination of the efforts of many individuals. Judges, editors, assistant editors, graphic artists, layout artists and office administrators have all brought their respective talents to bear on this project. The editors are grateful for the contribution of these fine people:

Jeffrey Bryan, Kurt Cobain, Keith Crummedy, Lisa Della, Chrystal Eldridge, Ardie L. Freeman, Hope Freeman, Howard Friedman, Julian Friedman, Robert Graziul, Diane Mills, Eric Mueck, Jacqui Spiwak, Cynthia Stevens, Caroline Sullivan. and Ira Westreich.

Grand Prize Winner

Marian Gagne

Second Prize Winners

Louise Rosenberg
Alice P. Smith
Marie Andrea
Charlotte Mitchell
Magda Herzberger

Cecilia Haupt
Jean Franse
Margaret Taylor
Lydia Kapell
P. Marguerite Forcier

Third Prize Winners

Willie D. Schempp
Susan Tausch
Rebecca Baumgarner
Nicole Larsen
Chantelle Cooke
Cathy Adams
Abdul Latif
Jennifer Lynn Stevens
D. P. Dresbach
Jay Murphy
Gloria Hockenberry
Eleanor Otto
David Williams
Hilda V. Finkbeiner
Carl Dallinger
Ruth G. Boyer
Vahe Kazandjian
Dorice McDaniels
Juliann Grandchamp
Neela Graham

V. Ursula Galley
Shirley Brezenoff
Rafaela Wintham Barker
Michelle A. Morgan
Margarita Isabelle
Auburn Lamb
Ling Fan Peng
Charlotte Riepe
Constance Washburn
Inkeri Eerikainen
Ethyl Treatman
Ed Rains
Dorayne Levin
Gregory M. Dultz
Patricia A. Craven
Sait Mohan Das
Virginia-Anne Edwards
Lynda Lambert
Victor M. Navarro

Steve Bertrand
Shrell Lott
Lucille Hughes
Mary Lindsley
Lynn Lewis
Amanda KC
Kerri House
Joan Gordon
Jeanne Zastera
Jennifer Lane
Jean Candee
Doris Marshall
Harry Dowdy Jr.
George Braman
Richard A. Duncan
Ruth Warner
W.R. Elton
Pierce Ketchum
Paul E. Garrett
Sister Mary Baldys

Congratulations also to our Editor's Choice Winners.

Grand Prize Winner

In Marrakech (Morocco)
In Marrakech, unmindful of a changing world
Life still is coloured as the Ancient Scribes
Marked down — where mixed flags unfurled
In this market town for Desert Tribes.
Burnoused Arabs who stealthily glide by
Bronzed Tauregs and Senegalese more dark of face
Than nightfall — in this ancient "Place to Die"
Name of this restless seething marketplace.
Moorish Mosques with acorn tops — not far
From Minarets. Gardens lined in glossy tile
Where Roses and Hybiscus bloom behind gates, that bar
Homeless men with vagrant souls, a while.
Mystery, Intrigue — where a History of Terror hid
Slaves cemented in the walls alive, in Tears.
As in the day of the Caliph el Raschid -
The same — unchanged in full a thousand years.
Days of Arabian Nights — when life was cheap
By values measured of today. For who can know
The Value of each persecuted Slave? Now we weep
That man, unlearned and cruel, would cause such woe.
—*Marian F. Gagne*

A Mother's Lost Love

A new baby girl cradled safe in her arms
  a brand new life to shape
to love, to hold and comfort her child
  these are things she could not escape.

As time passed by, this baby grew up
  into a woman with a mind of her own
one day the mother just turned away
  never wanting her child to come home.

Contempt and disdain replaced closeness and warmth
  not understanding all the reasons why
no hug or caress when needed the most
  just feeling like I wanted to die.

Someday she'll see that I'm still the same child
  that she nurtured and held to her breast
till then I will grieve for my mother's lost love—
  a love that she's chosen to test.
    —*Irma Clar*

The Merchant Marine

We leave family and friends, to travel the sea.
A brave gang of professionals, that's who we be.
We manned our ships, and moved our forces,
As the master plot and planned our various courses.
No matter where, no matter when,
We travel the globe to the very end.
Some voyages are long with restless days,
As we go about our work in subtle ways.
Each member assigned a particular task,
From engine room bilge, to the top of the mast
Nothings more amazing, than this large mass in motion.
From dock, the channel, to open ocean.
Crossing date lines and time zones we venture on,
Knowing you're one day closer to home.
Takes special kind of people to sail the high sea,
That's the person I choose to be.
Very seldom talked about and rarely seen,
We the sea travelers, called:
The Merchant Marines....
    —*Charlie M. Belton*

The Bridge

Big Cove, Alabama Creek's bridge
A bridge between Culu and KaSann, Viet Nam
The bridge we were guarding near KaSann
Reminds me of my home in North Alabama

No North Vietnamese troops to ambush
No tigers caught on the Constina
No monkeys swinging from trees
No Rock Apes throwing rocks

The Planet of the Apes
Seems a sophisticated Monkey
But the Monkeys near KaSann
Knew what was going on

How can it be
I don't know what is happening
Because there are no Apes
To tell me what is happening
    —*John W. Miller*

Advice To A Naturalist

Nature has her own society;
A certain form of stubborn snobbery;
Exclusive chambers, private doors and keys
With secret guards and bouncers posted here
And there, invisible, formidable
And cruel. We think that finally we've made
A friend of rolling hills, the rocks and brush,
And so we wander through in innocence,
Investigating native plants or flowers.
The following day we are alarmed to see
A rash that covers every inch of skin
And itches to the bone and peels and burns.
It's poison oak, my friend, a foe of man,
Which serves as sentinel of untouched land.
Oh, that's not all, the rose has thorns and
Snakes hide everywhere. Please don't disturb
The buttercup, a bee awaits you there.

So on days when fragrant flora tempt,
Remember naturalists are not exempt
From mother nature's ploy to stay unkept.
    —*Grace Matthes*

A Bard's Lament

The world of poetry is a challenging one,
A constant search for words to get the job done,
While the verse is composed a line at a time,
It's a carefully penned ballet in meaning and rhyme,

This process of birth can be agonizingly slow,
As a single thought waits for the juices to flow,
A progression of fluent imagery and prose,
Imagination runs rampant right down to the close.

A visionary smorgasbord, a creative delight,
Offers food for thought for the mind's eyesight,
As the fanciful whimsy flows forth unrestrained,
We each interpret the message therein contained.

Whether a light and capricious, transitory theme,
Or a many-faceted, thought-provoking, idealistic dream,
A poem, after all, is just a collection of words,
Put together objectively by those of us called nerds!
    —*Frances Runyon*

Deer At Night

When I'm out driving at night and see
a deer, startled in grazing,
lift its head and stare at my
headlights shining brightly,
  I remember how we often went
  in the car, spotlight in hand,
  to observe deer steal out of
  the woods, their minds intent
    on food and drink under night's cover.
    We never meant to harm them,
    but just to find and count time,
    each one our new, natural discovery.
    —*Charlotte A. Schroeder*

A New Love

What have we here all wrapped up and wee?
A delicate, small bundle of "She."
Such golden hair, so button a nose.
Arms reaching out, wiggling toes.
A face so beautiful and soft to the touch.
A bundle to hold and love so much.
Of parents' dreams and hopes realizing,
Mixed up with tantrums and big surprising,
Raising a child, how to share, how to love,
Takes all you can give, and help from above.
A run for the door with no looking back,
There will be many times that take you of track.
Just hang in there and positive be,
Your joy will be found in the bundle of "She."
As parents, her life will be on center stage,
Beginning each day, she'll turn a new page.
So treasure forever the pleasures she'll bring,
That will gladden your days and make your heart sing.
From now on, as you daily work,
She will be know as your labor's "perk."
—Dorlene Bressan

No Escape

The irony of it all hasn't escaped us.
A doctor and a nurse losing two children
   In violent accidents
The doctor a trauma specialist;
Inventor of emergency medical equipment.
The nurse manager of the company
That makes his new medical equipment.
Of what use were we, a doctor and a nurse?
Of what use the new emergency medical equipment?
Our son loved driving automobiles,
Mainly he loved driving trucks.
Our daughter was a rock hound
Long before she was a geologist.
And the instruments of their destruction?
The things they loved the best!
Our son's pick-up truck hit a telephone pole.
A rock fell on our daughter while touring a mine.
And a doctor and a nurse couldn't help them,
New technology couldn't help them
   Escape
   What fate had in store.
—Gloria M. Borschneck

It's Good To Be Alive

I have woken up one Morning,
A dream has drawn me near,
To the Final Conclusion,
Of everything I hold so very Dear.
Will I sink?
Will I be able to swim?
My life is not yet fat and ugly,
But is so very Lean and Trim.
The shore is close,
Yet it can be far Away.
It is where I long to be most.
I will walk not crawl up on the Beach
And to living,
I will begin to preach.
Then I will turn around,
And for life I will Grasp and Reach!
—Fred Pickrell

Super Vision Of My Heart's

Once I had a vision for the town that I love;
A dream so right that I knew it came from God above.

I knew it'd work again though it had been tried here before,
And submitted it completed to a friend who really knew the score.

I wanted it researched and re-checked out again,
Before I sent it to my judging editor who would really comprehend.

Who could make my borrowed fantasy a real concrete fact;
Although a character script and mural was all that it really lacked.

I put all that I knew about it into this first-run trial balloon,
Let a trusted friend be the first to pilot while still in silk cocoon.

One for a seventy-foot mountain mural absolutely so grand,
That it would've made even great "da Vinci" take notice firsthand.

Another for a character, outdoor dramatic script,
With a law'n' order love theme to make even John Fox, Jr. flip.

But, alas, even my grandiose plan to put hometown on the map,
Encountered strange financial winds above and a great
   thunderclap.

So sadly I had to put down with my balloon when victory was in sight;
On a strange mountaintop I had to "Light" my "Heart's Delight!"
—George Lynch

The Wind

And then a warning in the shadows comes when
a dry leaf sounds dry stepped on
A wind blows over the mountains
and some days you can smell the smoke
it must be real
Turn off the TV and breath the paradise lost
Nature building walls; too much life
a little soul
adds a molecule
a dust particle
and now it burns
disturbing the serenity
in the canyons
destroying their memories
Staring into the ashes;
all past years lie there
hidden.
Is this the end or
the beginning?
—Inkeri Eerikainen

Me

I saw an image yesterday, of who I do not know
A feeling of connection yet the face I can't recall.
For it was tired and aged, no aspirations showed.
Her eyes were sad and lonely, she had no place to go.
I caught her staring at me in a most pretentious way
With shocking penetration, but yet I had to stay.
Her cloak, it was concealing, as a phantom in a dream
This replica of someone still remained unseen.
Black clouds began to gather, lightning streaked the sky
Winds of change admonish impending fate is nigh.
A violent storm erupted, unruly winds prevailed
The cloak was blown asunder, a likeness was revealed.
An image sorely beaten, a soulless form exposed
Flashing recognition...
Devastation takes its toll.
—Debra Petrovic

Sweet Love

Back then when you looked at me, you saw a wide grin
A few missing teeth, a cowlick where my hair stood on end
A lop-sided eye, the one that winked real well
suspenders to hold up my britches, so they wouldn't fall
   down and show my tail
Worn out tennis shoes, one sock up and one sock down.
I'd fight anybody to hold your hand and stayed
   mostly on the ground
And yes, I'm the same young man who carried your books
I guess the suit and tie has altered my looks
My teeth finally came through and plugged all the holes
Other than that, I guess I just got old
The cowlick is gone and I'd love to have it back
At least I had hair, now I wear a very thin track
What happened and where did you go?
A million things crossed my mind, but fate plays a
   doh-cee-doh
it was not to be and I had living to learn
I was taught quite well and I have earned
Squatters' rights to precious memories, small tokens
Soft words spoken and promises unbroken.
   —*Glenna Sloan*

Do They Know?

Like a song with no beat, her life is so complete.
A flower cannot live without the rain.
As her heart cannot with all that pain.
She closes her eyes to picture a dream.
Only to open them for it to fall like a toppling ream.
Some nights she cries herself to sleep but each
morning awakes to the same.
Why must she constantly play this cruel game.
The sun will rise the sun will set.
Yet her needs will go unmet.
Another way out she does not see.
I just wish they knew that girl is me.
   —*Ann Mitchell*

A Snowflake's Gift

Reach me a snowflake, if you will,
A fragile one, so crisp and still,
With edges formed so firm and clean,
All white, with such star-glistening gleam,
That all who gaze upon its face
Can see in life their special place;
And once in time hold this flake up high,
A silhouette against the lightened sky,
Then tip your head so gently nigh
To watch the wispy flake and sigh;
for the flake that's held is as you and me,
Its walls e'er slowly melting free;
As it becomes yet something new,
So nature's planned for me and you.
Oh, reach me a snowflake, if you will,
That I may learn what it can tell,
A story e'er so plain, but true—
The snowflakes gives us nature's cue—
That tenderly touched and held in view,
I become me and you become you.
   —*Jean Lacy-Tang*

A Fragile Thing

Love is like the petals on a rose
A fragile thing to keep and hold;
Like the evening star, ever immobile
   with each passing year,
A rare gem set in platinum and gold;
Like the ebb tide as it flows out to sea
   at evening time;
Love is like the petals on a rose,
It comes in many colors,
Pink, yellow, red and gold.
Pink for the innocence that leaves
   with the passage of time.
Yellow for the memories to hold so dear,
Red for the passion that grows with love,
Gold for the love that lasts through
   the long years.
If you pluck the rose, remember
It is a fragile thing, like love,
tend it carefully, or it will droop and die.
   —*Emeline (Caretti) Shannon*

The Plight Of A Bird

I was sitting outside on a warm summer's day.
A gentle breeze was blowing through my hair.
A bird flying low,
Flew into my head.
He landed in my lap,
And saw stars all around.
He looked up at me, then down at the ground.
Tiny and fragile was he,
As I scooped him up in my hand.
He looked up at me with a tear in his eye.
"Don't be afraid. I will not hurt you," said I.
I stood up and asked him where home was.
He looked towards the big oak tree in the neighbor's yard.
I walked him over to the tree.
He went in his home,
And I went in mine.
   —*Joanne Verde*

Rose Marie

Been paintin' up a portrait 'bout —
   a girl stays on my mind.
B'lieve I've gone and captured her—
   likeness, she's so fine.
Red lips complimenting —
   her fair-complected skin—
Big brown eyes conveying —
   a beauty from within.
Photogenic features —
   her hypnotizing gaze
Commanding all attention —
invoking all your praise.
Sultry and seductive —
   she looks right back at me.
With beauty overwhelming —
   the Masters will agree.
When my work's completed —
   a final nod from me—
Gonna tag right on my signature—
   unveiled for all to see.
   —*Frank T. Torpila*

My Foolish Heart

I reminisce the year just past, and what it brought to me:
A girlish stirring of the heart with no purpose I could see;
I felt as happy as a lark, and smiled the whole day through,
The spring was young — and I was young, and just because of you.

You came to me one gloomy day when I felt all alone,
And left your Presence in the room, long after you had gone;
I'd caught a softness in your voice that made me think you cared,
And hours later, I still felt the moment we had shared.

My captive thoughts then fantasized; they played the fool I fear,
with happy scenes I'd never see and words I'd never hear.
I paid no mind when Reason came and tried to fill my brain;
I wanted just to dream my dream, and hear your voice again.

Then Conscience overtook my thoughts and told me sternly, "no!
This thing you find so beautiful just has no place to go.
You have an honor to uphold — what are you thinking of?
Now, hide this in your secret heart, to be your secret love."

So now, like Emily Dickinson, I brood my days away;
I've traveled on this road before, and I know well the way.
But, as I ponder on it, this has happened not by chance —
It's had some purpose after all; lift up, my heart, and dance.

—*Emily June Frick*

A Writer's Key

Some call writing a talent — not so — it's a key —
A key to unlock another world — a world of fantasy

In the real world when sorrow and grief have me
at the edge, a golden key unlocks my mind
filled with words — the words can carry me
to this perfect place of fantasy.

I may find myself walking on a beach — endless
blue water — white sand warming my feet.
The problem that brought me here exist no more.

I find myself feeling insecure — even putting myself down,
a golden key on a chain reminds me of just how lucky I really
am. It has unlocked barriers and allowed me to do anything —
be whatever I choose — go any place I've longed to be — places
where no enemies can enter — fear vanishes — I'm free to be the
person locked inside constantly searching for peace of mind.

I believe in this key with all my heart — I know someday it
will unlock a door — behind it will be the answer of where to
find my fantasies here in the real
world.

—*Juanita Farrow Trotter*

Observation Of Dying Love

In the shadows I hear voices crying, like
 a lone wolf under a desert sky.

I hear him say "why do you treat me this way,"
 she only says "you don't know me today."

 The moon has no mercy on lovers tonight.
 Lost in tears and memories they fight.

I hear him say "baby please don't leave!"
 but he knows it's a senseless plea.

 Their hearts they beat, their tears
 they fall and the night is so long
 but life will go on.
—*Christopher Ware*

The Lady At Midnight

She sings a plaintive song;
A lonely melancholy tune to the moon;
To the willow; to the inner sad one;
Capturing moonlight which turns to sadness;
Alone!

Soft, silvery moonbeams, filtered
By the tender willow leaves, patterning
their blessings on the face;
A beautiful face, of the lady at midnight!
Alone!

Passing the tree, I observe, the lady's tears
Touched softly, as a moonbeam slants through
To light her need for love,
Alone!
I seek the willow now! The moonlight on
Slightly parted lids, gains the very presence;
Close in; in my arms; together!
Loving!

—*Hugh Phillips, Jr.*

My Invader

I started me a flower garden,
 a long, long time ago.
And oh the joy it gave me;
 to see my flowers grow.

Our world would be a dreary place,
 without the birds, the flowers and trees;
When our Saviour made our world,
 He saw a need of these.

One day, when I went out;
 My pretty flowers to see
There growing among them,
 was a little cherry tree.

I started to reach for my hoe,
 I said "Tree, you've got to go,
There isn't room here, you see;
 for my flowers and a cherry tree."

But, I had a second thought, you know;
 and I laid down my trusty hoe.
Now I have a garden with a tree,
 It's grown much too big for me.

—*Bee Lansing*

Insanity!

A drowning in a pool of devil piss;
 A look into the abyss
And not being able to comprehend what we saw,
 A time when one's psyche is flayed raw
 Salted with melancholy's kiss
And then wrapped in a dirty material gauze;

It is a deep exposure of humanity's flaws,
A chaotic realization that something is amiss,
 Prints in our minds from some devil's paw,
To be constantly whispered to in a devil's hiss

—*David Williams*

Why My Girl

God blessed me with one granddaughter
Who is caring, loving, and kind.
Why she is so ill is always on my mind.

God blessed her with beauty and poise,
a loving smile an a beautiful voice.

She never complains but thinks of others
and family to her is one of her treasures.

We all love her for what she is.

God bless her and keep her as our family
is small and without her I'd be no
grandmother at all.
  —*Jane Seals*

Jennifer's Lullaby Of Jesus' Love

Hush, little Jennifer don't cry and I will sing you a lullaby,
A lullaby of Jesus love, how he came to earth from heaven
above. He was born in a stable in Bethlehem, He was born to
redeem the soul of man. His holy birth was like no other, He
was born of the spirit to a virgin mother. Shepherds in their
fields that night, seen a heavenly host what a beautiful sight.
He's lying in a manger in Bethlehem, peace on earth good will
to man. Three wise men came from afar, to worship him they
were led by a star. They came afar their gifts to bring, and to
bring, and to worship him their new born king. At the age of
twelve he was very wise, and taught in the temple to the priest
surprise. At thirty in the river Jordan, he was baptized by
his cousin named John. He turned water into wine, His mother
to please, and blessed little children at his knee. He fed
the hungry and blessed the poor, and cleaned ten leopards of
their sores. He walked the waters and calmed the waves, and
called a friend Lazareth from the grave. He caused the lame
to walk, and the blind to see, He cast out demons and set
people free. But men became angry as He walked this sod, for
He told them He was the Son of God. So they nailed Him to a
cross at Calvary, He shed his precious blood for you and me.
They buried him in a tomb of a friend, but in three days He
arose again. He rose to conquer death and sin, won't you open
your heart and let him in. He will teach you of his love, and
a heavenly home he's preparing above. So hush, little Jennifer
don't you cry, and I will sing you a lullaby, Hush.
  —*Delores I. Fulmer*

Dead Reckoning

I stand separate from the rest
A mammoth structure casting shadow to crush unsuspecting pests
A foundation of webbed steel and shell of concrete
Set deep within the bowels of earth providing an insulating retreat
A lifetime of darkness and emptiness: no spirit to be found.

Guards of Intellect and Reason stand watch over this perimeter
Each movement examined centimeter by centimeter
No inlet to provide the Peeping Tom a glance
Warning to be made aware: perpetrators stand no chance.

No entrance, no exit, no existence
A reflection of the universe...no resistance
Ironically, it is innocence that slips past all my defenses
Genuine concern may fracture this mammoth structure of senses.
  —*Christopher L. Burford*

The Birth Of A New Nation

He was a man unlike any other—
a man trapped between two worlds,
where neither could ever fully accept him.
With his porcelain and rose complexion,
and his strong Negro blood, all men
either feared him, or admired him
for exactly what he was—a drifter.
He could wander from one world
to the other with an amazing ease,
that he alone could achieve.
The slaves admired his intelligence,
just as those who kept him in bondage, feared it.
His very existence went against
that which the entire south was based.
A magnificent blow to the mighty south's solid
foundation. He, by mere existence,
disproved the southern justification of slavery.
He wandered through life, seeking the love
of one woman, and the support
of one nation, united at last.
  —*Doris Lee*

Caring

There are so few words we share
A moment or two at best
But it is in the smiles we bare
Our friendship comes to rest.
A fleeting encounter now and then
When our eyes meet to know,
Someone cares and reaches out
When there is nowhere else to go
A common bond, a human need,
That's all there is to see.
Yet, without this touch, as it were,
My life would empty be.
For each new time my heart looks out,
To see if you respond.
And when it does, I feel at once...
A wondrous dreamer's bond.
  —*Jo Tambo*

Antelope Star

Isolation, fascination, a moment without pain
A one way ticket to heaven in a glimpse afar
Such creation, my drama's contemplation, my minds walking cane
To be so young yet so old tell me please/antelope star
Moving so fast, yet forever still at twilight I cried last
night like an opera singer free of gravity my voice crying out
Time a merchant without patience, keeping the seconds of
our lives can't imagine how it is to wonder about you crashing
down like a gypsy caught in emotional eclipse, darkness
sharpened my sights to wish for rain could never cloud
your announcing pose
In silence all the universe sand there is no price
On the light letting of your kindness the mercy of your
throne as an infantile whisper escaped my lips in limbo
Caught between the racing of my heart and a homeless sigh
Like a telegraph wire immuned to distance was my hope
You would never leave my soul's cushion, up in the autumn
sky!! antelope star, a fragment of segments moan
Antelope star, an attraction beyond intervention blazing
cold antelope star, a derby hat worn by traveler's bold
  —*James A. Olivera*

Scott...My Missing Heart

Who is this man that appears to be a phantom of my dreams?
A passing thought, a familiar term- that slips up from
out of nowhere.

It seems so long, long ago, and yet, he's here with me.
Never have I known anyone to bring such calm.
Who said so much without a word.

And oh! when those words were said.
Those long awaited precious words- "I love you!"
It was as if time had stood still all those years- waiting-
waiting for the right moment.

Where is he now?
Does he still feel the way we felt that night?
Does he still long to hold me as I do him?

I do not know. I may never know.
But I will go on- feeling him near.
Sometimes for days on end, other times-
just a passing thought, a familiar term- that slips up from
out of nowhere.
—*Christine R. Hughes*

The Mother Lost

Is it possible to love a person you never knew?
A person responsible for your being,
but not responsible for the person you are?

Yes, it's possible because I love a person like that!!

I lost her a long time ago and had no memory of her love;
But somehow I knew she had loved me just as I knew I loved her.

She was a mother lost, with her love for me forgotten and wasted;
But I found the memory of her love still within me and that
love began to blossom and was wasted no more!
—*Cheri Lynn Hunter*

Who Am I?

I look in the mirror, and what do I see
A person unsure of herself, is that person me
The one who is gazing so earnestly
Seems to be different from the image I see

A life full of hopes, a life full of fears
Visions and dreams, misty eyes full of tears
Why do I seem different within and without
My image just stares, sensing my doubts

My head is full of luxuries that I have enjoyed
My heart feels so empty as if there's a void
Why do I feel this way, doesn't anyone care
Isn't there someone, somewhere with whom my feelings I may share

As I continue to stare into the mirror awhile
I notice my image beginning to smile
I hear a small voice say to me, friend
Remember what matters comes from within

When life gets you down and into the mirror you stare
The one staring back is the one who really cares
My smile now is much bigger as I stop to realize
To go far in this world you first should be, special in your
own eyes.
—*Jodi Ann Hilmer*

Nature's Young

Majestic and tall, with branches spreading wide,
a pine tree stood alone in a field by itself.

Two small trees planted deep into the ground.
One adopted by the pine tree.
The other adopted and mothered by me.

I watered and cherished my adopted child.
Summer passed and the tree withered and died.

The small tree, adopted by the pine, spread its
branches to touch its mother.
With loving arms they embraced each other.

Harsh weather came and the majestic pine bent
in the wind, protective arms surrounding her baby.

Spring paid a visit with a smile on her face.
There in a field, majestic and tall, holding hands,
mother and child embraced.
—*Judith Kay McElwain*

Gods Is Nigh

Upon majestic mountain, stream below,
a place I visit often so.

Lush valley floor, multi-green,
a peaceful spot to dream serene.

Glorious beauty through eyes of mine,
behold fir, cedar and assorted pine.

For the sun the berry bush gropes,
Squaw carpet drifts down rocky slopes.

Flat stone path leads to a stream,
lighted rays of golden beam.

Water lilies yield to warm sunshine,
intertwined fingers of the wild grape vine.

Song birds sing and rendezvous,
white plump clouds adorn sky blue.

Wild aromatic scents to heaven high,
Celestial like haven where God is nigh.
—*Jessie Paulsen*

Love-Look What You've Done To Me

I was a girl with many dreams and
a pocket full of hope. I knew
nothing about love and I didn't want to
know; But I found out all about it and I
though he was the one, but you left
me cold and lonely love. Look what you've
done. Now my heart won't be the same and
his memory will haunt my life. I'll look
back and see his face with every tear I'll
cry. I might not ever be the same, but
then again I may. Love look what you've
done; why couldn't you stay away? Why
did you have to happen and come into my
heart? If you would've left me alone
my world wouldn't be torn apart. But
now I feel the cold wind blow as
it softly whispers his name-love look
what you've done to me; I'll never be
the same.
—*Juanita Mouton Brasseau*

Civilization

Torn,
   A rose without a petal.

Blank,
   A night without a star.

Shallow,
   A play without a story.

Fleeting,
   A wound without a scar.

The human world is incomplete,
But not in the eyes of man.
Many move to a single beat,
Afraid to anger the clan.
Perhaps one day the world will know,
If someone spreads the word,
The value of letting each spirit grow,
Freeing voices long unheard.
   —Amanda Schaffer

Somebody's Boy

While walking down a lonely street
A sad little boy I chanced to meet.
I smiled at him as I passed by,
His answering smile was sweet and shy.
He looked as if he needed care
From his worn-out shoes, to his tousled hair.
His little face was streaked with tears,
And looked too old for his few years.
My heart went out to the little lad
I wondered about his mom and dad.
Surely there was someone who really cared
Whither he went, or how he fared.
I saw him turn in at an open gate
I hurried on as it was getting late.
But I couldn't forget, in my home that night
The little boy in his sorry plight.
I knelt by my bed and asked God to care —
For a dear little boy with uncombed hair.
   —Agnes Foutz

Too Many Brains Spoil The Fun With Lionel Trains

It began with Lionel Electric trains for Christmas
A set of tracks to show the movement of colorful cars.
A house full of guests absorbing the Holiday excitement
And their children displaying the oohs and ahs.

It didn't take long for extra interest to develop
And churn ideas as fast as the trains were travelling.
The higher the switch was moved more ideas were grooved.
The house was filled with varied mental unravelling.

Before long creativity took over the setup of the trains
The floor no longer dominated the simple layout.
Trestles of books raised the tracks around
But causing a problem turn-out.

The cord no longer reaching the wall
Another outlet was sought.
The chandelier the perfect solution
But not the short person selected to complete the thought.

Standing shakily on a chair trying to plug in the cord
Suddenly, a twenty-two scatter emptied the room.
Just the dangler hanging onto the pulled-out chandelier was left
Soon stormed by his father finding the near tragic scene of doom.
   —Edward Francis Branau

Jewels Found At Night

A silhouette -
A shadow on the land,
White gulls -
Water breaking on the sand.

Wind blowing -
Bends the prairie grass grown high,
Moon rising -
Lighting up the youngest night.

Crickets singing -
Their summer concerts loud for all,
Fire dancing -
The lonely mistress last we saw.

And after night, the road we had taken-
Forgot the way.
   —Heather Lynn Finkenbiner

How Can She Tell Them?

Awakened one night from a fitful sleep
A shot rang out from close in the street;
A man lay dying in a pool of bright red,
Clearly was seen, he'd been shot in the head.

Rain was now falling, the street agleam.
Police and ambulance came onto the scene.
A life was ebbing, no matter the cause,
By hoodlums who make and live their own laws.

A neighbor, running had called nine one one,
Too late it seemed for the damage was done.
Was it for money, for fun or for drugs?
Too many, by far, are street wise young thugs.

The search endless, no justice be reached;
Loopholes in laws span too many a breach.
What gain this violence, outside my door?
The victim died at a quarter past four.

Officers go to visit his home; where,
A young widowed mother waits all alone.
How can she tell her fatherless sons
Their Dad has been killed by a street thug's gun?
   —Frances Wilber Hellmers

Untitled

You are:
   A sight for the eye; an eye that has never seen before.
   A thought for the mind; a thought of calm and tranquil
waters. A breath for the mouth; a mouth of new born child.
   * You are all of that and yet more than that *

You have:
   Intelligence; to understand and yet exceed others.
   respect; to give and to receive from others.
   love; also to give and to receive from others.
   * You have all of that and yet more than that *

You will receive:
   A warm heart; one that will give you love and affection when
needed. A kind hand; one that will guide you through your
worst times.
   A loving friend; one that will stay with you in bad times
and in good times.
   * You will receive all of that and yet more than that *
You are more than any man could possibly want
I am nothing of which you desire or need
Yet I wish to have you, to love you, to cherish you
Forever!
   —Joseph Tugend

The Sign Painter

I see you clearly in my mind's eye:
A solitary figure framed against a New Orleans sky.
The scaffolding, lashed against the building, is as steady as
    your hand,
Which moves with the powerful certainty only total confidence
    can command.
The tune you whistle will that evening lift me up,
Like the sound of a long awaited band,
As I go rushing toward your arms with outstretched hands,
Knowing, even then, that they would always open for me.
Now, forty-odd years hence, it is the quintessential you I see:
A consummate craftsman at the absolute peak of his skill,
Joyfully lost in an American moment, freeze-framed still.
Below, festive corridors welcome like royalty the holiday throngs
Of postwar shoppers who glance up, momentarily, and then
    move on.
They do not know that the power in your hand
Will one day flow through me like a river,
Easing the pounding of my troubled heart,
Rushing me forward out of the dark.
—*Barry W. North*

Joy

Joy, the participant of happiness, a principle of peace
A spirit of thought, unto thy pleasure increase
Joy, the instillment for tomorrow, a path for today
A call of togetherness, within thy joyous way
Joy, the king of continuous, the queen of prosperity
Through moments of clover, with circumstances to see
Joy, the vision of sight, that darkness can't blind
Like heaven it's peace, that evil can't find
Joy, the picture for love, that sadness can't steal
The flower of strength, from a rose that's real.
—*Jerry Edwards*

A Gypsy's Christmas

Christmas is a manger where a blessed baby lay.
A star-light when angels and shepherds
Kneel to pray.
Still today it means the things He taught
In his stay upon the earth.
While with ageless joy and awe and wonder
The world still celebrates His birth
I looked back into my childhood
again; I heard my mother say
Christmas joy is yours forever
When your heart learns it this way

C-stands for courage to make the right stand
H-stands for helping, at which folks are grand
R-is for righteousness, our true guiding light
I-is for inspiration, to try to always do what's right
S-stands for sharing with all who are in need
T-is for trustworthy, may it always be our creed
M-is for the manager where Baby Jesus lay
A-is all the things He taught us during His short stay
S-stands for the sacrifices made by you and me.

So we all may share a Christmas, filled with human dignity.
May God bless us all - this Christmas
Then this special gift, I wish for you
May your heart know its joy and wonder
And keep Christmas all year through.
—*Rev. Georgia Milton*

Untitled

I hope the sounds keep coming on
    A steady stream to run
Until the job be done upon
    The subject under sun.

I hope the sounds keep coming through
    My head and never mar
The subject carefully tuned anew-
    Beyond the outer star.

Well, here I set to write with will
    That strengthens as I move
From region unto region, until
    The expectations prove.
—*John K. Crawford*

Feelings

An inborn sense given to us with intense satisfaction enjoyed—
A thrilling perfection of an innate gift given and not to
avoid, sensitive emotions by a powerful but natural receiver—
Answered by human warnings of a gifted believer. The feeling
to see, hear, touch or smell brings awareness, sense
impressions transmitted through beings from genes inherited—
Guilt plays a part as our conscience signals are employed- A
knowledge of right from wrong as compulsion's destroyed,
Messages in transit through skin give vital sensations—To act
according to faculties to do or not to do is wrong exploration.
Feelings are there for many reasons and felt in a big city on a
dark night—A time when fright overwhelms us as our bodies
shudder with fright. Natural abilities bring heartfelt
appreciation for a gift of art—Applause for an act that you
give from yourself and returned with feelings at heart.
—*Ada Sweet*

My Little Sister

When you were just a little girl,
A tiny little thing with long blond
Curls; with eyes of blue and an elfish smile,
And Oh! So busy all the while.

Sometimes with a little face of dirt,
Or for us to kiss a little hand that was hurt.
The mail man would come by, and she would
holler, "Hi, mister" That's my girl;
"MY LITTLE SISTER."

It's your birthday, I can't believe Forty
Years have passed; But my thoughts keep going
Back to the years; Of happiness and tears.
Of that little girl with sparkling blue
Eyes and long blond curls;

Of that happy "Hi Mister," That's my girl;
"MY LITTLE SISTER."
—*Evelyn Erreca*

At Last, To Rest

I climbed into my bed so soft,
A place of gentle warmth,
To soothe the aching limbs that bore
So many heavy loads,
Of daily chores,
And bags from stores,
And who knows what there was,
That put a strain upon my brain.
But all that's in the past.
And here I lie,
Oh lucky me!
To have this place to rest.
—*Joan Doddis Meears*

A Christmas Story

Long ago in the fullness of time,
A tired virgin gave birth to a child.
He grew to be humble, meek, and mild,
    Although He is a king.

Peace on Earth the angel said,
To shepherds who ran with joy.
In a stable discovered a baby boy,
    Although He is a king.

Wise men still seek this child today.
At His birth three came from afar,
Following God's own guiding star,
    Because He is a king.

God's fullness of time approaches once more,
As the Earth is torn by human greed.
    Satan plants his wicked seed.
    But Christ is still the king.

Sometime soon the skies will part,
As our king returns in all His glory.
His power will finish the Christmas story.
Each knee shall bow to the King.
    —*Jane Clark McKee*

lying under a giant oak tree
  a two hour freeway ride

flat on my back in my softly rocking hammock
  bumper to bumper traffic

looking up through soft transparent green sunlit leaves
  tense, tense, immobile anxiety

the wind wrestles her branches
  an irrevocable gray blur, erratic trash

the quiet sound of the mighty silver trunks gently swaying
  rude, mean, uneven displeasure

clear blue sky twinkling through abstracted patterns
  red brake lights flash

it's awesome laying here resting in peace
  a gunshot rings
  the snake of traffic snarls

i close my eyes
i rest my case
    —*Janet Mackaig*

Clouds

They are stampeding through the sky—
A vision that enthralls—
Great white horses running by

A mob that runs until they die
Or break in sudden squalls
They are stampeding through the sky

Laboring bodies that mystify
Of the wind they are just thralls
Great white horses running by

There is only white within the eye
The air resounds with panicked calls
They are stampeding through the sky

Manes and tails flying high
The excitement never palls
Great white horses running by

Pounding hooves that seem to fly
With each step lightning falls
They are stampeding through the sky,
Great white horses running by.
    —*Angela Thompson*

The Purple Ensemble

Clashing resoundingly with an orange blouse
  a white hat set on the head above it,
  purple suede shoes ready to beat out good rhythm,
  and oversized mauve hose that sag and don't fit.

Fitting too tight over buttocks that shake,
  of a length that is not quite chic,
  gracing a figure that should be girdled more tightly,
  So that its wearer doesn't look too thick.

Traveling in the ensemble would be uncomfortable, as could be,
  if the wearer were not brash,
  but Sally of the pepper Batch Johnsons got away with it,
  because she was just plain "trash."
    —*Elnorist E. Dial*

Untitled

I have dreams for myself, and hopes,
A wish I strive everyday to make come true,
And although people say "Oh it's impossible" and
"You'll never make it," I hold my head high and Try to do

Everything in my power, praying, hoping
that one day something will happen and
My dream will pour down on me, hold my hand,
And I will know I have succeeded.

It may be discouraging, and sometimes I feel
So much frustration at not having enough
to grasp my dream, missing the single element
that always keeps me one step behind, my heart
tearing at the knowledge that I might never do it,
While the optimist in my keeps my spirits up,
reassuring me that I can.
So I will press on, doing all in my power to fulfill my
dream, and in the meantime, giving
myself the undying courage to keep on trying.
    —*Evelyn V. Trester*

Dear God And Johnny Ray

Lord, help me find a way to tell Johnny Ray
  about his daddy running away.
Lord, let him understand that Mommy loves him,
And don't want him to hurt for his daddy day by day
Johnny, the going got to rough, and Daddy couldn't stay.
  I love him but we were in his way
Johnny, I love you too and in my arms you will stay.
I wish Mommy still had your sister, Angelia Kay
  Johnny, she went away with the Lord,
    That's OK!
Because in the Lord's arms she will stay.
I wish we were all four together today,
But Daddy wanted to go away
I hope he's happy as you and I will be someday,
Because Johnny the Lord will help if I pray.
Lord, let Johnny Ray understand
and not turn out that way.
I want him to know and love his daddy anyway.
    —*Angie Daveler*

Silence

After the song, I lay in bed thinking
about the year of 1978. The child brought into
this man-made world. All that confusion
five years ago. The same child in her room
crying for help. All of the sudden the lights
blink. Maybe, because of the storm, or it's
all just a dream that I had last night.
"Click." The silence is killing me. Too late,
too long, too far away. Silence is a
loud ring in my ears, that won't go away.

—*Elizabeth Adelaide Lettsome*

Cherished Memory

As I sit here in solitude
Absorbing the surrounding wonders
A beautiful river I see.
Water racing past the rocks
So happy to be free.
My eyes fall upon a figure
Standing all hunched and tired
Fishing pole in hand
Waiting, waiting for that big catch
Tears fill my eyes and my heart does ache so
For on this fine figure of a man
The years have taken their toll.
Hold on to this memory
It is so very, very special
For this figure standing by the river
With fishing pole in hand,
Is the great and gentle man
I am proud to call "my Dad."

—*Glenda McDaniel*

A Child's Sincerity

Beyond all things of beauty and wonder, above all dreams and achievements
Above all everything, I hold you there, as my friends, my guides, my parents
In my heart, I keep a place, for the two of you to stay
I ask Jesus to never forget you each night as I pray
There are many things I love in life, but above them all stand two
Now, forever, for as long as I love, above them all are you
My future is yet unknown, but I know you'll be with me there
My actions are sometimes uncalled for, but my love is forever sincere
Everything I know, I learned from you
Everything I do, your love helps me through
My friends, my dreams, my hopes, time changes all things we know
But your pride and love have not once weakened or let go
I am both proud and thankful to have you as my Mother and Dad
And am happy that I can cherish all the wonderful times we've had
There is nothing in this world that could ever replace your love
Among all that I've known, I hold you both above
MOM AND DAD, I LOVE YOU ALWAYS!

—*Jennifer Jeanne Patenaude*

Treasures On Earth

Oh birds, such beauty bring.
All colours and your songs of Spring!
Flying 'neath the skies so blue.
Indeed, at times I envy you.
Your freedom and your wondrous flight,
your roosting in the silent night,
flitting gaily tree to trees
and soaring high on gentle breeze.
A world without you, ne'er the same.
Let us spare ourselves this shame.
Let us all these species save
for us that Mother Nature gave.

—*Edna Burns*

Never Yield

"To late! To late" the chicken squawked, and she fluttered
    across the field.
"Go hide! Go hide!" the rabbit growled, but his voice was
    very meek.
"Don't move! Stand still!" piped up the squirrel, "It's only
    a passing cloud."
"I can't stand still. You silly thing. I'll just go underground."
"I'll bury my head, here in this sand," the ostrich gobbled
    aloud.
"Oh no you won't, `cause your body is out. You're acting like
    a clown."
"A perfect target you will make. Stop being like a fool. If
    I'd follow out your bad advice, my body'd soon get cooled."

This last was said by the gentle cow who calmly chewed her cud.
    She gazed at all and further remarked, "Just gnaw your food.
    Forget the sun. There's no place you can run."
"I guess you're right," a small duck quacked. "I'll settle my
    feathers and take my nap."

And…so the missile's frightening cloud shot across the skies,
The animals looked for means of escape, the fate that would end
    their lives.

But we, the peoples of Planet Earth are living from day to day.
All we can do to meet "The bomb" is stay…and maybe pray.
Unlike the chicken that ran away, we will keep on making
    appeals, until one day it will be too late, because
    we will never yield.

—*Helen M. Ostrom*

Old Glory

We honor old glory as she waves
    Across the land,
For those stars and strips we shall
    Forever stand.
As she waves she sends a message
Saying, "This is a country free,
We live that other countries may be
    Able to see,
When all band together with love upon
    Every hand,
That we had built upon solid rock, not
    Upon sinking sand."
Let us continue to stand with pride and
    Watch Old Glory wave,
Over the land of the free, and the home
    Of the brave.
And say, "This is my country, make it your
    Country too,
That all may live in peace forever, under
    This blessed Red, White and Blue."

—*Hazel Lee Armstrong*

Everlasting Friendship

A laugh warming the soul and heart
A gentle teasing; a gentle sparring
Quiet strength; a will of steel
An understanding of faults and foibles
Unwavering trust in each other
Acceptance of the other's inner self
Believing in one another
Supporting each other's dreams
Bringing laughter in times of sadness
A bond unlike any other
Sorrow for the other's pain
Joy for the other's triumph:
A friendship everlasting.

—*Jennifer Mack*

True Life

And now another lesson claimed
Adorns the timeless crown of life
We sift through days for yet an answer
That causes less the clouds of strife

Pure luck will raise its head by chance
And thus a fortune nips your heels
But not your life will richer be
Not till the spoils are spilled

So cast your dreams so tightly held
Pure joy will cleanse the senses all
The golden skies await your cry
The valleys announce your call
—*Fred Essex*

The Young President And The Old Pope

Two kindred spirits meet
After a brief pen-pal
Relationship solidifying
Their concern
For the weak, the poor and hungry
Trapped by the jaws of
. . . inequity
They well know the clarion call
Of love and peace toward all
But in the search for answers
In a world seemingly gone mad,
Hope shines brightly
On the young president
And an old Pope
As the bright and morning star
Begins to ascend from the east
To welcome them both to the
. . . NEWDAWN!
—*Bob Forest*

Lest We Forget

Who said, "Life is a bed of roses?"
After all, don't roses have thorns?
Just try to pick them without care,
Then, wish you hadn't dared!
Living it one day at a time,
Sweet Jesus, is all we can ask,
Even if we don't make a dime,
Sometimes, getting through the day is a task!
Dare we not lose and forget...
Our keen sense of humor,
For humor comes to our rescue, so yet...
We can turn loose and laugh with fervor!
Life is one big melting pot,
Tribulation brings patience,
Patience brings peace
Peace brings love and endurance!
All striving for the same goal...
Just to get up there to heaven,
And hear from the good Lord above,
"Well done! Thou good and faithful servant!"
—*Anna O. Thompson*

Voyage To The Magellanic Cloud

Out of the darkness from the storm
   hide conspicuous patches of light
     after the rains rhapsody pacifies the spirit
       like a song
Follow each note as they fall
   tear drop by drop
     can you hear it
       kissing the ground when they land
         in puddles
           or spill into oceans
             whose waves slap sand
'Neath lips pressed hand to hand
   while sheets of wet lavishly lament
     amidst languished thunder
       from corpulent clouds asunder
Decades wail listless
   as the last rains fall
     watering into flower

       the beauty between two hearts
         growing over its wall
—*Dena Beth Lesser*

Wasted Life

This man expected to be successful in his future that lie ahead. But the odds were against him with so much unemployment instead. He was among the others searching for jobs all over town. It was the same everywhere the recession had shut things down. His savings had all vanished and life had been tough so far. Hardtimes had fell upon his life and then worst of all he lost his car. His dreams of a good job had evaporated into a haze. He was in a serious state of depression losing hope with passing days. His life became a catastrophe—he lost all his self-respect and pride. He just give up and lived like a bum something inside of him died. Unemployment had claimed another victim his life just came apart. He carefully guarded his belongings draped over a grocery cart. He pushed that cart daily roaming up and down the street. From one trash container to another he might find something to eat. He would find a corner under the bridge where he could make his bed. Dreams of what he could have been would swim around in his head. If he didn't survive the elements another night to see the light of day. No special words would be expressed for this bum that passed away. Buried on a hillside with no marker on his grave. Just another wasted life that nobody helped to save.
—*Betty Joan Burkett*

The Star Bird (The story of the human soul)

Mid the fire and ice of earth's dank primeval birth,
A star bird struggled against labour's heaving walls.
It knew naught that it had come from a distant star,
Or its wings were woven from heaven's lighted halls.

As epochs passed the planet eased its birth travail,
And ruby flames were cooled by ocean-crested waves.
Mighty verdant trees rose to rent their umber veil,
As the star bird slumbered mid winter's frozen caves.

When grasses bent in the zephyrs of endless time,
Great cities raised their lofty and masted spirals.
Bronzed sinew broke the stone and heaved the wooded pine.
And the star bird stirred mid soul's unpainted murals.

One lighted dawn earth overcame its wars and rage.
And human life stilled its sorrows and shrouded pain.
At last the star bird unlocked its chains of night's dark cage,
To fly deathless toward heaven's boundless main.
—*Elizabeth MacDonald Burrows*

A Season Of Change: Spring

"A season of change: Spring" is really here
All afresh, my favorite time of year.
With all its beauty and life anew
Full of hope and vigor that dreams do come true.
God's landscape, so well and carefully laid
Bringing forth awe for all that He's made!
I look upward and see that brilliant sun
And once again know my work has begun.
Gentle breeze and the clouds drifting by,
All coming from that wonderful blue sky.
Flowers are blooming and in great array,
With so much beauty to begin each day!
The trees have grown and grass has turned green,
Among all God's display that can be seen.
All will soon fade with the summer storms
Spring comes and goes, a change of season forms.
We, too, like the seasons have much to change
Our thinking, ways, lives and rearrange
To keep all seasons, love, protect, cherish
Work to see that Spring will never perish!!
—Doris C. Daly

1-900

Sitting up dialing 1-900 numbers off your television set.
Body all hot, broke out in a nasty cold sweat.
Look at you, got your lips all wet,
thinking you're talking to the woman on T.V.
Ah man give me a break please, she's on the phone only to get paid,
you like a fool think you really have it made.
Her job is to put you in the right mood.
Sir you don't know who you're actually talking to.
Trying to satisfy your unnatural fantasies.
Jesus is what you really need.
Selling that dope to pay your debt.
Give your life to Jesus and all your needs will be met.
There's only one time around in this life.
If I were you I'd get my soul right.
Sir you think everything's just a big joke.
That's how it is with a lot of folk.
There's coming a day you'll have to leave here.
You'll have that one last look in the mirror.
You can't take your smoke,
you can't take your dope,
you can't take your woman, not even your man,
no not in God's plan.
If I were you I'd take time to think,
because you can be gone in one quick blink.
Thinking you're something, for you, life will stand still.
I'm here Buddy to give you the real deal.
Jesus died to save your soul,
He rose to cleanse and make you whole,
if I lied and said there's another way paid.
I'd have to give account on Judgement Day.
If God didn't give you breath, you couldn't breathe.
He gave His Son so even you can be free.
So if you believe the things that I say:
Repent of your sins, and receive Jesus into your heart,
He is the only way why not leave 1-900 alone.
Call up Jesus on the real telephone (prayer) ring TODAY!!!
—Anita L. Bumphus

Beautiful People

God made all of us beautiful,
all in a different way.
He made us black and white, red and yellow
and we all are equal, each girl and fellow.

Brothers and sisters all are we.
For each other — much love there must be.
We are God's creation of beauty and grace,
each person created has his own unique place.

Above all animals, oceans and hills,
man stands alone with his special skills.
He can build a bridge, conquer space, split a gene, love and create.

More precious than gold, fame and power,
man stands alone as God's spiritual tower.
Into us all He has breathed a soul,
which will live forever and never grow old.

So whenever you see your sister and brother,
remember that their soul is your same color.
For God made all of us beautiful,
All in a different way on the outside,
but, all in one beautiful way on the inside.
—Emilie Joan Caldwell

Sunset Insanity

Landscapes change from plain to gold.
All is well, though childhood sold.
The clowns are coming through the mouth of the canyon.
Bright colors frame the sky, and all is well and entertaining.
They seem to respect the concept of a journey unto the other side.
Antipodes in my mind, though they may be, accepting my presence
Only in their inability to dispute me...the master of this domain.
"Enter my Kingdom," I say to myself.
The sweet familiarity of certain sadness, memorized.
My mind is my castle and I am its slave. My soul is my servant,
   the child I have raised.
Ironically my life versed to form some cruel joke, so the gods may
   laugh.
And yet unwanted, unfriendly and devastatingly unfamiliar is the
far less captivating existence we call reality.
For what is reality but poor confused facts?
I stepped outside myself and found an overwhelming sea of voices,
joyous in the freedom...Liberation!
—Brandon A. Cebulak

Champions

My champions march on other fields.
All my heroes are gone.
Champions three, like musketeers,
Beyond the earth they left too young.
Like the dawn, the one a son,
One in midday's prime,
The third, a patriarch of heavy years -
At the dusk of life.
Eternity balanced against life's scale
With burdens weighing down a ton.
Memories remain, bring tears and pain,
My champions have gone.
—Diana Richardson Metcalf

Unseen Logs

Fallen logs are like those on rivers not left free
and controlled help loggers and industry.
Beavers use branches and wood to build dams to survive and be free.
There are logs for cabins, homes with wood for heating as well
as others to use and see; piled high outdoors in case of emergency.
The unseen logs we sometimes carry not realizing having the weakness
or strength depending what impresses us between as we see in others;
often not realizing it is in each of us more or less as we see in
our understanding of human weakness and strength.
Left in our limited strength regenerated through faith and
times of earnest renewal of pause and meditation are the logs of
our life's journey.
—Geraldine T. Tobin

Anxiety Resolved

When times are sour and nearly spent
And darkness shades the firmament
When the brightest cause appears as doom
And fear pervades the entire room
Let faith with pride be sent

When all appears to be as dust
And all around has turned to rust
When our love of life fills with dismay
And hope has surely lost its way
Let vision guide your trust

Yet, when a small one finds his hutch
And escapes his old tormentor's clutch
When the future shows in all its glory
And fulfills the mission of our story
How sensitive is our touch

Now, distress dissolves in apathy
And we are pleased with what we see
No storm tossed seas to swamp our boat
No trial of strength to stay afloat
Masters of our fate are we
—John Probasco

The Wall

Upon this wall are rows and rows of names, people that fought
and died for the country that gave them freedom. They are
heroes that have been forgotten by their family and friends,
left unknown to others as their memory fades like a passing
rain. The memory of their laughter and tears lingers in the
corners of their family's hearts and minds. It was only
yesterday they were playing war. Now they are playing with
real guns and killing real people; barely leaving their toys
behind. We lost so many of our young during those years,
making history, was it worth all those innocent lives? Then
there are the fortunate-so they were told-they were the lucky
ones that got to come home. They came back to a world that was
full of hatred and of rage, back to a country that did not want
them here. Their hearts and minds have been scarred forever
with visions of blood, tears, and death of friends. Their
lives have been filled with nightmares that will haunt them
'til their dying day, turning their lives upside down from a
nightmare into a living hell. You can still hear their
screams and prayers in the wind on a cold winter's eve.
The wall is the Vietnam Wall and the people are not forgotten
by me, they are just a memory.
—Jennifer A. Davis

Runaway Slave

Leaves rustle, twigs snap
and dogs bark behind me.
I must find a hiding spot
maybe a hollow tree
maybe under a pile of leaves
or maybe I should just run for my life,
Leaves rustle, twigs snap
and dogs bark behind me.
faster and faster I must run
for I shall jump into the icy river
so no one can follow my scent,
Leaves rustle, twigs snap
and dogs bark behind me.
down the river I go splashing to keep afloat,
dodging rocks
hitting waves
now the river becomes silent,
Leaves rustle, twigs snap
and dogs bark behind me.
now I must run again
for I see my freedom at last,
over the next hill lies my freedom thank God Almighty! I'm
free!
—Alysia McLain

An Ode To Love

God is always love dear heart,
And, even if our dreams did part,
My prayers are heard by him above
To reconcile my immortal love.
I knew the moment you were gone,
That my love would linger on.
Yes, I've had my so called escapade,
And, for my very fickle fancy paid,
But please try to keep the memory of,
A once beautiful romance my love.
—Jacqueline Andersen

Message From Heaven

Yes! I'm safely home in heaven, loved ones;
And even though you bade me tearfully not to go;
I loved you so — T'was Heaven there with you as well,
But here there is no death, no fear, no grief, no pain.
My soul soars, in freedom, with langs unfettered wings.
Air whispers softly past me, as my happy spirit sings,
So when you hear a song, or see a bird in glorious flight,
Or other nature's wonderments, that meant so much to me;
Be filled with joy, for I am there beside you,
Caring, as I always will.
There are tasks still waiting for you,
Ah! so much you've yet to do.
Try to look beyond life's dark days;
Waste no time in idle mourning,
For I love you dearly still.
When your work is all accomplished,
God will light for you the way,
To this rapturous place called heaven,
Oh! what joy that special day.
—Chris Dowdall Schult

Why Our Mom, God, Why?

We constantly ask the same question about our dear mother each
   and every day.
How could our Creator be so unfair and take her from us in such
   a cruel way?
Yearning for a little serenity we continue to practice our
   faith and pray.

Only the Lord has the answer for His actions which can weigh
   heavily on one's mind.
Understanding the meaning of God working in strange ways may
   never be defined.
Resigning oneself to accepting the Lord's will is hard
   especially when it's so unkind.

Many innocent people are falling victim to this ravaging
   illness called HIV.
Ominously referred to as AIDS, it's more deadly than any other
   disease could be.
Morally monogamous for over 40 years our sweet mother died when
   she was just 63.

Good, bad or indifferent this epidemical killer strikes
   indiscriminately without strife.
Our mom was infected with contaminated blood during emergency
   surgery to save her life.
Drugs shared intravenously was not the cause as she was proudly
   a mom and an honest wife.

While the five of us go on without a mom, our invalid father
   continues to suffer and grieve.
He's a paraplegic and mom gave him more strength and courage
   than anyone could ever believe.
Yet her killer persists in taking down the path of destruction
   it continues to weave.

   —*Diane Ayon*

Unfeigned

I circled the earth today on the wings of a Dove,
   And everywhere I lighted I found love.
Across shepherd's field the music rang.
   In the upper room, a lovely voice sang.
I noticed the soil was red in places,
   And the emerald green rivers reflected faces.
A tender touch from a man who stood tall,
   Carried me onward past the Great Wall.
Then, what seemed to be endless moments for me,
   Snow capped mountain peaks and ocean was all I could see.
I came upon land, and dropped down, under ground,
   Where curio shops full of gifts were found.
I hastened to rise to continue to fly,
   Toward the high rising structures of my homeland sky.
Lost in the dark with a million people, cold rock and steel;
   I remembered loving kindness, Oasis, and stopped to kneel.
The Dove gracefully continued winging His way,
   To carry me back where I should stay.
Filled with joy being greeted with open arms, laughter and
   tears...and Love Unfeigned

   —*Bonnie (Richmond) Clapham*

I Felt Dachau

I thought I heard the crying,
   and felt the chill of fear.
I smelled the stench of dying,
   Reality was here.
As I trudged, alone, the bleakest
   terrain I've ever known.

Other souls who passed me by
   seemed strangely saddened too,
And only whispered to each other,
   unlike most travellers do.
The pall of solemnity was there
   for all of us to share.

The ugliness and horror of the place
   hung low across the ground,
And permeated every bit of space.
   Babies cried, old men made sound,
And women moaned aloud.
   This was hell I'd found.

I saw it, and I smelled it, and I heard the sounds.
I really cannot tell you how, but I know I felt Dachau.

   —*Betty Fern Thakray*

Springtime Reveille

When I awake at daybreak
And hear a robin sing
Among the apple blossoms
And lilacs in the spring
As a soft breeze blows their fragrance
Across my window sill,
I can hear the distant drumming
Of a partridge on the hill;
Then the clear notes of the oriole
Salute the warm spring air
While the brook is swiftly rushing
By green willows bending there.
I rejoice that it is springtime
And I am here to see
All these wonders of creation
God has given you and me.

   —*Eleanor Kimberley*

The Last Switchback

Sweat cools in the shadow of the foothills

He stumbles, weary
and hears the echo of his footsteps
a pounding in his ears

Behind him the sun
searching for bits of mica and glass
glares briefly in his eyes

The trail he follows
curves by the palo verde, nursing
a young saguaro

And he pauses there
tepid in the canteen, the last drink
takes the chill away

He recalls the stone
still stroking a heel, desensitized
He waits to dig it out

As he waits alone
with only the view for company
above the last switchback

Until the chill returns and shadows fall

   —*Judith L. Ward*

Summer

How soft, how gentle summer, when earth
and Heaven meet.

Flowers released from winter, rise up the
sun to greet.

The gentle fall of rain is but nature's
cry of joy, stirring golden harvest and
greenery into birth.

The trumpets sound so softly with a
gentle stirring breeze, calling out
to nature, your magic now release.

Put on your finest showing, splash
color everywhere.

Your artistry in motion is beyond compare.
   —*James A. McMullen*

On His Blindness

When I consider how his time is spent,
and hers and theirs and ours and so on,
I have to laugh at them all who wonder why
God created men and women but meant
to create persons — you know it, he sent
us long-shore-persons to load our supplies,
middle-persons to raise their market price,
salespersons so sellers can pay their rent.

Who could be so blind that he, she, or they
could miss the need for fisherpersons and
firepersons? All personkind was planned
say his own spokespersons — necessity
had no part in it, nor did your cursin'.
So cut the crap. Stand up like a person.
   —*Adam E. Carr*

Eternal Power

There is a power that formed the world
And hung the moon in space,
A power that of a common blood
Made every man and race.

A power that spoke and at his word
The darkness fled away.
God spoke and light came forth
And changed the night to day.

The power that made the Jordan roll
And calmed the mighty sea,
Is the power that can save a sinner's soul
And sets the captives free.

The power that makes the roses bloom
And helps the songbirds sing,
Is the power that forms the snowflakes
And the beauty of the spring.

The power that touched a virgin's womb
And the Son of God was born,
Is the power that can change eternal night
Into eternal morn.
   —*Clyde W. Painton*

Spare The Switch, Spoil The Child

A scene in my home caught my eye that day. Danger lurked near and I began to pray that what I was seeing was just a mistake and there was no need for me to make a big fuss about the imminent doom from two evil men in my living room.

I watched in horror as guns each man drew. My children squealed in delight, "Bang! Bang! I got you!" I shielded them from the murderous blasts and waited in shock 'til the moment passed. I began to scream, "How can this be? I don't want you here. Now please, just leave!"

My children looked at me, now in fright. "Mommy don't cry, we'll be all right." I shook my head, who could I tell of the horror I witnessed? I wanted to yell at who let this happen, who was to blame. Deep in my heart I felt guilt and shame.

My children had witnessed to a serious crime. How many more would they see in a lifetime? These events could scar them, make them sad. I couldn't let that happen. Something had to be done and right away. No wasting time, I meant that day.

Now that's all behind us; that frightful time when my children
   witnessed that horrible crime.
They are glad I was there and saved them that day
   and in that same room they romp and play. And they
seem to have forgotten what they used to see. And I'm quite
content to have burned the TV.
   —*Emma Melinda McCullough*

Reach For the Stars

If you don't succeed, try again, Mama once told me
and I did, I jumped that rope until I got it right
Patience is a virtue, Mama once told me
So I waited a whole hour in the lunch line
Letting the other kids go before me
Beggars can't be choosers, Mama once told me
So I ate the vanilla ice cream even though I wanted the chocolate
Take time to stop and smell the roses, Mama once told me
and I did, on my way home from church last Sunday
Reach for the stars, Mama once told me
So I built a ladder as high as the clouds, but it broke
So I tried again day after day
Waiting to build it right
When I had no more good wood, I used the bad
When I had no more new shiny nails, I used the old
Soon my ladder stood strong and tall, but before I climbed it
I rested in the grass while the warm sun soaked into my skin
Last night I climbed it
To give my mother a kiss goodnight
   —*Anastacia D. Lepore*

You Are There

When many pressures cloud my daily life,
And I feel that no one's caring,
Just when I think there's no use going on—
A single ray of sun breaks through
Reminding me that I can lean on you.
Whatever happens one things stays true—
You are there.

When the night's too deep and dark for me,
I lie alone without sleeping.
When fear's cold fingers try grasp my heart—
My soul sends out a silent call
That reaches out beyond this body's wall,
The answer comes, the voice is strong yet small—
You are there.
   —*Flora J. Mentry*

How It Is

When the day is getting rough
And I feel I've had enough
I just go outside and look around.
All I need to do is look,
And it's there — just like a book
From the sky and right down to the ground.
Nature runs her realm just right,
Through the day and in the night—
Sun and moon and stars and wind and rain
Work together for the beauty and the worth
Of all the creatures of the gorgeous earth.
Altogether bringing growth and gain.
Down across the field is light,
Birds are singing; all is bright,
Happy is the pattern of the day.
Leaves are waving in the breeze,
Animals are in the trees
Now life is simply wonderful, I'd say!
How could I have felt another way?
—*Beulah Gill Braithwaite*

To All Parents Of Murdered Children

A missing child's found murdered,
and I know from where I sit,
that her family's descended
to the bottom of the pit
where once I fell —
to the darkness of hell.

And there is nothing I can do
except to send my heart to you
(a heart that's known that darkness, too)

and tell you that, in being lost,
I found some truth, 'tho rued the cost:

this truth is only that the Light
is holding onto your baby tight,
embracing her for all of you,
and at the same time,
  holds you, too.
—*Diane E. Ramey*

Magic Song

Beautiful music box song, you are
  altogether precious to me;
When I hear your cadence, I am
  again a child;
I skip through Marigolds in
  fields of Meadow Grass;
I feel the tinsel of parades; I see the
  spun glass figures of boats and planes;
I am on by-gone Merry-Go-Rounds; on
  Wooden Carousel Horses;
I throw my care kite of adult woes
  into the air
And let the wind lift its triangular
  body far, far from my sight.
—*Irene Cupido*

Be Still And Know That I Am God

"Be still and know that I am God;
  and I know the way that you have trod.
Just love me, trust me and obey,
  For I have great plans for you today."

"You have been within my care always,
  even though, so oft you went astray;
but I have you back within my fold,
  and you shall walk my streets of gold."

I am still and know that you are God,
  and you know the way that I have trod.
I do love you, trust you and obey;
  Lord, help me to do your will each day.

I'm so glad I'm in your care today,
  but so sad I ever went astray;
I am happy to be back in Your fold;
  and to know, I'll walk your streets of gold.

Lord, I want my loved ones there with me,
  to walk beside the "Crystal Sea;"
where joy and peace will ever flow,
  since you washed our sins as white as snow.
—*Eunice H. Hite*

The Empty Chair

I look at it, it is empty,
and I look back, but it's not;
I smile with it and feel silly,
Looks back at me with a nod.

I focus on it with silent cries,
It stares back and dries my eyes;
I am here, it softly sighs,
I will not leave, that'll suffice.

I drill and venture every day,
Pleasant memories have engraved their way;
I cuddle and secure them in a special way,
I store them safe, so they don't fade away.

I look back then from day to day
I reminisce a laughter that brings a tear;
These dear shadows cover every sphere,
They're wrapped with thread of gold-silver fare.

Yes! That chair is empty every day,
Yet from it, a radiant smile is directed my way;
And a pair of shy eyes glance at me and say,
Don't fret, I'll always be here, to occupy my chair.
—*Arpine O. Sanasarian-Hovasapian*

Waiting For The Dawn

The curtain of darkness will be descending soon
And I look out my window I can see the moon
If looks very lonely up there in the sky
But not half as lonely as you or I

Because we can't be where we want to be
Darling if you're dreaming I hope its about me
And now as I finally close my eyes
And hope for sleep to come
Its almost day break and soon will come the sun
It won't be long now before were cradled in loving embrace
Sharing our sweet love that nothing can replace
Even though the time passes swiftly when were together
We hope and pray one day we'll be together forever
—*Clara Harrison*

Who's To Blame

Once again another child has been slain
   And I wonder aloud, who's to blame?
Is it the parents, the government or me?
   Who's to blame? I can't say.

The shame of it all the children are so small
   A simple act of play can carry them away
Who's to blame? That it is that way?
   Nary a day goes by that some Mother does
Not cry oh Lord why, why, why?

My child is gone, and now I am all alone
   Once again I wonder who's to blame?
Their are children living in fear for
   The drug sellers are so near and I
Wonder who's to blame? Oh what a shame.

How much longer will it be before our
   Children can be free to once again be safe?
To never again have to run in haste to duck
   And dodge gunfire and be chased?
Who's to blame from whence the drugs came?
   Or is it us all for refusing to make that call?
     —Barbara K. Bynum

Lost

I feel so all alone,
And I would just like to find my way home.
but as I look around,
No where is it to be found.
One moment of rest,
So I can get out of this mess.
In a world that has gone mad.
I'm only another tender soul to be had.
God has forsaken humanity,
Leaving them to wander and rave in insanity.
Hope is no more.
All that's left is blood and gore.
Pity is no longer to be,
Instead, only monsters have glee.
Tragedy is our crowning feat,
To love and respect is to be beat.
What started as a dream,
Escapes our lips as a scream.
And a heaven on earth for most.
Unfortunately turned out to exist only for ghost.
An idea that would have been for our good,
Are like ashes after burnt wood.
Behold, this terrible cost, for now all mankind is lost.
     —Jacqueline E. Madison

The Pain Of Neglect!

My cousin passes away
And I'm not told!
The letters I wrote her are
Unanswered, months old!
Then her husband calls me and
says, "She's long gone!"
He tells me he is lonely
And he sounds forlorn!
No time could I find to visit Harry
And Yetta and give them a smile!
I'm treated like a stranger and I'm
heartsick all the while!
     —Herbert Miller

Autumn Reflections

The grass is bare upon the ground
   and in my certain corner,
   I sit with cat upon my lap,
   and yearn for winter's cover.

Northern creatures need a rest
   from summer's frenzied pace.
   The bulbs and bees and apple trees
   need snow, and time, and space.

Within our structured lives is found
   the need for calm reflection,
   and autumn's tang can bring to mind
   desire for white perfection.

When raindrops freeze upon the eaves, or snow drifts down
   with stealthy sound, in sparkling crystal prisms,
   we faint of heart are loath to start
   our slowed metabolisms.

Then, spring's a welcome fragrant breath,
   and birth's a new elation.
   Once more we join the vital force
   and end our hibernation.
     —Elizabeth Haynes McAnally

Experiencing God

In knowing God, I embrace my soul
And in this moment I am set free.

Inside my life I have felt so alone
Because love always eluded me.
Deep in the night I have felt so cold
Impatient to resolve life's mystery.
Searching myself, I have felt so lost
Running away from self discovery.

In asking God,
I have found a way to be led from behind shadows
In knowing God,
Faith dispels the grey, lighting the flame His wisdom bestows
In trusting God,
I find the strength to pray, casting out fears and sorrows
In loving God,
Hope defeats dismay
For He is the answer to all
That is unknown.
     —Janet Eskew

The Tangled Tree

Shaved sympathies have sucked me slowly, in savage streams,
and into such a state.
Courage and kindness, cuddling a contest, 'how crazy is
it really to hesitate?
A lettered lip, loved me once before in a lilac lane, where,
I fell and once was sore.
A God of gentle gifts gave me a name in shiny
nickels, and guarding me, was another grave, this of grated icicles.
....Sound swords, spare my skin.
While, wicked mountains wander here within...
Drooling dandelions can, definitely, dare my depth.
But, never break the bone I hold within my breath.
So, tempt me a tiger to trace a tangled tree.
The tiger fights fierce, yet, finely, it still bleeds.
And, I have a craving, rekindling my courage in a concept.
Found, far beneath the fences, where, fevers are far-fetched.
     —Cathleen Erickson

You'll Never Know

You'll never know me
And it's not anyone's fault.
For life's peculiar nature
Destines us to remain apart.
Not by great distances, but only short steps.
Two different life styles, and a world of regrets.

So you'll never know
Just how much I care.
And just how much I long
To share your joys, your sorrows,
Your todays, and your tomorrows.

So you'll never know
Because I can't be there
To stroke your face or hold your hand.
For all those endearments are forbidden to me.
Since you have a mistress of formidable size,
That prevents my approach for even one fleeting moment.

And I, timid and shy, will remain
FOREVER—a fan
  —*Grace Ann Bartolomeo*

When The Cottonwoods Are Green Again

Johnnie was called to defend his country,
And Johnnie was in love with Sue,
And Sue was in love with Johnnie,
And they vowed that they would be true.

Now there were three Big Cottonwood Trees,
Standing in a row,
The day was cold and blustery,
And their branches were covered with snow.

Johnnie was saying his last goodbyes,
And Johnnie said to Sue,
"When the cottonwoods are green again,
I will return to you."

But the fortunes of war are ever changing
And difficult to foretell,
And the day before the battle ended
Was the day that Johnnie fell.

Now the cottonwoods are green again,
And the summer sky is Blue,
And a gentle breeze moves through the trees
And keeps repeating, "Johnnie and Sue,
Johnnie and Sue, where are Johnnie and Sue?"
  —*Evelyn M. Wehrmeister*

Daydreaming

Turn back, oh time, roll back the years,
and let me fall in love again.
Just to live those precious moments
as I did away back when.

To have that special someone
To love day after day;
Something to fill my heart with joy,
As I finish my earthly stay.

A hand to hold when life gets weary,
A smile to warm a lonely heart.
Someone to be close beside me
Whose life I feel I am a part.

Only dreams of days gone forever.
For never again such times as these,
Tied with a ribbon and locked away safely,
They're in my chest of memories.
  —*Inez Spradling Grouf*

Never To Be More

Come nestle in my arms, my love
  And let us dream awhile
Forgetting worldly cares and thoughts
  On this our private isle

Come let us life a life time
  In a few secluded hours
Drifting quietly o'er oceans
  Under skies that's only ours

Let us lie on sandy beaches
  When the moon is sinking low
And dream the dream of lovers
  As the moonbeams softly glow

Let our love roar like the ocean
  As it breaks upon the shore
For this may be our lifetime
  Never, to be more.
  —*Cecil Harrison*

In Search Of Faith

I stand on the ground between the Light and the Dark
  And listen for the sound of the Truth.
I look down into the depths of the earth
  And see the fires that beckon to all,
Whispering promises of a comfort
  That is actually too hot to bear.
I look up into the reaches of the sky
  And see the colors that should be strived for,
Calling out to me with a voice so strong
  That tells me no burden need be carried alone.
I fear the Dark and the fire
  And the devils that wait unseen;
But I know I am not worthy
  Of the Light and the angels it holds.
There are many who hear the voices
  And have faith in the words that they hear.
I stand on the ground between the Light and the Dark
  And listen for the sound of the Truth.
  —*Jerry L. McClure*

The Musician

She played each key with deliberate ease
and listened to the melody that floated to her ears.
As each note was struck,
a chord seemed plucked within her soul,
and I wondered how she could create
the notes that touched the soul
and bring them to life with deft fingers.
Each sound that arose
was like a beckoning voice
urging those going by to listen.
So I stood on the corner
as she weaved a spell
with the clarinet held lovingly in her hands.
The mellow tones washed over me
creating images in my mind
of the notes dancing merrily around her.
And as the song ended,
I watched the glow around her fade
until the beginning of another song filled the air.
  —*Eleanor Calasara Tinio*

My Love

I climbed a beautiful mountain
And looked down at a raging sea
Then I looked toward heaven and cried aloud
"Why did you take my love from me"

From out of a sudden silence
Came a voice from heaven above
"Please do not grieve my child
For I too gave up someone I love"

"He was young, obedient and pure of heart
Yet was crucified on a tree
He suffered and shed his blood for all
So that by Faith they could be free

"The one you love is now an Angel
Freed forever from pain and strife
He has received by Faith, my Gift of Grace
The gift of Eternal Life"

As I slowly climbed down the mountain
The sea again began to roar
And the air was filled with the songs of birds
And I knew that I would grieve no more

—*Jean Bell G. Chinchillo*

My April

She was like my child from the beginning
and love abound without ending.

As I watched her grow through the years
alone came many tears.

Broken jaw and hospital stays
that quickly went away.

Cute as a button in her ballet ruffles
then came jazz with all that razz.

Eyes dark as the night but
oh how they shine so bright.

A smile so warm and friendly that
can conquer any enemy.

Laughter so light and free
and I pray it will always be.

May all her dreams come to pass
and she finds a love that last.

She is the daughter I will never have
but I'm so glad she is my child.

—*Jean Osborne*

Homecoming At Christchurch

A dove cries in the distance,
And my heart kneels
Here beside your resting place.
Sunshine steals the shadows,
And I can feel
Glory on your face.

   Sadness touches like a kiss,
   And memories mist through this lonely space;
   Finally, I must turn away,
   But my heart lingers
   Forever here
   In silent listening grace.

—*Jenna V. Ownbey*

Silk Purse State Of The 'Art'

'Infinity' counters our predestined demise,
And 'Metaphysical' defuses terrestrial ties.
'Light-year' increments the immeasurable skies,
And 'Paradox' lays benchmark to the affluently wise.

While 'Technology' races with time, as it flies,
'Humanity' calls cadence with desperate cries,
As 'Destitution' entrances indigent eyes,
And 'Sentiment' endures what assessment denies.

'Specialist' ornates the physicians disguise,
And 'Corporate' upgrades the barristers prize.
'Expendable' motivates labor to rise,
As 'Compassion' endorses what justice implies.

'Explicit' heralds pornographic emprise,
While 'permissive' allays what discretion decries.
'Pollution' evades ecological pries,
As 'Self-evident' now demands compromise.

'Sumaritans' earn synthetic applaud.
'Sacrifice' stands vigil on our blooded sod.
And if 'Posterity' fails as an adequate prod,
Our 'Complacence' shall summon the wrath of 'God'!

—*Glen Wagner*

A Brand New Creature

Jesus, I want to lift up my body to You, so You can shape it
and mold it, and make it brand new. Lord, may I give You just
one piece at a time, so You can wash it and clean it, and make
it shine. After I've given You each section of me, and you

hand them back for me to see. I can't wait Lord to learn how
to use each part, to worship and praise You with a brand new
start. The first thing I'll do is give You my head, when You

are done, it will contain all that You've said. Then I can
give You one eye at a time, so I'm able to see You, Take my
ears Lord, and clean them out, so I can hear Your voice

clearly. My nose is stuffed up, I need You to clear it, so I
can smell the sweet fragrance of the Holy Spirit. Lord, please
make my lips, and my mouth extra clean, My tongue can sure a
scrubbing from You, then I'd be able to speak the words that
You do. Here You are Jesus, my arms I can give to stretch out
in praise. My hands, they do need Your touch, so I can write
and proclaim that I love You so much. My legs and feet need
a lot of Your care, to walk straight to our neighbors with
Salvation to share. Oh! No! Lord, the last thing to clean is
the biggest part, my old wicked ways that lie in my heart.

—*Deborah R. Spine*

I Thank Thee Lord

I thank thee Lord for another day.
And my love ones near and far away.
For each blessing I receive from thee,
My health, my home, my family.
The clothes I wear,
The food I eat,
The words I say or hear,
The things I see and do.

I thank thee Lord for Godly parents,
Who truly loved, worshiped and served thee,
And taught me to love, worship and serve thee too.

Lord, most of all, I thank thee for thy love, mercy and grace.
And ye taught me to love instead of hate.

—*Helen Miller*

Inside Me Hides My Sweet Inner Child

Inside me hides my sweet inner child,
And no one can tell she's sad and mild.

For she was hurt when she was only nine,
And it lasted for a very long time.

She went into hiding and hung her head in shame,
And no one could even remember her name.

Her innocence was robbed late one night,
But she was very brave in this horrible fight.

Her tears and cries have been hidden by masks,
With my adult smile doing this difficult task.

Please don't be sad as there's plenty of hope,
For she's learning new ways in life to cope.

She's getting one day at a time,
And she must remember she survived the crime.

Her anger, guilt and shame will die,
As she is given permission each day to cry.

She grows stronger and stronger every day,
And I try to help her in every way.

I'm here to hug her and hold her and kiss her and such,
Because I want her to know that I love her very much.
—*Debra S. Kaminski*

Invisible Tears

A tear fell last night,
And no one saw it;
You may wonder why,
And say to yourself; but, you do see tears.

Well, a tear fell last night,
In someone's heart;
They lost a loved one or a friend,
The pain was private and silent.

A tear fell last night,
From an animal's eyes;
Lost and deserted no one cared,
No one saw or heard the wild lonely animal.

A tear fell last night,
When someone put their feelings on paper;
When your reading something special,
Or listening to a special song.

So, you see a tear fell last night,
And you didn't see or hear it;
There are those that you do see,
And the silent invisible tears that you don't see.
—*Elsa L. Chase*

Seamen's Ship Ahoy

Furry's tale of a fatal tide's undertow with increasing force
And rough winds entrapping seamen beneath as bellowings blow.
Seamen's ship ahoy faces escape in aftermath of great remorse,
As rising sea surf robs their identity and thoughts alone show.

Storm's enraging magnitude cries the sea birds inner marrow,
While sponges absorb diverse sounds the reef crevices sleep.
Entomb surrounding each passage becomes increasingly narrow,
Men like vagabonds, swallowing sea water their lungs now seep.

With the sinking sand each story tells of seamen sail no more,
A gift of gab diverting it's course only in silence will speak.
Now bodies entrenched memories claimed among the ocean's floor,
Immortality takes on wings for each fatality someone will weep.
—*Doris Natalie Yinger*

Carry Me Back To The Valley

In fond memories I recall the old home place
And of my childhood days away back then
In my mind I see our family all together
In that home in the valley once again

In the evening we would sit on the back porch
And listen to the whippoorwills sing
And gaze at the stars far above us
And hear the lonesome whistle of the train

Oh how I'd love to relive those moments
That we shared with each other back then
As we roamed o'er the fields and the meadows
And fished in the creek around the bend

Oh carry me back to the valley
Let me travel down that road once again
That leads down the hill to the home place
Where we lived and played way back then
—*Betty Breedlove*

I Wrote The Song

When I was born with promises, of futures all galore.
And promises of greatness, and a whole lot more.
I chose a path which led me, not knowing what's in store,
That took me down a road, I'd never been before.
Because of this it came to be, fame and fortune eluded me.
The promises of fame were lost, and promises of fame were tossed.
There was nothing left for me, for life is only once you see.
When I realized that time was fleeting, and that there was, no repeating.
It was too late for me, no time left for succeeding.
I wished I could have made it, But I wrote the song and played it.
I only hope some day, that all of you will see, and grasp the opportunity.
Be wise and seek your destiny, and go on to complete it.
For that's how it ought to be, God knows we need it.
So I say in sympathy, to all of you yet to be.
Take heed in what I say today, Don't play the song, my way.
—*Carmen Bozzone Michels*

Contemplation

How small I feel when 'ere I look around
And see the towering trees with roots so deep within the ground
It dawns on me how very little is the ripple I will make
Compared to the splash the reentry an astronaut will take.
I am but a mere dot over a tiny "i"
Under the vastness of the never ending sky.
And yet, there must have been some wonderful plan
For God to have created each insignificant man.
Even a tiny ant contributes in his small way
During the short time on earth that he may stay.
I ask myself, "Have I wasted all the years I've been around
In my search for things beyond my reach,
Have I passed by treasures on the ground,
Has the gift of love and understanding, which each of us
possess, been sadly neglected by selfishness and my unrest?"
"At the end of life's journey will it all have been a waste
because in my rush for glory, I trampled others in my haste"?
"Is there still time I wonder, to change so that I too may see—
the beauty and strength of character to be found in a towering tree?"
—*Gladys F. Stone*

Lover's Image

If you could look into my eyes
and see what's on my mind,
'tis images and thoughts of you,
that you would surely find.

Of bedroom eyes, smooth silken thighs;
and the fragrance of perfume.
Of sweet soft lips, round sensuous hips;
and a dimly lighted room.
Of sultry breasts, gently caressed,
till passion burns like fire.
Of stifled cries and ardent sighs;
and the moist warmth of desire.

But far, far more, you'd also see;
than mere bodies intertwined.
You'd also see two lovers joined-
at heart, in soul, and mind.
—*John C. Krebs*

Alone In The City

You flee remembered places
   And seek oblivion
Amid anew sights and scenes
And strange and unfamiliar faces.

Then, one day you hear the sound
   of birdsong
Through the weeping of the wind
   among the trees,
You walk a magic mile and see
Someone has hung a star, and at the Center
   lit a giant tree.

A young girl pausing in the snowy fog
   To give from mink pocket
Change to the blind man
Standing on the sidewalk with his dog.

Amidst the clamor of Broadway stands Cohen,
   And further, Gandhi strides in bronze —
A sight familiar from a world afar —
Staff in hand he walks determined for Calcutta.

While browsing, you chance upon a room
   Reminiscent of a lost Isfahan.
Tiffany windows gleam; Impressionists smoulder
   and flare -
Moments yours alone, but that a world may share.
—*Dorothy Ludowyk Joseph*

In Awe

He took His brush this evening
And splashed across the sky
A fiery burning sunset
As the night drew night.

There was crimson, gold and yellow
And a plum color too.
It was radiant and colorful
He used most every hue.

The sun slipped below the sky line
The colors grew so bright
The sunset lingered on
As the sun gave up to night.

Then a burnt orange glow caressed the sky
The sunset slowly faded
As I watched I knew my Lord's as near
As the splendor He created.
—*Anne Terrebonne*

Color It The Ugly American

Once, we were a nation filled with pride
And seldom had dealings to hide.
We took the time to help each other
Considering a neighbor as a brother.

Slowly morality began to sway;
Truth and honor fell to decay.
Marriage vows ebbed and wandered
And the family crumbled and floundered.

Corruption flirted with city and town
While politicians shed moral gown.
The going surely got pretty tough
When plenty still wasn't enough!

Our leaders seemed to fill with greed
As "me-first" became their creed.
They appear to govern without aim
Clothed in a mantle of utter shame.

Paroled murderers roam our streets
And boastful criminals laud their feats!
Plentiful drugs tempt, befoul and kill—
All this has made our nation ill.

Shout, people, in righteous indignation!
Rise against this sad proliferation.
We must recapture our unsullied name
Thus erasing the ugly American blame.
—*Edna Van Dyke Loughney*

The First Christmas

Night when glorious star shown down
And shepherds quaked upon the ground,
Hearing angels loud proclaim
The birth of Christ-announce His name;
God of majesty and power,
Born to earth this very hour.
Babe so helpless, wee but hale-
Born to blaze a sinless trail!
Yes, His sinless life here trod-
Son of Man and Son of God!
Born to rescue man from sin,
Let Redeeming Love shine in.
Brought us hope and peace and grace:
Made in Heaven for us a place!
—*Gladys Grant*

Optics

I would be your mirror
And show what silvered glass
Cannot reflect.
See... yourself.
You love the chaste beauty of truth,
Not in hope of gilded heaven
But because you hate filthy lice lies.
You are compassionate
But not that you may escape damnation;
You understand that human lives
Are equations
That sometimes equal zero.
You know you are the sanctuary
of Earth's skills,
The master work of the great designer.
Only integrity may be your door keeper,
Only the choicest may enter and abide.
See... this is your image.
—*Annie Ruth Waldsmith*

The Tears Of A Cloud

There are days we can look and see the clouds all and puffy
   and soft
Quietly floating about in the sky
Did you ever wonder what is their purpose
Because some days we see them happy
and some days we see them cry

You see when a cloud cries we can see his pain
Because when a cloud cries God makes the rain
We can feel their tears as they fall down on us
But they too can bring healing-they end the dust

There were tears in the eyes of the clouds tonight
They fell on the earth and we called it rain
But I can't help but wonder- are the clouds unhappy
Maybe they are crying for us
Do they cry because they see someone in pain

Now I hope you remember the next time it rains
And you see the tears of the clouds
the thunder and lightning shows you their crying out loud
And when you hear the pitter patter of the rain
They are crying quietly because they too can be proud
And me in my mind I like to believe
that somewhere and in this very way
God tells the clouds I need you to cry today
Because I want them to know I understand I share their pain
   —*Carolyn Sue Pritchet*

Jesus Has A Place For Mom

God had let me know that time was short.
And soon Mom would be accepted into the eternal supreme court.
It seemed like my whole world stopped when the doctor said she
Didn't have much time left, back in June.
But I never thought that the end would come so soon.
I never realized how empty you feel when you lose your best friend.
I never thought that the good times would ever end.
It was so heartbreaking to see Mom so helpless in bed.
Then to think it was just days before their 43rd Anniversary
   of the day she was wed.
She wanted to tell me something so I bent down and she kissed
   my cheek and told me "I Love You."
As tears welled up in my eyes I never thought anyone could feel
   so blue.
I could feel it when Mom was carried off on angels wings.
And was about to be presented to our Savior, The Almighty King
   of kings.
Now that she's in heaven with God, Jesus, Mary and all the
   saints on this day.
Already I miss her so much, I want to be with her, this I will pray!
She doesn't have to worry any more, she's peaceful, happy and calm.
I can imagine Jesus opening up His arms and smiling, now
   that He has a place for Mom!
   —*Alan B. Campione*

Judgment Day

When you get what you want in your struggle for self
And the world makes you king for the day.
Just go to the mirror and look at yourself;
And see what that one has to say.

For it isn't your father, or
mother, or wife;
Whose judgment upon you must pass.
The fellow whose verdict
Counts most in your life;
Is the one staring back
through the glass.
   —*Juli M. Lowrey*

Solstice

As Capricornus horned the sun
and stayed it on its wintry round,
so I stood still, bid Halcyon,
whose mystic magic powers bound
the chafing wind and chilling sea
into a tranquil nesting place,
wrap her enchanted wings 'round me,
becalm this tropic tempest, raise
a spell of warmth. Then spoke forthwith
they tyrant of my soul: 'Tis myth.
Yet now when frost-weeds crystal through
the wall of ice that crusts my mind
and forms the framework of my view,
that self-same coldness like a kind
companion comforts—all I know
of intimacy that its loss
would leave me frozen out and so
displaced, I dare not dare to cross
the threshold of that frigid door
for fear it leads to nothing more.
   —*D. P. Campion*

My Solume Prayer

Dear God above please hear me
And take away the pain
That has me so aroused
Only emptiness remain
Inside the scars are very deep
My heart burst into flames
And kindle all my inner thoughts
Interfering with my sleep

I press my way to work each day
Whenever alone I stop to pray
Oh Lord, I need your help this day
To take away my pain
And when the day is over
I head straight home and then,
I lock my thoughts inside of me
And thrive on TV to win
The victory over the needs I have
For this unfaithful friend
Has quickly made me realize
I shall be whole again
   —*Cathy Jones Easterling*

European Vacation

The gray clouds of Northern Europe hide the sun,
And the rains of autumn cleanse the Earth.
Once, where battles beat the ground,
Men died so farms and tourists won.

Where once the tank and gas cloud rolled,
Men suffered and went mad.
Today the cars and trains uphold
Our way of life and fad.

The summer sun brings piercing light
To bear on you and me.
The land is rich with fallow crop
For those across the sea.

Armies lurk behind the trees,
And missiles hide in lees.
Planes fly high up in the sky
Where light ignored their pleas.
   —*Gerald A. Somers*

The Night Sky

At twilight the breeze has wafted
   and the air is still and calm.
The birds are singing their evening song
   and whistling with gay aplomb.
Little brown rabbits hop toward their burrows
   to snuggle together and sleep until tomorrow.
The clouds are disappearing out over the hills
   and the sun is setting with colors that thrill.
Yellows and pinks with rosy red hues
   combine with various shades of blue.
Slowly and surely the darkness descends
   then the sky starts to sparkle from end to end.
The big dipper is up there as bright as day.
   How exciting to see the Milky Way!
The Seven Sisters are glistening and bright
   as they show off their beauty in the Autumn night.
The Northern Cross is radiant above
   and it reminds us of the One we love.
As an exploding star shoots across the sky
   we feel fortunate to have seen it streaking by.
How wonderful to see the various sights
   that come alive in the dark of the Arizona night.
     —*Jean N. Parsons*

A Country Morning

When you wake-up in the morning
And the "dawning" is very near
Do you get that special feeling
That the 'World's Awakening' you hear.

You can almost feel the trees stretch
   their limbs and sigh
And watch the grass and flowers shake the dew
That's when somehow you just know
God made this world for you.

The chirping little birds
And the flowers opening wide
The drew drops on the window sill
Are places the sun rays hide.

Then you see the winding lane
With the meadow full of hay
The breeze that rustles all the leaves
And you know it's a wonderful day.

You do not hear the honking horns
Or the sirens on the road
You may just heart "Little Tinker Bell"
Or the Prince that was a Toad.

That's why I like this "Country Outing"
On the city's busy street
For each and every morning
My day is made complete.
     —*Jenny Clark*

Youth

You're like the wild wind before a storm
and the restless breezes as it stirs
among the trees.

You're like the sun, the moon and the stars,
so beautiful and yet untamed you're like the
strength of a Lion And As Fleet As A Young
buck running before the hunter. The smile of an angel
and the innocence of a young child clothe you.
You are the universe wanting to expand beyond
new horizons. Stand still young one and grow into
the beautiful young man God intended you to be.
     —*Grace Higdon*

Sea Serenity

The vastness of the infinity of the ocean,
And, the great eternal sky from where God's ocean feeds,
Meet, and seem to touch in the background almost as one.

Gazing the sea, only a few leaping fish I see,
And, beautiful birds that like the shore and humid air—
Such wondrous view, on earth of salty sand, where I be!

Rippling waters of the surf are swashing up to me,
Little waves that hum a tune and roar louder with glee—
A kind of entertaining sound, coming from the sea.

Waving water's nearing and is reaching for my hand.
And, shells are washing onto the beach from ocean's strength.
There is moss grass from the sea floor, landing on the sand.

A bitter taste have I, the surf splashing mouth by chance,
Of strong briny water meant for creatures there who live.
A sip of sea—salty, sandy—I experience!

God's air has a fresh scent, like no other where on earth,
A special purity from just the sky and water —
Sea type of atmosphere, so valuable the worth.
     —*Judith A. Obuch*

Thanksgiving Day Awakening

My mind recalled the wistful look, the uncertain glance
And the need of love that showed so clearly there,
When a cold wrinkled hand reached out to touch;
That his heart might decide, does this person really care?

To search out my motive for coming, as he-
Had nothing to give, and what could I possibly gain;
By placing my warm coat 'round his shoulders
That his frail body might be sheltered from the rain?

Walking the river path that day, feeling the rain on my face
Wondering why things had not gone as I planned;
I was reminded of the abundance God had trusted me with,
As I warmed that small wrinkled hand

What had this poor soul to be thankful for?
No earthly possessions, not a roof, not a coat nor a bed,
With guilt I recalled the warm blankets, the fluffy white quilt
And the soft feather pillow where I nestled my head.

Yet it was I who had murmured and grumbled, but now-
The sweet smile on his face caused me to understand
And the reality of Thanksgiving flooded my soul,
As I clung to that dear wrinkled hand.
     —*Eleanor M. Carpenter*

Imagine That...

Imagine that everyone loves each other
and the world is filled with peace
Imagine that all of the wars have stopped
and there are no boundaries
Imagine that hate no longer has meaning
and fights have come to an end
Imagine that any place you go
you can always find a friend
Imagine that people really care
and the smile they wear is true
Imagine that people appreciate
all the little things you do
Imagine that life on earth
is all peaches 'n cream
Imagine that all I have said
for now, is only a dream
     —*Jennifer Davis*

Untitled

The pen has an unequalled power,
   and the paper has passion of such.
One of which words transcribe,
   to view, to feel, too much.

The pen of power, a realist though,
   to paper transforms such stuff.
One guided by mind to hand,
   Thoughts, mere words, enough.

Mythical passion plays through the pen,
   As clouds in endless sky.
Cover to cover of our lives,
   Poetic pens will ask us why?

On paper like the ground we stand,
   firm in our belief.
Transformation, thought and soul,
   Love, loneliness, and grief,

Pen to paper, unmasks our heart,
   commutes the vital thought.
Expressions of our dreams,
   and time that can't be bought.
     —Donald G. Layman Jr.

My Little Girl is Growing Up

One day God sent a little girl to her Mommy and Daddy
   and they decided to call her Tammy.
It seems like only yesterday to your Mommy that you were
   so very, very small.
She fed and nursed and diapered you and wiped away your tears.
She cradled you in her arms and kissed those little pink fists
   and watched those little bright eyes until you fell fast asleep
She salved your hurts and cuddled you and kissed your skinned
   up nose and would hold on to you when you stumbled and bandage
   those stubbed up toes.
Just today she packed your lunch and watched you get on the
   school bus.
Standing there reminiscing to herself and thought how far away
   you were going from her.
She prayed to God to keep you safe because you are so small
and all alone and with all the memories both sweet and sad
   she wipes away a tear.
My little girl is growing up.
Gosh!
She's in the first grade this year.
   —Joan Akers

Untitled

   I thought my poems had to rhyme
      and they didn't
I thought my paintings should look like something real
      and they didn't
     I thought God was a man
        and it wasn't
      Standing among the stalactites
       of my confessions of a deeper mind
   I hear a mesmerizing drip, drip, drip.....
I realize how easy it would be to lie down in this cave
   and wait for him to come and pick me up in his arms
      and take me home.
     I thought I had to wait
      and I didn't.
   —Camille Bird

We Thank God For America

We thank God for America
And this land that is free
A place to live, work and worship God as you please
And raise your family
I am proud to be a part of the greatest nation
This world has ever known
And I will fight, to keep this my home

When I look at our flag flying free
I give thanks for this nation
And this country that is free
The most democratic nation
This world will ever see
It is founded on a constitution, and a bill of rights
That give liberty, justice and equal rights to all

We give a helping hand, when ever there is need
And count our blessings, that we are not in need
We never plan to receive anything back
As we cast our bread upon the waters
Our blessings will be great
We thank God for America
   —Edgar H. Kleckley

Threads For Life

Life is sewn from a bobbin called time
And though it seems to change its pace,
   it has a content chime.

If your wish in life is to fulfill your dreams;
There are four threads with which to weave
   your patterns and their seams.

First, there's truth that's true wherever it is found;
Measure your stitch by its strong embrace
   and be guided by its renown.

Then there's the bright and flashy thread of love
That will bind and tug your full emotion
   like a hawk or better as a dove.

Thirdly there's the tread of faith; believing more than eye can see.
Bringing the facts to your loom of life
   that there's more than you and me.

Then lastly there's the thread of hope
   that looks beyond today
With its final touch for your tapestry
   of strength to find your way.
   —Don Nason

My Vow

Today is the beginning of our life together
and through God's will it will last forever.
I give my life to you to guard and take case of,
but most of all, I give you all my love.

I'll stand my ground in defending you,
and beyond a shadow of a doubt, I'll die for you.
I love you with my heart and my every drop of soul.
As long as I'm alive, I'll never let you go.

I've stood by you from the start through the laughter and tears
and I'll stand by your side through all the golden years.
I love you so much that words cannot express
my feelings of love and of happiness.

I'll be there until the end no matter what you do.
And through thick and thin, I'll always stand by you.
Today is the beginning of the rest of my life
for today is the day I'll become your wife.
   —Alisha Pickering

The Most Precious Gift-The Word Of God

I give to you the word of God...May you read it through
and through...May it comfort you in sorrow...May it lift
your spirit too...May it help to lighten your burden...
And when your cross is hard to bear...May you lift your
eyes unto the hills...And pray a fervent prayer...May it
bring to you contentment...As you live your life anew...
Seek God first and other things will be added unto you
...May you feel His presence daily...Every morning, noon
and night...May He give you strength and courage...To
always do the right...May your home be nice and cozy...
May God reign forever there...And if it be the Father's
will...May He answer every prayer...May you read the
Holy Bible...May you worship God above...May He comfort
you and keep you...In the shelter of His love.

—*Florence E. Allen*

Seen And Unseen

His presence had brought light to the darkened store
And to her life as they cleared not the dust from the displays,
But the leavings of the customers
Who had taken everything live with them,
Willing the remnants to those seeking life.
Mornings had been smoother because of the light
Covering left on each of the items
By those who unconsciously deposited themselves
After desire lacked the fruition of purchase.
There was no afternoon because people
Preferred to look at the cliquefaction
Unsullied by the corporal presence
Of those required to preserve the
Infinity of each creation.
Eternity to her was embodied in
The strong arm which moved effortlessly next to hers.
It gave action to the strength of the voice
Which paralleled that of the physique.
She prayed not for the perfect sale of sales
But for the everlasting life of lives.

—*Frank A. Langer*

A Patch Of Green

When native pasture turns to brown
  and trees they lose their shade,
I have to pause and thank my God
  for all that He has made.

Especially for a patch of green
  on a cold and wintry day,
That gives us just a little hint
  of what's in store for May.

The old oak trees have watched it all
  for nigh a cen-tur-y;
They know Texas bluebells in the spring
  are quite a sight to see.

When my time on earth is over
  and they lay me down to rest;
May it be beneath an oak tree
  in the pasture I love best.

—*Dee Dunnam*

A Boy And Spring

Tulip and daffodil soon will be seen.
And trees will have buds once again.
The robin will chirp his song,
And spring will be here again.

The woodlands will put on new beauty
After a winter of ice and snow.
And the beauty, that only spring has,
Will start young hearts to wonder and glow.

A boy and his dog will walk down country lanes
And school, will be far from his mind
For he can learn more in the great out of doors,
Than in all of the books he can find.

But youth has only so many springs,
And they pass so swiftly by
And it don't take many of them to pass
Until he's a man, like you and I.

So let him wonder down spring's lovely path,
And see all of life's beauty, he can.
So his life will be full of the beauty, and love,
That he, in his boyhood found.

—*Dorothy Abshagen*

The Tomb

I laid in the tomb where Jesus laid the day they crucified him
and tried to imagine what it was like as he saved our souls from sin.
It was lonesome and cold inside the tomb the three days his body
laid there, but now there's a holy feeling without darkness or despair.
The Roman soldiers stood in fear as they realized
what they had done and pulled their cloaks tight
around them as thunder rolled and God hide the sun.
Woe to the man who deceived Jesus with a kiss upon his face.
Judas played his part well in the prophesy that left him in disgrace.
An angel of the Lord rolled back the stone
  and was found sitting there.
The women who came to anoint Jesus were filled with fear
  and ran in despair.
Now they are as one in heaven, Father, Son & Holy Ghost.
This is Jesus, who saved us from our sins,
  the one we hurt the most.
Jesus spirit lingers on, as a guide to show us the way.
Just follow his footsteps through the land where he preached
  and stopped to pray.
He is the rock on which I stand, O Blessed Easter Day.

—*Eris M. Baker*

Joan Eileen

When I think of you and the love
and warmth of the charm you bear —
a new promise of time and life
awaken in my soul.

Lovely and fresh to the day
your eyes of hazel expression
evoke a feeling of freedom
to change a day from boredom to seeking.

Seeking roses and love —
Devotion and thought —
Right ways to make
something from nothing
Joan Eileen — true to be
something to herself and
something to me.

—*Corinne Collins*

Someone You Can Love For Me

I think I'll dial that number again
And try to become 1-800-thin.
This time my body will behave.
I'll ignore the ravenous rage

That grows inside me when I'm not satisfied.
Never mind how many times I've tried.
The pounds will melt. They will go away.
Then I will have a body to match my pretty face.

The price is never too high, you see,
If I can make you love me for me.
When I look in the mirror I'm afraid you'll see
Something else that is wrong with me.

I've thought about being strong and asserting myself,
But when I look in the mirror I'd see no one else.
My reflection cannot keep me warm.
Or embrace me in its loving arms.

I've said it before and I'll say it again.
No pain is too great if you will be my friend.
So I'll keep hurting myself until you see
Someone that you can love for me.
—*Jennifer L. Thompson*

Mandi E.

Mandi, Mandi you're so divine, you're so very sweet
and very, very kind; your smile refreshes me like the
early morning sunshine.
Whenever I see your smile or your presence in my face it
makes me have joy in my heart and a smile and a tear come on
my face, and makes me say, "Oh how you're the most beautiful
of your female race."
Cause Mandi, your presence radiates any place like the
luminaries of the day and night that's why I always take
exquisite delight in you whenever I'm in your presence because
your effervescent charm makes me want to express my likeness
for you, how so true.

And your voice is so melodious to me that it sounds like
a sweet lullaby being sung to me. As I say to thee oh
Mandi E, you are the girl for me… Oh ma cheri.
—*Cleveland Adams*

Gardens

I paused to look at the garden gate
And viewed with awe the pale blue slate
Guarded by her sentinels tall
Stood the nymph of the water-fall.
The Ghost Tree stands besides the lane
Leading to beauty that is never vain.
Boxwood hedged, clipped and neat
Invites a rest on the low placed seat.
Behold a vista of a garden sight
That bathes the soul with sheer delight.
The broad leafed Maple beckons you
While shyly nodding to the Irish Yew.
Strong and bold against the sky
Stand Atlanta Cedars to thrill the eye.
Over the hedge and through the arch
We hear the song of the meadowlark.
Pools of vibrant Heaven's blue
Reflect the Birch's silvery hue.
Glancing to the blue above
I know it's gardens I'll always love.
—*Gladys Shearer*

I Would

I would climb the highest mountain
And walk the fields in bloom,
Take time to stop and smell the roses
As time passes by much too soon.

I would reach for the stars
Twinkling high above in the sky,
Oh, I would do so many things
That I have now let pass me by.

I would take one step at a time
So very slowly in order to see,
All the beauty and wonderment
That God gave to you and to me.

I would take one day at a time
To learn to achieve and understand,
The problems that surround us all
We, all of the people of the land.

I would not stop to ask how or why
Nor would I turn back the pages of time,
I would only bow down my head
And thank God for the blessings that are mine.
—*Dorothy A. St. Louis*

Spring Comes

My eyes look at the dying night
  and watch the morn be roused;
I know this day will fleet to dusk
  and all too soon obscure,
But as last winter hours null
  to the ecstasy of spring,
I'll once again be sweet-seduced
  by my seasonal paramour.

Listen, winter, — enough of you!
  just blow yourself away.
You cooled and chilled and chafed and cut
  and left me but a cringing thrall.
Now, - spring will quickly spirit me
  and apterously I'll float
And thaw to life and stand alert
  and shed this hoary pall.
—*Josephine Salerno*

Why?

Their eyes were huge in tiny faces
  And we could see the shoddy places
Where they lived in misery. We asked
  Ourselves "Why should this be? The
World is small and we are one. It's 1993!"

The world responded - hands outstretched
  To send the help they needed. But other
People, not so kind, had many selfish things
  In mind and their cries went unheeded.

Then others came from many lands to open
  Up the door. It was no easy task; they
Tried and many of them fought and died
  To get the precious store.

Where is the justice, where the peace?
  These children should not cry.
To solve this ageless puzzle then, and
  Build an ideal world for men - so
Many have to die!

And so it is through all the years we're
  Always asking "Why?"
—*Helen M. Brenon*

Great Ideas

In books and magazines we've read,
And we have often heard it said
That great ideas must "trickle down"
From persons of power and renown,
Reaching downward gradually,
To everyday folks like you and me.
But, great ideas, perchance, may rise
From intellects of any size;
At a slow and steady rate,
Upwardly they percolate.

Ideas that speak of Education,
Of Health and Wealth and rising Taxation,
Of Civil Rights and Integration,
Of War and Peace and Immigration;
Ideas that speak of our relations
With Leaders and Workers of other nations —
As such ideas move up and down,
Through every city and every town,
Their "Pros-and-Cons" may help us to see
New ways of defining Democracy.
—*Dorothy S. Handler*

The Silver Thread

A silver thread came shining thru the blue,
And when it touched earth, behold, a bird was there
  To bring joy without measure.
"Good morning" he would chirp, "let's start our day,
Soon as you're ready, I'm waiting,
To get our routine on the way!"
During the day he would sing away while I did my work,
And then he would say, "How about me?"
So we had our little evening chat, and then time for bed.
As it is said, "All good things come to an end",
The silver thread was broken and I lost my little friend.
—*Ann Mahalko*

The Poet's Wish

    A poet lies awake at night
    And wonders if he'll ever
  Be understood for all the things
    He probably should have never
      Written with a pen in hand
      For all the world to see.
    And wonders if he'll ever manage
    His thoughts, inside, to free.
  For the easiest thing a poet knows
      Is what he wants to say.
  But the hardest thing for him to do
      Is find that special way
  To make the reader feel the pain,
    The joy, the thrill, the rush;
  The raging screams of thoughts within;
    And the gentleness of the hush
Which finally comes when the words are found,
    And are allowed to be get free.
Yes, the poet's wish is the grandest of all,
    It's "To give others part of me!"
—*John M. McBryde*

Untitled

Unaccustomed to the way,
And words of meaning soon betray us.
Dangling, as our participles
Precede the principles of trust.
Disciplining to and fro,
We cast aside both friend and foe;
To learn enough, when once one taught,
A poignant lesson, begrudgingly sought.
Irony has had its jest,
And karma's sting hath maimed its best;
To thwart an unencumbering nymph
From the parasitical lifestyle it had known.
Oh, spare this interim of inanity!
My eyes do blind me, yet still I see.
This broken face feels envy not, But only misbegotten lot.
Twas' never a fortune to blithely possess,
Our journeys compel us towards paramounts of hope.
To cherish the more, and grieve the less; We find ourselves within
each other, and yet inadvertently scuff the soul of us,
Atop the hardened surface of indignant love.
—*Heidi Ann Lehan*

Prejudice

Prejudice is a thing that has been around to long
and yet somehow it is still going strong
it has got to stop and we all know it
brotherly love is one way we can show it
does color of skin or difference in speech.
Make one any better then those that we meet
we did not choose what we would be
God made that choice for you and me
there is good and bad in every race
look in the heart not the color on the face.
We must learn to live by mistakes that were made
and make our world a better place
for each and all of every race
there was a beginning and there will be an end
lets make a difference in the old, old trend.
—*JoAnna G. Gardner*

Drug Abuse

I've often thought about what drugs do to your mind
And yet there're so many, all of a different kind
A lot of people don't think about the drugs that are used
And the way your body is totally abused
You see so many young kids on the street
And the drug pushers walking their beat
They get them hooked on one thing or another
Then they push it on their sister or brother
Its like a chain reaction that keeps going on
And you don't realize it until that person is gone
Then you feel the sorrow in your heart
And you wish you would have never let them start
The war on drugs is great
Just don't let it pull you down and be your fate
Please get yourself clean
You know what I mean
Even though you think it's fun
Take the time to think of what the drugs have done.
—*Cathy Durrett*

All Of Grace

It's all of grace!
And yet we humans try to keep
A set of rules, that leave us weeping
At our own inadequacy.
It's all been done,
The victory's won,
The debt is paid for all eternity.

How to be blessed?
Look to The Lord Our Righteousness.
He is the vine.
As branches, we
By faith, can see
The law's fulfilled by love divine.
—Dorothy R. Atwood

Renew Your Faith

When things are topsy-turvy
And your smile becomes a frown-
If your way looks dark and dreary,
And a true friend can't be found...

If a the road you used to travel
Has a closed sign on the gate,
And the answer to your problems
Always seems to come too late...

Just turn your thoughts inward
And you will surely find
The answer to your fervent prayer
And perfect peace of mind.

For God, who loves His children
Will never close the door.
So place your faith and trust in Him
And find your way once more.
—Helen M. McAfee

Technicolor

Looking through the glass to imagine
another world, imagine what would be:
The plastic figures running along in
the rain. Hurrying along the road to no where.
Imagining the same figures going by
over and over as if I were watching
an old movie. No sound. No color.
Just black and white and a blurry gray.
Running back and forth.
Running to each other.
Running from each other.
As the rain patters on the windowsill,
and the trees move with the wind.
Looking yet not seeing.
Listening yet not hearing.
Touching yet not feeling.
—Cynthia Paino

The Hot Summer's Day

We walked along the shore today
And watched the children at their play.
We gathered shells as we went by,
And the sun was hot in a cloudless sky.
I held your hand and you smiled at me
And it was just as it used to be.
I turned to kiss you, — and then I knew
It was only a dream I'd had of you.
—Helene Brozaitis

Iris

In the long rays of June I walk
Apart to see the iris bloom
They burn an ultraviolet delight
On winter's pale inverted gloom

The light blue curling lips
Speak ocean depths of wondering
In images of sudden grace
Imposed on dark profundity

A question dies in being born
The words concede their due respect
The sun derives what iris feel
In lilac, lavender and blue

Why should the human colors speak
Less openly as though our feelings
Shy in loss of surety
To symbolize unspoken lines

The image of a feeling lies
Concealed from conscious light
Though what we sense is warmth
As bright as scarlet in the heart
—George Beecher

Boredom

A small yard without horizons.
Apartment buildings shut them off.
A tiny piece of sky
that is more luminous than it should,
too joyful, too blue,
that's mocking this little yard's the tenants,
my cat, myself, my parakeet.
In his basket in the corner
my cat, purring with pleasure, sleeps;
through the wires of his cage on the wall
stupidly my parakeet watches,
And I, in the yard, sat in an armchair
I watch the swallows crisscross
this tiny piece of blue,
I smoke a cigarette, daydreaming
of trotting round the globe,
of jolly adventures
and deeds great and small,
without ever being able to extinguish
this idleness, this boredom that kills.
—Apostolos Divaris

Return Of Halley's Comet, 1986

Out of the bubbled galaxies' dark mix
Appeared the faint-lit flagellum at night,
And after years, three scores plus ten and six,
It boomeranged within our earthly sight.
An omen of black doom the ancients told,
A harbinger of old Jerusalem's fall
In days of Caesar's Rome, the historic bold
Defeat at Hastings and Anglo-Saxon's fall.
But now two million miles in endless space
Within the sight of all the learned world,
The comet swings across in flashing pace,
A mix of ice, rocks, dust, and gases swirled:
A fuzzy, flaxen blob to naked eyes,
A trailing, lighted orb across the skies.
—Iwao Mizuta

Phantoms Of Darkness

The invincible phantoms that are all around.
Are cautious and cunning, seldom found.
With telepathic eyes, they project your fate.
They leave you in wonder,
Sometimes left filled with hate.
Telekinesis can be fatally applied,
Be careful its painful, once its been tried.
Its not that I'm sure, of what I say.
You can't catch a phantom,
When you are the prey.
So while you are sleeping,
And the lights are dim.
Be wary of phantoms,
There relentless and grim.
—*Joseph I. Doman*

The Angels Are Crying

Have you heard that the Angels
Are crying when everyone sleeps
They know that their tears
Can't feed the hungry children
They know that their sorrow
Can't comfort the sick and dying
They know that their hands
Can't stop the wars that plague the world
They know that their love
Can't bring world peace
For only the Angels know that God
Will show His divine love
When the time is right
so if you should hear Angels crying
Let us wipe their tears with kindness from our hearts.
—*Beth Lambert*

What Are You Doing With Your Life?

What are you doing with your life?
Are you happy? Are you sad? Do you
need something to make you glad?
Are you living a life that's filled with strife?
Are you rich? Are you poor?
Somebody's knocking at your door?
Are you having fun, and your life are torn?
Are you running around, drunk with wine?
Are you living a life that's filled with love?
Are you hoping for something from above?
What are you doing with your life?
Are you living a life full of fights?
What are you doing with your life?
Are you living a life that will make you bright?
Are you living a life that will make you right?
What are you doing with your life?
—*Geraldine Stewart*

Lost In Time

Keep on drifting into the space of time
as I fall then rise to the gentle sound
of the rhythm that my heart beats to
keep gazing onward for what's ahead,
No one knows, not even I, here the echoes
of the past, the newborn baby cries into
the night, for the fear of love is ahead
for all of us to feel, we can grow to the
gentle touch of a hand on hand or fall
when love has let us down, love can't
slip by for it may me lost in time
and never return, be gentle with
love for it is the reality for us all
—*Connie Rouch*

There Are Too Many Lonely Hearts

A heart needs another heart to be complete, the nature has
arranged. How sad, that so many in this world...without this
blessing emerged wind blows through their minds—sadness lurks
in sight...When loving words they never heard, through their
lives flight; Grey is the sky around them...no light-house in sight—

Yearning after friendship, caring, even a little shaft of
sunlight; that will chase away hard sadness-spells from mind...
Giving hope of finally finding, happiness and peace, before
it's too late— A song of caring and sweet love...could take
away the unhappiness-spell; another heart that is lonely as
well—would "mend" the sadness - well. The wind then will blow
away...all the misery their faces tell-and only happiness, and
sweet love, from the "Wishing-Tree" will-fall...

Unfortunately the laws of nature...so many have left alone—
Peace, happiness, love - and good fortune, they never in their
lives have known; Although in their spirit there is a
continuous yearning after what's HOLY and GRAND: In their
lives they are always surrounded—with sorrow bringing--demand.
Without...the so traditional FINAL EMBRACE, in their grave
they - finally land.

(-there are too many lonely heart's in the WORLD).
—*Aino Kohaloo Kabe*

The Flying Dutchman

Thou spectral trader of the highway seas!
Art riding yet within the dawning's gold,
Lifting thy canvas to the laden breeze,
Fretting thy prow along the tracks of old?
Art stealing through the ev'nings purpling grey,
Thy stern-light flick'ring in the sifting mist,
Chasing the traffickers that run the day,
Blest to their haven-roads and Heaven-kiss'd?
And art thou in defiance of thy God,
Lab'ring thy timbers to the storm-rack'd Horn,
Destin'd not once to ground in harbor-sod
Thy keel, but roam forever shunned and lorn?
   So must thou, prisoner of eternal Time,
   Haunt the high-seas in penance of thy crime!
—*Basil W. Wilson*

Dedicated To A Dream

I sit in a corner with my eyes shut tight.
As a tear rolls down my cheek.
I try to open them and look around,
But it hurts so much to peek.
I listen to the sounds of the fights outside,
The railroad tracks is where we divide,
The rich is on the other side.
As I sit in the corner all alone,
I wish that I had a better home.
As I sit by myself with my eyes shut tight.
Maybe someday I'll see a brighter light.
I'll wake in the morning and go to school.
And no one will call me a stupid fool
I'll be a wanted child have a mom and a dad,
There will be no more hatred, and no one will be sad.
As I hear another gunshot and another door slam.
I soon remember where I really am.
I live in poverty, as I hear another scream,
My wish of being cared about was only a dream.
—*Ann Brillante*

Birth Of Spring

The hot evening all hung heavy,
   as boiling clouds rolled back;
And lowing cattle went hurrying
   to shelter in an old farm shack.

Excited people fled to their homes,
   disturbed by weathers foul state;
While humid air lingered,
   adding anxiety to the long wait.

Finally the slow fury broke fast,
   as swift wind filled the breeze;
And lightening danced in and out
   among the low weeping trees.

Pounding rain lashed the roofs
   all through that reckless night;
But people awoke safe and sound
   to clear skies and morning light.

God had spoken to nature and
   nature quickened the earth; —
Beautiful springtime was born
   and fair April gave her birth!
     —*Hassie H. Stone*

Child In Pain

The voice came from above,
As gentle as a dove.

Go to sleep my child in pain,
I'll keep you dry from the rain.

For your journey has been great,
Through hells flaming gate.

For you have been through the test,
Now's the time for you to rest.

I will give you strength within your soul,
For you must continue to reach your goal.

For the storm inside shall be calm and mild,
As your God shall heal the pain in the child.

So my child of beauty it's time to wake,
Hand in hand our journey to take.

A life of dreams, hope, and care,
For you have something special to share.

So wake my child with that tear in your eye,
Dust yourself off and look to the sky.

So whenever you have doubt about me,
A sign will be there for you to see.
     —*Charles E. Harvey*

Little Boy's Gift

At my kitchen window I stood,
As he came walking through the woods.

Through the yard with toothless grin,
Dirty face and grimy chin.

Shoes unlaced, socks not matched,

As he saw me, out he drew,
from behind his back a gift so true.

A bouquet of beautiful wild flowers,
Taken from many unsuspecting boughs.

Yellows, whites and purples too,
"A present," he said, "because I love you."

I hugged and kissed him and prayed silently,

And when one day you took him back,
I prayed that understanding I would not lack.

For in God's kingdom where he lives now,
Is an eternal rose, love to him I vow.
     —*Anita H. Cole*

Footsteps

His moccasins crushed the desert sand
As he followed the footsteps of another.
As the sun settled he studied the evening stars;
They were his calendar, his time, his friends.
He shared with the moon his loneliness,
His gratitude for life; all that he needed
His Great Father provided.

No longer is La Mesa Desert his alone,
Nor his the stars.
New strains of man lay claim to reaches
Beyond the desert solitude, the friendly stars;
Beyond the boundaries of imagination
Man searches, not the footprint paths
But through the galaxies of outer space
He seeks another generation.
     —*Constance E. Washburn*

God Must Be Sad Today

God must be sad today, I think,
   as he looks upon His Earth,
     and each Man, ... and Woman,
   created in beauty and in love
     ...in the Beginning.

The once settled lands, expansive and free,
   undisturbed in tranquil pose
now plead for mercy from throngs of thoughtless hands.
The once living waters in rhythmic concert
incessantly moved from sea to sea,
writhe now for mere breath from toxic wastes' discarders.
How long, I ofttimes ponder,
before humanity is roused to somber realization
of the myriad of wonders spread ev'rywhere before us
in His manifold creations.

And when he sees life being throttled
   by cruelty and neglect,
     can you not sense the sadness he grieves
   as He must wonder,
     ...is this the end?
     —*Faith T. Irving*

Never Too Late

What resolutions did we make
As January opened the door
On a year of new horizons—
To date, how do we score?

Did we resolve to love our neighbor—
Not to curse or talk about others—
To help the aged, sick, and poor —
To treat all people like brothers?

How many of the resolutions that we made
To improve ourselves in some way
Did we respect and faithfully keep —
How many did we break in a day?

But it's never too late to try again,
And really persevere,
For every day is another beginning
Of what could be a happier year!

—*Elsie Walush*

Dreaming

Dreams often can and do come true
As once they did for me, and you.
But comes a time when morning's light
Awakens us, restores our sight,
And though we try hard as we might
The dream, with closed eyes to renew,
It's gone.

I sail a sea of endless storms.
No harbor waits, no lady's charms.
But then, perchance, when time is right,
Our souls may sweetly reunite . . .
Another dream, another night
May bring you to my empty arms
Again.

—*Daniel L. Fleming*

A Tribute To Pastor Bob Kurtz

Six years ago we voted you in
As pastor of our leaderless church.
In great surprise and utter chagrin
We bid you God-speed and start our search.
In private many tears will be shed
Though we now other sheep must be fed.

We're grateful to you for many things:
A great speaker devout and sincere
You lifted our hearts like they had wings,
Inspired us with bible verses dear
Suffered with us through our deepest pain
Assured us our struggles were not in vain.

Your radiant smile given to all,
Some tender hugs and those warm handshakes
Voiced your concern every time you'd call.
And come you did brushing off snowflakes.
A man of God we found you to be
In our hearts you'll stay, a fond memory.

—*Albert M. Maier*

The Bountiful Sea

Frolicking and tossing
   as the locks of a damsel
Eternally stirring
   un-hampered and free
Alive and aglow of the sun's radiation
Yet calm and serene
   is the mode that I see
Only to rise
   an invincible force
Rushing forward in madness
   striking all in its course
Then in thunderous assault
   as a giant osprey
Pounces heavily down on an unwary prey
Now a leap through the air
   with a jubilant bound
Foaming and spreading it covers the ground
A magnificent spectacle
   sprawling gloriously a creation of God
   the bountiful sea

—*Ed Rains*

O, Little Donkey Did You Know

O, little donkey, were you aware..................
As the long miles you wearily trod.................
That the burden you did bear......................
Was to be revealed as the Son of God...............

Another donkey, a kin to one of yesteryear.........
Did a palm-strewn path proudly trod...............
Shouts of "Hosannas" reached it's ear..............
For it was carrying the beloved Son of God.........

How soon, that same throng of men.................
Did change their cries to: Crucify, Crucify........
O, little donkey, did you know then................
The son of God would be led forth to die...........

But, we who live many centuries after..............
O, little donkey, did you know then................
That we could greet Death and Satan with laughter..
They are defeated, the Son of God rose again........

O little, donkey, we are by your side..............
The road to Bethlehem we plod......................
Prayerfully, to return again, our hearts open wide.
Joyfully, Welcoming, the blessed Son of God........

—*Alice L. Horrocks*

The Wait

The porch light wasn't on last night
   at the house next door, hushed upstage
      while we waited...
   for the hands
      (that buried two sons)
   for folded eyelids
      not successfully hiding
      chips of light
      galaxies forgot to reclaim...

The trees heard
   her moving with spring
      toward our needs
   over Love's trumpet
      recalling its own
   when we were spotted —
      frozen
   in her sunshine.

—*Floyd Hansen*

The Mariner Returns....

Harbor lights can be seen in the distance
as the Mariner heads for the shore,
he's returning home from a journey
that's been traveled for ages before.

He has shown great valor and courage,
he's mastered the sails, wind and lee,
when tempest-tossed and discouraged
he has weathered the billowing sea.

When he chartered his course for adventure
and ventured through waters unknowns.
He knew not where current would take him
nor what tides might divert him from home.

As he crosses the bar to the mainland
past the lighthouse, the rocks and the shoals,
the stout-hearted sailor's returning
as Norsemen, so brave and so bold.

He enters the channel from starboard
his pilot he's taken aboard,
he is welcome with warmth and affection
to Snug Harbor, his own Flekkefford.
—*Harry Robertson*

Beyond Life's Sunset

I gazed with the eyes of an artist, out over the water so still,
As the sun was slowly sinking behind yonder hill.
Such peace seemed to surround me and everything was so serene,
This was the most beautiful sunset mine eyes had ever seen.

And I thought of the twenty-third Psalm, beside the still
  water he leads,
Then a pain pierced my heart as I remembered a loved one who
  lay suffering, indeed.
As he lay suffering and dying in such pain and agony,
I was enjoying this beautiful sunset, and I turned away so guiltily
And then I felt someone's presence, and I knew my Saviour was near,
And as I turned once more, these are the words I seemed to hear.

Beyond life's sunset a new morning shall dawn,
There all of their sorrows shall forever be gone.
And we shall be happy in the Saviours great love with a
beautiful son rise in heaven above.

—*Argie Willbanks*

Why Momma, Why?

A child looks out at the empty land,
At the scarred and crusted land,
I'm hungry, Momma, I want to eat!
A baby squeezes his mother's breast
But shriveled it hangs and dry,
The man beside her shuffles away
His only cover is shame.
Why, Momma? Why?
Cries cut through the arid air
And the sand clots red with blood
A shriek! The woman falls like a broken rod.
Talk to me, Momma, I don't like this game!
The child pushes against her body
Get up, Momma! I don't want to play
But now it lies quiet and still.
The child wails to the empty air
Why? Momma, why?
—*Juniya Rozenfeld*

The Eyes Of A Lady

They're big, bright and full of love
As they greet me in the morning.
Innocent as those of a dove
And flashing a look of trust as she's turning.

Who can know what she would say
If she could only speak
Of life she sees from day to day
And observes in a manner oh so meek.

She is not so very small
And neither is she big
She watches in the trees so tall
Each bird upon his twig.

And when she catches sight
Of those she looks upon
Her eyes will say "is it alright?"
A look of sadness she will don.

This lady with big brown eyes
Is the loving, trusting dog
Who, every day in every way
Tries to show her love through life's fog.
—*Frances R. Scholze*

Old Home Place

The house stands patient — silent and sad,
  As though waiting for its family to return.
Those walls which once heard our laughter and tears
  And shared the dreams for which we'd yearn.
The broad porch is still shady and cool,
  Its banisters seem longing once more to enfold.
The children who once skated and played on its swing,
  Not dreaming that they would some day grow old.

The windmill, too, stands quiet and tall
  Even though the gentle breezes swell.
I can almost hear my sick grandmother call:
  "Can someone bring a cold drink from the well?"

The big barn sags — almost ready to fall
  Which once was straight and red and tall.
Wide cracks in the walls let the breezes play,
  Where no longer the horses and cows wait for hay.
The hayloft where once we loved to climb,
  Finds it hard to remember a happier time.

"They're just buildings and cannot feel,"
  Is what I'm sure most people would chide.
But as I wander about the old home place,
  I can sense the sorrow they're trying to hide.
—*Avis Pitts*

Worship

Last night I caught my breath
At the streaked orange sky,
The twilight dark enough
To display the half-moon in the autumnal heavens.
I stood in the coolness
Entranced by the ethereal light
While thrilling to the core.
"Am I close to God?" I asked;
I know I am
When nature puts on a show of this dynamic,
And I am spellbound at the beauty and the generosity of God.
Beauty and love — they're almost one,
And I am uplifted by my chance to worship.
—*Helen Pierce Callihan*

Simple: Guardian Of My Heart

Such loyalty in a cat, so bold,
As to meet me at the end of the road;
Where upon a rock, between some logs,
Simple crouches down, aloof from the dogs,
Who have come to walk their children home.
Could it be they know they are not alone?

She looks at me, gives her tail a lash,
And then off she flies, as quick as a flash!
Through the back woods she darts like the wind,
And when I get home, to me will she sing
Of the dark woods, and how she did play,
Stalking and chasing gray squirrels all day!

Oh Siamese, with your eyes so blue,
To me so much more than a dog is true.
My cheek with your tongue you do caress,
When sad times in my life do me depress;
Then dance and play all over the floor
Till I smile, then laugh, and I am sad no more!

—*Anne Evans Gibson*

Life Or Death

Is it life or is it death?
As years multiply,
   What happens at the end?
Struggle for everyday life,
   Is it worth it?
      As body systems fail
      Do I wail or do I throw away those pills and let
      old grim reaper take over?
How do I die?
I want dignity, love and acceptance.
How do I live when my broken body fails?
How do I die, who cares.

—*Judy Hauschulz*

To "Mom"

You have witnessed my creation
As you brought me out, to live
What a Sacred Innovation
That only God, to you can give.

When I ever needed helping
And you saw me in despair
Wherever I went or wandered
I could always find you there—

You have helped me in my yearnings,
And have shown me how I can
Conquer hardships, make my earnings
And to be a real Man—

You gave me all the tools to fight.
The foes of Truth, with all my might;
You taught me that the Wrong is Evil
And that Truth is always Right.

You have left my life so early
But, the memories that I share
With you, my Mom, are always living
In my heart, and everywhere.

—*Ali K. Maksad*

My Daughter

   Hazel eyes and Tawny hair.
At first glance, you'll think she doesn't have a care.
She wears blue jeans and crazy T-shirts.
You'll hardly ever see her in dresses and skirts.
She likes loud rock music and staying up late,
and junk food is about all you'll see on her plate.
She likes to party and dance till dawn.
When the others are beat, she's still going strong.
But you have to know that deep inside.
Beats a heart of gold and a lot of pride.
If you need a helping hand, she's always there.
She'll be a great friend, if you treat her fair.
Her temper flares from time to time.
But I want you to know, I'm proud of this
daughter of mine.

—*Annabelle Aronhalt*

A Second Chance

In December of 1988, I thought I almost had a death date.
At the hospital when I arrived,
I was gasping for air to stay alive.
I was there about a week, and then I was released.
Knowing I was coming back home made me feel relieved.
I knew God had given me a second chance,
So I started looking at life with a different glance.
Before 1988, I was timid and more of a home body.
Being home with my family was just fine with me.
Then in 1989, I went on a diet and lost some weight,
And it helped my self-esteem feel great!
In 1990 I started taking this class and that class,
And I have turned into a different lass!
I've taken Computer Literacy, WordPerfect, DOS and Windows,
   and Graphic Arts.
I'm learning Oil Painting, a little Spanish and so many
   different parts.
I enjoy my computer and high technology,
And everything in my life is much more precious to me.
Now I have a spirited stride, am more confident and outspoken.
I'm thankful to God for giving me a second chance as my token.

—*Betty Lou Bremer Kruger*

Patience And Priorities

The sea gull sits and waits
At the water's edge,
His grey and black feathers
Ruffled by the northeast wind
Blowing steadily!
No deep water for him today,
Too cold!

He'll wait 'til a kindly wave
Brings him a morsel
Or perhaps some human
Staring down from the glassy condos
Will take pity and throw him a crumb.
We should, you know,
He was here first!

—*Julia M. Phillips*

The Winds Of Change

The winds of change direct life's many turns,
at times soft and gentle, like a spring rain.
Silently without warning, they swirl and churn,
like a raging sea; waves crash and sigh, never the same;
yet they remain, caressing the sand,
leaving us to, ponder life's master plan.

The winds of change weigh heavily on my mind.
In our quest for life's greatest treasures, how are we to find
the strength and courage to run towards the sun?
Where it shines bright within our souls; Love awaits.
Nurtured tended like a flower; it grows.
With each passing day, like water falling over a dam,
the feelings change and overflow.

The winds of change blow against you and me,
bringin' forth great challenges full of mystery.
Let your inner voice guide the way,
keep close your heart, and you'll never stray.
Let the winds of change fill your sail, make your life your fairy tale.
We must try our best, to make the most of our quest.
Let the winds of change blow over us, and we will do the rest.

—*Cathy Adams*

Autumn Music

The autumn rain is falling. Hear the lilting cadence swell!
Autumn rain is autumn's music, autumn's liquid philomel
Rhythmic as a drum beat the crystal legions fall
Lightly as elfin feet tripping to a madrigal.

Autumn's music can bewitch us, set our vagrant fancies free
It can charm us and enrich us with its roof-top symphony
Now and then we hardly hear it. It breathes a scarce-heard sigh
(Perhaps a requiem for the spirit of a flower about to die!)

Then, at times, it roars triumphant in a sudden gale of sound
Just as though it feels incumbent to beat its drops into the ground!
In spells of gusty bravado it seems to lash and spit
Defiance at the coming snow to which it must submit.

But it's mostly gentle music, with enchantment intertwined,
Bound to lull the restless spirit or to soothe the troubled mind
So, about your peaceful firesides, listen to the lyric din!
Hark! The music of the raindrops; let its magic enter in!

—*George A. Hymer*

Awakening

At some magic moment, the call went out.
"Awake, awake. It's time."
Responding to the urge, nature slowly stretches,
And sends forth its color guard.
Crocuses peek up before the sun
Is warm enough to melt the winter snows.
Tulips, daffodils herald the ground forces,
While forsythia, magnolia, and plum bushes
Decorate the background.
Trees respond with unfolding leaves
Of pale green, red hues, and dangling seeds.
The apple trees followed by dogwood
Adorn the fields and forest trails.
Insects emerge from hiding
And hum their searching calls.
I am awakened from my winter doldrums,
Energized by the dramatic show;
I leap forth to join the surging force,
Marching to the music of my soul.

—*Adele Lynne Wagner*

Remembering A Dream

I remember those days dreaming and hoping, wasting my youth away;
I remember dreaming and wishing the past would evaporate into clouds of darkness;
I remember dreaming of a better life, a life of serious friends
I remember how my dreams kept me from crying into the depths of sadness.
But if I dream no longer, then what puts that tender smile upon my lips?
Could it be, somehow, that I am happy, no longer alone;
Could it be I made a friend for life?
Yes, it possibly could be;
My dreams are no longer remembered, they are a miracle that a have made my life come true.

My dreams are remembered, forever.

—*Jennifer McGregor*

My Children By Day

Children, my children only by day, When night falls, they all slip away, to places where adventures of every kind await. Some sit in

darkness, brave yet afraid of the light illuminating, the dark murals of poverty, hunger, cold and disappointment. Some walk aimlessly seeking

themselves, their mothers, fathers, sisters, brothers in dangerous places. Some sit quietly, anxiously fearful of being noticed by one who is abusive, brutal, and controlling. Some sleep in their crowded

spaces, listening yet desperately wanting to drown out sounds of gunfire, screaming sirens, mournful weeping. Others find themselves warm, secure, happy in their rooms, feeling loved by all who touch their lives. Children, my children only by day.

Hear my message, absorb all I say, I hear your silence or loud cries for help. I feel your despair, sitting there hungry, tired, and confused. Asked by the system to follow the rules. I am your friend,

I love and care. I am your mother when your God-given Mom's not there.

I want you to know you are somebody, you can achieve, you must not just hear this, you must believe, you're beautiful, intelligent, creative, resourceful, a person of worth. You are this nation's future you will help save the earth.

Power, you have power to be anything you can but dream, what your mind
creates, your hands can bring to reality. Eat, drink the knowledge served by day, savor the taste in every way as you sample and nourish your body and mind daily with me, your teacher —
    the one who wishes for you, my children, happiness,
    prosperity, success, love, and peace of mind.

—*Correll L. Townes*

For Phil

You taught me,
as you told me
how
when you were a child
your mother taught you,
and together
we,
like bees and butterflies and hummingbirds,
sip the sweet perfumed nectar
from the honeysuckle blossoms.

—*Irma Wassall*

If You Would Only come Back To Me

If you would only, only, only come
back to me baby thing would be so
different I would love you, love you
like I never, never love you before
I would even tell my friend to stop
come around so much so I can be
with you more I would even let
you love me like you want
to if you would only, only, only come,
come back to me baby thing
would be so different, I would
love you, love you like I never,
never love you before, I would
even let you love me like
you want to if you would
only, only, only come, come
back to me baby thing
would be so different if
you would only, only, only come,
come back to me baby.
　　—Annie Nelson

Thanks Mother

As a child, we didn't have much food to eat,
barely any clothes to wear, or shoes upon our feet,
never knew where we'd be come sundown,
come sunup, we'd be moving to another town.

We didn't have many friends,
we never stayed long enough,
to really get to know them, then,
Oh Lord....those times surely were rough,
But....one thing mother taught me, early in childhood,
"Always, always, be thankful, girl,
someday, life will be good."

Mother was right!
She taught me of a King in Heaven,
that I was His child, for me, His life was given,
Now I have a friend, who'll always be near,
to comfort my heart, and wipe away all my tears.

Thank you, mother, for sharing with me,
your friend, "King Jesus,"
Now...I'm a child of the King,
He's building me a mansion,
on streets of pure gold;
Yes, I'm a child of the King,
With great riches untold.
　　—Glenda McKee-Abbott

Beauty

Beauty - A treasure hard to define
Beauty - Faceted - Cause divine
Beauty - Beholden in someone's eyes
Beauty - Of sense - given the wise
Beauty - Of form - movement, grace
Beauty - Granted the fair of face
Beauty - In nature - music - song
Beauty - Inhaled - heady and strong
Beauty - Described so many ways
Beauty - Eloquent voiced in praise
Beauty - Is felt in friendships dear
Beauty - The smiles as they appear
Beauty - Surrounds us along life's way
Beauty - Brings joy each and every day
Beauty - Is love - a point of view
Beauty - A glimpse from God - real - true
　　—Constance M. Johnson

Happy Anniversary

I'll spend some money tomorrow for sure, on the both of us.
Because I love my little wife, and don't want to have a fuss.
I will buy some gifts for her I can't hardly afford to get.
Oh, yes! It's something I want her to have, and maybe a set.

I think I should only get one or two, or should I get four?
Yes, she'll let me know later, too, if we need to get more.
Now she knows, that it's wrong to get more than we really need,
But to surprise her now, I'll go ahead and take the lead.

My wife likes the finer things, and everything to be just right.
And I do my very best, you see, to please her with all my might.
These gifts are awfully cute when they're looking up at you,
But I gotta get going now, cause there's quite a bunch to do.

I spoke before of a set for my wife, or maybe as many as four,
So few she doesn't know yet, but she'll probably want some more. She's not familiar with the type, nor does she know their sounds, but I just know she's going to love, our new little coon hounds.
　　—Jimmy Lee

The Saviors Love

Jesus' love can't be measured in handfuls so small,
because in rivers it flows from him to be received of all.
His love reaches beyond sin and shame,
For he wants to remove the stain and take away the blame.
His love out weighs the hurt and all the pain,
for you see every soul he longs and wishes to gain.
His love over rules the cursing mocking and hate,
Because he has one great desire and that is
To make you his heavenly mate.
His love rises above the horror of his torture,
agony and pain,
For he does not want his blood shed for you in vain.
What Jesus is really saying to one and all,
the reason I gave my life on the tree,
is because I created you, loved you, cherished you
and never, never wanted you to fall.
Amen
　　—Harold D. Jordan

My Precious

Let me look at you sweetheart,
because your little hands will soon be much more than little.
Say "Cheese" Mister Baby, so I can add another
　window in time to my scrapbook of photos.
Run and catch the ball Connor - because you'll
　soon outgrow those choppy strides in your sprint.
Keep talking, I'm listening - even when no one
　else understands your words.
Just touch the world, sneak a cookie when I'm not
　looking, pet all the animals you can reach and
　ride your horsey fast!
Sit in the snow and taste the rain - jump in every puddle,
　and keep telling me every time you see an airplane.
I'll be quiet as I watch you sleep - these soft but deep
　wrinkles at your ankles are the same as when you were born.
Your tummy so round, just boasting of your bedtime snack.
Your Angelic face, so content.
You still have that unexplainable sweet baby breath, the same
　as the first time I held you.
No matter how big you grow, you'll always be my precious
　baby.
　　—Jennifer D. Weiler

It Feels Like Rain

Never has my heart,
Been so savagely blown apart;
It feels like rain inside,
Why have you attacked me so bad,
God knows why you've made me so sad,
Why does all your pains and anger
   vast on to me?
I am the one who loves and cherishes thee,
Will I always pay for the sins of
   another?
Do you remember, I am the woman you
   call mother;
Never has my heart,
Been so savagely blown apart;
It feels like rain inside.
   —*Eileen A. Souza*

She Loved Her Lover's Brother

I once had a friend named Elizabeth,
Before a yuppie she became. With
Expectations beyond her means;
Transparent mind, and liquid dreams.
She altered her nose for a sweeter face;
And so it's upped a little higher. No
More would she wear designer jeans, but
Fashion's best is all she sought. She
Ridded her man and wedding rings, and no
Weeds in her garden grow. Slinking around
Like a midnight cat, she searched for her
Prey discrete. Upon the town with her
Flirty look, seeking eyes, for hers to
Meet. For pleased she's not by her lover
Alone, but, alas, her lover's brother.
Her Seer had spoke to her of faith; "To
The ones you love, be fair." And now
She tastes her bitter fruit, for nought
Remains to love. Where there she sits in
Her ivory tower, remembering all her vains.
   —*Jewell Hahn*

Another Life

Before I knew the mass of body human,
Before I knew of the intricate species,
I was an independent soul of the universe!

I would travel on gentle winds,
I would see through avian eyes,
I would perch on strong limbs.

On sunrise I would soar with the sun!
On sunrise I would seek a slow stream,
On sunrise I wouldn't keep to my soul!

In the afternoon I would find a clear meadow,
In the afternoon I would feel a sweet breeze,
In the afternoon I would enjoy my solitude!

At night I would seek and gather aromatic seeds,
At night I would seek a sturdy tree for rest,
At night I would perch and gaze at the mountains!

In aeons of time I evolutionized and settled,
In aeons of time my soul still soars afar!
In aeons of time nature still havens my soul!
   —*Deanna LaVoy-Lewis*

Hymn

I hear terrestrial symphonies playing,
Before the harmonious void above,
With the softest of purest melodies
Languorously wafting up into heavens heaven
where the ancient stars, in their depths sublime,
Resound - forever in vast thund'ring choruses -
Upon the eternal consciousness of Universal Love,
which, infinitely, enrobes all universal things and beings
Just as, even, lovely Aurora - sweet mistress of
All our early mornings - caresses the dawn
within us with her quietly saffron robes and bids
the outer worldly dawn to (with a sensuously
full-blown kiss) take celestial flight into
the heights of colorfully full - blazing noon while
the golden sun beneath his azure sky with his hours,
sprays all the bright world below,
with the bliss of Radiant Light..
O mortal! seek the source of this zenith,
This light, which once found and tasted shall be like
heavenly healing nectar!
   —*Jerry A. Wills II*

Moonfall

It came out of the twilight
Before the rising of the sun and moon
A solace so healing, a solitary feeling
So true
It's wonderful to feel like you're really with someone
Together.
Will I find her,
Somewhere in the night?

In secret sadness I wander
A rainbow in the depths of night
Will she ever find me, unseen and undiscovered?
Silently gathering the lamenting moon
In the hoping dreams of the midnight sky
It brings me to a sacred sorrow
I see the silver stars cry, and I know
There is no tomorrow.

Somewhere in the night, a distant droning
The forests breathe and shiver.
   —*Alex Simpson*

I Must The Eager Ivy Trim Anew

I must the eager ivy trim anew
Before these creeping trilobed layers of vine
Mat wall and road and hug the vast milieu
Until the world and heaven intertwine!
But — wait! I know this nonsense cannot be —
My transient thought ensues the summer heat,
So stop will I and cool beneath a tree —
The task at hand I later can repeat.
In memory the banks slept clay and bare
Awaiting youthful plantings in their quest
For reaching, clutching, mantling unaware,
Caressing earth with evergreening zest.
When I no longer match your seasoned strength,
Then others must your tendrils bound at length.
   —*Gloria Hockenberry*

The Journey We've Made Together

Remember what our lives were like
Before we had TV?
On radio was "Hit Parade"
Park dances they were free.

Glen Miller and Big Bands were in
And phonographs were too.
The melodies we hummed back then
We long to hear anew.

We were the depression babies
We fought in World War II
We came back to a GI bill
The good life was our due.

Building roads, airports and houses
Were engineering teams,
Slide rules then turned obsolete,
Computers filled our dreams.

Those dreams we dreamed continue on
From in our sturdy core.
New generations carry the torch
We held up high before.
—Betty Lemke Bobrow

Only One Judge

If you feel the need to judge all as they walk down the aisle
Before you do — try walking in their shoes awhile.
"God will judge all on the same principle —
Therefore thou art inexcusable, O man, whosoever
Thou art that judgest; for whereas thou judgest
Another; Thou condemnest thyself; for thou that
Judgest doeth the same thing."
What if—their church should have no walls; ceiling or floor
No corners within—or any name on the door
And not be a 'one day house of prayer'
So they could carry it in their heart——everywhere
And only have one judge————and— "He" won't giggle—
point—or nudge. Doesn't care what kind of clothes they wear
How their make-up looks—or their hair
If they wear a fur coat—or holey underwear.
"The Lord seeth man not as man seeth
For man looketh on the outward appearance
But the Lord looketh on the heart."
Lord—forgive us our trespasses—as we forgive others who
Trespass against us.
—Harriet (Shove) Bedard

Kitten Smitten

One sunny morning outside the breezeway door,
Began this constant meowing for hour after hour,
I thought this little kitten just roamed in from somewhere,
Having no thoughts that someone had dumped him from nowhere.
Checked the neighborhood for anyone missing a kitten,
His big blue eyes, purrs and rubs, causing me to become smitten,
Our male Burmese cat was starting to mother him,
Seemed we all became attached, this wasn't just a whim,
The husband appeared home from being up north hunting,
Accused me of adding to our Zoo by going pet shopping,
Explained that with no car and all pet shops 20 miles away,
There was no way I could have been looking for this little guy.
Chato, the family cat who'd been left home with us,
Adopted little Sam with no additional fuss,
Showing it's very possible for a beautiful Burmese,
To help raise and adopt this little orphaned Siamese.
—Eloise M. Houvener

Little Flower Of The Grassland II

In the evening when family flora
Begins to remember the forays
Fauna laments the rape of wilderness.
Even though nature's indictment grows
The shadow of human beings looms large
And the horizon bids adieu to Little Flower.

Little Flower of prosy prairies,
Disband salamander's posies!
Invoke the mythical Phoenix!
Rise again as bright as a star!
Beckon the glossy galaxies
That gravitate heavens afar.
Blend the aeons, creatures, billions
Land gentry and chameleons
In the Garden of Paradise.
Flora's genus realizing
Nature's harmonizing beauty
Self-sacrificing soul's duty
With ne'er an utopian disguise.
And solar rays greet the matrix!
—Don Eischen

True Love

In times of sorrow, let us always
    believe in the beauty of life,
    the power of goodness
    and the right to joy.

Let the moments of meditation that have
    linked us together give us strength
    for our daily tasks, strength to endure.

Tears are the price of love.

Pain is evidence that you have had
    a great share of life's blessings.

Something of ourselves dies with our
    loved ones.

But then, something of them remains
    living with the living, forever.
—Al P. Alpert

The Immaculate Reception

The strong are weak and weak are strong
Beneath heart's desire each pulled along
Striving, with love the aim,
Oft lost or found, but ne'er the same.

Sweet is love to friends she knows,
Yet sweeter still is she to those
Who long to meet her, shake her hand,
Joy she brings understand.

Life's too long to live without
A love as child dreamt about,
Yet oft too short is life to find
True love before life's left behind.

Though ever searched, thought lost or found,
True love on earth does not abound,
For to truly love we know not how,
Our love for self will not allow.

Still true love is ever sought,
And though all search, she's never caught,
For love that's true we cannot conceive,
Only God loves true, and we all receive.
—David M. Wilmouth

The Contented Hawk

He sail with ease across the sky
   beneath the cloud above where I
set watching his most graceful movement.
   "I wonder if his soul is content."

I wonder if he ever try
   to figure out who made the sky,
who sent him that gentle breeze
   to glide him above the rocks, the trees.

Who cast the sun upon the sky
   that might see wherever he fly.
Who gave him life and liberty
   a heart, a soul and set him free.

I pondered long in pensive mood
   without a moment solitude
until that bird that caught my eye
   cried aloud, "I try, I try."

Tis now I know his soul is content,
   for he know tis God from which it is sent.
     —*Esaw Wilson*

Snug Harbor

Quiet cove, in whose reflection'd depths the little fishes play
   Beneath the keel of some great ship whose sides of rust
And storm-scarred decks have seen a better day,
   Or round some schooner whose tall masts are skyward thrust.

Smiling inlet, where in summer, laughing boys carefree swim and dive,
   Where, on whose soft swell, some duck or weary gull may ride
And plunge to try its luck and on thy bounty thrive,
   Then slowly, on grey wings rising, will seaward glide.

Safe refuge from November gales, the fishing fleets in thee do seek,
   When autumn's sweet halcyon days have passed them by
And Winter's lashing rains and bitter, icy winds may shriek
   Thy shelter to them all impart thou unstintingly.

O Lord, who surely fends me constant from above.
   Keep me ever in the Snug Harbor of Thy Love.
     —*Jack C. Allworth*

Oh Beware My Friend

I hope you listen to what I am trying to tell you Today... beware.

Because if he hurt me he can hurt you. Please don't put your heart First like I did...beware.

Just because you may be Lonely now and want someone to be close to and hold you. I can understand but ...beware.

I love you as a friend, That's why I am telling you Today so...beware.

But if you are still not Listening to me and you are Listening to your heart In stead still...beware.

I am just looking out for my friend. I tried to do my best, to tell you this while crying so... beware.
Signed...Broken Hearted
     —*Charlotte I. Griesel*

On The Brink

I stand on the abyss of thought...
Beyond reach clear, precise and profound images
Merge into classic patterns.
Nearby dim, imperfect and obscure shadows
Strain, crack and break.

Sadness infects my soul
Doubt confuses me

I'm aware that something is going wrong
But.... no way to stop it!

Outside the sun
Inside the gloom

Don't worry about me
JUST those I love.
     —*Glenn Crouch*

Day Of Daze

Confetti in the bathroom floor
Bill collectors at the door
Petticoats draped on chairs and beds
Pains and aches in tummies and heads
Pulled off hose found in spots
Wilted flowers not in pots
Unopened presents everywhere
Day-afterness in the air.
Can you guess what I describe
The day after she left, the bride.
     —*Helen Gersbach*

Calling

Many times while I am out walking
birds are singing and calling me.
They often call me by my name.
Why is it, that they know who I am?
In the valley I see them dining.
Father has set them a table to share
grapes and berries amid friends.
Though not understanding it all,
This one brought victory and glory.
We rejoiced with Thee from within,
of families and such wonderment,
and a treasure most precious of all,
is realization of the One amid them,
to save, to forgive, to heal and bless.
His lovely flowers upon the hillside
wave and smile, looking up to Him
Who has baptized all whom are His;
for whomever are willing, do come,
hearing His song, calling their name.
     —*Eleanor D. Garcia*

Why I Sold My Car

I started to town the other day.
   Before I got there I lost my way.
I drove here and I drove there.
   I didn't have much time to spare.
I prayed to God to please help me.
   Then very plainly the right way I could see,
     —*Dorris L. Thompson*

Who Am I?

Who am I in the world of man
But a minuscule part of a grandiose plan?
Like a grain of sand or a bit of dust
Tossed about by a windy gust.

What role have I in the scheme of things
And is there some message that I should bring?
Have I a contribution for humanity
Or would that be construed as my vanity?

How often I have been put to life's test
For reasons which are not yet manifest,
Thou insignificant in the world of man
I am an integral part of God's greater plan.

—*Carol Frederick*

The Light

There is a light — not a bright one,
    but a relentless one.
One that calls, that beckons,
    one that seems to pull
      the soul away,
    leaving an empty shell.
But there is another light —
Its soft sweet hues of gossamer
      brilliance
    can fill the world
      with colors no man
        will ever see.
Deep swirling clouds of this
    shimmering light surround us all
That is the one light on earth
    that guides us now
It is the perfect light of hope.
    And it is toward that light
      that all of us
        must follow

—*Glenna S. White*

Crossroads

We travel along the same path for many days,
but after a while we went our separate ways.

We begin our lives and remember each other
cause we used to be as close as sister and brother.

We were very different, but still the same
and no matter what, we'll remember the other's name.

We became great friends and earned each other's respect and trust
Our friendship won't ever get broken; nor turn to rust.

Cause one day, now or later, we will cross paths again
and see what the other did and when.

Just like the beginning, we'll split up once more
until we are together like the time before.

We can never be completely kept apart,
Because like best friends, we have a piece of each other's heart.

—*David K. Toyer*

Come Again Eternal Christ

O come again, eternal Christ, we pray;
    But come again no longer in a manger
    To grow amongst men, as before, a stranger.
Be born, instead, within us, Lord, we say:
Born born as Wisdom in our minds, O Lord;
    Be born as Love within our hearts, O Christ;
    Be born as Truth within us sanctuarized.
Be living God within us, loved, adored.

Be born within us, be our God within;
    And let Your Star ignite our Inner Light.
Become the Splendor underneath our skin,
    So that men walk in radiance, black or white.
Inscribe, O Lord, upon our brow, Your name
And end, oh, end our sorrow and our shame.

—*Benito F. Reyes*

The Garden Of Love

For love is like a garden green, with many flowers that grow.
But gardens take a lot of work, and so does love, you know?
You see it must be cared for, and nurtured everyday.
For if it is neglected, your flowers will go away.
Then once the weeds have taken hold, it's hard to get them out
The ones that grow so rapidly, are pride, mistrust and doubt.
And then the roof of bitterness, will rise just like a tree.
Consuming everything that's left, it's all that you will see.
So take these tools, and use them well, to make your garden grow.
Use caring for your shovel, understanding for your hoe.
Then use the rake of tenderness, to pull the weeds of doubt.
Let truth become your sprinkling can, mistrust will soon be out.
And last of all forgiveness, is the plant food you should sow.
It kills the roots of bitterness and weeds of pride can't grow.
So take these simple tools my friend, and use them every day
Then love will be your garden green, and never go away.

—*Joseph Mushinsky*

Living Alone

Loneliness can be such a sad theme.
But I am one who likes living alone.
It's an answer to my dream,
A humble place to call my own.

No one to tell me me when to be home,
Nobody screaming "Your stuff's in my way!"
Won't interrupt anyone when my shower's done
'Cuz I'm the only one that's here to stay.

A new place to hang my hat,
I can create my own decor:
A dorm room with a welcome mat
And an open door.

Mickey Mouse will perk up my walls.
Checkerboard carpet to cushion my feet
A machine to answer my calls
And a stereo would be neat

Friends nearby to keep me company
Just a few doors down
Michelle, Vickie, Debi, Jodie, Tanith, and Tiffany
So many friendly faces won't let me frown.

Being alone is not such a sad thing.
I enjoy the privacy.
And it's a lot better
Than someone threatening me!

—*Heidi D. Hawk*

No One

The songs play...
But I have no one to dance with.

The snow falls...
But I have no one to keep me warm.

The sun sets...
But I have no one to share it with.

The roses are in bloom...
But I have no one to give them to.

I feel like being held tenderly...
But I have no one to do the holding.

I go to bed...
But I have no one to share it with.

Until I met you...
Can I give you my love and so much more?
Your heart is locked and I have the key.
Let's open the door.

I want to have no one...
But you.

—*Christopher Trejo*

A Bright Future

You reach out to touch me.
But I pull away from you.
You say oh it must be him.
I tell you to please leave him out of this.
He has nothing to do with us.
There is no us.
There hasn't been for awhile.
Not since she came along.
You are her husband, you made your choice.
It wasn't me.
So don't blame this on him.
It was all your decision.
Nothing you can say can change the way he makes me feel.
I finally have something worth keeping.
You may be out to have a fling, but I'll
be in love for the rest of my life with him.

—*Frances Moore*

If I Were A Poet

If I were a poet, I would write about you,
But I'm not a poet, Will these lines do,
Twined through the years of weep and sleep,
Of love and happiness, lies and deceit,
The cries of the poor, their hunger we see,
And the cries from their bodies awaken our sleep,
They linger in our minds forever and a day,
The bloody hands of life, the rich man's pray,
If I could hold, and tend to their needs
I'd give all of my self for it's the master I'd please,
If I were a poet, I'd unchain the evil hours and endless nights,
With words of love I'd unveil hunger from sight,
If I were a poet, I'd unlock all heart's that weep,
I'd open the eyes of the world to see their needs,
But I'm not a poet, I'm just a heart that weeps,
I write in the lines unavailing the truth the needs,
When hunger cries, bodies ache there is no sleep. In the darkness
Of love give hope to life the golden keys, If I were a poet, the
Unsung song I'd sing, The gem of sweetness belongs to the hearts, that
Weep within. I close my eyes and slumber, through the nightmares of
Yesterday. A lost race the scarlet fears unlocked echoes of evil ways,
The tearful cries the out stretched hand, I saw the dying lay. I am
Not a poet my eyes see a world of tortured people crying in the winds.

—*Clara C. Purtee*

A Letter To My Father

I was never able to know you,
But, I'm told you were an honorable man.
You fought for our Country,
And were killed in Vietnam.
I sometimes felt lonely,
Not understanding why,
Everyone else had their father,
And mine had to die.
You fought in honor with all your might,
You did what you thought was right.
No one really knows the purpose of that war,
So many lives are still a mess,
So many lives, no more.
I have a lot of respect for you,
And can only hope that someday,
Everyone else will too.
I pray that you can hear me,
Say these words to you,
I know you're at peace in heaven,
Somewhere in that sky so blue.

—*Christina R. Palmenta*

Stroke

Dread word we hate to hear
But it happens to someone every year
Gradually we learn to cope
Hopefully we do not mope.

Lying in the hospital bed
Our main ambition is to use the head
Rehabilitation helps to learn to adjust
Retraining is an absolute must.

You are not sick, so don't complain
Hard work is required to sustain
The status quo you plan to maintain
Exercise is the way to go, necessarily so.

In time you can return to former ways
It is up to you to stay
Set a goal, make a plan
And soon you will be dancing with your man!

—*Catherine Rickards*

A Powerful Tool

"Prayer," is such a little word
But, it's a powerful tool;
It quiets us, when we are sad,
And helps us when we're blue.

It's one sure way, of being close
To God, our heavenly father;
He likes to hear our voices, each;
He never says, "don't bother!"

Yes, prayer can be our friend at night,
Or in the morning hour;
Anytime, you bow your head,
It has the same sweet power!

It calms our nerves, and dries our tears,
It can even help us sleep;
It's God's sweet way of showing us,
His love that runs so deep.

—*Janice E. Leitz*

Dr. Lyle Griffith

You are quick, alert and decisive,
But kind and compassionate, too,
You have chosen a path of sorrow,
That is fraught with grief as you go,
You have given the best gift of life
That a man can give to his brother,
But onward you go determined to win,
'Gainst obstacles that stymie another.
They tell us each man that's successful,
Has a wife that is faithful and true,
Who nourishes, cares for and loves him,
Encouraging him onward to go.
You have a star waiting in Heaven,
For a crown when the bell tolls for you,
You will hear the words "faithful servant"
For those who have followed through.
—*Edna Rush*

Maple Seed

The world is wide, and miles are long,
But love can travel on the wind,
With a breath I'll follow you
And say hello, where have you been?

You've traveled roads, I've never walked,
Seen canyon walls, God painted so.
Met many friends, and with them talked.
You'll learn from listening as you go.

We never was a man to wait,
For fate to pat us on the head,
But search for what is farther on,
That's how you grow, by learning so.

Say Hello, to the hills for me,
Work, and wait and search and see,
Perhaps when the time is right,
God will show you what's to be.

The world is wide, and miles are long,
But love can travel on the wind,
With a breath I'll follow you,
And say Hello, Hello, again.
—*Dorothy Seiber Rhea*

The Bitter Spirit

I remember breathing and wanting the air to clear,
but my lungs, my chest, rebelled against the false
reasons I gave, for sending air of life into them.
I remember walking, and the desire to go limp creeping in.
I remember eating and my throat refusing to swallow.
I remember crying and refusing to draw a tear.
I remember searching for the one responsible for
my existence, to return all the damaged parts.
Then, I remembered, that the one I was searching
for, was not responsible for my Bitter Spirit.
It was an outside force, of a human
Nature, that had my spirit confined.
In that moment of despair, it all began
to come clear, that just because I took
time to care, the chains of confinement
Were no longer there. The one for whom
I searched, than found me, and with an
embrace, held me, and held me.
—*Barbara Breland-Davis*

Susan

The road's been tough that is true,
but never was there a time I didn't love you.

We've come through so much never thought I'd see the day,
make her grow up I would constantly pray.

Now your about to become a bride,
it's hard for me to stifle my pride.

The lump in my throat is tough to keep down,
the day will be special with you wearing my gown.

My hopes and prayers will all now be,
Give her a marriage like God gave to me.
—*Janet S. Hahne*

Lonely is Spelled Without You

I was once very much in love
But that was in my past
Now as I look all around
I ask how long will this last
I once had a name which no one knew
A name can hold much pride
The name that I now must bear
Will be with me till I have died
Lonely is spelled without you
Lonely just means I will be blue
If you should ever need to find me
Just look in the yellow under lonely
Now everyone shall know my name
She has spread it far and wide
When I first heard I knew I was to blame
I hung my head an I cried
—*James Walker*

Are You Waiting In Paradise?

Soon I'll be leaving this world,
But the exit I haven't yet found.
Is there a great bridge to cross over,
Or a tunnel that leads underground?

Do you sense my impending departure,
Are you waiting for me even now?
When word gets around of my passage,
Will you know when I take my last bow?

I hope that my life here was fruitful,
I hope I left more than I brought.
But time has a way of advancing
And mine is about to run out.

Oh, yes, I am definitely coming,
Though I'll need a few years for Goodbyes.
But I'm praying when life here is ended,
I can join you in Paradise.
—*Catherine Geeting*

I Love You

I wish you were with me at all times,
But there are miles between us,
Phone calls are all we have,
Words over the phone are not enough,
Saying "I love you" means a lot,
But actions speak louder than words,
I wish I could show you,
How much I love you.
But the only thing I can do,
Is tell you over the phone.
—*Joanna Toney*

Praising God

Many songs, I have heard, down this path, I have trod.
But the ones, that are scarce, are the ones, praising God.
What else, can we expect in this ole, satan's place.
Though most people, think so, loving God, isn't a disgrace.

Praising God, in his greatness, praising God, in his might.
Praising God, for his mercies, the one, who'll make all things right.
Praising God, for his kindness, praising God, for his love.
Something, so precious, surely came, from above.

It may be, out of style, oh but that's, alright with me.
Cause his promise, to our people, it shall surely, come to be.
All of satan's, stumbling blocks, they shall soon, pass away.
To that glory, land we'll go, there forever, we shall stay.
—*Frank J. Vaughn*

Victory Of Peace!

Rumbling! Armageddon's drums again and again,
But the wound after truce is pain.
Hark! The moans, the groans as croaks the frog,
Far and near around the Martian morgue...
Where are their dreams of the triumphal throne?
Now their souls hover on the hoary bone.
Rome is on fire, the sanguinary stream does flow;
Caesar's sword, the fiddle of Nero, no hero.

Alas! Hide the armor and alarming din,
For it is the sound of horrid sin.
Let's leave doom and darkness behind,
Pray the Lord to save mankind!
If the victory of peace will come anon,
The Ares' shadow shall be gone.
Then a happy, happy way we will go,
To live in joy and harmony, no foe, no woe!
—*Jim H. Lee*

God's Creation

We can look upon the ocean and see beauty, peace and might
But this can change to fierce tumult before a new day's light
Yet wild or calm or peaceful, we wouldn't change a thing
For this is God's Creation, we accept what it can bring.
Gaze quietly upon the sky and meditate and wonder
Then watch the dark clouds gather and hear the distant thunder
Though winds may blow and storms may brew the sky remains a curtain
For this is God's Creation to enjoy in awe that's certain
Now look around at people, no two are quite the same
Yet deep inside we're all alike, with just a different name
Our moods may change from time to time our zest may rise and fall
But we are God's Creation and our love must be for all.
—*Betty Davies*

My Friend Jon

Right now I have lovers on my mind
but usually I am mistaken
about them so I put them aside.
But my heart seems to keep you
my friend Jon in mind first all of the time.
Since you are constantly in it I am going
to resolve myself to at last being here for
you while I grin and bare it.
Since I can only handle one love
at a time and my love for you
mostly consumes that time here is
my friendship I hand to you,
my guide and the others will have
to come second.
—*Carolyn Milazzo*

Peacelessness

I think I've been here before
But this time you are holding my hand and walking me into the light where—
our souls can heal.

And then again, you've been here before.
Was it hard for you?
One would think that after living under artificial light your whole life—
through, that you might be blinded by the real thing.

Of course, the warm glow of it all just makes us calm in the world's still——
waters.
But then again,
you've been there before.
—*John F. Daniel*

The Rose

I saw a red, red, rose today — I couldn't help
but to stop and think of you. Its beauty so
lustrous and rare, like a brilliant stunning gem.
The wind blew lightly through its green leaves
playing a winsome melody that could only be
compared to your sweet voice whispering for all
to hear. The many fragrances of its perfect
blossoms in the air...sending spectacular images
that only you alone could bear. The bright
and pure sunshine shining off its wondrous
petals — reminded me of your radiant eyes that
are full of loveliness, mystery, and surprise
It always stands so glorious and admirably for
all to see, with the grace and eloquence that
belongs only to thee.
—*Amy Williams*

Problem Resolution

There are so many problems in life we must face,
But we have to fight the battle and run the crooked race.
Of shouldn't and shoulds, decisions to be made,
Often we wonder, if we will ever make the grade.

Some days, every little thing seem like climbing up hill,
And after pushing onward, we're like wheels of a mill.
Just grinding passing time, into power as we go,
Leaving footprints with no answers, into new fallen snow.

Hence, we blame the other fellow, hoping to free our minds,
Of the remnants little problems, we wish to leave behind.
But we have to get a grip on the matters now at hand,
Try to find some answers, and take a firm stand.

Hiding doesn't solve them, face facts as the chips fall,
There is a lesson to be learned, with each beck and call.
Never let it get you down, meet conditions head on,
Clear the mind, before you know it, the old problem's gone.
—*Gloria M. Little*

Dreams

I reach to touch you.
But you're not there.
I try once more.
But still I cannot reach you.

Your body seems so close.
I can almost hear you breathing.
I hear you say, "I Love You."
And finally, I have you in my arms.

Suddenly I awake.
Holding my pillow with all my might
Just so you cannot escape.
I go to sleep with a smile on
my face, feeling secure.
—*Chris Osborn*

Why Can't I Touch You

How do I touch you?
By entwining rhythms of thought
Through space and time
All beats chime
The note of love.
I don't have to touch you to feel you
The roots are deep
Springs so potent left alone to steep
Stew I always knew,
No knight with armor
Rode by my castle
Mills though creep through the floor,
With rushes of air,
The elements break open the door,
Crossing the threshold,
Wanting you more, I try to stay warm,
By my heart's burning fires,
Vibes wired for your love
I don't have to touch you to feel you.
—*Camella Ward*

Before The Cock Crows

There's a full blown moon and the whip-poor-wills
Call to a boy in the Ozark hills.

He leaps from his bed and he races out
In a world of silver with a happy shout,

Following his hound to a hidden wood,
Treading on tracks where a wild thing stood.

There's some strange presence____there's something unreal
From the fairy world he can hear and feel

That now can lead him passed the river's bend
Down the moon's path to the rainbow's end,
To a pot of gold, adventure in store!
The boy waits there breathless on the forest floor.

And then of a sudden, a great black cloud
Covers up the moon with a fearsome shroud.

The spell is broken, and the world is black,
Some dreadful thing is breathing down his back!

The boy and the hound race back to his bed
Shaking as he pulls his sheet overhead,

Waiting for the cock's crow telling night is gone,
That he'll be safe with the coming light of dawn!
—*Daphne Huntington*

Friendship

Did you ever feel this fleeting thing
called friendship?

It touches your life once I awhile,
this friendship.

It's very rare and hard to find,
but it touched our lives
Yours and mine.

This mystery,
this fleeting thing,
this friendship.

Did you ever notice when it touches your life,
it's stays forever?

And no matter how far apart you may be,
it's there.

It's touched our lives,
this mystery,
and bonded us together.

Now through time and space
our friendship's there,
the two of us forever.
—*Arlene Finger*

This Battle Called, "Life"

We are all in the same boat, in this Battle of aches and pains, called
   "Life."
My joints ache in a deep, burning pain, but thank God, I am not lame.
I am just crippled up, in a slight, little way, yet I get up,
dress myself and walk some every day! My steps are slow; I
shuffle a bit and when I have a pain, I just bite my lip and,
if others are looking, I just grin and smile and pretend
"everything's copacetic", for a while, but once out of sight,
I really let go and say: "Dammit to hell, I just stumped my toe!"

Now, God, up above, knows me real well and "forgets" my weakness,
when I fail... to be the person I should be and I ask his forgiveness,
but I can't get on my knees... "Coz", I've got Arthritis;
a pain in the neck; a "catch" in my hip, but what the heck!
I take my aches and pains, wherever I go and here I am putting
on a show! Others want to see me, at my best! Sometimes,
"Forcing a smile", is quite a task! Yet, it does me good, for
others to see, "A Happy-Go-Lucky-Smiling Me"!
—*Dorothy Mauldin, OWG*

Times Past

As I climbed the hill
The thought came to me
How many times, I came this way,
To see the old oak tree,
Standing tall, and still,
Surrounded by quiet beauty;
Since childhood, a much loved spot,
'Til now, time has changed, it not-
Our bittersweet memories
Of cherished old places,
Sometimes are the absence of familiar dear faces—
Knowing, they worked and played, in the shade of the tree,
Which is still standing, is a reminder to me—
Time moves swiftly, touches all and is soon past,
Teaching us to treasure, things that will last—
Truth, love and mercy enduring and steadfast—
For earthly joys, and sorrows, someday will change.
To eternal life.
And endless
Tomorrows—
—*Frances Moss Taylor*

To My Brother - Marty

This yellow rose I'm placing at your head,
   Came in a dozen and one and the card read:
"In Loving Memory of Your Brother - Marty"
   You see it was one year ago today,
Good-bye, I had to say,
   For you, no more golf,
No more church,
   No more aches, pain or cough,
No more search,
   I don't know what you were looking for,
Oh, How I wish I could have opened that door
   You must have had a good reason,
Because you picked the season
   Why so far apart did we grow?
   I guess this no one will ever know.
   Listen to me well,
For as brother you were swell,
   I love you now — I loved you then
God rest your soul
   My Brother
     My Friend
       —*Dawn H. Barrell*

Vacation At The Beach

In the wake of early dawning
   came the sunlight peeping through,
   changes on the blue horizon
   marked the hours I spent with you.

Walking, talking, of the beauty
   where the skyline met the sea,
   ripples on the foaming water
   brought our souls in harmony.

In the rapture of contentment
   Mother Nature close at hand,
   sandy beaches stretched far beyond us
   one side ocean, one side land.

As the cool breeze chilled our bodies
   and we watched the sea gulls soar,
   mighty were the waves before us
   beckoning like an open door

In my mind thus activating
   all exquisite forms in view
   came the facts of realization
   why the ocean beckons you.
      —*Emma Noon Reed*

Big Daddy Diamondback

He just sits there under palmetto fronds;
Coiled up ever so peacefully, even to
prodding he doesn't respond;
he just rattles a little and hisses a lot;
If you give him a little more flack;
But that's just the way it is, with Big
Daddy Diamondback;
He lays there silently, his head flattened out;
Quietly sleeping not worrying about;
Who watches his slumber, who spies on his nap;
He knows he could end you with a quick and fatal snap!
But He has not a care, he's a snake so laid Back;
For that is only way to be, for Big Daddy
Diamondback.
      —*Daniel E. Ragsdale*

A Saturday Evening In October

Whipped cream on warm pumpkin pie
Camomile steeps in a mug
And "Wind Across The Water" breezes through my mind.

Woodwinds dance with guitar strings
Gabes "good night Dad" tells my heart
Of evenings with family when life can be so kind.

Heli studies in our room
Josh finds his sleep in a song
While from a warm night sky, the full moon winks and smiles.

Home made pizza mountain bread
Laughter filled the early night
With happy voices that have come so many miles.

This night, this home, this feeling
Words that flow through pen to pad
And whisper to me of the joy I find in life.

Then silence, all is quiet
A fine day has gone to rest
Thank God for two fine sons and such a lovely wife.
      —*Donald F. Lake Jr*

Just In Case

Clutter, clutter, everywhere
Can I throw out anything, DO I DARE?
It may come in handy someday
So I leave it where it lay, "JUST IN CASE."

Those long-awaited books and magazines
Stacked so high, saved from my teens
Those articles clipped and stored
To look at later when I'm bored.

You see! I may want to read them someday
So I put them neatly in a pile and there they lay.
   "JUST IN CASE"
While the piles grow and the shelves overflow
The clothes gather dust that no longer fit; but just sit

The days, months and years go by
While I look at the clutter and sigh, then a voice is heard.
"Let us out of here," someone whispers in my ear.
"Get rid of those things so near and dear, that you never use,
   Do you hear?"

"Possessions Possessions possess you, there's no room for
   something new; but as I ponder I spy something irresistibly blue
I can't resist, "so make room just once more, it's such a dandy
   and will be handy" so what do I keep?
Why naturally, I keep everything, "JUST IN CASE"
      —*Carol M. Santell*

Snowflakes

Snowflakes falling down a lane.
Church bells ringing clear and plain.
Snowflakes knitting a scarf of lace
Around a sweet young face.
Snowflakes: crystal blossoms blooming bright
Ethereal designs frosting the night.
Snowflakes angelic messengers float
In a cathedral silence packed with rapturous motes
Snowflakes weaving tapestries
Golden to samite as doorways to twilight
Snowflakes radiant with fire of ice
Sketch their intimations of Immortality
For man's delight.
      —*Bess Eileen Day*

A Nation Cries

Standing on the battlefield, through the mist of time.
Can you feel the vision...see the dividing line?
Here the battle rages on throughout the night.
In a fit of passion, boys pursue the fight.
Brother killing brother, every mother cries.
As each minute passes another soldier dies.
In the name of freedom the war rages on,
To separate the union, humanity is gone.
Battle after battle blood is freely spilt.
The dying of a nation...who will share the guilt?
So the army marches on; fields are trodden down.
Who can claim the victory? Who will wear the crown?
Can there be a winner when fighting from within?
A nation is torn apart...divisions can not win.
Offer then, an open hand to lift up one another.
Build up, don't tear apart...each neighbor is your brother.
—*Debra Ann Bishop*

Untitled

Come closer to me
Can you see what I feel?
Hold out your hand,
And feel the tenderness in my touch
The love in my heart.
Do you feel my love for you?
The bond that I feel between the two of us.
Look into my eyes
See a world of love and happiness
Enter into a world of everlasting peace.
Look
Listen
Feel
Become one with me
—*Julie Kuhns*

Zen Of Tea

Always in the gentle music and sound,
  candlelight tenderly gleamed.
In a tranquil and dim corner.
  I meditated with scent of tea and people's murmur.
My spirit was far away from the noisy world,
  entering into a wilderness with leaves green as jade.
My spirit lingered like mist in the woods of bamboo trees,
  my heart following the breeze the flower scent...

In a brief lifetime, brilliant or mediocre
  success and failure;
  everything is vanity of vanities,
  vanishing eventually into wind and clouds.

How much stupidity could there be in this world,
  human cruelties, battles and sufferings never ceased.
One could easily let go his burdens
  this empty life's ecstacies and agonies.

Only this moment
  revelation in a blink is transparent.
The existence is holy bliss,
  with tea scent and melodies...
—*Jane Hwa Hu*

Mommy, mommy help me! A precious little child cried.
Can't you hear my silent screams? Can't you even try?
I can't hear you, I can't see you. Once again she cried.
I feel nothing in my heart. A mother's love denied.

Mommy, mommy help me! A precious little child cried.
Can't you see he's hurting me? I need you by my side.
I can't hear you, I can't see you. Once again she cried.
I feel nothing in my heart. A mother's love denied.

I sure must be a bad little child and deserving of all this harm.
Because if I were very good, my mommy would comfort me in her arms.
I can't hear you, I can't see you. Once again she cried.
I feel nothing in my heart. A mother's love denied.

So now this little child is all grown up. But the precious little child is still inside.
The mother is still not the mommy. She never even tried.
The adult and the child went hand in hand when their mother died.
They said goodbye to Mother—then they merged as one and they and they never even cried.
—*Judy A. Lindmeier*

Someone's Going To Call Me "Grandma"

Someone's going to call me "Grandma!"
Caren and George's "Bundle of Joy"
A child of love of the "children" I love!
A precious girl or boy.

A tiny, brand new baby...
To set our world a-whirl
Sharing giggles and grins dressed in diapers and pins.
A precious boy or girl.

A baby is a ticket to forever
For all who lived before.
Our loved ones who've gone, now, will live on...
A link to our ancestors of yore.

So many generations...
From every corner of the Earth.
English, scottish...et al,...short, fat, slender or tall.
In this baby and the miracle of birth.

And...I'm going to be called "Grandma"
By this precious bundle of "genes!"
A child to love and watch grow as the years come and go...
Who'll teach me what being "Grandma" really means!
—*Carole L. DeRuiter*

Dream

Commitment
Caring and sharing to start the dream

Affection
Brightened with respect

Honesty
To make life joyful and kind

Passion
To make us real warm and secure

Trust
To keep love strong

And Love
To keep life's dream alive
—*Julie Ann Bailey Lipman*

Scenes Of Life

I've watched the sun rise in the morning,
Casting rays of amber and gold,,
Above the majestic mountain top,
As the day was starting to unfold,
I've raced through the meadow,
In the warm days of spring,
With the wind blowing through my hair,
Pausing to pick the wild flowers,
That seem to bloom everywhere.
In awe I've watched a mother bird,
Quietly sitting on her nest.
I've sat and rocked my babies,
Peacefully sleeping on my breast.
Now the evening shadows are falling,
Soon the darkness will come.
These things will all be forgotten,
When I move to my permanent home.
—*Ina Price*

Fishing With A Friend

We like fishing using worms and/or a spinner bait,
Catching small ones, big ones, but every once in awhile
one gets away, which we hate.

Telling fishing stories about the big one that got away,
But tell the truth, maybe we did not catch one all day.

Using the best fishing tackle, like hooks, nets, and
line that's ten pound test,
And bragging to one another who is the best.

With blue sky above and clear cool water below,
Sometimes fishing can be fast and sometimes fishing can be slow.

But to feel that tug on the line,
Then to bring that bass in looks mighty fine.

To have the peace and quiet of fishing is one of the
good things it will bring,
Which will keep me coming back at the start of every spring.

We must all take care of the land, rivers, and streams,
So others like the children to come, can fulfill their
fishing dreams.

Also we must always be thankful to God and mother nature
for the beauty that they lend,
When we go fishing with a friend!
—*Charlie Rutherford*

Autumn Leaves

A gentle breeze that blew today
caused the leaves to leap and play.
They scurried round upon the ground
as tho in games of lost and found.
Their coats had changed from flat to round.
Their moves were slow when on the grass,
but on the walks, or driveway fast.
And with lifting of the breeze,
they all seemed settled, at ease.
Some bushes standing tall and straight,
with branches closely shutting in
A scraggly leaf clung her and there,
with all the other branches bear.
Some still on bushes clinging fast
declining from their perch to pass.
These ragged leaves would go
with the coming of the snow.
—*Alice Ostrowicki*

Grandma

Grandma is so special
Cause she has so much love to give
And she always seems to know just when I need
An extra hug or kiss.

She has a little cookie jar
That's always in my reach
And it never seems to empty
Full of magic it must be.

Grandma takes me shopping
And takes me to the zoo,
She sings and reads me stories
Shows me pictures in a book.

She tucks me in at bedtime
And listens to my prayers,
And tells me little stories
You can't find in any book.

When I grow up I wanna be like grandma
And when grandmas little just like me
I'm gonna give back all the hugs and kisses,
Grandma gave to me.
—*Edith Young*

Hard Times

The little house where I once Lived,
close to the railroad Track.
A place that I always called Home,
but most called it a Shack.

Cracks were wide in the Walls,
and holes were in the Floor.
When the rain came tumbling Down,
the water then would Pour.

The house only had two Rooms,
the roof was made of Tin.
There was no insulation To,
keep out the cold north Wind.

We never had much Money,
but we had food to Eat.
Some bread and water Gravy,
but mostly wild Meat.

Pallets were made on the Floors,
a place for us to Sleep.
We played a battery Radio,
these memories I shall Keep.
—*John H. Turner*

Long Walk

Through the stillness I walk alone.
Cold and heat press hard against me, touching bone.
My own breath—a pounding drum.
That fills my ears and tasks my lungs.
It breaks the stillness.
Far above, but not that far.
Clouds like specters glide.
Shimmering phantoms, fallen angels
they pass me by.
I try to touch, I try to grasp
but I cannot reach.
They pass on by.
Through my eyes I see the giant.
Ageless still yet ever dying
its timeless vigil keeps.
I come by close and am permitted
to touch its greenwood cloak.
—*Eugene A. Marino*

Spirit, Soul And Body, Trust God

Gentle spirit within me
Come forth and see each day!
Now it's safe to frolic forth
Rejoicing as you play!

I know that you have hidden
Your pain far, far away
And kept your personal distance
To survive within the day.

With you, spirit, I have chosen
To allow God's light through
Now my soul trusts in God,
And what He wills this body, I do.

Continue to strive for excellence,
And learn all that you can;
But now you need not know what's best
You are part of His greater plan.

My gentle soul has come forth
To praise the beauty in each day
For now we live within the truth
That will not go away.
—Clara Hill

North Shore Hospitality, World War II

Come see my lilacs!
Come have tea!
My garden's full of lilacs,
Do come see!
Any afternoon between two and three,
I'll be waiting for you,
Do call on me!
My house's on the corner of Ravinia and Skokie,
You can't miss it, it's easy to find!
Look for a big house, two stories high,
Grey with green shutters and a bright red door!
My fence is white picket with rose trellis gate —
The gate's always open,
So come right in!
Come see my lilacs!
Come have tea!
My garden's full of lilacs,
Do come see!
—June Allegra Elliott

Table

If you want to solve a matter
Come sit at the table
Converse and share our wandering thoughts
at this barren, naked, table.
Mix some drinks and sit a spell
Carve up words like meat.
Shut anger down to a snails pace
Dern, we forgot to eat
Chew on words and spit them out
Chatter 'till you freeze.
Solve the problem until finality
then go ahead and sneeze
Frozen words, thaw them out
Heat them in your mouth.
Salivate their outer shell
get up and head for the south.
At this table is a bowl of conversation
dish up the subject and discuss
the put on wings, fly words out
then table all matters and collect dust.
—Frances Marie Surls

Someday

Someday I may live to see all men,
come together all as friends.
No mater what color, race or creed,
they'll all work together for those in need.
In need of someone to show them how,
to start to walk as of now,
someone to help a blind person to see,
and others to help the poor in need.
Who are all human like you and me.
—Cheryl Mari Lakey Loring

The Child Inbetween The Woman...

The child inbetween the woman,
Comes with two faces...
It is the child the Woman's reflection
no longer displays,
Except in the eyes of her aging mother...
And, it is the child the woman wants to
someday bear and love,
Wearing the eyes of a mother she's known...

The child in between is the woman,
The mother...
A womb both full, yet, vacant,
Sometimes, biological,
Other times, simply symbolic...
Here, the very core of the child in between
spreads and blossoms...
In synch with the woman or mother you must be.
—Brenda Eileen Figueroa

Emily

Euphoria
  compressed
    into giggles
Emily straddles
a loose leg
and clutches . . .
her dark hair
  deepening
    into jet eyes
that laugh
quietly
questioning
    the visitor's thoughts

Energy unbounded
  Emily
  dances
  circling, pleading
  to those enraptured
  before falling,
  kneeling
  and with baby yells
  soliciting
  desires inchoate
  from a cross-stitched sky
  Emily waiting . . .
on a stilled wind.
—Cheryl Block

Azealy

Azealy shakes her head,
concern marks those green eyes.
What is Momma doing?
Who is this fair-haired, brown-eyed
stranger kissing Momma's sweet lips?
Daughter walks in the room,
asks questions with no words.
The stranger just consoles her,
no explanations, no sorrow,
only sweetness in the new arms.
Azealy leaves the lovers
still shocked at the scene.
She looks at her own body—
could she be attracted
to another like herself?
Sleep fills her eyes,
she drifts off to the sounds
of her Momma and the beautiful lady.
—*Darren Griffin*

Untitled

Lifeless hollows in an empty face,
Constantly running an endless race,
Against the devil and his ways.
It stares back and does not.
Many years it has fought.
It screams its soul cannot be bought,
But it has gone. It's already gone.
Oh, when will come the dawn?
It has become the devil's pawn,
In his attempt to rule the world,
Simple insults are thrown, they're hurled.
It yearns for its freedom to be unfurled.
But it's too late, its fate is sealed.
It cries each night, it must be healed.
Its only weapon is deeply hidden love that it wields,
With all the strength left in life and soul.
It has lived, now it will pay the toll,
Down to the pits of hell, a bottomless hole.
And in its last strike of fear, it calls its name before it's done.
"If I say my name, can I run? You know who I am- I am human!"
—*Jennifer Gregerson*

The Rebel

There are those who sit in patience's seat,
  content with what life gives,
Not to wander on rebellious feet,
  like I, in whom a restless spirit lives.
Yet, the mist of morning, is not always gray
  because the golden rod
Blooms along a country way
  but not every friend is dear,
And not every poem complete,
  but I pray, dear Lord, teach me
To take the bitter with the sweet.
  Sometimes I feel like the restless tide,
That keeps the mighty sea in motion.
  But still 'tis the sweat upon my brow,
That becomes a healing lotion.
  Then diligent work will smooth my way
And hope will dry my tears,
  and help to bring a brighter day,
Throughout the coming years.
—*Eva Darrington Rule*

God's Allegorical Reality

The Gods - being those in the universal sphere
Controlling the forces of nature - like here
Realized as so many here do now
Existantance would cease without this plan of the plough

So the host of heaven gathered and agreed
Sending prince Lucifer with his third of greed
Their mission - to thwart good if they could
While the remaining were to choose the right and good

The Lemniscus is a sign of eternity
As also Uroboros and Kundalini
While rhyming and timing are known as poetry
Each another form of semantics to me

For as it was above - tis now so below
No matter the temptations - be they fast or slow
Earth's time is limited - as many are aware
Too many thinking too many just don't care

And as eve made her choice to disobey
We each now have many choices each day
So pray for peace people every where
As we continue to try to share and care

  Or to quote Alexander Pope:
  "To err is human - to forgive . . . divine"
—*Beverly E. Vincent*

Resurrection Of Roses

Wooden sculptures brood in frozen breath as
cool clouds portray the crispness of winter.
Structures of skeletons are the season slaves,
white Death dominates earth with cold evidence
of still branches and bold, bare landscapes.
Suddenly, an echoing of existence rustles,
brittle trees slowly ache and arise with life
petals pop brilliant shades of jade and blue.
Stripped twigs are caressed by ruby jewels,
endless spirals of spinning yellow twist while
soft, secular beauty sings and speaks fertility.
Somber shadows slink away as winter wanes.
—*Chantelle Cooke*

Autumn In The Ozarks

When there are multicolored leaves
Corn and wheat is bound in sheaves
And hibernating spiders weave
Their web homes in the autumn...
Song birds then will all take flight
To places where it's warm and bright
While a harvest moon shines silver light
It's autumn in the Ozarks

There...in the quiet backwoods deep
Nestled in the hollows steep
Trees and flowers prepare to sleep
It's autumn in the Ozarks

The Smoky Mountains autumn's fair...
While the Rocky Mountains autumn's rare
But here and now I must declare...
That only heaven could compare
With...autumn in the Ozarks
—*Hazel H. Wells*

The Climb is Nearly Over

It seemed so high so far away.
Could the climb ever be made someone might say?
Marvel of all miracles not surprising to us all,
You've climbed and near reached the mountain top without a
   single fall!
Fears did not hold you back or waver in your stead.
Your beautifully and unreservedly kept your calm instead.
Searching many times and overwhelming it sure must have been.
You sought out strength and courage and never questioned when?
Holding to this moment and seeking the mountain's path,
Circling the rocky crags and precipices you reached out to the last.
In those precarious moments where faith and hope seemed dim,
A light would shine from the mountain top and fears would flee again!
Standing tall on the mountain's crest you see the world stilled by awe.
Nestled is the valley below where you didn't take a fall!
Through love and friends and family, you've defeated every
   obstacle in the way.
You've climbed your mountain and given us a proud example
   of who you are today!
—*J. J. Johnson*

Life

Life is often like a river
   Coursing down through time
At first 'tis but a rivulet
   Then youth, cascading in its prime.

Sometimes 'tis like a placid pool
   Unhurried its tryst to keep
Then 'neath some towering, darkened cliff
   Forbidding, cold, and deep.

Now plunging down some precipice,
   Through cauldrons, awesome, wild
Then stretching out o'er sunny plain
   Calm, benign and mild.

Till flowing on in course now set
   Fulfilling destiny
It comes at last to journey's end
   In the ocean of eternity.
   —*Francis Phelps*

Respect

Respect, an expression of deference
   Courteous, respectful, high in esteem,
Seemingly abandoned completely
   By the whole world, it would seem.

Always taught throughout the past
   In the home and in the schools,
It was always an inclusion
   Of a mothers golden rules.

Today it has lost its meaning
   Look around and you will see,
There's no respect for others
   For their lives or properties.

It's time to re-examine
   Some priorities in growing up,
Re-establish the word respect
   Down play the word disrupt.

Respect should always be included
   In our vast vocabulary,
Its meaning taught at the earliest age
   And then practiced regularly.
   —*Gilbert L. Hilderbrand*

The Goddess Of Love's Demise...?

The Goddess of love is under siege, a demon harbors doom,
Courtship, in spite of tradition, may be bound for somber
   tomb.
Sweethearts tend to worry when their hormones are excited,
Romantic chase must be chaste, instincts stand indicted.
Impulsive sex is branded "X," and is socially taboo;
Saying "No" is the way go, permissiveness is through.
By purging carnal urgings, so that feelings are suppressed,
Allows for rationality and consequences get addressed.
A devil-spawned view of death has reared its ugly head,
Causing couples to fearfully spurn a dormant lovers bed.
The love-lamp flickers dimly, doubt shadows its pale glow;
Cupid has lost his careful aim when blinded by a deadly foe.
There are better odds for bettors at the tracks of Hialeah,
Than prevail in the avoidance of Aids, Herpes, and Gonorrhea.
Condom use has been advised, causing many a doubtful frown.
But when we face reality, it's the only show in town.
Accepting such a mandate may turn some hearts to stone,
However we'd wisely listen lest the Goddess be overthrown.
The counter-act of condom use my keep the games alive;
Compromise may do the trick — the Queen may yet survive!
   —*H. Bud Holmes*

Octoberfest In Knightstown

Fall, fun, festivities
Crafts of all kinds - what a delight.
Games by R.A.F. III and friend:
   Three chances at
     mini bowling darts with pop cans
     or shooting darts at a board or
     tossing a ball through a hole.
   If you win - take fists full of candy.

Will you have your face painted?
Choose: a ghost? A black cat?
   a teddy bear? A rainbow?

There's cotton candy, hot dogs, and
   pumpkins to buy.

Clowns to excite the hearts of children,
   willing to stand in long lines for
   receiving the magic of balloons —
   - A heart with a teddy bear holding on
   - A fantastic sword and sheath
   - A seven color high, high hat for Rebecca.
   —*Julia Strain Fangmeier*

Endangered Species Pray

Organic melodies stack on the ceiling
Crowded with pipes. Fingers hack on tusk
In one lit eyeball staring dusk
From the nails and tales of healing

Before the beggars fallen, kneeling
In fields of corn. Pick and bicker husk
For husk to offer him in stench of musk
From hours of stealing and praying and peeling

His skin. The bang of every chord
Is met with a crossing of their sword
To hang him on the wall and press their hands

Together. The elephant left the maternity ward
And fell to the ground in the name of their Lord
To hear the rotten teeth chatter where he stands.
   —*Gregg LaBranche*

The Beauty Of God's Creation

Highways and right-of-ways encircle the beauty of God's creation. Interstates equip motorists for traveling life's fast pace. On the map, highways appear to be gift wrapping on our great nation. All about those roads, nature is shining with such a happy face.

Faithful workers busily care for the beauty of God's creation. Employees work faithfully to complete their trying task— Spring, Summer, Fall, and winter—there're things to do each season. All workers should know the Lord because they often face risks.

The forests and orchards are part of the beauty of God's creation. The colors are breathtaking! All colors are dazzling and beautiful. I like to think of each tree as waving, "I'm part of God's creation." Man's inventions get rusty and antique; trees are always beautiful.

Little creeks seem to say, "I portray the beauty of God's creation." "My water flows over the rocks so clear and so blue" And the water's ripple is saying, "I too am a part of God's creation." Such beauty causes the Christian traveler to say, "Lord I love you!"

Out across the fields we see the beauty of God's creation. There are birds, cows, and there stands a many-horned deer. All nature makes us feel that truly God is near. Looking across the woodlands, we feel like having a celebration!

—*James H. Duke Jr.*

Life After

On infant knees the days crawl past,
creeping spiders burdened by mesmerization.

Suspended in this void I wait,
an amber globule bedded on a petri dish
while my inmost eyes examine my intentions.

Did I mean it when I said,
"I'm happy for you"?
Or was that merely masque
to protect my confusion?

After these twenty years or so,
can I still feel for you?

Am I humane or a fragment,
splintered, so many iron icicles
on an empty battlefield?

Dare I search myself so far?
I am, I think —
content to be,
whatever there is
left of me.

—*Janice L. Dunn*

Wind Tune

How shrill the worn wind whistles
Circling us with lassoes of sand,
Binding tightly our wraps around,
Forcing our short steps to stop
Until it unwinds its woodwind tune,
Letting us loose — momentarily—
Then fiercely it lashes out again
To sting our legs with staccato notes!

—*Jeanne Claytor*

ISP

Like lemmings they came, from near and far,
crossing oceans and borders and boundaries
and barriers of race, color and creed.
Black and yellow, red and white,
Muslim and Bhuddist, Christian and Jew,
they came together in one accord.
They laughed together, and cried.
They broke bread together.
What miracle is this? Who are these hordes?
Hundreds of people from distant landsat must be said.
and different cultures?
They are poets.
The International Society of Poets.
They are one!

—*Ella M. Dillon*

No Meat In The Pan

With howling of wolf and moan of the wind,
Cruel winter arrived with a cry of its own.
For at the barren land frozen with snow.
Only cold bones laid, the bison was gone.
No big medicine as conjuring gods,
With beating of drums and shaking the skulls
Brought buffalo back. As the Indian falls,
Strife and despair made a prey of the land.
No white man gave a damn if the Indian starved
All buffaloes were skinned and the meat left to rot.
While in a freezing shack as cold shadows went black,
The fire was lit...but no meat in the pan!!!

—*David G. Acosta*

"A Special Gift"

Take these precious pearls of wisdom
Cultured by the sands of time
Strung one by one on silken thread
By these two hands of mine

Add precious memories to above
To help us to grow strong
Add memories that let us know
What's right and what is wrong

Add precious love to all above
To give us daily hope
Mix with pearls of wisdom
Strung on a silken rope

Add precious choice to all above
Be careful when you sift
It's meant for you and me my friend
This very special gift

Be sure to mix it all with care
Stir well with all above
And know this special gift from God
Who watches us with love.

—*Delores Wilson Reece*

Tapping Through

Into the world
   daddy's arms
      mommy's lap - tap

Take first step
   terrible twos
      walk, talk-clap - tap tap

School days
   not your will, mine
      teen flap - tappity tap tap

Stage, robe
   tassel left, right
      graduation cap - tap tap tap tap

Marriage years
   children and tears
      household trap - tap tap tap

You've paid your fare
   you're there
      your face - the map - tap tap

now the final nap -
   Tap
      —*Jacqueline Burks-Shiver*

A Poem

You see them there, those ghostlike words,
Dancing above your head,
As locked inside this darkest night,
You lie unsleeping upon your bed.

You reach out to grasp them
And know the pain that they are gone
And as the silent moments pass,
You pray their return with the misty dawn.

Yet you search the shadows and shake awake
All the dreams that know you well.
For certain, one will supply the words,
Yes, surely one will tell.

Might this poem go a secret to the grave
In a crushed heart held still?
The words eternally unnudged from the tongue,
Unable to take love at will.

But comes that precious moment, rare,
Your soul writhes and then, and only then,
You humbly step behind yourself
And let beauty flow through the pen.
   —*Dawn Hilliard*

Ripples

Ripples made in a stream like those of a pebble dropped,
Circle out to encompass a broad expanse before their action is stopped.
When ripples are made in the stream of life by the deeds that
  we create
Take care they abound in the acts of love and not in the acts of hate.

Ripples of God thru His church on earth, rebound both far and wide,
Calling all people to live for Him so His love in them may abide.
Will you heed His call; make a ripple for Him; no matter how
  large or small?
Right where you are, you can circle out, who knows, maybe
  farthest of all!
   —*Juanita Derringer*

Through The Window

Through the window I have watched you
Dancing in my heart.
Tell me your secrets of beauty and mystery!
You're always changing through the seasons:
Summer, spring and fall; none as beautiful as
The winter, for you lay a blanket of snow on me.
I'm always watching you through my window,
Since the accident with my car put me here.
I was completely paralyzed, except for
My heart and soul calling out to you.
I love to watch and listen to the birds call
In the morning and afternoon; I imagine
I am not this heartless, boxed-in room;
I am by a beautiful waterfall,
With nature calling to me everywhere.
Eventually I am dragged from my world and reminded
Of what happened to me by a loved one's visit.
Then I no longer hear the birds, but instead
I hear God keep pushing me to continue
To love the world and love myself for who I am—
A strong, powerful woman.
   —*Jamie Goff*

Ecstasy

Running through the meadow
Dancing through the trees
Like a mirror is my reflection
In the brook below my knees.

Singing birds and butterflies
Freely come and go
With their enchanted melody's
Entwined with nature's soul

The azure sky, white puff's of clouds
Above my head I see
The shadowed reflection of the sun,
Between old oaks and me

In one hushed moment the graceful gait
Of a tiny little fawn
A doe and buck also appear
Then in one split second are gone

Deeper and deeper, this pulsating love
The earth, the sky, and me
Spinning, whirling, to the sun
Ecstasy
   —*Jeanne DePorter*

Savor

Why do we not stroke the sun in
days with little pardon?

Softly I kiss these velvet lips
As sweet years move over our tongues
And nothing is lost
Here in the sunshine
As we consummate our passions in gentle rapture

The heavenly texture of wind
is speaking its ancient voice;

Stirs our blood with the remembrance
Of exquisite tastes-
With the promise of an alternative to fortitude
With the savored knowledge
That this is our only light.
   —*Casey Schuck*

Color Him Alex

He was so very tiny, as I held him in my arms
Dark hair, dark eyes and cheeks of pink
His heart-shaped mouth opened in a yawn
Tired from his journey into this big world
We counted his toes and fingers, as all new parents do
There were ten of each, and we marveled
As their smallness was measured against the size of ours

   Color him Alex-God's special gift

We went through all the trauma, as all new parents do
The sleepless nights and all the fears of wondering what to do
But the days went by and Alex grew
And we were filled with pride
His first smile, first sounds, crawling, standing, his first steps...
Each time our hearts swelled with joy and love
And now, today is his birthday
It seems like only yesterday when
We held that tiny baby in our arms
And yet, we can't remember life without him

   Color him Alex—one year old
     —Alice Gosch

Where Are You Now?

Where are you? Whom like the sun invaded my threshold of darkness. Filling it with warmth and illumination. Where are you? With whom I briefly danced under neon lights; With whom I shared the foams of an excessively chilled and bitter champagne, smoothed with sweetness and desire by the touch of our lips. Where are you? With whom I laughed in silliness! And, Where are you now? When I need you to talk with and share our ideas so as to learn more about each other. When I need you to hold me as the touch of your hands heals the pain of my body and soul. When I need you to listen to my dreams and tell me of yours, and together, to make them a reality. When I need you to dry the tears from past sufferings And work toward a brighter tomorrow. When I need you to take my hand in yours And guide me through the unknown wonders of Life! Where are you now? When I am here in need of you. Anxiously awaiting your return, prepared to overcome the obstacles that have torn us apart at the very birth of our union.

   —Angela M. Carini

Last Moments

At my last moment of Breathe.
Dear Lord, let your words be on my lips.
As I pass thru, this dark ole, world
May I have an example been.
May I have felt others, despair
And been of some help
To somebody some where.
And have shed a tear, or two.
Of grief and joy.
That I am now in your arms
Forever more.
As the shadow of death.
Passes my door
I have you and want no more
   —Beverly Marski

Soft Over An Ocean Night

I see flowers but of you,
deep down in the future,
"Sight of You"
I see your color in my sight.

Soft over an Ocean Night,
What a delight it told me,
Deep down on the shore
soft as a peach, pretty as a beach,
you are my dream over a soft ocean beach.
   —Charles R. Childs

The Beginning Of An End

High in the mountains he dwells,
   deep inside a dark, and lonely cave.
He'll spend the rest of his days,
   living in the style meant for him.

The tribe calls him an old woman,
   because of his aging ways.
His time has come to travel alone,
   for his few remaining years.

He has served his time as chief
   of council, and other important matters.
His youth is spent, he now is old,
   no more can he toil the laborious tasks.

His people will come for his body,
   when all life is drained from his living being.
But his soul will continue to live on,
   in a most spirited way.

He's now looking forward to the time,
   when he will be reunited with his ancestors.
In the happy hunting grounds,
   for the beginning of an end.
   —Aileen Jennings

Demons

Spirits they called them, in bottles they dwell
Demons so evil, called up from hell.
Each one ensnares you, beguiling they be,
Eases your pain briefly, denies eternity.
Satan is clever while he steals your mind,
Ruins your body, your soul he entwines,
Lures and binds you in chains more each day,
Denies God still loves you and leads you away.
Away from the glories our God has in store,
You drift out so slowly, so far from the shore.
Our God reaches out for you, He puts out His hand.
Oh, grasp it, beloved, while you still can!
Fight all those demons, don't let them destroy
All the gifts that God gave you, your health and your joy!
We will fight with you, help you and pray
That God will assure you our love surrounds you today.
Oh, please, please remember Satan wants you in hell.
Please let us help you so together we'll dwell
Someday in heaven at our fathers side
Where in his full glory we'll together abide!
   —Barbara F. Ahearn

Beauty

Reflected in the plainest face,
Detected in a simple sigh;
Not always in the object viewed,
But deep within the viewer's eye.

A rose to some is just a flower,
Others cherish its rare perfume;
A grecian urn can give delight,
So, too, the fabric from a loom.

A poem needs a special art
To magnify the poet's heart;
It need not be of words sublime,
But cadence in each thoughtful line.

Beauty is where you wish it found,
It matters not the form or guise;
The eyes but see the poem viewed,
The mind wherein the beauty lies.
—*Juliann M. Grandchamp*

The Tale Of A Lonesome Heart

Creases line the sunken-in brow,
Devious smile plays upon crinkled lips—
Innocent eyes narrow.
Black hair tousled,
Fine boned nose rests between cheeks,
Thin wrist holds large knuckled hand
That swipes at a teasing fly.
Crumpled on a bed,
A cloud seems to hang over her—
As if thundering and lightning.
Gray ovals circle her steely eyes
Pounding headache is shrill and doesn't cease—
Wishes to be alone.
Fury screams and
kicks in the pit of her mind . . .
Wishes so hard to be alone,
So hard . . .
Granted? She's speechless.
During her mind's tantrum—
She was already alone.
—*Colleen Williams*

They Burned Our Flag Today

They burned our flag today!
Did the fiery glow enthrall
Those who taunted Freedom's Call?
How high the flaming torch arose
Against the darkened sky!
For shame! A far-off land incite
To burn our Country's flag for spite!
Will the flames of fear imbue
The intolerant to spew
The Sparks of Hatred here?
Why? the questioning voices heard
Why desecrate our Country's flag
with garish deed, and slanderous word!
With fiendish force and cowards cries!
They burned our flag today!
—*Anah Patton*

untitled

changing times

forgotten promises   hope scarred with flames
              dignity lost   children fears
too much hunger   so much hatred   too many are dying

in
the
last
few
thoughtful
years

how much more until we see   beyond
    apathy   separatism   prejudice   ego   pride
      ignorance   fear   criticizing   analyzing
to love of each other   right now
—*bev kelly*

Dear Lord, I Pray

Dear Lord, each day as I pray
Direct my paths along the way.
Keep within me a clean mind and
a pure heart that I might think
and say that which pleases you.
Give me wisdom to know your ways
In all I do and in all I say.
Help me to decrease that you
might increase in all my life.
Fill my heart with love that I
shall keep thy commandment to
love others as you have loved me.
Help me to look beyond the faults
of my family, neighbors and friends
So they can look beyond my faults
and see you through my life.
With your divine help and love
I shall be able to press onward
toward perfection and be acceptable
to my blessed Heavenly Father.
—*Annie McInnis*

A Sorrowful Future

Pain for shadowing my tears as the beauty
disappears.
Emptiness fills my soul as destruction takes
ahold. What was here is now gone as in each
passing dawn.
Ever lasting tears I cry for fear
No golden sunrises or blue skies
No eagle soaring or butterflies flying
No life to be given or taken.
As we are digging our own graves
Slowly now I watch mother earth disintegrate.
—*Dawn Tomasello*

Perishable Love

God done gave us a forever love, Revered Mouth said until death do us part; Death never cross one's mind 'cause the heart flutters instead of beats, I'd searched high and low but none suffocates my every breath like this addiction; Life once taken for granted seems so precious now. Love and matrimony makes two into one, Legs can't move without a head and vice versa; Contentment of knowing someone is in your corner fulfills a need I never knew, when the world is cruel and sorrow fills the air I know you are there; Time brings fourth sometimes offspring and new friends from this relationship of love. Love is a struggle with many pitfalls and triumphs, Reverend Mouth said let no man bring us apart; No one loves you like I but God states he's a jealous God, All I vision is your loving embrace and tender kisses assuring our emotional high; Life once taken for granted seems so precious now. Unlike Adam I would give two or more ribs to stay immersed in this love affair, Eyes sometimes deny the metamorphosis time and health plays; Death feast on the circle of friends and family, I'd rather die a million deaths to see your love again; God done gave us a perishable love and what we made of it can never expire.

—*Byron E. Turner*

Torture

How dare you shout at thee!
Do you find yourself so self-righteous you can judge me?
Only hatred and contempt I feel,
is it not conformity to which you kneel?
Trying to stay different yet joining from vanity.
All the violence I control, battling for sanity.
you owe your judgmental life to me,
still you dare shout at thee!
Without me you could not exist,
without you, never, would I resist.
Puddle size lake to a vast ocean,
as dangerous as an intoxicating potion.
Never blessed for you to leave my thoughts,
freedom from you is what I have sought.
It is you, you have induced these negatives you have built.
Murmur your torture, for I realize, you are my guilt.

—*Cynthia Collins*

Success Is Most Evasive

Success is most evasive
Do you go this way or that way?
We work and try not to be lazy
And when we cannot find success, what can we say?

We struggle on in poverty
Listening to the mockingbird's song
Where is the road to successful prosperity?
Where did I go wrong?

On how we long to be a financial success
Wishing the money to go to Hawaii or Paris or Rome
Trying to feel, while we're poor, we're blessed,
As we listen to the mockingbird's song.

We try to be patient, hard working and strong
As in times the rose in kissed by the buzzing bee
At times folks can't seem to get along
The road to success is not plain to see.

Will we be poor in our golden years?
Will be have many friends and things?
Even working hard and not be lazy,
Success is most evasive.

—*James T. Carter*

Lost People

Listen! Do you hear it! It is coming!
  Do you hear it! It is here!
The sounds of our lost forefathers;
  crying in the wind!
Listen! Do you hear it! It is coming!
  Do you hear it! It is here!
Sounds of our lost forefathers;
  Shouting in the pale moonlight!
Listen! Do you hear it! It is coming!
  Do you hear it! It is here!
Sounds of our lost forefathers;
  Crying in their shame!
Listen! Do you hear it! It is coming!
  Do you hear it! It is here!
Sounds of our lost fathers;
  Crying in the wind!
Listen! Do you hear it! It is coming!
  Do you hear it! It is here!
Sounds of our children;
  Crying in the wind!
Listen! Do you hear it! It is coming!
  Do you hear it! It is here!
Sounds of their children;
  Lost in the wind!
Listen! Do you hear it! Do you hear it! It's is here!
Sounds of our lost people;
  Crying in the wind!

—*Flora Billings Wilson*

The Symbol Of Our Freedom

When you hear the stride of marching to the sound of fife and drum
Do you swell with pride and pleasure as the marchers closer come?
Look with pride upon our soldiers, sailors, airmen, and marines
As they stride so firmly forward, in dress whites and blues and greens?

Sweethearts, brothers, sons, and fathers, placing duty over all,
Following their nation's banner anywhere their country calls.
Silent prayers we're sending upward; not a single eye is dry
As we stand so proud and humble, while Old Glory passes by.

She's the symbol of our freedom, and we look on her with pride,
Remb'ring that to defend her many thousand men have died.
So my friends, do not disgrace her in your speaking or your deeds
She's the symbol of our freedom, let's all follow where she leads.

—*Bessie G. Clipner*

Love

What is love?
Does anybody really know anything about love?
If not
Then why do we write about it?
Why do we say "I'm in love?"
Is love a true feeling
If love is a feeling
Than why do we always have to search for it?
If we do have to search for it
Then with whom?
But the only true person in the world
Who really knows what love is.
Is the Lord.

—*Christine Jette*

Who Do You See?

A melancholy mood sweeps over my soul as the storm wind hard
does blow. I stare into a looking glass to be greeted by one I
do not know. What I see is not the keeper of my soul it is a
prison with walls of flesh and misfunctioning parts. Yet the
sentence is not live and die alone, but freedom by prayer and a
power not my own. My pick and shovel are faith and trust; my
plans all detailed in one Holy Book. My assignment is not to be-
moan my task, only simply listen and do as asked to deny myself
whether people or places or things I don't need to take up my
cross and follow indeed. The climb is slow, the pain intense at
times. And loneliness the hardest payment for the crime of choosing
my own way, which points me straight to my judges court where
sin did condemn and flesh distort. But what I find time and
again is not condemnation, but a true friend eyes emblazoned
with love freely given no judgement, no chains, no walls of a
prison. Only strength for today, hope for tomorrow, and when the
day comes eternal freedom from sorrow. Consequences for sin are
born with me still yet freedom from weight was paid on that
hill. What lies ahead on my journey afar is held in the hand of
the Hanger of stars. The adventure ends not in valleys so low,
but continues as onward and upward I go. Knowing I'll fall as I
go on my way, the blow is lessened as I hear Him say, "Fear not
my child for I Am the Way."
—*Amy Little*

Silent Sounds

There are so many sounds it seems I cannot hear,
Does darkness say "Good Morning to daylight drawing near?
Do raindrops sound like crystal as they dance upon the leaves,
Do acorns say "Excuse Me" as they fall from out the trees?
Do tall trees whisper "Thank You" as they drink the summer rain
Or is it just the breeze rustling through the leaves that makes
  the sweet refrain?
Do little caterpillars sound like marching bands
As many tiny feet scurry 'cross the land?
Do rainbows say "Wake Up" from vantage points on high,
To all the world beneath their glowing banners in the sky?
Do spiders bow politely, say "Thank You" loud and clear,
To fronds that grow more densely on the evergreens each year;
Providing spots to spin each web that catches dew at dawn,
Does grass say "Ouch!" as puppies bounce across the shining
  lawn?
In forests deep where rays of light filter through the leaves
And a myriad forms dart in and out here, among the trees,
Do fairy sprites play with delight, can you hear them laugh,
Or is it just the wildlife scurrying on the path?
Or are the legends I've been told...of many happenings of old!
Of goblins, fairies, sprites and more...still milling 'bout the
  forest floor?
Are the shapes that dart through merely butterflies,
Or is that quiet flitting sound fairy laughs and sighs?
—*Colleen Sullivan-Rusch*

The Man

Twas his love that carried me away
deep into passions and fantasies
I dared not desire
Forces were created when our two souls collided
Our bodies were made for each other,
and our minds were becoming one.
His love carried me places
I'd never been and never dared to go,
but yet here he was making all that a
women wants real....
  "He was a man."
—*Anna A. Recupero*

Then And Now

Throughout the ages of change and progress for most
Does quality of life share their needs of hope?
Not much time to rest nor to know what is the best
For whatever reason one should dare hint
But everyone seems to know it's too much government.
Not so long ago, a hundred years or so
The world of small communities was apt and great to know.
Security and happiness afforded by stewards of the soil
And friends at church or school shared task of daily toil.
There was no need for the bold to venture very far
Few roads and bridges lest encroachment of tyrants from afar.
Two or four wheel carriages neither pulled nor shoved
But drawn by special member of family as gift from above.
The horse thrived on travels, care and hay along the way.
With or without aching bones in travels of weather exposure
Was the price gladly paid for their way of life and composure.
And perhaps to endure pain with or without liniment.
Was the substitute for too much government.
Whither away so fast today on the ground or the in the air
Of course rejoice there is choice - simply serve, care and share!
—*Archie G. Rich*

Never A Burden To Me

You were never a burden to me
Don't ever say these words to me
You're someone who meant the world to me
So don't ever let me hear you're a burden to me
The love you gave will never be erased
With your child-like embrace
You took care of my needs
You were on constant watch of me
Never out of sight of your light
You were a beacon on the darkest night
You were never a burden to me
Don't ever say these words to me
You touched many lives
More than one can say
Yet as we lower you in your grave
And as my hand releases its grip
What can I say to someone who meant the world to me
But that, you were never a burden to me
—*Andy Harris*

The Secret Of The Land

America is the country made of dreams
Dreams made in the faraway country,
When sameness makes you restless
And the escapes is the only way.

Is it worthy to leave the cozy little life
And start fighting your way through
A lot of injustice and unhappiness
While wondering what's that all about?

It takes years and even lifetime
To understand, and feeling uplifted
By given experience of life
So free, unusual and moving.

And finally the understanding comes
And finally you know the why and when
Feeling all that richness, no stagnation,
By unlocking the door to the secret
of the land.
—*Hedy Wolf Formanek*

Don't Mind The Tears

As you read these lines, which are for you, I note,
Don't mind the tears, that fell as I wrote:

To lose this love, my heart still cries.
With memory of you, tears fall from my eyes.

This is not the way, I thought it would be.
I pictured us together, forever .... an eternity.

The picture of us, that hung on my wall,
Is stored away, where memories don't call.

Ah memories — you left me a lot.
I'd like to forget them all, but you, I fear, I will not.

Maybe I'll love again, once or twice.
(Damn these tears, they bother my eyes!)
I think I'll just runaway, far away from you.
Go places, see people, and be someone too.

That love we shared (and no one can agree),
Was the best time of my life,. . .just you and me.

"You're young," they say, "You will forget."
But til this day, I miss you so, I regret.

Forgetting you will be hard, and I guess I already knew.
But...please, don't mind these tears, that fell for you.

—*Eufracina Isabel Herrera*

When Someone Has Fallen

O when one of God's chosen one has fallen,
don't point a finger and throw stones.
Remember the story of David, he was God's Gem,
how the enemy tried to rot his bones.

O when your day of trouble comes in like a flood,
don't you know there's a rock and redeemer.
Remember our sins are covered by God's Blood,
His perfect laws will cut down the schemer.

Oh how can we know what sins are lurking in our hearts,
don't you know we have all sinned and fallen short,
Remember the story of Mary Magdalene's brand new start,
His loving ways heals the cancerous wart.

O when someone has disgracefully fallen into temptation,
don't condemn, this just maybe God's Gem.
Through all the worldly ways of aggravation,
someone has been planted to save the world from sin.

O may there be songs of joy when comes the victory,
don't you know God finishes His Holy Revelation plans.
Remember the divine story of Job how he made history,
Jim Bakker's pleasure is truly in God's hands.

Scripture...Micah...Chapter...7...Verse 7—8—" therefore I will look unto the Lord; I will wait for the God of my salvation: my God will hear me." Rejoice not against me, O my enemy: when I fall, I shall arise; when I sit in darkness, the Lord shall be my light unto me."

—*Elayne Gocek Walden*

My Dreams

Dreams!
Dreams!
In my youth I had many dreams.
I dreamed of places I wanted to go
And things I wanted to do.
I dreamed of going to Switzerland
To see the high mountains
And perchance climb a few.
I dreamed of going to Rome
And of its architecture take a view.
I dreamed of going to Paris
To learn more about the trends in fashion and flair.
But, as time passed, these special dreams
Gradually vanished in the air.
So I concentrated upon my smaller dreams,
And was refreshed with a greater awareness
That these were the ones closer to my heart,
And that if some or all were to come true
I'd be proud to be a part.

—*Dura Ward*

The Well

The well had stood for many years
   Dug by sorrow and filled, with tears.
Shadows play on the walls within,
   Echoes rang out off stones wore thin.
How deep it ran was a question often pondered
   As the soul it harbored searched then wandered.
However there was no end it seems to reach on forever,
   No drink for a fool or refreshment to the clever.
Manifested by years of life in itself,
   Part of the poor somehow showered in wealth.
A lot of the time it seems almost dry,
   Retrospectively it filled to the brim in one single cry.
The well stands for the thirsty to think,
   If ever the needy pay heed then drink.
Memories are the cement holding the stone.
   The stones themselves are answers shown.
Most all of us have a well to ourself,
   To keep emotion alive remembering our mistakes for better health.
How does one dig such a fine old well?
   Its something not given and you cannot sell.
One life makes it for better or worse.
   Maybe to praise perhaps start a good curse.
Shame if it wasn't there that old battered well,
   Thirsty would we be in our own type of hell.

—*Albert Joseph Arnett*

Spring Cleaning

Sweep away the clouds of gloom that may come your way,
Dust off your disposition, be more cheerful day by day;
Wash the windows of your mind and you will really see
That life is worth the living, I am sure you will agree!

Vacuum all the corners where some hidden thoughts may lie,
Mop up all ill feelings and leave that ocean dry.
Launder all the words you speak before they get away;
You will be much happier, more cheerful every day!

Iron out all your differences that you may have with others;
Mend family broken fences now with sisters or with brothers.
Clean out all the dusty clutter, you've kept hanging round,
A better person you will be, with happiness you've found.

As you go right on through the year to do exciting things,
You can have a happy time and a heart that truly sings.
We are given time and space and fields of life for gleaning,
But every year the time comes round when we must do spring cleaning!

—*Ada M. Spencer*

Dandelions

Names of stone immortalize the hillside upon which they
dwell. Passersby scan the etched identities for
remembrances of the years gone. I, too, search for
the visions of yesterday hidden behind the silence
of tranquility...Memories of the warm comforts of
laughter enveloping a young girl's soul...Images
of a golden princess adorned with dandelion jewels
waltzing with her aged prince beneath clouds of
marshmallow...With champagne music transforming their
reality into a rapture of wishes and stars.
All brought to bear upon the forgotten stone elusive
amongst the shadows of existence. Walking ever near,
I know there will be no flowers, no granite pillars,
no stars of bronze, only a name diminished by time.
As the princess places the dandelion upon the prince
of stone, their world is once more transformed into one
Of caressing laughter, glistening jewels of gold, magical
violins enchanting the gods of wishes, stars, and dreams
Immortalizing the memories upon which they dance
beneath the pillow of white.

—*Julia Hanson*

A Wishful Thought

My love for you grows each day,
Each time I see, I love you in a new way.
  My heart cries out for you,
I need your love - one that is new.
  Your eyes so clear,
Make me forget my traces of fear.
  The looks you give,
Are those I will remember for as long as I live.
  For when you are around,
My heart is filled with a wondrous sound.
  Some day, I hope we will see,
The perfect vision of you and me.
  There's no way my feelings could be wrong,
Our relationship could be so strong.
  I'm searching in my mind,
For the words to leave behind.
  So please don't go away,
But with forever stay.

—*Jennifer Diane Tippin*

Different Wings

  From misty mores to rainbows bright,
each was created for our delight.
  Each, created in such wonder and love,
from a touch of the Master's hand above.
  Whether, rippling brook or waterfall,
His mighty hand has made them all.
  God fills our world with these lovely things,
and to mostly all gives different wings.
  Flowers float like butterfly wings,
and like every masterpiece of bird that sings.
  These flowers fly on silent wings to Summer's ground,
and like Autumn leaves never make one sound.
  He puts silver wings on snow and rain,
as they lightly dance on our windowpane.
  God, even gives the sky some wings,
as clouds go drifting by like airborne things.
  To even quiet and gusty winds that fly by,
and that fierce lightning that streaks across the Summer sky.
  Wings to every bug and bee that buzzes by,
also to the days on wings that seem to fly.
  As does his light that reveals the grandeur of all things,
while we rest so safely, "under the shadow of his wings."

—*Emeline Pennock Morris*

They Cry For Peace

They come from the East, they come from the West.
  Each with their own voice, history is being made,
    in the final quest for Peace.

They speak each one for their own people in this final
  quest, for Peace. Their leaders cry, "Oh God that no more
    blood be shed, it is by Your Mighty Hand that we have
      been led. Let our people see their leaders prophesy,
        let each our proud nations flags fly free
          with our land of love and liberty."

The world is in a turmoil, each seems to go their own way,
  but when all is said and done each is striving for the
    final quest, for Peace.

Their leaders gather together in one final place,
  America, Israel, Palestine side by side at the conference
    table with one thought in mind—Peace.
      Trying to overcome past hurts and differences
        to put them at rest, for the one final goal
          all mankind yearns for, the final quest,
            Peace.

—*Enid Jo Williams*

Curl And Becky

Two little old ladies full of love and grace
Each wore a bonnet of black taffeta and lace
At church they sat by a window
Each time in the same place
These little old ladies visited far and wide
Curl with Becky always at her side
Curl talked while Becky sanctioned
Every word pure gospel so Becky said
And all agreed with the little old lady
With the bonnet of taffeta and lace on her head.
I grew up and years went by—
Then I returned to a new congregation many had gone.
I never heard a word that the preacher said
Tho' unashamed I wiped the tears from my face
For all through his sermon there by the window in her usual place
Sat Curl and Becky wearing their bonnets
Of black taffeta and lace.

—*Julia D. Simmons*

Sounds

Ours, is a beautiful town, bustling with familiar sounds
early settlers created sounds of conformity, while new
freedoms were being found. There were rhythmical sounds
of men building houses, and new roads, soon, to be named.

Sounds of the horse-driven buggy, and the trolley-car, vie
for preferential treatment at city-hall; while awaiting the
court's decision, the towns-people are amused by bob-o-links,
challenging passers-by, to imitate their perky calls.

Arriving at city park, you hear the innocents at play; some
crying, some giggling, and some laughing hysterically,
while chasing their pets, commanding them to stay.

Sounds, coming from a boisterous, brazen group, disrupt the
area, bullying everyone nearby. Instinctively, we recognized
those troubling sounds, and reluctantly, hurry to leave,
but with tearful eyes.

Take heed! Sounds of hate, sounds of violence, we have
mesmerized, immunized, immobilized, and - reduced you to
silence. In spite of the disenchanted who disturb the peace;
our planet will produce beautiful sounds, for future
settlers, yet to come, whose love of country—"Do unto others"—
Sounds that will never cease.

—*Audrey Bickart*

Memories

Memories are heartbeats sounding through the years,
Echoes never failing of our smiles and tears,
Moments that are captured sometimes unaware,
Pictures in an album or a lock of hair.

Images that linger deep within the mind,
Bits of verse we cherished once upon a time.

Through the musty hallways of the days we knew,
Ever comes the vision beautiful and true.

Memories are roses blooming evermore,
Full of fragrant sweetness never known before.

Life must have a reason goals for which to strive,
Memories are lights that burn ... to keep the heart alive.
—*Bridget K. Sinko*

Love On A Higher Plane

I am seeking a love eternal,
Emanating from the Spirit of God,
Joining heart, soul, mind, and body,
Man, woman, Trinity --
One.
God breathes His holy breath upon us,
And we are one.
My heart longs for you.
My soul pants for you.
My body aches for you.
Come to me, my love, and issue forth the
    seed of righteousness.
Burst forth and bloom perennial in a fallow land.
Take my hand and lead me till we reach
    that higher plane, where you'll
Walk with me and talk with me,
Laugh with me and love with me,
And pray with me and stay with me -
Till together we cross Jordan and lay down
    our love at its source.
God is love.
—*Ernestine Collins Meade*

Healing Tears

A river flowing throughout the years,
Embraces wonderful healing tears,
Delicate as crystal and pure as gold,
New as the day and centuries old.

Fresh as dewdrops on the morning rose,
Quietly they dwell in secrecy close,
Sharing thoughts and sorrows deep,
Teardrops surface that you may weep.

Gently they fall and caress your face,
Wondering dreams with perfect grace,
Fearless they are and dare not cease,
Until they shower your soul with peace.

Oblivious to person time or season,
They may appear for many a reason,
The teardrop army at watchful rest,
Alerts to battle at your request.

Drink deeply from the river of tears,
Anointed water that vraves the years,
Medicine of nature, refreshing and pure,
Healing tears, the flowing cure.
—*Jean Manning*

The Song Of The Red Rose

I'm a charming red little flower,
Enchanting fragrance is my power,
Mother Nature has so made me,
As beautiful as I can be,
And I grow on sunlight and rain,
Like people live with joy and pain.

God gave me thorns to protect me,
From the hummingbird and the bee,
Time goes on, my petals unfold,
I'm still attractive, though I'm old,
And I grow on sunlight and rain,
Like people live with joy and pain.
—*Connie R. Raquepo*

Sensations

The caresses of your eyes linger in my memory
Enfolding, delighting, exciting, thrilling me
With your nearness, intoxicating my senses
Like gardenias in a night garden expelling perfume.

Your lips have burned invisible scar-prints on mine,
My body remembers the closeness of you
Pressed against mine, every hollow and curve,
The firmness of muscle and of bone.

My fingers tingle from the touch of your skin
The soft down of your chest, matted against my cheek
The firm burnished pressure of your arms
Holding me against your heart, and time...

My ears glow with the remembrance of your voice
Silken-soft strands of sound, love-words, muted
Murmurings of joy and belonging, weaving a
Tapestry of treasured togetherness.
—*Ethel M. Cummings*

RVR

Ragged rabble dwell in broken hues
Enrobed, endorsing immortality
Manifolding man's regality
Brought by painterly and magical muse...

Rembrandt had discerning wizard's eyes
A hand with pencil captured living souls
Nobly limned within exquisite goals
Depicting features we immortalize...
These modest proffered views do poetize.

Vagabonds and kings, or verily, Christ
All painted, etched and drawn in solitary
Now recognized as being extraordinary
Remain eternally emparadised.
Incessant labor was his daily mode
Joining palette, oil and pigments rich
Nimbly stroked the colors that bewitch...

Painting master, he bestrode art's road
Imagination dwelt in thoughts profound
Ne plus ultra, he will yet expound
Xerxes-like from his esteemed abode.
—*Dean Lowell Qually*

Unbearable Sadness

She lives in her dominators shadow with thoughts of those brief episodes of yesterdays happiness, slowly dying of loneliness. Always hoping, waiting for that change for nothing lasts forever. Sadly though, it goes both ways. She's trapped in her prison made to look like a house. Each day the walls seem to move closer, ever so slowly. You can't see them move but you can feel it. Trapped in a dirty town with it's orange night sky, fall into a dead sleep hoping for a beautiful dream. It doesn't happen. Her mind is full of nightmares. Wakes up to the darkness of her room, watches the red glowing time pass until finally she falls asleep. Only to wake up to a new day that feels like yesterday. The dominator has the power to do as he pleases while we have to abide by his rules spoken or un-spoken. The pain she feels could be the unbearable sadness kept within herself. She doesn't want to die, only to be happy for a long long time.
—*Alesia Trowbridge*

If The Light Goes Out

If I should slip within that dark abyss
'Ere time has drawn my cycle to a close
I'll dwell on all those well-remembered scenes
That inner eye has treasured up for me:
Dew-beads upon the early morning rose,
Shade and sunlight playing tag on distant hills,
The pageantry of stars and sunset bloom,
Sequioa challenging the vaulted sphere,
Waves weaving strands of lace along the shore
And trace of wings against the paling sky.

So shall these visions linger with me still,
Though I must walk alone the pathless night.
—*Dorice McDaniels*

Miles and Miles of Smiles

To hear a note sing,
especially on an instrument of peace.
It's like flying on a gossamer wing,
universal songs supplying the breeze.

This boss of brass you can touch,
no matter which horn you hear.
The sound can never be too much,
seven notes so clear.

Making laughter and smiles,
a feeling that says its alright.
Music for miles and miles and miles,
soaring on an eternal flight.

Whether the trumpet, cornet or fluglehorn,
turning heads gets attention.
Waiting for each note to be born,
less distraction more retention.

The greats are dropping like flies,
luckily they left a legacy behind.
Peace to diz and miles in the heavenly skies,
a real master of brass is a rare find.
—*James Stewart*

Alpha And Omega

The creator, our God, melchizedek and lamb.
Eternal, saviour, sacrifices and "I am."
Overseer, planner, perfecter and shiloh.
Prophet and priest, our healer and so-
Enforcer, petitioner, the high and lofty one.
The prince of peace, our maker, the son.
The cornerstone and rock, bread and wine.
The word, and refuge, tree and vine.
Redeemer, ransom, comforter and then-
He's alpha and omega, beginning and end.

Our example, counselor, wisdom and might.
Our cloud by day, and fire by night.
The firstborn, Emmanuel, heir of all things.
Messiah, almighty, reverend, and King of kings.
Witness, surety, and captain by far.
The holy one of Jacob and Bright morning star.
Our judge, Pardon, mediator and our stay.
Resurrection, bridegroom, teacher our hope today.
Our guardian and shepherd, Elohim, our friend.
He's alpha and omega, beginning and end.
—*Durwood T. Thompson*

Snowflakes

Merry little snowflakes, softly gliding down;
Ethereally, without a single sound.
Ricocheting, unrestrained in their flight.
Reflecting God's glory, oh what a sight!
Each little snowflake, a shape of its own;
Frolicking and spinning as 'tis wind-blown.
Soon to accumulate, in mounded array;
Here come the children in gleeful play.
Snowmen and snowballs their young hands will mold.
Wintery pleasures of happiness unfold.
Miraculous snowflakes drifting down from above,
Bringing from God, His message of love.
If all the world would heed and declare,
A hope for World Peace would be everywhere.
—*Doris M. Halliwell*

Deason's Fourscore Years

My hands are not in decay
Even though I am eighty years old today
My hair is not long, but it is silver white
You can bet a silver dollar that is right.

My birthday, but not many are coming
My big hands to shake.
Yes, Yes, one thing is surely coming,
That is my big birthday cakes.

Although not many are coming
Yet, I shall enjoy their songs.
For many will surely come along
Because it is at my house they belong.

There have been eighty years since birth
So I have enjoyed them all on God's Earth.
When I was young, during the depression,
I spent too much of my young life rushing.

I can truthfully say inside my body will say,
You are just starting upon your way.
Very young in the years of time to be,
You will be just a few hours old in Eternity.
—*James Deason*

An Evening Whisper

Moonlight cascaded with candlings — as soft winds lulled the evening with a sonnet of silence.
Echoes of two hearts bedazed as one — as desire became the soul unto deep passion.
Our silhouettes layered the carcass of the night — as we quietly molded among the entwined darkness.
And, with our hearts drifting into a catacomb of reality — fantasy thus became our eminence unto love!
With a sonnet of silence filling the lone night — we lain among the emotions of an evening whisper — echoing our names.
The tallowing remains of candlings seemed to mien our existence—
as we blanket'd ourselves with the last remains of moonlight.
Within the aura of passion's touch - we clutched to the image that stabled our thoughts.
And, within the last beam that has fallen from the moon — we deepened ourselves within an evening whisper.
As the soft beam of gold cascaded our kiss — it sparked against the dark — just as we exchanged those passionate acts of desirous affection.
And with the passionate acts burning in our souls — the last ember of the candlings smoldered — as the moonlight cascaded
               the fervor of dawn.
   —*George D. Kovach*

Led By A Child

An old man was walking, one evening getting late,
Every step was painful, for age had slowed his gate,
He neared a broken parkbench, and here he stopped to pray,
He finally got down on his knees, long ago he lost his way.

No hurry to get anywhere, he had nowhere to go,
Many years he had been gone, his family left him so,
He closed his eyes and bowed his head, his lips began to speak,
His words came out both soft and low, his voice was very weak.

Dear Lord up there in heaven, I need you so tonight,
I've traveled far as I can go, have I won or lost the fight,
Please come and get me take me home, I've traveled my last mile,
I've no more purpose here on earth, I have to rest a while.

Someone took him by his hand, and as his words unfurled,
He opened up his tear-dimmed eyes, here sat this little girl,
She did not help him to his feet, just held his hand a while,
Her eyes to were filled with tears, someone had lost a child.

They just sat there together, until the tears had passed,
They then smiled at each other, now they were home at last,
His last words were thank you Lord, as her head against him pressed,
Her hands clung to him tightly, for they both are now at rest.
   —*Elroy Thornhill*

Peace

Peace is a state of silence that,
Everyone longs for constantly,
Americans, Africans, Asians, Europeans, Latinos and the rest of the world,
Can hardly wait to rejoice the silence: no sound of fire, no sound of pain from hunger and abuse.
Only the sound of freedom will ring
Every country on God's great earth will rise and sing:
Thank you father, there is peace at last!
   —*Clara Jo White*

Would You?

You've given me all I ever wanted.
Everything that money could buy.
You've given me diamonds, bracelets, and roses.
You've given me so much: Why?

All I want is your love and affection.
Sometimes a hug and smile.
But those are things you fight to hold on to,
and I see once in a while.

I've never been wealthy before.
I won't miss it now.
But I miss the love I've always had,
and to often my life is sad.

If I gave back the diamond rings, the watch,
and bracelet to?
If I took back the trip to Holland and Paris,
France would you?

Would you love me with all your heart and
make my life complete?
Or would you buy me another diamond and rely on it to speak?
   —*D. Rosena Jones*

After The Storm Was Over

This was the blackest day I'd ever seen.
Everything was so still, so calm.
The birds were even gone.
But their it was like a demon of the night.
At ten after four it had taken everything in sight.

As we looked up we saw that black funnel cloud hanging down
As we run for shelter it hit the ground.
Taken all our worldly possessions.
Thirty year of working hard, saving things to retire.
Now they are gone and we're alone at the sight with no home.

We've nothing left of our former life
Just an old spoon and a knife.
We were all wet thru and thru but we had no clothes to change into. We're all broken hearted as we walk around this sight.
There's nothing left but the gas light.

We've only each other to hold on to.
But our love will see us thru
After the storm was over we were left in a field of clover.
For that swirling cloud had cleaned the ground.
There was nothing left as we looked around.
   —*Bessey Nichols*

Big Wind

Just yesterday, you soothingly caressed the night. Causing everything you touched to tingle with delight. Big wind-big wind, you smiling sailor's friend. They don't know, in an instant, you can change your grin.
Big wind—big wind I respect you, just listen—to the way you blow. As soon as you pass, I'm gonna pray, you don't come byhere no more.
Big wind—big wind why'd you hurt me? Big wind—big wind why'd you hurt me? I worked real hard all of my days, trying to have a little something to show. Now you come howling along,
and I ain't got nothing no more.
Big wind—big wind you smiling sailor's friend. I worked real hard of all my days, trying to have a little something to show. Now you come, you Big! Old! Wind! And I ain't got nothing no more. Big wind-big wind! Big! Old! Wind! Big wind—
   —*Charles L. Butler Jr.*

The Beauty Of A Smile

It's nicer here, it's nicer there, it's nicer just about
everywhere, and all because it's you I see
who gives that great big smile to me.

A warmer welcome couldn't bring more happiness
causing my heart to sing, and joy without measure
it surely yields the lightness of spirit I now feel.

It costs nothing, but means so much, it's as sweet and
gentle as a loving touch. Its good to know it's a gift
we possess, to pass on to anyone life's spiritual zest.

And so we can lighten our bit of turf, and bring brightness,
fun and mirth, to a sometimes sad and unorganized
world, which deals in crime for the sake of gold.

It's wonderful to know that to give a smile can change
life and make it worthwhile. Can lift from the doldrums
a spirit who strives to raise his consciousness to a
better life.

So let's greet each other with a smile, as we traverse
life's busy miles. And remember, it's nicer here, it's nicer
there, because God taught us to give and share.

—*Dorothy Flood*

Spring's Simple Pleasures

New flowers will begin to bloom,
    everywhere soon.

Bees, with all their newly found power,
    will fly from flower to flower.

    The gentle breeze puts everyone's
        mind at ease.

    The soft spring sounds make
        many hearts pound.

All you must do to view nature's beauty
    is to walk out and look about.

        For every change in season,
        there's always a worthwhile
            reason.
  —*Angela Eisenhoffer*

My Silent Tears

When I was just a little girl —
evil showed his face in my world.

For years, my mother's brother molested me—
my home was not a safe place for me to be.

My family was not able to see—
I needed them to protect me.

What is a child supposed to do—
when an adult has power over you?

He stole my innocence; he spoiled my youth—
There is no forgiveness; there is no excuse!

I thought that I was only to blame—
I felt guilt, anger, and great shame.

I've shed my share of silent tears—
I sobbed alone; and no one could hear.

To suffer in silence can only sustain—
heartache, misery, and years of pain.

I know that I don't stand alone—
others feel the misery I've known.

Strength and courage are my savings grace
I'm on my way towards a better place.
  —*Cathy Adams*

Morning Rain

I awoke this morning to rain everywhere
Except in my heart, your sunshine was there.
Touching me gently, I felt your hand
Like the raindrops falling outside on the land.

I felt your caress and longed for your kiss,
My whole being awaited the fulfilling bliss,
That breathless moment so divine
When I am yours and you are mine.

Then I knew that quiet time, that quiet place,
Where we shared each other in love's embrace,
Was only a fantasy inside my head
You were not there, I was alone in my bed.
  —*Helen S. Gates-Kirk*

As Long As One Can Breathe

Fallible Creatures Immune to Love
Exhausted Dreams of Unpainted Lives
Destructive Fear Colors the Soul
Forsaken Testimonials Within Your Eyes

Childhood Innocence Pleading for Contentment
Premonitions of Heaven Nowhere to Find
Only Dead Hope to Harvest the Love
Diverting Thoughts and Delaying Time

Losing Sleep in the Dead of Night
Wondering Souls Playing the Cost
Chilling Blackness in Early Light
Nothing Feels like Feelings Lost

The Depth of the Ocean is Shallow in Thoughts
As Powerful as It May Be
Yet the Burdens of Life Scar Our Minds
Staining Crosses for All to See.
  —*Darlene M. Howell*

Tao

Thirty seven points of light
Extracted from a beam.
Reflected values.
This is a world of illusions.
Illusions unseen.
Have you ever tasted death?
A great gray wolf awaits in its hills
Overlooking a valley of souls.
His eyes glow red
As a mist covers us.
We walk a path of tears.
Yeah though I walk through his valley
I will have no fears
For this is the place of conclusions.
  —*Pete Floyd*

A Circle Of Life

A simple smile.
Eyes as big as the morning sun.
The laugh of a child
So happy you can't help smiling.

Walking along the park trail
You see children playing at the edge of the pond
The excitement in their bodies
Makes you smile the whole day.

There isn't anything more special than
To have a child take you by the hand
And walk with you down the park trail
Take you by the hand and walk with you
And teach you the joy of being.

To have the opportunity to share
My life with a child is the
Greatest part of living.
The things we can learn from each other.

To live fully is to forget
What you have learned
And become child-like.
Only then will you understand.
—*Anna Maria Bronco*

Redemption

Tears regretting smiles pat the bitterness away
Eyes reflecting mirror holding shadows born from dreams
Souls will live in worlds split and darkened by mishap
Whom our angels find amusing stealing laughter from the throat
Evening leaves descend without single observation
Changes life's disguise that takes ages to decipher
Lacrimal conclusions invade presently the body
Of the sacred temple that was guarded selfishly
Ivory-tower solitude exit into worldly pleasures
Enter guilty pleads from sorry ice-blue lips
Climbing back to tower safely rotting from within
Mirror glances: "Coward, choose the sword of El Cid!"
Remember narrow path how arrival here attained
Hopeful memory: "Please brush away the dust!"
That penetrates the pores like a lovely woman's smile
Cleansing the spirit from conventional bourgeois bullshit.
—*Andre' M. Janssens*

For The Love Of Nectar

I heard this sound a mellow drone
   faint though it seemed to be
As I spun around there he was
   Hovering not noticing me
He was so handsome and iridescent
   roaming from the left to the right
That his jewel-like colors and brilliant plumage
   seemed to change in the light
He appeared so intent as he darted about
   controlling his rapid speed
Stopping at one to withdraw its splendor
   that he was forever in need
As he shifted about while kissing the flowers
   that were of tubular design
I couldn't help notice that at the time
   he seemed so simply divine
The flapping of his wings were humming a song
   but he couldn't utter a word
He just merely flittered around for the love of nectar
   was that hummingbird
—*John Michael Mailhot*

Just Fun

I never thought I'd
fall. I thought it'd be fun and then
be done. He held me so close I
thought our bodies would melt
to one. It was so cold, he was
so warm. It was so wrong, but
it felt so right. I only hope there's
a net at the end of this long fall,
maybe he'll be there to catch me
at the end of it all. He's so far
away, but yet he grows closer
everyday. This isn't a stumble,
nor a trip. I fell of the end of
a very steep cliff. Maybe he'll
be there and maybe he won't.
I only wanted some fun and then
to be done.
—*Brandi Mahan*

Incomplete

Leaves like tears
Falling at my feet
Now a moment to breathe
The day before I sleep

Falling star natural wonder
Calling me a sure reminder
Man's capacity to love exists
But never compares to nights like this

A dream cast on golden sands
Music we've made with mere hands
In our voice a song thru the land
Gifts to treasure we'll understand

The depths from the watery ocean's deep
The heights from solitary mountain peaks
A tree bends in the wind as tho' to speak
Whispers the very secrets that it keeps

No one will know pain I feel
Heading home has all been real
As I turn and step to the street
Aware of being incomplete
—*Brian Mulhern*

Inspiration

Shimm'ring ethereal moonlight,
Falling from the storied windows,
Faintly through the gloom discloses
Pointed arches heav'nward straining.

Through the dim and silent nave
Steals a still, mysterious figure;
By the foremost niche it pauses,
Sinks to earth, and bows in prayer.

Then from high a knell resounds,
Tolling, hopelessly, defeat, but
Through the tumult wells the organ,
Telling hope, and victory.

"All is not lost," it seems to say,
"Keep faith, and wait, though come what may,
Tomorrow'll bring a better day,
When human hearts from love will fay."
—*Dwight Smith*

Outside Baltimore

Waking to the grey sunshineless light that
   falls over my bed covers
I rise and go to my window with its
   suburban snow view
The perfect white on the parking lot, like my
   own typing paper, and then the cars
   come to write their poetry
I dress like the day, grey and black with
   hard boots, so as to stomp
   the people down
I go outside where the air covers me in
   softness that I am unable to
   reach through
The smell of snow long gone from the air, and
   the snow on the ground turned into
   slush, like the slush that fills the sky
I long to be two months and ten miles
   forward, sitting at the Inner Harbor
   in the spring sun
   —*Jennifer P. J. Monroe*

Free

'Tis yet a trickle of surety
Falls slowly in innocence and grace
The beauty of their elegance
Shined in their eyes

I tell no lies to you my friend
No lies, at least till the end

In the end, we'll tell our souls
In the way our souls do tell
We'll make our way to heaven's gate
And pray we end not in hell

Only when the raven crows
And the Lord silenced
Shall we be envious or prude
Or selfish to only one's own

Only when we are free within
Only when we are of one in our soul
When we are alright with ourselves
Then we can be...

   —*April L. Medendorp*

Untitled

Fallible creatures immune to love
Exhausted dreams of unpainted lives
Destructive fear colors the soul
Forsaken testimonials within your eyes
Childhood innocence pleading for Contentment
Premonitions of heaven nowhere to find
Only dead hope to harvest the love
Diverting thoughts and delaying time
Losing sleep in the dead of night
Wondering souls paying the cost
Chilling blackness in early light
Nothing feels like feelings lost
The depth of the ocean is shallow in thought
As powerful as it may be
Yet the burdens of life scar our minds
Staining crosses for all to see.

   —*Darlese McCraw Flowell*

More Beautiful

I hear you say: "I'm not all that beautiful of character or
   fame,
But, thanks so much, for mentioning my name.
Your kind words of love brought tears to my eyes,
So sorry to have worn such a successful disguise!"

"`Cause down underneath is the true little me,
With frailties a plenty, and weak as can be.
When it comes to have followed the straight and narrow path
Fragments of rocks lay bare the truth of life's past.

Rocks are like problems that come thick and fast,
Few are overcome, while all too many last
Until the rocks are found to be
The sure way to build a God fearing beauty.

As God fearing beauty is taken into account,
This sure foundation sets firmly the amount
Of God's love and of service, specified
In the good book that tells how rocks are rectified!

So we pray to the giver of life yet to be:
God make us more beautiful, more beautiful for thee!"
   —*Irene C. Pemberton*

My Life

My life has been so exciting—
Family, friends, business associates and trips.
My family has always been there for me and loved me no matter
   what.
My friends shared my joys and struggles while I was growing up.
My business associates have been my strength.
They've seen me fall and get up again.
They had faith in me, even times that I didn't believe in myself.
Now I'm sharing my future with them.
I knew success wasn't far away — I had to work for it.
I have so many things now:
My trips around the world: Australia, Europe, Hawaii and more.
I have two houses: one near Wildwood Crest, the other in
   Australia.
Most importantly are the wonderful people I've met through my
   business--
many of them have become my friends.
There is a special man in my life — he treats me like gold.
Waiting for him to come along was well worth it.
My life is so fantastic now.
I'm traveling everywhere, and I don't need to work.
I'm enjoying my life now.
   —*Christine M. Kachurak*

Fairytale

Out in the meadow where the marigolds grow
Far beyond the fir trees standing tall in a row
Rings are hidden: not many, but a few
Enough to be seen in the not-quite-dawn dew
This is where elves dance through autumns and springs
And fairies fly lightly on gossamer wings
They're almost like fireflies, they sparkle so bright
Like faraway stars on a wintery night
And while one is peering through the cobweb-like mist
The day comes at last, and the earth is sun-kissed
But alas, the lovely fairies must flee from the light
And hide in the flowers to wait for the night
   —*Heather Cathcart*

Crystalized Tears

Teardrops glistening in my eye
Fans dying embers of love to lie
Within the bosom of my heart's desire
Can one cruel word put out the fire?

Teardrops fall from my eyes again
Gems of crystallized pain
Each one, a hope oxidized
Each one, a treasure unrealized!

Can you heal this would from cruel remarks
Or stanch the flow of tears wrung from
an aching heart?
Or, will the passing time reveal
Your face, etched in my memory still?

If the memory of the past could be released
These crystallized gems would
slowly deliquesce
In the future I could conceive
Patterns of a new love to cleave!
—*Aretta Nash Seal*

Mission Of Virtue

Upon the crags the flowers bloom!
Far below the river ripples all day long
And tires not even during the night.
Let your song be one of praise
That it may reach the crags,
Where the flowers, too, shall lift up
Their voices in making melody to our God.
May the river within you run deep and long,
Satisfying the thirst of all
Who seek refreshment.
Though jagged rocks may batter you
With insults as with labor pains,
May your white steeds ride through the storm
With honor —
And may you not know unkindness
Without understanding,
That you may direct those surging pulses
Into gentle brooks and rivulets
That serve rather than destroy.
Then shall your signature stand as evidence
Of a vision published; a testimony of
Refracting euphony and Heavenly desire.
—*Beverly Lyon*

My Little Hill

There is a little hill outside of town, not very
far from here. On which the earth and sky doth meet
beauty last all the year. It lies from the other
hills, secluded and alone. I go there some times
when I am sad, that hill is all my own. I stand upon
the very top, quite bare from the trees. I look out
from the country side, and listen to the breeze. At
night the heaves is a dome, the stars they glide
by. As ships sail the charted space, reflecting
lights against the sky. There is something very
restful, in the stillness that I find. And little
care and worry, sort of vanish from my mind. The
little hurts, the little pains, my spirit could not
drop. All seem to disappear from me, when I have
reached the top. And every heart should sometime go,
where all is quite and still. Life's road is not so
weary, when you have...A Little Hill.
—*Arlie U. Bobo*

Journey

Far away into space we travel, farther from our fears,
Far from the present standards of society,
and the hostility and the speculation, of our peers.
Where out in the infinity we exercise our capabilities,
without inhibitions, and we find new dimensions in our minds.
We inhale our thoughts with good intentions,
and the kaleidoscopic room revolves multi-million times.
As something foreign in our systems sends us strange sensations;
time is unlimited and we feel inexhaustible.
Our spirits loose their reasoning, and we seek compassion.
We speak as though our loves and lives have been very full,
and people stare at us, without comprehension.
All thought is mangled, the loudest voice is but a murmur.
Who is the manslayer of our children's minds?
All the chants are misleading, promising some odious treasure,
Where is it that we seek the answer that one must find?
—*Debbie Wood*

The Perfect Architect

Perfect Architect of the Universe, loving
Father of al men
You set the Earth in order for
Man before you fashioned him.

You hung the sun for heat and light
Reflecting on the moon at night
Dense forests laid providing him
Fresh oxygen sustaining him.

Supplied abundance of fresh water
To sate his thirst and bathe his body
Thou madest cattle and fish ror meat
When perfect setting was complete
You fashioned man, a loving feat.

You bade him, "Multiply and subdue
The Earth I have prepared for you."
You came to Earth in Cool of day
To walk with him in Eden's way.

Then Satan lied and Adam strayed
He ate of fruit, thus disobeyed
So Jesus came, God's love displayed
A way to Heaven by Him was made
Fulfillment of the Plan God laid.
—*Ada Amburgey*

Truth

I am still angry, mad and upset,
feeling as frustrated, as I can get;
you see the problem, is still within me,
when am I ever, going to clearly see.

I know the truth, comes from within,
however, I must not want begin;
for I'm still letting people validate me,
people who don't care, but won't let me be.

I need to learn, to see the truth,
and not to listen, from those uncouth;
seeing myself, from within not without,
will give me the strength, to turn me about.

I want to be free, to bask in the sun,
to live life to the fullest, to have some fun;
no more suffering, no more pain,
learning He's with me, makes me feel sane.
—*Carol A. Brook*

If I Surrendered My Love
It seems like I'll never get over this hurting
feeling, it's hard to explain.
As if my life is revolving through a merry-go-
round I'm fighting desperately to stay focus.
But I must admit there's a lesson among all of
this or is it?
I just know it's hard to love again because if
I open myself to pain again will I last.
I was always told had to hurt a little bit to come out right.
So I guess I had fool written all over my face
because where are you now?
Simply no matter how many tears I cry the problem
remains the same; a broken heart.
Now I have to trust my instincts and better judgment
to avoid another lonely experience.
I ask myself where did I go wrong? What will I do? And how
will I know
But it's you that I'm really scared of this time I
wanna make sure this loving feeling is real.
So I ask you if I surrendered my heart to you will
you follow instructions — handle with care.
Because if I give my love to you I expect you to give
it back to me unconditionally.
—*Darrell Brandon*

Nightmares
Total, utter, complete
Feeling of a hollow shell
No one here, no one there
No one to really care
No one, no one, no one
Empty, lost, quiet
Feeling of a hollow shell
Thoughts are empty, mind is hazy
Everything is... nothing is right
Nightmares of blinded, dark mazes
No way out
Wake up sweating,
Open my eyes - black
Distant radio sounds
No screaming - just shaking from fear
Scared to go through the nightmares - in reality
Snakes, slugs, maggots - all around me
Maze - no clue as to what's ahead
Inching my way to no where
From hell? Back to hell? Who can tell?
—*Jenn Hlavach*

The Statue Of Hope
  The beauty on the pedestal
Fills the world with light,
This mystic glow, this awesome shine
Shows majesty and might.

  The structure made of solid brass
The dress of solid gold,
The necklace made of silver beads
All are centuries old.

  Her sandals made of brilliant bronze
Are chipped and worn away,
Her anklet made of diamond stone
Was shiny in her day.
  This guardian from Roman times
Resting on a slope,
This thing that you have heard of
Is the statue of all hope.

—*Jesse Dorland*

Ever Still No More
My heart's afire with thoughts of you
feelings haven't changed they must be true
tragic moments
twisted thoughts
unbelievable fate
both not sterile in any way
chastise by honest devoted care
aeons of time, I'll always be there
passionate moments
flipping thoughts
determinable fate
evolution some day
life's passing me by
no baby birds needing to fly
restless moments
see through thoughts
expected fate
I will love you anyway
ever still no more
—*Howard K. Geffner*

His Majesty, The Racehorse
One may not ever possess this mighty steed.
few have pride enough to care for his humble needs.
A caring hand must pick the pace with strength
to soar and prepare for the flight, springing
with power in a flash of bright — unknowing
of his might.
Guiding hands, lightly so as not to unwind
til time is right for needed burst to finish first,
with his speed and heart.
He returns his love to who cares.
In awe each time our eyes behold
The graceful racehorse.
—*Holly Lason*

Fiddler's Green
Will we go to the "Fiddlers Green"? Oh, yes! To the
    "Fiddlers Green" we shall go;
With Life's cruise complete, and our mem'ries replete
    With the good times - the good times, you know!

The good times extol, for they're burned in our soul,
    And don't mourn for the lost when its found;
Sailing on seas where the wind's a warm breeze,
    And the hurricane's only a sound.

    Forever a-sail, with no hint of a gale,
      The place of a seaman's own dream.
The good times we've seen were a promise between
    Earthly cares and that Heavenly Beam.

So when the clouds fall, and the nightly shrouds pall,
    And the future looks dark ever-more,
Remember well, love, the good times we spoke of;
    Know I'll wait on the Far Distant Shore.

I'll wait on the strand of that Far Distant Land,
    In the Heaven where sailors abide —
In "Fiddler's Green," with calm waters pristine,
    Once again, we shall sail on the tide!
—*George W. Crampton*

Find Me...

"Find Me"...He said, as He parted the veil,
"Find Me"...He said, "Be strong... do not fail!"
"Find Me"...The words, echoed through my mind.
"Find Me"...He said, "You are one of a kind!

Find Me...Oh, Find me... I'll always be there.
If you kneel humbly, you'll find me in prayer.

Find Me...Oh, find me... my light will help guide,
Trust in me, daughter, then walk, by my side.

Find me...Oh, find me... through reading my books.
The scriptures will tell you, where, you should look!

Find Me...by listening, to your teachers, who care.
Find Me...by believing...by knowing, I'm there!!!

"Find Me"...He said, "Look inside... for my light."
"Find Me"...He said, then was gone, from my sight.

    I do love him...
    And I promise today!!!
  I will find my Heavenly Father...
 I will have faith... and choose His way!
—*Gwen H. Hall*

Hi

Flashback Generation of power, romance, freedom, and love.
Flashback Generation and only we know where we're coming from.
So many different standard's upon which we are judged,
Flashback Generation of the season of love.

Trying to be so different and not do the same old things usually only tales back to repeating what we've seen. We're a generation like no other, like none you've ever seen. We're looking into the future for what yesterday will bring. AIDS and the OZONE LAYER guess which one's going away? The Flashback Generation will solve these problems one day.

I'm writing this poem to let you know who we are, well we're a brand new generation and we could be the best by far.
—*Angelica M. Smith*

Dancing

Hold me closer when the music is sentimental.
Fling me and swing me with an occasional twirl
When the words are incidental
But the melody seems to swirl.
Take light, quick steps when the tune is catchy.
And swiftly glide when the music flows.
Let the beat and the rhythm enter your ears
And send the message down to your toes,
And as you do, may we move as one
Until the song is over and the dance is done.
—*Elizabeth Vickery*

Night Memory Of Maui

Irregular waves crashing,
Flowing into ribbons of white foam,
Silhouetted against the night sky,
Rushing toward shore.

Slowly creeping up the sand embankment,
Poking watery fingers into cracks and crevices,
Leaving behind Earth's history:
Coral, shells, and recycled sand.

Nature's art work,
Nature's history;
Creation impossible by human hands
Left on the sands.
—*Jeannette Vollmer Schulz*

To The "Arts"

Oh wings of Love of lace so pure
Fly up high so I can live
To touch the flowers and feel the breeze
Thinking of tender babies and delicate trees

Where everything of purest thought
Ascends above the human mind
Where no intruder can want to go
To shatter the dreams that we have sought

My love my love I miss you so
Oh let me rise to touch your hand
To have a love of understanding
That you will know me before I am

Hush dear shadows that are not dark
Feeling the light that pulsates softly
And know it is from your inner heart
To touch the colors of the "Arts"

Oh pictures pure and lovely so
by great artist "Raphael" and "Michelangelo"
To see what is within their heart
by feeling the colors of the "Arts"
—*Carla Marie Huff*

In Lilac Time

In lilac time ... I reminisced
Fond mem'ries I did trace
When lilacs perfumed springtime air
With petals soft as lace

In one bouquet ... There was no doubt ...
I saw my Mother's face
T'was then I sensed her presence
And felt her warm embrace

Her countenance was radiant ...
As fresh as morning dew
More lovely than a rainbow
Or the lilacs' purple hue

I knew these blossoms were her choice
From spring's enchanting bowers
Then ever-so-softly she spoke to me
Through language of the flowers
—*Hazel H. Wells*

A Good Wife

There is nothing more precious in this life
  For a man to have than a lovely wife
 And most sensible men don't have to be told
That a good wife is worth far more than gold.

  Although I know most of us men forget
   To pay our wives a deserved compliment
But that is something we should not fail to do
To thank her for what she has done for you.

   For one kind word somehow, someway
  Spoken to her perhaps may make her day
 And may well be one of your best deeds
To provide her with the lift she needs.

As she too may have done more than her share
 Keeping up the home with its wear and tear
   And doing much work we seldom see
  That makes a home like it ought to be.

But of course there are many other things
  That in a home a good wife brings
   And this is the very reason why
Our appraisal of her should be sky high.
—*Harold R. Snider*

Lonely Heart

A lonely heart can do no wrong
for no one's there to hear its song.
A song so lonely, it cries in the rain
So if there's anyone there
They'll not see its pain.

A pain so great.
It cuts like a...dull, rusty switchblade,
For there's no one there to share the night.

A night so empty
As the sea is wide,
And will I ever know
What I've never felt inside?
As empty inside
As the night is long,
And a lonely heart that beats so strong.

—*Dean Huffstutler III*

Revelation Day

Revere the stars that lighten the night
For shining brightly below the heavens above.
Earth's mankind takes note
That the stars, the moon, and the sun
Present the awesome works
Of the Mighty Hand.
Such elements of the Creation are these,
Leaving mere visions
Of the yet unseen
Until the day when Gabriel's call
Lets man see the Lord's eternal realm
As it meets all eyes —
At the momentous, mighty,
Sounding of the trumpet
When the canopy of the Universe is lifted
And the reign of Our Savior begins.

—*James William Stallings*

The End Of Waiting

Forever, it seems, I have waited
for someone just like you.
You've captured my heart
in a way that few could ever do.

So content am I to be with you
as we walk the shore along,
just listening as the birds sing
their soft, lullaby songs.

Come share a glass of wine with me
as we enjoy the sunset's radiant hue.
Watch as night's soft velvet curtain
descends to conclude the sunset view.

Then take a moonlight walk with me
on the beach, on the soft white sand.
As you might have, when we were young,
reach out to touch me and hold my hand.

Hold me close as we say, "goodnight."
Let me feel the warmth of you.
Please know how very glad I am we met,
and how very much I've come to love you.

—*Carroll M. Martin*

The Balm Of Poetry

Poetry..is man's outlet
    for stress and fear;
    a way to keep the mind
    steady and clear.

    It brushes away "cobwebs"
    and dusts corners;
    it makes hearts lighter,
    and comforts mourners.

Poetry..also brings laughter,
    a smile or two—
    it chases away storm clouds,
    and cheers, when blue.

    It's a balm for tears,
    and soothes the soul;
    it brightens a dreary day,
    and helps us feel whole.

Poetry..draws families closer,
    and sometimes, friends, too;
    and just for a few moments-
    makes all things — become new.

—*Evelyn Ver Dow Hayslett*

The Comfort Of My Love

Let me give you the comfort of my love
For that is all that I possess, and all that I can give
My dreams of love are a living nightmare
For in my heart I know that you do not want me
The emptiness in your eyes when you look at me
And the silence that shouts the unspoken truth
From you who will not speak
Ask me to die, and it would be easier
Then to feel the loneliness when I am with you
Tell me it's a dream, my love
A twisted version of reality
Your smile would bring me back from the abyss
I am saying that which I am afraid to admit
That I am nothing without you
Let me dream with you
And walk with you
If only for a little while
And let me give you
The comfort of my love

—*Alexandra Smith*

No Chance To Choose Thank God!

If I could ask the creator
for the perfect woman for me,
I'd ask for beauty, strength and character
and also simplicity.

She'd have to respect the creator
and all that he has made,
She'd project a love and compassion
that times passing could not fade.

Her persona would be so impressive
She'd be loved by all so dearly,
Pretentious she'd never be
for what she does, she does sincerely.

But I have no chance to choose her
and I guess it's plain to see,
For God has already sent her
my mother eternally.

—*Joseph M. Hogan*

The Sad Refrain

Dear God, I thank thee with all my heart,
For the blessings you gave me,
Health of mind and body,
A peaceful, happy home,
With my life's loving, endearing companion.

Eight children born,
One died in infancy awaiting us in heavens,
Two attorneys-at-law, two doctors of medicine,
One BSEE and BSC, one civil engineer,
The youngest, a Ph.D.

At age 74, the bitterest cup: "My God, Thy will be done!"
My life's endearing companion breathed his last.
  "A loved one from us is gone,
   A voice we love is stilled,
   A place is vacant in our home,
   Which never can be filled."

Standing in heart-rending grief, longing, dreaming;
My beloved in his usual white double-breasted suit,
Appeared, approached me, embraced me, wiped my tears,
Consoling me saying: "We have our children."
  —*Esperanza H. Escalante*

Untitled

Every night I say a prayer
For the one I love to get well
Just rest your head along with mine
And I shall make it all well
It is alright to cry
Alright to pray
We are born believing
A man bears beliefs
As a tree bears apples
Just believe as I believe
God's protection is man's hope
There is no ill which may not
be dissipated
like in the dark
if you let in a stronger light upon it
With a little said it's soonest mended
Just rest my friend
for morning awaits
The rays of the newborn sun
Shall mend all sorrows.
  —*Jamie C. Musloski*

It Matters Not

It matters not...the color of the skin
For the blood of life...runs red within.

The same God created all
To work and laugh and play
To see and hear and smell
To taste and feel and touch.
Like variety in the garden
He choose to make us such.

So whether the skin is black
Yellow, brown, red or white
God placed us here
With the power to choose
The wrong or the right.

Then, let us show love
Each for the other
And care for the needs
Of our earthly brother.

Yes, it matters not...the color of the skin
For the blood of life...runs red within.
  —*Julia Irene Hardy*

The Sad Good-byes

As we waited at the station
For the train to appear,
My heart and mind grew weary.
I knew the time was very near.

As the train came to a stop,
We quickly said good-bye,
Like thieves on the run.
God only knows how hard I wanted to cry.

The train slowly pulled away.
Through the windows we waved good-bye.
I could see the sadness upon his face,
As he took a deep sigh.

As I sat down, I hung my head
And began to think, could this be the end?
Or would there be another time,
As the train pulled around the bend.

I buried my face in both hands
And for many miles I felt bleak,
But I kept on holding the kiss
That my son had planted on my cheek.
  —*John Petrali*

The Weeping God

I dreamed that God was crying
For the world that wasn't trying
To rid itself of grief and pain
But goes on looking how to gain
The best for self without regard
For how it makes the living hard
For helpless, hopeless, homeless man
For thoughtless, careless, mindless plan.
But then I dreamed how can this be?
Then awoke to realize he cried for me!
  —*Darrel Maxson*

Humanity...?

To beautify the human race,
For trinkets that are seldom worn,
We murder, butcher, and deface,
For elephant's tusk and rhino's horn.

The leopard's skin and tiger's pelt
Many uncaring backs have worn.
The snake and alligator shoes
That some unfeeling feet adorn.

Rarest trophies for the hunter,
Heads hanging on the study wall.
They stare with fixed attentive gaze,
Gathering dust there in the hall.

How quickly we forget the days,
When hunter, once the hunted felt.
Human scalps of red, gold, and brown,
Adorned the mighty warrior's belt.

If once again roles were reversed,
How very quickly we would see,
Instead of gain at such a price,
A lesson in humanity!
  —*Ginger S. Belknap*

Untitled

One more day gonna roll myself a fat one
For twenty nine days been doing cocaine
Don't like doing powder but it don't pollute the blood stream
But it leaves me feeling edgy and depresses my brain
Cause the boss's been hinting that I'm gonna see the doctor
And I'm lucky that he does understand
That I always get the job done though I do the marijuana
And he knows I never do it on time
So he never talks about it till the doctor man's coming
And I keep his operation running just so fine

Some folks say that I shouldn't need to wallow
In a drug fed stupor, I should just say no
While they belly to the bar and they take another swallow
Put the key in the ignition and the gear shift in go
Call it simple relaxation or mental masturbation
Does it matter why I like to light up?
Does choosing hemp instead of liquor somehow make me less
   than human
Billy Bennet says I'm nothing but a bum
You can lock me up forever for this forever simple human habit
But I ain't no thieving junkie I just do it for fun.
   —*Chris Manley*

To Happiness In '94

We wonder what life has in store
For us in nineteen-ninety-four.
Have we done everything we should
Doing for others what we could?

If we've done this and even more,
We'll have God's blessing evermore.

If sometimes stormy winds might blow,
or if life's problems we might know,
Trusting in God, he'll lead the way
To find a sunlit happy day.

Then in the year of "ninety-four,"
We'll have much happiness in store.
   —*June Briner*

Easter People

We are the Easter people,
   For we walk the paths He trod-
From Gethsemane, to the hills of Calvary,
   Where we stand on hallowed sod.

From the star in the east on that silent night-
   To the cross, where His voice was stilled.
Like shepherds and kings, His praises we sing,
   And our cup is overfilled.

We are the Easter people,
   And we bask in His glorious rays.
Christianity is in our soul, and it is our goal
   To embrace its heavenly ways.

In our joys and in our sorrows,
   We know Christ is always there—
For we are the Easter people,
   And we've learned how to care and to share.
   —*Barbara J. Cuyle*

God's Poem To Man

Man does not know and has no true cares
   For what it is that gives me these tears.

The earth which was green is now turning brown;
   The trees which stood tall are all but cut down.

The air which was as fresh and clean as could be
   Is now so polluted it's not fit for me.

I planted this garden and spread out the seeds;
   Put man in charge to keep out the weeds.

Knowledge I gave him and provided the tools,
   And all I ask is that he follow my rules.

My plan I know will soon come to be,
   But my gardener, however, you must pray that he may succeed.
   —*David James Rooper*

The Sea

My heart belongs to the sea.
For whenever I gaze upon its watery splendor,
I feel freedom's breeze.

My soul belongs to the sea
For whenever I gaze upon its still serenity,
my spirit is set free.

My love belongs to the sea.
For whenever I gaze upon its perfect beauty,
I see tranquility.

My life belongs to the sea.
For whenever I gaze upon its mysterious depths,
I know life's true meaning,
within me.

My vision belongs to the sea.
For whenever I gaze upon its perfect pattern,
I sense the inner need.

My growth belongs to the sea.
For whenever I gaze upon its majestic power,
life's fullness is blessing me.
   —*Jeffrey Levine*

Memories Of Grandma

Memories are all I have
For you have gone away.
Though I cherish each and every one
I'd rather you could stay.

I know that you are happy,
And wild and young and free,
Yet I miss you now so very much,
And I'd like you here with me.

I remember all the times we shared,
You were always there for me.
We laughed, we loved, we cared a lot,
We were as happy as could be.

You always had a gentle hug,
Sweet smile, and tender touch.
Your being there, your understanding,
Always meant so much.

The time will pass, my heart will heal,
The pain will be no more.
And memories I'll no longer need,
When you meet me at the door.
   —*Candi McCane*

Sin Against Morality

Today the wind blows uncertainly
For young people to be insecure
Not knowing what the future may bring
Making songs of rap to sing
And sinning against morality

Marriage today is seemed forgotten
Living together or shaking is highly acceptable
But God knows it is not appreciable
For he said a man shall leave his mother
And father, and cling to another
Which is his wife and no other
The two shall be one, for forsaking all others
Which is not sin against morality
—*James A. Dingwall Jr.*

Fickle Flower

The sun rises to warm and nurture at first,
Forces the laughing, rainy, clouds away.
The flower rejoices in light,
Slowly the sun rises, higher and higher it climbs,
Laughing, scorching, burning the flower; killing, strangling.
The flower prays for clouds,
Still no tears from heaven fall, none to comfort,
Only the laughing sun,
Laughing in victory over the clouds, over beauty.
Slowly the flower cries, weeps for lost life.
Cries for clouds, comfort,
Yet none shall come,
Oh foolish flower, dreaming of comfort,
Poor flower, depending upon many, laughs the scorning sun.
Laughing forever at the pain of flowers?
No say the clouds who come to fight,
As many have come before,
Who shall win? Only ruthless time holds the secret.
Gently, tears heaven fall,
Only for the flower to change once more.
—*Heidi Lynne Rabe*

I'll Stay On The Lord's Side

I'll stay on the Lord's side
Forever and ever with Him I'll abide

He said that if I wait on Him patiently
One day He'll come and His face I'll see

Yes I'll stay on the Lord's side
That up in the clouds with Him I'll ride

I'll walk in His way, I'll obey His command
And if I grow weak, He'll help me to stand

I'll look to Him always; I'll seek His word
And about my loins His truth I'll gird

Yes I'll stay on the Lord's side
I'll follow him always and not backslide

To sin and evil I'll say nay
That I'll never, never go astray

I'll look to Him in every way
And He will save me on doomsday

Yes I will stay on the Lord's side
That one day heavenward I'll glide
—*Jeri Bello*

New Years Eve: December 31st, 11:59 P.M.

Forget the hurt.
Forget the dirt.
Forget the pain.
Forget not being sane.
Forget the persecution, you received in the institution.
Forget the hate, before it's too late.
Forget the sickness.
Forget your hit lists.
Forget the meanness, the world with no tenderness.
Forget the lies, even the unapproving eyes.
Forget the crime, you paid the time.
Forget the threats, you paid the debt.
Forget the enemies, there's nothing more they can do to me.
Forget the harassments, they can no longer embarrass me.
Forget the price, you paid so high.
Forget the cost, it wasn't all lost.
Forget the bad news.
Forget you've been used.
Forget the tears, it's a new year.
Move on with your life, after all it's past midnight.
—*Beverly Nyoka Ghupta-Williams*

Do I Forgive?

Someone said,
"Forgiveness always starts
When you ask the other person
To forgive you."
My starled ego countered, "No."
Yet there things I need to know.
(An introspective search will find,
recessed, the thistles of my mind.)
Is there bitterness,
A blast of blame?
Or sparks attached to someone's name?
Am I, from malice, really free?
What do I find inside of me?...

What loveless thoughts prevent our seeing
The Selfhood of
Another's being....
—*Aimee McKinnon*

Poe's Soul

I curse the day that I was born; for I was born alone.
Forsaken to be a lonely man without love and friends to give a hand. Though my mind was a genius by a forgiving God up high; I never knew what I possessed, thought it to be, a lie obsessed. Though a love, I had acquired by some fortunate beguile, it tore beneath my beating heart before my life had a happy start. A drunken fool, I then became without knowledge of whom to blame. I roamed to find what I had lost or to gain, whatever the cost; but a fool, a drunk, I had become a poetic bum, drinking rum was how others did see me, and their words were salty as the sea. The lonely nights slowly fled, leaving me a sleepless fool, without a bed. And so, I took a pen to hand while singing sonnets which slipped through sand. I wrote words that tore apart, my lameness body with a torn heart. And yet, it was a soothing relief to put in writing my words of grief. And from then to now I search the path to show how my being really was, a poor soul without a cause.
—*Diana Redwine*

Petra

Citadel of temple tombs,
Fortress of cliffs and crags,
Plain of narrow river gorge,
Petra, carved in living stone,
Stands strong.

Home of ancient Edomites,
Host to flow of caravans,
Prize coveted by Arab greed,
Petra, gateway in the wilderness,
Stands guard.

Tomb of kingdoms come and gone,
Edomites, Nabateans, Moslems, Franks,
Forgotten, lost for centuries,
Petra, roseate region of the dead,
Stands mute.

Soul of Islam zealousness,
Spirit of Christian faith,
Torn and cradled in history's march,
Petra, eternal shrine,
Triumphant stands.
—*Florence Weber Mann*

Spell Bound

A full moon in the distance
Frames her lovely face
Cat-like eyes reach out
In a possessive embrace

Radiant is her smile
With a touch of sin
Hair as dark as Hallow's Eve
Given life by the howling wind

If her magic weren't so black
The cauldron held no brew
She'd seem to be an innocent
All evil would fade from view

For bewitching is her manner
And when her beauty fails
The clouds of dark descend to reign
Her wickedness prevails
—*Christina Pruczinski*

Freddie, Tha' Shoeshine Man

Apop-pop, Apop-pop-pop!
Freddie, tha' shoeshine man;
He goes 'bout his business ever' day
'N' he always has a grin.

Apop-pop, Apop-pop-pop!
As the sheep slaps that cow!
Apop-pop, Apop-pop-pop!
But Freddie's gettin' older now.

Apop-pop, Apop-pop-pop!
He don't think 'bout nuthing' but today.
Apop-pop, Apop-pop-pop!
He got mouths to feed 'n' bills to pay.

He's been doin' dis forty years now;
Makin' the sheep slap that cow!
Apop-pop, Apop-pop-pop!
Apop-pop, Apop-pop-pop!

His fingers gettin' weak 'n' he don't understand;
He got arthritis now 'n' no pension plan.
Apop-pop, Apop-pop-pop!
Yes, that's Freddie, tha' shoeshine man!
—*Johnny Rogers, Jr.*

In The Meadow

The air was crisp with scents of spring,
Freshly bloomed the April morn,
Winter passed so cold and gray,
Melting into thoughts forlorn.

Apple trees all dressed in white,
Cause to start the springtime chore,
Drawing those to their delight,
Carrying back next winter's store.

Birds aflit and chirping tunes,
Calling mates to treetop perch,
Gathering twigs and seasoned hay
To build a home in tangled birch.

Grazing cows meander loose
Without a slight ignoble care;
Sweet and tender meadow shoots
Satisfy their cravings there.

I just stare in wanderlust
While seated 'neath a sturdy tree;
Imagining the world becomes
As peaceful as this time for me.
—*Jonathan E. Fennell*

They Put Me In The Mix

I'm between races, "I" — know where I came
from. And all I know is what's done is done.

This is something that I can't fix. Because
"they put me in the mix."

I'm accepted by some. But living with,
race — rejection has not been fun. Its
hard for me sometimes. I don't know
which race is really mines
  I'm human as anyone can be,
  there should never be a race conflict,
  For "we" all were created by "thee",,
The mixing salt and pepper is always
right — but, when races are mixed — they
are scorned on sight. Why don't
mankind do what's right?

  And learn to embrace the simple love
  for each other, regardless of the race of
  the father or mother.
And be proud, of the mixture of all human
races and walk with heads held-up high
and smiles upon their faces.

Yes — I'm mixed and I don't
really give a damn, 'cause I'm
proud of the person, which I am.

I- can dream and think, beyond
any poem such as this — I'm
not ashamed because "they put me
in the mix."
—*Morganna*

Hold Me

Hold me when I cry; it's just my sanity slipping.
Hear me when I call, or I'll be lost (another breath in the wind)
See me, alone in this place (no one understands)
Taste the moisture in the air, feel it set in your skin
Help me. Listen ... Please?
Don't be afraid if there's a whisper at your window tonight
It will just be me — saying goodbye.
Never again will my heart beat alone.
Never will I be empty again.
—*Brian J. Walsh*

Where Are The Children

Here they come, one by one
From early morning, till day is done
Hey mom, will you lend me a hand
My room's a mess, you are so grand

Dishes in the sink, waiting for a washer
Don't ask the kids, they think it's torture
May as well do them yourself
Put that book back, on, the shelf.

Gotta go now, time for the game
You can't go, oh, what a shame
Gotta cook and clean the house
Don't forget to iron my blouse

I'd like to sit and chat awhile
Gotta go mom, that's not, my style
I'm much too busy, can't stop now
Someday mom, I'll come for chow

When young, they step upon your feet
Tug at your clothes and are so sweet
Step on your heart when they are old
Where are those children, you used to hold?
—*Bonnie Macy*

Feeling Things

Reflected vibes of things past felt must now erase
from eyes mine often met,
but never knew, nor dared embrace.

Yet, tonight, in baring my lonely heart
and filling it with yours,
I find its gap more closed than apart.

I'm feeling things I've never felt before with you.
Some glow reflects its warmth and beats with force
'til blossoms sprout with growth in forward course,
and whole, once more, I breathe sweet life anew.

Yes, I'm learning things I've never learned before about you.
When earth is cold, you culture flame divine;
bright stars replace dark clouds which wasted time.
On ground, you lure me fly the sky with you.

Now, I see you feeling things I've never seen you feel before.
—*Florence Raush Ehlers*

Truth Will Set Free

This is a time for sound narration,
From one that speaks, to bear in mind,
The stand is taken, this declaration,
And then to impart, revealing find.
A people in clamor, as held apart,
The issues that render'd, now in view,
Would be any place, then want to start,
For a task that is, as our right to do.
No one has come, amidst this pall,
Sensing to chaos, of scheme in guise,
Show this, the right, then to recall,
And then with a purpose, will demise.
This is, that, which voice, and to be,
To intone and pen, th' sound is clear,
A call to heed, saying to fore-see,
Know of that hour, and yearn to hear.
Then to you, and this would record,
Of whom we hear, thus now, will be,
Th' price to know and can afford,
At best, said then, truth will set free.
—*Eugene F. Tonelli*

Ode To The Artist

How do you manage to instill life on paper
From inanimate brush, paint and water?
In what way do you allow me to hear
The chatter of the crowd in your painting?

On another wall soft tendrils from your flower
Dangle downward, pulled by gravity
Touching, almost touching
The ivory-colored picture frame.

The cat lying golden with sun-streaked hair
Brings summer warmth
Into the cool spring kitchen.
Lazy, purring from a porch etched into eternity.

Black-clad monk, sad facial features,
Eyes cast downward,
Has silently watched from the same quiet spot
For seventeen years.

The joy your colors bring is overwhelming,
And the peace and comfort your images leave,
You'll never, ever imagine.

Accept these words then,
As my humble token of appreciation
For what you have given.
They are my meager gift in kind to you,
Artist, master of the easel.
—*Joyce Green Sells*

The Treasure Of My Mind

I walk the heartbeat of life
from the cradle to the grave.
In search of my inner-self with
hopes to find my soul.

I look within. I look without
as I examine my life in time.
In hopes to find the inner-key
to the treasure of my mind.

The journey's short. The journey's long.
The heartbeat of life is tough at times,
but I know deep within that someday I shall
find my soul. The treasure of my mind.
—*Eugene B. Hill, Jr.*

Another One Just Like Me

We mate as does everything in nature-
from the one-celled amoeba, hydra, paramecium-
to the insects and fragrant flowers -
to the buttercups and roses, daffodils,
sun flowers and towering trees-
to birds, reptiles and animals-
they mate in a world of reproduction.

Find a mate, a true romance-
watch how the love buds accelerate-
before you know it, the deed is done-
the union of the sexes- impending birth-
to the beasts of the field, all kinds look alike-
the world is in a state of reproduction.

"Another one just like me," in repetition-
from acorn, egg, seed, cocoon-
man imitates nature when he reproduces-
he also produces products of mass production-
not one of a kind but thousands of varieties-
everything and everykind separate and unique.
—*Professor John Buckland Erdell*

Bear In Waiting

His glassy eyes stare down at me
from the top shelf of the bookcase
where he has been exiled.
Once my constant companion, now
set aside, forgotten in the process of
growing up.
His worn, torn body bears the scars of
years of patient stitching.
He is my oldest friend,
a bear named Pooh.
Can he even forgive me for
casting him aside,
into this stuffed toy limbo?
Fear not, Pooh.
You are not forgotten,
Just waiting for the day
When my own children can hold you.
 —*Eileen Kelly*

September. Ballet.

The leaves on the trees, dancing in the breeze.
From the tree tops, to the roots. Aground,
A square dance or perhaps a virginia round.
The squirrels are running to and fro, and nutcracker suite,

Cold storage, no defeats.
The roar of a lion, the hibernating of a bear,
"The hall of the mountain king," when the saints come marching in,"
The leaves of the mountain trees in gold and red,
Wafting to the ground, form a beautiful spread.

Seen by few in the daylight dew,
The water still flows in the brooks,
"Let's take a look," though it might be a mite late,
We might find, "a swan Lake."
 —*Florence G. Axton*

The Role Of A Flower

The heavenly flower mysteriously follows life's way
 From the very moment of our "Birth-day."

At Confirmation and Graduation, it's there to say—
"Congratulations" on your well earned goal Today.

So proudly it will caress you down the aisle on
 your wedding
To remind you of the new life you'll now be
 heading.

There shall be fun and sorrow as memories unfold
And (the Flower) it will share our joy or loss untold

The flower's role is ever important, we can't deny
 It's God, ever silently by our side.
 —*Anne Son*

The Choice

It's a wonder-filled world for me,
How great to be alive!!!
I have turned my face to see the light
Where dark shadows disappear.
Thus, I learned the truth that sets us free
And the choice was mine,
It's a beautiful world I see.
 —*Eleanor R. Lofton*

Life

Dedicated to President Bill Clinton and family.
From within Her illustrious womb we all must pass,
and fall weeping into Her tall proceeding grass,
where none can see ahead, only behind;
taking one bold step at a time, we hope to find,
that illusive Golden Chalice few are destined to hold;
stealing a sip of Her burning wine before it is cold;
warming our waning lives with a measure of hope;
for we know it is useless to whine and mope.
So willingly we accept Her small and meager measure,
for of a truth we know it is our only treasure.
For too soon She shall point us to an open space,
where we in spectered awe will behold the face,
and view the Field that all must see,
of bold, relentless, Eternity.
 —*John Demps*

Reconciliation

To a mother once forgotten,
from your son far away.
I ask your forgiveness
for now and yesterday.
I long to call and say I'm sorry
to put aside the fear and worry.
Who was right? Who was wrong?
I do not know,
for it was so far away and long ago.
A lot of pain and sorrow
have hurt us over the years-
It's time to end our hurting
and time to stop our tears.
From a son to his mother,
some warmth to stop the chill;
I always loved you
and I always will.
 —*Brian Turner*

Early Autumn

A chilly, blue day stands before my face.
Frost had edged the windows with lace.
I bundle up so as not to freeze
And head outside—the day to seize.

Green, yellow, orange and red greet the eye
As autumn leaves begin to die.
In the darkness escapes a sigh
For all the colors going by.

To the east a ball of flame
Has entered upon my little game.
As it rises a little higher,
It sets the leaves of the hill on fire.

A warmth spreads to my feet;
Now this autumn day is complete
And I can go on with all the chores
Knowing life is a little better than before.
 —*Holly Dobberpuhl*

Untainted Rose

Glaring from a magnificent portrait
   frozen in time, for mortals to see
A brimstone rose, in a midst of thorns
   keep taunting and beckoning to me

There's not a pedestal worthy enough
   to signify the serenity you possess
You're not another ordinary rose
   revealing a revelation of sheer loveliness

Lilies, poinsettias, and golden daffodils
   somehow, they play second - fiddle to you
For the frenzy hypnosis you're creating
   is like a simple fairy-tale come true

The delirious vibrations that you transmit
   when you blossom out in vivid bloom
Can turn a humble man into a savage
   or exonerate him from instant doom

It will be a recession in heaven
   before you lose your infinite virginity
So let the summer breeze nip your petals
   and let your innocent dreams run free

   —*Grover J. Garrett, Jr.*

Sweet Butterfly

Fragile little butterfly -
Gaily plucked from out of the sky.

Fascination for your beauty -
Never once a thought to duty.

Calloused fingers groping, clutching -
wings too delicate for touching.

The bold pursuit - the crude abduction
Alas! the ultimate destruction.

"No harm intended", so it seems -
Just selfishly pursuing dreams.

"So sorry" to have made you cry -
You are the dream.
  Sweet Butterfly.

   —*Helen Anastas*

At The Break Of Dawn!

At the break of dawn they come,
Galloping across the bright pink sky.
Carrying on their backs all the dreams of the world.
Their horns shining in the early morning light.
Announcing:
They are the Kings and Queens of majesty and light.

No one owns them, and no one dare try.
Because to own the unicorn you must first own the sky.

You must rule all that you see,
And be all that you can be.

You must let your heart open up to the world
and you must let it fly like a bird in the sky
at the break of dawn.

And once you have done this,
Then you can truly claim your right to the unicorns
At the break of dawn.

   —*Diana M. Blount*

HEAR O NATIONS Of The WORLD

Hear O Nations of the World,
Gather your tribes around the LIGHT.
Follow the path of ONENESS
For all are of the Eternal Source.
Call IT what you will: Spirit, God, Allah, Yahweh, Brahman.
Know not what has been revealed to you,
   has been revealed to many in their
   own tongues and ways of understanding?
Are you so special, so set apart,
   that the source of Life is yours alone?
Oh, foolish children - the River of Life
   flows through all tribes...Through all times.
It replenishes Itself, and cannot be contained
   in clenched fists or limited thought.
Unbind your minds... your ways of being,
Stretch as rays of morning sun... reverent and expanding.
The Great Spirit will guide.
Leaders, wear moccasins of truth, guiding younger
   nations through the thorns of rivalry and fear.
And as the eagle soars, release a new beginning for this day.
Fly with keen sight, knowing Father Sky and
   Mother Earth give freely to all their children.
So must we, give freedom, respecting each other's ways.
Our sacred earth-path is within ourselves —
   round the wheel, to the four corners of wisdom,
   that one day we may join the Elders.
For in time all will return to Father Spirit
   within the Great Mystery.

   —*Carol Conley-Klahorst*

Mirrors

Life
generally is an illusion
and understanding depends upon
moving mirrors

Unless
of course
you happen to ignore
reflective glass
thereby never noticing
yourself as you pass under neon signs
and brightly lit carousels

Too bad for those who never
dare to glance
they shall be surprised
when they finally notice
that there is someone standing by

A friend
whose only existence
is altered by
the mirrors of chance

   —*Carolyn Jean Custer*

Love Falls, As Fall Leaves

Autumn arrows shoot through the sky,
Hitting the stars and making them cry.
Leaves, like feathers, float down from above,
Covering the ground with tears of love.
Lonesome hearts and naked trees,
Go hand in hand through winter's freeze;
But spring will bud and hearts will blend,
In summer's heat, love never ends!

   —*Jeanne C. Franklin*

Fragrant Lei

Plumeria and ginger ride the wind tonight,
   gently from Lahaina's fragrant gardens—
The sky beyond the breaking wave
   is darkening,
Where once we watched
   the dancing flames of
Summer's sunset beyond Kaanapali—
Yes, my love,
Sweet is this night perfumed by
   invisible flowers, and
Sweeter still, my thoughts of you—
Our hearts caught in
   love's invisible lei,
Our hearts warmed in
   love's invisible fire!
      —*June Allegra Elliott*

Thanksgiving

Oh Lord! Who gave us life,
Give us hearts replete with thankfulness.

We thank Thee, Lord, and do Thou bless
This home, a place of loveliness.

These friends, their kindness manifest
Their thoughts and hopes to Thee addressed,

In gratitude for things bestowed,
As each pursues his chosen road,

Good health, good cheer, the mundane things
Conferred to fashion a heart that sings.

We thank Thee, Lord, for all of this,
The gift of life, the wind's soft kiss.

And on this day reserved for Thee,
With reverence, we make this plea.

Oh Lord! Who gave us life,
Give us hearts replete with thankfulness.
      —*Ida Sagers*

Hospitality

Hospitality traced to world's start
   God sent Son with loving heart.
Abraham and wife showed they cared
   They fed travelers and thus shared.

Cure some weakness in time with love
   Prepare haven through spirit above.
Hospitality requires honor and affection
   Added to prayer gives greater perfection.

God's hospitality comes to those who care,
   He repays those who their gifts share.
All who claim others as sister and brother
   Have knowledge that God dwells in the other.

Cure problems one at a time with love
   Accept balance from the Lord above.
Added prayer gives strength and score
   Thank Father, Son and Spirit ever more.
      —*Bertilla Burger*

The Soul

Now here we are under one big sky
God's own creatures only He knows why
People all different as snowflakes can be
All only human with souls we can't see

What does it look like this invisible thing
What inner peace does it really bring
These questions as old as time itself
Could the answers be lying around on a shelf

Would there be a way of reaching one's soul
Is it something we could touch and repair the mold
Or a cut deep within with a surgeons knife
Would release the energy and restore the life

For we all have a soul I'm sure of that
Some hidden some hurt some buried so deep
Some elusive and always just out of reach
Yet the thought of its absence can never bring peace

So how to recall it the question remains
If lost can we find it and stake our claim
For what's rightfully ours we all have the key
To regain the essence and set it free
      —*Donna DePaolo*

Ken

That last look, that final word, The hurt,
   Good-bye may be forever
   Yet no one seems to know
   You hear that word good-bye
   You know not where to go
   My cousin left me standing
   Not knowing right from wrong
   Just staring at a casket - soon to be gone
To me good-bye is forever
A neverending path
Curious as to what lies ahead
Behind life's mysterious mask
For my cousin
I'm sure he's found the way
Good-bye means forever
Forever after to stay
When I sense forever is near
It's not a time to cry
It's merely turn my head to you
And whisper... good-bye
      —*Hollie Heffley*

The Women That Are In Demand

The women that are wanted are good women
Good from the heart to the lips
Pure as the Lily is white and pure
From its heart to its sweet lip tips

The women that are wanted, are women of sense
Whom fashion can never deceive
Who will follow whatever is pretty
And dare what is silly to leave

The women that are wanted, are wise women
They are wanted for Mothers and wives
They are wanted to cradle in loving arms
The strongest and fairest lives.

The clever, the witty, the brilliant women
There are few who can understand
But oh, for that brilliant home woman
There is a constant steady demand.
      —*Iris Hunter*

Papa's (Reflections) Dearest And Greatest Love

One day bent from age, my hair white, setting with great grandchildren in the evening light, they will ask "Papa who is your dearest and greatest love?" How can I tell them about the woman I love? How can this story be told, to great grandchildren that are not very old?

If I could tell them my hearts desire, they would know great grandmother was not the one that set the fuse that started this fire. My love had the most beautiful face, her sensuous body moved like satin on lace. My Angel with golden loops through her ears, has been my Gypsy love all of my years.

I fell in love with this suntanned girl, eyes of green, teeth like pearls. An Angel had kissed her on each cheek, leaving two dimples perfect and deep.

Her hair was gold with a hint of red, soft waves and curls formed a halo around her head. Her body lean and smooth, responding to my every move.

Our souls and hearts we did Wed, this was not done in our marriage bed. We loved and cried and God how I did pray, that she would be mine some sweet day.

Forget her? No this could never be, she will always live in the heart of me. So to the children I will say, "go my darlings catch fireflies and play. You all knew from the very start, that you are Papa's special love from the very start."

—*Juanda Hurst Mouren*

Grandchildren

Most precious that a thing can be
Grandchildren sitting on my knee
Their souls quite bare, no hidden set
What you see is what you get.

They wash away the stains of man
And give you joy no other can
They early learn that hearts are love
and shower sparkles from above.

They let you know when they are sad
And quick to show when they are glad
Their trust is free, no strings attached
Their love complete, a gift unmatched.

Though they share these wondrous lights
Their beams will shine on different sights
While some illume the higher planes
Others glow on darkened lanes.

Thank heavens they have come along
To spice my life with children's song
And I'm as lucky as can be
For the joy they bring to me.

—*Arnold J. Lau*

If Dreams Came True

A dream, a wish, a vision, too, these expectations formed and grew in minds of heroes from the past who fought so moral rights might last.

And were those dreams the same as mine, or does euphoria fill this mind? For this is what we all would see if dreams were real for you and me.

Bright golden fields not far away where children of all races play and none are harmed or hungry there as joyous laughter fills the air.

A lovely place beside the sea where women seek tranquility as all their hopes and dreams are found within this hallowed, fruitful ground.

A mountain peak that men might climb to find concurrence of each mind, for all are equal in God's sight and only He dictates what's right.

A quiet nook around the bend, a place where freedom has no end, where mankind goes to meditate as love suppresses wrathful hate.

In every corner of the world a universal flag unfurled would represent how life might be if dreams came true for you and me.

—*Elizabeth Haldane Sawtelle*

God's Garden Of Colors

This is God's garden, this is our home, flowers grow in this garden, all shapes, sizes and colors, They grow together in peace, harmony, and love

There's even wild life in this garden from the tiny Ant to the largest Elephant, they come in all shapes, sizes, and colors, they live together in peace, harmony and love

The fruit and vegetables we eat come in all shapes, sizes, and colors, they grow in smaller sections of this larger garden, they don't fight about where they will grow, or who they will grow next to, there is only peace and love

The sky and the water copy each other, they like to be the same color you see... and trees of all kinds, different shades of green, they don't quarrel because a pine tree has moved into the neighborhood they live in peace

And then there is man, made in all shapes, sizes and colors, they kill out of hate, they separate out of ignorance, there is no harmony, no peace, this is God's garden, this is our home, it's the only home we have, there is no where else to go, man must learn to replace hate with love, violence with peace, disharmony with harmony, ignorance with knowledge.

Then and only then will this garden be complete....

—*Colleen Farlow*

Traveling In God's World

We have traveled so far in this vast land and God has helped guide us safely home. I have set in green valleys and felt emotions of reverence as I've looked with awe at the majestic mountains. I've watched a chipmunk play close by and heard the distant call of a wild animal that inhabits the wilderness. I have been inspired by a waterfall or a babbling brook, the wild flowers with all their beauty, the blue sky overhead with soft white clouds floating by and I have wondered how anyone can deny God. This beauty could not have just happened God has painted masterpieces all over the world. When I set in the sand on a seashore watching the waves, tides coming in, tides going out, the white peaceful soaring of a sea gull overhead, a ship in the horizon and the soft breeze blowing thru my hair I feel God's presence everywhere.
—*Jeanette L. Smith*

The Open Door

Watching from the open door.
Guiding us. As only he can
asking us to trust him more
and to love our fellow man

Standing is his father's holy light
Helping us to get, what we need
So our lives can shine bright
if we just trust Him, to Lead

Listening from the golden door
always ready, to help us again
asking us all, to pray more
He's loved us, since time begin
  Light
In the beautiful blue sky
Looking from his open door
within, the white cloud, so high
For he loves us, forever more.
—*Freida Hoffman*

Spirit Is The Secret

That's the Spirit friends, you've got it.
Guts and heart and brains to fit.
Don't ever think that you can't lead.
Believe in your self, that's what you need.

Break forth like thunder in the sky.
Never stop too long to ponder why.
Success is only one step away.
My friend the choice is yours today.

The future has never been so bright.
Opportunity knocks both day and night.
Hesitation brings thoughts of vain defeat.
But you are made of stuff that can't be beat.

Go to it with gusto and all your might.
You'll find success with such delight.
Never mind the tears or fear
For they follow hard trails year by year.

Catch the spirit as she goes by
Because you've got "it," is the reason why.
The way you are traveling is where stars have been.
The spirit is really what matters my friend.
—*Elbert P. Green*

My Lord And I

We often walk together, God and I
Hand in hand we go - heeding neither time nor weather.
He leads me down the path of joy - I have found the road
That leads to heavenly treasure.

When the clouds are heavy and the skies are dim
He takes my hand and I follow Him
I'm so thankful that He never lets me go.
He charts my course when morning lights the skies
And we're together, He and I.
When that day comes when I say "Goodbye"
To my earthly friends and family - will they sorrow not
Nor show great grief - for God will be beside me!
—*Florence M. Craven*

The Attainment

Infinitely small and weak, man stretches forth a quivering
    hand to God.
Hesitating, he takes the first, faltering steps toward eternity
The spirit groaning, writhing in its development,
Mind straining against the boundaries of familiarity,
Pushing forth to the birth of totality.

Physical existence fading in the realization of omnipotent
    magnitude, he views his world as home no longer.
Instinctively moving forward, he clings to the dregs of his past.
Seeking security in the ignorance of the ancient,
He is irresistibly drawn toward his origins.

Looking back, he sees his future aeons behind him.
Looking forward, he sees his past spread forth in a panoramic
    view of chaos and delight.
The circle closing, past and future blending irrevocably with
    the present.
Precious choices made, no recourse presents itself.
The beginning has become the end, and the end is now the
    beginning.

The future awaits participation by the human spirit.
Formed from countless generations of prejudices and mistakes,
    yet like the phoenix rising, man emerges as a priceless
    gem, capable of the most wondrous act known in all
    creation. The act of expressing love.
—*Donna Butts*

A Friend

Each person young, old, big or small,
Has built around himself a wall.
It's high enough to block the view
From all including me and you.

Outside he paints some lovely scenes,
Inside his visions and his dreams.
The whole world sees the ones outside
But very few the ones he hides.

Those are reserved for those rare few
Who qualify as you might do
If you don't judge or criticize
Or give advice or otherwise

Betray his trust. It all depends,
You may become his true real friend.
—*Floyd W. King*

Don Pancho's Ghost

Tell me, have you seen Don Pancho?
Has he come this way today?
Long he's traveled on this roadway
In an endless come-and-go.

Early mornings, he goes northward
And heads southward every eve,
Hating what he's going toward,
Missing what he hates to leave.

Saddened heart, he's just a grieving
Ghost of shadows in-between,
For he's not among the living
Or the life he had foreseen.

He had run away from danger
In the country he had known.
Now he finds himself a stranger,
In his new land and his own.

Should you ask him what he's seeking,
What has taken him so long,
He will answer, softly weeping,
"For the place where I belong."

—*Giselle Sierra*

Time

Time has not softened the pain carved in my broken heart, nor has time helped to dry my lonely "tears." Life as I once knew it, is never to be again, no not without you "here." Time has not eased the ache of "missing you" hours you do not roam my mind, are oh so very few. Yet I find beauty still surrounds my daily life, yes the "beauty" of each cherished yesterday I shared with "you." Time has not silenced your "velvet voice" like a classic song it is "music" to my ears. Nor has time dulled the "golden glow" of precious memories I have amassed thru your oh "too short" years. Time has not faded a treasured portrait etched so colorfully in my heart, a picture of you, one of my "greatest loves." Yes I make it by each hard tomorrow here on earth, with a "gift" of love and strength sent to me by two "guardian angels" up above. Time has not blurred a thrilling "vision" of you walking in my door and up and down my stairs. Nor has time dimmed a bright recurring dream I have come to "relish" one in which again in my empty arms you "reappear." Time has not allowed the "love and devotion" I have planted deep within, wither away or "die," Only those "lucky" enough to have been "blessed" with you in their lives, need ever ask me the reason "why." "Time" does not heal "all" wounds.

—*Joan Nolan*

The Wailing Cries Of Sorrow

Lord, you who search the thoughts and heart of man,
have heard the wailing cries of sorrow,
in the silence of my soul.
If all the tears I've cried within have become Sacred
tears, for your sacred thirst: Every moment of misery
and every tear has been worth it!
For what has more life than a tear in sorrow?
Tears of grief and sorrow spring forth from the depth-core
of the heart.
May my sacrificial offering of heart-rendering-tears,
be a sweet aroma without blemish before 'Your Sacred Eyes'!
And, by your grace, may I forever be your humble servant.
A faltering, stumbling, believer.

—*Gil Hernandez*

Spirits

One day;
   Have you ever held a perfect rose?
   Its infant blooms, its first blossom
   And it has no thorns —

One life;
   Its soul lives within thy kingdom of heaven
   Its body grown upon thy end sinful ground
   And nature allows harm to be done—

One heaven;
   For thee suffers greatly, never wilting mindly
   Its body lives numb, for thee cannot stand alone
And whom;
   Who can stand against my winds of spirit
   Comprehending death in vows
   Knowing I'm a soul of love —

And when;
   From thine time to fine lines I write
   See my dust fall thy land of death
   Watch my body fade to dry ashes—

And last;
   Who'll be there to lick away your teardrops?
   Is it sweet or sour to taste?
   Are you going to hold me in your arms tonight?
   Then kiss me once and forever more —

—*Christopher Cookson*

The Silhouette Of God

He lies alone, content and unafraid.
He always goes back to where
He once had laid.
His bond with God that none can compare.
His love for God that knows no limit
With that he takes care.
He lies in the shadows,
Praying before sleep.
The shadow of a church steeple
Contentment he'll always keep.
He died one cold winter night
Alone that he was.
He went to be with God,
For all he loves he does.
He looked down upon the earth.
Giving protection just in case.
In the shadows a small boy lay alone.
Another to take his place.

—*Charles F Martin*

Lord Can

The Lord can turn your heart around.
He can turn your heart from heaviness
into joy.
Joy is something you can not express

He can make you smile
Smiles comes from the Lord.
How you smile is because
after you are heavy and
you go to God.
And then you will begin to smile.

—*Betty Huyck*

Repo Souls

God loves his children,
He cares for their souls;
Not one shall he let go,
Not one shall be lost from the flock,
Not one will he fail to redeem;
Their lives leased for an instant of time,
On death to return home in a flash,
Repossessed by angels in white,
From worn, torn and broken bodies;
Never again to feel pain,
To suffer indignity,
To be threatened,
Nor to be ignored,
Their purpose on earth accomplished.
—*Austin Thomas*

We Are The Giants

We walked into the abdomen of a big bird,
    He carried us soaring aloft the earth.
        We are now in the endless sky,
    Surrounding with various clouds and sunshine.

  There are miles and miles of white cotton spreads,
Floating in the mid-air to cover the world's unknown beds.
    The crystalline cliffs hang above the snowy carpet,
Hastily, the swift cirri like hundreds of horses gallop across it.

    The sun shines on the universe eternally,
      Its radiance sparkles in the space powerfully.
  Our big bird pierces through the celestial bodies,
He is a libertarian fleeing from the earth's gravity.

    We seem to fly among the stars and the moon,
      There is no other superman coming soon,
  We are the giants in the universe at this moment,
      And proud of being as superior human.
—*Diana M. P. Chang*

I Fell In Love

I saw Charlie at the Burger King.
He caught my eye. I said to my daughter,
I'll make a pass at him and I did try.

Then the time did fly!
We went places at Sr. Citizen's Center and Saturdays in town,

We each had a need.
God surely knew this indeed.
Not any man did I ever love so dearly as Charlie,
except my husband the father of our daughter.

There was a magnetic spark between us which enabled us to have
a good rapport. I don't know which one learned from the other more.

The Whirlwind Romance lasted four months and God called Charlie
   away.
But the memories still linger today.
—*Donna Belle Rowe*

Crosses To, Bear

Blood, dripping down his, heavy "cross."
He knew no, pain, for he, felt no, loss.

For dying for self.
He lived for me.
"Making" it easier for, all he see,
that (selfishness) is greater (pain) then (death),
for it, brings (years) of, unhappiness.
—*Christina Y. Acevedo*

My Jesus

He doctored an old lady back to health
He caused the lame to walk
He caused the blind to see again
He caused the dumb to talk

These are a few of the miracles
My Jesus did perform
Before they placed upon His head
A heavy crown of thorns
And hung Him on a cross to die
Which He did for you and I

He never spoke a word
He never shed a tear
I guess He did it His way
As He hung on the cross that day.
—*Doris Tyner*

Mans Flight

Man was told he could not fly!
He dug in his heels ... it was "Do or Die"!
Various contraptions were tried ... but alas,
They failed so miserably ... showed no class.

Orville and Wilbur soon remedied man's plight
When at Kittyhawk they made their first flight;
It didn't take long for the fad to catch hold,
Then men became fliers, both brave and bold.

As planes skimmed the rooftops ... clipped the trees,
Flying caught man like a contagious disease;
Thus used for travel, to haul cargo, or fight,
Man soon had the urge to speed up his flight.

They built the planes bigger, stronger and faster,
Controlled automatically ... or with man as its master;
Then up came the jets with their sonic boom,
And quick as a flash, man aimed for the moon.

The moral I give, is to never tell man,
There're some things he can't do ... cause he can;
It was said he couldn't get off the ground, but by chance,
Man soon learned to fly by the seat of his pants!
—*Joan Crawford Hammond*

A Gift Of Love

God looked down from up above.
He gave me something, very special,
A precious little bundle to love.

I'll love you forever, in a gentle way.
I'll give you my arms, each
night and day, to rock you and
cradle you, until you can lay,
your delicate little body, asleep
this day.

So hushabye, sweet baby of mine,
sleep ever so peacefully, all thru
the night, Jesus will hold you
firmly, in the palm of his hands,
He'll adorn your tiny body, with
his loving light, so have no fear
or fright, He'll keep you safe
forever, each, and every night.

So hushabye sweet darling baby
of mine, I just wanted you to
know, of God and his love. I will
always remember, his gift from
above, that came, from his, undeniable love.
—*Elaine E. Smith*

Grandpa

My grandpa is a special man
He helps us kids anyway he can.
He acts so tuff around us all
And he stands at least 6 feet tall
When I was little he was just so neat
When I fell down he'd set me back on my feet
He taught me important things about life
And I saw him cry the day I became a wife
So he's not so tuff I thought that day
He's a proud man who finds words hard to say
I'll cherish my time that I have with him
I'll remember his stories and his funny grin
He may not realize how much of a part,
that he's given to me that has touched my heart
And I'm so glad God choose him to be
My grandpa who's so special to me.
   —*Jenny Abernathy*

One Who Left Us Too Soon

In the cowpoke heaven up there above
   He is drifting along with his cowgirl love
There are things to do on that fenceless range
   Where time moves on without any change....
There is stock to move forever on
   Across those plains of the great beyond;
But the ponies will never be weary and sore
   From working away at that endless chore
For they'll pause to rest in the dusky haze
   And on heavenly grass the ponies will graze.
Our cowpoke sweethearts will murmur then
   Of their cowpoke dreams and lovers yen;
Or perchance they'll break into a reckless race
   Over the miles of infinite space
Until they're stopped by cowpoke friends
   To bring the race to a laughing end
Happily they'll all jog along
   Joking - or singing a cowpoke song.
He is at peace away up there
   Where cowpoke souls their love can share
   —*Barbara Perkins Cleary*

What Is A Husband?

What is a husband?
He is many things.
He is a lover, friend, and confident,
When in the shower, he tries to sing!

He is the provider,
And general supervisor,
The family guider,
And usually the family miser.

He is a loving and caring father,
Who wants only the best for his family.
He gets into quite a lather,
When someone disturbs one of his family.

So you see, a husband is many things,
But mine is the best you see,
There was and still is, love in our wedding rings,
and the vows we said, "I love thee!"
   —*Joan A. Wagner*

True Love Or Not True Love

He treats me the best
   He is the sweetest
   He is a wonderful guy
   He makes me feel good.
      Then why am I so
   confused about what we
      are doing.
   I care about him, but is
this that which will just fade away.
   He's not all that cute, but
      he is the only man
   who has ever treated me
         this way.
      He wants to marry, I
         am not sure.
   I really don't know how
         to tell him.
   I wouldn't want him to
      throw his life away
   for someone like me, of
what use would I be to you.
   I wish I knew if I loved
         you!
   —*Jerry Cox*

The Cripple

God put the cripple on earth for a purpose, as he did you.
   He is whole. You do not include or care to purpose.
   A person can be a cripple in many ways. An unbeliever
   in God is a cripple, it can go without say. Cripple as
   cripple shows. Need anyone say anymore of close.

God might have put the cripple of limb and not of soul to
   help guide the way. There can be many defects in any
   clay. Many do not accept and many
   flawless bodies fall. Perfect is as the mind sees. Many
   accept God's will without plee.

A cripple body can't be as bad as a cripple soul. A soul
   has to be flawless in order to join the foal, God is perfect
   and must be accepted for anyone to be whole on that day.
   I will never be perfect in body, but on that day in soul.
   God always tries urge us all before he does (enclose).
   Salvation can be perfect just you ask those who should know.
   This for everybody can be so.
   —*Geneva Hood Davidson*

Soldiers Last Song

I'm coming, coming, coming home
Have I been away so long, too long
That heard was Song of Songs
Soundings of Paradise Park.

I'm coming, coming, coming home
From long ago and far away.
Home, from across frothy foam
Going from, and long to stay.

Carved in darkest marble — etchings
Home is here, the price we pay —
Quiet sounds of song a catching
Traces of its morals — weigh.
   —*Charles G. Harding*

Lures

When my father was the age that I am now,
he often descended in winter to his basement bench
in search of solace by the furnace
while the stoker rumbled with coal.

Surgical scissors in hand and thinking of summer,
he snipped strands of feathers: blue macaw,
wood duck, black turkey, peacock and teal.
Matching their length, he carefully placed them
together between his thumb and forefinger,
then wrap them with marabou silk.
They formed wings like the bow of the hook.

In spring he would practice casting on the long
green stage of our lawn. Using only his wrist
he would whip the air until it whirred and sang,
then crack the line into fluid loops
of calligraphy old as bone.

Remembrance of him catches me now like a hook
as I sit in this fragile boat and rock
on the summer's edge watching my lure
as it bobs over the dark gray water.

—*Jean Musser*

Trigger Happy Ray-Gun

A prez was named Ray-Gun. He was loving so much gun.
He played a lot cowboy. He had nothing but one toy.
This toy was named gun-gun. For him it was a lot fun.
He sent troops to Lob-None. To make a peace, but in John.
He teased Russia, the big beast. Both in Middle and Far East.
He said to his wife, none see. You need a gun, but fancy.
He said to kids, in white house. Don't be scared like a mouse.
Let us spend all for gun. Let us make war, just for fun.
A man got him in out door. Shot him, but made little sore.
Even did not take his life. Did shake friends, and his wife.
Said this shooting everyone. Will make decide our Ray-Gun.
They will gather every gun. Weapon and gun will be gone.
We will have all new life. Without pistole, even knife.
After healing was over. Ray-Gun announced all over.
I am still gun lover. Even people will suffer.
I am Run-Old Ray-Gun. I give much more to Bay-Gun.
This is U.S. slogan. You don't like it? Go Iran.
(Go to hell).

—*Habib Emami, M.D.*

Street Scene

In front of the welfare hotel
he sits in a wheelchair
at the middle of the sidewalk,
clearly a nuisance
to those rushing by.
The evening sun casts
eerie shadows on the Vietnam Vet
still clad in army greens.
The name on his pocket
has faded to illegible.
An open magazine rests on his lap,
he bows his head almost in reverence
to the image of the woman
on the centerfold. Smiling almond eyes,
the warmth of woman's touch.
His gaze is fixed upon the page.
He is transported to another time.
His fingers caress the image of the woman.
His heart aches,
almost as much as his missing legs.

—*Giorgetta McRee*

I And The World

The sun opens up and his eyes shine with laughter
He touches me

The world rushed here and there and he fights to stay equal
He touches me

I walk past with a pounding heart, he glances my way
He touches me

I wait with worry as the wind caresses my face,
I think of him, suddenly he appears from behind the bend
He touches me

He sees me and smiles, I see him and cry
He touches me

He rushed toward me, the wind fighting back with strong force
He touches me

He brushes my arm and my skin burns with fear
He touches me

The clouds open up and cry over the world
He touches me

He shields me with his coat and wipes my tear-stricken face
He touches me

He looks in my eyes of sadness and smiles
He touches me

He has a quizzical look, I explain
He touches me

He holds me to him and kisses my heart
He touches me...

—*Jennifer Hale*

The Roach

Tonight I killed a roach. So what? you say.
He was a big one — fat and juicy — meant to be a tasty treat
for insect eaters,
or else for other roaches, who dispatch their kind
 With grip and flip and smack of lip and rip and dip and sip.
So what? I'll tell you what: I customarily kill roaches with a swat
That gives the roach a fighting chance to get away
Provided that he's smart enuf or fast enuf or knows a nice safe nook.
But this time I got modern and I used a spray,
And when it hit that little fellow — well, he shat.
He shat four times — huge drips — he knew this was the end.
He knew the meaning of the phrase "to scare the shit out of,"
tho maybe not the words.
I know the terror that the little fellow felt, 'cause I've been there —
I thought I was about to die one time, and got the shit scared
out of me just like this little guy.
So who could possibly be such a sickly sentimentalist
And give a second thought to some dumb roach he killed?
Well, I confess I did — in fact, I cried.
But maybe not so much for him as for myself.
He knew his time had come; I know mine's coming.
And maybe if I shit someone will cry for me.

--*John Bryant*

My Father

I placed him on a pedestal when just a mere child.
He was tall and handsome and his manner so mild.

His smile could always warm me from head to toe,
And a hug or kiss brought a very special glow.

From child to teen conditions limited the time we could share,
But there was never doubt that if I needed him, he would be there.

The years have passed and he is still handsome and tall.
My love and respect for him have not changed at all.

He is still on that pedestal because that is where he belongs.
He is kind and wise and has a special way righting most wrongs.

He has time for me when I'm happy and always if I'm sad.
He is like no other, this special man I call Dad!
—*Donna O'Malley*

One Solitary Life Of Jesus

He was born in an obscure village.
He worked in a carpenter shop
until he was thirty.
He then became an itinerant preacher.
He never held an office.
He never had a family or owned a house.
He didn't go to college.
He had no credentials but mineself.

Nineteen centuries have come and gone,
and today he is the central figure
of the human race.

All the armies that ever marched,
and all the navies that ever sailed,
all the parliaments that ever sat,
and all the kings that ever reigned
have not affected the life of man
on this earth as much as that
of the life of Jesus Christ.
—*Elmer J. Bryan*

Guilty Of What

Day by day he walked among men
Healing the blind, deaf, and lame
Forgiving all their worldly sin
Never pointing a finger of blame

Miracles were done where ever he went
Like turning the water into wine
Demons into the swine was sent
He fed five thousand at one time

What about the raising of the dead
And the love he spread around
Followers going where ever he lead
Because peace in him they found

Day by day he walked this land
Knowing what lay ahead
Nails waiting for his hands
And thorns for his head

Guilty, guilty, guilty, they cried
Fists in his face they did shove
So on the cross my Jesus died
But what !!! Was he guilty of ???
—*Dorothy Marlene Reed*

At Sunset In May

As I sit on the deck near sunset,
Hear the rush of the tide coming in,
And farther out the ripples
Break with the sight of a fin
Of Orcas, going Southward
Thro' the Straits, in their usual way,
To get to other places
At the end of a nice Spring day.
And, as the sun is lowering,
The horses in pasture graze.
The sky is turning orange
With a hint of mystic haze
That enhances distant foothills
As they blend with the blue of the seas,
And leave a painted backdrop...
For black silhouettes of trees
Whose stiff or lacy branches
Stretch over a cottage small,
Demurely sitting placid
Beyond the poplars tall.
—*Emelia L. Bave*

Thanksgiving Invitation

Today we got a telephone call that was
Heartfelt by us all. Dad
Announced that Grandma wants us
Near on this Thanksgiving Day.
Keeping this invitation in mind and
Savoring the thought intended—
Giving of oneself to all is
Indeed for her an achievement.
Victory — in that she's saying she cares
In an indirect way — oh! the
Natural instincts of a mother and
Grandmother who has never learned to weigh the
Affection and devotion of others directed to her through the
Times — and now the time draws nearer
To her departure-and
Hence the
Emotions will begin to rise — nothing should be
Left undone when our
Mother and grandmother goes
Away because there will be no time left to
See our dear mother grandmother Thelma
—*Dorothy Jean Jenkins*

Fifty Years Of True Love For A Special Couple

True love is . . . holding hands when you're young and two
  hearts beating in "two-step" time,
It's . . . feeling "alive" when you're together, and your
  souls seeming to entwine!

It's . . . being like a part of you is missing when you are apart,
And it's a feeling of bliss and contentment, when you're
  back with your sweetheart!

It's . . . marriage —— then the pain of separation, like
  when he's called to war,
It's . . . the ecstacy of happiness and joy when he comes
  home, and you're together once more.

It's . . . dreaming dreams and sharing thoughts and having a family,
It's . . . being there to comfort one another when tear-filled
  eyes cannot see.

It's . . . caring and sharing, and a "love-lite" that keeps
  right on a-burning,
It's . . . being strong enough to last 50 years —— and
  more — as this ol' world keeps right on a-turning!
—*Elva Nell Johnson*

The Time Before Remembering

In the time before remembering when we were but a Spirit in
Heaven above.
God, Our Heavenly Father, sent us on a journey, with great hope
  and much love.
He gave us each a spirit, to guide us all the way, to fill our
lives with hope and faith, that's still in us this day.
He gave us great tools of creation, our minds, and hands to
  help us along the way.
He said" take care of your bodies so you can stay well and strong."
Then he sent us to our Earthly home, as we come through at our
  bright.
He said "All will be forgotten as you begin your life on Earth"
He didn't promise us a life free from trials and pain, but he
promised to be with us, till we come back home to him again.
So, if we have done well, and our best, we know we won't have
  long to wait.
Our Guardian Angel will guide us, as we meet him at the gate.
—*June Dawn Ferrier*

Personal Prayers

Precious Lord hold my hand
Help me to understand
The task thou has for me to do
"Dear Lord God, I worship you."

Souls are lost and saints are ill
Draw them to thee their hearts to fill
With that great love, and comfort give
While here on earth they still do live.

And may their journey to glory be
One they will want to come to thee
No sorrow, pain, or heartache there
Only love and peace we all will share

To meet our savior "Face to Face"
What joy that will be in eternity
"Holy Spirit" be our guide
Bring us safely to thy side.

"Heavenly Father" with open arms
Meet us on that golden shore
Where we die to cross over
To live with thee for evermore!
—*Goldie E. Patteson*

A Childish Blessing

The little one cast an eye of woe;
  Her body a tale of fire below.
I placed my hand upon her brow;
Then held her head, like I knew how.
Trading a glance, her eyes still I see;
A fever, cool hands, seemed to draw unto me.
My voice spoke with love, about her sick plight.
When finished she turned and then left my sight.
Oh! Miracle true; was the next thing to view,
Such laughter and stride;
Come play, watch me ride.
I had a strange feeling, I wanted to cry.
Let's call it a blessing, I hope you all try.
—*Janice B. Cassidy*

The Dancer

He sees her dancing in a room filled with sunlight.
Her body twists and turns
to the erotic rhythm dictated by the music
He studies her as she moves,
graceful as a swan, light as a butterfly
Her body, young and long of limb, yet that of a woman
Her cream dress accentuates the golden glow of her skin
Her chestnut hair is pulled into a loose knot
Gentle tendrils curl about her face,
softening her smooth, classical features
As the music slows a young child runs to the woman
His daughter? Her daughter
She lifts the child high above her head
Laughter fills the air
A woman's ... happy yet strangely sad
A child's ... joyous and carefree
She continues to hold the child, dancing around the room
She makes the child a part of her dance
Together they float ... and almost fade ...
as he closes his eyes and lets out a shuddering sigh
—*Christin Olson*

Come Back Friday

Dianne had to have her own little hound.
Her Daddy took her to the dog pound.
The homeliest puppy that she could see.
That was the only one it could be.

Part snozzer, part hound that's what he was.
A veritable ball of warm wiggly fuzz.
Twas Friday the thirteenth the day he came.
So naturally that was his logical name.

Now Friday was friendly and right down smart.
We loved him and held him close to our heart.
When anyone came, he was sure to bark.
Even if a car in our driveway did park.

Monday evening the insurance man came.
Cause Friday was barking, Dad called him by name.
Back to his car the man was making his way,
cause "Come back Friday," he heard Dad say.
—*Ada Thomas*

The Window

She awaits the regal lady, hair of snow, eyes of sadness and light.
Her house sets on a carpet of green, tranquility she weaves within
  a dream.
I follow her through the cottage so blue, through rooms that reveal
  sounds and sight.
I say tell me which way to my happiness, and do you have the key to
  eternity?
She smiles as I open the window to see the world beyond my thoughts.
I smile when I see the sun peak over the clouds for me.
Come here I am awaiting the golden rays of your love.
Come here I am awaiting the warmth of life from above.
I fall to my knees and realize the Power I behold.
The Creator of Heaven and seas, the Creator of all and me.
I thank thee for this vision, insight to my soul.
I thank thee for my answer to help attain my goal.
Amen.
—*Angel Malisa Castro*

America The Beloved

America was built on a moral foundation.
Her freedom was born of the pain of war.
The pages of her history books stained
With the blood of the brave men and women
Who fought for the God given ideals that made her great.

Anguish sweeps across her soul as she faces
Her deadliest enemies, moral decay and spiritual decline.
And allowed to fall.
I hear her voice trembling, praying, crying, dying.
America, in mourning for herself.

As God watches over the America that our forefathers
asked Him to bless, He speaks, but no one listens.
He weeps and mourns, but no one sees or hears.
And so it will be until we build America up on her
true foundation of Biblical principles and restore
our precious families.

America's light has been dimmed, but through her darkest
hour, in spite of her weakened spirit, we know her, for she
is a part of us. Our hearts hold dear the vision of the
Original Dream. Old Glory flying high in a crystal sky too
blue to name. Proudly and with ease.
Displaying her colors of Red, White and Blue on top of
our buildings, in front of our schools and homes.
In the late afternoon, before the sun went down, they
were gently laid to rest for the night.

An eagle circles a meadow with ease, sailing on the wings of
the God breathed wind. Sparkling sunbeams shining down with
blessings on our land we peacefully called home.
—*Carol Ann Tetreault*

Study In Copper

She sat on the hard board, lis'ning, her face wrinkled and old-
Her long snowy hair was a thin cascade,
Across the tunic's bright fold,
Her thin hands, work thin, lay quiet in her lap,
And scuffed shoes, peeped from beneath the voluminous skirt
Mid'st the dust where a small dog did snooze:
Outside the lightning crackled - the air hung heavy and still,
While an infant's cry 'rose, sharp and shrill:
As a man preached lovingly from the BOOK
A gentle breeze sighed through the throng,
Beneath the rough roof, and a quartet sang
In tones so deep and strong!
Her dark eyes never left the face of the speaker,
As life's words were told,
Then, standing straight, by the old man at her side,
Sang the hymn, triumphantly bold!
Off into the stormy black night she vanished, a stranger?
Always to be — No, really close kin, a sister with copper skin,
Through the love that turns the KEY.
—*Doris Pack West*

A Friend Indeed

Her warm, friendly face strengthens me,
Her sweet smile encourages me,
Her sturdy soul supports me in everything I do,
Her kind words coax me through life,
Her good judgment keeps evil out and good in,
I mold myself to be like her,
I strive for her wisdom and gentleness,
I challenge myself for her greatness,
And I will not give up until I am
a mirror image of this wonderful being,
my mother.
—*Jennifer Remillard*

April, Arn, D. & D.'s, And George

If George Strait could only see me?
Here I sit, on a Monday night, playing his C.D.

The music, he sings, has a clear sound.
It makes me feel like I'm out of town.

I feel April dancing with her smile.
She's so much fun and has style.

When we two-step it's like flying.
I feel butterflies, I'm not lying.

Some of our turns are not quite right.
She says it's her, I say it's me each night.

We will just take our time and learn
Practice makes perfect, we will get that turn.

All I know is, when we are both on time.
It makes us happy. It makes us shine.

Dancing at Denim and Diamonds is fun.
I'm glad it's with April, she's the one.

She's cool, graceful, and forgiving.
It has changed my life and makes me feel like living

I'll always remember the hours on the floor.
How we stayed until it was time to close the door.
—*Arnold L. Raether*

Along The Way

Along the way I met a guy
His color was not mine
He spoke of problems with a sigh
I counseled him real fine

Along the way some girls were there
they had no goals in life
and when I spoke to them of things
they soon began to care

I built a home along the way
I built it all alone
I worked too hard they used to say
they loved our summer home

So many problems I resolved
for friends along the way
and some they thought could not be solved
I made them all go away

And now that twilight time is near
I reminisce each day
about the friends that were so dear
and lost along the way.
—*Andrew L. Pezzica*

The Policeman On The Highway

I saw a policeman on the highway,
His job was directing traffic all day long,
I guess he stopped when he had time to rest.
I watched out of the window as he kicked his feet.
I guess they were falling asleep,
After a long day of standing on the street.
Thank God for Policeman, and there little feet.
Imagine without them, what would happen on the street!
Policeman cannot be beat!
So remember to say hi, to the policeman on the beat.
Remember always be protects us all before he sleeps.
—*Joan K. Merritt*

Little Johnny

Little Johnny cries himself to sleep
His mama left and his sister weeps
Little Johnny afraid of life so sweet
Cause he knows that he's in trouble deep
No where to run, no where to hide
No one to love you, no one to abide
Little Johnny has no where to go
His Papa never loved him so
Little Johnny's livin on the streets
Having no strength to get upon his feet
Little Johnny cold and lonely deep
If he only had a family to keep
But there's no where to run,
No where to hide
No one to love you
And no one to abide

—*Jill Miranda*

Phoenix

Bravely sings the Phoenix
his melancholy dirge
as he is tested in the crucible
he trusts the searing pyre.

Deathlike shroud is shed.
Rising crimson but alive
he's soaring to majestic mountain tops
praising the cleansing fire.

—*Betsy J. Bramhall*

Weary

Idle pleasure, pure extravagance.
His mind fed on these simple little
Choices for his life.
His mind was filled with the exuberant life,
That his heritage provided.
But his heart was oh so weary.

For awhile, her smile peeled away at this weary.
Years of freshness with her.
Now he couldn't even utter her name.

His pride and ignorance helped with shielding himself away.
He settled nicely into his tired life.
Time developed a man filled with agony.
A man longing for the cool memory of her.

He wanted so to travel to that place,
Where happier years, blew away his present
state of weary.

—*Jonette Holmes-Daniel*

This Void

This void embarrasses me deafening silence transient storm
hopelessly abysmal inconsequential and insipid as our dreams
overtake me livid near death swallow hungry swallow dry
this void pink and violent as flesh then red as lymph
quivering lively autonomous and obstinate a way out an
empty excuse interminable exit a gap resplendent pallor
on blank palms upturned exposed like a criminal exposed
like a vein bleeding eyesore inexorable and paltry as life
itself superfluous a sunspot imperceptibly burgeoning
emptiness upon emptiness distresses me this void in the
process of explaining I have filled it can't remember
if it was yesterday sprawled nude as winter on newspaper
throw it out into space let the stars devour it this void
cripples my senses reeling backwards i inherit the void

—*Jay P. Murphy*

Thanksgiving

I am thankful to God for salvation and the Bible that tells us
His plan— how Jesus came down from His glory to die on the
cross for 'man'. Then I thank God for my parents, who've long
since gone home to their Lord; I'll never forget their
teaching—to love and to honor God's Word.

I'm thankful my husband found Jesus before being called home to
rest. I know we will meet up in Heaven—God's ways are always
the best. For my family, all grown, and their families, I'll
be thankful to God all my days. I trust they will never
forsake Him but follow His guidance always.

For friends, old and new, I am thankful; and for brothers and
sisters so dear; for a home where Christ is the center, and a
church where God's Word we can hear. For my homeland I'll
always be thankful—America—land of the free! These are only
a few of the blessings which God gives to you and to me.

For sight to behold all life's beauties and ears to hear
melodies sweet— for sun, wind and rain, too, I'm thankful—
e'en winter's cold snow and sleet. All things are God's gifts
to His children; each serves some real purpose in life. So
pause and start counting your blessings; take rest from life's
burdens and strife.

Each one has some cause for thanksgiving, if only sweet
memories to hold. When once we start counting our blessings,
they multiply so many-fold! If you do not know my dear Savior
—have no home or family or friend, be thankful that 'Life' is
still with you—accept Him ere reaching life's end.

—*Dorothy V. Garka*

Flying Lesson

For John Gardner
   His strong hand squeezed my eagerness.
     Feather-touch the stick
       to see the nose lift;
   Feel the dropping fetter-chains
      of gravity.
   Feather-touch, he whispered gently,
    That's how it's got to be.

    And I imagined barnstormers
     selling thrills and joy,
   riding piggy-back on pillow winds
    of soft-brushed sky-canvass;
    biplanes in wheat field beds,
    weary pilots wing-sheltered,
 a star-winked sky their company.

   My son runs through a wheat field,
  balsa plane thrust to invisible winds,
    Feather-touch, I call, and a summer
breeze remembers, that's how it's got to be!

—*Elizabeth D. Brownlow*

Through My Eyes

If the world could really see,
Human beings would realize,
We all come from one tree.
But we should really harmonize.
People choose to divide themselves,
I know why they are afraid,
Like library books on shelves.
Look what a mess we have made.
Things are changing I know why,
We now understand what is wrong,
His word is strong and we should cry.
Let us all sing out in song.
Profess His name Jesus in a crowd,
No matter the size sing out loud!

—*Edward Nolden Murdock*

Winter Friend

Come share the winter with me.
Hold me thru the cold and be my sun.
A winter friend is warm and true
Come share the fire and let me warm
You in the comforter of my love.
Stay with me and wait for the spring.
Our winter memories will keep us thru the
Madness of spring's coming fever.
Winter friends are rare and when you have
One they are a treasure
Spring friends burst forth and blow away like
Spring blossoms.
But the bud of a winter friend is
frozen in time.
Come before winter just at the edge of autumn
And lets warm each others heart.
—*Cyntra Gaye Smallwood*

Undying Love

Hold my hands and tell me how much you love me dear
Hold my hands and tell me you'll always be right here
Put your arms around me and whisper in my ear
Soothing words of comfort — love and not to fear
Place your kiss on the back of my hand that no longer knows
how to move
Show me with your actions all the Love I need you to prove
I feel so alone and I'm so afraid cause I don't know how to cope
I need your arms around my neck like love on a soft tough rope
Just gaze into my eyes and you'll know my love's still there
Just gaze into my eyes there's no mistake that I still care
Put socks on my feet that are cold and still
Put socks on my feet that won't move at will
Do you know how much I love you? My God do you know?
Not in all this world is there a wind so strong to blow
God put us together a long time ago
Now it's time to let all that love show
Do me the little things like kisses on my cheek
Don't think because my mouth's not straight I've turned into a freak
These very things that happened have always been my fear
In a tiny corner of my heart there's always been that tear
—*Dolores Cipolletti*

A Rainy Afternoon

I tried to clean the desk, Lord.
Hoping to get rid of some stuff
But when I read old cards and letters,
It really was too tough!

The memories were flooding my mind,
As I read letters written so long ago;
Thinking of happy times and sad
And I couldn't let them go.

Some friends are with You now
And some I never see,
But the bond between us
Will surely ever be.

I gave up cleaning my desk, Lord,
And put the letters back in place
And wiped away the tears
From my old and wrinkled face.

I just look forward to the time
When we'll all meet up There
And then I can tell them
How much I really care!
—*Jean D. Wisner*

O Beautiful Sunset

O beautiful sunset, at the end of the day;
How absolutely splendid you show us your display.
You're a breathtaking beauty, sometimes it is true;
With your exhibition of colors, how they do come through.

Sometimes you're red, purple, pink, or blue;
Sometimes blazing orange, or golden in hue.
No two are the same, you're a magnificent show;
As the sun disappears, you send us your glow.

Just look to the West, if there's few clouds in the way;
A performance of splendor, will appear that day.
Sit and admire a spectacular view in the sky;
It'll give you a lift. It'll make you feel high.

A sunset can be intoxicating with joy;
To excite the beholder, be it girl or boy.
The young, and the old, can enjoy the sublime;
Just gaze at the sky, whenever you've the time.

The big ball of fire, slides smoothly away.
It slips beneath the horizon, at the end of the day.
Then the show is over, it's taken from view;
The glow with its warmth of color is through.
—*Florence A. Klabunde*

No More Weepers

Reluctant dreamer with emerald eyes,
How do your pennants of life and love arise
When, all around you, a veil of smoke
Seems to take the form of a bluish cloak?

Silent screamer with dreams tied down,
How do the remnants of life and love abound
When, all around you, a mist, silvery grey,
Seems to make night darker and a mockery of the day?

Lonely weaver of plots and wishes,
How does your lover like your kisses
When she is lost within the fold
Of a fairy tale yet untold?

Banish weepers and their tears of pain;
Warn them not to stain their cheeks again.
All the pain that they've received
Is nothing but the face of joy deceived.
—*David B. Arnold*

Burbank's Way

Luther Burbank told all the world
  how he worked with plants.
He said: "I walk and talk
  with Jesus: He tells me
  what to do."

Burbank showed all the world
  how he wrought change in one plant.
As he sat before his glass-caged cactus,
  he said: "Prickly Pear, you don't need
  spikes; so, just let them go."

Burbank sat one hour each day
  five and a-half months, patiently
  talking to Prickly Pear Cactus,
  persuading. Two months later,
  Prickly Pear plant shed its spikes.
—*Clara S. Dick*

To Forgive Is Divine

A disciple asked the Lord one day,
"How often must one forgive?"
And the Lord said, "Seven times seventy if you like me would live."
So if someone asks you to forgive, and you find this hard to
do; think of how you've treated God, and remember,
He forgave you.

If we want to love as God loves us, we must care for every
soul, no matter what color their skin may be,
or if they're young or old;
And though we bring many gifts to God, and pray with all our might;
yet we hate our brother, we'd better go make it right.
Regardless of how much we give to God or what we'd like to
 believe,
If we're not willing to forgive, our gifts He'll not receive.

For we are all sinners, you know - come short of the glory
of God. We will make many mistakes while on earth we trod,
But He will forgive our many sins until the end of time.
To err is human, but to forgive is divine.
 —*Earline Moore*

Precious Baby

How precious the sunset on lips sweet surprise;
How precious the dawning in dew sparkled eyes.
How precious the interim set between these
In arms oh so precious — desiring to please —
As velvet of night forms its envelope rare,
Surrounding two souls caught up breathless and bared.
How precious my Sweet One in true light of day,
As sunbeams surround; dance their flagrant display
On "This Precious Baby" desire hath wrought:
The 'Greatest of Treasures' mere man ever sought!
For, song of a bird lasts but 'moment' it came;
Man's spent soul desires a longer refrain.
 —*Glee L. Stevens Weiner*

Remember When

Remember when you were young.
How things were different,
or so it seemed.
You thought winter would never end
and summer was much too short.
You couldn't wait to grow up
to leave home
to be on your own.
Remember how mom and dad were there
To carry the burden of your care.
They fed you; clothed you;
were always there for you.
The strong arms of father
and gentleness of mother.
It's no wonder as we age
that we dwell on our youth.
It was a time when we were protected,
cared for,
and troubles seemed few.
 —*Joyce Upchurch*

Maternal Stranger

I look at myself and wonder
How this unknown person looks
Her thoughts and dreams past and present
The things not found in books
The decisions she made long ago
The courage that she had
I want to tell her it's okay
And that I'm not mad
She made a mistake and
Did what she thought best
And what she gave me was wonderful
Something she never would have guessed
I hope one day she sees me
So secretly she'll know
That what she gave to me was great.
The chance to live and grow
 —*Jeni Mills*

Winter Fury

So cold the icy air - did
howl and blow in the night
All sleeping were the bears
the "hunted" out of sight.
Beware the winter my son—
winds of chill and snows that kill.
Respect the polars' hungry fun
lose the winged-of sabre bill.
Burning well - his Father's tongue—
on marched boy in impish trust.
Toasts of victory 'ready sung
Before his weapon thrust!
From subtle den the polar came
Fear sent boy upon his seat.
Fast took he, a marksman aim....
 Death fell at his feet!
 —*Dorothy M. Carani*

Politics—Or—Potluck?

Animals have fleas and ticks—
Human critters have politics—
We spray the beasts for pesky bugs—
Eliminate from floors and rugs.
For politics there ain't no cure—
Grit your teeth—try to endure—
Look and listen to pick the best man
Register and vote any way you can—
Through a storm of flying mud and dirt—
Try to decide (a prayer wouldn't hurt)
Now you think you know who is the right man—
Competition says "No—he's the one to ban!
He steals candy from babies—you can't vote for him!
Now your left hanging way out on a limb—
So you close your eyes and jab the book—
And vote for the guy—you thought was a crook!
Then if he does well—you loudly pro-claim—
You know he's the one—to get the job done—
Now it's time to get ready—for games and fun—
Yep! It's hard to believe? Well—
That's politics!!!
 —*Ginny Mae Neff*

Friends

Together we share our lives...the happiness and the pain, the hurt and the joy... My friend.
We give when not asked...a comforting word or simple glance a caring touch, or tender smile... My friend.
Our thoughts encircle each other's world...our loves, our hates our turmoil, our peace... My friend.
For there are no favors between good friends... just constant faith and treasured thoughts-moments of truth and hours of warmth...
My friend.
Remember when-we shared a laugh-a silent tear...a book...a glass of cheer... My Friend.
Inside our hearts is a place for us...as the years pass and years come... My friend.
Enclosed in our minds-our lasting friendship...yesterday's memories...today's sharing...tomorrow's dreams,
Special times remain forever...ours....
My dearest friend.
—Andrea M. Probsdorfer

If I Love

If I love only myself,
I am a tightly wound rose bud.
If I love God,
I start to open my petals.
If I love another human being,
My blossoming petals will increase.
If I love our families, then our children, their spouses and our grandchildren,
I blossom more.
If I include friends, and neighbors,
My blossoming continues.
If I love strangers, and my enemies,
I become a full-blown, beautiful,
Complete rose.
But if, I keep the knowledge of this love
To myself; and never express the loving words,
It's only loving myself...I'm one dimensional.
—Bonnie Lee Weishoff

An Evening of Harmony

As I savor a splendid meal, so tasteful that it charms my feelings,
I am ecstatic with joy, the food lifts me and the spirit within is delighted,
As I view what is before me, looking outward into the scene, I am
Favored with sparkling music that sets the wonderful mood of the evening;
There is before me a snowfall, so gracefully descending from the heaven
Wind driven, but ever so lightly, the clear white flakes, glistening as they fall;
I am overcome with this magnificent scene of beauty, a joy to behold!
And the scintillating music continues, and my heart follows each melodious note;
The snowflakes fall on the barren trees, filling the branches with gleaming white;
Illuminated by the street light above, a scene that fills my being with rapture;
All this is enlightened by the vibrating sounds of a mandolin, and it is a song of long ago,
A joy to have known and had lived, a memory deeply etched in my stirring heart.
—Joseph De Cicco

Singing In The Fire

With heart swept toward a quagmire
I asked why deal with me so, silence reigned in the room broken,
   by the log in the fire.

The log gave answer, letting loose
a sweet soft sound like the
tender trill of a robin, somewhere
   beneath a window sill.

The song, gnarled up when all was well,
birds twittered on its branches, sun
flecked leaves with gold, hardened
   since and grown old.

The fierce tongue of flame came
consuming its callousness,
the heat of fire brought from it,
   a song of sacrifice.

The old log with forgotten melody
gave way to the heat of fire,
releasing notes of trust, while
   singing in the fire.
—Doris M. Lee

Absence Of Love

As you and I spend more time together,
   I begin to feel like it could last forever.
Those sensual places deep within me,
   soar with delight every time you're near me.
Your presence lifts my spirit to the sky,
   as high as bluebirds fly.
From this altitude, the fog clears...
   I realize I'm shedding purple tears.

Love came around, reaching for one to be found.
   Empty-handed and with despair,
     the morning arrives with sorrow.
Pain from longing of forever,
   truth arrives in the meadow.

Reacting from the absence of love,
   I try not to unfold.
If I do that, I'll walk around in a daze
   I'll just want to fade away.
But harmony stays together the next venture will be better.
—Joanne Papadopoulos

Music Magic

They say love makes the world go 'round
I believe it's spinning to a tune
And with every revolution
Up comes that old devil moon

Moonlight and music together
Affords romance a chance
It can all begin
With just a glance; a dance

It's music that stirs our emotions
Like the fun there is in jazz
The restfulness of symphony
The friendliness of ballads

The love and feeling there is in blues
The thrill to songs old and new
And those melodic strains that let us dream
Of a world that lives in harmony
—Claire W. Dougherty

Fool's Repent

Oh dear Jesus, I call out to you
I call to you once more
Although I am wise, I am a fool
So please don't close your door
I have lived a wayward life with little concern
It has cost me everything, A lesson I have learned
My river too abundant, life has become stagnant and still
My love for life is running dry
I go on, but on without will
So I beg of you Jesus in my most desperate hour
Give me strength, give me hope and peace of mind
Let me stand at your watch tower
For ignorance has been my only crime
Oh dear Jesus I cry out to you
Carry me my Lord, carry me just one more time.

—*Gregory Sturgill*

Wounded Soldier

We met during the war
  I came in wounded.
I'd been fighting for months
    through the pain
    (It wasn't that bad)
Yet you put me in intensive care
  I was dumbfounded.
    What emblem did I wear
    (I had to wonder)
To earn from you such deeply felt devotion?

In time, my wounds were healed
  Thanks to your mercy.
Restored, I returned to my station
  and took up my arms.

  So far, the war goes well
Yet, now and then, in the midst of a skirmish
  I consider some reckless maneuver
    (Incredibly.)
  For the loss of your loving touch
    lays heavily.

—*LJ Davis*

God's Love

There are no words that can express the love Christ has for me.
  I cannot feel the pain He felt while hanging on that tree.
    He came to know rejection from the friends He loved so much.
    He even felt that Father God withdrew His loving touch.

There is no love like Calvary love, exchanged for sinner's hate.
  The stripes, the nails, the thorn-pierced brow, the death that
    was His fate
tell at what price that love was given, but can we yet perceive?
  He did it all for you and me, salvation to receive.

Unworthy, I, in filthy rags of my own righteousness
  can find forgiveness, peace of mind, as to His side I press.
What tender love, when heart of flesh replaces one of stone;
  when we deserve no mercy, yet He takes us for His own.

Shall we receive that love in vain, and fail to love Him too?
  Can we, in careless freedom, forget what we must do?
Until we cross that span of life, that leads to heaven above,
  I want to live for Him, and strive to give Him back that
love.

—*Coralie Lee*

Help Me — I'm Falling

I have so many thoughts in my head;
I can't seem to put it all together.
I feel so alone, yet so many people exist within me.
Sometimes I'm me; sometimes I become someone I don't know.

I'm always so frightened of myself and living,
I just can't do this anymore - I'm giving up.
Please help me - someone - anyone;
Help me - I'm falling deeper and deeper into the darkness.
I'm scared - oh, so scared!

Space and time; sights and sounds -
None of it makes any sense - confusion reigns.
There must be a light at the end of the tunnel,
But if there is, it's not on, someone please turn it on.

I don't know love or happiness, only confusion, sadness, despair.
Give me some answers - something to hold onto-
Peace of mind, hope, goals, dreams,
Please help me - I'm falling
Deeper and deeper into the darkness.
It's black, empty - nothing - blank,
Help me - I'm falling.

—*Debbie Webster*

What America Means?

America is more to me that her houses, lands and trees;
I close my eyes and hear the tread of those millions, now dead,
Who roamed her hills and forests deep, giving us liberty,
A birthright to keep.

Those ancestors of ours, in homespun jeans,
Were dauntless as Saxon Kings,
Ne'er more bravery was ever found than their defense of home
and town,
Wielding mattock or ax, driving the British ever back.

Oh such spirits of men born free,
A heritage left for you and me.
Will this be lost in apathy and ease?
How loathsome that benumbing disease.

Let us arise and take our stand.
Bring God back throughout our land.
Not this time by wielding the ax,
But with Sword of the Spirit let us rise and attack!

—*Ina Askew*

The Witching Tree

Hidden from watchful eyes, when I was six,
I clung to the arm of a tree so big
It tickled the clouds with its branches!
Draped in my shawl of lacy green,
I entered a secret world where witchery
Conspired with sunlight and shadow
To create a wonder-land:

Where leaves whispered secrets when the wind blew
And birds sang while building their nests,
Where petals bowed and danced with buzzing bees
That tumbled in and out of perfumey blossoms
Like fuzzy little acrobats at a circus,
Sprinkling gold dust confetti upon the clouds,
To leave forever their magic in the witching tree.

—*Anna Mae Hoffman*

My Friend

If I wanted to fly
I could if I wanted to
but not without your strength
when I look into your eyes
I know you're part of my life.
You lead me to where I should be
And I can't get lost unless you're not around.
My friend will always be there
to listen and to hear
She helps me through the bad times
And celebrates the good.
We'll survive our fights
even though we fight a lot.
Our friendship is to strong
to strong to let go
And I hope you know
that I'll be there for you
And I know you'll be there for me
Because you're my friend
And always will be.
—*Jenny Turner*

Falling Out Of Love

Since the first day I met you, you were so sweet and kind that
I could never get you off my mind. Now as days go by I just
sit and wonder why. Remembering the good times and the bad.
Looking back at the first time we kissed, the first time we cried
the first time we loved and the first time we lied. So many
memories to keep close to my heart but it still happened.
We did fall apart. You promised to always love, you promised
to always stay, you broke both promises that's all I can say.
So as time goes by all I do is think about you and that's when
I start to cry because I know your falling out of love with me
and I don't understand how that can be.
—*Elena DiTrolio*

Your Dear Friend

I just had to come over to see you today
I could not find you, you had gone away.

I was sitting there forever watching the clock
I couldn't take it anymore, so I went for a walk

I heard something beautiful around the bend
A man at the cemetery playing a song for his friend

I stood there and listened as the music filled the sky
Then the man turned around — there were tears in your eyes.

Seeing your pain, I didn't know what to do
I could only give you a hug, after all you had been through.

Although that person's life had to come to an end,
You will always have fond memories of your dear friend.
—*Amy Barrington*

Heavenly Surprise

I crossed the Threshold through blackest night
 I entered the portals, golden and bright
And then I thrilled to the glorious sight
 Of Moslem, Brahmin, Buddhist, Jew
 Of Catholic, Shinto, Protestant too....
 And I smiled as I knelt with them to pray
For I thought to myself how this very first day
 Each one of us could be heard to say....
"And I thought mine was the only way!"
—*Charlotte Knight Harrison*

Mother's Mind

Did I tell you who I saw today?
I did?
I don't remember telling you.
Don't roll your eyes like that.
You think I'm getting senile.

Can I tell you what she said to me?
You heard?
When was that?
Are there so few pleasure left
That simple words seem so important?

Did I tell you where I'm going soon?
You know.
You won't want to come along.
My voice will be still.
Your rolling eyes will fill with tears.

Did I tell you who I saw today?
I did?
Come sit beside me, hold my hand.
There are few pleasures left,
And soon you might forget.
—*Jean C. Lockwood*

One Fine Day

I took a walk, on a beautiful day
I didn't get far, I'm sorry to say.
From out of the direction, that I approached.
Came 4 beautiful horses, drawing a coach.
It shone so bright, and the horses were well cared for, an awesome
 sight.
As I heard the driver's command, the 4 steadily prone animals to stop.
well trained, without an extra clop.
I thought, a unique sight, this can't be
perhaps I'm hallucinating, or maybe a dream.
From inside the coach, came a voice of despair, "I'm lost, and
don't know where to go." "How can I help you?" was my reply.
"For what city, or town? In what direction or what land of renown?"
Hop into my coach, and be my guide, take me from this frightful town
and let's head to that land of renown. I hopped into the coach,
and to my surprise, there was the devil, in full disguise.
He appeared to me as a damsel in distress with all her good looks,
and most wonderful figure too. Trying to tempt me, in her brilliant
way. Luring and teasing, she slid me so close, I opened the door
and ran from the coach. As she rounded the corner, I heard her say,
"I'm going to get you." one fine day.
—*Frank H. Wiest*

There's Someone Above Who's Listening

At night when I go to bed,
I don't close my eyes until my prayers have been said.
I pray far family members whose health is bad,
and friends who has done me favors,
with problems that I've had.

Nearly all my prayers are answered, you see
but it's not that I'm all that good, as could be
all my life I've been blessed with good health,
can't say that I've had too much wealth.

I'm a plain old country grill, from a family of eleven
we had little to eat or wear, but it was heaven
I retired from union camp after 37 years
Gonna throw away my clock, and have no fears.

I'll always believe there's someone above who cares,
or I wouldn't have answers, to nearly all my prayers.
—*Iva Lou Heape*

This Body I Call Me

I came into this world, with everything intact,
I don't mean to brag, merely stating fact.
It's served me quite well, this body I call me,
And though I've abused parts, it's still plain to see.

My eyes function with ease, unaided by glass,
And the heart beats strong in this human mass.
Though I fill lungs with smoke, occasionally drink beer,
Eat fatty foods and things others fear.

I've enjoyed my life, even through sorrow and pain,
Might will live it differently, if I could again.
But that choice isn't mine, so this option I decree,
I'll just plan ahead, where these body parts will be.

There are many people who didn't have the same start,
Or somewhere along the way, had a bad body part.
A heart that won't function, bad liver or spleen,
Eyes in their heads, yet the world is unseen.

My brain functions fairly, and it's told me with grace,
Just because you die, not all parts should leave this place.
There are many that could use them, just think what a gift,
My used body parts, giving someone else a needed lift.

—*Hugh W. Ruckdeschel*

I Dream

I dream, and the world is beautiful!
I dream that there is no pain.....
I dream that the sun will always shine,
That lives will no longer have rain.
I dream that sweet music
Will live in my heart
And find there a dwelling place.....
I dream that warm feelings
Will live and survive
In a world made of satin and lace!

I awaken
I awaken from a lovely dream
A fantasy 'tis true
Where love and kindness are everywhere
And the skies are always blue
I see the world as it really is
A sticky, murky brew
But I have no time to sigh and cry
I have a dream to pursue.

—*Beatrice Siegel*

One Lost Soul

I wasn't there
I escaped from here
I went to where
I do not know
Strangers said "Try over there"
And I'm still nowhere
I reach out to those who were there
As much as it's wanted I don't belong
So I reach for the ones who are here
I accept how little they don't want it, I don't belong
I am told I don't look how I appear to be
I plea for someone to tell how I look like me
I search for one person to answer my inquiry
But if you weren't there
And you can never be here
I shall try a little longer to persevere
To find that soul that is me
As I won't pretend to have been there
And I'm not wanted here.

—*Barbara J. Bartow*

Love

As I stood over the pieces of my broken heart,
I feared tomorrow as my world fell apart.

And suddenly I looked up and saw a bright light
of love and new hope as He came into my sight.

Everything got quiet as He came closer to me,
the love that was glowing, nothing else could I see.

When He held my hand I began to understand,
the love He was giving was not a command.

All the walls around my heart began to melt,
as He looked into my eyes, His love is all I felt.

I looked at the tears run down His face,
the peace and joy I could never erase.

As the tears ran down I saw a big grin,
the love He was giving would never end...

I finally see that God holds the key
for the love He was giving was made just for me!

—*Curtis Donald Lee*

The Friend

I gaze upon you with a heart that can't deny, a love that
I feel for you, but through my eyes I lie
A love that's pure and gentle, accepting and true, a love
that burns with passion, ignited by a miracle called you
I live my everyday pretending I love you as a friend,
and cry as I think, that this will never end
I will never feel your touch except in a casual embrace,
or your tender lips against me, other than a peck beside my face
I will never share your hopes except by infatuation, or the
fulfillment of your dreams in my imagination
I will only feel your pain in a platonic way, and your
disappointments with a hug or maybe words to say
So much I long to give you if only I was able, but I am
forever cursed by that cancerous friendship label
I do believe in miracles praying for them often where your
concerned, hoping to hear someday, for me you secretly yearn
Please don't get me wrong, I'm not one to complain, I
treasure what we have and wouldn't trade it for anything
It just that in my lonely life I dream of something
more, like the blessing of an intimacy with
you to experience and explore
I will try hard never to disappoint you in all the ways
I possibly can, to love you with all my heart, but pretend
its as a friend

—*Bill Eardley IV*

It's Really Over

It's really over
I feel nothing for him anymore.
How/When
It died off completely,
I do not know,
But I do not want him.
I do not want to be with him
I don't want to kiss him or
Feel his body pressed next to mine.
I don't want to smell him or
Taste his tongue in my mouth.
I don't want to feel the sweat of his body pouring
    down over mine.
I don't want to hear him breathe as he sleeps and
I do not want to wake up in the morning with the
    stickiness of his passion between my legs, and
I do not want to fix him coffee.

—*Amanda KC*

A Little Girl Again

Along a country lane I walk, a little girl once more
I feel the dust beneath my feet I hear the future roar.
I see the cotton fields of white and then the leaves around
my door. I view again the days gone by
where willows weep and children sigh
I taste again the melon sweet
and milk flavored by bitter weed and deep with in my heart
I find strength for my every need.
I view again the swimming hole
where branches low on the water hang
And breath again the moist air
as it was refreshed again by rain.
I see the big tall men who stand
and say that they are my sons
I wonder where the years have gone
as through this life I've run.
Once an adult and twice a child
Oh gladly do I greet
This day of childhood once again.
As I walk happy street.
—*Charlotte Kirkland*

The Gift

Through a window an autumn breeze cools the air.
I feel warm inside as it blows my long silky hair.
Sitting there my saddened heart begins to uplift,
As though I've been given a very precious gift.
An overwhelming sense of serenity somehow,
Provides me with strength to face my burdens now.
My heavy cross becomes less difficult to bear;
Gone are the unwanted feelings of despair.
As I rise from my pew, bells begin to ring!
Praising the Lord, the choir continues to sing!
That is when I thank God up above,
For Sunday mornings and all His blessed love.
—*Eva M. Crist*

A High, A Low, A Rainbow

You see I touched a rainbow,
I felt its warm moist charm;
And that gentle grace it had,
Was meant to still and calm.
Seven colors bright as stars by night,
How they twinkled in the sun;
A signal to the inner eye in each
new day begun.
I dare not lay my body in the
fullness of that glow;
For it is known to young and old
That rainbows come and go.
Next time I find a rainbow
In it I'll bask and twist,
I'll inhale its very essence
And drink deep its pure sweet
mist
—*Forrest J. Baroni*

Friend

The day you walked into my life.
I found a friend indeed.
For you were there through
All my strife,
And helped with all my needs.

I found the truest happiness
That I have ever known.
You see my friend, because of you,
I'm never quite alone.

Of all the crazy fun we had;
The good times and the bad.
Of laughter shared; yes, even tears
I'll remember all my years.

No matter what you do or where you go.
My thoughts will be there too.
You gave so much and never knew
How good for me were you.

I know not what tomorrow brings,
But through the thick and thin.
The greatest treasure that I own
Is to be called — your friend.
—*Glennie M. Klingbeil*

Those Spectacular Trees

Whether it's spring, summer, winter or fall
I gaze at those trees, and love them all
While walking through a city street
Or riding along a country road
There are those wonderful trees, great beauty to behold

Snow tipped branches in the winter
Glistening in the sunlight
The whistling wind, cold and bitter
Visions of beauty in the moonlight

Signs of spring begin to show
Wonderful colors of the rainbow
The maple, the oak, the birch and the pine
All seem to be standing in line
Showing off their beauty for all to see
Whether in the country or the city

Finally comes fall with different colors
Yellow and rust, red and brown clusters
Soon winter will be here and some of this color
   will be covered with snow
Nature will soon display another side of the rainbow
—*Julia Lombardo*

The Moment Of A Sunset

As the sun became lost behind the horizon
   I looked at him with a smile.
Telling of his love for me
   he said he'd wait and travel many miles
to win my heart and possess my every thought
   I would someday belong to him.
Nothing could keep me from his love
   because he believes his dreams will win
the only love his heart has ever known
   she is engulfed by his depth.
Lost in his affection and needing his near
   the love they share is felt in every breath.
—*Darcy Erin-Marie Long*

Are You Really Concerned?

To whom it concerns,
  I guess I'm okay.
    To who it concerns,
      Is it what I did, or something I said?
        To whom it concerns,
          Do you really understand
            The way I feel, that wasn't my plan!

To whom it concerns, this is how I was born.
My parents really do care
But, my life is permanently scorned.

To whom it concerns,
I might not do everything right.
I am not perfect
But people tell me I am bright.

To whom it concerns,
  I really don't understand.
    It takes a few minutes
      But sometimes a life time....

To whom it concerns,
  It's a learning disability
    That is plain to see.
      I am just a person
But please........Oh please
  Just accept me!
—*Cheryl Zander*

The Game

There're no losers in the game of life
I guess we all break-even
We brought nothing with us to this place
And that's how we'll be leaving

We chose our teams and battle grounds
We chose our occupations
We sometimes moved so swift with grace
We sometimes faced frustration

Choices were made to move ahead
Some people paid the cost
We healed the wounded and buried the dead
And we all felt the loss

Are we strong enough to finish this game,
Or weak enough to die?
When will we all return again
To get another try?

Is time itself our opponent
In this ancient game?
If life and death obey the rules
I guess we'll keep on playing...
—*James Michael Rice*

Love Isn't Love Until

My husband's been sick; I can't count the number of days
I know what love is from friends who do and say...
"Love isn't love until you've given it away."

It's easy for all to say "I will help"
Whatever you need just give me a call.
I spent a forenoon calling one after another;
They're all going to the basketball game together.
Disappointed slightly, I turn to prayer with God
He answers quickly as the phone rings..."it's Cobb;"
You want a day off? ...I just lost my job
Yes, love isn't love until you've given it away.
—*Betty Lou Pollestad*

A Change Of Scene

Drowning in the summer steam and heat
I had almost forgotten the kiss so sweet
Placed by an early autumn breeze so gingerly on my cheek
The tell-tale equinox occurs in little more than a week.

Gazing up at the September sky
Watching marshmallow clouds roll by
I know that summer is over for this year
As I listen to the approaching autumn whispering in my ear.

Cooler air, a crisp breeze
Grayer skies, falling leaves
The trees in seasonal masquerade
Garnished in rich scarlet, gold, and plum shades.

And so I wave a cordial good-bye
To the departing September sky
Soon arrives autumn, October, and Halloween
To me, a most welcome change of scene.
—*Christy Armentrout*

First Love

I thought our love would never stray
I had been so sure of it that day.
We met one sunny afternoon.
He wasn't handsome, until I saw his laughing green eyes.
I was in his spell, under the blue sky.
He was much older than me, I could see.
We went out that very night.
It all seemed so right.
He taught me what love was all about, when he held me close.
I had no doubts.
He took me by surprise one day! He said
he was going away!
I felt so sad, I longed to beg him to stay.
I did it his way-
He never saw the tears, in my eyes,
When I kissed him goodbye.

Today my little girl is three,
Folks say, she looks like me.
When she smiles, I see her father's
Laughing grey eyes.
—*Diane E. Reilly*

My Best

For Mason Scott, my closest and dearest friend
I have had many friends over the years
To share the laughter and the tears.
To have such friends I am truly blessed,
But only one has been my best.

It's important to always have friends you love
And feel on their list your name is above
Their other friends; yes, all the rest.
But only one has passed that test.

My best friend has helped me through times
When I had scarcely little than a couple of dimes.
He's there for me when I am depressed;
No one can cheer me like he does, I guess.

Family and loved ones I've held so near—
None can compare to a friend so dear.
He goes for it all, never settling for less.
He'll always deserve from life its best.

It's warming to know he's a child of God
And that when he leaves the earth he has trod
Heaven is where his soul will rest,
And he'll still go on being the best.
—*Christina Howard*

Edgar

While musing through poetry and prose,
I happened on but a few of those
that caused you many a weak, weary night
but filled your readers with delight and fright.

And I queried now as you might have then,
does the world think me a raging manic?
Should I even dare take up my pen;
Is my heart one of tell-tale panic?

Yet you wrote of the beauty, Annabel Lee,
was she your wife, mother, mind's ideal?
It matters not, your words fill us with glee
and with us she stays, in moments surreal.

In life you never a fortune amassed,
fame, too, did not come 'til death you passed.
Despite your genius, you died destitute,
and our praises now seem a meager tribute.

In death, as in life, you loom a true myst'ry,
found as you were not by friend, not by foe,
our only clue now, your words for our hist'ry.
"A Gold Bug," "Monkey's Paw?" What E. A. Poe?
   —*Byron G. Cornelius*

My Wishing Well

In a corner of the garden,
I have a wishing well,
Many hopes and dreams, I have placed in there,

For, to it, my wishes, I tell.

I wish for health and happiness,
for those whom I hold dear.
I wish for peace, and joy, and love.
Throughout each of their coming years.

Then, I wish for others,
The same things, the whole world through

Then I bow my head, and ask for God's love,
To help make my wishes come true.
   —*Jane Menzie*

Amanda

I have reached the age of eighty,
I have laughed, and loved, and cried,
Believed in those I trusted,
Stood tall, and kept my pride.

I have shed a million tears or more,
My heart has died a thousand times,
For loves I lost, and hurts I bore,
Tho thru it all, the sun still shines.

Tho life has not always been easy,
It was never meant to be-
For sorrow can bring a courage,
That others might never see.

Then came my 80th birthday,
And, a gift of love from above,
God sent a miracle baby-
Born on my birthday, to love.

Amanda! Amanda! Amanda!
My dear granddaughter, thru wear and tear-
Gave birth to you, on my birthday,
With only forty seconds to spare!!
   —*Dede DeVries*

Mourning Bread

My mourning bread rises in the warming oven.
I have made them by the dozen.
Like the dear departed, I gave them all my lovin'.
My mourning bread waits for the oven.
My throbbing temples, I am rubbing.
The water boils for the tubbin.
My mourning bread cools on the tables.
The homemade jellies are set out by their labels.
Tents are set up & secured by their cables.
We've eaten our sorrow & buried our dead.
The sun is going down blood red.
I drag my feet in shoes of lead.
My mourning bread is down to the heel;
Not enough for a meal,
Not even for my hound, Neil.
   —*Jane Pierritz*

The Knocking On The door

It was deep in the dark dreary night.
I heard a knocking on my door.
The pit of my soul on fire with fright.
Turning the knob, I didn't feel right.
Outside, rain began to pour.
It was deep in the dark dreary night.
Nowhere did I perceive a light.
My heart throbbed even more.
The pit of my soul on fire with fright.
Such an evil and blood curdling plight.
Silently crying, I felt so unsure.
It was deep in the dark dreary night.
What will be this deceiving sight?
Crashing thunder continued to roar.
The pit of my soul on fire with fright.
It was death, smiling, eager to fight.
I, too weak, fell to the floor.
It was deep in the dark dreary night.
The pit of my soul on fire with fright.
   —*Jennifer Lyn Kafaf*

Lonely Little Poor Boy

It was many years ago, and some folks think it strange,
I knew a lonely little poor boy who never had a name.
His trousers needed patches, his eyes blinked back a tear
Yet he skipped along with confidence, his life to him was dear.
He splashed his bare feet in the grass, after every summer shower,
He'd set beneath the willow tree, for long unnumbered hours.
He loved the beauty God made, and sprinkled from above.
The sky, the stars, the white clouds and the cooing of a dove.
He liked the wind to blow his hair as he stood on the river bank,
He dropped a pebble here and there then watched until they sank,
Then one day a furious storm came raging through the meadow,
The lonely little poor boy was crushed beneath the willow.
His lifeless little body lay there upon the ground,
No one came to claim him, no kin was ever found,
He now was laid to rest where the willow tree once stood,
God came to take him home, just like I knew he would.
   —*Elizabeth A. Hall*

The Ides Of June

If I could live my life anew,
I know exactly what I'd do.
I'd rise at dawn and on my knees,
I'd thank the Lord, I'd say "Lord, Please,"
"Give me this bright and shining day,
To be Your creature all the way;
I'd recognize my duty first,
And then the next and last, the worst;"
I'd voice some mortal "wills" and "won'ts;"
A tidy list of "do's" and "don'ts!"

I'd count lost the day the sun descending,
View thus my good intentions ending.
With all You have to do, I know,
Sometime I must "go with the flow."
Now with the setting of the sun,
When beauteous night has just begun
I'd look up at the brightest star,
Drink in its beauty from afar,
and thank You, Lord, for helping me;
Without You, I would cease to be.
—Clara L. Frieze

The Shadow

Through my eyes only
I look beyond the storm
Through the rage of burning heat
To a reach that was beyond

I had to look into the calm
Where I could survive
I walked upon this raging path
Through this mask I am blind

I reach out beyond the point
To someone or something deep inside
The smell of death lingers near
Watching from both sides

The mighty sound upon the wind
calling through the mist
The words of free upon my face
Just beyond my grasp

The shadow come in many forms
From the darkness of the pit
But death can't come in soul of man
That was not born to quit.
—Ann Pruitt

Going Home

Goodbye, My love
I must leave this place
A distant star has called me home
I shed this flesh
To don a brighter light
Grieve not one single moment
For you will join me there
When you feel its ancient magic
A perfumed wind
Brings forth memories of happy times
And loved ones will not be far behind
To join us in our Eden's rest
Then when we are called back
To the masses
Our combined love will make us whole
For, you see, we are never parted
It's only the flesh
That think it's so.
—Elizabeth Ann Cramer

Mom, I'm In The "War"

I am standing in a river of sand, bathed in grit
I look up, and see an immense ocean of sand
  as I look again, I see vast landspaces
    "of" sand, sand — always sand....
The chill of night-time is heavy on my body
I become aware of the stillness, and my loneliness
  the endless security measures
    the empty, empty space, beyond my view
    the limitations of my movements,
"and" on the horizon, the heavy equipment.
    the "landships," and "airships"

I am weary with obedience.
  But "i" am your son, and sometimes ——
    your daughter.
  I "feel" my red, white, and blue flag
    "encased" around my breast!
  I am brave and courageous.
    I will come home to you.
    I am an American!!
    and I am your child.
—Gloria Duff

Slow Time

I've heard as you grow older, time really flies.
I may be mistaken, but I think otherwise.
When I was younger, there weren't hours in the day
To say all the things I wanted to say.
Tho I worked very hard, I couldn't find time
To do all the things I had in mind.
Time raced by at such a fast clip
There were many things I had to skip.
Now I'm retired. Time goes very slow.
I wait on the corner to ride on the bus.
Is it ever coming? I'd like to cuss.
I wait for the postman to come to the door
With a note from a friend I simply adore.
I wait for my wife to buy just one thing more.
What is she doing? buying the store?
As I get older, time really slows up.
It takes the waiter forever to refill my cup.
Time really goes slow, or to me so it seems
But I like it that way, I have time for my dreams.
—H. J. McFadden

A Dawning In Denver

As dewdrops sprinkle the ivory roses,
I meditate peacefully...
Feeling ever so gently,
The early freshness of a glorious spring day.

As the sun peeks through the breathtaking valleys,
Warmth is given to me...
By this grandeur,
Which shadows my journey's way.

As cotton clouds patch the sky,
Comforting the blue horizon...
An eagle in flight soars with grace,
Over the silent bay.

As a rusty seasoned barge passes slowly on still water,
Wisdom abounds...
From its infinite destinations,
Guided by the sun's ray.

As mist blankets the mountain peaks,
God's image emerges in splendor....
And cool breezes flow through me,
Where guardian angels lay.
—Beverly Withee

Sixty Years

Sixty years after school?
I must be an April fool;
Yet I know this cannot be;
For it was Holy God who created me!
I am one of the very few
Who still find "creative" things to do.
My wife I visit everyday,
In the "Nursing Home" not far away.
I know her time and my life too
Shall soon be done; but shall renew.
It's great to see my lifetime friends,
And look forward to life that never ends.
We all have had our "ups and downs."
Some tragic accidents too;
But if we keep our faith in God,
That's all that we can do!
I thank each one who came today,
And for their Godly souls I pray.
Have a good time and lots of fun;
And my "congrats" to everyone!
—Charles C. Beland

Untitled

My heart was silent, but now it sings;
I must be patient...I must go slow,
For if I push, my love will go;
There are so many things I
want to say, but I must guard my words every day;
We have both been hurt, we know the pain;
So patient I'll be so love will come again
Maybe together we can ease the pain,
Replace it with love, then joy we'll gain.
If only I could say what is on my mind;
But I must be still for it is not the time.
I sit on the edge of near and far, gazing at the moon among
the stars. My emotions are mixed, my blood runs hot...
There is a fire inside that burns for nought,
The feelings I have, I thought were gone,
Buried deep, in the past, I feel alive with purpose again,
and whatever force is in control. I pray it never ends.
I try to look beyond this day, but the feelings are strange,
and I don't know quite what to say...I feel...I care..
I love this day...
—Jim Christofic

My Best

For Mason Scott, my closest and dearest friend
I have had many friends over the years
To share the laughter and the tears.
To have such friends I am truly blessed,
But only one has been my best.

It's important to always have friends you love
And feel on their list your name is above
Their other friends; yes, all the rest.
But only one has passed that test.

My best friend has helped me through times
When I had scarcely little than a couple of dimes.
He's there for me when I am depressed;
No one can cheer me like he does, I guess.

Family and loved ones I've held so near—
None can compare to a friend so dear.
He goes for it all, never settling for less.
He'll always deserve from life its best.

It's warming to know he's a child of God
And that when he leaves the earth he has trod
Heaven is where his soul will rest,
And he'll still go on being the best.
—Christina Howard

Back When

When I first saw you way back when.
I never thought of Trying them
You had this took a savior faire
The way you were just standing there

As time passed on, the feeling grew
Although, It was you who never knew
All the feelings I had buried inside
I never spoke a word, I swallowed my pride
Then once again in that same place
Two years later appeared your face
There was something about that night
It seemed right, but not quite

On that night after two years past
I never expected that you would've asked
But come to find two years ago
You felt the same as I had so

On that recent, unforgettable day
We had a conversion least to say
We decided to start what would have started then.
On that cold night way back when.
—Jessica Dean

Lovely Trees

I planted just a tiny little tree,
I placed it where all might see.
This little twig became a part of me,
As I watched it grow into a mighty tree.

Barren plains as far as the eye can see,
Not even a shady tree for you or me.
Give me a home by a bubbling stream,
Where I can plant a tree and dream.

Lovely tree's so graceful and so proud,
Their mighty root's anchored to the ground.
God grant me the joy and the wisdom to see.
He created them for you and for me.
—Guy V. Ryan

I've Played Second Fiddle All My Life

When I was very young
I played second fiddle to my twin brothers.
They were in the limelight;
I was always shunned.

I got married at an early age
And for thirty five years I played second fiddle
To the whiskey bottle.
You can see, I've always played second fiddle to someone or
something all my life.

Now I am alone
But I don't play second fiddle anymore.
You see, I play first violin with Jesus
Because I am very special to him.

I'll never play second fiddle again,
When I can be first violin.
You see, that's the way with Jesus—
You're always first with him.
—Bobbie Jones

The Hall Of Mirrors

in the Emptiness of Solitude
    I reach for your hand
        shattering glass and sky
  to touch your face
    only to see my blank reflection
        hypnotized
      by a thousand illusions
    calling my name
      enticing me with the Feathers of Forever
        delusions

the intimacy that we shared
    became the void that I feared
      as we groped blindly
  through the maze
      becoming confused
by our own reflections

    I may never find my way
        out of your Hall of Mirrors
—*Alyssa K. Beaty*

Daddy's Girl

Although I never knew you,
I really wish I had.
Cause with all the men my moma knew,
Not one could I call "Dad"
And though you died before my birth,
It seems that I can see
That you are walking by my side
And watching over me.
There's times I lay awake at night
And want to speak to you,
But I know, Dad, that is one thing
I'll never get to do.
Fourteen years have come and gone
Since you left this world.
But just remember that I love you
And that I'll always be daddy's girl.
    —*Geryle Wallace*

Remember

Remember when we three were small, not too big, not too tall?
I remember, and I always will, Sis, me and brother Bill.
Remember?
Remember when we took the wig off our doll, put it on Bill
and made him bawl, he looked like a girl, tears and all.
Remember?
Remember when the grasshoppers came in a cloud of black and
ate the tarpaper off our shack? Ate our clothes off of the
line, your pajamas, Bill's and mine.
Remember?
And then when we went to school to try to learn the Golden Rule
The things we did, the games we played, the lessons we learned,
the friends we made.
Remember?
And now we are old and getting gray,
  I'll remember till my dying day————
Yes, I remember and I always will, Sis, me and brother Bill.
    —*June Benn*

I Remember

I remember his laughter and funny little jokes.
I remember that smile that couldn't be broke.
I remember the good times, and the bad ones too.
But, most were good I wish this were too.
I remember so vivid the look on his face.
I knew he would be happy in his new place.
The tears stained my face as I started to cry, the
memories of him swelled up so high.
I never knew how much I cared,
because that day I felt so weird.
I will always remember his
laughter and smile, and
every time I think of him I
know it's worthwhile.
Because one day I'll see
him again, in the sacred
land we call heaven.
    —*Jenny Racette*

A Tribute To Mother

Oh mother, when I think of thee
I remember the love you impart to me.
The gentle hand that parts my brow
The watchful eye that says you are nigh.
Your faithfulness, patience, love, and concern
Are just a few of your virtues I've discerned.
For though holiness you've shown to me
How to seek the Lord and draw close to Calvary.
To pray in the spirit being honest and sincere
To know by trusting the Lord I've nothing to fear.
That is why I'm thankful to God for you, Mother
A Mother so dear
    —*Gertrude Jackson-Carter*

Sweet, Sweet Innocent America

Sweet, sweet innocent America;
I remember thee ... so grand in thou beauty of laughter;
So nurture your land; I remember thee of times past ...
Sweet, sweet innocent America
How I weep for thee now; my tears so sad to express!
Your slogan, wonderfully stated
One Nation Under God; Your currency proclaim your devotion;
Yet I hear a cry! "weeping!" why do you moan?
Sweet, sweet innocent America

By chance I came upon your burden; idol temples sat boldly
upon thy soil
Sweet, sweet innocent America

You bring to mind, of two sisters, Aholah the elder, and
Aholibah
I read of their whoredoms, Ezekiel 23 tell it marvelously
Sweet, sweet innocent America
Your nakedness is discovered
You have become as the other nations;
O how I weep for thee, thou time has come
Sweet, sweet innocent America.
    —*Doris Marshall*

An Untalented Author

They asked if I had talent and of course
  I said no.
But then I started "thinking" that I would
  like to show
A little hidden talent which I'm sure
  that I could find
If I just searched deep enough in the
  channels of my mind.
I started my search immediately and I
  prayed along the way
that I would find my talent to show
  to you today.
But I guess I'll have to keep searching
  cause my talent I can't find
So I thank you for your patience, you've
  all been very kind.

By an untalented author…
   —*Betty J. Shumaker*

Wide-Eyed

I came into this world one night…Wide-eyed.
I said show me everything you got, this place called earth.
So he took my hand and led the way,
To the greatest adventure that I could imagine.
He said.. this is how you tie your shoe, swing a bat,
drive a car.
He meant.. this is how you show you care, love your
child just being there.
I didn't know what my father was saying, then.
But now it's evident that he's my friend.
I'm grown now and it's my turn,
To share and teach the things I've learned.
As I watched my son come into this world,
So alive and wild.
I knew that the legacy had been pasted
down to another Wide-Eyed Child.
   —*Craig Bruce*

Once Upon A Summer Time

Once upon a summer time
  I sat upon a cloud
I looked up and I looked down
  I even laughed out loud

Once upon a midnight black
  A silver star I kissed
The shimmer dust touched my hem
  I twirled through starlight bliss

Once upon a wintertime
  A snowflake floated free
It settled on my upturned hand
  The pattern I could see

And once upon an Odyssey
  A sailboat drifted through
I scampered out and rode the sail
  The craft I set anew

Once upon a summertime
  A golden prince came by
On wings of fire we flew beyond
  Just my prince and I
   —*Celeste Kusnell Granieri*

The Winds Of Winter

The winds of winter are on their way
I saw the geese fly south today,
It won't be long before we have ice and snow,
And the winter winds once more will blow.

Goodbye dear sun that keeps me warm,
Farewell gentle rain that does no harm,
In spring you gently stir the earth
And all around is a grand rebirth.

The summer heat it warms my soul, like red ripe cherries in a
  crystal bowl,
Weddings in June and grass that's green, the prettiest flowers
  you've ever seen.
Children bronzed from summers sun, water fights and chewing gum.

We are tricked by fall, a cunning fellow,
He turns the hills and trees to gold and yellow,
Then sneaks around in dark of night and covers everything with
  frosty white.
I think he does it just for spite.

Winter, summer, spring and fall, I guess I really love them all,
But each year when summers past, I really wish I could have make
  it last, just a little longer.
Life goes by so fast and I know, the winds of winter once more
  will blow.
   —*Helen Harding*

I Brought A Rose For You Today

I bought a rose for you today
I saw the roses flare
It caused my heart to sway
I chose a small and delicate one
For you, I bought a rose today
I could only pay the purchase price
As fire beauty was plucked from the stem
I handed the folded bills away
To a merchant with greedy hands
That yielded the rose I bought today
I looked at its fair beauty
Swelling tears came into my eyes
The rose bound by its duty
To speak, pleading anthems of love
Stalk plucked, it would die and lose its beauty
While red petals fall, no, are placed
Upon the milky white smoothness of your breast
There, the heaving breast would sway
And cause the flaming petals to blush in shame
I bought a rose for you today
   —*Glenn Smith*

What I See

I look at my children and what do
I see? The image of love looking
back at me.

The sparkle I see in their big blue
eyes is like the brightest sun in the
bluest sky.

The sound of their laughter brings
to me the worlds most beautiful
symphony.

I look at my children and what do
I see? The angels that God has
given me.
   —*Barbara Hadbavny*

My Love Gift

Although you deserve much more than this
I sealed the box with my love and a kiss.
This gift may leave you very fast
But my love for you will last and last.
This may be only a very small token
But words of love are often spoken.
You will always be my beautiful bride
Who held my hand and stood by my side.
As we made our vows to stay together
As long as we live forever and ever.
Some loves may come and some may go
But our love will continue to grow and grow.
The time has come to see with your eyes
If you really like this little surprise.
I don't profess to be a poet
As you can see these words show it.
These words of love are all very true
For they come from the heart from me to you.
—*Joseph R. Tomaino*

Who Am I?

When I look in the mirror,
  I see a reason for living.

A person with a lot of love,
  and that is unendingly giving.

A person with many good points,
  and bad ones I'd love to change.

I can be very serious,
  and sometimes a little strange.

I have a loving heart,
  just like a lovely dove.

And I will easily give my life,
  to someone that I love.

I have an open heart,
  but can be closed at times.

I love being around people like you,
  that can open up their mind.

You made me realize something,
  that maybe I'm not so bad.

The reason I'm writing this poem,
  is to show me what I have.

I'm glad you opened me up,
  made me take a look and see.

That deep down inside,
  I really do love me.
—*Emily Morrison*

How You Feel

"What time is it?" said the young man in hurry,
"I must there in a scurry."
Oh how I worry.
I smile at 60
even better at 50
It's not how old you are
It's how you feel,
That makes the meal.
—*John F. Baptista*

Looking Back

Looking back at the past
I see a world of you;
Looking back at the past
I think of our love that was true.

Looking back at the past
is what I always do;
I think of all the different things
that I did with you.

I think of all he love we had—I think of all the love we had,
that you and I shared;
I think of all the songs we liked
and how much you really cared.

I think of when we said goodbye
and when you kissed me last;
I think of how it is today
and I think of how it was in the past.
—*Betty Lee Conley*

Lack of Love

In the inventory of my memories
I see pictures of grief.
I remember those painful silences,
the forgotten tenderness, the loneliness,
my needs to be loved and the necessity to love someone.
Impossible to make that disappear.
I made the utmost efforts to please
I was turned away, I feel rejected.
In vain, I will accept what I cannot either change or forget.
I have to see calm restored.
Even though I forgave, even if it's my turn to love
Will I survive all the bad memories?
Will I get over the pain?
Will I recover from the lack of love?
I don't know…
Some wounds won't heal up
because the hurt always come back.
—*Daniele Tangway*

Special Love

When I look into your eyes
  I see the love shining through them.
The love that two people share
  when they really care about each other.
A love developed through time and patience.
  The time it takes to get to know each other.
to truly understand the ups and downs,
  the ups and downs of the others personality.
The patience it takes to make it through
  all of the hard times.
the times of misunderstandings and sadness.
  The surviving kind of love,
That's the kind of love I see
  when I look into your eyes.
The special love that you and I share.
—*Carrie Cross Paulsen*

Early Morning On The Farm

I love the early morning; the air is clear and still.
I see the pristine day break, the shadows on the hill.
The sky is softly graying; the nighthawk hovers low.
The rugged forms of mountains stand starkly in a row.

The dew is soft and gentle upon the new-mown hay.
The creatures of the nighttime seek shelter from the day.
The breeze is light and pleasant; it hardly stirs the grass.
The surface of the gray pond is broken by a bass.

The silos stand like statues, full-outlined by the sky.
The trees are dark and furtive; above them mallards fly.
The fields are etched in furrows; the docile cattle laze.
The dog has flushed a pheasant; she races back for praise.

We come upon the barn-cat; she rubs against my legs.
I scratch her ears and shoulders; she arches, meows and begs
Before us starts a kill deer; she feigns a broken wing
And lures us from her chicks' nest. I softly start to sing.

I hear a rooster crowing, the sun begins to shine;
A tractor starts to rumble, the dog begins to whine;
The pigs begin their squealing, the cattle start to low.
I love the early morning. But now—it's time to go.
 —*Duane S. Chipman*

Hey Beautiful I'm Thinking Of You Again

I feel so alive every time I am with you.
I see your face within my mind throughout the day and
 throughout the night.
I feel your soul within my heart.
You walk like an angel.
Your voice is as sweet to my ear as honey is to the taste.
Your hair is of gold and shimmers like the sun.
Your eyes are like the stars that dance upon the heavens.
Your lips are as red as the petal of a rose, and appear
 to be as sweet as the dew that is upon them.
Your smile is enough to brighten up the saddest nights.
Your body is beauty in the truest of form.
Your beauty is so intoxicating that if I were to kiss your
 sweet lips, I would be inebriated forever.
Let us knit our souls together this night, and I shall
 show you I will love you this night, forever and then
 beyond.
 —*Ian Walborn*

When I Sleep

I lay my head on pillows to sleep
I seek reality and you to keep
In slumber hours I hold you near
My heart is full and my eyes are clear

The days are nights, irreversible theme
I woke last night from a terrible dream
I dreamt you left, never to return
My eyes would cry and my heart would burn

Daylight haunts my sight and mind
For you in daylight, I can not find
Nightmares start when I awake
My eyes will open and my heart will ache

But when I sleep, I am conscious to you
Reality starts and my dreaming is through
And the only time, I do not weep
is when I am with you and I am asleep
 —*John Brodbeck*

Taken after Psalm 23

The Lord is my Upa
I shall not want
He provides me with
Moose, caribou and beaver. The fish, duck and goose.
He leads me to camp
Where lakes are calm and smooth.
He restoreth my soul. When my heart is heavy
In the cold of winter,
I take the dog team and go.
The air is brisk and still.
It helps awaken me.
The trail is good, the snow is hard.
He leads me in the paths,
For his righteousness sake.
How white and spotless the sun
Like after my sins are forgiven, My sight is clear to see.
The awesome beauty of thick snow frost on the trees.
Beauty is clear and white. It sparkles by the ray of sun.
The sight overwhelms me. Surely god is with me. In Alaska my
friendly village, Surely his goodness and mercy are with me
forever.
 —*Agnes Simeon Lovell*

Mommy

The sun is shining it's a beautiful day
I sit in the park watching the children play
The proud mothers watching nearby
My jealous lonely heart wants me to cry
The smile on my face doesn't hide the pain in my eyes
An empty pain that is hard to disguise
A child to call me "mommy" is the only dream I need
I can see you, I can hear you coo
Innocent eyes, sweet little cries
Your daddy's nose, ten tiny toes.
Mommy's smile, you would be our precious child
I'll help you up when you fall down
Soon a smile will erase that frown
I'll comfort you from every storm's thunder
As you grow I'll watch each day with wonder
I wish just once I could rock you to sleep
But alone I rock and silently weep
Tears welling up in my eyes as I kiss my dream goodbye
When the angels I dream of flew away from me
I swear the wind under their wings whispered "mommy"
 —*Betty Haverland/Reynolds*

Destitute Of Ship

As I navigate my vessel
I spy a storm on the horizon.
Weeks of calm water
and kind winds have been mine,
but now the hour of desolation
creeps upon me.
Upon impact of the storm
I feverishly tow the line,
but its methodical omnipotence
is more than I can control.
My ship torn from me
I struggle to keep my head above water,
and with the hours drifting into days
I wonder...
Will another vessel come my way,
or am I destined to drown in a sea of loneliness?
 —*Brian W. Lundy*

Good-Bye (In Memory Of Rick H.)

I feel so sad and lonely, I'm not sure what to do.
I still can not believe God said "your time is through"
you were so young, never mean to anyone.

I don't believe I said goodbye, don't believe I told
a lie. I wish I knew something I could of done to make your
life a longer one.

You were only thirty-seven still in your prime, but
I guess your heart couldn't keep up with the time.

God didn't let you stay for the game, now my life won't
be the same. Now I know they will win they will win just for
you... Dallas Cowboys, great playing in Nineteen ninety-two...

—Jessica T. Hayes

A Special Thanks To God

This morning as I rise from my bed
I thank God that he let me awake;
I was not dead.
As I started to wash my face
I could feel God's love
and all His grace.
As I made my way toward the front door
I felt I had to tell God
So much more;
As I made my way on my trip
The words of love kept pouring
From my lips.
I talked to God as I travelled
And felt my feet
Touch the gravel;
I talked to God in a gentle and loving way
And I felt in my heart
That he would lead me everyday.
I asked God to be my guide
And His love and honor
I would not hide;
I asked God to guide my feet
With His grace and honor I would never get weak.
As I made my faraway journey I gave God My Utmost honor.
Smile.

—Frankie Lewis Folk

I Think I Know

I think I know why willows weep on summer lawns,
I think I know why raindrops cloud a sunny day,
And why the doves call forth as morning dawns,

I think I know why dewdrops cling to flowers fair
Before the sunlight dries them from the sleeping vine,
And why the moon is sometimes dark and does not dare

I think I know why children's laughter turns to tears.
I think I know why dancing feet at last are still,
And why the joy within me can be rent by fears,
And why the swordsman who can love can kill.

It could be that the soul of all creation's lay,
Once surfeited by heaven's bounteous gift of love,
Must rest in fitful sleep and turn away

It must be that the Lord who gave us hands to hold
The infinite beauty He so eagerly bestows,
In haste to bless, just chose too small a mold
To bear His gift which, like His generous heart, o'erflows.

—Hazel S. Loney

The Memories Of You And Me

I once smiled more,
I think, many months before.
When Summer time warmed the air,
When wild flowers hung from your hair.

I once smiled more,
When in your arms I closed my eyes.
On those lazy days, I couldn't cry,
For way back when, I was yours.

Oh how time, I now pass by,
It couldn't ever be the same.
In my eyes, you hung the moon,
When way back when, you were mine.

I couldn't ever give enough,
As to say how much I loved you.
The unbelievable promises of love and friendship.
For a time, they were coming true.

And not too far down in my heart,
It's where I felt it start.
Ours will forever be,
The memories of you and me.

—Glenn P. Camley

Something To Remember Me By

I couldn't think of what to give anyone when I was gone.
I thought what could you receive or hear that meant a lot to me
Could I leave money and make you happy for a few days or give
you something from my heart. So, I decided to give you a
poem, "Something to Remember Me By." A few lines of reading
to make you think of me. First of all let me say, I love you
each and everyone in my life. I owe you a part of what I am,
God, family, friends, and everyone in between. You seen me
grow and even cry, won't you remember me once in awhile.
Think of the good days we spend, don't shed a tear for me.
I'll be with you somehow. I give you my best, "Something
To Remember Me By. Everyone I know, you are very special
to me, oh yes, you are. I take something good from you.
Wherever I do go. Even if it's not in skin, believe me I'm
with you someway. I leave you memories of yesterday.
I know I'm not dead yet, but one never knows when their time
is near. So I leave you my poem," Something To Remember
my by. I give you the red blood from my soul. Whoever reads
this, remember you mean the world. Till we meet in land or
air, I want you to take a few moments and think what I
left behind. I now go to make you think about,
   Something to remember me by....Goodbye, see you
   Somewhere, some time...

—John Paul Padilla

Pressure Shot

Ten seconds left, the score is tied,
I threw up the ball in hope for some pride.
The ball fell short of the rim
And made my heart turn within.
The crowd was still humming deep in my heart,
My throat was incapable of making a remark.
I walked off the court with my head down low,
The tears in my eyes started to show.
A rejoicing chill ran up my spine,
When I looked up and saw that
The crowd was still mine.

—Jonas James Weller

A Mother's Good Friday Lament To Mary

O, Mary, Mother of heartbreak,
I, too, have lost my only son!
Give me your courage and teach me
That not mine, but His will be done.

My heart is filled with loneliness
And cries to you today in despair,
For my sins caused your Son's crucifixion
The cross should be mine, not His, to bear.

Let me share your grief at Calvary,
Your desolation and your pain—
For then the joys of Christ's resurrection
Will bring me happiness again!
—*Caroline C. Kwaterski*

A Wise Man's Peace

Racist hate breeds like wild flowers.
I try to protect our youth from its power.
The days grow longer.
And the flowers grow stronger.
Their bitter smell hands in the air.
As I slowly rock, my rocking chair.
I cry sweet sorrow when the night has begun
I await the morrow when the mowing's done.
For days I continued on at this pace.
Always fighting this endless race.
One dust I grew angered at the sight of those weeds.
so in the moonlight I cut them, then fell to my knees.
Now understanding these mindless attacks.
You see in the morning they all had grown back.
Now I happen to be the talk of the town.
I know I will never lit it down.
See they just don't seem to understand.
That mowers, like me, are in demand.
—*Nada*

The Quintessential Silence

When I move into the silence,
I try to still my mind —
Find for my psyche the presence
Of the Father of all mankind.

Yet it is the company
Of the Son, Christ himself, I seek.
It would be a great blessing for me
If I could join the company of the meek.

What a flood of quiet joy He brings
Into the silence when He joins me there!
My tired heart truly sings
As He lifts my every care!

Can this peace be real?
Can this strength for the facing of each day
And this bonding form a shield
Against each hazard on my way?

The silence seems to enfold me
As my ravished spirit heals.
It is as if I've found the key
As the Son of God beside me kneels.
—*Florence Anderson*

My Papa

My father is gone, but yet he was not.
I turn to see and there he is
always there, always for me.
He is my "Grand" father and "Grand" is he!
He was the one who was there,
there for me.
I love him so dear and what he means to me
I shall never forget.
Now he is gone and if only I would of said...
if only he would of known
what all he had meant.
For now time is gone and I'll never have
that chance to tell him that...
You were my father and such a grandfather you were!
Thank you for being there, being there for me.
Thank you for letting me be your granddaughter and
a "Grand" daughter I hope I was to you!
I shall miss you papa, never shall I forget you.
Thank you... thank you for being My Papa.
I Love You!
—*Britt Meredith Gjertsen*

Crying Angel Eyes

As I glanced up from my reading
I turned my gaze unto the skies
And there to my amazement
I saw crying angel eyes

As I gasped and stood in wonder
The angel spoke words clear and wise
There was a message from this being
With the crying angel eyes

You've been given gifts of beauty
You've been trusted to obey
But you've failed to honor nature
Must you throw it all away?

I see children without comfort
I see homeless souls and ill
Will you not redeem yourselves then?
Have you no concern or will?

As the vision slowly faded
I felt the guiding spirit rise
With a prayer that we be willing
To dry those crying angel eyes.
—*Chris Johnson*

An Ode To Annie

When some evenings seem to be long,
I try to think of a memorable song.
Those memories that thrilled the past,
The Janes, the Marys, and the last!
That Ann, oh, she created something new,
She had everything I had to pursue.
Wow, that is my Annie, and there is only one,
A wife, a cook, and full of fun.
Together, we have been a long, long time,
And may the years continue in such beautiful rhyme.
—*Hal H. Ebersole*

Somewhere In Time

I stand alone
I walk the shore to see what I can see
The only thing that's out there
Is the deep and darkened sea.
I stop! I hear the sea gulls cry
They glide across the deep blue sky
As if to say "I'll lead the way
To a better time. A better day."
Out of nowhere appears a cloud
The voice I hear is very loud
But softly spoken are these words
"Listen carefully and observe.
For you my child were sent to earth
To live a mortal life
To learn, to feel, to touch, to see.
To experience the strife,
And on the day of your return
You'll tell of everything you've learned
While being tested for future use
In the ways of the universe.
    —*Juanita Marble*

Brother, Brother, Brother (My Love)

Brother, brother, brother (my love)
I want you to know today I'm hurt.
I never thought I'd ever hear
The things I heard today
Coming out of the mouths of your friends in the world.

Brother, brother, brother (my friend)
Am I really your friend? I'm mad.
I really thought you could come to me
With whatever you needed.
I'd pray with you and help you through your need.

Brother, can I describe the distance in my heart tonight?
Where do you rank me when I first hear from the world
About the trial you're going through?
Maybe I don't understand - there is so little I do -
But do you understand how all this makes me feel?

Jesus, cleanse my heart from all stains of bitterness;
Help me understand why here all alone I am.

Brother, brother, brother (my love)
I've said what I'll say - let's be reconciled today.
Yes, I understand, forgive you, and, yes, I still love you.
    —*Jeff Stoneking*

Marriage

if you held me
i would love to fall
silently to sleep
but butterflies flutter
keeping my eyes open
staring deeply into your
hazel eyes. i see my own
reflection. i see a
white gown flowing gently
on a deep burgundy carpet, as the
sun sets and pink candles
light my path to you.
waves beat along wet
sand. i see in your eyes
my eyes aglow with passion, with love.
  the butterflies move
   quickly as i realize strong
   arms wound around my body
  i kiss you and eyes close
  to dream further.
    —*Christieann McCabe*

A "`GI's" Lament

Saddened by another war
I watched our forces depart
For a land so distant and hostile
For a cause that's dear to our heart

Youth with its fighting ambition
Eager to achieve its goal
Unaware of destiny's calling
As events of war unfold

'Twas like re-living one's own turbid past
And having known the score
To watch those young and eager lads
Walk a path I trod before

Our hope for all who went away
Was justly cause for concern
But as all of us have learned before
Some will not return

In passing, I would hope once more
This "Cause" will seal gun's breech
For I feel I embarked a second time—Via T.V.
For that far and hostile beach
    —*Donald M. Foellner*

Her Eyes

A Poem For Pat
I went to see a friend tonight
She wasn't there within my sight
But in her eyes she saw me there
She felt my hand and knew I cared

Her body is gone; she did not speak
But I know she felt me touch her cheek
She heard what I had to say
And knew that I was there today

It may not have been her I saw
But in her eyes I read much more
I saw the way she used to be
And I know that she saw me

My heart hurt much for her pain
And the peace I hope she will gain
Tonight I went to say my good-byes
And I know she saw me in her eyes
    —*Isabel M. Peck*

My Heritage

I am an American and
I will ever be
Proud of my heritage of freedom, equality,
And justice for humanity.
Lives have been lost in so many wars
Across our land and on far-flung shores.
Our fore-fathers fought in the war to be free.
The blues and the grays gave some equality.
All other wars were said to be
For justice toward all humanity.
I am an American.
I must do my part
By loving this country with all my heart;
Respecting its flag and obeying its laws;
Defending it in a common cause.
It is our heritage — yours and mine
Upheld by a touch of the Divine.
A birthright from peoples of many lands
Who have formed this nation with hearts and hands.
    —*Joyce Ellsworth*

One Day At A Time

Dear God, just for one day at a time
I will promise
To see your love in all things.
In the calm, in the joy and the
Peaceful things.
In the burdens, the pains and the stings.

I will look to your love in the moonlight,
And in the wave of each swaying branch,
In each breath, in each step and each movement.
Dear Lord, I will pause each day to give
Thanks to you.

Though the turbulent waters surround me,
I will be as still as a calm peaceful lake.
For if you are in charge of this temple,
Then the reward will be so great.

So, with my new mind I will sing praises unto thee.
And, I will rejoice every day,
For if you and I are in this temple,
Then the joy and peace will be made known.
—*Edward Maloy*

Yesterday, Today Or Tomorrow

Yesterday, today or tomorrow
I will wonder what life's all about.
Tomorrow today is yesterday
And today is on the way out!

Oh what today means to me when
I think of the memories just past.
The next thing I know it's tomorrow
And today will just never last!

The past, the present and future
Are the times I think about now.
I have built on the past for the present
As the future will come anyhow!

Oh you thought you had problems
When you think of the yesterday just past.
Today has its precious moments
With the future tomorrow at last!

Life goes on all around us,
While time seems to go on its way.
The past and the future will care of itself.
As for me I will have a great day!
—*Doris J. Erickson*

Ricecakes On The Moon

The man said: "Stand Tall"
I tried, but; I was too short.
So I laid down instead and
rolled newspapers to swat flies with.
The toaster rang and I ran over to the tree
and picked the toast.
The Pretzel gods were taken away
in rubber elevators,
never to be eaten again.
—*Clifford J. Jaksha*

My Wish

Ageless, life, why can't it be
I wish it could be true
So many things I'd like to see
So much I'd like to do.

To listen to the singing birds
To gaze up in the sky
To look around the countryside
To watch the clouds pass by.

To hear the water rush along
the bubbling brook so clear
To walk along a shaded lane
To think of memories dear.

All this and more I pray will last
Forever, could that be?
I never want to let life go
It means so much to me.

As I travel through each wondrous day
Every precious thing I see
Reminds me just how wonderful
An ageless life could be.
—*Ann Marie Szili*

A Letter To My Son

Dear son I am thinking of you tonight.
I wonder why you never write your Dad
and I are lovely and blue, because we do not hear from you.
Your old ford is still sitting out on the lot.
Wright where you left it, in the same old spot.
The winter weather has faded the pain it had.
But Dad got it to running, we thought you'd be glad.
Now your old car runs like new though weather-beaten and worn.
The fender has a dent, the upholstering is torn.
But that old mercury stays side by side.
With the fastest car you could ever ride.
Son if you don't write how will you ever know.
How that old mercury can get up and go.
Your dog walks by our side when we walk down the lane.
But he seems to know things aren't the same.
So many miles away you are tonight.
The way your Dad and I worry it is a sight.
Son please write.
—*Georgia M. Drusch*

In A Days Walk

I walk alone most everyday
I speak not, there's not much to say;
So many people I see, none I know
They see me past, they see me go.

I see smiling faces, hiding their frowns
I know they've been let down;
I feel their heartache, their pain
The flowing tears, so much rain.

I take in their sorrow as I pass by
I try not to cry;
I hear their cries, I see their dead
All these images are in my head

None is aware what I see
They only see me pass and think nothing
more of me;
As I walk alone everyday
I'll speak not, there's not much to say.

I'll still capture their pain
I'll see their rain
All these images, I see again and again.
—*Gwendolyn Cloyd*

To God Be The Glory

With out His love for 'little ole' me,
I wouldn't have the sight to see.

Our Japanese garden so perfectly done,
Just as He gave His precious son.

I feel the warmth of His ever-present love,
Ascending on me like a lonesome dove.

At times I want to kneel to pray,
To thank Him for another day.

Our bird feeder is a place of action,
Where God's creatures get satisfaction.

The flowers are a gorgeous sight,
Colors so vivid — what a delight!

Bird sounds so pleasantly heard,
The presence of our majestic Lord,

May this garden be a source of pleasure,
To everyone who seeks His good measure.

I ask —How dow we deserve this place?
My child He says — by my loving grace.

Forever I could go on with this story,
However, it's to God I give the glory.

—*Beverly A. Biddle*

Fly Me Away

If I could only for just one day, meet you on the other side
I wouldn't stand a chance in this world
cause I think I'd never want to leave, and that my dear I can't deny

Cause living in this world, it's alright, and it's o.k.
But, to dine with thee above the clouds, would take my sorrows away

Sometimes I feel like leaving, when I stare at your photograph
And it echoes in my mind
I could still hear your voice, and the way you laughed

Please take me with you, don't leave me here alone
Fly me away beyond the stars, beyond the thunder dome

I want to be there by your side
But, will you still be there
When the angles fly me to the sky
And I walk up heaven's stairs

Hush my love, don't say a word
I'll set your mind at ease
All systems set for takeoff
I think I'm gonna leave

Fly me away beyond the stars, beyond the thunder dome
meet me half way in heaven, I think I'm coming home.

—*Billy Barnum*

Zest Of Life

The zest of life you are sure to find,
If you have a feeling of love for mankind,
People will respond to a smile and a grin,
Treat them like brothers and sisters
And they will treat you like kin;
For love of life is a state of mind,
Which you may have very easily—or be left behind;
So why not live life to the fullest,
Without a frown or a smirk,
To be complaining all the time about things you can't change
Is a silly quirk;
For if you approach a person with a cheerful attitude,
He is infected—and that's the end of my platitude.

—*Austin Thomas*

Universal Pledge

For The Shapers of Destiny
I/We Pledge
To honor oneness of the universe;
Bonding of all creation
Interconnected life, earth, air,
Fire and sun, water and sea.
I/We Pledge
To seek understanding and wisdom,
Compassion and charity,
Integrity, maturity,
Justice, peace and unity.
I/We Pledge
To co-creatively generate
A humane and sustainable community,
Truth, love, beauty, an intimate soul,
Earth and humans
As one interwoven, sacred whole.

—*Arvetta M. Souza*

If I Could Pay You Back

If I could pay you back,
I'd forever be in debt
I'd owe you for the life you sheltered
And for all you taught me, you bet.

For taking my mother's place for me,
Filling in for my father too..
And teaching me solely what a child should see
If I could pay you back.

I'd start by giving you back your life,
And making it as easy as I could..
Void of all unpleasantness and strife
And full of love for which you stood

If I could pay you back,
Your working day's would be over..
I'd fill you up on big Mac's
And gild your life with clover

Nothing would be too good for you
That I could readily afford,
I'd thank you for all the wisdom..
That without you I'd never have learned.

And for teaching me so vehemently,
That alls' good in life must
Be earned!

—*James S. Carr*

To Tiger Tom Tom

Where did you go when you went away?
I'll always wonder why?
Did you go to distant places
Under a foreign sky?

What did you do when you went away?
What did you hope to see
Or did somebody take you dear
Far away from me?

Now you have returned
I know not how or when
I only know I love you, dear,
And glad to have you back again.

—*Donna Marguerite Strough Barnes*

A Letter To Santa

Dear Santa, (if you're listening)
I'd like some snow that's glistening,
And lights up all around the tree,
And my family's hospitality.

Some Christmas cheer for everyone,
And hustled work that'll soon be done,
I'd like the little children, all,
To have what their hearts are hoping for.

I'd love all folks to come to terms,
With age old grievances to be resolved
I'd love the hungry's mouths to be full,
And a cozy place to keep them warm.

I'd like the lonely to be with friends,
And heartaches gone where love begins,
I'd like the sick to 'all' be well,
And hear the sounds of 'Jingle Bells'.

But most of all; I'd like to wish,
Our dear "Lord" a birthday gift,
'A Merry Christmas and heavenly peace,
To the brightest star that shines in the east.
—*Bunni Koblentz*

Far Away From City Lights

I'll share my land with the coyote.
I'd rather hear him howl at night
than hear gunshots in the city.
I'd rather hear a frenzied kill
of a pack of four or five, knowing they'll eat,
than hear the senseless kill of a drive by.
I'll share my land with the coyote,
the ancient guard of Earth,
and be proud to stand by him
as he gets too crowded by man.
I'll share my land with the coyote,
he'll guide me to safe shelter,
far away from city lights
that burns red on wet pavement.
I'll share my land with the coyote,
until extinction comes upon us,
like a hot wind
from a dry gun.
—*Gregory M. Dultz*

College Bound

I didn't want to work but I needed some cash
I'd spent my last buck, even exhausted my stash
I needed a way to get money, not knowledge
So I took out a loan and started goin' to college
I buy my booze, I bought a car
I don't go to class, I sleep at the bar
My diet consists of cold pizza and beer
I've really got a good thing goin' here
Most come here to learn the tricks of their trade
But I just go for the financial aid
When I stumble to class, the skirt next to me
The one with "the eyes" and the exposed knee
Fondles her hair and nibbles on her glasses
I wish I had her in all of my classes
I'll skip my last one, it's such an awesome day
I'll go back to the bar and really "par-tay"
I'll check out some chick with a really nice smile
I comfortably fit into my indulgent lifestyle
I just call up the bank and they send money to me
So I'll keep on goin' 'til I get my Ph.D.
—*Brian Albrecht*

If I Could Hear My Mother Sing Again

If I could hear my mother sing her favorite song
If I could go back to yesterday when I use to sing along
she sang "I must tell Jesus the great—
isn't friend I'll ever known"
he understands that I cannot bear all my burdens alone
I'm leaving on the everlasting arm that guides me day by day
and clinging to the old rugged cross on a hill so for away
then there were the days where everything went wrong
Mother took the hymn book down, and mother sang a song
she just sang while she worked and
at church with faith so strong
we were the proudest of all when
mother got up to sing a song
so often I look at your picture that I
have hanging on the wall
tears fill my eyes as so many of the good times I recall
she always sang about how beautiful Heaven must be
now through the windows of Heaven so plainly I can see.
Mother going through the hymn book singing
for daddy, Reva, Lorena and me.
—*Audra Jerlene Hughes*

What Doth It Profit

What doth it profit,
If in pursuit of power, one achieves this end,
In so doing loses dear ones - the respect of fellow men?

What doth it profit,
If one obtains great riches in terms of worldly need,
But forfeits his integrity for avarice and greed?

What doth it profit,
If one's ambitious vanity leads to worldly fame,
When the price is true humility - the end eventual shame?

What doth it profit,
If one attains mere beauty in physical form apart
From that of noble virtue and purity of heart?

What doth it profit,
If one acquires knowledge for knowledge' sake alone,
But has no moral guidance to call his life his own?

What doth it profit,
If through unceasing striving, one gains each self-sought goal,
But in exchange relinquishes his own immortal soul?
—*David C. Janson*

Sonnet #662

I may withdraw and shut myself inside,
if not in my own; slug-like in some shell
imparting apprehensions to myself:
barricaded—my heart again denied.
I may want love naked close by the side
entangled in passion sharing my breath,
muscle-bound passing through the door of death.
Intimate orgasms bodies entwined.
Vulnerably afraid I stay distant;
denying these desires that I hold—
merely working hard, storing bits of gold...
Wishing you'd penetrate my resistance
no ones held me in bed or in my house
nor carried the load when it's weighed too much.
Sometimes I miss the presence of a spouse
the camaraderie and pleasant touch.
My life is enriched with work and good friends.
Yet, still I'm alone when every day ends
longing for love while light to darkness blends.
—*Diane Cole*

Look For Men Like Mine

There are certain things to look for in a man
If someone has hurt him it was to you he ran
For your sympathy, loving, tenderness, and care
The rest of your life keep him if you can

But if he runs from you
Saying he doesn't agree with things you do
Don't bother with chasing after that man
Just like chocolate, you're better off
without him, too

Me and my man, for instance
saw true love at our first glance
For years we've longed for one another
And now, today, we have our chance

We plan to get married someday
The little things we do or say
Brings us still closer together
Day by day we'll find our way

The future holds many surprises
for him and me
In a helpless love forever we shall be
Nothing will ever break us apart
The end of our relationship, no
one will ever see.
—*Heather Nicole Morris*

The Artist

Have you ever thought what life would be...
If work, eat, sleep was all we could see?
To enjoy the beauty of a tree...
And run in the grass, happy and free.
Painting pictures for others to see...
Lifting spirits in humility.
Listening to music, we all agree,
Unifies hearts—on land or sea.
The power of art colors history...
In shades of culture and destiny.
Art has a responsibility,
To inspire—awaken energy,
Blend the human with divinity.
Rhythm and poetic prophesy.
Let's do our part, for the world to see...
The need for the work of you and me.
—*Dawn Cahoon Kniff*

Heavens Nights

The heavens open.
　Illumined by starlight,
The moon casts a radiant glow.
　Tranquility descends, harmonious cosmos
Absorb the night.

The heavens roil.
　Angry clouds, black with rain,
Thunder claps, lightning streaks.
　The storms, in majestic magnificence
Absorb the night.

The heavens hush.
　White, soft, fall the flakes,
Blanketing the earth.
　Pristine snowscapes
Absorb the night.

Alone in the universe,
　I drink from the cup.
Nectars,
　The heavens offer me.
—*Helen P. Hansen*

A Poet! Who Me?

You will never know who I really am,
if you don't read the thoughts I diagram.

My body must stay in an environment that's small,
its defected parts are none God can recall.

Yet space is no problem for the likes of me,
for the pen is the wand that sets me free.

You may never see my face, or hear my voice,
but that really was not my choice.

So I present "me" in the way God lets it be,
after all that's really the only way we see.

Reality is only moments in time,
it's our memories that keeps life in line.

The rhythm of life is a sensual tune,
awakening my thoughts in their cocoon.

If they emerge rhyming passionately,
then you will understand I'm not a mystery.

A poet, who me?
Only if you can believe in what you can't see.
—*Iris T. Stark*

Late Love

Love comes in many ages
I'll bet you didn't know,
And in the early stages
Sometimes it doesn't show.

You don't have to be young and slim
Gray and fat will also do,
As long as you are there for him
Older love can be so true.

Remember too, that it's been said
Love's better the second time around,
And if you've long ago been wed
Don't be afraid to just respond

So make the most of every day
There's so much love to share,
Don't let precious time get away
Before you show someone you care.

When you come to the golden years,
Remember you never have to be alone
And there's no time for lonely tears
Just as long as you have a phone!
—*Dolores M. McCandless*

Introduction Please

I've never met a wise man,
I'm sorry this to say
But, I've met a few smart men,
who passed along my way
Talked they did of money schemes
and the great success they made
Told me of the worth of things,
yet, how little they had paid
Faulted, they seemed to say,
are they who have much less
The measure of man is his pocketbook —
to this they do confess
For now — I've had enough of smart men —
the purse is all they see
So, if you know a wise man —
Please! Introduce him — to me
—*Charles K. Santens*

Autumn!

No, no not the Fall. I haven't fallen. I'm not defeated.
I'm Autumn! I'm also known as Beautiful Indian Summer.

I have polished the air to give you a better view of my
magnificent splendor. I scatter my gold, toss in some amber,
the red of rubies, and a bit of lingering green for the
emeralds, and casting on the floodlight of canary yellow I give
you brilliance. I do it all for you.

And to accompany the wealth of color of my jewels I brush the
sky with azure topped with white fluffy castles.

And when you walk through the radiance of my gems dropping
around your feet listen to the rustle, the murmur, even the
sigh of music I do it all for you.

At night you see on display in the sky the Great Golden Disc
of Harvest Time, filling you with desire to reach up and
encircle it with your arms.

No, not Fall. No failure. No sadness here. Not in my
gorgeous splendor on parade! But I'll rest awhile and again
next year and all the years that follow, I'll return giving
you shining, warm, happy, glorious Concerts of Color, all in a
spectacular pageant. I do it all for you!

—*Dorothy J. Everett*

Desperate Flight

The story that forever is told years of mysteries unfold
in a beautiful and yearning twilight
a story of one mans desperate flight
The searching of a lady fair the agony when she was found not there
He sought her for years only to add sadness to his tears
He came upon her one evening in his heart he had no hope of leaving
On his knee he bowed down in the sand
The rose of her wishes in his hand
No one knows the mystery of that fateful night
but lest you forget this was a desperate flight
The finale of this tale is all one knows
Out of this world he went to the heavens for her soul
With a lifetime of eyes set upon a beautiful vision
into the stars his spirit had risen
Forgotten a life of anguish he embarked upon a quest
to lay down his heart and for once to rest
His pursuit across the universe was in vain
Yes my child it sounds insane
of lovers passing in slight
but ye remember it was a desperate flight

—*Joseph Lunsford*

The Wonderful Spring

I awoke with the kiss of the sun on my cheek,
In a moment was up and ready to greet
A beautiful day at its very beginning.
The birds were bursting with joy in their singing.

I dressed and walked out to my garden where
A delicate perfume filled the air.
The dew, unleashing all of the fragrance,
Enhanced each bloom with a glowing radiance.

The rush of the breeze that makes the leaves dance
Way up in the trees, I could see at a glance
That they welcomed the day with pure delight,
Like a bird that is free and happy in flight.

Happy the heart that can harmonize
With all of the beauty that's in front of our eyes,
Thanking our God for all this perfection
We lift up our eyes in complete adoration.

—*Helen Pearl McDonald*

The Lonesome Drifter

Just cowboy hills and indian lakes
   In a place that time forgot.
A lonesome drifter on his great roan horse
   Came riding, riding at a slow trot.

It was on a beautiful morning while
   The birds still owned the day
That they crossed the shallow creek and rode
   Into those sloping, purple hills they say.

They watched him trotting toward them,
   Whistling low on the early wind.
She watched as he steadily approached them,
   Yet knowing it would all soon end.

He never stopped along the way or ever
   Slowed from that same drumming trot.
Scooped her right from the rail where she sat,
   Raced out at a full run before the lot.

   Never knew where he came from and
   No one ever knew his proper name.
   They just called him the lonesome drifter
   As he carried her away on his horse, the traveling flame.

—*Jimmie Nell Bush Sutton*

Vision of a Dream

In a vision — of a dream!"
In a vision — of a dream
when sleep falls over me
I have vision — sometimes
as I rest my head — on my pillow
I smile
a joyful day — spiritual — it seemed so right
I heard a song — from way back then
it came through my mind
I whisper, whistle and hum and sing —
all through the day
when sleep falls over me — at times
I rejoice — a joyful song
I recall memories
it brings gladness to my heart
in a beautiful voice — to be heard
a sweet — brilliant sound
in a sudden light
flaring flames of fire
in a vision — of a dream."

—*Ingeborg Strausbaugh*

Hope?

The waves of the wind cross the paths of time,
In an ocean of an effort to seek all of mankind.

To wash away the pain and suffering of old and new,
Replacing it with comfort and tranquility; all true.

Memories of hatred, prejudice, all fall away,
Laughter, color blindness, smiles, are here to stay.

If only all of this could become reality,
Still very apparent are hurt and hate; unfortunately.

Just look around and see and listen and hear,
See and feel in everyone's eyes the eternal fear!

Serbia, Croatia, Somalia, and still in the Middle East too,
Everyone is dying — Muslim, Atheist, Christian, and Jew.

—*Jean I. Rauschning*

Lunar Influence

Behind the draperies rough and coarse,
in back of panels sheer and fine
the magic moon plays 'hide 'n seek'
like illusive day-dreams through my mind.

I am intrigued by summers' nights,
an aesthete of her moons,
they mesmerize. Subconscious thoughts
cause me to hum the clair de lune.

Impassioned by earth's satellite
I kiss those visions sensory,
of full lips and skin so warm
reality and time escapeth me.

Ageless youth's a fruitless goal
when 'all the world's my oyster' still.
I have but to part the curtains on my soul
and in the hush possess a whippoorwill.
—*Carmen Riley*

Peace! Be Still!

This rushed and hurried world of ours,
  In desert, land, sky and towers.
The world's so filled with abuse,
  counter-attack, revenge, criticism and blame.
If only we could focus on peace
  Instead of inner and outer turmoil,
  Which really puts us to shame.

Ethnic group against ethnic group,
  Religion versus religion, state against state,
  Nation against nation, city against city.
We have problems forgiving,
  And this is a pity.

Do we really live in a civilization
  mis-using the words freedom and peace?
These deep-rooted negative feelings,
  we need to release.
We should practice harmony
  and love in our hearts.
Feelings of unforgiveness and reacting
  to every event in life keeps us apart.

When we can truly establish concern
  for ourselves and others,
The rage will be over and we can feel the calm,
We then can gently whisper, Peace! It's Still!
—*Ethel R. Whitaker*

The Lost Key

I lost a key — I knew not where,
  In desperation I looked here and there.
It was the most important key of all,
  And a tragic loss on me to befall.
For many doors were locked to me,
  When losing this most important key.
And in my searching — I paid a high cost,
  For it was the "Master Key" that I lost.
All across the land I searched in vain,
  Down many paths that led to pain.
Many times I thought I'd found the key,
  In someone else — but it always eluded me!
And then one day — to my surprise,
  A thought in my mind began to arise.
After all my searching — I finally found the key,
  And it wasn't lost — it was inside of me!!
—*Jane Masterson*

Pray, But A Dream Be

To near the waking hour spent
In dream alone, 'twas now I sent
There be the sight of child like jeers
But reflect did they adulthood fears

'Neigh down a lone forsaken path
My mortal being now was cast
See faces carved of granite stone
I walked this trial so much alone

The stage beset with shattered dreams
There lost a new found love did seem
Was then when tears now filled my eyes
In retrospect I could but only cry

For 'twas the loss of a cherished friend
More so had we met the lovers end
To wake now with mine eyes still filled
And soul to spine with a wintry chill

Perhaps but a nightmare this vision be
By chance but a dream is what I see
So forgive me love for whence I fail
Let your special smile now tell the tale
—*Herman J. Mosteller Jr*

Time

Time you travel on and on
in flight from aeons ago
There is a time once spoken of
when time would be no more
There has been time for every thing
What, when you have no face?
Will all things timed mean nothing
where will you go in space
If there will be time for nothing
there shall be nothing to do
Oh time forgive, I am guilty
of wasting so much of you
—*Johanna Morris*

More Than Life

I look at you often, in sunshine on in rain,
  In happy days and sad days —
In quiet moments of peace, or in hurried moments of unrest.

I look at you often, and my heart leaps
  And at times it seems to stop —
For you have touched it just by being there.

I look at you often, and I still see the girl I met,
  The one who truly touched my heart —
And I see the woman of my life; the mother, the lover,
  the gift.

I look at you often, and I know you look away
  In embarrassment and fear —
That I may see you different than what my heart tells me.

I look at you often, and I know that I am blest,
  And you are all that I want —
That there is never time enough just to be where you are.

I look at you often, and my breath is gone,
  And my soul is weak —
For I know with all my heart I love you more than life!
—*James J. McCarthy*

Two Trees

One tree, nearly leafless, stands stark and bare
in late October's warm, soft glow
The winds of early autumn have already wrested
summer's growth of green
So soon it presents a winter scene
I liken those lost leaves to those who in their weakness
find no anchor for the storm.
Beside this stands another, countless leaves still
clutching firmly to the limbs
Swaying softly in the gentle breeze, it seems
to find joy in another Indian summer day
It sings a joyful hymn
I liken it to those whose roots go deep
to living water
Shall I be like the leafless tree,
succumbing to life's storms and giving up too soon?
Or like the tree with plenteous leaves,
life arms of praise
through autumn's latest days?
—*Joy Moad*

A Hermetic Silence

A silence of mercurial yellow covers my soul
In magenta-pallid adumbrations
Of sapphire-chrysanthemum, Moreau-deepening light
A sage of Norham-pealing blue turns upon the sable—
Crimson waves of my inner soul in venetian—
Adamanthine curves of wisteria-sunset mirrors
An apricot-cascading windmill of psyche-lambent
Petals perpetuates the apocalyptic renewal
Of silver-infinite, jade-masqued solitudes
A mausoleum of Salisbury-auburn odysseys
Dreams of Chartres-liminal mirages
And scarlet-breathing, corinthian-pilastered
Oblivions as the amber-conceiving evening wind
Permeates sibylline-fated deluges of genesis-warm,
Astral-mazed dawns.
—*Hugo Walter*

The Poet

The poet is an adventurer
In many places and climes,
A solitary wanderer of all times
Here and there and everywhere.
He is the creator of worlds of all kinds
Those that have been and others yet to be.
These may be on land or sea.
He is never alone entirely
For he can create his own company
From what he sees or feels
He is an adventurer in both time and space;
A strange creature of a strange race.
Yet he thrives upon both real and unreal
From his store of never-ending zeal.

The poet is an extra dimension
Of whatever life is meant to be
An extra length or breadth
of time and destiny
Whether human or divine.
He is an unsolved equation
of all time.
—*Charlotte J. Chambliss*

Send No Rose

Send no rose to grace the hillside,
In memory of me.
A rose is a thing of beauty,
Only when we leave it be.

Plant a pine tree upon a hillside,
Where the squirrels run and play
Where the wind will whistle through it,
On a chilly winter day.
Long of a needle let it be,
Tall and graceful, ever green.

The sun will set upon its needles,
The snow will grace its boughs of green,
On a hillside a thing of beauty
Like no one has ever seen.

Send no rose to grace the hillside,
In memory of me.
Plant a pine tree, long of needle
Through which the wind will softly moan,
A thing of beauty in my memory,
When I have gone on home.
—*Elizabeth Phillips*

Woodstack Hotel

As soon as wood is stacked up on the porch,
In move the tenants, at the cooling-down
When tempered autumn can no longer scorch.

Here comes the bobbing lizard as the clown
With - a dash, sunning, giving us the eye
Or giving lessons to the little fry.

The mantis on patrol is brown like wood
And lashes out a anything that moves,
While spiders nest inside for livelihood.

The friendly crickets like to leave the grooves
To ride the shuttle for a chance to roam
And do their noisy concerts in the home.

The stack is central with its woody smell
And it allows us all to winter well!
—*Jo Lea Parker*

Shattered

I once held this fragile chalice
in my hands and caressed its beauty
shamelessly.

Confidently I would close my eyes,
knowing that when I opened them, you
would still be there.

Never will I forget your soft and
delicate shape.

As a ballet dancer you posed
in front of me, giving me the unique
opportunity to travel on the same flight....

As you got closer, the air became
purer and you touched me ever so softly.

On a rainy day, I came back, only
to find you on the dusty floor, shattered.

It is not your beauty that I miss, it is
your absence in my life that I regret.
—*Elvanelga C. Isenia*

Holding You So

These loving thoughts I send to you;
In my heart they slowly grew
Until they appeared like stars in the night
Shining softly in a world of blue.

The river of life flows on and on;
Our roses blossom and then are gone,
But bloom again in eternal spring.
In my heart of darkness I feel the dawn.

Love unfolds and nothing can sever
Or come between what we feel forever —
Holding you so all else fades
But the quiet joy we know together.

Far removed from the world's great sin,
We abide where the gods have been —
The compassionate gods that even as we
Loved and wept — then loved again.

We are one with the trees the north winds bend
And the rain-filled clouds the storms shall send
To renew the earth and flower the plains.
We are one with the beginnings that never end.
—Edward E. Abbott

The Lion And The Dove

How different we are — it seems, yet still alike,
  in one important way. . .

Our love, each for the other, is a living-
  breathing entity.

It possesses the strength of the mighty lions
  of the jungle. . .

A virtue which is needful for it to survive
  the trials of Earthly existence.

It also encompasses the serenity and peacefulness
  of doves in flight. . .

A refuge from cold reality.

As the lion and the dove — both part of the sacred
  chain of life — fulfill each other's needs;

So, my love, do we.
—Debrina Peek

A Precious Stone In Our Heavenly Father's Crown

You can be a precious stone
In our Heavenly Father's Crown,
A blessing to all you are around.
Are you a jewel in His crown —
Worn in a royal way,
Accepted by the beloved Heavenly Father,
Known and read by all men,
Your steps ordered by the Holy Spirit?
Then and only then can you be
Placed on the Royal Crown
And have a position of beauty and grace.
You are a precious stone
In our Heavenly Father's Crown
A blessing to all you are around.
—Dale Ann S. Verma

Valentine Letter

  As I look into your eyes, I feel like I'm
in paradise.

  As the tears roll down your face, oh how I wish
I can embrace.

  To feel your warm soft touch, I see your love
and just how much.

  Oh can't you see my dear sweet Valentine, if I
only had a chance to live for a few, I'd ask to be
with you.

Eternally yours
 From your Valentine...
—Cindy J. Matthews

If This Is All There Is

When dragons of doubt seem to turn me about
In proving my faith in God's story, or insisting on who has the
  Glory,
Some may declare this is all that is here.
Come, live for yourself and drink up the beer!
If my life is snuffed out this day with striving and trying to
find the way to a better place on some distant shore, wondering
as this life ends, is there no more? If all ends up with one
final splash with nowhere to go but to dust and ash; shall I
change my way of thinking, and love only myself as I am sinking
into oblivion..the end..if there is no more, once we come in
and then out of the door?

No way, Jose! I still choose to love like the Lord Teaches me
from Above. No if..no why's or concrete proof of where we go
when we're removed. God's way is so clear when honored and
tried, for what really lives is love's awakening inside. And
when we love others as He loves us, there is no need of proving
Him a must; because in our every breath in all our days, His
love proves best in every way. So regardless of how short life
is..or how long, when we love unconditionally today, we cannot
go wrong!
—Anne Robinson

A Lonely Grave

There are no poppies there to blow—
In Sicily the cacti grow
Along the roadside, row on row,
And trail into the hill.
The rocks and bushes hide the way,
So minutes later none could say:
"It was upon this rill."

There by his side I saw him fall,
So young to answer to the Call!
'Twas thus we laid him there....
We dug the grave and let him down;
No music played to ease or drown
Our sorrow - just our prayer:

"O, God in Heaven, grant him rest,
Please keep this spot forever blest,
Please guard him close we would request
For one we honored so".......
In Sicily (the Lord knows where)
Our fallen comrade's sleeping there
Where thorny cacti grow.
—Arthur L. Walters

Ode To A Free Spirit

I felt a unicorn under my hand
   In soft white flesh and not marble
     It had come to stand

I felt the heart beneath
   The breast it rested on
     And wished that this treasure
       Could be mine alone

I felt its spirit
   And the freedom it owned
     And the love with which
       Its head was coned

I pledged my heart to its beauty so rare
   And wished that my hand could always
     Be resting there
      —*Charles E. Grady*

The Sea, My Saviour, And Me

At dawn I send up the incense of my prayers to the throne of God,
In that moment I feel the moving of the Spirit that indwells me
It leads me into the understanding of the depth of His love,
And I rejoice in the gifts given by the Father up above.

In the beauty of His nature, I can see the Master Artist's hand,
As the sunrise flings fiery darts into the azure blue skies,
Their rosy glows reflects upon the white-capped ocean waves,
And all the birds of the sea sing their songs of praise.

I love the gusty playful breezes, and the warm sand under my feet,
As my spirit soars to my loving, precious Saviour Jesus,
And the sea brings me joy that I have never known before,
As the rolling surf rushes in to caress the waiting shore.

I will spend the rest of my days in praise and worship,
To my heavenly master Jesus, whom I will always adore.
Then when my life is over, and Jesus meets me on the other shore,
I will live, and love, and sing my praises to Him forever more!
   —*Junerose Smith*

Early Morning Advent

To the beautiful scenery that appears
in the early morning atmosphere
I rise,
to welcome the wisdom that starts the day
and make me wise,
knowing that early rising
brings happiness, health, and wisdom to me
Rising to see the morning twilight
slowly transforming into day light
and to view the rising sun
seeping from beneath the eastern horizon
and emerging through
and to feel the sweet sun burn of early morn
shining henceforth at the break of dawn
Early rising make me learn
why early bird catch early worm
revealing many startling secrets
that has been hidden by dark night blankets
confirming things I once wondered about
freeing me from uncertain fears and doubts.
   —*Frederick Williams*

Unknown

I shall live on forever
   In the lives of my Honor Guard
Although I am nameless.
   I was but a boy when I received
Greetings from the President
   Of this great nation.
I took my place in that first battalion
   Which sailed on the luxury liner the Queen Mary.
The spirit ran high
   There was a cause but what?
Our days in England were few
   Even fewer in France.
My youth was cut short
   Although it was my choice to live.
My lifeless form joined my fellow Americans
   At Chalons-sur-Marne that was in 1914.
Later I was permitted to come home
   And I was accorded the honor of President and statesmen.
On November 11, 1921
   I was placed in a tomb
Symbolic of all soldiers like me.
   The inscription read as follows-
     "Here rests in Honored Glory
       An American Soldier known but to God"
Although I am nameless I am not alone
   A sentry guards me day and night
But God, I wish I might have lived!
   —*Claire McTavish*

A New Day

Beneath each roof lay tired heads
In the quite stillness of the night.
The stormy winds had ceased.
Bright stars shine forth in radiant light;
Both man and beast are out of sight;
The night is dark and long.
But soon the birds will burst in song,
The cocks will crow, the dawn will break,
The sun will shine, the mist will fall,
   And souls will rise
     To a New Day.
      —*Enola Arnold*

Stargazing

There is one star
In the star filled night
That seems to beckon me
And my gaze turns always to that place
In the quiet endless sea.

The sea of heaven
Of cosmic space
The core of life's own yearning
And I turn my face to that far off place
And sense my soul's returning.

Returning to touch
In that timeless sea
All that has been or is yet to be
Caught up in a dream transcendentally
Roused, when the star winks back at me.
   —*Elsie Nelson Fought*

Wadda Ya Think

You can buy a home for any price,
  In the town or the country way,
Now I've picked a place that's cozy and nice,
  But first listen to what I say

Don't ya think we're both a lot the same?
  And that we should have the same last name,
Then we could have our own kitchen sink,
  Say, Wadda Ya Think?

And don't ya think we'd help the mailman some?
  With just one place for our mail to come,
And everything always in the pink,
  Say, Wadda ya think?

For the folks who really know,
  Say that married life is great!
You've got me on the go,
  And I want you for my mate.

So I think I'll make my move tonight,
  I hope you answer my question right!
I'll be your ball and chain, be my link,
  Say, "Wadda Ya Think??

—*Abe Levine*

Our Fathers' God

Our fathers' God is still the same
  In this greet age of space,
As when He brought the world to life
  And set the stars in place.

He still brings joy to all who seek
  His blessed will to know,
A joy to meet the tests of life
  In this old world below.

He still brings peace to troubled hearts,
  Who only darkness see.
His peace alone can change the world
  And make us truly free.

He still brings comfort to the ones
  Whose hearts are filled with fear.
His strength alone can cause the clouds
  Of dread to disappear.

Our fathers' God will be our own
  If we will do His will.
His comfort, strength, joy and peace
  Can be our children's still.

—*Florena M. Elgin*

Psychoanalytical Query

What could have happened to me
In some long-forgotten time,
That I should be afraid of the moonlight?
Summer moonlight, dappling
Black leaf-shadows on the ground
And the incessant shrieking
Of a whippoorwill
Turn my bones to jelly
And my will to water.
I would as soon venture out alone
Into black darkness.

—*Dicie Selman Woodard*

Otherwise

Every man should know for what he was born,
  In which place to live, which law to abide,
  Which bread to eat, which obstacle to turn,
Every man should know for what he is alive.

Otherwise...if you are a man with no personality,
A pig could look at you and say: "You are just like me."

Every woman should know for what her heart beats,
  Why her blood goes through a cycle every month,
  When to say yes or no, when to stand up on her feet,
Every woman should know for what she was born.

Otherwise...if you are a woman with no dignity,
A cow could look at you and say: "You are just like me."

Every teenager should know the golden rules of living,
  The respect for the elderly, the use of the mind,
  The games of growing up, the talks of a human being,
Every teenager should know for what he is alive.

Otherwise...if you are a teenager with no responsibility,
A monkey could look at you and say: "You are just like me."

  After all...when good human morals are gone,
  The difference between people and animals is none.

—*Albertino Simao*

Mystery City

Your beauty shines in my heart more
  indelibly than moonlight on the ocean.
Your purple gorges, your delicately sketched
  mesa hills etched by God
Were far more memorable than the skylines
  of the cities I abandoned you for.
When I gazed at the setting orange sun,
  twirling over San Francisco Bay,
I saw only your sunsets, flaming like
  Nero's doomed Rome.
Night transformed into day by neon lit
  Las Vegas, Nevada
Could never upstage your jeweled sparkle
  twinkling 'neath the background of ebony
  mountains; canopied by the diamond Milky Way;
  embracing the enigmatic Rio Grande.
Who are you? You know who you are,
  my adobe-sprinkled wonder.
You are the one who inspired my soul.

—*Eve Cobos*

Defiant Mist

Defiant mist descends; it floats,
inhaling, over rim's barbed crest;
descends through day's old sun into
a ponderosa shadow, tick-
ling needles free from hundred feet
high, frosting raven wings and squirrel
tails, lying rest at Mogollon's
hem. Decomposing pen on forest
tablet
 -chilling Nature's peace.
I am that mist, defiant, far
away, foreseeing my descent.

—*Chris Dutton*

Curacao

We met on a jet to Curacao.
Inhibitions didn't last
We became acquainted fast
For we couldn't let a single second go!

Everyday we did play in curacao
Living happy loving dreams
Just like fantastic themes
From a South sea Island movie show.

In the sun we had fun in curacao;
But time on us ran out
And we had to turn about,
Without a backward look to spoil the glow.

With a sigh we said good-bye to curacao.
But sealed was our fate
For our love was too great.
Now we want the whole wide world to know

That tonight we're on a flight to curacao.
There's a ring on your finger
And this time we'll longer linger
On our honeymoon in wondrous curacao!
—*Andrew A. Johnstone*

Escape!

I feel in hibernation.. a moth, sealed
inside my cocoon-being; a prisoner -
   Seeking out, but am not able to break through
   my barriers of confinement - to fend my
     being in a callous world;
       the webbous bands of living!
It is not a strong structure that keeps me
   prisoner within. Some may think it but delusion,
    to be intactile within my airy nothing,
      weeping for lost hours,
       envisioning barren days.
I make further attempts at release from my entrapment,
   but, now - I feel my time has come!
I break the chains of my confinement; to conquer
   on my own! To fly freely! Reaching new heights!
     Without fear! Without temerity!
I emerge as a butterfly,
   soaring on waves of mild breezes!
    I am free! ... I am woman!
     —*Dolores E. Teufel*

At One Time

I am helpless without your driving Sony
Intentions glimmering in the hazy red dam
Cadillac evoking lazy absences through
smooth clean hotel photographs flesh (a friend of mine)
looks at Sand pumice a device allegations
flinch back at me black even more Sally rides
Reporters fall asleep whitely war killing
War, war in the shadows cha cha aims cha
electrically colored slate bears a strong mouth
similarity to you moving but that coming home
doesn't mean I don't embrace blind
the moon and pile on more rain
   —*Candace Hill*

Have You Ever Been Thankful?

Have you ever been thankful for being a human
Instead of a Doberman pinscher or hound?
For instead of the warmth of a cozy, soft bed,
You would sleep in a box or on ice-covered ground.
Instead of a strawberry punch and a steak,
Your master would feed you with dog food and scraps.
Your pail would be filthy with water and dirt,
And life would be mangy with boredom and naps.

Have you ever been thankful for being a human
Instead of a pig or voracious old hog?
For instead of a plate of delicious spaghetti,
Your trough would be filthy and worse than a bog.
On a miserable morning your master would kill you,
And scald and dehair you for succulent meat.
Your master would bleed you by slashing your throat,
And your flesh would be butchered for humans to eat.

Have you ever been thankful for being a human,
For having a life-span of eighty or more?
And with knowledge of science and change of your habits
Your life can be longer than ever before.
If the doctrine of reincarnation is true,
Let us pray that your soul will be human forever
For it's sad to be anything other than man,
To be mastered by humans so cruel and clever.
   —*Alfred Leon Wallace*

Retreat

I have no fear of enemies that lurk outside my door!
   Intangible foes, deep within, frighten me so much more!

External forces, evident, are easy to evade.
   The covert ones, insidious, unable to keep bayed.

They strike from highest battlements, with weapons obsolete!
   Engaging mental weapons frail, I flounder; I retreat!

Opposing forces' constant clash destroys all reverie,
   Reducing me to molten ash and meager memory.

The battle rages endlessly, niggard of any rest.
   The mind, the body overrules; real pain pulsates the breast.

"Call off the insurrection!" cries the fighter deep within.
   "Allow the resurrection! Let release to peace begin!"
   —*Joyce A. Poirier*

Comes The Dawn

When night has come and stretches endless
Into deeper night not dawn
For no light shines and all is cold
And all that's gay is gone

Hope fades too, no longer strengthened
By anything that's warm or bright
As closing round is only darkness
To never end this empty night.

The day had brought no word from you
So why wake for another
Why do tears not drown me
Or the darkness smother...

Then comes the dawn, your words come back
A sunburst glorious tune...
As I recall the day you said
We'll be together soon!
   —*Carol C. Larson*

I Wasn't Looking

Going down life's road you go around many corners. You came into my life when I wasn't looking. I was feeling down and out. You came along making me feel up again. It happened so fast when I wasn't looking. I gave up on love and happiness until you came along. I found love and happiness when I wasn't looking. This corner I nearly missed. I could only make this corner when I wasn't looking.

—*Barbara Handy*

The Ghost Of Time

I slip through the channel of night
   into the light beyond
For I am the Ghost of Time
   where space is my universe.
I search for the manifest of life
   and the meaning of Christian love.
Always reaching, grasping, probing
   to find a haven of peace and glory,
Where rest becomes eternal.

Time is the light everlasting
   and life is the essence of love.
Together we become an essay
   with the most commonplace bond.
We hold fast to the truth of living
   ever ready to calm troubled waters.
The bridge between Heaven and Earth
   is our pathway to eternity
Within the realm of God.

—*Dorothea M. Petrut*

Devils Avenue

There's a street where a teenage haven
is, a favorite rendevous.
Where our young are lured and driven.
It's called the devils avenue.

Under city lights they promenade
Ego-sensed with power, to give a
nightly mascarade, called the children's hour.
Some perform in innocent beauty
they have nothing else to do.
On the street of colored rainbows,
the devils avenue.

Finding thrills is easy.
And this leads them to
Where the users, and the takers wait-
on devils avenue.

Rejected ones and runaways, prance about in false bravado.
Most of them living — in communicade — looking for easy
street listening to there peers.
God's mercy on our children, the devil sheds no tears.

The traffic after midnight is in human revenue.
Witness the new generation, on devils avenue.

—*Helen Heywood*

The End

Beneath the wind turned wave
Infinite peace:
Islands join hands; beneath heaven's seas
Lies eternal happiness and love.

—*Debra Brown*

A Different View

The world when viewed through the eyes of Chelsea
   Is a vast and mysterious place.
   To discover a bug, cricket or frog
   Brings delight to her cherub face.

Chelsea finds joy in the most simple things
   An hour spent digging in sand.
   Or raindrops falling upon her face
   Just walking holding my hand.

A little squirrel scampering up a tree
   Makes her shout with glee.
   Her mirthful laughter rings out loud
   As he jumps from tree to tree.

A trip to the zoo is an experience
   With which nothing can compare,
   To her great pleasure as she shouts
   "Hey! Nana come look at the bear.

Take some time and view the world,
Through the eyes of a little child.
You'll find out things look different
And your worries forgotten for awhile.

—*Jo Sansbury*

What I See

I look around and all I see
Is an insecure girl, who is me
Afraid to look behind the door
Of a past filled with twisted souls
Afraid to see what the future holds
For it may bring me sorrow or more

I look around and all I see
Is a shattered world around me
Broken hearts and broken dreams
To last for eternity
People wandering aimlessly
Searching for the truth of reality

I look around and all I see
Is a little girl staring back at me
Pleading with herself
For someone to help me
Open the door and look beyond it
To see how far I've really come
Although there's more for me to see
I'm not afraid to look at me

—*Frances M. Chance*

Crystal Snow

The most beautiful sight I have ever seen,
Is crystal snow that is made by a fanciful Snow Queen.
It sparkles like stars and glistens like glitter,
Nature's own quite and most beautiful baby sitter.
It lays soft and gentle, covering a sleeping world,
An ever-changing blanket of swirls and twirls.
It appears soft and fluffy, but it hides a cold and frozen river.
The reality of its striking beauty may cause a sigh...or a shiver.
The Snow Queens' greatest creation,
   This I know,
 Is Montana's Crystal Snow.

—*Deborah L. Reed*

The Tear Thief

Where is the tear thief tonight?
Is he courting a fair maiden
  or dueling an evil lord?
Is he helping just one person
  or an entire nation?

Where is the tear thief tonight?
I created him
  and he has left me here.
I forged him
  and he refused to help me.

Where is the tear thief tonight?
He is doing what I created him to do -
  steal the tears of a should-be happy person.
He is out there in the night working
  while I wait for him to never come and
steal my lonely tears.
    —Ian Glazer

Cross Of Thorns

Just as the pain of the radiant rose
Is in the piercing thorn, not the soft bloom,
And the deepening gloom of fading fall
Is in the barren branch, not the fallen leaf,
And the bitterness of northern winter winds
Is borne from captured ice, not the newly-fallen snow-
So is the silent sorrow of death's demand
Buried in grey grief's loneliness, not the murmured amen.
    —Bill Otto

Is This Heaven?

I wonder what heaven is like!
  Is it blue and rose and gold,
A place where true friends meet,
  And confidences are not sold!

A place where saddened hearts
  Find solace and sympathy;
And sorrow's tears will vanish
  Like rain - drenched clouds in April's sky.

A place where time drifts by
  Like a lazy river — so timelessly
We may ponder and dream till night,
  Falls it's curtain — so heedlessly.

I think in the morning's rose,
I think in the evening's blue
I think in the mid day's gold
of a Heaven like this — do you?
    —Dorothy Dickson

November Storm

The gray flannel sky of November
Is ripped by a blade of light.
Then the thunder breaks and the city quakes
With the violence of the night.

The dignity's gone from the elm trees;
In panic they're shaking their bones.
The tamarack's hair is whipping in snarls
And the juniper weaves and moans.

Then the water spills and washes the air
And the elm trees' leaves. The tamarack's hair
Hangs limp and straight in the sodden calm,
And the juniper's sigh becomes a psalm.
    —Helen Scott

What Would The Animal Say?

Porcupines Declaration of Independence
Is signed with a penetrating quill in essence
It is saying your predatory presence isn't welcome
You critters who want some whiskers come, get some.

The eager beaver hastily builds a dam
Often resulting in a colossal log jam
With incisors sharp as man's power saw
All he has to do is clamp his teeth, and gnaw.

The pungent aroma of a skunk carries for miles
If down wind of it, concoct your own wiles
A skunk when badger-ed by any thick skin
Badger gets whiff, leaves sheepishly feelin' chagrin

A mink would say that stole you stole is mine, me
When you trapped me, took it out on my hide-see!
Some animals are killed, stuffed by taxidermist
I'm certain it isn't at their own personal behest.

A mischievous child's play is horsin' around
Trying to get your goat, at this he's profound
When caught in the act, trying to weasel out anyway
Being compared to people what would that animals say…
    —David Glen Cook

Monarch Of The Meadow

A tree, lone in its meadow
  is the jewel in Nature's crown
Blest, the leaves that house the breeze
  and limbs with nests of hatchlings' down

Can that tree with its great might
  withstand all man's brute force
And live to see new Season's life
  or be torn from Mother Earth

We all must know — mankind must see
  that to tear it from its place
Our souls would be diminished
  should nothing stand, but space

Pray let it live and cause it care
  whilst its sojourn here on Earth
As reigning Monarch of the Meadow
  rules this kingdom's greatest worth
    —Irene G. Messerall

The Most Awful Era

The most awful era in my life's span
  is the present time when age commands.
With bone and sinew as hard as steel,
  there comes a time when men are killed.
I've walked thru this world as tough as nails,
  and frowned at my failures without any tears.
What I've did a hundred million times,
  becomes a feat for sure that wasn't timed.
A slip of the foot a slip of the toe,
  the smallest molehill and down I go.
I've been the toughest vine that ever grew,
  and I've never backed up from what I could do.
I've swam the rivers, I've manned the rail,
  if there was a course to chart I was always there.
A man only dies once in his life.
  and that's when he steps back from the strife of life.
I've toiled the fields, I've fought the fight.
  a family with God is a family's might.
But of the tallest trees that once stood so strong,
  they too were felled by something, that was ever so small.
    —John L. Roton

The Fog

I look out my window and I see despair
Is this what hell is like?
A curtain shrouds the color of life
The fog saps my energy
It is a blanket, not warm and secure
But heavy and cold
No sparkling whites to reflect the sunlight
No deep, rich blacks to give me anchor
Just grays, heavy and cold.
Will tomorrow hold the colors of life
Or will it become another foggy, desolate memory.

—*Judy Giles*

What Luck!!!

I found a four leaf clover
It brought me lots of luck

......All Bad......

First I crashed my car, into a speed limit sign
When the cops got there, they found my bottle of wine

They took my drivers license, and clipped it in two
Then they looked at me, and I cried "Boo Hoo"

After the cops left, a wrecker took my car
It was on the way to impound, didn't make it that far

The front tire fell off, my car crashed to the ground
I'm never coming back, to this seedy little town

When all was said and done, and I payed all my dues
I won't drink and drive...I have to much to loose!!!

—*Deborah Lee Bull*

The Forgotten Veteran

"Anybody home?" asked a strange, new voice!
It came from a man in a vested suit.
"Reckon there is," came the reply, within!
As he searched for his oversized boots.

Advancing from his cardboard castle,
Behind a stubbled face, beamed a smile!!
He was surprised to have such a visitor!
And, motioned for him to sit...a while.

Too many Indians! I knew there were!!!
There's no way he could have survived!!!
The Good Book says the Babe will return;
Then, he pointed towards the sky!

Coffee, Captain?!!! It's so hot, here.
I'll have the 'Corporal' bring you a cup!!
Honesty! Morality! All those little children!!
Sir, your Battalion is sleeping! Sir, wake up!!

Age and loneliness had taken their toll.
He worried about this country he had served.
In silence, the President just stood there!!
Amid sounds from the parkbench, nearby the curb.

—*John H. Blackburn*

Untitled

Friendship is a gift from God.
It cannot be bought, borrowed, nor traded.
it can only be given and received.
Friendship is the roadway to the heart.
It is one of the greatest gifts from God
And its greatest asset is love.
Friendship can be a comforter, a provider, a moment of compassion.
It can be whatever one needs when one needs it.
Friendship is so available,
Yet so many of us take it for granted.
Help us, God, to be more like-minded of you,
Trusting some of your words in our lives.
And we will, indeed, become better friends to ourselves,

But most importantly to each other.

—*Diane Hill*

Only Good Christians Can Govern

As a political power structure maneuvers for strength,
It disguises it's intent atop a christian banners length.
If not a "good" christian you should not rule,
So says the Christian Right as they all drool.
They claim the present dilemmas prove the "Godless" fallibility,
As presented by this movement in seeking overall credibility.

It is inferred that only they can properly govern,
So we must vote accordingly so as not to be put asunder.
The Great Crusades and yes the Spanish Inquisition,
Are to be looked upon with favor, in a new dominion.
We are to look up our government as made up of "Godless" men,
And place only those into power who they favor — Amen!

—*Anthony Torres*

Four Legged Friend

Stumble in at 2:00 a.m., trying to let you sleep
It doesn't matter where I've been, out of bed you leap.
You never ask me why I'm late or try to bar the door,
When I come home slightly drunk or smelling like a whore.

You always welcome in my friends when I invite them home.
You never bitch or call me names when I forget to phone;
And if by chance I don't come home or seem to lose my way
I say I'm sorry and treat you well and by my side you'll stay.

I've seen you jealous time to time when another has my eye
But all the times I did you wrong, I never saw you cry.
You're always happy when I come back, no matter where I've been
Whether I have been alone or shacking up with friends.

All the times you've gone with me, the attention that you get
The people flock around you, most you've never met.
Tonight I'll bring you with me, but I cannot bring you in.
You'll have to stay out in the truck and wait on your old man.

Once again it's 2:00 a.m. and you are all alone,
Maybe I will make it up and bring you home a bone
You never care or seem to mind, if I am late again
You'll lick my face and wag your tail,
Thank you, my four-legged friend.

—*Gary Arrants*

My Dream For America

I have a dream of America as it should be.
It has been quoted, "As the land of the brave and the free."
In our country people have the freedom to stand up and say,
I'm gay,
But in some places people are not permitted to pray.
I dream that some day our school children will again be allowed
To start their day with a prayer.
That they may stand straight and tall,
And look to a future that is bright.
Without fear of guns, of knives and
Drive by shootings in the night.
That our streets will be safe again
From the evil that stalks by night
That there will be love, trust and
Friendship as bright as the morning light.
That we may be proud to be an American
And hold old "glory" high. Proud to hold
Our heads up our faces to the sky
Where lives the maker of the earth,
And in Him we place our trust.
—Helen H. Horsley

The Horses And The Road

Life is one way road
it has no return,
but detours,

On the other hand,
we absolutely need
to go back to our farm
and hoop the horses
to the matter of watching the road
and keeping carefully
its left and right turns.

It occurs some times that we don't pay attention
to the furious horse of destruction
which looks as if he were just crossing the road....

In reality, he is awaiting for us to ruin our lives.

We ought to stop,
observe the horse carefully;
he might not expect
we would make another definite detour.
—Elizabeth Paz

Wedding Day

On this the day of your wedding,
it is a beginning that marks an end
a start of a new life as one,
with your partner, love and friend
Ending the uncertainty of being alone,
and loneliness that marks the time
A start of brand new memories, making it a sweet upward climb
Where your love will live eternally,
and grow more than you will know to forever shelter from harm,
but always remember to let love show
Let it live in everything you say and do,
Let it become everything that you are
Never stop it from becoming stronger,
Never let distance make it too far
Let your two minds become one soul, and two hearts one love
Never searching again, it will be sheltered by God above
So on this the day of your wedding,
Let it be a beginning that marks an end
a start of a new life as one
with your partner, love and friend
—Danielle Tjomsland

It Is Morning

Oh day dark cold and wet.
It is morning and the brightness I have not see yet.
Where is the sunshine that was promised to me.
I kept looking but nothing I can see.

I know the sun is out there, but I cannot see it from here.
I can feel the warmth but is nowhere near.
Could the clouds be moved away to let it shine.
Let me see it for one moment and I will be fine.

It was not promised to me to see everyday.
But please remember I am not yet dead, so help me I pray.
Remember its morning the dawn of day.
Just show me today, and tomorrow you can take away.

Oh thanks for the sunshine now I can see.
Everything I have I will give unto thee.
From today, this morning, I am all yours.
I can see the trees, the mountain and waves splashing along
   the shores.
—Grantley Crawford

Beyond Our Control

We don't choose when our feelings die
It just happens
It's beyond something planned
And is it something to question

Where there is death, there is new life
We must go on to new love
We can't forget our feelings
Although sometimes we try

Leave your thoughts behind
And new feelings will come to life
Do what's right for now
Because tomorrow is all of our todays

When we have forgotten all of our questions
And answers are received
What should be done with all these answers
Do we dare ask new questions
—Joan Sullivan

Once Stood So Tall

There stood a building so big and strong
It looked as if nothing could move it at all.
But all of a sudden, the sky was so black!
So black you could not see.

I saw this building in front of my eyes,
Only to turn my head and turn it back again,
Just in time to see, the building crumbling before my eyes,
Sad it was, it stood so tall
Such a beauty it was to all.

For the wind did blow, and the rain did come, and the hail did fall.
Knocking out windows and blowing off shingles,
My how they blew all over,
With bricks flying through the air looking so small.

But all of a sudden, the wind did lay,
And the sun did shine,
All that was left, but a pile of rubble
That was once the building that stood so tall!
—Eunice Arnold

Untitled

Every time I look at my little girl
It makes me feel high above the world
Cute little bundle with a smile on her face
Makes me feel like I can win any race
Her eyes look at me so loving and true
Makes me feel warm and wanted too
Her eyes close slowly, and drifts off to sleep
These are the memories I will always keep

—*Elvin L. Westhuis*

The Missouri Flood

The Missouri flows along,
it makes no song.
Midst sunlight and shadow,
midst sunlight and grief.
There seems no relief.
What will come tomorrow?
Gods hand is in the breaking,
and the remaking.
To teach us greater love,
and greater caring for one another.
For we are but like clumps of clay
That floats along the old Missouri.
For like this our ending has its way.

—*Annie R. Forrester*

I Love You

I need to hear the words "I love you"
It may seem silly, but it's true.

This is what makes my heart jump with delight
an, I love you, before we say goodnight.

An, I love you, from a friend so far away,
an, I love you, from my grandchild each day.

And as I close my eyes at night,
a silent I love you, in my heart
   from my Lord,
as the day fades out of sight.

—*Catherine Dunham Retkowski*

Chances

My attitude was stinking
  It plainly showed
    People began not to like me
      No matter where I would go

Then one day something happened
  I'm no really sure what, but the same day
    Kept happening over and over
      It never seemed to stop

Give me just one chance I pleaded
  I will surely change, and I will care for others
    A better person be
      If my plea is granted you will see
        A better me

I got to work
  To others I did give
    My mind was on helping others live

I lost myself in giving
  But what I found was living
    It was plain to see
      I found me

—*Emma Lee Hill*

Pray For Peace

Pray for peace is all I ask
It really is not a difficult task

If a few loving words spoken from your heart
could help mend the world and prevent it from tearing apart

Why not give prayer a chance and see
If this world could not better be

A world in which together we all can live
And learn how to better give

Love from one heart to another
And call everyone sister and brother

How nice to have a world in the end
Where we peacefully sleep after saying amen.

—*Jacquelyn C. Garner*

Wandering—Whispering—Winds Of

I heard the wind go whispering...as it wandered through the trees.
It sang a haunting melody...as it brought the evening breeze.
It spoke of places far away...as it wandered through the trees.
It spoke of places far away...as it wandered through the gloom.
And it filled my heart with glory, till there was no empty room—
My thoughts went gently wandering along the sands of many seas
Of days of going here and there...wherever I should please.
The moon shone bright as sunshine as it lighted up the night.
Then my whole world was brightened
by a glorious-beauteous light...
My soul lifted high above me...as the wind sang in the trees.
For it filled my soul with sunshine...from many happy memories.
I remember! Oh, I remember!!! some glorious happy times...
Oh, I remember! I remember!! all the days of "auld lang syne!"
And the passing of life's ages slipped away on the evening breeze
For my whole life passed before me as the wind whispered in the trees,
So that my heart was moved within me...and I was once more young
    and gay—
As the wind sang softly, whispering... in the twilight of life's day.

—*Catherine G. Curtis*

Home

Last night I dreamed of a beautiful place.
It seemed as though it was way out in space.
The rooms inside were spacious and fine,
And one beautiful room was all set to dine.
The bedrooms were pretty - as pretty can be,
All decked in bright colors, just to please me.
The lawn was so green, and the trees were in bloom.
I finally woke up, and right there in my room,
Were some of the same things I had just seen.
They were right there before me and not in a dream.
How lucky I felt to have such a place,
And find it's right here, and not out in space!

—*Anne Browne Graf*

Crystal Blue Morning

Your eyes are the color of crystal blue
In the early morning, just after dawn.
Your smile is like the bright sunshine.
On a rainy day, it's just what I need.
When the sky is blue.
And the sun shines,
I feel the warmth.
The warmth of your heart.
You are my crystal blue morning.
Bringing life to my sleeping world.

—*Charmin Rothgeb*

Peaceful, Quiet, Beautiful

As the sun sinks lower into the deep blue sea,
It seems like the world comes to a cease.
It is peaceful, quiet, beautiful.

The clouds fluffy and soft.
The stars slowly coming into view, twinkling their eyes at me.
The sky first red, then pink, then finally midnight blue.
The day has ended and the night is beginning.
Slowly the silvery moon begins to rise
from the deep blue sea on the other side.
It casts an eerie light, but yet,
it is peaceful, quiet, beautiful.

I don't want this feeling to end.
But, it seems like the feeling of death,
thinking this may be your last breath.
But, if I were to die I would like it to be here,
in the deep blue sea, with the fluffy clouds, and the twinkling stars,
and the midnight blue sky with the silvery moon, because
it is peaceful, quiet, beautiful.
—*Jessica Marie Street*

Reality

The time is passing by,
it seems to move in slow motion,
yet I know reality.

The slower I go, the more things happen.
If I were in synch, would this be the same.

I keep trying to catch the movement
that has already passed me by.

I'm not lost in drugs, simply
in the lack of anything,
that means reality.

If the pressings of reality
would let me slow with the motion I feel,

Would the motion be real or
would I still be out of synch.

If I could drift on the motion
could I form a new reality.

When and Where is Reality.
What and Why is Reality.
—*Janet Leonard*

Common Ground

The pain you felt I understood, for truly I had been there,
It strained my heart to see you cry, so lost feeling no one cared.
Your very fiber crying out "won't someone please love me,"
"I am not bad, I'm just alone, oh why can't you see?"
Your hunger for belonging, an itch you could not scratch,
Relationships a plenty, but never one a perfect match.
Being hurt so many times, you throw up a wall,
Pretending to be a giant, and yet feeling oh so small.
Not knowing what to do, to find the perfect girl,
You run with crowds, who mar your vision of the world.
Your laughter hides a broken heart, an endless aching need,
But please hang on tighter, for I know you will succeed.
For out there is a person, who needs the love you have to give,
As she's been lonely, lost and searching and wants to start to live.
I know these things are true and believe me I have found,
That our lives are intertwined for we have walked on common ground.
—*Jean Stevens*

My Bonnie Lassie

Your smile is like golden sunlight
It warms me through and through,
Your words are as gentle as raindrops,
When they fall on my ear soft and new.
Your laughter rides on butterfly wings,
And flutters about me;

Like nobility around kings.

Your eyes are like a thousand fireflies
Twinkling in the night; illuminating my life
Whenever your image graces my sight.
So no matter the month or the weather
October, December, or May,
I know the moment I see you

I will have a daffodil day!

For your "Bonnie-Lassie" charms...
Refresh my heart anew,
Like a beautiful rose at dawn...
As it silently collects the dew.
—*Jacqui E. Murphy*

Old Photographs

While rummaging through the attic, a corner box I did spy.
It was filled with old photographs, of days that had gone by.
I leisurely took them out and glanced at them one by one.
Reminiscing of younger days, and remembering all the fun.

They took me back to my youth, of friends and old places I'd been.
Doing things together, that we will never do again.
For now we have all grown, and went our separate ways.
But through these old photographs, I can keep my younger days.

So I'll put my youth back in the box, and seal it with a lid.
So when next I go back in time, the way I just did.
I'll wipe away the aged dust, that has helped preserve my past.
That is captured on these old photographs, so through time my
   youth will last.
—*Debbie Robinson*

Give Me The Old Time Salvation

Give me the old time salvation,
It was good for Enoch and Elijah, Jeremiah, and Isaiah;
Give me the old the time salvation as Job and David,
It gave them joy in their souls.

I want the old time salvation, it will give us
Grace and keep us in Jesus all through life,
I want the old time salvation, it was good
For all His disciples and saved all their souls.

That old time salvation will do when grieving,
It will comfort and keep us true to Jesus.

That old time salvation was good for Daniel,
And the three Hebrew children and saved them all;
That old time, salvation was good for Moses
And Aaron and saved them from all opposition.

Give me that old time salvation, it was
Good for Peter, James and John, it saved them,
Give me that old time salvation, it will
Give peace and joy in our soul and take us home to heaven.
—*Elmer R. Green*

Full In Fall

"I had a rendezvous" with George,
It was in early autumn.
As I arrived at Valley Forge,
The trees were mauve and auburn.

As I made halt at yonder church,
The leaves of grass were swaying,
"The spot we root in, and a birch,
Is right where he was praying…"

Though Switzerland has higher peaks
And Holland smoother beaches,
Here 'round the hills liberty speaks
So all can hear her speeches.
—*Joseph F. Cserepy*

Remembering

As I remember my home in these years,
   It was never filled with heartaches and tears.
A palace it was not, but to me it seem to be,
   Happy times for mom and dad, my brother and me.
Wish I could recall every day of way back when,
   I went bare foot in the summer way back then.
My brother plowing the peanut patch,
   And waiting for the baby chicks to hatch.
And down the road about half a mile,
   Is the church I went to as a child.
Passed the church at the woodwards was the fishing hole,
   Where mom and I went with worms and a fishing pole.
I could feed the stubborn ole mule we had,
   The ole mule that could make my brother so-o-mad.
My brother would pick his guitar and sing,
   On the front porch sitting in the swing.
Mom would pat her foot and hum along,
   With him singing a gospel song.
Dad would sing tenor with his son,
   Relaxing after another days work was done.
—*Jean Stephens Johnson*

The Fear I Feel

The days are lonely the nights are cold,
It will get better or so I'm told.
The fear I feel deep inside of me,
Is pushing to get out pushing to be free.
My heart has been wounded my feelings torn apart,
And people wonder why I have such a cold heart.
I've felt the cold of night creeping upon me,
Shutting out all the light that I can see.
I know what its like to feel all alone,
To feel my heart harden like stone.
But what people don't get is I feel pain too,
I feel it so deep sometimes I don't know what to do.
They say it's all a game that I'm playing for fun,
But they don't know why I really run.
It's for reasons so big and reasons so deep,
Reason that keep me away from my sleep.
And I'm just learning now how to talk it all out,
Then maybe someday they will know what my pains all about.
But it's been so hard for me whose kept it all in,
And there's so much to tell I don't know where to begin.
—*Jennifer Bullock*

A Piece Of Land

I bought a piece of land today, I will not farm it, I'm sad to say,
It will not hold a house for rent, but I still feel it was cash well spent.

I've waited all my life to buy, this piece of earth, I cannot lie
Upon the hill and under shade, where thoughts of me shall never fade.

My wife and I shall here reside, each other's thoughts we shall confide,
Until each voice at last is hushed, and last respects for us are rushed.

This placid ten by ten by ten, shall welcome us, its owners then,
My wife in bronze, myself in steel, into our clothing they will seal.

Then lower capsules six feet down, for to await our heavenly crown,
Into their cars they file back, and leave the work to spader Jack.

He works the land for which we paid, the others gone while we
   have stayed,
Awaiting visits children pay, although they've grown and moved away.

A tear of memory they will shed, while placing daisies by my head,
Don't mourn I'll whisper in the breeze, and love will echo through the
   trees.
—*Brett S. Gayer*

Time

Time is so precious yet so annoying. You can't see
it, you can't feel it, it's everywhere, yet its no where.
Your day begins with it, your nights end with it.
Time stands still, but yet it flies by so fast. Time can
mean life or death to some. There's a time to love
a time to cry, a time to laugh, a time to work, a
time to play, a time to sleep, a time to pray.
Time is around us everywhere. We can't stop it.
We can't make it go away. Time is one thing the
whole world has in common. Everything and everyone
exists and comes together with time. There
is nothing you can do or say against time to
make a difference to time. It just keeps
on ticking away, every second, every minute of
every day. It never pauses to be refreshed.
It never stops to take a rest. No one knows
where those used seconds, minutes and hours
goes. No, no one knows.
—*Betty Mae Eaton*

The Rainbow

Have you ever gazed at a rainbow?
   It's a bridge between Earth and sky,
That's silhouetted in all its glory
   After the storm passes by.
Its colors are tinted so subtly,
   And varied in texture and shade,
It had to be fashioned in Heaven,
   Such splendor man never made.
Can it be just the reflection,
   Of the sun shining through the dew?
Or is it God's gift to man,
   A glimpse of Paradise breaking through?
Is there a pot of gold at the end,
   Where it tenderly touches the Earth?
Nay! The treasure lies before your eyes,
   For who can measure its worth?
Nothing on Earth can compare,
   To its beauty arching the sky,
Nor the feeling of awe it inspires,
   Truly Jacobs coat, floating on high!
—*John Munck Probasco*

Autumn

Summer's gone - so bright and clear,
It's a changing time of year
Time when autumn comes along
Sings a chilly, breezy song.
Clouds appear and skies are gray
Air grows cooler every day.
Trees no longer green alone
Leaves are every lovely tone.
Red and yellow - orange too
Autumn paints them every hue.
There are feelings - rather sad
Some are good and some are bad
Thinking of the winter snow
When the frosty winds will blow
Harvest colors of the fall
Make me think - it's best of all.
—*Amelia Lucas*

Uphill

From the time you are born
  It's an uphill fight
    One of tact
      And one of might
        To mix the two with deadly skill
Will have a great effect on the space you fill
    Your future may be paved with stone
      The path you chose
        You may walk alone
          Battles won
        And battles lost
       And much to do
      Before the frost
    Love to give and joy to share
    A wish for peace and freedom
      Everywhere!
  From the time you are born
  Until the time that you die
  You will have good cause to stop
    And wonder why…AF…92…
—*Andrew J. Foster*

Altar Boy

I smile as I serve Father McKelvey
In my white surplice and black cassock,
The nuns say my smile is quite angelic;
Yet between responses I can still taste
The wine I sampled while vesting for Mass.
I spy Betty Sue's budding breasts
Protruding beneath her summer voile dress.
Thank God no one can see my tumescence
Hidden in the folds of my full cassock,
Am I hypocrite or a healthy youth?
Ora pro nobis Madre Dios.
—*James G. Dunn*

To My Son

In your joy I have joy.
In your love I have love.
And in all your yesterdays and tomorrows
I will remember and plan.
Can there be more
Than this between a father
And his son?
Can there?
—*Eric v. K. Hill*

The Rose And The Weed

Everyone…enjoys the rose.
  Its beauty, we are all captured by.
And its color…fills us with wonder.

But the weed that grows next to it.
  It's shunned, and considered ugly!
And is pulled and killed…
  The moment it peeks out of the ground.

On looking close, it too has color.
  And a beauty all of its own.
It too has a good reason, to be here
  Like the rose, that's loved by everyone.

The weed too is loved by someone, somewhere.
  For all things, wanted or unwanted…
Were placed in this garden we live in.
  By Him who created, and loves us all.

Look deeper into the weeds.
  And you too may capture the inner
Beauty they hold…and will someday understand.

There's very little difference,
  About the rose and the weed.
The rose…with its visual beauty;
  The weed with its inner beauty.

With your eyes, you'll see the roses.
  But listen, listen!
Very closely…for the sounds of the weeds.
—*Charles Moran*

Hunger Pain

The growling in my stomach worsens.
Its been such along time since I last
  tasted food, that I can't remember what
  my last meal was….?
Killing time in silence, sitting on the sidewalk,
  clothes ripped and dirty - panhandling for a
  little spare change, as I look through a
  magazine that a passing person threw away.
The pain in my stomach is now unbearable!
I look at my cup to see if any kind soul has
  given me any money? The cup still sits
  empty.
So with a small pocket knife I keep for
  protection, I carefully cut out the
  pictures of food that I like from the
  magazine.
With little thought I assemble them on a
  make believe plate —
I say a small prayer…and then begin
  to eat.
—*Daniel Albert Young*

When Is Life?

When do we come upon the decision to live?
Is it when the sun fills the sky?
Or when the leaves on the trees sprout?
Living is when…,
We are breathing easily,
And that can only be done when…
We are lighthearted about,
The sun in the sky,
On a cool day of life.
—*Cassie Goodspeed*

Moribund

The school still stands where I once learned,
It's bricks effaced with the passing of time.
And the nicely paved streets that once showed
great works in cobblestone have been choked
With low budget coatings of black topping.
The neat private homes that lined this street
are but sorrow today.
Somehow the whole scene reminds me of a human
skull, lifeless, with missing and corroded
teeth- where there was once an endless smile-
perhaps brought about by the caustic servings
of life.
And over there, on the corner lot, there once
stood a home, a hope and a dream that never did
last. There lived the girl that would share her
life with me, then life served its acrid portion
to me. Now all that remains there, beneath the
heap of rubble and weed trees, is a chimera of
a shattered dream— and it won't let go.

—Humberto Cappas

The Haunting

Who's there, I call, as I'm awakened in my sleep,
It's dark and quiet, not even a peep;

I know you're there, I can feel your presence,
so speak I say, as my body grows tense;

My legs tremble as I fumble through the dark,
to try and find my dog with no bark;

the stairs squeak as I reach the bottom,
and my eyes squint as I try to spot him;

there's something out there I can feel it in the air,
I feel a breeze as it runs through my hair;

I want to scream, but instead I hide,
from what I fear is now inside;

something falls, my heart starts pumping,
my hands shaking, I reach for something;

I try to run but my legs will not move,
I'm screaming but there's no sound coming through;

Help me I say, and then awake,
to the sunlight beating down on my face.

—Debbie Chadwick

What's Happenin' To Our Young Black Folks?

What happenin' to our young black folks?
It's definitely ain't no joke. Drugs and crimes
controlling 'em and it's takin' 'em out on a limb.
It's a cryin' shame. Because it's tellin' 'em this
Is the way to reach stardom and fame. What's happenin' to
our young black folks? I wish I had a clue, as to
what we must do to get back on track. Because I stress
if we don't, it show we have no pride about ourself.
And that's a well known fact.

—Evelyn "Sugar" Gregory

College vs. High School

I know that we have to go our separate ways,
It's just I don't know what to do or say.
I love you so much and I don't want to let you go,
and I've tried so hard to let you know.
We will still be together just farther away,
And in my mind I'll always want you to stay.
Two years in college is not that long,
and I hope in time that we will still be strong.
I will never forget you,
and find someone new.
Even though we will be farther apart,
You will still have a place in my heart.
When college is over and school is out,
You won't see me upset or in a pout.
If we're able to get through these next
years together,
hopefully we will be able to last forever.

—Julie Herzog

The Cry Of Three

Sandpiper's flight descends on reef:
Its lonely cries like disbelief ...

'What traced in sand, then washed away;
So quickly gone, what did it say?'

Illusions shadowed by device;
Drunken mumbles, bells of ice.

Pushing, pushing as life tires;
Yoked uneven, our desires.

The sand, the sea; sandpiper, - three
Together cry 'it's me, it's me!'

And, 'leave us not without a note,
Else, 'here lies who?' unnamed by quote!'

Did you see who passed by here,
Or was it late, perhaps, last year?

Swirling, falling all the while,
Never gathered in a pile ...

'What traced in sand, then washed away;
So quickly gone, what did it say?'

—Carl J. McKelvey

Gorgeous Flower

A gorgeous flower I did see growing up above the window sell,
Its lovely petals seemed to sing as the wind blew them away
from me. That gorgeous flower some how reminded me of life
and how fragile life can be. It was so perfect then within
a moment it was not there, Its petals had blown away and
there it stood bear and just a stem of green, no more flower
just a seed, left for it to return again when fall comes
around once more.

Gorgeous flower back again more gorgeous then before, the
wind did blow again but your petals stood still as the wind
blew you once more, but your much stronger no more helpless to
the wind oh, gorgeous flower standing tall you stayed much
longer then before, but your gone once more, your not gone
forever, just sleeping, I know your still there, waiting to come
back more gorgeous then before. Gorgeous flower buried down
deep within the ground you'll keep coming up as long as you
stay strong...

—Gloria R. A. Balogh

Fall

The light is different in the fall
It's not like summer's light at all
The inside of a pearly shell
Describes the fall's light very well.

The color changes in the trees,
And later on, they drop their leaves.
The marigolds are gold, and small,
And have the very scent of fall.

Yes, fall is like a golden dream,
And lake and valley, field and stream
Are all suffused with yellow lights
And then descends the winter white.
—*Alice Lincoln Woodruff*

Happiness

Happiness is not composed of things.
It's not something to be bought or sold,
but it's something that each of us brings;
the way that our stories are told.
I may write it, while someone else sings
in a voice that is so clear and bold.
It's not something just belonging to kings.
If it were, then I'd tell you to fold.

Happiness is all a state of mind.
It's not something that comes and is gone.
Events and good times that you're hopin' to find
can happen, but then we move on.
Sometimes memories are hard to leave behind
but if we'll just keep rollin' along,
I don't think you'll find it to be such a bind.
I think you'll find it to be a new song.
—*Gerald L. Miller*

Untitled

Everyone knows I am different
It's special to be this way
at least...
That's what they say.

...Sometimes...

I feel so young and all alone
they tell their stories, meanwhile, I'm the quiet one
They say it's good to be this way
should I keep it, until my wedding day.

...Other times...

I want to go out
and do it, get it done
so I will no longer
be the quiet one.

...It hurts...

Sometimes as you will see, people make fun of me.
They do it in humor, not meaning to cause pain
Don't they understand?, to me it's not a game!
Guys—or so called men, say it is no big deal, they say it
doesn't matter
You know what? That's really not how they feel.

...Someday...

I hope I will be the one, able to say, no I'm not a virgin.
—*Jennifer Mueller*

Born For Baseball

Welcome to tonight's game at the Metrodome.
It's the place the Minnesota Twins call home.
And a place where the fans come to let off some steam.
After a hard day at work, many come to see our team.

Now we all have a favorite player, and mine should be of no
surprise.
An excellent team player, he is #1 in my eyes.
After all, he won The Rookie of the Year award in 1991.
Proving to himself, and also to his teammates that it could be
done.

He plays second base with everything he's got.
And at the plate he's no different, his bat is blazing hot.
And as he's leading off of base, you'd better be alert.
Cause he's always willing to steal, while sliding in the dirt.

He was meant to play baseball, of that there is no doubt.
Now do you know who I am talking about?
Just look for #11, he is always on the run.
Whether batting or fielding, he will get the job done.

Do you give up yet? I will give you one last clue.
I have heard that he was "Born for Baseball" and I believe it's
true.
For as long as he stays healthy and productive in the game.
Surely, Edward Charles Knoblauch, will make Baseball's Hall of
Fame.
—*Jamie Likes*

The Virus—AIDS

Here I come again so you better watch out,
Its your partner, your friend, your acquaintance
you have to ask about.
I was injected into you out of love — so you thought.
But you were so naive you didn't see, and that another
life I just bought;
Now a little boy around the age of nine met in the woods
one day, when he came upon a needle and decided to play.
Also a woman about the age of 35, who needed some blood to
survive. But I snuck in again and not even the blood could
keep her alive.
So you see I'm the one your mother warned you about,
Or did she?
Maybe if momma had told you this isn't the way it would be.
But its too late anyway nobody can go back into time,
And the prisoners like you who didn't know I'll still
be able to claim mine.
—*Amy Linsalata*

The Astronauts

The lords of earth are spinning avenues
in the solar mother's vast vacuum.
Out of the web, spidery spacemen sling
their gossamer threads at footless anchorings,
bridging dark and light dreams to be assembled
bit by bit in sterile, silent berthings.

The silver-suited cadre bobs about
With torch and wrench bolting beams together
into glinting nests where firesome birds will roost
Ere winging starward,
While the twin-horned moon, aghast,
ogles at the astronauts at work.
—*Carmichael Strange*

Where Are You Going?

Where are you going
I've already been there
With the slavery and lynching
And the K.K.K. everywhere.

Where are you going?
I've already been there
With the drug dealers and child killings
It's one horrible nightmare.

Where are you going?
I've already been there
No respect for our elders
Who live in constant fear.

Where are you going?
I've already been there.
Living in the projects
With a feeling of deep despair

Where are you going?
I've already been there.
I hope the situation will get better
If people take interest and show that they care.

—*Burnardine Flanagan*

And Mom Became Mother

Just what is a mother, supposed to be?
I've asked this question, quite ardently.
Of myself, and of others, of all, I do ask.
Yet, finding the answer, a most difficult task.

Mothers do have faults, they're not an exception.
Of course! they are human, we admit through a sigh.
Still knowing this fact, our Mom, should be perfect.
As near to perfection, as God's Angels on high.

We need our Mom close, for her loving support.
Though giving her understanding, we tend to fall short.
Seems we ask more of Mom, then we're willing to give.
Let her voice an opinion, we retort, our lives we will live.

Oh! then let us face problems, or run into a snare.
Our Mom should drop every-thing, just to be there.
As adults, we're still child-like, if supporting such dreams.
Emotions must grow-up too, and accept life's change of scenes.

We must quit our searching, for a Mom, so close to perfection.
And when faced with her faults, don't hold tight to rejection.
With respect and acceptance, this new relationship will grow.
And Mom became Mother, for there comes the time, to let Mommy go.

—*Gloria P. McMurry*

Nowhere With Nothing

I've been everywhere and seen nothing at all
I've been nowhere and seen every time they fall
I've looked into the eyes that cry and never shed a tear
I've dreamt inside a heart of gold that would never let me near
My life is so completely full yet I have nothing real
I'm going nowhere, have nothing to prove, and never do I feel
My nights are full without someone who says so many things
and days are screaming silently without promises to bring
My world is dull with shining eyes of beautiful misery
How do I love, when love is hate and no one's eyes can see?

—*Amanda Ramsey*

Waiting

I'm dry bones on a beachhead
I've felt no dredge, foot, or human spit
Not once in all these wasted years.
I'm a No-No in Never-Never Land.
Such patriotic exuberance that day
Gun butt heavy at my youthful shoulder
Helmet branch a-swishing at my sweaty brow
Wouldst the Creator given me a circle of eyes
Knowing my mission here—now in the shadow—
Am I to be the raven-picked voiceless one?
Lord, stifle not my thought of victorious summit heights
Now the stabbing, wailing, human degradation at the lowest
Sgt. Evermore—U.S. Marines—they read
I knew then, my tears would never flow again.
My Soul cries out—who will relegate this voiceless one
Who has so much to say
Will not the lion tend the lamb
Before God's Mighty Day
Soul Brothers-all-waiting for the dawn of peace
Waiting for our advocate—will there ever be?

—*Delphine Draxton*

Lightning

Blazing bolt, let your energy thrust down;
Jolting, searing, scorching the ground.
Rip thru the sky, your force so unyielding;
In spasms of power; white mountains yet building.
Rending the air with your static charge.
Sabering the night, some forked and some large.
Expel all your fury in a moments quick passage.
While I gaze in awe, from my high-placed advantage,
And share in the rapture your celestial power.
Feeling a part of that magic—
  In my high, lonely tower.

—*Craig Lancaster*

The Sounds In The Distance

I hear the sounds of people shouting and singing. I hear the joy bells ringing. Beat the drums, blow the trumpets. Come let us make merriment and glee. Praise! God Almighty we are free.

I can hear the demons screaming, see the millions flee. I hear the people singing, Praise! God Almighty, we have won the Victory.

The mountains have fallen, there is no more sea.
The New Jerusalem has come down for eternity.

The lame are walking, the dumb are talking. The blind eyes can see. The weak will be strong, the wicked will perish for their wrong. God's children are singing a new song.

I hear a voice from heaven, a trumpet sounds. Thrust in the sickle, it is time for the harvest to be bound.

A voice sounds from heaven saying behold the tabernacle of God will dwell with men. You will live in a new world without sorrow, death, or sin.

I hear the sounds in the distance as they make merriment and sing. Glory to God in the Highest, we will reign forever with Jesus Christ, our Lord, and King.

—*Dorothy Johnson Jones*

To Share The Moment!

Joy, however written is forever!
Joy interprets one's emotion and passion!

The mid-morning sky is a clear
translucent blue, that portends the arrival
of winter - but, it is not
yet cold.

A relentless wind blows upon my face.
It is magical and triggers compassion
from another time and place
- now gone forever.

It brings with it memories of a friend's
smile, my cherished old rag doll,
and most of all a little girl
all grown up now.
—Helen Trouton Golightly

Just Appearing

How often you come to mind,
　Just appearing
　　As the evening breeze
　　　Softly sweeps past my face,
　　　And is gone.

Or, like the sea, crashing
　To the shore,
　　You rush to mind,
　　　And once kissed,
　　　Ebb silently from the sands of thought.

And like the wisher's star,
　Afire though afar,
　　Seems closer with each glance,
　　　And, like your hand once to touched
　　　The feeling ever present on my mind.

How often you have gone,
　Aloof, like the cold of night,
　　Until slivers of dawning sun,
　　　Come, just appearing
　　　Through the shadows of unchanging love
—Herbert T. Smith

Our Youth Today Adults For Tomorrow

I know you feel that things don't always go your way,
Just do your best and hang in there anyway.
Above all stay in school, get your diploma and a good education,
Because a few years down the road some of you will have to
　lead this great nation.
Stay away from drugs, gangs and a life of crime,
There is only one thing this can get you and that is a lot of jail
　time.
There are only one thing drugs are good for of which,
Is only to make the drug dealers rich.
I certainly hope this message for you is quite clear,
For as our youth today we want you to know we hold you all
　very dear.
—Eldon L. Stolzenburg

The Easy Way

This life we have is ours to use
Just figure out the trails to choose
The easy way's not always best
You can miss friends and opportunities
Put yourself to the test.
If we have to work for what we get
We appreciate, much more, and yet
Most people would choose the easy way
No work of all, just romp and play.
But, God says by the sweat of your brow."
No matter how hard, you'll get through is somehow,
Keep him as your friend, your troubles tell.
You'll come out on top, therefore, live your life well.
Then in the end, how proud you'll be
You worked your way through.
The trail you chose was easy, you see.
—Betty Bratsky

A Moment In Time

A moment in time, of above I ask.
Just give me one moment, one from the past.

"A moment," He said, "Is never returned.
You receive them just once." This I have learned.

I beg of you please! I ask only for one!
If you give back this moment, I will get back my son.

"That moment" He said, "Was tragic indeed,
but a moment in time I cannot return to thee."

"Each moment is precious, some tragic it's true.
Remember the moments so special to you."

"The moment of birth, a first word, a first step.
These are moments in time also kept."

"Moments of laughter, of smiles, and of love.
These are special moments, given by me from above."

"Remember these moments I have given to you.
Remember them all, so precious, so few."

"One moment in time is all that you ask.
I'm sorry, my son, but that moment has passed."

"But I give you the memories and the will to survive.
It's up to you to keep special moments alive."

"Make each moment special. Never wish one way.
Each moment is special in it's own special way."

One moment in time is all that I asked.
God would not give it. He said it had passed.

Hard lessons to learn, I cried to above.
Lessons about time, about memories, about love.
—Don Olesen

Life

Life is like a poem
It has a beginning and an end
In poems you find rhymes
In life you hear chimes
Life is sometimes confusing
and we the people must understand
poems are like that too
So you see
In a new poem you find a new challenge
and in life there's always
something new.
—Cynthia Saint Felix

Turn Your Mind Toward Jesus

As you're sitting and you're thinking
Just how rough your life has been
Then you think about your headaches
And illnesses suffered now and then

Then you pause and start to wonder
Just why your Journey is so hard
While others seem to glide along
As if each step is a reward

In your mind is a constant question
Why are you suffering so much grief
But you wonder if you're being tested
Til God grant you his sweet relief

Surely he knows about your troubles
And also knows what tomorrow will bring
For he's the conductor of all action
Since he's the composer of everything

So just turn your mind toward Jesus
For he has promised to always be
Close beside you during your sojourn
Now and throughout eternity
—*Bennie Townsend, Jr.*

Colors

Colors are the greatest things
Just think of what you see
If everything was black and white
How dull this world would be

You wouldn't see the sun's bright light
Or the moons silvery glow
The twinkling stars above so high
You'd never ever know

The green, green grass the purple hills
Falls leaves of red and gold
The rainbow with its many hues
An eagle brave and bold

A peacocks stately tail
A blue bird on the wing
You really wouldn't get to see
So many pretty things

So next time that you do see
Some colors gay and bright
Remember what they'd look like
If they were black and white
—*Donna M. Long*

An Etheral Embrace

Oh how "The Talents" of others in their extensions
Keep alive, the spark of "hope" in times
  of chaos and extreme tensions
Beautiful creational blessings, are felt
O'er miles time and space
The essence of pure Grace.
An "Etheral Embrace" to those beings
Who share their concerns and feelings.
The "Aura of Love" will protect their
  sensitive hearts
From caustic snares and thoughtless smarts
Enjoy, the Warmth therein
It is Precious -Precious -Precious
—*Dorothy E. Gaines*

Untitled

My thoughts, the paths for which I walk
Keep my feet worn bare of soles.
  I cling to times of peace on earth
As they shoot me full of holes.
  My streets don't end and I can't pretend
That I'm fond of where I am.
  I think of rhymes at early times
Of green eggs and ham.
  We all grow old and we all are told
Of the evil that comes with age.
  But evil don't tell us as it shells us
With all the hatred and the rage.
  So the time is now that we must bow
And make amends to all.
  But, before we go, we all must know
How to walk before we crawl.
—*Edward Hedrick*

Harley's Prayer

Oh Lord my Father in Paradise,
Keep my spirit clean and nice.
Let me lie to not one man,
for lies are like pollution upon this land.
Keep me from temptation, because my flesh is weak,
Lift up my heart and let righteousness be it that I seek
Protect me oh Lord, I pray for your love,
Keep me from harm like you do the Angels above.
I pray to you Father, for your mercy and grace,
Abandoned me not, but prepare for me an eternal place.
I beg for your forgiveness in the name of Christ,
for he bore my sins and paid the price.
—*Harley Campbell, Jr.*

Only If I Could

If I could, I'd hold you from the fears of the night. I'd keep you in my dreams. I'd love you eternally, and I'd never let you go, only if I could.

If I could, I'd hold you in my arms forever. I'd fight to make you mine. I'd do anything for you, only if I could.

If I could, I'd sail half way 'round the world to find you. I'd walk across the rays of the sun. I'd chisel your name in a mountain side, only if I could.

If I could, I'd swim across the Sea of Darkness. I'd catch every star I saw. I'd jump over the moon to show my love for you, only if I could.

If I could, I'd paint your picture across the sky. I'd tie a ribbon around my heart to show I was yours. I'd be the one you love and trust, only if I could. I only wish I could.
—*Becki Lynne Andrewski*

Prayer To The Great Spirit

You who rule the land and waters
Keeper of the herds and fishes
Protector of all men and creatures
Hear us when we call upon you.

Oh, Great spirit look with favor
Guard and guide us on our journey
For our spirits lift we skyward
Following in your heaven bound footsteps.
—*Jacqueline L. Childs*

Care Seeds

Lord, help me plant a seed of
kindness,
Show a little of God's love;
For, we're all needful children
Of the blessed Father above.

Just one little seed of kindness,
Could flower into love;
To make this world a little brighter,
And make the heart soar like a dove.

The human heart is lonely,
And needs concern to make it sing;
If only this we would remember,
Much needed happy music,
We could constantly bring.

Someone's burden and cares
Might be easier to bear,
If we'd all just remember,
To one another's burdens share.
Some people don't care; Sad, but
true;
But to me,...tis just as criminal,
Not to show we care, when we
really do!!

—*Helenjean Hays Speights*

Glistening Beauty

White and shining I see the moon
kissing the bough of the pine
in this most beauteous season
of wintertime.
It's almost like the kiss of a lover
on the lips of the one he loves -
so intimate and alive with a
glistening beauty.
See the shaft of moonlight as it
kisses the bough of the pine
in this most beauteous season
of wintertime.
Listen to the silent beauty as
their hearts entwine!
Look at the glistening beauty
of the moon and the pine
in this most beauteous season
of wintertime!

—*Elizabeth J. Frye*

My Love

My love for you is like a rose,
It grows from day to day.
You mean so much to me my dear,
In all so many ways.
Your eyes are like the stars at night,
that show me the way.
Your smile is like the sunlight,
That brightens up my day.
Your lips are like a blooming rose,
Waiting to be kissed.
All these things I say to you,
Are all the things I miss.

—*Gustave Walters*

The Last Flight

Last night you came again
knocking, knocking at my door.
I answered to darkness,
darkness once more.

The shadow calls again —
voices echoing beneath the deep blackened pit.
We fly once more my shadow and me.
I know now—twas when I was a child,
there was so much darkness that frightened me so.
I pushed you away never knowing who you were.
So alone, and nowhere to go.
But now you've returned again and again,
and I fear you not, because you are my friend.

The stages of life that we have passed,
have all come alive like a snake in the grass.
It slithers upon you all slippery and sleek,
and betwixes a gaze through the phase we defeat.

The shadow will corner the past to your door
knocking, and knocking forever and more.
Oh shadow my shadow come fly with me,
from the floor to the door and over the sea.

—*Cindy L. Auman*

Jack And John Two Living In One

Known to many as both
Known to all others only as one
One more serious, the other more fun
Some places someone calls the other,
We both look but they're talking to another
Kind of makes me wonder,
Which is liked best?
Is there any way to test?
Sometimes someone thinks the other is my brother
My answer makes them wonder, is there another?
Could he really be his brother?
Imagine the thunder if I did ever meet my other.
What if it ever happened, I wonder?
Which one would be strong enough
To control the thunder?

—*John G. Wharton*

Night Shadows

In haunted dream, I walk unpeopled
lands, their silent streets.
Who passed before? what shadow to
entreat?
Where shall I travel in night of
sleep?

Coloured variants fade at dawn,
Shall I fear what cannot be seen.
before,
Canyon'd wall in distant, drawn.

These nights of dreams, to memories
past, beyond my time.
Awake!, awake! ere I fall.

Held now in arms, I must recall.
Who are the shadow'd ones that I
meet? where do they go?
Who knows? but it is they, I often
greet.

—*Donald D. Gardner*

Northern Spring

Spring bursts and burgeons as snowdrops pop through
   last layers of white, and crocuses march yellow and purple,
     close to protective houses.
Forsythia, quince, flowering plum and crab trees radiate sprays
   of yellow, pink, white, rose, and fuschia against bluing
     skies.

The grass begins its resurgence,
   inspiring the sharpening of mower blades
     and reconditioning of engines,
Whose petroleum emissions and cacophonous voices
   will soon blight our senses.

Spring rains bring flooding and nurturing moisture —
   and draw angleworms out onto sidewalks
     where they exude musty, wormy odor.

Assured of Spring's timely arrival, eager robins return,
Digging for food — sometimes through
   late blankets of surprise snow and unyielding asphalt.

Trees bud and leaf — a soft, bright greening,
   the beginnings of summer's delicious, cooling shade.
     —Carol Frances Rush

Poinsettias, God's Christmas Magic

Within the stable under the shining star
Lay Jesus in a manger with three Kings visiting from afar
There was a little boy with a White Flower all in bloom
All was very quiet as he began to enter the room
When he laid the Flower at the foot of Jesus' bed
The points of the Flower started to turn bright red
Everyone was amazed at this sight
Not understanding God's handy work that night
As the magic of God's blessing started to begin
The white of the Flower represented cleanliness from within
Turning the Flower all to bright red
Was showing them Jesus would save them all from sin
   —Barbara Jo Schuckmann

In More Peaceful Times

   I seem to recall before ambition came,
lazing on afternoon meadows beneath skies once blue and clear;
   or chatting on some friendly porch, smoking pipe in hand,
   Once in more peaceful times that were.

   Of bonfires, sea shells and windswept beach,
hand in hand walks with a woman true;
   of family unity around a glittering Christmas tree,
   Once in more peaceful times that were.

   I seem to recall when honesty was but a spoken word,
the shrill morning song of some tiny bird;
   of serenity before ambition came;
   Once in more peaceful times that were.

   Now that ambition has come and gone,
youth is but only a jaded dream;
   and I wish for life's simples joys that once were ours
   Once in more peaceful times that were.
     —Brett W. Bartholomaus

Arrows

It was early October, that the arrow of love was ripped from my heart,
Leaving a distorted illusion of the happiness that love brings.
I lay dying in a pool of frigid sorrow, remembering the brightness
of that love remembering the gleam, the sparkle, the moments
in which
Had been my heavenly shadow;
I had gasp my last breath, when father time gently restored my life
Like the slow blooming flower on a warm spring day,
Birds in song flocked around me, lifting my tattered spirit high into
The heavens releasing me into the warm rays of the sun.
I was then cradled like a child in the arms Venus, like a soft
Tender kiss she whispered into my heart
And once more I am free and happy in this world that can be so
Unhappy...
   —Bythford C. Smalls

Ahab And Jezebel

The ancient atriums of Ahab, unhallowed halls of hatred,
lie buried in the hot oppressive desert sands.
God forgotten, golden calves begotten
this son of Omei bowed his knee to Baal,
cowed by his lust he fell under the spell
of Jezebel the Queen of Hell.
Painted and primed with plastic smile,
filled with guile, she sat on Jereboam's throne
but sighed at the sizzling thighs of Moloch.
Together these specters wander and weep
for horror can never sleep.
Memory is their fate while they wail and walk and wait
for God's final judgement of their deeds
of greed, idolatry and carnage.
Their sins, like howling hydra-headed monsters,
devour death day-by-day until they stand
hand-in-hand before Jehovah and damnation falls
and thralls them with their hatred.
No more waiting, no expressing of desire
only cursing, accusing and eternal fire.
   —Edwin B. Fountain

White Ash

Once, I received tobacco for my pipe.
Life began, a good light was given,
I began living.
The coal was radiant and warm.
From it, I drew pleasure,
often and regular.
And inevitably, later, the coal died.
Slumped in sorrow, I silently cried

Despairing, sighing, I drifted back to my beginning,
and suddenly lifted up strong,
remembering how I began...and gave,
knowing it was good, giving until my heart was full,
feeling more whole, though only partially so.
And then, a spirit appeared and gave new light,
strange and bright, for my dark wooden bowl.
The coal, now warm and radiant, the sky!
The earth! And all the living, with color, splendor!
Brilliant candor

This tobacco gift I will love...and love
and love, until the last becomes white ash
   —Dale J. Sprague

Song Of Valiant Spirits

In early pearl-dewed hours before dawn's coral rays,
Life offers sane solutions to benefit our ways:

Though weary soldiers die in wars
  and vital problems plague our land,
our ingrained courage seldom wanes,
  for Hope rewards our stalwart stand.

Though jobless young men look for work
  while single mothers seek relief,
and aged souls walk painfully,
  still, prayers are answered with belief.

Great music, poetry and art —
help lift our spirits thankfully
  and forge our future bright again.

  Thus:

Molten sunrise sparks ideas,
  Challenges for fresh beginnings.
    Morning's energy increases,
      reaps consistent daily winnings.

—*Charlotte Riepe*

Time's Tides

Sleeping, milk-filled, on silken breast
Life's tides, undreamt, unknown
Daddy's finger clasped with minute hand
Security against the sleeping tide

Crawling, standing, walking all alone
With daddy's help he knew the thrills
Daddy's hand his rampart still
Against the rising tide

From primered-hand to capped-head
Learning, learning of life's tide
Now down-chinned, he stands
Eager, in challenge of the risen tide

From yearning, he fell to love
And stood beside a white-gowned bride
His chosen made a stalwart help
To stem, defy, overcome the roaring tide

Now, white-capped they rest
Life's tides a distant dream
Of life's storms surmounted
Hands clasped, they view the ebbing tide

—*Frederick I. Schofield*

The Wind's Web

A wind blows through the night,
  like a bat in its flight.
Its soft breath leaving a fine mist
  at some points its gentle and
  caressing and at others it shakes
  its might fists.
It connects with every thing, every being,
  every apparition in the shadows.
It's like the depths of my soul it surrounds my
  heart and my lungs, breathing life into
  my being.
It's now blowing a soft breath and is rattling
  against my bones.
I stand alone in my endeavors hoping the
  night I long for will become one of my
  treasures.
The wind's breath is always weaving its web.
My soul envies the wind's web, for its always
  free and everlasting.

—*Heather Muth*

Gettysburg National Cemetery

Why does the wind blowing here disturb me so,
Like a host of souls in anguish, crying for peace
To angry world? But the world keeps turning away.
After all, it is only the wind, not a voice from the grave
  crying, "Cease,"
"Cease, my brothers, to hate your fellow men,"
And the wind has been blowing ever since time began.

Why do I feel that the pain was much greater here,
When battles still rage, and there have been wars before?
Here, brother and friend turned into foe in an instant's time,
Creating a pain greater far than the wounds of war.
But the world doesn't bother with troubled thoughts like these.
The wind has always blown through the maple trees.

Why do I walk as though treading on hallowed ground,
Softly, in fear that my steps might disturb their sleep?
Wake them to hear the cruel sound of war again,
The rifle, the cannon, the soft sounds of women who weep,
And the whispered prayers, "Forgive us for we have sinned,"
But the world doesn't hear. It's used to the sound of the wind

—*Angeline Maine*

The Rainbow

When the storms of life overwhelms me
Like a ship I'm tossed about
Like a ship without a captain
I begin to worry and doubt.

I'm tossed by the raging waters
I'm tossed by the waves and wind
Like a ship without an anchor
I long to find a friend.

I struggle to hold on to my faith
And do the best I can
To live in peace and harmony
And love my fellowman.

Suddenly, my ship becomes quiet
And my doubts begin to calm
I hear the voice of Jesus saying
Come to my outstretched arms.

Be not weary in well doing, my child
In all the good you can do
In all long-suffering and patience
There's a rainbow waiting for you.

—*Hattie Martin*

Wild Whispers

My fingers pass through her silken hair
  Like an obsessed weaver of dark desires
Parting strands of a chestnut waterfall tress
  Displaying a Canova visage blessed
I rush to savor this truth confessed
  Her breath beholds this secret scent
Delicate faint flowers that now unfold
  Lips of probing petals soft but bold
Pressed full force against passion's gate
  Kisses that have surely sealed my fate
Warm designs patterned across a slender throat
  Brief angel secrets of tender notes
Unleashed pants that lock this embrace
  Heedlessly I succumb to pleasure's haste
Waiting to accept her sweet sung sting
  My pleas to Venus's ears shall ring
Hoping she will hear this man's crescendo cry
  Without a trace of doleful tears or fears
Only the whispered hush of a lover's sigh

—*Davan J. Dodrill*

Redwood Majesty

The timbered mountains pierce the azure sky
Like bosom buddies of nature to defy
The beauty of existence of great renown
Wearing billowy clouds upon their heads as crowns.

Majesty profoundly expressed in each silent tree
Enchants the soul in harmonious dignity
In vastness of terrains' unending crest
These citadels of time immortal blest

The world as stately markers, history told
Challenging life in creative beauty as they unfold.

Unrelenting earthly storms of nature condemn
But cannot conqueror these giants, nor stem
Their growth, in centuries of strength and worth
For God blesses their endurance with noble birth.
—*Gladys Taft Johnson*

A Poem Is Born

Is there some verse within me waiting to be born,
Like the first rays of golden sunlight on a frosty morn?

Can words gush forth to form exciting metered rhyme,
And like a golden sunrise be forever on my mind?

I hear a poem that's calling and longing to be free,
Demanding my caresses like the sun that's bathing me.

The pen moves deftly onward as the words I swiftly write,
Before they're lost forever, like the sun gone down at night.

At last the work is finished, a masterpiece to treasure.
And like the sun in heaven, its depth I cannot measure.
—*Jack A. Wallace*

The Little Things

It's the little things that will count the most today,
Like the smiles you give away.
(You'll never run out because it's true
Someone will give them back to you.)
Stopping to give a hug so tight,
Can make another's day more bright,
And did you ever stop to think
How fast a child responds to a simple wink?
Or a waved "Hi!"
As you pass by?
Oh, the little things do so much good
But we don't always share as we should.
God gives us chances each passing day
To lift our spirits and find reasons to pray,
But we are so busy with what each day brings
That we overlook the most rewarding little things.
—*Eulaliah T. Hooper*

Quiet Heart

In the quiet of my heart, in its own secret space,
Lie dreams never lived and passion never faced.
In the hope of each tomorrow, as I go about my day,
Lies the wish that I will see you, that you'll come along my way.
So once more we'll be together in the sunshine or the rain.
Able to face "whatever," through the laughter or the pain.
In the quiet of my heart, in it's own secret space.
Lie the memories of you and the vision of your face.
—*Dawn Welch*

Ritual

Unobserved shadows
   linger upon silken dreams
of demented heroism.
   Incendiary passions
  cause torches to light in passion.
    Bodies dance in undulated rhythm
 caressed by the dark winds
  Ancient faces stare into the warmth
   of youth
    so devastatingly sensuous
  Long cascading waves of dark tresses
   awakens sleepy eyes
  Monotonous beats claim
satirical chants into mindless mumblings
   circles of black magic
    form within the velvet burgundy air
as
  Potent potions swirl into an oblivion of
    constricting throats.
—*Ghazzal Dabiri*

Look At Me

I love the way you move your
lips as you think
I think that I need you more and more
then what I've ever needed you before
Before I die I have to say...
I love your walk your talk and your smile
But I feel constricted as I try to say it
so I change the subject and begin to walk
As I pace the room with that mortal
thought and as you lie there in the bed
I hear the heart monitor stop...
So I say it knowing its to late
but I say it anyway even as they pull
the sheet over your face and slowly begin
to walk away I love you
—*Darrell Lundin*

Kenny G

    Warm, moist
   Lips touching lips
   Strong, tender
Hands caressing shoulder—caressing thigh
   Movement, so fluid
    So rhythmic
  As bodies sway in time
   The pulse
   The feeling
   The song
  Over and over
  In our heads
  Through our hands
  In our hearts
  Lost in you
  In pure tones
 Sweet notes that melt
   And we melt
   into one
—*Charlyne McGraw*

Horns Of Plenty

Rain on the Plain
Liquid treats for thirsty survivors.
Extremities coiled around a horn, not raised
in adulation but prophecy.
Eroding death in the dessert, upon the earth's
crust and below.
Treasures of excavation, precivilization.
Shadows of behemoths, no longer cast.
Horns of plenty, of blood, of triceratops.
Impaled in time, in cavities, in tyrannosaurus rex.
Thirsty survivors, harvesting immortality.
Fossilized godlings being godeviled to a new grave.
—*James Lore*

Release Me

I just got a letter from Hank today
Listen; I'll tell you what he had to say:
He reminded me 'twas four months ago
It's time you dry your tears, let me go.
We enjoyed life on earth for many years
You can't call me back by shedding tears
God was with me as I crossed the divide
We walked hand in hand-side by side
Now don't you think of me as dead
Let me enjoy the wonders God has prepared
As I was led to the Heavenly Throne
Well done, Hank, Welcome Home
—*Alpha Arme Peterson*

The Robin

Prancing, dancing, the robin hops about,
Listening for worm beneath foot.
With her built-in receiver,
She is quite the retriever.
—*Dick Finn*

On The Prairie

On the prairie in the sunshine
Little Sioux Boy, picking flowers;
Dreaming dreams about the woodland
Of the antelope and coyote,
Of the gentle winds and showers.

On the prairie in the twilight
Little Sioux girl sings of sorrow;
Dreaming dreams about a warrior
Fallen in his line of duty;
Wonders of her own tomorrow.

On the prairie in the future
Bride and groom stand in the heather,
Dreaming dreams about a family;
Of the children they will parent;
Of their love-life now together.

On the prairie years to follow
Little Sioux sibs play and wonder;
Dreaming dreams about their childhood;
While their parents watching gently
Reminisce, and smile, and ponder.
—*Irene Bakker*

To Just Say No To Drugs, You Must Say Yes To Life!

How to say yes to life when the world don't give you room to live?
You Create The Room!!!
How to say yes to life when You Have No Conscious Of How to
Live? You must have a monstrous desire to Be! Once this
desire has been awaken, You will experience a whole new
Revelation!

How do you say yes to life when you finally come to be and
there is no light. You get on your knees and pray that the
Holy Trinity: Father, Son, and Holy Ghost will enter you. From
then on A Light will shine and the rest will Depend On You!!!

Now that the Light of God has entered me, How do I rid myself of
all the fears that have enslaved me over all the years???

Have enough Faith In Yourself, to believe you have All The
Powers Within You To Do Whatever Necessary, to give you the
strength to Live Freely In This World that God Has Made For You!!
So to just say no to drugs you must say yes to life!!!
—*Celestine J. Custer*

Graven Years

Prolonged like inherits insanity.
Living an unknown life of dead heartbeats.
Pumping blood to a vacant moribund brain.
 -Cruel Life -
Looking in a mirror and seeing the reflection of
 a stranger.
There must be a better way.
To leave this life through haziness and
 scrambled days.
Leave your loved ones, once and for all.
Than to catch glimpse of them that is
 dark and dull.
O' the sorrow I feel for their unknown pain.
To live a normal life and break their back.
And then in their last years go insane.
—*Douglas Alan Karaszewski*

Life

Living the life is sometimes easy
Living the life is sometimes hard
Living the life is really simple, not complex
As it is, because life is living and living the life
As it is, or were, is very special, very precious to us all.
So enjoy the living of life while time is on your side.
—*Arthur Guy Cornish Jr.Poetry's*

El Rosario

Tia Maria Luisa, what are you praying?
"Lolo, I am praying El Rosario to the blessed mother,"
Tia Maria Luisa, why are you praying?
"Lolo, this is between God and me.

Tia Maria Luisa, are you afraid?
"Lolo, no I am not afraid, because El Rosario is my serenity
"Lolo, my browns eyes, do not have tears from you,

"Lolo, you are good"
Tia Maria Luisa you are more good than me,
"Lolo, we are both good"
"Lolo, I will pray from heaven, and do not cry for me."
"Lolo, when you feel sad and have anxieties
"Pray El Rosario, and it will help you, and
Remember I am your beloved Tia Maria Luisa!
 Amen.
—*Dolores Maria Bolivar Brauet*

Master Spirit

In this tenantless heritage
long made juiceless by truant nurturing
who will cause our seedlings to flower
In this dry and dusty time
who will till the hardened souls
of transplanted vines.
Alien soil does not give reason
to puny and parched creepers
Who will be the plowmen
in days to come
For gentle harrowing makes ready for planting
Seasonable mulching cultivated by prudent
gardeners strengthens roots
Purposeful pruning brings forth lush
and fragrant blossoms
Who will be the Master Spirits
the vesselled mentors
from whom cascading pearls will quench the
thirst of perennials yet to bloom
—*Janis J. Dickerson*

Ode To A Downhill...Er...Skier???

'Twas there at the top, he stood in the cold,
Looked over the brink, and thought, "Am I too old?"
  The dug in his poles, with sweat on his palms,
  And started downhill, for he had no qualms.

  His leg bones creaked like an old wooden slat,
And his skis threw up clouds of the wintery mat.
  Faster and faster, the slope he descended,
  A tree loomed ahead, would it be rear-ended?

But no, for his flabby old arms made their move,
And flailing, he missed, and was back in the groove.
  "Not bad," he thought, "for a man of my years."
  "I know I could challenge each one of my peers!"

It seemed for awhile, that he'd be at the bottom,
  But alas and alack, a snowhole just got him.
His ski backs turned skyward, and so did his nose,
  His body soon followed, increasing his woes.

  He buried himself in the welcoming white,
  His wind-blown ski-tips marking the site.
  Though help soon arrived, he had time to muse:
"I would have been smarter, if I'd taken a cruise!"
—*Douglas M. Walsh*

Evening Reflections

This evening I sat on my patio
  Looking and listening to the surf
As it crashed on the shore.
  It was dusk and the western sky
Was splashed with every shade of
  Red, orange and gold.
A few sandpipers on their
  long, spindly legs
Were still playing on the shore.
  Running out as the tide receded
Scurrying to shore when it returned.
  I thought of years long past
When I lived in the north country
  With the beautiful change of seasons.
Sometimes I miss that
  But not for long....
Icy roads...blizzards.
  The sky is now a somber grey.
The sandpipers have all gone away.
  And it is night.
—*Caroline Feder*

Desert Storm War

On a snowy sleepless night
Looking out my kitchen window
There was a wondrous sight to see
As the old hoot owl sang his song to me.
Shadows dancing in the snow. The moon shining all a-glow.
Gave life to the dark grotesque figures below.

Then my mind wondered to a foreign land.
Where our boys are fighting in the desert sand.
Their nights are filled with a different sight
from a missile as it shoots across the sky.
Shadows they see are planes overhead.
That carry the bombs that leave the dead.

I'm sure their hearts grow weary,
each time a plane takes to the sky.
But if they look to God He'll bring perfect peace
Soon he'll bid the bombs to cease.
If they remember God always walk beside them.
He's their Lord and dearest friends. That ever
Cross they carry God will lift the other end.
—*Bea Bon Durant*

Hope For Tomorrow

Hope, Is there any such thing in this world that we know?
Looking upon everyone's face as people go to and fro.
Broken homes, Heartaches, seems as if there's pain everywhere.
Asking within ourselves, Is there anyone who really cares?

The answer I knew not of for many long and trying years.
Searching for answers and looking to all my peers.
All that surrounds me was such hatred and strife.
Not ever realizing after Death there is Eternal Life.

Not a human on this earth could help in any way.
So I bowed my head in prayer, Please forgive my this day.
Never before such Peace and Joy had entered into my heart.
I now know the Risen Saviour and from Him I'll never depart.

This precious Saviour name Jesus, who I've come to love and
know. He has given me a Hope of a Heavenly Home to go.
Satan thought He won His battle by blinding me you see.
But the blood of Jesus Christ has given me total Victory.

The Holy Spirit Lives within my heart each and everyday.
For the answers of tomorrow are to bow your head today.
Don't flee this passing moment of salvation to depart.
Just start this new day over and ask Jesus into your Heart.
—*Barbara J. Terrell*

Winter Is Here

Everything is covered with new fallen snow,
Looks like a diamond field in the moon's glow.
There are no children playing,
A little red swing is swaying,
As a breeze goes past.
Winter is here at last!
Tomorrow, a snowman there will be,
To greet the people like you and me.
A warm fire is sparking and leaping,
On the hearth the cat is sleeping.
I snuggle deep into my chair,
Without a worry or a care.
—*Doris Clough*

Poetry's

the fond embrace of mind and heart,
locked fore'er in wedded intercourse.
—*Herman Eutic*

Aimless

Lost within the blue eternity filled white visions floating about
Lost within the green growth topped with color
Suddenly the blue eternity became brushed with orange
as the large glow sunk deep into the ground
all musicians refrained from sound
The deep endless pitch black melted over all forms of life
Especially mine — I became afraid

For better or worse seems such a promising phrase,
While blinded by all those colors
Lies and alibies were painted so well, even sealed
Within eight years the paint faded - love lost truth revealed

There I stood in the deep endless pitch black
Afraid, yet hiding so well from the beautiful offspring
Adhered to this creature that has no more thought than an insect
yet enough love to fill every wicked man's heart

A strong hand more gentle than my own came forth
I became lost within the blue eternity filled with white visions
   floating about
About lost within the green growth topped with color.

The strong hand encouraged me to stand alone with him in the deep
   endless pitch black
I did and I was not afraid—Afraid not was I and why?
Afraid not was I and why? Perhaps all those colors
   —*Cynthia Russell*

A Tribute To Gizmo

As all puppies are - he was beautiful and warm. A bundle of love and great joy Saddened to see within weeks of his birth Like a puppet on a string - his head bobbed all around He went backward instead of forward and appeared to be deaf. With unconditional love, massage and herbs, Gizmo progressed very quickly He was loving, unique and smart as a whip. Keeping in mind — We have lessons to learn, I realized Gizmo had come to teach. Several months later, came the start of strange actions I wondered — was Gizmo in pain. With a heavy heart and tears in my eyes, I asked God for a sign I needed to know — was it time to let Gizmo go I questioned myself — did I love him enough Or would I be selfish and keep him alive? God Answered with the blooming of an iris God gave me the strength and lifted my heart Now both - Gizmo and I have a new life We soar with eagles in the heavens — we are free Gizmo Gizmo, child of God — I thank you for sharing your life with me For the joy you brought — the wisdom you taught But most of all — I thank you for your love.
   —*Joanne Toth*

Our Precious Years

Life is given that we may share
Love and helpfulness and so prepare
To live more fully in a super sphere
Where truth is known and mysteries are clear
Where all our dearest dreams may find release
In an abundant flow of love and peace.
So whether glad and bright with joy,
Or touched with tears,
Let us treasure and make the most
Of our precious years.
   —*Gladys Mixon*

A Vision Of World Peace

In this trouble world of ours
Lurks a virus still unknown.
Dwells deep within existing souls
Waiting timely to unfold.

When revealed it's mind controlled,
Our actions direct it where to go.
Good and evil they're on their way
Spreading contagiously every day.

Evil virus leaves its mark everywhere it ventures.
Everywhere it ventures
Corruption, greed and hatred
Has time without dimensions.

Good virus has peace on its side,
With love and care for all mankind.
Fighting evil best it can
With abilities of virtuous man.

If scientists of noble prize
Creates a vaccine of knowledgeable size,
To destroy the evil within the soul
Before it commences to unfold,
Perhaps we'll achieve our peaceful goal.
   —*Josephine S. Luporini*

My Belly

   It seems I've been squashed
Made a little shorter thru the years
      With the result
   That my height settled in my belly

   Now my belly has found many uses
      I can rest my hands there
   When I need to be contemplative
   I can use it to bump other belly's

      It acts as a shelf
         Over my belt
   Keeping the rain off my boots
      But most of all

      It is something
   That adds to the laughter
         I have
      As I wander thru life
   —*Curt Kurtz*

Elegy for Gayla McGinnis

   The smile that could melt Antarctica; the liveliness that made the apathetic involved in a cause.
   Cheerful, light conversation and perpetually hopeful spirit is with us mo more. She was and will be a continual joy to remember.
   There was a time in human history when holy men debated whether or not women could claim to have souls. I know completely within my heart she had it and that it was open to all. Petals of the lotus flower were here and now are cut down.
   An ex-psychotic, meeting her and knowing her uplifted my being in the darkest times of mood swings that threatened to render me useless.
   She never wanted me to know that she had passed on. Gone is a kind, gracious woman.
   —*Carl Cassner*

A Morning Prayer

Let me start each day with a smile
Make me so thoughtful not to hurt others.
Let me not utter idle words in vain.
Lord forgive me if I have caused any pain.
Make each day a happy one
Let it be filled with hope
Help me not to be hard or cold
Help me to know; help me Lord to know!
Forgive me for the sins I've committed.
For all the hurt and pain I've caused.
Forgive me for the years I've wasted.
And for all the people I've lost and loved.
Lord help me give others the love
Thou hast given me!
The joy, and hope for all mankind;
Good Lord help me "please; please help me!"
—*Freddie Mae Johnson*

The Storm

Listening to the storm outside,
Makes me think of my storm inside.
In my heart and mind; my body and soul.
I see the rain falling from my eyes,
Feel the lightning flash thru my heart.
I hear the wind blowing thru the trees,
Like your voice blowing in my soul.
My body left alone, to wither and die,
Like the leaves blown from the trees.
The pain in my heart,
Must be what the tree feels when losing its branches.
A part of my life is gone, never to be replaced by another.
And when the storm is over,
The grass, flowers and even the trees flourish from the rain.
But my tears do nothing to soothe my pain.
My storm just keeps raging, my mind going insane.
—*Elaine Jones*

The Pencil

A tool for the mind
Manipulated through the hands
Held and massaged gently
As it leaves thoughtful trails behind.
Sometimes it must be sharpened
Its point made more pronounced.
Sometimes there are mistakes
And erasers make the marks extinct.
A pencil can lead a sorry life
Shrinking away in scribbles.
A pencil can be a powerful voice
Writing words to which we work.
The age of a pencil is sometimes great
Often small
Depending on its use.
And as the mind behind the pencil
Its errors long out live it.
And as the life behind the pencil
Its work just might survive it.
—*Eric Laird*

Friendship

As we travel on life's highways
Many folks we chance to meet
It may be in our daily labors
Or upon a busy street.

We may meet thru recreation
Or perhaps in social trends
But soon we learn to know them better
And we speak of them as friends.

Then we share each other's feelings
Share our joys and sorrows, too,
And this bond of love keeps growing
And we've formed a friendship true.

But the world goes on forever
And true friendship never ends
And my life has been much richer
'Cause I've known you as my friend.
—*Georgia S. Cramer*

Jesus, You're Alive!!!

While walking along earth's shores and among us;
Many miracles You lovingly performed...
You are so mercifully helping prepare the just
For the soon approaching darkness of the storm!

You could have called ten thousand angels
And made your enemies disappear!
Instead, You showed no malice nor anger
As they beat, mocked, and crucified You, my dear.

You even asked Your Father in heaven
To forgive for they know not what they do...
Is that why You said we must forgive seventy time seven,
Even that person who has been most unfaithful to you?

Thank you, Dear Lord, for teaching courage as soldiers pounded
Into Your precious hands and feet those gruesome sharp spikes...
For giving that most wondrous and truly important message.
No grave could ever keep you down, Jesus! You're alive!!!
—*Belva Carey*

Mothers Know

My mother told me years ago
   Many things a lad should know.
To be kind and thoughtful in what I do;
   To read God's word and know what's true

To greet my friends with a little smile
   And a firm hand clasp that is worthwhile
To let them know in word and deed,
   They can bank on me in time of need.

To look to God for all good things,
   He knows our needs and always brings
Some token of His wondrous love,
   To humble hearts from Heaven above.

To watch my step in all I do,
   To take my time and think things thru.
To stay with a task once it's begun
   And never leave till the job is done.

To be brave and courageous in times of stress,
   To shake my head when the mob says "yes"
To stand my ground and fight for the right
   And see justice come from darkest night.
—*Harry A. Stocker*

Shadows

In the darkness of our shadows lies
many things. Some of which we fear,
others we treasure. I used to only
bury my worst fears and memories in
my shadows. And I would never let
anyone see into that side of me.
Hiding in my shadows was my anger,
fear, hate, and loneliness. I have
since come to a point in my life
where I can open up and face my
darkest shadows. To my amazement
I was able to put them aside and
put new things in my shadows. I
am no longer afraid to face my
shadows. For inside I have placed
my most prized possessions. There
deep inside me is peace, love,
content, and happiness. For the
first time in my life I truly
believe in myself. And I have found
that a shadow is merely a mirror of
ones self.....

—*Jeani Ethridge*

Why?

So much asked in one little word,
Many whys of the mind have never been heard.
The children's question, from age-old mothers and babies,
The miracle of life and so many "maybe's."

Asked where we live in wondering force of nature,
From rippling stream to mountain-top glacier.
Questions ignite the beginning of wherefore and why,
Never fully answered til the by and by.

Ask "Why me" of accidents and disease,
Of greatest loss and pain with no ease.
Ask "Why they," those of sexual abuse,
Of orphans, disabled and fear induced.

These musings on why lead me to believe,
I have been blessed in what I've received.
They've taught me strength and to always try,
And never, never give up asking why.

—*Betsy H. Leach*

A Prayer

Pray night may offer more than dreams -
may discard fretted tapestry and frayed seams
of worn-out day by weaving new designs
for tomorrow's fresh beginnings;
Pray no sweet sleep or favored innings
to devisers of crooked paths or signs
which stumbling wayfarers fail to see,
or to merchants of poisoned beauty who
tempt the innocent to folly - pray you,
dear night, clear away all yesterday's debris
leaving a true and shining path free
to lure lost travelers safely through.

—*Irene Prater Dell*

Wherever You Go Whatever You Do

May the Lord always protect you,
May the Lord's face beam with joy because of you,
May the Lord be gracious unto you,
May the Lord show his favor unto you,
May the Lord grant you his peace forever.
Wherever you go, Whatever you do,
In the name of Jesus Christ, May God the father always be with you,
May he answer your prayers and may his guardian angels
Always be there to protect you,
Wherever you go, Whatever you do.
As you go through your day,
May God bless you in every way,
May God grant you wisdom,
May God grant you knowledge,
And every good thing found in heaven.
Wherever you go, Whatever you do,
In the name of Jesus Christ, May God the father always be with you,
May he answer your prayers and may his guardian angels
Always be there to protect you,
Wherever you go, Whatever you do.

—*Elizabeth Skerencak*

My Life My Own

All I want is my own life - with no one to bother
me and not to see or know
of the next one's sorrow all I
want is my own life and as good as possible a tomorrow,
all I want is my own life.
When I work all day one thing I must say
all I want to think about is my own
way, I do not want to know of the next ones
sorrow, so please again don't tell me of the
next one's troubles cause all I want is
my own life, all I want is my own life.

—*Judith Schmidt*

His Rose

He reaches out to me and he hands
me the rose,
So beautiful, so red, its fragrant
aroma drifts through the air and it
seems to linger under my nose.
A tear slides down my cheek and
onto my lips.
I lick my lips and taste the salt
from the tear.
Its bitter taste brings me back to reality.
I now gently lift the rose from my lap,
and the once red petals turn brown
and float to the floor.
The rose is dead and so is he.
And I know I must go on, and I
will, but it hurts so much.

—*Dina Teierle*

Heart Beat

I hear the soft beating in the night...
louder and more distinct in my dreams
fainter and further from me in the light of day
It grows quieter in the time to come...
older and older, fainter and fainter, softer still
until the dreams that belong to it are silent
Hushed...
in the still of night, never to be heard again.

—*Amber Forland*

Finest Epitaph

Towering high are my thoughts wrapped in us, the gift you've given
   me with a slice of time
To jumble together echoes of birds and bees making music
   in my mind.
I've laid down my time, poured you my mind running liquid gold
Creating the finest epitaph of love words ever told.

In your lips I lost my way hearing who you are and all you know
There, your voice reached out and grabbed me,
   your style will never let me go.
From your eyes I fell in your moving black pools
We shared are everything: mind, body, soul.

Instead of honey savoring my morning tea
Drops a tear, wading dreams and wants of you for company.
I lull the cries of the child you've given me, suckling milk I hold
I wonder his eyes, chance upon a miracle; his twinkle;
   "sky blue"—mirroring—the finest epitaph of love
   words ever told.

It doesn't matter we never shared this life or a season
   my love wasn't measured it was spawned.
On memoirs of sweetness swaddled betwixt the hours,
   dusk to dawn.
   —*Denice Jane Babb*

Crumbling Hammer And Sickle

Storm clouds, dark and threatening, massing over Red Square
   Memories of Budapest and Prague uprisings
   Death's scent fills the late summer air.

   Old faces, weathered yet stalwart,
     Unwilling to relinquish the past
     The Old Guard's dying notion
One desperate bid for power, one last gasp.

   Lenin's statue, stone-faced, keeps watch
   Seventy years of socialism withers away
   Revolutionary words, "Peace, Land and Bread,"
     No longer hold sway.

   Images of Red Army soldiers goose stepping
     Countless ranks now a distant scene
Tank columns advancing, subduing the masses
Crashing human barriers, wiping the streets clean.

   Fifteen republics no longer in union
Leaving their Mother, pursuing a separate path,
   Seeds of discontent become a rushing tide
Symbols and banners swept away in its aftermath.

   Russian will and desire hold firm
   Clinging to the ideas of truth and freedom
     Sounds of the crumbling Hammer & Sickle
     Echo throughout the Soviet Kingdom.

   Once blindly loyal soldiers join the cause
Refusing to silence the voices of the country
   Soldiers no longer with an unceasing will
   Soldiers no longer dying for the Party.
   —*Edward J. Kula*

Untitled

Give me a dragon to slay,
My adversary clearly in sight,
Liberate me, from the political steps,
Upon these mens lips fall forth
knives of illusion.
They vanish away the truth, these weapons of cowards
   —*Deborah Meshirer*

Ode To Mad Men

Hammen, Hitler, Hussein
Men of hate who are insane
Each came upon the scene
In their own time and place
With all their power
You brought fear and horror to the human race
You planted the seeds of hate
You wanted to flourish
But evil men have no courage
You tortured, you killed, you maimed
You brought only pain
With your seeds of hate
You sealed your fate
Your aim was to bring you glory and fame
Instead history will record your shame
You brought death and destruction
With fire and flame
And you will be damned in hell
As the world rejoices with ringing of bells
As we celebrate peace in the middle east
   —*Anita Friedlander*

Fantasy Valentine

   You are a dream fantasy come true.
Men of the world wish all women took their cue from you.

   A real lady from which fantasies are made.
Keeping me entranced with your body on parade.

   You are my Fantasy Valentine.
   Your love and devotion are truly divine.

I need not close my eyes to dream, fantasize, or scheme,
I need only open them to see you and my life is supreme.

   It is ecstasy having you to love, hold, and cherish.
   The ultimate dream of the perfect marriage.

   You are my Fantasy Valentine.
   To have and to hold; knowing you are mine.

   You are a vision felt deep in my heart.
   A river of love tying us together; never apart.

   It is easy to tell you were made just for me.
   Your beauty and love setting me free.

   You are my Fantasy Valentine.
   The love you give to me is truly sublime.
   —*Donald C. Howard Jr.*

Innocent Sunshine

Innocent sunshine from another time.
Little boy
Strains to hear the pretty language.
Intangible favor.
Old books.
Transfixed distractions.
Thought dreams.
Therese and Isabelle.
The Fox.
That Cold Day in the Park.
Innocent sunshine
Offers a hazy illumination.
Wistful
Yellows.
Happy little afternoon.
Wooden doorways
Bear no malice.
Small arousal.
   —*Joseph Verrilli*

Say What

Woof woof woof!
Meow meow!
Meow woof, woof woof meow!

My dog says; "Woof,"
My cat says; "Meow,"
I say; "Say What?"

Say say, what what what,
Woof woof what,
Meow meow what,
Say what meow meow woof!

My dog, my cat and I say;
"Shhhh quiet, quiet, let's all be very quiet
before we get yelled at,"

By my Mommy who says;
"I don't know and I don't care,
if you guys won't be quiet over there,
I'll just go and get out of here."
—*Jackie Land Anderson*

Mother's Spirit

    Your clear mezzo
Mesmerized me in church the other day
And I find your wise counsel speaking to me
   ...Still...in the back of my mind.
Your warmth is felt where you once were
And the light of your courageous soul
Glows and floats about me wherever I am.
Your presence is sensed dimensionally, electrically;
    Comforting and caressing,
   Loving even from beyond the grave.
—*Jeannie Carlson*

Space: A Junk Dealer's Paradise

There's entirely too much junk in outer space
Metal and garbage galore
I think it would benefit the whole human race
If we didn't send up anymore!

You see, the rockets they're crashing
To Earth, here, there, and everywhere
I think it would be quite smashing
To instead shoot up a few prayers.

They will say "new horizons"
Are what they are looking for
Good Heavens! Would space aliens
Descend on our shores by the score?

I will tell you the secrets
Of all of the universe
God placed sun, moon, stars and hung planets
So why should we travel from Earth?
—*Dee Maddux Bauchspies*

Untitled

Fire and smoke clouds the sky, as
mother earth starts to cry.
From deep with in her broken crust,
flows tears of red like rivers to the sea.
Soon she'll rest, her tears will dry to
leave behind new wonders for the eye.
—*Jimmy R. Sandifer*

Poetry

Bardic shards, bits and pieces of earth,
Meticulously matched
To make an artifact
Fringed with Joy

Concave receptors
Arching heaven and earth,
Focusing truth
On the pavement of the mind.

Lightning flashes,
Illuminating earth's horizons,
Fading our partitions
In a vision of the whole.

Light constellated in a pattern
Of providence, when
Faith, o'erleaping the abyss,
Finds firm footage in bliss.

Strains of the creation song
Caught on the banks and shoals
Of the crystal sea,
Tasting of eternity.
—*Grace R. W. Hall*

The Past

We sometimes live our lives
mingled with the past.
Hoping we can capture
a memory that will last.

Our lives they change so drastically
and crisis never ends.
And we must grow and follow
the path that changes us within.

Never try to relive or change
what has been done.
For you must look ahead to life
and use the lessons you have learned.

Find the happiness in life
that lies ahead for you.
Life is very precious
don't sit there feeling blue.

Learn to laugh and sing, my friend
don't let the moment pass.
For you may miss today's reward
by dwelling on the past.
—*Janice Tucker*

Untitled

Once upon a time there was this guy
My love for him would never die
For my daddy, my arms will always be open wide
Then this day I met another guy
My love for my daddy didn't die
I had to let my love divide
Together in my heart they are one
  in my mind they are mine
I'll love you, daddy
  Til the day I die
—*Cindy Sue Foster*

My Family

My dad a carnation,
mom a red-stem rose.
With their love created
a beautiful bouquet to show.
Flowers of eight we blossomed,
growing within its bounty.

Holding each close to their breast,
releasing us slowly out into the wind.
Knowing within their hearts
we shall be gathered again.
A joining tear forms like dew,
upon the empty vase they hold.

They surrender that vase unto God,
and He now holds it in His hands.
One by one He will pick us up,
this is all apart of His plan.
The vase is not empty,
It now holds a yellow rose.

Watered by the tears of those left
waiting, still to follow.
Samuel J. Gorzelsky, God
forever holds you.
—Diane Marie Bernardy

My Special Grandmother

I had a special grandmother
Mom to most of those who knew her,
She was a very down to earth person
Not one for fancy things or fur.

She never had much in her life
But her belief in God was strong,
She shared what little she had
With others who didn't seem to belong.

As a child to her house I would often sneak
Knowing she would find the time to listen,
I often thought she must have a halo
And in the dark it would glisten.

She dealt with a lot of sickness and pain
Always taking it in her stride,
She always had faith things would get better
A neat lady with a lot of pride.

Now that she's no longer with us
And I think of her so often,
Wishing she were here to thank her
For the many hurts she softened.
—Edna Coon

I Know Not What Tomorrow Will Bring

I'm thankful God to be alive today. Even though,
my heart is filled with Pain and dismay. I know
not what tomorrow will bring. If it should be
happiness sorrow or pain.
I'll keep trusting you to give me strength
to see me through.
If it should be your will that I have more years
left to live.
I will be thankful for the time that I have left.
If my time should come tomorrow, there
will be no more pain or sorrow.
—Agnes Johnson

Memories

Dream of things that use to be
Moonlit nights upon the sea
Summer meadows filled with light
The buzzing sound of bee's in flight

Rain drops falling from the sky
The night winds wailing, lonesome cry
Flitting wings of a bat in flight
Crossing the path of the moon at night

The suns first rays, its final blaze
As each day draws to a close
Dusk as it deepens into night
Stars as they flicker into sight

Love that came, my heart to snare
And stayed to light my life
A husband and a child to hold
These memories shut out the cold

My thoughts still wander thru the ways
The dreams and songs of yesterdays
When I was young and dreams were new
And there were many things to do
—Charlene F. Nichols

New Dimensions

We have been given a treasure
More precious than mounds of gold;
It brings us a new title
And excitement of life untold.

It brings unending pleasures
And happiness in smiles and tears;
It gives life new dimension
And dreams that will last for years.

We relive past years of memories
And marvel as we review;
For now that we are grandparents
Life seems to start anew.

For we enjoy the caring
Of a new life and joy so true;
So thankful for the privilege of sharing
This new life, our children with you.
—Eleanor Biggs

Broken Lullabies Patched

Broken lullabies can be patched.
More than hearts can imagine.
Or minds can comprehend.
For His greatness exceeds every fount of living,
As God is always ready to mind.

Broken lullabies can be patched.
All of man's needs for peace, love, joy, and rest.
Just give Him a chance.
Put God to the test,
For God gives His children His very best.

Broken lullabies can be patched.
When we are one with God.
The bountiful gifts, are ours without end.
All God says is remember me.
I'm the one, My Son, I did send.

To mend and patch those broken lullabies.
The burdens to heavy to bare.
There's no need for impressive prayers.
For the minute we seek Him and sigh.
He is already there to patch our broken lullabies.
—Betty M. Rush

My Best Friends

They don't own houses Work or drive cars.
Most are well-dressed in fur, others
Ragged and scared.

None speak a language few humans recognize—
Yet all speak freely to me thru their eyes

They have a wisdom Man merely sees
They live in a kingdom Of the wild and free.

They know not of dishonesty or lies—
Except, what they see but don't understand
In our human lives.

Why can't we, as humans, fall a step
To our knees — or lift our eyes to
Some towering old tree?
"See" the true joys in life
Is, Simplicity

"They" were on the Ark with Noah—
And since time began—
Domestic and wild, God's children—
The animals—
My best friends.
—*Bobbie T. Christian*

Glimpse Of Thoughts

If I were a girl either way a boy,
Mother will buy me a very nice toy,
But how can it be we are very poor,
If no money can't buy in the store.

If I'm bad troubles always haunt me,
My family uneasy won't feel so free,
No friends around lonely with shame,
Life shorten tomorrow is uncertain!

If I'm still young what shall I do?
I should be good to school I must go,
To learn all things to make me shape,
So my parents' burden I help to share.

If I expand my thoughts for the future,
I look around me to deal with nature,
And men like me to share their love,
Power and glory who have faith in God!
—*Gerardo C. Edra Sr*

A Troubled World

Earthquakes, raging, by the sea,
Muggers, stalking you and me.
People, that should be in jail.
On the streets, out on bail.

Children carrying guns and knives,
Stealing cars, and taking lives.
Foreigners, running everyplace,
And missiles, pointed, at our face.

Weather patterns all awry,
Satellites, roam the sky.
Life on earth is getting rough,
Someday God will say enough.

I don't think it will be long,
Till He'll be back, to right the wrong.
Time on earth is growing late,
When man will know, his final fate.
—*Bernice Ann Morgan*

Breathe So Quietly

Overwhelming world
Moving hastily along
day and day
Uncontrollable and impatient
I find myself in a spin.
Smothered by chaos- - - Stop!
To turn off.
Step out of these ugly feelings,
Put them in a box and walk away - - - Run.
Disappear into myself and fly freely
Search for an inner peace
So deep I can feel the moon shine above the sea,
Hear how gentle life can be,
And breathe so quietly - - - Content.
Give birth to a new attitude - - - Stand Tall.
Polished with a wealth of strength
To walk back, open the box,
And redress my world - to move on -
In control
Breathing quietly.
—*Denise Ricker*

The Golden Years...

Dedicated to Cousin Bud
Much has been said of growing old,
   of golden years without the gold.
Your bones they ache and creak so loud,
   you lose your sense of being proud.
Memory grows dim on certain facts —
   it's hard to keep your mind intact.
That golden hair so long admired —
   no longer a part of your daily attire.
Your youthful skin so full of dew,
   lined like a road map now hangs on you!
That trim looking waist no longer is seen —
   in front of a mirror you no longer preen!
Your sight grows dim, your sinuses drip;
   the ears on your head are there just to grip!
With hearing loss you you your best
   without that aid that you detest!
Your balance is off, your control almost gone —
   don't cough or laugh if you're not near a john!
All said and done, growing old is a blast!
   Hang in to the finish, hold on to the past!
Memories are golden — they'll see you through,
   And when you check out — no time for adieu!
Though you'll be missed and some will be sad,
   they'll be consoled by whatever you had!
Endure to the end whatever your lot —
   old age beats dying so give your best shot!
—*Jane H. Putta*

Flashbacks

Moss...fiddlehead ferns...
Mushrooms... purple skunk cabbage...
Brown woods greening up.

White caps disappear...
Distant heat lightning ... stillness..
Ozone in the air.

Ruby cardinal...
Topaz sugar maple tree...
Flashing sapphire skies.

Clear black ice booming...
Stinging snow...grey wolf howling...
Back-to-back blizzards.
—*Joan M. Jones*

Emptiness

Upon the completion of accomplishing successfully
Much that they have planned to do
There are those who find inner emptiness,
This feeling of emptiness does not mean failure,
It means that one has more abilities,
Talent, capabilities, know-how
And is ready to accomplish new things
For one is not limited to accomplishing
What one has materialized,
Yet many stop themselves, become remorseful,
Sad, self-deprecating, unappreciative of their accomplishments
For they are looking outward instead of inward,
Inward looking must be thorough, decisive, deep, independent,
Alert, aware, confident, comfortable,
With the aim to find what more one wants to achieve,
It does not mean to give the control
Of oneself and one's direction to a person or a group
For to do so may mean failure to achieve what one must;
To feel empty does not mean that one is empty.

—*Guen Chappelle*

Dedicated to Bobbi Pressley, My Best Fried

I can call you,
  My Best Friend.

You are a special person.
  I can share my emotions with.

You laugh with me,
  When I react crazy.
    Laughter of a clown.

You listen to me,
  When I am confused.
    Words of friendship.

You talk to me,
  When secrets are shared.
    The bonding of friends.

With a friend like you; I can't lose.

  You're one in a million.
    My best friend.

My treasure of friendship.
  That's you!

—*Deborah Burgett Setty*

Of Circe's Dilemma

In my predicament, I must disclose
My charms are worn down to the knuckle-bone;
What rotten luck - a siren so moss-grown
That she can't net the man who might propose!
Of course, if I were like a bramble-rose,
I'd twist and bind my quarry tight - and own
That all through life he'd never be alone—
But would this be a creature I'd oppose?

To no avail, I've neatly cast each spell,
Just hoping someone might deliberate;
Yet, in the interim, I now concede
That my allure has struck a horrid knell,
And Vanity must soon inoculate
A miracle — to remedy my need!

—*Dorothy Krueger Burman*

Untitled

I sit here and just stare at the wall.
My eyes are bloodshot from the hours I just spent crying
  because you left me.
I never realized how much I cared about you until you were gone.
I don't know how to go on without you.
You were such a big part of my small life.
You gave me all the confidence I needed to go far in this world.
I felt so close to you, yet I never even realized that I
  loved you until just now.
But I can't love you.
I promised myself I wouldn't do that.
I promised myself I wouldn't ruin another great friendship
  by letting love get in the way.
So I'll stop loving you now and start getting on with my life.
It will be hard, but I'll get used to it…
  My eyes are back to normal now.
  And I stop staring at the wall.

—*Jennifer Baker*

A Tribute To My Father

Special: a battered screw driver at my place that was used by
  my father and more valued by me than delicate lace;
Special: a metal lockbox on one of my shelves that has his
  hand-written notes of the college expenses paid for me;
Special: a striking table with singer legs that was designed
  and made especially for me by him;
Special: a cluster of damsum plum trees at the back of my
  lot that were grown from the ones once dear to this man; and
  a row of blue hydrangeas in front of my home that were
  regenerated from the ones he raised.

All about me are tangibles of the things that had my father's
touch, all of which remind me of the father who loved me much.

but more special than these: a love for God expressed by him
for me to see, a love for family he passed on to me, a love
for work he instilled in me as I worked along his side, a
love for others he forever responded to, a love for learning,
a love for music, a love for fun.....

All of these intangibles are within me because I was touched by
my father's touch, all of which remind me of the father who
loved me much!

—*Grace Jones*

That Faithful Friend Of Mine

I was lonely and forsaken
  My friends all gone their way,
I ached and felt forgotten
  By those I thought would stay
How sad it is in golden age
  Grown old and all alone
We never thought we'd turn the page
  Life's book was all unknown
Have you ever felt the quiet
  Of a house with no one home,
A threat of future still unmet
  Like the calm before a storm?
And what I thought were problems
  Vanish 'neath your hand
You take the time to listen
  And you always understand.
And I count myself the luckiest
  That any one can be
Because I know beyond a doubt
  My Savior Loveth Me.

—*Forrest J. Binion*

I'm Hurring

I must not delay much longer to achieve my goals in life, for
my growing aches and pains dampen will, and foster strife; I
must fulfill a promise I've made, in youthful days many times
to be remembered as many times delayed. There are also chores
and duties I must hurry to complete... Some of need and some
of fancy that could make my joys complete, but I recognize one
duty, far more urgent than the rest... That demands my first
fulfillment as the dearest, and the best. In my simple mode of
living that prevails from day to day, I've failed - in love and
duty - the hearts for whom I pray; the hearts of faith and
caring, who have loved me through the years. Are partners to
my struggles and companions to my tears. Theirs so little time
for past regrets and less- to make amends, for time - can heal
the deepest wounds, in chosen cherished friends. So little
time to share my love and beauty here on earth, for swiftly,
pass the waning years, and the strength - to complete my given
tasks.

—*June Davignon*

"Ariel" My First "Grand-Daughter"

The first time I saw you Grand-Daughter dear I knew I had lost
   my heart
I saw the dreams of your parents fulfilled, you were pure love
   from the start.
You made all the gurgles, faces and sounds, that little babies
   must do.
But Grand-Pa held you with reverence and love and prayed your
   dreams would come true.

You know your birth was a special event, I want all the world
   to know.
You made me a Grand-Pa proud as can be and set my heart all
   aglow.
I was there, dear child, for such a short time, but still I
   was filled with love.
As I watched your Grand-Ma, holding you close, bathed in loves
light from above.

I also saw that your mother and dad, as they held you close to
their breast, surrounded you with the tenderest love, I knew
you truly were blessed.
Ariel my sweet and wonderful child grow strong and honest and
free. Your parents true love will always be there,
just like your Grand-ma's and me.

—*Charles Crispin*

I Walk In Sadness

Today I walk in sadness
my heart is full of pain.
The tears flow from my lashes
like softly falling rain.
He sleeps upon a quiet hill
his grave I cannot see.
His spirit is within me
and beckons to be free.
The memories come to comfort
of times that we have shared.
My heart swells up with love inside
because I know he cared.
This man, he was my father
who lies there now at rest.
Of all the men upon the earth
I know he was the best.

—*Joyce Mustain*

Memories Become Shadows

Like the endless chain of time
   my heart repeats this weary line
   where, my darling, are you?
As pages of a book do fade,
   as sunshine mingles into shade,
Memories of oft spent days
   become like shadows in the haze.
Many happenings trite and true
   recall my longing, dear, for you.
The light reflected in the skies
   Gives me faith that love never dies
While past and present intertwine
   to form the
     pattern of life, divine.

—*Beryl A. Lyons*

The Touch Divine

Last night as I sat alone in my room
   My heart seemed full of despair.
When suddenly I heard a voice in the gloom
   And looked up as Christ stood there.

He said, "Fear not, I am always here,"
   And laid His hand on mine.
As I felt His wonderful presence near
   I knew perfect peace divine.

His face was beautiful to behold
   From His eyes shone the holy light.
His smile of understanding told
   There was nothing to fear from the night.

So now when trouble assails me
   To Christ's hand I'll faithfully cling.
In the darkness I'll always be able to see
   The dear face of my Heavenly King.

—*Jean C. Paul*

My Children

Tissued from fertile essence of my kin,
My intrinsic marrow ingrained within,
I'm the architect of God's greatest gift.
In the sea of life I set you adrift.

First your helpless state recruits my lifeline.
Then your fears, your joys, your tears become mine.
A tiny seed sired with love and care,
You rise to bloom assured yet unaware.

The passing years open your eyes and mind.
You start to wonder, you question, you find.
The lifeline now becomes a cord of thought,
Embodied as only the heart hath wrought.

As you stand tall aside of other men,
If only you'd be what I've never been.
My life has now merged with my pride in you,
And now you architect the gift anew.

—*John J. Destefano, Jr.*

An Invited Guest

At first, I thought something was wrong,
my lack of pleasure with the throng.
Was I a recluse, sure and true?
What could my alone desire imbue?

The imaginings and thoughts I feel
are shaped on Nature's pottery wheel.
An idea is molded, formed, and styled
by Beauty's landscapes tame and wild.

The tiny flowers demand respect.
Diminutive powers they reflect.
A Master Designer crafted these
and sculpted mountains, caves, and seas.

God's invitation I accept
though I fear my perception is inept
to gaze at glorious fields and streams,
to ponder Earth's amazing schemes.

My heart and mind find one conclusion.
Science and Faith bring a strong infusion
to a searching soul upon a quest
of discovering Truths as Creation's guest.

—*Julie Jarrett Hall*

Death's Door

The wings of time, have taken hold,
  My limbs grow weak, my body old,
My hair has turned to silver gray,
  My pace has slowed from yesterday.

Sometimes I sit and reminisce,
  I feel alone, my friends I miss,
I know my strength is fading fast,
  Each breath I take could be my last.

I reach out for a helping hand,
  But no one comes who understands,
My soul is longing to be free,
  I've only God to comfort me.

I close my eyes in somber prayer,
  The gates of heaven drawing near,
I feel the warmth of God's embrace,
  An angel's kiss upon my face.

The golden gates have opened wide,
  I am about to step inside,
The pain no more for me to bare,
  God's grace and love for me to share.

—*Carol A. Holbrook*

Desperate Days

My soul is in anguish.
My eyes are filled with tears.
I cry to the heavens to take
Away my fears.
To take away the desperation that
Destiny has given me.
To take away the pain in my heart,
For only God can set me free.
Yes, the desperate days which followed
Me are like the shadows in the night
But despite the darkness,
God will bring the light.

—*Barbara Wirkowski*

My Little Black-Capped Chickadee

He's out there singing in the tree,
  My Little Black-capped Chickadee.

It makes my heart feel so gay,
  To hear that song on a snowy day.

That cheerful little melody,
  Really means a lot to me.

He seems to greet me with a grin,
  When I feed and talk to him.

In the lilac bush he lingers there,
  His splendid music fills the air.

It sort of lifts my spirits high,
  Like an angel singing in the sky.

A-pecking on those crusts of bread,
  Then he sings and cocks his head.

Chick-a-dee, chick-a-dee,
  Chick-a-dee-dee-dee.

That pretty tune I love to hear,
  Just a drifting in my ear.

I write these words in memory,
  Of My Little Black-capped Chickadee.

—*Carroll R. Buffum Sr.*

The Sounding Place

I must go back to the sounding place
My love is there forever more.
I heard her whisper, O love of mine
I stare and stare at the shore.

I must go back tot he sounding place,
I'll compare this moment to a …
soaring eagle in the sky
My heart is working overtime
I'm like a bouquet of roses, when they die

I must go back to the sounding place
Where birds sing along with the ocean breeze.
I hear her laughter in the night.
And violins playing beautifully in the trees.

Oh yes! I must go back again this day.
Where a world of dreams unfold.
Her beautiful shining eyes sustain me,
My love story must be told.

And I'll go back to the sounding place once more
A well-spring of her love is in the air.
Kissing my lips, there's nothing to compare.
My treasure, lovely adorable lady fair.

—*Eulah Stanley*

In All That's Voiceless

In all that's voiceless truth resides:
Nature's words and love's dark eyes,
In memories and faith's good hope
Like old moon riding stormy skies.
Ever voiceless our sun resides:
Reaping days with payment death —
All truth flows on that good tide:
Man's words are apt to be the lies.

—*Jean Candee*

Splendor

I dance on billowy clouds of splendor,
My mind drifts with the wind,
My eyes focus on shapes of circles and squares.
I feel on top of the world; nothing can bring me back.
I look down to my ankle; there is a chain
Made up of heartbreak, hardships, and hard times.
My mind becomes black with distrust and hate.
But… I see a light. A little spot of hope.
I grab for the light, it's coming closer.
I can see the clouds drifting above me,
I can feel the warmth of the sun,
I can taste the sweet air in my mouth.
Soon I am back on those clouds,
Those clouds of splendor.
—*Andrea L. Eatherton*

The Mind

The wind blows through the window, an echo calls out your name.
  My mind rolls searching backward, my love, you will remain.

It could not be the love I've known, I won't settle for imitation.
  My mind knows of what used to be, or at least my imagination.

I dreamt you up one winter night, your smell lingers in the air.
  As I reach out to embrace you, I realize you weren't there.

Each tender moment spent with you, memories come back to me.
  Yearning for one last tender touch, before you set me free.

My eyes are overflowing, the tears stream down my face.
  My heart it slowly breaks in two, the pain I must embrace.

I'm overcome with thoughts of you, I ache for another start.
  Yet I know You'll never be again, the true love within my heart.

Controlled by such emotion, as a vision comes crashing through.
  I realize time heals nothing, I'm still in love with you.
The final tear falls to the ground, on the memory I did recall.
  I'm thrown back to reality, my heart turns into a wall.
    —*Cristina M. Coveney*

The Meaning Of Intelligence

Intelligence is just a word, of what out minds would say,
My mind says, it's some chemicals, that we call D.N.A.
Two simple strands of molecules, all twisted very tight,
With no predestined harmony, to say just what is right.
Now how they got together, was not by laws, but rules,
Of universe attraction and chance, their only tools.

When these compounds grow and swell, they colonize into a cell.
The chemical environment, decides how cells will grow,
The end of each cells growth, determines what they know.
The sequence of each chemical, that's found in D.N.A.,
Decides what rules to follow, in forming R.N.A.
The cells thus formed, create a life, by moving in conjunction,
For life in its most meager terms, is nothing but a function.
A coded set of rules I say, intelligence is made this way,
Just simple little chemicals, that follow all the rules,
And coded information, their universal tools.
Our sun, and all the planets, are chemicals I say,
The galaxies, are the cells that formed, as they go on their way, the universe, is the body, as endless as is time,
As for the word intelligence, why it's not worth a dime.
    —*Jack Frederick Collier*

My Wishing Star

As I lay here looking up at the evening sky,
my mind was full of thoughts of you.
  And wondering why I'm so confused about
What I feel for you that I've been questioning it?
  Is it so wrong for me to love you so much?
Even if I don't know how you feel.
  Then with a blink of an eye, I saw,
A shooting star I wished on that star
  For you to be apart of my life.
I'm hoping that someday my wish
  will come true, until then
I'll keep wishing on my stars for you!
    —*E. Hoffmann*

Peaches And Cream

  If I was a pauper and you were
my Queen, would you enter my world
be part of my dream, would you
walk through the forest, would you
dance by a stream, would you stir
up my fantasy, eat peaches and cream.
  If you saw the contents that rest
in my heart, you know I could never
see us apart, our love takes our lives
to the extreme, each day's sorrow brings
joy so it seems, rest with me now eat
peaches and cream.
  Some souls stay bitter some souls stay
sad, no life is better than the one that
you had, when your world becomes
troubled on me you might lean, I'll
show you my feelings, my soul seldom
seen, lay with me now eat peaches
and cream, stay with me now,
our life's but a dream.
    —*David P. Plante*

Silence Of Night

Deafness…up until a few days ago,
my son was just hearing impaired,
He could hear via the help of his hearing aid.

We were blessed with twenty eight wonderful years,
though I will admit, at times frustrating,
of dealing with louder than normal T.V. sounds,
louder than normal talking voices.

Oh…. what I wouldn't do to have it be this way again.

Now, communication takes a whole new meaning,
as we strive to learn the language of sign.
We are new at this, like lost babes in the woods,
but learning ever so slowly, the beauty and poetry in
the motion of hands.

My son says, his new world of silence is a peaceful one,
and at peace with his Maker, he does seem to be.

The least I can do for this brave son of mine,
is to hide my sorrow and to shed my tears in the
silence of night.
    —*Beatrice H. Limon*

A Moving Respect From The Freeway

Traffic leaves me behind on the outside lane
My stares flow over a stretch of cars;
a length of floral colors
turned to the compassion of a brief visit
on the Memorial Gardens cemetery

My imagination runs faster than my driving

I see trees there — I do not observe them
I notice the cortege dedicated to the absence
of an old man - or not so old, or a child
labeled before time, maybe a woman
aged in life's excuses - or one younger
ahead of herself - the depth of sleep;
one of these trembled yesterday.
in an avenue of life

My eyes are faster than my driving

The liquid ambers; bent, swaying, support,
are full of color turning leaves;
with the help of the low winds spread tints
over the lot of graves

I leave my thoughts for the bereaved
—*Francesca Aragon Azevedo*

Essay In Time

Shackled to the desk and locked to the clock
My tortured brow bent in time
And twisted over the tick-tock
Rectangular whiteness

Persecuted into leering at the clock
Perched, looming darkly above the desk
A vulture with one cramped talon flexing
Gripping the seconds that coil around
The tick-tock instrument of death

Waiting to release the tick-tock
Dammed blue blood, the impending feast
So painful and slow, with a plethora
Of cursed corporal linear curves
The slaughtered words flowing from the pointed tip-tock

Tensely waiting to pick the tick-tock flesh
With sweeping words rolling counter clockwise
Onto the blank page and into the grave
Over my blank mind and under a blank tombstone

The myriad of thought ring, wake up!
And flatten into words that tick-tick through
The frightening abyss
With the carrion of an essay in time
—*Jonathan D. Lipson*

Times

Old friends, not here anymore, I miss their faces,
New buildings going up, supplant familiar places,
Things aren't the same as when we were young,
The music, the songs, not the type that were sung,
Youth busy, making their world, day by day,
The old falls back, for a new better way,
We don't even love the same anymore,
There's a deeper, richer love than before,
Old trees, under the weight of years, have fell,
Life tried, proven and known too well,
The young hasten on, and the rivers run,
To find their place in the morning sun.

—*Alma Roberson*

Shattered Life

Each time I close my eyes, I try to picture
Myself in a new life without you. God knows
it's been very hard to do
For many years my life revolved around you,
day in and day out you and the children were all
I ever thought about.
Now that you're no longer in my life, I feel as though
my heart and my life has been shattered and you
act and conduct yourself as though it doesn't matter.
What kind of person is it that has the heart to break
a wonderful family apart.
In time you will realize what you have done
and you may love will end up the lonely one,
for you will someday feel the hurt and pain
that my heart feels on this very day and by
then we would both have gone our separate ways.
—*Cathy Bordayo Cunningham*

Tribute To The Dolphins

As I stood upon the warm white sand with
nature's beauty all around me

I looked across the sparkling sea with
its endless wonders abounding.

It was then that I noticed among the
white foaming waves

Two magical creatures as they affectionately
played

Appearing to understand and have compassion
for one another

As I think of this now I chill and I
shudder

At the thought that we humans should love
and respect

The way the dolphins did the day I
watched the sunset.
—*Dana Gruetter*

Dearest Daddy

He lays in green pastures,
   near the meadows he played in.
He's now in just memories,
   instead of with me.
He was always there,
   when he could be.
He always made sure,
   that I knew he loved me.
He and mom were give the job to raise me,
   but he won't be able to give me away.
He loved kids very much,
   but he won't get to meet mine.
He laid there as I said,
   "Daddy I love you, you have to get better.
   because you have to give me away.
   Daddy I love you very much good-bye.
   I'll always remember you."
—*Julienne Wright*

Priceless Negro

A man of strength and of deeds,
Negritude and gratitude;
Is like an amaranth in a Jardin,
And when the rest cease to blossom;
He remains the only handsome.
Unlike an adonis or an apollo, oh no!
For his ancestry is of helot, and not a hero.
Yes, indeed, like a negro.

And when in the pit, he prevails with not a bit,
Rather much of wit.
His virtue well will shield-
In the most erring field.
His pedigree of great heroes-
Oops! Negro-heroes.
Yes of Louverture, Dessalines, Petion, and Christophe.

He retains the rage of X, the bravery of Douglas,
Words of Marley and conviction of Garvey;
Hands like baldwin's, thoughts like Hughes',
Mind of Du Bois and the heart of King, Jr.
Call his an immaculate hero, an autocratic nigger, or "un negre perfait,"
For once, or ever twice, your wish you were this priceless negro.

—*Aderson Exume*

Time

Time has a habit of ticking away
Never caring if you want to stay
In the midst of a breath taking scene.

Time keeps on flowing along with the tide
Never caring what you feel inside
When you wake from a beautiful dream.

Time has a habit of slipping along.
Find a love, but too soon it is gone,
And there isn't a thing left but time.

Time is illusive and quick as the breeze.
Watch the wind as it plays through the trees.
Are we all just a figment of time?

There is never enough, No! There's never enough time
Just twenty four hours in a day.
There is never enough time, No! There's never enough time
Life is so brief, but what can I say?

Time is a thing with no reason or rhyme.
Tell me, what will it gain from its crime
When there isn't a thing left but time?

—*George Bullock*

For My Valentine

I will love you for what little time we have,
no questions asked, no demands made,
nor any limitation...
There is just this:
I will love you for what little time we have
with all I am...with all my heart
and all my soul,
with all my hopes and all my dreams...
This time is precious and will never come again...
But oh! the splendor and the gladness
and the blessing that you bring!
I will love you and I'll sing you songs of spring
for what little time we have...

—*Charlotte J. Kaems*

The Family

The uncle and the auntie dear
never give me pause or fear,
because their eyes shine brightly
with love that comes not lightly.

I've known them forever, it seems,
for they have addressed my dreams
when uncle talks of roses grown,
and auntie smiles and makes it known
that she and he are happy.

"How are you feeling my dear Sweet?"
That's how they are whene'er they meet,
for the wishes of their hearts are glad,
when neither one is feeling sad.

Oh, how I wish I'd known them long,
when they sing their merry song —
of youth and joy, when they were young.
'Tis where they feel that I belong.

Oh, happy song.
Oh, happy song.

—*Douglas L. Bishop*

Inspiration

Listening to the teaching of God's word
New thoughts, new realms did unfold
For I knew as I listened intently
There's much in this life to be told.

For into each life God has given
Deep gifts of lasting delight.
If we only learn to disclose them
He'll give us much deeper insight.

As I give forth my talents to others
In words, in actions, in deeds,
To those who listen, believe them.
To those He gives deeper beliefs.

For from His words He has promised
Greater deeds will gradually come.
They may not be born in my thinking
But expressed through some other one.

For inspiration is only the kindle
To commence a much deeper glow
Bringing forth a brighter ember
That perhaps, I myself could not let go.

—*Alberta A. Cox*

Heaven

No right - hand seat at banquet hall,
No starry crown or streets of gold -
Only this, dear Lord, that I might
walk hand-in hand with those I love,
That together we may share our joy
in meadows knee-deep with flowers.

And might I, with untired feet
climb the heights I've so longed to reach?
There boldly and from mountain-top
hymn my song of heartfelt praise?
And, oh, to see your loving face
and sit, adoring at your feet!

—*Alice Dommer Berg*

The Night God Stepped down on Earth

I can imagine that wondrous
night, that God stepped down on earth.
In the form of man born of
woman by natural human birth.
I can imagine the wondrous
sight the shepherd must have seen
In all their glorious assembly
to announce the newborn king.
I can imagine the animal world
as they gather all around
they knew that something grand
had happen, that night in
Bethlehem Town.
I can imagine the heavenly host
as they shouted out with joy
the coming of our blessed Savior
as a tiny baby boy.
Yes sometimes, we all ponder
and try to think of that first
glorious and wondrous Night
that God stepped down on Earth.

—*Frances Sneed*

The Greater Love

Sweet is they love to me, Jesus my savior,
No greater love could be; you died for me.
My sins were washed away, I was forgiven,
And on "The Cross" thy blood; my soul set free.

No greater friend could be, than thee my savior,
No greater love could be, than thine for me;
And now each cross I see, I cry and cling to;
Because it was "The Cross", that gave me you.

Oh Lamb of God I kneel, kneel here before thee,
Giving my soul to thee, It's lonely free.
These tears I shed for thee, pearls to the mem'ry,
Of "That Old Rugged Cross," my rosary.

No greater happiness could come to me, Lord,
No greater ecstasy than thy touch, Lord.
So back to thee I give, the soul you set free;
For life without your love, could never be.

—*John Boyd Finch*

Melancholy Manor

No smiles brighten its faces.
No laughter lightens its rooms.
Speech is rendered in terse commands.
The morrow arrives in dark gloom.
The rain, prayed for, receives no thankful ovation.
Illness, pain and grim demeanor mark the hours.
No love nurtures the human condition.
No ears the songs of birds.
The seasons fly into sober inevitability.
Curses fly like the chanticleer's crow.
Joy long has fled.
Sorrow lurks in its somber habitat.
The flowers of summer dry into dust.
Crickets murmur like dim, nightly buzz saws.
The moon's silver-cream face glows unseen.
Natures glories display in vain.
Alienation separates.
Jealousy, malice and envy lurk darkly.
Ye who dwell therein, arise.
Only one life for you! Spend it wisely.

—*Dorothy M. Schreiber*

This Hour

5 o'clock is tea time, or is it wine time, or time to dine?
No matter what the time is — this entire hour is mine
'Mine' to take a nap in, or, 'Mine' to read a book
Or, 'mine' to sweep the floor with — or find a shady nook
To run and hide my worries in — pretend they're not around
Or else I'll have more wrinkles and develop an ugly frown

Yes, this hour I have is mine — all mine to do with as I choose
And, if I choose to waste it what've I got to loose?
It doesn't seem like much to loose — just one hour out of the day
But, what if it turned out to be the last hour here of my stay
I wonder how I'd spend it? With whom would I choose to play?
Or, would I choose to just be "alone" — just God and me today?

To close the final chapter of this book — "My Earthly Stay"

—*Betty McLendon*

Somewhere Out There

Somewhere out there, there is a little baby crying.
No one to care for her.
Somewhere out there, a mother pines her loss.
Her only child to a drive-by-shooting.
Somewhere out there, a boyfriend contemplates suicide.
His girlfriend was killed by a rival gang, because of him.
They were all innocent.
Violence never solves anything.
Why can't people see?
The pain, the agony, the loss.
How bad will it get before we kill ourselves off?
In a matter of one lifetime, we learned how to create life.
We also learned how to destroy ourselves.
If this continues, who will be the next generation?
The people who survive the savage gang wars!
Why can't we all just get along?

—*Amy Elias*

The Flood Of 1993 In Springfield, MO

The torrential rains continued to fall,
No relief was in sight,
The roaring of the water could be heard
In the darkness of the night,
Amid the rush of the water,
Frightened people were awakened,
Trembling with fright,
Where will we go, what can we do?
Were their anguished cries,
Our homes, our place of security,
  is being destroyed tonight
My sister and brother in law,
  Willa Murlean and Richard Everett, were so awakened with
Thoughts of what can we do, where will
  we go? Where will we spend the night,
With water covering their bed,
They fled for higher ground.
Tears come to my eyes, as I viewed the destruction,
My loved ones were trying so hard to be brave,
Now they have no home, no place to call their own,
  just a rented place.
Now may God bless them and help them,
  through these trying times.
And help them to forget the flood of 1993, and bring peace to them.

—*Almeda Utterback*

Woman In Bosnia

There is no peace to be found,
   no stopping of the sound
of gunfire, of death all around.

In the awful battle, I spoil
   myself; my senses must recoil
from the brutality of this bloody soil.

There is no place within me
   for life; could there ever be
in a carved out, hollow tree?

There is no peace any place,
   no peace, no grace;
no peace, no rest, not a trace.

There is no place I can call my own,
   but through my pain a light has shone.
A ray of sun, a hope begun.

Far away, I hear a healing voice
   too faint for me to rejoice
of any chance I have a choice.

Will someone come to plough and sow
where seeds of peace alone will grow?
   —*Annette Ansari*

It's Not Easy

"Ah What is this these eyes behold, pray tell me, pretty one?
   No, 'tis not easy growing old.
     Do I see tears in those blue eyes—
     and why the sad and mournful sighs?
Come my Dear, sit awhile—and Hey!
   though our steps are slow, in Spirit we are young.
   and though we're wrinkled now and gray,
     our love and Faith will keep us strong.

Don't you weep for us now, we're together,
   We'd have it no other way;
We could never live apart, you see
   our lives and hearts are intertwined.
'Twas planned for us by God's design.
We bid you fond adieu my child, it's time for you to go.
   Our paths may never cross again
     but you must flourish and grow___
     until a time like this, and then you'll know,
   It's not easy growing old."
   —*Juanita Creech Gilliam*

A Woman's Lullabye

The pain that is a woman's
No man on earth can know
for it's in the very nature
Of her she-ness that it grows.
It has the essence of a womb
The same soft swell as breasts
The crescendo of her labor pains
And the smell of a newborn baby's breath.
It's everything that is of her
And everything that is not
At the very core of femaleness
Is the longing, aching, empty spot.
So sing her a song of motherhood
And girlhood long passed by
Sing a soft and gentle tune
For she needs a woman's lullabye.
   —*Alice D. Carter*

Pictures

I touch your picture,
No warmth or love comes through.
And yet the memory of the other
Causes me to cradle it
As if it were you.
I close my eyes and see your smiling face,
The warm embrace of the child I once held.
I miss you more as time goes by.
How can that be?
The pain is so great you see.
I touch your picture,
The warmth and love comes through
Only in the memories of my heart.
My mind riddled with pain
Soothed only by the feelings my heart recalls.
The memories I desperately need to ease my broken heart.
I touch your picture,
For one brief moment transported back
To the warmth and love of other times,
Your smile, my child and son, in memory now…
   —*Beckie A. Miller*

They Knew All Along

Can I come home Mom and Dad?
Nobody here likes me like you do.
No one treats me the same as you,
They don't love me just as I am.

I thought I could do it on my own,
Thought I'd be all right, I'd survive.
Well, on the outside I'm all right,
But my inner self could use nourishment.

I need some support, some encouragement.
Can I come home for awhile?
Can I again be the child,
And let you take all the responsibility?

Will you shelter me from the world,
Tell it to go away and leave me alone?
I'm tired of fighting and always losing so
My energy's down to the last spark.

Can I come home Mom and Dad?
Soon I'll grow restless and return
To my grown-up life alone, but
Sometimes I just need to come home.
   —*Beth Vonder Embse*

Groundoun

Ground-hogs Day, named for a big fat rodent
Not a swine as the name might make you think
But one of POGO's pals from the Big Swamp
Who got his name from time his species spent
In frontier cook-pots from which squeamish shrink
If told what they've just ate after a chomp.
His weather predictions are never wrong
Since it's six weeks to the Spring Equinox
That translates to just six weeks more Winter
Or time to tune the lyre for a Spring Song
Pessimists, optimists pull-up your socks
It's the cold seasons' final dull splinter.

This rat can predict a Spring Solistice
As well as any T. V. Forecaster,
As long as he's stirred up on Feb the deuce,
Perhaps not with precision of the Swiss
Nor can they make Spring come any faster
Even if they give the old girl a goose.
   —*Joseph E. Barrett*

Unchain Your Brain, Let Freedom Rain

It happened centuries ago, and we weren't here. Neither you, nor me.
Nobody wants to talk or hear about slavery. Not you, not me.

But, you're a slave now! Just how could this be?
Yes! Everyone's tired of hearing and talking about slavery. Both you and me.

You're a slave indeed. But don't believe me.
Too much's been heard, read and said about slavery. By you and me.

Think, look, listen, if not dense — you'll agree.
It's nineteen ninety-three and we're still in slavery. Both you and me.

That's why we just can't forgive and forget about slavery, you see,
Because you're a slave to your superiority mentality.

How up-lifting it would be to end this slavery of you and me.
But you're a slave driving to impose inferiority upon me.

True, it was handed down to you and me by ancestry.
There's yet one big difference between your being a slave — and me.

You persist in being a slave by choice, but not me.
My eternal struggle is for equality, harmony and to be free.

But you're a slave to the endless task of keeping me in captivity.
The ultimate questions now seem ironically to be.

Will you choose to...? Thus, I be forced to..., or

Will we "Be damned," if we leave posterities in slavery?
—*Ardelphia Hickey*

Taurus

No one understands the Raging Bull,
Nor ever will.
He lunges forth and whirls back.
He stomps the ground and tosses his head,
With horns that threaten,
And his eyes are filled with Rage.
His nostrils are flared and muscles poised,
For a purpose that only he understands,
And that's the way he likes it.
—*Darrel Robert Safko*

To My Mother

I no longer have to see the despair in your eyes,
Nor the wretched smile that you tried to disguise,
The pain that you felt within your heart,
Nor the torment that you carried from the start.

I know that you're now happy at last,
No longer to endure the things of the past,
The pain, the suffering has come to an end,
The broken heart is now on the mend.

You're dwelling with the Angels with God on your side,
You can now hold up your head and walk with dignity and pride,
No longer the indignitaries that you had to endure,
You're now resting in the heavens', with all that is pure.

Your face is before me with each morning I awake,
I feel your presence within me, with each step that I take,
I know you're smiling down at me from heaven above,
And that you'll be watching over me with affection and love.

—*Carmela Mariano*

Creation

Twas the dawn of creation and all through the land
Not a creature was stirring, they were still just a plan.
Then the Spirit of God, God the Son, God the Father,
Moved upon the face of the water.
He held up his hands, said "Let there be light,"
From the darkness divided, behold day and night.
This was the first day, the works just begun, for
There still was no moon, there still was no sun.
But God was not finished, He then made the heaven.
This was day two of a total of seven.
On the third day God gathered together the seas,
Created the grass and the fruit bearing trees,
The moon and the stars to rule over the night,
To rule over the day, the sun would shine bright.
For signs and for seasons, for days and for years,
The sun rules the day and hides our night fears.
On the fifth, living creatures and the birds of the air.
"Be fruitful and multiply," He said to each pair.
To the two by His side, He said, "Let Us make man
And give him dominion of the beasts of the land."
So in His own likeness, He gave his man life
And from one of his ribs, He made him a wife.
On the seventh God said, "Behold all looks good."
He sat down and rested as all of us should.
For the seventh is holy, we call it the Lord's Day.
And we'll keep it holy, forever I pray.
—*Charlotte J. Byerly*

Heros Are Never Forgotten

Heros are never forgotten,
not by man or God.
While some men run and hide,
shaking all over inside
Afraid that if they fight,
they might lose their life.
Heros don't think of danger,
that there is for them.
For God showers them with favors,
giving them great courage,
with unmeasurable strength
Allowing them to do impossible task,
unheard of by average men.
Because of their love for life,
God reserves a place for them,
where only angels live.
Heroic acts become immortal, both for God and man.
Locking their deeds in history, so people will understand.
What it takes to be a hero, is to be an outstanding man.
With endless love for God, country and fellow men.
—*Felix Bourree*

The Thought Of Life

Deep in secluded thought,
of all life's perils and blessings brought,
To continue to fight a battle within,
Facing life's obstacles, determined to win,
Sometimes discouraged, life's in vain,
Seeking God's grace new courage to gain
For in seeking God, there is power in prayer,
Knowing the answer when life's unfair.
Whether unfair or life's at its best,
Remaining in hope, God's perfect rest.
Rest from the cares and worries and strife,
That often we face as we go through life,
But again in christ, new hope we find,
Granting us faith and true peace of mind.
—*Clara Jane Conner*

Forever

Nothing lasts forever
Not even time ask it of the moment
it just left behind.

Springs come and summer's show
but listen to winter ask you
where did they go?

Autumn leaves dance across the ground
where lies it's greenery?
It couldn't be found.

Mountains roar up to the heavens
with such a great fuss
not knowing their ending
as a pile of dust

Where lies tomorrow but in yesterday
"a dream" called reality that's
faded away.

Nothing lasts forever!
"Not even time, ask it of the moment
it's just left behind.
—*Hamus Khan*

My Everlasting Gift

Lord help me today to serve my fellowman
   Not for me, but for Thine
A happy greeting, and a smile, this which is free!
   Without these, life is not worthwhile.
Let my gleam be a beam of a glow
   That shows a life worthwhile.
Let my hands be a symbol
   Of what you have given,
To make my life worth living.
   Without Thy help,
My eyes could not see
   The beauty in front of me.
Without the fine tune in my ear,
   I could not know what the eye sees, the smile says
The gleam gleamed, and the glow glowed.
   These things are mine
Because of your love,
   And the seeds you sowed!
—*Eldora Anderson*

Rebekkah

Her name is Rebekkah
Not from sunnybrook Farm
she's quite a lady
Who has lots of charm
she's funny and witty
In her own sweet way
Once you get to know her
She will always make your day
She's the sweetest little girl
Whom you can always depend
When you want to hear secret things
When in need of a friend
So if you meet her
And a friendship starts to grow
You will always feel at ease with her
Because she is a wonderful person to know.
—*Barbara C. Mazrolle*

No More Heroes

There is no such thing as heroes
Not in my mind
I used to believe, but then I learned
   that there really is no such thing

There is not one person in this world
That can make everything "right"
A "role model" for all to follow
One that we can all be proud of

A white knight in shining armor is not
   to be found, either
No one gets "rescued" their way anymore
Only in fairy tales - and this is reality

I had a few heroes in my day
But life took them away
You see, my daddy - he's gone, never to
   save me from harm again
And my knight in shining armor rusted-

   Rather fast

There are no such thing as heroes
Only in make-believe
—*Georgianna W. Zboray*

Hobo Eulogy

I've walked those lines so many miles, my legs have ached at night
Not knowing or caring where they go, sometimes I walk just for spite

There's a lesson to be taught if you're willing to give the time
But it can only be learned out there, and you have to walk those lines

You can take the memories with you or let them lie instate
For there's always new ones waiting, if you want to chance your fate

Some things you may not understand as along the lines you tread
Like blind curves, trestles, and even the darkened tunnel ahead

The clickity-clack over the cross-ties, that lonesome whistle at night
That disappearing shot across the desert, is an unforgetful sight

You'll recall the moist mountain shadows, the dusty flat fields
But for every connecting rail you pass, the adventure builds and builds

The noise from the city lines will deafen your waning ear
Then you'll treasure the gentle quietness that's out there in the clear

The rushing noise anticipates that pushing wind in your face
In a few short minutes it's gone—so you begin another pace

For me it's a way to slow life down—this world's too fast as it is
And I believe God placed those thoughts along those lines,
And it's just another mystery of His!
—*James Allen Hayes*

Courtney

C - is for caring, so cute little grand,
O - is for overwhelming, obviously smart,
U - is for untarnished, little one.
R - is for respect, that you rightfully deserve,
T - is for thoughtful, caring heart
N - is for nice, new young face,
E - is for expressive, a happy child
Y - is for youth, young and special, that's Courtney,
   pure, precious, pride and joy.
—*Joyce J. Williams*

My Prayer

God grant our prayers that we may have peace
Not only that the wars must cease
But peace in heart and soul and mind
And restore dignity to all mankind

Oh cleanse this earth Almighty God
Arrest the sin that runs rampant on our sod
The addicts who have gone astray
Please help them Lord to see the way

Our sins of riots and rape and greed
And homeless people who are in need
The judges who have turned there head
When crimes were committed and blood was shed.

Yes man has progressed in every field
Yet humbly to God we should yield
We're very proud man can perform a heart transplant
To left our soul in only something God can grant.
—*Edith Taylor*

The Beauty Of Nature

Have you ever really taken time to look around?
Nothing as beautiful has ever been found.

Nature acts as protector of all of Earth,
It'll start to shield you and protect you
at the second of your birth.

If you're kind to Earth, it'll be kind to you,
Earth can make your best experiences shine anew.

People don't know what Earth has to give,
But it has given the ultimate, the chance to live.

There's a side of Nature that we seldom see,
It's Nature's fury, pure havoc when set free.

When you have a chance, look around our home,
All of this beauty in a huge dome.
—*Brian Stewart*

Tomorrow's Child

The weeping of a planet's people once graced
Nothing returned whence removed from its place
Timberland destroyed, waters contaminated, now...burning the sky
Without clean air tomorrow's child will surely die

With fire and shot inner cities discharge destruction
Only from love and peace can we begin reconstruction
First fill the hand, then heal the heart
Bring us together, that's where tomorrow's child will start

A new beginning, time to rebuild our lives
Men must take responsibility and live with their wives
Put down the drugs, stop lusting after greed
Show tomorrow's child, life begins with good deeds

Life's breeze carried by hope in our hand
Know by sharing which brings change across the land
All but no difference between race, creed or color
For tomorrow's child will be someone's sister or brother
—*Joseph Wayne*

Boredom Creeps In

As children, we get up in the morning and run out to play, nothing to us is boring.

As young adults, the days are quite routine, but at night we feel like we're soaring, and sometimes it just can get boring.

As adults we finally get married, and wonder what life has stored, the days are very hectic, but at times become a little bored.

As older folks, we find life is adoring, and think there's time to do some exploring, but life has gotten the edge on us and ————— Ahh, everything
  Seems
   Too
    Boring!!
—*Gloria J. Brown*

Untitled

The few words I said in anger hurt you deeply
Now we are both carrying the scars on our hearts
The same hearts that once shared a special bond
The hearts that once held love now harbor hate

What happened to us, how can we feel this way?
Did we make a wrong turn, or have we changed so much that we don't know each other anymore?

I miss your gentle touch, your love and concern
You were always there for me when I needed you most
The time we spent together means more to me than anything I have every known
Now that we are no longer together, I can feel the void left in my heart.
I can't go on this way, so I know I have to tell you something-
I am very sorry, and never meant to hurt you
I pray that you can find it in your heart to forgive me, but I understand if you can't.
I will never forget you, and my love for you will never die.
—*Amie Zischke*

Standing Before The Judge

Maiden:
O Judge please let it be
That this gent in marriage accompany me
I beg my dear Sir, leisure hours we have spent
Abomination if no proper intent.
Gent:
Her virtues are no delight
My intent was only one night
Engagement naught, is upon my brow
Twas the ale, that vexed my mind some-how.
Judge:
Out of his snuff-box it was a pinch and whiff
Twas his nose he gave that disgusting gift
With a cough and a sputter
Guilty, guilty, guilty, was his mutter.
Judge:
Appointment there will be to wed
Marriage now is upon your head
For in my book I now shall write
Tis a devilish man that spends just one night.
—*Judith I. Tucker*

My Reflection

O' wind where are you, I need to fly away
O' sun where is the warmth to fill my day
O' soul where are the raiments of my beliefs
I feel them falling, engulfed by grief.
The cries of torment that fill my nights
In this mirror image, there are no lights
The anguish of loss I feel no more
For my flesh of this world, is but a sore.
The image is glass, I tell my self
Put it away upon the shelf
Tomorrow will bring the sun I know
Melting away the things that must go.
To feel the peace my soul cries for
Must I leave and close the door
No! wit to say I remain intact
I need not leave to return back.
I must look in the mirror, know face to face
Retrospectively, put things into place
For its not this world I must surpass
But my own reflection in the glass.
—*Daris Riggs*

Torn Between Love And Hate

And God asked, "Do you take this life, to be good,
  obedience,
    cheerful,
      and kind?"

And the Devil also asked, "To be mischievous,
  dishonest,
    hateful,
      and non-refine?"

And man said, "I do."

And here we are torn between two walls
of love and hate for me and for you.

"Oh, God!" we say
when trouble's at hand,

And at the same instance we're at
the throat of our fellow man.

We all have two things in common, and this I know;

They are birth and death, so—
  so, why not live together in love
    and harmony.

And there's plenty to go around for you and for me.
—*Berry L. Sweeting*

Eternal Spirit

Our family fell to pieces after she was gone.
Now she is surrounded by loved ones and
strangers who all get along.
She has left us with only memories
and her spirit to help us
get on with our lives.

Though our hearts are heavy with sorrow,
we know she is in a better place
where there is no pain,
no anger, no sadness.
Love embraces us as he arms
had in the past,
she is still here watching over us.
Her name lingers on every tongue
and echoes in every heart,
she will never leave our sides.

—*J. J. Peto*

Prayer For Peace

Spread thy wings, O dove of peace,
O'er the nations of all this earth.
How hollow: "He has not died in vain:"
Soar on through storm or rain,
    We pray for peace.

Man has his choice of the sky wherein may fly—
Bird on wing or some destructive thing,
Where sunshine may light the earth,
Or flak blacken out God's gift to man.
    We pray for peace.

Earth may yield to the horn of plenty,
Tilled by the lovers of soil and nature;
Or man may choose to flood with blood,
God's universe, where stand crosses row on row.
    We pray for peace.

Oceans, whose only song was a melody,
A zephyred breeze, horizons kissing sky.
How man's will can change this all....
Yet peaceful it can be if only you would try.
    We pray for peace.
—*G. W. La Prell*

Here Is A True Story

Here is a story and it really is true,
Of a newly married couple named Bob and Sue.
Long before the first week had all passed by,
Sue heard her husband breathe a deep sigh.
The money we had, has all been spent,
Perhaps even foolishly, was his lament!
We've boxes and boxes of china and spoons.
But no mouse trap, no fly swatter, not even a broom!
Lest Bill and Donna come to this same tragic end,
Here are a few dollars for extras from some Noble(s) friends.
Love, and best wishes always,
Melvin and Addie Belle Nobles
—*Addie Belle Nobles*

Forever Autumn

As I rest here, this day, underneath the stretching bough of a tree
Hovering gracefully, gently, over you and over me,
I realize how long a period of time has passed
Since my brief, yet so sincere visit of last.
The flowers Nana brought for you dance, as if alive in the breeze
Just as you are, wild among the shrill whisperings of the leaves.
"I've missed you, Mom."
And the air with its seasonal chill is already here.
Together with its bright, crisp autumn palette;
A whited sepulchre of yet another passing year.
It seems an eternity since I've heard the sweet notes of your voice.
Yes, mom, of course there was a good reason for this dark,
  veiled choice.
Though, let us not dwell upon such ill-defined ideas; No, not now.
Let us only be together; you, me, the constant creaking of the
  bough.
For I have this day, come to tell you that I love you.
My mother - to me transcendental; to me so pure.
How I wish I might kiss again your soft lips, so very like to my
  own,
When I say, "Happy Birthday, my darling Mother," 1955-1974.
—*Jennifer Lane*

The Coelacanth

The Coelacanth slumbers in Neptune's bed chambers dreaming
Of ancient Crossopterygian fisherman who spearless and
Stripped of their neoprene, stand naked to the epoch.
Down ten thousand fathoms a heartache begins to rise
Headlong toward the surface like some antiquated submersible
That too soon has severed the timeworn ties of ballast.
It rises upward, festooned with hitchhiking barnacles,
Throwing off kelp beds like chains of painful memories.
As recollections start to bend in the coelacanth's veins
Sea anemones drunk on nitrogen bubbles chortle and
Tap dance upon the cortex of its primordial brain.
An agonizing anguish courses through its antediluvian hulk
As the scintillating surface beckons it like a burning bush.
A shower of foamy brine trumpets its marriage with the air,
As hoary gills burst in the gasp of a surf sounding sob.
Methodically the tumbling tide pitches it onto the shore
Where it's cradled in a coffin of brilliant burning sand.
Azure waters lap furtively at the decaying corpse
Like pallbearer's hands insidiously clutching bronze handles
Hoping for a surer grip.
—*Edwin R. Gilweit*

I Will Seek No Angels

Strangers in the distance beckon, silver silhouettes, familiar denizens
Of childhood dreams and eldervisions.
Love like nothing ever known, majestic, draws me,
floatingsoaringflying
Groundless golden skyrise of rebirth. The new beginning—
secondchance—
 draws near,
But Jacob Marley's chains stretch taut from Atlas' ball of dirt.
Reality returns, it din and labor dulling dreams, hope and courage
 drowned in humdrum.

If Creature man must spend each day much like another, I will do the
 same,
But live all my Todays as my Tomorrows, not
The Yesterdays of sagging souls—did He create the World in shades of
 gray?
But sweet ephemeral precious beauty—forettick, unsulliedstream—
This time conscious of her virtue, innocence a priceless gem.

Not for me, a tarnished Heaven! Not for me the rainbow's rust!
I'll pledge my faith to Peter Pan
And walk the nights with Lincoln's ghost

And when I set out from the Valley
Where bluebonnets flourish and bison play,
When daylight darkens on the whisper of wings, I will seek no angels
Save the spotted owl-lets who fill the sky, numbered as the stars,
And if you chance to hear His call, watch me take my leave, you'll see
My God and I together soar among them, free as wind.
—*Holly A. McCoy*

Dreams Of The Night

In the still, secret, seclusion
Of the darkness drawing near
A colorful, floating fantasy
Lingers from ear to ear

It seduces you with its illusion
You're soon to fade away,
Just drifting in a timeless world
Like a non-rehearsed play.

Before your feet can hit the ground
The robin starts her song
To celebrate another day
Now the dreams of the night are gone....
—*Gail Ranae Brensike*

Goldenrod

I catch the ripples
of dewy condensation
that form on skin as fair as a new daisy's petal,
with my tongue...
and delight in the free spirit you are
and the copulation sustained
by the riveted moondance of your creation.

You have unearthed fields and meadows
of fruitful, vegetative wonder
by the manipulation of your mystical eroticism...
surpassing the splendor of the moves
of the serpentine in the forest
with your superfluous drive.

And the fertility and passion
of the Goldenrod
consumed by encounters seeped in droplets
sweet as plum wine...
dispel thoughts of all
but you
in the abyss that is my soul.
—*Bianca Mihalik*

Embers Of Eden

Did he go east, or was it west
 of Eden here today?
I've lost my innocence because,
 he said he knew the way.
A newborn was I, but I knew
 the rib from which I came,
So trusted in his word and now,
 I'll never be the same.
I thought his love was perfect then,
 my love would make it so,
But when the innocence was lost
 I saw perfection go.
Now Adam is not here with me
 in Eden, I'm alone.
No longer innocent, but lost,
 and where has Adam gone?
—*Jean Franse*

It's Time

It's time to think of days gone by,
 of first grade tears and
 twelfth grade cheers,
 of friends who stay throughout
 the years,
It's time to say good-bye.

It's time to have that future plan,
 set the goals for life ahead,
 learn to listen to what's said,
 use the knowledge of what's read
and say I know I can.

I'll have my Lord beside me,
 showing me the way,
 to live and work and play,
 while guiding me each day,
with love that keeps me free.
—*Jacqueline R. Smith*

Reflections

Before me lies a thousand fears
Of future incarnated years;
Of memories buried in a haze;
Of bondage in a Mortal maze.

Before me lies a thousand shoals
Of moaning, musty, naked souls;
Of yawning chasms spewing fire;
Of wraiths depraved, aroused desire.

Before me lies a thousand dreams
Of stranded love, misplaced scenes;
Of tainted replicas of my past;
Of trials before the Saintly Caste.
—*Betty Jeanne Wilhite Everett Brewster*

Idealistic Youth

To my brother.

Dreaming, day-dreaming ... in ecstasy,
  Of gallant swordsmen and charming knights
Rescuing ladies — o, romantic century!
  Ladies fear and endless sighs.

Those days of you are gone forever:
  Bold encounters and daring feats —
Only a cherished past — to remember.
  Wake up! Be alert to today's needs.
—*Isabel O. Neidig*

Friends

I think of you often, the way it used to be.
Of how much I loved you. Do you remember me?
A friend I wanted, nothing more.
I'd never had a real friend before.

The first time I saw you, I did have doubt.
There's no possible way this will work out.
I didn't like you, you didn't like me.
Thought friends we would never be.

Then, our first days together I began to see,
That I could care for you. Do you remember me?
But in time all good things end.
Just as it did with you, my friend.

So, as the years pass by, we lose and gain.
Friends are the best things that we can obtain.
I hope you'll remember me now and then.
And the special time you were my friend.
—*Barbara Howell*

Please...

No plastic posies on my grave,
No artificial flowers;
No iridescent rose that glows
For hours and hours and hours...
Just place a real, a live bouquet
Well watered with your tears,
And I'll sleep peacefully, my love,
For years and years and years...
—*Doris J. Bunch*

The Master Speaks

And the student humbly spoke to the Master....

  "Tell me, dear Master, what you've learned of life,
  Of human bondage, pain, and strife.
  Speak of the knowledge received during the fight
  To let go of self and experience the Light."

And the Master spoke to all who would listen....

  "Life is a paradox," the Master began:
  "...the more you give, the more you get,
    the more you get, the less you need.

  ...the more you let go, the more you receive,
    the more you receive, the less you want.

  ...the less you indulge, the more you enjoy,
    the more you enjoy, the less you desire.
  ...the more you know, the more ignorant you are,
    the more ignorant you are, the wiser you become.

  ...the more you die, the more you live,
    the more you live, the more you hurt.

  ...the more you hurt, the less you care,
    the less you care, the more you love."
—*John Charping*

On Little Cat Feet

Again one night I experienced a slight tread.
Of little "Cat feet going round my bed.
"Little cat feet", as Carl Sandburg wrote.
Of his poetic words I've taken note.
But my little eat feet weren't in a fog
But close to me in a slumbering bog.
My own little cats were in another room.
I made their shapes, throughout the gloom.

Are these little foot falls of eats I once knew?
From another time and dimension, I once knew
That wander nightly into my view.
Who think my warm bed, as a welcomed home
Even in the half worlds they seek to find.
A loving place, one warm, welcoming and kind.
—*Betty Perotti*

Reflections 1994

The space ship voyager, in its probe of millions and millions
of miles has not revealed to us a place called heaven.

The scriptures say: "Now we see through a glass darkly—."

Perhaps, heaven really is "all about us." But as mortals we
Cannot see the souls of our departed loved ones.

Yet, there are times when we feel them near. Suddenly our
Faith in eternity becomes firm and we can sing!

O God our help,
  Our hope,
    Our guide,
"And our eternal home!"
—*Evelyn Butler McCulloh*

Memories VI

Realms of time bring us rare gifts
of remembrance

Oft' in our dark and lonely moods
Our mind creates an image
So that we can be with you.
Through the holiest depths
our memories thrill 'til we almost
look to see thee rise, like a soaring
bird to the free blue skies.
A star sent down from the heavens
above and all undimmed by the
shade of love but, oh it's sweet,
'tis very sweet,
In these fairy realms of dreams
to greet. Thou truly ar't far away
though we know not where
your steps now stray.
A rainbow pictured by love's own sun
on the clouds of being
God's chosen one.
—*Gina M. Moore*

Mountain Memories

I sing of seasons in the past
Of summer's heat and winter's blast.
The gray wolf's song on icy nights
And the eerie flash of northern lights.

I sing of springtime's buds and rills
Of rainbows arching distant hills.
Of summelt's trickle from weary gray snow
Seeking it's way to the streams far below.

I write of summer's happy hours
Of shady nooks and fragrant flowers.
Of birds a-winging from the south
Warm zephyrs bringing hint of drouth.

I sing of autumn's golden days
Of morning's mist and evening's haze.
Of frosty rime on brook and glade
Where fall's bright leaves began to fade.

When crystal crusted the mountains high
And dark clouds gathered in the sky
Then Indian summer's harvest moon
Showed early winter was coming soon.
—*Josephine O. Ritchie*

Widows Years

It starts with the loss
Of the one you let be boss.
Then comes the start of the grief
There doesn't seem to be an relief.
It begins with shock and tears
As you look back over the years
You have the wonderful memories
But you have to see ahead through the trees.
Everyone keeps saying give it a year.
Is this a magical time when I will cheer.
I think not, but I really don't know.
My year is about over and it doesn't show.
It went by so very fast.
It will be a year in my past.
I will go into my remaining years,
Maybe with just a few less tears.
There is a little bit of relief,
I know there is less grief.
Yes, there is a widows year,
But it certainly is not a time to cheer.
—*Ann Marie Meverden*

An Easter Prayer

O Father, give us understanding
   Of the things we cannot see,
Give us faith and love unending;
   Make us messengers for Thee.

You made your Son a revelation
   Of Your own divine estate;
He taught us how a resurrection
   Can save us from a bitter fate.

He came to take the mist away
   And leave us free to choose,
To climb the heights or go astray,
   A goal to win or lose.

He built a life, pattern for us;
   O let us strive, His likeness merit,
And make each step a moving forward.
   Eternal life? God, let us share it.

O God, let zeal and wisdom sway us,
   Inspire our aims, our every breath,
We pray Thee in the name of Jesus,
   Immortal conqueror of death.
—*Fannie C. Brown*

If Only

I dreamed I was Merlin Wizard
   of the worlds —
     Magician extraordinaire—
Who made a magic potion —
Sent by breezes - wafted on the air
Dissolving hate and disillion.
Each smelled what he liked best —
the farmer new mown hay
   and fresh turned earth—
Filling each - with the love and resolution.
I - with all the rest
With smells of family dinner —
   home - love in all its worth.
All men were brothers
With prayers that never cease —
The name of the potion
Was — the word called "peace."
—*Helen J. T. Brumbaugh*

Nail-Scarred Hands

How sad to read the story
   Of those nail-scarred hands and feet
     How Jesus must have suffered
       As many looked on, but few wept.

Jesus, however, did not complain
   For He knew it had to be
     So He suffered it all in silence
       Yes, He died for you and me.

He gave His life for all our sins
   There on the old rugged cross
     Can't you just see Him and understand
       He really cares that much for us?

What a glorious time it had to be
   When Jesus, on the third day
     Arose from the dead to reign
       On high, and is there yet today!
—*Helen E. Bean*

When The Birds Came Tumbling Down

Generations of birds had nested in the trees
   Of vast, majestic forests, offering security and ease
To nurture babies; with food in great supply...
   Seeds, nuts, berries, insects flying by.
It was nature's paradise of freedom, joy and song...
   Until progress destroyed forests; moving ruthlessly along...
Paving streets, building houses, erecting poles with wires high;
   Human beings were everywhere; noisy traffic raced on by.
The birds settled on the wires, where once had been their trees,
   Finding little sustenance and shivering in the breeze...
Then, labeled "Public Nuisance", by the people down below
   For soiling on the sidewalks, plans were made for them to go.
The famished birds pecked the toxic grain,
   That progress lavished on their town...
And the wires were still with eerie calm
   ....When the birds came tumbling down....
Across the land, the people moved,
   With New Technology given birth....
Until.... the Chain-Of-Life forever torn
   .... There was nothing left on earth....
    —*Dona K. Soler*

Locked Out

I trudged home through the storm leaving a wall
Of white behind me. Once I turned the key
And opened up, a pigeon set to flee
The bitter cold and blustery snowfall
Ran past into a corner of the hall.
Secure at last it stared askance at me
Who could not fail to understand the plea
That I must help it live or death would call.
I flung open the door and chased it out
Of the apartment building. Tenants know
We do not need a bird strolling about
Where young and old or what we are must go.
At dawn I wondered, who are we to flout
The frozen pigeon lying in the snow?
    —*Carrol McNeal*

Fall

For many of us, fall is a favorite time
of year, a time when we revel in the
splendor of the autumnal foliage.
But it also brings with it a certain
amount of sadness.
Soon the trees will shed their summer
coats, and their bared limbs will serve
as a reminder that winter will soon be
upon us.
Leaves scurry along the ground seeking
refuge from their impending doom.
Squirrels whisk about burrowing food to
carry them through the long months ahead.
And as we look skyward, we see formations
of our feathered friends heading south
to a warmer climate.
But for those of us who must stay and
weather the storm, and for what seems
to be an eternity we all wait, and watch,
knowing that with the passage of time,
we will soon rejoice in the first signs
of spring.
    —*Carolyn P. DuEst*

On Love And Peace

Do away from harmful rivalry instinct.
Of your neighbor and of yourself you think,
And forget envy greed and jealousy,
For as mankind we are brothers born to be
One with care for love and peace possible.

Put aside all differences which are
(Inborn or acquired onto time this far)
Due to race or culture or language mode;
Tolerance we heed to the best we could...
Oh, that we foster brotherhood in our hearts!

Then the candle we lit amongst the lights,
Bright in daylight brights, bright in darkest nights,
Shines full in our heart and soul all the time
Throughout the length of years through any clime
With life of happiness fostered by peace.

Then we know our existence in this world,
For HE made us the object of the WORD,
And we are here to magnify HIS deed
As to shine more the life to live we need,
That LOVE is our world and our PEACE the price.
    —*Amadeo Abaya*

Going Home

When all God's children are gathered home, won't it be great
Oh God I pray, no one will be late
On that great tomorrow, He is sure to come for everyone
God the Fr. God the Son.

For that great tomorrow, I cannot miss
Eternal love, eternal bliss
He loves us so, wherever we go, we'll be so happy there
With God's love everywhere.

Oh blissful day, when Jesus came to say
I am the truth, I am the way
I must hurry on down the path of love
He will surely come for me from heaven above.

I think about that great plantation from day to day
In joyful triumph, the great great way
Where we'll walk with Jesus, hand in hand
In heavens glory land.
    —*Grace Stuffle*

The Lonely Cowboy, Auld Lang Syne

      Following this dusty trail,
  Oh, so lonely, searching, yet to no avail.
    Leaving Donna behind, never no more,
    His feelings of being unable to score,
   Behold, an old acquaintance he does find,
Their trails, once again, doth entwine, "Auld Lang Syne."
   Sherry, beautiful hazel eyes, of scarlet hair,
   Her hands, still the touch of loving care.
  Her smile, more beautiful, than spoken word,
    Like that of a beautiful mockingbird.
It's been a long time, since seeing this friendly smile,
 in the riding of this lonely trail, a true reward, for
every dusty mile. To once again, to share a few moments
of this new day, As he was traveling on his onward way.
It was nice, their acquaintance to once again renew, her
eyes, showing a sparkle, like a fresh morning dew. "The
Lonely Cowboy," feeling their friendship, would carry to
the end. Riding on out, following the trail, going around
a bend. Not looking back, within his mind he knew, that
   their friendship would always continue.
    —*Bobby Clark*

If The Beastie Boys Can Do It, So Can I

Chillin' in our kitchen
On a cool autumn day.
Just me and my person
And C. A. A.
A lotta talk
A lotta laughs
And a lotta lox.
Got the N. W. A.
In the box.
Got my hands in the fridge
My finger's on the bagel
My person's gettin' hungry
And there's something on cable.
Some shows got class
Some shows got trash
Cable's got the kinda shows
That keeps you on your ass.
—*Amy M. Whalen*

Loving You Lord

Loving you is like a cool, cool drink
on a sultry, dusty, sunshiny day.

Like drinking hot chocolate on
a cold, blustery winters night.

You are as comfortable as
my favorite easy chair.

As exciting as an eagle in flight.
As beautiful as a rose in
its first bloom.

You are as dazzling as a sunset
in the evening and as
refreshing as a spring rain.

You are as soothing as a mothers hand
and as strong as waves breaking on the shore.
You are everything to me and More.
—*Darlene Tallman*

Evening Memory

In my memory, I walk again,
On forest trails
Climb rocky hills, beside a cold, cold brook.

Thru unshed tears
I see the distant hills
Across the valleys trees.
I hear the owls, talking to one another
As dusk, the bark of the deer
When they discover
They are not alone.
The thrush, deep in the woods,
Sing that beautiful song.
Darkness falls, the velvet night is black.
Now the tears are shed.
Now the deep knowledge
The awareness—
That memory
Is all there is.
—*Agnes Hunter*

Revitalized!

Know you a sound more joyous, snow still being
On the ground, that that faint note
From Valiant scout of feathered friends - to quote:
"The harbinger of spring" Scarce heard - not seen.
When energies seem totally out-drained,
Each move a chore, the winter's zeal - stout chain
Of resolution - broken; snapped in two;
It's life to me, that chirp, is it to you?
It says, "Take heart! A better time is truly
On its way". It says, "Mine's but a sample
Burst upon you growing quite unruly."

That cheerful call injects a medicant.
I will hold on - no longer say, "I can't!"
—*Harriet C. Meyerink*

Answering Suicide

Does His blood run thin
On what we have done?
Though we take a whim
That life's on the run.

Free will is ours...
Responsible: our choice...
Ownership of our lives:
Such is his voice.

Does grace always keep pace
To those who once asked?
(Leave that to God.)
Go on with our task-
(To tell all:) Grace is his grace!
G-od's
R-eaching
A-ll
C-laiming
E-ternity
A-men!
—*Ira Fortna*

My Greatest Love

Dedicated to: Mr. Joseph Bruce
Once again, my love, it is time to put on exhibit, my
feelings and thoughts about you.

My love for you, flows like a river, and its destiny,
Is eternity. The hours that we are apart, take fleet,
and fly us to each other's waiting arms, for our love
has the image of paradise.

I feel that our love is strong enough to put a hurricane
At peace. Our love plays on every wave of restless sea.
Our love is engraved in the sands of a seashore, and when the tide
rolls in, and
Rolls out, our love will still remain,
Engraved in its sands.

The Universe will be our home. The stars will be our toys.
Your love has challenged me to climb to the highest mountain,
and proclaim to the whole world, how much I love you, and
how much you mean to me. Our love has taken on the voice
of a meadowlark, and each day, it sings a new song.

Winter, summer, fall, and spring will be my witnesses,
and verify the fact, that each one of their days, will
find me, loving you. Fling yourself to me breathlessly,
and let me experience the depth, and the worth, of your
priceless love.

I know within my heart, my soul, and my mind, that I want
to spend the rest of my life, with you. I love you. God speed.
—*Alma Jean King*

The Rome Story

Somewhere in the burnt-out ruins of ancient Troy
Once lived a happy kid known as Helen's boy.
When the day of judgement came with Achille's men
Paris friends spirited the love-child out of ken.
Their instructions were to transport this child to Thrace
Where no one there would be familiar with his face.
They followed their instructions without any doubt.
They took an oath to never let this secret out.
They were to care for this child and forever roam.
And somehow bring this boy back to his mother's home.
As they wandered they were joined by the friends of Troy
Soon the boy became a symbol for their deep ploy.
They formed the scheme to rebuild and relocate Troy;
The son of Helen became their tool and their toy.
They vowed that their city will stand eternal;
That they would stand against forces infernal.
Bringing the boy back to Sparta would be suicide;
Rather they would bring him to his kin folks to hide.
They traced the spartan breed to their source way up north.
In that direction the hardy band then went forth.
—*James G. Khing*

Devoted Companions

Two souls, motionless, gazing into the whispering stream.
One a fortress upon whom a fragile vessel would lean.
Reminiscing about days that slipped into the distant past.
Precious secrets, joyful tears and a bond that
   would eternally last.
Hazel eyes sparkled remembering lazy Sunday
   afternoon along the sleepy lake.
Blue eyes shimmered recalling rainy days and the
   sweet smell of a chocolate cake.
Ambitions of new tomorrows, open horizons and
   mysterious places.
A delicate flower, awe-inspiring sunsets and smiling faces.
Two separate lives bound together with tender care.
The path ahead filled with laughter and tears two
   souls would share.
—*Heidi R. Sauer*

One Beautiful Movement

Look at the spider spinning her web
   One beautiful movement in artistry
Look at the butterfly flying free
   One beautiful movement in melody
Look at the flower blooming in your eye
   One beautiful movement of the bumble bee
If you can see, what I can see
   Your one beautiful movement loving me
Look at love and it looks at you
   One beautiful movement to see
In the tunnel of your eyes
   A whirlpool loving me.
Look at me and I look at you
   One beautiful movement to see
Waterfall rainbows hugging on the window sills of our minds
   If your that spider spinning her web
And the butterfly flying free
   Then your the flower blooming in my eye
And you can see, what I can see
   Your one beautiful movement love-ing me
—*Francis E. Delaney*

Saga Of A Tree

If I were a tree,
one can see,
the impact it would be on everyone.
Imagine me—a Tree? and then again, back to me.
Compare me to a tree,
a tree-standing alone
at peace with everyone.
a Tree——
beckoning the weary Traveler to rest,
and shade him from the sun,
and perhaps to pluck a fruit, to boot.
A tree, like me grows old and gaunt.
Never complaining, never in want.
A tree, can be struck by lightning,
or felled by an axe.
A tree, that is used to make shelter
could also be left
to rot by the Sun.
That is the Saga of a Tree.
But, what about me?
Once felled, can one see
to what use I could be?
—*Ben Rubin*

The Pedestrian

Perhaps you started crossing a street
one day or night, and then from well
you don't know where a car approached
in sight.

You closed your eyes or held your breath,
you might have even jumped.
With shrieking cries of fear for death
you screamed and yet weren't bumped.

You might have looked around then
to face a staring crowd
of people that had watched you jump
and who were laughing loud.

But just the same it scared you
and how your heart did pound.
You made the crowd of others laugh
of how you got around.

The squeaking brakes had quieted.
The horn stopped its blare.
You looked each way and crossed the
street and went we knew not where.
—*Eugene R. Henry*

World-Side

In some yet distant time, when we shall meet - and part again -
one doubtful moment will I hold your eyes with mine;
one infinitesimal moment, then we shall stand friend to friend,
the world-side of our lives will speak of usual, formal things,
and be the greater part of each...
without a trace of anything remembered.
Then we will say a casual goodbye
with scarce a pang of realized regret.
But when I find my bed at night to ease my heart and mind
in blessed sleep,
a timeless moment will possess me then;
for I shall know you only in that instant when your eyes
crossed mine —
while we both lived — and while we both remembered.
—*Albertine Thomas*

Life

To be born free of U.S.A.
One gets married and the pleasure of
Loving each other.
Special when children
comes (Overjoy to give life.)
Extra special to make it to good parents.
To respect yourself and to know God
is peace with everything and yourself.
Double extra special for God
to come and clean this earth.
peace for all.
Always.
—*Erminia Pia Thomas*

Sequel To The Stars

The dancing stars awakened me
one humid summer night.
So I waltzed out to the meadow
and danced with them in delight.

My white skirts dragged across the grass
as I ran upon the hill,
and continued to dance with the blinking stars,
oh the feelings they made me feel!

The locusts buzzing in the trees
made music just for me,
and God made tiny, flying stars
for all the earth to see.

The moon followed with us
as we danced across the field,
that's when I decided to give thanks
so upon the grass I kneeled.

The blinking stars around me
proceeded to ever gleam,
as I said "Thank you, God, for these wonders
that now my eyes have seen."
—*Amy D. Krambeck*

Forever Loving You

I've lost everything, including the
one I love. Over time, I'll find another
to replace you. But for now, I'll cry
for your lost love. I'd never
cry in front of you, for you would
think me weak. I've lived through
more then you could ever imagined. I've
lived a thousand before this,
and I'll live a thousand after this.
But never will I forget, of my love
for you. You showed only hatred to
me, but it made me love you even more.
Some say that time heals all wounds.
But time, is something I don't have.
Even if I did, only love could mend
my broken heart. A love which you'll
never have for me. Sometime in the
future, I'll look back and remember
that boy who I loved so much. And I'll
remember only you.
—*Jessica Snider*

The Last Gang-Member

Thoughts trigger inside my head
one minute he's here, the next he's dead
Always un-able to understand why
Now all I can do is helplessly cry
If I told you once, I told you twice
But you never listened, just rolled the dice
Why did you have to join? What was the point?
Thought it was cool to make money off a joint
Joining a gang, I said, would cost you
Now you leave us behind, All of us blue
Late at night the streets you would roam
Because it was love you were missing at home
So, so-long my old friend, left with a tear in my eye
Wishing we'd never have to say goodbye.
—*Amy Sabbatis*

Beyond The Blue

As I stood in the shadow watching children play
One small boy with tear-dimmed eyes slowly walked away
He kneeled beneath an old oak tree like he was going to pray
I had to stay and listen as I heard the small boy say

Dear God I hope you're not too busy so I can have a talk with you
I'll try not to take much time I know you have a lot to do
I'll try to speak quite clearly so you'll know just what I say
You see I'm feeling lonely and I was told to pray

You see I was so very small when my Daddy went away
And it was hard to understand that he had gone to stay
My Mama always told me and I know that it is true
That someday we will meet with Daddy somewhere beyond the blue

She said that Daddy told her just before he went away.
That he was sure we could feel closer if we would take the time to
    pray.
He said he would be waiting and watching from above.
Just his soul was going with him he was leaving all his love.

It won't be easy waiting but I'll do the best I can
And each time when I get lonely I'll talk with you again
I will try to comfort Mama until our time down here is through
And again we'll meet with Daddy somewhere beyond the blue
—*Herb Trewhitt*

Kite

Way over my head, and motionless there
One small paper bird hangs up on the air.

It's coming alive and then darting when
Those long wooden bones are filled up with wind

That tugs, pulls, then fights and strains to release
The gossamer thin, long white cotton leash.

This afternoon, somewhere on some other street
The bird had been roused from long winter sleep

In a toybox nest with marbles and bears
On this, Spring's first day, to challenge the airs

And brush vivid strokes on a canvas so blue
That the orange kite looks red, and seems smaller, too

Than down on the ground in little boy's hands
That fashioned the bird and made fast the strands

Of string and cedar and paper and glue
That ran up the street until the bird flew.
—*Dean A. Clark*

The Friendly Red Barn

A large, friendly Red Barn stands upon an old abandoned farm,
One that watched children, puppies and kittens, frolicking in the sun.
What happenstance was there - why did everyone desert the friendly barn?
Perhaps the residents grew restless, desired a greener view,
And less hard, back-breaking, sun-up to sun-down toil,
'Cause, before you could wink an eye — the children, puppies and kittens grew,
Leaving behind, the friendly barn and fields of well-worn soil.

The lonely, handsome Barn remains silent. Its secret never revealed to a soul.
And now, the emptiness, so still, you think, oh dear, how sad.
Plaintively the Barn cries out "All is over — something has gone afoul."

Please — wait — Listen! A sound, there, just beyond the door.
The family, children, puppies, kittens, came home, grown up, true, hurry into the house.
Enter through the door tread noisily, happily across the floor,
And breathe a sigh of relief — then seat themselves, quietly as a mouse.

Once more the Barn awakens, as if from some very bad dream.
Alive again — still — not quite believing, that now,
They're all at home, and like a ray of Sunshine, beams,
Upon them — settles back, refreshed and life is refurbished, anew.

—*Dorothea S. Seely*

Aliapaens The Montana Monkey

Fossil hunting in Monarch on a prehistoric devonian corral reef.
One treasure trove of death from past aeons life, truly magnificent grief.
My quarry is an ancient, familiar specimen from the deepest, darkest cryptozoid.
The modern offspring of this hominoid are still savages to avoid. mentalis aliapaens.
The carnebrivorous primate, or missing link, father and mother to homo sapiens.
An earthly scourge born to mayhem, pillage and rape.
A genetic crossbreed mutant of haminid and interplanetary treozopape.
Petrified crinoids, fish, shells, sponges, and other organic skeletal remains.
Are all there to be exposed if we dare to live within nature's constrains.
Aliapaens and the turtle, turpinsaura, dived for the edible mollusk, monoplacohora.
While drunk on fermented juniper coneberries, a la Coniferora.
But alas, my search revealed no clues of Aliapaens protruding from sedimentary rock.
Once again, the new discovery of an old hominoid was stopped by a clock.
How insignificant mankind's existence in time seems to be.
When compared to the inhabitants of this long dead, (un) tranquil sea.
Whose species (If God did not in his wisdom create) evolved anew to perpetuate.
Into universal life forms no mere human can comprehend or speculate.
We the ancestors, of aliapaens, possess its worst traits of distinction.
And therefore, homo sapiens will follow a decadent path to extinction.

—*Darold L. Bennett*

So Close, Yet So Far ... From Sadness

I'm just a cloud away from claiming heaven as my own,
Only a kingdom away from sitting on the golden throne.
Just a seed away from growing the final tree on earth,
Only a door away from witnessing my child's birth.
Just a rock away from scaling the highest peak,
Only a day away from lasting another week.
Just a robe away from clothing the highest priest,
Only a dessert away from devouring the greatest feast.
Just an hour away from the greatest sleep,
Only a foot away from the riverbed so deep.
Just a musical note away from writing the perfect tune,
Only a grain of sand away from the steepest sandy dune.
Just a petal away from touching a perfect flower,
Only a second away from living a perfect hour.
Just your heart away from taking you in my arms,
Only your brain away from taking away all that harms.
Just a touch away from a hug that never ends,
Only a 'yes' away from a love that never bends
You're a dream I'll never have, for away from your thoughts I'll always be.
Inches from ever touching, or holding you...so patiently I'll wait for the day when you come to me.

—*Drew Rogers*

To God Be the Glory.

To God be the glory for anything I can do.
Only by His grace have I received
What I pass on to you.
It may be by my hand these words are written,
Their wisdom comes from a greater intelligence than mine.
This world is so much more than what we have seen.
Don't doubt the workings of the unseen world.
Some fortunate people have had glimpses.
We need to trust, not only our eyes, but also our instincts.

—*Edna R. Oakleaf*

Inspiration

You lift my spirits with only a gentle word
  or a soft touch of your hand,
You listen intently to my worries
  and love me like no one else can.

When I am by your side I get a feeling
  of devotion and integrity,
But when I am in your arms, we drift off
  into a never ending world of serenity.

You inspire my every thought in all you say and do,
And it is because of this, that my dreams
  are able to come true.

The warmth that embodies your soul
  transcends into mind,
As the sun's gentle strength glistens
  across the ocean kind.

We have become one candle in the night,
  and I give you a life of dedication.
For all that you give to me, my love,
You will always be my one and only
  Inspiration

—*Christie Gagnon*

Angels' Whispers

You hear a soft voice calling you to arise,
or gently calling your name,
You awake in wonderment!
Could it be an angel's game?
You may feel a slight breeze brush against your skin,
or catch a glimpse of a wing fluttering by.
Messengers of God, they are, leading the way for you,
With a delicate touching of their souls to yours.
Spiritually you hear them whisper softly,
while gently prodding you after your pleading for direction.
If you ever feel an angels wing, or hear an angels whisper,
So very blessed are you, for you are chosen by God
To be an angel's reflection.
—*Dorothea Colangelo*

Evening Shadows

I could never obstruct the passage light,
Or give sable ghosts competition at night
I belong too much, to the forces of man,
As I think about living, lying here on the sand.

My eyes focus upward, blinking pictures in motion,
The gold flush of sunset, edges clouds of commotion
Seeing phantoms and figures, with bodies and faces,
I feel to be soaring, in those lofty places.

I don't think it spooky to be alone, these few hours
The ghosts I believe in, are as Spring is to flowers.
And because of my feelings, I breath a deep sigh
At peace with all creatures, on earth, and in sky.

I rise up, becoming, aware of the time
The sun in its setting, is no longer mine.
I turn and walk back, 'cross dunes toward tomorrow,
To loved ones - to needing - to happiness or sorrow.
—*Florence Rolle*

Friendships

A friendship has no eyes to see by,
  or guide it along the way,
No road nor path does it have which in to follow,
  what lies ahead is ground untouched,
  with each step taken a path behind is laid.
No man can write the future, but knows what he as written.
  however, to look behind is to ignore the present...
  with no hope for a future.
If to expand, one must first open the mind to explorations
  and adventure, if walls along the way are met it's
  because the mind has placed them there in fear of the
  unknown around corners winding turn.
But to stop is to wilt ... and thus, "the end."
For not can one retrace steps taken on a path once blazed
  by travel, nor, is any two travels that in the same
  as taken in past by or with another.
Each travel forms and carries its own history,
  not to be confused, compared, or looked upon when
  breaking new ground with that of another in present
  time, for each is its own anew.
Yesterday lies the past which not can we travel again,
  for the mind puts all that was to memory.
Therefore it is today that we must adventure forward,
  and travel within the present if we are to succeed
  in our journeys toward tomorrow and arrive at futures
  awaiting mysteries.
—*Don L. Meeker*

Voices

It couldn't be that life alone was merriment
or misery, for all the things are looked
upon as angles in a body.
As water flows, the sun emits the atoms
of its being, upon the earth they also
Fall and spread by wind along our faces.
The golden dust is seldom found to
Leave eternal traces, but it was seen
by many, that found they were, but all,
in the strangest places.
One could search, and all in vain, if it
were not for feelings. They lead you
through the treasure-hunt, but rarely
to the treasure.
For if you search, it is in vain,
the treasure is before you, just
spread your eyes and reach your
hands - towards - ...
—*Annelyn Kayson*

My Valentine

If you could know the love in my heart
Or the thoughts that race through my mind
Then you would know how much I love you
And you would be my Valentine

So won't you take this heart of mine
And say that you will be my Valentine
Can't you see that I love you dearly
All my life would be filled with bliss
If you would seal this card with a kiss
Because I am yours sincerely.

Some may send a box of chocolates
Or perhaps a bouquet
But I give to you my ever lasting love
That grows stronger day after day.
—*Bert J Vanorse Sr.*

Poetry

To read someone else's poem,
Or write one of my own,
Makes me feel less alone.

To share a poetic thought or two
Is a very worthwhile thing to do.

To hear a poem read gracefully
Is pleasing to my ears,
And calming to my fears.

To come upon a poem quite unexpectedly
Is a nice surprise for me.

Poetry is food for thought
That's gently penned
And finely wrought.

A poem can speak to you and me
Of what we neither hear nor see.

Poetry is for anyone anywhere,
Ageless and timeless
For those who care to share.

A poem can please, or tease,
Or bring us to our knees.

Poetry is food and drink.
It's how we feel and what we think,
Rare as a peacock or common as the kitchen sink.
—*Janet M. Held*

Let The Little Children Play

Little dark-eyed children played and laughed and ran so young and free.
Others lived and cried aloud in fear or grief or searing pain,
all victims of the mushroom cloud. The world would never be the same.
That day man took a giant stride towards his possible demise.
That day so many thousands died as just one plane sped through the skies.
Dark-eyed children still do die. Blood flows on rubble, grass and sand
as greedy powers vie to dominate their fellow man.
The mushroom cloud's man's badge of shame. It's the symbol of his lust
for pow'r to kill, coerce and maim for what perversely he calls just.
We must turn it all around. Every man deserves his place.
A path to freedom must be found for all men of every race.
One world this planet must become. Be not content with two or three.
If greed and pride be overcome, we all can share equality.
We must ban the bomb for good and all weapons great and small;
so we can live in brotherhood, with fear for none and peace for all.
Let the little children play with a smile on every face;
with eyes of black or blue or grey they'll look with love on every race
Let the little children play. Let the wild flowers grow.
Let the leafy willows sway as the gentle breezes blow.
—*Jack Davis*

Brilliance

Some people say bright brilliance is the diamond in a ring.
Others say bold brilliance is to hear the opera sing.
To some the brilliant glitter, glass and glory of the earth,
Is bedazzlement and brilliance in its grandest form of worth.

Be'times I sit and ponder 'bout the brilliance of the earth.
My mind reflects the blessing of a tiny baby's birth.
The brilliance of his soul caused all eternity to ring,
And bursting bits of truth and light, intelligence to sing.

His brilliant soul embodied and ennobled all that's pure.
His brilliance spoke of love, and that with him you are secure.
Like the beauty of a rose, or the bounties of the field,
His brilliance spoke of giving and the sacrifice he'd yield.

No brighter light or brilliance on this earth will ere be found
For to know him is to know that love is one eternal round.
No blackness, hate, or bitterness will dare to round him stay,
Because the brilliance of his love bursts darkest blackness into day.
—*Cathi Goff*

Love Is You

Love is you, Love is me, Love is our son and daughter, Love is our family.
Love is the thought of you, constantly on my mind,
Love is knowing you will forgive, if ever I've been unkind.
Love is holding my hand, wherever we may go,
Love is that certain look in your eyes, that lets everyone know.
Love is knowing you are there, at the end of each day,
Love is your help and understanding, come what may.
Love is the little things, that only you know how to do,
Love is in my prayers at night, when I thank God for you.
Love is yours, and Love is mine,
Love is what we have already known, but so many will never find.
Love is us Kitten, just you and just me,
Together we are one, and our Love will always be.
Love is my life Kitten, I give it to you,
Love is my whole world and that is why,
Love is You
Together forever, till death do us part, you may leave my side then, but never from my heart.
—*James F. Crowley Jr.*

Book Of Life

A leather book, bound in gold,
our life's story, is being told.

Our meeting and courtship, is chapter one,
He was in the navy, handsome son of a gun!

We met in our teens, at ghouls pavilion is where,
Life's secrets we vowed, we'd always share.

He was fifth, of fourteen, I was second of a family of ten,
We dated and wrote love letters, for six short months, and then.

On the 30th. Of June 1947 we tied the knot,
Blessed with six children, grandchildren 15 is all we got.
Now it's only the beginning, of chapter two.
of 38 years of marriage, together we had very few.
A wheelsman aboard large freighters, sailing on great lakes.
Loneliness, determination, and sacrifice, is what it takes.

As life's pages turn, on to chapter three,
all that's left, now, is the kids and me,
A page from life's book is missing, in chapter four,
Because our loved one is with us no more.

Unwritten words, as we come to the end,
When he died, I lost my best friend.
—*Eldrus Goetz*

Ships In The Night

Like two ships passing in the night
   our lives so swiftly crossed. And yet,
   there was a ripple in the water. I felt
   your presence against my soul.

It rocked me so gently yet profoundly.
   The impact was deep and strong.
   I reached out and you touched me,
   leaving your imprint upon my remembrance.

I knew better than to think that it be
   anything other than what it was
   a comforting provision of Almighty God
   for a time in life such as this.

I brushed your hand lightly in response,
   with understanding and with trust,
   knowing that you too needed to be
   affirmed by the ripple of the wave.

And so, we both sail on, richer for having
   passed this way, firmer in our belief that
   He provides and cares... even, mostly,
   through weak and broken vessels such as we.
—*Gail O. Tiska*

Autumn Leaves

Walking through the park
On dry grass
Late in the afternoon, I pass
Ruddy-cheeked children
Running and shouting.
Inhaling the apple-wine air, I breathe
So long ago
When I was there
Playing in the park after school.
Burning my youth to
Crisp autumn memories.
—*Jeanne Zastera*

Anniversary

Sixty-five years ago on September Twenty-Two
Our marriage vows we took
Through all the years we were true to them
Our love showed with each look.

We met each new day with plans we made
It was fun because you were there
Then God took you from me and left me alone
No more, on this earth, could we share.

Your presence still surrounds me
Tho' I do not feel your touch
I can hear your voice say, "I love you,"
That's why I still love you so much.

Your gentle voice still guides me
In the many things I do
But you can't be there to help me
As you always used to do.

Just why God took you from me
I can not quite understand
Someday may we be together
In Yur great eternal land.
—Edna Dame

Highest Praise

Warblers abound at my green mountain dwelling, notes trilling out of little breasts swelling; calling to far off neighboring fellows, singing as though they are tiny wind bellows. All of their songs are in the key major, praising in trills their LORD and my SAVIOUR. Who, but in humans, are unhappy singers, in the animal kingdom, no sadness lingers. Joy exudes from little hearts bursting for gladness and thanks and little souls thirsting for God's great goodness, as well, ample bounty-noting each sparrow's fall numb'ring county by county. So warble on little patrons, warm our hearts with your singing. Thrill us and cause us to praise with thanksgiving- the Creator of all who saw fit to make you and bless this earth with your wond'rous ballyhoo.
—Barbara N. Moulder

The Reality Of Dreams

One little stone came rolling down,
Out of the darkness of night;
Trying to escape the nightmares it had,
The nightmares of horror and fright.

It would dream of the wars which had come and gone,
The wars which had taken brave men;
And before the stone could have time to wake up,
Another war would start again.

The stone had begun as a boulder years back,
A boulder so big and so strong;
Couldn't the humans see what had been done,
And that destruction of nature was wrong?

The boulder had been hit by the shrapnel of years,
It exploded to make hundreds of stones;
The humans had been killed and buried nearby,
And reduced to nothing but bones.

The little stone had frightened itself close to death,
It was glad that all was as it seemed;
To wake up in the darkness of a night like tonight,
It was glad this had just been a dream.
—Faye-Linda (King) McGovern

Lonely

A Marine in the middle of the night
Outpost on a bleak Korean hill
Thoughts of home broken by snow and fright,
Interspersed with profanity against the winds wintry chill.

A prisoner squatting behind sixteen iron bars
Having paced too long in his eight by eight
Thinking of women and fast new cars,
Wondering how long he can bear his fate.

An old maid with friends - yet so alone,
With alcohol tries to find comfort and care
Like a queen bee without her drone,
Frustrated and crying - needing to share.

A young child confined to a bed
Missing friendship at school and play.
Eagerly awaiting someone's time while being fed
To talk of dreams and wishes this day.

None of us are alone - for He is there.
Just the same, we need another
To share our thoughts of when and where,
To feel the strength of a mortal brother.
—Joe Reynolds

Morning Sky

Light filters through the darkness
Outside my window;
It unveils branches, then twigs
And green leaves restless
In the early morning's breeze
They dance against the sky.

A lone star shines bright
Then disappears into the light.

The moon still glows gold
Unwilling to let go of night,
But must resign.
A stronger light has come to reign.
The vanquished moon recedes
Into a chalked silhouette
Upon a sky of blue.
—Edna Norton

I Think It's Going To Rain Today

I think it's going to rain today,
Outside the window the trees do sway
The wind comes up and takes to flight leaves of various colors
orange red and yellow swirls dancing in the air
While clouds of darkness rolling in bring doom without a care
The inhabitance of the forest sensed the storm drawing near
and retreated to their hideaways to feel secure and
get shelter for their fear
Then the rain came crashing down the silence then did end
The mighty branches of the trees against their will did bend
As if to say I've had enough the sun shown through the rain
and thrust its rays through the sky to
Disburse the clouds on high
Now it is all over and the forest is renewed
The many eyes of wild life reluctantly protrude
Although the ground is dry again the storm away did blow
The wind will carry it back this way to help the forest grow
—Jeffrey Everleth

Untitled

In the window it peeks
   oval and or round silently
   making no sound
   brown, blue or green
In the window it peeks
My bedroom with walls closing in
   In the window it peeks again
Tucked in all soft and warm
I can sense the calm
In the window it peeks
Outside a branch tapping ever so lightly
   In the window it peeks
I close my eyes for a second when
   wakened suddenly by shadows of
two peering across my face
   In the window it peeks
Morn was nigh I first opened one eye,
   then the other
I can't remember if it were a dream
   or something other
All I know is as I sit on the edge of the
   bed
I shutter to think, when I'm to sleep
   In the window it peeks
     —*Janice E. Rowell*

Home

I have traveled this old world over,
Over the mountains and over the sea,
I never found a place to call my Home
Until I met Jesus, the man of Calvary.

In the morning I'll see Jesus,
In the morning I'll be Home,
In that city of many mansions,
I will never be alone.

There will be Mother, Sister and Brother,
And dear old Daddy too,
In the morning when I see Jesus,
And all my friends I knew.

We will have a celebration,
On that Hallelujah Square.
I'll sing and shout and praise His name,
With all my friends up there.

I will know no more sorrow
No more heartaches, no more pain
In the morning when I see Jesus,
My Savior, and my King.
     —*Clay Perry Sr.*

Glory

To God be the glory for anything I can do.
Only by His grace have I received what I pass on to you.
It may be by my hand these words are written,
Their wisdom comes from a greater intelligence than mine.
This world is so much more than we see.
Don't doubt the wonders of the unseen world.
Some fortunate people have had glimpses.
We need to trust, not only our eyes, but also our instincts.
     —*Junerose Smith*

Another Lesson From Life

The year was nineteen ninety
Overhead, a sky of blue;
This story I now relate
Is so beautifully true.
There, in a strawberry field
A hen pheasant on a nest.
Though kids were seem to touch her
So calmly she did rest.
"If pheasants are fearful of humans,"
Some did ask me why;
"Though she could have been harmed,
Steadfastly she did refuse to fly?"
Three days later I did return,
My curiosity was turned on;
All the eggs had hatched,
Mother hen and chicks we're gone
Had she been created a human,
I seek not to be a cynic;
Would she ever be seen
Headed for an abortion clinic?
     —*Harry A. Fry*

One, Two, Three...

You know square and angle
pair and triangle
tractor and factor
But do you know the most famous
problem of all
Algebra with no one to call

Math was a breeze
with addition and subtraction
sum and difference
I passed it all with ease

It became more advanced
with multiplication and division
product and quotient
I came through it with a little provision

Next comes Geometry
with circles and ovals
with all different degrees
I'll need all the help I can get, please.
     —*Catrina Wiggs*

Outsiders

The outsiders are our human brothers,
Part of what make us what we are.
Equal within our diversity
The humanity of all mankind.
Have any of you met or spoken
With any of them? Its unfortunate;
Too many of us are prone to speak,
Or think of others in a manner of
gross disparagement some of them
May be your next door neighbor.
Outsiders are persons who carry the
same human diversity as we do.
They raise their children, live in houses,
drive cars, pay their taxes, love their
wives, I caught one of them watching
me, one eye closed, tears
in the other eye.
The outsiders are our human brothers,
part of what make us what we are;
Outsiders have an equilibrium for life.
     —*Grafton E. Lucas*

The Marvels Of Trees

We all fail to realize the marvels and greatness of trees.
Particularly, we do not recognize the many comforts and benefits
that trees bring to you and me.
Trees are nature's best cleansers of industrial pollutants and smog.
This permits most of us to work and live in comfort,
without having ailments, and jog.
Our homes and the furnishings therein are derived principally
from trees. These make our lives more a pleasure and a breeze.
Trees provide roosting and nesting for our many birds. The songs
of birds being pleasure to some beyond their words.
Newspapers and books add to our pleasure and enhance our
   knowledge,
education and skills. This is possible through the processing of
   tree pulp through paper mills.
There are many marvels in God's many and great creations. Of these
the tree is among the greatest in providing ease and comfort
to the inhabitants of earth's nations.
—*Charles W. Morton*

Here I Sit

Here I sit, lazily in the grass - here I sit, with a 72-hour
   pass; I must return to the sanitarium today
      to kill the TB germs and do what they say.

Here I sit, with the kids at my knee - here I sit, it really is
   me; no more sorrow for days ahead, only gladness when I tuck
      them in bed.

Here I sit, near each one I treasure - here I sit, and gives me
   such pleasure to see them playing and laughing today,
      as I listen to each lovely word they say.

Here I sit, wishing never to leave - here I sit, knowing I will
   grieve, waving goodbye to them on the porch
      will be like putting my heart to the torch.

Here I sit, beneath the maple tree - here I sit, as they
   chatter to me, trying not to show them the tears that I've
      shed while putting them fondly in the memories of my head.
—*Jeri Haase*

Covering Up

This world is one big masquerade
People think they are hidden when
   things are done in the shade
This world could be a very lonely place
Especially without God and his amazing grace
Don't you be the one to slip
You could end up in Satan's grip
Don't think the things you do are cool
You could end up as Satan's fool
But always remember the Golden Rule
Use your bible it's the daily tool
Jesus is the only cool
—*Debra S. Stevens*

Pioneer O Pioneer

   Shocking frozen corn at down
         or
Shocking droughty grain of Depression
         Era
   Shambled my spirit of pioneerin'
         with
      John Barley Corn
—*Alice H. Senter*

Mrs. Conger

Ninety five years old with a broken hip to mend
Perhaps a younger body she wishes someone would lend
"Good morning Mrs. Conger," professionally said I
"What?" - was the only word she gave in her reply
"I say good morning to you ma'am. How are you today"
"Ha?"
I offered her medicine with the hope of feeling better
She could not decide upon the medicine
Or her great-grandson's letter
And then from her I suddenly hear
So calm, collected, deliberate and clear
"Don't work too hard"
Staring quietly at her with her hand in mine to hold
I wonder how it will be for me when it's my turn to grow old
As I leave I turn to see her
Sitting in her chair
Doing what she was doing
All the time that I was there
Moving this - moving that
Always adjusting something
—*Jim Krikorian*

My Legacy - I Leave You

I'm sixty, right now, and my life has been full.
Perhaps not successful, but, nonetheless, not dull.
I've borne three children, whom I love and adore,
married a man who has five more.
The grandchildren, there's ten, and one more to come,
this may seem inconceivable, even a burden to some.
But, if not for these little ones, my life would be gray,
they bring sunshine and laughter, with their smiles and their play.
There's Frankie and Christina, so angelic and sweet,
and Vito, his smile, with dimples complete.
David and Kevin, Corey, and Jamie,
Megan and Julie, and can't forget Amy.
The eleventh in just weeks, with more in the future,
from Michael and Peter, given time to mature.
These children were raised with respect and with love,
with discipline, honesty, and belief in God above.
My legacy, my dream, is for these children to create,
a better world, without war, nor hunger, nor hate.
I hope and I pray, they'll contribute to this earth,
With all they have learned, from the time of their birth.
—*Constance Rose DeRosa*

Beta Waves

Oh, how I'd love to sit a spell in there
Perusing all the flickers of his brain.
I'd watch to see how he selects his fare
Surveying convoluted brain terrain.
I'd sit so quietly that he'd not mind
That someone's perched upon a brainshelf high.
Solutions to all problems he would find
While I eavesdrop on ev'ry wave, and sigh.
How much I'd learn if only I could share
His images and lasso some for me.
It's fascinating watching his thoughts flare
But maybe it's not right for me to see.
   Intrude upon the master poet, no!
   Just dream of delving into things he'd know.
—*Charlotte R. Mitchell*

Desert Storm

Death, destruction and darkness
pervade their universe, blinding the sun
in the land of scuds and shrouds,
stealth and strategy coolly planned,
the newest level of mechanical precision,
sophisticated weapons, remote control
to be unleashed on command.

Satanic powers, grim and grisly, decimate life -
the life of the innocent, the life of the warriors -
all victims of the great war machine.
Nation against Nation seeks a diabolical solution.
Man's mad, inhuman behavior supersedes
     all logic
        all costs
           all godliness
The purpose forever elusive; a pact with man, not God.

—*Jane S. Peters*

The Flower

Fate plucks the Flower of Life...
   Petals floating...
     Gentle water flows...
Summer night cold...
   Gray Wolf watches prey...
   Vulnerable memories... weeping dreams...
For strength builds...
     Realizing weaknesses...
   Yawning sun morning wind shiver
   One petal holds firm.
     Friendship root.

—*James L. Boynton*

Hope

Come to my side, my lovely child...
Place your hand in mine...

We'll talk of things that bloom and grow...
Of stars that brightly shine.

We'll listen to the sounds of night...
Dark, warm and thickness reeling.

We'll talk of joys and some fears...
And you'll tell me what you're feeling.

We'll reach for the sky and touch it not...
And wonder of its infinity
Earth so near, Heaven so far.....
Ever questioning it's divinity.

My child, you sweet and precious stone...
In your soul lies mysteries unspent.

I'll feel your energy and refreshing delight...
As through my spirit your origins are sent.

Come to my breast, oh entity mine...
And go with me through time.

For in you I see a beginning, an end...
The oyster is yours sublime.

—*Jodi Medley-Lopez*

Ice Storm

Trees became crystal castanets
played by a vagrant wind.
Snow piled high on wire fence
geometric beauty to behold.
A squirrel tried to climb a tree
He wisely went around the trunk
to the ice free side.
He flicked his tail and with a bound
was out of sight in his hidden home
safe from natures pranks.
The sun came out, the music of the ice
became soft plopping sound
as it dripped and dropped
to the forest floor.
Crystal diamonds soon were gone
replaced by buds and leaves,
Til next winter when
mother nature will again
show her jewels
diamonds and, snow flakes and icy curls.

—*Agnes Phillips*

The Sweet Sin Of Silence

Satin eyes cry tonight, left me in the cold
Played this game way too long, now it's time to fold
Mocking sun laughs today, it hears the red sirens
Made a desert from my soul
The sweet sin of silence
Starry eyes used to shine, faded from the cold
Rejected love crushed by feet, dried on all their soles
Gonna change nature's plan, I'll stand in bold defiance
Life is mine the turn is mine
The sweet sin of silence
At night you'll pray
That the day will come when you no longer run
When your worries fade away
When you are six more feet
Under the sun
Calloused eyes close tonight, free now from the cold
Satin sheets cover my skin, life is hard to hold
Precious stones left uncut, they never had the guidance
Lost my grip, I lost my mind
The sweet sin of silence

—*Heather E. Brown*

Help Me Lord

Help me Lord be kind and gentle
Please help me Lord every day
To watch and pray so I won't stumble
In life's journey on the way.
Help me Lord to live your love
Help me Lord please leap the way
To always live and share your love
To be with you every day.
Help me Lord a poet to be
And share your love in poetry
Cause that's the way our life should be
To live and write your poetry.
Thank you Lord, thank you God
Help me thank you on my way
Give praise, honor, and glory to God
For all you gave me on my way.
Help me Lord when life is done
Help me Lord to be with you
Lead me to your kingdom come
Forever Lord cause I love you.

—*John V. Lisovich*

Touch Me

    Touch me and tell me what you feel
Please, honey, share your thoughts with me.
Find the part of me that is real.
That I don't let everyone see.

    I need to be touched and to be understood
No matter what I may say.
I need your embrace if only you could
Even when I push you away.

    I need to be needed... but not too much
dependency isn't my style,
commitment with freedom, closeness with space
and the anchor that is your smile.

    I know what I am and I know where I am
and I know all that I could do
But I still need your touch for it says so much
That you know where I am too...
    —*Grayce B. Upshaw*

The Necessity Of Your Love

I need love like an air — need to stroke through your hair,
Plunge my eyes in your eyes meeting lost Paradise.

Need to breathe with your breathing, feel breathtaking cool seething
On our lips, in our lungs, on the tips of our tongues.
Need to feel with my fingers — how you, trembling and springy,
Give a sweet stinging part and a dart in my heart.

Need our white eight-winged souls to be poured in one bowl
And become in a flash our one blood and flesh.
Need your heaven affection would perform resurrection,
Let me feel like newborn never leaving lovelorn.

Eight long years I had fears, lonesome nightmares and tears -
An unbearable pain: we were parted in twain.
Now you saved me and granted to be loved and enchanted...
And our love never'll die - here on earth, there on high!
    —*Andrei Dmitriev*

Needless Trip

I rounded inspiration point
   Poetic license close at hand.
Aboard my trusty penmanship
   I headed for the land.
The land of all my longing
   Far beyond the synonym sea;
Where I could free my imagination:
   The land of poetry.

Oh, how I yearned for the thrill there
   Of a parade with my own viewing stand
Thousands of words rhyming thoughts there
   With all of English at my command.

Slid into compatible harbor
   No strangeness to greet me...instead...
Vibes familiar the kind I encounter
   Each time that I rhyme in my head.
I felt deja vu disembarking
   And realized my trip need not be.
With a heart to its source oft' returning
   The land of poetry was me!
    —*Gloria Mercedes Beacham*

Truth Of The Matter

My eyes closed and the void crept upon me,
Possessing my whole being with beastly hunger!
This was my escape; my chance to avoid
The hateful lot of humanity, performing evil deeds,
Leaving behind them unbearable, woeful sobs of victims.
Deeper and deeper, I fell into this pit of unconsciousness,
Drawing from it, like blood from a venomous snake bite,
Those things I wanted and needed. Love, most needed,
Was not to be had. Ah! Could I have been wrong?
Was my escape not so perfect? 'Tis so! 'Tis so!
Like death, there is no escape from truth.
Truth is 'what is' and death is that which 'will be'.
Love is the bridge spanning life from one to the other.
    —*Dolores La Bianco*

Care For Me

Today you're carrying me in this
   pouch,
Tomorrow I'll be out.
I hope that you have planned so,
many things that we can do.
Teach me - Show me - Train me,
so that one day I can do it on my own.
Love me - Encourage me - Embrace me - Help me
understand the ways that life game goes.
Discipline me - Explain to me - Correct me
when I am wrong.
Feed me - Hug me - Pray for me - Keep me
   from harm.
    —*Jesse Thaddeus Chapman*

Sweet Reality

Imagine your imagination is a blank canvas for your extremely
   productive
Mind! Inspire those creative juices to flow,
Let's contemplate what we may find.
Imagine you're gazing up at billowy clouds, yo-ho, what
Do you see? Pirate galleons ragin' on froth, or a child
'Neath a gnarled bonsai tree. Imagine
There's no such thing as child abuse, that atrocity
Is forever unheard of! Innocent infants
Are born to nurturing to nurturing parents, who adore, protect,
   cradle, and love! Imagine
Willie Wonka's factory has eliminated hunger and starvation!
Precious
Children enjoy the sweets of life, now
Till the end of creation! Imagine we
Have the insight usually acquired through ripe old age. We
Listen with our hearts to folks who've earned
Their wisdom on a previous page! Imagine actions
Speaking louder than words, though it's a proven fact of life.
Be
Kind to one you simply can't fathom; don't prolong
Hatred and strife! Imagine you've extended your wings
To soar where few have dared. Whatever you do, always
Give it your best, the result shows how much you cared!
    —*Julie Toth*

Majestical Prophesy

Mystical array of prophets bringing forth a majestical
prophesy marching towards humanity, who long awaited
messages brought forth to Earth to sail upon silver blue
clouds portraying the masses.

Listen quietly and the prophets shall read from The Book of Life.

Never march ahead without looking backwards. A new day is
a gift from a long-time eve. Remember to love is as sacred
as the first offering. To make others happy, to bring about
laughter is as joyous as a warm summer day. Always remember
it is important to give knowledge to those that seek it. To
heal the mind, as well as the body and soul, is something we
all must heed within one another, through one another. To
offer the bread's and wine's to feed the hungry and quench the
thirst is something we must never forget.

I approached a prophet and expressed a desire to have The Book
of Life, I was told, "You are The Book of Life!" I thought
about what they said and knew each of us within oneself
through oneself, truly is "The Book of Life."

—*Deborah Mae Post*

Nature's Haven

Forever shines brightly my haven in the sky
Protection that warms me to perfection in sweet supply
Giving me a glow that baffles my dreams
Moves me to the point of passion within its seams

Calms my soul to the tune of a babbling brook
Engulfs me comfortably in its smallest nook
Fleets my heart into the midst of a forest
To the daily lives of the animals as they move in chorus

Shaded by the care of its trees
Grasping hold of the freedom I felt, from its ambiguous decrees
Nature runs through its blissful pace of motion
Relaxes me in its arms, like a magical potion

Here no one's in a hurry
Where minds are free to scurry
Into nature's beauty you have embark
Feel its energy, the warmth of its spark

—*Earnest B. Haynes*

Jehovah's Finest

The Creation was his delightful loving game,
Psalm 83 verse 18 gives us his wonderful name.
Jehovah overwhelmed with his creative love
Drafted our creation for here and for the above.

Yes! I love a sunburnt country rich with flowing lands,
Expansive sweeping plains, mountainous regions fill his hands.
Yes he loved the far horizons and the jewelled sea;
Her loving beauty and exuberance was charming me.

I rafted rivers of coolness and echoes were calling,
As I drifted dim gorges and heard creeks falling,
When it breathes and mountain flows over moss and sedges,
Yet graced by their beauty are the banks and the ledges

Greatness are the trees that spiral into the sky,
Then sweetness of flowers to a gal from a guy.
The warmth of a hand that clasps as you walk the beach,
It brings your heart to heart with sincerity to teach.

The every thought of you as I forgot to do,
Had little ordinary things that everybody ought too.
Learn about the greatest things I have described above,
Because they come from our creator with the warmest love.

—*Edd David Mcwatters*

As Simple As A Tennis Ball

I kicked it once or twice or two, but then I let it still. And after
pulling back my foot, I kicked it with my head. I watched as it
flow through the air, then on the ground it hit, I thought if I
should pick it up, but I just left it sit. About 5 years on down
the line, I was walking through those weeds, round and small and
fell to scrape my knees. I picked it up and held it, and I
remembered back to the day, when I could've prevented the
incident, but instead I walked away. It made me stop and think
about mistakes we lay aside. Instead of dealing with them like
we should, we shrug our shoulders and ask why. The ball was round
and simple when we kicked it aside with ease, but it grew and got
in the way, just when we didn't have the key. Just like mistakes
we made long ago, we long ago forgot, but we snagged upon those
memories, and now were forever caught.

—*Darlene Balls*

The Robin's Song

I was kneeling in my garden
  pulling weeds one summer morn,
When a robin perched a-top the line;
  his song was message born.

"Your mother will be leaving soon."
. . .The tears streamed down my face.
"I know, I know. . .I know," I said,
  "Oh Lord, please grant me grace."

"I don't want to let her go," I wept,
. . .My thoughts aloud I hurled.
"It's time. . .," he sang right back to me,
  "she's suffered in this world."

"The plans I've made for her will
  heal the silence of her pain,
"And win the souls of many more;
  "she's laboured not in vain."

"Oh thank you Lord, for calming me,
  when my fears give way to race."
"You're not alone," the robin sang,
  "I am here to take her place."

—*Barbara Jaeger*

The Flower

I feel like a flower growing from a seed.
Pushing hard, reaching full face into the sun.
My petals of color make me proud and happy.
I depend on a rain drenched bath
To freshen my life, to help me grow.
Have I made people gasp at my beauty?
Did I go unnoticed when I hung my head?
I was the flower, who, over all other flowers,
was remembered....
The brightest, most colorful, most admired...
wasn't I?

—*Ann Martin*

Glory

To God be the glory for anything I can do.
Only by His grace have I received what I pass on to you.
It may be by my hand these words are written,
Their wisdom comes from a greater intelligence than mine.
This world is so much more than we see.
Don't doubt the wonders of the unseen world.
Some fortunate people have had glimpses.
We need to trust, not only our eyes, but also our instincts.

—*Junerose Smith*

Your Journeys End

As you adventure life's tough roads
  put your hand in Gods to lighten your loads.
Praises to the Lord we shall sing
  for the flowers that bloom in spring.
Even for the sorrow, pain and tears
  praise be to God with joyful cheers.
For if bad times hadn't past by,
  we would never know if we were high.
And being high on love and laughter,
  your sure to reach the dreams your after.
All the people that pass your way
  wish them happiness to brighten their day.
Give of yourself all you can
  to teach others how to lend a hand.
When your life's journey has come to an end.
  Thank God for all that has been.
Be glad you kept your eyes on the Master
  for there's no greater reward than
  life ever after.
    —*Bernice Myers*

Unending Touch

An unknown place of unending time.
Quiet and peaceful,
Ominous and perfect.

A peace glow from the fire.
Champaign filled glasses nearby.
Satin sheets on the bed.

One on one we care.
Nothing else matters.
As we touch love fills the air.

No words need to be spoken.
I watch your eyes for a sign of emotion.
A small grin,
A bashful look;
And tonight your mine.
    —*Cynan*

A Cry, Off A Mountains Sky

A-lways striving for Salvable's Perfectous Living;

C-ontained in Souls, of unconditional giving.
R-uling of pathways;
Y-ielding its rest in the end, within…

O-rdered by another's labor of love,
F-orever searching into the Red Stained Skies Above.
F-inding your abiding place, amidst the stars kingdom;

A cry to be heard, by those who sing them…

M-ourning begins our Tenacious Journey,
O-ver Foundations unshakable ground.
U-nderneath the sole's of all-mankind;
N-igher and nigher, unto higher and higher ground.
T-rudging through the muck and mire of despair;
A-polite gentle breeze of comfort for the weary soul.
I-nto Palatable Heights of pure chaste, fresh air;
N-ever doubting,
S-erenity's hold…

S-urely! We do prevail, from the Highest Fountains Why!
K-neeling over Eminence Breath, of the Horizon's Virgin Dawn;
Y-ou and I, will soar into the Mountains Sky…
    —*Billy J. Powell*

The Fire Ring

The luminous coals on the ashen bed,
Radiate their presence in yellows and red.
A blue flickering flame occasionally raising its head,
But in the morning, they will seem cold and dead.

A poke, a stir, a fresh log will bring
New life from old and the fire will sing
The crackle, roar, pop, and ping.
Of new life, around the fire ring.
    —*J. Daniel Marsh*

Oblivious

He hears the wind if it lifts one lone leaf
Rain when the first tear falls upon the pane
The rose's flower drop a single petal
A blade of grass drink to life sustain.
He hears a cricket when there is no sound
The hummer sip a drop of nectar's gold
A fly warming itself on the screen door
The faintest swish of butterfly wings fold
The spider tossing out his silk lasso
A flake of early snow kissing the ground
The first peach bud of the spring opening.
He is so sensitive to change and sound
He knows, under the ground, open of seeds,
Yet never hears her heart cry its great needs.
    —*Elizabeth Robertson*

Twinkling Light

Drops of rain, gently falling on moist green leaves.
Rainbows forming across the sky.
Feeling freshness all around.
Experience the tenderness of a young warm heart.

While drops of love are all about.
Bringing people to warm and kind relationships.
On breezing nights and star filled skies.
Wishing on a twinkling light and hoping it comes true.

Days and nights are all in one.
Singing songs of love.
Show me is a state of mind, and seeing is so right.
Bring the gentle rain drops, hoping for our rainbows.

Joy of touching someone's face, smiling back.
Delight in seeing a child's first step.
Flowers growing through the snow.
All from wishing on a twinkling light.

Tenderness all around swallowing you in strong arms.
Tell me of a love so true, and awaking to you.
Facing all that makes the world, and smiling at it.
While drops of rain, fall gently on wet green leaves.
    —*Anne Marie Madison*

Peace

The roar of the ocean, the quiet of the colorful sky
Quiet meets the roar, blending into peace.

I sit and wonder of our chances of ever capturing the secret.
Will peace ever quiet the roar of the world?

The roar of the ocean, the quiet of the colorful sky

I sit in awe, peacefulness embracing me.
    —*Colleen L. Davis*

Argumentative

Imaginations bear apple seed
Realities into fruition
Confusion results sometimes
Unable to think
Interesting conversation
Terminates endlessly hours
By the bye people interrupt
Increasingly talk difficult
Inevitably results anger
Fists clenched table beneath
Blurred and tear stained reflections
Compose emotion uncontrolled
Ultimately anger on the back burner
Exchanged peace offerings
Hand in hand walking blindfolded
Unknowingly into future encounters
—*Wink*

Happy?

Happiness!! Most I know are
really a mess.

So why does it seem that happiness
is truly a dream?

Absurd as that may sound.
Look, not much of it around.

Most people that are happy
seem to be happy about the wrong.

Just doing what they want
as long as it feels pleasurably good.

In the end the feeling of happiness
is not their friend.

For most the hope takes on the impulse
to surrender to dope, drugs, or too much drink!

God - help us all - Amen!
—*Curtis M. Crouse*

September's Swan Song

Going out in a blaze of glory,
Red-gold flames line the river bank,
Reflected in Red River's flowing water
Where summer swallows dipped and drank;
Haunting is your cool perfection,
Heard in the wild goose flying south,
And echoing in my heart's chambers
Mourning the loss of beauty, youth;
Yet so graceful is your dying,
Painting pictures shot with gold;
I gather them for winter albums—
Wherein your song is my story told.
—*Joanne McKibben*

The Little Fisherman

The boy was clad in cut-off jeans,
Red hair tousled by the morning breeze.
Wading along the rivers edge,
Sometimes out of sight by the grown-up hedge.

His face already tanned by the warm spring sun,
Searching the waters was his way of fun.
He carried a pole to jab and poke,
Might step in a hole and get very soaked.

My father is a fisherman, he boasts with a smile,
Out in the ocean he goes for miles.
My dream is to own a boat and go to sea,
The very best fisherman, I will be.

Thoughts were broken by passing gulls,
Out from shore lay a decaying boat hull.
Should I explore? What treasures can I find?
All of this passed through his mind.

His knowledge of the waters was something to hear,
Telling about tides and currents, showing no fear.
He pointed out markers showing the way to the sea,
This little fisherman in cut-off jeans.
—*Jackie Scarbrough*

Very Rare

I lifted up my face toward heaven, and I thank God, for making these red roses. Now I can bring you some. God is so gracious, that he is always doing things for us. God love you thy servant of His. You are very special, and very rare. Like that rare diamond, I saw in a jewelry shop. That is the reason I pray that you always have a red rose. So that joy, and happiness will fill your heart. Life is a beautiful thing. God hold all life in his hands. He put life here in this red rose bush, so it may grow into something to behold. Every time I see one, I want to pick some and bring them to you. You keep a walking with that smile upon your face. May God always be with you.
—*Dorthea Darby*

The Key

Have you ever looked into a mirror of no reflection? or loved someone non-human? Neither have I, but that mysterious sight and your unidentical personality has me running in circles. Circles which are only known by me. The certain way you calm me down after we fight or the position of your beautiful facial features before a tear. Makes me wonder how I know so much but still so little when it comes to you.

Help me learn, and mold my knowledge. Locked away in you is a key which one day I will get and finally be able to open you up to new horizons. But until that day comes I will always be here for you. Awaiting the final page of that dusty, old novel in you to be turned. And the book to be shut!
—*Elizabeth Sloan*

Light And Dark

The air is crystal clear this coolish day -
Refreshingly clean and light.
I feel, I hear, and see the breeze,
I hear the music thru the trees.
Then I see the darkness creeping in
As dark as ...
The blackest inky night -
Then I pray
And dawn breaks in
And suddenly...
There is light!
 —*Charlotte Borsos McKinney*

Sometimes The Rainbow

Clouds stain the moon,
Releasing the redundant of rain.
Tavern light finds the lively crowd,
Playing in a dangerous world.

Smoke laces the man on the mike.
Standing is a lonely man of fate.
Thunder stills at the break of dawn,
The sun is shining through the rain.

Leaving, feeling no transgression,
His wealth by others worn.
Fast driving is an obsession,
Then appeared the rainbow as to warn.

Life flashes before him to instill
The other side of pain.
The sobering feel of the wheel,
Brings truth and justice then.

Sometimes the rainbow,
The heavenly fathers creation,
Leads him to the stained glass window,
The prisms of the sun.
 —*Harriet J. Warmack*

Remember Me

Remember me when your all alone,
Remember me when your walking away
Remember me when your feeling blue,
But please don't remember me when your thinking of her.
 Remember me when your days are long and your nights too short.
Remember me when the moon is bright and everything seems clear.
Remember me when you look at heaven above
But please don't remember me when your reaching for her.
 Remember me when your lonely
Remember me when you think of the one who loves you only
Remember me when you look in a picture book.
Remember me when you see a smiling face.
But please don't remember me when she's on your mind and in your heart.
Remember me when you think of all the times we sat alone and cried.
Remember me when you laugh.
Remember me when your love was for only one.
Remember me when your day's are past.
But please don't remember me when she's by your side,
 But remember me when she says good-by
 because I'll be there to welcome you back.
 —*Debbie Elias*

Remember Me....My Love

Remember me when times get rough,
Remember out love when things get tough,
Don't dwell on the fact that we are apart,
Just keep close that feeling of warmth in your heart,
Shed tears if you must to help you cope,
Don't let those tears drown your hope,
Keep thoughts in your mind of days that have past,
Of laughter, of sharing, these memories must last,
When the darkness falls and the tears seem to flow,
Pray to God for strength and it will be so,
Be strong my love this I ask of you,
And know that I'll be remembering too,
for while I'm away I'll be working to prepare,
for the days ahead when again we will share.
 —*Brenda Hartley*

Golden Memories

Years bring such memories.
Remembrance of the past.
Such visions that last
The love of family,
Friendships that endure,
Our thankfulness for such people
Gives meaning to life.
To cherish the many memories
That radiate beauty around us;
To shine and enrich our lives
With thoughts to treasure
In full measure,
And as the years enfold,
When did the silver change to gold?
 —*Hilda Smith*

Intriguing Eyes

Haunted by dreams invading my sleep
restless passion that runs so deep
quench my desire - stirred by your fire
awake me with a kiss.

Intriguing eyes.

Followed by specters without substance
uneasy obsession reaches the distance
sate my yearning - aroused by your burning
embrace me with your arms.

Intriguing eyes.

Tormented by shadows I set myself free
seeking this place I hunger to be
excite my emotions - sprinkled with potions
revive me by your visions.

Intriguing eyes.

Intriguing eyes
forever watching me.
Intriguing eyes
don't reflect the truth they see.
Intriguing eyes
 —*Annette H. Baldao*

Untitled

A separate place in time,
Retrospectively -
An image was created
A unique intelligence, never before seen,
Wailed through many ears
With its distorted power of feedback.
No one to listen.
No one to hear a silent cry.
Blinded by fame,
An incomplete life was lost,
   Now and forever.
But in the spirit of -
   the sound lives on
& continues to wail into the bleak future.
   —*Jennifer A. Landry*

First Friends' Reunion

Like so many of life's events,
   reunions come and go.
Recalling "best" friends,
   as well as those we hardly seemed to know.

Looking back when we only thought
   about what lay ahead.
And, what we knew about the world
   was only what we read.

One common beginning —
   at the same time, in the same place.
Each experience memorized,
   so no one can erase.

Together facing our differing
   personalities as they unfurled.
Never realizing how significant this would be
   out in the real world.

Now we find ourselves in another time,
   wishing our past we could re-live.
If only for a moment,
   let it be laughter that you give.

So, enthrall us with that priceless story
   that only you can tell.
Stories we've heard so many times,
   yet love to hear so well.

Repeat each memory over again
   before the evening ends.
But, most importantly, get re-acquainted
   with those who were your first friends.
   —*Judy A. Westenfelder*

The Deserted Beach

It's cold and windy and wide as can be,
Sandy and full of shells and sea life.
No one walking or running today,
Alone with the reflection of clouds.
Alone with the wonder of nature,
Its beauty to behold, its colors so inviting.
Yet alone, lonely and deserted.
   —*Helen S. Brooks*

Our World

Our world is slowly dying
right before our eyes.
Do you ever wonder?
Why there are no eagles in the skies?
The forest turn to roads
and rivers turn to streams,
is anyone out there listening
to all the animals screams?
The man with all the money
you know He doesn't care.
It won't be to damn funny
when we don't have any air.
You can drive on down the highway
and see the acid burnt trees.
There won't be any flowers
if we don't have any bees.
People must stand up,
save what we can.
What will you tell your kids
if the whole world is turned to sand?
   —*Dennis W. Brown Jr.*

Omissions

Omissions occur when you relinquish or forfeit your innate right to put forth effort to try... Omissions suffocate the natural voice of the heart, rendering it inaudible deadening the cry... "I'm not responsible" flows in torrents and is far too comfortably said... "There's nothing I can do" quickly alleviates, (not the other's plight) but our very own dread... Did you peer behind the veil as you cautiously circled along its edge? Or was your solemn vow, "I can't get involved!" your real "self-protective" heartfelt pledge? Was his, her or their problem labeled, just an unfortunate calamity? Oh, did you never learn or consider beyond the surface the "uncommon responsibility?" Did your well-concealed fear stifle any saving deeds, till none were done which could have made a difference? Or was so high the value of other people's opinions, the food which fed and nurtured your diffidence? Did you raise your incorrect socially-conditioned mind above the atrocities and name it "law" keeping peace and safe distance from the foe? When the tumult was raging in the depths of you, voicing "this should not have ever been let go"... When you fully understand you're fighting something, you should not have ever fought... When you crystal-clearly comprehend through-out your being, lessons that were never taught... If we don't believe by now, when we omit a tender word, a gracious pure feeling or dismiss a call... For "silence" is an utterance we will be most accountable and will forever fall... For all that we have accepted and become placidly resigned... Remember, oh, remember, when man chooses himself, he chooses all mankind.
   —*Agnes Theresa Reap-Williams*

After Fall.

oh the still cool waters of after fall
rippling miles of rows to the waiting shore,
purged with early winter's silent call,
unconquered but broken to her once more
in the blinding mist of Autumn's impuissant fall.
moored captains and I have stood braced before
her troubled waters cast in settled evening grey.
weathered perhaps deeper than we best ignore.
watching Winslow's ferry, white with distance and spray,
sound her warnings to clear all before,
harbour bound for strangers impatient with delay,
all waiting like foreigners with little to know
of what ills these straits this forbidding October day.
   —*David D. Gillespie*

Dirge

Toll, toll, oh bells of the world;
Roll, roll, a vast dirge, on thou tides of the sea.
Cry out for him that is with us no more.
Let rain fall gently over the city of his repose.
Lower the flags, oh peoples and nations.
Let minor keyed music wing through the air.
None can return him, this leader of men;
Not one can encompass the void of his passing.
Extol his virtues in solemn-toned voice.
Weep, weep, oh ye nations —
   harken to the throb of deep-throated drums,
To the metered marching feet;
   hear the sobs of parents and children.
Sorrow with mankind, all nature;
Flow slowly, thou rivers and streams;
Sigh gently, winds on the plains; shine dimly, oh glorious sun;
Rise sadly, thou swells in the oceans.
The enemies of man have won a battle;
The tides of the war surge over and over.
Toll on, toll on, thou funeral bells;
Roll on, roll on, thou funereal drums;
On through the ages in the lingering memories of mankind.
   —*Dorothy A. Fick-Cox*

A Story Of Youthful Passion

Into his outstretched arms she moves, with delight
rouging her cheeks, parting her lips.
Few words are spoken in the humid haze of their sheltering
night - only young lovers urgent questions, his "Where? When?"
and then her, forgetting to breathe, pleading to know "Why?"
His trembling hands, unable to heed her soft command to stop,
caress longed-for mysteries of breasts and hips
as tears mat her lashes, pool in her eyes, and drop.
"Oh, please understand," she whispers, "I've never before been
held like this. I'm trying so hard to resist."
His searching hands clench and are fists.
These young lovers, hidden from others sight,
crying for forbidden pleasures, sharing their natural plight,
murmur their fears, their splendid dreams of someday,
bittersweet love words
into a darkness too complex, into an ageless night -
"Will you love me forever?" "Are you mine alone sweetheart?"
Eternal questions, eternal pledges of "Yes, yes, until death us do part."
Can their love last a lifetime, through all joy, sorrow, pain?
Poets sing of it always, knowing that brightest blossoms follow rain;
so youthful passion, sustained by a bond of love, may forever
flower, bear fruit, grow.
It is only one part of living yet, perhaps, the best of it
anyone may know.
   —*Charlotte Ladshaw Garrett*

Heavenly Voice

Sitting alone in the Garden
Sad and at toil with my mind
All at once I knew I love Jesus
The one I had left far behind

All at once a voice from our Heaven
Seemed to whisper so deep in my soul
Welcome back a lost child in torment
I welcome the back to my fold

But remember thy always of damnation
And the sins you have sewn through the land
For someday you might cry for salvation
But find I'm not holding your hand

Take heed and listen oh sinners
And learn these things that are true
I will take you seventy times seven
Then no longer can I plead for you.

So come and pray to our Father
And let him know that all is well
Stay with him for to know Heaven
Or it might mean the torments of Hell
   —*Snake Sneer*

The Awakening

When I awoke this morning
   Safely sleeping thru the night;
I thought of all the blessings
   I've enjoyed throughout my life.

God has been very good to me
   In all I've said and done;
He's guided me thru the perils
   That have come to everyone.

Many things I could not see
   He took my hand and guided me;
My life has truly been real blessed
   With friends, and health, and all the rest.

So this, dear God, I must confess
   There's no one anywhere, has been more blessed.
   —*Frances H. Ryan*

Cat Fishin' On Cache Creek

I left the bright lights, out on ol' Broadway,
Said goodbye to the hippies, out in Frisco Bay.
I've been in ever city, and ever little town.
Left all the cowboys, said goodbye to the clowns.

You can't call me, you can't find me.
I'm nowhere around.
I'm cat fishin' on Cache Creek,
Waiting for the sun to go down.

I've got trout lines, pole lines, limb lines too.
Sold my Lincoln for an old canoe.
Thirty years of singing, in a club all night,
Is nothing like the feel of a catfish bite.

So don't try to call me, don't try to find me.
I'm nowhere around.
I'm cat fishin' on Cache Creek,
Waiting for the sun to go down.
   —*Frenchie Clements*

Behind That Smile

I was watching a little girl smile one day when the Holy Spirit said to me—"Behind that smile is a whole lot of pain that only God Himself can see. That smile hides years of mental torment, rejection, physical pain and abuse; she has told no one about her anguish and suffering—why? She feels that the world doesn't care so what's the use. Behind that smile the little girl hides a fear that goes far beyond the normal fears of life; she sits back and laments will she live long enough to realize her dreams or perhaps become some kind man's wife. She wonders why a God who says He loves her allows her to go through day after day. She wishes He would hurry up and send His son—Jesus—to whisk her up in the clouds and take her away. Behind that smile the young girl ponders over several ways to get attention—excel beyond others, wear bright colors or she could pretend to be extremely glad. If none of those work, she'll try other ways—feign an illness, cause a stir, be mischievous or maybe she'll act real sad. That smile cries out for love from someone who is both naturally and spiritually strong; for you see, this little girl craves plenty of praises when she's right, but she also needs someone who is kind and gentle; someone who is willing to take a chance. Anyone who is able to make that smile genuine can watch his or her spiritual life advance. Behind that smile the little girl still has hope and a heart that has a lot of love to give. She also has a lot faith, fortitude and inner strength and a fighting urge to live."
So to this little girl I say, "Hold your head up high, trust in God, and remember that weeping may endure for a night. It won't be too long before you see the morning, and in your life, God's Son will be shining bright."
—*Deborah Ezell-Gray*

Context Of Youth

Bewildered youth it's questing why
Scanning the future A war torn sky
Forced through time's intimidaty
Piqued insecure in troubled morbidity.

Ascending descending from brooding obscurity
Portending eternity or a dubious maturity
Pondering events all of life's mystery
Of a glorified past stymied by history.

Unplotted uncharted unsung and unsaid
Absorbed engrossed engulfed in dread
Life's forces gaining momentum and speed
A tempo awakening processes of need.

Generations of mentality of thought and creed
Overcoming miraculously cruel thought and deed
Mediocrity Anonymity Immortality Fame?
Timeless Forces and Faces Relentless Remain.

—*Eleanore Bosco Cramer*

Dreams

Do you know what dreams are made of?
Scenes of darkness, hate and fear?
No! Far more than that, beloved
Sounds of music, laughter, cheer

Strange and yet familiar places
People whom we've met before
Many of them not acquainted
Passing through a golden door

Have you ever tried to follow?
Tried to enter all in vain?
Felt the anguish and the sorrow
For you knew you must remain?
Yet, my love, I almost made it
Almost made it through that door
Golden portal of my dreaming
Shall be there forever more

Do you share with me this feeling?
Shall we meet, and hand in hand
Some sweet night, together dreaming
Enter that forbidden land?

—*Dorothy Drew*

Woodsman, Spare My Life

I am the spreading chestnut tree
   screening you from the summer sun,
The heat from my hickory fire-place log
   keeps you cozy and warm.

As you trudge through the woods
   do you hunger and thirst?
My branches are heavy with fruit
so filled with juice and ready to burst.

I am the chair that rocks baby to sleep,
   The shelf holding grandfather's clock,
I'm also the handle of your mother's broom
   And the door where friends often knock.

I am the willow who weeps to hear
   the beating drums and marching feet
of those who carry the burdens of war,
Standing firm, like me, with no retreat.

I'll be your cradle, your home, your coffin,
   I am the bread of kindness, cherish me.
   Tread softly, all you who pass by,
   Harm me not listen to my plea.

—*Berniece Cover*

Soul Searching in the Shadows

Slip into the shadows of the night.
Shadows cover and move, but no one's there.
Trace your steps into the past,
Decide, if the present can compare.
Thoughts can rise up and claim the space,
Where once our foolish actions filled—
Mindless, carefree, constant motions,
That now one wonders why they thrilled?
Where are you going? Have you already been
Down all the roads, that lead somewhere—
Somewhere important and worthwhile to be,
Now that you find yourself here?
The night has the answers in its misty arms.
Seek out the reasons, and look for the truth,
For all those memories, and shadowy faces,
That you thought you knew from base to roof.
Slip into the shadows, that stretch from you.
Pull them around you to make you complete.
Don't let any light escape in the night,
Or, tomorrow will evaporate, who you are, in its heat.

—*Joyce Hughes*

Forests

The beautiful trees that cast
Shadows on the ground from the early morning sun.

The golden needle grass that
softens each step you take.

Animals scamper to their hearts content.

The brilliant sun shines through the
branches of the tall pine trees.

The crickets chirp their song as
the night comes near.

—*Ann L. Chandler*

Life

Shall we be sad or shall we be merry;
Shall we laugh in the sunlight or weep in the gloom,
Shall the world e'er greet us with a face that is cheery
Or one that is mournful and sad as a tomb?
There may be joy and there may be sighing,
Those we meet on life's byways are ne'er the same;
Some stride with quick life and some with slow dying,
Walk thou with each brother and be kind in His name.
There must a time come when the glad will be wailing,
And the sad will be happy a space on the way.
With laughter and tears is the life of man builded,
With the mists of the night and the light of the day;
Then let us puss on serene in His mercy,
Thru rain and thru sunshine to the end of the way!

—*Delmer R. Hite*

Hidden Delight

Do you wonder where the stars that guild the night
Seclude themselves in safety from our piercing morning sight?
Do you know that after dark while it's still growing light,
Those stars do quit the fleeing dark, descending in earthward flight,
To spill their glistening glory into a silvered pool of fresh delight?

The secret of those daylight hidden stars I know.
Come off with me and through the green and grassy woods
  we'll go,
To find a pool of depthless light where murmuring breezes blow
Midnight's mercuric magic to a sparkling silent show,
And there in silver sanctuary Argus' splendors wink and glow.

—*Irene Nibarger*

Playmates

Two little girls with their dolls in the shade,
Shared little secrets and laughed as they played.

Two teenage girls saw sailors leave by rail,
Wrote many letters, waited for the mail.

Two young brides settled many miles apart,
But each held memories deep in her heart.

Two young mothers saw their children grow,
Loved them, cared for them, and then let them go.

Two older ladies shared news by letters,
Never together, friendship grew better.

Now two widows are sitting in the shade,
Through tears and laughter, talk of when they played.

—*Elizabeth Terwilliger*

The Wren

When into the garden the Wren comes to settle
She bubbles and bubbles like Mommy's tea-kettle.
A wee little bundle so active and nervous,
There's no other birdie so willing to serve us.

It's really a pleasure to have her around,
For even her chatter's a right welcome sound.
Her nest-site she chooses, it seems, on a whim,
Then sets about building with vigor and vim.

At times it's a nest-box, old hat or old shoe;
And sometimes a coat with a pocket will do;
Or any old kettle or can she can find
Will suit little Jenny, for she doesn't mind.

Ambition is never this garden friend's lack.
No job she selects is too big to attack.
So after she's chosen a spot for her nest,
She builds her home eagerly - gives it her best.

The single intention in Jenny Wren's mind
Is to fill up that home-site with all she can find.
She gathers in rubbish and grasses and dregs
And fashions a nest to hold eight tiny eggs.

—*George H. Boyer*

An Ode To Moms

There was a dear lady who lived in a house that was not new,
She had lots of children, but she knew exactly what to do.
  She gave each one a job to help make it a home and keep it
    clean,
And taught them the art of working together as a team.
  As they went about doing their daily tasks,
They learned good habits that would always last.
  They were pleased with themselves and each other too,
And we've never bored for they found plenty of constructive
    things to do.
  They also learned to love and respect all others
And were ever so proud and grateful for their dear, smart mother,
  Who taught them not only to be alert and clean,
But how to implement what the constitution of the United States
    of America means —

  A nation whose foundation is built of Christ, the solid rock
Against when the storms and fury of mortal mind can never shock
  Us into thinking God is dead or asleep,
For over all his creation constant watch doth He keep,
  Loving and healing us with His perfect peace!

—*Florine H. Hall*

Special Lady

I walked with a lady who is gracious and sweet,
   She knows not the meaning of despair or defeat;
Her warm tender smile like sunshine in May,
   Scatters clouds of gloom away from the day.

I walked with a lady who is valiant and strong
   She assured me that life is a continuing song;
That things are never as bad as they seem,
   And that struggle and strife will build self-esteem.

I heard a special lady speak,
   Of adversity and how unique
When the road of life seems difficult to climb,
   That hope is the essence to glorify time.

Then when I'm feeling down and out,
   This special lady will free my doubt;
Now I count my blessings without measure,
   For a special friend and a blessed treasure.
     —*Josephine Cordaro*

Marriage

In love with my lady, today's so special,
She looked "radiant" so beautiful and bright.

The glow on her face, made my heart race.
I said to myself this love is stronger than mace!!
We have become one, in God eyesight
so everything feels — so right.

Never let anyone, come between me and you
If we do, we both lose. Always be
trueful to each other, that way. Our love
will grow.

Communication is the key that unlock the door.
So keep it close to your heart.
And give honor to our God.
Marriage is the beautiful blending
of two lives, to hearts and to lovers.
   —*Gregory Coleman*

Autumn Fantasy

When mother nature starts her autumn show,
   She sets the whole country-side aglow.
And with winter waiting in the wings,
   this seems to be her last fling.

She paints the country like a fairyland,
   with just a touch of her hand.
Leaves of bright red, yellow and gold,
   And beautiful colors that seem to unfold.

Trees with apples that are blushing red,
   with nothing but bright blue skies overhead.
The witches' brooms sweep the clouds away.
   While the toothy jack-o-lanterns adorn each day.

A great beauty like this cannot last,
   and colors soon will be fading fast.
When the leaves slither to the ground,
   no longer will this beauty be around.
     —*Harley Allen*

Letting Go

Filled with hurt anger and pain
She sits in her room listening to the rain
As it's falling hard and fast
She wishes she could put her feelings in the past
Her feelings are strong and she knows they're right
As they leave her thinking all through the night.
Knowing that he never knew what love stands for
Just shows her, she can't be with him anymore
It's time to say goodbye and to let him know
The hatred she feels makes it easier to let him go
She cared for him once and she always will
But it's time for her to go on,
It's time for her to heal...
   —*Crystal Blackwell*

In New Light

She sits there silently questioning her life.
She stares out the window into the night.
How deep, how dark, how cold it seams,
The night, just as those in her dreams.
The darkness closing in upon her.
The fog will be gone the morning after.
She doesn't notice the first of the morning light.
As of now it is not very bright.
She is wrapped up in her thoughts.
She hasn't yet found the answers sought.
The sun has almost broken through.
Soon the sky will turn pale blue.
The sun will soon shine upon the land,
She will look again at the ring held in her hand.
It does look different in the sunlight.
She now feels that everything might be all right.
What a difference the dun does make.
The gloom of darkness it does take.
   —*Cynthia Carraabine*

Black Rose

      Worrisome weed
   she torments my sleep-garden
     a poisonous whisper
    dripping down sable lips
    she thirsts the night through
      inky, insatiable
     bleeding arid lust
     dream-soil stained
'neath her witch-blanket nightshade
     frolic faceless fears
   a cancerous kaleidoscope
   of writhing patterns pitch
   demonic nether-children
   retch forth from her womb
   former mindscape serene
    now playground insane
  daybreak delivers dancing light
     dreams depart, dust
  enchantress and her legacy
    now lay in ruins rust
   —*Don Simpson*

Blind Memories

Imprisoned by a wall of fate
she travels through a misty place
that leads her back towards the gate
of no return, a struggling race.
She does not stop to feel the pain
or learn the causing source;
she takes both leaps and bounds and gains
the weight of blind remorse.
She never knows just why she slips
upon the rock beneath her feet;
the day will come when she will trip
on why she cannot weep.
Will she listen and will she hear
the inner voice that questions fear?
—*Dorayne Levin*

Vincent's Butterfly

What happened to my butterfly?
She was so pretty and so free.
Did you clip her wings?
Perhaps she was captured and forced
into a cage and hung on the dying willow tree.
Surely, imprisoned, she will die.
She was fragile, but her wings were
strong and she could rise to distant
and secret hiding places;
taking her away from all that made
her sad and weary. To forget the pain
and the accusing faces.
Did you break her lighted spirit?
Are you hiding, my butterfly?
Behind a cloud, behind a tear, looking
back in time, crippled by fear. Silent.
And now, I have passed into the space beyond.
I see where you are, I feel your thoughts, your pain.
Take heart, Rise! Take flight. Please try.
I will wait for you, my butterfly.
—*Carol A. Schweickert*

Mother's Fur Coat

My mother had a nice fur coat, that kept her nice and warm.
She wore it when the snow came down, and when the wind blew up a storm.
She liked the coat an awful lot and wore it a long, long time.
She even loaned it to her daughter once, and she wore it for a time.
Her daughter gave it back to her and she wore it many seasons more.
The coat was starting to show its wear, so it was put into a bag to store.
When mother departed from her earthly home, to a better home indeed,
The bag with mother's coat was found, when searching through her things.
To throw it out would be a shame, with all the memories it brings.
I let my mind go to and fro, as to what way that I should go,
I want it saved some way to show her love for that old coat
So I asked a seamstress friend of mine if she would help me out.
I wanted her to make for me, a bear so firm and stout.
It took about a week to sew from a portion of mother's coat,
A fuzzy, fuzzy, Teddie Bear was made from Mother's Fur Coat.
—*Joyce L. Duitsman*

Mama

Saint Peter will be sad when he sees my Mama at the Pearly Gate
She'll make him sweep the golden street each day after.
If he won't, Mama will do it by herself, I'll wager.
This would cost him peace of mind,
He'd be filled with guilt, and pine—
For where would Heaven go that very day?
Peace and guilt can't dwell together, Oh ho, never!

Joshua made the sun stand still
Yet, who'd move Heaven and earth but my dear Mama?
She is ninety-four years old,
And she weighs just eighty pounds,
But who would ever guess—
She is mightier by far than winds, or sails, or oceans are!
So, nothing can I do but be her daughter.

Mama, this verse was written all in fun,
But if there were "Emmys", you'd surely have won.
Since I was a baby you've held my hand,
And taught me the things I should understand.
Now, I am a mother, and I too can do
All the wonderful things for my children, too.
And this is the role that never shall end, called "Mama!"
—*Edris Guenther*

Gayle

Who is this girl named Gayle?
She's a gift from above
An expression of love
She's warmed our hearts a hundredfold.

Nature is her best friend
Music her company
Her style reminiscent of old.

She's witty and clever
with a flair for surprises
    beyond measure
With pride we answer the
    question why?
This green eyed freckle faced Gayle
Lives to be me — myself — and I.
—*Betty Ciavarella*

Hurray For The Fourth Of July

I love my dear country, the land of my birth;
She's the greatest, most beautiful country on earth!
America is the land of the brave and the free,
Where each person can be what he wishes to be.
You may forget dates and events you learned in history,
But never forget the brave patriots who fought to make us free.
They pledged their lives, their for tunes and their sacred honor
And helped mold our great nation's destiny.
This year is the one hundredth anniversary of Miss Liberty,
Her golden torch will always shine brightly on land and on sea.
She is the symbol of hope and a better life
For the millions of immigrants who come to our shores
To seek a safe harbor from oppression and strife.
When you watch the parade on the fourth of July
And see the flashing bands and the stars and stripes pass by,
Remember all the courageous who gave their lives
So our beloved America might enjoy liberty.
For they are the patriots who hold freedom's bannerhigh
And keep our Old Glory flying against the blue sky.
May God bless America! Hurray for the fourth of July!
—*Elda Schwarz Wright*

Why?

Why did God make the sun come up and
shine it's lovely light?
Why does the moon come out to give
such glowing light each night?
Why do some girls have their babies,
to laugh and smile and coo,
while other girls never give a thought
to a life that will never come true?
Why are some people so mean,
hateful in every single way,
while others are the nicest folks, in all
they do and say?
Why are some people so rich, never
willing to share their wealth,
while others work with all their might,
have nothing to show but bad health?
Why do some people have all the luck,
never sick, feel bad or cross,
while others are always down and out
because of some great loss?
Why does God who created us all,
let all this come to bear,
doesn't He look down on His children from above,
to give us all the same care?
Well, my friend, if these answers you find,
will you please share with all who cry,
For Solomon, the wisest man of the world,
Could not answer this little word, "Why?"

—*Brownie Lawler*

Strength, Oh Glorious, Fortuitous Strength

Year by year, the walls around me close.
Shrinking endlessly, reducing in size and space.
But strength, oh glorious, fortuitous strength is by my side.
When teams of life are picked, He is on mine,
Backing me oh so gracefully, when no one knows He's there.
From places unknown and unwanted, He comes.
No name, no identity, no trademark.
A silent beckoning, a call in darkest night.
I await Him with patience,
Knowing when He arrives, all will be right.
He comes in a pounding and rushing of blood.
A name He doesn't need, just to know He's there is enough.
My entire being is based on Him.
The life which flows like a river through me, He is there.
I need Him like a potent drug.
If anything goes not right,
He's there, right beside me.
That feeling allows me to breathe freely and
live life to its fullest.
There He will remain, in my heart, and in my soul forever.

—*Hope Warren*

A Thanksgiving

Rags, heaped upon chilled bones, a mattress.
Sidewalk grates, bed frames, radiating warmth
    up from the earth. A place in heaven
until a large, mean, someone discovered his berth

Driven out into a world more cold than the night
to earn his street place in such a glorious spot
        not yet his, he prayed.
Thankful for a kindness: He could keep the rags
    and go unmolested. Unexpected bliss.

He was grateful, too, the night was almost gone.
A frozen early light misted the skyline and dimmed
the frightening shadows of the nocturnal world.
    Another day. Maybe there will be a sun.

—*Donald F. Withee*

Sounds Of A Silent Day

The elevator hummed as I moved upward,
silent in my thoughts.
I dwelt on sounds of laughter, mountain apples
and strolls along the sea.
The click of my heels as I walked the corridor
echoed back at me.
The solemn faces of nurses and doctors greeted
me at the door.
The room was filled with a breathless hush.
The sound of silence hung heavy as I closed
the door.
I left the stillness behind and ran out into
the street.
Children were playing kick ball. The sun glared.
My heart rolled away with the hapless ball.
The silence drowned the children's laughter.
I was left alone with the silent day.

—*Doris Hartsell Brewer*

Untruthful Truth

Untruthful truth? Balboa or Cortez,
"Silent on a peak in Darien...;"
Is truth what all? Or one man sees and says?
Truth? Says it all: all life: if only in
One white-tail'd moment of, insight to cheer,
One breathless view of beauty, oh-h 'tis gone,
Around a curve one comes upon a deer,
However brief, then, something lingers on:

Truth glows in memory's (bad history?)
Soul food's kind light, man's life too often dark;
And day that rains to day eternally
Too soon: o'er flood of time, where's Noah's ark?

On ship nam'd Poetry. I float my case,
Love's truth? It's my desire; your beauty, grace.

—*James Madison Whitehead*

Tropical Paradise

A wave caresses lonely shores, a gull above an inlet soars. A silent song of wind through palm, a wind that's cool and always calm. A human ne'er on these shores strode, nor made a camp nor built a road. No other life 'cept field and bird, no sound of humans ever heard. No painter's brush could paint a scene, of solitude and so serene. Of waves that kiss the pure white sand, or palm that sway on fertile land. Or rays of sun through foliage pass, to twinkle on green blades of grass. An island circled by the sea, where fish and bird and all are free. No filth or dirt on shores washed clean, no trash or sickness nor things obscene. No fighting, poverty, hate, or war, where life is free and nothing more. Someday this lonely isle unmarred, will be invaded, hurt, and scarred, by someone too engrossed to see its beauty and serenity. They'll mar its shore with signs and highway, ruin the soil with cement and byways. They'll cut the palms and kill the gull, and build their scrapers straight and tall. Pollute the water, kill the fish with oil and whatever else they wish. A bustling city hard and cold, is what the birds must now behold. Where once the giant palm tree stood, are pillars of concrete instead of wood. So hope the time should ne'er arise, that humans come to paradise.

—*Duane S. Nelson*

Love's Fountain

Love, for some, is like a bottomless sea gliding, sliding,
    silently.
Or it may be a bubbling brook, rapidly flowing, with much like a
    tumbling look.
But, for me it is a beautiful fountain, its water showering,
    sprinkling, spraying.
A little of it you may get if you reach out a few drops to
    catch.
In its water reflection you will see all of us holding hands
    universally.
For love's fountain is laid out and made from the master's most
    beauteous landscape plan,
Which is every thing that is created, lives, and breathes on
    the face of this land.
We will always have love for we are drinking from this
    fountain's never run dry cup.
Come, baste, or saturate yourself in love's fountains
    sprinklings of joy and trickles of memories, which flow into
    the basin's structure.
Love we will always find if to love's fountain we there
    eventually walk,
No matter what language we talk.
    —Janette C. Thomas

Labor Day 1967: A Sonnet Instead Of A Bonnet

Ho! Little black girl, why do you pull at your head?
Silky the skewered lock you clutch
So, brittle cracked pearl, sigh and make the ground your bed.
Milky, harpooning-it's your brain you touch.
On your bright brow a dimpled bud
Wet red bloom on tarnished spires
Burning frost of untimely blood
Turning all to tiny sparkling fires
My baby, he's shot my baby,
Beseechingly clamors the woman who bore this life
Innocent player on noxious stage maybe
You'll feel better to know he was shooting at his wife
Still you grasp your white pony tail frownless
Leave it be and go as you are crownless
    —Ed Stewart

My Mother's Hands

My prayer today, I know Dear Lord, will seem unusual to most.
Since all my life I have been taught to pray for
rest for all your Host. To pray that Labor will be o'er
for those who reach The Kingdom Shore.

But as my mother slept one day I saw her hands were seldom
still and was reminded of the days, before she'd started
down the Hill. When every sunrise held anew some labors
for her hands to do.

Those eager, busy, lovely hands, that held my very LIFE
within. That wiped away my childish tears and snatched
me from the jaws of sin. E'en now I feel their soft caress:
Those hands so filled with tenderness.

And so, dear Lord, I'm sure she'll be, much happier in
That Kingdom Grand, if pleasant tasks be found so she can
occupy those busy hands.

My prayer to others may seem odd.
But knowing Her, I pray, Dear God.
    —Bernice Hauser

A Mother's Sorrow

A burning flame sears through my heart,
Since death unkindly did us part.
How could what grew within my womb,
Be transferred to a lonely tomb?
I lift my head in silent rage,
For taking him before he aged.
I clutch my arms around the air,
And I am only too aware
Of what it's like to feel despair...
For nothing's there........nothing's there.
What angry force could cause such strife,
And take the very gift of life?
Did someone really judge me bad?
And, therefore, take the child I had?
This pain of mine will not be gone
As life around me still goes on.
And endless thoughts, the woeful kind,
Will always burn across my mind.
And how long will I have to wait
To meet you, love, at Heaven's gate?
    —Carol A. Martin

Underneath The Learning Tree

It was a long time ago you see...
Since I sat underneath the learning tree...
Let's see now... I must have been two or three...
When my mother began speaking words of wisdom to me...
I would ask her questions about the birds and the flowers...
    ...Everyday...
    My mother would answer my questions for hours...
As I travel through time these... memories come to mind...
    ...Of songs and rhymes...
    ...Of prayers at bed time that were said...
Of the right and wrong things that I must... do and never do...
Now I have children of my own...
    They are angels that God has given me on loan...
Underneath the learning tree... they'll be...
    Like it was with my mother... and me...
Because my learning began at my mother's knee...
    She was my human learning tree...
    —Bunny McCall

Tombeau

All of the meter and the rhyme
since man began to think and seek
are wafted on the wings of time
to merge, to coalesce, to speak.
My deathless words, uncarved in stone,
become an epitaph for me.
Such are my words, my thoughts, alone
that hymn me for eternity.
Words that have meaning to my soul
will speak to kindred spirits when,
at last, encountered in the whole
can make my musings live again.
One phrase, one line, one memory,
and I shall speak eternally.
    —Frances M. Church

Best Friends

I can't believe it's been so long
   since the hour you were first born
it must have been a beautiful day
   on that sunny August morn!

Jean Francis is the name you were given
   what a cute little baby girl
So happy to be let out in the world
   anxious to give life a whirl.

So many years have passed since then
   and with them laughs and tears
you've always been there by my side
   to listen to my dreams and fears.

Store bought cards can't say what I feel
   there couldn't be a better friend
We'll still be together in our rocking chairs
   best friends till the very end!

   —Donna L. Stokes

Zephyrs

I hear evening winds
Sing praise to God at Evensong.
They shout laudamus te here!
Whisper pianissimo prayer there!
Sun reflects mystic holy light on
Chapel windows stained glass bright,
As Zephyrs join monastery chant,
They blend their songs with
Dulcet organ sweetly,
Loud chapel bells ringing,
Riotous birds singing.
What a lovely Canticles cant!
The last fond echoes of sing songs
Are heard,
Together with melodies of the
Nightingale birds. Remain Zephyr Winds!
Please dear God! Let them stay!
Permit such joys to remain, I pray! Oh
Give us Lord, another Zephyred day!

   —James B. Long

Christmas Love

As the carolers pass our window at night
Singing their songs of joy and holding their candles so bright.
We look and smile and sing along
Because we love those Christmas songs.

People are happy this time of year
Because they know Christmas is near.
If you could see the children I've seen
Then you would wonder what Christmas really means.

Some of our children with their faces so bright
Have no food or even a place to sleep tonight.
Can you feel the pain they must feel?
As Christmas comes they wonder, is Santa real?

If Christ was here what would he say?
Could be, to love and help your neighbor on this Christmas Day.
As we decorate our trees so bright
Just think about these children tonight.

When you buy your gifts for someone you know
Stop and think of these tiny faces with no place to go.
Their Christmas could be so cheerful and bright
If they had one small gift on this Christmas night.

   —Gregory Meshaw

Untitled

my
Sister is like a lovely little insect that flies around the room
lighting for only a moment
on any piece of furniture that will show Her off

She has tiny wings that i cannot see that carry Her
From the couch to the chair to the floor
and that beat so quickly i'd swear they weren't even there
except for the gentle breeze they create when She passes by

i love the way my Sister smells
like something very clean ... like baby powder ... and i follow
behind her every chance i get just to breathe in Her subtle
bouquet

i could stare at my Sister's face for hours ...
such exquisite beauty ... Her cheeks lit with some inner light
that makes the air around Her glow like a halo

how i love my Sister

i often think that the only way I could ever express my love
would be for me to hold Her in my arms so tightly that we
would merge
together into one

Then my thoughts would be Hers and
Hers mine

   —dennis parsons

Summer Rain

   The summer rain falls silently outside my window, as I
sit gazing at the million raindrops that fall from the dark
clouds above.

   Each drop of rain carries its own crystal clear beauty,
but the beauty is far out weighed by the deep sadness felt in
my heart when I watch a single drop turn into a shower.

   This same sadness I feel when watching the summer rain
is the same sadness i feel when I'm away from you. Because
like the rain you go away too soon.

   —Jaime Warden

A New Day

A new day is on the horizon
Skies are blue above
Birds are singing to their mates
the world is bursting with love

Trees are swaying to the music
flowers are smiling up to the sun
Butterflies are softly floating
calling, "everyone come have some fun"

Squirrels are gathering their nuts
in the cool moist air
Rabbits hoping about
Inviting all, come to the "carrot fair"

See the graceful deer
poised for a portrait of natural art
While that ol' moose just stands there
Refusing to leave a cool marshes heart

The brook keeps marching on
creating bubbles on its way
While all the creatures on this earth
rejoice in a bright new day!

   —Jean Epperley

Sleep

I dreamt of angels
Sleeping next to you

I dreamt of angels sleeping with you
Sleeping next to you I dreamt of angels
Angels soft and angels sweet
Some large others petite

Angels floating effortlessly
Angel wings fluttering dynamically
Sleeping next to you I dreamt of angels

Angel smiles soothing relief
Angels happy angel glee
To accompany them was my plea
Flutter and whirling through the sky
My absence my alibi

Roaming with the clouds
Dissipate in pleasure
With only an angel allows
Soothing smile angel relief

Sleeping next to you I dreamt of angels
I dreamt of angels sleeping with you.
—*Airec Lenn*

Purple World

My mother draped in a purple apron,
slicing a can of cranberries
and eating raisins.
Cranberry juice runs all over the counter
to the purple grapes in the glass bowl.

My father sits on the purple sofa
fondling his purple heart,
remembering how the purple haze of a grenade
kept him from seeing the enemy.

My sister weeds her garden
of purple roses
to avoid our father's face
when he sees her first hickey.

My twin sister watches Grape Ape,
singing to her purple-haired trolls,
wearing her mother's purple wig
to play in her fantasy.

My family in a world
with my purple crayon.
—*Anthony Michael Guadagnino*

The Rainbow Of Flowers

Take a walk on a dirt travelled path,
Slightly covered with grassy green growth.
Kick the loose stones off to the side.
So, here 'tis narrow, further it's wide.
Oh! Sweet fragrance, perfume in mid air.
Rides carelessly near on gentle breeze.
Fragile wild flowers, bend to and fro.
Boast of their freedom, for all to know.
Tiny buttercups, daisies, others sky blue.
Bunches clustered everywhere, seek no fame.
In a vase, they could brighten any room.
Not daring to compete with roses in bloom.
Bedded on distant hill or plain.
Free to grow or wither at will.
This rainbow of flowers, first sign of spring.
Brings cheer to us all, like a bird on a wing.
—*Connie K. Fiamella*

Angels Unware

As I was walking down the street, a stranger
smiled, how are you today? Hastily I made my
way. Will I be late the light is red.
People surround me oh! "Get out of my way."

Arriving at work the day is hectic. Phones
ringing the paging system is driving me mad.
Lunch is a glorious site finally I can rest
and get off my feet. The subway roars to a
halt the door is open a stranger asks are
you okay?

My day has come to an end I'm finally home.
The phone is ringing, the dog is barking well
let's take a stroll. A stranger approaches when
suddenly he asks are you alright?
I bid you sweet dreams and good night.

How wonderful the day when I recall the
stranger who greeted me throughout the
day. Least beware for have we entertained angels
unaware.
—*Irma Jean Martin*

Save The Whistle Of The Whippoorwill

Candle glowing
Smokey hill
Weeping willows
Dance and still
They are after the moonlight
Of the rain-filled night
Where in the village lonely
I can see a tiny light.

Skilled the lights
To give enough to lead the pathway out
Of the village lonely, still
Save the whistle of the whippoorwill.

Save the whistle of the whippoorwill
Against that cold dark night
Save the whistle of the whippoorwill
Which keeps the lantern bright.
In the winter of a thousand years
The lantern guides the way
Save the whistle of the whippoorwill
Which tells the lantern what to say.
—*Erica Farneth*

December

Flakes like down, drifting then swirling in the wind,
    smother the world
Through the day, rising in mounds like leavened dough
Clinging to branches, pines transformed
    by a somber white shroud
Night's whistle rising and falling as the
    white sheet is unfurled
Nature transformed magically o'ernight by snow
Morning's grey shows crystal encased tree-fingers
    against the cloud…
Sun breaking through crevices and
    round the edges of clouds curled
Suddenly lighting all I see with its glow
Revealing snow-captive diamonds and
    ice-locked tree limbs proud
A magical time is winter sudden transformations
hurled at Nature stripped of her gala fall gowns
    and bare of toe
Still unflinching she stands in her new gown of white,
head unbowed.
—*George F. Bergman, Jr.*

These Dreams

These dreams —
   so big
   so deep
   so wide —
They are trapped inside
   a mind too small.
Or, are they held captive
   by a world of insignificant walls?
The heart and
   the soul
     together join and wage war
to fight limits set by fear alone.
These dreams —
   these desires
   these plans
   these hopes —
They stay locked up tight
And are set free
   only at night, as I sleep,
   when dreaming is allowed.
     —Christine Ann Bosinski

All Night Counting Stars

That time of youth so brief, so brief,
   so brief for ripened cherries,
for wading in willow streams.
For moments of crimson lips
   and clover.

From the petals of frosted
   purple asters,
from walnut groves and mountain springs
ice-thorned winds torment
   the fearing heart
and the taste is bitter
   of green persimmons.

New glass on the pond
   and scarlet haws on snow
the fox wanders, wanders in hunger.
All night counting the stars.

Song of awakened birds,
golden breath of sunrise clouds
   a tear prisms the dawn
in blue bewilderment.
     —Emma Crobaugh

Christmas In The Country

The snow has stopped falling, but will start again soon.
So, bring in some wood to help warm this old room.
Build up the fire until the flames are hot white.
That should help us through this cold dreary night.
We'll have to rise early, so set the alarm.
Were the horses and cattle put up in the barn?
First thing we'll do tomorrow, come dawn,
Is to chip some ice from around the old pond,
So the cattle and creatures some water can find.
Then we'll go looking for an eight foot tall pine.
We'll drag that tall tree home on the sled,
The one that Dad built and we painted red.
Then by Great-grandpa's grave we'll stop for awhile.
Then we'll chop-n-split wood to build up the pile.
But for now let's lay down and try to keep warm.
As the snow starts to fall and the night starts to storm.
     —Joey Jackson

God's Fearful Storm

The harsh rain wound across the street
so coarsely, yet still keeping a steady beat.
   We wonder how it comes to thee,
it's fierce strong winds still whirling free.

The woe of the night reflects
from each pair of cautious eyes.
   As if each raindrop
held a sin full of lies.

God faces each day
with storms such as this,
He releases each raindrop
as each sin he forgives.

The storm that continues
in this world is yet one.
The struggle to overcome sinning
and see yet a glimpse of the sun.

Though people still sin,
and God releases the rain of fright.
   Behind that storm cloud,
is the amazing sky of heaven's light.
     —Candi Biggs

Today

Today is the first day of the rest of your life,
So fill its every minute with happiness, not strife.

You and I are free born folk and can make our choice
So praise the good, ever rejoice.

That you can live in a land of liberty and
good can come your way
Be the best person, do your best from day to day.

What happened yesterday is over and done
The hours have ticked by, they are over and gone.

Tomorrow is out there yet to be lived to the best,
But, it is what you make of today—that is the test.

How will you choose? What will you do?
Rely upon God and He will see you through.
A day, an hour, a minute passed,
A task, a deed, is done at last.

Keep on keeping on 'til the end is in sight,
Strive to make it all come out right.

If we do our best in each and every task,
What more, what more, can anyone ask?
     —Emma D. S. Trent

Not Yet! Not Yet!

I had a visitor today— my wide-eyed younger self.
She looked at all the dreams and goals I had stacked on the shelf,
And raised her brows, and shook her head, and questioned why
   the waste—
Had I set back these precious aims for years without a trace?

With shamefaced air, I must confess—I laid my goals aside
For worry, work, affections! claims, for simply lack of pride.
I buried talents in a field—I weakly fled my fate—
And now I see—Oh, tell me, child—did you return too late?

Is it too late to show the world the treasures I possess?
To speak the words I could have said, long-silenced by life's stress?
I will no longer grieve my youth—I'll to herself be true
And seek those ends, and voice those dreams, and spread them
   out to view,
Retrieve those aims; dust off those goals, and send them forth anew.
     —Edna Inman

This Day

This day is one I will never forget
So many memories but none to regret
The ride to the church was short but seemed so long
I just can't believe that she is really gone
Then almost as if in revue I went to open the door;
so she could get out too
Instantly I realized it was only me;
This is the way from now on it would be
This day as I walked through these door's as old as a century;
Everyone turned to look as I made my entry

My heart seemed to be beating so very loud;
As I looked out across at all the somber faces in the crowd
Ever so slowly I approached the casket so shiny and gray
I would never ever forget this day;
Looking down on her beautiful face
I knew no one would never take her place;

All was silent and not one soul would speak;
As a single tear ran down my cheek
I bent to kiss her crimson lip's so cold
Her hands gently lay across her I would never hold
I just could not seem to pull myself away;
There was one more thing I just had to say
As I gently pulled her raven hair away from her ear;
I softly whispered I love you my darling angel dear
This day finally ended and came to a close; In my heart she will always be and I am sure she know's
—*Ashley Falon Winthrop*

Something Nearest To A Kiss

Thoughts of you abound in my mind,
  So many that I ponder of the kind;
That together make me truly feel,
  As if only you could be so real;
In temperament and physical traits,
  You run the gamut of different weights;
From sensitive to strong-willed,
  I see a woman completely filled;
With humor, spirit and sheer intelligence,
  Combined with natural beauty and common sense.
Qualities so rare for this day and age,
  Have brightened so vast a world stage;
Where my soul longs to take my heart,
  And draw it in to play the part;
Of passion and desire so forbidden,
  That in your presence it must stay hidden.
Thus, fate has dealt this true romantic,
  A folding hand where I must pic,
  Between pure ethics and holy bliss;
So here on earth I will always miss,
  SOMETHING NEAREST TO A KISS...
—*Daniel Ray Voboril*

To Live To Die

People seem to live to die.
Some come as quick as some die.
Why not live to live,
than live to die?
Seems a waste!
Are all the beautiful things on earth
passing us by? Or are we killing
the importance of life for no purpose?
The greed of money seems silly to me.
I do not see the point to kill
for a green piece of paper
that is spent on bills before it's
used for one's own enjoyment of life!
Greed is a terrible disease indeed!
—*Chanie Herring*

The Drapes

We swell, I swell grow old and still struggle
so much older that we fear the end
not because we did not succeed, rise, fly high
not because our cause failed our passions
not because we lost, for we had lost nothing!
not because we had chosen a sour course
or found ourselves alone outside easy comfort
nor unable to bear the uncertainty
O' no! For we were even more cautious
with our rulings, flag flying, small prizes
O' no! all these were revealed as simple now
like the early days of school, small desks and numbers
simple tidy succession of rites, rules
just one after another like counting
one, two, three, on our hands, as it were
as well when we fell moved freely outside the margins
those arbitrary lines, set by God's,
packs of dogs, whimpers of impotency
or something more convincing like O' BEAUTY!
we took such deviation with rich ease, for no this we did not fear.
—*Jayne Blair*

Enter An Angel

You come across my mind as some sorta fantasy
So take a part, of my poor broken heart, and toss it into the sea; you leave so many wonders deep inside
Because heaven cries, from cloudy skies, where love cannot be denied.

I've walked in the paths of angels
Protected by their light, lost in the night,
dancing in dreams unmangled
I've been sheltered under their wings
Where happiness is shown, in the things
I've known, what causes our hearts to sing?

You can't believe in the rainbows I've given
It glows in the dark, this burning heart,
upon the dreams I'm driven; you choose to take full advantage.
Of the things I do, just for you, over the hurts I couldn't bandage.

I tell you I'm just pretending
What is love, that an angel must rise above,
the feelings I've been sending
I believe in the heaven as too where we met
As if it's a crime, to enter your mind,
with thoughts of me in your head.

You say so many things you can't remember
No tears abound, on frozen ground,
it feels so much like December
You'll never be able to forget me dear
Where the snow is falling, hear the angels calling...
Thank you for being here!
—*James M. Jones*

Blind

Hear the birds singing
Smell the flowers so sweet
Feel the wind in my hair
The sand between my toes

Hear the water splashing
On the shore
Hear the mournful call
Of the foghorn
A little baby cry

Knowing I'm blind and cannot see
But happy with all the sounds I hear
—*Edith A. Handsaker*

Modern Life

My parents have split 'cuz my Dad is not fit,
So that I, the young son, was not taught.
It's fun to shoot pool so I dropped out of school,
But you know, it's not really my fault.

I live on the street and push drugs for a treat,
And I sell them where ever they're bought.
They cause you some pain, and may mess with your brain.
But you know, it's not really my fault.

I've picked up more crime 'cuz I've found it pays fine.
And I know that I'll never be caught.
I rob and I steal, and don't care how they feel.
But you know, it's not really my fault.

I roughed up a bum, but he carried a gun,
And he wouldn't fork over, but fought.
He hadn't a lot, in the end I got shot.
But your know, it's not really my fault.

My mom, through the years will have nothing but tears,
When rememb'ring the life that she brought.
I'll not be the boy who is bringing her joy.
But you know, it's not really my fault.
  —*Jack C. Page*

God's Mysterious Ways

They showed they didn't want you
So you came to live with me
They tried to break your spirit
But God set your spirit free.

They made you feel a "nothing"
But God had other plans
So he removed you from them
And placed you in my hands.

With God's great power to guide me
I encouraged you to see
That you could accomplish anything
With your ability,

You'll soon be off to college
To major in psychology
Knowing that with God's help
You'll be all that you can be!
  —*Florence Flett*

Still They Ride

On a warm summers day the music is heard,
softly at first but starting to grow,
making way for the children, their faces aglow,
reflecting the sight of the horses ahead,
painted in colors of blue, green and red.
The children ride with the proudest of smiles
on horses equipped for countless miles.
On a cold winter's day no music is heard,
no smiles, no laughter, not even a word.
The children are gone, the porch lights are dim,
no swing in the tree, just the oak's bare limb.
The old ones have taken what was not theirs
without thought, consideration, or so much as a care.
This is the legacy the old ones have left,
to the children has been given dismay and death.
On a warm summers day the music is heard
resounding through the laughter and chatter of the crowd
seeming to float through the air on a melodic cloud.
Locating the source is a sight to behold as children laugh and play on
brilliantly colored horses of silver and gold.
These horses are the finest, full of grace and pride,
and in this age of injustice, still they ride.
  —*Jonathan Boyer*

You Must Go On Without Me

I died just the other nite.
Some say it was suicide
But we all know how the story goes.

With my switch blade knife, and the
    street lights bright.
I have gotten to big before my time and
    I knew all my dreams wouldn't come true.

You see I was fast much too fast to know
I couldn't go slow until my power showed.
Now I know all my doors became closed

I was bad, I was never good
But there was something I never understood.
But I would get even anyway I could

Now I am gone, and I have paid my dues
When I finally got the news I already
    knew this day would come soon

I was hooked on drugs, and my switch blade knife
Some damn guy went and took my life
I knew I had to pull threw

Broken down with my broken dreams
With a wink of an eye, you can hear my screams.
You must go on without me.
  —*Fannie Thomas*

Love And Disappointment

Despite the reasons, contrary wise, is it now so long?
Somehow depths of love forgotten, I feel I don't belong.
A love that's pure and beautiful, once we thought was right.
Where's it gone, put on hold, the dimming of loves light.

Suddenly a pain so real, does roar within my heart,
No reasoning or conditions, separated by miles apart.
To love another human being, it entangles our mortal souls,
Difficult to feel this love so rare, anticipating goals.

Letters and mutual feelings, we found our narrow milieu,
Then my loving faithful wife, all letters ceased from you.
We each did promise caring, our love to always dwell,
Sure of awareness, predisposed, this must be truly hell.

Then suddenly our wondrous world, violently did explode,
My heart so very full, ripped apart from the overload.
A world serene, so exquisitely fine, now I feel quite lost,
Love diminished, where's it gone, all the good it tossed.

My reflection glaring back at me, and from my lonely stare,
I truly hurt, now love is absent, is it because I'm not there?
Questions fill my weakened brain, no answers soon to come,
I'll continue loving you my wife, now my broken heart does run.
  —*Daniel S. Mincy*

Alone

I don't ever think I'll have
   someone like you;
To call me up at night and
   tell me things that we should do.
As you can see, I'm lonely and blue;
Please tell me, "What can I do?"
To ease the pain when I
   see you walking by;
For you dumped me for a
   friend of mine.
You may not think it
   hurt that bad;
But I must say I was
   pretty mad.
I have forgiven you for
   what you did;
I must admit that I still love you.
Even when I have someone new;
I'll always be alone
   because of you!

   —*Chrissi Guth*

Just In Case

In case you didn't know it, with you I have it all.
Someone to depend on to catch me when I fall.
Someone to tell me I'm okay, when disappointments come my way.
Someone to help face myself, instead of hiding on a shelf.

In case you didn't know it, you are my closest friend.
You're always in my corner, my causes you defend.
Whenever trials darkens my days, you show me brightness that's
   your way.
When sharing with you my hopes and dreams, you never
believe they're
   too extreme.

In case you didn't know it, from you I've learned the best.
To stand alone for righteous sake and be different from the rest.
To take pride in my virtue, that's my precious gift from you.
To patiently wait on God's will, sit straight and just be still.
Just in case you didn't know it, there's a fact I'm proudest of.
At times in you I see myself, yet our diversities show love.
I pray this prayer daily, to our saviour sitting high
It's uttered from my heart, not just said with a sigh:

   Thank you for this special person, there will never be another,
But mostly God I thank you, for making her my mother."

   —*Beverly Lynn McCrory*

Lazarus!

When you chose not to heed my sister's call, Lord
Something in me died!
How cold and dark it was down there Lord
And cramped and smelly too,
And like more than twenty years, it seemed
And not a matter of days;
So stiff with fear, and ever so lonely
Or share the pain of parting.
With no one to comfort me
But then I saw a beam of hope—
A streak of light as the stone was lifted;
And heard that firm yet tender call
In such familiar accents say:
"Lazarus—Come out!"
Though dead to the world
I was pleased to comply—
I could not but obey that summons.
And then another well-known voice:
"Had you been here, my Lord,
My brother would not have died!"

   —*Fidelis*

"Just Being Together"

You push me away and say just let go.
Something on your mind I have to know.
Your worried and still say, "I'm all right."
Let me help in your struggle to fight.
You ask for no guidance, no help or support.
God, help me break down the walls to his fort.
Your pain is so intense and your fear is on the rise.
I see the suffering when I look in your eyes.
You feel you need to let go but I want to be your strength.
I don't want to say good-bye. It will only leave us in pain
and memories that will be difficult to pass by.
You know we belong together by fate.
If I lose you, there will be nothing to compensate.
I know you need me and I need you. Your apart of my heart and
leaving would cause a break.
When we are together our chemistry is clear.
You know the reality of our very deep love and the happiness we
share is and forever will be here.
Sure we have our ups and downs but the love we share is
eternal. You will never be alone. We were meant to care for
one another, a fact I've always known.

   —*Janette Taylor*

My Mother

There was something awe inspiring about a giant of a maid,
Something solemn and pure and good
None can name it, but it lingered,
Felt by all who passed he way.
None could listen to her tone
Lest he feel inclined to pray.

When the brooks and trees were silenced,
When the wind had knelt in prayer
As we gathered around our chosen,
To mingle in her song, and praise,
She's the one whose care abideth
Thru early dark and dreary days.

And we felt ourselves uplifted
From the earthly common clay,
To be a fruit of this rare colleen,
To be guided by the hand unseen
Through song and story, through dance and dreams,
To know and feel the breath of God.

   —*Cornelius J. Nichols*

A Yearning

I have no fear of dying.
Sometimes I yearn to go,
To be with my Father and Savior,
It's the truth and I want you to know.

Don't cry if I must leave you.
Please don't bid me linger here.
I know my dears that you love me,
But I need to depart it is clear.

There is such a lonesomeness in me,
Deep, deep down in my soul.
I'm yearning to be home with the Father
Then I can truly be whole.

I know there are grand vistas out there.
Worlds that I've yet to see.
I know there are glories, just waiting,
And who knows what form I will be?

So put a smile on your faces,
And bid me a joyous adieu.
Send me off on my greatest adventure;
I'll claim that special mansion for you.

   —*Jean W. Goodhue*

Looking Back On Life

I'm looking back on life though I'm nowhere near the end.
Sometimes it's been an enemy but it's mostly been a friend.

It wasn't always sunshine but it wasn't always storm.
It wasn't always freezing though it wasn't always warm.
It wasn't always good times, though there weren't too many bad.
I haven't always had a lot and a lotta times I've been had.

I've done a lot of taking 'cause I had a lot of give.
I've faked my share of aching, gonna hurt if you're gonna live.
I've done a heap of living and I ain't by no means done.
If I've seen a lot of hard times, I've sure had a lot of fun.

One thing I wasn't gypped on, love's one thing I've always had.
I've still got my darling mother though I've lost my dear old dad.
I've had my share of loving and I've also loved a few.
Some of them have played me false but mostly they were true.

If today the good Lord calls me and he says my time is near,
And now that judgement day has come, is there anything I fear,
I'll say, "I've tried to cause no pain, my debts I've always paid,
And since I am God-fearing, here I come, Lord, unafraid."

I'm looking back on life though I'm nowhere near the end.
It's sometime been an enemy but it's mostly been a friend.

—*Claire Waeber Hicock*

Words

We use them when the dawn we greet
Sometimes they're salty—sometimes sweet
Depending on our nightly rest
We use these things which suit us best.

Yes, these are instruments we use
To calm a fear or light a fuse
To build a dream or tear it down
To coax a smile or fix a frown.

They offer pray'r or curse a cause
They mend a mind or render flaws
They cry for peace or wars they start
Which tears all nations far apart.

A two edged sword these things can be
They cut—they tempt—and disagree
Or humble as a child in need
They tumble out and scatter seed.

I think these wondrous precious tools
Will make us bright or simply fools
But used the way they ought to be
'Tis God who speaks thru you and me.

—*Alice S. Brown*

The Candle

I carry an eternal flame,
Somewhere, down deep inside.
I am a woman - soft and sure -
And cloaked with sensuous pride.

No wonder that I wear a smile,
And shed a beauteous glow.
I walk with sunlight every day.
I let the blessings flow!

I would not trade my female garb
For all the gold on earth.
For I am proud of what I do.
I know my womanly worth!

So love me now, while days are new,
And trust is e'er the same.
And you will feel the gentle warmth
Of my eternal flame.

—*Jo Piper*

Little Children

Watching from the deck, as you run and play in my yard, happy, free,
Sometimes wishing you could stay that way.
Only a moment, then I know it was not meant to be.
These busy, innocent, wonderful days.
So full of joy at everything you see.
Who knows what you will grow up to be...
All is new, to feel, to touch,
   to explore — God's world.
For you He gave His son,
Thinking that when this world is deep in sin —
Maybe through you a new world will begin.
Where love, hope and peace will fill man's heart,
And everyone can have a part,
You must listen for His voice,
On this earth so full of choice,
For hurting, hungry children there should not be.
They need a chance to live —
To fulfill the plan God has for them.
Precious children, run and play.
The world will be yours — someday.

—*Betty Jo Pursell McClure*

Listen

   A melody flutters on the wind of the night
   Soothing with powers much stronger than sight.
   It echoes through chimneys, and rings in our ears,
   singing in our joy, and crying in our tears.

   A small child laughs 'neath a streetlight in the dusk
   singing out her happiness, her hopefulness, her trust
   Her song has played forever, gleaming softly in our eyes,
   It's gentle truth has echoed in our smiles and our cries.

   An old man walks along the street and hears her song-
   Tired feet and rumpled coat; the day has been so long
And yet he stops to listen, take a breath and breathe a sigh
   Unsure of how the melody had made him want to cry.

   Thankful for the growing dark, he wiped his tears away
and shuffing down the road again, he could hear the music play
   The beauty of her laughter, the whisper of the wind
He captured all within his heart, and listened, deep within.

—*Jennifer E. Showen*

Discernment

Maliciously aligned powers have neatly arranged
sources of action cursedly defiling humanity.
Not just today:
But throughout all history.

Relentlessly seeking destruction of reproving truths
while exciting opposition in guise of individuality,
love is denounced, more, love is proclaimed:
Seditious, full of ambiguity.

Appealing to unimpassioned reason so convincingly
multitudes led astray so incredulously
forsake principles of law written eternally:
Revealed in boundless hate and abject misery.

What then the remedy
For those holding so tenaciously
Deceived by masters of sophistry
Victimly blinded by devises of bondage, of slavery?

Freedom lies within service of love-
Springing from intelligent appreciation of His character above-
Dependent upon perfect accord as principles of righteousness,
that are quite simply impossible to ignore...

—*Cheryl Bogowitz*

Sahara

Emotions tripping through
Space, blown by time into another
Sunrise, dancing upon
Lashes, reflecting liquid remaining from
The early frost, so as to
Catch, first glimpses of
Morning, supposedly the last
Chance, to thread what is left
Unsewn, are the seams of
Life, coming apart in the
Middle, falling through
Dimensions, only recently
Discovered, still uncovered
Untapped, are the resources of
Intellects, leading one's heart
Astray, like cats in the
Alley, darkness and insecurity of
Hearts, leading one's intellect
Array.

—*Barbara Leigh Voyt*

His Power

The starry heaven reach beyond the time and space of man.
To make us wonder and to dream of an unknown hand.
That fashion all the splendor of a moon, that silver glows.
With radiance for all to see his majesty it shows.
For who but one above us all in might and
power could string the stars in velvet blue
and give with beauty, life, such as me and you.

—*Janice Sherfy Owens*

Stil'Amor VS Chellmurr

In reflections beneath my Lovemere-Tears...
　...Sparkly-Transcendence yea snared ... By Old-Fears,
　　Whippy-Windsong screams ... of Silent-Sirens,
And Lighthouses that never really blink.
　　Still-Amor Arrears; Wavy-Clears.

Thus when I'd find a Fragrant-Flower
　Adrift in fields of cologne...
　　　...Well-borne pollens....
　　　...I can hear them laughing ... even now.
　Trees without fruit, a pointless-moot,
She's ....A Dawning — Dream to be,
　So lovely in Feminine — Garments ... Pretty,
　Tho' may never uncover a-cloak .... Pity,
As beautiful as her birthday-suit.

Through what we'd want
　And that which we can't,
　　Oft widest gaps-revealed ... between,
　So if you must stay-put ... for — now,
Then travel-widely
In your thoughtful-feelings ... and dreams.

—*Carter P. Cate*

Oh It's Something To Be Irish

Oh it's something to be Irish
Something whimsical and gay
Thou you kill you own ambition
In you contradictory way
Though you'll never own a house or lot
Nor ever gain renown,
You have something that's the envy of the richest in the town.
For when God breathes the breath of life onto the lowly cloud
He smiled and for the Irish pat a singing in the sad.

—*Joan Therese Camp*

My Special Garden

Dear friend please take my hand and walk with me thru my special garden.
Listen to the songs of the beautiful birds. Feel the cool breeze blowing against your face.

See the pretty flowers smell their sweet fragrance. Listen to the water fall cascading over the rocks, falling into a bubbly pool below.

Enjoy the deep, blue sky and the warm sunshine casting funny shadows on the walk way.
Breath the fresh, clean air, and let your mind be filled with peaceful, restful thoughts.
Thank you Jesus for being my eyes, for I have been blind since birth.

—*Evelyn Block*

One Precious Moment

We came to be joined as one
spend our life together, a new day to dawn
now our todays, are yesterdays, tomorrow
nothing of life or love for us to borrow
lets' reminisce of what was, will be
the destiny of our love is eternity
our life together has been bumpy and long
through the years we have become oh ever so strong
let me be the first to say that I truly meant my "I do"
for ever so long our loves' been tested, still remains ever so true
in my suffering and my pain you have been there to help me through
that is why forever I will love you
for all this and more for us to lament
we would have shared on this earth one precious moment.

—*Edward P. Almada*

Fruits Of-The Spirit Of Christmas Jesus Nature Of God In Humanity

Spirit of love shed abroad in our hearts by the Holy Spirit—
Spirit of the joy of the Lord which is our strength—
Spirit of peace that passes all understanding—
Spirit of endurance that tolerates—
Spirit of gentleness to endure all things—
Spirit of confidence, faith that never gives up—
Spirit of meekness, strife never can intimidate to do evil—
Spirit of patience, bearing up without complaint sustained by
the spirit of truth dwelling within creating righteousness
of God continually in spite of the failing mortal self—

—*Berta McGlothlin*

Life's Levels

Life grants us the four of its seasons.
Spring hearts but the child's call.
Youth finds its rhyme in life's summertime;
Middle life has its realm in the Fall.

Three levels there are in lifehood;
Each higher than any before.
All must be scaled in life's passage,
For beyond them arise no more.

When we come to the last act of Action,
And doing's no more to be done;
We have found but the beginning of knowing,
For reason is yet to be won.

When the world's finally wrought into thought parts,
'Til nothing remains that is whole;
There begins but that final beginning,
When all is rejoined in the soul.

—*Floyd George Steele*

World Peace

The world is ours for peace;
Springs of joy ripple thru the Cosmos,
The now of God unfolds as we beheld the
Mideast performance of Rabin and Arafat
Another emanation—Mandela, South Africa
This train of peace events will reach out
    to all areas of conflict.

An eternal flame flashed thru the earth,
Expressing light, life, love, and worship.
    Above all—universal peace.
We are the catalysts for the new earth—
    We are now embarking with hope anew:
        All missing dimensions
        Will coalesce, integrate
        And at last form one
        Humanized Society.

—*Adele Haddad*

The Horizon Of Humanity

The horizon of humanity forms a skyline of decadence:
Stain glass windows in cathedrals with bingo and roulette
Alters where ceiling vaults are ornate with the neon light
Of the faith healers and empty verses blaspheme its sacred
Halls.

Outside the homeless are "indigents," mere obstacles
In the rush toward success.
Street alleys are graffitied with human blood
Proclaiming self-righteous vulgarity and naive independence.

The home is no longer trimmed with white picket fences,
But barricades of barbed wire and iron spears.
Flower beds become deceiving snares,
Good fences no longer make good neighbors.

The horizon of humanity form a skyline of deterioration:
Vain, unsightly, selfish-dead.
Though we pray in casinos and worship in taverns,
Though we adorn ourselves with rich fabric, adoring less our
Human fiber.

Yet, above the horizon of humanity also hovers hope—
The sun whose golden communion reminds us of a sacrificial
promise:
"Take and eat. This is my body which has been given up for you;
Do this in remembrance of me."

—*Jack M. Talbot*

Walk With The Lord

Walk with me my Lord please take my troubled hands
Stand by me my Lord through these most tiring of all times.
Help me my Lord for these days brings sorrows and much grief
Console me my Lord please give my soul a little joyous
    moment of peace
Walk with me my Lord walk along at my side
Uplift me my Lord when in the dumps I do feel safe to hide
Caution me my Lord when decisions I do tend to make in a haste
Protect me my Lord as I go along life trying bitter sweet paste
Walk with me my Lord even though at times I am standing still
Quiet me my Lord when in an uproar I do sometimes hastily rebel
Guide me my Lord when my eyes seem to have gone blind
Carry me my Lord with your strong loving and outstretched hands

—*Barbara P. C. Greaves*

The Old Oak Tree

I can see it now, in my minds eye
Standing so tall it seem to almost touch the sky.
The leaves were shimmering in the morning breeze,
In my grandfathers' old oak tree.

On weekends when the weather was bright,
Grandma gathered all her little tykes, with
Baskets filled with goodies galore.
To the shade of that old oak tree we'd go.

We'd spread the cloth, upon the ground.
Fried chicken, cookies, lemonade and all
We'd sit upon the checkered cloth - It looked
So delicious, we could hardly wait.

We'd all join hands - while grandma prayed.
Thanking our Lord for such a wonderful spread.
We ate goodies a plenty - till we thought we'd burst,
Then grandma knew we all had enough.

Grandma loved her little tykes, all twenty-one.
She read to us from the old bible every day.
After the chores for the day were done. We all
gathered around her chair that old oak tree,
And listened to her stories about Matthew, Paul,
Mark and John.

—*Delsie Eaton Brown*

The Sermon In A Crust Of Bread

I saw her bending ore her food, (though I didn't mean to stare), I wondered why someone would ask, a blessing ore such humble fare. Then glancing up she saw my face, and read the question in my eye's she motioned me to come to her, which came as a surprise. I walked across the crowded room, until I stood before her chair. She said, "Please share my meal with me and I'll tell you why I bow in prayer." I smiled at her quaint charity and with an arrogant smile, sat down in curiosity, to listen for a while. "For years," she said," I did not know, my Father up above." "I took for granted everything, He furnished me with love." "Then when He saved me from my sin's, I saw all things anew." I worship Him and thank Him now, in everything I do." "This food you see is all I need, though to you it may seem spare." He feeds me now with 'the bread of life', that takes away all care." "I have a greater hunger now, that food can't satisfy, I find it in my Savior's words, and my need He does supply." I walked away a humbled soul, much wiser than before. The sermon in a crust of bread, changed my life forevermore.

—*Judy A. Knox*

Destiny

Ascending toward the sun with wings
Spread wide, graceful and carefree
as he soars higher and higher. With
nothing between him and his destiny,
except for himself, he continues to
fly like wild fire.
As the sun starts descending behind
the blue sea, he will return to where
he first took flight, for even he is
unsure of facing his destiny.

—*Angela L. Dosier*

Time to Say Goodbye

He sits there so calm,
   staring out of a window.
He see's the rain and the dark clouds,
   there's a far away look in his eyes.

It's cold in the room,
   like on a snowy day.
And the only sounds that are made
   is the beating of the machines,
   that is controlling the life beside him.

He doesn't know what to do,
   he is lost and confused.
The love and pain hurting inside,
   he can't bear watching life die.

The time has come to say goodbye....

Machines stopped suddenly.
   Silence has now filled the room.
Nothing to be heard, nothing to be said.
   the emptiness in his heart hurts too much to move.
His daughters life now removed.

All he does now is stare out the window.
   —*Jennifer McDougal*

And Flowers Too!

Cool trade winds blowing
Stately palm trees swaying
The air is crystal clear!
Jagged mountains looming
Puffy white clouds flying
Such wondrous beauty drew me here!

These islands are still growing
Volcanos erupting, lava spewing
Coral beaches tanning us to spice!
Blue-green water cleanly sparkling
Brown bodies surfing and snorkeling!
What else could be such Paradise?
   —*Joy J. Robedee*

Lavish Love

See how the little babes play. I know our love is forever to stay.
So much love I have to shower upon you.
We can sing and dance to songs by the who.
Yes just us three, and our happy family.
We can go in our car for a nice drive.
See how happy we are, the two of you girls, and me your
   Champion, our love will forever stay alive.
Lost in a fantasyland of lavish love.
Time is frozen still as we fly to heaven above.
My two living angels truly from heaven you are.
The most beautiful girls ever created, like a shooting star.
Now the great star war is won.
My blues and depressions are forever gone.
Oh how I love my angels two.
Presents and flowers I want to bring to both of you.
Yes I struggled and prayed so hard.
The good Lord heard my prayer and gave me two living angels
   to make love to in my backyard
I will forever thank God above.
For giving his greatest gift to me, Lavish Love....
   —*Gerald S. Szewczyk*

Ghost In The Darkness

The end, there is no escape
Stealing thoughts and secrets, a mental rape.
Too tired to run and too scared to fight,
I'll never survive this never-ending night.
No longer is there a line between wrong and right
Please, please, why is there no help in sight?
Alone to face the darkness.

Is the danger real?
The evil, no one else seems to feel.
So simple to begin, so hard to kill.
It is stealing my spirit, my soul, my will.
The nameless terror that waits in my dreams,
Silence smothers each of my screams.
Alone to face the ghost.

How did it start, a simple joke?
Too late to take back the vow I broke.
On my shoulders the guilt lies
I can still hear the echo of his tortured cries.
My fault, so why is he dead, the one I loved the most?
Alone to face myself, for I am the darkness and he is the ghost.
   —*Cindy Beck*

The Mind

      Creeping out of curiosity,
   stepping across known and unknown boundaries,
    gathering an abundance of facts and fiction,
reaching beyond simple truths into complicated realities,
    frustrated by its own inconsistencies,
   surrounded by a multitude of diversions,
alternating between a conscious and subconscious state,
    capable of solving great mysteries,
     yet stumbling over the very obvious
   —*Charles Beatty*

The Bull Rider

He's in the chute! 2,000 pounds of meat-tenderizing, bone-stomping Brahman manhood. Eager to pulverize and main. An atomic bomb on the verge of exploding. Eyes rolling, nostrils flaring 'n blowin' snot! When the gate swings he has 8 seconds to show his stuff 'n he's ready. 8 seconds—an eternity in hell!

Ease on down there, cowboy. Wrap that bullrope 'round yer gloved hand 'n hold on with a grip of steel.

It feels right. It's time. Open the gate—!

A breathless pause 'n then that bombastic explosion of rider 'n beast!

Yahoo! Ride 'im, cowboy!

Balance, Balaaaaance. Score them points!

"Damn this twistin' devil! Gotta stick till the horn. Damn, ain't that horn ever goin' ta blow? Arm must be outta the socket. Son of a—!"

"There's the horn. Where's the clown? Hell, he ain't even close.
Gotta take a header 'n run like hell."

"Come on, come on. What's my score? Damn, 78 'n jest a dislocated shoulder. That ain't bad, fer a Sunday outin'!"
   —*Frances R. Long*

Dangerous Liason

Fantasies and fairytales,
Story books and life in hell.
As a child you knew the name,
When you grew up it wasn't the same.
Fantasies are dangerous,
Especially between the two of us.
Fairytales were written by Grimm,
And always involved a mortal sin.
Story books have a happy ending,
Never divorce, or time, or mending.
So it remains a life in hell,
Trapped inside an old ink well.
Filling with passion, pain and danger,
Turning you into a total stranger.
Take the pages and tear them out,
Burn them quickly and never doubt.

—*Julie Pugh*

If I Could Choose The Dream

If I could choose the dream I wish to dream and write the story line, it would begin on a summer's eve with you lying by my side...

Stillness prevails, only the faint echoing of night sounds are heard. Long blades of grass fold and bend to nestle below us, while millions of stars form a kaleidoscope of wonder above. The whispering breeze cools our skin where love left it moist like dew. The moon in nearly perfect brilliance illuminates the night, it's reflection shivers slightly across the glassy lake. Whiffs of fragrant flowers, scents of pine, and you, tickle my nose. My finger tips trace the contours of your chin, your neck, your chest.

The world at this very moment feels perfect... still, and at peace. Our lips touch, glowing embers re-ignite into flames of passion. A love never before experienced is born.

With my head again cradled in the safety of your arm, I can feel your raging heartbeat, slowing, regaining it's natural rhythm. As my eyelids begin to flutter, I hear you whisper, "I love you." If only I could choose the dream, that I wish to dream.

—*Beth Gade*

Do Something Nice For Someone Each Day

While sitting here in my living room, my mind just seems to stray. My memories take me back to so many yesterdays. This memory lingered with me for many, many years years. And when I think about it my eyes still fill with tears. I really love to go fishing, and the sun was beaming down. I heard a tractor down the road and this is what I found. Sitting on that tractor was a kindly dear old man. Trying to drive that tractor with wild flowers in his hand. And in my mind I pictured his wife of many years. And I know when she would see them, her eyes would fill with tears. He probably had worked in the field all day, he really looked wrinkled and old. But seeing those flowers in his hand, what a wonderful story was told. His loved one was waiting supper, no doubt, and had probably felt lonely all day. Just waiting for her love to return, and the flowers just made her day. So some kindly deed done for someone each day would make this world quite a place. You know, just a smile, or a kind word or deed, no matter what ever it be, will bring happiness to some dear soul. And that's the way God meant it to be.

—*Grace E. Porter*

City Of Disgrace

Walk with me to animosity
streets filled with hostility
the blind man picks you a flower
the deaf woman hears your screams
I'll show you around this miserable town
ignorance is all to be found
take my hand, I'll show you this land
I was born here and lived here since
product of society, with no repentance
Help me in my search for tranquility
it is far from here
I walk forever to the end of this city
Serenity is miles from near

—*Christine Duncan*

Reach For A Star

My child reach for a brilliant star
Stretch very hard, it is not too far
The race is run with hope in your heart
Hills and valleys challenge from the start
Your momentum will rise and fall
You are special so always stand tall
The race is won by those who stay
So quicken your pace, look up, it is a new day.

—*Jacqueline Kristensen*

Etowah River Run

Rain water wild to the base of the tree
Stringy toed roots shrink from an angry touch
Slush swirled and cleansed into a boiling scourge
Creamed coffee liquid pours from thunder rolls
Orange sherbet tassels swing over air on
The flashing flow of trapezed trumpetivines
Slowed and harnessed under sun splashed shadows
I Ching patterns float free from deep mired mud
Chase ghosts of jade green dragons slithering
On to a distant sea of corn cob lights
Points of silver kernels race the sunset
Eternal mirrors searching for the way.

—*Constance Joy Alexander*

Building The Good Life

Oh, Lord, help me build my life—
Strong, to combat a world of strife.
Let me use the material close at hand —
To strengthen, mold, as you planned.
Let me not "make do" with shoddy pieces
Like jealousy that weakens the creases;
But strengthens each joint with faith and love
With a healthy trust in our Father above.
Nail it all together with spikes of self-control;
Secure the beams with a compassionate soul.
Coat it all over with peace and contentment;
Stick a lot of joy down in the cracks of resentment.
So when the storms release their force
My sturdy residence will resist its course.
Resisting the storm with faith from above.
Hatred will be shed off my roof of love.
The winds of distrust and shadowy doubt —
From my walls of trust, be turned about.
Yes, Lord, help me use your building Plan,
For when the battle is over — It will stand!

—*Joan Ulmer*

If You Could See What I Heard

I heard birds singing in the trees, and the sun silently
submerging into darkness over the ocean's floor. The
howling in the dark signaling the close of the day. The
glare of the sun sparkling so beautiful over the water with
its rowing sound enhanced the melody. The orchestra blended
peaceful and yet despair.

The birds and the waves moving each in its own ceremonial dance.
The view was something for the eyes to see. The branches took
another form as they swayed, touching their tips with fun and laughter.

I sat quietly enjoying the scenery. The sun disappeared into
darkness, the birds cease to sing, the waves rolled out to sea
and it was time for me to go home after enjoying a symphony of
a life time.
—*Helen Mack*

The Owl

Its evening call sounds from afar.
Such a quiet sound,
but an eerie one.
The darkness hides its flight,
as its voice becomes louder.
Who is it calling?

I do not hear the swishing of its wings,
as once again it
makes its nocturnal visit.
I locate its sound, but cannot see it.
In vain I watch and wait.
Where does its flight start or end?

Finally, when I least expect it,
I see it, its wings spread in silent flight.
It appears before my car,
escorts me down the gravel lane,
pauses on the overhanging limb,
blinks its eyes in the moonlight, and tells me,
"you may see me when I desire,
but not because you watch or wait."
—*Don C. Kittinger*

The Medicine Man

Sun and clouds, soon turning into moon and stars - they seem to fly,
Such are but swirls of paint, brushed against sheets of sky;
And the desert mountains with their rivers grand,
These are but stroke of paint, brushed sheets of sand:

Sky against earth, earth against sky,
These are the mysteries of the man - so sly!

A burst of yellow fire begins his day,
He torches the horizon and sets it aflame, while
   screaming red flowers run out to play,
Higher and higher the flaming orb sails towards noon,
Hanging by hidden puppet strings, strands from his magic loom.

Then he prays down a shower from heaven's bowl,
Turning hot rays into a showy display of rainbow,
But spectral arcs soon melt into layers of sunset golds reds and pinks,
While desert flowers drift off to sleep - and twilight
   predators awaken to crawl and slink.

As night descends, the fiery orb collides against earth and sea below,
Exploding into fireworks - a lightning show at dusk, aglow,
With beacons of light rising, falling and streaking,
To the clash of thunder clouds clapping - and soon, joyfully weeping.

Then, upon seeing the first falling star disappear in flight,
The medicine man fades into blackness, out of
   sight - or, so the story goes, in tales at night.
—*Garret Bradley Sparks*

Through The Hills

It's joy to travel through the hills
   Such lovely sights to see
For Autumn has arrived again
   And painted every tree.

Each wears a lovely coat
   Colors of every hue
No man could use a brush
   And paint what God can do.

So, I watch with wandering eyes
   As the seasons come and go
Time just rushes on and on
   God is every place, I know.

It's joy to travel through the hills
   But sometimes, I wish that I
Could live among those hills
   Instead of passing by.
—*Agnes Lys Dillard*

Soul's Journey

From the dark bosom of goddess Nile,
Suckled long on the milk of despair,
With anguished cries most dark and vile,
My soul in torment, filled the air.

Called forth - a journey to be had
In wilderness with heavy load,
To find a balm in Gilead,
To travel down a narrow road.

Into the land of milk and honey,
Seven times through Jordan clean,
My soul refreshed in Presence sunny,
Such love and peace never seen.

Yet, in the glare of life's reality,
I find I love me more than Thee.
—*Janet M. Johnson*

The Seasons Of Life

Spring. A slow awakening of nature. The warming rays from the
sun ad intermittent rain cause hidden patterns to evolve.
Flowers nourished will soon display the colors of the rainbow,
Violet, indigo, blue, green, yellow, orange and red. The
miracle of miracles, a child is born. From a water bed to a
strange new world. The first cry is for love and all through
life that will be the foremost need.

Summer. Nature in full exquisite dress. Crops maturing and so
with food we will be blessed. The child now grown, active in
sports and pondering a skill to contribute to life and finance
his goals. Vacation, an interlude to get away from it all and
nourish the Soul.

Autumn. Harvest time, the reward for work well done. Nature
slowly moving toward a long deserved rest. Leaves falling at
nature's behest. The child now grown, education completed and
a chosen career begun.

Winter. There are those who realize the zest for life begins
to wane. The weather is cold and snow covers much of the
terrain. The once new born child, now ageing, realizes there
is so much in life no one can explain. Many leave this world
for the longest of rests. The adage "one day at a time" proves
to be the best.
—*Ethel Raeuber*

Ancient Indian

Tired old eyes that always glisten
Sun-burned ears that try to listen
Fought a man named Jesse Chisholm
   Now sit by the fire

Cross your legs and sit down slowly
Hear the thunder rolling lowly
Think of Custer and Jim Bowie
   Your big job is done

Painted pony now stands weary
Faded blanket now looks dreary
Think of years and deeds more cheery
   Take your time to go

You have known your son's grandchildren
If your eyes see dimly...will them
Face the East where wind is buildin'
   Know you've had enough

   —Billy Greywolf

I Walk

   The narrow passage between the big trees
Sunlight pencils in through the leaves of the tall trees
   The mist is rising as the sun rises
  I watch the dew, drip from the fragile leaf
   Standing like a statue in among the bushes
   The graceful dancers wait for its cue
 The rushing babbling sonnet of the nearby creek
    The sweet scent of nature's perfume
 The moving spirit of the wind carries new life
The spring showers give drink to the ever growing earth
   And I stop, and I listen, as I stand in wonder
     At earth's magnificent being
    I will treasure each step of each day
     I am allowed upon this earth

   —Josephine Rose

Sea Of Souls

In the darkness of the night,
Swift winds blow and sails twist and turn,
As ships set sail to ports unknown,
Filled with human sufferings bow to stern.

Upon the sea of love they sail thru night and day,
As white caps and waves of sorrow strike at their side.
Ever onward they glide thru torment and strife alike, to
Distant ports of Heaven and Hell thru waves of pity glide.

Their course now set by the old man of the sea,
Who guides them along their pathways bold and strong.
Only to have some snatched away by waves of sin,
And unrepented souls to Satan do they now belong.

The old man of the sea of love, does battle royal
Against the mighty sin filled human tide,
Of satan and his followers who seek to sink each ship,
Until the port of Heaven is finally reached and do reside.

The port of Heaven is all tranquil, peaceful and bright.
As each ship enters to unload its cargo of souls so plenty.
While the port of hell is dark and gloomy, all littered
With hopes and shattered dreams of lost souls many.

   —George W. Rogers

The Flight Of A Dove

I followed the flight of a dove
Swiftly it flew; my eyes were fixed
On it's straight course, so high above,
And I watched with emotions mixed.

Birds have their nest and so have I
A home that is shelter and rest;
A man only walks, a bird can fly
To a home on the highest crest.

I followed the flight of the dove
As it flew on its' homeward way;
To rest I know in a nest of love,
Built only of twigs and clay.

I pondered anew the flight of the dove;
The wonder to me, and God's reason why
A man only walks; a bird can fly.
We must reach god's heights in a different way,
And walk on towards heaven on our feet of clay.

   —Adolph Zielsdorf

To Be A Child Again

  If only I could be a child again, I would be a happy child.
Swinging on the playground reaching for the stars with my size
    four tennies pointed up.
   Leaning back to see my hair fly in the wind.
   Laughing, wondering what tomorrow will bring.
 But each time my head would reach the sky I felt close to a
    being, holding me from the heavens.
Each time picturing my father. Wondering why he went to sleep
to never again awake. Wishing I could go where ever he has gone
   but knowing someone needs me here.
 Wanting to stay a child forever but tragedy makes me older
  before I am ready, missing everyday that goes by.
   Loving who I have, missing who is gone.
  Wanting to rewind each day to play it over again,
    while going nowhere in the future.
 Needing to release the child inside my soul but she's not
to be found. Wanting the child to be free to blow in the wind
    like a tumbleweed.

   —Joanna Spires

Peaceful Moments

Finding peace in this busy world is easy to do.
Take a walk in the garden,
See the beautiful morning glories glistening
With early morning dew!
Listen to a mockingbird sing in the magnolia tree,
The lovely song always brings tranquility and calmness to me.
Go to the rose garden and pick some lovely blooms,
Then watch the hummingbird zip over flowers with a zoom.
When you visit the mountains, take time to sit
on a rock by a waterfall,
This magical beauty and sound brings
calmness to us all.
Go to the beach and watch the sea gulls soar,
The sound of the majestic ocean brings us peace,
As we listen to the mighty roar.
Watch a full moon rise on a clear night,
What a relaxing and tranquil feeling as we
enjoy this breath taking sight!
When I hear the choir sing, "How Great Thou Art,"
Then my heart overflows with "Peaceful Moments"
from the start.

   —Annelle Stuckey

Dear Mr. Mailman

Dear Mr. Mailman please just for one day
Take all of my junk mail and throw it away,
Your load will be lighter and mine will be too,
Just one day is all I am asking of you.

So many things people want me to try,
Youth creams and condos and jewelry you buy,
And vitamins, flower bulbs, siding and more,
Like magazines, furniture, products galore!

Here sits my wastebasket filled to the top
It seems there's no way I can get it to stop
Piles of trash mail to get rid of each day
I glance at it, tear it up, throw it away.

Only one day I am asking of you,
One day when my third-class mail doesn't come through
So dear Mr. Mailman please just for one day
Would you take all my junk mail and throw it away?
—Jean Westerman

The Image

There's a mirror hanging on the wall,
Take it down and look inside;
Take a good look inside yourself.

What is it you see, you ask?
A person that's got a will to live.

Maybe you think; maybe not.
Keep on looking, the power of the
mirror gets stronger the longer you look.

Don't look at the outside of the image
that appears in the mirror,
but inside yourself.

Grasp hold of that real you,
pull it out;
Show it to the one's you love.

That's the real you.
Loving, caring, honest you.

Now take the mirror,
Hang it back upon the wall,
But leave that image there
and walk away with
the real you.
—Beth McCullough

Great Grandpa

Sittin in my easy chair with my feet propped up.
Taking my pills according to the Doc.
My stocking caps in place; my pipes filled up.
I'm a sipping Sanka from my coffee cup.
All the kids with their kids came bursting through the door
Now I'd like to ask, who could ask for more?
Hearing as they holler, Hi! Hi! Great Grandpa.
Sittin' here a thinking, there's not a finer bunch around.
Thinking, except for me, they couldn't be found.
Kinda nice a knowing all my laboring days are through
No. 2 don't believe I'd change places with you.
Holy Mackerel! Here they come again.
Hugging and a kissing and a hollering bye.
Watch but for the little one!
She just slobbered in my eye!
Another Sunday over and the visiting's through
It's so quiet around here I could get blue
Instead I'll close my eyes and take a little snooze
No! I don't believe I'd change places with you.
—Anna Lee Kirkpatrick

The Bible Is Being Fulfil

We are traveling life's highway
   Taking one day at a time.
Sometimes the road get mighty rocky
   And the hills are hard to climb.

It makes me very sad, when I see how
   It is today.
We are not taking life serious at all,
   There is no time for delay.

We are living in the end times.
   The Bible is being fulfill,
So please take life serious
   And do the masters will

Prayer has been taken out of the schools
   No thought is given to the golden rule
Children are taking their guns to school
   And they call it being cool.

Prayer is out of the schools yes!
   Prayer is out of the church also
Prayer is out of the church's amen corner
   They don't pray there any more.
—Bessie Seward

Mountain Autumn

The forest has turned into a vibrant vivid array,
Tall aspen's stand as if in a giant spray—
   of colorful flowers,
Here and there still a columbine is seen,
   Even the grass is losing much of the green.

The land scape is turning to various shades of gold,
   Aspens tall and slim sway against the blue sky,
Bright and beautiful they stand proud and bold,
   In the mountain even down low--
     then on up, up high.

'Tis Indian summer near deer and elk browse,
All of God's nature of the mountains seem to peacefully drowse,
   While leaves bright flutter in the breeze,
As the vivid bits of color bid farewell to the trees.

Beautiful mountain autumn soon you will be over,
   No more foliage will be left to cover
     the trees, crags and ravines,
All leaves and fruit will soon be gone
   from the swaying trees, flowers, and vines
—Edithe Zeigler Holmes

Dreams

It happened once, on one unknown evening,
that God wanted the people to have a small gift...
He thought about the rainbows with the seven colors,
Or maybe the spring waters, for a thirsty person.

Or maybe the bird, with the golden throat?
Or maybe the forests with the lucky fern-flowers?
He wanted to finish the travellers' big melancholy
And golden the night sky with the millions of stars...

And then - the dreams - he left on the Earth,
As big and as wide as the surface of the ocean.
For the possibilities to grow with in the hearts.
For this sincere gift - thank you, dear God...
—Anna Ludwiczak-Cadd

His Love

His love makes oceans roar,
tames waves kissing sandy shores.
Placing stars within dark skies,
they become his light and my guide.

His love strong like a mighty oak,
never bends for the breeze.
As mountains strive to touch blue
skies he tries hard to please.

His love shelters me from fear
a sentry protecting when he's near.
Should hurt fill my eyes he wipes away the tears.

With love I partake his nectar quenching
all my thirst.
Thriving like a flower within his
tender word's.

His love my life, I'll remember in sweet review.
Every tender whisper of I love you.

His love I've found among Multitudes one of a kind.
A love of grate magnitude, forever mine.

His love of a husband, most faithful, my best friend.
As a father forgiving to the very end.

His love as GRAMPY or POPPY which-
ever it maybe, he gives to his grandchildren,
in a Heart's Beat.
—*Joyce Sweet*

The Stars At Night

The stars at night
   Tell about the flows of water in the daylight.
   And the bees and birds are quiet.
   So we can see any falling stars.
   When the moon comes up to shine upon.

You may look up when a plane flies over, drawing
   attention to Jupiter or Mars.
   Twinkle, twinkle, say the stars,
   We are for you to study.
   Can't you see our brightness,
   Tucked in the heavens.

Some nights the clouds are gray covered,
   A dreariness sets upon us.
   Nothing to see, so off to bed we go,
   Turning somersaults for a show.

The morning brings a warm glow,
   Sunshine gives us a thought of the garden.
   Flowers are blooming profusely.
   From the dampness of the night.
   Quietly we wait for the evening star to appear.
   At last again we see the beauty of
     The stars at night.
   —*Jane B. Cox*

Black Cats At Midnight

Childhood memories,
Sunny flowers succulent,
Black cats at midnight
showing wear
like old clothes hiding in a closet.

Anger was difficult.
Powerful people could have it.
Not me.
I withdrew,
A butterfly into a cocoon.
—*Jean W. Mosher*

Yesterday

Earthen vessels buried in sand
Tell many a story about this land
Ancient bones bleached white by sun
Piled together one on one
Indian relics on pioneer land
Buffalo robes, weathered and tanned
Fables of brave men and terrible beasts
Ancient tales of tribal feasts
A land commandeered by our pioneer sons
We hope, bequeathed with honor
Gallantly won! Pioneers, Indians, gone away
We saved the arrowheads and pots of clay
Grim reminders of yesterday!
Shadows speak and perhaps, they say,
"We are the ghosts of yesterday
Our prayer was for another way"
The Indian's pain has not gone away
The pioneers shut bitter memories away
Who's to know?
What can one say — how it really was — yesterday!
—*Donna M. Crebbin*

Time

I have a watch that talks to me
Telling me the time wherever I'll be,
With each tick the seconds fly
Sixty ticks makes a minute go by.

Sometimes I'm fast and sometimes slow
But my watch will always know,
Just how long I take each day,
To do my work or when I play.

Sixty minutes make one hour
My watch comes off when I shower,
Some are made real waterproof
Causing some to feel aloof.

Twenty four hours makes one day
Twelve hours for work or play,
Twelve hours to sleep or rest
Spending time to do what we like best.

Time never stops but we sure do
We wind our watch and take our Que,
My watch has told the time of day
It's up to me to plan time my way.
—*Eva Cook*

The Poet

So quietly and softly words are written
telling of the visions that we see
speaking in a language of the heart
the feelings that might never come to be...

Emotions that are splashed across the page
like colors warm and glowing to the eyes
fill the reader's mind with anticipation
as images unfold with great surprise...

Reflections of a world not viewed before
of the splendor and the majesty untold
are printed on plain ordinary paper
to touch a heart as they lovingly unfold...

Who paints the pictures deep within the soul
and writes the words that no one else could say
who with their hands can touch all God's compassion
who but the poet can pen a beautiful day...
—*Donna Marie Lovell*

Pearl Brevelle Francois by Jocelyn Johnston

Dear Mom:
Ten years ago you left us
And oh, there was so much pain
Our eyes would fill with tears
At the mention of your name.

Sometimes a word or thought
Will remind us of a day
When you were right here with us
As we walked along life's way

We still feel your presence
Though we can't touch or see your face
Yet we are comforted to know
That you're in a better place.

We will always miss you, Mom
Your smile and loving embrace
But your spirit lives on within us
As each new day we face.

We just wanted you to know
That until we meet again
We'll hold your memory in our hearts
As God holds you in His hand.
   —*Your Children*

The Shadow On The Wall

Quiet lies the garden which resolutely surrounds me, soft and tender are the flowers ladened with dew as they glisten in the early morning light. I lie softly, like the shadow of the vines against this garden wall, and listen to the world outside my garden. The noise and clamor growing increasingly louder try to penetrate my sanctuary.

Through a crack in the wall I catch a glimpse of that world beyond, and I tremble, for all I see is war, famine, disease and death. The stench of the deluge wafts through the crack invading my nostrils and I stagger from its pungency.

I cling tenaciously to the wall hoping to add strength in preventing that world from penetrating into my garden. But the crack grows larger, and I watch as my garden is trodden to dust and the devastation is more than I can comprehend.

I linger, pondering what more could I have done to stop it all, then as the sun began to set I was reminded that I was but a shadow, resting softly on the wall.
   —*Arthur Ewing*

Generations

You come to me in tears today
that I can quickly wipe away
and with a soft warm loving kiss
can rectify what is remiss.

This time will pass and you will grow
and I would like you now to know
that troubled times may come along
I watch each day as you grow strong.

I'll guide you in my humble way
and hope on a clean path you'll stay.
For life has many twists and turns
by trial and failure each one learns.

As years fleet by you know they will
for time we know does not stand still,
and I can see the day so near
when you reach down to dry a tear.
   —*Elizabeth L. Frantz*

Untitled

With the touch of a wire, a cry is heard
Tenderness she receives, as soft as a bird.

The words of caring that gave her so much
A tear drop falls, as her heart it is touched.

The sweetness of sharing, that is seen in you
Shows me the friend, in you is true.

A ways in a number, and often in sight
But always with-in me, through all of my flights.

I see in you, something I've forgotten to be
The beauty in you, brings it out in me.

Though often forgotten, inconsiderate sways
From others I've taken, in unmeaning ways.

But then to see you, the warmth reunites
That only a special friend, so dear, can ignite.

So for you my friend, there always will be
A place in my heart, through eternity.

  With the touch from a friend,
    There is no end...
   —*Connie Tuominen*

Trinity Church

Our Father:
Thank you for Trinity, a lovely place
Where we can worship in dignity and grace.
Bless us here each Sabbath Day;
Help and guide us on our way.
Bless those who are ill and cannot be here;
Fill their hearts with hope and cheer.
Bless all those whom we hold dear.
Some old and some young, some far and some near.
Bless those less fortunate than we.
May they not homeless nor hungry be.
And may our father up above
Let them know they have his love.
Give our leaders wisdom to know right from wrong
To keep our country respected and strong.
May we have peace in home and heart
And o'er the world in every part.
And when we go to our final sleep
May the good Lord our poor souls keep.
   —*Hazel S. Russell*

Courage

You gave me the light,
that guided me through the night.
You gave me the courage to fight,
for what I believe to be right.
You gave me the light.
As a candle flame does burn,
for freedom I did yearn.
I wanted to be me,
to do this I needed to be free.
You gave me the light
that guided me through the night.
You gave me the chance to learn and grow,
and happiness I would know,
my flame did grow.
As my closeness to you did grow
a special love I would know.
You gave me the light. That light,
guided me through the night.
You gave me the courage to fight,
for what I believed to be right.
   —*Cindy Cerka*

Love

It's been said down through the years
That being in love can cause one tears.
That love is blind and causes one pain
Some have said love drove them in sane.

But it's not love that has done these things
Love never ever causes pain,
Love does not drive you out of your mind
Love is gentle, sweet and refine.
Love does not hurt for love is kind.

Loves makes you do the things you can,
To help your friend and fellow man.
Love comforts, consoles, and heals griefs
Love causes us to live in peace.
Love does all it can to see you through
Whenever life lashes out at you.

Love never seeks for itself
But gives and gives, and helps and helps.
Whatever it is that man defines, that hurts and crushes and
Leaves one crying, it's not real love at anytime — for God is love,
And Love is kind.

—*Josephine Carr-Merritt*

Friendship Is Like A Tree

As I look around, I am reminded
That friendship is like the planting of a tree.
The more attention that it receives,
The better off it will be.
The lack of proper attention,
May lead them to their doom.
But with the proper amount of care,
They can burst into full bloom.
Whether it be a friendship or a tree,
They both require a lot of tender loving care.
For they each have a lot of conflicts,
Of which you must always be aware.
Yes, I know it is true,
That friendship and tree do not rhyme,
But they do have something in common.
They both need a ray of sunshine.
You ask, Where do the rays of sunshine come from?
Well, the sun furnishes it for the tree.
And friendship gets its ray of sunshine
From the trust that you place in me.

—*John Ralston*

Walk With Me Lord

Walk with me Lord by the river
That I may enjoy its great flow.
Walk with me Lord in the mountains
That I may watch trees softly blow.
Walk with me Lord by the ocean
That I may see waves hit the shore,
Walk with me Lord 'cross the prairie
That I may its beauty adore.

Walk with me Lord while in sickness,
Put your great hand on my brow.
Walk with me Lord in my wellness
As I send you my thanks, here and now.
Walk with me Lord through my lifespan,
Teach me thy kind, loving ways,
Walk with me Lord, everafter
And I'll praise you the rest of my days.

—*Eileen M. Taylor*

Nearer To Thee

I pray every day, dear Lord,
That I come to know and love you more;
That I am sensitive to your touch,
And that my faith will soar.

My heart longs to be nearer to thee,
For to be close to you makes my soul sing.
I pray to be stirred to greater heights,
To always have "audience with the King."

I've learned how truly lovely you are,
And you're the only one worthy of my praise.
I've known the sweetness of your touch,
How I adore your gentle, loving ways!

I want to love and praise you more each day.
Move me always upwards towards this goal.
I love the quiet peace that is mine,
When I feel you near, and you edify my soul.

So, be with me sweet Jesus, in all my endeavors
and keep me always in your sight.
Let nothing take me out of your hand,
For without you, dear Lord, there is no light!

—*Gayleen Lucas*

Your World

There are times, when you don't notice
   that I'm not there
Your world is so full, I barely make it to its inner fringes
You are almost a total person
Not really ever needing any one else
Just being around you, makes me breathe faster
From the energy and excitement you generate
I keep hanging on because, the times you do open up your arms
and let me in is well worth the wait for it
You are like a comet, that only comes to earth every so often
You crash down on us mortals and dazzle us with your charm and
   vitality
I have often accused you of not being totally human
It's not a joke, I never knew anyone quite like you
I race to keep up with your tempo,
And it often takes me days to recuperate
   From the madness of being with you
We really met during quite a painful time in my life
God I didn't know it was almost worth it to have known you
When I hold out my hand to you, you go right through my fingers
But the brief instant, that we do touch is magnificent,
And breath taking, when you do stop to look earthward
   Your eyes will meet mine

—*June Ann Johnson*

A Christmas Poem

"There isn't any Santa Claus," said Erica one day.
"That is only kid stuff. That is only play."
I looked at her with sadness and told her, "Come what may,
Santa lives within our hearts and there he'll always stay.
For the spirit of St. Nick my pet
is something that you can't forget.
It lives with you both day and night.
It guides you in the path that's right."
"Here's your present Mommy." And as I smile and pause
Erica whispers shyly, "It's from me and Santa Claus."
This Christmas there is happiness for Erica and me
because we know that in her heart Santa Claus will always be.

—*Celia Volkman*

In The Hollow Of My Hand

In the hollow of my hand there is a special place
That joins my heart and life line
Our memories we will chase.
Hand in hand we wait at this intersection
For the days to pass by
But we cannot hurry the passage of time
No matter how hard we try.
Sometimes words may elude me when all I try to say
Is how much I love you each and every day.
Tho many miles separate us
Our hearts are linked as one
For mingled in the memories of sadness and pain,
I see your face; I speak your name.
Our paths are lit with shining beams
Helping us to find those elusive dreams.
Yesterday is gone only memories can be found.
Today is here and will leave without a sound;
But tomorrow will come and you'll hear me say,
"I love you my friend
Forever...and a day."
—*Gladys L. Leturgey*

Untitled

Did you write that promised letter
  That laid heavy on your mind,
  Or did you put off writing it
  'Til a better time you'd find?

Did you say, "Tonight, I'll write
  When I am feeling better,
I'll have more time to concentrate
  And write a longer letter?"

But when the evening shadows fell
  And all gone off to bed,
Your mind was wandering somewhere else
  On other things instead.

And so the days and weeks passed by
  And you forgot to write
That letter that laid so heavy
  Upon your heart that night.

Now, maybe when you write it
  At a more convenient date,
The time your friend receives it
  Might be a day too late.
—*Elden W. Sherman*

My Cabin

Here in my cabin I find the rest
  That men pay wealth to gain,
And stretch my legs before the blaze
  Upon the hearth, and listen to the rain
That beats upon the glass. Content am I
  As an Arab on the desert all day,
Who pitches tent at eventide and finds
  Shelter, and time to pray.
Here I am master. Here I dream
  The dreams that come to all
Who heed the voice of Nature, and
  Answer her silent call.
My dog for companion is enough for me,
  And like the eagle alone that soars,
So, too, soar I and rest,
  In my cabin, in God's out-of-doors.
—*Barbara Williams*

A Requiem For A Son

I awaken at dawn, and I remember
  That leader of men, my son,
His valiant three-year fight against cancer,
His courage throughout that terrible ordeal
  and I weep!

The dawn brightens and I remember
  A tall, blue-eyed, fair-haired man,
  A man who could laugh and make jokes,
  A man who put the needs of others ahead of his own
    And my heart feels lighter.

The morning goes on and I remember
The days of his youth and the happiness he brought us,
His marriage and his two sons now in their twenties,
How he loved his sons and sacrificed for them
  And I feel happier!
As twilight approaches, I remember
  The long journey he now is on,
  Where will it lead him?
I have faith he will reach a higher plateau
And because of my faith, I rejoice!
—*Edna Mae Lowell*

Never Ending Blindness

Here it comes again,
That never ending blindness.
Seems a misconnection,
Always said so mindless.
  It pierces oh so deeply,
  But yet is not revealed.
  Instead it stays unanswered,
  Hoping to be healed.
A never ending blindness,
Is quite a ravenous wave;
Constantly it's striking,
The shore that is its slave.
  The token of a lifetime,
  That is worth its weight in gold.
  That never ending blindness,
  Will always have me in a hold.
—*Liz Wilkinson*

Our Marine

Who would have guessed, when he was born;
  That someday, at twenty, he'd become a marine;
But there he is, handsome, tall and proud,
  And the happiest boy, that he's ever been.

He had lots of drawbacks along the way,
  But he overcome them and grew strong;
Strong enough to want to serve our country
  And show that he does belong.

He loves chocolate cookies, this marine of ours,
  He never seems to get his fill,
He'll empty the cookie jar very quickly;
  So grandmom will make more, still.

He loves to laugh and tell jokes, this tall marine of ours,
  He does sound effects, with each one he tells;
He keeps us all in stitches and laughing,
  Even though we know some of them well.

We are so proud of him, this tall thin marine;
  He means so much to all of us;
As he takes his walk through life;
  You can be sure, when he comes home, there'll he a fuss,
—*Clara Ewald*

Rainbow Children

God held his seed in celibacy until he found a plan
that promised universality to soothe his troubled land.

The attitudes of war and strife, of hate replacing care,
He buried deep in nature's womb transformed, to learn to share.

The pain that all that struggle brewed deeply challenged sons
and daughters, as hearts reviewed their lessons taught
and wisdom chose their "aughta's"

Then suddenly, a heavenly light reflected o'er the scene
and magically turned the tears to Hope, redefining what they had seen.

Each special light became a child well loved for its own hue.
And all held hands to form a team to learn to act anew.

Creatively, from God knows where, a newer child evolved
who passed the universal test, with God's request resolved.

Humans now can freely choose to honor Mother Nature
so Rainbow Children find their place in our Universe's pasture.

America, now can fill its role as the Rainbow Child of nations.
A jewel in the crown of kings, a seed for Peace's salvation.

We share responsibility, as history's deposit
to love our children, young and old, designing future's logic.
—*Carolyn Ashe Stokes*

Him

He sits and stares
That quiet pensive face
No smile shines
Among the lines —
His brow forever etched
From summer sun and rain
Solitude is his great forte
   Toil is his need.
Great strength remains
Through strife and stress
In time that is and time that was.

When day is done
And evening falls
To gether we are again — just —
Him and I to end the day
The way it had begun.
—*Genevieve Paone Berry*

A Parable

There was a field of golden grain
that quivered in the wake of rain,
and bowed to earth before the wind
as though it had been disciplined.

The feathered sheaves were tumbled hair
that hid the silent meekness there;
and raindrops coursed down through, to fall
like tears of shame, beyond recall.

The dark night passed. The wind was gone.
The red-streaked sky of early dawn
looked down upon the golden yield
and saw the penitence revealed.

And then, with mercy gently worn,
the sun, forgiving, bathed the morn.
The humbled grain, caressed and warmed,
was slowly lifted and transformed.

There stood a field of golden grain,
with proud sheaves reaching once again
to thank the heavens that blessed their days;
to spend their gold in growing praise.
—*Doris Newton Whitney*

In Your Arms

It's when I'm there,
  that safe I feel

It's where the warmth
  of your love is real

It's there when I'm asleep
  that time stands still.

It's there in the night
  that I'm completely content and fulfilled

It's where I always want
  to begin and end each day

It's there all of my life
  that I want to stay.
—*Carol Ann Deignan*

Flow As A River

Be as a river
That stops for nothing
To reach it's destination.
It rushes over rocks,
Boulders, and such,
That hinders it's flow
Not even one drop.

It flows over the falls
Like a stream of unraveled ribbon.
Then, settles down to a gentle flow
With little ripples and wavelets,
But still on it's way
To reach a lake or sea.

So be a river and know in your soul
That you too can reach your goal.
—*Eileen Nebeker*

Courage

Courage is a challenge
That takes knowledge and skill.
But we will never be defeated.
If we have the wisdom and will.

If you have life's beauty and wisdom,
To do what it takes to succeed.
Then climb until you reach your goal,
You will have all that you need.

You may walk through the lowest valley,
Or climb up the steepest hill,
Your walk or climb will never defeat you,
If you do what life has instilled.

There is A Harbor that shelters me,
However when I feel despair
It gives me great comfort
Because I know someone is there.

So do not stop or be weary,
The climb will be hard it may seem.
But we have to strive for it,
If we want to accomplish our dream.
—*Glendola Skaggs*

Rocks

Hush, 'tis nothing short of wonder,
   That the rocks can so enhance,
That the dreamer ceases searching,
   Relentless yielding, not by chance.

Some are washed by gentle hands of lovers,
   Others know the pang of anger's wrath,
Nature forces shun their recognition,
   Forcing them along a troubled path.

Prisoners doing penance beat upon them,
   An outlet for frustration they provide,
Men carry them in little "good luck" pouches,
   With pebbles and slingshot, Goliath died.

Precious stones that grace my ladies fingers,
   Diamonds and rubies their rare beauty display,
Gold runs through their veins like a river,
   Phantom mysteries, in rocks, locked away.

   —*Faylene Otis*

Years Come And Years Go

Years come and years go
That thought makes me feel so very low
When you're young life is great
But age moves in so
You think maybe it's just too late
Is there really a thing called love
Does it stick around as you grow
Years come and years go
Does love come and love go

   —*Janet K. Thomas*

A Touch Of Spring

What is this fascination
That traps me in your eyes?
And when you smile, why do the heavens
Send a youthful glow
Erasing years of living from my face?
You look at me and only see
The outer shell of wrinkles and grey hair;
A false facade that hides the fire
And spirit burning deep within.
And I can only smile a false-toothed smile
And pray the feelings trapped inside
Do not seep through,
I only know, if I had met you long ago,
We would have made the earth sing with our song!
Oh, God! Don't let my eyes betray me!
Let me enjoy this touch of spring
That for a moment makes my poor heart sing!
Help me accept this wrinkled shroud
And be content to just sit back and let him go
While praying he will never know.

   —*Anne T. Oxley*

Stupidity

S is for something we never should do.
T is for things we say that aren't true.
U is for uppishness found in a slob.
P is the Prying that produces the snob.
I is the Ego that goes with the me.
D is for Dumb-bell we sometimes can be.
I, once again, that word said before.
T for the things that make us a bore.
Y is the you that goes with the me.
  Put them together, get Stupidity.
    'nuff said

   —*Duane Hougham*

Just Yesterday

"Wasn't it just yesterday," said the owl with his spots quite shaken,
"That we had homes, clean air, and food and the rainforest had not been taken?"
"How true," chimed the eagle so lonely and weary,
As she looked left and right her eyes sore and teary.

In the murky sludge below a saddened manatee tries to float,
Avoiding nets of fishermen hauling toxic fish aboard boat.
Poor opossums and squirrels hit hard by pollution's wrath,
React so obscurely they're led straight to carpaths

Wasn't it just yesterday that schools had windows, tiles and learning?
Now tight buildings with carpet fumes keep pupils' senses burning.
As toxins fill their frail little bodies, discipline is needed aplenty,
No wonder Johnny hasn't learned to read and Johnny is now twenty.

Wasn't it just yesterday, as I secured the gas mask across my face,
That I could actually go outside and be a part of the human race?
Wasn't it just yesterday that I heard the sweet songs of birds,
Smelled blossoms, watched animals romp — today there's not a word.

There's nothing left safe to eat, wear, or do,
Who can stop this from happening — ONLY ME and YOU.
Don't make today and tomorrow become our toxic end,
Wasn't it just yesterday the earth was our dear friend?

   —*Carol Bailey*

Thinking

We live our life each day, the best
That we know how, to pass some Test
Are we humble, patient, prayer'ful
Do we treat others gently, careful?

Am I loving to my children
Who are married, on their own
Or do hurts and unshed tears
Take precedence in what is shown?

These hurts are not just words that's said
But from aches and scrapes that bled
Bodies seem to cram it all
Into life - like Adam's fall

Can I accept this part of living
Along with fun and some achieving
Look up and grin if things go wrong
Appears that life is a happy song.

   —*Erma Roper*

You Can't Go Home

The path is overgrown
That we once walked by.
I'm going to grit my teeth;
I am not going to cry.
The highway has widened.
The animals are shy.
I am going to think of other things.
I am not going to cry.
The home I will always love
Is no longer around.
The tree I once swung from
Is a stump in the ground.
Home is where you make it;
That much is clear.
You can't go home if it is no longer there.

   —*Bertha Snyder*

Tender Are The Leaves

Tender are the leaves
   that whisper words of love.
I can hear him now as he answers
   when I ask, "How much do you Love me?"
"Ten bushel baskets full with
   the tops, bottoms, and sides out."
Yes, tender are the leaves
   when they echo these words.
Love that is infinite
   and I'm not worthy.
My love for him was a heartful
   and running over.
Life with him became a new thing -
   I was a new person.
He spoke words of love,
And the tender leaves whisper them
   to this day.
I hear them in the silence surrounding me.
Though he is gone from me - I still
   hear his words in the rustle of Tender Leaves.
   —*Edna Kleis*

In Her Heart

Oh! My Darling, My Darling, I grieved,
   That you must depart.
I'll cherish you forever, My darling,
   Deep within my heart.
I bore you sweet and comely, Oh!
   Such a loving child.
You were a special daughter, dear,
   As the years sped by like miles.
One fatal auto mishap, then,
   Cut that precious life so short.
Neither reprieve nor recompense,
   Is found in human court.
Only our God up in Heaven,
   Can repay or make things right,
And I pray to my Heavenly Father,
   That I might "see" with his "sight."
   —*Jean W. Goodhue*

Arrival

I had been saying for a long time
   that you would be coming down the trolley track
   with those bent straw flowers waving,
   big smile like it was only yesterday
   and what's all the crying for, anyway,
   your bones clacking tunes.
Old Judah Street scarecrow.
   You wouldn't take me by surprise, I said;
   I wouldn't let up remembering.
   A thousand million projects later, still I
   started every morning with
   a glance to the rising North
   and a listen for the two-step bell.
Time flies and crawls, somersaults and spins
   but never has it caught me unaware
   until today.
I wonder. Did I really think you'd come?
   That clickety-click seems such a
   sudden sound.
   —*Christine Taylor*

Wishes And Dreams

If wishes were horses beggars would ride,
That's an old adage that never has died.

It seems that wishes are dreams in our heart,
And it is dreams that set us apart.

For where would we be if dreams didn't exist,
Think of all the happiness dreamers would miss.

So I'll take the wishes, dreams and happiness combine,
And I'll be a dreamer until the end of my time.

For it is dreamers who make wishes come true,
And I am a dreamer who wishes happiness for you,

And the wishes and dreams I have for mankind,
Will always be, my state of mind.

So my prayer to God, is set me apart,
And keep dreams and wishes here in my heart.

And the happiness this brings will live after I'm gone.
It will be the legacy, I leave everyone
   —*Helen M. Pybus*

Eric's Bouquet

Four petals form a lucky clover,
   That's what most people say.
If that be true, I'd gather so many,
   You'd have a forever bouquet.
Each clover would bring you its own
   special joy,
     A gift to cherish and treasure,
Like the joy you give to all of us——
   That there is no way to measure.
Courage, strength, gentleness, love,
   These things will be yours I know,
For deep in your eyes, I can see them all,
   And you'll need them as you grow.
You'll need them and more to reach rainbows high
   You'll need them to climb mountains tall.
You'll need them to see joy all about you—
   In everything great and small.
You'll need them to reach for a sunbeam of gold,
   Or a marshmallow cloud floating over,
So keep in your heart, these gifts I impart,
   My love and a lifetime of clover.
   —*Jean L. Bourassa*

In The Still Of The Night

In the still of the night when the world's asleep,
that's when I find God in meditation deep,
I thank him for his love divine,
and for all his goodness towards me and mine.

I tell him of my love for him
and ask him to accept for an offering
the words of my mouth and the meditation of my heart,
my whole life for what it is worth.

I tell him all my heart desires,
and ask him to hear and answer my prayers.
I listen for his still small voice
for his loving words makes my heart rejoice.

So in the still of the night when there's no one else around
I call on God knowing, he can be found,
He is always there to give me a hand
for all my thoughts he understands.
   —*Julia L. Fhynn*

The Inner River

Behold! Immersed deeply within
The abysmal chasm of thine inner being
Flows an ethereal, crystalline river
Of life, love and truth eternal.

Thy primordial self emerges a transparent dewdrop
Reflecting luminous expressions of mandelic design
Until, unified and whole, thou art one
With the fluid, auroral prism of universal flow.

Surging ever onward toward thy destiny,
Moment upon moment through the seasons of centuries,
Embrace with exhilaration each wind-born challenge,
The rippling joy of each breakthrough discovery.

Thy current flows perpetually in transformation;
An endogenous blending of diverse
Yet cosmic-interconnected tributaries seeking
Enlightenment en route to transcendent communion.

Hark! A glowing celestial sunrise awakens the dawn.
Whirling rapids of prismatic light rays
Cascade breathtakingly into an efflorescent
Lotus blossom waterfall of infinite revelation.
—*Denise Marie Travaglini*

The Storm

    Bashing "violently" against the shore—
The angry waves "crushed" through the sand, as if settling a
    "personal" score.

    Faster and higher, the waves grow in intensity, and pace—
    "Competing," as if in a life/death race.

Winds and rain joined together in battle, to build up strong
    force—
    Causing damage and change to "everything," in its course.

    Darkened sky, "screaming" winds of pain—
    Untamed power, "spears" of murderous rain.

Lightning "cracks" the sky, followed by thunders sound of a
    whip—
Pieces of driftwood are "forced" to shore, like "caskets" of a
    ship.

    The "battle" of the storm seems like "forever," in time—
But, only "minutes" have passed, since the sun last "shined."

    As if on a "cue," the storm moves out to sea—
The "aftermath," is accepted—the shore, is now again "free."
—*Jo Ann Marti*

Man's Star

Flowers wash their faces with the rain to refresh themselves
The atmosphere is wet while the heart searches for ownself
The physical world around us is not in a good shape
Very few are there to survive for good reasons to face
One shall learn truths in life to ward off inner storms
To cope with the devastating effects it may be the only norms
To life is short and shall explore other permanent avenues
After all speaking in sweet and soft tones surely gives good
news
The bright sun obscures the lesser light of the stars
Shadows of the darkness shall never prevail on the man's star
To have higher realm the intellect shall provide the best light
Heart and conscience come forward for the finest and pure light
Speak with a tongue above that of a mortal man
One learns his own fate and the nature becomes man's fan.
—*Abdul Latif*

The Children Of Tomorrow

I guess it all begins the day
The baby comes home from the hospital, in many ways.
The baby is hugged, squeezed, cuddled, and kissed,
Center of attention, you can't miss.

As parents, we teach them what is right and wrong,
We make sure they eat well, to be healthy and strong.
We teach them what is good and bad,
To grow up as a young girl or young lad.

They grow up too fast and then move away,
As they travel in many directions, to earn a day's pay.
They are looking for a future in this fast moving world,
To establish themselves as adults as they toil.

Their future is our future too,
What is decided now, can have effects on us later.
Just as we were their teachers, our ideas, when they were young
Maybe it's our turn to listen and accept their ideas, as we
get older.
—*Fred N. Long*

The Beauties of Nature

Every day I look out and see
The beauties of nature each day brings.
The sky is blue; The grass is green.
I often hear the birds sing.
There are beautiful flowers in people's yards,
Daffodils, pansies, and lilies too.
When people water them, they bloom.
They are purple, yellow, pink and blue.
After it rains, a pretty rainbow appears.
Red, yellow, and blue are the colors you see.
I enjoy looking at the sunset.
At times it is as pretty as it can be.
I love to watch the birds
As they fly in the shape of a "V."
How wonderful it is to see all the animals
Roam on the land or swim on the sea.
We really do live in a beautiful world.
I am so grateful for this.
If the earth didn't have such beautiful things.
The world we live in would really be amiss.
—*Darla Mae Seely*

Christmas Prayer

Lord, open our eyes that we may see
The beauty of your nativity.
Open our hearts, that we may truly love,
As you graciously taught us from above.
Open our minds that we may understand your word.
Open our hands that we may labor in your vineyard
And freely give back to you a goodly portion—
A portion we should never discard.
Open our lips that we may speak and sing your praises.
Make us thankful and appreciative for yester years' Sages.
Sages who taught us to use the green bounty of your
fertile earth aglow—
Rather that than the use of pagan practices of human sacri-
fices—
So demeaning.
During this season, keep us mindful of the thoughts behind
Christmas,
and its true meaning.
In your name, Jesus Christ, we pray. Amen!
—*Dr. Dorothy K. Hunt*

Just A Kid

I sat upon the ground, seeing the sun.
The blessed light of day had just begun.
I could see the clouds in various shapes.
They seemed like curtains, or maybe drapes.
High noon came, gosh it was hot.
But I cared not a single jot.
Evening came that others thought chill,
For me I never seemed to get my fill.
   But then I was just a kid.

Now I'm intrigued with mundane things
Like making money for what it brings.
Over the years I'm older, no one to blame
I'm sure the sun and earth are much the same.
I wish God could grant me the wisdom
To see great things with the vision.
   That I had, when I was only a kid
   —*Clark Ryman*

Quiet Listening

Seashore sings a beautiful melody
The blue sky listens almost cloudless
The waves speak to the dismal sand
The sand awaits the wind's turn
No visitors pass it's simply calming
The beat of the tides, a quiet drum
Chill from the wet, warmth from the dry
Comforting to see and as just to feel
Slowly wipes away misery and grief
Though never stay that way
   —*Colleen Ford*

Growing

His heart yearning, hands reaching, thoughts racing,
The boy longs to embrace a timeworn toy,
Yet it remains beyond reach of small Troy.
His heart thumping, hands sweating, thoughts racing
Troy questions the journey he is facing.
Decisions to be made haunt the young boy,
Success in his quest would fill him with joy;
Failure would hurt. He found himself bracing.
He took his first steps. Troy gave it his all.
Unaided and alone, Troy faced his fears.
He knew he had to try, or he would never know
Whether he could walk, or if he would fall.
Once success was his, Troy began to cheer.
This is Troy's secret: Despair is our foe.
   —*Crystie Stewart*

Tuning Nature Together

Look at the top of the tree gently swaying,
The branches are mostly bare
As the wind blows the dry leaves to the ground.
We are reminded with each fallen leaf
A change is approaching the air
With the coldness of night time,
Shadows reflect the sun's last flare
The earth is quiet with a gentle whispering sound.
Nature is preparing us for
The next season of weather.
We watch with awe and wonderment
Tuning life's nature together.
   —*Esda L. McGill*

The Beauty That Is God's

The beauty that is God's, man cannot duplicate,
The bright blue of the sky above,
The tall straight pines with their gentle whispering,
The beautiful clear stream with its quiet murmuring,
The sweet voices of the Lords little creatures,
The loveliness of the smallest flower that grows in His garden,
This is the beauty that is Gods.

The serene darkness of the night sky.
The myriads of twinkling stars,
The bright golden moon sailing over head,
The peaceful quiet of the night creatures voices,
This is the beauty that is Gods.

Did you ever see a sky so blue or full of shinning stars,
Did you ever see a tree so tall,
Did you ever see a stream so clear,
Did you ever see a flower so frail,
Did you ever feel so close to God,
As when you are in the midst of the beauty that is His.
   —*Doris Graham*

Striving To Seize

The artist that tries to capture the scene,
The brilliant sunrise, to the roll of the sea.
The poet that tries to master the art,
writing the words locked deep in the heart.
Both trying to express what God has created.
Trying in vain, sometimes feeling frustrated.
To find the key that will unlock the door
and release the creativity that once flowed before.
For it is a gift to pass through each generation.
For someone to experience their creation.
To share in their picture, or feel their thoughts.
To touch someone's soul and to live in their heart.
We are on this earth such a short period of time,
Someone else will surely write a better rhyme.
Yet another will paint a greater masterpiece.
Forever striving to seize God's beauty for eternity.
   —*Cheryl L. Becker-Wiech*

The Beauty Of Fall

Across the meadow I can see, the trees in autumn's dress,
The brilliant yellows, the fiery reds, against the greenness of the pine.

And as I gaze, my heart is lighter and I am lost in time,
The sky is an azure blue, ablaze with white fluffy clouds.
The sun is shining brightly, as it accentuates the beauty while my soul cries out aloud.

Oh, Lord, how can man doubt that you designed it all,
Because not one of us can create a tree, that the leaves change color in the fall.

Nor can we change with wind, or the fall of needed rain.
I do not understand the vastness of the universe.
I just believe and thank You God, for your creations I can't explain.
   —*Elaine Ellis*

The Ragman

It was old Manhattan with the noise and all the hustle.
The busses trains, and subways, the flurry and the bustle.

Saturdays, I did my work and then relaxed a bit.
I'd drink my tea on 68th and sometimes I'd just sit.

On the busy morning, in the distance I could hear,
A noise above the others that used to bring some cheer.

Clip clop, clip clop, whoa, although quite far away,
I heard that old familiar cry "any old rags today?"

Clip clop, clip clop, soon he reached my street.
Clip clop, clip clop, I heard the old horse feet.

Some rags were given freely, others bought and sold.
The old rag man came down the street in summer and in cold.

In and out past cars he'd go, yelling loud and clear.
"Any old rags, any old rags? So everyone could hear.

The children ran or walked behind, so closer they would be,
They loved to hear the old man say "any old rags for me?"

Life became a slower pace in noisy old Manhattan.
The sounds and call the ragman made will never be forgotten.

I wonder if the ragman's there, it would be fun to see
That horse and wagon on 68th and hear "any old rags today?"

—*Genevieve Ostrander*

A Mother's Day

A Mother is a special woman that has our children to bear,
The child could be short or long, thin or fat, black or white,
  bald or with hair.
They carry our babies in their womb nine months of a year,
and protect our bodies for this span until we're born without fear.
When our children scrape a knee, run a fever, or get into a fight,
they call that special woman in their life to make things come out right.
A mother has special love that is sincere and so tender,
that puts her in a lofty place above the ones in her gender.
She could be young or old or somewhere in between,
but when you se this special woman she's like nothing else you've
  ever seen.
She works, cooks our meals, and cleans our home with her best,
with what seems to be boundless energy doing it with zest.
She gives us loving care with each hug and every hold,
and shows us the pattern for our lives to shape and to mold.
A mother's day is twenty-four hours long, three hundred
  sixty-five days a year,
For if it wasn't for this special woman none of us would be here.
So on this special given day in the month of May,
this day is put aside for these Mothers to have in their own way.

—*Anthony Coppolella*

I Am Me

I am a child—not just any child.
The child that I am is me.
My own unique eyes, my ears, my smile,
Is what most people see.

I'm gentle, kind, a mystery;
At times like a bitter pill.
Yet through my actions and my speech,
It's clear that I have a will.

The person that I am is me;
With ways some may not understand.
God made me special in his sight,
And weaved me into his plan.

—*Ethel K. Grinkley*

The Rainbow Bridge

For back in the mists of ancient time
The Chumash Indians tell
How Earth Goddess, Hutash, created them
on Santa Cruz Island to dwell,
They lived in peace and multiplied.
But their talking kept Hutash awake:
So she told her husband the "Snake of the Sky"
A rainbow bridge I will make:
Across to the mainland my people may go,
But they must not look down:
If they become fearful and look below
They will fall through the fog and drown.
The people crossed over the rainbow bridge
But a few fell and though they were dead.
The Goddess took pity - They did not die,
She turned them to dolphins instead.
   "Now the dolphins are our brothers"
    The Chumash people say
    As they watch the friendly creatures
    In the channel waters play.
—*Jessie V. Hartman*

There's A Beautiful Place Called

There's a beautiful place called "Heaven," above
the clear blue sky.
Where the loving thoughts of kindness, will never, never die.
There the righteous all will gather, in that home up above.
There we will meet "Our Saviour," the one who gave us love.
If we keep "The Ten Commandments", as the bible tells us to.
We will meet "Our Heavenly Father," away up in the blue.
He will come in all his glory, when he descends from the sky.
For everyone shall see him, in the twinkling of an eye.
When he takes us home to Heaven, oh what a glorious day.
For there will be no more sorrow, sickness or death,
for the former things has passed away.
Yes there's a beautiful place called "Heaven,"
above the clear blue sky.
Where the loving thoughts of kindness, will never never die.
To be a righteous person, this we can well afford.
For our award will be, is to live forever with "Our Lord."
—*Fordyce Green*

Free Questions

Free will! Free to choose!
The Cleric proclaimed.

Splendid state of being, agreed
The Layman in unexamined deference.

Free? The Skeptic questioned. Are we

Free to disobey our genetic mandates and
Hereditary decrees? Defy our biological
Overlords? Shun our sovereign instincts?

Are we directed by the subconscious?
Held back by inhibitive hold? Cast in
Inescapable roles by sacred dogmas instilled
From birth? Predestined by a benevolent
Will or driven by an evil one or both?

Does the power of place and time and chance
Compel our behavior? What of environmental
Determinants? Irresistible impulses? What
Forces, in totality, push and pull us to act?

Saith the Philosopher: We make choices and
Think ourselves free but cannot choose to stop
Wanting, yet little know what makes us want.

—*Harry K. Dowdy, Jr.*

My Cries Through The Shadows Of Darkness

So many things I've wanted to express but I never had the courage.

Frantically searching for the Why's to no avail.

Perception of my life is like an empty brook even after the snow has melted away.

Blame is not yours to have for the way I perceive my life to be.

Hurting during my experience, I wondered if anyone could hear my cries.

Reaching and praying for a second chance to say: "I'm human with mistakes."

Even though my life seems to be meaningless to me, yours is still in bloom…

Wait…I hear the birds chirping! I feel the warmth of the sun gazing into my life!
Tears of joy are flowing from my eyes.
Suddenly I know there's a greater force up above and within me.

My letting go and accepting His love I am learning that communication is the key to all of life's ups and downs.

I will let His love save me from another mistake and Prevent the final curtain of my life from happening by my own hands.

—*Diane Koudela*

Flowers

The rose is pure red,
the daisy is sweet white and yellow,
but what color are we?
The flowers you know,
they grow together.
The rose, the daisy, even the sun flowers,
they grow together, they grow by one another.
But why don't we,
because maybe we're too busy…
Fighting,
lying,
crying,
being scared,
murdering,
I wish we could stop the hate,
but do you think maybe,
it's too late?
Maybe not,
stop the hate,
maybe,
it's not too late.

—*Erin Payne*

Loneliness

As I sit here and watch
The darkness fall across the land.
And as the mountains slide slowly by.
I feel an incredible loneliness overcome me.
I feel as lonely and abandoned
As the barren mountains surrounding me
The loneliness grows each passing minute.
My life does indeed feel barren
In the vast playland for America.
I feel like an outsider looking in on what can never be mine
And as the darkness settles in,
I wait for the loneliness to overwhelm me.

—*Amber Rurup*

Tommie's Lament

I'm huddled in a rut, in
the dark like a shut-in
waiting at night by her window.
Watching the night,
waiting for first light,
and wondering which way will the wind blow?
There's a yearning inside me,
trying to guide me,
but I'm afraid — I don't want to hear it.
So I dig in more deeply
in this rut that can keep me
away from the yearning. I fear it!
I fear what it brings.
It will change many things
and I'm so scared of the things I don't know.
So it's better to lie in
this rut I will die in
than to climb out and venture to grow.

—*Dorothy Anderson*

Of Gold, Diamonds And Love

Dearest one, my love for you, is pure as pure fine gold;
  The depth of feeling that I have, in words cannot be told.
Purest gold will tarnish not, but will forever glisten;
  And so my love will shine for you and seek to always listen,
To hear that music to my ear, to hear "I love you too."
  And now will wait so patiently to hear you say "I do."

The diamond is the hardest gem that God has ever made;
  Nothing else will scratch its face: not wood, nor stone, nor blade.
So our commitment now will stand against time's rigid test;
  Outside forces will not mar this bond by heaven blessed.
A diamond's glory is not matched by any other thing;
  The rainbow colors shining through will all their beauty bring.

So too, love's vibrant colors shine when we're alone together;
  I desire to live with you and love you now forever.
Accept this gold and diamond ring as token of my love;
  Throughout each day and lonely night, it's you I'm thinking of.
I wish to hold you in my arms; to you I'll always cling.
  Now wear for always on your hand, love's symbol in this ring.

—*Bob Kiefer*

Chains

I feel heavy.
The chains around my neck are getting unbearable.
I've tried to cut them loose.
And I have succeeded.
But they always seem to come back again.
And once again, I am burdened with fear of being me.
Will the fear ever go away?
And if it does, will it take the chains with it?
What do I do until then? Suffer?
Is that the only solution?
What else is there?
Suicide? No, I can't.
I don't have enough courage for that.
But what if I suddenly got that courage?
Would I do it then? No.
I'd use the courage and turn it into strength.
And I'd use the strength to cut the chains.

—*Amy Ferrill*

Knights Of The Unemployment Line

As heirs of Eve and Adam,
The dragon exacts his fare;
To toil on earth, to inherit its dust,
To fade without a share.

His shadow touches everyone,
All dread his swift return;
His breath will leave you paralyzed,
His trail will leave you burned.

Do not let the dragon smother you!
Do not let him stay!
Take up your arms, fight his charms,
Embrace another day.

As in the days of Arthur's Knights,
and legends of St. George;
Gird yourself with resume,
let "interview" be your sword.

For the dragon preys on lack of faith,
He robs all of enjoyment;
He uses many pseudonyms,
Yet his true name is "unemployment."
—*Alan Tavassoli*

Another Place - Another Time

Love me tonight, my sweet - while moonlight drips upon the earth
And clouds sail like magic carpets over our heads
Let our lips meet in softness and gentleness -
Forever saying all that needs to be conveyed.
Let us walk hand in hand down the road leading to the lake
And let this time linger, literally coating my brain-
As an insulation against the lonely times.

Hold my hand - press it tightly so that the imprint of yours is forever
   there;
Hands will remember - feeling loved through the years
Let us walk as One while we are young and wind whips our cheeks
And never let us forget these moments -
A partridge drumming - peeping frogs and shining stars,
A banjo and a ukelele playing in harmony
All this will not return - wonderful perhaps but not the same.

You will return time and again with a clarity that sears my mind
Before the coals burn out after opening an old scar;
I shall leave you with brimming eyes and an apple blossom in my hand
To be pressed in a book - to last as long as I
Through the years let us be as phantoms in the mist
As we walk the road of remembrance.
—*Evelyn Kimball Blake*

Canoe

Water flows by as the shore drifts away
The ebb rippling while the sun draws you to bay
Floating, floating, floating away
Your thoughts leave you while you stay, stay all day
Shimmer of the wood of the bow
Underneath the life glimmers while you lay a long while
Floating, floating, floating to and fro
Feelings of tranquility permeate your soul
While the rays of light bounce all around
and the sight of a jay passes your way.
—*Cynthia Soroka*

Myra

Myra was young and free,
the extremity of innocence, a vessel of fair beauty.
Her lingering scent of lavender would permeate the air,
soft eyes of jade in silence spoke amidst a flame of flowing hair.
Her never ending presence was reaching out to me
intensifying what I see,
submerging my being with the universe harmoniously.
She was like a walk through the forest,
like the renaissance of spring borne after a long sleepy
winter's departure,
once a gentle bird tender in my hand,
than an untamed ocean thrashing violently toward land.
She had a lust for life, so vivacious in her mirth
and the love she had for me surpassed anything on this earth.
—*Anne R. Burkholder*

Dream

I saw them in the shadows,
   the faces were not clear.

A mural of feelings passed my mind,
   knowing everything he would do.
Perhaps memories of another year.

He held the hand of a young girl.
   Was it the girl I used to be?

Our eyes met quickly and looked away.
   From sadness? Or just yesterday?

He touched the petal of a flower,
   to feel the velvet leaf.

Awakened from my dream,
   I had faith in my belief.

It was a lovely picture painted,
   not one of grief!

Shadows of days gone by,
   placed deep in my dreams eye.

Arising to a new day,
I brushed the trace of a tear away.
—*Jackie Della Monica*

The Girl

When a boy meets a girl for the first time in life
The feelings in his heart are so unsure.
When he takes her by the hand, or how his heart begins to pound;
Could it be that this boy has found the girl?

When he whispers close to her sweet little words of praise
Something in his soul says, "She's the one."
As he turns her cheek to his, kissing her oh so tenderly,
Could it be, that his search for her is done?

Only one girl in life will be made for him
Though many other girls would often do.
When he finds the perfect one, she will make his life complete.
For he knows, her love for him is true.

Little girl did you know you are the one for me?
The look in your eyes tells me I'm sure.
Take my heart, take my soul, take my life and make them yours.
I realize — "I found the girl!"
—*Jacque Buchanan*

Visions Of The Future

Harken, all America!
The few, bastion of many.
Pols deliveries are eloquent,
Needs not met: Fall into promises.

One thing's sure we now have
Hope for a better tomorrow, with
Peace, joy and security. As we rest,
  At twilight, happiness.

No more empty words, lost in midair.
If we all work together, hunger,
Sickness and ignorance shall
  Not prevail.

In this land of ours, the homeless,
Everywhere, shall have a house to
Call their "home"
   —*Gilda M. Perez*

When The Fire Dances

Draped in hues of gold,
The Fire dances in brilliant whirls.
He breathes and speaks of words so bold.
He feeds upon His hosts with brittle whispers.

He is a hope of Light in the darkness,
Comforting Warmth in a cold world.

The tame infant god slumbers in His cocoon—
But once the furious Butterfly spreads His Wings,
His rage is unleashed—
He tastes the flesh of every flower—
Every leaf—
Every life.
His licking flames are fatal.

I wonder if the Maker of Life ever intended
For a butterfly to bring death—
Or if careless mortals ever meant
To free it from its silky prison.
   —*Channaly Oum*

To Nona

You were my first born: Oh, what a thrill.
The first time I saw you my heart stood still.
Now you are all grown up with children of your own,
and they have given me a wonderful love
That I have never known.
You have always been a joy to me
and I am sure you always will he
Time goes by and quickly too
But time well never change my love for you
No matter what life hands me I will never be alone
For you will always be beside me, this I've always known
You have so much sadness I thought—you couldn't take
And when I looked at you my heart would break.
But God sent you a true love and Happiness too.
And now I can see a wonderful change in you
but you will never change the way you look at me,
and I know that cherished I will always be.
and Nona you are still my little girl as before
and as time goes by I will simply love you more.
   —*Della Harrison Kromer*

Your Love

Your love is like a candle glowing in the wind,
The flame is so strong it will not come to an end.
Like your love this candle will comfort and guide
  me through the night,
To make sure everything is all right.
The flame gets brighter day after day,
And like this flame your love is here to stay.
   —*Carolyn Patenaude*

Driftwood And Mountain Climbers

I sat beside a stream one day where Driftwood and Debris,
The "Flotsam and the Jetsam" all were drifting down to sea;
Drifting, drifting ever downward to where angry breakers roar
And dash and crash all drifting things against the rocky shore.
I knew the waters far upstream were limpid and serene
And drifting down the river started out a pleasant dream,
But just around a bend or two a Cataract took toll,
And then the Falls, where not a piece of driftwood came out whole
I thought upon my life that day and turned myself around,
Determined that the Easy Road no more I'd travel down;
I asked the "Lord" to make of me a Climber who keeps on
And scales the Heights and looks afar with glad exultant song!
I asked that I might lend a hand and lift up others too.
Because until one climbs the Heights he'll never get the View,
Where undreamed Grandeurs stretch away as far as eye can see,
Surpassing all imagining, and fill with Ecstasy.
Where everything is Clean and Pure, Untrammeled and Untrod,
And those who Seek, reach out and clasp the outstretched
Hand Of God!
   —*Elsie V. Johnson*

It Is He That Is Passing By

The rains came and turned the garden green.
The flowers have water drops on their petals.
The clouds in the sky take shape as the sun comes
peeking through.
It is He that is passing by.

The day is a new creation.
He lifts His arms and the breeze passes by.
The birds sing their canticles of joy, for it is
He that is passing by.

Did you feel Him, see Him, touch Him or hear Him?
Oh, it was He, that is for sure.
Did He say that He would not leave you?
Then believe for it is sure; yes it is He that is passing by.
   —*Addie Monaco*

It's Only A Dream

Everything is a dream, a dream full of mystery
The fog enshrines the forest so that I can't see
The path which will lead me home
I remind myself that it is all a dream
But my racing heart tells me different
I hear it coming and knew what my fate was
And I tried to remember that it's only a dream
I turned slowly around and then knew
For certain that it was not a dream
Because I was facing myself in the mirror
The stringy hair, the bloodshot eyes, and
The pale yellow skin that outlined every
Bone in my body, faced me with menace
I saw in my right hand, a bottle of rum
And I smashed it against the wall
As I slowly turned away from the
Horrifying image and the alcohol
   —*Chris Wright*

God's Love

Consider with me for awhile
The fragrance of a rose
the wonder of a newborn babe
Perfection from head to toes
Christmas lights seen by the eyes
of an innocent 2 year old child
Crocus blooming in the spring
On a balmy day, sunny and mild
The joy in the eyes of newlyweds
Repeating their wedding vows
The expectant look of an honor grad
Hearing applause and taking bows
Receiving cards on your birthday
From dear friends, tried and true
The catch of your heart when a little one
Says "Mam-ma I love you"
Consider and search our world below
Then lift your eyes above
All of these many wonders pale
In the presence of God's Pure love.
—*Ethel M. Vogler*

My Mom

My mother's hand, her tender touch
the good night kiss I miss so much,
Mom was gentle with loving care, you
could hear her laughter everywhere.
When asthma struck her so hard to
breathe her smile and laughter did
not leave. God, took my Mom
with loving care, now her smile
and laughter no longer fills the air.
God, took her laughter and her smile
to shine and brighten up the sky.
—*Dorothy Kasian*

Different Stages

Upstage I am no less happy than you — I am no less fulfilled.
The grey hair in the midst of my scalp speaks softly of love
in every stage.

I am a baby, a child, a woman who longs...
Bewildered, it is hard to determine the difference between
relief and sorrow but already my mask in physical love is
twice removed.

Clearly, my sexual desires held by a splint need air
and to you I look for ventilation.
My fantasy includes sexual bodily actions and reactions
to a higher intensity.

I am good. But I want to be better.
I want many things including empathy and understanding.

Deeply, tears well from trying to improve myself
but to strive, learn and solve is satisfying.

My wounds are not fatal...I beg you, help me withdraw
the blade.
—*Christine Grace*

Showers Upon The Bounty

God always send the rains down upon
The growing vines of life,
So, it was on today, that He decided to run
The water over those vines, and make them ripe
For the up-coming harvest.
God always mails the raindrops equally,
And with nutrients, for the fall fest,
As He gives the Word to all, to be
Fed with the bounty of love.
God always posts the showers, inside
And out, as He takes His peaceful dove,
Sits him on the vines, and stays astride
The harvest, and waits for the bounty to mature,
Spontaneously, while being photographed, as
    a mighty picture.
—*Eva M. Roy*

In The Dark

Echoes in the dark keep tearing at my heart
The happy days of yesterday keeps me from falling apart
My thoughts are rushing back when you belong to me alone
I never dreamed I would be alone
I wish you would had never left,
Wait for me by the garden gate.

Hand in hand, face to face, together forever in another place
But 'til then, echoes in the dark will keep breaking me apart
My broken heart may never mend
But I can always remember when
No matter, I will be waiting by the garden gate
No more echoes in the dark
—*Joyce A. Shannon*

Liberty Alight

We honor the statue they call "Liberty," lovely, lonely lady in the harbor." Huddled Masses who longed to breathed free," once swarmed below her, looking up, awestruck, full of apprehensive hope, tearfully.
"Liberty," the English said we could not comprehend;
Generosity, they said, the French could not afford to spend.
And yet—and yet, this Century has seen her bid farewell to her own, some who never would return, who died abroad on teeming shores, saving French and English lives from tyranny.
And Why? ...... Why die to defend???? For Liberty!!!

"Ah," but she seems to say, "Liberty is not for all.
"In all the span of History, through centuries of toil, of slavery, of man's inhumanity against man,
"There always has been tyranny. Liberty's torch has only burned through flickering moments brightly turned
"Before the tyrants overran and crushed her out again- and yet
    again, again
"Liberty is not the rule in life.
It is the bright exception for a dearly purchased price.
"No man can breathe free unless he stands tall....for Liberty!"

"Do not appeasers stop to despise. Teach them yet to see
    through wiser eye
"In everyone there's good and bad, but some look up while
    others alas are cruelly had.

"Only those who govern well, keep pride and greed at bay and swell "with God given freedom's dearest chore: to see that others share freedom more." Sweet Liberty!
—*Elinor Van Dyke*

The Beauty of Night

The firmament showeth the handwork of God,
the heavens, his glory declare.
The sky sifts silvery moonbeams to earth
while in sleep, the world forgets care.
The vast blue dome of the heavens
seems upheld by the tall stately trees,
The hills lie quietly dreaming
while the earth cools beneath the night breeze.

Then soon will hasten the daybreak,
the sun arise in the sky.
A new day to live, and live better
than the day so lately gone by.
So forget all your heartaches and sorrows,
forget the failures you've made.
The night gave birth to the morning,
the new day, for which you have prayed.

—*Elnora Wilson*

Lionel (In Memory)

A rainy day in April, the day that Lionel died
the heavens seemed to open up like teardrops falling
from the sky.

God took his soul with him to sit at his right side.
At fourteen years he was wiser and older than most,
he was like on old soul.

Lionel will always be in our hearts missed and loved
by all; he was a nephew, a son, a grandson, a
shy young man who stayed alone. The ocean swallowed
him up on that rainy April day, like the pit of a
bottomless well. His soul looks down from above, as he
walks through the valley fearing evil no-more. He's at
peace now sleeping in the kingdom of the temple
Forever more.

—*Joyce Evans*

Lady Bay

Oh, Father, who lives in that House?
The House in the Middle of the Bay?
The House with no yard, no place to play? A Long Time
Ago—
A Father and his little Girl named "Bay"...
Chased a crab across the deck, the only House they knew
For the Boat provided the Captain and little Girl well.
Will you build a House for Me? A cry heard and a promise made
    before..
While pulling their nets for food from the see.
One Summer Day a cloud blew in and covered the Sun
Even the Gulls and Porpoise moved out
The waves grew large and the caps foamed white
The storm was everywhere and bolts of lighting became their only
    light.
The nets became hung, soon water filled the cabin floor
Masts became tilted and sails torn by the Wind...
From the dark water came screams of fright.
Hard rain, kept his daughter from view...
When a wave covered her and the currents pulled...
His cries became swallowed by the storm and it's fury.
Years had passed, his heart still broken
But his promise was finished for her Home was done...
Raised high above the waves that took her Life.
From Bon Secour to Bell Fontaine, Mobile to fort Morgan..
You can see her home on a clear sunny day. Still many questions
    w ho,
in that House does Stay? The Captain's only Daughter; "Lady
    Bay."

—*Charles W. Weinacker, Jr.*

Little Joys

Harvest the little joys around you:
The hug of a child, unrehearsed, spontaneous,
The excitement at the touch of a loved hand,
The taste of honey fresh from the hive,
The feel of marble polished like glass,
The full moon casting its arc-light spell,
The shaft of sunlight piercing the forest,
The painted leaves of the autumn,
The sound of waves crashing on the shore,
The salty smell of the sea,
The stretch, mobility, and power of limbs,
Small riches, all yours for the taking.

—*Harriet L. Axelrad*

American Blues

Of the hideous deeds of the past, the young swell in the sin of
the inner city. Life's forces, abandoned in the after birth,
seldom retrieved, and always forgotten. Their rearing cursed
in the blame of a society living in absolute denial of its
plight, refusing its destiny, inconsiderate, as it seeks out
the utility of freedom. Like a brazen hussy that has forsaken
her children, and given way to shame and injustice. Knowing
that the once diverse range of her neglect, her strong hold on
the damned, now rages in a unified battle cry of poverty and
deceit. Blind youth go sailing in the cesspools of the inner
city, as a mother adorns the exotic customs of the day, and
becomes a harbinger of sluts. The neighbors stealing quietly,
and efficiently, the very soul of a once beloved family.
Fathers toss in the graveyards of greatness, for the shame that
is called freedom. Old mothers weep in places where only the
good can go, and the great one prepares in HIS promised way.
Men turn their backs, as souls are bought and sold at the
auction blocks of despair and complacency, as unknown
generations wait in the dark recesses of humanity, for a day
when freedom and truth will once again become the champion of
time, and peace shall reign supreme. Still the mother, the
mother of freedom, waits for the return of the glory that was
her youth. Sheltered in the strength that once beckoned the
souls of many, and harbored the cry of freedom for all.
FREEDOM.

—*James A. Thomas*

Hope

It's autumn now, Thanksgiving's near.
The last leaf fell, I shed a tear.
The air is crisp. The wind blows cold.
A reflection shows a face grown old.
The heart feels young with spirits high,
But hair light gray, the question; why?

From birth to child, a youth soon bold.
To become an adult is best we're told.
My children watch, but don't understand
The responsibility in becoming a man.
Years pass by, our times not free.
A few more days is often the plea.

Then a ray of hope! We all will win.
All God's children will live again.
As the last leaf falls, now I don't cry.
Because I now can see the reason why.
A new life to live more wisely spent.
The spark I needed was Heaven sent.

—*Gary M. Homan*

The Torture Of A Memory

The last leave is torn off the once life-filled tree
The last spark of the once astatic fire dies peacefully,
The last petal of the wilted rose fades back into the ground
The wind briskly wisps the leaves and ashes randomly around.

The deep, dank clouds hang over the horizon in fright
As the last ray of hope is replaced by the thickness of night,
A widowed man walks with his cane in the dusk of fall
Never letting go — just holding on to it all.

The beauty of nature hides from the winter sky
Reminiscing past losses gathers tears to the eye,
Hope and dreams were formerly easy to revive
Back when a majestical sparkle dwelled within the eyes.

These long somber days are so sorrowful and cold
And the blackness of my soul was all once gold,
But the last straw has drained all hope from thee
And now it's all no more than the torture of a memory.
—*Jo Pelland*

Switzerland

Another time, another place...
The love in your soul, etched upon my face.
Naturally we two joined as one,
The joy of God's love destined to become
Ours.

Exquisite love, chilling plight,
One to remain, one to flight
In the spiritual spiral about to unfold.

Under a lonely pale sky stripped bare,
I catch my breath, feel you there
Standing on the mountain, haunted blue eyes...
The air crash that claimed you, brash surprise.
For you were my sunshine, eternity.
Fate intervened, brutality.

So alive in the springtime...
Pungent earth flocked with goats, daisies and dew.
Your hair burnt gold, eyes sea-green blue.
Reborn as the mountains are capped with fresh snow
Like the tired yellow daisy hard-pressed to grow,
Too zealous to die, now I shall follow.
—*Jill Josette Shaw*

Deceased Love

Out of the light and into the dark came
the man who made the spark, from the ledges
which he stood came a cry from the good.
Into the darkness that seeked for light came
an orphan not so bright. He brought his
sword to her head and said with this you are
dead. And to the ground she fell with pain from
her death his life will gain. The ground shook
and the dirt broke free and down went the man
like a tumbling weed. The clouds broke loose
for the sun to shine and up from the rumble came
a vine. And there was the orphan great to be
alive, jumped into the air, and fell to die.
—*Cassandra Jenkins*

Graduation Day

No one can ever take away,
the memories you make today.
From the day you're born to the day you die,
you make memories that make you laugh and cry.

You have friendships to look back on,
all the laughter and the tears,
the things about those times that made you laugh,
throughout your high school years.

Saying good-bye is not forever,
there will be another day,
when we can share our common memories,
and once again have lots to say.

So until then, if your heart is empty,
fill it up with something sweet.
The memories of your childhood,
are the best things you can't beat.
—*Cheryl Angyal*

Moon

Tell me about the moon he says.
The moon, ah the night Jasmine's sun.
Without it's silvery light their perfume would not smell as
    sweet.
It is the light that lends brightness to the shadows and
    guides the night-walker on his path.
The moon the lover's hiding place.
For under the moon he knew she was the one for him.
As they gazed at the silvery moon rising over the horizon he
    fell in love with her in the night air.
Tell me about the moon he says.
To do that I would have to tell of the dreamer's soul and
    all the mysteries of the night.
—*Jennifer Heindel*

Spring Is Here!

April showers bring May flowers, so they say,
The moon descends, the sun brings a new day.
The sugaring is completed, the buds have appeared,
Yes, 'tis spring now and so many had feared,
That it'd never come, at least not for awhile,
Let's rejoice in the fact, and wear a nice smile.
Not long until we plant gardens and spruce up the yard,
The work seems quite endless and often times hard.
But to have the health to conquer such things,
Is a blessing not to all this life brings.
To get up in the morning, to a bright sunny day,
With the understanding that all of life is not play,
Even if the morning brings rain or even some gloom,
Don't despair, for it has to end soon.
Yes, rejoice and be glad and do not fear,
Wake up now, don't you see, spring is here!
—*Carol Tifft*

Remember Me When

The stars hang like diamonds in the sky,
The moon reflecting in your eyes.

The wind bending the big oak trees,
The summers soft cool, cool breeze.

When heavens are colored so brightly blue,
Clouds so white and quite a few.

The rain on the roof softly sounding,
Making hearts skip and pounding.

The dusk responding to the shimmering lake,
The future brighter, it seems to make.

The favorite song, singing in your heart,
A vision of me it will impart.

A softly spoken, "I love you,"
Remember, it has been said to you too.
Snow falling all around,
Looking like love dressed in a gown.
Remember me when each season is due,
The memories are for me and you,
Not a season can go by then,
That you can not, "Remember Me When"
— *Dorothy McCroskey*

The Color Of Money

The color of money is green for greed.
The more you have the more you want.
The more you want the more you need.
The more you need the more you worry.
They say money can't buy happiness but I'd like to give it a try.
I'd rather be miserable and rich than miserable and poor.
Money is a cliche that we buy and sell.
Avarice is the root of all evil.
Money makes avarice.
Money is the root of all evil.
Still, I'd rather be miserable and rich than miserable and poor.
— *Chris Boka*

In The Mist

The mountains high peaks fill the air with rough edges.
The morning dew arrives, spreading its fog along a winding stream.
Birds song awake with the sun to feather the warm earth with serene contrast.
The salmon spawn upstream scaling the rocky shore with an ode of current.
The swift wind releases the trees with the smell of pine, filling the smooth lake with perfume.
Red violets blanket the hills with rows of color, exhausting itself from spring fever.
While the climbing of distant geese flock to migrate the murky marsh.
Pillars of clouds converge on the scene to shadow the illustrated glimmer.
The smell of fresh air is on exhibit to infuse and frame.
While the sunset plunges into the mist leaving the shine of capture.
— *Donald Jones*

The Man I Love

I lay and listened in the stretches of
 the night
As you talked of things you'd like to do.
The moon traced your features with her
 ghostly fingers
And revealed the rapt look in your eyes.
It was in moments like this that I came to
 understand
A little of you - the man I loved.
Then I knew the courage with which you
 faced the world -
The bigness of your heart -
The things you longed to do for those less
 fortunate.
— *Frances E. Tolson*

Welcome Fall And Winter

Summer time is almost over, the kids are back in school
The nights and days that were so hot, now are turning cool
The locusts, crickets, even the frogs
Have hushed for the winter and returned to their logs
The days are getting shorter, which makes the nights so long
The leaves have left the trees, and we miss the song bird song
Soon the winds will whistle, the snow will hit the ground
Once more we'll hear the children's laughter as again they play around
Winter has it's beauty, same as summer and the spring
We all should be so thankful, no matter what they bring
Be thankful for the beauty, "GOD" makes at any season
Don't fret at whatever may befall, you know he has a reason
So if you get the "Winter Blues" and in the house you have to stay
One thing that will enlighten you is to get down on your knees and pray
Yes thank "HIM" for all he has done, and
will do from day to day
and don't forget to thank him for our freedom in this U.S.A.
— *Elizabeth Unangst*

All Goes

How hard you worked, to write it down,
The notes and chords, for me!
So you could play, when I would sing
So perfectly!... for me.

And so I sang and you did play
But what remained of this?
A piano in an empty room?
Torn music, that I miss!

The pages scattered, on the floor...
Not needed anymore!
Sere, petals of a flower's sore!
Forgotten, near the door!

And now, I see:... what for the work?
Nothing is left — for spring!
All goes away, ...you are no more!
And I, ...can no more sing!
— *Irene Belikoff-Sherr*

My Garden Of Life Needs To Be Replanted

I will rebuild my garden by pulling out
the old weeds roots and all, I will recheck
to see that no other trace of the past will spoil
my garden; I will rake out any stones and
other unforeseen objects.
Next I shall dig three inches deep and set the dirt
beside each row.
In the 1st row I will put in my seeds of Happiness.
In the 2nd row I will put in my seeds of Generosity.
In the 3rd row I will put in my seeds of Love.
In the 4th row I will put in my seeds of Laughter.
In the 5th row I will put in my seeds of Understanding.
In the 6th row I will put in my seeds of Kindness.
In the 7th row I will put in my seeds of Faith.
In the 8th row I will put in my seeds of Patience.
In the 9th row I will put in my seeds of Hope.

After each row I will put the dirt back to cover up the seeds,
thanks with the help of God, I have recreated a new and better
Foundation of Life.
 —*Estelle Gertz*

Where Is My Brother?

Where is my brother?
 the one that I so miss.
 the one that teaches me so much.
Where is my brother?
 the one that assists me when I am down.
 the one that never lets me down.
Where is my brother?
 the one that tell me of the world.
 the one that is my best friend.
Where is my brother?
 the one that mother so grieves.
 the one that God so grieves.
Where is my brother?
 the one that died in war.
 the one that a country so forgot.
Where is my brother?
 he has gone away.
 he is embedded in my heart.
 her resides in my soul.
  —*Allen Spry*

The Grand Old Flag

It is the grand old flag that we proudly hail.
The one that stood proudly the through the stormy gale.
The one that stormed onward as it heard the disparate wail.
Yet some today would it's grander furiously assail.

That grand old flag has stood for many years;
Through all of the shouts of joy and stormy tears.
It stood as a wall of protection when many had their fears.
It stood as a symbol of freedom through all the years.

Each flag has it's story to tell to all who would hear.
A story of love, and faith and of sorrows and tears.
Of soldiers who proudly marched out to war;
Because they knew it was something worth fighting for.

So on this special day, wave your flag proudly and high.
Show all around you of our courage that won't die.
Wave that grand old flag up in the sky.
I am proud of its freedom for you and I.
 —*Alice May Shutt*

My Mother

My mother, mother so dear to me,
The one who taught me many things,
You were the one who dried my tears,
The one who made my special meals,
My mother so dear to me,
You understood me,
You taught me what truth meant,
And lying and friendship,
You were always right,
And when I had a problem,
You cared and listened and knew what to do,
You'd never tell my secrets because you knew what that meant,
Even as the years go on and on,
And I grow older,
Your always there to listen to my sorrows,
And dry my tears,
My mother, mother so dear to me,
With all my heart I love you.
In memory, Ruth L. McGill my mother.
 —*Cathy "Cat" Michele Vaughan*

You!

Don't worry there's nothing you can do
the only thing you can do is worry
about me and you.
To many careless days have been
going by, now the Black Forest has to die,
"and that's a fact"
You still keep pushing dirt in the
Atmosphere "you don't care"
The war against AIDS and human being
began, the hunger gets bigger in the slum,
"You forgot all about Sudan!
Love and care dies under civilized dust,
Evil and sadness grows in us!
Start to worry there's a lot more you can do,
not only worry about me and you!
"Don't forget the world depends
on you too."
 —*Andreas Gobor*

Question To God

I had a long talk with God
The other day

I asked him some questions
About following his way

I said, "Lord will I haft to give up
My house, and my car

Will I haft to go over seas
Lord, will I haft to go that far"

Then I said, "What about me
Lending a hand over here

I could do a good job Lord,
But over there I've got a fear"

Then God said, "My child, follow my lead
And from dungeons and swords
You shall be freed

And when it's time
To come home to me
Jesus, my son, shall carry thee"
 —*Bary Lee Herrington*

Life's Tapestry

No it isn't meant for me to see,
The other side of life's tapestry.
I see only what my eyes behold,
What I see and hear and what I'm told.

Out of a grieving, broken heart I cry,
"Oh, father, have you left me here to die?"
The troubles come upon me one by one,
There is no end it seems, what can be done?

My troubled mind I feel must be relieved,
So I bow my head in quiet reverie.
Then as my troubled spirit quieter grows,
I think upon his word and my heart knows,

Our Father sees the beginning from the end,
He is not blind, he truly is my friend.
Our lives are like a lovely tapestry,
The threads we see are all a mystery.

All tangled and knotted and sometimes cut in two,
The colors are pain, sorrow, joy: red, purple, blue.
We must remember that our Lord can see,
The other side of life's tapestry.

—*Joyce Porter*

The Old Stone House

My friend opened the door and ushered me in
The owner walked toward me across the hall
I suddenly felt I'd come home again
It was the strangest feeling of all!

Had I lived here before, had I loved here before
In the not so distant past
Else why these feelings of peace and joy
And that I had come home at last?

It was a big old stone house at the top of a hill
With a sparkling creek running below
Had this been my home in the century past
What person had I been—I don't know!

All I do know is this—the house grabbed me and held
To this day I can't break it's control
It calls me back from all over the world
It owns me—mind, heart and soul!

—*Ellen Carlstrom Adams*

Behind The Glass

It's time for all the world to see,
  The picture of my soul;
All my thoughts of love and life,
  Of years that to quickly go.

My baby's grown before their time,
  Just days ago it seems
They walked threw my heart and mind,
  Where now their baby's go.

Of flowers and trees and birds that sing,
  On winters icy snow.
Or on the lake a new sun set,
  With hands two lover's hold.

The gold or silver in your hair,
  Old pictures in my mind;
Of years ago are just today
  Old lovers that's left behind.

—*Jimmy L. Blazer*

Battle With Creation

If space fought with gravity, stars and the sky;
the planets, the earth would not survive.

If the air fought with the wind and breeze;
nothing could stir or move and even breathe.

If the clouds fought with the rain and the snow;
no more water, rivers, oceans and seas could flow.

If the land fought with the mountains and hills;
no more grass, trees and leaves that shades at wills.

If the sun fought with the moon;
the day, the night, the cold, the warmth would end soon.

Let the battles of creation speak to us,
Stop fighting each other and let's trust.

—*Jean Maish*

Prayer

The prayer of thought which is
The prayer of self
The prayer to feel what
We can not understand,
But try to feel what is
Right in the power of God.
We as a people of righteous
Are always trying to find that peace
From within, of which the answer
Seem so come from with prayer of sincerity.
The prayer that can make us unwind
From the un-nature spirits of the world
From sin as we know it.
The prayer that keep us as ourselves
Of being human with the true thought of mankind.
The prayer that keeps us from being so sad
Of what we see toward the end of our lives.

—*George Cox*

Taxes

Went shopping today - what a trip
The prices made me do a flip
The Government says prices are coming down
But they have not shopped in this town
The prices keep going up and up
Don't know if I should eat or drink from a cup
Then they tax me on what I earn
But do they ever learn
They tax me on what I save and spend
But overseas tax money they lend
Now they want tax on tax
And the Doc, he says Relax
If as those countries don't pay back
And I could borrow as they I'd sure relax
For then work I'd need not do
For Uncle Sam would be taxing you

—*Ernest E. Moutoux*

Triangles

Intermediate particles of our being;
The point of possibility;
The relics of Caesar's time,
Of old ancestors of mine.

The life — a rude, rough course;
So is the universe, till
We in our rugged-edged being
Connect to the sculptured, rounded
  edifice of time.

—*Alexandra C. Carpenter*

If You Don't Use It; You'll Lose It!

You can never go back... When today is gone, that's it!
The rest is stored in your memory bank
For time immemorial—or as soon as—just a bit of it.
You remember yesterdays by referring to your think tank.
Do it now! While you can.
You've heard this saying—I'm sure—since time began...
"If you don't use it; you'll lose it!"
Be it time, strength, energy, brains, or whatever,
Use it often or lose it forever.
Be you young or old—at any age—never be undersold.
When your mind is used to its fullest potential,
Reaching the hardest goal seems inconsequential.
We learn through trial and error
To make our lives rich, full, and even better.
They say, "In one's life cycle we reach the highest plateau.
Each growth level brings with it plenty of woes."
Those of us lucky enough to reach the golden age knows well
The meaning of the words "Use it or lose it" to be very true.
By practicing this saying, the successful person could easily be you!

—*Frances M. Pappacoda*

Of Cheyenne Autumn

At the massacre of Cheyenne Autumn
The ricochetting of yellow leaves cry...
With her carrying only memories
Of the past will keep her dreams alive
With the unborn growing inside
She will tell when the time arrives
To share the recounting
Of her old world
When the buffaloes fell
At the attack scattered old ones
Remembering it will not die
As she runs her appaloosa horse
From the massacre of Cheyenne Autumn...
Her baby will be born when the buds burst
At the encampment of green grass grows tall.

—*Judith K. Buffalo*

The Seed Not Sown

The town seems the same as yesterday;
The same white houses stand in rows,
The same sun warms the roofs of gray,
And pauses where the greenery grows.
The same trees, rooted long ago,
Still stand in silent symmetry,
Year after year the branches grow
Still stretching toward infinity.
Things seem the same as yesterday,
But listening, there's no living sound,
And looking, there's no child at play—
Just silence settling all around.
There is the quietness of sleep,
Suspension of all daily needs.
The wagon-ruts, not now as deep,
Are overgrown with beggar-weeds.
And there's a feeling in the air;
A searching for the seeds not sown;
A sense of changes lurking there.
A waiting for things unseen, unknown.

—*Catherine F. Douglas-McCargo*

Sunset Sonnet

A vein of gold 'mid shades of dark is shining from the sky.
The sea, a blushing red beneath, reflects the glory from on high.
The darkening clouds all raise their peaks like mountains wild and high,
While peace reigns quietly ever all, the earth, the sea, the sky.
Like ghostly galleons far away, the clouds sail o'er the sea.
Enchanting is the end of day, which brings real peace to me.
The Lord pulls down the shades of night and tucks the earth to sleep,
While sun hides bread and shinning face and sinks into the deep.
The father comforts fretful man with evening's peaceful kiss,
But ne'er a mother's loving hand gave me such peace as this!
Beyond the sunset's golden hue lies Heaven's golden shore,
Where the Son of Righteousness will shine forever more.
There golden skies and golden streets will ever more delight,
And the glories of the setting sun will never change to night.

—*Bernard Stanton*

Sudden Storm

The old house moaned at the peak of the storm, blowing in from the sea. A moaning, groaning blast that struck...the time? A bit past three! Suddenly, strange quiet hushed down the fury of the storm... but yet again, she struck it up...lashing away all morn.

We rode her out, the house and I, trees bending backs to the wind. A devil wind that stormy night...'twould stop and then begin. All night and day she really blew...we felt the mighty blast... coming from nowhere into our somewhere, and said 'how long will she last?'

Three days, three nights, the angry storm unleashed both wind and rain. Then, and then, it whimpered away, out back to fields and plain. But there, she sent a mighty power...making the land a lake, forcing the pigs and cows...birds, fowl and folks, other plans to make.

So, such is the way of the sudden storms that thrash and whip the sea...making us wonder just what's out there? Out there... where minds don't see. This the fury, the great surprise... strikes our hearts, opens our eyes! Wakes us up...is this our God..cutting us down to size? Such is the way of the sudden storm, blowing in from the sea...a moaning, groaning blast that struck...the time? A bit past three!

—*Chloris B. Brownell*

The Children Pay, For The Sins Of The Fathers

They came from clay, primordial soup,
The sediment defined, Adam called them by name,
Apollo, his fiery steeds, circuit the heavens,
Python, magnificent creatures, vengeance decried,
I shot an arrow into the mist, the toll I cannot bear,
The battle rages, my blade, sullied,
Delphi, O mystic place, the great beasts vanquished,
Nothing remains, if so, forgotten,
Temples aligned, their veneration complete,
Mysteries left behind, omniscient earth,
Pagan rituals, misleading, delusions abound,
The epitome of man, shattered, just a dream,
Fading tomorrows, our enthusiasm wanes,
A euphoric state, to be expected, unsure,
Alpha and Omega, the beginning is the end,
The Children Pay, For the Sins of the Fathers.

—*Charles T. Chilcott*

Lumiere De La Chandelle

Into the room where I had stood,
The shadow of a youth came.
She wore a woven, woolen hood
Glistening with the evening rain.

The room was stark, bereft and bare
Of all that had been before—
Yet the transient wraith took a chair
Quietly closing the door.

Into the room where I had wept—
The sentient girl cried aloud,
You are aged and badly kept,
I within am young and proud.

She said, remember....grace will come
To stand again at your side.
Let not your lips touch bitter rum
Or you despair with paths not tried.

From the room and into the hall
I snuffed the bright candle flame—
Shadows lapsed and gathering my shawl,
I left to walk a country lane.
—*Francine M. Tyler*

Never Say Goodbye

The moon is shining on the dark earth.
The shimmering light trickles down your
silhouetted body.
 I can see your muscles tense at every sound.
 You are so perfect, so innocent, so blind;
This complex world seems so simple to you;
You do not see the dark shadows, you only
marvel at the good things in life.
 This is what draws me near to you,
because I see death, hate, and cruelty, but
you see love, life, and innocents.
 You make my world come together, when
before I use to fall apart.
 Now the dark doesn't scare me anymore, the
only thing that scares me is you leaving.
 I need you by my side to see the beauty of
the world.
—*Jacqui Byrne*

Twilight

Shadows are falling and it's twilight time again,
The sky has just a glowing light before darkness settles in,
The birds have flown up to their nests to spend a quiet night
The flowers hold their heads down low to rest from bright daylight,
There is a lonely quiet that seems to fill the air,
So I'll just sit awhile without a worldly care.
If fate is kind I hope there'll be years for me to see,
The sun come up and set again with time that can be free —
I will not fill my thoughts with life's unpleasant things,
Just hope I can enjoy the peace that twilight brings —
—*Eleanor Henry Hummel*

Beautiful Sunsets

Reds purples and blues
The shining crystal clear waters.
Azene, turquoise gold, the calm
sounds lapping against the shores.
Birds and breezes whispering in the
trees. Its as if time stood still.
It's as if this is the way thing
were meant to be.
—*Julieth Willmann*

Our Walk Through The Woods

Spring is upon us. The sun is shining so full and bright;
The sky is so blue that it seems to say "It's to God's delight."

A walk through the woods is a sure case of pleasure to me;
God's wonderful work is so plain that even I can see.

As we walk in the woods at a slow but steady pace;
The breeze from the air blows wildly across our face.

The trees are growing leaves which at first are little sprouts.
This is God's creation and with us there should be no doubts.

Nature seems to have a beautiful sound all its own;
Birds jeeping, squirrels chattering and even me throwing a stone.

Back to the house we walked until another day;
And back to a wheelchair where I stay!

This little walk means a lot as you can see;
To know the Lord will walk with even me.
—*Green Jarrell, Jr.*

The Beauty In Life

The brilliant sunset left me breathless
The sky lit up like gold
I could hear the whispers in the wind
Of secrets left untold.
The water, iridescent glass
Shimmered like visions of broken dreams
Caught up in all of that beauty
Lost to how much it means.
I thought to myself, "How can all this be found
In a world that's so twisted around?"
People discover the essence of life
But forget it when they get scared
Yet all of that can be rediscovered
When the beauty in life is shared.
—*Anna Race*

The Field

In the field the mighty field,
 The Slugger waits tonight,
On the mound the mighty mound,
 The Pitcher stares in fright.

As the pitch is thrown in the air,
 The swing of the Slugger's bat is heard everywhere.

In the Field the mighty Field,
 Strike one is called tonight,
At the plate the mighty plate,
 The Slugger stands upright.

At the mound the mighty mound,
 The second pitch is thrown,
The Slugger swings with all his might,
 "Strike two" the umpire moans.

At the plate the mighty plate,
 The third pitch is thrown.

In the Field the mighty Field,
 In the bottom of the ninth,
The wind is the only sound heard,
 On this lonely night.
—*Chris Michael Mieth*

Trapped

I climbed upon a mountaintop on a silent starless night
the snowflakes started drifting down, a beautiful wondrous sight
I crept into a cabin sitting there among the pines
and built myself a fire and composed the following lines
the silence is astounding, not a soul is there to see
I find myself a rocking chair and enjoy my company
I think I must be trapped up here, the snow is coming fast
the mountaintop is treacherous, I'll probably never last
the fire's burning low, there's no more wood in sight
my rocking chair has just collapsed, I'll never last the night
the roof has started leaking, snow melting on my head
I wish that I had stayed at home snuggled up in bed
the howling wolves are circling the cabin just outside
I know they want to eat me, and I've no place left to hide
I have a lousy headache, my arthritis hurts like hell
my feet are frozen solid and there's no one here to tell
a realization dawned on me, my poem won't be read
by the time I get back home, I'll probably be dead.
—*Charlotte McKay*

Upon The Midnight Hour

Sleepless dream upon the midnight hour,
the sounding of your heart,
the sweetness of your warm desire,
but alas we stand apart.

I walk down by the sunless sea
to catch the rising mist,
to taste the salt upon my tongue,
the pleasantness you have kissed.

The shadow of an eagles wing
before my eyes has flown.
I wake to questions in my mind
that I might walk alone.

I pray the gods to guide us,
to lift my saddened heart,
bless us with a new love —
we shall never be apart.

Bind us with a silver thread
the winds can never break,
and rest my soul in a peacefulness
that no man may ever take.
—*Dale L. Wilson*

Tale Of A Sea Traveler

Moon beams fall upon the distant shore.
The sounds of the serf echo off the earth's floor.
A warm ocean mist fills the air.
Seabirds pause to usher me a silent stare.
Soon they lift their wings in flight,
As I watch them vanish into the night.

Tiny sand crabs scatter across the beach.
Sail boats sail too far for human hands to reach.
Trails of a child's footsteps climb the walls of sand hills.
Beneath my feet hide small shells,
With many shapes and intricate designs,
That with all of my mind,
I can not fathom,
How this could be,
That God would create such an exhibition of perplexity,
All for me!
—*Gwen Washburn*

Man

God knew what he was doing when he put us together. It's only the spirit of man that lives forever. God knew what he was doing when he made us from sand. And he only knows the frailty of man. So are we to think, we're so mighty and great? It's only the spirit that keeps us in shape. For we are just a form made from sand, made to perfection by God's great hand. And after He finished the great roll, He breathed into man, and man became a living soul. But this is just the start of God's great work, for without Christ, we're still just dirt. But with Christ in us, the hope of glory, we have a new life, we can tell a new story. We can tell the world a Savior has come, we can have a new life, through God's only son. We can be free in the spirit and feel His great love, And someday together all live above. We can more than conqueror, this flesh of man. For you see God has made us more than just sand.
—*Ellen Jane Hobby*

The Storm

The night is bright—with thousands of stars tonight
The stars twinkle—the moon glows against a navy blue night
Crickets, play softly—bats are in flight
Suddenly, a breeze picks up in the peaceful night
The breeze begins stirring a soft chill
The wind picks up violently at God's will
The warmth of the night is now gone
You hear only angry roaring wind
The wind over powers trees and makes them rock
Back and forth with great power—back and forth
Drops of ice hits the earth
A flash—a roar—then Boom!
Lightening to some is music—To others it's evil
Now the temper of the storm—drifts onward
Thunder fades—winds and rain quiets
Finally, a single ray of light—breaks through the clouds
Bats and crickets are now replaced—with birds songs
The smell of pollen fills the air
—*Joe E. Workman Jr.*

The Prairie

The prairie is so still and quiet in the fading darkness
The sun begins its ascent on the edge of the sky
An orange glow splashes across the desolation
The chill of night slowly gives way to the day's warmth
Solemn silence is everywhere on the prairie
The wind now beings its assault. blowing hard across the land
The grass sways and moves like waves on a golden sea
Tumbleweeds move like ships intent on a journey to nowhere
With the wind as an only companion the prairie seems so lonely
The ghostly winds fade away as the sun begins its descent
The pink sky mixes with the features of the prairie's face
Night's darkness begins to envelope the land
The calm comes once again to the prairie.
—*James E. Robo*

The Graduate

Now that all is said and done
The race is run
The battle won,
You stand atop your own plateau
To laugh at all your tales of woe.

With surer foot and steady hand
Take time to note the height you stand,
For as the mountains in your mind
Beckon onward ever climb.

Recall no mountain touches stars
And your dreams make you are.
—*James A. Radosevich*

In Memory Of

Although he's gone, and sorely missed,
  The sunny smile, the lips you kissed,
    His cocky manner, always there,
to hide the fear, he couldn't share.
For courage was his middle name,
He treated life, just like a game.
  I know he's there, way up above,
and looking down upon his love,
to spread his courage, all around,
and blessing you, without a sound.
  So, smile awhile, and do recall,
The very best years, of them all.
  Your special day, will surely be,
a very happy memory.
    —Helen Anthony

Love Of Children

The children of the world can unity and peace prevail.
The symbol of serenity and peace are children. Create a
worldly vision of high expectations, a soul of light and love
which illuminate lives. Let land of opportunity ring out and
let's reach for the stars. Every ecumenical particles of the
outer atmosphere of the highest entity, will eventually dissipate at
the end of eternity. May the future of the world's children
illuminate our lives and many gold treasures be found at the
end of their rainbows. Children who create the fantasy of a
life time will reach their ultimate destiny and reap the
richest rewards.
  —Adrianna Rolando

Four Little Words

Dedicated to my granddaughter Amanda
The telephone rang and I said, "Hello."
  I heard a little voice that I love so.

  Four little words rang through my ears,
  I touched my cheek and felt the tears.

  Four little words that made me feel glad,
  That took away all that was sad.

"Can you come over?" "Grandma," she said to me,
"Cause Grandma, it's you I want to see."

  I couldn't believe what I heard,
  I'll always remember those four little words,

"Can you come over?" "Grandma," she said to me,
Believe it or not — she's not yet three.
    —Alice Pike

Crazy Horse

Badlands!
  There he stands.
Crazy horse,
  Mounted on
A steed of granite.
  None braver brave,
Nor warrior chief
  Ever rode or fought more fiercely
For his belief.
  Alone on a full moon trail of a burning past,
He rides in chiseled silence,
  Of echoed war cries.
Companion to the lone wolf,
  Searching for his brothers.
    —S. M. Yates

My Child

Yesterday you were just a child—playful and happy as could be;
Then suddenly within a few fleeting years, you became an adult
  and now you are ready to venture into the world.
God's love will always embrace you, His wisdom will council you
  and His light will illuminate your path—making clear the way.
As you passed through our home, we did our best to instill the positive
  life to you:
"Self-esteem, self-confidence, and respect for others."

There is never enough time to be with those whom we love,
Or say all the things that should be said;
Because time is so ephemeral and everyone must move with it!
Life for parents is often a "bittersweet" experience because one day
  our children must move into their future.

During your fleeting years at home, you were a blessing to your
  parents;
You were a loving and responsible child;
It was necessary to remind you to study your school lessons; you were
  perfect in every way!

My child now you must go into the world,
Become a magnificent person and make a meaningful contribution to
  Humanity!
    —Randolph Sturrup

Trying Is The Key

Afraid to venture to the unknown?
Then you will never know
The awe that's felt from your success,
And just how well you show

Afraid to try because you'll fail?
That statement troubles me
For fail you have, if you haven't tried,
Trying is the key

Afraid that you might foolish look?
To a fool guess we all do
And you are a fool, if you care so much;
How someone looks at you

Afraid to see what you might see?
Well look, don't turn away
For you'll see exactly what you are,
Your own conscience is your prey

Afraid to say what you might say?
Well think, be sure, then speak
For your thoughts are yours and your alone,
And you are your best critique
    —Saundra Songer

Up From Bondage—For Those Without A Song (For Song)

The way of bitterness is sad
There is no sky
Nor soul's unfolding warmth...
The more to draw Thee nigh;
We cannot see
We cannot give
Unyielding depth —
We cannot live!
To harbor shaft in place of heart,
Which neither gathers nor emits is wrong—
And damns the wound wherein it lies!
O God - belay that bitter cup
And let Thy tender shoots come up!
    —Myrtle Trott

To The One I Love

As I answered the phone, on August 5th, 1992,
the voice on the other end of the line, belonged to you.

My speech was to be the same, as all the times before,
somewhere along the way, our conversation became much more.

You told me about your life, from the time you were a young
man, in turn, I told you about my life, because I knew you
would understand.

As I listen to the sound of your voice, so sexy and sweet,
I knew you had to be the most precious man, I could ever hope to meet

I never wanted that call to end, with so much to be said,
I had so many thoughts and feelings, swirling around in my head.

The day we met was the sweetest day, I'll ever live to see,
you were the most handsome man, like I knew you would be.

You had a special charm about you, and a smile to behold,
I knew you were the man of my dreams, I didn't have to be told.

You stand tall among men, honest, proud, and true,
there's nothing for you, that I wouldn't do.

You my darling, are a living legend, and so very special to me,
you are the man, I want to stand beside me, for all the world to see.
—*Alice M. Farrow*

A Child Alone

You know those billboards you see along
the way? I cried when I saw one yesterday.

There was a child, whose wounded eyes accused,
those poor dead eyes saying, "I've been
abused!" This child whose life has never
seen, love, trust, or dreams redeemed.

That tortured child was familiar too.
I cried then, because I knew, that tortured
little child was you.
—*Cheryl G. Palermo*

Missing You

I miss those long cold nights —
the way it used to be,
me touching you and you touching me.

I get so lonely not having you here—
thinking back to those nights,
wishing you were sincere.

I long for your kisses
And the warmth of your touch.
Just having you near — it means so much.

There is not one thing I can say or do
to take away the pain that you
have been through.

I just wish that I wouldn't
have gone this far.
Now it feels uncomfortable the way things are.

So I have to be strong and set you free.
But, if you ever need a friend,
you can always count on me.
—*Julie L. Sheets*

The Housewife's Tea Party

To break the boredom of her life,
The way things seem to be,
She's called a very special friend
To come and have some tea.

The ironed tablecloth lays on
The table set for tea,
She sets out all the snacks she's baked
And says, "Please join me...

    And she says these words to Death so sweetly...
    As she folds her napkin once more, neatly...

"Won't you have some as I have mine?
We'll share the treats discreetly.
And when our tea is over, then
My tears will end completely."
—*Barbara A. Carr*

I Tasted Life

I tasted life with you a while
The way we taste fine wine
I held you close and loved you
And I thought of you as mine.

And love is really blind
But oh, the taste was sweet.

We filled our glass to the brim
Who could know that we should wait?
The glass was running over
And the joy was much too great.

We tasted joy, then fate
Turned the taste to bittersweet.

I drank in all your goodness
And I gave you all of me.
The glass was drained much too soon
And now what is, must be.

For now, you've set me free
Oh God, the taste is bitter.
—*Jan Tate*

Promises

The organ played in sonorous tones
The wedding march from Lohengrin.
With soft touch on her father's arm,
The bride in lacey white came down
The aisle to join her waiting groom.
They listened to the pastor's prayers,
The scriptures and the homily.
He said his vows with vibrant voice.
"For better, worse; for richer, poorer;
In sickness and in health," she spoke
Aloud then paused to take a breath.
Her eyes shone brightly through warm tears;
No words came out her open mouth.
The weighted silence hung in air
And pastor only heard the rest,
'So long as both of us shall live.'
With rings exchanged, now man and wife
They knelt, were blessed and stood to kiss.
A man behind me whispered then,
"They're both HIV positive."
—*Hilda V. Finkbeiner*

Love In The Golden Years

We began our life together more than fifty years ago
The white hot flame of youthful love
now softened to a glow
A glow that warms and comforts
When sadness comes our way
Our lives enhanced by sharing
Whatever comes each day.
The bond of love that bound us through the years
Grew stronger in the sharing of laughter and of tears.
We've had our little arguments, that's a part of married life,
But we've always stood together, united man and and wife
It's said these are the golden years and if that is true,
I'm glad that I can share these golden years with you.
—*Dorothy A. Crites*

Christmas Is My Favorite Time Of The Year

Christmas is my favorite time of the year:

That's when, there's much joy and "Cheer."
There sits on my table, a "big" juicy "Turkey."
And everyone's face is happy and "Perky."

After dinner, everyone will sit,
and talk, of the year, that will soon pass.
And the new year, will bring.
New hopes, and dreams, that will last.
Everyone, will give a big hug,
and a kiss, as they depart.
Will new found love in their hearts.
—*Juanita Strothers*

The Past Left

I find I'm standing in one spot
The years have started to roll
I have to move with what I've got
My life is paying the toll.
I can't go back, that's not for me
I've weathered the storm half-way
I made a vow, I still agree
I'll find happiness someday.
What makes me stop and second guess
The answer I know so true
The answer is none the less
I'm only part way...not through.
So now I make that final step
The move that was the best
The past is where it should be kept
It's finally laid to rest.
—*Helen L. Hite-Smith*

The White Coats Are Coming

They move in a hurried manner
Their time is always too short
They think they know all the answers
That is if they don't get caught
If you really want to survive, the person
  you must truly see
Is the one who's inside of you, the one
  you always call "me"
Rely on yourself, get involved, keep informed
Because if you don't, consider yourself warned
Health is a tricky business, your life a one- shot deal
Become your own advocate or you may literally keel!
—*Judith Katz*

If He Knew

Two lonely people, searching for a star.
Their paths crossed by chance one night,
in the small town's local bar.

A look, a few drinks, and some friendly conversation,
Soon they were whisked into a whirl revelation.
Fun, laughter and nights of ceaseless passion,
Soon they were consumed with lust and love,
as is usually the fashion.

Reality struck a sudden blow,
When she confided in him her news.
He turned his back, walked away, leaving her desolate and blue.

She carries the secret in her heart,
Weeping silently thinking of the truth,
Would he, too, turn his back and walk away?
Would he still love her, if he knew?
—*Judy Kay McVey*

A Poet's Duty

I study the Market to see where I can go.
Their samples give me a headache.
They say they want to bring poetry back,
but to who, a select few?
Just mention the word
and people give you the vague look
of a concentration camp.
Because poets are putting together words
that thoughts just can't stand.
They have gone too far
into reaching inside themselves.
It reminds me of pulling the guts out of a chicken.
I was ready to hang it all up
until I saw the eyes of everyday people.
I won't allow them to be cheated.
I will bring back the simplicity
like it was meant to be.
I will plug in their cord to my outlet and give them light.
It is my obligation,
and their right!
—*Carolyn Barnhardt*

Our Knights Of War

All their yesterdays are past
Their tomorrow may be too.
We hope the conflict will not last
Our Knights Of War are fighting for me and you!

Many young boys from this school
Must now be men ready to fight.
Why must this world be so cruel
I remember when their future looked so bright!

Now they look across the roasting sand
That looks like a vast shimmering sea.
If I could I would give them a hand
For there is not where I want them to be.

What will happen I do not know.
When once again they are at their homes' doors,
With love and pride my heart will glow
For our Knights Of War.
—*Fred Rice*

Precious Friend

Friends I love mean more to me
Then the great pearls of the sea.
Like the pearl's lustrous glow,
Bud of rose, or flake of snow,
Sound of harp, or the soft wings of a dove.
All are gifts sent we know
To all people here below.
Heavenly gifts, are but symbols of God's love.
Precious friend take my hand
And I know you'll understand
Why this friendship will always remain true.
Sometimes when you're far away,
Every hour of every day,
I just close my eyes
And breathe a prayer for you!

I will be a faithful friend
Til eternity shall end,
Pressing on from day to day,
Keeping touch along our way.
Praying universal peace comes, friend of mine!
—*Eunice C. White*

The Droopy Tulip

Today it's bright and sunny,
There are flowers everywhere,
The tulips, jonquils and hyacinths
fill the bed they share.
There's such a range of colors
from yellow to bright blues,
A bountiful assortment
from which my friends can choose.
They're happy and so healthy
and growing by the day,
To bring us hours of pleasure
in every little way.
Except for this one sad tulip,
stem bent down to the ground,
Just doesn't have the strength
to take a look around.
I staked her up and watered her
and said a little prayer,
So she will have a lengthy life,
the rest is in Gods care.

—*Frances Bucaro McCliment*

A Confederate General's Last Stand "Gettysburg 1863"

I can hear the Yankee drums beating ever so softly out
   there somewhere in the fog shrouded trees;

I know at daybreak that this old southern General will
   lead my men into combat; but right now I feel pretty
   weak in my knees;

The cannons will bellow, and the smoke will fill the sky.
   Good men on both sides will surely die;

After the battle is over and all the blood is spilled and
   the wounded carried away;
Will it somehow make a difference in life, for those who
   survive some future day.

I sure pray it will, because for this old General in
   charge now, its a frightening nightmare.
The only wish I have is the ones at home really love all
   of us enough to really care.

—*Floyd Simon*

Time Affords Many Changes

   Many changes have I seen in my ninety-two years,
There have been great accomplishments, yet cause for many
Tears. Long before my time was the great year of
Seventeen-Seventy-Six, when fifty-six names to the Declaration
of Independence were affixed.
Knowing that their lives were in jeopardy, they stood bold,
Though tortured and killed, the World's greatest Nation did
Unfold. Great inventions: telephone, electricity, planes,
Computer, and many others, have been great blessings and means
Of contact, until all are as brothers.
But, there are now wars and rumors of wars in every direction,
And within our own nation there is even insurrection.

   Time is now changing, and changing very fast,
We no longer believe, not trust the Lord, who sustained in the
Past. It was the Lord God Host, who gave us our dear
Nation, and only by trusting in the cleansing blood of Jesus is
There Salvation. I realize that Truth is not considered very
Popular today, but, may we be faithful witnesses to tell it
While we may. Christians have a hope of escape which is a
Consolation, while all others shall suffer through the Great
Tribulation. There shall be seven years of torture, chaos and
dearth, before the Lord shall return, with His saints, to bring
Peace on Earth.

—*Alva McGregor Crisp*

Fear

There is a feeling trapped in this soul.
There is a voice, menacing, becoming yours,
an obligation to him not chosen
an insecurity in yourself since the beginning
a wolf tearing down your walls
a smell of fear, intense, rising,
obliged to care for him!
   Setting his wrist!
   Sewing his side!
Touched by him, holding him ever so slightly,
there is a clamoring from your spirit,
an inexperience brought to life
shouting at you
hurting, pulling, flinging, destroying,
but you cannot take leave.
There is a screaming voice,
yours.
Oh, there is an uncertain feeling,
set yourself free from your shadowy cage!

—*Jennifer L. Dreyer*

A Time For Parting

A time for parting, a time to say Goodbye
   There will be loneliness, heartaches, tears, — but why?
Loved ones are left behind, weeping for the loss and grieve
   But when Heaven's Gate opens, we have to take our leave.

Our time on earth is, for some, a short time or while
   For God gives to each, his destined mile
And when it's time for parting, God may take us alone
   He calls, and takes, a loved one for His own.

Covered under a world, of drifted snow so white
   Hidden in the Heaven's resting place, is this son tonight
At rest, he is not dead, we know, but in his Father's care,
   Dispelling gloom, or even regret, a prayer to his shine of
     Light over there,
God will see you through this time of parting.

—*Alma A. Carlson*

Sightless Vision

A form of sight is limited to what the mind thinks is actually
there. With my mind I can see all things.
I don't have to wait until autumn
To see the beauty of red and gold trees.
I don't have to wait for
The sun to come up to see the bright yellowish glare
that streaks across the skies.
When I close my eyes, that's when I see best.
Now, I'm consumed in visions of warm and tender smiles of happy
   people.
The innocent, carefree expressions of playing wondering
   children.
In my mind, harm is so far away,
And love wraps me up like a thick soft blanket.
—*Ellen K. Gordon*

A Winter Ride Home

The night air, bitter cold, crisp
There'n going to be snow falling tonight,
I can smell it in the evening air,
I feel it in my aching bones.

Though the horses' trot is brisk,
And the sleigh being very light,
It feels as if we're going nowhere.
Off in the distance, the aromas of home

Hasten your pace, onward, lets persist
I see the windows, cherry and bright,
Homeward bound my trusty mare,
To the warmth and love of home.
—*Cheryl Sass*

To Sit Alone

I sit here alone my God and I, sit and wonder why
There's a haze o'er the clouds as we Soar thru the sky
O'er the miles the clouds are as valleys and crevices
   in the depth of the sea.

I sit here alone my God and I, I sit and wonder why
Such beauty's out there everywhere
Thru out God's heavenly home
There's no reason I should think I sit here all alone

For God is here each step I take
He daily holds my hand, to let me know He's here with me
To help me understand, there's beauty in each thing I see
   and as he holds my hand.

The haze will leave those clouds someday and thru eternity
I will spend my time with God in his home up in the sky
Never more to sit alone, or sit and wonder why.
—*Helen Rae Wegner*

Lament

My lament is my sorrow for things that will never ever be.
They say the place is where the heart is, my heart is in my
yesterdays.
Yesterdays of tomorrow that never were. My heart lays broken
in a dark corner of a un-known place.
Dreams and glories that never came to pass.
Oh, how I grieve for people lost in my yesterdays.
Today is now, yesterday is gone in the smoke of the past,
Tomorrow trouble me. Made to feel sad for my yesterdays.
Is my heart truly locked in my yesterdays! How I long to
break free of the past and fly happily into my tomorrow.
—*Gail Tamara Taylor*

Love and Hope

To: Steve Ray
   There's a long narrow path, each soul will soar down;
with each step they shall take, a new clue shall be found;
A new piece of the puzzle, that will join together,
to be used for eternity, and can last forever.
We learn from this lesson, held deep in our hearts;
judge no one from outside. Give each a fair start.
So many are scared, to admit that they're wrong,
until it's too late, when the answer is gone.
The truest of love, two people can share,
so many unknown, it's found very rare;
but when it is found, a bond that's unbroken,
true love from the soul, an emotion unspoken.
Intertwined by a strength, unconditionally tight,
held together by hope, with the help of the light;
with the wisdom of honesty, true hope did arise,
and the care of your words, that were seen in your eyes.
When the love that was felt, pull two people together,
it's the magic of hope that will last forever.
In the world of today, people pass love by,
but hopes always been, love found you and I.
   "I'll always love you"
—*Carrianne Shortt*

A Twist Of Faith

Where there used to be a spotless home
   there's dust and clutter in every room.
The manicured bushes and lawn somehow
   are the weeds and wild overgrowth just now.

A work-a-holic all my life
   homemaker, mother and a wife.
Deserted since a stupid fall
   with broken knees and disks, that's all.

"Why me?" I look to God and cry
   a quiet calm within replies
"You gave your time, love, work, energy true
   a pillar, a presence, a helper, you.

To get all your attention back to Me
   You had to stop cold in your tracks, you see.
My Life wasn't all just doing and show,
   there was even a borrowed tomb, you know.

Frustration was part of my life you see
   so offer the idleness up to Me.
Take help from others, a crushing blow —
   keep sharing your faith, not just what shows."
—*Eva Bass Bishop*

Summer Clouds

They look like snow on distant hills — like castles in the sky
They build gigantic figures — that catch and hold your eye
Their rolling waves of snowy white - against our heaven of blue
Make them a wondrous beauty — with attractions strange and new

Sometimes you look above you — and oh! what holds your eye—
A little row of lattice-work — of clouds up in the sky.
They stretch across our universe — an hour perhaps two—
Now our lattice work is gone — instead, there's something new.

This time a quite new wonder — it's a monster too I'd say
But look! he isn't staying long, the winds too strong today.

When the wind is sleeping — and a breeze doth take its place,
These huge white ghost like figures — come creeping into space.

Now they're o'er our city, with a sun kissed amber hue
I'll bet the sun is setting, to hide our precious view.
—*Crystal Grace Clark*

Graduation

It's just the beginning, not the end;
There's much more to learn, around the bend,
As you leave the classroom and enter the realm
Where sickness and death preside at the helm.

You'll learn how to cope with the stress and strain
Of tasks done over and over again.
Your feet will hurt, and your back will ache;
But there's meals to serve, and beds to make.

And patients are cross, and doctors gruff,
And you're tempted to say, "I've had enough!"
But you'll carry on, and the joy you'll feel
When someone whispers, "You helped me heal"

Will compensate for all the pain,
And the many times there was no gain;
And the Lord looks down and says, "well done -
You've carried on, just like my Son."
—Ida Mae Rodgers

Magic Garden

The gate is closed and locked you see.
There's no one here, just you and me.
There is so much for you to see.
Here in my Magic Garden.

I saw a Pooka yesterday,
a Zenner and a Gonderlay.
They all wanted me to play.
Here in my Magic Garden.

The meadows, they are soft and green.
The creatures gentle as you've seen.
It's like living in a dream.
Here in my Magic Garden.

We can come here every day.
Our parents, they must stay away.
They couldn't see it anyway.
My secret Magic Garden.

What a delightful thing to do.
To share my special place with you.
I'm sure you'll love it as I do.
My wondrous Magic Garden.
—Charles Atkinson

Refuge In Oxford

Such praise, but these scenes are texts of beauty!
There's no painting half as alluring
Nor any depiction by novelist Faulkner
Can array the soul as God does without words.

But, why must these things become a creepy dust,
    laden with fears, crumbled with tears,
        withered frames that are rivets of pain,
A conscience without consciousness of fear.
But, thus, is the formation of such a mental state
    in minds that mate,
And this very earth buffets these endearments in
    accordance to a given faith.
This invalidism of beauty lies within
And corrugates the soul.
The tentacles of mankind become a medium of love
And Christianity is increased two-hundred fold.

The dogmas of trees contain the wisdom of God
But how many men understand?
—Charles L. Nelson

Kellie Marie

For Kellie my love
There's nothing you and I won't be able to work out and solve;
Anything on me you will be able to call!

You arrived on Oct 28, 1991. Oh what a very special day
You couldn't have had a better doctor than Dr. James Gay;
Money or words couldn't thank him enough, that goes without say

Oh yes, to me you mean so much
It's so, so nice to now feel your soft gentle touch;
And be able to hold you in my clutch!

For you my little one, I'll always do my best
My sweet little girl we'll keep a very tight nest;
I'll always put you first, never mind the rest!

Yes, you see you're #1 "Kellie Marie"
You've changed my life for the best, so much clearer I see;
For you I'll always be there, even when you fall and skin your knee

This world is rough, but we'll make it you and I
Honesty is the best, always remember never lie;
Never be afraid to show your feelings or cry!

Kellie your nickname is "Bug"
I love you so, I'll always keep you warm and snug!
—Brenda J. Sawyer

Destiny

Every time I touch you
there's such a strong feeling there
No one has ever taken the time
to know me, to love me, or to care
When I look at you there's
a special warmth in your eyes
The love we share has grown
and its now something neither of us can hide.
I'd give anything to be with you,
to have you hold me in your embrace
Destiny brought us together,
the love we receive from one another
could never be replaced
If I had to live life without
you by my side, I wouldn't be able to live
Because without the love you share with me
my heart would forget how to give. There
are no words to fully describe the feelings
in my heart. And I pray to God every
night, that we will never part...
—Jennifer Ramirez

Best Friends

Best friends are truly a "gift from God"
They love you no matter what path you trod
They share in your happiness and in your pains
They share in your losses and in your gains
You help each other in any way you can
With loving and open hearts and hands
You know that with life's busy pace
Things at times get out of place
So when sometimes things are in a mess
You offer to help and give it your best
The friendship is strengthened along the way
And for it, you give thanks to God when you pray
Life is always easier to bear
Knowing that best friends are always "there"
It helps to know you can always phone
So you're never really alone
They are really God's angels from above
Sharing His acceptance and love
—Bonnie Jean Hern

Hillbilly Blues

In that hillbilly country! In that hillbilly country!
There's that place where you should be.
And though you show that true love, and that true rock and roll
You share that hillbilly love and their true songs.
And though there's this crooked old man, and his crooked old dog.
they both live in this shabby old shack.
And though the two get along with this pearly white goat, it
provides them their milk and cheese.
But as the two take a stroll, where it's down to the mart.
They barter for some food in exchange for their milk.
But while the two hit the hills to their home up above.
The old man starts to play that hillbilly music, all over again.
And while you hear that music from the hills,
where you hear those songs of old.
Its a place where you'd want to be.
And though you hear that rhythm of the beat that's coming from
the hills.
The crooked old man sings his blues away.
But as the dog hears the beat while the old man sings.
His dog starts to howl away.
Up in that hillbilly country.
—*Dale Hendrickson*

Tired Ole Heart

   God Bless the little children,
     They are such a special gift,
   Whenever my grandkids come to call,
   They give my tired ole heart a lift.

   They are very important in my life,
     And I'm proud as can be,
   When they walk through the door,
     And have come to visit me.

   They are such a joy to have around,
   They make the old feel young again,
And warmth comes to a tired ole heart,
     Every time I see them grin.

   When I hear them call me grandma,
     I silently say a prayer,
   Giving thanks unto the Lord,
And ask, He keep them in His care.

   For they are the golden thread,
That keeps my life from falling apart,
And they are the warmth and inspiration,
That deeply moves this tired old heart.
   —*Betty A. Macy*

Our Children

Our children.
They grow beyond our ken, become strangers to us
   And grope forward in their own way, deaf to our experience.
Some grow to greatness, some to plodding mediocrity
   But showing a sturdy courage facing today's obstacles.
Others fail us, and themselves, abysmally.
In that instance, self-doubt creeps in.
Did we do too much? Too little?

Inventory of ourselves is not a bad thing if done without
   a convenient memory.
To probe too deeply in the ruts and furrows of ourselves
   proves uncomfortable—full of shame and regret.
But wait—apologies and atonement aside—
Whether near and loving or distanced in soul and body,
   They are still our children.
And, after we tire of sculpting our todays with our actions
   and ideas, they are the molders of our tomorrow.
I, for one, am grateful for it.
I am growing weary.
   —*Jewel Kindred*

Untitled

If our ancestors came across an ocean to find freedom, why did
they persecute and seek to destroy all that did not believe as
they did? They created that which they claimed to want no part
of a place to live that was just like 'home'. They didn't
understand the People, or how they lived, and didn't try to
learn. They just destroyed all that was not their way, in their
eyes the only way. At least the People were willing to listen,
and let each believe as they chose. Now, we, with our
ancestor's example, look to the stars and beyond. Who would let
us find them, if they knew what we had already done; destroy all
that is not our way. If Mother Earth is truly to be saved, the
People will have to show us, if those left of the People still
remember the secrets. And, if they don't, we can only blame
ourselves. We did nothing to change our destruction, and we
still hold the People captive. Are we really more advanced?
Show me in our souls, our spirits, are we better than the
People? Perhaps all that they did was not right. Have we done
so much, that we have no guilt? Or do we choose not to face
the truth? We declared "all men are created equal." In my
eyes there are, but I don't know how to show this to all.
   —*Anna Flanagan*

My Flower Garden

Kindness and consideration, little acts of love,
They say are watched by someone, and registered above!
Someone in authority says each good act you've shown
Plants a lovely flower, every kind you've ever known!

Here the story veers a bit, as an explanation,
Maybe things will clarify with some concentration.
Grand-dad was a Florist, Horticulturist, in town.
His roses were most beautiful-anywhere around!

So every little kindness I do down here on Earth
Has a bit of selfishness, a flower, each one's worth!
For every little kindly act, maybe God will see,
And leave a note for Grand-dad, to plant a Rose for me!
   —*Florence Bland*

A Walk In The Woods

I wander through the woods, lonely and depressed,
thinking of the news I got
this morning as I dressed.
Daddy sat me down; Son, he says to me,
when you wake up one morning
you'll be surprised at what you see.
On the trees the leaves will disappear,
only branches will you see.
And with those words he left me
To run and ask the trees.
So here I am a-walkin'
through the forest grand;
now you find me talkin'
to the trees upon the land.
I tell them all my troubles; Boy, they say to me,
Didn't your daddy tell you
that the leaves come back in spring?
No, says I, as I shake my head, he never told me that,
I thought that you were dead and gone and never comin' back.
With that I left the forest, with a smile on my face
as I went to tell my daddy what a silly mistake he made.
   —*Christina Ables*

My Mom

Moms cuddle you when you're young,
They tell you "no" when you stick out your tongue.
They watch you grow up into an adult,
Moms remember all those crazy insults.
Moms love you no matter what,
Even though you drove them nuts.
We remember all the hugs,
Even though they never got rid of all the stained rugs.
They remember every time they dried your tears,
And how they loved you year after year.
They remember every birthday,
How young they wished you had stayed.
Moms remember how they kissed all of your mistakes away,
They wished you would still be their little angel to stay.
They knew they had to let go,
That's how moms are, you know.
In their heart, you're always their sweet little precious
angel, you see,
In your heart, you will always let yourself be that "me."
They love you forever,
They will leave you never.
They are there never to depart,
You see, I love my mom deep within my heart.
—Billie Cook

?

Tires squeal to a halt, wild eyed they pour out of the truck
  They're in luck.
Rushing over to tables piled with treasures and junk.
There's Mom's battered but sentimental trunk.
Aunt Ellie's old lemonade pitcher with a crack
Son's toy engine, red caboose with a circle track.
The clothes so neatly stacked are scattered.
As eagerly they seek for bargains that matter.
Granny's rocker, faded foot stool, cross stitched sample of the
Golden Rule.
Odd sets of dishes, hand painted vases, lovely porcelain dove
Afghans knitted, crocheted table cloths, quilts pieced with love.
Odds and ends gathered from 50 years of wedded life—
They're buying a find—old tarnished silver knife
That cut our cake—also tins for apple pies.
I smile and heave a sigh for years gone by.
To no avail for it is my "yard sale."
—Helenmae Manon

Dreams

Have you ever noticed that in dreams
  Things aren't always as they seem?
  Colors, clear or blurred together,
  Depend upon the dreamy weather.
  Flowers hear and rain falls there
  Around your fuzzy teddy bear.
  You live again in the days of old
And dream up stories that remain untold.
  You learn to fall and then to fly,
  You ask the questions and don't know why.
  Look into the eyes of children unborn
  Or know the danger and not what to warn.
  Dance with the devil, sing with the sky,
  Sit on the mountain, watch the world go by.
  Be a great hero, or no one at all,
  Speak to the animals, know their own call.
  See the old railways, ride the pony express,
  Soar with the eagle, put your faith to the test.
  But don't ever forget, when you awake,
That dreams aren't just memories, they're chances we take.
—Janelle Yates

I Want You To Know, Son

Son, there are some things that I'd like to say.
Things you may not hear often, but I think of every day.
You are the foundation on which I've built my life.
You help me go on, even through toughest times.
Almost everything I do is because of you.
Sometimes you think that I work too hard,
Or that I'm almost always on the go.
When you feel this way just say, "Mom, take it slow."
And, Son, when you feel left out because I'm so busy,
Get my attention; say "Hey, Mom, remember me?"
When I was carrying you, Son, I knew how special you'd be.
You're the greatest blessing that God's ever given me.
You've brought so much joy to so many hearts.
Your sensitive, caring ways brighten my world each day.
Though sometimes I fuss when you want to act up,
Please remember, my Son, it's because I love you so much!
My Son, I pray to God each and every night,
To give me strength and guidance, that I may raise you right!
—Connie Murray

Thanksgiving

I know as I, you all give thanks for the
things you've enjoyed your lives long.
Friends, family, pets and such, the strains
of a heartwarming song.

The blue of the sky, in mid-July, when the
sun is shining so bright.
The sights and sounds all around us, a bird
with its wings stretched in flight.

The happiness spread by the children, as they busied
themselves in their play,
To kiss them and tuck them in bed each night
always made us a most perfect day.

So think of the countless blessings bestowed,
thank God for the pleasures of living.
Remember the treasures enjoyed on this earth
and make all of your days thanksgiving.
—Herbert Cook

Plates Awaiting

The forks and spoons sat by the plates,
thinking long and hard,
dinner must be late.

The water glass breathed a sigh,
not to be chilled by passersby.

The platter wondered if time would come,
for those to boast,
about the juicy, tender roast.

Serving spoons lay in their spots,
waiting for the food from pots.

The ticking louder of the clock,
reminding all of dinner not.

The time had come.
The time did go.

Where were these guest of dinner at?
With food still warming in the pots,
all the plates and all the pots,
think their dinner guest,
FORGOT!
—Della Koster

Second Chance

If I spent one more day
thinking, retrieving, wondering
I would drive myself insane.
But, for now I don't care.

If I really wanted to tell you
I would, I could, I should
But I don't think you'd listen.
Yet, now I wish you'd hear me out.

If I tried to figure out the past
I'd regret it, I'd hate it, I'd hope to forget it
Because I made a big mistake
By not informing you on how I felt.

If I ever got the chance again
to hold you, to kiss you, to love you...
I would grab it and take you back
Because now, I'm sorry we said goodbye.
—*Holly Jeanine Guardiano*

The Clock

Patiently ticking away endless time,
This accountant of life reticently performs
   its never ceasing task,
Without thanks from the life it governs,
It works faithfully until its days are done.

As all things reaching points of obsolescence,
It is replaced by the new and improved,
A journey that shall continue into perpetuity,
Until extinctiveness is reached.

Clocks, appearing as clinical and arduous instruments,
Are so characteristic of their makers,
Steeping the atmosphere with irony,
For having man as its creator.

Such a masterful organism to be without life,
Yet, exuding prophetic subtlety.
—*Howard H. Mackey Jr*

A Cheatin' Truck Driver-My Husband! Where Are You Going Darling?

You pulled up in your diesel and said, "You're not going to like this, but I'm going Saturday morning truckin'."

Then in the dark of the morning, what was this excitement in me when I saw you gettin' up to leave
-it wasn't because you were thinkin' of lovin' me...

You promised you'd be pullin' in home around three...
-oh, why couldn't you be here now, lovin' me...

They said at the yard, your pickup was gone and your rig was in the repair shop — my heart wanted to cry out — don't! — stop!

My mind told me what my heart didn't want to believe...
-you were goin' cheatin' on me...

As the hours slowly passed by, all I could do was lay down and cry, listening to every passin' diesel and looking for your pickup in the night...these hurtin' feelins just aren't right!
-babe, look what you're doing to our love...

After talking to you all night long in my prayers and almost hopelessly blue — on the phone, it's my darling, you!

Through every sobbing tear I heard myself saying, "Babe, I never stopped to realize how much I've been hurting you — come home darling!
—*Donna Lee Mello*

Night's Surrender

Dark evil lies in corners of the night;
This evil, yes, darker than the blackbird.
Witches and warlocks hide from human sight.
How can the sins of night seem so absurd?

But in its wickedness of dark does lie,
A painted picture of white by moonlit brush.
Small creatures hidden now let out a sigh.
No more is this dark world of night in hush.

A ground that's frosted of the moonlit splendor,
Reveals the inhabitants of evening.
Creatures show that virtue won't surrender,
Even though the vail of death is falling.

Evil nightfall spells that always fail,
Let the beauty of creatures prevail.
—*Anne Mauro*

Life's Auctioneer

How much am I offered, what do I hear?
This is tho chant of life's auctioneer.

How much of yourself will you give today?
Will you pay the price or just walk away?

I have a treasure worth more than I ask.
It'll take just a moment from your busy task.

It is old as time and we still call it love,
To have it is rare, it's a gift from above.

What am I offered? How much do you care?
Life will give back the amount that you share.

Will you speak gently to someone who's sad?
Will you lift up his heart and make him glad?

Do I hear a voice? How much did you say?
Raise your hand high and your heart will obey.

Come share your joy and your compassion, too.
You may help someone find life that is new.

You will value this treasure I'm offering you.
It gives strength to be kind in all that you do.

Join in the bidding for soon you will hear
"Going - going gone! From life's Auctioneer.
—*Elsie Brayman*

Red Man Black Man

The sound of nature fills the air. It beckons me to listen, in this moment to share, a time of life long since gone by when eagles soared across the sky. When mighty warriors, swift of feet, lived and hunted o'er this land they thought was their's to keep. The sound of nature fills the air. It beckons me to listen, in this moment to share, on the bank of a river, maybe this one where I sit, was the place for docking very large ships. Ships with cargo not of food and grain but of men and women snatched from the bosom of their mother-land; to be kept in bondage yearning to be free—as I am now enjoying the beauty that surrounds me. The sound of nature fills the air. It beckons me to listen, in this moment to share, the message of this river as it runs beneath my feet, the secrets that it holds and will forever keep. Maybe, if we're still enough lessons can be learned from the history of our land, from all the twists and turns. That God has provided for each of us a place, to pursue our hopes and dreams no matter what our race. The message is clear amidst the sound of nature that fill the air, it beckons each one of us to listen and with some other person this truth to share.
—*Brenda C. Smith*

My View

What of this aggregate
  This totality of me,
Gathering disparagement
  By failures' spree?...

To look beyond to view
  But to maintain my own.
Not to see them or you
  In lieu of my nature's tone.

Disparagement as views maintain,
  Not the object but the source.
The demand of self to wane
  As only through life's course.

To be surprised as new appears,
  Belongs, indeed the view.
As encroach the other, defined, the peers,
  Alas, it's 'me and you'.

The view beyond, to really look,
  Sees something unique of them.
Not the same as me, of course
  But now by part of her or him,...
I view, I see and I learn of Love!
   —James M. Huffman

New Moon - Full Moon

Thank you Lord for letting me view
This wonder - this celestial ball
That reminds me once again
You are my All in All

I know you are beholden to your creator
The same as I
They call the years I now live "golden"
Seeing you - I know why
How do you hang so alone in space
Able to shine, with a smiling face?
Your countenance ever so bright
Even in the darkest of night.
Is it because you are so high?
That your light reflects
Our Lord so nigh?
   —Alvera Victor

Gospel Songs

When you hear
those old and dear
gospel songs,
they just seem
to reach down into your soul.
With gospel music, people experience
many emotions: Peace, Joy, Happiness,
Love for God, and His Holiness.
As humans, there are emotions
that we all go through —
Heartache, pain, joy, sorrow and strife.
These are some things
that may happen in our life.
When you hear or sing
those beautiful gospel songs;
Both old and new,
those songs seems to comfort you.
When you're saved,
you know that Jesus cares for you.
And, He loves you, too!!
   —Donna L. Jarrell

Untitled

Abby Rose, don't cry so
Those tears may stain your cheeks
Save that salty potion for toasting
Celebrate!
Live your pain, don't drown it out
(feel the steely edge?)
Tears will only rust it
Leaving dull and wasted sorrow
When you stand upon your father's grave
Don't wet that ground with grief
Save those precious little gems
For when your child is born
Then as you bathe that gentle being
In the tears so long you've saved
You'll finally know the meaning of
Your Daddy's special gift
   —Joseph Britton

Untitled

How many times had I walked to the shore gazing out to the sea,
Those unknown places and pleasures calling out to me.
My life was content, secure, my home warm and safe;
But my soul longed to wander to a far and distant place.
And now, as the ship moved away from its moor,
I knew my course had been set, I could go back no more.
I thought of my home and the friends I would leave behind,
So many thoughts, so many memories raced through my mind.
I stared into the dark deep waters below feeling fear... hesitation;
What lie lurking there, what dangers would haunt my destination?
Then my eyes lifted to the sun, the clear blue open sea,
And the fear melted to hope as a calm came over me.
For whatever lie ahead now, whatever life dealt out to me,
It would clearly be of my own choosing as to my destiny.
My heart was content in knowing it would never wonder again,
About what life could have offered, or the way things might have been.
   —Dane Smith

Warped Ambition

Judas
Thou didst not know her
Nor her tender love for thee
Else thou hadst ne'er betrayed her Son
For paltry sum
Of thirty pieces silver.
She knew his worth.
'Twere better thou with her
Thy bargaining hadst made.
And then
If thou hadst willed
Thy sin
Like even that of Peter's
Wouldst now resound
Not to thy shame
But to thy everlasting fame.
But now alas! 'tis all too late
Thy greed for gain and pride
Were means fulfilling prophecy
Thou Decide!
   —Dolorine Mathaller

I Wonder Why

The farmer said,
"Thou hast bloom, beauteous and fair.
O lily, yet not rare:
In the open fields where're I go
A million I find as fair as thou.
Blue butterflies do come and go
Flitting here, there, then over thee:
The meadow's blossoms all seem to say to the butterflies,
Come hither, hither here's the nectar for thee!
But at daybreak lovely and fragrant
Thou has the sugar the butterflies want;
And yet with a cold blast thou swingest to and fro;
A sip thou deniest them as they fly by,
Please tell me why!"
The flower answered,
"Cast thy magic wand, I pray thee,
Upon him who is far from me, lest he forgets me;
Its for him thou has sowed my seed,
All, my all, must be for my own blue butterfly."

—*Angeles Trinidad-Aradanas*

Rainy Days

A rainy day can be great —
Though the best of it comes late.
A birthday in which to age.
A day not to stay home caged.
A simple call from down your way;
Which speaks words I need to hear you say.
Your voice thrills me more—
Then all the goods from any store.
To hear you say how much you care;
To you I give my life to share.
A rainy day can be very sunny—
Just to hear from you honey.
A rainy (or sunny) day can be dreary,
Because no word from you makes me teary.

—*Ella Majors*

Time

You mark the beginning of creation,
  Though you are yet to come tomorrow.
You thrill the child with anticipation,
  While you fill the old with sorrow.
You are a healer to the wounded,
  And a brutal foe to the lonely.
You are the factor on which life is founded,
  While life's span is set by you only.
You are the force that brings wars to their end,
  While your infinite span breaks warriors' hearts.
You are to change an inseparable friend,
  While everything it builds you tear apart.
But with all your power given from above
You will never be able to conquer love.

—*Jeff Ridgely*

Even So, Father, For So It Seemed Good In Thy Sight

We know not what God's tomorrow my demand
They may call on us to let got the hand
Of one we've walked with many a mile-
Never more, this side, to see his smile;
Nor, feel the tender caress
That brought such happiness.
When that time comes, Lord, help us say:
"The Lord gave and He hath taken away."
"Blessed be The Name of The Lord,"
And, looking not back, go forward.

—*Betty Gentry Christner*

What Happened To Dr. Mayer When I Really Wasn't All There

The people who lived in my former Irvington slum
thought that Dr. Mayer was really dumb
They wanted him to go straight to hell
as they pushed him downstairs, he fell
sprawling flat upon the floor
not being able to get out the door
When I saw him just lying there
I really did happen to care
I cushioned his head and stroked his beard
telling him that I was not to be feared.
We both expressed our prevailing love of each other
despite family enforced separation from one another.
While waiting for an ambulance, it was Dr. Mayer
who told me that every night he said for me, a prayer.
And that when the going go tough, he would always be there
Perhaps not in person, but always in heart
We would never be too far apart.

—*Chris-Mary Repiscak*

Mirage

If the lake could mirror my
  Thoughts today,
I'd see your face as the
  ripples play washing ashore;
While the swaying leaves
  whisper your name
In their gentle breeze,
  As they upward soar.
The golden rays of the afternoon sun
  Kiss my cheeks, as you've
sometimes done tenderly, sweetly.
  The sailboat glides with
  smoothness, then wild
Into a turn, and changing mild—
  Discerning, discreetly.
As twilight dims and stars appear,
  I feel your presence ever near
    Tho we're apart.
  A peaceful tranquility comes with night,
A deepening yearning, burning bright within my heart.

—*Jeanne S. Agnellini*

Memories Of You

As my lonely nights and days go by, only memories of you linger through.
As I walk by a flowing stream, I remember all our happy dreams.
As I see two crystal clear champagne glasses sparkle, I remember our happy faces shining all so bright.
Now I've come to realize that you no longer love me, so now my lonely days and nights grow longer.
Although we once have sworn that we would always be together, that now is just a fading memory.
I'll always remember what we once had and shared, I'll remember the good times and the bad, now I'm trying all so hard to forget you, but those memories of you I'll always treasure.

—*Josie Lea Vallejo*

Brat

You were one of our favorites for so many years
Through a lot of laughter and a lot of tears
Being part of your family was your choice alone
You came out of nowhere and made this your home
Such a little puppy you brought us your love
I'm sure you were guided by heaven above
We've seen each other through ups and downs
At times all of us behaved just like clowns
Then came the time your age started to show
Every thing you did was done very slow
Your ears failed you, your sight was no more
Still you found us by sniffing the floor
The day finally came after fourteen short years
You were laid to rest through a flood of tears
Someday I'll see you, we'll be together again
Nothing or no one will part us then
Until then you'll live on it my heart
That way I know that we will never part
   —Betty Smith

A Leap Of Vision

On dusky spheres spreading defiant night
Through daybreak's walls blazing blue light;
Bursting earthly images I imagine,
   A leap of vision:

To hear the voice of Creation
In a deep rolling thunder,
And be beyond our sun
Where eternity dwells in wonder

To touch the Infinite
While dancing with starry flows,
And in their wondrous orbit
See supernal essence create endless Cosmos

To hold lightning in your hand
And behold Universes seething in a sea
To encompass ultimate reality and
Become the witching hour beyond Eternity

To fly on a Moonbeam's mane
Where galaxies swirl in a pond
And there, on that celestial plane,
   Live Beyond!
   —Ernest L. Davis

The Beauty Of His Love

In nature's beauty we can see,
This tall specimen called a tree.
The beautiful colors in the flower
Some are short and others tower.

The beauty in the lakes and rivers,
The ocean's depth give us the shivers.
The small fishes is mountain streams.
The mammoth whales of ocean dreams.

His love shows through all creation,
It abounds in every nation.
Some in the desert and in the plains,
The most spectacular on the mountain range.

The beauty of His love shown through,
When He died on the cross for me and you.
His true love really shone the best,
When His resurrection gave eternal rest.
   —Edward D. Gompf

It's My Place

It's my place to become whomever or whatever I choose to be;
Through Jesus' blood we all have been set free.

Sure, there's hard trials and tribulations in running this race,
But, John Newton said it all in his song, "Amazing Grace."

Martin Luther King shouted out loud, "Let Freedom Ring."
Romans 8:37 says through Christ Jesus we can conquer all things.

Proverbs 3:6 states,
"In all thy ways acknowledge him and he shall direct your path."
God will provide whatever we need, if we would only ask.

It's my place to become whomever or whatever I choose to be,
For nothing is impossible through Christ Jesus for you and me.

Rosa Park road a bus, and she refused to stand.
She sat boldly in her seat, for it was part of our Master's plan.

We boast about our hard times, what's right,
What's wrong and what's fair; this is true,
but let's take a stand for the world to see God in us
and what we can do.

It's my place to reach down and give my brother a hand,
For God looks at our heart not race, creed or color of any man.
   —Bertha Hall

In My Heart

   She'll remain with me
Through life and through death
   She'll be watching over me
Through good and through bad
   She'll lend her shoulder to me
Through joy and through pain
   Just as before
Only now she is above feeling no pain
   Crying no tears or feeling alone
She'll remain in my memory
   From start to end
She'll help me to see
   From dawn to dusk
She'll help me to learn
   From my mistakes
She'll always be there
   In my heart.
   —Donna Irene Rowe

"Roads Apart"

Through his eyes the world is kind.
Through my eyes I see only blind.
With his touch he feels love and friendship.
With my touch I feel only hardship.
His smile is true, the lines that form
Around his lips for years have never faded.
My smile soft but short, lines not yet formed,
Only anticipation.
His walk long and with stride,
Mine hastened by sounds going by.
Different as he and I are,
I know where I've come from
Even if I do not know where to go.
The road that led together now must part.
In him still kindness, love,
And understanding of humanity.
In me a need to feel and see
The life ahead of me.
   —Diane Peterson

The City

The city I know best-poverty, sickness, and death.
Through the crowded streets of the city you go-
Driving round to and fro.
   Horns honking, sirens blazing-it's enough to make you lose control.
The crowded streets, the polluted sky-but you live for it
You reply-
   "I love this place yet I do not know why. Could it be the people, the places or just the brown sky?"
   Hustle and the bustle-on the city it thrives,
The bums and the bankers-yet they do not know why.
The glamour! The excitement! That's just a lie,
Under its layers there's nothing inside.
   —*Brian Gordon*

The Old Oak Tree

It started with great grandpa, when he planted a twig. And throughout the years has grown so big. That old oak tree, has served so many, for many of years. Even though its branches have mostly all rotted it stands there still. The swing is still hanging, but the ropes are all worn. The barks all tour away, and mostly all gone. You can still see places where we curved out little hearts. And there is nothing left of our tree house it has apart. The moon use to shine so bright through its branches which look at like monsters at first glances. And when the wind blew, the shadows were so scary on the wall. So up from my bed I went running down the hall all through the years so bravely, you've stood. And now for this winter. I crown you fire wood. That mighty oak is now ashes and dust. To keep those old termites from making a fuss. Again the cycle starts one more time. And some of your little acorns have done just fine. Soon they will be as big as can be. They're shade the whole yard just you wait and see.
   —*Annie Raines*

Does Anyone Hear My Cry?

As I watch the wind blow gently,
thru the trees, here I sit.

Wanting to know,
Does anyone hear my cry?
Wondering, what do I have to do...

To have someone to love me.
To hold me gently, like the wind,
blowing thru the trees.
The wind, blew gently across my face...
Did the wind hear my cry?
As I watch the wind...
My tears dry,
The wind as all around me...
Holding me ever so gently.
   —*Diana L. Gladman*

Chosen Seven

Chosen Seven selected in prime;
This had been planned for a long time.
Schemes and plans had been selected,
Chosen seven had been elected.
Their flight into orbit they wanted to claim,
It was a dream of fame.
Was a thrill soaring into the blue.
Only an instant all was through;
Chosen seven had trained with culture,
Will be history for the future.
   —*Alyce Marie Oellien*

Have You Ever?

Have you ever heard the wind blow—
Thru the trees — on a rainy night?
And heard rain drops a-dripping?
Like little feet a-tipping—
Thru the leaves on a rainy night.
Have you ever seen a tiny beast—
peeping from its den—on a wet dawn?
As the sun rises like a golden eye—
And starts its run—across the sky—
To leave a world warm and dry-when it's gone?
Have you ever seen twinkling stars come out—
Like winking eyes—that are gleaming?
Thru pale shadows—that cross the land—
Where trees—like sentinels—stand—
To watch over a world that is dreaming.
Have You Ever?
   —*George A. Bailey*

Grandma's Boy

As the sun brings warmth and brightens my day—
thus too — my grandson's smile affects me the same way.
As the flowers and nature bring beauty to my being—
I've been made aware of what he is seeing
Thru those little blue eyes just barely three
and realize how very much he means to me.
A tot so lively — he drives others around him — wild —
But he is grandma's boy and a special child.
As I grow older and remember my own —
I know this little boy's not mine — he's just on loan
From parents who love him as much as I
Who know that as the years swiftly go by
Grandma won't always be around to enjoy
Their little treasure and now grandma's boy!
So each day we two discover the world together
Two children — a grandma and a small boy — as if
we had forever.
   —*Heidi Gehlen*

God's Smiles

In trouble and in Grieft's God
   Thy smile has keep me all.
      all the way.
And joy has God's love which around
   my path lay all around us.
      The hours of pain and yielded good
         wick days refused.
Like herbs through retiring
   spread ever where when we are
      bruised. But God is with us
         all the way.
   —*Beulah Malleen*

Thinking of You

Thinking of you I'd often smile
Those telltale eyes no alibies. I'd
often wonder, I'd often grin, It's you
my love the heart to win.
Thinking of you, your like a rose
give me consent, I would propose to toast,
to cheer to hold your hand
make me the happiest in the land
Thinking of you, is but a kiss
I love your charm, the tenderness
and with this thought there comes a ring,
you'd be my queen if I am your king.
   —*David Dadonas*

A Young Man's Cry

The moon was high in the sky. He pulled me close to hold me tight. And as we stood there in the cool night. I felt him shaking in my arms. I pulled him closer to hold him tighter. I looked up into his eyes. His tears fell upon my forehead. Like rain falling to the ground. The moonlight made his flowing tears glisten in the night. As the tears ran down his cheeks.

"I feel cheated," he said, but only in a faint whisper. "It's okay to miss her, it's alright to cry." I stated to him softly. I only wish I could say I understand. But I know I never will. The pain is just too great, and deep inside his heart she'll always love you as much as you love her. He looked at me from behind a sheet of tears. "I know," he said, and hugged me tight. "I bet you've never seen a grown man cry before" he smiled. Although for all that he's been through is enough for ten men. He cried like a lost little boy. At sixteen though, it is a young man's cries."
For Adam, with Love.

—*Jamie Lynn Warner*

Night Of The Lonely Soul

Have you ever stood at the edge of
   time and space
   alone and utterly lost?
Have you listened to your song
   of memories that tears a cry
   of despair out of the depth
   of you, that echoed lost and forlorn
   through the cold void of space?
Have you ever experienced the acute
   agony of sadness that stripped
   the essence of you bare and
   left you in the shadowy
   valley of desolation?
Have you cried in soul shattering
   agony for help and only the
   cold silence of space echoes back your cry?
If you have, then you walk with
   the soul of all who have lost
   the flame of a loved one
   through the portals of death.

—*Brooke W. Adkinson*

Waiting Until Midnight

Shadows fell upon the earth; the light faded from its glory.
Time echoed as if to quicken its rate; the minutes ticked as
   fast as a bat senses its prey.
I sat still, but my mind raced with wonder.
I felt calm, but my nerves clutched my fear.

What will become of me? What will happen to my soul?
The time for me to depart was close; I knew that the end
   was only a few hours away.
The window closed, and that showed me less hope.
The door slammed, and her power crept closer.

Now darkness covered the night; no moon captured any remaining
   brightness.
Please let the time come to a halt, for her spell will
   otherwise make me what I'm not.
I felt rested, but soon I'll drift into sleep.
I sensed terror, but fear won't faze me.

Where will she send me? Where will my soul helplessly travel?
The clock struck midnight as she approached me; she touched
   me, phased into me, and gave me my death.
She pumped me; the succubus killed me with lust.
She guided me; hell awaited my cursed soul.

—*Adam Altman*

Time For Legacy

Dwell not upon the past
Time enough to reside therein
Eventually residing amongst immortals
Beethoven, Florence Nightingale, Debussy, Galileo,
Michelangelo, Shakespeare, all dwelling
Within God's realm
Beyond today, future is tomorrow's dream
It may or may not exist
What will be, shall be.
"Now!" Time for Legacy.
Dwelling amongst the living
Immortal I cannot be
Contributing to humanity in the "Now!"
Validates existence for today
Whilst poems are read, songs sung, writings read,
humanity serves amid life's symphony
Time and distance will merge
In the interim, kindred spirits shall intermingle
Prepare for a new birth
Legacy is born when we enter the realm of the past.

—*Dumas F. Frick*

Girl Behind The Wall

   Lookin' out from the crack losin' track
Time goin' bye - blockin out the cry
Knowin' who you are you can't run far
Girl behind the wall hear my call
Afraid of a shadow from within
Budding with goodness - battling sin
Reachin' out for today so much to say
Girl behind the wall hear my call
Grieved by others' words not much
More to lose beaten and used
Girl behind the wall hear my call
Listen to my voice singin' loud
And clear
You gotta love first the one
In the mirror
Girl behind the wall hear my call

—*Cheryl Thomas*

Time Passing Quickly

The clock tics softly as the hands sweep by.
Time passing quickly and here I lie.
Flare-up again, how long has it been?
Without any pain, I don't know when.
Time passing quickly and here I lie,
watching the people living their lives.
Scurrying and hurrying and moving around,
flare-up again, got to lay down.
Time passing quickly and here I lie,
can't go along, just waving good-by.
Maybe tomorrow, wait and see,
have a good time and don't worry about me.
Time passing quickly and here I lie,
God only knows and he knows why.
Tomorrow comes quickly, ever so fast,
could this be my day of peace at last?
The clock tics softly as the hands sweep by.
Time passing quickly and here I lie.

—*Debra K. Berger*

Time

Time stands still when there's nothing to do.
Time stands still until you have a drink or two.
Time has meaning, new found freedom.
Time is nothing when you rule your own kingdom.
Time is nothing, but yet everything you need.
Time takes advantage, discovering greed the end.
The end is very near.
So close to the eyes, yet there's no fear.
The end is harmless, assurance and surprise.
The end is coming, don't despise.
The end is so close, won't take but a second.
The end is over in the drawers cabinet.
The end is sharp with little pain to see.
The end is blood trickling down from me.
The end is over and now on its way.
The end is will begin all over, tomorrow's a new day.
—Jaime Schuetz

Christmas In The Country

Christmas memories in the country, this time of year,
Time to look for Santa and his eight reindeer.
The hard ground was covered with pure white snow,
Artistically layered and it's glistening gave off a glow.
Jack Frost painted the barren trees a glitter of silvery white,
The sun shining down from above gave off a brilliant light.
Frost on the windows of the house, oh what fun,
Draw pictures, make faces, before it melts from the sun.
Children coming home for Christmas, planning meals and treats,
Hastily preparing the food, making bread, the meats.
Packages beautifully wrapped, nativity-set placed
under the decorated tree,
We'll catch old Santa with deer, just you wait and see.
Lunch of cookies with milk, placed near the tree, for when he comes,
Should we ever catch him we'll ring bells and beat the big drums.
The children when small would look down the long dark lane,
Santa we couldn't be sure, sometimes we heard an airplane.
Dad got out the classe sleigh and a team of horses harnessed,
with bells,
The enjoyment of all, plus catching snow-balls with yells.
Memories of Christmas in the country, this time of year,
Oh what a blessing for families and friends we held dear.
—Dorothea Ruth (Urban) Lux

The Empty Chair

Like the hourglass on the doctor's desk,
Time will run out for all the rest,
It ran out for you, dear lost father,
Each year goes fast, your memory is farther.

You taught me music, and to love sports,
You encouraged me with friends, my cohorts,
You drove me to school when I was late,
I never suspected your moribund fate.

We used to fish, as was our wish,
We'd go in a boat that was always afloat,
You weren't buried at sea, but on the land,
You were a mystery to me, the "leader of the band."

This passover we toast and have a chicken roast,
You used to boast, but with modesty
That you knew Walter, studied with Toscanini,
And taught me religion, like the parting of the sea.

I miss you now, but mostly on holidays,
Passover is here to my amaze,
I conduct the seder, as you taught,
But grief is with what I am most fraught.
—Alfred Elkins

First Fire

Creeping, anonymous, gently stroking my soul;
tiny sparks, at first unnoticed,
sloughed off, unrecognizable, yet persistent,
gently tapping, tugging shyly at my inner being;
pitching no tantrums,
yet determined to burn and blaze within me
throughout my life;
then, at the last, remain an ember
between the pages of my book,
an ember waiting (hopefully)
to stir another still sleeping poet
to awake, recognize, and fan
to a blazing inferno,
their first fire.
—Jane Taylor Overton

A Daughter

A daughter's a blessing in more ways than one
  To a mother and father or even their son.
A mother is happy to have everyone meet
  Her daughter. A miss, sincere, so sweet,
Who'll stand by her side when cares come along
  To help close the blues with a beautiful song

It's a thrill, to be sure, for a mother to know
  A daughter will chat, confide and will great
From maidenhood sweet into womanhood fine,
  Possessing the virtues and merits sublime
A daughter, indeed, is a princess divine.
  So thank you, dear God, for giving me mine.
—Betty Brobst Fenstermaker

Fate

It is my fate to love you
To attend to your wants and needs
To wait patiently for a smile
or a look that could lift
my spirits or restore my soul.
It is my fate to miss the words
as they cascade across your tongue
and fall to earth around my feet;
or float wistfully to the clouds.
When you are away I am empty.
I am alone and isolated.
Cut off from the reality of life.
I can only sit and wait
for you to return to my life and me.
It is my fate to love you.
Beyond this life, beyond this world,
to love you for the smiles you bring
to an otherwise drab and ordinary person.
—James R. Anders

Small Child

  When you were a small child wasn't it so grand
to feel a fluffy kitten sometimes lick your hands

  Joyous and wonderful to walk in pure white snow
or sometimes run down a hill as fast as you could go.

To sat and watch a bird build it's nest so high
or tried to jump and catch a cloud from a moving sky

Oh! My friends when sorrow comes the world starts
closing in how I wish with all my heart I was
a child again.
—Anna Kirby

What Is A Son?

A son is a man child sent from above, God's gift to his mother
to care for and love. The image of God placed in her hands, a
beautiful brown-eyed baby to be formed into a man.

My son is so precious, my arms love to hold. I thank God for
trusting me with, his valuable soul. I learned as I held him,
he wasn't really mine. God only loaned him to me for a period
of time.

To make my life happy; with joy to fill. He's special in every
way, I know he's God's will. He is molded very quickly, by
example more than words. Will I show him love, honesty, and
determination, and not only let them be heard?

He soon grows from baby to a busy little boy. His work is his
play; his tool his toy. His mind so inquisitive, his tender
heart never a bore. God's word in his reach, his soft hands
did explore.

A pleasing personality, a music loving child, very obedient,
patient, and kind teenager with a heartwarming smile. Sensed
at a young age, life's road he must trod. Perceiving it
mandatory to be controlled by the Holy Spirit, in order to be
transformed into a shepherd of God.

Called into the ministry, God's sheep to feed and attend.
Guarding and guiding them from straying into sin. With fervent
prayer, compassion, and preaching he reaches for the lost.
Enduring persecution, rejection, and hate has reaped a harvest
of souls. Leading them to the cross.

With love, dedication, and tenaciousness he will overcome. A
God-fearing, Bible-believing, faithful man, I'm proud of you
Rev. Michael Owens — my son.

—*Frances Owens*

Special Person

It takes a special person
   to care until the end,
Tote bedpans, change sheets,
   and still wear a grin.

This old man, bent and broken,
   warehoused here to wait for death,
Doesn't know how mean and cruel
   are the words that pass his breath.

It takes a special person
   to care and still be kind
To this old relic of the past
   who's lost control of body and mind.

Remember, Special Person,
   this pitiful soul I brought you
Was once God's fine creation,
   a man so kind and true.

So please be kind and patient
   and do the best you can
To take care of my precious friend,
   to me he's still a special man.

I know God will surely bless you
   and hold you in His love,
And you will wear a crown of stars
   when you reach Heaven above.

—*Barbara S. Barker*

Giving

It's true God gives us lots of time
To carry out his plans
But are we making use of it?
and do we understand?

There are those of us
who like to wait
until we've pleased ourselves
and things we know that we should do
we place upon the shelf.

Did you give someone help today
So they would know you cared?
Did you say it won't come true
The awful things they feared?

The man upstairs is keeping count
Of things you didn't do
And when you see him
   face to face
You know he'll question you

So each day do a deed
   that's good.
Make someone glad their
   living
You'll never miss a thing
   you loose
And that's because of giving.

—*Evelyn Carter*

Yesterday, To-day, And Tomorrow

Yesterday is fast
To-day is now
Tomorrow is coming
Where were you yesterday
And what about to-day
And wonder where you will be tomorrow
Who is to say
Was yesterday a good day
Did you do a good deed in any way,
Just try to do better to-day
Continue with dreams each day
It will surely be worth while
To make the best of each mile
To have lived yesterday, and now to-day
With visions in the future
For all the on comings, of tomorrow
It's a great life for all
Who have seen many yesterdays.
Lots of todays, and hopes for the tomorrows

—*Connie Ayers Hall*

The Key To Life

As we search thru out our life
To find the key to end our strife.
We make it too big a task
When with this question we do ask:
"What is the key to life?"

As we go thru life's plan
We search to find what truths we can.
We make it too big a task
When with this question we do ask:
"What is the key to God's plan?"

Before our life on Earth is done,
Our search has been joyfully won.
What we thought too big a task
In answer to the question we did ask:
The key to life is: God's Son!!

—*Clynis A. Benson*

Seashore

We left our home in Maryland
   to drive down to the Bay
Watch sea gulls soaring overhead
   where children love to play

First we saw castles made of sand
   an interesting surprise
Long tunnels deep that soon collapsed
   with disappointing cries

We came to watch the steamboats pass
   with wakes of foamy white
Together splashing through the surf
   was everyone's delight

We dug for clams without success
   then how could we resist
A foot race on the beach to face
   invigorating mist!

Sunset calls for an oyster roast
   the appetite now craves
A good fresh oyster on the shell
   as sunbeams dance the waves.

—*Clara Evelyn C. Cummings*

Childhood Dreams

To quickly learned life is not what it seems
To easily awakened from childhood dreams
Every memory is still locked in the heart
All the feelings that seem to never part
Expectations low and hope continues to fade
Searching for light, still trapped in shade
Pain is deep conquering from within
Losing touch, insanity is sure to win
Afraid of love always slipping away
For any happiness there is a pride to pay
Hurts to remember, hurts to forget
So much of life is filled with regret
Tears fall hard, never seems to end
Words that need spoken, rules that bend
Promises from long ago went unkept
Been such a long time since misery slept
There is no place left to hide
Emotions are stored, better left inside
To easily learned life is not what it seems
To quickly awakened from childhood dreams.

—*Angela M. Diobilda*

Goose Chase

Up here is down from there;
To get in is to get out.
The central point, I do declare,
Is a question of doubt.

I hear a sound
Sharp and clear,
Is the mid-way
In my ear?

A speedy chase, is this trip is real?
A search for tomorrow.
No time to look back
Or review pain or sorrow.

This world turns
And dark is light;
Catch a wild goose
In it's flight

—*Eva D. Patterson*

God Granted My Request

Lord, I asked you years ago,
to grant my one request.
Let me live to see my children raised,
and help me to do my best.
Lord, you have granted that request,
for which we give you praise.
Not only are my children grown,
but you have given me extra days.
Now I am enjoying my grandchildren,
that you gave to me.
I want to thank you for these blessings,
I know they come from Thee.
I asked for my children this same request,
that you granted me.
And help them to teach their children,
that Jesus they may see.

—*Jim Smith*

Thank You, My Love

It's been a wonderful experience
to have the most incredible night with you
It was a night made in heaven
thank you for the dance that we have
it was so incredible, that at last
we could have that dance together
I miss you, I love you, I'm yours.
The roses that you gave me
meant so much to me, nobody gave me
flowers before, only you, the man that I loved.
You in your sporty clothing,
I in a beautiful red dress,
just like the color of the roses.
You could not believe your eyes.
He said to me you look more beautiful than ever.
We stood the hold night and morning together.
It was wonderful the warm kisses,
the hugs, the love making, your words.
Thank you, Elisamuel, for letting me know
what really love means, thank you, my love.

—*Diane Gonzales*

Love And Memories

   As I walk along the river's bank and my mind begins to wonder,
Overhead dark clouds gather as they start to thunder.
   Even if the sun did not shine and the sky was filled with rain,
You take away all my earthly troubles and all of my life's pain.
   It's you that gives me hope and faith,
It's you who erases all my hate.
   It's you that makes everything shine bright,
It's you that makes my life so right.
   And even when death takes me into its embrace
And I am finally set free,
   The only things I will take from this mortal world,
Is your love and memories.

—*Michael Zamorsky*

Departure

"Good-night," I said, then kissed his brow-
   This boy not yet fifteen.
He oft resisted, but not now,
   Bed-tucked and quite serene.

He looked at me, the eyes so grey,
   And whispered from his bed:
"Good-night, dad,"....then went away...
   No more "good-nights" were said.

—*Joseph J. Mauceri*

John, A Professional Business Man

John had super standards,
To his business he had grade A in his cards.
John always coordinate with his employee.
It was always a sense of good will,
He succeeded always in the business he was in.
It was always willing to give and take
In his order of the day,
John charmed his way.
The variety rules he had it didn't matter
But his business was attractive and never bad,
John had willingness to go on, and on,
With his employees he had,
Their sweetness that he won,
His patience is more than important precision,
All of the above is for his own satisfaction,
A dedication from his Mom,
John is now a professional business man.
—*Catherine E. Pawlowski*

Ode To Life IV

"But, Still, Life! I want to contain you!
   to hold you! Impossibly
    embrace you to my breasts, alone
     waltz with you through infinity…

"Ah, but Life, you cannot be held.
You cannot be embraced. Your
   vastness
  can only be viewed in the awareness
   of the moment

"Even you cannot design a cup
   deep enough to hold your wonder
Even you cannot find a far enough horizon
   to conquer
"But, Life, in the silence
  of an unsuspecting moment…
    You come to me
     and I know."

Ode To Life V

"And, Life!" I implore, as you stand
   at the inner chamber door
"What can I give, other than the gifts you
   have already given me?

"And your response bursts   my cup
   and you become the sea of me
    filling my tributaries
     beyond capacity

"Now, in cyclic wonder…I am
   given to fill your estuaries,
    knowing at overflowing,
     I ride a new tide
"'Til my arteries give…
   and the sea of me and fresh air meet
    still, another ocean…
     another journey."
—*Ann R. Essance*

False Pretenses

The flames licked upon my heels, ordering me to bow down,
To kneel, yet I refused, I chose to defy
I chose to speak out, speak my mind.
They told me I could not, I couldn't be true
I had to stay quiet, I had to be you.
Yet again I refused, I rebelled
I had something to say, words to tell.
So I spoke my mind, I let it free
All the time knowing what was in store for me.
Tried and convicted, like I committed a crime
When all I was doing was speaking my mind.
We had our rights! We had freedom of speech!
Never knowing it was out of our reach.
We always say we're true as can be, but we lie; you are me.
What can we do, but hide all mirrors
Scared to see our true faces any clearer.
And you asked me why, why did it have to be?
But what could I say? Welcome to reality.
When all is said and done, all I can do
Is look in the mirror and say, "At least I'm not you."
—*Amina Akhtar*

Little Things…

I could help you walk,
To learn to talk, to giggle, laugh, and sternly balk.
At little things.

To ride a bike, to skate the block,
To skip, and hop, and write with chalk…
All little thing…

To play the keys, both black and white,
Or blow soap bubbles thru a pipe…
Such little things..

All adding up to where you'd get
To ride the bus that went to school
To learn about the Golden Rule…
More little things…

To leave our love, to journey forth
When college called without remorse…
No little things…

And then there came a harder time.
To let you go your way, I mine,
To live a life rewardingly filled…
With little things.
—*Dorothy V. Smith*

Life

    Life is beautiful in every way,
      To live for God each and every day.
  Let us give our best, coming from the heart,
    In giving our best, we will do our part.

     Life is the beginning to the end,
Like the blending of love. and the blowing of the wind.
     Take the time to balance the scale,
  The quality of the sides will complete the sale.

    We should all think about our life,
    Make it beautiful, with no added strife,
    To falter repeatedly by the way side,
  Prepare for your safety, with a safe ride.

  To make it right, we must rely on the cross,
  Our souls will be saved, with no added cost.
  Those who live by God's Commandments alone
  Have no problems when it is time to go home.
—*Florence Daughtry*

Alone

What trepidation exists between my mighty bones?
To live or die; to go or stay...
To heave to or shove off.
What is this death, this bereavement, this separation that haunts me night and day?
To live or not to live. To die, to go away or stay...
To play and have fun. To run?
None of it makes sense to me except my mighty Lord.
Without the God of my youth, I should surely perish.
Without Him, what exists for me that is pleasurable?
Naught. Is He all I know, shall have, will have before I die?
What of the many days I still care to call my youth? A sleuth could not find happiness in these bones though I am contented.
What else to ask of life? The spice of my living has never existed.
Philosophy—the thinking, reasoning, the why-where-fore to be of me? Yes, that I like. But what else?
The physical universe leaves me cold. To bold are the humans who call my space home.
They would eat me alive if I did not fight for my survival....
Arrival? The unknown shore. I shall get there alone...and I shall always doubt, very much, whether or not you really helped.

—*Jeanne Albers Rennell*

Time

So many years have I to spend with you
To love, to laugh, to weep and then we're through.
Spending days that are bright, days that are blue
And all too soon we bid the world adieu.

So many months have I to spend with you
Winter months, stark and cold; spring months, bright and blue;
Summer months, fruitfall and growing;
Autumn months with their golden harvest hue.

So many weeks and so many days
To work and share your loving ways
So many hours and so many minutes
To enjoy the world and the life in it.

So few seconds in a moment of time
Our past fleeting spot of glory
Will anyone remember sometime
To tell the world our love story?

Time goes on, the memory fades.
The body grows weary, the eyes become dim
The only hope we can ever have
Is God's promise that we have from him!

—*Beatrice Harnago*

Unconditional Love

To love without reservations and implicitly
To never question incidentals of one's origin or where one is employed
To extend affection without affliction
To love unconditionally...without mitigation
A goal seldom achieved; but, a goal often set.

The love of a mother for her newborn child
The love of a sunset when life nears an end
The love of a friend when life's gone awry
Without reservations and implicity.

—*Alice H. Chastain*

Untimely Goodbye

Avoiding doctors all her life, she thought herself immune
To pain and sadness and despair, in the end her mortal ruin
The hospital beckoned, she dared not go, afraid of what lay ahead
The virus was slowly wearing her down, in weeks she would be dead
"My beautiful pool days are over", she moaned
Her positive outlook on life had gone
A purple haze above her head, her breathing began to slow
An eery sense encased the room, she gasped aloud - "Oh no!"
We sat and watched with bated breath.
She loved her life, no matter what, believing it would never end
Death came to her as a mortal foe, not a welcome guest or friend
My life has been forever changed, I love her more each day
And now I know, for the sake of Mom, I'll live my life "My way."
I'll look at what I have right now and dream of what lies ahead
I'll love as much as I can bear and hope that my love will spread
And when my time to go arrives I know it will be okay
I'll smile and pray and thank the Lord for this, my final day.

—*Erica Goodstone, Ph.D*

The Crimson Carpet

It was great-grandmother's
To pass down
To every generation within sound
Of the need for warmth and grace
Who provided for it a special place.
Many come and many go
But few there are who really know
The secret of its jewel red
And the intricate pattern on which they tread.
A yarn of an adventurous one
Who to a foreign land did run
With the love of her youth
Celebrating the joy of truth.
An eye for things keenly wrought
From the blood of others who also Heaven sought.
The woven pattern is the tale
Of the years lived out by every male
Who finds his heart in loosing it
To another whose soul is likewise lit.

—*Holli Johnston Traylor*

Vietnam Moving Wall

Hundreds come from all over this country
To place their hands on this wall,
To touch the names of their loved ones
Who have given their lives to the call.
We can feel the energy within it
As we place our hands to the stone,
Our loved ones reach back and touch our hearts
And we suddenly realize, we're not alone.
If the spirits of all these thousands of soldiers
Were inside this wall looking out,
They would tell us how much they loved u
And that freedom's what their all about.
A father's tears trickle down his checks
As he touches the name of his son,
Remembering the boy who grew into a man
And served his country as his father had done.
This wall is a part of American history
And will remain in the hearts of us all,
The freedom that each one of them gave us
Keeps our nation the one standing tall.

—*Joseph A. Weaver*

Sonnet To Dixie

Please hear my song as I lose touch with strife
To praise my sister, Dixie Dear, my queen.
She's been an angel to me all my life.
When I found birth, she'd almost reached thirteen.
She claimed me as her child, her baby boy.
At that time we were far from mother dear.
Sis fell from school, stayed home to deal my joy.
With her there near, I had no cause for fear.
We lived that style until I reached age three.
Then mother came and took me far away.
It took twelve years for me to ramble free.
I tried and tried to find my way to stray
   Back where my Dixie and I fell apart,
   But Dixie, all this time, dwelt in my heart.
    —*Ben Hicks*

We'll Meet Again

When I start to die, I am going to try
   to put up one hell of a fight.
I was given birth, to leave this earth
   but I want time to be just right.

I will not give up, to drink that cup
   filled with coffee every morn.
Greater than wealth, has been my health
   since the moment that I was born.

If I should get sick, I know of a trick
   that might let me get well again.
I may lose the battle, so don't tattle
   wanting to live was never a sin.

After I leave, you just want to believe
   that I put up a hell of a fight.
If it could've been done, I would've won
   to be sure everything was right.

As I go to my grave, I want you to save
   tears that are falling that way.
I will learn to love, our heaven above
   knowing we'll meet again someday.
    —*Howard Golley Jr.*

Rain

  The old trees lift their branches toward a paling evening
    To raise a humble offering toward a rainwashed sky.
  Now everything is rainwashed and all the branches pearly;
    The earth is darkly damp and smells of life.
  The mountain stream is rushing, its curdling mud is boiling
O'er the boulders' hollow rumbling as the torrent hurtles by.
  See, now the leaves are fresher as they droop above the water
    Their colors ever brighter for the rain.
  The evening spreads its shadows, merging with the greenness,
    Enveloping the stillness of a forest washed with rain.
  The evening air is vibrant with the song of thrush and warbler
    But it cannot still the torrent nor the rain.
    —*Betty Evans*

The First Computer

These modern times are the age of the computer.
They might even turn out to be your tutor.
And as one programs information into the machine
Very shortly we will be witnessing a scene.

But this amazing creation is far from new.
There's been one assigned for me and you.
And for centuries it has been fulfilling its roll.
The first one was originated when God gave man a soul.
    —*Dante Gramolini*

Daily Blessings

Oftentimes I pause each day
   To raise my eyes above
And thank the Lord for all the ways
   He has of showing love.

He blesses me with food each day
   To keep my body strong,
A place to sleep and clothes to wear
   And fills my heart with song.

And all the wonders of the world
   Are there for me to share
With splendor far exceeding what
   I search for in my prayer.

My joys are wrapped in blessings
   That fit me like a glove
And yet the greatest joy I've known
   Is having Him to love.
    —*Bob Day*

We Are Indebted

Hosannas to the protesters of the plight of the masses,
To researchers who toil to salve our suffering,
To keepers of the peace,
To resisters of hate and wrongful action,
To kindlers of faith and learning.

Hallelujahs to clear sane minds,
To harbingers of health, cheer and laughter,
To givers of understanding, compassion, love,
To creators and inventors.
To the courageous who brave the unknown.

We are rich with the balm of companionship.
With the yield of the earth and the beauty thereof.
We are blessed with the brilliance and spiritual
   goodness in man.
We are the doers and the indebted.
    —*Florence K. Wiener*

Lord — I Pray

Lord, I pray for the inspiration
To say what needs to be said!
Words that will sink so deeply
Into my loved one's hearts and heads!

Words that will fall on attentive ears
And stir action in sleeping souls,
To awake from the apathy and indifference
That over this sinful world rolls!

Lord, you said to "come ye apart
Into a desert place and rest for a while"
How I pray that my loved ones meet you there
Where His love and peace overcome life's trials.

Though we live upon this earthly place
We must not let it claim our souls,
For it is up to Heaven we must look,
As we labor to meet life's spiritual goals.
    —*Alice Tohill*

Special Friends

It should be my job you see.
To see the world outside for thee.
From the first morning's sun-lit ray.
To through-out, the entire day.
From gentle winds, to the rustling breeze.
As the wind blows thru the swaying trees.
To feel the air before the rain.
To telling you of the storm I see.
How it's building clouds up in the sky.
Then throws the lightning, with a tremendous thunder cry.
While lighting up the entire sky.
So let me tell you of the majesty.
That nature throws each day at me.
Thou the greatest pain that there is for me.
Is that nature itself you cannot see.
—*Charles L. Cunningham*

The Clown

I crawled into my soul
To see what I could find.
To my surprise, I am told,
A clown of the oddest kind.

We headed down my rocky road
Looking for chips of silver and gold
Somewhere along life's weary path
They chipped away till all had past.

My funny little clown and I,
We traveled far and wide
For those sparkles, sweet and bright,
In my soul of tormented night.

His great pockets of clowns
We filled with magic I had found
With jewels jingling each step,
We finish picking all the rest

I hopped out of my soul
A look into the mirror,
The funny little clown
Most certainly did appear.
—*Jane Kurtz*

A Man's Life

You came into this world, so fair, to live, to die, our souls to spare. With words so true and deeds so fine, the lame to walk, sight for the blind. Chastise the "good", forgive the bad, You started as a very young lad. And grew in statue, poise and fame, but never wanted material gain. You ignored our weakness, forgave our flaws, and offered Life to one and all. With steps so slow, You took a walk, with slight hesitation and little balk. With whips they beat You, and thorns did scratch. No reasons they found to make their attacks. But walk You did to Calvary, where on some trees they did hang three. You in the center, with thieves beside, one was ignored, for help the other cried. Again forgiveness was your mark, the one who asked, You took to heart. And then You died, all hope seemed lost. Your garments to win, the dice were tossed. But as You promised, You did arise, in glorious praise and alleluia cries. Death no longer wins, You are set free, and life eternal is available for me.
—*Jesse E. Smith, II*

A Picnic At Sunset

What would you give
to spend time alone with me
on a white sandy beach,
the horizon melting the sea
and the sky together
in endless shades of azure.
White caps rolling into waves
as they crash into the dock pilings
when the tide rolls in.
Just the two of us
picnicking on a blanket,
basking in the warm summer sun
in awe of our surroundings
as the sun begins to set.
Shades of purple, crimson and gold
with the sunset reflecting its golden trail
of liquid light
in farewell of another day.
—*Jennifer Merth*

Katey Brown, On Wind Swept Streets

Listen children while I asleep
to stories told on wind swept streets
where icy rains like rivulets fall
on sidewalks paved along concrete walls.

Hear the clock strike half-past twelve
the hour when all seems well
for grace and wit will cast their spell
to lend a hand to this ghostly tale.

A maiden fair in a snow-white gown
her face streaked by tears that reached the ground
knelt beside an earthen mound
that bared the name, Katey Brown.

O! Katey Brown, Katey Brown
the stonecutter's chisel
etched in sound
the name, Katey Brown.

For you see beneath that earthen mound
lay a maiden clad in a snow-white gown
her name - etched by sound - was
    Katey Brown.
—*Jamieson Steele*

My Country

From the Canadian border on the north
To sunny Texas in the south;
From the deserts and the plains
To the Mississippi mouth;
From the Appalachian mountains
To the rockies in the west;
From the Atlantic to the Pacific,
With beauty we are blessed.
It fills your heart with wonder
When you see an eagle soar;
When you view the deep Grand Canyon
Or hear the great Niagara roar.
Look at the Statue of Liberty with
Her arms stretched open wide,
To welcome all the strangers to
Whom freedoms have been denied
This is my United States where
I can worship and vote without fear.
And with all her troubles and faults,
I thank God that I live here.
—*June Bennett*

Duff

If we could go back
To the days of our youth
Oh much wiser we'd be

We'd solve all the problems
Before the mistakes
Then simpler life would be

But oh if that's possible here and now
Well we'll just have to figure out how

'Cause first there's a problem
Right after mistake
That gives us a problem somehow

Now without the problems
That come from mistakes
Our minds would soon be still

And learning and growing
Touching and feeling
Together would add to nil

Now if these words are confusion
Bringing you disillusion
And causing you to repeat

The words I'm displaying
All together are saying
Off your Duff and onto your feet
—*Joel Thomas Newcome*

Blind-Battered And Abused

From my first slap on my small white butt,
To the hard core be stings I got as a teen,
I was blind-battered and abused.
From prehistory to this history,
I was kicked from basement to bedroom,
I was blind-battered and abused.
I shall be praised by many,
And despised by few,
I was a child,
Beat-broke and torn apart.
And at times I was turned inside and but,
I was blind-battered and abused.
For God sake,
Let it end,
For God sake,
Let me die…
I am so God dam tired.
of being —.
Blind-battered and abused.
—*Denis Allen Trehey*

Precious Moments

Nothing can compare
To the precious moments we share.
Whenever you hold me in your arm
I feel safe, secure, without any harm.
Your kiss is tender and sweet
You lift me off my feet.
Your look is so sexy and soft
I find myself aloft.
I look forward to being with you
For now I'm happy, never blue.
These precious moments are so dear
To none other can compare.

I need you and
I love you.
—*Judy C. Brogdon*

The Price Of Freedom

Sold! I heard the auctioneer exclaim,
to the woman in back, getting soaked with rain.
I shoved the box of rags, under a nearby table,
I'd pick it up later, when they had sold the
things from the stable.
When I came home, I was completely empty handed,
Except for the box, I felt I should have
abandoned.
I thought what the heck, I might as well look.
Somewhere in the box, I might find some coins
or a book.
As I dug through the box, my eyes filled with tears,
and I turned back the time, some twenty odd years.
For at the bottom of the box, lay the faded
red, white and blue.
of a tattered old flag, that reminded me of you.
Of the blood that you shed, so that I might be free.
I wish you'd lived, I wish it could have been me.
—*Betty Wineland*

Time

Let us not turn our thoughts of now,
to tomorrow.
For tomorrow, cannot be begged, stole, or borrowed.
Only anticipated.
And yesterday, a lifetime away,
from today.

To peer into the looking glass.
A view through a fish eye lens,
Frozen in timelessness, caught for a moment.
In our thoughts.

As the future lies waiting in the wings.
Un-seen places, un-known faces.
Un-spoken words, never heard.
But known, within the framework of our hearts, and minds.
And time.

Lifetimes roll away.
Like water, from a ducks back.
In the end, all is connected.
Somehow.
—*Brian M. Jackson*

The King Who Crys

The Saviour stood before me; I to my knees,
to view His pain, His bitter begging pleads.
Here was God, crying to His child.
In my visit to heaven; no imagination enough wild.
To feel His crushing pain upon my very soul.
a life altering message, to better my role.
The pain was that of a thousand mothers, losing a thousand sons.
Each very precious, losing His precious ones.
Look at Him He cries, and He is our God.
Shuddering me to the soul, for what is the odd.
What does it take to make a King of Kings cry?
A million folds of compassion, I know that is why.
Don't hurt Him. You wouldn't if you knew.
And those who realize are much to few.
"Chose me!" He begs. Have you ever seen a King who begs?
Our King does, breaking His back and His weight bearing legs.
Believe me, He cries in heaven, and the angels can't console.
He cries for His children the ones that satan stole.
—*Gabriel B. Santiago*

Steady Ground

Mountains on a Reservation, I'm thinking about an Indian dance
To ward of evil Spirits, each man takes his chance
Sun comes up to glory, sun keeps going down
Pinewood River is flowing, I'm standing on steady ground
Steady Ground
Steady Ground
I don't need Walls or Bridges, as long as I have two hands
passed down from generations, ancestors in the sand
deep seed rhythm is calling for something I haven't found
there's only one way of knowing, I'm standing on steady ground
Steady Ground
Steady Ground
I'm looking for a change of Season, I'm moving one step at a time
Eagle high above me, the River of life on my mind
carry me with reason, please don't turn me around
as long as I keep on trying, I'm standing on steady ground
Steady Ground
Steady Ground
Steady Ground
—*Albert Paul Thomas Waugh*

Daddy's Smile

What I would not give to see the smile on Daddy's face,
To watch his caring lips smile down on the little ones in
his embrace,
To see it stretch so very wide when we all come home to stay,
To feel its radiance as he watches his grandbabies at play,
To know that smile is always there for friends and family too,
To be assured that it is filled with love for me and you,
To experience that smile complete with all its laughter,
To be confident that it will be there today and every day after,
What I would not give to see the smile on Daddy's face.
—*Bette Delay*

The Waves Crash Down

I love to visit by the sea,
   To watch the waves as they break free.
They crash and then spread out of reach
   And go in and out along the beach.

I feel refreshed; I feel so young...
   A grateful song it should be sung.
The sea, the sky, a perfect blend.
   I wish this day would never end.
—*Janet B. Dole*

De Kooning

The last surviving school of modern abstract expressionists
Today has an artist who paints a while longer; yet exists
In the world of art...
Willem de Kooning, who in the quiet year of 1993,
Still lives, age eighty-nine, with Alzheimer's, soon to be
An immortal glory of remembered historical classic art,
Paints women like ice aegean primate females, where style starts.
Three years ago my father visited him, when he was strong
He would paint a work, once a day, as he has been for long.
De Koonig is probably the last of the Picasso avant-garde
Ergo their generation passes, and their memory is in regard.
—*Anatole Kantor*

The Dance Of The Hours

Today that the morning is fresh, blue and exuberant
Today that seems to be a player boy the morning
and the sun looks that wanted to go running
behind the clouds, in the far away extension,
Today, I would like to laugh..........

Today that the afternoon is golden and lightened,
Today that the fields are singing a song of life
under the concave sky, that is reflected on the sea.
Today that seems the death was sleeping,
Today, I would like to kiss..........

Today that the moon has an ashed color,
Today that the wind says ambiguous thins
at whose step bristle its mistletoe the sea.
Today that the hours have a more slow sound,
Today, I would like to cry..........

Today that the night has a tragic doubt,
Today that the leisures in the shadows, a mute question
in what something sinister, seems is going to happen,
that the chest is washed by the nude sadness,
Today, I would like to die..........
—*Carmen Garcia*

G.L.A.D

Glad to care for one more child
tomorrow -
   Their friendly smiles make my
life worthwhile;
   Laughter fills my heart with the
"Love" I've been missing???
   Hugs and toys with many little girls and boys -
   Memories of joy and special times ***
"Thanks go up above" for making me
Glad to be me - (G.L.A.D.)
And I know "someday" all the caring
I have shared in my lifetime; will
bring me "happiness" to last a long
time in the future
   A time when I can have children
I will call my own -
     "A Family"
—*Grace L. A. DiBella*

Banana Pudding

   He was ten and taking his Saturday night bath,
tomorrow they would all go to Church.
After Church, dinner would be served.
Many dishes would be on the tables,
Displaying the skill of those able.
Connoisseurs would stalk the tables,
making their choices of the dishes.
   Of deserts, there were many,
but banana pudding was the favorite.
They were on one table at the end.
The center one was a beauty,
of banana pudding, he had never had his fill.
He placed a big spoon in his pocket,
for this was one time he would satiate his desire.
   When the preacher had finished grace,
he had already taken his place.
He grabbed the center pudding and began to run,
across the road and into the woods he went.
He sat under a tree and began to eat,
till his desire for banana pudding was spent.
He lay under the tree and gave a sigh of content.
—*Gerald O. Merritt*

We

We're two old fogies—up in years
Too darned busy to be filled with fears.

We watch for the postman to bring our mail
We don't deal much with courts and jail.

We're bit stove up and too plump to run
But we aren't convinced we should carry a gun.

We have some clothes and a comfortable house,
Plenty of food and a cat named Mouse.

We have a lot of books and three TVs.
We respond to requests if you just say please.

When Girl Scouts with cookies come to the door
We buy what we can—and sometimes more.

We greet our neighbors with a friendly word
And we often gossip of what we've heard.

We have a van and we have a car.
We travel some, but we don't go far.

We don't live in church nor in the gutter
We don't play golf, but we love to putter.

We have no computer, no yacht, no boat,
But you'll always see us in line to vote.

We're living our lives the best we can—
Just one old woman and one old man.
 —Effie B. Hutchison

Brother

Toiling on the farmland, herding in the pasture
Tooling down the highway, swinging through life's journey
Flying with the eagles
Piloting his ship among the clouds and sunshine
To find his way, to make his mark, to build his legacy
He chose a soft landing in the orange groves
An extended lay-over in his golden years
A time to mellow, a time to bask in the sunshine
To walk the country greens;
Commanding attention to honor, pride, success
Hard-won by a farm boy
A Tuskegee Airman who championed the cause
An Air Force Colonel embodying strength of determination
Commitment, loyalty, sensitivity, love of family, friends
Brother in truth and deed
To persevere, to rise above it all;
And when he was summoned to stand down
His mission here completed
The final entry of his flight path logged
He flew away to soar with the Lonely Eagles.
 —Lois Williams Young, Ed.D

The Woman I Love

The sunset's golden fingers
 touch your wandering eyes
The globe of fiery orange
 mirrors in your sky
Across the sea, around the world
Behind mountains, hills, plains and trees
 in villages, towns and boroughs
Over oceans, lakes and cities
From space and orbital views
Above the atmosphere blue
Every setting sun
 becomes a sunrise too
 —David Quamme

Ode To Absolute Safety

Looking from a gorgeous sunset,
Toward the ultimate storm.
Full spectrum astern so come about
But even rain sometimes feels warm.

Overtaken anyway by
freezing watery gales.
Get below and batten down
Play it safe under these bulging sails.

Hiding from the hurricane,
You'd stay down there night and day
And hold fast until it passes
But another one's on the way.

Heels to butt with arms around shin,
You're on a shaky trek
'Cuz cringing below is about as safe
As being up on deck.

I rather stand tall on the bridge
'Cuz there's always a storm somewhere
But when you sacrifice spontaneity,
Paranoia strips you bare.
 —Ben Sedgwick

The Diary

Memories written on white paper,
Traces of tears that tried to wash away the pain.
Of broken promises, misplaced dreams,
and illusions oh how life was
"suppose to have been."
Evidence of broken lives,
all written across the page.
Thoughts of confusion
you plainly can see.
Memories, written on white paper
Before my eyes to see.
Tears fall quickly
still blotching up the page.
As haunting memories reach out
with a stabbing pain.
Once again reminding me,
some things never change.
 —G. Jujuan Barnes

Memory And Time

Memory runs reversely on the
tracks of time;
as it tries hard to find
the rare and special moments
that time left behind.

It sees a lot happiness,
as it goes backward through
the years.
Occasionally, it stumbles upon
a scene that displays both fears
and tears.

It explores the realm of childhood,
which is filled with fantasies and mirth,
Then discovers the state of reality,
where it met time at the moment of birth.
 —Arlene V. McMorris

Gray Skies Are Blue

Gray skies are blue when I'm thinking of you
Traffic jam's turn clear when your heart is near
I find the perfume that you wear so, sweet
As the rhythms in my heart skips a beat
Live the way that you want as long as your heart is true
I never thought that I could find a girl to love me thru
Just big, tall, or small girl your love is good
Turning around as fast as you could
Telling the world you'll my girl
Is as true as a real man should

Pick me up with a smile I look at you
Wondering just what to do as my life cling to you
Walking right by and sitting right down
As all of the other girl's that I've found
Are not like as nearly like you
Couldn't we've be together for a moment or two
I surely believe the things two of us can do
So why not lift your eyes up to the sky
And feel the rhythms of love run thru and thru
Not just mention to you the gray skies blue
—*Floyd T. Wright, Jr.*

The Lonely Fisherman

I am a lonely fisherman so very far from home.
Treading the murky waters for the source of my income.
There is danger beneath the waters in this dirty river bed.
In various shapes and sizes and very much to dread.
Be careful not to stumble and fall, beneath the mire.
Or eyes will be upon you and you'll be all that they desire.
—*James Clary*

Dead Leaves

I felt most sad last night.
Trembling like doves, unable to reach them,
That grimy pain from wandering so much,
That clear brightness of canvas
In silv'ry nights not finding you,
That roving tune of rippling secrets o'er the sea,
All made me cry.
What wouldn't I bestow in sad nights
Like this one
To take even if only
a nearly malcontent caress
Or a wan beam of light
In the slanting twilight
Of my sorrows!
I know not; I am falling asleep
With the beads in my hands.
—*Carmen Chiesa*

Untitled

As the water flows freely
  trickling down on the rocks
I feel the crisp, cool water
  of Autumn drenching my socks
Pulling my feet away quickly
  and sensing the tingling in my toes
Which they felt like knotted bows
As I walked with swishing noises in my shoes
  I started to get the blues
When in the hot summer months
  The brook was warm and smooth
I could then walk across the
  rocks in my socks and shoes
—*Janice Rowell*

Faith Of Two

Clouds came over and determined to stay,
Try my optimism and weary my soul.
A never-ending rain dance keeps time in my heart,
Encourages the blood to flow through my veins
Yet, waits patiently for the showers.

The spirit is dry; the hope has turned brown.
If there is no water soon, the young cannot survive.
The arid environment does not nurture well,
And the saplings are pitiful imitations of the future,
Horrible reflections of the past turned around.

Keep the chant low and steady for I must believe
That somewhere, someone sends the same prayer.
If two of us in accord are heard
Through the dusty thickness, drops must fall,
And the choking will vanish as the clouds.
—*Jacqueline McCauley*

The Tears Of A Clown

I find myself in this world
trying to be someone — something, of value.
At times I feel lost in this great abyss,
drowning like a rock flung into the sea.
I feel as if I am sinking, quickly, with no way
to jump up and reach the surface. There are days,
though, when I feel like a leaf that just sits on
top of the water, and floats so effortlessly and so
peacefully. There are moments when I want to cry,
tears that never end, tears that burn with pain, like salt
in a wound. Suddenly though, there dawns the sun, that
renews the soul and gives to it life and the happiness of
a butterfly that has just emerged from its cocoon. There
dawns the day when the crying stops, and the tears stop
burning. The day when freedom comes, the ultimate liberation
from life and its pain. This is the day one lives for, the
great moment of happiness, the great moment of joy.
—*John M. Santone*

Trapped

To be awakened in the middle of the night from the cry of a baby
Trying to program your thinking to the infant's cry
Knowing the cry could only mean there's something wrong
Why is such a cry made at this hour of night?
So alert, so distraught, so overwhelmed with fright
On the outskirts of the outer limits of a predawn awakening
Needing all resources to bring the situation in control
The quiet awaken my senses to the fact of the security needed
The joy, that came with new life brought forth
The adrenalin flowing, the excitement exhilarating
I'm ready for the task at hand
Awake now, realizing finally, the baby is asleep
I think, I think
The sensation, too strong
The thought, overwhelming
Seemingly caught in a time and space voyage fantasy
What—reality too devastating, sleep or awake?
I'll never, I'll rest, I'll rest
Tomorrow, oh tomorrow
I will rest, it will be over.
—*Anderson D. O'Kelly Jr.*

Fantasy

In a fantasy world I live
Turning the pages, within my head.
Believing what I want to be
Seeing what I want to see.
Writing my life as I see fit
Working in scenes naturally.

Believing in a world of make believe
Hoping to be reality.
Dreaming on and on, that's me
Living a life that can not be.

Retreating there when things aren't right
Using it as reality.
Comforting myself in the darkest times
To shield the light of mortality.

Believing in something that can not be
Living a life with no stability.
Yes, it's me that you don't see
Hiding behind reality.
—*Jeanette Treaster*

The Fateful Two

In that special place so long ago,
   Two lovers fatefully met,
With smiling face and tender hearts,
   Beneath an amber sunset.
A lovely lassie and a handsome lad,
   Were they, the fateful two,
and hearts of flame pulsed together,
   Cupid's weapon deep and true.
Then in the beauty of frosty winter,
   At the alter in a citadel,
They fervently pledged undying love,
   To angelic wedding bells.
The years a drifting brought joys and sorrows,
   like the skies bring sunshine and rain,
But the anchor tossed in the storm of life,
   Held fast, not anchored in vain.
So hearts that bound on earth below,
   Bound reverently in heaven above,
As the fateful two stepped beyond the door,
   Love perfect and pure as the dove.
   —*Jean Manning*

Burrow Of Bud Poems

Dedicated to Bud Ehlin, Uncle of the H.S.C. at N.I.U.
Uncle Bud is the fellow who is kind of mellow.
That no one can paint yellow.
Because he stands like a pillar and sleeps with
out his pillow.
Unlike the devil, he is the guy you can follow.
Just don't stand in his furlow, because he plows
this under.
Stubborn like the mule and sharper than plow.
He is the one, when we are done, that wins, the
call of bud maestro.
   —*John L. Thompson*

A Country Girl

Bury me under a bed of roses
Underneath a tall, rose tree
So I can smell that lovely smell
for all eternity

Bury me under a huge, wide garden
underneath a garden wall
so I can watch the bright, new flowers
grow colorful and tall

Bury me in a blue-grass field
with lavender and lace
so I can feel each wistful breeze
bend every blade with grace

Bury me in a spring-time forest
with open trees and sky
So I can touch each pussy willow
and feel each bug go by

Bury me near a silvery lake,
under a silv'ry, bright, white moon
So I can hear each bird and toad
like in the month of June

And if all this can never be
If this should prove too tall
The, wish I wish above all this
Don't bury me at all!
   —*Judith M. Plytynski-Young*

My Best Friend

My best friends cares for all that lives.
Understanding and love is what this friend gives.

Tear filled eyes as trash floats down a stream,
Only sometimes finding happiness in a peaceful dream.

When together the world lies in the palm of our hands.
Yet, we never make selfish inconsiderate demands.

Not always concerned with self-centered needs,
Putting each other above all or any greeds.

No one is perfect and this we understand,
There's no need to criticize or reprimand.

Knowing of heartache, death, and pain.
We share our bleeding hearts without refrain.

Letting down my guard and opening my soul,
My best friend always wants me complete and whole.

Always responsible, never letting me down,
Making me laugh removing my frown.

Jealousy inevitable, yet over come by our care,
Only proud encouraging sentiments we share.

Never divided by money or uncontrolled lust.
Always bonded together by strong will and trust.

My best friend is smart, kind, and true,
I find all these qualities in all that you do,
That makes me see my best friend in you.
   —*Jeanette Barger*

Daydream

Daydreams, buoyant lilt on the battle's beach
Undreamed sunsets to seek, to paint the hues of music
for the soul
The tour to evolve, self-portrait's bole
Unveiled quicksand for hurrying footsteps
Drifting entrance of a transparent cloud
Untraced image with life's breath to cling
Reality to surge on folded wings
Whichever it may be, it is mine to redeem
A wanderer of the future with no guilty dream
—*Anna B. Kemmerer*

A Soldier's Endeavor

The house that stands seems a common place
Until I raise my eyes to a flag's pure grace
And I kneel in awe to a soldier's call
A soldier who never sought glory at all.
A flag never flew from his residence
And on special occasions he would sometimes comment,
"I only do a job for the USA
I try and do it well throughout every day
I never waste time on a job of imperfection
For any job can ba done well with effort and concentration.
Thus I try my best to make money for the Boss,
That way I know for sure my efforts are not lost."
—*Dortha Mae Parker*

All I See

All I see is the future like all that has past,
until this moment in time.

All I see the promise of a dream I can't keep,
that has stored itself in my mind.

All I see is the light that sometimes is darkened,
whenever I'm closing my eyes.

All I see is the truth as I listen to people,
telling me little white lies.

All I see is a reflection of a man in the mirror,
but he looks nothing like me.

All I see is the living as it dies all around,
not knowing how it feels to be free.

All I see is the sea as it crashes to shore,
exploding with a thunderous sound.

All I see is the sky as the sun passes by,
on it's endless travel of round.

All I see are the stars and opening arms,
that leave me waiting for more.

All I see is the rain, all the tears and the pain,
as I'm picking my heart off the floor.

All I see is a hole, deep in my soul,
waiting for someone to fill.

All I see is the eyes filled with love that's disguised,
waiting for the moment to be real.
—*Jon Lee Lauer*

It Could Have Been Me . . .

Do you remember when disco fever was in
Up all night listening to Grease and Bee Gees albums
When we saw Star Wars in the movie theater
and dressed as L.A. cheerleaders for Halloween

When we swam in your pool all day and went to slumber
parties at night
Riding our bikes all over creation
and skating to the beat of Roller Boogie

Do you remember our fights; the times we didn't get along
When we didn't talk for days on end and hated one another's guts

Do you remember when we grew apart and became vital enemies
Finding other friends and attending different schools

It seems like a lifetime ago
Yet at times it seems like yesterday
When, we were inseparable,

Now, we face the ultimate separation:
I here, and You there

Every now and then I seem to miss you in a strange funny way
I only wish you could have known . . .

It could have been me.
—*Jacalyn Glinbizzi*

It Will Be All Right

He was just a little fellow with hair of golden blond, curled
 up on a tattered blanket with trash all around.
 the three year old in her arms was restless in her dream.

The father made the circle each day hoping to find work, he
 would take anything, ditch digging, gardener, shipping clerk

His auto plant had closed six months past, the landlord had
 evicted them and the money didn't last.

He walked very slowly past the schoolhouse down the street, he
 knew come evening the family would not eat.

A voice called out from near the schoolhouse door, Sir do you
 mind, I have all this food and more.

I don't want to throw it all away, the children didn't eat it
 all at school lunch today.

The father gladly took it with tears in his eyes, and then the
 words he heard were a wonderful surprise.

"I know of a job, maintenance down the street, you can live in
 the building, though the rooms are kind a beat."

The father smiled and thanked the man again, the future now
 was brighter than last week it had been.

He walked a little faster back to those he loved, silently he
 thanked the God Lord up above.

She's seen the smile on his face, the tears in his eyes, he
 hugged her and the children, then told them his surprise.

They would make it now, with a job, shelter, food for tonight,
 he knew the Lord had heard him, and it would be All Right.
—*Doris June Winkelman*

God Loves All

Life on earth wouldn't have meaning
Upon God we all are leaning
Without the Lord to save our souls
Never on earth could we feel whole
God won't forget a single need
For all of our needs His heart bleeds
We are all alike, boy and girl
We are more precious than a pearl
Within our hearts we all feel pain
Upon our heads we all feel rain
If someone cuts us we all cry
If someone shoots us we all die
God is after the heart that's His
He has taught us what mercy is
A broken heart still reaches out
A gentle hand erases doubt
Love is stronger than any storm
The meaning of love can transform
The heart that is so far away
The heart that lives just for today
—Hope Rubinstein

In Memory Of Robert Burns, Scotland's Beloved Poet

Oh had I met you Robert Burns
   Upon the bridge of Ayr

Had I known your highland Mary
   With her face so meek and fair
Oh had I met you Robert Burns
   Upon the bridge of Ayr

Had I rambled in your cottage
   Had I slumbered in your chair
Had we strolled the banks of Afton
   Above the haunts of care

Oh had I met you Robert Burns
   Upon the bridge of Ayr

Had I known your highland lassies
   With their pearls rich and rare
I would have loved Clarinda
   If I were only there

Oh had I met you Robert Burns
   Upon the bridge of Ayr
—John J. Hoey

Dreams Vs. Reality

She had dreamed a thousand dreams
of a life full and challenging.
It was the endless work and long days
she had so much trouble managing.

Her dreams left her only with wants and a smile
of days fulfilled, dreams yet so be realized.
The harsh reality of life delivered the tired truth.
Those dreams of her life were now idealized.

A woman, yes, but so many more obligations.
The needs of others, the world does come first.
Today's woman just keeps on going and going,
as she watches her childhood dreams burst.

The burden on women today is very heavy.
So many roles to fill, and the expectations to do them well.
No one gives her credit, for it is expected.
She cannot stop, no time is allowed to dwell.

So many dependents, more than she chooses,
yet she plugs along, her head held high,
fulfilling demands that leave her empty.
At day's end, a silent tear glistens
As she looks towards the sky
—Susan M. Catalano

Stranger Mountain

Wild Honeysuckles spill their fragrance
    upon the mountain,
Yellow Bells and Violets stretch to reach
    above the molded leaves,
A swift stream makes a fountain
Flowing against a huge rock in the stream.

The chatter of a Pine Squirrel
As he darts across the road,
The wide spread wings of the Eagle
Soaring above, looking down for food.

A Doe and Fawn, bedded down,
In the shade of tall pine trees,
Waiting to got to the stream
Until they feel the evening breeze.

To see the Bluejay and Woodpecker
Hear the cooing of the Evening Dove,
To know this steep and rugged mountain
Cradles Cougar, Bear and Bobcat
    tenderly and with love.
—Jamie Stalcup

Photograph

There we were, on worn oak step;
Various pieces of cord wood stacked four generations deep.
The family dog, who someone must have called,
stands frozen in joyous gait.
Some of us smiled, some only looked - a few stared far away...
I balanced on my mother's knee, that mild afternoon of May-
too young to savor the love all shared and gathered that day;
Though now looking back, I see the warmth of color-
'mongst the whites, greys and black.
Countless days they've warmed my soul,
countless days I've wished them back,
as life's fire grows steadily dim.
The cured timbers of old are ash —
that burned while I was young,
and so the strands of life are strung,
until the pile is nearly done.
The green wood smiles though —
when set to stack on worn oak step.
Already they warm each other, as I once did.
This old picture is worn, and I grey too,
but will pass this onto my children —
before fire, turns to ember — to sleep,
so they too —
may have that day to keep.
—John E. Vadala III

Love From Within

In many faces I see the exhilarating quest
of a moment to hold in time and in place
a truth among lies to find footprints that will
match with their steps.

For one has not found yet his shape in the shadows
and that one word that will explain
the emotions through the motion of this living carrousel.

In hours of discontent the smiles seem to contain
a numbed comfort of the eased pain;
that voice screaming inside, disappears, no longer is,
and the tiredness finds a sleepy search.

But I've flown with the wind, and I've talked to the birds,
I've cried with the rain, and I've slept with the moon
and they've shared their wisdom, with this simple man;
the answer is love my friend, love from within.
—Maritza Becerra

I Am

I Am Jesus, God's only Son,
Victory on the cross I won;
I Am the door to Eternity;
No one enters except through Me.

I Am the Shepherd sent from above,
To tell the world of my Father's love;
I Am Alpha and Omega, too,
I'll ever be right here for you!

I Am the Lamb that was crucified,
It was for you I bled and died;
Come to the cross without delay,
My blood will wash your sins away.

I Am coming to earth again,
So I can take you to where I Am;
So be ready and watch for Me,
For behold—I come quickly!

I Am Jesus—the great I Am,
The Son of God and the Son of man;
I am the Truth, the Life, the Way,
Now is the time—come while you may.
   —*Jeanette Olson*

Mending

One thing for sure without reservation,
Vietnam almost destroyed our nation. . . .

People divided on what was right
Proposing peace not wanting to fight.
Others patriotic willing to go and serve
Wanting our rights and freedoms to preserve.
The division is healing after many years
At the expense of human blood sweat and tears.
There are many still paying the price-
In the hospitals, on programs seeking advice.
On how to live normally and fit once again
Back into society and forget where they've been.
To forget the war and get on with their lives
Be more peaceful and get along with their wives.
To loose the anger, frustration tearing them apart
To heal the wounds and broken hearts.
To feel peace and finally rest
And not feel guilty for doing their best.
   —*Charles R. Hampton*

An Open Wound...

   The sounds I hear — echo of my voice,
    visions I see — mirrored from my thoughts.
   A tingling feeling throughout my body.
         An invigoration...
         An open wound...
   My heart bleeds with sadness dipped in anger.
Its difficult to swallow the bloody tears that coat my throat.
  A lump forms within the shallow tunnel, a bitter taste of
         a bitter taste of anguish.
      A subtleness of a drifting emotion,
 a bundle of feelings grinding in the pit of my stomach.
         The walls are rotting away.
   Nervousness that the memory will soon be devoured.
      The tears erupt from my swollen eyes.
         My head aches — My hands will shake.
   I want to mold a new beginning, shatter the past,
     before the erosiveness taints the sadness...
   —*Frank LaTorre*

Loneliness

Alone, but surrounded by people
Voices ringing, like bells in a steeple
No stranger, for many have seen your face
But in their company you have no place
Being an island not yet discovered
Sunken treasure, never to be recovered
A sparkling diamond viewed only as a stone
Priceless value left unnoticed and unknown
Having time with no time to spare
Full of feelings but no one to care
A tunnel of emotions settled deep within
Standing on the outside of experience looking in.
   —*Deborah A. Bosch*

Wailing Winds

Winds drifting 'cross the earth
Wail for babes too weak to cry.
Scarce born, death calls,
And they become but little heaps of dust
On mothers' breasts, dry as parched ground.

Guns, prized more than milk, rain death;
The wombs of power bear monsters;
While famine rapes the land
They thrill to thunder's roar,
Not of clouds but bombs;
A hail of hate brings desolation in the land,
The grind of misery goes on,
And death stands guard
Beside beds in the sand.

Where has the human spirit gone,
The healing hand, the cup of water cool,
Full breasts for babes,
A cradle, not a bed of stones?
How can we staunch the hate
And hush the wailing in the wind?
   —*Carl A. Dallinger*

Burning Bridges

I've never been one to burn any bridges—not the ones that I've
walked on. I've always liked to know my pathways are open
Even back where I came from
but now I'm doing my best to burn all the bridges that were built
by me and you. Those are the bridges that I hope I never see again
They only lead back to you
So for the first time in my life I'm gonna make those bridges burn
I need to see them come apart as ashes
Then I'll know I can never return
Now I'm doing my best to burn all the bridges that were built by
me and you. Those are the bridges that I never want to see again
They only lead back to you
With the smell of fire in the air I'll start out all alone
But somewhere down this road I know
I'll find my heart a home
That's why I carry this torch, burning all the bridges that were
built by me and you. Those are the bridges I'll never need again
I'm never coming back to you
   —*Andy Cook*

Jesus Take My Hand

Jesus take my hand my heart, my all I give to you.
Walking beside you my Lord, I know I'll make it through-
   this old world of sin and pain, and sorrow too;
  Take my hand and lead me, I want to walk with you.

   I need someone to guide me along life's way.
Someone who will understand, even though I slip and stray.
   Someone who will still love me when I am blue;
  You're my rock my Jesus, I give my all to you.

   When I'm weak and lonely, you come and comfort me.
You tell me that you love me, and that you've set me free.
Although I don't deserve your love, my Jesus here I stand,
  Please take my hand, and lead me to the promised land.

   —*Dorothy Morris*

Balance

   Alone, the slate-blue Heron
     Walks with measured tread
  In mirrored shallows of the marsh
     Which meets the gulf.

Muscle-still it stands from time to time,
    Its head held high,
Then clearly shows its skill as fish darts by.

 If man and countries kept as skillful pace
Ecology and peace might balance in this place
     We call The Earth.

   —*Cornelia James Dorgan*

Dancing In the Shadows

Dancing in the shadows,
Waltzing with fear.
I keep dancing in the shadows,
Wishing you were here.
I am dancing in the shadows,
Ignoring all of the anguish that's welded into a single tear.
As I dance in the shadows,
My eyes flood with pain.
I stop dancing in the shadows,
as the sky is filled with a hard, cold rain.

   —*Danielle Louis Rudin*

The Painted Prayer

In my mind's eye I painted a colorful prayer
Of beautiful flowers in the garden of sorrow
Our gentle Jesus was there praying with care
He accepted the cross for souls of the morrow

Then with me eyes still closed
The painting turned to reality
With Jesus I became engrossed
For I loved the man of Galilee

As my Jesus was still praying to his Father in paradise
I saw descending from the blue sky a fluttering dove
From the deepness of my very soul I began to ecstasize
Is this our creator come down to this earth from above

I gazed at Jesus's eyes that were so mystical
As though he saw through a dark thunder cloud
When the darkness banished in the skies locale
I knew heaven was at work and I humbly bowed

Then the colorful painting became very magnetized
My sweet Saviour walked slowly and directly to me
He touched me and I became spiritually hypnotized
I look his hand and walked into the painting to Thee

   —*Ray Gordon*

Autumn Hike In The Blue Ridge

   Mountain mist lifts slowly
  wan sun's warmth moseys toward midday
   gone is the sizzle of mid-August
  the dog tiredness of summer is over
   spruce's greens are darker, smokier
 oaks, maples and dogwoods stately now
   royally arrayed in hues of saffron,
    scarlet and burnt orange
flashing their brilliance once before they die
  the leaves enact a cosmic drama
    even older than the earth
   scattered leaves litter the trail
spaniels toss the downed leaves high overhead
    as they scamper up the trail
    dry leaves crunch under boots

  In the spring, there were promises
   flowers spoke of a coming harvest
in the autumn, there is a redemption of promises
    a harvest that will last
   under the leaves lurks decay
   leading to winter and to death
    and again to spring
 Shiva is dancing in the leaves today
  free admission and ring side seats
   for those with eyes to see

   —*Jean Cameron*

I've Died Inside

I may be alive on the outside, but inside I'm dead. I may want to be alive on the inside, but I'm dead. I've been hurt too many times, that my inside died the day you walked out. On the outside I go on, but inside I'm at a dead stop.
  For my heart can not take no more pain.
  I feel like I was a train, you hoped on just to hop off down the line. So this is why I say I've come to a dead stop. I can not run on, or to stay on track.
  So that is why I've died inside.

   —*Joanne K. Ferrell*

Addictions

There's this hollow, empty feeling deep within.
Wanting to consume…eating me alive, merciless,
  perilous, all empowering.
I can hear it sweetly, melodiously, calling me by name.
Succumbing to it means giving up, giving in.
Embracing it would be soothing as it rocks me to sleep,
Holding me close, stroking my hair, and singing me songs.
And Oh! How I miss the songs of times gone by.
Please, … let this feeling pass by my door.
For, I must secure the lock in place,
  bolting the doorway of my veins.
And listening, …carefully, …quietly, to a new song..life.

   —*Cheryl Chernick*

Cavan

O Cavan of the lakes and hills.
To your sweet name my heart doth thrill.
Forested beauty of gorgeous green
To me, oh so much do mean
Beautiful Ireland forever in my heart
Of your beauty, I will always be a part
God's country you truly are
Although, across the sea, you
are never very far.

   —*Dorothy Shelley*

Untitled

Lonesome tear from her eye
Wanton lust for companionship
A shoulder to lean on
Someone to care, share and be there
A quiet drive, a mellow walk
Come from afar, an old beau
Television his companionship
Taking without giving
No offer to help or promise to be there
Her lonesome drive and walk, he is absent
He left as she shed a tear of joy
To live without him to answer to
To walk and talk with the Lord
He who cares, shares and is always
    there.
    —*Francie A. Frank*

Fire Prayer

Around the snapping, crackling fire we gather feeling its
    warmth, protecting us from the chill of the night, keeping
    back the dark.

We gather to listen to you respected and wise one of how we
    are to care for, respect mother earth and give thanks for
    all creatures in the waters, on the land and in the sky,
    for everything has a spirit even the trees, water,
    grasses and rocks.

Oh wise one tell us of the spirits, the old ones of long ago
    who protect and guide us along this path of life.

As the fire burns lower we in its circle lift our hearts and
    arms up in prayer, giving thanks to you Creator God for the
    gift of life and love, for those you bring into your
    lives.
    —*Josie Kruttlin*

Montara Is Forever You

A small coastal town where I once grew
was a little girl's paradise for me and you.
As Springtime awoke it tickled our senses
with tasty wild strawberries and blackberries.
Our eyes danced with lemon-yellow Daffodils,
Poppies, and multicolored straw flowers too.
The fragrant scent of Honeysuckle lingered in the air.
Shetland ponies we rode, just me and you,
through those fields of color that nature grew.
Secret dreams we told, just me and you,
that only the following Swallows knew.
Ancient Eucalyptus towered with Pines and Cypress
was home for the red tailed hawk and deer.
Quail and cotton tails were hidden here,
along with me and you, as games of Cowboy and
Indian were played, who won we never knew.
Adventure filled our souls, just me and you.
When I go back and walk quietly I here,
a giggle or two, and the swallows
telling each other untold dreams of me and you.
    —*Jennifer Lazzari*

September Morn

The sky on that cool September morning
Was beautiful to behold.
The sun was peeking through very dark clouds,
And looked like pieces of gold.

The rays filtered down through mountainous clouds
That appeared to be canyons of red;
I watched with awe as the colors changed,
And I said, "My God isn't dead!

The sun burst forth from behind the clouds
To light up the lake and the land;
My heart overflowed with love for my God
Who gave us a world that's so grand.
    —*Bonnie Jean Vaughn*

Sage

The Himalayan mountain path
was rocky, curved and steep.
Not all who came continued on.
I heard that near the top in caves
Yogas meditated daily,
pondered life's great mysteries,
and spoke to those who traveled by.
Soon I found myself within
a circle of devoted followers,
and at the center I saw him sit —
the legendary sage.
I came up close, my quest at end.
"Where do I find God," I implored.
"Seek within," he answered, and closed his eyes.
Stunned to silence by the simple reply,
I wandered slowly down the hill.
    —*Brent Webber*

Why Did I Fail You So?

Why did I fail you so?
    Was so afraid or just mislead or
    tempted inside my heart I would fail
    or could fail after being called or
    being led to being a missionary.
Because of my weakness I refused.
I could have been stronger.
    I listened to sermons by women preachers of
    the methodist faith.
One had been a bar singer and gave it up
    and followed her calling.
Another a Baptist Missionary.
    She told of her experiences with such love.
I sang in public for you dear Lord
    when I was very young.
I felt so great giving that testimony for you!
I was a very gifted pianist and devoted Christian!
    —*Ellen Martha Finleyson*

The Sea Shell Poem

I am a lonely sea shell washed away into the sea, as the waves continue to rush up against me; I will no longer be. I was once a living organism who could fill smell and see, now I am just a fragment of what use to be. My life ended so suddenly without a sign or warning, now that remains are only traces of time that suddenly slipped away.
    —*Jacqueline C. Graves*

Andre Restieu Discovers Chartres

When I was just a child of ten, the hallowed light
Was streaming through the ancient, stained glass windows, bright
With all the brilliance of antiquity. These
Perfect images remained with me. They pleased
My emerging soul, in such a vibrant, yet holy, way
That I can still behold the beauty of that day

And when I pilgrimaged to study how a color
World was made I went to Reims, to Notre-Dame,
Lyons, Poitiers before I even gave a thought
Of what it was I was soul-searching: technique wrought
By gifted artisans of years ago; their same
Strict measures of perfection would be the only way.

So then to Chartres, where the windows are the best,
(The experts say), and after many months of sketching,
Rendering what I thought would meet the secret test,
I must agree that these are miracles. So stretching
Mind to capture how this work was done, I knew
That here was where the essence of the art came true.
   —*Auburn J. Lamb*

The Monster Number Two

For years I worked for "Smoking Bear"
   Was the name Ed called his market
One day I came to work and found
   "The Monster" came and parked it!!

"The Monster" has re-vamped everything
   Making Miss Judy lose her flow
I heard a costumer ask for jumpin' jacks
   She answered "sugar I really don't know"

Little Angelic stood looking oh so sad
   There was no room to clean no more
Lorraine played the tune of "Monster Mash"
   And customers hurdled across the store

Christina's eyes were very wide
   said, "This monster" turns me around
With his tail spread over the floor
   A place to walk just can't be found

Evening time "The Monster" did trap Jason
   Midnight came it got Lisa and Tweety
I'm trying my best to hang in there
   Because our new boss Terry is so pretty
      —*Ina Smith*

Heartsong

The rhythmic beating of her heart
Was the staccato of a trip hammer;
The anticipation was growing,
Suddenly the time had come
For her to burst into song.

She started slowly with a hushed voice,
As if she was a little unsure.
But that was only the beginning of
A masterpiece, which happens once
In a lifetime.

The tempo grew stronger and faster
She remembered every word.
As she sang, you could almost
Follow the flight of a bird,
High in the sky

The trills went ever upward
Fading, fainter, so high
Then without warning came back
To be a part of her, who had
Sung from her heart.
   —*Hazel Maskel*

Fabric Of A Nation

The strong, resilient fabric of this illustrious nation
Was woven from the vision and inspiration
Of intelligent, courageous pioneers,
Who, by conquering their tribulations and fears

Boldly built homes upon empty prairies, planting lush, verdant fields,
Envisioning their families reaping the fertile yields;
Not without trial and conflict was this fabric loomed;
Not without sacrifice of bloodied flesh entombed,

Yet, transcending rubble, grief, and deprivation,
Their nobility of character and total dedication
Is blended in the length and breadth of blood red bars,
The strong, rugged threads of fifty United Stars.
   —*Glory Posey*

A Cloud And I

I stood upon the hill today,
waving weeds below said "Hi,"
bending, so their seeds could lay
in shadow or sun to root or fly.

A white cloud whizzed past
I climbed on its hump with glee,
before I could breathe we were sailing fast
Toward just where I wanted to be.

We flew over the town toward the sea,
sunlit ripples were the only waves.
The wind blew gently, my cloud fell low
my spirit and I in a glory daze!

I fell too, out of dreamland town,
my head on the pillow recalling
my flight of joy when I lay down,
with all cares and fears receding!
   —*Alberta Schilling*

The Sassy Magpie

The big, tall pine tree,
Way high up in the sky
Makes a perfect refuge
For the big, black, sassy magpie.

Hearing a clutter, clutter and chatter
Looked out on the lawn,
To see what was the matter.
Couldn't believe what I saw
Before my eyes.
The big, black, sassy magpie
Diving and pecking at Amos the cat,
Right in his eyes.
My entire life had never seen
Such a sight as that!

Amos gave a big angry dive,
Chasing the big, black magpie.
Turning round and round
And summer sets on the ground.
Again I looked out,
And there was no cat
Or bird to be found!
   —*Jessie Taylor*

Parents

Naked, without a penny in our name,
we all came into this world, to start the game.
Parental love, that goes without say,
let us become what we are today.

But all too often we forget,
what we once, in our parents had.
Only children of your own will give you a clue,
what our parents once went through.

The daily bread, we all do need,
was hard to bring home, indeed.
Much too fast we grew out of shoes and cloth,
there was no time ever, for them to dose.

How often was there a sleepless night,
when they sat, and held their sick child tight.
They gave up for us, their daughter and son,
their best years of having just fun.

Dear parents, don't you ever believe,
that we do not appreciate what we've received.
It is just too hard to put it into words:
We always will love you, until it hurts!

—*Annegret Meier*

The Happy Birthday Poem

Happy Birthday from everyone.
We all hope you're having fun.
Today we hope you're feeling good.
It's your Birthday so you should.

Today's the day for joy and cheer.
It happens only once a year.
So sing the Happy Birthday song.
And be happy all day long.

Birthdays are a joyful time.
That's why I wrote this rhyme.
So just remember what I say.
Have a most Happy Happy Birthday.

—*David Vanderburg, American Author of Poetry*

Beautiful To God

Regardless of what we do or say
We are beautiful to God.
Each of us He made in his own way
And our personalities he approved with a nod.

As we go about in our busy days
We tend to forget to thank Him
And give Him the proper praise
For all He has done for us without a whim.

We may not think of ourselves
As beautiful with the way we feel or act
But God overlooks that as He shelves
The books of our lives in his pact.

We are more beautiful to God
In the way we treat each other
As He would want us to with a nod
Of His head concerning one person to another.

—*Connie Harden*

To You This Prayer

We are God's children, first and foremost.
We are not alone —
He is "always" with us.

It is up to us, to lift our hearts
And lips in prayer, asking for His forgiveness,
Love and help to bear our daily cross.

God "will" answer our prayers,
By embracing us and our thoughts to Him,
Through this Act of spiritual communion.

The fulfillment of Prayer —
Results in ecstatic happiness,
Making our hearts feel lighter and
The "burden of our daily cross less heavy."
While the River of Life once again,
Resumes to flow — F-r-e-e and e-a-s-y,
With or without its Ripples.

—*Anna Toma Anderson*

Note To Sandra

As the time continue in proceeds,
We are shifted into other dimensions,
Our every element of existence shall
 either fail or succeed,
The constant struggle for survival does prevail,
Our need for life and freedom is an ongoing concept,
This puts our human relations to a test,
For we fear the disease of loneliness,
Our only cure for this is our eminent death,
We thrive on the caring of another,
Even though our species is continually
 committing genocide,
Strengths do we possess shall always be,
In heart and soul shall we always
 be part of each other,
For our friendship is one from
 the works of time, trust, and
 love...

—*Joan Bickford*

Untitled

I remember
We both could see
Their vacant eyes, their measured dreams.

When does it begin?
The compromise,
The loss of self, while other eyes

Judge you,
Your eternal depth;
They think they can reach, think they can guess

Who you are.

I remember
When we both knew
What it meant to live, and to be true.

When did it begin?
Your loss of faith
In yourself, in the human race.

Though it's hard
With your surrender,
I still live, I still remember

The dream that you forgot.

—*Carin Marzano*

Tell Me Why

Tell me why my Lord
We discriminate against our brother
When we were all made in Your likeness
To live with one another

The Jews and Irish catholics
And now the blacks & browns
The feud between the sexes
And so it goes around

We try and trust Your wisdom
But fail along the way
To see we're all Your children
To be judged by You one day
   —*Dolores Von Bieberstein*

A Rain Bow At Sunset

In truly loving someone
We do not judge with word or action
But listen with loving heart
With never an infraction

Our learning goes on until the end
That is God's plan
Which will always transcend
Constant and continuing
Unlike the shifting sands

Much to much to mention
Amie world turmoil and tension
He provides the answers
That can not be found by man
The oneness we feel
And trust in his plan

These are my thoughts
Like the contentment of a summer breeze
Or wind whistling through the trees
Or a lifting melody
In a true life's parody

All our lives are planned by design
With the knowledge that is predestined
By the unseen that is divine
   —*Betty Flanagan Porter*

Protection From Above

   We are like ships being tossed in the sea.
   We keep sailing on to our eternal destiny.
      "O Lord, help us to look and see.
     Open our eyes to see angels that be.
    They fly over us, like in Desert storm.
    They protect us from Satan and all his form.
    They are warring angels sent from above.
They fly over us with power, yet gentle as a dove.
    Your Holy Spirit in us gives us power.
Through us, you love those in the world this hour."
    God will lead and guide us all the way.
He dwells in us with love, truth and power today.
     His Holy Spirit is our guiding force.
   Like radar, he guides us through each course.
He says to the winds and waves; "Peace be still."
   There is a calm assurance from his holy hill.
God gives us the assurance, we have eternal life.
   We can live together without all that strife.
      In this life, where is your stock?
      Is it in Jesus, the solid rock?
    —*Al Thomas*

Frosty Snowy Day

Our world is covered with frosting
We look like a fluffy white cake.

Bushes and trees are the decorations
Their beauty beyond our ability to make.

Frost gathers itself on everything
Even the very smallest branch.

Let's feast our eyes on the beauty
Displayed by home, farm and ranch.

We grow accustomed to surroundings
For granted their beauty we take.

Let's look with the eyes of a painter
What a beautiful picture 'twould make!!

Tomorrow the scene will be different,
More beautiful, perhaps to see.

Let's keep today's scene in our memory
So a little more pleasant we'll be.
   —*Alice Rogers*

Painfully Watching

With each day that passes by,
   We pray his soul, God won't deny.
Though his body weakens day by day,
   We can only hope he has no pain in anyway.
And as he slowly deteriorates before our eyes,
   Some will mourn while others cry.
But with each breath that he takes,
   Peace with God, he shall make.
The long suffering he can no longer endure,
   As his hours on earth become fewer.
Happiness he will soon receive,
   And at last his soul will be at ease.
When God reach down to draw him up,
   To him he'll say servant, you've done enough.
And when all his work on earth is done,
   Asleep he'll fall to that place beyond.
But in our hearts he'll forever stay,
Although he's now gone away.
   —*Deloris A. Fuller*

Impressions Of The Sea

The restless waves rush in like a heartbeat
Washing foot prints engraved upon the sand
Salt air, pungently, surrounds our retreat
Treasured sea shells remain in my hand

The cry of the gulls, livens the air
Unending, their heedless call
They circle above the shoreline, where
Sand castles stand proud and tall

Drifting along with the rolling waves
Seaweed clings upon each bower
Above these ancient rock formed caves
Rise, the massive cliffs that tower

Gliding across the vast, blue waters
Are the sails of gleaming white
Where adventures loving seafarer
Guide the helm, beneath the sunlight
   —*Joanna Manoogian*

They're Human Beings, Sir

When a nation goes to war, we think of men readied, with gun in hand.
We, seldom think of the one's who go, wearing a red cross band.
The medical men and women, are the lifeline, of any war.
They are faithful and compassionate, realizing, how important
  their duties are.
We, are taught from childhood, that we must love and care.
To help the sick and needy, and be willing, ready to share.
When American's become warriors, and realize, they may have to kill.
It can't help become a problem, as they question; is this God's will?
We, go and defend our country, confident, our medical teams
  will be there.
They have saved so many of us, their dedication and, knowledge
  is rare.
It's strange about us Americans, when we come across an
  injured foe.
We, treat him just like one of us, he's almost a "G.I. Joe."
God teaches us to be forgiving, and this embeds within the heart.
But, to aid an injured enemy; some might think it's not too smart.
A newsman saw this happen, and asked our soldier his "true feelings."
He summed it up, for all American's saying;
"They're human beings, Sir, just human beings."
—June Berry

Let Me Soar

As we seek into our hearts
We sometimes speak to harshly

As we fly high in the sky
We sometimes fall onto our brothers

As we fall into their arms
We sometimes are not caught

When you see me in reality, do not speak harshly
When you hurt my heart, it is alright, I am strong

When you see me falling
It is alright to let me fall

I am trying to soar
Remember, I too can land on my feet

When I am healing myself
It is alright to comfort me

When things are truly dark
I am trying to soar

Remember then how you have soared
Remember, by my side
—Carol Heaton

We Laugh In the Same Language

We laugh in the same language.
We cry the same understandable tears
And we sleep with the same annoying snores.
It says in the Bible that long ago
God created the Tower of Babal
To make different people, fear each other
So that later on we would become friends
With one another.
We laugh in the same language
But misunderstandingly
We say to those from whom we differ
"What is that strange sound you
say in my ears?"
—Carolyn Milazzo

The Mother

In the garden of life
We spot just one flower
Its petals so delicate
Its beauty so rare
A softness, a gentleness
A comforting flair,

A fragility that's entwined with an enduring strength
An essence of power
A definite charm a wisdom, a caring,
A protection from harm.

A heart that is filled with a love so sublime
A deep understanding
Of life's ups and downs.
A guidance, a giving
A smile from a frown

And when faced with adversity that may make one cower,
In the garden of life we spot just one flower
Its petals so delicate its beauty so rare.

'Tis a mother, our flower
Someone to treasure 'Tis a mother of course
Who loves you forever in the garden of life.
—Janice Pacht

Love's Gratitude

While living as young lovers do
We stop to think of persons who
Were there when first our love began,
And those who gave a helping hand,
Who brought our lives from separate ways,
And shared in our beginning days.

To them we owe an awful lot
Of thanks, for maybe we would not
Have met, if they had not been there
To recognize the things we share
In heart, and brought us closer in our love.
These are the friends we're thankful of.

Now, many years of marriage stand
And as we dream here, hand in hand,
We throw our hearts to people who
Have all along been standing too
Beside our marriage, from the start.
We're truly grateful, from the heart.
—Deborah R. Moe

What Mom Took

Most often when we think of mom
We think of what she's given
The softness of a loving touch
A gentle guide for living.

But sometimes when I think of mom
I think of what she took!
She took a child and taught it how
To live this life with pride
Then took those "kinder garten" tears
And kept them all inside.
She did all this and more-
And never asked for thanks,
A little love, this mom took.
But, now, number one she ranks!
—Bonnie B. Mangrum

My Friend From The Motherland

My friend from the motherland
We toiled through the creeping sands of
the land which we loved and both had a
helping hand.

My friend from the Motherland of Africa
Our relationship was bonded in the precious hands
of the Creator who gave us truth and a spirit
of roots for freedom
    From
    Land to land
    And
    Hand and hand
United States, South Africa, Nelson Mandella and Afro Americans
"We can stand up! We can stand up!" To promote equal
opportunities, prosperity, better health care to shape the
nations and enhance better education!"
My friend! my friend! from the Motherland!"

—*Janette S. Smoot*

When We Grow Old

We used to play together, we used to have fun.
We used to hate each other, but now we're as one.
As the years went by, we grew together.
We said our vows for worse and for better.
There we were young and in love,
We had nothing, but the heaven above.
You got a job, bought a house and car,
In this world we've gone very far.
We had three kids, we raised them right.
We never let them see us fight.
The kids grew up, and moved away.
I guess I have nothing more to say,
"except" when we grow old, we grow old alone.

—*Brandie Leigh Hancock*

Changes

Once upon five scores ago
  we walked to Sunday School
from home to church to and fro
  to learn the golden rule

We learn between Genuses and revelation
  to stop, listen, and hush,
For words to build a biblical foundation
  that came from the burning bush

Great teachers explain it universal
  to make their self understood
Withdrawing from a brief rehearsal
  on speaking of Noah's flood

The old and new biblical life
  may come forth with another change,
What is a husband? What is a wife
  with Mrs. taken from name?

—*Ed Lewis*

Fireflies

Rising from my darkened patio
Were phosphorescent lights, spiralling upwards
in flashes of "on-and-off" for a moment's view
Of one of God's special creations that man cannot mimic,
As they rise like glowing bubbles of chilled champagne
Circling upward through a dusky stem of a crystal flute,
With an aura of ethereal beauty,
Disappearing in a ceiling of darkness.

—*Edna May Hermann*

Campbell Clan Memories

The fishing trip was an annual affair.
We went to Lomola Lake, to breathe some of that fresh clean air

Brother Stan took some steaks for our supper that night.
We also had a jug and the old man got pretty tight.
We cooked the steaks by the campfire out there in the rough.
Dad started to complain, "My steak is really tough!"

We all said the steaks were pretty good.
He claimed his tasted like a piece of wood.
He said that kind of steak for a ton he wouldn't pay a dime.
He finally finished it but it took a long, long time.
He took his doubled up paper plate to the fire,
Then on his face came a look of ire.

"Well, I'll be dammed," he said, with a voice that shook.
Then he held it up so we all got a look.
It sure was a funny sight as he glared around.
We all laughed till we fell to the ground.
We all agreed it was a terrible fate
Grandad Campbell ate the bottom out of his plate.

—*C. M. (Red) Campbell*

What Happened To The Golden Years?

What happened to those golden years
  We were told did lie ahead?
And that we faced with no fears,
  What we unhappily found instead.
Was that unless you have good health,
  (Or endowed with some wealth)
It was not all peaches and cream,
  But just a beautiful dream.
The price of gold is up we know.
  But, how high is it going to go?
Our incomes are going down-hill,
  Getting harder and harder to pay each bill.
I'm worried about my children and theirs,
  Praying for a better world for my heirs.
Lord, please turn things around,
  So we again can get our feet on the ground.

—*Gladys Stockl*

Let Freedom Ring

We hope before we leave this earth,
we'll see mankind have a rebirth.
We hope that men will realize
that our God, gave all men, the right to choose.
He doesn't use force to get us to come, to heaven,
with Him. He let's us choose right or wrong;
and gave us the "Good Book" to make us strong.
So, why do we impose rules and regulations on
people of other nations. Sometimes, it may be?
necessary, when they are imposing their wills;
and threats on other people's lives. However, we
should also; realize not all people, want
the same things, that we hold dear! Some of
these people still live in great fear.
We all belong to the good God above He created us,
with all his love. He sent His son to save us
from sin. Do we not owe our very souls to Him.
Should we not treat our brothers, as Kin;
and share all our goods with him? Wouldn't
it be great to see all mankind
free? Wouldn't that
Be a great surprise, to see this
part of history, unfolding, before
our eyes, that all men would he fully recognized?

—*Doris Kuenne Campbell*

Solutions

We the people of this earth
Were given certain rights by birth.
To freely walk with our fellow man,
To share our lives wherever we can.
Now wars and destruction, famine and disease
Have polluted the world over land and seas;
Fear and hate, mistrust and greed
Are other foods to this pollution we feed.
We have seen the problems we can feel the strife,
Yet we know there is an answer somewhere in life,
I only wish that people would take the time to see
Another solution possible; extending hands across the seas.
The fears we have of the different sides
Maybe would slowly, completely subside.
If this one lesson we do not miss:
You can't shake hands with a clenched fist!
I know we have struggled, I know we have tried;
Some men have lived others have died.
Now only man alone can truly say
For a life of freedom the price he would pay.
—*Dorothy Moore*

No Matter What

    If only I had known
  what a blessing that day would be
    when you came into my life
  and my world became "you and me."
      I'm amazed,
That of all the people I should meet,
    I would find the one person
That would make my life complete.
When I reminisce about all those memories
    we shared in loving bliss,
I'm thankful for all that we have become
  for "you and I are now as "one."
    Once again I realize
      that our love,
  no matter how wise, or how rough,
     will always be there
       no matter what.
    Now "you and I are "we"
    and this love we share
     is truly meant to be.
—*Caroline M. Sullivan*

The Boy Behind The Man

What a funny boy
What a character
Such a child at heart
Such a playful soul
A smile of a thousand words
A face of mischievous wonder
The heart full of love
The mind thinking extraordinary thoughts
With simple pleasures
With a touch of sensitivity
Like a man but still a boy
Like a lion but only a teddy bear
Though quiet at times
Though shy at times
He is the wonder of it all
Alex!

   —*Carolyn Henley*

Praise

  At the dawning of morning or the of day
   What a marvelous privilege to be able to pray
  Prayer provides answers, it's a gift of his grace
  And prayer has a partner; there's power in praise!

  In joys and in laughter, or most trying of days
   I find it refreshing to pause and just praise
  When prayer comes not easy and blurs into haze
  I find it renewing to pause and just praise.

He's my light! My deliverer! He lengthens my days
Against him there's no counsel; He is worthy of praise!
So I'll abide under His shadow, undergirded by grace
And not oft as I ought, I will pause just to praise.
   —*Jane B. Cox*

If I Were

If I were to write a song
What beautiful verse it would be
The sun would be shining, the birds singing
Not a thing in the world would be wrong

The children are all playing
While the mothers would be laying
Out in the sun, if only for one
Brief little moment a day.

If I were to write a book
It would take place in a faraway land
Where everyone played in the sand
While at the colorful sunset we'd look.

At night the children would lay down their heads
And dream of the stories I told them
When they awoke to start again
Their adventures would never have ended
   —*Cami Beckerdite*

Questions, Questions Question

What color is the bumble of a bumble bee?
What color is a lion's roar?
A dog's bark sounds blackish-brown to me.
How does a vulture make his motor soar?

What color is the inside of a cloud?
What color is the thunder's crash?
If I could catch a rainbow's end,
Which color would I hold, or would I
Just have a rain storm's splash?

What color is a mouse's squeak?
Why does a grasshopper jump?
His noise sounds like golden straw to me.
How heavy is a camel's hump?

Mom tells me I ask too many things!
But how else am I to know?
Where can I find answers to all of these?
O, yes, what causes winds to blow?
   —*Dorothy Moore*

What Indeed

There are so many trees to see
What is one less I said within me
Fish in the sea countless numbers abound
They will always be there, plenty
To go 'round
Clean water there will certainly be
Just as the air, Mother Nature
provides
But something happened, what
Could it be, now she is angry
I am just a human what could
Cause her to be angry with me?
—David A. Bernal

Karon

What is the morning without sunlight?
What is the night without moonlight?
What is the night sky without stars?
What am I without you?
Without sunlight the morning is dull—
Without moonlight the night is dark—
I don't want to be without sunlight moonlight or stars—
But I could have all if you would be mine through:
All the sunless mornings—
All the moonless nights—
All the starless skies.
For I am like all these things, and you are my sunlight,
Moonlight and stars.
You brighten my morning—
You light up my night—
You are the brightest star in my Heaven.
Please give me my sunlight, moonlight and starlight—
By being mine through all the dark days and nights.
My love is as bright as the sun, mellow as moonlight,
and will last as long as there are stars in the sky.
—George H. Klavitter

Snow, Snow Melt Away

Snow, snow melt away.
What is this season; spring or fall?
You know little baby crows must grow tall.
Nature will make you again next fall —
So snow, snow melt away!

Baby crows need water and seeds and bread you know.
They like to hear the soft winds blow.
Robin Red Breast will soon be here you know,
And you don't want her to find snow again this year —
So snow, snow melt away!
—Jean I. Fuhr

Winter Wonderland

The drab condition on the ground.
We detest the disorder all around.
But, low and behold, overnight,
A snowstorm came covering the blight.
That which was so detestably visible last night,
Has become an extremely beautiful sight.
The snow has transformed the most drab, wa may be sure,
Into the most beautiful perspective so attractive and so pure.
I have been transformed into winterwonderland today,
That which was so drab and unsightly yesterday.
—Howard Beymer

A Thought

When I read my Bible I can see
What Jesus said to you and me,
"What you do for the least of these,
You do for me," and it does please
Your heart and theirs, and He knows,
Whatever kindness anyone shows.
The little we do to help others.
A smile, a kind word to our brothers.
"I have no brothers," did I hear you say?
We're all brothers on judgement day.

"Suffer little children to come unto me."
If we think as children how good it would be
A child doesn't know hate or bigotry,
Unless its taught by adults you see.
So let's put aside our worldly way;
And prepare ourself for judgement day.
Give everyone a hug, a kind word, a smile,
It will make your life and theirs worthwhile.
Thank God every day for His gift.
He really gives our life a lift.
—Connie Ludolff

Life Cycle

I wonder if you'll ever know
What joy it was to watch you grow.
If only words could tell you so.
How sadly now, I let you go.

At first I gently took your hand
And helped your wobbly legs to stand.
Then off to play, away you ran,
And suddenly, you were a man.

I often wondered what you'd be,
When I held you upon my knee.
Oh, the questions you asked me,
As if the future I could see.

Raising you brought pain and fun.
Now all your growing years are done,
And most of your young goals are won,
So go, and be a man, my son.

Just remember, when you see,
Your bouncing baby on your knee,
And your heart swells with pride and glee,
That's what you'll always be to me.
—Bonnie Ziller

Mom

You will always be my Mom I don't care
What they say
That is one name you deserve and they
cannot take that away
You carried me for nine months and your
back was in pain
No one else has felt your pain
So to try to strip you of the name Mom
has to be insane
Although you came upon hard times and
You did what you thought was best for me
Mom for into the future I know that very
few can see
That is why you will always be mom to me
—Anthony Mercorelli

Innocent Eyes

They have been taught to obey their elders. Never question
what they say or do, just follow orders. Their tiny faces look
up to you with trust and respect. The love for you is ever
eminent in their eyes. They ask not much of you, just a kiss
and a hug. All they ever wanted was to know that they
were loved. But look at our society, the crime and the pain
that is bestowed upon their souls.
They do not understand why you
treat them as you do. The questions pasted across their
innocent faces, but never uttered from their quivering lips.
Why do you hate me so? Why are you hurting me? Have I been
bad? I promise to be good. I want my mommy and my daddy?
How is it possible for us to go on as if none of this is going on
around us? Their helpless bodies have been cast aside as if
they were not human, but just a possession. The night grows
cold, no sounds are heard. Their lives have been cut short,
for what purpose. In the distance the angels wait with open
arms for the next child to embrace.
—*Anita Yatso*

Waitangi Dawn

Weeping Waters, WAITANGI, why do you weep?
What truths lie locked in your chambers deep?
Is it Man who first sailed seas unknown your way?
    To find your Bay?

Heaven's Dark-before-Dawn is a silence vast
A finely meshed net holding things of your past.
The Dawn-Glow breaks.... Perhaps like that day
    Man found your Bay.

Breaking-Dawn opens a flaming pathway of light
Brimming, turning over a sleepy startled night.
Bringing life to myriad isles where hills 'n rays meet
    Love nestled at your feet.

Early Dawn whispers... "Awake, E ara e."
Silver winds dance low on silken skin of your Bay
Sending ripples inland where land and water meet
    Love touching my feet.

   New Morn moves horizons on edge of memory
   Winking smiles...a waltz...whips of melody
   Mounting a Prelude to Love on tenderness borne
    In Waitangi Dawn.
—*Amy Kaleiho'opi'o C. Tam*

Who Is His Real Mother?

I heard a thoughtless word today;
"What would his own real mother say
If she could look upon him now
With golden hair upon his brow?"
I am his mother, can't you see
I've changed his diapers on my knee
I've loved him whether sick or well
And kissed his bruises when he fell
I've ironed his shirts and cleaned his ears
And shared his hopes and calmed his fears
Adopted is a word of doubt
It leaves all love and honor out
I am his mother that you see
Our hearts were twined in infancy.
—*Judith M. Smith*

Time The Same

Another time and yet the same
When all creatures — the environment
Are listening to the Muse's song.
The poetry pageantry perseverance
of marching Marionettes
Responding to the needs of earth mother
Attending to her global peoples
Heeding their pleas for mercy—salvation
Reacting to each soul's vibrations
With compassion toward all creatures.
"We" organize. "We" synchronize.
"We" march in unison to fulfill
The cries of mother earth
Attending to her needs
Nurturing her children
Caring for her creatures.
"We" are the performers of this time
Acting with great care to ensure
A long life. A wholesome existence.
Another time and yet the same.
—*Dorls G. Libby*

I Wonder

I wonder how He felt that day so many years ago
When all His friends and family pretended not to know.
I'm sure His heart was breaking—His mind was surely torn
To hear His fellow-man, behaving with such scorn.

It started several years before-in a manger very small
He was sent by God above—to save us one and all.
As He grew He listened to the stories about God
In the temple He did stay to learn of His great love.

By trade He was a carpenter—working with His hands
Until the time had come, to continue with God's plans.
He traveled all around the land—Disciples at His side
To teach the meaning of God's word all over far and wide.

He loved the little children—this was plain to see
He gathered them around Him and taught them patiently.
He healed the sick-the blind to see-miracles galore
They traveled everywhere to teach—the word from shore to shore.

A woman at the well one day—a drink she gave to Him
She knew he was a special man—a very special friend.
With all His special talents—and love so deep inside
I wonder how the people felt—when He was crucified.
—*Betty Huber*

Hands

The hands of the babe are shut tight
When he emerges from the dark womb into the light
Little by little as the days go on
More and more his palms are shown
Gradually the hands begin to grope
Open and close as if tugging a rope
Soon grasping and holding the utensil and toy
Cuddling and relinquishing all things they enjoy.

These hands that learn to create and acquire
In time amass fortune to fulfill man's desire
For these hands time passes too quickly
And all worldly goods they've attained so avidly
Now are relinquished to those they love best
And with open palms are laid to rest
Nothing to take with them to a place unknown
Only the good which their life has sown.
—*Anna Lee Nissel*

When Angels Light
In memory of an angel named Jason.
When angels light upon this Earth
Their wings encircle all
Gentle children, pure in heart
Gliding with the wind at dawn.

Cleansed by love their world appears
beautiful and bright
They touch our hearts with gentle peace
to guide us towards the light.

They dance between the raindrops
to watch our fears away;
and give us strength to face the world
by lighting each new day.

To lift us when our knees are weak
In God we all stand tall.
On a quiet hill they hold our hands
to lift us when we fall.

In the silent comfort of a prayer
They hear our hearts despair;
and whisper simply "Do not fear
My love is always there."
—*Dawna Lee Holloway*

The Vows Of Marriage
Shall I remember you at Christmastime
when dove-white spreads of snow deny the green
of fields in spring and apple trees in bloom
when long-speared summer grasses reach their prime...
perhaps in autumn, when the moon's ripe sheen
recalls the marriage vows of bride and groom
who pledged themselves to love through death and doom
in happiness or dangers unforeseen...
and promised then eternally to hold
each other close despite ill-fate and mean
disasters—always shielding love sublime—
anointed through two wedding rings of gold?

I keep you in all seasons—warm or cold
set deep in mind—in ev'ry place and clime.
My heart shall wear you like a precious stone...
forever to remember you—my own.
—*Eleanor Otto*

The Ultimate Journey
My heart of some greater purpose knew
when first our eyes met.
Sensing this tryst was not casual,
upon the ultimate journey we set.

Your gaze beckoning me to respond,
my heart pounded with anticipation.
Though my mind insisted upon reason,
my body surged with sensation.

Through these feelings we grew closer,
closer than even we could know,
toward that ultimate journey;
our souls mesmerized by the light's glow.

If only we had known from the start
where this predestined journey would end,
would we so eagerly and with abandon
have allowed these indomitable spirits to blend?

The angels sent each to the other
friend, lover and traveling companion to be
on this our ultimate journey;
earthly bonds our souls to flee.
—*Brenda Gentry Thompson*

Tribute To A Hero
Our beloved leader chose to say
when he took the leader's stand,
"Seek not what your country can do for you,
But what you can do for your land."

Now the day is o'er for him,
As dusk is hov'ring near,
The soldiers kneel to say a prayer,
For their comrade brave and dear.

Their hero now lies motionless,
As though he's sound asleep,
Dreaming of home and battles won,
For an everlasting peace.

God grant the angels sing to him,
Their eternal vigil keep,
Let us not fail, to lead all lands,
To realms of love and peace.

Seek not to take, but seek to give,
To God and country, let us lift,
Our aim in life, that he may know,
His life and death, were not in vain.
—*Abi Zinn*

Laura
Dear little Laura was going on seven
When her mamma died, and went to heaven,
She said, "Dearest Laura, I'm going away
But I'll be with you again-some day."

The tears on her pillow had dried,
But most of the night, she cried;
Then in her dream an angel came,
She brought her a gift and called her name.

The gift was a moonbeam of gleaming white,
It whisked her away into the night.
What a beautiful view of earth from above,
A feeling came over her of purest love.

Then she saw ahead, the brilliant light
Of Jesus Himself, in a robe of white.
And mamma was there and angels by the score,
They were singing hymns on that beautiful shore.

Mamma was happy and her love was so strong,
Laura knew, surely, to call her back would be wrong.
So she rode on the moonbeam back safe and secure,
To wait upon Jesus and His love that is pure.
—*Annette Mates*

Ocean Of Love
Upon the shores of love I stand
Watching the waves crash on the sand.
Can our love withstand such storms?
I wait and look.
  The sea calms; the waves cease,
And serenity is all that is left.
Love must live through the test of time
  And all the weather's change.
Only then will it grow to bud and bloom.
The blood red rose divine.
—*Joy Nicole Thompson*

The Lamp Of Hope

Like a flickering flame in darkness,
When hope's at its lowest ebb,
Love could reach out with the softest hands,
To ease the things we dread.

We never know as we pass through life,
How faint the light they see,
These Mortals all about us,
God's children same as we.

We could help them fuel their lamps,
To give a brighter light,
Dispelling the darkness in their lives
Replacing it with hopes light.

A kindly deed, a helping hand,
A loving word or two,
Might turn the darkest clouds for one,
Into skies of blue.

—*Jim L. Stoeckel*

An Old Piece Of Clay

I was looking through some boxes the other day
When I cam across—an old piece of clay
Memories returned my heart—back to when
that old piece of clay—was formed
By my child's little hands

A little piece of clay
Brought tears to my eyes
As I remembered her
How hard she must have tried
To make something special
For her Mommy that day
And I felt my child's love—in that old piece of clay

I can still see her—as she was back then
Her tiny little fingers—working with a grin
A little frown forming—as she tried to make
Each part so perfect—as the clay lost its shape

Each tiny impression—touched by her heart
Brought memories of her life from the very start
It was if I could almost—feel her hands that day
And the love she felt—in that old piece of clay

—*Darlene Sams*

Portrait Of Tears

How could I think of how I should be?
When I did not know the existence of me!

How could I imagine my own way of life?
If I could, I would have made the right sacrifice.

For three decades, I've wandered a path not clearly.
How could I not feel my own love?
For if I had, I would have awaited sincerely
for clear guidance from above.

How did I accept to live the life with lives inflicted in pain?
I only gathered from them pictures of actions they alone can claim.

It has been from my beginning, till maybe my end,
I'll forever seek and search for forgiveness to amend.

I'm the portrait your eyes will forever see,
You will wonder of my existence and what caused the death of me

Yet, you will wonder over fragments of what remains,
as you look upon this portrait filled with pain

The question which will be asked, How did he die?
You will wonder, then notice
the portrait designed
with tears from my eyes.

—*Gary Allen Herman*

Red

It was a beautiful day in the fall,
When I met a man whom I thought had it all.
He said he was called red when he was growing up.
I said I was called skinny bones and milk when I was a pup.

It was off to Victorian Christmas we went,
On a cold winter's eve we spent.
I asked to take his arm not meaning any harm,
But little did I know the magic would soon become tragic.

Our really first date I would not highly rate.
I sobbed my heart was breaking
As red told me of his hurt and aching.
I learned a lot about myself, felt like I had been on a shelf.
Falling in love with this man really wasn't in my plan.

This man called red still lays his head
Not far away as distance would be, but far from me.
He dropped out of my life because of his strife.
His burden was too heavy to welcome a friend or a wife.

Yet, it was a beautiful day in the fall
When I met a man whom I thought had it all.

—*Barbara Cotter*

Unspoken Words Of A Dying Man

You were always there,
When I needed you.
Though I never realized it till now.
I gave you courage, my love,
my strength.
Oh my love, I need you now.
You are in my every thought
and haunted dreams. I was your
teacher and you were my student.
I need you more than I
can ever express, your
loving smile and your gentle
hand makes my pain less.
I never stopped to look at
my priceless jewel,
Right before my eyes.
Together you and I will
combat my pain. My deepest
regret is not telling you
how much I love you.

—*Barbara Grandchamp*

To My Dearly Departed Child

I have to keep busy trying to breathe.
When I pause my womb aches
to the heart.
Tis bitter-sweet
to give up a child;
for its good, give up a child.
Love's umbilical cord is torn,
ripped asunder with your
first breath...
worse than divorce
to give up a child.
Meaning finds no air
to survive in.
But, somehow, when I hear
you are fine
I breathe just a little easier.

—*Beryl Khabeer*

If

A caterpillar crawled on my shoelaces
When I was just a little kid
It delighted me
I stroked its fur
But fun is fun
And somehow I had
To remove the caterpillar from my shoelaces
The work was slow and tedious
Not as exciting as capturing a firefly
Or scratching a cat between the ears
What would it be like
If
Caterpillars purred also?
—*Gertrude L. Anchelo*

The Wander Lust

The wander lust was on me
When I woke at peep of day;
How I longed to be a gypsy
To take my tent and away.

The morning breezes whispered softly
The road never seemed so wide;
The birds flew beckoning onward,
All ready to sail was the tide.

How wonderful a gypsy's life must be,
To roam the land and the deep;
Never owning a trip of ground
Or a roof under which to sleep.

Now I have friends and country
But it is the gypsy's life I crave;
To live and roam as the gypsy does
And in the end find a gypsy's grave.

Some may envy my learning.
Others may envy my wealth.
But I envy only the gypsy,
Here drink the gypsy's health.
—*Hallie C. Compson*

Hindsight

To Alisa Lynn Van Veghiel
When in the arrogance of our youth,
we brush aside sweet, gentle truth,
and on distant goals we set our sights,
and feed our souls on bitter slights.

Unaware that there shall come the day,
and the heavy price we'll have to pay,
when as our eyes and footsteps falter,
we lay our souls on God's great alter.

In retrospect we will weigh our chances,
and look around us with covert glances,
at our fellow travelers deep in strife,
and wish we'd lived a more Christian life.

As we'll gather under darkening skies,
and pray that God will hear our cries,
as in time, to each of us he'll turn,
to display mercy or condemn to burn.
—*Howard W. Wood*

See And Do It

It never fails,
When it comes to little boys.
They see a mud puddle,
And stomp right through it.
Every time they're sure to do it.

It never fails,
When it comes to little boys.
They see a little girl's pigtail,
And grab ahold to pull it.
Every time they're sure to do it.

It never fails,
When it comes to little boys.
They see your back turned,
And they make faces, call names and pick.
Every time they're sure to do it.

It never fails,
When it comes to little boys.
They see you coming angry,
And they flash that big smile and bright eyes.
Every time they're sure to do it.
—*James Nelson Deitz*

A Message To Daddy

It's hard to say good-by
   When it's time to go;
We're never really ready
   Because we love them so.

It's comforting to recall
   The good times you have had;
And usually among them all
   There's some to make you sad.

It's hard to know just what to say
   or think or act or do;
But knowing others feel your pain
   makes it some easier, too.

Yet no matter what time of year
   Whether spring or in the fall,
We need to be ready to say good-by
   For life ends for us all.

And some day we will all reunite
   Above the sky so blue;
We're looking forward to that time
   When we can be with you.
—*Cindy Wilson*

Banner Stars

Are we aboard when life moves on?
When shade and shadow, and gold bloom paints dawn?
The river of life measures our mood
From the shock of our dreams, that it wood.
We believe in the future, singing soul music.
Dealing out hurt from our mood, we are ecstatic.
Breath to breath, our infinity with life,
Is like a spray of flowers, we take from strife.

Are we aboard when life moves on?
When strains of music, and beauty are drawn?
Like a wayward wave moves back, we stall.
Have we a flower in freedom's hall?
An echoic throbbing, like many feet walking,
Are the steps we learn from the grand music, we sing.
A flotsam moves, exposing driftwood art.
Banner stars flash power to us, and we start.
—*Audrie M. Fiskaali*

Love's Quest

Tis not time to cease to live
When love has stopped to give
The passion, lust, and fire
That has now begun to expire.
You have but one short life
So do not live it in strife.
Love laughs at the brevity of life
For this lone reason:
Life has but one short season.
Love will never take its last breath
For it has no master named death;
Nothing can outlive love,
Not even the stars above.
Do not waste the time God has given you by crying
Over a lost love till the evening
Of your life has disappeared.
A broken heart is not to be feared.
It is real life, not just fairy-tales,
Where the fool often fails
To realize that other lovers exist.

—*Darlene Fry*

Elusive Sleep

In the small hours of the morning
When my troubled mind roams free
I stroll once more down a lonely lane
To what was — or still may be

I run through caverns — full of hope
To where the dreaded future lies
And gather remnants of my youth
With heavy heart and tear-filled eyes

What fancies take me to that house
Decayed and gone this many years
Where Mom and Dad with smiling eyes
Once more could brush away my tears

"Oh carousing youth" without a care
Without a thought to payments due
I tried to hold those passing years
But like a fleeting dream they flew

The thoughts of love that might have been
The joyous friendships of the past
And of all that vanished with the years
For how could those precious moments last

And as the son breaks in my room
  and all the shadows fade away
The phantoms that possess the night
Have left me for another day

—*Charles Saber*

A Show Of Seasons

Seasons present to us a show,
 When spring arrives winter must go.
 It seems spring has hardly begun,
 Before dawns days of summer sun.

Each season brings its own delights:
 Winter's magic of snowy nights,
Spring's verdancy with bright flowers,
 Summer's sunny, long, lazy hours.

Then comes crowning glory of fall
 When trees get dressed as for a ball
 And monarch butterflies in flight
 To Mexico are a grand sight.

—*Jean Young*

The Gardener

Gardening is something that many like to do.
When Spring comes around you start in all anew.
You need to till the soil to make a good seed bed,
Then you check your neighbors garden, cause you don't want him
  to get ahead.
By doing a little planning you might keep from getting
  trouble bound,
Cause some plants grow up straight while others spread
  out all around.
You check your seed can to see if you have any usable seed.
Then you go to town and buy the rest of what you need.
Now when it comes to planting there are some things you need
  to mind,
You need to check the Almanac and do it according to the Sign.
There are plants that take special care such as poles for the
  pole beans.
And there is a custom to cage the tomatoes, so it seems.
Finally there comes the bragging day when you get your first
  red tomato.
From then on your bragging is, how big your veggies grow.
Now you have an abundance, more then you can use,
So you call to your neighbor but he politely does refuse,
Cause the neighbor up the street has already filled his larder,
And you find that getting rid of your surplus just keeps
  getting harder.
Now, wouldn't it be something if you could just FAX them far away,
To some on this earth that is going hungry on this day?

—*Bruce Elliott*

Silver Wings And Earthly Kings

It was just a year ago today, as I lay fast asleep,
  When suddenly I was wakened, by the patter of little feet.
An angel whispered in my ear, at last the time had come,
  And I must leave my heavenly home, before the morning sun.

The next few moments were busy spent, bidding my friends
  good-bye
  And though I tried to hide it, a tear dropped from my eye.
It was at this moment the Lord appeared, and calling me to His
  side,
He spoke but for a moment, but calmed the fears inside.

The next thing I remember is clinging with all my might,
  To a friendly little comet, streaking thru the night,
And as it plummeted down toward earth, I could plainly see,
  A reception committee dressed in white, waiting there for
  me.
A year has passed since the day, I shed my silver wings,
  A happier one never felt, by any earthly king.

And now dear Mom, the time has come, the sandman's on his
way.
  My heart is filled with happiness, on this very special day.
And so before I close my eyes, and into slumber do depart,
  I'd like but for a moment, this message to impart,
May the Good Lord watch over and protect you, may you never
  shed a tear,
And may you know Joy and Happiness, for a hundred million
  years.

—*James P. Curran*

Here's Tyler

I was playing with my friends by the throne,
When the Great Father looked at us and said,
"I have a mission for one of you. I want you
to go to earth and make a young couple's dream come true."
Then He pointed straight at me.
I was scared as scared could be
He said, "never fear, I'll always be near."
"Here I am, Mommy and Daddy.
And here I stay until my Father calls me away.
We're going to have lots of fun
Because everywhere I go
You'll have seats in the front row.
When you are old and gray
And your steps falter a little more each day.
I'll be right there with a helping hand.
Until you cross over to the Promised Land."

—*Eula M. Moody*

The Railroad Crossing

I stopped my car and waited
When the red light blinked one day.
My patience seemed to be on end,
As the minutes slipped away.
It seemed the train was slowing down
As the freight cars squeaked on past
I watched, and started counting...
They seemed to fly so fast.
The rails swayed easy with the load,
The hypnotic sound did rise
And childhood memories flashed back to me
Before my very eyes.
The old freight train kept rolling on
My heart lightened, just to see
They had not changed with the years
The changes were in me.
The squeaky wheels, the lettered cars
Were there, for all to see
Just like they were, when I was small, and
The engineer waved at me.

—*Dorothy Rednour Andersen*

Evening

In the stillness of the evening
When the sun has gone to rest
When the purple shadows deepen
That's the time that I like best.

As the light grows slowly dimmer
All the birds are in their nest
Cheeping to their sleepy young ones
Settling down for a night of rest.

Then the crickets start their chirping
While the bull frog croaks his song
Lighting bugs flit here and there
While the tree frogs sing along.

The night is all aglow then
There's a golden yellow moon
As the stars begin to twinkle
On a lovely night in June.

—*Julia Bartins-Pavlic*

Summer Distractions

It's awfully hard to settle down and write a rhyme or two,
When the sun is shining brightly and the sky is oh so blue.

It's difficult to contemplate on the matching up of words,
When the flowers are gay, I'm led astray, with the singing of the birds.

I try a little line or so to see how it will sound.
I conjure up a thought or two and toss them all around.

"It isn't always easy to make a rhyme with reason,
One that is appropriate for every day or season."
Then the breezes in the trees make me stop to listen.
I wonder down the creekside, oh how the water glistens.

I pick a flower here and there and check a nestling bird.
Find a family growing there and I utter not a word.

I move along and try again to put some words together.
Find a pretty stone or two and then a bright blue feather.

See what I mean, it's very hard to keep my mind on rhyming.
Maybe I should change my ways or maybe just my timing.

Next thing I know the pictures clear, the words are flying free
I change a word right before or there and then I stop to see.

How does it look, how does it sound and does it tell a tale?
Will it be good, will it be bad or will it make a sale?

Then I put it all together and add a bit of spice.
Now I have a little story that I feel is very nice.

—*Eleanor J. Hand*

When A Person Must Stand Alone In The Sun

There comes a time when a person must stand alone in the sun.
When the tall trees behind her, in whose towering shadows she stood,
Are fallen, clear cut by lumberman's saw.
Trees are floating on death's river; she shivers and weeps in the warm sun.

There comes a time when a person must stand alone in the sun.
When leaning back, there are no longer arms to support her,
There is an eerie emptiness, where once there was presence.
She must embody wisdom, courage and strength, though she still feels like a child.

There comes a time when a person must stand alone in the sun.
When she must rely upon her own judgement, her own vision.
The sage has vanished from the forest, and the giants of banyan swamp are silent:
She has only the quiet, frosty breath of the mountains to comfort her.

There comes a time when a person must stand alone in the sun.
Combing back from the presence, her face glows with hidden Light.
Opening her mouth, she utters the words of her Soul, wisdom of the Primal Lord;
Opening her hands, she gives her gifts to humankind.

There comes a time when a person must stand alone in the sun.
Having walked down the final wind in the road, she beholds a door.
Outside this door, she is a mortal being of flesh, wracked with pain and sorrow.
Through this door, she is a radiant daughter of light, clothed in robes of deathless thought,
   creatrix of her world and experience.

—*George A. Boyd*

Southern French Sunflowers

I miss the sunflowers in southern France,
When the wind blew, they'd dance a dance,
Between the train that ran through them
In the afternoon.

I'd walk down to the bottom of the steps
And down the path that led
To the strawberries and pick and eat
Their sweet strawberry juice.

When the summer sun was shining,
I was happy to be free and alone
And I imagined this French garden
Was my secret home,

Where the crazy world stopped
And my thoughts grew quiet
As the southern French sunflowers
Drew me back and forth
And lulled me to a peaceful sleep
In the strawberry patch,
In the garden.

—*Jennifer Lynn Stevens*

Yesterday

It wasn't very long ago;
When, trees and, grass.
Were green and, the little dell,
Where I once sat:
Wishing: You were there with me.
And little birds, made it,
Their favorite place where little flowers grew,
And, this, "was only yesterday:"
Not, so long ago but soon
The leaves will turn
To red and gold and,
the "grass no longer green"
And, the "little dell"
Where I once sat will be,
Covered with snow and frost, but,
I will have my memories
of only yesterday,
Not so long ago.

—*Ellen Londgrof*

First Love

I didn't think I wanted a dog
When we went to get you, "J"
But Dad said the "kids" must have a dog,
And I had to say O.K.

The lady said she had two Pugs
And after she went out,
I sat down on a footstool
My mind still full of doubt.

Then two small Pugs came bouncing in
Both fawn, black-faced and full of charm;
One ran across that little room
And jumped into my arms.

And from that moment on, sweet "J,"
Of me, you were a part;
Not only were you in my arms —
But also in my heart.

—*Edith Whiteman*

The Boy In You

I wish I had known the boy in you
 when we were young for awhile,
I bet I'd have been your best girl, too,
 when life wore a smile!
You could have borrowed my best jump rope
 to hang your tire from a tree,
I'd even have swiped my Mom's face soap
 and bathed your old dog for free.

You'd surely have been my very best beau—
 name etched in ink on my wrist
And we'd have been like engaged, you know,
 right after our first real kiss.
I missed out, Hon, on that boy in you
 (but bet he sneaks out for fun)
He runs the train set, like "Daddys" do,
 down on the floor with our son!

—*Jeanne Thomas*

Remembering

Dedicated to my son, Mike
When you lose a loved-one, it is so sad: When you lose a parent, you feel so bad. But when you have a child to die; It's a different feeling; and oh—how you cry!

There's an empty feeling — a missing part, Like a piece has been torn away, from your heart You remember the good things, all of his deeds, You remember his wishes — and all of his needs.

You remember all the little things he'd say. You kissed his hurts — along life's way. You remember his laugh, a grin, or a smile, When he gave you a "hug" every once in awhile.

You remember when he said, "Mom, I love you so!" When he showed concern, when you felt low. When he said, "Mom, you taught us kids Love," You felt that you were in "heaven above!"

You remember after his baptism, his falling tears - You remember the "love" he gave, through the years. You remember so much, there's so much more; Then — he's gone — through "Heaven's door." You wonder then, why things went wrong, You ask "Dear God — why is he gone?"

—*Dory Guess*

Emptiness

 The emptiness of the soul
 When you lose the will to love
 Is an incredibly scary feeling
 As you pray for help from above.

 When you lose the sense of trust
 And the ability to let anyone close
You walk around as an incomplete person
 A coward, a fraud, a ghost.

But how can you learn to trust again
 To give your heart away
The fear remains, too strong to ignore
 During the harsh reality of day.

 To become complete
 And to cleanse the soul
 To trust and to love again
 Is the ultimate goal.

—*Carolyn D. Gregersen*

God

There's always one person who's there
When you're down,
He's there.

When you need companionship,
He's there.

When you need someone just to look for advice,
He's there.

When you need someone to hold you and say "it's okay,"
He's there.

When you're having a bad day, and you need someone to talk to,
He's there.

If you trust him,
He's there.

If you have faith,
He's there.

If you totally believe,
He's there.

If you believe in the heavens,
—*Amanda Stutchman*

That Old Red Kimono

That old red kimono so easy to wash and wear
Whenever it needs mending, I carefully fix its tears.
Not so long ago it was new and so pretty,
Now, like me, it is getting old...what a pity.

I would not part with it for any price..
To me, it still looks very nice.
Like a memory, it becomes a part of you.
You keep it along with you until you are through.

Now it's faded and doesn't look so red.
It's tired and worn out...a long life it's led.
It's been a constant companion of mine.
I will dispose of it ...in my own time.

—*Johnnye L. Kleckner*

Angels

"Oh Lord," I cried in deepest despair
"Where are you, Lord? You are not there."
"O child of mine," He said to me
"I've had to bring you to your knees.
I've had to break your heart into
That you might know what I can do."
Then Lord you did a wondrous thing
I want to laugh, and shout, and sing
You sent your Angels from above
To wrap me in your tender love
They dried my eyes of all my tears
They took away my deepest fears
They lifted me above despair
They told me "Yes, the Lord does care."
Now my Lord, all I can say
"I'll sing your praises every day
Thank you for your gentle care
For letting me know you're always there."

—*Judy Rickett*

The Prison

Is prison just a house of stone
Where bad men are really kept?
Or is it just a place of steel
Where many souls have wept?

No it is not a "prison pen"
As some would understand,
But it is where all struggling souls
Can stop and renew their mind;

When rushing on in the current of life,
Many rivers we all must cross,
And some get carried down the stream
Until their footing they've lost;

To rescue them, is it such a thing
That's counted all for nought?
To rescue them from the currents of life
Till the lesson, well-learned, is taught?

Stand still, O, soul, thy struggling cease!
Let the rescuer's strong arm,
Encircle thee, there, in thy lonely cell,
And deliver thee from thy harm!

—*Anna M. Lampe*

Santa Rosa Plateau

There is a place I relish wandering
   where carpeting the hillsides in the spring
Bright lilies, lupine, poppies open wide
   along the zig-zag trails through countriside
Nodding Monkey Flowers, tall Paint Brush
   are next to Miners Lettuce, crisp and lush
While shaded vernal pools are sometimes seen
   with Salamanders, Tree Frogs, glossy green

Birds and flowers undisturbed we see
   like sparrows, pink Owls Clover, Filaree
Living wild where no man can destroy
   Cougars hide, while deer watch a skipping boy
There, majestic thoughts flood to my mind
   and this Preserve I trust we'll always find!

—*Dilys Raley*

My Inner Feelings

Oh God my father
Where dost thou come from
Thou comes from the depths of my being
Thou comes from the grandeur of all that is
Thou comes from the depths of hell it self

Oh father
How can I love thee
When thou art so great
And I am so small

I long to hold thee, to kiss thee
For thee to kiss me on the cheek
That I may feel thee
For thee to squeeze me
Oh!!!
I am so alone
Hurry to me before I will for I love thee

—*Franklin J. Rourke Sr.*

Nostalgia

Lazy thoughts and sunny slopes
Where doth they prance at one time
Before man came and began to climb...
To reach his ladder of success
His ego he must effervesce.
To show his neighbors and his friends
How much he has before it ends...
Now you tell me for what it's worth
Is this what I inherit at my birth?
Not soft warm grass and rolling hills
When nature cured many ills.
Not noisy brooks with babbling water
All these wonders I could not alter.
So with lazy thoughts and sunny slopes
I leave thee...
I close my eyes and see,
The antelope is running free...

—*Helen Donchez*

Sounds Of A Battlefield

The bluff slopes flow down around stone markers
where each of the cavalry met his final retreat
Their cries of battle, their guns, all silenced:
caught in gray-brown soil below a magpie's call.

I see hovering mists of the Yellowstone going west,
as then, down the stilled ramparts of Siouan lands.
Silence river-creeps along Little Big Horn Valley;
silence deepening, flaking off into sudden sounds.

A man, standing where one had fallen, chipping off
holiday mementoes of stone from one site marker:
flakes of white-gray marble falling to
a white hand and the Indian's alkaline earth.

A magpie takes away its wing-mix of white and black.
The clouds drift higher between banks of sight.
The little Big Horn flood carried quiet time away;
a sound of decay falls marble-broken underfoot.
Wings carry over a vulture's rocking float; sage-
brush sweeps this coliseum of a general's last mistake.

I move downslope toward another's hasty mistake.
There I see new history chipped on a death marker.

—*Carl Cunningham*

The Ruler

    Taken into a world
   Where everything is white
    The confusion awaits you
    Morning, noon, and night
    Your ruler is a substance
  and your life becomes a lie
    The ruler will control you
    or even help you die
  It helps you have a good time
  But loves to watch you suffer
    The ruler wants you fully
Your father, your brother, your lover
    It needs to hear you call
   You can't forget its name
  The ruler needs to have you
   Just simply yell out cocaine

—*Dawn Wilkin*

Shifting Winds

Grandma's garden was an exact square pose
Where flowers conformed under her care.
The rows, stiffly straight in the summer air,
Bloomed with violets, the pinks and the rose.
Grandma nurtured with songs of her yesterday
While she worked with the sunlight on her crown
Till strong breezes seized and tumbled it down
While I swung on the garden gate in play.
Today I went to see a tangled perfection.
Where weeds bloomed benignly, asking no pardon,
Blending with the conformity of Grandma's garden.
I stood in wonder in this complexion.
The winds blow, where they will, continually.
As even now, they nudge the gate and me.

—*Anna Bernice Coon*

Adrift

Wherever the storm-clouds gather,
Where forceful winds blow free,
Over missel-moor with a hollow roar,
Or turbulent over the sea;

Wherever the darkness falleth,
And one with its heart tonight
I'm tumbled as rampant torrents
Descending a craggy height.

Across a barren wilderness
Where reigneth but solitude,
(Save for a sad, a keening wind)
A wasteland shapes my mood.

I go with a vagrant's purpose,
Trekking on, never seeking to rest;
O blow, ye winds a-wandering:
Your will's my sober quest!

—*Cecilia Roseline Gregg*

An Old Shoe Box

An old shoe box with a bright blue lid
Where in the young lads treasures were hid
A slingshot responsible for a broken window or two
A toy top held together with glue
A bag full of marbles, colors bright
A ball of string for a kite's flight
Some baseball cards from a cereal box
And from the neighbor girls head some golden locks
The box tho a little worse for wear
Was handled with tender loving care
These precious belongings of a freckled face lad
Were much the same as his dad once had.

—*Doris Brubaker Walter*

Memorial Day Tribute

Does it feel like you are holding your heart in your hand
When you bow your head to the flags and flowers
as only those who served could understand
As only survivors who have read the long list of names know
that these minutes seem like hours
As we press our palms to our faces in prayer
Remembering those we knew who are not with us today
As we slowly walk away from the silence there
Keeping inside the feelings so difficult to say
Just emotion cascading down the cheeks of those who stir
Remembering quietly...the ones who were

—*Darlene Fremgen*

Traveling! Leaving With Jesus

Alive for eternity
Where joy's everlasting!
With "Jesus in heaven I'll be"
Safe with my "Saviour"
  I can't wait, to see.

With "Jesus" I'm leaving!
Traveling, daily!
Gradually reaching "eternal" destiny!!
"Jesus" I follow!
"His footsteps leading way"
Naili scared, hand I, hold!
In her "precious name" I pray.

Alive in heaven glory.
With "Jesus Christ" my king!
"I'll praise! "God!" forever.
  "Gods family we will, sing!
No sorrows, no death's ever occurred!!!
With "Jesus" I'm leaving!
  Behind all sorrow.

In "Heaven with Jesus" living we thout, worry!
  "Eternally!"
    —*Beulinda S. Murley*

As We Dub You, We Are

I work for the city, I work in the drains
Where most of the water must go when it rains,
And where all the dross of the dwellings must go,
To make all the sewage to run thus and so.

I lifted the lid of a manhole, one day,
And there saw a woman, her eyes all agley
With mending some clothes in pursuit of quick cash,
As the sewage flowed by, with her needles aflash.

I said, "What are you doing down in that hole?"
She looked up at me with such mirth in her soul,
I quickly burst forth with surprise in my laugh.
I wondered if she thought me daffy, by half!

She said, "What's the word that you see on the top?"
"It's sewer," I said, and I spoke without stop.
"Ah, no! It says sewer, now put back the lid."
I had to agree, so that's just what I did.
    —*James G. Billson Jr.*

Metamorphosis

In the darkest recess of my mind.
Where old memories are hard to find.
Stood a mental trunk filled with pain and woe.
A place where awareness was loath to go.
It was covered with cobwebs of forgetfulness.
Sealed with tears, and no return address!

He kissed my cheek and walked away.
His soul flew home to God that day.
Pandora's trunk was opened wide,
And all the pain that was inside
Has come to haunt my every day.
My love, Why? Why couldn't you stay?

Days drag dismally, depressing my soul.
I search for reasons, and for a goal.
I struggle with each hour of my life,
Lost and lonely, no longer a wife.
My prayer is that when I cross the bar,
We'll be together beneath the morning star.
    —*Ann Aldrich Barlet*

Montana's Flathead Valley

Vast flower-dotted prairies end at a narrow cleft
Where once a gigantic thrust divided a continent
Revealing kaleidoscopically a broad well-watered valley
Ringed by timber-covered mountains, their jagged white tops
Promising streamflow to rivers, creeks and lakes
Where fish jump high or hide in sheltered pools.
Massive pine trees climbing to eye-blinding blue sky
Were more than seedlings
When the first white man passed this way.
As eyes feast upon this widespread panorama I wonder:
Will hearts of progeny four generations hence
Respond as mine does now and behold a still unspoiled diorama?
    —*Helen Christensen*

Trials Are God's Kisses Too

Somewhere in Heaven,...God has a place,
Where souls are supplied,...for the human-race;
Of all the riches,...that heaven can boast;
The soul of man,...He loves the most.
The worth of a soul,...is a precious thing.
The sacrifice...was the King of Kings,
To pure the soul,...He must take out the dross;
The cost has been paid,...He died on the cross.
For if we suffer,...and we find we're at fault,
It's to put more worth, in the inner-soul-vault.
For in each trial,...there is a lesson to gain;
This school for the soul,...is never in vain;
For when one trial...has obtained its goal,
We're one grade higher,...with a richer soul.
For faith must grow gradually, to be solid and strong.
Each trial...is only a bridge,...to help us along.
For God,...loved us so much,...He died in our stead;
But, He also knows,...each soul must be fed.
And each test we pass, He's pleased, oh so much;
He sends a reward,...tis, His sweet tender touch.
    —*Audrey Jean Webb*

Beyond The Horizon

Beyond the horizon,
Where the sky -
Meets the Sea, Is a paradise waiting,
For you and for me.

Voyagers have tried,
For many years -
To reach the Horizon,
And conquer their fears.

Where Heaven and Earth.
Seem to meet as one,
The end of a search -
And a victory won!

But everyone learns,
As they sail the sea,
The horizon - keep looming
Endlessly!

So we assume -
That's one place we go -
When the Soul is our Captain
Not our mind - in control!
    —*Adeline Fleischer*

Precious Time

It's sad but true that no one knows
Where time so swiftly passing goes
Time where hours are mostly spent
Doing good have come and went
Where, it's such a mystery
To such a lowly one as me

A month, a year, perhaps a week
Where has it gone can no one speak
Ah time with its fleeting ways
Cannot be measured by months or days
But rather like the shifting sand
Is measured by the masters hand

For he who holds it in his hand
Can measure width, breadth or span
When we have used our allowance
It's what we've done for him that counts
Then can we honestly truthfully say
We've wasted not one single day
Of precious time and bravely stand
Before he who holds it in his hand.
—*Alene Stamper*

A Feeling We Share

My mountains with all their grace,
Where trees, creeks, critters, and flowers all have a place.
Comfort me and put peace in my heart and a smile on my face.
After awhile there, my pain you'll find no trace.

Safe here in God's arms I am truly saved.
Trails to beauty you will not find paved.
For love I want, here I no longer crave.
For those that want it, it is a free as God gave.

The air is fresh and clean with smells of nature and flowers.
It helps one gain strength and power.
As the trees and world above you tower.
Safely you can spend many hours.

The brooks run fresh and clean.
No rat race here will you find, to make the world so mean.
Togetherness all around can be felt and seen.
The earth is covered with a blanket of peaceful green.

A place of comfort anytime I can go.
Here I write the best I know.
A peaceful place to let my feelings flow.
Where pain rides out on winds that blow.

At times I am glad not all can see.
The great gift God gave you and me.
For I can still alone there be.
Thank you God for setting me free.
—*Billie Jeske*

Dream Land

I want to go to a place far away.
Where all my dreams come true
and things go my way.
Where the waterfalls are funning
and the trees are swaying,
and everything is worth all of my praying.
I want to go to a place far away,
where all my dreams come true and
I can go there day after day.
—*Barbara Grow*

Lovely Minnesota

Traveling westward again to Minnesota's grand retreat,
Where we love to visit once more among woodland breezes and "tom-tom" beat
From woodlands that edge fertile fields here's pure air for us to breathe
Where summer's heat and winter's cold reach such degrees, hard for us to believe.
Our eyes feast on long and broad, fertile fields within great plains of earth.
Punctuated with farm houses, barns, and grain bins of great worth.
This state earned pride with astute and historic politicians,
Who even express concern for the inmates of prisons.

Your state has a remarkable record of growth in enterprise,
Enriched by ideas to betterment from the thrifty and wise.
When here, we delight in all the family members of Jerry, our son,
To hear tales swapped about fish, deer and Minnesota Twins scoring their runs.
Ferns, tall trees, white clouds and beautiful flowers greet our gazing eyes,
In this glory of Nature's rendezvous under these wide, open skies.
Of forty nine states travelled, Minnesota stands out.
To help one understand what pioneer life was all about.
Hats off to people of energy, endurance and beauty.
Who keep their eyes on their goals and seldom shirk duty.
We salute your good attitudes about home, church and school,
As we see you keep living by the known Golden Rule.
Now time has come to thank you for rest, fun and food;
We must return home on our journey to Penn's Woods.
—*Charles W. Miller*

Lord, Let Me Live In This House

Lord, let me live in this house on the top of the hill;
Where your light will shine out for all to see;
And may these hands of mine be your hands
Drawing the lost and wandering ones home to Thee.
Let this house be a haven from the storms
That beset them on their way;
And may they find your love and peace
Within these walls, Dear Lord, I pray.
Then when they venture forth once more
Upon life's turbulent sea,
May their faith and love be anchored fast,
I pray, Dear Lord, in Thee.
Walk with them, Lord, each step of the way;
Hold fast their hand lest they may fall;
And guide them into that perfect day
Where there's peace and joy - and a crown for all.

I thank, Thee, now, Lord, for this hill-top house
Where I can let my light shine before all men;
And they who see it will glorify, Thee, Father,
And believing, will take heart again - Amen - Amen and Amen!
—*Beulah Lockhart Parsons*

Christmas Poem

Christmas is a happy time of year
When we are with friends we hold most dear.
We all sing Christmas carols loud and clear,
When Jesus was born and Angels sing,
We lift up our voices and let them ring.
Families gather around the Christmas tree
To see what we receive from he or she.
We look at our gifts and wonder what could they be.
—*Cornelia Schulz*

Our Nations Bond

Whatever the language or the skin, we find a bondage there,
Wherever there's humans or it's kin, we are duty bound to care.

The white man's sword, the black man's shield, our foreign
brother's reason, we make a mighty force at any time or season.

Who can come against us, when we stand for liberty,
What terror can defy us, when we for peace agree.

What shout can be as strong as the shout for peace on earth,
What evil can endure our mass powers and their worth.

Let us always stand for justice, unafraid and so profound,
Let us for the victory, march on the chosen battleground.

If evil forces try us, on the shores of Tripoli
Let us united, meet our foes, on land, in air, or on sea.

A United brotherhood are we, an America, the brave,
We strive, arm in arm, you see, our continents to save.

We won't take down, or deny freedom for the oppressed,
We'll always rally to the call of those that are distressed.

So in the name of justice and peace on earth always,
We'll fight together, for one cause, throughout our endless days.

—*Dorothy E. Jenkins*

Deprivement

I long to return to the home place
Which all my roots embrace:
The salt box farmhouse with red sloping roof,
The green shuttered windows, close and snow-proof,
The winding clay path leading up to the door,
The rose-smothered summers, the noisy hay mower,
The vegetable garden with feasting for all,
The welcoming love of the picture-decked hall—
How clearly I see them with memory's eye,
So dearly I love them; how hard not to cry!
Without a return to the home place
I'm a ship without a prow,
But I cannot return to the home place;
It's a super-highway now.

—*Anne Marron Rensel*

The Garden

Life is a delicate-scented flower,
Which God adores on His heavenly walks,
And tends with love from His holy bower,
But Man is the rust upon the stalks.

Nurtured by His beneficent care,
A miracle wakens the budding seeds,
All things in this great bounty share,
But Man is the rank, unsightly weeds.

The earth is a garden of exotic splendor,
Gently pruned by hands Divine.
Man reaches up for this grand provender,
As a clinging, choking, strangling vine.

Life's path runs through a verdant field,
Dew-kissed in the rose-tinged dawn.
As the earth brings forth its nourishing yield,
Man is the crabgrass on the lawn.

The world is a great, majestic tree,
With rain-dappled leaves and ripening fruits.
Its golden harvest intended for thee,
But Man, the fungus amongst the roots.

—*Hunter Bridgeford Fleshood*

should one break free

As one whose life has been tied to rigid rules of science
    which carried over into rigid rules of verse
he wonders what it would be like to escape these rules

can he learn to appreciate the freedom of unfettered verse
dare he venture into a new would devoid of structure
should he desert the beauty of rhythm and rhyme
which ring like music in his soul
should he try to follow the thoughts of others
or perhaps even express his own
in the absence of pattern

would it be as a train running on its ties
    rather than on its tracks
or would it be as a graceful gull coasting on the wind

let him venture into this unstructured world of words and thoughts
let him meander where there are neither paths nor signposts
where neither are needed because there seems no destination
and then let him return to his safe world of "sines and cosines"
of integrals and differentials
    and of engineering tables and standards

and having made this trip into uncharted lands
how is he upon his return
perplexed serene or enlightened

—*Edward W. Clautice*

The Pauper

Lying High on twenty mattresses
which, having toiled endlessly to stack
when you half-year toppled them
with a Mocking tear (and a Bitter laugh)

present, Long time from that Evil deed
Peace atop my perch
but one Small pin in my blade
or a stitch in my side
(or a stab in my heart)
pain whichever way I lay

One hundred feet above, I clamber down
to find what caused that Tiny kink
ah, here 'tis
between first and second mattresses

I try to flick it away
or grab it and cast it out
that stone is still Out of Reach

how did you get it there
in the first place

—*Aron Borok*

Love's Accoucheur

Within everyone lives a weaver of poems for those
Who take the time to listen to his sweet song-
Woof chosen, versed in various times, through wove
With heart-threads, bound fast and written to last life long.
Is there prettier music heart anywhere on earth
If not from the blending of two hearts into one?
How magically this weaver works a mystical birth
That gives rise to such savory sounds when done.
What wizardry that enchants young hearts;
Glances exchanged flood senses foretelling the song
They will sing when from friends they finally part
And enter a world to which only they can belong.
Yet the sounds of life added by friends do enhance
The work the weaver performs spinning love's trance.

—*J. Roston Jacobs*

The Far Horizon Or Journey's End

On the escalating steps of time
which in my daily life I climb.
I pause to view the years behind.
Days of pleasure, so deceiving,
times of sorrow left me grieving,
numb and sore, unbelieving.

Time is a thief, it steals my friends
it can never make amends.
I wonder how my journey ends?
May my soul with angels guiding
reach and touch the far horizon,
as the early sun is rising.

Day has ended; when the sun
sinks in the west night will come.
Then my soul, its journey done
hopeful, rises up to heaven,
knowing sins can be forgiven.
Pray my soul will go on living.

—*Charlotte Smith*

The Wind's Pursuant

So bland, the tastes of passing winds
Which once enthralled my breath
The nipple touched by tongue tip
Melts as lips enclose.
Yet eyes shut, hands behind me,
I lick the biting wind;
A taste much like a phantom
Who's face flows without form.
Unsure when scents accost me
Of what bloom is their source,
I suck the wind which pushes,
I lick the wind that pulls...
And though winds flavor is not full
And at my feet fresh lilacs grow,
Like hair my craving blows
A trail into winds flow ....
   The fruits I left behind,
   Unknown as those I seek.

—*Joseph Layden*

Guise

With my mind's eyes, I see a goddess
which only Zeus himself could have created.
I see a vision of beauty
unmatched even by Aphrodite.

Mannered by the three Graces
of splendor, mirth, and good cheer.
As she walks the rainbows of Iris,
I see inspiration even Apollo would fear.

I see a glimpse of hope
coming from a mountain of faith.
I see a morning rose covered with dew
blooming on a bright sunny morning.

But O what deed has been done to the gods,
for she is cursed to walk amongst mere mortal men.
What flaw stems from flawlessness?
This I cannot see.

—*David M. Kane*

The Enchantment Of Nature

   The trees above are littered with leaves,
which sway and rustle with the wind.
   The sun overhead exerts its warm rays upon the ground,
and cotton-white clouds dot the brilliant blue sky.
   Numerous voices of birds are heard,
as they are seen soaring across the expanse sky.
   A single leaf drifts silently upon the surface of a
waterfall, swirling and moving, lost in the current.
   Foam arises from the crash of the fall,
leaving only mist to rise in the crisp air.
   Flowers are blooming in full color,
and the green carpeting of the woods forms a collage of green.
   In a different realm I seem to feel,
for I am enchanted by nature's beauty.
   Suddenly, as a crash of thunder erupts from the sky,
the whole of nature is illuminated.
   Rain pours upon the ground,
converting the dampened soil to rivers.
   The waterfall crashes and falls steadily,
and the sun is blocked from the ever-darkening clouds.
   Streaks of lightning shoot across the sky,
forming bands around the charcoal-colored clouds.
   Winds blow at intense speeds,
an annihilating all things in its path.
   Slowly, the storm begins to recede,
until all is still once more.
   Again it is peaceful, but a path of destruction remains,
as a silent reminder that not all things are as they seem....

—*Elizabeth Anne Thompson*

Sounds That Steal Loudly

Vibrations from dancing feet are felt
While crystal rounds of chandeliers
Mirror images above youthful heads,
Where others, preceding, simply watch,
Remembering the rise
And feeling the fall of the beat of time,
Recognizing something
In the repetition of reminders,
Which stronger sounds have overcome.

The steady movements still hold charm
And clamor for more lively measures,
For some, now unwillingly undone.
A loud voice hollers,
In order to be heard,
"Isn't anyone at this table
Going to dance?"
As the crescendo rises,
Some of the guests do, too.
Leaving by a door,
Resembling an entryway,
Used many times before.

—*Jo Anne Allee*

A Limber Latin Limerick

There once was this alcoholic ex-Marine named Barrackass,
Who persistently strong-armed a little, lively, lass from
   Caracas-
Soon searchers found his "Ying-Yang" and seeds
Tossed from the roadside among the tall weeds,
Seems our lively little Latin Queen, with kitchen knife keen,
   had wind-rowed old Barrs' "Warrackcus"!

—*Harold O. Smith (Ole Shep)*

Award Of Honor

Highest award a wife can give her husband,
who for twenty years has given this honor
for his country and to every individual
around him. His honor has seen me through
the darkest of hours! As we ascend with
clasped hands down a different path of life,
May the richness of this honor forever lite
the way for all mankind.

—*Clara M. Gange*

Mysteries Of Mother Earth

Who spins her on her axis? Who knows if she will stop?
Who knows if she will quake or spew? Who knows if she will drop?
Our mighty earth holds secrets no one can understand.
Is she a concept of a God and formed by his own hand?
Was earth's origin a gas that gathered years of dust?
Is she one of many worlds? What theory can we trust?
Do you listen for earth's secrets on quiet summer nights?
When stars are twinkling brightly, do you see her secrets' lights?
Are we divine creations or does nature hold the key?
Did someone send us here to live? What is our destiny?
What is the purpose of earth life so many want to know?
The earth's our home for a short span- then, where do spirits go?
The hope of all mankind has been that death is not the end.
Will there be life again for all sometime, somewhere—what then?
Do you ever get the feeling as you ponder earth's great power,
That earth's creator knows the law and governs every hour?
Technology has changed our world; new-age answers we now find.
Yet-earth's mysteries are still hidden from the ever-querying mind.

—*Joyce Johnson Merryweather*

Show Me the Way

The world is full of people
Who like to tell you what to do,
But they need to be "shinning examples"
That goes for me, as well as for you.

It's not so important as to what you say
As it is to what you do,
I'm not in the "watching business"
But God keeps his eyes on you.

Many times, I get all mixed-up
When you tell me what I must do.
But wouldn't it be must easier,
If I could do like you?

Don't draw me a road map to heaven,
When your life could best, "show the way"
I have trouble in following directions, but
When you "show me", I can easily find the way.

A reader can read a book
And tells you what it says.
But when a person can "show you how to do it"
It's more convincing in many ways!

—*Hosezell Blash*

Untitled

Who is she who walks o'er there with hair of flaxen wheat,
With her gentle lips of rose and temperament so sweet?
Would that she could turn this way and soothe my racing heart,
With just one look upon her face of finely sculpted art.
The hazel depths that are her eyes shoot arrows through my soul,
Wounding me in such a way I'll n'er again be whole.
Alas I fear I'm lost to man, a poor fool who's in love,
The hapless willing victim of a softly cooing dove.

—*A. A. Kinzie*

Ode To Cupid

How cruel, O Cupid, that Thou shouldest smite a man
Who seeks to hide within the fortress of his soul
And wishes not to be given to the throes of love.
But Thou, O Son of Venus, dost not care for mortal man,
But with thy shafts of love, keener than the sting of wasps
Or Orion's blade, fitted to they bow,
Doth bend thy bow with unrelenting aim
And within his fortress a man is wounded
And made to bow before his queen of love
Pledging the vows of Juno.
Let him who will jest at these lines.
But he will smile most broadly,
And scoff most loudly,
Who idles on the bed of ease, or drinks long
And deeply of the intoxicant of leisure dreams,
And never venturing into the fray,
From his bivouac of life, received into his bosom
The darts tipped with the flaming fires of love,
And being thus transfixed, lies bleeding
On the arena of life, or being healed
Carries the scars upon his soul.

—*Charles W. McCulloh, Sr.*

Mother's God To Be With God

She was one of life's noblest characters,
Who treated everyone just the same.
We loved her with all our hearts
And mother was her name.

Even when we were naughty,
She would give us a chance to explain.
And she was always ready and willing
To help us bear any pain.

When we were downhearted,
She was there with us all the while,
To give us encouragement,
With a hug, a kiss and a smile.

When we often failed to thank her,
She never really seemed to mind.
She was that sort of a person.
Who was always loving and kind.

She was the sweetest lady,
That on this earth ever trod,
But now she is in heaven.
Mother's gone to be with God.

—*Byron C. Casey*

Julie

Laughter, amid squeals of delight echo as she encompasses the whole room. Her hands caress his face eyes as tho drops of rain glistening in the sun. Their eyes lock and they become as one.
   Who is this person she has stolen his love.
Lips touch, hand tousle his hair, soft sounds emit from her piquant lips. She shares his lap, tossing her sun kissed hair like shafts of wheat blowing in a windstorm. His every word is treasured even in tears she hushes as he speaks. He need only to say her pet name squirly to make her feet run to him.
   Who is this person she has stolen his love.
He kisses the tip of her upturned nose, she sighs and hunches her shoulders and revels in it all. Saucy, unrelenting in her love for him. We must share him forever. Our eyes meet she is all I have said. Why am I willing to share him with her forever? One sentence it takes to expose her.
   Who is this person she has stolen his love.
She daringly answers Gram its Julie!

—*Dot Chasse*

Blind

So many things happen in the world today,
who's right, who's wrong, who's to say?
Different beliefs, different lands,
so many people with empty hands.
How can we help, what can we do?
Don't ask me, I wish I knew.
Men play with tanks and rifles like toys,
armies of soldiers, bunches of boys.
Millions starve while others hurt,
no food, no shelter, no shoes or shirt.
Some have more than they'll ever need,
killing off others with foolish greed.
You have your God, and I have mine,
people die while we dance and dine.
Now ask your God, your higher being,
how can we act blind with all we're seeing?
Come take my hand and I'll take yours,
and let sweet peace bathe our shores.
Colours, races, religions aside,
we're all the same, on the inside.
—*Brett A. Beliveau*

Forever More

Reach out to "Him," the Lord our God
Whose love can now abide
Free like the soul of Abraham, whose love can't be denied
Once commith love, give it away, like thunder in a storm
Call out his name to all who play, and keep them safe and warm
go now into the light my child and here the words I say
For peace of heart will come to you, upon this blessed day!
Reach deep inside and come out strong
With grace and will abide
And with the gifts God gave to you, you cannot run and hide
you must rejoice in great esteem and call him loud and clear
"Oh God" you know I love you so, come now and hear my prayer
That peace will come from you above, and love will now abide!
I will not cry I will not hide.
Just want you by my side
Forevermore, forevermore
I need you here today!
to teach me how to come to you and teach me how to stay
close by your side....forever more!
—*Jo Linda Jennings*

Where Angels Fear To Tread

I do not sit with men of lies,
Whose thoughts and acts I do despise.
Tumult, some nations, to us bring,
While muttering but empty things.
They serve a God who bids them do,
Unholy things to me and you.
The god they serve — we do not know,
But by their actions they do show,
They hate the good; they love the bad,
And love of God, they never had.
So I decline, that for a time,
I sit with them, to drink and dine.
That you may know my thoughts are true —
I wrote them down to send to you.
—*Goldie L. Amnah*

Dedicated To Cerita

You came in to my life on the 24th of May.
Whose to say that you would be with me to stay.
Such joy you brought to my heart.
I couldn't bear to be apart.

Your big brown eyes shine so bright
Tears streamed down your cheeks when you cried at night.
Your smile is as wide as the sky.
And when you ask no one can deny.

You were barely a year when you started walking.
And before we knew it you were already talking.
You are as curious as an old Tom cat.
And there are times when you are such a brat.

Through all this you've been such a joy.
And though I've had three, I was glad you weren't a boy.
And it was you that made this all come true.
I dedicate this poem to you.

Now that you've learned the truth of your birth
Just remember you heard it here first.
And even if you didn't come from my tummy.
You still get to call me Mommy
—*Annie Raines*

A Time Or Two Before

Why does it take war to make peace?
Why are all our children fighting in the streets?
Why are we taught to be #1,
When today we're looking down the wrong side of the gun?
What happened to virtue, heroes, and prayer
And where's the reward for the people who care?
It doesn't make sense to me anymore,
Haven't we been through this a time or two before?
Why is our country just looking away
When wrongdoers live in our midst everyday?
And, why is it that people are starving in our streets,
When we produce more food than we can eat.
What happened to parents, teachers, and rules
What happened to family, home and good schools?
Were parents so busy and teachers so scared,
That children grow up feeling nobody cares.
It doesn't make sense to me anymore
Haven't we been through this a time or two before
—*Cynthia Schustereit*

Peace Forever

Why can't we have peace on this planet of Earth?
Why can't we be friends of one another?
Must we always bear each other's throat with disdain?
Why can't we be peaceful and learn to refrain from violence?
Why must we draw blood-to remember from where we came?
Let's try to learn how to remain at peace!!!
We need peace on this planet
Or we may never have time to explore the universe
For extra terrestrial life or find ourselves,
Please eliminate the external strife in our lives
   on this planet of Earth.
We would like peace within
Then give peace on Earth to our friends.
—*Brenda A. Sprague-Fuller*

A Golden Christmas Hug

All I want for Christmas is the love of heaven hidden deep within you,
   you see-
That is the greatest gift from God you could give to me
For it is eternal and it is everlasting
Of course all the gifts of Christmas are as special as can be
Red and green lights silver bells and packages of all sizes and
   colors placed under a winter white Christmas tree
But it is your Christmas hug that remains in my heart as the season's
   golden memory
So slip your arms around me for then in spirit we are one not two
And that's what I want for Christmas it's A Golden Christmas Hug
   from you
For it will carry me thru to April, May and June and all thru the
   summer and then to Autumn too
And then on to next December when Christmas time comes due
So, I can say once more
All I want for Christmas is a Golden Christmas hug from you
You see a Golden Christmas hug won't be hidden underneath your tree
Is that special gift at Christmas time heaven gave just to you and me
For your Golden Christmas hugs last from year to year
They carry us thru the good times and they are a shelter for our tears
For all I want for Christmas is a Golden Christmas hug from you
To end the old year and bring in the new
And seal the bond of friendship and the love of heaven
I have found in you
   —*Judy Heikes*

The Wonderful Man

I want to tell a story
Without pictures you can see
Using only imagination
Come follow along with me

It's about a strong and gentle man
With a family of his own
A wife, two sons, and daughter
Who placed him on a throne

He's changed my life in my ways
And touched those of my brothers
He's a respected and admired man
Who has touched the lives of others

He's the best you'd ever hope for
And the best I've ever had
He's the wonderful man I've been talking about
I love him, he's my dad
   —*Debbie Andree*

Hatred's Reflections

Fools are they who think me a game
Who think me naught but a toy
For I cater to the whims of no mortal
To none do I bring joy
I respect no one's values
I honor no one's beliefs
Violence and misery are my eternal gifts
To none shall come relief
For those who dare to play with me
Let them now beware
The heavy price that I will bring
A price that they will bear
Black or white, rich or poor
None has meaning here
For to walk with me will bring a fate
That teaches one lesson: Fear
   —*Emory M. Biggers*

Penance

Am I really to die a lonely man
without the knowledge of love
all of my affairs and passions of fire
burned out with the next day's sun
names of the past are forgotten
such as the traces of youth
my heart lies cold and empty
now I must face the truth
that love, to me, was a religion;
a faith in which I didn't believe
pleasure was my sole reason for living
and living was the excuse for my grief
lust was the food I fed on most
an appetite which could never end
and still today my soul goes unfulfilled
but never to be fed again
for the chances that I had to change my ways
are never to come around twice
falling in love is just a dream to me now
so like the real joy of life
   —*Brennan McDonald*

The Meaning Of Life

You are my life — my reason for living.
Without you, there would be no Yesterday
    - no Today
    - no Tomorrow
    - no Forever More.

From the tiny seed of our first meeting
   there was born the bud of friendship, and
   from that, the full bloom of Love.

Unlike the beauty of the Rose, which bursts
   into bloom and fades in a few short days,
Our love has continued to live and grow -
   and the rich color of its passion has
   withstood the test of time.

You have shown me the true meaning of Love
    - by the way you speak my name
    - by the way you look into my eyes
    - by the way you hold me close
     in all too rare private moments.
   —*Dianne Gibbens*

Thank You Lord

Oh, thank you Lord For sparing my life.
And also that of my Wonderful wife.
And now that you've granted me this second life.
You have my promise to praise you daily, as I have seen the light.

Oh no more acting as a fool.
I am yours totally, and I will follow your rules.
This I say, and I do not jest.
You will always be first, above the rest.

And as I close this verse to you.
I know, you know, my love is true.

Praise you Jesus, Praise you Lord, Amen.
   —*Charles Ruhland*

Old Age

I sometimes ponder night and day
wondering just what could I say
to a beautiful woman that I might see
at old age if it comes to be

I might let it stay a while
'til it starts to cripple my style
thou I'd just as soon go forth
with the angel of death leaving behind all
fame, fortune and good health

Some would like to live on and on
while others would just as soon be gone
and I guess that's a matter of degree
at old age if it comes to be

Now I know that I shouldn't ponder
or even wonder yet it does
bother me a might
for I've seen many crickety sights
holding on tight and in their prime
was their true delight

It keeps me awake and often I lay
wondering just how I might pay
those who offer their services for a fee
at old age if it comes to be

—*Freeman Edward Moore*

The Rose Is All I Have

The lavender petals were lovely contrast to the pink gown you wore.
It was for the last time that the sweetness of your smile and
the fragrance of the rose blended together - and soon it
too will fade and its petals fall; but memories of sharing
years with you will not fade as the rose they will grow as
reminders or timeless love. How fragile you both were.

You gave so much for so little in return.
There was no limousine parked at a mansion. There was no
servant at the door.
There was no fur wrap for cover against the chilling winds,
nor pretty lacy stole for a summer's night.
There were no diamonds to grace your slender fingers, only
an orange blossom band.
There was work to be done at dawn and never finished at
evenings dim glow.
There wasn't the continued hum of children's laughter, only
the drumming of an aging heart.
Was there really so little you received?
No, you had my love, tho young, was constant.
>Body>You...just always gave too much, my Mother.

—*Dorothye B. Abraham*

Dear Mr. Major

Dear Mr. Major
Why don't you deal with your Irish problem
- now and for all?
For neither north or south
They simply must not fall,
They both love the Christ
Mention Him and they shout
Many are Saxon, - maybe, some are not -
- but their language is the same
With here and there a change,
Dear Mr. Major - why can't you proclaim
And stop their notorious actions
  of waste and shame?

—*Imogene V. Lee*

God, Here We Are

Two lost souls groping in the dark
Worlds apart, his night - her day
What came over their friends to think
  that day could be one
Only the Almighty created such circumstance.

Both prayed that they needed someone
Both were answered, they never knew why
All it comes down to is they are
  God's children

Who asked and believed in the power
  of prayer.

God, here we are at your disposal
Show us the way to follow your commands
For we belong to you and whatever else we have
May we be worthy of your generosity.

Praise, oh praise the Almighty...
The source of all things beyond our imaginings!

—*Ann Casanova Palabasan*

For Our Love Of 49 Years!!

Another time — another place — questions in our mind,
Would anything be different, or would these ties still bind?
The ties that happened yesterday — bringing us together,
Destiny holds us here — many obstacles to weather.

A touch of joyful happiness, perhaps a touch of sorrow,
A glance from eyes that promise a very sweet tomorrow!
Hopes and dreams stored deep inside, we can't let them go;
One by one we pull them out and hopefully watch them grow.

Growing together over the years — what a great delight.
To have someone to share this love morning, noon, and night!
We wouldn't want it different, these "ties that bind" are real,
They keep us close together, with a trust as tough as steel!

The bonds pull tighter still, if adversity looms near,
God in His infinite wisdom has helped us year after year!
We don't need perfection, with faith we will sustain,
And faith will bind us closer, together we'll remain!

—*Agnes M. Dobias*

If I Knew

If I knew what God had in store for me,
Would I continue to be someone just like me?
If I knew the answers to all the problems I face each day
Would I be wise enough to make the right choices some way?

I don't pretend to know the answers to life's sorrows
And struggles anymore than you do
I pray each day to learn to live to be a better person
But sometimes I take more steps backward
Than forward, just like you.

I'm not content to leave this world
Without leaving somewhere, somehow my own style and imprint
Not anything pretentious you see just so someone
Who lives on loves and remembers me.

—*Della Hurn*

An Owner's Shame

You were my owner, my friend
Yet you brought me here to meet my end

I'm locked in a carrier looking out its steel bars
For I fear I'm not traveling very far

A gentle hand lifts me out then whisks me to another room
Suddenly setting over me is my fate my doom

I begin to shake, whimper and cry
The hand holds me close "Shh" says a soothing voice

With my sad brown eyes I ask why am I here
And the soothing voice answers
Because your owner didn't want you my dear

And as I leave this room to go to that special place
The last things I will remember are a gentle touch from a hand
And a soothing voice belonging to a beautiful face
—*Dawn Bowman*

A Tribute To My Parents

Mother and dad I did all for you that I could,
You always knew I would.
The "Holy Master" has never once done anything wrong,
It's by his 'grace' I'm yet able to continue on.

Bye, bye, is something my parents just wouldn't say,
They would rather tell me to just have a good day.
As I write this the tears are rolling down my face,
Through the precious blood of Jesus I can keep the pace.

Sometimes I just can't help but cry,
I'm your baby dad! you wouldn't even tell me bye, bye.
Mother I am your thirteenth (13th) child,
At this moment I can't even force a smile.

I will forever love both of you,
Yes, I'm yet asking "God" for strength to endure.
No! No! No! The "Holy Master" has never once made a mistake,
I will stay with "Lord Jesus" and dare not hesitate.

Naturally mother and dad your leaving left me so lonely,
My strength and courage come from the "Holy Master" only.
You wouldn't tell me bye, bye,
I won't say it either, I'll only say bye.
—*Ella Smith Dixon*

Untitled

Jay, how could I ever thank you for all the things you do?
You are an angel sent from up above, you are a dream come true.
Sometimes I'm not as grateful or as thankful as I should.
If I could make them up to you I hope you know I would.
My love for you goes beyond that farthest destiny, beneath
  the deepest sea.
How could I ever express in words what you mean to me?
You are the most important person in my life, you always seem
  to care.
We've had so many wonderful times, and so many more to share.
If anything should ever happen and we should ever part…
Know I'll always love you and keep you in my heart.
No matter what you're doing or what you're going through,
stop for just a minute and remember… I love you.
—*Joella A. Huie*

Whispers Of Love

You are my love, my joy, my treasure
You are my hope, my light, and my pleasure
Knowing that you always care
Knowing that you'll always be there

I'll kiss and hug you all night long
Your words you whisper like a sweet melody's song
I have a love that is alive and true
I have a love that is fresh and new

I'll love you until the end of times embrace
For I can see the love all over your face
You mean the world to me
My heart beats for you like the rushing sea

I love you for who you are
Because you are my bright and morning star
You are the one I hold through the night
You are to me, my mornings early light
—*Jerri Dean Hyche*

A Loving Parent

Though your life on earth is over
You are still my paternal parent
Without whom I would not be here
As I now am, and I think of you often.

I think about the fact
That I owe you so much
For what I am and for
The good qualities you inspired.

No one is perfect
But you were a Christian,
A bible teacher, an Elder,
An Example and a friend.

While I live you will not be forgotten
And when I lay beneath the sodden clay
We will meet again in that land beyond
The chilling tide of departing from life.

We who are left and remain
Should mind our relationships so
That when our loved ones are gone
We will not have to have regrets.
—*Charles Andrew Campbell*

Two Vows Of Love

"My love,
You are the flowering spring of my being,
The medial path of my life;
And should my finale come swiftly,
My captive soul shall dwell eternally
Within your embrace!"

"My love,
You are the Titan of my day-and-night dreams,
My thoroughfare to happiness;
So I, Dulcinea, pledge my love,
And the whole of my existence shall stay
Within your embrace!"
—*Barbara Lummus*

The Need Of God

Sweet God how I need your blessings, I feel
You are the only One that can heal
The anxiety that I possess;
I feel that I am gradually drifting away
From what I need and desire each day,
Without this inner joy
Life is irrelevant as a breakable toy.
Your guidance is what I need
Or I'll wither like a weed;
Please, God, let me come to you
So that I may do,
What I feel is right
And allow me to see the light
Of your everlasting love.
—*Henrietta LaVerne Johnson*

A Grafted Blue

Replenished by ravished lightning, teams of spirit blended.
You are, we are my love, silhouetted diadem.
Walking a dream, dancing in him.
New gardens, vision any man would hold.
Fancy dancers feeding flowers a necklace
Of treasures in the pocket of a heart
And tinted souls in polished walls of memory.
Spilling stories into a running waterfall,
Blessing a pot of glory.
Depth of darkness, silence heard, presence is, never alone.
He is everyone loves me, awareness incomplete.
Hit hard by pellets of fire, molded in a lions tooth,
Beauty devoured the beast.
Walking a dream, where the wind opens doors of a new golden street.
So many small nothings carried into lands afar.
Separating colors of the rainbow, light lifted echo in heart.
Lady love memories became a carrousel of laughter
Saddled by the elated face of an angel.
Riding on through the night, tenderness captured thought.
Delight in eyes of the star that played in merriment of grafted blue.
—*Bonnie Simmons Peter*

You My Child

You are not an extension of me,
you are your own.

You were created by God,
a miracle in your own right.
You come by me and of me,
but you are you.

Like a flower you will unfold in your own unique fashion.
Therefore I will not expect of you, but accept of you.

Alongside of you in person or spirit I will always be.
I am for you and you too must be for yourself.
Remember you are special and your possibilities are as
endless as time.

My love is with you always.
—*Jean A. Sutton-Mortonson*

The Leaving

My love - my long lost love
You control my destiny
With sudden loss that I feel
Inside this broken man.
You reach into my tortured soul -
The echoes of my mind -
Cross somewhere from here to there
With the emptiness you left behind.
My broken heart cries out for you
In a symphony of tears -
A river through all my life
That time can never heal
In dreams I think of times gone past
When you were mine alone.
But, dreams are only fleeting things
That come and then are gone.
You left me with a loneliness
A void - a space in time.
The hardest pain I have ever felt
Was the leaving you left behind.
—*Garry Groves*

Fallen Star

He was famous and full of pride,
you could see it in his every stride.
Everyone would shout his name,
to show they shared his fame.
Their teamed had won the game.

Teachers helped him pass his grades,
after all "heroes" shouldn't fail.
Everything for him was made easy,
he never studied, this was a shame.
They wanted to win another game.

The school year came to an end,
he was no longer everyone's best friend.
His family gave him clothes and car,
no work was good enough for a star.
So he began stealing seeking new thrills.

For stealing and causing fear he felt no shame,
the Judge was not impressed with his false tears.
He was given prison years a time to learn,
respect is not free it must be earned.
In prison the "hero's" just a "fallen star."
—*Elizabeth Keefe*

My Tribute

I clutch in my hand a tiny key.
   You don't know it, but it's there.
I've cherised it these many years,
   No one knows, nor cares.
   "True love never dies."

I hold in my hand the key to his heart.
   He holds the lace edged satin pillow
With sweet heart roses o'er his heart.
   After 24 years I placed a stone - engraved,
   "In Loving Memory:"

"His sun has gone down, while it is yet day."
—*Grayce E. Kuhn*

Untitled

A lot of times on a weekend night
You go out drinking and leave me in fright
You are no longer the man I fell in love with
I wish it weren't real I wish it were a myth
You scare me so bad
I don't like to see you drunk it's sad
I wish you realized how pathetic you are
Every time you stumble out of a bar
You are so cold insensitive and mean
You say things to hurt me it's not fair not clean
When you suggest that you want to sleep with a whore
I don't feel good enough for you anymore
You are such a shame
You have only yourself to blame
Your problem has gotten out of hand
Like ocean waves raging over the sand
I wish you didn't drink and cause me pain
You make me worry you make me go insane
Every time I'm upset and I cry
I wish the alcoholic part of you would die
—Diane Zona

To My Suicidal Friend

Sometimes I sit and wonder why you said goodbye.
You had a life ahead of you, you were to damn young to die.
Your dreams were coming true,
Your hopes not far away.
You had a boyfriend who loved you, and friends who needed you to stay.

Did you stop and think of the times yet to come?
Did you live day by day and try to have some fun?
What of those who needed you,
Who prayed for you night and day?
What of those who loved you,
Who wished you hadn't gone away?

My friend, you are dead now
And no one can bring you back.
I wish I could have staved you from your own immoral attack.
I wish you could have seen the world from a different point of view.
Especially for someone
As suicidal as you!
—Dusti D. Howard

Mystery Rose

Mystery Rose who in heaven thou art,
You have given me hope and belief in my heart.
Oh, Blessed Mother who reigns above,
Please, show my heart the way to love.

The Blessed angels guide my path,
and lead my soul from the fire's wrath.
These Holy Spirits allow me to live,
with the endurance of faith, and ambition to give.

God in heaven, our souls you may spare;
we worship your name, knowing how much you care.
Though we know not what our Lord might say,
our prayers are answered every day.
It may not be in the manner we choose,
but the response we are given, is the one we must use.

Oh, Mystery Rose on beads we declare
our innermost hopes and fears.
Through your grace we receive heaven's miracle of peace
that endures throughout the years.
—Darlene C. Radzanowski

Don't Treat My Heart Like A Book

My heart isn't an open book.
You have torn this heart of mine into.
Don't treat my heart like a book with pages.
A book doesn't have feelings, but a heart does.
Give my heart love and kindness.
I'm willing to give you another chance.
Don't treat my heart like a book.
You can write a book over.
You can't mend a broken heart.
If you need to mend something, try mending socks.
If you ever do me dirty again I'm going to sock you
One.
I'm going to hurt you where you never been hurt.
So watch out Darling it can be fun or rough.
You decided which way you would turn.
I rather make love than fight.
A book can tell a lot of things.
My heart is a story book within itself.
Let's make our love a story book that comes to life.
Let the whole wide world know, how we love each
Other.
So, please don't treat my heart like a book.
—Joyce Ann Carter Kennedy

Mother Time

Mother Time, it is a shame, you've slept your life away.
You haven't helped Father Time, to keep the time of day.
Wouldn't you think that Father Time, needs a nice long rest?
He has been faithful and done his level best,
To keep the time as perfect as it can be.
But you are sleeping very late, my dear, dear lady

Sleep on Mother Time, you are having your way;
You've already slept thousands of years, they say.
You haven't shown any willingness before,
To carry any part of Father Time's timely chore.
Just nestle there, in your flowery bed of ease.
No need to wake up now; it's just too late to please.

Father Time could have used your help, many centuries ago,
But selfishly you slept there and never made a show.
Father Time has the strength to do the job quite well,
He does not need your help now, as far as one can tell.
Sleep on, my dear lady, Father Time will win this game,
Not right for you to wake up now and try to claim the fame.
—Etta J. Strickland

Baby

I looked at you with tear-reddened eyes,
  you held me tight and told me no lies.
  You picked me up when I repeatedly fell,
  and by the look in your eyes, at once I could tell.
Every word that you spoke, every breath that you took,
  made me open my eyes, and into my heart look.
I never understood what true love was meant to be,
but when I took refuge in your arms, I could finally see.
  My heart cries out when at times you are not near,
  but I know and I trust, and with you I don't fear.
  The touch of your heart against my buried soul,
  the warmth of your eyes brings joy untold.
  My happiness outnumbers the stars in the sky,
  and my faith in you is what I live by.
In these simple words I write, yes baby, they're true,
  I guess what I'm trying to say is...I love you.
—Jeani Griswold

The Morning Paper

When you wake up in the morning,
You look through your eyelids,
And see the sun.
You open your eyes,

It's for real.
A yawn to start the day.
You stretch to feel the reality.
As you drag yourself to wash up,

You feel like sleeping again.
But once you splash on that cold water,
You know you'll have to stay awake.
After you get dress and find your shoes,

The smell of coffee leads you downstairs.
You take that first sip of fresh coffee
And that first bite of a raspberry danish.
Then comes the eggs and toast.

Another sip of coffee to wash it down.
Finally, you get to your Morning Paper.
"Good morning," your spouse says, "it's six o'clock!"
You don't get to read your Morning Paper after all.
 --Harri Lau

Achievement

To reach an achievement
You must have a vision
Always look forward to anticipation
Look within for inspiration.

To make your dreams came true,
It's entirely up to you.
Whatever you do, Your accomplishments
 will amaze you.
Success is achieved in many ways
You must have a goal every day.
Strive for the est, believe in yourself
you will reach the top.
For what you have cannot be bought
It's knowing who you are
That makes life worth living
To sum it up, It's all in the giving.
 —Helen L. Merryman

A Ballad Of David Koresh

(With apologies to "As time goes by")
You must remember this,
A Koresh is just a Koresh.
An F.B.I. is just an F.B.I.
Those terrifying things are here
Without a single thought of beer.

When adversaries they do stew
It's rarely, rarely, "I love you."
No matter how the land may lie
Those horrifying things don't die,
They linger, all are here
With nary a sultry draught of beer.

And you can't put that in your eye,
Nor flee or fly or rise On High.
Whatsoever the Prophet foresees,
As time goes by, Pharisses.
 —Glenn Abercrombie

Your Child

One day you learn about the child inside.
You now have choices that you must go through,
 But keep in mind that you were there too.
 So don't be rash or he'll be gone.
Please give him the chance to be born and live on.

 When he grows up into a fine young boy;
Love him with tenderness, but be firm with the law.
 Then when he is a teenager and driving a car.
Give him the sense to know what's right and what's wrong.

 And as he gets older you will soon see;
 that you have no choice in what he does or see's.
And when he's an old man and his health is decreasing.
 Pray to he Lord that he will be with him.
Then when he moves away and you hug him good-bye;
 Never let go for he will surely die!
 —Alison M. Wolbeck

A Child

The national anthem comes on.
You raise your hand listlessly
As you look over
to see only one person singing.
His eyes sparkle with joy,
As he belts out his nations song.
One person.
Our pride and joy.
Our only hope for the future, is a child.
 —Alyssa Wolford

A Touch Of Love

Every time you look at me you create a fantasy beyond belief.
You release the imagination in me and I begin to dream.
Every time you look at me I'm a child holding the moon
gazing far above.

You touch me...I'm lost in a wonder land chasing a rainbow.
I fly high to the sky and swing on a golden ring.
I hear angels singing your name and see graceful lingering
saints placing stars around your feet.

Leaping tiny pink fairies playfully sprinkle love beams
upon the pillow as you sleep.
Oh, what a revelation tis is I'm at peace.

Every time you look at me I float on the mist of joy,
rising above the clouds, touch eternity and cling to spring.
Our love has no bounds we are freedoms wings,
 —Barbara Annalisa Kelalis

His Love

When you come to the close of a long long day,
You are troubled and know not what to do
Look up to Jesus and earnestly pray
His love will carry you through.

No night is so dark, nor road so long
But Jesus will show you the way.
In your heart He'll put a new song
And turn all your darkness to day

So put your trust in the one who cares
Believe Him and serve Him true
He is the one who will answer prayers
And bring joy and peace to you.
 —Carrol Rowan Bailey

Time Is Short

      When your age is ten
      You should recognize a friend
      At twenty you will see
You must work hard, nothing is for free
Now comes thirty, you face the future
      A future you must nurture
      At forty you are on your way
      Your hair may be turning gray
Fifty is half way, you can still move swiftly
      If you are prepared for sixty
As sixty arrives, the count down starts
      A time for theater and the arts
      Seventy does not leave you much
      After seventy you may need a crutch
      Eighty, ninety, one hundred
      You have one chance in fifty
   —Finley A. Brees

The Ferris Wheel Ride

Life is like a ferris wheel:
You start down low and then go high.
You look around and see the world;
Things look bright when you are high;
Then you start down, soon to say good-bye.

You look up where you have been;
All that is left is only a sigh.
The ferris wheel goes 'round and 'round,
Rushing you up
And then rushing you down.

This is life as you go your way,
And soon you begin to slow down one day;
Then when you look up you look beyond
For Heaven will be higher
When you are gone.

You will never be down low anymore;
Yes, you will be higher than before.
What a thrill it will be then
To know life there
Will have no end.

The ferris wheel ride
Will be over and done,
And you will ride high—
The victory won!
   —Edna M. Spriggs

Don't Wait Too Long

Don't wait too long before
you tell me you care.
Time lost is never really found.
When you have the opportunity
to do what you have to do,
for God's sake don't hesitate.
How little we know that time
will come again.
Don't let pride interfere with reason.
Say what you feel, think out loud
before it's too late.
Are you sure tomorrow will be soon enough?
Don't wait too long to do, to say, live
the things you want to.
Maybe later, who's to know it will
then be the same then that it is now?
Love is not half as impatient as need
and passion.
   —Ben Carpenter

The Orphan's Song

Oh! when you hear my merry songs, and see my gladsome smile,
You think not of the grief, that tortures me all the while.
You know not that my heart is sad, that it bears many a woe;
You see not all the scalding tears as they silently flow.
And when I sing my heart-strings seem as breaking to the strain
The songs were sung to me by those, I shall never see again.
My flute is all the friend I've left, its tones seems sad and low,
And what to others seems of joy, to me is full of woe.
It sounded sadly to my ear, the time my parents died,
And at the death of each dear one, a strain it always sighed,
So low and sad, and full of grief, I hushed my breath to hear,
As if 'twas touched by angels hands, that floated very near.
Alone! Alone! no friend among the cold and heartless crowd,
Who at the merry songs I sing will murmur long and loud.
Not one among the many forms, that each day I see!
Ah, no! a whisper comes from them: "There's none that cares
  for thee."
And often will my bosom swell, and the hot tears will start,
And a heavy load seems placed upon my aching heart.
When I think of those I loved so well, I cannot still a sigh,
And the happy days gone by.
I think of other days, and wish that I like them, had gone,
For every recollection brings, the thought, "I am alone."
   —Edward V. Buerkert

Karen

You meant a lot to me.
You were my hope,
My spark...My life.
You guided me through my 11 years,
Shared my joy...Shared my sorrow.

When you got married you moved to L.A.,
But you never left me.
You visited me weekly in New York City
No matter what the weather:
Rain...Snow...Hail...
Nothing stopped you.

And one night, it was
Raining...Snowing...Hailing
But you came to see me anyway.

It was dark.
The cab driver couldn't see upcoming car
I don't blame him.

By the time we got to the accident
You were dead.
The blood pouring from your eyes...Your ears...Your mouth.

The tears came.
Spilling down my face...Pouring by the millions.

The pain came.
It was like a bullet ripping through me,
A bullet which wouldn't come out.

The realization came.
No more guider,
No more fun,
No more Karen.
   —Adina Levine

My Memory Book

Upon the shelf, should you chance to look,
You'll find my greatest treasure, a memory book.
The pages are yellow and frayed from lots of wear,
You might even find some teardrops there.

I take it down every now and then,
And relive my life over and over again.
Places, as a child, that I called home,
Look how far away I've managed to roam.

Memories of good times long since past,
My, how could the years have gone so fast.
A pressed red rose, faded autographs, letters of love,
Pictures of loved ones who've passed on above.

I hear their sweet voices, I feel their warm touch,
Their love and their friendships, I miss very much.
Tickets from the theater, valentine's from a beau,
yellow ribbons from my hair, as off to school I'd go.

Anytime I need that special feeling
I know just where to look,
I go to the shelf and lovingly take down
My old memory book.
　—*Edith Piercy Zimmer*

Your Choice

During this Holiday Season
You'll have a very good reason
To be filled with joy and pride
If you have Jesus on your side.
Jesus came to God's great earth
Through the miracle of a virgin birth
To show us how to live God's way;
He even taught us how to pray.
Your future looks so very grim
Unless you choose to live like him.
Don't you think it's very odd
That the fool still says there is no God?
You are headed for disaster
If you don't accept the Master.
Come to Jesus, live on the level.
Don't show allegiance to the devil.
Believe in Jesus and rejoice
That's your only reasonable choice.
I earnestly hope and pray
That you will accept Jesus today.
　—*John O. Johnson*

A Day With My Friend

The day is young,
　young as a summer breeze.

Outside its hot as a slow breezy summer day,
　inside its cold as a winter storm.

For myself I sit outside and watch the sun come up,
　but for my friend she stays inside eating yogurt.

Later on I'll go ride a horse for an hour or so,
　she might go swimming for a couple of hours.

Now the day is old,
　old as a winter's storm.

For my friend and I
　we sit outside with a cool winter's breeze
　at our sides.

And drink a couple of cokes
　to watch the sun go down.
　—*Jennifer Kahanek*

Are You Ready?

　I hear footsteps in the hall
　Your cadence fills the room
　It is the march of many feet
　And the sealing of the doom.

　The prophets told in yesteryear
　　Of your coming, yes, 'tis true
　Your second coming, the time is near
　　When we'll be home with you.

　It will be a time of rejoicing
　　It will be a time of delight
　For didn't He say a thousand years
　　Is as one day or night.

　Will you be ready for His call?
　　Will you be ready still?
　Have you said, Yes Lord here's my all
　　I'll carry my cross up the hill.

　Oh, do not hesitate my friend
　　Please get your heart in tune
　Who then can tell the time, the end
　　Oh, give your heart! But soon!
　—*Clara M. Crist*

The Storm

You've got to be in these mountains high and feel the wind in
　your hair.
You've got to walk on the mountain path and look at the sea—
　down there.
The wind is wild—the sea is churned, the fishermen out of
　their form. The hand of God is out to us all.
We are facing another storm. The trees will bend—till they
　seem to break. The sea will splash up the walls. The birds
take wing and the folks get home but they have weathered
　so many squalls.
No one can know the length of time this fury stays with us all
Then nature calms down and peace will come. Leaving wrecks in
　its wake large and small.
It's the hand of God we feel these days. He is testing us here
　on the ground.
Not a punishment—no—He is testing our faith. We must trust
　and His love will abound.
The aftermath is a soft calm breeze that is much like the touch
　of his hand—caressing us all in a gentle way.
Restoring faith in ourselves and peace to the sea and the land.
　—*Ann M. Coyle*

Hooray For Heredity

Dad, you're the main trunk of our family tree
Your line will continue cause the main limb is me.
I'll plow with you on this farm that Ol' Grampa left us free
Fate gave us Grampa's great genes — Hooray for Her-red-ity.

One glance in the mirror shows I'm your perfect clone
We both already know that you're Alzheimers prone.
Aw, there's no need to panic —it's the non-violent kind
We can keep right on a plowin' till we both lose our mind.
I'm no longer concerned that you like your Bull Durham —
'Cause those gen-er-ic cigarettes I really go fer-em.
Then there's that dandy affection you have for home brew
It's now my handy excuse when I "tipple a few."

God bless you, Dad — I'll be like you all my days
Reckon I'll get to love farmin' even love farmers ways.
Maybe we'll send out some comfort to all us common men
"Great genes are a treasure one can own now and then."
Grampa's genes may have us harnessed and we won't rise above it
But we can pull hard on those tugs — live our life and just love it.
Now you've got grand kids a comin'up — looking just like you and
   me.
A brand new crop of "sod-busters" — Hooray for Heredity.
   —David S. Bowen

Chriss

My face, the smile you have painted across mine,
Your lips pierced on mine each kiss wild and divine.

My eyes, see that glow you've brought me,
You've made my eyes shine, you're all they want to see.

Your lips perfectly shaped to kiss my skin in every way,
Your eyes say it all leaving our lips without a word to say.

Your touch and kiss is my every cure,
Your body so built, I feel so safe and secure.

You've made me so happy, just me and you,
You turned my world right side up, and made everything new.

How your hands could cure almost any given pain,
You're the sun behind my dark days of rain.

Even when you are standing right next to me,
I still miss you, you're still too far to see.

Don't ever leave, you are my life below and above,
It is plain to see Chriss, you are the one I love.
   —Heather M. Larsen

You're Like The Wind

You're like the wind that blows where it will
You're like the wind that blows til the end of time
That's the way you love that's the way you live
You've like the wind
The wind says a storm is coming
but you never see it
The wind says spring is coming
but you never feel it
You're like the wind that blows where it will
You're like the wind that blows till the end of time
That's the way you love, that's the way you live
The wind says a change is in the air
Things will be different, people will care
You're like the wind you only hear yourself
You're like the wind that blows where it will
You're like the wind you will feel what you have done
But like the wind your loves and your life will be gone
   —Helen S. Henry

Give With Love

   Be kind and thoughtful
Your Love will then shine through
 By bringing happiness to others
   Joy will come back to you.

   Be kind and thoughtful
Remember the helpless and poor
 A friendly hand is what they need
   But your Love is needed more.

   Be kind and thoughtful
   If a problem child you have
 Love can melt their little hearts
   Joy will turn away the bad.

   Be kind and thoughtful
To the elderly who are lonely and sad
  A visit can brighten up their day
But your Love will make them glad.

    Give Praise and Glory
   To God and His dear Son
For the Love you've given others
Was given to you from Him above.
   —Arlene D. Schonfeld

Releasing Your Shadow From Darkness

Touching the shadow
your shadow
how dark and wild it may be
Become-Closer
Closer to reality.

Touching your shadow
begin to embrace
with Life and Honesty.

The honor of your grueling past,
in which you slave upon
Need not; to hold you back.

How wonderful
to learn from your mirror.

   Reach out and taste
   Reach out and hold
   Reach out and love
   The shadow of your past,
   What a special feeling
   In releasing the self of
The darkness that shadows your past!
   —Dorothy S. Oehmke

Dear Father

Time passes many things fade away...
Yet no matter what differences we have created,
there's one thing that time can never change...
We belong to each other...
You are my father and I will always belong to you...

And though we do not see each other, know that I have
never ceased to embrace you with much love and compassion
in silence...

From my heart to yours...I love you.
   —Duedene K. Mowat

Playground...Sugarite Canyon...

I caught your downswing, then I flung you back,
your tiny toes stretched out to touch a cloud.
You laughed while soaring on that one-way track

And rode, it seems, right up the chimney stack
of the nearby schoolhouse. You were so proud.
I caught your downswing, then I flung you back.

You, who loved to fly into the distant flack
of birdsong ringing from the feathered crowd...
you laughed while soaring on that one-way track.

You were one with the early morning pack
of swift strong wings that then through heaven plowed.
I caught your downswing, then I flung you back

Again and again. You asked little slack
and swung into the wind (by fear unbowed)...
you laughed while soaring on that one-way track.

The raging years have proved no cul-de-sac
to one with sacred memories endowed...
I caught your downswing, then I flung you back...
you laughed while soaring on that one-way track.
—*John W. LaRocca*

Hey I Know You

Hey I know you
You're the girl I once laughed with
But I don't laugh anymore

You're the girl I once loved with
But I don't love anymore

Oh but I still remember
And a smile comes over my face

There are tender moments in my heart
That can't be taken away

Why just the other day I had a dream of you
But then I cried
HEY I KNOW YOU
—*James R. Alderson*

Missing You Today

Missing you today!
You're the topic of conversation
between God and me today.

I pray that you are healthy,
and that your job is going fine.
I pray that you think of me,
for your always on my mind.

I understand your reasons for leaving
and why you had to go.
An opportunity of a life time
a chance for your abilities to show.

But God understands this mother's heart
and how I miss you so.
He knows the pain in
having to let a child go.

Missing you today!
Your the topic of conversation
between God and me today.
He knows how much I love you,
and is carrying my love your way.
—*Joyce Kay Williams Remy*

Untitled

Wake up little Susie;
You've done had your snoozzee

It's time to stop an take a break;
Have some sausage or pancakes

Egg McMuffin, Hamburger or French fries;
Or for desert, you can have apple pie

Milk shakes, soda pop, or coffee if you please;
Oh have some Florida orange juice freshly squeezed

So come on folks, don't polk around;
And we thank you, for going Greyhound.
—*Junior L. Miller*

Reality

Reality — flee from me
You've hurt me enough, now let me be
How could you lie to those of us
Who trusted in your every word.
You promised joy, tranquility too
To all who faithfully followed you —
All we had to do you said,
"Trust in the goals I've set for you."
Reality please answer me
What's happened to all you promised me
I never had time to see them grow
My children how they needed me
A faithful pupil I tried to be
Doing all you required of me
Reality why did you hide —
And twist your answers into lies —
Oh foolish me, why didn't I see —
Reality laughing at me. No more tears do my babies shed
For far away from me they've fled. My goals attained,
And here I be — A perfect pupil of reality.
—*Gayle W. Grassi*

Awareness

I've learned to love God's precious things,
A baby's smile and butterfly wings,
The azure blue of summer skies,
The river passing softly by —

The morning sun, it's early rise,
The bird calls and their early cries,
The squirrels that gather round my door.
The camp robber who always begs for more,

The busy beaver builds his dam,
And moose surround me where I am —
Ah, this is heaven, and maybe more
To have them near, and still adore,
Their sly and curious ways.

It fills my life and fills my days,
So from the mossy, fem-filled floor,
My friends appear forevermore,
And try to enter at my door.
—*Patricia E. Sherwood*

God's Thread

Everyone can take God's Thread and with it make
A beautiful pattern to last for all time.
For God's thread will do whatever we want it to
In your life and in mine.

These patterns we make into eternity we'll take
For God's thread is a gift beyond compare.
We can take it and weave it or else we can leave it
We can use it or leave it laying there.

There's thread for me and you in colors of every hue
We can choose what pattern we will make.
When God calls us one by one to see what we have done
Will you have the right pattern to take?

—*Patricia Drummond*

Just The Ringing Of A Bell

Far away in the foggy mist, I hear a familiar sound.
A bell, a single church bell, ringing a lonely sound.
I wonder at the reason for such a soulful round.
A shiver of dread creeps up my spine and sends my fear unbound.
Is something wrong, is someone lost?
I really dread to hear, and yet some strange unknown seems ever
  to grow near.
I wonder about my nervousness, my dread, and my fear.
After all it's just the ringing of a bell that I hear!

—*Sylvia Hendrix*

When The Gaslight Glows

The moon shone from the jet black sky,
  A bluish-white ray on the cobblestone street.
The only sound was of a horse and carriage;
  reverberating through the area, it passed through
  the moonlight.
The silhouette of a horse and a hook-mustached man with
  a bowler hat sitting atop the carriage, became a shadowy
  feature on a stone wall.
A gaslight illuminated a portion of this road, it gleamed
  all night;
The nightly torch of the city.
When it radiated, stray dogs and nocturnal strollers became
  enraptured in its gothic luster.
A policeman patrolling the block stopped to lean against the
  post of the gaslight,
As the cathedral bell tolled midnight.....

—*Michael Riccardi*

Dying

A last flame flickers in the burning out candle;
  A breath of fresh air inhales only once more.
The brain becomes dim and clear alternately;
  Finally the sheer harmony brings
    calm, holy, and whole.

The blooming bud falls down to the dust
  after an unexpected storm;
The transient boat is sinking into the eternal ocean
  before the waves rolling on.

The midnight of the deep winter
  without tomorrow, without spring;
The exhausted souls walk alone in the life journey
  without faith, hope, and love.

—*Ling Fan Peng*

A Vision

Standing amid, the most beautiful scenery,
a breath taking view, of God's Planetary,
suddenly the view, moves away,
leaves a huge picture of like today.

Looking up, at the picture so tall,
I find it not finished, from wall to wall,
the top and middle are complete,
both sides are empty, down to my feet.

Torn ragged pieces, are scattered around,
skin color of people, of all do abound,
"two hands," come down from above,
one on each side, of the picture I love.

Each hand, takes a torn ragged piece,
places it to the picture complete,
each piece, becomes a beautiful sight,
when attached to, "the picture of right."

A voice from above, saying these words,
"I am putting all the pieces together,"
"It won't be long now."

—*Norma M. England*

Case History

We were all playing around, like kids out of school, Which was a diabolic violation of all safety rules. When somebody shoved me, like a big dumb fool, I stumbled over backward across my stool. With the end result, I fell flat on my back, And I was sure that I heard my tailey bone crack. I tried to get up, but found I could not move. My hand was all twisted, and my head had a groove. My foreman grabbed a bicycle, with me across his lap, We headed down the road, to see surgeon Snap. "Surgeon Snap is not in," said pretty Miss Louise. "But we've made arrangements for emergencies like these." "Pardon my intrusion, I don't mean to be blunt, I'm afraid you'll have to settle for trainee, Dr. Hunt." Dr. Hunt was called out on a bicycle wreck. So we finally ended up with Dr. Nubbenspeck. He took me into a room which had no label. Turned me upside down, across a big cold table. He fingered my backend, which made me sneeze. Then loudly he called for Miss Louise. "Go quickly," he said, "and summon Surgeon Snap. His time is up anyway, for his noonday nap." Surgeon Snap came in, rubbing red, sleep eyes, Said, "call the orderly, quick! before he draws flies."

—*Zeddie Gillenwater*

A Tribute To A Dog

There's an empty leash upon the wall
A dog house, forlorn and dark
Never for me will he wag his tail
Never again will I hear him bark.

He was just a black cocker spaniel
But his love and devotion to me
Could not be counted as the stars at night
Nor measured by the sands of the sea.

Just a dog? My, beloved friend
Who had lived for fourteen years
Whose passing he left me with loneliness
Choked with emotion and blinded by tears

—*Velma Fitzpatrick*

Afterthought

Late rain has spilled magnificence across
A dooryard path, and perfumes of the night
Fester in recollections of things past:
Magnolia blossoms, April sunset, loss.
I cannot close the book lightly to toss
Its contents from my mind or glance to right
And left saying, "It was a tragic last
Chapter," or "The world is full of dross!"

The aromatic evening turns to dark,
But there are birds that will not sleep at all
This vernal night, stealing the rainy peace
Of many a bed with daybreak's restless spark
So shall I lie, a creature of recall
Awake with thoughts of you that will not cease.
—*Robert M. Hukill*

Reflections

The future lies in our hands right now
  A dreamer's dream may
    come true somehow
As looking upon the past today
It brings tears to my eyes in a sad sort of way
The good times, the bad times, the situations
  we've been through
The friendship will last no matter what we do
  The road to success will leave us no time
    for a dream to come true
    we must master the mind
It must take time for friendship to grow
  But in my heart I'll always know
  That pictures will just be there to see
    But reflections will always
      Remain in my memory.
—*Kate Farrell*

The Stain Of Destruction

The horrid sky lingers motionless
A fury of darkness which scowls down upon all
A eagle that swoops down upon its prey
"Attack, Attack," its wings whisper
Causing an uprise of bitter winds that scorch the warmest heart
Oh how the howls fill my ears
Timeless wailing for evils of long ago
"Can you stop what must become," its wings whisper
The ponderous sky lets forth its wrath
Which falls and falls till it collides upon the earth
It soils the earth with dark crimson
Oh how the leaves weep
Till the mist of eternal sleep grips all
Nothing escapes from its unseen hands
Which sings I must destruct
—*Mariah Nunez*

Childhood

A touch, a smile, a kiss
A giggle, a crawl, a step;
A favorite book or special toys
These are the simple joys.

One day, one month, six months, a year
Crying, colic, teething, sleep;
Observing the way little people grow.
Where did all the time go?

Making memories for the future
So, we can reminisce about the past.
Indelibly etching in our minds,
The love we felt, that will always last.
—*Kelly Costa Whitmore*

A Place In My Heart

I have a place in my heart she may never come to,
  A handful of wishes that may never come true.
    Endless hours we may never share,
  An empty feeling when I think that she cares.

I can't figure out what it is that she likes,
  I keep telling myself I'm just not her type.
The things that I thought, but was never quite sure,
  I can't find a way to stop loving her.

I have so much love that she doesn't seem to need,
  A broken heart that may never bleed.
  Two crying eyes that hold back the tears,
  Not even a chance of holding her near.

I may never know the feel of her touch,
  Trying to please her a little too much.
  What I wanted so badly, may never be.
When I close my eyes she is all that I see.

I can't turn her head with all that I've tried.
I'd beg for her love, but I do have my pride.
  Hoping for a day that she may realize.
I just can't see it when I look in her eyes.
—*Timothy Gene Sims*

The Encounter

One afternoon there hovered over
A helicopter, needing cover
Flown by Captain Bruce A. White
Retired, and Kind, ...and full of fright!

He didn't crash...no! Thanks to Bunky!
It's nice to know a Super Monkey
Watches out for folks who fly
To help them safely from the sky.

Captain White was soon enthralled
What wondrous things his eyes beheld.
"I've circled 'round the world and seen
the mountains high and valleys green...

...the sky above and oceans blue...
But never seen the likes of you!
Who are you guys and what's your mission?
Of both, I'm sure that I've suspicions."

The SHUMS took Bruce and with him shared
Their history, plans, and how they fared
The vast and empty miles of space
and how they built that unique place.

They asked the captain to request
His only child who's called Celeste
To join their cause and help them work
At healing ills on planet Earth

So now that men have joined the team
It's safe to say that we may dream
Of futures bright and Earth restored
And peace for all-the SHUMS' reward.
—*Sammy Gouti*

Life's Promise

Innocence of youth gone by and reflections of days past.
A life remembered as a seedling struggling for light in the
Darkness, with tall trees and rocks shielding the way.
After life's storms take their toll, God's light appears.
Unlike the rolling stone, the moss that life's beauty brings
Gathers spiritual growth and maturity from trials and
Tribulations of things not seen, for all loss is gain.
And from above — love. Patience and understanding as only
He can give. With age, our faith growing stronger, our
Mainstay for each day. Falling logs and forest plants — as
Nature changes towards life's end. Our reward of eternity
Is within our grasp, if only we will follow him until the last.
  —Karen A. Peters

The Little Wooden Cross

In the valley of the angel, in the mountains way up high
a little wooden cross was carved and here is the reason why.
In honor of Christ our Lord it was made for the one who
believes, for the one who has fate.
It will bring true contentment from the worry of the day,
happiness and peace if you believe in Him and pray.
There is no sorrow that He cant not feel no pain you endure
that He cannot heal. — The little wooden cross is a bridge
to His almighty love it carries every blessing from heaven
above. — Christ is your savior, your friend in need trust
in His wisdom. His kingdom He will lay at your feet. — He
gave us this earth for work and for play and to live our
life in a righteous way. - Whether rich, whether poor to
Him it's the same for we are all equal in His holy name.—
At the end of life's journey only His glory will count,
as we pass through the valley of the angels,
where the little wooden cross was found.
  —Ursel Blanco

Real Verses Unreal

A rocking horse cowboy travels many miles going nowhere!
A live horse cowboy can really travel any distance from here to
  there!
The rocking horse is fed coins for its ride, and the coin
  pushes a button inside!
The cowboy riding a live horse who is fed food-strengthening the
  stead for its ability to move!
The penny fed horse sustains only the one who owns the horse-
  He rides his car to the bank of course!
Both horses has need for water to satisfy its things
Horse of life, to satisfy its horsely thirst
The other to cleanse body no need to quench its thirst!
One pretends to go somewhere, but the other wins the race
  getting there first!
Much like humans, don't you agree
Feeding food to the pretentious horse, or feeding coins to the
  horse that lives
Brings efforts such as failure for sure for
Neither were made for food such as this!
Life's pretensions are really short lived!
  —Mary Evelyn Parkison

Untitled

Like a flash before my eyes here I am
a wife and a mother. Most excellent way
of life I've come to discover.
Looking at my son I wonder, what his
life will uncover. Hoping he has common sense,
so he can handle youngsters' nonsense!
  —Loretta Yezuita

Last Red Rose

December, I cut a red rose from my garden;
A long stemmed rose perfuming the air.
The rose cast an image on the crystal top table.
Bright and clear I saw a form, the form of a child.
The child hiding the cup, the empty cup,
There upon the table top.
Blanking out my memory of past ages,
Seeing a picture, my mother, a virgin rare,
No earthly care.
She cared for me, she loved me,
She listened silently, singing a lullaby.
She bore a gem, the price was paid,
That all may sing and sing and sing.
The rose I cut was smiling.
I caught the image there.
Polished cleaned and bare, innocence,
Dew, that lingers there within the rose.
She formed a perfect image melting the stony past;
Creating within, the red rose that lasts.
  —Margaret V. Hunsinger

My Love

You are my one and only true love. We have
a love that is very strong. Our love will
keep us together. Sure you treat me mean
and sometimes I treat you mean, but neither
of us means it. We started out as friends and
ended up falling in love.

You are my bow-hunter and I am your Susie Q.
Because of the love we share, we were able to
overlook each other's quirks/faults.
We discover all the time how much we
have in common, sometimes we even think
alike. Yes, you are definitely my
only true love.
  —Susan Boland

A Loving Heart

A gentle hand
A loving and patient heart
It was there from the very start.

I never forgot for a single minute
I didn't grow under her heart
  but in it.

Each day, I will treasure and cherish,
For she was once there.
To nurture me ...
She continually showed me she cared.

Mother, I knew from the very start.
Your gentle hands
Your patient and loving heart.
  —Linda S. Lia

Friendship

It can be earned, but never bought
A working relationship which requires much thought
Rarely, has anyone ever reached its border
A mixture of love, honor, understanding, and trust
Are the ingredients necessary for a gift so just
Human frailty constantly challenges its integrity
But, if given the proper care, becomes a gift of longevity
  —Margaret E. Coles

Asylum In The Sky

Dear Mental Case,
   a message from your King
   who suffered what you suffer,
   long — and some of everything —

This sinful lord
not unlike you
took many a stand
in the "Psycho-Blue."
    Be true to Thine Own Heart
    Silence during the evil time
      — Courage —
    in the End and Start.

Over a score ago
then Our Sister came
an Angel of Mercy
Dymphna is Her Name

Ghost of God in Her
He is seen to say,
He will, "punch you back,"
She lights the Way —

the Truth is the Word
Our Minds must try
the Life we seek —
is Her Asylum In The Sky.
   —*Robert Michael Moreno*

Windows of Light

Windows nearly covered share a glimpse of life inside.
A momentary glance reflects existence not denied.

A minute ray of light appears beneath the shades so drawn.
An obscure gleam intensifies, enabling hope to spawn.

Emergence of a mending soul creeps slowly into view.
Illumination glimmers like the early morning dew.

Visions unseen now exist, as energy unfolds.
Dreams enhance reality, creating future molds.

Shades of the past have been removed, reflecting light anew.
Windows nearly covered now come fully into view.

The weightlessness of radiance, dancing with delight;
Envelops windows in its wake, euphoric in its sight!
   —*Mildred L. Taylor*

A Poet's Thought

A poet's thought is as fleeting as
A moor's fretful mourn on a faraway dock,
A smile in which to bask in,
A piercing sea gull's cry,
The moan in a lover's tryst,
A light sprinkling of rain,
A secret's giggle,
A moment of truth,
The sudden prickling of terror,
And the whistle of a train just passing through.
It is as fleeting as a moment's chance to put it down on paper,
Then, forever it's gone, never to be recaptured again.
   —*Kathleen A. Dube*

Have You Ever...

Have you ever fallen from a mountain;
A mountain so high, you just wish you hit the ground.
Have you ever fallen in love so deep;
That you try and find your way back up again.
Have you ever been so down and sad;
That the only hope you have is the highest one above.
Your heart is so broken down, you do not know what more to feel.
It will be a time when all you want is the end.
But the end is far away, and the best is still to come;
And when the best comes, all these experiences will be a loss
   in your memory.
And all you will ever want in life will be at your reach.
So that you will never fall again.
   —*Victor Candiotti*

Wildflowers

As our eyes met and our hearts touched
A mystical flame, softly and gently compelled
our two ardent yearning souls together.
Drifting unleashed without bounds, internally
In the garden of wild flourishing desire.

The beckoning light gently allured us there
Softly and tenderly drifting, heart to heart
Through passion's misty ethereal meadow.
Of desires unfolding, receptive wild flowers.

Passionately reaching, gently touching
One petalled flower and the another;
Arousing each tender somber petal
With fervent incandescent fire.

With passion rapidly soaring —
The surrounding forest, hills and valleys
Awaken, and amorously surrender
To the singe of the compelling fire.
   —*Nina Ruffner*

Nobody

I'm just a nobody
A nobody I'll always be.
I dream that I'm somebody
But I'm just fooling me.
I know that I haven't the talent
But I try and maybe some day
The impossible might happen
I can dream, wish and pray.
Once you face up to the truth
You find it a little bit better to bear
Your just one of the million of nobody's
That are upon this earth everywhere.
Be content with what God has given you
Strive always to do your best.
No one can ask for anything more
Time will take care of the rest.
Your still just a nobody
A nobody you'll always be
No more you dream of being someone
Your just plain "ME"
   —*H. L. Garber*

Sunset

It is twilight;
A pale moon hangs in the distance...
The sun is fading
After another day of lighting our world.
The pale blue sky turns to pink;
Then orange, and a deep sad red.
The world is hanging onto
The last ray of shining golden light
Before we are plunged into impenetrable darkness.
The moon grows strong;
She sheds a cold silver light
Upon the darkening land.
The stars appear
As the sun sinks deep
Into an abyss of darkness...
Another day is past.
—*Sarah Lewis*

Why Love Hurts

God gave love to all mankind
A part of life each must find
When God decided to create man
He had a beautiful and wonderful plan
He wanted it perfect for all to see
To give us His love for all eternity
Man did wrong from the start
God must have felt the hurt in His heart
God was angry that day
Since then, we all have had to pay
God took away what he wanted to give
But still, he allowed us to live
Though He was angry, he did love
And watched over us from above
He felt a feeling, the first that he had
That love can hurt and make us sad
Why do we do the things we do
And saying things not meaning to
Why not just say, I'm sorry and I love you
—*Wayne McGhee*

The Winds Of Heaven Blew

One May-Day morning the world stood still.
A Primrose sprang up, on a lofty hill.
The dry earth cried, and tears from inside
Sparkled as dew on petals new.
And, "The Winds of Heaven Blew."

The Primrose flourished, and a Mocking Bird sang
High on the hill-top his melodious voice rang.
Butterflies flew sweet nectar to sip;
A Humming Bird too, came for a dip.
God's creatures were nourished...
Over the lush green hill they flew
And, "The Winds of Heaven Blew".

The lonely Primrose petals fell one by one;
But many seeds scattered abroad, ere
May's setting sun.
Both hill and valley shall bloom in abundance,
For the earth cried tears of sparkling dew
And, Ah yes! "The Winds of Heaven Blew."
—*Roxie Oxford McCoy*

Dream Sea

In sleep I descend into worlds undefined,
a puppet of my subconscious; in the Dream Sea am I.
Tossed by the waves adrift in my mind,
the Captain of my ship; alone sail I.

On the tides of tears of which I have cried,
broken dreams and lost love; form the sea and I.
In a quest for harmony now forever tied,
through time and eternity; sail on sail I.

To the ticking of the clock, one heartbeat at a time,
alone in my abyss; are the sea and I.
In search of tomorrow where my heart may find,
a safe harbor by night; so sail on sail I.

Till my dreams become reality in a flower's bloom,
your love as the blossom; for the sea and I.
Where in first morning's light with dreams gone so soon,
still with flower in hand; no longer alone need sail I.
—*Terence P. M. E. Sullivan*

Madonna Lily

The hardy lily with white flowers bold,
A purity demanded of her life;
This is a time her bulbs are in blue strife.
Tragedy; - path to Golgotha, I'm told.
Silent dreams stare onto blanche petals gold,
The dream of Erotic summons by fife.
Her love beckons me East by season's knife.
She is under shelter of a Word old.
Triumphant will be her love in the spring.
Circadian rhythms will show her bloom.
Stare at the resurrection ground she'll bring.
Sunshine, her mother, will become her room.
Her trumpet petals; a song saying sing.
A cipher of her beauty is my doom.
—*D. D. Yates*

The Way To Calvary

A crown of thorns upon His brow,
A purple cloak they gave Him.
A scepter reed, they did allow.
Oh woe, oh woe, unto them.

They knelt and mocked our Lord as King,
These cruel heartless sinners.
His cries, they will forever ring
In the hearts of His tormentors.

Oh the wooden cross was heavy
On that hill so far away,
But our Lord was ready
Upon that awful day.

Each step he took was agony.
His love was there for us,
And in His heart was pity
For those who did not trust.

There He was scourged and spit upon
On the way to Calvary.
For you and me our Lord did groan
Upon that cruel tree.
—*Valda M. Harrison*

She Stood

She stood upon the hillside, sunshine on her hair
A ray of sun toyed with her eyes, then gently settled there

She did not move as he came closer, her gaze was left untorn
Her thoughts were wrapped serenely, on her face they were adorned

Peace was in her expression, a quiet calm within her breast
A gentle, hushed stillness had on her features come to rest

Her feet were still beneath her, a statue there she stood
Relenting freely to the beauty, as she alone could

He did not draw much closer, attempting to join her there
For he knew that only at a distance this serenity he could share

So, thus, he stood beside her, sharing as closely as he could
The bit of heaven she had found as on the hill she quietly stood
—*Nancy J. Schuessler*

Corn Pudding

My mom's name is Edna May,
A real great cook the neighbors would say.
When she was mad everyone knew,
Because on your plate a huge pile of corn pudding she threw
Gross to look at, gross to smell, but grossest of all to eat,
A crusty clump of puss from which corn would secrete.
Mix together corn, flour, butter, salt, and eggs then bake,
The aroma so awful, guaranteed to give you a belly-ache.
The strictest house rule was to eat everything on your plate,
Regardless to if it was something that you love or you hate.
Soon we would ask, who are you mad at, what did we do wrong now?
Not a word, but another plop more corn pudding, then
A raise of her left eyebrow.
Once I tried to sneak some under the table to my dog, Taffy,
He jumped up banging his head, spun a few circles
And for the next half hour went daffy.
Corn pudding is so bad that it is not fit for man nor beast,
If you ever eat at my mom's house, when she is mad,
Bring a guest, better make it a priest!
This pudding is the worst, rottenest, grossest food I ever ate,
Thank God, I'm now grown and will never ever again
See corn pudding on my plate...
—*Teri L. Theberge*

Memory Garden

Memory Garden - an enchanting roam
A rendez-vous set in a tranquil zone
Solace and peace reigns there.

Embellished with treats of special thoughts
Boughs flowing with tid-bits of bons mots
Cameos of life delights strewn everywhere.

What 'ere the need
A planted seed to blossom
For a friend in need.

Sadness and despair borne, I'm well aware
Yet, my "Memory Garden" continues to grow
No weeds — only good deeds to sow

Along the pathways, I pause
Adjust the "name tags" — nurture the blooms
The atmosphere, forever in tune
It's always Spring there.
—*Lucille G. Williams*

And When

And when the last dinosaur surrendered to oblivion
A rift was created which mammals then competed to fill.
Amongst themselves a pitched struggle for supremacy
Above all others was fought across their earth.
An old idea played within an older theme.

Arising as the winner was quite a phenomenon
Anemic hairless apes had won the reptiles' will
As the ruling life form till the next catastrophe.
All thought the position much more than it was worth.
Age - old curse it truly is, to rule above all supreme.

Across the land all others were tamed, studied and
Absently hunted and protected into extinction.
Almost all of the lessor species died unnoticed
Although small consequences built upon each other.
Ancient lines of life left the tangled scheme.

After plants disappeared in a blur from the land
Animal kingdoms passed quickly without distinction.
Alone the mammals held empty court in short-lived bliss.
And when loneliness of spirit took the last mammal away
Another rift was left to be filled with another's dream.
—*Thomas M. K. Stratman*

The City; 1983 and 1993

Splintering echo rends the waiting air;
A roof crashed in beneath the wrecker's ball.
Another good old house is leveled to the ground,
Its memories a heap inside its basement hole.
Street after street of houses, all torn down.
Heaps of rubble, once neat neighborhoods.
In time, the heaps of rubble leveled out,
And grasses grow where once the houses stood.
Grass turns to fields, and pheasants roam about,
And Nature once again, turns bad to good.

...1993
Where once the "heaps of rubble" stood,
Is built a fine new neighborhood;
But don't come here, unless you can -
"One hundred, thousand dollar" man!
—*Marjory A. Treumuth*

Success

Success seemed certain at twenty—
a rowboat ride in the sun-splashed pond
of shallow experience.
Craving the distant ocean's salt spray
and shimmering aqua vistas of more,
I waded ashore,
waved farewell to small Pondopolis
and sought a deeper, colder lake
of college and life's exams.

Success seemed elusive at thirty—
a sailboat decade of choppy happen-chance.
Muted colors of chosen and unchosen regrets
aimless cruising by a coastline of mud.

Success seems relative at forty—
comfortable, more cautious, slightly blurred
as the speedboat of time skims along.
Clinging to a hand to hold, friends of old
I plunge past possibilities—slow down!
Where is that rowboat now?
—*Sue Buck*

Aloha To The Name Of Lili'uokalani

Aloha to the name of Liliuokalani
A Royal Majestic Queen of Hawai'i
So dedicated is the name of Liliuokalani.

Stand firm for our nation, oh Chiefs of our land
Voices are heard it's the kupuna now and ever
Together for the right of our beloved Hawai'i.

Be grateful ye blossoms, for our Heavenly Father
His love to behold now and evermore
With endless pride hear the voices of our children.

Bloom endlessly for the name of Liliuokalani
A Royal Majestic Queen of Hawai'i
So dedicated is the name of Liliuokalani.
"E Liliu e—E Liliu e—E Liliu e."
"A Tribute to the Last Queen of Hawai'i"

—*Katherine Kamalukukui Maunakea*

Plateau's

In a stagnant place, goals lie defeated and disarmed
A screeching halt has come, the plateau of ones life
In a stagnant place, where one stands very still
Foreboding, and so painfully, ohh so painfully alone
Disappointments come to the good, as well as the bad
The plateau's of life, are setting one aside to know
Goals are never reached, without ascent and struggle
From the valley so low, to the top of the mountain
Where all experiences gather, one achievement at a time
But when in the valley, it can be wonders sublime
Reaching up to God letting Him guide, by wisdom's hand
Gently, He carries you over the roughest of exteriors
Trees, rocks, mountains, and many jagged edges
Bringing you to His smooth, wondrous loving interior
Settling you so very high above, the plateau's of your mind
The stagnant place, now stands far off in the distance
No more foreboding, and no more painful being alone.

—*Martha J. Fanning*

Behind Crumbling Walls

Behind crumbling walls lives concealed
A shattered, weary soul deprived of grace
Invisible to its true self and the human race
Society's outcast breathing in shame
Stripped of a name, where lies the blame?
A chained, embittered spirit dying inside
for soulfulness and understanding
Ever questioning life's immortal scars
Revealing a face, forgotten, ravaged by time
sorely in need of healing, life is a crime!
And life's cruelties cannot be left behind
Oh, how the heart feels, indeed no one knows
for behind this face is a rose yet to bloom
A flower still infatuated with life's cryptic ways
Despite these walls is a self desirous of
A heartwarming story, and music to soothe the soul
Its rhythm to conquer the inner storm
Oh, this self would die to abandon these walls of decay
If only it could see through the eyes of yesterday
to once more feel alive in time and space
and see the world as a less lonely place

—*Ljubinka Dimeska*

A Single Rose

To my adopted adult son.
A single rose, beside the pathway growing,
  Lends beauty to the lives of all who pass;
On slender stem, its crimson petals blowing,
  It nods among the bushes, o'er the grass.

Just so: A single life touched by Christ's beauty,
  Lends loveliness to all who linger near;
Whose lives are lifted up and cleansed of sadness
  By Him, to whom each heart and life is dear.

You are that rose — Christ's own beloved disciple —
  Shedding His love on lives of all who pass.
Because you love, and give Him all the glory,
  A crown awaits you in His heaven at last.

—*Marjorie M. Miller*

Time To Care

What makes a friend we ask ourselves
A smile or laugh some tears
Respect for someone's privacy
Perhaps allay ones fears

A bond cementing days and years
To which one can respond
Just trust concern for fellowman
Of whom you may be fond

What designates ones loyalty
To be one of a pair
You need not ask what will I get
By helping if I care

To just bestow what you can share
So someone yet may learn
We all have different ways to do
But it can be returned

Remember when you share a smile
You know if it were you
That fond expression as it's caught
Are shared with others too

—*Virginia Pedersen*

No More

No more hugs, no more kisses.
A stranger replaces the one that she misses.
No more love notes, no more "I love you's."
A feeling of loneliness has brought on the blues.
No more tender glances, no more soft caresses.
Bitterness and coldness is all she possesses.
No more surprises, no more roses.
Only false and pretentious poses.
No more sparkle in their eyes.
Dark angry clouds fill the skies.
No more love making, no more snuggling together.
Just freezing cold winter weather.
No more caring, no more protective arms holding her.
Alone she feels so insecure.
No more thoughtful gifts, no more holding hands.
Sleeping together is all they can stand.

—*Melissia Bryant*

The Old Man And Me

A sunset by the sea, the old man and me.
A sunset by the sea, what does he see?
The old man and me staring out upon the bright blue sea
The old man sees the cities, ports, and trees.
The lands faraway.
Remembering days gone by of old wooden ships, white sails
Full of wind.
Then he sees me and I do see the teary eye of longing for
Times gone by.
But joy for the love of me, both standing by the bright blue sea.
The old man and me
—*Sidney Lee Phelps, Sr.*

The Man On The Cross

There on the cross for all man to see
A symbol of beauty precious to me
A crown of thorns pierced His head
And from His hands and feet He bled
The King of all Nations looked to the sky
As His gentle eyes began to cry
Vinegar touched His weary lips
And pain shot through His finger tips
While people mocked His words below
Only a few did really know
The man whom they were making fun
Was certainly Our Father's son
Then on the ninth hour the earth shook
And His spirit and soul God took
A man so perfect in every way
Died for us on the cross that day
Born to save the world from sin
Soon He will be back again
And may someday we touch His hands
The hands that bled for the sins of man
—*Rebekah Elizabeth Basford*

Winters Wonder

Winter comes to the land, the cold wind blows
A thousand tiny lights sparkle in the new fallen snow
Bringing with it the magic of the season
With its fairy tale wonder of rhyme and reason

A light wind begins to softly whisper through the ice
laden branches of the trees
Causing them to release their winter songs into the breeze
Then the wind picks up and hides their branches in white snowy
  swells
And the songs ring out like a hundred tiny bells

Millers pond, now frozen with an icy lace
Etched with delicate lines never to be duplicated or replaced
The stars seem brighter, from the beauty far below
With the complementing shimmering of the clear clean snow

A celestial wonder lays over the land
Brushed once more by the master's hand
—*Phyllis Doebbler*

Angel

One fateful day in "93"
a tiny kitten came to me.
She makes us happy
as Angels do and her
name proves to be quiet true.
A friend to three and great
company for free,
who but God could have sent her to me.
—*Tamra Stewart*

Lest We Forget

Christmas is a joyous time, celebrating our Lord's birth
A time to sing, a time to praise the gift God bestowed upon
  this earth.
Our thoughts are deep as the organ plays yuletide music full of
  praise
For the Savior kind and all forgiving, whom we're apt to
  forget in our zest for living
Christmas is a time indeed to help all those in their time of need
With a gentle reminder to those we've met, to give thanks to
  their Savior, lest they forget —
Chimes are ringing on this Day of days, the multitude gathers
  to sing their praise
On a clear Christmas morn with heads bowed in prayer
    Asking forgiveness from our Lord up there.
     We feel God's love through our answered prayers
     We are full of compassion, and feel free of cares
     We happily receive Gods grants and yet —
     We must too give thanks, lest we forget —
Each day He is there with arms held wide
  asking us simply, to abide —
In Him — with out stretched hand to hold
  while He gently gathers us to the fold.
At close of day we kneel — to thank Him for His Grace
In anticipation of our great Day —
When we shall behold, our Dear Lord's face.
—*M. Bernice Mac Donald*

That Sad Day

It happened that day, the gruesome crash.
A truck and a car, it happened so fast.
A girl died almost instantly,
no pain could be felt.
By her grave her parents knelt.
The other three kids a girl
and two boys were taken to the hospital.
Their families hearts destroyed.
One day later the message said.
"Sorry Mr. And Mrs. your son is dead."
As for the other two, there to be fine.
My heart on the other hand will never find,
a way to mend the bind.
In two days two kids died.
Two friends of mine.
—*Natasha D'Andrea*

On The Edge

You, a dream, on the edge of night,
  All eternity laid bare,
Before us, the horizon,
  Hammered gold,
Thinned only by the encroaching stars,
Lost in the birth,
  Of a rising moon,
Alas, too soon,
  The end.
Gone, with the blessed,
  Restless wind,
One moment,
  In an expanse of time,
A dream, perfection,
  Achieved in grace,
You, on the edge of night.
—*Roger W. Bridegroom*

This One Of The Turtle Clan

Of ancient spirit and man's inhumanity,
A turtle soul formed.

On spirit wings, the turtle flew - she saw, she wept,
O'er her mother earth.

From ancient spirits, Her teardrops fell on her languishing
mother earth.

Turtle soul, with braided hair, it's time to touch that
earth - with spirit whole.

Turtle soul, with braided hair, it's time to touch that
earth - your completion.

Whole turtle soul, on wings of ancient spirit, now
Touch all humankind.

Turtle soul, on wing of ancient spirits, touch the
Ravaged earth - heal her.

Turtle soul, the drum! Feel its ancient message,
eternal - breath of life.

Turtle soul, listen to the drum! Hear its ancient
Message - eternal.

Come to light on earth, to walk its human paths, bridge
Of spirit to man -

This one… of the turtle clan.
—*L. A. Pedersen*

Untitled

On your 50th anniversary celebration,
   a Valentine's Day gala,
Your most cherished anniversary ever,
   remember:

This is a golden time for you both,
a time to be cherished,
a time for family and friends,
a time to remember forever,
and a time to celebrate the years to come.

A time to remember the 50 years
   you've been together,
to think about the family you've had together,
the families they've had
and the families they will have in the years to come.

Take the time on this golden day to remember,
   the good,
   the bad,
   and yet to come in your lives.

May the love you've shared in these past 50 years,
last for the rest of your lives,
and go with you through eternity and beyond.
—*Vicki Broekhuizen*

Looking Back

High upon a lonely hill
A crying soul keeps very still
A heart that drums a lonely beat
Remembers love once young & sweet

A leaf floating down in air
Comes to rest in golden hair
Laughing eyes now filled with tears
Mind deep in thought of love-filled years

A trembling hand reaches out to touch
A cherished locket she loved so much.
—*Marilee K. Stevens*

A Valiant Sacrifice

A valiant lad shall rest in peace,
A victim of a warlike horde.
His heartbeats stop, his breathing cease,
A mortal blow from a flaming sword.

And in this final fleeting moments,
Before the fireball took his life;
What curious thoughts passed through his mind,
Through all the blood and pain of strife?

He must have thought of country dear,
His motherland, whom he is fighting for;
Pride, ambition, hope and fear,
Sentenced him to die in war.

He must have thought of his dear home,
His girl he'd never see again;
His mother's tears, his father's pride,
This boy amongst the fighting men.

He must have thought as he was dying,
Why he killed them, why he bled?
Instead of laughter, weeping, crying,
Instead of peace, was war indeed.
—*Tomas D. Estolloso Matic IV*

Death Of A Citizen

Mourning life, existing still, resigned to a lengthy demise,
A victim of his own free will, a citizen painfully dies.

The fault seems never in himself, as a witness he takes the stand
Putting involvement on the shelf and going through motions bland.
Feeling no need, he sadly retreats to a wasteland of his own…
Like a leper. Humanity he cheats, confined in this world self-sown.

Reason ruling answers not, for intimacy with God he lacks,
Depression replaces his Camelot while misery his body attacks.

Larynx closing, he barely speaks, our citizen becomes a taker
With feelings unreliably weak, he sits, waiting for his Maker.
Will war or weapons change his death? The answer is quite simple
Self-will must leave the throne of wrath where Ego is the temple.

Lacking heart, existing still, with only The Media for eyes,
A victim of his own free will, a citizen painfully dies.
—*Mary L. Shriver*

Destiny

Of destiny's enchanting call,
A voice so intense, encompassing all.
Choices given, haven't a chance,
In fate's unending twisted dance.

Loves and dreams that imagined much,
Compelled by a force more strong than touch.
Preordained by celestial rule,
By the powers that be for star-crossed fools.

To undertake this perilous path,
Of pitfalls, blunders and life's mishaps,
Is to see the light, to be awakened,
To the joyous revelry of destiny taken.

Tis a fingertip hold on a delicate web.
The moons strong pull on the waters ebb.
Too short a time in the clearings mist.
A world made of fog and ethereal bliss.

Reflecting upon those things we considered,
An afterthought of promises, undelivered.
Cast out our musings, hopes and dreams,
For nothing is ever as it seems.
—*Pamela J. Lakan*

Walk To School

On a cold and blistery day,
A walk to school two miles away.
  We march in single file by three,
To keep wet grass from soaking me.
  With coats pulled tight around our necks,
We brace the worst that's happened yet.
  There is a trick that lies ahead,
A creaky bridge that must be tread.
  A mere foot wide and slick with frost,
It lies ahead for us to cross;
  Where any slip could pitch us three,
Into the creek with hapless glee.
  But now it's past and we can see,
A clearing where there seems to be,
  A better path for us to climb,
So we can reach the school on time...
  —*A. J. Del Ianziti*

Storm Front

Clouds roll over, sunlight fades
A whirlwind of fear surrounds all thoughts
Eyes fill with dreadful tears
People yell and gasp "take thee not"

Voices scream into the dark
No creature is salvaged from its wake
Eyes close, hands clasp
Children give the Lord their souls to take

Eyes close into a deadly sleep
No more can the stress be withstood
Demons appear, dressed in black
Their evil replacing all good

The storm soon ends but the people know
No more can their lives be the same
Rebuilding lives, reliving dreams
They once had before this deadly game

The raindrops begin to calm
The sun begins to shine through
The people begin to gain faith
But hope is the best they can do
  —*Megan Susanne Aepli*

Combat Of Power

  The war has ended in the dark of the night,
a young blonde girl shivers with fright.
  She stands so still on the bloody battlefield,
each side was determined neither would yield.
  "Why?" she ponders as she stretches forth her hands,
"Why do they fight over these green prosperous lands?"
  The child is youthful, innocent still,
she doesn't understand why humans kill.
  Twenty years later quite a beautiful flower,
she now understands that we kill for power.
  Our greed gnaws at us eating away our life,
thus causing bickering and strife.
  Instead of helping one another with respect and care,
we learn to hate each other and never to share.
  If we don't help our fellow man with kindness and grace,
then we'll prolong the fighting obliterating the human race.
  —*Rae Lynn Palombi*

The Gamekeeper

  He whispers a song about you and me,
about friendships that last from land to sea.
  He whispers a song of wars and
fights of disagreements on long winter nights.
  He whispers a song that we all know
about what happened many years ago.
  What he whispers one girl does not know
of goodness in summer and of happiness in snow
of days that come of nights that go will she
ever understand, who knows?
  It's all a game that we must play a game of love
and death of things to come, all it take is one
little breath....
  And the game never ends.
  —*Rachel DeSpain*

No Name

It sit here thinking
About the many splendors
  of God's universe
We try to focus on why
  these marvelous works exist
    for us to see
The sands of time pass through
  The hole in the hour glass
Drawing us nearer to the time
  chosen for us to rest in eternal peace
The deterioration of mankind
A never ending fight for
all creation to coexist
The rape of the ecosystem
Time passes on at a tremendous rate
The vision is locked in place forever
The Splendor is burnt into your mind
If you missed it it's to late
The sands of time have just run out
  Eternal rest is upon us.
  —*Petar E. Szymanski*

Scalpels Of War

Incisions of fire, viewed as exquisite
Accuracy against evil, the utmost requisite

The surgeon masked, but without gauze
Cockpit the cape, gravity without laws

Ethers of ebony inkwell the earth
Fireflies of lasers author their worth

Needles of steel pirate the breath
Closing the cannons pungent with death

Swords and sabers rattle old bones
Warriors and horses awakened by stones

New knights above, gallant ones below
Steeds of silver, armor of peridot

Sojourns into clouds, sojourns into sea
Traversing the terrain, paying highest fee

The targets carved, removed and cut
Accuracy within measure, weaponry the glut

Saving the innocent, sparing the child
Holding the old, damning the wild

Thy entity above, whom we implore
Gather these souls, for peace evermore
  —*Nancy Nelson Gayle*

Sea Of Life

As you sail your little vessel
   Across the storm-tossed sea of life,
Plagued by troubles without mercy
   Blown about by winds of strife,
Remember who rides these seas beside you,
   Who steers your ship beyond the wave
And sets your sails forever after
   Throughout your life unto the grave,
"Oh ye of little faith," he cries,
   "Be brave and all these winds will cease,
Fear not! I am always with you,
   I bring you my love and peace."
     —*Winifred Byers*

Violet Raindrops

The rain began to fall that afternoon.
Across the street, a juke box blared a tune.
Wet tires began to sing, as traffic splashed along;
Their music was a steady droning song.

Upstairs, a tiny boy too young to go to school,
Began his solemn vigil perched upon a stool.
Round eyes looked out the window fascinated,
Seeing more than just a city desolated.

What made him marvel, as he gazed,
Upon the dismal scene amazed,
Was not the city's dull monotony;
But what a child's Wonderland (imagination),
In rapt magic, really let him see.
     —*Robert C. Crissman*

The Blessing Of Poetry

God in creating man and the universe,
Added a blessing with the name of verse.
With it, people using this blessed skill,
Would open vistas of sky, sea and hill.
These would be themes of everyday life,
That would bring joy, peace and many things nice.
Joy—by it, people would work with eagerness,
For their hearts would be happy and reaching out to caress.
Peace—not only in the mind and soul,
Also by verse others would behold,
God's beauty in all nature and life,
Rewarding us with a feeling so nice.
And all about us reflections of God would appear,
And poetry would capture them whether far or near.
Then when all is quiet and a calm prevails,
Before us a copy, in verse, of nature unfurls.
And as from God came this wonderful blessing,
We reflect and look beyond to what God is bestowing.
Then our prayer will be as we read and reflect,
That God be praised in poetry in everyone's respect.
     —*Brother Michael Holmes, S. C.*

Unknown Reasons

    A falling drop of water,
     A trickle of liquid,
  A transparent globule of moisture,
    All shed for unknown reasons.
    Falling drops from the sky,
  Trickling liquid showering down,
  Transparent globules pouring about,
    All shed for unknown reasons.
   Like a rain shower from the clouds,
Or the water from a river flowing rapidly,
   Come tear drops from the eyes,
    Shed for unknown reasons.
   —*Tina Marie Bells*

Gleaning

I walk a well-trod road each day
Adding to my loaded cart
With just one light to lead my way
And bruises from my heavy heart

I gather things along this path
That might be in another's way
Discarded feelings from the past
Could I ease your load today

There's always room for one more thing
A thought, a word an unkind deed
Please share with me and let us sing
Lighten your load! It's what you need

It's twilight and I must be leaving
There's many miles I have to go
Searching, grieving and retrieving
My loaded cart with time must grow
     —*Margo Carlson*

Walking In The Footsteps Of Socrates

On a blistering hot summer day,
after a climb to the fabled Acropolis,
we entered the Agora in Athens, the "city of classics."
Dust clouds rose like thick gray fog to grip the throat
and blur the vision, where fragments of ancient walls
scarred the market place. The streets were over run
with tourists, and foreign archaeologists dedicated to
unearthing rare artifacts from tombs of ancient history.
Peddlers, in temporary stalls, hawked their wares,
from exotic perfumes to tangy red pomegranates and
pungent pickled fish.
Twenty-five hundred years ago Socrates, model of an
exemplary life, symbol of strict moral ethics,
with his companions, frequented this place,
mixing philosophy with good humor and spicy gossip.
In this ancient place where, daily, wars were fought and won,
and ideas widely explored, Democracy was born.
In a building in a corner of the square, Socrates,
the Great Philosopher, was convicted and sentenced to die
for refusing to compromise his principles.
Calmly he drank the lethal hemlock cup and
"lay down to die in peace."
His philosophy has survived the centuries;
his final act a lasting symbol of his courage.
     —*Viola Zumault*

Rude Awakening

A tiny green plant did sprout one day
After a rain in the month of May
And as she grew she looked all around
To see just who shared her plot of ground
She found herself surrounded by flowers
So she began to while away hours
Deciding which kind of flower to be
Finding fault with each one she would see
The daisy is too painted for me
And a shy violet I wouldn't be
The peony I would find much too big
The marigold seems to wear a wig
As time went by and she grew quite tall
She received a shock to end them all
She saw flowers around her going to seed
And knew at last she was just a weed!
     —*Nina D. Simmons*

After We Are Gone

After we are gone, my dear,
   After we are gone from here,
From the here of joy and strife,
   From the here we all call life

Our friendship still will linger on,
   It will live in the lilt of a song,
It thrives because of tender care,
   No weed of disrespect is there

We've shared our laughter and our tears,
   Through long and understanding years,
And, when we have found our final peace,
   Our faithful allegiance will not cease.
   —*Nona Fairhurst*

One Day We Will Stand Before The King

We need to get ready for the Lord to come
Again the signs of his coming is very soon.
When we see Him face to face. Cause one day
We will stand before the King.

They say that He will come in the great white
Clouds. So the time to get ready is right now we
can't wait anymore. Cause one day we will stand
before the king.

So let us make a watch towards the eastern sky.
And tell everyone we know that our Lord will be
here soon to take us home. Cause one day we
will stand before the King.
   —*Lacy E. Geist*

Houses Of Age

Yellow, Reds, Whites, Blacks and Browns,
All are wrinkled with Time.

Each herded to this common ground,
Without rhythm, reason or rhyme.

Endlessly filtered through bingo, crafts and sing-a-longs,
Held captive without chains in sterile, solitary rooms.

No bars or menacing guards but captive by the throng,
Better for one and for all, society assumes.

Unseen for convenience, bastions of culture are forced aside,
Gray inactivity sets a tangible tone of finality.

Through their cold, clear dividers the future arrives,
Our genealogy dissolves in the wake of its progeny.

Lifetimes of experience rotting in disdain,
Venerable purveyors of wisdom ignored, society's demise begun.

Multitudes of knowledge lost, instead of being cultivated and
   reclaimed,
Hidden, our unheard captives hunch and die forgotten.

Society's Pillars dismissed, collapse is near to all,
From our pontificated parapet we fall.
   —*G. Mark Blaschak*

Untitled

Thursday morning
   and a sky, cool, crystal blue.
A flock of geese, heard before seen,
   take flight in a wandering, distorted circumflex—
     like a child's first letters scrawled across a page—
      Until, finding their bearings,
        they engrave initials on the air.
   —*Leslie L. Vavra*

The Clouds

Foamy are the clouds of spring,
All birds are anew on wing.
Clouds turn creamy when the sun is gleaming
And gleeful children are singing.

Heavy are the clouds of summer,
When the days are growing warmer,
Bushes are thirsting for water,
The soil is as absorbing as a blotter.

Thin are the clouds of fall
When days are dull, and when the
Church bells slowly toll
In the distance they seem to roll.

Cold and icy are the clouds of winter.
The last flowers of the season are chosen
For the portrait of the painter,
Before everything is frozen.
   —*Oscar M. Duke*

I Walk Alone

A single soul left cold, shivering, and in pain
All emotion extracted, only emptiness remain
Torn and twisted, left mangled and shot
A path traveled searching, wound in a knot
Oblivious to the suffocating, eyes look away
A soul that is battered, left to decay
A cry is released, quickly stifled by shame
Painted with blackness, each day lived the same
Inner turmoil continues, forever confounded and condemned
As a blanket of darkness encases, the search has come to an end.
   —*Stacy Blasberg*

God's Holy Carmel

God's holy carmel is a Heavenly place
all filled with His love and Divine Grace
an earthly refuge where God's chosen stay
guarded by Angels each night and each day

God's Holy Carmel is His special abode
where the cares of this world are put to unload
and unloaded they are by each Carmelite's prayer
surely God loved us for He put Carmel there

How special God's love for His chosen must be
where surrounded by walls for no one to see
He shuts out the world with it's care and it's strife
and calls His beloved to this Carmel life

Tis a wee bit of Heaven that God put on earth
all whom are chosen were chosen at birth
as God smiles down from His throne up above
a Carmelite prays with a soul filled with love

Saint Theresa, I'm sure keeps doing her part
doing good on this earth is close to her heart
and God in His infinite mercy and love
allows Saint Theresa to guide from above.
   —*Margaret M. Frees*

For Robbie

There I've gone and done it again
All for a bit of privacy I thought I was trying to defend
I never want a lot of or any attention
But there I stood causing a great deal of the aforementioned
I fussed and I fumed almost all day long
And when I got home I realized I had been wrong
I stayed in your office ranting and raving
Acting like a child intent on misbehaving
The origin of the outburst I've yet to pinpoint
But for some reason I felt that something was out of joint
Now, for all the commotion that I did cause
Just goes to show you I do have my flaws
This one is for you to SHOW to those you wish
BUT if I see extra copies, I'll really get pissed!
—*Martha L. Acosta*

God's Angels

God's angels come on wings of wind—
   All heaven praise His name!
 He sent His Son in love and peace—
   Man turned away in disbelief—
   Angels sent in love and light—
   Next come with flaming sword!
     The time is now!
     The hour is near!
   Who has ears let him hear—
    Who has wisdom—
    Let him understand—
   The seal is broken—
   The time is here!
—*Sharline Maria Thomas*

A Tragedy Of The Heart

A chemical called dopamine runs rampant in my brain
All I feel is sadness and pain.
Any affect I seem to display I have learned as an art.
Oh world how I long to play a part.
I am stuck inside a void, Where nothing is enjoyed.
Some would say I am simply in a shell.
I call it however, a veritable hell.
Suspended in a sea of despair,
Pieces of me are everywhere.
I have become Michael Jackson's "The man in the mirror."
Everyday I awake in torment and fear.
How can I change, I don't like this thing I've become,
A desperate creature who thinks she is eccentric and dumb.
I am a composite of this world's misery and pain.
Of what value is it if one has an abundance
   of what is material but emotion one has to feign?
Wondrously we have explored the secrets of universal space
Yet the mind, the psyche is the most unchartered place.
Madness is a tragedy of the heart.
I confess living is a struggle and coping is an art.
—*Kathy Sims*

A Dancer's Dream

    A child stands in fifth position.
     A young girl dreams of performing.
       Tip-toe, tip-toe, tip-toe
    She turns and darts across the floor.
A professional dancer entrechats gracefully in the air
      To Tchaikovsky's Swan Lake,
     And just like fifteen years before,
        Lands in fifth position,
       Bowing the audience goodbye.
—*Kasia Lyson*

Once More

Nature groaned. Nature coughed. The world came tumbling down.
All man's effort laid across the bulging of the ground
Death reached out to take its choice from the motley crowd
Buildings creaked their protest - pitiful but loud
Cries rang out against the air from victims trapped inside
Cement crashed towards the earth and all the sounds subside
A world gone mad is suddenly once more still again
Man stares out in wonderment trying to guess the end
People scurry out like ants who've had their nest disturbed
Life no longer gone about quiet and unperturbed
A lesson taught throughout all time now stands on review
Man, though conqueror he be, can just so much do
Nature's rule, like nature's plan, is not to be denied
Centuries over, off and on, many men have tried
Then the heavens open up. Rivers rise to crest.
Rumblings shake the world apart. Winds blow down the best.
Man, once more, is humbled down to where he first began
When, a million years ago, the world took on its span!
—*Nina B. Doughty*

Sharing With You

I'd wish to share with you
All my wonderful dreams,
All my happy hours,
All my sad and bland days.

I'd wish to share with you
My fantasy filling our empty rooms
Chatting softly and harmoniously
As an unwritten melody.

I'd wish to share with you
All the parts of my body
In a wealthy trade of your pretty eyes
And your always passionate lips.

I'd wish to share with you
The short time of my whole life
Travelling all over the world
In an endless and happy cruise.

I'd wish to tell you
All my ugly and good secrets
And I'd ever wish to listen yours
With tender and eternal love.
—*Oreste Flavio Perdomo*

Thou Art Worthy

For Thou art worthy oh Lord to receive —
All the glory and honor and power.
Thou did'st create all things I do believe,
From birds to bees and each falling shower.
For Thy pleasure oh Lord Thy created —
I too am included in that great plan.
So now all Thy works are consecrated,
When all else fails, Thy Holy Word shall stand.
The freedom of choice to serve, you gave me
With all the pain you bore that lonely hour—
Taught me to be humble, making me free—
Oh Lord made Thee worthy of all power.
For Thou art worthy oh Lord I believe,
A rock of strength that's present every hour.
For Thou are worthy my God to receive
All the glory and honor and power
For Thou art worthy my Lord I believe.
—*Marie Stewart*

Our Friends

As we walk upon the face of this Earth,
Almost at the time of our Birth.
We are the people, that meet on Sunday, to show our respect,
We see our best friends accented in circumspect.
The greatest of all Friends, from Clover.
With all the kindness and sincerity of A Drover.
Adversity has been, long ago dispossessed.
And we are all, most certainly are at recess.
Our fortune is not in gold, but in sacred Friendship.
In Boston, 1976, A.P.T. Boat Convention A relationship.
We can give cause, and evaluate the positive, on Record,
With all the glory of memories that we can accord.
Along with an event to celebrate, when the Faris's came to Florida,
Very important to us, all the way from South Carolina.
Protocol has been drafted, and in Gold,
We invoke the essence of time, for we are all on Parole...

—*Walter J. Lewis*

Deadly Grace

Devious with such insouciant,
along its course of travel
As destine bears deadly grace,
with unsuspecting sorrow
Protruding mirror allows faults glare,
as this one is glace
Thoughtless from all cares,
soggy with solace
Fright appears at first glance,
oblivious is on the move;
with a hellish dance
Presenting sunder as thee given,
imprinted into memories of time
Taking completion from the need,
as isolated pictures become dust to clean
Left with vexation as tribulation,
for one's decree
While filling their decanter
with evildoers seed

—*Linda S. Mowry*

A Gift For Richard

Snow is falling, the first of the season,
already the trees and the ground are all white.

There's a wise old owl sitting in a tree,
hooting, feathers puffed up, what a sight.

A little stream runs freely in its earthy bed,
slowly being etched as snow continues its flight.

Changing of the season, a grand and glorious thing,
all so serene, clean, and bright.

I wonder if snow is God's gift of love,
a cleansing, making all things right.

Thank you Father for letting me see and feel,
allowing me to walk free in thy precious light.

—*Sandra Fulton Lanier*

How Quickly They Go

If I could only slow my days
and make them like before — when I was young,
then I'm quite sure I'd have the time to see
that all my songs were sung.
But that is not the way of life
and one cannot role back the years.
They give what fate ordains
and write their sorrows with our tears.

—*Wilfred H. Faulkner*

Center Thought

Most will agree marriage is addition and multiplication
Also divorce is known to be subtraction and division
Many never thinking of the many fractions
Because they have me, myself and I loving you vision

They destroy what first was a love attraction
Where it becomes a messy and hate faction
With their little ones becoming scattered fractions
Mom and Dad please renew this love attraction

Remember the vows, until death doeth we part
Mend, not break these little ones' hearts
For to be as they, we have heaven on earth
As parents we were the ones that caused their birth.

—*Lee Wells*

What do I, have to do, to let you know, that I am God

There are times, when I have shown you a lot.

And even perform miracles for you.

When you were in need, I was there,
Also, in trouble too. So, what else,
Do I have to do to let you know, that I am God.

Do you remember, when you called on me, Lord, Lord,
And, I answer: Yes, my, child, who, was I then.

Do you, remember, when you ask
me to watch over your children's and
your home, and even paid your bills too.

Who, was I, then.

Through, all that, I've done for you.

What do I, have to do to
Let you know, that I, am God.

—*Shirley Crowder*

Family Matters

I came into your lives with a swiftness likened to the wind
  Although I came with light, in your mind my
    Presence was like a darkened shadow.

  My entrance was love, yet your fear gives me pain,
    My giving to you is not for personal gain.
    Draped with the knowledge of experience,
    My pleasure is to set happiness in a place
Where your sad memories will give love an embrace.
  The higher purpose for us for me, is to grow in
      Heart with unity.
    Now Daliah and Hayley, ask this I must,
  Simply put stepdaughters, I ask for your trust.

    Family to me is a cohesion of hope
With the desire to be strong, as bloodlines lose importance
      When sincerity comes along.

    Family to me is not fatal intrusion,
    With a mixture of ties meant for confusion.
      We are a force destined to be,
      Perhaps this is why family,
        Matters to me.......

—*Melinda Rosellinni-Rogow*

Our Precious Lord

I have a friend so wonderful although unseen by all,
Always there to help, me whenever I might call
A simple prayer is all it takes, to get a problem solved
Regardless of what be the case, or who might be involved
If only you can start anew and put the old behind
You too can have this special friend he is one of a kind
You may have guessed he is "Our Precious Lord,"
Without Him life must be a bore
Please do it now, don't delay, invite him in your heart to stay
No greater friend could ever be than "Our Precious Lord"
  just trust and see.
    —*Patricia L. Carstens*

Safely Launched Eternally

Mother of one, but grandmother of six,
always trying to pick up or fix.

Ruth grew up in a well-known family,
given strict Biblical homily.

A gracious hostess; knitter, seamstress too,
or engrossed with superb quilts to do.

Faithful through husband Martin's long illness,
accepted with humble willingness.

Often endured hidden burdensome trials,
Not knowing she faced many more miles.

Shocked by Grandma David's untimely death,
Just ten weeks before her own last breath.

Their courage and compassion would both win,
even when their commitment waned thin.

No investigations; cause for upset,
time softens the deep pain of regret.

In truth's power their lives now richly blend,
those left seek strength to work for that end.

If depressed by stress we'll learn a choir song,
Above all we must trust and go on.
    —*Katie J. VanRaden*

My Guardian Angel

In memory of my nephew Nathan Bridges Callahan Peterson,
who died from an accidental shooting while target shooting
with friends.

The leaves have turned, the wind has chill
But no one knows just how I feel
I used to love the seasons change
But now it's different, somewhat strange
They always say that life goes on
But part of it stops when someone's gone
The never-ending grief inside
Is something I try hard to hide
If only I had seen the loss
So much I'd change at any cost
All the I Love You's I never said
Now I can't because he's dead
I hope and pray that he can hear
The silent weeps of my hearts tears
I hope he knew the love I had
I hardly said it, now I'm sad
Every night while I'm in bed
I say a prayer within my head
That God will somehow let him be
A Guardian Angel over me.
    —*Susan Ivey Boston*

Are You There Lord?

My heart trembles, is that doubt in my soul?
Am I coming close to losing control!

Are you there Lord?

I am frighten and confused,
that on my way home to you, my way I might lose.

Are you there Lord?

Worldly things are trying to drag my feet from the path,
which beyond awaits satan and all of his wrath.

Are you there Lord?

It's been one of those days, when every thing seemed to go wrong
and I feel as if I'm in a place where I just do not belong.

Are you there Lord?

Today I really need a friend
to help me face this trouble that never seems to end.

Are you there Lord?

I try to do the best I can, but there are things I just can't
understand and my heart cries out for a peaceful land.

Are you there Lord?

I stand here meekly, my head hanging low;
life has beaten me, my heart is full of woe!

Are you there Lord?

Softly a voice comes out of the blue,
"I was there child, where were you?"
    —*Mildred Ayers*

Monkeypod

Palace of woodland timber
Amid fields of iris splendor
Freely thy roots grow
Impoverished vine stately slender
Thy moist limbs reach upward
Clearly thine eye hath seen
Palms upward in silent embrace
Tasting rain within thy face
As dripping water spans the place
Clouding mystery of Raintree Country
Thy silent secret, no soul reveals
Scattered throughout the forest range
Written under Monkeypod's name
Growing circles inner change
Coloring bark light and dark
Tracing Monkeypod of Raintree glen
Patterns of pen and ink pictures thoughts to see
Forever visible ancient scenes of Raintree.
    —*Lynn Mitchell*

My Mother

  For those whom I've admired most
    Among those was my Mother,
      The one who cared
      The one who shared,
  Oh, she could match no other.
She stood so tall at five foot two
  And though her bones were aging,
Had strength and courage to carry me,
  Through life as it was changing.
Yes she would have to be the most
    Among those I admire,
And though she's gone to peaceful rest
  Still her teaching I desire.
    —*Lynn M. Hoffman*

No Need For Envy

There's no need for envy
Among God's family,
For each of us are made unique,
Our mold is formed especially.

No one else can do the things,
Performed by only you.
Your special traits are yours alone,
In what e're you choose to do.

So really there is no need for envy,
We all should be very proud,
For we are one of a kind people,
Proclaim it long and loud!

Our work while here upon this earth
Is to love and exhort one another,
Altho' we're unique and one of a kind,
We are God's family, of sisters and of brothers.

So let us fill our hearts with peace,
The world is waiting just to see,
If we can walk with heads held high,
With no malice, and with no envy.
—*Martha C. Page*

Posterity

I saw him standing there so near to me
An aged man planting a seedling tree.
His hair gleamed white; patterned facial lines.
It seemed so futile, this planting a tree
He would never live it's full growth to see.
He paused then heaved a deep and weary sigh
Then turning, appraised me with his piercing eye
He seemed to sense the question both'ring me
"Young men, you wonder why I plant a tree
We both know it will live beyond my time
Will grow and shed its verdant shade when I'm
Gone. But, my son, those who lived before me
Saw fit to plant shade my shelter to be.
And so for you who follow after me
I build for the future and so plant this tree."
—*Katherine K. Sibrel*

Goddess Of Love

Goddess of love,
an artist's eye view, a woman!
Qualities of a Goddess
  most likely she could possess.
A likely instrument for love's purpose
  to be transferred disguised in a dress,
A good idea I must confess,
  capable of giving love's gentle caress,

Effects of love's touch is seen everywhere
A mother's love beyond compare,
  no sacrifice to great for her to bare,
  her child is worth the dare.

Goddess of love so shared,
  how a mature love by you is fed.
Out of each other's sight
  they refuse to be led.
"Your gift of love making; this love's special
  powers will not leave them ever!"
    They said!
—*Mary Ann Tomasic*

Interlude Of Spring

Warm breezes blow, 'tis spring I know;
an ecstasy is mine.
Each season has its proper place,
in scheme of grand design.

I hear the warb'ling of a thrush,
beautiful music to make;
with cadenced notes, melodic sound,
an interlude to take.

With freshened breath, the earth now stirs,
awakens from winters sleep;
seems that it is indeed aware
of promised life to keep.

Summer soon comes, with burning sun,
to scorch the tender leaf;
but for a moment now behold,
springs interlude, though brief.
—*Rodney Perkins*

Prejudice Equals Pre-Justice

Fear is power.
An inner force promoting hatred.
Coming out to overwhelm, to feed mistrust, instill dislike
Fear can turn you against even yourself.

Ignorance is fear.
Lack of knowledge, defense against the unknown
Racism, bigotry, sexism, taught hatred
Ignorance can turn you against even yourself.

Power is abused.
Unquestioned authority instills terror through violence
Fear is not respect it generates intense hatred.
Bitter love, even for yourself.

Think about it before casting stones
How different are you from those you abuse?
Destroying others lives, is that what you treasure?
Is it what you would want, even for yourself.

Freedom is power.
A driving force coming out to inspire
To feed life, give substance, promote happiness.
Freedom to believe, even in yourself.
—*Susan G. Landeck*

As Love Passes

My soul screams at felt injustice
and crumples from foul deeds
Heart yearning for primal emotion
a touch burning trails of fire
raking coals down my spine,
scorching the skin.

Music soothes the pain only
when soft refrains of a heartbeat
light feelings aglow—immortalizing
thoughts and actions passing before.
A time remembered, then forgot
A place revered, then abandoned.

Forlorn the heart slowing, stops
as my blood dries on the knife
the red pool drowns my cries
as death smiles in triumph.
—*Kathleen A. Muja*

Young Lovers-Aged Strangers

Young lovers, so many years ago.
An outlook of newness!
A world of unknowns!
Excitement of a life-time to be spent together.

No doubts, they could conquer all!
A life-time to experience and explore.
Love would carry them over the milestones of life.
Good times, bad times, they would conquer all!

Years have passed, time has taken it's toll!
Good times, bad times, they experienced all.
From the birth of children, through the labors of daily day living.
Life, death, happiness, sadness!

Young Lovers so optimistic!
Now aged with the affects of life.
Young lovers so full of excitement.
Now filled with disbelief and discontentment!

Young lovers now aged strangers!
Young lovers filled with optimism and an outlook of conquering all,
Replaced now with matured anger and resentment.
Young lovers now aged by the times of a life their love could not conquer!

—Kathy Smith

Epitaph

Gloved fingers daintily clearing away
An overcoat of sapling,
Vine and gnarled metal—braided
As a sheet of twine-
From the stone retaining wall
Whose longevity upholds
A remnant of home,
She slips along, in shadow of these lives
Now bound to one inanimate and gray,
Regretting her own intrusion;
Wearing a crown of songbirds
(They flutter, scold, so near above her head);

In search of answers. A need to separate
Fact and myth is bringing her this way.

"Nonconformists; … recluse,"
They echo in her mind. These explanations
For his decision to "withdraw" …

Everything—different—united here as one.
Nonconformist; … recluse …
The wall supports her now.

A lone vulture circles overhead,
Partaking of death; to survive?
How familiar to one who seeks a dead man's point of view.

She gazes in the mirror; turns to leave.
Her questions remain, etched in stone.

—Laurel J. Walden

Teach Me To Dance

While mind remains alert
And cues transfer with clarity to feet
Help me to dance with grace
Of drifting autumn leaves.
Before eyes dim the memories
Of river's rush
And ears forget the sounds
Of crashing waves
Then like the Sacred Nine
Teach me to dance with beauty and for fun.

—Rae Egland

From Bud To Bloom

It is an innocent infant, brought forth, when life begins;
An untampered life who knows nothing of virtue or sin.
It is a child who is guided by established roads and paths;
A child initially taught to feel; taught when to cry or laugh.
The toddler stands looking for guidance and understanding;
The eyes tells us, trustingly, that on wisdom they are depending.
It is youth we walk beside who longs for a meaningful chat;
Sometimes in need of assistance; sometimes seeking a reassuring pat.
It is the young adult who is often filled with doubt;
In search of responsiveness to learn what life is about.
It is a person we mold by what is said and done;
A life shaped by reasoning from the moment breath has begun.
What greater gift can we ever give than to teach one how to think?
What wonder is more magnificent than bonding with a solid link?
What better being can develop than one who shares from the heart,
Nurtured by love and truthfulness right from the very start?
The pendulum from infancy to maturity is often measured in years;
Perhaps it would be wiser to count the laughs and the tears.

—Libbie Richman

A Promise

Right now I stare at your picture
And all I think about is making love to you
This very eve;
This very day
I pledge my love undying and true
Tender and warm; gentle and kind
To you Kamaria of the moon
Bringing to vision a peace of the mind
Allowing tranquility…security
Of a heart so longing of you…
I beseech all the universe
The power from above and high
To let me be with you silent if loud
Honest but true to the love we share
To let me care and provide for you the same
Tranquility; same peace of the mind
Warm when cold…faithful and undying
A heart, a soul, a man … a lover ….
A husband.
I love you.

—Kemal Catalan

The Beauty Of The Stream

It has a Soft, Soothing Flow
And all People Wonder where it does Go
As it Passes over Rocks and Flows Down Hills
Many Children Play in its Wonder And Enjoy its Cool Chill
People sit at its Side Deep in Thought
Wondering of all the Dreams that They had Sought
It Passes from the Small Backyard Grounds
To a Massive Force where Life Abounds
If it Must Through the Air it will Pour
And at this Sight all Emotions can't Help but Soar
As it Finds its Way over Rocks and Through the Ground
It Produces a Most Hypnotic Sound
And to Find A Calm Spot and Relax for a Time
All Troubles will Flow with it from Your Mind
And Perhaps What Makes You Stay there for so Long
Is its Beauty, With the Birds Singing their Euphonic Songs
Just Relax Yourself at its Side and Dream
But these are only this Man's Writings,
On the Beauty of the Stream

—Mike Tetto

Road To Nowhere

I was looking back on my life
and all the things I've done to me.
I'm still looking for the answers,
I'm still searching for the key.
The wreck I've made of my past
keeps haunting me.
It just won't leave me alone.
I still find it all a mystery
Could it be a dream?
The road to nowhere leads to me.
Through all the happiness and sorrow,
I guess if I had the chance I'd do it all again.
Live for today, not tomorrow.
It's still the road that never ends.
The road that leads to me.
And eventually the road nowhere's
gonna pass me by.
The road to nowhere leads to me.

—*Tanya Griffeth*

All Good Things Must End

Just as the darkness covers the end of a shining day -
And as the ocean blankets the shores of the white sands.
Autumn turns winter, and the once green leaves, now browning, fall.
The death of color is seen as bare branches in a cold chill.
And as mountains crumble and become just hills,
The once beautiful flower begins to die and starts to bend.
For all good things were meant to come to an end.
So, live, love and be carefree.
Before you know it, life as you know it, will come to an end.
You can't relive it - can't forgive it -
Just live for all that you can be.
As you grow older, time grows colder, giving less each passing day.
Do those things that bring you joy - live life to its fullest
  in every way.
For all good things were meant to come to an end.

—*Nancy L. Kovaleski*

When My Last Fly Has Been Cast

Yea, I have fished the rocky rills of the mountains
And cast lures into quiet lakes and ponds,
While enjoying the beauty of flora, fauna and fountains
On journeys to valleys, vales, deserts and mounds.
Oh! God's beauty I have seen throughout my many years
In search of that trophy, that denizen of the deep.
It caused me to traverse many places from ponds to piers,
Providing many memories my heart shall ever keep.
Yes, I have taught fishing to man a man and boy,
Though I'm not a pro, nor a man of renown,
I did it from pure pleasure, just a sport that I enjoy;
A God-given right that I learned on my own.
Now that my years have advanced along the way,
I've proven that life is more than toil, work and wishing.
To aver that a thing is a God-given right is also to say
That He does exist, whether we are working or fishing.
God is a fisherman, too, a fisher of man down to the last;
And I will be one of His number, that's just how I feel.
I, then, will be happy when my last fly has been cast,
And God takes me and gently lays me into His Holy creel.

—*Kenneth D. David*

My Tormentor

Whosoever stacks the wall of bricks around me now
and covers me completely 'till the daylight I shall miss?
Interred 'neath the bricks I lie.
My tormenter, did this.

The bloody hands are clean for the inspection which they wait.
And bronzed in wroth, do I now shake with knowledge of the deed
I tremble with undying thoughts,
My tormenter, does feed.

I'm blindfolded and led to execution in the woods,
the grip around my arm familiar, hands I once had known.
Who leads me to this final hour?
My tormentor, alone.

A massive terror do I feel engulfing me at once.
Mine eyes do see the visage, accidentally did it show,
and in the wreckage of my mind,
My tormentor, I know.

If any bell would ring for all insidious acts I've met,
then now I hear it toll, aloft the bellfrye of the end.
Who raised the sword, that struck my neck?
My tormentor, my friend.

—*Virginia-Anne Edwards*

It's A Great Life

If the weather is cloudy, and it looks like rain,
And everything else seems so gray;
Don't waste the time to gripe and complain,
Tomorrow may be a better day; because it's a great life.

The world may seem like a difficult place,
Maybe you're trying to please everyone in it;
Don't fret, put a smile on your face,
And remember that God's love is infinite, it's great life.

Thank God for flowers that bloom around your feet,
Enjoy the delightful song of a little bird -
Admire the green green grass so fresh and sweet;
And be aware of how you speak each word, you'll see, it's a great life.

The world is so full of beauty,
Look around you, it is everywhere -
If you will allow love to flow warm and free;
Then everyone could gather a share, because it's a great life.

Just be kind to people that you meet,
Be glad to spread happiness along the way;
There's a time and a reason to laugh at defeat,
If you'll take a look at yourself and say, "it sure is a great life."

—*Viola M. Crider*

Creation

The Lord made the heavens and also the earth
And everything in it and all that it's worth.
The clouds are his chariots, the winds are his wings.
He's surrounded by angels, who praise him and sing.
The Lord took the darkness and separated it from light.
The light was day and the darkness he called night.
He created dry ground and he called it land,
Then the Lord made the seas and surrounded them by sand,
He created the moon, as well as the sun
And he was pleased with it all, when each thing was done!
With his hand he sprinkled stars that would twinkle in the sky.
Then created the birds and made them to fly.
He covered the earth with an abundance of trees
And flowers bursting with color, and then he made bees.
He put fish in the ocean and animals on land,
But one thing was missing, and that was a man.
So the Lord created Adam and then he made Eve.
And then he was pleased with all he'd conceived!

—*Sherry Howell*

The First Snow

When falls comes
   And everything seems to die,
I look forward
   To snow. It makes everything alive.

It seems to cleanse
   All the dirt from summer
And brings its brightness
   To make the land glitter.

Oh! I love
   The first snows of fall.
They bring joy
   And hope for all!

—*Nancy Jo Norville*

Where Eve Once Stood

Where Eve once stood we will stand, with good
and evil both at hand;
And will we too His will deny and thus the consequence defy?
Ours the choice to heed the Word, or shut it out—
Unseen, unheard.
Knowing God alone is good; Here we are, where Eve once stood.

Have we shut a certain door, where we left an apple core?
Saying, "God, don't go in there. You might catch me unaware!"
Choices face us every day—to yield to sin or to obey.
With temptations all around, can we in God's grace abound?
There are two ways; one bad, one good.
Here we stand, where Eve once stood!

—*Virginia Foster*

Generosity

What glorifying image, incites great delights,
And exalts its fervent desire, with binding pleasure?
What hopes and expectation, stir noble insight,
To glamour, in its gracious, glowing stature?
Surely, it's the reflection, of noble, unseeming profile
That stimulates life's sophisticated, glorious spell.

Great involvement, worthy of super blessings.
Generosity - the hope, and goodness, or sublime heart.
With cherished love, great concern, for ardent caring,
To retrieve humanity, from insidious, painful hurt,
Of despair, frustration, and distress encroachment,
The sordid wiles, of shrewd, grimy, entanglement.

Hail generosity, accentuate with dazzling splendor,
Radiating, exciting delights, ideal grandeur,
To dispel the ravaging, intolerable, girded obsession,
Of deceit, indifference, and rabid selfishness,
The ghastly image, and lust, of greed's ambitions,
Schemes, so wild, that undermine cherished happiness.

—*Uldario P. Custodio*

Contradictory

I went to church on Sunday
and I found myself in a night club on Monday.
I prayed to God on Wednesday
and I cursed out loud on Thursday.
I participated in Holy Communion on Friday
and I was in a gambling party on Saturday.

I went to Sunday school
after I had drank liquor like a fool.
I saw the church minister
but I had just had an affair with the church's spinster.
I once held my hand on the Holy Bible
but for my bizarre past I am liable.

—*Michael Leroy Porter*

To Be A Child

How wonderful to be a child and run through meadows free
   And feel the clover underfoot and chase the bumble bee

   To feel the soft dew in the air
   And feel the wind blow through your hair

How wonderful to be a child and watch the cottontail
As he zigs and zags across the field over hill and dell

To chase him through the meadows green until you're out of breath
How wonderful to be a child and never think of death

How wonderful to see the world through wide open innocent eyes
And smell the flowers on the hill and chase the butterflies

To get so excited when you find a brand new tree to climb
And never thinking past today just living one day at a time

   How wonderful to be a child and only think of now
   And feel a loving kiss at night upon your tired brow.

—*Sharon Ruth McEntire Raybal*

The Dream

He takes my hand,
And flies toward the dawn,
I become a child.
He shows me the land as it was,
The fields and the trees,
The clear rivers and lakes,
So pure.
Their beauty so brilliant,
That I am blinded by it.
He turns then to the sun at its peak,
And I grow old,
The trees and fields replaced by concrete and steel.
The rivers and lakes filled with death and decay.
My heart breaks, I wish to see no more.
But his hand is firm,
And I am forced to see as he then flies toward dusk,
The burden on my heart lifts,
For there before lies the future.
The world reborn, new, and once again free.
As I am led back to rest,
There is hope in my soul,
And hope for all.

—*Stephenie L. Carter*

Mama, Daddy And Heaven

They walk the streets of gold today,
   And for all eternity.
From frail bodies racked with pain,
   They have been set free.

Oh, to have the faith they had
   In the One who loved them so,
Through all their years of life on earth,
   Even through their pain and woe.

They are happy there in heaven,
   Just as God has promised all—
Who have such faith in Him,
   And will answer when He calls.

Yes, they're walking streets of gold now,
   No more sleepless nights, or hurting days,
Just thanking Jesus, and serving Him,
   In a thousand different ways.

Mama and Daddy will welcome us
   When we reach heaven's gates.
We'll all gather around the throne,
   And sing to God, eternal praise!

—*Wanda Hendon*

My Dream World

If everyone could see the beauty in a flower
    and forget about that dollar
If everyone could see the rising sun
    and realize what fun
      it would be
    to just be by the sea
    If everyone you meet
    could just be sweet,
    Look at our good side
    and then let the rest slide,
Wouldn't this be a great place
    for all of us to face
Because today everything
    is going to be alright
Like the birds in flight
    Everyone could be free
      Free to be you
        and
      free to be me.
—*Sallie Korte*

Friends

      Friends come
      And friends go
    But the best ones stay
  They may go down a different road
    But they're still there
    When you need them most

  No matter how selfish you feel
Or how much you want them to stay
    If you're a true friend
  You would never stand in their way

    We all have our own lives
  And can't revolve them around our friends
Therefore we do what we feel is right for ourselves in the end

  So all we can do is cherish the great times we've had
    And look forward to the time that our roads may meet
      Parting doesn't always have to be so bad
    But one thing it will always be, is sad
—*Sarah Williams*

Untitled

If you can take whatever life may hand you,
and from it try to fashion something good,
If you know others may not understand you,
but you keep right on doing what you should...
If you can watch a friend go off without you
and know that you can take such things in stride,
If you are kind and just to all about you
and let the Golden Rule become your guide...
If you are wronged and still can be forgiving,
believing it is better to forget,
If you think there is too much joy in living
to waste your time on anger and regret...
If you accept a failure and not mind it,
but stop to learn the lesson it can teach,
If you resist temptation when you find it,
remembering the goal you want to reach...
If you can hold your own when you're not winning
and know you can't achieve the things you plan,
If you can proudly make a new beginning
and never lose your faith in God and man...
You'll find success is waiting if you're willing,
that happiness is there for all who try —
Your life will be rewarding and fulfilling,
and nothing good with ever pass you by!
—*Thomas J. Seidler*

Two Rivers

The streams runs slowly at its source
And gurgles gaily round the stones.
On farther down it picks up speed and force
As the stream broader now, begins to carry
Parts of the land itself, as it scurries on.
Sticks, grass, bushes, even huge boulders
Are carried to lie in some strange, new place.
Mighty in its course it rushes onward
Toward its goal, the sea.
So is our river of life.
It runs so slowly at its start
When we, as children, join its gentle flow.
The days drag by, an endless stretch,
From birthday back again to birthday.
Downstream it tosses us atop the rapids
Rushing us through days too short.
Bearing us onward in that dark raging stream
To our goal, the sacred promise of God, eternal life.
To the mansion that awaits, the crystal sea, the throne,
Oh blessed, divine glory, eternity.
—*Margaret Sutton Hadden*

Wee Amanda Marie

  Did not see her until three weeks old.

    With your new born eyes so blue
      and hair so silky and black;
        coming from God's Hand,
      seeing this world anew,
  wonders upon wonders, with a knack,
knowing someday to be in God's promised land.
    Tis for thee, Wee Amanda Marie.

  May the years in between be mellow,
    with time on your side,
    to grow and learn His love;
  that we are placed here, on Earth's Pillow,
    for knowledge of Jesus having died,
so that, with belief in Him, can fly like a dove.

    Tis for thee, Wee Amanda Marie.
—*Rodney Bessire, Sr.*

God Spoke. God Breathed.

God spoke. Light was divided,
  And Heaven and Earth were born.
The waters were divided,
  And the earth with seed adorned.

God spoke. Each grass, herb, tree
  Endowed with continuing seed.
Sun, moon, and seasons allotted,
  Fulfilling every growth need.

Then life came forth from the waters,
  Fowl freely flew with new hope.
Mist watered the earthly garden,
  And all because God spoke.

There was none to tend the garden.
  God, from dust, made a man whole,
God breathed the breath of life in him,
  Man became a living soul!

God speaks today through His word,
  He breathed a new spirit in me.
My living soul communes with Him
  And I'll live eternally.
—*Ruth C. Grace*

Whole And Free

The seasons ever come and go
and here you silently sit the same
For every passing face seems to show
that you have no relevance in the game

Sun bathes your face in its glow
Sometimes you don't even know your name
And every effort that you make to grow
seems always halted by your need to blame

Sits the moon in a heavenly sky
The night so illuminated and still
All about you love does softly fly
Yet thoughts of self-pity dash your will

Here is my hand, take it please
It too trembles like your fearful heart
Yet, I fight when life brings me to my knees
My courage has made me an integral part

Before this Season does bid farewell
It will reveal us to be whole and free
A happiness beyond mere words to tell
shall be the possessions of you and me
—William R. Johnson

Desert - Bent

There was weary, old Slim with sand-blasted skin,
And his old burro, Jim- bent to the desert sun,
Weathered and worn, patched and torn
Shuffling the sand in this endless land.

Old tired Slim like mangy Jim,
Was skinny and lean as could be
But though picking were scarce, and comfort unknown,
They planned it their home, eternally.

The dirty, wrinkled hat on scrawny slim
Seemed to grow out of his wire-thin frame
And stiff-legged Jim; a little bit lame,
Appeared molded to the rough terrain

An inseparable pair with so little to share,
Except nature and life in the rough
With rocks and valleys and miles of sand
And grovelling each day for the magic stuff.

Some day I know when men will pass by
A lonely, desolate wind-swept hill,
There will be cactus slim beside prickly rear Jim
Bent to the wind, petrified and forever still.
—Mandalie Thompson

In Remembrance Of Mark Nevin

It's Sunday, my dear
And it's nice to have Mark here.
I cannot compose like Mark can,
But I can hear the beauty of his land.
I cannot tie notes with chords sublime
But I'm attuned to a higher rhyme;
For the Lord who marks the beat for Mark
Is the One who's ever in our heart.

My Life He spared through those who cared,
And a stronger faith was fully shared.
A "Right Now" Messiah brought Claire to me;
The "I Am" before Abraham is ever here:
I know - because it's Sunday, my dear.
—Karl Van Bibber

Crimes Of Passion

You used to take the time to tell me you were all mine,
And how my body was so very fine. The privilege of
holding me close, listening to me breathe, the way you
used to tuck me in was so very sweet. You swore you'd meet
my every need and that you would never leave.

Three years have flown by so fast I prayed the fireworks
would last the smoke, now cleared, I fear I am your task.
You hardly hold me close at night, I ask to make love but
instead we fight. The covers now lay loose around me and
I become your second thought as I lay and watch your back
breathe lightly.

It hurts to know I'm on the lowest rung of your ladder
because all the little things used to matter. I no longer
appear to look so nice, instead I'm a bitch with eyes full
of ice. I'm no longer worthy to be your wife, there are no
more moonlit cornfield nights, small needs are your biggest
strife. Am I just an object in your life?

I fear the gate on the garden closed as neglect chocked its
only rose. I speak my feelings line by line but you tell me
it's a waste of time. Now as the covers lay loose around me,
I long to be held oh so tightly, but instead I lay and watch
your back breathe lightly and a tear falls silently...
—Mary Frances L. Heller

Forever My Love

You are the stem
and I am the rose
Together we are one
alone no one knows
You keep me standing
alert and awake
You help me grow
While upon your shoulders
my life you take.
Forever my love you will always be.

Without you I'm nothing
but petals and dust
You keep me living
to me you're a must
Our love is a rose
both petals and stem
a bond meant to last
for all eternity
Forever my love you will always be.
—Teri Keens

Islands

Somewhere in the South Pacific
And island surfaces,
Breaking the plane of last resistance,
A treasured token from the sea,
Unnoticed, unheralded, and unable
To proclaim its own existence,
Except within the minds of windward souls
Not yet marooned by their imaginations,
Who feel the presence of a trade wind blowing,
Flowing gently, calmly
Encircling their deepest emotions,
Reminding them of how islands ought to be,
As if to say, "Don't you think it's time,
Islands of the human kind,
To break the lane of your cool indifference
And surface above insensitivity?"
—Robert Hall

I Believe

I believe in my God,
And I believe in his only son.
And I am preparing for the time
When my work here on earth is done.

I believe in the Holy Bible,
It is God book, you see.
And it comforts and teaches
Us to be all we can be.

I believe in the songs we sing,
As we sing praises to our Lord
And the prayers that we pray,
Peace and contentment is our great reward.

I believe in the Beatitudes
And the Psalms, especially the twenty third,
And the Lord's Prayer that from
Our Childhood we have all said and heard.

I believe in the ten Commandments
And I strive to keep each one,
For I know God is my Savior,
And that He gave us His only son.

I believe Jesus died for me,
Just as he died for each of you,
Died on the cross for our sins,
This no mortal man would do.
—*Willie Johnson Cummings*

Moments Of Friendship

You brought so much love out of my heart
And I can still remember right from the start
You never left my side — you were always there
Though tired and worn was I — you didn't care
Because I was the light that shined in your eyes
But the day would come and I would soon realize

That time would allow only a speck of sand
And you would no longer reach for my hand
Though I smiled and laughed when you were here
How life left its mark and would bring my first tear

But remember that I will always be
Full of the wonderful days of you and me
And wait for the time when once again
I can call your name — "Sam, my friend."
—*Toni Acuna*

Taps For The Soldier

I heard taps blow at setting sun,
And knew the battle had been won,
Ere dawn, a new charge I would keep.
I heard taps blow, and fell asleep.

I did not leave, nor yet retreat,
My tour of duty was complete.
Then, from Headquarters came the word,
I did not leave, I was transferred.

Duty came first, I had no choice.
I heard the Great Commander's voice,
Ordering me to His High Brigade.
Duty came first, and I obeyed.

I am not gone, I'm uppermost
Within the ranks of Heaven's host.
Not sealed within a catacomb,
I am not gone, I've been shipped Home.
—*Vivian Coffey-Tomlin*

To My Children

If I had riches and wealth untold,
And I could bequeath to you all the world's gold,
You would still be penniless my child,
Without knowing God, and having His promises to hold.

The things of his world, doth rust and decay,
But the legacy I leave to you will never be that way.
I leave to you, the Word of God, which will never pass away,
And the knowledge that He loves and watches o'er you day by day.

I leave to you the beauty of a child's smile,
And the fragrance and color of the flower wild,
I also leave my love and pride in you,
For all the kind and good things, that I've seen you do.

But most of all my child, to start your "Heavenly Treasure,"
I leave to you the many prayers that are without measure,
The ones that have asked God to guide you, and be very near
  and dear,
And bless you with the wealth of knowing Him, so that you
  never have to fear.
—*Kathryn L. Reiff*

Guilty Or What

When someone silently called out for help,
and I heard every syllable, yet did I help?

As in anger someone shouted at me,
did I, oh, did I reply in the same?

When someone was lonely, and I knew it was so,
Did I, God, did I try to fill their void?

As some in the past had refused my love...
have I just stopped trying, or held on fast.
Going to battle to anchor my love.....

When in the past, was I guilty, guilty of these,
and oh, so much more?
But I am humane, not perfect you see.

Dear brother, dear sister, take a glance in
your life, and all will see, not only me is
guilty of these!

But all isn't lost, there's hope for us yet!
Get down on your knees, for repentance plead.
Cause God's there waiting, for you and for me.
Forgiven we are, we're free, we're free.
—*Sylvia Helton*

Rainbow Man

I see colors, drippin' from the sky like water on bubbles
and it seems like to me, I'm livin' a dream
Then I feel the summer sun and see all the work that never gets done
and I know it can, cause I'm a rainbow man.
Livin' on the road and always on the go ain't's easy
But I make it and I get by the best I can
If I ever need someone, God's above me
And I know he'll always love the rainbow man.
I can almost see another town and feel raindrops start fallin' down
Can it be? Well, I guess it can
Soon to be I'll be there with work to do everywhere
And there'll be happiness again for this rainbow man.
—*Thomas E. Hill*

My Final Breath

Life is full of many turns
and not knowing which way to go
we listen to our elders
for they've seen all and know...

But when loved ones are left
standing by the way side
do we then listen to our hearts
or close our eyes to hide...

Leaving you behind was pure hell
and if it could be done again
I believe we'd still be together
strengthening what we had then...

But we were both young and innocent
each stubborn and ungiving
now I wish I'd given more of myself
for as man and wife, we might still be living...

I know I still love you very much
and will until my timely death
in my heart I whisper your name daily
confessing my love for you with, my final breath.
—*Mary Moffet*

I Walked With God Today

I spent the day with God today
And oh, what joy it brought;
My heart was filled with wonder
By the lessons that He taught.
We walked o'er hills and valleys,
And rested by the streams,
And all around He showed me
The grandeur of His dreams.
The flowers and butterflies that die.
Though dead, return each year—
God's promise to His children
That they too will come back here.
He made me understand how
Every form of life depends
On another of His creations
So that each may serve its ends.
But the most important thing I learned,
As we walked along our way,
Was — God expects us to take care of
And preserve His gifts each day.
—*Mary Leah Blake-Miller*

One Day

One day there will be no wars...
And one day hate will be no more.
One day many cures will be discovered
For all types of diseases...
And one day there will be food and
Shelter for all and not just for me...
One day there will be a good educational
System that will teach all to respect
The Histories of other cultures, as well as,
Our own.
One day there will be true justice
For all...Rich or Poor...
And one day we will all experience
Love, Peace and Joy
One day....One day....
—*William B. Thomas*

Grandma's Cedar Street

First filled with love and hope some myth,
And plans and schemes of future dreams, all possible to cope with.

Through the years the contents changed.
The hope endured; the love matured; but dreams no longer ranged.

Souvenirs stored as time went by:
A teddy bear, some Navy wear, clothes no longer one could buy.

Army patches, high school letters
Earned in sports of many sorts, some still complete with sweaters.

Surely everything is pure antique!
Is there a time, a reason or rhyme, to throw away things so unique?

One thing's sure: Grandma won't!
The wedding dress; pictures, no less; throw them away?
Don't!

Everything is of the best.
Results of schemes, and plans, and dreams
That's Grandma's Cedar Chest.
—*Vera E. Putnam*

Memorial Day

Speak loud and clear of flag and glory,
And play the fife and drum.
Tis now a stone tells our story,
The battle finished,
Our twilight has come.
Heap words of praise upon the stone,
Its letters etched so bold,
For neath we lie in tidy row....
Forever still, and cold.
Comrades in arms, from all walks of life,
Of every size and hue....
Sleeping soundly now,
Through each new war,
Beneath the granite pew.
Remember this day; our silent rest,
Hold it close to Americas breast.
Hear these words, great America,
This prayer, hope, and plea.
Because for you America,
We gave our all to thee.
—*Paul D. McCreary*

To Be Like A Tree

If I could only be like a tree, I could stand and grow tall
and proud but wait maybe I am like a tree after all. We
were both born of a seed. The tree outside has grown straight
and tall, and I next to it seem so small, but I, also, seem to
have grown straight and tall. My beliefs are like its roots,
firmly planted in the soil of life. I have not been able to
grow straight and tall without learning to bend like the tree
bends its branches in the wind of the storm. Just as the sun
nourishes the tree as it grows and grows throughout the years,
I, too, am nourished by the sun. The sun warms me and shows
me the way with each step I take. As the tree grows older
with each year that passes, its beauty continues to live on as
it grows stronger and strives to grow in an upward manner, as
it tries to touch the sky. I, too, like the tree will bloom
with each year that passes. But my blossoms will be the peace
and beauty of life, I feel within me. I will strive like the
tree to always grow upward and tall trying to reach the sky,
with my beliefs planted firmly in the soil of life.
—*Pamela J. Senn*

Love Lives On

If tears could be bottled up.
And sadness locked away,
I'd do my best to spare you,
any hurt that comes your way.
I'd gather up some sun beams,
so shiny for your hair,
then make a wreath of
flowers and gently place them there.
I'd shield you from all danger,
I'd pray that you would know,
that a lovely rose is
living, just beneath
the fallen snow.
—Rebecca McGraw

Sentry At The Spring House

Where the poison ivy halts the wood land path
And salamanders by pale moss take a bath
A Spring House up the creek to Patapsco Park
Encloses a bubbly sprinkler in the dark.

Foot steps quiet through the forest stop at the brink
Of the Spring House where curious deer take a drink.
Under cold, vaulted rocks there creaks a rusty door
Inside which thirsty travelers placed a cup before.

But that happened long ago when times were dull;
Now the changed opening hosts a grinning skull.
What is the story the skull would have us heed?
If you can tell us, please proceed.

But as for what I do myself,
I leave alone what's on the lonely shelf;
Then back off to say a little prayer
Not to meet who left that dark hole's surveyor.
—Linda Marie Fahey

Paradise Almost Lost

I looked today into the heart of this, my native land,
And saw so much of agony and grief, and broken dreams on
  every hand,
That my soul recoiled in horror from the anguish and the dread,
And I wished my eyes were blind, and my hearing dulled and dead

The shining dreams and brilliant hopes of a people unafraid
Have been stifled 'neath the blighted bigotry of greed upon
  them laid,
Until the golden sunshine of our destiny is darkened in the skies,
And the clouds self-indulgence, unrestricted pleasure and lies
Have almost destroyed our hopes of being free.

Those who should be our statesmen are leading us astray,
Making truth and honesty and solemn vows stumble in the way,
As we deny to these, our brothers, the freedom we once sought,
Content to lose the legacy for which our fathers fought.

Return America, land that once was hope to all the world,
Of peace and prosperity and equal chance beneath our flag unfurled;
Regain the heights that once were ours in the eyes of all who sought
For the chance to stand and proudly win the battles we have fought.

Come, o my country dear, and lift your eyes to Heaven's light,
See reflected in the stars the destiny that spans the height,
And leaving dishonest, greed and self-indulgence all behind,
Grasp the shining promise that will give us peace of mind.
—Margaret D. Coolbaugh

Untitled

Looked up to you when I was three
And saw you looking back at me
Proudly
I'm twenty now, you're someone new
It's different now, what can I do?
Nothing
How did we drift so far apart
But still be close in both our hearts
I love you so much from the start
But your new You tears me apart
Help me
I'm trying hard to understand
About you and your brand new friend
It's hard now
You'll always be my shining star
No matter how apart we are
Inside
Even if we'll never be
What years ago we used to be
We tried.
—SerenaAnn Kirby

Storm

When I look out a window
And see a wind tossed tree,
Or grasses flattened to the earth,
Or spindrift flying free,
I feel a wistful envy
Of the wild things all outside
While folk like me stay dry and warm,
Safe from gale or tide.

From the inside of the window
The drama of the storm
Speaks to a regal savage
Who lurks within my form.
She yearns to fling the portals wide,
Confront the storm which valiant stride,
Confront the terrors of the night
And overcome their awesome might.

But, no, the gale-swept tattered night
Split wide by flaming streaks of light
Eludes my reach - be silent, pride,
It's watched, but can't be felt inside.
—Portia Griswold

Waterfall

Cold spring water falls from above
And splashes down hard to the ground
Sun shines through the tall green trees
Makes rainbows all around

So powerful this waterfall
It's beauty has no end
Peaceful hours alone out here
I've found a real friend

Forever flowing, it feeds the earth
As it runs out to the sea
Why we destroy it day by day
Just makes no sense to me.

Our world needs help, now can't you see
We have to give it our all
So our children's children will be able to see
This beautiful waterfall!
—Robert J. Wesner

What Life Is Left To Us

There are songs yet to sing
And sleigh bells to ring

There are rainbows to chase
And sweet fruit to taste

There are doors to open and doors to close
And sunshine sparkling on winter snows

There are corners to go around
Hills to go up and hills to go down

There are "I love you's" to say
And a sunrise each day

There are dreams to dream
And strawberries to sample with thick, sweet cream

There are shoulders to hug and lips to kiss
There are letters to write to those we miss

There is laughter to laugh and tears to cry
And sorrow to bear when "loved ones" say good-bye

There is love in abundance, here and there
Much love in which to share

And beyond this place and all future time
Lies a world alone .... just yours and mine
—*Rosetta J. Duke*

The Year 2000

In the year two thousand, I will be still alive,
And so will other humans and animals.
There still will be vegetables and minerals,
And mundane life as ever in the sunshine.

Not the earth will tend to stop revolving,
Neither the seas to dry, nor the air to condense;
Each day will be a new one, no last hence;
And the world, humanity, will face no ending.

Wars will continue to erupt here and there
As an ordeal to test Man's thirst for peace.
Poverty, ignorance, and diseases will not cease
For egoism, greed, and cruelty will not care.

But anywhere on the globe at any moment,
There always will be conscience, common sense.
The elites still will vow the innocents' defense,
For people to be prosperous, happy, and consentient.

We still will have much more progress to make
And many more stars to explore and conquer.
To prepare for the twenty-first century to enter,
We need self-reliance striving for our own sake.
—*Thanh-Thanh*

Birthday Party

A little old lady turned ninety one day.
And that's pretty old, whatever you say.
And then when she knew she would be all alone
Did she sigh? Did she cry? Did she groan?
Did she moan?
Not this little lady - she leaned on her cane
and opened a bottle of ice-cold champagne.
She sipped and she sipped until it was gone.
And then she stood up and yawned a great yawn.
She called to her cat and he came with a purr-
She held him and stroked his soft silky fur.
She went to her bed and slept all night long
And dreamed of the mocking bird's beautiful song.
She woke in the morning all full of good cheer
And ready to start on her ninety-first year!
—*Phyllis Drummond*

Memories

You came into my life quietly
  and softly as peaceful fog
  on a silent still river.
Your eyes, twinkling as you smile;
  remind me of clear, blue Alaskan
  skies.
Your hand in mine, a comforting
  surprise, belongs, as if mine
  were always waiting.
Your arms, strong and tender,
  keeping out the world, feel
  as if this were the home I
  always longed to be.
You brought into my life a special
  tenderness, and a hunger for more.

Memories of your kisses, soft in
  my hair, your fingers, tracing
  my face, your body, pressing
  close and warm are my special
  treasures.
—*Roberta J. Falter*

Fall

Yes spring has come and gone,
  And summer's nearly past.
And soon the radiant colors of fall
  Will shine threw at their best.

The leaves will turn from shades of green,
  To yellow, orange and red.
And before we even stop to think
  Their leaves will all be shed.

The chirping of the crickets
  And the singing of the frogs
Will soon be hushed to silence
  As they sleep deep in the bog.

In slips the chilling evenings
  And the days will soon grow short
And soon the summer's fishermen
  Will bring their boats to port

Yes soon the hand of winter
  Will be knocking at the door
And as the months of snow pass by
  We'll long for spring once more
—*Sally Raugh*

Sabbatical

I'm going down river
  And round the bend
Over the hill
  And through the glen,
Going with a song in my heart
  Going West to get a new start.

Going to see the cave
  Where the red-man dwells
Where thundering hooves
  Mark a cattle trail,
Going to view with a stranger's eye
  Mountain peaks that scale the sky.

I'm going to cross that "Great Divide"
  Where brave men flourish-
  A coward dies!
Going where God's land is best
  Tomorrow, tomorrow, I'm
  Going West.
—*Pat Calhoun*

In Heaven And Going To Hell!

Come, my friend, sit here with me
And tell me - am I wrong
In thinking we are sinking down
To a depth we don't belong?

Our winds no longer burst with sounds
Of the laughter of a child
The fields of green have turned to dust
Dry weeds spread vast and wild.

And mournful souls in deep despair
Hide in a darkened hall
So disheveled, so addicted
They scream, they curse, they fall.

Life, too, cut short by the blast of guns
Or a screeching auto wheel
By those who seem to lack remorse
For the beauty that they steal.

So, tell me — am I really wrong
In all that I am fearing?
Is our grandeur and serenity
Rapidly disappearing?
—*Miriam E. West*

Just In Time

I was lonely when you came
   And thanked whatever Gods may be
     For your presence. ——

You rekindled dying sparks among the embers,
   Hidden in the ashes ——
Bringing fresh and glowing flame,
   With warmth and sudden touch of life,
     Vibrant and discerning ——

The soft touch of your body meeting mine
   In love's embrace,
     Like the sound of waves
       On distant shore;
   In tune with all the universe!

Love meets love, if only for a moment
   Dwelling there ——
And all seems right and bright and warm
   As deeper meaning winds its way
     Through all of being,
       Dispelling all the loneliness that
         Ever was!
—*Robert F. Taylor*

Tell Me Why

Please tell me why a baby cries
And why the sun comes up each day
And why earth's beauty always dies
Like flowers in the month of May.

Please tell me why forever stays
For such a short time, then it's gone
Why we lay waste to all our days
Why morning always follows dawn.

Please tell me why the seasons pass
The colors in a sunset blend
Why true love doesn't always last
And why the scars of time don't mend.

I want to know, please tell me why
I have to know it's not a lie.
—*Vicki Alexis Pardallis*

Dedicated To The One

I look at the swans in the lake
And the birds in the sky,
They were meant to be as one
Knowing that together they can get by.
Couples walk along the street
Holding hands and staring into each other's eyes
Knowing that someone will care about them
Until the end of time.
Even the stars up in the heavens,
How they glisten so at night
Shining over all the love they find below them,
Making all those hearts in love shine bright.
Watching the world go by
Makes it plain to see
That everybody's in love,
That is, everybody but me.
I've been in love with him before,
But then he broke my heart in two
And I'm willing to give the pieces
To be mended by you.
You glance, then turn the other way to look at another
Because everybody has someone but me.
—*Lydia Murdza*

Indian Summer

Frost last night
And the leaves loosened their hold
On the limbs of the trees.
This morning when the sun
Came out and breezes stirred the leaves
They came floating, tumbling, turning
To the ground.

Some I noticed had forgotten
To change to their autumnal dress
So that green as well as yellow and red
Strewed the walk under my feet.

The sky is clear blue
And the moon forgot to go home to bed.
The sun in warm splendor is shining
On the Fall-plowed fields
And dry shocks of corn.
The scent of the dying year is in my nostrils.
I walk the field in the sun!
—*Karen S. Burr Zelle*

A Fable

Courtesy and Kindness met on the street one day
And they chatted very softly as passersby went on their way,
They smiled at each person as he or she passed by
But no one turned to look at them, nor did they catch their eye.
Everyone was hurrying as on his way he flew,
Each one glared at one another and thought — "how could I
   speak to you?"
But one gentle little soul braved where angels feared to tread,
Smiling at one another as by her each one sped.
Each busy shopper barely noticed her and none returned her smile,
As she met them in each business hurrying up and down each aisle.
Courtesy and kindness looked in sadness and shed a tear or two
And turning arm in arm they walked away and faded from the view.
—*Marie E. Gingrich*

To Marry A Navy Man

He's the father of my children
and the man that I adore.
But while in the United States Navy
the world he did explore.

He wasn't there for Thanksgiving or Christmas
or even a first communion.
But when he came home we were over-whelmed
it was like a family reunion.

My car and every household appliance
had their own ears and eyes.
They watched my husband leave for sea
and that's when they deliberately died.

As a Navy wife sometimes I wondered
why I even bothered.
It's not just being a lonely wife
you're also both mother and father.

If you're ready to marry a navy man
be prepared for "sea duty strain".
When you say your vows for better or worse
remember you married the man, sea duty's the pain.

—*Sue Koch*

The Howling Moon

"There are times when the wolves are silent
and the moon is howling."
    The Last Whole Earth Catalog
how she wishes things would change
they won't — they always stay the same
scars will fade, bruises heal
so confused it seems unreal
shattered vase upon the floor
walked into an open door
soft in the dark the night wind cries
she tells her friends still more lies

—*Nancy Meilahn*

Composition Of Nature

As the days are short
And the nights are long.
Fall arrives with a melody of songs.

Crisp cool mornings,
With the sun beaming down,
Silhouettes of many,
Appearing on the ground.

The delightful wind,
Gracefully, humming through the trees,
Oscillating the branches,
With the harmony of the breeze.

The chirping of the birds,
And the squirrels at work and play.
Nature is creating a magnificent display.

Spectacular sights,
And sounds of life,
All do appear,
On this crisp fall night.

—*Patricia A. Van Horn*

Sweet Life!

Our Father in Heaven, or God who is Life!
And the Only giver of Life!
The Eternal Creator**-Our Lord Jesus Christ
I love You and the life you gave to me!
I vowed 52 years ago to die a martyr
For Your Sweet Love!
And Your precious Gift of Eternal Life!
God or life is in the air we breathe
God or life is in the earth we walk on.

Satan and his mean, cruel, miserable, lying children
Have persecuted Me for 52 years!
But I must try to make them see
And understand You and Me!
That we love them truly and want them to see
How stupid and foolish they be!
Because they won't love and obey You and Me!
My Sweet Love Truly for all eternity!

—*Rhea Rebecca Kullberg*

Storms Of Life

When the dark storm clouds gather
And the rain falls from on high
When the sun shines through the raindrops
There's a rainbow in the sky.

When the rainbow lights the sky
And the storm clouds disappear
Then the sun shines much brighter
And the day is bright and clear.

The world seems topsy-turvy
Threats of war in every land
There is so much of evil
That I do not understand.

Little children joining gangs
Taking drugs and smoking pot
Promiscuous living, the norm
While family values are forgot.

When these storms of life beset me
And my heart is filled with fear
Lord, help me see your rainbow
Through the veil of my tears.

—*Virginia Sewell*

A Fantasy Of Power

I've been stuck with a knife,
And it's twisting in my gut,
Walking next to death, I swear,
"This is the final cut,"
I wake up in a box, the lid weighs a ton,
I notice the growth of my hair and nails,
How long has it been since I've seen the sun,
I'm dying to get out and be released,
It's just like birth,
I claw through the lid, and behold,
There is the earth,
Digging through the dirt with a mad, wild rage,
Trying to escape from this seemingly psychotic cage,
Then I suck the cool night air into my lungs,
I suddenly realize what has already begun,
As the pale moon's light hits me,
There is an emptiness in my mind,
This is something that happens to all of my kind,
It is the middle of the night,
There is a full moon in the sky,
It is the hour of the wolf,
I shall never have to die.

—*T.F.W.*

Yesterday

Time is like the wind
and the songs that it sings.
You can not hold them in your hand
They fly on invisible wings.

Oh yesterday, not long ago,
we fell in love.
How we danced and romanced
'neath the stars above.

Then we were wed in harvest time,
in that quaint little town.
And all the folds came
from miles around.

Our children played on carrousels
there in the park.
Old friends we loved, sang and danced
And the band played 'til dark.

Now the kids have grown,
Old friends have flown
And now comes the dawn.
Oh where has yesterday gone?
—*Pat Kenney Martens*

Night Magic

The moon has appeared in the Eastern Sky,
   And the Stars are shedding their light.
The coyote howls from the distant hill,
   And the soft breezes fall on the night.

The fireflies are busy casting their spell,
   On all who, by chance, would observe,
That these tiny creatures are blessed with a gift,
   That, like many, is seen and not heard.

The gentleness felt when the Spirit encloses
   Is almost too great for one to contain,
But the contentment that fills this being of mine,
   Has, for too long, been on the wane.

Hush! Listen! But no, there is no other sound,
   'Tis only my heart that is pounding,
Proclaiming anew these, long dormant, feelings
   As they rush to the surface resounding.

This Night Magic has long been a part of my life,
   The peace that it brings I still treasure,
But only when shared with someone I love,
   Can my soul be filled beyond measure.
—*Sara J. Hester*

Autumn

As Earth dons its autumn colors,
And the warm winds gently cool;
This marks the end of the summer season,
For this is nature's rule.

What brightens my eyes and warms my heart,
Are these colors and the cool, cool air.
But deep in my mind and in my soul,
I know the realization of winter being near.

When the birds fly south,
And Jack Frost lays his blanket of white;
In my memory and in my heart,
I will hold the thoughts of autumn tight.
—*Lisa Nickels*

Dearest Mom (Happy Birthday Mom)

When I think back to years gone by,
And the years that you've been gone,
I think of how much I miss you, Mom,
Without you, I'm so all alone.

I think of the things you taught me, Mom,
And the prayers you helped me pray,
"Lord give us this day, our daily bread,"
That prayer, I can still hear you say.

Mom, I think of you quite often now,
But much more on your birthday,
I wonder how you are, Mom,
Since heaven is so far away.

I just can't help but wonder, Mom,
Do you hear me when I pray?
If only I could just drop in,
Or if I could just hear you say, "Hi Son,"
On this your special day.
—*Ralph L. Cranford*

Dearest Mom (Happy Birthday Mom)

When I think back to years gone by,
And the years that you've been gone,
I think of how much I miss you, Mom,
Without you, I'm so all alone.

I think of the things you taught me, Mom,
And the prayers you helped me pray,
"Lord give us this day, our daily bread,"
That prayer, I can still hear you say.

Mom, I think of you quite often now,
But much more on your birthday,
I wonder how you are, Mom,
Since heaven is so far away.

I just can't help but wonder, Mom,
Do you hear me when I pray?
If only I could just drop in,
Or if I could just hear you say, "Hi Son,"
On this your special day.
—*R. Locke Cranford*

The Crimson Pest

They flew south this winter, birds of every kind,
And there one sat, bobbing on the nearest pine.
Wearing black o'er the eyes, feathers of bright red,
A yellow beak, and a plume atop its head,
The cardinal noisily chirped and eyed
His glass-mirrored image. I surmise
He saw an intruder in his domain
Or potential mate in that reflected pane.
He swooped against the window from a bush,
Approached as if in an air raid or ambush,
Circled high from hidden limb, and dove again.
That pesky masked-bandit, bombardier then
Dropped a mess on my rain-washed car.
Dressed in coat and tails, he went so far
As to flirt with the windshield's reflection,
Chirping and cooing with great affection.
If there was a way to hurry nature's clock,
I'd bring the spring with its migrating flock
And send my seasonal, fine feathered friend
Back to the northern hemisphere again.
—*Marilyn Jane Vedder*

We'll Grow Old Together

When your hair has turned to silver,
And there're lines upon your face;
I will love you then as now, dear.
Age is never a disgrace.

When your hair has lost its ebon
Mine no longer will be black
We will both grow old together
And not wish our vain youth back.

When age lines are on your visage
I'll have lines in my face too;
Do not think I'll love you less, dear,
I'll grow old along with you
—*Susan J. Carr*

Second Hand Smoke

Of all the troubles round about;
and there's plenty, I've been told.
There's Aids, Cancer, Heart diseases,
and of course the common cold.
But there's another problem that bothers me,
and I tell you, it is no joke,
It's the choking wheezing feeling I get,
from second hand smoke.

It seems it's everywhere you go,
that puffin and blowing of smoke.
May come from a cigarette, pipe or cigar,
Don't matter, it will still make you choke.

So think about it everyone,
how that plague harms us all.
We really want to stay healthy,
and to disease don't want to fall.

So love your neighbor one and all,
and so on his rights don't encroach,
and help keep his body clean and free,
from second hand smoke.
—*Luana McGowan*

Dogs Are The Warm Fur!

Dogs are the warm fur that envelopes my heart!
And they give me unconditional, accepting love from the start!
A dog's pure smile can melt a person's soul quicker than any piece of chocolate! And a dog's warm personality makes them an ideal domestic mate! Dogs are to people emotionally what Jesus Christ is to them in the spiritual sense! Loving dogs and praying to Christ can help humankind be less tense! Dogs are a loving breed, no matter what! This includes every type of canine friend we have, from the specialized breed to the variety known as the Mutt. The eyes of a dog are the bright, mirrored reflections of the Maker's tender soul! Since dogs are sinless, they're able to help people be healed and whole! A dog's soul can tenderly and sweetly lick any emotionally pain away in an instant! With child-like innocence, we don't ever again need to emotionally suffer and pant! Dogs and other animals often show people the way they should treat each other! Something - whether human or animal - like a sister brother!
—*Laurie C. Thornton*

Two Loves Have I

Listen to the tale of two loving, tender, terrific, talented
and trusting partners whom I choose to hail!

Their romance became a spark in 1990 taking place at no less
a "mystery" party..

Soon after, the flames grew magically hearty!

Now, Cyndi and Kevin, "the world's best engineers" are movers
and shakers sharing that rare combination of blends —

Their wave lengths so tuned in to sophistication and
organization, there is ne'er a need for any amends

Observing their sharing and caring and planned comfort zone
days, we can just blink with pride at these two we have raised.

As 11/20/93 unfolds, our warm memories will remain bold

Of that sweet little darlin' standing tall in her pale wedding gown

And her smiling handsome groom focused on that joyous sound....

"I do, do you?" — "We are man and wife"—

In his own time, The Lord has made today our celebration of life!
—*Marilyn A. Rieti*

My Grandmother

My grandma showered me with T.L.C.
and was as sweet as could be.
The years went by so very fast
as she talked more and more of the past.
She spoke only good of everyone
forgiving the faults they had done.
She loved for us to take her for a ride,
As she sat there with love and pride.
My Grandma was very dear to me
and as kind as could be.
The day that my Grandma died
all I could do was sit and cry.
I think of her each passing day
and all the love she sent my way.
My children never got to see
the kind of Grandma you were to me.
I'm a Grandma now you see,
as I ask "How can that be?"
Can I ever be a Grandma like you?
Grandma, I'll do the best I can do.
I love you is all I have to say,
and we'll be together again some day.
—*Nancy J. Sahr*

Bereft

The winter is so cold once more,
And lonely as a memory...

The warm, sweet cloak these shoulders wore
Is torn, and sagging emptily...

The heart is numb and clothed in lead
As pain-sewn winds freeze every tear...

The leaves of hope have fallen dead.
Another winter...another year...
—*Sylvia Anfang Trotiner*

Verses For A Tree

The winds came off the river then as now
And whispered up the roads the work of life;
The old hills smiled to greet another spring
The young roots searched the secret heart of earth.

A century gone, forebears planted well
And watched their seedling burgeon into tree;
'Till now it stands a tower and a sign
Of goodness harvested through long full years.

So we have come to make a second planting
Another copper beech to catch the sun;
And burnish summer's light in green-gold leaves
That always blossom last, and all at once.

We give our tree to earth and air with gladness
Its roots to water, its branches to the sky;
We lock within its life our dreams and visions
Of all the promise that our plans shall spark.

May these green days be prelude to long summers
Of golden goodness ripening through the years;
May this our tree be ever our thanksgiving
For lives begun in God; For lives well-done.
—*Miriam Elizabeth Allen*

I Wonder

I wonder why, the sky is blue
And why, the grass is green,
I wonder why the birds can fly
The loveliest sight I've ever seen!
I wonder why, the ocean roars
And why the earth shakes so!
And hurts so many people
That I won't ever know.
I wonder why we each must pay
For the things we say and do,
I wonder why we just can't play
And tally up when life is through.
And each could go his separate way
To heaven, or to Hell,
And pay his debt, in one lump sum
To that man, who tolls the bell!
But I'm glad, things are, the way they are
And we don't always get our due,
How else could I, then be blessed
With a lover, such as you!
—*Miriam McLain*

You Can Only Know

As surely as summer brings warmth
And winter brings snow, you can only
know ———what "God" wants you to know.
 otherwise
 everyone would die with every answer.
—*Tim Hornacek*

Webs And Dreams

Yesterday a spider created a web.

He worked toward his goal determined
and without distraction,
His labors tedious and consistent,
His movements exact and precise,
The web was perfect,
a fragile masterpiece

Today it is gone.

Tomorrow he will begin again.
—*Pamela Bruster*

The Artist Of Autumn

The golden days of autumn, have once again arrived
And with this special season our spirit seems to rise.
In the air there is a chill that brings us sweet relief,
From all the heat of summer, which almost had us beat.

As we look upon the trees arrayed in vivid colors,
We recognize "the one" behind what seems to be a portrait.
The color scheme, is one that "we" could never hope to match,
'Cause He has done His works of art for centuries in the past!

By now, I know you realize, the one I'm speaking of.
He sends us "every season," and paints each one with love.
The extra time He spends on fall makes all His earth
Rejoice and call this lovely season.
The greatest of them all!!
—*Thelma L. Meadows*

To Young To Go

Jason we know you are in Heaven for you have touched many lives
And you are by far not alone now for you have the Lord and your
 Best friend Kris with you always
 And here on earth we have memories of you J
 Smiling and laughing and sometimes tears and sadness
 But those memories we will hold with us always
 And we miss you and love you so very much
 That we are screaming but nothing is coming out
 No words to describe this pain and a longing to see
 Your smiling face again
To hear you coming a mile away in your car with the music
 Playing boom boom boom
 Oh how we long to see you again
 But out lives will be entwined forever Jas
 J is for Just missing you
 A is for Always thinking of you through the
 S is for Sadness we have of loving
 O is for Only you and of
 N is for Needing you always

 But never a Goodbye Jason
 Love your family and friends
—*Rebecca Lamkin*

Babe

When you come into my life I held you in my arms
and you brought so much joy to me.
As time went on I saw the hurt you have inside,
It is always on my mind.
Oh, Babe, I wish you were mine.
There are times you feel alone and there is no love.
I hope you know I'll always be at your side.
The love for you will never be left behind.
I know you are holding on strong.
With me is where you belong.
Babe, don't ever hold your love inside.
I know you are down and I see you for a day,
I know you want to stay.
Babe, I don't know what to do,
I want you to know I love you.
There are times you need love and don't get it.
Babe, I'll give you all the love I can.
You light up my life in so many ways and brighten my days.
I want you to know that I love you so,
I'll never let you go.
Babe, you mean so much to me.
—*Sherry Corish*

Let The Sun Shine Through

I'm happy as a Leprechaun
And you say you wonder why?
It's 'cause I changed my attitude
When I heard this lullaby.

We Irish are the proudest lot,
We dance, we sing, we play
For the pure delight of dreaming,
"It's a happy St. Patrick's Day."

We Irish are the proudest lot,
We work, we teach, we pray
For the good of all humanity
In a most comprehensive way.

I'm happy as a Leprechaun
And you wish you could be too?
Just tap your toes, wiggle your nose,
And Let the Sun Shine Through!

The Irish in me just had to come out ... or is it the child in me?
—*Rae Kae Powers*

To A Mourning Dove

Oh, mourning dove, I hear you
   And you speak for me as well
With your melancholy call
   You say it better than a tolling bell.

But you are such a slender beauty
   And as sweet as you can be
A shy but friendly bird
   That is why I really cannot see,

Why such as you should have
   A call full of sadness
Such a lonely sounding cry
   You should be full of gladness.

Or do you call that way?
   To be in tune with melancholy man
And to express our feelings
   So much better than we can.
—*Marie Andrews*

Angel Of Peace

Fair as the sunbeam that tinteth the dawn,
Angel of peace, thou has't tarried so long.
Who ever with a watchful eye;
From that bright portal of the sky;
Who guides the planetary sway, of solar-suns, the milky-way;
And numbereth the holy stars above,
Fly to us now on the wings of a dove.
Too long in heaven thy tarrying has been,
Too long the discords maddening din.
Too long men and nations have lived by the sword,
God's holy word they have trampled, ignored.
The God of our refuge, our strength, our shield,
The scepter of peace his Angel shall wield.
Oh then, may the heart of man be changed.
With the peace of heaven that falleth like rain.
Like the river of waters ever onward that flows,
Where love for thy neighbor continues to grow.
Healing the Nation's cleansing the seas;
Blessed Angel; oh breathe unto these; the gift of thy peace,
   love and harmony.
—*Mildred R. Winters*

Mary Birthed Jesus, Oh Holy Night

A star in the heavens began to glow
Angels sang sweetly soft and low
Follow the gleam of heavenly light
For a miracle happens this special night
City full of people no room no room
Mary told Joseph birth would be soon
Make a bed on the hay in yon manger
Kindly innkeeper said to the stranger
Angels sang sweetly come follow the light
Mary birthed Jesus, oh holy night
Humble of birth, our saviour be the man
Come and adore Him, God's son of man
—*Maxene Gonzales*

The Artist's Perfect Touch

Nature awakes with a decree
Announcing spring with her dynamic glory;
She has broken free from the blast
Of winter's dismal prison clasp.

Spring periodically evolves a treacherous scene
While billows of black angry clouds convene;
They pour forth floods which clasp
The earth with a torrential grasp.

But as the furies of the sky become peaceful and quiet
A cloak of solitude reunites;
Soft, clean breezes whistle tunes of delight
As they rustle thousands of young tender leaves as though
   with foresight.

Nature's gift can now be seen
In trees and grasses with shades of green;
She has painted these with her artistic hand
And has left the earth with a new carpet, colorful and grand!
—*Katherine Gant Maxwell*

Another Chance

    As dawn breaks this early morn....
    Another day of hardship has now been born
I gather up the newspapers that kept me alive...
    For one more day I know I will survive
I slowly glance at my child's innocent face...
    Thrown into this life that is such a disgrace
    He understands not for he is only three...
    Continually questioning where his Daddy can be
    Once a happy family productive and secure...
    After his death it has all been such a blur
    With no education and no money at hand...
On the streets it left me in this prosperous land
I try to button his torn and tattered sweater...
But my frostbitten fingers are affected by this weather
    Rapidly I accumulate our meek possessions...
    Trying to ignore my severe depression
I did not choose this life and I know not where to turn...
    Survival for my child is all I have to learn
    As I pass by a window with a sudden glance...
    I know God has given me a second chance!
—*Margie Cohen*

A Thin Blue Line

Flashing squad car lights chase with screaming siren sound
Answering a call to where a body went down
Blood flowing in the street is epidemic in our day.
With hostility raging inside people who chose the wrong way
Bitterness and hatred festers in their soul
Not regarding law and order and no remorse for
who they hurt and how they stole
Citizens are protected with a thin blue line
By patrol officers cruising to defend what's yours and mine
Gun shots echo in our violent streets at night
Where drugs, booze, and hookers congregate in hopeless plight
Another shot just rang out and another body fell
And another soul is burning in the eternal flames of hell
—*William Shuttleworth*

The Representative

Dear Lord, if I have forgotten to mention,
Anyone's needs in my prayers today
I do believe you know who they are
And what they might really wish to say.

Often we ask a great deal from thee
but give very little or nothing in return.
Yet still your torch of loving care and kindness,
Will always and forever burn.

O' Lord, you have heard and answered many of our prayers
Still there are so many of us waiting in line.
If we can learn to have more patience and wait our turn.
Our prayers will be answered, when You Will the time.

We sometimes do not merit.
Many of the blessings which we receive.
But you grant them to us anyway.
Along with your reprieve.

Now Lord, we are really very thankful and grateful
For you being so thoughtful, generous and kind.
We will always love and praise thee.
In our heart and soul and mind.
—*Marguerite Rosario*

Light-Catchers

    Life-long memories like chips of colored glass
        are carefully stored away
           until retrieved for creative fun.
Intimate union with a welding metal forms light-catchers,
        mosaic designs of permanence
          I cannot live without.

        Bits of gray sorrow
     subdued by patterns of yellow joy,
      Books read and poems penned
        translated into songs
       of love, peace and grace.
    Colorful birds, flowers and trees
       created to remind me
       of friends and love ones,
        my faith and my God.

   All make up for me a constant window
      full of light-catchers
       which give back to me
        glimpses of things
         greater than myself.
—*Mabel D. Gilmore*

Memorial Day, (1993)

Free elections in the nuclear age
are needed in this uncertain age.
How big Memorial Days are we to have
to make free elections on the whole Earth?

Our struggle for free elections
goes on, as ever, no big exceptions.
If any exceptions there appear,
in proper time they should disappear.

Problems we have, in the meantime,
this certainly is not our best time.
Domestically, some families and local bosses
do not see horizons beyond their centro-egoses.

Yet, the United States of America
remains the main hope even in Antarctica,
in the nuclear age to survive,
with free elections in peace to strife.

To control nuclear weapons is urgent,
in free elections, we must be respondent
to the dictatorial threat that we all face,
for future generations to remain on the Earth.
—*M. Synek*

The Beauty Of The Morning After

Cornfields that once proudly swayed with the breeze
Are now flat on the ground massacred as the trees.
Coconuts with battered palms lying head to head
Soaking in tears of defeat.

Last night they fought like the soldiers at Bataan
Against the mad Japanese fleet.
They used every weapon prayer and strength.
It was not enough this typhoon was a winner wind.

As the sun peeps through the far eastern skies
A hungry bird with a worn-out beak flies over
The scene we call "The Morning After"

The skies seem bluer without clouds,
The air smells like deepwoods after a spring rain,
The sand oh! the sand so white and clean
Like each piece was polished and then rinsed by the rain.
The water so quiet like a passionate man after a rage.
For these things we willingly submit to this fury of
the pacific.
—*Nenita T. Davis*

Early Morning Ritual

I hear the whir of the dragonfly's wings
as he watches his shadow in the pond.
The breeze blows him gently off course'
his life span is not very long.
He hovers in the air as he meets his mate
a pretty damsel fly.
He can chase ripples in the pond
or soar high in the sky.
A tender mosquito is a breakfast feast,
a morning cruise on a floating leaf.
New morning, new day, no cares, no strife,
he lives to the fullest
that's the meaning of life.
—*Madilene Stark*

Fall In Colorado

Glorious blue skies overhead
are perfect backdrop for the red
and gold and yellow, brown and green
before our eyes the changing scene
of fall in Colorado.

Each flower vaunts its brightest hue
to show off 'neath the sky's clear blue.
The birds are gathering their clans
to start their autumn caravans
in fall in Colorado.

All nature joins in lovely song,
inviting us to sing-along.
Red and yellow, blue and green
a vibrant sight that can be seen
each fall in Colorado.

Soon cooler winds will chill the air,
the leaves will scatter everywhere.
Indian Summer comes and goes,
prelude to the singing snows
of fall in Colorado.

—*Mary Arthur Tatom*

Christmas Eve

It's night time now, the stars
are shining, air is crisp and cold.
Hearts are filled with love and joy,
there's beauty to behold.

The fireplace is glowing,
decorations hanging there,
there's a feeling that we can't explain
floating through the air.
There's music playing softly,
of carols old and dear.
Christmas cards, displayed with love,
bring messages of cheer.

Children gaze at packages all
wrapped beneath the tree.
Sleep will not come easily to
hearts filled with suspense and glee.

But at last we all retire,
looking forward to the morn
when everyone can celebrate
the day that Christ was born.

—*Sandi Chaussee*

Harvest Fruits Of The Master's Hand

Fulfillment, hope, and pleasures unplanned,
   Are the harvest fruits of the Master's hand.

An unexpected encounter with "one of His own"
   Can lead you or guide you to paths unknown,
Bringing you discovery, or challenge undreamed,
   With trials of heart and soul supreme.

"One of His own" is near every day of your life—
   A sick child… troubled teen… someone's dear wife.
Frustration, grief, and pain may take their toll,
   But much you can learn from each precious soul!

You're "one of His own," always focus on this,
   And your true mission in life you cannot miss.
You'll find He provides you with much to share
   When He gives you courage to love and care.

Fulfillment, hope and pleasures unplanned,
   Are the harvest fruits of the Master's hand.

—*Neysa E. Seed*

The Immortality Of Thought

If brass and stone and earth and trees
Are victims of mortality;
If hurricanes with all their force
Must chart a self-destructive course;
If light, might, grief and joy fall preys
To be dissolved in numbered days
Like snowflakes falling to their doom,
Far mightier flakes shall be entombed
By time, which measures and transcends,
Mute witness to their births and ends.

Can thought, less fragile than the wind
Survive the crush of time within?
Or dare aspire to out-pace
The march of time's destructive ways?
Thoughts will from mind to mind commute,
Claiming new life in new abodes,
And in their flight through time and space
Defy the predator's ruthless pace.
My thoughts, frail begins, won't cease to be
Though time in time shall smother me.

—*B. Washburne Hall*

Here's To Your Health

What is your current condition?
Are you bending the rules?
Do you practice good nutrition
Or do you gorge like a ghoul?

The pressure is on; the diets are out.
You must exercise properly
Or risk getting gout.

Drink lots of water to clear out the grime.
Eight glasses will do it
If you don't drown - in the meantime!

Take your vitamins daily
with reverence and ease
And you'll have the gusto
To do as you please.
Learn to relax with yoga and such.
Get eight hours of sleep.
Don't worry too much.
Pray about good things,
Dream to the end
So you can get up and do it all over again!

—*Nancy Torrence*

God's Other Child

Who are you to question the way I love?
Are you so one-minded that you think my being didn't come from
   above?
Can you believe that I chose this path in life?
If so, then you do not know of my fears and strife.
I am any color, either sex or any age.
No matter, what is important is my rage
At "straights" not accepting me as I am.
I don't hate you, why do you hate me? Damn,
You have the arrogance to call me "gay,"
If you were to walk in my shoes for just one day
You would see the sadness and the fears
That have been my plight for thousands of years.
You are my brothers and sisters, why do you hate me?
Can't you see that I am only who I have to be?
Please, try to evaluate me as an individual,
Not as a loathsome homosexual.
I am a child of God, the same as you.
If you can understand this, perhaps you can accept me, too.

—*M. L. Namia*

harmonium specter

One rainspattered morning
as a dream finished dreaming me
i awoke with a leftover
vision-question lingering
in the amber morningmist
of my meadowlarked consciousness:
could kokopeli
that ancient flute player of hopi
myth and memory have been
a smiling woman with hyacinth
in her hair for i had seen her
softly seated on a sunflower
slope of autochromed luster
(on a mystic mountain i've seen before
only from another-life distance)
wearing a brown brocaded skirt
of animal pageantry and beckoning me
with mindwaves of pure honeymilk music
to come with her to the center of
beauty beyond today's pandemonium
—roger wilbur

Love Wasn't Blind

The search is for Love,
as a gift from Above,
so a writer becomes simple clay.
Look and you'll find,
love's always in time.
I'm its memory,
this I can say.

Know you're in love, when in love you find,
Love means the most, to those who are blind.

Love is just this,
that I might help some see.
Being blind in life,
there's still light to be seen.
And in the light,
being blind we'll see,
faith's more than dreams, life naturally.

Know you're in love, when in love you find,
Love last forever, never-ending, past time.

For soon I'll be gone, I'll have left this behind,
with hopes you see clearly, love wasn't blind.
—Mark Albury

Fantasy

I stir, not yet awake.
As dawn is formed with shafts of gold
And creeps to count the blades of grass untold;
It reaches to my window, open—bare—
No curtains hanging there.

Awake,
I sense the vast array
Of flowers bent to greet the day;
Beneath the weight of one so small—
It seems it is no bird at all.

He spills his song and floats upon the wind.
I watch it, lost to view!
And wondrous be to take that flight;
With arms out-stretched in weightless lift
To see the world along with you!
—Pearl Wentworth

Spread Your Wings

When I was little you were always there for me,
as all big brothers should be.
You calmed my fears and shed my tears,
you showed me laughter and joy too.

Though quite a few years separated us,
we always seemed to grow together.
When I was little, you were my hero,
you always filled my life with hope.

When you went to college,
I thought we couldn't be close anymore.
You showed me truly, though,
we'll always be friends forever.

Now I can say I look up to you in many ways,
both as you fly and as the person you are.
As you wear your blue uniform and polished shoes,
you now become my inspiration.

Many people say we're alike and I really hope it's true,
because nobody means as much to me as you.
—Lisa Breton

Friendship

Is—as high as the sky
as broad as the land
as strong as the wind,
as soft as the sand.
As bright as the sun
and as twilight is—grey.
As rose as the dawn
and as dusk is to day!
Ever omnipresent, ever retreating
like the unconscious rhythm
of a heart that is beating.
As a closed garden wall
can shield and embrace
As wide open prairie lends exuberant space—
Friendship is taking and
friendship is giving.
When heart and soul and spirit to blend
how great it is, I know, to be living
How great it is to have found a friend.
—Kathryn M. Ellison

Derivation Of A Topological Poem

...a topological poem
as derived by...

   ...a definition
     that demonstrates, language is an art
     drawn upon a composition
     of algorithm

   ...an algorithm
     that reveals, processes are iterative
     drawn upon a song of
     science

   ...a science
     that calculates, patterns which will hold the truth
     drawn upon a history of
     mathematics

as derived by...
...a topological poem...
—Toni A. Williams-Sanchez

Man Of Afghanistan

Afghan proceeds slowly in desert heat unconscious
as dromedary to the beat and flow of
life, his mind on truths, not desires relating to
self. He watches the gazelles leap ghostlike and skim
over sands where no breezes move and no flowers
scent, all is peace as he scans blinding horizon.

Beast and master sway gently as mirages of
lakes shimmer on plain. Pious Moslem evading
destiny as earthly body illumes to the
divine with fairy-tale feeling where he has no
personal ideas, no private goals, his dreams
revealing different path and waking—being
another sense of time.

Time that is merely a state of mind beginning
and ending with each full day irrevocably
ordained with its place from the Godhead, creation
itself. Though sweaty and dusty he's not of earth.
In celestial spheres beyond he exists
as far-off mammoth magenta mountains murmur
and minarets tinkle the faithful to prayer.

—Ralph E. Martin

A Quiet Sharing

We acknowledge love
As God's gift to us...
To be cherished, and held,
Unending.
Yet, if love is eternal,
A foundation to build upon,
Is it not also, unfailingly,
And even magically,
Glorious strength for the moment?

Does it not follow, then,
That it is far more than good, one's
Quiet sharing of life with another,
As we become aware of each blessing
And, together, accept adversity ...
Which may bring not only maturity,
But truth and reverence?

For this ...
This is lasting and, perhaps,
The most ennobling of all things
Achieved throughout the years.

—Lester E. Garrett

No Resolution Of Conflict

My heart beat rapidly
    As I drove to the emergency room.
In the darkness and rain, I made
    Mental excuses about why I didn't make it.
I was reluctant to come see about you
    My reasons; too painful.
Selfishly I prayed that you'd be okay
    Because I didn't want to be there for you.
You hadn't been there for me!

You need me and I choose not to
    Fill that need.
Though I am not prepared,
    I am here now.
Be well when I see you mother.
    I love you but,...

I don't want to care.

—Regina B. Holland

The Picture Album

The wind blew his hair
as he sat in an old rocking-chair
on the front porch, tears in his eyes,
his hands trembled,
as he slowly turned the pages
of an old picture album
much used pages,
some torn and loose.

He stopped at a picture
of a lovely young girl,
running his fingers slowly
back and forth over the picture.
His lips trembled,
as he slowly mumbled
"So long ago I loved you,
now as much as I did then,
wait for me,
for I soon will follow you
in that final resting place
upon the hill.
My darling wife, I miss you."

—Lucille Hughes

Going Home

I thought it to be a gentle wind blowing
As I lay in my bed knowing that you in your bed
Were dying, cancer was taking its toll.
then I felt the sound become that of a host of angels,
Watching and awaiting God's call to bring you home,
But in the morning you were still here.

Again, as I lay in my bed and you in yours,
To the sound of hovering angels was added
The strains of low sweet music as the host still waited
God's call to bring you home,
But in the morning you were still here.

Tonight you are not here,
And there is no sound of waiting angels,
Only a quiet stillness and an aching loneliness in
my heart, enjoined with peace and thanksgiving,
For God has called to His angels to bring you home,
And tonight you are there!

—Lucie G. Titus

Suffer Little Children

Suffer little children, come unto me!
As I look at all these sad little faces,
    this phrase comes to me.

Such sadness, such despair, such injustice
these children have to bear.
Deprived of all the necessary things of life.
Trying to exist in a world filled; with strife.
Forever hungry, never knowing how it feels,
    to have a stomach filled.
With eyes filled with sadness, each day they go on.
Never knowing the joy of playing, or being held,
    cuddled and loved,
They wait for life to be better, filled with such
    longing.
Only to find each day the same,
Another day filled with suffering and pain.
God, as I look at these children,
    I wonder how can this be.
And then I think, suffer little
    children, come unto me.

—Robbie Brading

My Love

I wake to the birds chirping, the sun shining and with you on my mind
As I open my eyes and turn to an empty pillow, you I did not find,
Even since that first touch which sent chills down my spine
Even since that first kiss which was so very fine,
You have made my dreams and reality so hard to tell apart
When I dream and then awake, I have to say, "Be still my heart,"
Now when I look in your eyes, what do I see?
I see a fire burning inside and it is burning for me,
It warms my body clear through to my bones
My temperature rises to a degree unknown,
No fire engine can put out the flames of desire
No medication can lower the heat of the fire,
My body quivers at your every touch
I want it more and more and need it just as much,
When your lips are pressed against mine
I feel as if I am standing still in time,
Every moment, as seldom or as often as it may be, that we are together
I live it over and over in my mind, so it will last forever.
   —*Tracy Craig-Clark*

Down By The Sea

Oh come, do come, please come with me,
as I take a walk down by the sea.

The sun is shining, the water is clear,
take heed to the sounds, what do you hear?

First comes the swishing of water and sand,
mighty waves then come to the land.

A rumble and roar as they turn about,
racing to beat each other back out.

The breeze seems to whisper a gentle song,
as it skips and dances, just going along.

The birds join in to complete the chorus,
what a wonderful, magical show just for us.

Down by the sea.
   —*Maryann B. Thibodeau*

Demons

Laughter fills the empty halls
As I walk down I hear them call
Seeing things so far out of my mind
And mentally can't be conceived
My mind is playing tricks on me

I try to scratch the surface
But who is that scratching?
Inside my head
This nightmare is laughing

Living life
But sucked up through the vacuum

An endless daydream
Beckons to me
Wanting so badly to be reality

So I try and try to climb that ladder
And all the while
Demons grab at my feet
Trying to grab a piece of my soul
Grabbing, twisting, they don't want to let go...
   —*Lisa Rawls*

Autumn Leaf

The air was chill this day,
As I wondered in the park.
Few days remained with weather like May,
For soon, winter would embark.

I strolled upon a carpet green
Of lusions grass, so cushion soft,
On which lay a leaf so clean
For it had just fallen from aloft.

This colored beauty, the first to fall
Lay gently on the grassy tips
Of sturdy blades, oh, so tall,
Displaying itself as the first one nipped.

Its yellow coat upon the grass
Trimmed in pink to rosy red,
Made such a delightful scene,
One forgot it dead.
   —*Vivian Mathews*

As One

They sit by the fire — two spirits ablaze,
As individual curls of passion, whirling, amaze ...
Each hope and each dream swirl about, swirl around
Combining through airs surrounding abound.

Entering their bodies with each breath taken through,
Flowing through souls together but two.

They sit by the fire — two spirits ablaze,
As combined curls of passion attract and amaze ...
The hopes and the dreams swirl about, swirl around
Entwining the spirits surrounding abound.

Entering their bodies with each breath taken through,
Joining their souls now no longer as two.

They sit by the fire — one spirit ablaze,
Full curls of shared passion, whirling, amaze ...
One hope and one dream swirl about, swirl around
To be lived by the spirits now soulfully bound.
   —*Leslie M. Kahn*

These Things You Are

You are as beautiful as the sunset,
  As lovely as the dawn,
  As gentle as the twilight,
  As peaceful as the calm.

As powerful as the redwood,
  As sturdy as the pine,
  As stately as the live oak,
  As limber as the palm.

As invincible as the ocean's tide,
  As robust as the river,
  As grand as the quiet lake,
  As flexible as the stream.

As unconquerable as the jungle's lion,
  As unyielding as the bull,
  As impressive as the hippo,
  As supple as the cat.

Splendid, comely, soothing, tranquil,
Forceful, durable, irreposing, lithe,
  These things you are;
  You are these things.
   —*Kathy Moody*

Playwidit

Searching, we are for many things. Peace of mind comes from within as mediate and grow stronger there are fewer disturbances to our search. Some people think we were all meant to be the same, that would be a boring shame. Variety is the spice of life made up of many individuals struggles and strive as they live life.
Ego's aside were going on a magic carpet ride through your mind; surprised at what you find? The cost just a little time. Fantasy in mind as we explore what was a mystery and is now folklore. We can go so deep, may be not so deep till your thoughts are strong enough to manifest themselves without speech, god like in their reach.
Remember your purpose, respect yourself and the world is truly a
   stage in which to play.
Must I seem so self indulgent? No, if you truly understand and can find beauty in this verse, matters of procreation and society can be worked out. There are those who think my projections are mere reflections of myself; you are me to a certain degree, but my respect for your individuality allows you to go free. I can't please everyone just someone; peace.

—*Richard Alvin Snow Jr.*

Of Choices

   The organ music swells in sad refrain
   As mourners gather clad in whispered woe
   To bid farewell and comfort who remain
     Beneath the pall of viruses we sow.

As silently, fear stalks throughout the land;
With anguished hearts, what can we do but doubt
That there exists a God who cares for man.
Then in reply, the Spirit's voice cries out,

   I sent a special child who held the key,
   In preparation for the coming scourge,
     To unlock knowledge for humanity
And quell the tide of Death's relentless surge.

   Before its birth, you sent it back to me.
   The world is how you chose for it to be.

—*Sara Graham Hawkins*

Dance With Me

Dance with me as I sit alone
   As my theories make me cry
Only the poet who writes the poem
   Can understand these lines

I ask to dance in only dreams
   For my feet would never agree
So I am still; and so my thoughts
   They make no sense to me

My style unique — you'd never relate
   My difference is unknown
The words I speak deny my thoughts
   And so they stand alone.

—*Rosamaria Amoros*

The Last Request

The blossoms fade, the rainbow's gone
As I live latter days.
These days are long with memory's song,
The nights with heaven's praise.

So Death be not indifferent
To Life's compelling hand.
It's but your cape that brings escape
From flames that time has fanned.

—*Parnell Pierce*

Autumn Colors

The colors of autumn are so wonderful to see.
As nature paints a rainbow among the leaves.
Happy shades of reds, yellows, orange and gold.
Each a delight to behold.
But no happier color could there ever be.
Than the blue of a clear autumn sky.
It is said, that beauty is in the eye of the beholder.
But it is plain to see as autumn comes to the land.
That true beauty lies within the paint brush.
Held by the master's hand.

—*William Baker III*

Call It October

One by one the leaves are falling,
as October unfolds each day.
Songs of insects attempt stalling
the passage of this month away.

Pet cat sits poised on little hill,
peeping into cornfield next door.
In distance dog barks with a shrill;
having caught a field mouse, sees more!

Walnuts fall fast from naked tree;
squirrels active storing their food.
Could there ever a creature be
who does not love October's mood?

How beautiful are lowly weeds
all decked out in colorful charm.
Unwilling now to do bad deeds,
red poison ivy means no harm.

Lazy smoke from trash fire scents air;
now and then a gentle breeze blows.
Nature's secrets are ev'rywhere -
choice ones only October knows.

—*Lowell "Ted" DaVee*

Raindrops

How shall I describe my love for thee—
As one tiny raindrop clinging, among a million others,
To a flower petal soft and smooth as your skin?

No—that would not do
For, no matter how long and how hard it holds,
That raindrop finally falls to the ground and is forced
To join the million other souls
Who also wished to cling to your heart with so much love to give

Perhaps, I could be that one, solitary, drop
Whose love makes it cling and stay
After all the others have perished
Perhaps I'll be the one
Who refuses to let go,
The one who will only let go when the sun's harsh rays
Shine on as bright as can be

Until, finally, I too are just a memory
Of a summer shower which raised and cared for you
With so much love

—*Stephanie Seifert*

Love

Love is a feeling, that hate cannot find.
As pure to the heart as gold to a mine.
And remember grief is forgotten where love is forgiving.
Love lives longer where kindness nurtures the heart that hope
is strongest.
Lighting the paths where love begins guiding us to the hearts
of our true friends.
Now erase all the anger that robs the heart, and vanish the
fear and take love sincere.
For Love is selfless and has no shame.
Love cannot be measured nor can it always be seen.
So while others glisten in the light of men, so do impostors gleam.
Harbor the hope that someday you may find.
Love that is tender and not given blind.

—Mary Anne Thomas

Behind The Attic Wall

Behind the attic wall it's as quiet as can be;
As quiet as a sleeping child or our old cherry tree.
Behind the attic wall where sleeping voices lie,
They plot their return cunningly. They give it one more try.
Behind the attic wall they wait in a deep sleep. They hide
   among the rafters and occasionally sneak a peek.
Behind the attic wall; the root of all your fears,
Lies the pasts of people's laughter, triumphs, and tears,
Behind the attic wall are cars, dolls, and stuffed toys,
And in them lay the spirits of little girls and boys.
They remember what it felt like to be gently cuddled and loved.
They want to feel the tiny arms; they want to be hugged.
They fight for our attention, with everlasting hope,
And once we leave the room it's with our rejection they must
   cope.
In that darkened room; the core of it all,
Are tears shed unseen - - behind the attic wall.

—Sarah Murphy

Predator

Sharp dragon-like amber eyes blaze, scanning.
   As scents draw closer, it sniffs the air.
Nose arched like a sheath, ready to bare fangs.
      Sharpened, lubricated;
      Greedy for the kill.

   The hunter stands motionless
Its stance subdued, anticipating the chase.
   Sudden movement triggers the attack.
      The animal of prey keeps pace,
      Driven by instinctive talent.

   Passion races through its veins.
In one lightening leap the beast strikes,
   Claws spaced even, razor-edged.
Contact is made between prey and predator.
      Paws firmly planted.

Alarming the sounds of silent circulation,
   Closed flesh erupts and spews forth its
      Slashed contents from the jugular.
Reddening with wonder, sight and sound over.
   The survivor reigns, over fresh meat.

—Susan Taylor Jackson

Thoughts

Everything that happen is not always meant to be,
As some would like to believe.
There's not always some good in all bad
That's very plain to conceive.
But why fret and ask "why me?"
Are you more deserving or less.
Problem will arise sometimes.
That will put your values to the test.
I've done things my own way,
And known at the time it's not right.
I've grabbed at straws, taken things
In my own hands, and taken quite a flight.
Is there still hope for a fool like me.
I know I've slipped and fell.
But will I once again see the light
At the end of this long trail.
Or is hope like a bird that flees in fright
If so, I'll hold onto hope with all my might.
But as selfish and hopeless as it may seem
My life can't be fulfilled without my dreams.

—Armittie Austin

An Annual Aura Of Love

January bewitched my life with a love most amiable and new....
As the days danced into February the passion developed and grew.
March blew in, its tempest caused emotions to dissipate,
   to fall away.
The bounty of flowers eagerly anticipated, would they bloom in
   April or in May?
Spring soon provided the stimulus, the sweet rose burst into flame...
June slowly dwindled away, a repent, a consent, a promise to share
   my name.
July produced explosions of grandeur, spectacles of such wondrous
   hue.
What has been created, perhaps the likeness of me or you?
August was about to indicate, punctuate, reiterate, would summer
   heat abate?
Would the thermal waves of ardor engulf and seal our painful,
   endless fate?
September, long, hot demanding...yet flickering with each volatile
   move.
Autumn, October, a simile, a carbon copy, an image...fit snugly into
   a groove.
November, dreary, dank, dark, November...full of screams and
   doubts and cries.
December's chilled winds rape the landscape, the birds screech their
   mournful sighs.
The heaven in all it's blue serenity is quickly overtaken by a bleak
   grey cloud.
Its passiveness sublime, its beauty gone...covered by a shroud.

—Millard M. See

The Lioness

   A lioness I
As in the darkness softly tread the silent house.
   To check my children
      Locked in slumber.
   I gaze with pride on them, my own.
To me entrusted, me alone;
   And joyful thoughts in prayers unnumbered
Fly to God, our loving maker!
   In total thanks my heart does cry
      And sing His praises to the sky!

—Virginia Campbell

The Queen Of The South

The birth of the beast is about to unfold.
As the Queen of the South gives life to its Soul.

Through the pains of her pregnancy, his reign shall begin.
And life, as we know it, will never be the same again.

He'll grow up quite docile, yet driven by desire.
And deep in his heart dwells an eternal fire.

Like an angel of light, he will stand at the door.
To the young and the old . . . to the rich and the poor.

Through his signs & wonders and with a bullet in his head.
He will deceive many people, till their blood he has shed.

He will unify the nations with works well rehearsed.
Then plummet them all and desecrate the earth.

Like horses with blinders, they will be led down the street.
To a place of utter darkness, to the gnashing of teeth.

Be not discouraged and be not dismayed.
This "All" must take place before the judgment day.

As the Queen of the South gave life to his Soul.
Hear now her cries of labor from the depths of Sheol.
—*Paul J. Tibbs*

The Window

I was gasping for air
As the waves whipped me around
I reached out and here is what I found.;
A window, with a ledge to hold on to
Like Jesus almighty hand
The water was deep and the waves were rough
The window seemed so grand
I thought I let go, and was on my way
The waves seemed to obey
I landed safe on the other side
The Savior, again, was my guide
—*Lori Souder Knupp*

To Kameron

The morning dew stole a tear from my face
As though Mother Nature hadn't provided enough;
Reluctantly, I let it go.

The rainbow, arching aristocratically over the far horizon,
Stole the pink from my cheek
Giving it a radiance that once was mine.
Not given a choice, I let it go.

The pitter patter of the rain as it gently falls to the earth
Mimics the precious throbbing in my womb.
Painfully, I let him go.

Little Kameron, you gave me a whole new world.
To know the miracle of life, even it's briefest moment
Propelled me to a higher level of love, patience and understanding.

Today I stand proud
Knowing a part of me glistens with the morning dew;
Arches gloriously in every bend of the rainbow
And thunders for the whole world to know you,
Kameron.
—*Monterey J. Harper*

Sisters True

I'm sorry we've never been as close
as we could have been,
Don't you think that's quite a sin?

Just think of all the fun and good
times we've missed,
When we could have given each
other a few hugs and got kissed.

Maybe it was the way that we were
raised by our mother,
I really don't know why we've ever
been at odds with each other.

Often there are times I think of you,
Then I realize how often you've
made me feel so blue.

I haven't figured out if you realized
what you were saying,
Or if you unconsciously knew what
you were really doing!

So, in order to not be hurt, I retreated
into a comfortable shell,
And there I've stayed so nice and well!
—*Rose Marie Patronella*

The Passing Of Summer

The Equinox is upon us late and soon
As we look back at yesterday and smile,
Remembering the burden of heat so intense.
The fantastic summer days were not without dust
For the sun, pain's furnace, literally slept in the sod,
Each day it came in waves to scorch the earth.
The heat once a melting agent has changed to cooler air.
The dewy freshness of dawn nips in with eager whispers
Of "where are the snows which drive out the heat".
Earth and skies are reflected in the dead grass of yesterday.
Weary flowers fill the air with a sad perfume.
Summer's noontide hangs with vaporous vitiate
As days of golden languor are hushed midst fluttering leaves.
We look forward to the sunbeams, in a winter's day,
Which gild the once vernal earth in a summer's day.
The morning sun will no longer sear the earth
Now protected by carpets of colorful sodden leaves.
A now weakened sun rushes to hide its dull glow.
Some call it autumn as evenings become long and dark.
We willingly welcome this change and put nature to bed
To sleep under its blanket of crisp, dry leaves.
—*Madeline D. Crane*

Time

As the days one by one travel across the horizon
As the years move from past to present
My yesterdays of memories fade into the distance
As my dreams of yesterday are laid to rest
As the wind sweeps across the earth
A breath of newness lingers
Yet takes some of today for tomorrow
Hopes of old still hold
Of a never ending tomorrow
Like the ever changing winds of time
My life goes on
—*Shirley J. Wright*

Autumn

There is no joy on our street
As when the happy children meet;
There is no tonic like the graces
Of watching all their eager faces.

As they rake the leaves in bright attire,
Burning energy like a gay bonfire,
Nostalgic thoughts caught up in the blaze
Respond and drift in a smoky haze.

A mother confined with an ailing child
Watches and forgets her cares for awhile
As the children outside in an engaging way
Draw the babe on her lap into their work and play.

The room grows dark about the window seat;
Outside, the twilight unnoticed grows deep
'Til the children are shadows, but in the house, unlit,
A reluctant pair still watch and sit.

—*Louella Urbanczyk*

My Mother My Friend

I can hear your soft words spoken so often in my head
As you have tried to convey your truths for me to see
So omit I might be spared
Some of the hurt in life's maze.

   I've tried my best to listen
   To hear the message of your words
   And though I've deviated often
   Perhaps one day soon you'll see a woman here.

Knowing that you helped along
That girl child you conceived
To brave the world of all it's risks
And to know I'm be safe alone.

   And Mom, I want to make you proud
   Forever needing you as my friend
   Being grateful to always have you there
   As you have always been.

And to let you know how much you're loved
How truly remarkable you are
My Mother, My Friend.

—*Paula L. Killion*

Starlights Way

Concern fills my thoughts...friend—
As you pass through each day—
Along the hardships life sends—
Go gently along starlights way.

Go swiftly with lightened heart—
Throughout the troubles of your day—
I am with you, to turn the hurts—
Go gently along starlights way.

Softly, softly, walk the bright path—
Beware the gray,
Of times alone; trust in heart and soul—
Go gently along starlights way.

Know inside your thoughts of tears,
That I hear the silence within—
Pass this life with no journeys astray—
Go gently along starlights way.

—*Ken M. Creson*

Shooting Star

From the windows of my mind, I stand and watch you
as you live life to the fullest. For you, time
has no beginning and no end. Each day brings a
flash of light, a flash of life to be lived

Life is not something to be endured but, life is to
be experienced as it is pulled in new and ever changing
directions. The past is a base to draw on and the future
is the rocky road we will call tomorrow

Like a shooting star you burn white hot

I stand here and reach out to you, pondering the
impossibility of containing such energy. Even a
brush from the trail can bring such pain. Pleasure
and pain are intertwined, and sometimes hard to
separate. We need one to feel the fullness of the other

A shooting star lasts only a moment, but in that
moment the whole world stands back in awe. The
power isn't in your time span but in the purity of your light

I'll close for now the windows of my mind and
climb through the windows of life. Following the
trail blazed by you... My shooting star

   —*Sue Flynn*

Time

The loud ticking of time
Assails my ears and fills my mind,
As it echoes in cavernous halls
Where mental images and memories fill the walls.

My life, for auction, on the block,
With each sonorous cadence of the clock.
The past keeps crowding in on me,
As though it's where I'd rather be.

The familiar faces of those who cared,
Are there behind in moments shared.
Is there enough time left ahead
For new places where I might tread?

It's easier to just slip away
By falling into yesterday.
Forcefully, life pushes me toward tomorrow's door,
That if opened, promises
        more,
           more,
              more...

   —*Marilyn McQueen Weishaar*

Untitled

If all the mothers of the world were to meet
at a crowded bus top or corner or market,
the problems of the world would then be nonexistent
and good guilt would rule the gaudiest Gatsby!

The sleepless skyline of cities and states
is the burning, combustible symbol of fate —
for no one can alter or mock out or tell
what the world would be like without risk of hell —
   for guilt would have no bearing
   and all we'd have is hearing
   and sight - two useless functions
   without a little guilt.

—*William Hulseman*

My Lord Is Near

I do not know my troubles come
At break of day or setting sun;
Though reason will not make it clear
I only know my Lord is near.

I do not know why sorrows tears
Pained my heart all through the years;
The answer may be void of cheer
I only know my Lord is near.

I do not know why failure comes
Heartaches beat like marshaled drums;
None can explain within this sphere
I only know my Lord is near.

I do not know what joys await
When I pass through that pearly gate;
With peace divine and no more fear
I'll know for sure my lord is near

—*Lloyd F. Brownbock*

Parliament

It's better to give, than to receive,
At least that's what I was taught.
Do unto others what you might want done.
Is that such a mind blowing thought?

The time by now is long past gone
for thinking I'm the only one.
United we stand. Divided we fall.
Which is it we want for one and all?

Why take advantage of one another
who is certainly some one's mother or brother.
This is not what they meant when
the fathers developed the parliament.

All for one and one for all,
is what they first intended to call.
Somehow, somewhere along the way,
now each one for self, is what they say.

—*Patsie Messinger Hunt*

John F. Kennedy

Who is this man named John F. K?
At one time, President of our US of A
He was only President for a very short while,
Then tragically murdered in gangland style.

The Kennedy motorcade was moving along,
When a shot was heard—loud and strong.
It hit it's mark - straight to the head of JFK
And soon he was dead!

   This happened over 20 years ago,
   But we remember it as tho it were yesterday
   And we dislike it so
   Because it happened on a city street of Big D
   Our beautiful city in US of A.

It was the shot heard 'round the world
And pierced the heart of every boy and girl.
The young, the old, the brave, the bold
We all loved this man named JFK
The 35th President of US of A.

—*Lou-Peck Cooper*

The Window

She looks out her window,
at the world around.
But what she seeks,
She's not yet found.

All pain she felt,
just faded away.
Just a shell of emotion,
is all that remain.

People saw her as perfect,
with nothing to hide.
What they didn't know,
is what happened on the window's other side.

No one could have imagined,
what lurked in her core.
All the pain and anger,
in this girl most girls adore.

There's more to people,
than what meets the eye.
The most important thing,
is what lurks inside.

—*Melissa Mast*

Urban Ocean

Waves of urban ocean roar
Atop a bed of asphalt surf-
A school of swimmers swims submersed
In a world for which they were not made.

A broken six-pack ring
Once washed up onto the beach-
There were no worms, no pearls to be found
When the fisherman's hook was cast into the sea.

The bait was but a token
Of future possibility-
Now the mammal's legs are lost
And Darwin's fish don't seem so bright.

—*Kris Curtis*

The Outer Cover

The cover permeating dark and gray
attracts few willing to stay.
Justifying, of course, from the outside
dreariness and doom awaits inside.

Why take the time to open that cover
expectations not wanting to discover.
What tragedy could possibly be precluded
giving worthiness to the wasteful time secluded.

What deranged state must one be in
daring to expense the chance within.
Perhaps that permeating dark and gray
deliberately intend to keep the shallow away.

Treacherous minds, fabricate the inside
those who destroy by observations outside.
Fantasy of love and beauty only exist
for those who search for reality's bliss.

When one explores for truth to show
then wonders of love uncover and grow.
Perhaps life will perpetuate like a lover
when we no longer judge it by its cover.

—*Larry H. Bange*

Victory In Death

I could not hold the fatal grip—
Away from my father who lay in eternal sleep.
His favourite five stood around him
Pondering, life without him would be so grim.

A heavenly smile his countenance lit
As the tears on the faces constantly drip.
The eldest one who loved him no less
Was absent, and too departed after he did.

He gave them all that he had:
Compassion, manners, talents and all
To become man and women —
Ever striving for the success of their call.

On the next to the eldest, it reflected most
Her mother she missed, cursing nature's course.
She made a vow to the father and the four
A loving home for their being, a shrine for their soul.

In hue of glory I see my father smiling
With his message; fare-you-well with my blessings
Victorious he lives beyond those hills
Ever loving, and watching over us still.

—Priti David

Fading Roses

All the love you gave us that never stopped, just slipped away.
   In our hearts those memories stayed.

In the beginning we saw the changes. We overlooked them
   we loved you the same.

Zooming around. Restless and scared. Remembering things.
   Never left your head.

Holding on, in our heart, to a beautiful rose petal falling apart.
   Bits and pieces, we pick them up. To see it
   crumble with each touch.

Each day we pray, in a way — God take this evil disease and
   throw it away. Give us you. If just for a day.

Impressions of crystal upon your face. Thoughts like a stone,
   A storm taken away. Leaving little for today.

Memories of our childhood days, you did so much, we can't
   repay. You've given us life, we have today.

Efforts we make today. Love you each and every day, in every
   way. And keep you safe and happy, we pray.

Reaching out, holding on. Touching each rose petal before
   it's gone. Hoping the shrub stays strong. Strengthen
   the stem for a rose to bud on.

—Odies Liddell-Donald

Just For You

The moment we met I couldn't help but see, the way I looked
at you and the way you looked at me.
We got closer and closer day by day, I couldn't help but care
in that warm, sweet way.
The things we went through some good some bad, some I wish
we never would've had.
Now it's done with and gone away, we both forgot each other
in that cold, hateful way.
I know that you dislike me now that we're through, but I
wrote this with love just for you.

—Nikki Mulvaney

Bent Knees

It is no mystery of the given symmetry,
   away with all misery in completion of history.
For all those who seek a strengthening of the weak,
   an inheritance of the meek forever they shall keep.
The candle so bright removes the darkness of night.
   Changing blindness into sight eternal burning light.
Into empty hours the spirit fills and inspires,
   giving courage and power to all who desire.
From this world of pollution and constant confusion,
   this is one conclusion that goes beyond the illusion.
It is never too late for no one owns or holds fate,
   we must learn to relate or otherwise will forsake.
The spending of a heart's time so precious in mind,
   a search for the sign of hope we might find.
Look not behind as life's mountain is climbed,
   so evermore kind is life's simple rhyme.
Life is short and not long, in a heartbeat were gone.
   Start each day's new dawn with prayer's life-giving song.
From within humanities crowds are sighs given so loud.
   Like rain's silent clouds feeling's spoken without sound.
The faithful will dare to escape the lion's lair,
   paying life's simple fare are knees bent in prayer.

—Paul R. Staples, Jr.

Precious Counselors

Watching little girls play, oh what fun that can be
Baby dolls, pigtails and those delightful tea parties.
Wee giggles and whispers…one big continuous surprise
So sensitive and soft spoken, they'll capture your heart with a smile.

Watching little boys play, now here's a real treat
Cars, trucks and mud puddles…dirty little feet.
Robust laughter and boisterous talk, always on the go
Why, without saying a single word, their glances will steal
   the whole show.

Now, watching these two play together…this is where the fun
   truly begins
And believe it or not, if you'll just observe, there are many
   answers for us bidden within,
The many compromises each one makes while still maintaining
   their identity
So willing to give…and receive…both sharing time so naturally.

Christ said to "come as a child" and the beauty of this is
   sometimes unspoken
Not only should we use this teaching in accepting our Savior,
   but apply it to areas of our lives that are broken.
So much stress is put on "self" today, as if no one else really matters
But the real answers to our relationship problems lies
Within the Lord and that precious little playground chatter.

—Kim Dlugosh

Have Faith In God

He's all you need, he'll be their
beside you in times of your need.
when everything else seems to go
wrong, He will love you where every
you roam. He God my master, I love
him so. He makes me happy more
than anyone knows. I love being
close to him when my heart in pain
for he is my savior and he does love me.

—Naomi Lanier

School, The Learning Tree

The classroom is a learning place.
Back into history, and even outerspace.
History and English, I desire to learn
Filing too, but-in its turn.

I'm really trying to do my best
Willing to help others, in this quest.
Adult I am, but I must be
Like a child again, at the learning tree.

I intend to press on, and never look back
For if I do I'll only be slack.
I pray that many will join its parade
And never turn it, into a comic charade.
Please fill the classrooms of every school
Allow the teacher to tap you, with her rule.

The harvest is great, the students are few
Age doesn't matter, each has their cue.
The learning tree is the place to be,
It's a guiding hand for you and me...
—*Mary Ellis Warrick*

Oh, Dear Jesus, Touch Me Gently

Oh, Dear Jesus, touch me gently.
Bathe me in your precious love.
Oh, dear Jesus, touch me gently.
Guardian angels watch above.

Oh, dear Jesus, guide me safely
When I wander from your way.
Wipe my tears when I am crying.
Keep me longing for that day.

Turn my footsteps toward a city
Never touched by human hands,
Filled with pilgrims free from sorrow,
Flowing strains from angel bands.

Flood my soul with love and giving.
Grant me strength to carry on.
Let your radiance be a beacon.
Let your glory be my song.

On that day when life's a vapor
And we climb the golden stairs,
Maybe God will leave the light on,
Just to show us that he cares.
—*Rubye H. Dowlen*

In Toto

Assuming that which I observe,
  be true,
At last, I summon up the nerve
  to view
    The image I project.
Mirrored back to meet my eyes
  and mind,
I both indulge and patronize,
  in kind,
    The vision I inspect.

I find me wavering around
  the brink.
I tread on dangerous ground I think
Where angels fear to go.
I am dismayed by what I see,
  and say,
"Is this the sum and total me?"
  and pray,
    "Lord, let it not be so!"
—*Loyed L. Arnold*

Visions Of You

Whenever, I see a vision of your
  beautiful face,
I will see roses, violets, and daffodils
  entwined with victorian lace.
Your benevolent shadow will fall
  in the world someplace
And that lovely area will know
  and feel your splendor and grace!

The mere mention of your name
  will be like a Schubertain refrain.
You have no love save for Him above!
Take my heart, do as you will;
  No matter where; I will
Know and feel the thrill.
Remorse, remorse, as you
  whispered adieu.

To the Lamb of God you must
  remain true.
Love, and infinitium, endlessly
  forever to you.
—*La Vena M. Drummond*

Angels and Your Love Song

Music, music I hear!
  beautiful music keeps ringing in my ears
  such sweet music - it's coming from above
  it's sending a message of love.
The angels are singing: it's your song of love
The words are saying: share, share together
  your thoughts, your cares
  true happiness are yours ever and ever
  as you live, love, and daily share
Softly-still singing: Love is free, costly, it could be
  throw away your fears, bury
  them onto the yester years.
The guitars are playing: a symbol of joy - as the
  melody of the strings entwine:
  seek, seek together you shall find
  songs of love, songs within your heart
  songs of good faith it's sacredness:
  never from you shall depart:
  its fruits - its riches beyond all measures
  are your most cherished of treasure
Signing off: the music keep echoing!
  Its the Angels and your love song now and forever.
—*Mary Grace Carbone*

The Summer Rain

A shrouded night, an ebony wave
  beautiful yet bittersweet
  roses upon a forgotten grave
Watch its fall; the summer rain.

A lover's passion, a rising sun
  pellets of a vengeful god
  each new drop a new emotion
Hear its stories; the summer rain.

A scent of damp, an eerie still
  engulfing any earthly boundaries
  chaotic yet a stubborn will
Smell its power; the summer rain.

A moist breath, a cold wet hand
  a serpent trapped in rising tide
  secrets not meant to understand
Feel its chill; the summer rain.
—*Scott Field*

Life And You

Life is likened to a winding land,
   Beautifully bright with flowers,
Butterflies fluttering from bud to cane,
   And fruit all glittery from recent showers.
Luscious fruit which I barely taste;
   Since I must hurry on down the lane
To seek more beauty; and in my haste
   I fail to see beyond the rain.

On down the road, less flowers I see,
   And the butterflies disappear.
And the luscious fruit is scarce on tree,
   And songs of birds I do not hear.
Once again I round bend in road,
   See naught but bleakness up ahead.
I cannot help but feel a heavy load
   And in my heart a lonely dread.

Then I saw you! Letting in new light
   Through ragged chinks that time had made.
I'm unwilling to give up the fight
   As time passes into the shade.
I know I am stronger by weakness,
   I know that my price has been paid,
And that time shall dispel the bleakness,
   And future and past have been weighed.
   —*Ruby Golliher*

The Child

Innocence
Beauty
Love
Eyes aglow with the twinkles of her smile.
Alert
Watching
Laughing
Dancing to the music of "Sesame" or "Zoo".
Reaching
Touching
Discovering
Eyes, ears, nose, mouth, hands, other children.
Warm
Trusting
Hunger satisfied
Head on the shoulder ready for sleep.
Eyes closed, another smile
Happiness
Contentment
Mommy. Daddy. Home.
   —*Kenneth W. Brown*

Untitled

Close your mouths, open your eyes and ears.
Become color blind.
Watch and listen to what's been happening over the years.
You'll be shocked by what you'll find.
The world is no longer candy and flowers.
The candy has melted and the flowers are wilted and dying.
Everything is controlled by superficial powers.
Each other is what they seem to be buying.
It's the people they are selling out.
They've made it so that we really don't have a choice.
Unless we get out and vote, we'll no longer count.
They no longer can hear our voice.
"Power to the people" is what they always say,
But the power of the people gets weaker every day.
We have to stand together and unite.
Forget the racial boundaries and take each other's hand.
Raise your voices and begin to flight,
And tomorrow the people will be in command.
   —*Kelly K. Bresnahan*

Closing The Ship Log

To write I must
Before my body is only dust.
If, very gifted, as many say
I must continue day to day
To use the gift before turning to clay.
I weather the storms in the sea of life
No longer with crew, nor first mate (my dear wife),
Alone I sail this ship into un-charted sea.
The compass was set long ago by me and my dear Bea
Into open sea, squall or calm, to be free.
With devastations, tossed to rocky reefs, we continued to sail
Aware until weighing anchor in the final port we could not fail!
Loss of our shipmates: Son, families, many comrades dear
In the treacherous sea of life we sailed on without fear
Of what lurked unknown beyond the buoys, we were full of cheer.
Alone as Captain, no first-mate since '86, I see not too distant closing the Log.
Last entry, a final cross, sealing tight, as the fog thickens, heavier the fog.
No further need of sextant nor compass to check
I hold the wheel firmly sailing the open sea. Knowledge of what's ahead, ship-wreck
Anticipated, before weighing anchor, sleep of the deep, I'll die Captain on deck.
   —*Perry W. England*

A Tribute To The Unknown Soldier

How many more "Unknown Soldiers" will there be?
   Before the war-makers can see!
Lives disrupted... tears and pain...
   Sacrifices all in vain!
What good do sacrifices make
   To greedy people who take and take,
Never giving...let the boys give all!
   Even life!...The bitter gall
Of scheming men sitting smug and warm.
   While our boys are facing death and storm...
And lonely nights... and bitter cold...
   Young boys growing old...
Fighting!... dying!...
   What's the use?
No end in sight....such sham!...abuse!
   Each day for them a thousand years...
What do war-mongers know of tears?
   If fight we must... let's fight to win!
Then off our conscience blot the sin
   Of the "Unknown soldier's" life we lost...
In God's name make it worth the cost!
   —*Virginia Carlson Knight*

Eventide

I love evening when the sun goes down
   Behind the strips of the motionless town
   Which towers above what lies beneath
   And belies the fact of pain and grief.
For the sun has a way of giving a glow
   That supersedes the gray of the buildings below
   Which although they stand stalwart and straight
   Are weary and numbed, accepting their fate.

I love evening when the sun goes down
   Behind the strength of the busy town
   Which permeates with the sounds of might
   And rescues the lonely from the fear of night.
For the streets have a way of inviting man in
   To experience himself, to be his friend
   To wander around or speed on through
   Seeking a place where souls renew.
   —*Vera B. Riley*

Telling One's Self

Telling one's self, I am a human
being, and I am me, but am I also.
False, and lost, like the birds, and the
Beasts, or am I as true
And real as life, and all powerful as
the sea, which then is me,
That I could know and identify, my
true destiny, and my very
Existence, so that I may shine forth in
the world, and be worthy
Of the true beauty, and air I breathe,
to conquer all, and lose
Not all, this I seek and believe, to be
my true reward, my greatest
Joy, and my truest freedom, which
can only happen for someone as
Human as me.
—*Samuel Cohen*

Dinner For Two

It was the fateful night...again.
Being polite as when we first met.
Sharing as strangers do,
Saying too much of nothing.
Sometimes...something. About Life.
Our talking habits mechanical and veiled.
With interrupted coolness and haphazard nods,
Eyes barely meeting, barely feeling.
Time slowly passing our awareness,
Remaining closed, silent to past secrets.
Our love diminished.
For we wouldn't change, wouldn't try.
Yes, it was that night when I asked,
"How long will we last?"
—*Merle K. Lai*

Seasons In The Adirondacks

First, winter with its temperatures sometimes reaching thirty
below. You think of anyone that has to shovel snow as a hero.
When the snow almost reaches the window tops, you think it
might never stop. Then spring with it's flowers, you could
look at them for hours, if you get enough sunshine and showers.
The two are an unbeatable combination making everything pretty
and green. Showers makes the air smell so clean. Then summer
with nice sunny weather, your family likes to spend time
together. You go canoeing on the lake. You hope it doesn't
rain for your family's sake. You want it to be sunny and
bright. That would be a wonderful sight. Last, there is the
fall which I think is the most beautiful season of all. For
that is your time to go leaf peeking. For the beautiful
oranges red and yellows on the trees, which I am seeking.
Even though they will soon fall, which leads to raking. So end
the seasons in the Adirondacks. Whether it be good or bad.
—*Mildred Beswick*

Pickings

The picker sweeps the field of grain
Beneath the winter sky;
The rose gray vault just frames
The hawk that scans the field for mice
And silhouettes the pheasant gold
In search of fallen corn.

The hunter aims, the pheasant falls;
The falcon dives, the mouse takes wing;
The farmer hauls his full load home
And leaves the fallow field.

The picker silent stands beneath a vault
That silent shares with falcon bold the winter chill.
—*J. M. Dodge*

What Shall We Leave Our Children?

Our forefathers carved out a nation,
   Bequeathed us liberty,
By writing our constitution
   For equal opportunity.

What shall we leave our children?
   Will we continue these rights?
Will we see each has protection
   From oppression, abuse and might?

What shall we leave our children?
   Our streams, now polluted, and death
Of fish, plants, animals, ourselves,
   With poisoned air every breath?

What shall we leave our children?
   Laziness, apathy, greed or deceit?
Or will we fight for what is right,
   Get rid of the drugs on the street?

Will our legacy be prejudice, injustice, hate?
   Or compassion and courage when
We all work together, before it's too late,
   What shall we leave our children?
—*Ruby Tippit Peacher*

Bloody Eyes

I stand in the white room
Beside an almost helpless form,
A fake smile conceals
The bloody battlefield.

To no avail

As our eyes meet, I know
Mine are fountains of
Faith's and Hope's blood.
Two soldiers ever losing
Mental territory to an enemy
Growing exponentially in might.

He stares long into the red pools

His gaze overflowing with inner strength
Is a panacea.
I fight to keep my balance
As the tide turns

My eyes will never bleed again.
—*Richard A. Duncan*

Golf Widow's Lament

On that rolling meadow
Best known as the golf course
I've walked, and searched, and called
'Till my voice has grown hoarse.

He's far our of my sight
But not out of my mind.
He's there somewhere, I guess;
The husband I can't find.

Now he's not a gambler, my man,
And never hangs out at the pub,
But for heaven's sake, I can't take
Each night a different golf club.

Listen you gals, take my advice;
Don't let that golf game get started.
Once He has mounted that golf cart
Your charms, and his arms are parted.

So turn that guy of yours around.
If you see a golf course ahead
That man with a club in his hand
Means romance is dead, baby, dead!!
—*Richard Penn*

Oh Mother Of Mine

Oh mother of mine, why do I love thee?
Because you are the best mother known to me
When I heard you were ill, all I could do was cry
I thought about the things you had taught me and
I know you didn't lie.

Oh mother of mine, with patience for children like us
For the noise we made was such a fuss.
When you chastised us, it made us so sad
Though it was because you loved us and
We were just being bad.

Oh mother mine, you'd make us take baths
So we would not smell
You raised us up to believe in God
So we wouldn't go to hell
Oh mother you taught us to have nice clean hair
You taught us to love one another and
How to share.

You were a poor woman, with very little money
Who shared her love with eight children
A love sweeter than honey
You taught us to pay no attention
To what people say
You said believe in God and
He will walk with us everyday.

Oh mother of mine, please survive
And I'll pray and thank God, you are alive
Oh mother of mine, please don't concede
I love you so much I'm not ready for you to leave.
—*Zack Marvin Gunn*

Old Friends

If one could change the outlook
between old friends, would it be for better
or for worse—
Could one explain, accept the difference it
would make and then again could two
Do the same to gain whatever at stake
Two free souls so long alone but always
within the friendship zone.

If one should say "I love you" could one
answer "yes I do" how long would it last
is anybody's guess—it's true, more or less,
would life become more humane, a warmer
plane, less insane as friends and lovers both,
would it be in vain a different point of view
no cause for blame, just happy to remain
Old friends.
—*Kathleen Kay Lewis*

Relatively Speaking

Insanity is emotion trapped
   between the expectations of man
reality is what we seem to perceive
   yet our dreams are elusive and grand

Chaos is the freedom of knowing
   that nothing is as it seems
our senses are fine as far as they go
   but there's so much we cannot see

Philosophy is a mind game
   if it only means what you want it to mean
theology is a power game
   maybe a few of those players are clean

Psychology is but another game
   which they use to blind our eyes
politics is the dirtiest game
   and a sign of our unholy times

It's all relative
   so they say
     but I want to know
       who's relatives are they?
—*Randy McQuilkin*

The Sea Wind

The wind from the sea, calls to me,
Bidding me come, and follow Thee,
Where we once walked, hand in hand,
Together on the sun-warmed sands,
I've walked alone, since that day,
That you set sail, and went away.
The sea birds call, and fly away,
Would that I, had wings as they,
I'd fly away, to that distant shore,
Where we would walk together once more.
I pray to my Maker, as I walk alone,
That you will find, your way back home,
He will answer, of that I'm sure,
For my love, for Thee is pure.
You had to go, you could not stay,
Still I'm sure we'll meet one day,
Whether here, or that distant land,
We'll walk together, hand in hand,
For Love is Eternal, it's here to stay,
And not even the Grave, can take it away!
—*Ruby Coggins Gordon*

Branwyn

Branwyn, I wish that I were there.
Branwyn, I remember your moon-fairy hair
Almost hiding your solemn brown eyes
That the impish smile on your lips belies.
And your butterfly hands that gently caress
My own, or a dog, our your pretty dress.
The attention you pay to a story re-read.
The stop-sudden stillness, when you are in bed.
The questions that come to your alert mind
When dancing, or playing with something you find.
Your quaint-serious manner that turns to glee
When you think you have pulled a trick on me.
I remember these things as I saw you last,
And pray that you don't grow up too fast.
But if it happens that you must,
That you keep your wonder, love and trust.
—Stella M. Reed

Spring, 1993

Today I heard a strange smooth song
break through the voice of spring,
ringing clear and alone in the morning sun,
before lost in the myriad sounds.

The rasping "ya-a ya-as" of bluejays
punctuated the wren's twittering descant
and the "cher-cher" of robins' reddish throats;
while sparrows flocked and flitted about
"cheep-cheeping" at spring cleaning———
all rose to crescendo at black hawk's "caw,"
then paused while that tender solo trilled again,

I tried in vain to glimpse the source
of that etherial lay, as I felt engulfed
in nature's orchestration,
'till my heart must stop in harmony.
—Lillian Twining

It Is Very Special

Every day as you come into sight, the days become brighter and brighter every time I see you. Poetry is more than just love, but passion is something to desire and you are more than the stars upon the moonlight sky as to say about your identity, I am speechless in words. I can tell by the look of your unforgotten eyes, the time that has passed between us, though the time seemed very short, but endless to seek in your magnificent wonders as you are like an angel from the very heaven above that shows the great wonders of the earth. You are one in a million that walks upon this very earth as the sun casts your shadow upon the very pathways in which you walk upon. Every move that you may make, let it not be nothing but a golden one as though every step you make is something very special. May I not say more, but may everyone be something special in their own special ways.
—Michael G. McKibbin

Time

When I was young, how time crept by,
but now I'm older, time does fly,
My children are grown, and I'm alone,
and now I think of the times gone by,
and wish that my time didn't fly, as my
time on earth is growing less, I often
wonder if I did best, the mistakes
I made, I cannot undo, but everything
is done, and I can try not to be
blue, Oh! My children how I love you.
—Peggy J. Koontz

The Silent Wind

A destructive force broke out in the streets of L.A.
Bringing a rage of confusion causing values to decay
The news media reporting full coverage local and wide
Where all can see that no one is walking side by side

A silent wind crept into the minds of many
Causing a wind storm that destroyed plenty
This eruption came from time, which had a losers hand
Provoking man to react to a devil's command

Many lives, buildings, and homes are gone
Leaving tears and bitter hearts turning to stone
How can we undo the unjust or right a wrong
By giving all people a chance to sing their own song

Human color comes into issue which is a sad thing
Watch the flowers unfold and see the beauty they bring
Humans are like flowers, blooming all over the universe
But our intellect is diminishing, going in reverse

Let none of us forget—L.A. Wed. April the 29th, 1992
A time to change minds for the better and a time to do
Let us hope and pray that all hearts with love be filled
And let the silent wind cease and let the wind be still———
—Mattie Simms

Snow

Grey-washed skies settle down around me
Bringing with them the quiet, soft snow.
The snow delicately cloaks the sentinel firs
Bowing their branches to the ground.
It catches and clings to whatever it touches
Making the glass covered trees crinkle
Under their growing crown of white.
Soon the street and grasses will be gone
Bound together by the crystal snow.
The white snow falls from the grey skies
Covering with gentle persistence
The individuality of the world.

If I stand long enough
I, too, will disappear
For I have already a fine coat of white
If I stand long enough
I, too, will become one with the sky
The trees
And the silent snow.
—Milly Kruper

Humanity's Journey

These three must align and entwine
Brothers Dark and Light seen and unseen
Along with Heaven's might
Peace in our time is from the Light
Tho never free from Humanity's plight
Our lusts come from being dust and
Must be heralded along its way
Progressive steps can never held at bay
We must all go along this way
Once for all time in every clime
Lest we lose our step never
To align nor entwine these three
Then to begin again the journey dark
With every step we make a mark
Seeking ever to align and entwine these three
Brothers dark and light seen and unseen including Heaven's Light together and forever we will be... Humanity.
—Wanda Gibson Richardson

Look Up

Stars know the way
  burning holes in cold distance,
  they shed on shifting dunes,
  where solders wrapped in fear
  gasp icy litanies to the prophets

Stars know the way
  they blaze the crack child's eyes
  in frozen memory of white that never ends
  patterning the mindless
  into blind harmony

Stars see all
  mingled tapestries of life and death,
  the global rage of living
    bloated pouches of hunger
      in the sudan
    bloated faces of obesity
      in stricken western eyes
  (the time of reversal has not come)

Stars know the way
  they grace the night
  with points of hope
  lit in the soul
  of the seeing
   —*Lila W. Duckett*

Untitled

An array of Autumn
Bursts forth in a blaze of brilliance
Bordering the country and causing celestial countenance,
Caterpillars spin cocoons in disregard. Dreams decorate the design.
Dancing dandelions are elegant. Essential energy escapes the
Evening's employ. Full-grown Flowers flourish into
Fancy graphics. God's great goodness gives harvest
Heap upon heap. Hibernating in imagination
Ideas impose identity through iconographic justice.
Jays jabber joyfully. Jonquils in jackets know kindness.
Kids kick leaves. Lamplight lengthens leisure moments.
Man masterfully manages memories to mitigate the night.
No one notices a niche
Now occupied by the old owl.
Often she ponders her prize.
Then pounces quickly with queenly qualities.
The quiet quadrant ruptures by riot rebels;
Then relaxes slowly and settles.
Squirrels skillfully scamper up sides of tall trees
Tending to tedious tasks. The tabloid unfolds
Until understood is an unequivocal eulogy to a
Vanishing Vanguard. The Victor is Winter.
  —*Martha Brock*

AIDS

Silence, stalks the mind
Burning rage in their hearts you'll find
The passion to live as long as they can
It is hitting our children, every woman and man
A recluse is what they become
Hidden from people, people they love
They need our support for ever more
Please, don't push them back through the door
I believe that they will find a solution
One that will wipe out this plague of pollution
But for now, I'm afraid it is here to stay
This disease took my cousin away.
  —*Kristine Elizabeth Miller*

Spring Is Just Four Days Away

The earth it wears a cold grey mask
but beneath this icy face,
silent hands begin their task;
all bleakness to erase.

Spring is just four days away
soon come the breezes mild
that will, so gently, the flowers sway
pure as a new-born child.

Also like this child of May,
in joyous colors blooming
Spring is just four days away
an April, May, and June thing.

Spring is just four days away
fold away this solemn cover
And as a child greet the day
embraced by a loving mother.
  —*Mark W. Haggerty*

Wandering Wondering

Generations come and go,
but does humanity grow?
Does it seek after graces,
which lead to holy places?

Why do some seek after pleasure,
and live life by their own measure?
Do those out there who care -
have discipline to share?

Does all perversion thrive,
to keep Satan alive?
Though he wants to confuse,
have us think what's the use?

Along with the hi-tech advance,
why can't they give morals a chance?
With war a punishment for sin,
why can't they all seek God again?

Have they forgotten what's real?
Has salvation no appeal?
Considering the state the world is in,
isn't it sad, to know what could have been?
  —*Robert A. Rowland*

David's Dream

Life was eighteen and looking bright
but ended quickly in that night.
I turned to God and asked for truth,
Why did you take him in his youth?
I'm so angry I want to shout,
but still, I'm left with all these doubts.
It's hard to understand your plan
for things like this seem out of hand.
Is the reason why he was called
beyond the reaches of us all
that no one here can understand
the mystery that surrounds your plan?
It's hard to let a loved one go,
yet holding on, it hurts me so.
The living must try to survive
by working toward a compromise.
So many dreams he hoped to share,
that I must ask you, Would you care
if I borrow a dream or two
and try to finish them for you?
  —*Robert C. Parbs*

Friends Need Friends

Do not ask to have yours load lightened
but for courage to endure

Do not ask for perfection in all you do
But for the wisdom not to repeat mistakes....

People need people and friends need love,
For a full life descends

Not on success or on worldly fame,
But just in knowing that someone cares...

Remember God is ready and willing to share
The burden you find too heavy to bear...

And finally do not ask for more before saying "Thank you"
For what you have already received...

For people need people and friends need friends
So with faith, let go and let God lead the way...

Someone who takes time to think of other people's needs
Someone who can always chase a little tear away...

Someone who's so glad to share,
So glad to help and give and care...

People need people and friends need friends
We are very special to help in the world we are in....
—*Virginia A. Taylor*

Atlantis

The name comes 'cross my mind and shapes my lips
But gets no utterance or sound except
In memory, when lovers walked, and tips
Of willow branches all our secrets swept
Into the stream of youth that knows no bounds,
But blends so silently into the wide
And faster current that flows past the towns
Where mundane adult duties must abide.

The erstwhile rivulet has reached the bay,
Which opens on to ocean's greater depth
Where two drops merge as one. And all the way
The chambers of my heart the secret kept.

So, now, the sum of life — the total's all,
And I am free at last to call out, "Paul?"
—*Louise Dodd Rosenberg*

God's Care

The time is long 'til close of day
But God is with me all the way.
He cares for me 'til setting sun
And gives me rest when day is done.
He watches o'er me through the night
And keeps me safe 'til morning light.
I do not know what I would do
If God did not love me so.
His loving arms around me stay
To help me on my weary way,
He gives me peace within my heart.
I know that He will not depart.
—*Vivian L. Holloway*

You're Still Here

Seasons come once a year
But Grandpa Dear, you're still here.
You're here when I laugh,
You're here when I cry,
You're here come rain or shine.
I wish I could have asked
For you to stay forever.
But when it comes to life,
There is no forever.
We all must die
Sooner of later.
But you, My Dear, died the sooner.
Your memory I'll keep
In my heart with a key
Locked forever.
Grandpa Dear, you're still here.
—*Patty Peters*

Peace On Earth

And goodwill towards men is loudly proclaimed.
    But, how can that be the answer
when hearts are such ghettos of sin, and so maimed;
    when minds have evil thoughts astir?

No. There will be no peace or goodwill on earth
    till sick hearts can no longer kill:
    sadly, for them, love has no worth.
    Peace, then, is for those of goodwill.

Yes. For these are the true images of God.
    Their hearts are clean, humble, and meek,
as guileless as doves and without any facade.
    Just they can turn the other cheek.
—*William C. Furby*

The Death Of My Mother

A thousand times I said "Goodbye"
but I always knew, I will see her again
But now oh God, I cry out "Why?"
my heart and mind is filled with so much pain.

When death walks in uninvited
and someone so dear...is taken away
the emptiness that follows and the fear
for in my heart I know
my loneliness is now here, to stay.

I ask the wind and the morning sun
to greet my beloved mother
wherever she might be, my heart is yearning
my eyes are burning, I have no tears to cry
"Oh God," I scream toward heaven
"Please tell me...why?"

I know we are just travelers here on earth
and someday...I too
must find my way home
but until this day...I know now
I am truly all alone...

...for when a mother closes her eyes
...her child has never again on earth...a home.
—*Maria Heiser*

Passing Strangers

I never knew your name
But I saw your face somewhere
I know we never met
'Cause I can't remember when.
This day I saw you on the train
You sat across from me
As I look upon your face, the sadness I can see
Then suddenly the tears begin to flow
I don't know the reason why
And I guess I will never know
Why I feel so hurt inside
Just by looking at the sadness in your eyes
I can feel the pain you held within
Was it a lovers' fight?
Did someone take their love from you?
Wish I knew why you were crying
And why I feel this way.
Something about you attracts me
But you will never know.
We were passing strangers; and may never meet again.

—Peter Marshall

I Don't Know

c don't know what this is
but I sure know how it feels
an empty heart, an endless ache
with you being my one and only heartache.
I'm consumed by what you make me feel
and I don't know if it's for real
I hunger for you so much
I can't be without your touch
I wish I knew what to do
for I don't want to be blue
but for now all I can say
is that I do want you to stay.

—Mitzy A. Ruiz

Too Lethal Too Late

"I'll just check his pulse", said evil nurse
But instead took a syringe from her purse.

Now it was to pay for his rejection
That she gave the illegal injection.

Then she packed her bags and flew down to Rio
But soon there followed a detective trio.

They brought her back in cuffs and chains
And now in prison she still remains.

"I should have checked his pulse," she's often said.
"For I didn't know he was already dead."

—Ken Wilkins

God's Medic's

This is strange, but God works' with the doctor's and nurses,
But he also has a secret army of doctor's and nurses he can
   command at anytime to work a miracle in your life.
You never forget that time.
When you were visited by God's Army of one or two doctors,
Females or male,
Whatever Chosen, this is only one miracle that may happen
In a life time.
But can never be forgotten.

—Ramona E. Hamric

Outspoken

It has always been a big world
But it's bigger now that we've
Stretched ourselves to the moon
And amazingly on into vastness of space.
And here I sit in a small town —
In living quarters small — very limited
In many things as well —
But sometimes I feel that this whole
Wide world rests on my shoulders;
The weight unbearable, pressing
And breath-sapping.
That's because I care. I have no
Elusiveness so as not to care —
I just do.
So when you feel alone you should
Take a second thought — So long
As I live....

—Mary Schacknow

Sinful Nature

The dawn of each morning tolls my knell.
But let there be no morning that does not know forgiveness.
How long must I say "Mea culpa, mea culpa?"
Must sin be so redundant?
My soul calls out for forgiveness,
Despite the fact that I cannot identify my sins.
Give my conscience succour, oh, Lord.
Oh save me not to wander in the ignorance of my transgressions.
We are sinful in our thoughts before our deeds.
Your love knows this, because it too was once frailly human.
Spare me the footsteps leading to gestures of sin.
And grant the thought that someday
We may join hands together in salvation.
And a hearty laugh shall make light of the burdensome past,
And may the morning glories rise around us.

—Michael J. Michanczyk III

My Guardian Angel

The leaves have turned, the wind has chill
but no one know just how I feel
I used to love the seasons change
But now it's different; somewhat strange
They always say that life goes on
But part of it stops when someone's gone
The never ending grief inside
Is something I try hard to hide
If only I had seen the loss
so much I'd change at any cost
All the I Love You's I never said
Now I can't. Because he's dead
I hope and pray that he can hear
The silent weeps of my hearts tears
I hope he knew the love I had
I hardly said it, now I'm sad
Every night while I'm in bed
I say a prayer within my head
That God will somehow let him be
A guardian angel over me.

—Susanne Boston

And There Were...Strawflowers

There are many flowers that beg for my attention
  but none vies more for my mind's retention
  than nature's own wild, purple Strawflower.
Suddenly, fields have exploded into a regency
of expressive blooms fashioning petaled lagoons.
They search the sky for sunny rays as rainless
  clouds smile to hide their deficiency.

Strawflowers question not their squatter's rights.
Cloistered from worldly care, wind-blown, they hum
  hymns from distant gods.
Were these a gardener's splashy border, they would
  merit and receive appreciative nods.
Lacking invitation, planning, planting, pruning,
  destain welcomes their overnight visitation.

Rashfully, they are scythed. Where I pleasured
  my eye on prolific medallions bashfully
  nodding to their peers,
a stark, purposeless ground agonizes the scene:
Soon to imprison thorny spears...totally unlike
  purely pastoral Strawflowers.
    —*Kate Hartnell-Stobbe*

Love For Me

Oh Lord you did it all for me.
But not only just for me.
Whosoever might believe on thee.
You wore a crown of thorns for me.
You wore a purple robe for me.
They spit upon you Lord for me.
You carried the heavy cross for me.
Oh Lord you uttered not a word
A nail pierced your hands and feet for me.
You said "I thirst," for me.
  You really thirst for me.
Oh, Lord your blood flowed red for me,
And there oh Lord, you hung for me
You died between two thieves for me.
  So why can't I live more for thee
  You did it all for me.
    —*Zana Cowherd*

Levity

I'd like to write another poem
  But nothing comes to mind,
I can't get one idea
  Can't seem to write a line.

I've thought and thought and thought
  But my mind's completely bare,
So when I take my pen in hand
  I just sit and stare.

Surely there is something
  That I can rhyme about,
Well, if there is it's hidden
  And I can't bring it out.

There's moon and June, spoon and tune
  Wind and rain and weather,
But they are just a bunch of words
  If I can't put them together.

So here I sit, the page is blank
  My mind is just as bad,
I think I'll call the whole thing off
  And take a nap instead.
    —*Ruth Poorman Eicas*

Improvisation Naturale

Speak to me not with artificial notes,
But permit Earth's great symphony
To perform her magic.

High on the top-most branch of a wild cherry tree
A red-winged blackbird, balanced precariously
On a too-vertical limb, is conducting today.

A cardinal on a sassafras sprout
Turns leaves of music which hum in the wind.

The red-headed woodpecker provides rhythm
Hidden in the leaves of the proud little elm,
While the bobwhite drags unrhythmically,
Like some sleepy choir boy.

One by one the number expands in a joyous chorus,
'Till all nature's creatures find their part—
  the frogs in the barnlot pond naturally sing bass;
  the wood's dove sings the alto line,
  while the mockingbird naturally sings a lilting soprano.

Improvisation Naturale is the name of the composition,
With each performer playing his part in perfect harmony;
A once-in-a-lifetime masterpiece forever recorded in golden
  memory.
    —*Vickie L. Warren*

Autumnal Meditation

As our days dwindle down and the summer's leaves fall, one can
  but ponder the meaning of it all.
Crisp golden fall Sundays, in subtle way, seen somehow attuned
  to that hallowed day,
When God took pause in His terrestrial labor day, for well
  earned rest, and time to savor,
The gorgeous flow of His earthly creation, so artistically
  schemed, evoking life's adoration!

And now as we gather, these aeons gone by, to offer our thanks,
  'neath His azure sky,

For our gift of life, family and friends, countless blessings
  that seem to portend,
Peaceful rest when our journey's done, and we bid life adieu,
  as the setting sun,
Reluctantly dim, join the ethereal stars, with memories
  ingrained, of the life that was ours!
    —*William H. Dennis, Sr.*

The Guest Of Honor Is Omitted

A birthday party was planned ahead,
but the guest of honor, they forgot to invite.
In all of their work and plans there was an oversight.
The party fun, gifts and food was so intense
that no one seemed to notice his absence.

There was a time so long ago
when two forces met on quaking ground.
There was dealt a mighty blow
and it was determined then that Satan would be bound;
thought the climax of history was yet to be.

The Devil still is given his due
but, Christ today is taboo.
Strange, wouldn't you say
as to which one is given preference?
Can it be, that Christ makes a difference?
    —*Violet D. Lange*

Imaginary Friend

I would like to introduce you to Nancy,
But the truth of the matter is,
She dwells in the long ago, golden past,
Where a child's imagination lives.

A spirit child with flaxen curls,
Hazel eyes and sun-kissed skin.
Not a mirror-image of me, by far.
I still see her as clearly as then.

She came in silence, crouching beside me
Beneath the spread of the maple tree.
A small girl, in an old, brown print dress,
Bare-legged and barefooted, like me.

It seems it was always warm fall days,
When Nancy was visible only to me.
Television and Disney movies were not invented.
—I don't know how she came to be.

Sometimes in children's laughter,
Her image returns to my mind.
As we braced small bodies against the wind,
Our spirits forever entwined.

—*Rose Anne Phillips*

The Gift Of True Love

Love has a way with being unjust
but then of course it's always a must
Love can cause suffering and pain
then the tears will fall like rain
It makes us hurt, it makes us cry
but it can be special if we try
It can bring us happiness too
Just by certain things that we do
The romantic words that we say
The cards and flowers we send each day
These things can make the tears end
They can help a broken heart to mend
But going to a place or store
and buying cards, flowers and more
or wishing on a star from above
is not the way to find true love
Reach in your heart and find what's true
find those special words and say "I love you"

—*Lindsay Decker*

I Sing A Sad Song

We have grown up together from youth,
But through the years have grown apart and aloof,
I have many times treated you wrong,
and for that I sing a sad song!

I kind of miss what we never had,
hoping to remember the good times and not the bad.
There were so many things I wanted to say,
But foolish pride got in the way.

Please forgive the anger I showed,
It was only a cover for the love I hold.
I'm not perfect, and never profess to be,
and for all we went through,
I'm glad you know me!

—*Stephen E. Spencer*

There Are No Words

There are no words to mend you heart
but to share your time of grief
and pray that God's loving care
will alleviate the strain.
There are no magic remedies
to help your spirit soar
away from life's tragedies,
sorrows and restrains.
There are no songs to pacify
a heart whose joy has ceased,
nor words to efface the emptiness
a tortured heart retains.
There are no words to comfort you,
for time will show the way
and as the seasons march on by
your heart will nurse itself;
fond memories will resurrect
without a trace of pain;
once again, your heart will sing
'cause God has cleared the rain.

—*Maria L. Canales*

Two Golden Rules

The game of life has many rules,
  But two stand out among them all;
These rules we must observe each day,
  If we must live harmoniously.

If we must do just what is right,
  And ask God for His guiding light,
We will be at peace with all we deal,
  And steer clear of the gates of hell.

This is what Jesus taught of old:
  "Do unto others as you would
Have others do to you each day."
  This means peace and security.

Let us tread our paths carefully on,
  With no fear of the worst to come;
With our great faith in the divine,
  God will provide in rain or shine.

Another rule we learned by heart,
  Will help us clear our daily paths;
"To err is human, to forgive — divine,
  Let love and peace reign over mankind."

—*Marciana A. Sevandal*

Chuzpah

Uncompromising suddenness of smile
breaks through the whispered sadness of your face.
The sun of gladness shines a little while,
then back to your extraordinary grace.

A thousand volumes I shall never know:
what came to you and to what had you come?
The want you suffered, good you helped to grow,
to virtue ever wise, to evil dumb.

You say it would not really help to tell
the reasons why you toss on darkened bed,
just let me wonder, worry just what hell
you have endured to choose the fifth, instead.

You hide your care, assuring all is fine.
make me aware I can't present you mine.

—*Mary Gribble*

Dear One

The Lord, our God, only true comfort gives...
Can fill a void and aching emptiness,
Be a companion through each day one lives
Like that love one the living sorely miss.
He hears the agonizing prayer of grief,
Waits to enfold that one in arms of love,
Console the grieving soul and give relief
And heal that heart with blessings from above.
So do not drown your soul in dark despair,
But yield your life unto His perfect will
And know that you are ever in His care
And that your life with purpose He will fill,
Raise thoughts from deadness unto life again...
If only you invite Him to come in.
—*Mary Jean Lane*

Hang On

The stray dog just keeps on running and whining:
Can someone know what is in its heart?

Days are nice and warm but nights are long and cold,
They that sleep in streets dream of snowflakes.

With quaking heart she opens the crisp envelope,
Out comes a pink slip that nips a dream.

The widow weeps as she reads a mournful dirge,
Her husband is dead; seems the end of her world.

Hang on homeless and broken ones, be brave and faithful,
God will never forsake you, God will make you whole.
—*Ursula De Peralta*

Just One Brother

A single soul upon this earth
Can stand side by side with another,
Take care not to suffocate or smother
Common regard, even spread some mirth
Upon the breadth and girth
Of the globe and try to cover
It with love, also, for his brother,
Thus endowing it with rebirth.
Oh! but how loudly we could shout
And proclaim the world at peace at last
If indeed all this could come about—
Spreading Good Will to the peoples vast.
Yes, only one person could pack great clout
If he could but free himself from his past.
—*Willye Hatch*

Help Save The U.S.A.

Fight illegal drugs in Amerryka
cannot let me be,
we just don't have no use for them
is our society.

Beat me up Amerrykans
destroy them by the pound,
knock me out from our lives
we don't need them around.

Fight illegal drugs in Amerryka
make them go away,
lets have some pride about ourselves
help save the U.S.A...
—*Kunta Kinte*

Believe In The Magic

Oh Listen To The Magic.
Can you hear it? Can you hear it?
It is the sound of silence, broken only
by a gentle breeze, rustling the leaves
on the trees.

Oh Look At The Magic.
Can you see it? Can you see it?
It hangs silently in the heavens and
shines a golden glow on to our love.

Oh Taste The Magic.
Can you taste it? Can you taste it?
It can fill your heart full of powerful
raging emotions.

The Magic,
Is the silence of a country night, sipping wine,
while standing on top of our mountain under the
twinkling starlight above.

The Magic Is You.
You enhance the beauty of it all.
—*Patrick B. Sheahan*

The Old Lady Speaks

She walked awkwardly down the street
Cane followed by left foot than right foot
Her back was bent, her face showed the wrinkles of age
Her hair was a silver gray
She halted her walk upon hearing the mocking voices of young men.
she slowly turned and jestered toward them.
A smile slowly formed on her face.
"Sons," she said, "You mock this stumblin' ole woman, eh?"
"Well I'll tell you. I've seen many a man
young and old laid out fine in his coffin.
Will you mock me then when I see you laid out in yours?"
The young men walked away in silence.
The old lady continued her journey, her eyes filled with tears.
—*Steven G. Alston*

They Want My Sanity

Can't let this crush me as I strive to live;
Can't take the stifling stress and strain they give.
Can't let them drive me absolutely crazy;
Can't let them take my sanity.
I do not know why they are hell-bent on snatching it.
Trouble lurks and breeds where they are hatching it.
They send a steady stream of strife, I won't be catching it.
Fighting fire with fire, you know that I'll be matching it.
I do not understand it,
This is not the way I planned it,
I hadn't planned to struggle relentlessly,
All-out and tooth and nail, nightly and daily,
Merely to hold on to my sanity.
They do not care, they must not know;
They must not have any sanity left to show,
And thus, they see me as their foe,
And wish for me to know the chaos,
The madness that they know,
And now, I know why they want my sanity.
—*Marcus S. Canada*

Rumors Of Angels

Rumors of angels all around,
   Captains of hosts with their armies abound.
Warriors and messengers sent by God;
   Commanded by saints,
These ambassadors of peace need not praise
   ...but prayers for strength.

Wearing only the armor of faith to
   defend the truth,
On golden wings they carry the good news.
Compassion is their password,
   Love is their goal —
Bringing the message of hope to the
   neediest soul.

Guardians of the vincible—champions of peace,
   Their loving vigilance shall never cease.
They battle the demons of darkness
   to the death;
Until armageddon there can be no rest.

Angels are not fiction nor fantasy,
They are as real as you and me!

   —*Sally Sterling-Heyns*

Untitled

A bead of sweat forms on my forehead which was
caressed, just hours ago, by the lips of my lover.

It rolls gently down my cheek, which was touched, just hours
ago, by the hands of my lover.

It slides down my neck, slowing, stopping, tickling my neck
as did, just hours ago, the breath of my lover.

It finds another droplet and joins with it, two becoming one,
as just hours ago, did the souls of me and my lover.

It speeds down my chest, splashing over my nipple, as did,
just hours ago, the tongue of my lover.

It falls over the ridge of my breast, following to the center
of my stomach, as, just hours before, did the eyes of my lover.

It slips past my navel, flowing through the light hair on my
stomach, where just hours before, did the trembling fingertips
of my lover.

This ball of sweat glides past my sex, to my inner thigh, which
was, just hours ago fondled in the hands of my lover.

It rolls down to my knee, tickling more, and drips down my
calf, flows past my ankle, and leaves me forever, as did,
just hours ago, my lover.

   —*Scott W. Mobus*

Silver Wings

High in the heavens, the surging wind
Caresses silver wings that lie within
Courageous souls who dare defy
And ensue the mysteries of the sky.
Where sunbeams weave their golden shrouds,
Embossed in lofty solitude—
Soaring through the misty clouds
And corridors of endless dreams,
Silver wings reach to embrace
Bright fiery comets ember streams—
Mercury, Saturn, Venus, Mars,
The moon and galaxies of stars,
Among countless wonders that transcend
To lure the odysseys of men.

   —*Mamie Lou Killin*

My Dad, The Firefighter

"My dad, so courageous, and brave,
Caring, and risking his life, for another life, to save,"
"The sound of the alarm, he acts swift, and fast,
Knowing in his heart, this call, could be his last."
Rushing into the fire truck, driving fast, away he goes,
Until he reaches, the fire,
Will be survive? "God," only knows."
"The weather is frigid, way below zero, at that,
   As "Dad," fights the fire,
Melting the icides, on his fire hat.
"High up on the ladder, he tightly holds the hose,
Letting go the speeding water, and the fire,
   out it goes."
"Arriving back to the fire house, saved
   from harm,
"Dad", is ready for another loud alarm,
"He's one of the "heroes," who made this
   world brighter,
"My "Dad", "The Fire Fighter."

   —*Mary Agnes Lynch*

The Pond

The cool, blue water of the pond lays amid a verdant field.
Cattails occupy the quarter portion of the pond's north shore.
They wave rhythmically according to the beat orchestrated by
   the wind.
Looking through their nodding heads, rainbow splashes of
   wildflowers are seen.
Jousting minnows and whirligig beetles make ripples at the
   cattails' feet.
Sun perch swim in the cooler depths in search of their daily repast.
A perch splashes sunshine as it leaps from the mirrored surface.
Pairs of blue-helmeted dragonflies hover above to investigate
   the commotion.
Squadrons of fliers land at the water's softly sloping shore.
Swallows and wasps vie for mud amongst the grass' green shoots.
Their frenzied activities occur beneath the broad wings of a
   soaring hawk.
The fixed gaze of the hawk is upon a rabbit finishing his drink
   at the pond.
The rabbit beats a hasty retreat to his warren as a shadow
   passes harmlessly by.
In a flurry of rapid wing beats, quail fly fast and low over the pond.
As this sudden flourish of activity winds its way down,
The raspy call of a red-winged blackbird falls upon the pond...
   now becalmed.

   —*Wesley Robertson*

Gossips Defeat

To be an object of concern,
Certain people never learn,
The meaning of a silent tongue,
Pleasant words, not poking fun!

Silence is golden, pass the word!
Scandal and gripes should not be heard,
It is better to not talk at all,
Than to make someone feel very small.

Lift people up, don't put them down,
Smile sometimes, don't always frown,
Be kind and wise, try for peace,
Pray for people you like least!

We can't see our own faults like others do,
Be kind, do unto others as you want done unto you!
Sometimes we offend people close to us,
Do a little better without much fuss!

   —*Mary Ellen Finn*

He Is Coming-Again

The decree went out all through the land-no one was exempt from
Caesar's command. The rich, the poor, the weak and the lame,
to the town of Bethlehem they came. Mary on a donkey and
Joseph by her side—looking for a place where they could abide.
The road had been long and not so smooth-beneath her breast the
baby moved. Mary needed a place where she could rest she
didn't care if it wasn't the best. The inn-keeper stood and
shook his head, "what more can I say-I have no bed!" Joseph
was worried, "we need a room, Mary, my wife, will be delivering
soon!" "I have a stable; its dark but warm, there your baby
can be born." The stars were shining so very bright as
shepherds were tending their sheep that night. The gates of
heaven opened wide-angels were singing as they filled the sky.
"Peace be to you for we have good news-a baby's been born He is
King of the Jews!" The shepherds were stunned and fell to
their knees, "In a stable—do not delay there you will find Him
on a bed of hay." Though this story is often told and it
happened so long ago. Listen to the message that it brings-the
heaven's will open and the earth will ring as angels herald our
coming King. The saints will be gathered from over the earth-
for they believed in the Saviour's birth. The Master is
calling and heaven we're; bound, will you be ready at that
trumpet sound?
—*Sandra M. White*

In Ebony And Light

In ebony and light,
Change is a song,
   sung by Time's ongoing plight,
while Seasons unravels glorious colors,
in the timeless birth of each new moon.
Life, is but a tick of the clock,
But Life's loves
   are eternally held in the arms of a heart.
In ebony and light,
I'll hold you through dreariness and night,
through growing shadows of Time.
Seconds will be held, tightly bound,
by threads of feeling
   and Belamy, Virtue's well-being, will abound.
I'll call you to my heart, eternally held,
through Change's life,
   Time will move on,
past the stilled movement of Life's loves,
eternally held,
   In ebony and light.
—*Melody Lynn Allen*

Charlie

Charlie was a man who was fun to be around,
Charlie would always make you laugh instead of frown,
If you had a problem, Charlie was always there,
But deep inside he had no burdens he wished to share.
Charlie needed someone; to whom he could talk,
He needed to get out and think on a walk;
Nobody knows why he took his own life;
He had unknown depression, burden and strife,
Nobody will ever know what he thought that night...
We will never understand; unless we look through his sight
Charlie may not of been perfect or led a good life
May be through this tragedy, we'll all see the light
From Valentine's Day '91 he'll forever rest in peace.
Charlie, I love you, this is coming from your niece.
—*Sarah Rodocker*

Pieces

Pieces of silver, pieces of eight.
Circles of love, surrounded by hate.

Outbursts of anger, traces of tears;
Moments of joy, fragments of fears,

The touch of a hand quiets the heart.
Yet shattered dreams keep them apart.

Pieces of souls, unknown be their fate.
Pieces of people—people who wait.
—*Nadia Giordana*

Soul Sunset

Golden lights blazing,
Circling cumulus cushions.
Rays radiating, reaching toward
   The earth,
Shooting, slanting in a downward direction.
Mounds of mountains
Blending with azureness,
Lending a backdrop to the performance.
Sparkling shimmers changing with time.
Movement.
—*Kathleen Marie Brown*

Gripped

Death's cold fingers
clasped my hand,
in her vice-like grip
she leads me on my journey.

Every flower of joy
has become a thorn of pain,
to be discarded at life's end.

Every moment past
is reviewed over and over and over,
for a symbol of meaning,
a reason...a why????????

Every moment born
is a reminder of the fear,
that hugs the depths—
the pool of my being.

Tomorrows, todays, and yesterdays
loose their meanings as distinct.
They are all one in preparation.
They are all the means of the journey.

And.....
When death's cold fingers
become the warmth
of embrace...
the journey is ended.
—*Paulette Robinson*

Your Best Friend Can Be Your Worst Enemy

You'll be there for them
But when you need them their gone
You'll talk them through their problems
But when you need them their gone
You tell them a secret
But they tell the world
You are your only "Best Friend"
—*Tesha M. Maden*

Warm Hands

Glimmer of a candle light flickers on the trees, mystical cloaked figure stands in the breeze. He comes from a secret place far away hidden without a trace. Quietly, softly he steps out of the past with an amber gaze his sweet spell he cast. He comes in pitch of night when fragrant airs float lazily in flight. White skin caressed by raven locks, time stands still on a handless clock. Serpent mist wanders through the trees, mist of dreams float on the breeze. High abode a castle sits draped in clouds dark as pitch. The nightingale sings out his sweet song to the moon bathed shadows, by morn he will be gone. The fish in their channels dwell, mist of rain falls on my cheek so pale. The rose scent airs sweep across my face and glideth with the wind with scarce a trace. He takes my lace cloaked hand to his lips with kisses that rain down my finger-tips. His eyes filled with a glimmer of dancing light, nor tis the sun as bright. With his mirth crackled lips, softly and sweet he looked at me and said, "my lady faire," and gently touched my rose blushed cheek. Here like darkness he stands this dark figure with warm hands.

—*Mechel Cisco*

Of A Cold Winter's Night

Out into the winter's
  cold, clear night-
With pail in hand
  by lantern light,
Grampa and I crunch through the snow
  to the barn to milk "Sally"
In her stanchion, alone.

The barn smells sweetly
  of new mown hay,
And crickets chirp softly
  in corners - away.

Slowly the cow turns
  her broad, dark face
And lows a welcome from her secret place.

Puffing, vaporous, warm, moist breaths,
  she stands quietly by,
And lets grampa go on milking
  until her udder is dry.

What a patient, lovely cow!
I think - how right
All things are, - Now.

—*Lucille Banford*

God Is My Lover

The eyes of my darling are upon me
and with love for me how they shine.
The eyes of my darling are upon me
and I know HIS love will always be mine.

GOD is my lover and I'll say being loved
by HIM is divine...when HE caresses me
with HIS HOLY SPIRIT I feel chills
touching my spine, and I am then Oh so happy!
No other lover could make me feel so fine.

Oh! Its wonderful to be in love with Jesus
In remembrance of HIM I take wine, and the
breaking of bread represents the eating of his body divine.

The small amount of wine I take...represents
HIS shed blood on the cross and those who live
up to HIS word their end will never become a
loss. Other lovers have disappointed me greatly
but GOD makes me feel like a loved queen...
therefore I'll be thankful forever for HIS blessings
upon me says Lorene.

—*Lorene Dunaway Thrower*

Color Me Equal

Color me white or color me black —
color me yellow or brown,
whatever color you choose for me,
remember beneath the skin you see,
no matter what shade that I'm to be,
the sweat comes out of my pores,
and my blood runs as red as yours.

Color me Christian or color me Jew,
color me Moslem or heathen,
but remember, I was put on earth,
the same as you, by means of birth,
how I choose to pray doesn't change my worth,
for this one thing is true
I die just as dead as you.

Color me homeless or color me gay,
or colored with an awful affliction,
but remember when you're judging me,
here but for the Grace of God you'd be,
so show compassion for what you see,
all I ask is my due,
for I feel pain just as you.

Color me different with a ring in my ear,
color hair that's done a strange way.
In the ghettos of life I don't stand alone,
and flowers do bloom in poverty grown —
and the choices I had were not always my own,
still I know when life's cycle is through,
you can color me equal to you.

—*Stanley R. Lefcourt*

1492

In fourteen hundred and ninety two
Columbus sailed the Ocean Blue,
In the Nina, Prita, Santa Maria
and the Santa Clara, too.
Why haven't you heard of this ship and its crew?
It's 'cuz it sailed off the edge of the ocean blue!

—*Stanley Livingston Schirmacher*

Sun Obscured

Through darkening clouds upon the sea,
Columns of rays descend.
They ride the waves and on them go
Ascending to heights again.

All else is somber,
Clouds wrapped in gray.
Only the path where the radiance plays.
Shimmering, glimmering, dazzling sheen,
A path which might truly delight Ondine
To tread it with spritely, fairy steps;
And there amongst radiant columns find rest.
Only to vanish and no more be seen,
When cloud patterns shift,
Awakening our dream.

—*Louise M. Finau*

A Word From Our Sponsor

T.V. dramas by the score,
  comedies, heartaches, reality and more.
Laughter echoes ever on,
  changing channels, national anthem is gone.
Award shows never seem to cease,
  someone always honored, with "the envelope, please."

Soap operas from noon till four,
  glamorous clothes, and secrets galore!
Doctors, and lawyers on every scene,
  displaced families and runaway teens.

Beauty pageants, such as Miss U.S.A.,
  music awards all have something to say.
Famous hair-dos all the styles which change,
  it makes more money, if bizarre and strange!
Advertisers tempting our every taste,
  dextrose, triglycerides are our own worst fate.
Additives, preservatives, artificial too,
  remedies passed down, through commercials we knew.

Television continually screaming singing out—
  and is this really what we're all about?
    —Stephanie D. Berry

Through All

Through all the pain that comes with life
Comes the sorrow and the strife.
Through all the wounds that will ever have bled
Comes the tears that will ever be shed.
Through all the poverty and the riches
Comes the vultures, the sons-of-bitches.
Through all the days and the years
Comes the doubts and the fears.
Through all the doors opened or closed
Comes the nakedness exposed.
Through all the times your need is none
Comes the time your need of one.
Through all the times I will understand.
Through all the times I will be your friend.
    —Lynne Montz

A Revelation

Life may be hard rough, and cruel, to one, and all, but why
complain, or curse the day, since all men born, are born not as
a king, or to rule as one, on a golden throne, and even though
you with your smile, and age, expect to live as one, and have
it made, yet you live on all the same, happy, or not, as you
are from day, to day, without a king's crown to own, or wear,
upon your head, from year, to year, but that you might bless,
and be blessed, this very day, and live your life, without a
worry's say.
    —Samuel Cohen

Fog

Fog is a veil on a bride
Concealing the city and all its buildings
Allowing the hazy lights to glow through
Its transparent flimsy material.
The headlights are eyes shining through the mist
Gazing in expectation.
Fog is a hint of things to come.
When the veil lifts
The city dances in excitement.
    —Renelle Perez

A Map Of Elimination

The areas that look as if no one reside
Consist of beings whom have become demoralized
It is sad to see them for they do not realize
That accepting a poisonous substance will subsequently become
  idolized
The attraction is fatal but still they continue to patronize
 Driving expensive cars and wearing gold jewelry just to be
  recognized
Dependency and violent behavior sometimes result in suicide
  and homicide
This poisonous substance is equivalent to genocide
    —Mary Woods

He Choose To Go!

There was a rage going on inside of his mind, for some reason he
  could not control.
It hammered his heart and beat his body and soul!
He knew he was young, but he wanted no part, of the pressures
  weighing him down.
Of a world that just was not for him, going constantly, around and
  around!
A strong young man, don't ever call him weak, for weak he never
  could be!
It takes courage to take one's own life but for him it had to be! He
  loved his family, specially his mother and dad.
He had a chosen family from God, the best he could of ever had!
He belonged to God, Just lent to them, for such a few short years. He's
  in heaven, there left in hell, drowning in a million tears.
It's the ones left behind, with missing piece, of a puzzle made in hell.
They go ever every moment, they remember them so well.
It is a piano, that keeps piercing, at there hearts, until there is no
  beat!
The wailing of why this could be, is a constant cry or weep!
Who are we to condemn the not chosen ones? The ones who chose to
  go!
For to get to god this young man thought, the going was to slow
He sacrificed his life on earth, to go to his eternal home above.
Never doubt for a moment, it wasn't hate, it was an unconditional
  love!
For everything within this universe, is a reason we can not see!
Just trust in God! Please understand, some things just have to be!
    —Mary Wyant Zebik

Perseid Storm

Your moment long past spent they now regard
Cremains, from an arc ablaze; the northeast skies
A dim stadium, present so haggard
A star the crowd decries your pale demise.

Players take final bows to moans not cheers
An audience numb, naught but booms and blasts
Titillate ears; your innumerable years
Reflecting and glowing, now deemed miscast.

Eons of distance, time warps perception,
And the hubris of their temporal strife,
Gives folly to your stellar eruption
Erenow lighted the way to afterlife.
    History lost, statistics past replay,
      Yauld corpses they, are doomed to duller clay.
    —Patricia A. Craven

Homeland

Who but God, but God alone
  could provide that special throne
    cradled in our mother's womb, no sins to atone.
A haven, a homeland of our own.

We are released the cord is broken
  received by gentle hands, a loving token.
Born into that cozy family place
So full, so very full of God's special grace...

My homeland, a country steeped in memories so great
The heather, the bracken, the moors the open gate...
The sight of wild primrose, bluebells daffodils
still dampens the eyes
A loving family sharing those special joys.

A homeland can last for some for all of life's span
For others, there will be so many moves to meet
God's special plan.
Whichever the case, memories will be so paramount
Fellowship, love, patience, sadness, put only
receiving Christ will count.

Our final home beyond the very needs of life
A homeland where there will be no strife.
God for us in Jesus Christ alone—
God with us the Holy Spirit, all our sins to atone.
    —*Lawrence Hutchinson*

Chromatics Of Autumn

Odd colors, splashed by an autumn sun,
Craft a wild, whimsical-colored world
Where green trees and grasses are one,
A neutral beige; with black shadows hurled
To unexpected places as the day goes by.
The chartreuse leaves of September
Silhouetted against the brilliant blue
Of an approaching October's sky
Cause one to sigh, and remember
Other autumns when there was You
And one had not yet asked, WHY?
    —*Ruby Nifong Tesh*

Sun Set

Your simple touch can burn my heart,
create flames to sooth my soul.
I just close my eyes, feel you body melt in mine. Hold you
tighter until were one.
Feeling you move inside of me,
my eyes see the mountains move.
I hear the oceans roar and feel the rivers flow gently to me
as the sun sets calmly in the sea.....
Creating a sight for two lovers to see.
Sempre mi cuore
Sempre mi Amore
    —*Therese Garrison*

Never Truly Gone

Gone from the world,
But locked in the memories,
Never forgotten by those who knew you,
Remembered forever and ever.
Through the good times and the bad,
You helped them through it,
And gave them courage,
So forever you'll be with them,
Never truly gone!
    —*Lynn Eisenhauer*

Whip-poor-will on my Chimney Top

The whip-poor-will on my chimney top
Cries and cries and will not stop.
Beyond the cabin are a thousand trees;
He could have perched in one of these.
Or on the clearing's house-size stone
And left my chimney top alone.
While the moon makes patterns across my bed,
His carrion cries ring overhead.
I hear the sound within his throat
That gives his voice a rasping note.
The whip-poor-will, my favorite bird,
I love the best when faintly heard.
Say, in the top of a tall beech tree,
Deep in the wood, some miles from me!
    —*Violet Hiles Ringer*

A Fight For Life

A small part of a mother's womb
cries out "let me live!"
You're fighting for the rights to kill,
a creation only God can give.
They know nothing of the world around,
But wait anxiously to see.
Just think of the many things
that child could grow up to be.
That's your baby, he has your face.
You could help save his part of the human race.
Before you decide to do this,
just think - he has your eyes.
After it's all over,
you'll hear the endless cries.
Believe me, you'll regret it,
this is not the thing to do
After all - how would you feel
if that baby wanted to kill you.
    —*Patrice Francis*

Unsung

The world is red -
Crimson contaminates from over the horizon
A night filled with hidden desires and veiled
Whispers seeping into the heavy air - languid
And dead. The stars turn into piercing eyes,
Laughing at everything I cannot hear.
Murmurs, the night is full of murmurs -
Discourses on the existence of man and wild,
Tempestuous verse, an explosion of speech.
All this is wasted upon me.
I am deaf to everything
That I cannot believe; a sadness
Slowly wells up inside me - to hear
Words never said.
I would trade my life, my soul, to forever live
In this sea for miserable blackness,
Colored only by beautiful words that appeared
In dreams and visions and
Inspirations, but that somehow people just
Couldn't seem to say.
    —*Sonesh Charnani*

Mom

For the iodine and bandages,
crooked bangs and pin-curled hair.
The cocoa on cold winter nights.
And tucking me in bed.
For the stories you read,
And the secrets you kept.
For the lessons you gave,
And times you didn't say "I told you so."
For the tears you kissed away,
And the smiles you gave.
Of the courage you showed,
And your unselfish deeds.
For your comfort in sad times,
And sharing with me in joy.
To just listening to me
And always being there for me

"I Love You, Mom"
—*Susan M. Dorie DuBeau*

Leftover Children

Who will love the children leftover from marriages
crumbed like brittle tumbleweed under the pressure
to excel in a world of throw away emotions?
Mommy's portfolio vies for space beside
Daddy's briefcase in the corporate office.
The heart beats cold in homes left abandoned
to the race for personal achievement.
What has become of the center of family values?
The board room table has replace the kitchen table
of gentle resolution.
Who will love the leftover children flown free form
as clay spun hob style on a potter's wheel?
Gone is the cohesive compromise that aligns
parenthood on equal par with the yuppie idealism
of the cutting edge.
Civil in separation; equal in divorce.
No justice for the leftover Children.
—*Virginia Thomas Wells*

Wonders Of Creation

Listen to the newborn baby's loud, first
cry, behold the colorful butter fly,
as it goes passing by,
Smell the delicate flowers of the magnolia
tree, taste the sweet honey from the busy bee,
See the fierce hawk, when it soars toward
the sky, look at the little bird trying to learn to fly,
Gaze at the lush, green valleys far below,
Peer at mountain peaks, sometimes covered
with pristine snow,
Watch the changing of raindrops, as they
began to freeze, feel the chill of a
cold winter's breeze,
stare at giant bridges that stretches
for miles and miles, glance at the happiness
of a child, as they began to smile,
Amazed at how ships can cross the vast
seas, wondering at planes flying, so high
that land with such ease.
—*Sarah E. Phillips*

Jared's Message

Damned train! Parked in the dark on an unlit track.
Damned alcohol! And the news; my son's not coming back.
Oh that dreadful night, what did it have to be?
No flashing signal for my son to see.
Volleyball on the beach, a cooler full of beer.
Commercials of enticement to the eye and to the ear.
Brainwashed, young and old; they all drink in the lie;
Trapped by the propaganda of the alcohol they buy.
But Jared's death has something clear to say to you;
All those promises of alcohol, simply are not true.
When He faced the terror of that crash,
And the awful fury of the fires;
He knew the glamour of alcohol
Was promoted by a pack of liars!
But you didn't get the message of the awful death he died.
You think you did him honor 'cause you came to the funeral and cried.
But in his memory, resist the pressure of your peers;
Who say there's no harm in a couple of beers.
You can mess up your life or lose it, going for the brew!
It happens. It happened to him! And it can happen to you.
—*Nancy Hayes Clark*

Lucienne My Wife, The Face Of France

Now at thy dying I in a clasp of death
Dance the dance or death
   Yet feel the warmth of thy loving hands
Thy kisses soothing like the wind
   Over the lonely meadows
And like the rustle amongst the majestic trees
   We run like children in Paradise
Then with joy and pride I kiss thy sacred brow
   As tears upon my cheeks so freely flow
Ever joyful within thy caring arms
   As with awe to the Heaven above
We embrace in never ending love
   Oh my love see the falling petals
Now bloom by thy side
   As in sleeps deepest dreams
I dance and sing as for thy love I yearn
   For when time apart
In agony my heart would tear
   As I cried forth for our love
To journey into eternity!
—*Serge York*

Spring Presage

The daffodils are up; I saw them
   Dancing in the brumal breeze,
Courageous harbingers to bloom
   While Winter yet may ice the trees.
But Spring approaches, verdant warmth
   Advancing on these Southern hills.
Winter may blast away; Spring's coming soon -
   Thus say the daffodils.

If with the healing balm of time
   The warmth of Spring brings Winter's end,
Perhaps a frozen heart may thaw
   Within the embrace of a friend.
And I, who long ago had ceased
   To dream of nights sublime may find
The courage to escape these bonds
   Of doubt and, maybe, love … in time.

Spring comes, and yet again my heart may dance —
   Thus say the daffodils.
—*Kathryn E. Darden*

Sorrow And The Angel

I saw an angel once...
dancing on a cloud as it rained.
So I spoke to her without speaking;

"If I am sorrow,
how can I touch a soul...
or ride on the wind...
or change like the colours of the sea?"

And the Angel said,
"Sorrow always has purpose...
for nothing lost means nothing gained;

A passionate heart plays magic on the soul...
so dreams can catch the wind...
and time changes spirit,
as a rainbow changes the seas colours."

Then the rain stopped...
and the Angel wrapped me in her wings,
and I was warm.
—*Laura D. Vannatter*

Loneliness

I stand on the bridge of life
Dark waters are cold below me
Standing alone in the grey mist
I think of suicide and the pain of loneliness
I ask if I'll always be this lonely
But no answer is there
The waves are still
And fog moves silently away
Not a sound is heard
No answer comes, just loneliness
—*Linda K. Humphries*

Jesus In Reeboks

I put on my Reeboks to go for my evening run
Darkness was gently laying her blanket over the sun.

I came to a hillside and a cry shattered the peaceful air
A man sitting on a rock and of me He was unaware.

I ran to Him as I thought surely someone very close had died.
Or perhaps someone beloved had told a grievous and hideous lie.

"Excuse me," I said "can I be of any help"
He looked up, I recognized His face, numb is how I felt.

I fell to my knees, my eyes cast upon His feet
There were angry wounds from sorrow so deep.

I took my water bottle and shirt and tired to clean away the pain
Poor, Jesus, once again He was here, once again we caused shame.

"There is no truth left, the ability to lie is as if divine power
Now all that I have taught, all I have preached has gone sour."

His wounds now clean I took of my Reeboks and socks
I put them on Him to cushion the wounded feet from the rocks

"Jesus," I said, "maybe you can walk now without as much pain.
He stood, took a small step and a smile from deep within Him came

He jumped a little jump and then He laughed and took my hand
And I would go with Him to find purity of truth somewhere in
  the land.
—*Peggy B. Browning*

Whimsical Season

Moon glow o'er the landscape spreads.
Dawn still sleeps in her misty bed.
Whimsical season ever changing,
Mother Nature's rearranging.
Tis Indian summer.
Dew drops quickly shrink and fade,
as dawn awakes with molten blaze.
No cloud atop the mountain floats,
it wears old snow like a tattered coat.
Tis Indian summer.
Trees of flame display their beauteous hues,
against a sky of topaz blue.
Curly leaves all dried and brown,
crunch under foot upon the ground.
Tis Indian summer.
Sunny rays have dipped away
and shadows shade the light of day.
Now there's a leafy silhouette,
on the rosy glow that panes reflect.
Tis Indian summer.
—*Myrna C. McFall*

Fall

Leaves turning golden, red, yellow, and brown.
Days growing shorter and nights longer.
The air grows cooler ...
Everything is getting ready for winter.
Squirrels are gathering and storing nuts for the winter.
Dogs, cats, and other animals are growing thicker coats
to keep them warm throughout the long, cold winter.
People are preparing for the coming of winter.
They're buying winter clothing and antifreeze for their
cars and trucks.
They're stocking up on firewood to keep their fireplaces
glowing warmly all winter long.
—*Marie Addington*

Como El Ave Fenix

Como el Ave Fenix me levanto
de las cenizas de un ayer sombrio
y al mundo elevo, en mi voz, un canto
en abierto y franco desafio.
Como el Ave Fenix me levanto
y acepto el reto impuesto por la vida
y he de luchar, luchar a cada instante
para cura mis alas rotas y elevarlas.
Como el Ave Fenis me levanto
para volar sobre la human a hipocresia
bus cando nuevos horizontes luminosos,
y restaurar mi corazon herido.
Como el Ave Fenis me levanto
haciendo una hoguera
de las cenizas que quedaron
para quemar en ella mis pesares.
Como el Ave Fenis me levanto
renaciendo cada dia y cada instante,
haciendo otra vez de las cenizas vida
y volviendo a nacer, otra vez YO.
—*Nora A. Vidal-Torres*

The Miracle Child

A child was born in Bethlehem, one cold
December night
   The stars shone down, the angels sang; it
must have been a glorious sight
   Three wise men came from far away, bringing
gifts, great tidings, and joy
   Not planes, not trains, not automobiles, or
any other toy

   Christmas is for giving; freely giving from
the heart
   Of reaching out and sharing our love; it's the
only way to start
   No toy could ever replace, the feeling that
comes from within
   When you hug and say 'I love you', to a
relative or a friend

   God gave us his son, His only begotten son, to
save us, one and all
   Could you have done this with your child? If,
on you, He decided to call
   Greater love hath 'no man', than God did
on this day
   Than to give to you, His 'Miracle Child.' He's
the truth, the life, the way.
   —Linda B. Wainwright

Childhood Preserved

There are some things you can't touch,
deep inside your ever existence.
Things that can't change, alter, or defer.
Things meant to be in memory, in thought.
Special places, a mind-set to never change,
no matter how often you return,
who you are with, or why you came.
Special scent, of time gone by, events had.
Scent of familiar, scent of life, scent of youth.
There's a feeling, over come by anxious flutters within.
Excitement, recall, warmth, comfortableness.
Fantasy appears with apparitions of exact moments,
exact words, expressions, I look down,
I am amongst the activity of yesterday.
The thoughts are sharp, of yesterday, pictures assist.
Like an early morning mist....the visions are fogged.
The clarity is lacking, but the lesson is learned,
the words are present, the souvenir is taken.
In A Childhood Preserved....
   —Karoline Keith

Bill

What is true love, and who should be the one to say?
Define best friend, spouse, lover, sweetheart or saint.
Who is there for me when everything is dark and I am lost?
Who will always hold my hand and dry my tears,
even when the times are years apart and people and things and
space have been between? I call in pain, and you are there.
And for the great things in my life for which I worked so hard,
who was the first to congratulate, praise, and celebrate? Even
the smallest, dullest, ordinary advance I make, you
give me credit and applause. I turn to you not just for your
support and praise. I turn to you because through all the ever
so many years I have known but one heart so steadfast and true.
   —Sali Ford Evans

On Great Lone Hills

On great lone hills, the barren, crusted earth
Denies the green which was its heritage,
Refutes the promise of the winter's end,
And closes out the coming of the spring.

On great lone hills of life, the frozen heart
Weeps for the dream which was its sustenance,
Cries to the wind against its bitter loss,
And wraps itself in silent suffering.

Yet from that silence, from that suffering,
Spring forth at last a hope. A blade of green
Finds strength to push its way through frozen earth,
To reach a searching tendril toward the sky,

And one heart dares again to look for life,
To bury broken dreams beneath the snow
And lift a trembling hand toward the light
With strength it found from walking great lone hills.
   —Ruby I. Denton

The Circle Of Life

The circle of life is when your spirit
Detached's from your body.
Then your spirit drifts far into time and space.
Only to return to another life time.
We are all in this time and space for a reason.
Sometimes we do not
Know this reason of life.
But when we know this reason of life.
The circle of life is complete,
Then and only then will our spirits
Go into infinity to join with the super universe.
   —Keith Scarpino

A Mother's Love

   A Mothers love is made of deep
devotion, sacrifice, and much pain,
   It is something that you
Really can't begin to explain.
   It is never ending, unselfish,
and loving come what may,
   And nothing can destroy it
or take her love away.
   It is sparkling and shining
like the brightest of stars,
   And you can feel it still with you
no matter where you are,
   I guess God opened up his ever
lasting hands, and made this kind of love
for us to never understand.
   —Latosha Scott

Bird Of Prey

In the pale azure,
Dark wings spread
Round and round.
The crisp air forewarn lean days ahead.
Cringing leaves on the tree tops
Reminiscence glorious summer past.
Round and round
Leisurely cruising
The hunt is on!
   —Tae W. Stout

A Handclasp

A name was spoken
Did she remember?
Yes, she did
It was Helen_____!

The hands were clasped
And suddenly
A weeping woman recalled the past,
And clung to the present without tears.

The future was no more
As she held fast
To strong hand
And she wept no more.

What is a handclasp?
It is strength
And power for tomorrow
Promise and hope.

She clung fast
And knew
It was Helen_____,
A neighbor and friend.
   —*Ruth F. Gilman*

Puppy Love

She was only ten years old when she
   discovered puppy love...
It was in the summertime when she
   was free as a dove.
She saw him on a bicycle, and you know
   how young girls are...
As she watched him ride on by, she
   thought he was a star.
He turned around and stopped his bike,
   and said "Hi" with a smile...
Then he sat down next to her and they
   talked for a while.
He said he's staying with his mom for
   only a month or so...
And I live with my dad, so soon I'll
   have to go.
As little walks and bike rides past, so
   did their numbered days...
They didn't really notice they were
   caught up in life's maze.
All too soon those numbered days caught
   up to the last...
With suitcases packed and good-bye's
   said, they can only dream about the past.
How can they call it just a puppy love...
   when my heart it hurts me so...
She knows it would happen to anyone
   when the one they love has to go.
   —*Stephen G. Claissie*

Work Of Love

There upon an auburn stallion he sits,
Erect, majestic and bold.
Gazing out over the land he tills,
Pride burns deep inside.

Life is his land,
The earth his soul,
The rich, dark earth his love.
Nowhere is there another life for him —
This place,
This land,
His home.
   —*Marilyn Mace*

Evil

Evil does not have to be death or crimes, it maybe
discrimination; which can rot the human mind.
It can look you in the face constantly without delight.
It will always make the human heart pound in fright.
It is like an eye staring and observing your every move.
The jealousy is overwhelming, as you live your life peacefully,
but with an exception, you will think "Why could something
act so disrespectfully?"

Evil uses prejudgments and ignorance whether or not you
should be accepted as a person of its kind.
Throws you, an individual, back in a box, laughing and
giggling, thinking "If only you would cry it could (evil)
win the fight, and you will be mine!"
You could be a person of color, grace, class, or intelligence,
but evil does not care and is not altruistic, for it continues
to stare in vain and disgrace.
Evil eventually makes you feel boxed in with bad omens cold,
an anathem as of unwant. Evil holds on with harsh chains.

Hopefully our society would just one day be carefree,
of such a sin and dishonesty.
   —*Montez Tiana Diamond*

Crossroads

Going on or jumping off?
Dismal shelter or unknown cost?
To seek a child who is not yet lost
He's the only one who knows.

Going on or jumping off?
The choice is simple and its hard.
To risk this world's uncertainties,
or plod dull safe trivialities,
either choice may spill the cards.

Going on or jumping off?
One stops to think and see.
What is it always that we search?
Is that the cause for all our births?
Why do we fool ourselves and flee?

Going on or jumping off?
The choice is clearer hence.
To live my life I've learned and grown,
To save my soul, sell what I own
To choose a way, stable my home,
The key is action, not suspense.
   —*Thomas A. Lucey*

Wade James

I don't want to say goodbye,
Even though you have to go.
My heart will surely die,
For your love is all I know.
And as my tears fall like the rain,
I'll stay close to all the memories.
The distance brings such pain,
But you must always remember me.
And when the sun will shine no longer,
And the sky seems an endless gray.
My love for you will only grown stronger,
Even though tomorrow's another day.
But when you're feeling lonely and blue,
Just close your eyes and think of me.
My thoughts will surely be of you,
Much more than just memories.
   —*MandieLee Manning*

Garden Bird

Dear friend,
  Do not cry in such a high place.
    My aged neck is no longer able to look up to see you,
      My garden is covered up with the grown up trees, I planted.
        It is our favorite paradise, so peaceful and tranquil.
          Come down here, close to me. The earth is
          wonderfully warm now.
            It is always receptive to all of us, living creatures.

      My friend,
        Do not hide in such a high place.
        It is so far-away for me to reach you.
          Come down here, to my flower bed. Talk to me for a while.
      I won't catch you. You are always free to fly away
    Into the heavenly lofty sky, into the unknown, perhaps you know,
  Your destination where I can not follow.

  O, my little friend,
 Sing the song once more for my destiny
Before you go for your world.
   —*Sachiko Asano*

Dear Howard:

Do you know how much I love you? Do you know how much I care?
Do you know that if you need me, say the word and I'll be there.
I love you for your courage to meet life's burdens day by day.
I love you for your compassion to help a friend along his way.
I know we both need someone when we are down and blue,
Someone that we can talk to and tell our troubles to.
I think we both know who He is, and we will both agree
He'll take the time to listen and be there for you and me.
I know that both of us can go when - ere we have a need,
To lay our burdens at his feet and let Jesus our case to plead.
But these young folks that now grow up, do they know that this is true?
Who will they depend upon, for courage and comfort too?
Who is going to teach them, if we don't do our part?
It starts with just a little seed planted deep within the heart.
First there is a seed of faith, then one each of charity and love.
The seed of responsibility and work, tis given from above.
The harvest is a testimony, they can now declare it's true.
They can now be busy planting seeds, it's something we all can do.
   —*Maxine Taylor Thomas*

Weeping Willow

Weeping willow
don't shed your tears
for the sun will come out tomorrow
Weeping willow
please, stop your crying
or the rain will disguise your sorrow
Won't you smile, for your not alone,
your branches represent my life
Can't you see, your strength
is there, just like our memories,
it is ours to keep
like the days that
surrounds us daily with it
whispers, its beauty and it's life.
For you and I are just the same,
Weeping, but living one day at a time.
"Weeping willow"
   —*Kira Melgar*

Untitled

Of yourself, be proud,
Don't always follow the crowd.

Who cares what others expect of you,
Do what you want to do.

Go where you want to go, see who you want to see.
Be the person you want to be.

Your dreams you should always pursue,
Follow them in what you say and do.

Live with just the simple things,
Like that which nature brings.

All the beauty of nature you should take notice to,
Soak in all its splendor like so few do.

Live the life that was given to you.
Accept the hardships and move on, like so few can do.

Learn to love the life you lead,
Don't look at it as some big chore or deed.

Love yourself for who you are,
And you will be able to go far.

Forget about material wealth
And you will be happier with yourself.

What is important is who you are inside,
Not what you have and what is on the outside.

What you think and what you feel,
Is what makes life real.
   —*Lisa Kingsbury*

Got To Have Heart

Got to have heart, keep an open mind,
Don't shut the door, true love is hard to find,
No mind if you're poor.
Never throw caution to the wind,
Never mind what others think,
Just keep an open mind.
Use your better judgement,
Love's what makes the world go 'round.
Got to have heart!

When it seems your world is tumbling.
And the world is down on you,
Shake it up, turn it around,
Throw your heart into what you are doing,
Make your dreams all come true.
Don't throw caution to the wind,
True love will come to you.

Remember what's important,
It's your world, use your better judgement,
Keep an open mind, it's all up to you.
You've got to have heart.
   —*Shirley Nielsen*

Abyss Of My Soul

Oh! Help me! Please help me: my soul it cries forth
Give me meaning for being alive. I'm old now disabled.
Sarcastic in view. This dilemma is as dark as the night.
All the lights I had found, have eventually all gone out:
They were weak and not stored with much truth. Yet
Somewhere in this abyss of my soul lies a key, that when
Found will unlock what I seek.
   —*Robert R. Weetman*

A Shack By The Tracks

A six room home along side the railroad tracks
Down feather quilts placed neatly against our backs
Grandma, Grandpa, Mom, Dad and eight children, in fact
Dad was a coal miner, Grandpa worked on the railroad
Mom and Grandma did all the home cooking in the abode.
The kitchen stove had an oven that warmed our toes
We even shared our food with the wandering hobos
The bedrooms were delicately heated by a coal Heatrola
Music ensued from the lovely mahogany Victrola
We played in the Lackawanna River, the thought makes me quiver
The wooden outhouse made the entire family shiver
Neighbors who shared, teachers who cared, therefore created a bond
Playmates galore frolicked in the natural swimming pond
An inviting ice skating pond was enjoyed in the winter
A homemade wooden merry-go-round gave us many a splinter
Grandpa made a grapevine gazebo with wooden benches underneath
The grapevine gazebo continued to keep us cool in the heat
Homegrown vegetables, fruits, ducks and chickens to raise
A despicable old rooster made us find many a maze
Was that really "A Shack By The Tracks?"
—*Pauline Tatiana Mizok Guman*

Sunrays On Your Pillow

The first-light sentries of each
down used to search for
grace, arraying rays of sunlight
in a halo 'round your pillow.

The halo formed, betokened feigned astonishment
to find the imprint of departed loveliness,
for the sentries never found you sleeping.
You had left your bed by dawn
to tend to family cares.

Now, after many years, you enjoy retirement
and the sentries light your pillow, finding beauty
where it should be found, enhancing the halo
of sunrays on your pillow.

Rest, and let the sunlight kiss your cheeks
on our behalf.
Let the sunrays speak our love
and gratitude.

But when the sun has left the sky,
its days work done,
your loveliness remains
for me alone!
—*Raymond F. Rogers*

My Sweetest Dreams

When I go to sleep at night, I often
dream of many things, sometimes, I
have good dreams, other times, I have bad
dreams, but the dream I dream most is my
dream of hope. Is to live in a world free from dope.
All of the bad diseases in the world will go away,
and be replaced with healthy happy and gay people.
My sweetest dream of hope, is a world of peace, no more
murders, no more hurting each other and no more hating other
races of people because of their skin color. But instead a
world of people who only love and help each others. Instead
of being afraid of each other. My sweetest dream is the dream
of all dreams that there will be no more homelessness. No more
poor people, but instead each and everyone of us will live in
big beautiful houses and all of God people will live just like
Cinderella we will all live happily ever after.
Thank you.
—*Ve'Lva Ma'ria Combs*

Long Live Kirsty Alley Forever

Long live Kirsty Alley forever, long live her hopes, long live her dreams, long live her future as actress, long live her love and trust to people inside and outside the motion picture and music industry. Long live her appearance on Saturday Night Live when she made all of us feel so much alive, long live her appearance on Cheers for all those wonderful and memorable years, when all of us watched the Cheers finale and broke down into tears. May the Lord bless her and keep you forever, I Paul Andrew Pease will worship you, and remember you forever. God Bless Kirsty Alley Forever, long live Kirsty Alley forever and always forever.
—*Paul Andrew Pease*

Memories Of Pearl

The silky slivers of priceless pearl
Drift slowly downward and so softly swirl
Each silky flake caresses my window sill
As memories of your smile my heart o'er fill
Memories like snowflakes drift o'er my soul
Memories of fun and laughter before love grew cold
I stagger and reel from memories that over power
My logic, my senses, and my will, hour after hour
The string of pearl like memories drift and fill
The empty hollows of my soul like my window sill
Cold days of winter soon follow warm days of spring
The emptiness follows after seeing you again
No place to run, no place to hide
Your memories are with me forever inside
I grasp for new meaning in life
But find little happiness, only emptiness and strife
This smile I show to all the world
Can only be touched by the string of pearl
—*Margaret Peel Burris*

One Alone

One tiny snowflake, so fragile and light,
Dropped slowly to earth from its lofty height.

One alone made no differences, it melted away.
Then as many more joined it, they determined to stay.

Each was so delicate and harmful to none,
But when they stuck together, their strength was begun.

Then they were in command of country and town,
As deep winter show covered the ground.

Soon they could stop the greatest of men,
By sticking together, any battle could win.

There is strength in number, now we all know.
Can we remember this lesson from new fallen snow?
—*Marjorie Allen*

Disillusioned Promise

The mist rolls in, but I still see your
Eyes, glowing in the night. They
speak to me, "Come closer, we shall make bright
what hides beneath."
I move, I reach, I grasp in search
but never finding you, my love.
From where you journey, that golden road
I never can stand, for when I
try, you are distant, worlds away
and I wake up, the
dream
disappears.
—*Tany Ling*

A Crystal Delight

One cold morning in early March there appeared a beautiful sight.
During the night the long winter had its last fling.
A view of sparkling beauty took over dear Mother Earth...
As all Nature was displayed in a magnificent rebirth.

The once barren countryside was now alive and gleaming,
Taking on a shimmering icy glitter of sheer wonder.
The dawning of the bright sun on this gorgeous day...
Created a spectacular scene of glistening colors in full array.

The lifeless trees were crackling in a gentle, peaceful breeze.
The small glassy bushes were also joining in their chorus.
The crystal branches caught the colorful sunbeams in their sway
As this wonderful landscape took over the sunny day.

The awesome radiance of this day was one to behold:
As the wonder of winter will soon be gone for another year.
But not before it went on for some days to come,
Making all God's creation as always...His job well done!
—*Lucille Flure*

Untitled

I thank God for the world
each and everyday.
Each day holds its surprises
each in its own special way.
Every part of this world is special
because God made it that way.
All the different colors
green, yellow, pink, white, and blue.
Green for every plant and tree
Yellow for the sun that fills our days
with light.
Pink for the sunset each day
Blue, for the never-ending, crystal blue sky
White for the fluffy, white clouds.
As you can see all the different colors
and parts of the world
Are important because;
God made it all in his
perfect, special way.
—*Tiffany DeArmond*

My Wish

I'm missing you more and more
Each day as tears flow from my eyes,
Wondering when are you going to return.
   So we can dance among the clouds,
Lie together on the sandy beach,
And I can have the love that I yearn.
   I wish for you to return.
I wish for your love and friendship
To be meant for one, to be meant for me.
   With no strings attached,
Like my broken guitar
Simply given away for free.
   A love that I could show my fears to,
And pick up in my arms and hold.
   A love that I could bend,
A love that I could mold.
   Mold into one that is so strong.
   A love that could never go wrong.
   I wish that with the love
You'd have for me, you'd never change your mind,
   And turn around searching for
Another love to find.
—*Shannon Le Barron*

Unity In Diversity

How beautiful are the eyes that see
   each other's heartfelt needs.
How wonderful are the ears that hear
   a broken spirit's pleas.

Refrain: All praise to you and honor, too
   for empathy and care.
As God's instrument, you have been sent
   in answer to our prayer.

Oh, how lovely are the feet that tread
   to those who hunger feel.
And blessed be hands giving bread
   touching, so as pain to heal.

How precious are the lips that speak
   words, of tenderness and peace.
And how heroic are the hearts which seek
   to befriend, that hate may cease.

Let us then, join hands and hearts in love
   and each other's burdens share;
So that in him we may all be one,
   dear Lord, grant us our prayer.
—*Sister Mary Marcy Baldys, CSSF*

Unity In Diversity

How beautiful are the eyes that see
   Each others' heartfelt needs.
How wonderful are the ears that hear
   A broken spirit's please.

All praise to you and honor, too
   For empathy and care.
As God's instrument, you have been sent
   In answer to our prayer.

Oh, how lovely are the feet that tread
   To those who hunger feel.
And blessed be hands giving bread
   Touching, so as pain to heal.

How precious are the lips that speak
   Words of tenderness and peace.
And how heroic are the hearts which seek
   To befriend, that hate my cease.

Let us then, join hands and hearts in love
   And each other's burdens share;
So that in Him we may all be one.
   Dear Lord, grant us our prayer.
—*Mary Marcy Baldys*

Untitled

   Snowflakes, tiny pieces of heaven
      fall to the earth.
      Ironically they melt as if
the soil is not worthy to receive them.
They vanish as quickly as they appear.

So much like the days we had together.

      It seems only yesterday
         that spring was here;
      the times I held you in my arms.
         But like the snowflakes
you too vanished as quickly as you came.
      Now I wonder if the soil
      that falls upon you disintegrates
      unworthy of my piece of heaven.
—*Sarah A. E. Hendron*

I'll Remember You

Looking through the pictures, faded memories. Birthdays, Easter, Thanksgiving, and even Christmas Eve. You always had a smile to share, words of encouragement too. I remember the days, I used to come in, and have nice long talks with you.

Life is so uncertain. We don't know how long we have. Sometimes we take it for granted. Other times we just let it pass. The moments you share with someone you love, should be made to last.....so I'll remember you. I'll remember you.

You looked so delicate. Fragile as a child. But in your last moments on earth, you still shared that smile.

I never told you enough, how much I love you. But now you've left this life behind and there's nothing I can do....except remember you. I'll remember you.

The good times we shared and the fun we had will always be alive. I'll keep those treasures close to my heart and etched upon my mind.

So, if you're up there listening, I'd like you to know—I love you, I miss you, and I will never forget you.....

I'll remember you. I'll remember you.
—Michelle A. Simpson

Exercise Your Mind

Exercise your mind as you begin to unwind
Embrace positive thoughts, seek and you will find—
The mind is powerful and needs knowledge and understanding—
The choices you make can be quite demanding
When you exercise your mind here's what you can do—
Relax, read always learn something new
Eliminate the tension and pressures on your mind, focus on
what it takes to overcome any bind!

Don't be negative
have no fear
Trust you mind
and keep it clear

Learn from your experiences and continue to create
Make up your mind and do not deviate — Use mind power, relax
let go —

Just exercise your mind,
the more you know,
the more you grow!
—Marilynn Carson

Doubting Thomas

In the dim and distant past
Ever since the world began
There has been entwined in the
heart of man fears and hopes for a world
without sorrow and bitter strife
which culminated for me
on the quiet trail at Gethsemane
When Doubting Thomas beheld
the Resurrected Christ with
our saviors unhealed wounds
all his doubts gave way to ecstasy
and the sight blessed him with celestial light.
Overwhelmed and believing
with living proof of man's soul
Takes flight beyond the earthbound sod
He immortalized the words
My Lord and My God.
—Margaret Tucker

Woodland Bedtime

The summer sun arcs downward in the West. Nature's creatures emerge from cool siestas and in appeasement of their hunger, frenzy abounds. A multitude of birds compete at the feeders. Pine squirrels and chipmunks gorge their elastic cheeks. Bits dropped by careless diners are gleaned from the ground. A spectacular "Star Wars" overture begins as the selfish Rufous denies himself his evening meal by attempting to thwart the timid hummers' chances for nectar. The cottontail delicately nibbles tender grass shoots. Later she sits by the door of her hidden abode twitching her nose as she surveys the evening world. As the sun sinks behind the mountain tops, eating ceases. The tiny, furry creatures scurry from sight. Birds flap noisily while trying to find their night's roost. Calls and answers bounce from tree to tree and raucous Stellar jays loudly declare their supremacy. The crescendo climbs and peaks! Did cymbals clang? The sky becomes rosy red; a few rays streak upward as if trying to hold onto the day. Diminuendo begins as sleepy birds' calls become softer. There's a faint snap as a pair of deer bed down. All is calm; the rippling stream can now be heard.
—Lucy Schweers

Winter Sky

Dreams of a winter sky
　encircle my world

　　like flurries of an innocent age,
　　passionate tears of the old man's soul
　　flash before my eye

And what of time to come?
　prayers of destiny, or
　betters yet -
　hopes of the listless young

So take heed of the wind,
　inhale the silence;
　swept over the calm sea,
　bitter frailty

　　though pious the frost in skin,
　　ravage sayeth fire, true heart within

but misty mired it reflects on you
　flakes of passion
　to devote or devour

As dreams of a winter sky
　encircle my world...
　　—Tim Curran

The Dream

The dream could never die
Even though the body was made lifeless
Strength was felt
Even though the multitude was weary.
Work was endless,
But the human spirit had the endurance of a lifetime.
Songs of a promised tomorrow
Were heavy on the burdened soul,
But yet, these songs never ceased to be sung.
On lips of a dying nation.
Sometimes in the cemetery behind the old church house,
Low and sorrowful singing can still be heard.
Died before they could realize their dreams came true
Their torture, blood, sweat, and tears
Helped pave my way.
Now it's my turn to dream.
The dream has been passed on.
—Melody Nicole Wilks

Finally Home

He touched the name of his father which was
engraved upon the stone —
And he thought how long his mother waited,
for him to come back home.
He was just a boy them, and didn't quite understand,
But it seemed like overnight, he had to become a man.

It was the first time that he touched the stone —
and the first time that he cried; as if twenty
some add years of hurt, were all bottled up inside

He himself had gone to war, and didn't come back the same,
And the love he knew, she took another name!
But his mother helped him through his hurt and shame,
Till he finally felt he was a man again.

And the promise he made so long ago, had been
etched in his mind and engraved on his soul,
And as he kissed his father's name on the stone;
He said father at last you're finally home!

And ashe turned around and he faced his mother's
grateful stare as she slowly maneuvered
the wheels of his chair!

—*Marlena Sabella*

Golden Moments

Firelight embers 'neath the blue,
Entwined with amber shining through,
Lacy leaves of antique brown,
Twirling, dancing, falling down.

Autumn mists and dewy frost.
Summer paradise now lost.
Artists paint their harvest sheaves,
Whilst berries thrive amidst the eaves.

Halloween and goblins mingle,
Ghostly tales that make you tingle,
Then will come old winter's glow,
With icy winds and magic snow.

Riding in a horse drawn sleigh,
Remembering tales of yesterday,
Thanksgiving brings us pumpkin pie,
To herald Christmas bells near by.

—*Kay Koontz*

Thoughts

Mind of mine,
  eternal tormentor
    and comforter,
how often have each of us
    p a u s e d . . .
to muse upon the other?
  Wandering back along our journeys,
I recall the peculiar events we've shared. . .
  many times I desperately clung
to pull you back to safety,
  then in turn,
you did the same for me.
  Apart,
in our oneness
  we are the struggles of humanity
    within humanity. . .
  Together,
in our oneness
  we are the struggles of humanity
    within the soul.

—*Peggy Nuckols*

Father's Masterpiece

Eternally, Father's mind centered on love's masterpiece.
Eternally, Father's mind knew unspeakable rebellion.
Yet, in perpetual love waves, Father created cosmos,
Produced angelic spirit, nurtured human soul to share awesome love.
Free will was gallantly bestowed in full view of pain.
By choice spirit and man rejected perfection, twisted creation.

Brilliantly, perfection outshone perversity, and an immutable
God forever changed form in love's masterpiece—a Son, a Savior.

Could God not feel paternal pain?
As no being could ever comprehend!
Father suffered supreme garden agony in pristine pure Son,
Blood-pressed in man's stead.
Boundless love suffered suffocating, nail-pierced agony in
marred Son,
Beloved in ultimate sacrifice.

Not insensible, but knowing resurrection, Father's longing
For unheeding souls was reflected in Son's forsaken cry that
Moved creation, made shamefaced sun hide, split rocks, split hearts.

And new blood-washed sons resound, "Abba, Father,"
And true, heedful children ever experience a
Gallant Father in His mystical body-exhibition of love's masterpiece.

—*A.M.C. Moylan*

The Four Seasons

Let's talk about Winter—it's a great adventure,
even though there's not much sun.
Your teeth are breaking,
and your whole body's shaking,
But you still have lots of fun.
Let's talk about Spring and the joy it brings,
flowers are starting to blossom.
The wind is not too cold,
and the air is not too bold,
Everything is looking so awesome...
Let's talk about Summer and never a bummer,
I like this season too.
The air is hot and tight,
and you start to toss and turn at night.
And the sky is a color of blue.
Now it is Fall and the whole joy of it all,
the season has begun to enter,
The colored leaves are falling,
and the heavy winds are calling.
Just think...next comes winter.

—*Roxanne Fortune*

Life

The sun beating down on untouched hills,
Ever-lasting is the urge to go beyond the next mountain,
Again, the road curves, and a new scene to marvel at is
  brought into view,
One sight, one story, one trail, rediscovered a million times
  in a life-span,
Looking out at the ocean, wondering what the next day may bring,
A new sight, a view, a sound, a discovery is made every second,
Great men go unknown, goals go unreached, man constantly
  attempts to surpass himself and nature,
Never succeeding, for nature is unconquerable, life, unpredictable,
It always breaks free, never contained, never controlled,
The provider, life, yes, the creator, can never be out-done
  by the created,
It is attempted, but will it never be accomplished?

—*Rob Spousta*

Where Will It End?

We have sunk to the lowest level:
   Every evil device we applaud,
Adopting the wiles of the devil—
   Electing to live without God.

Yes, we cling to the slippery border:
   Whatever seems right in our eyes,
Devoid of any semblance of order,
   To our shame, and, perhaps, out demise!

Notwithstanding the peril and gravity
   Of ignoring God's precepts, we are plumbing
The uttermost depths of depravity—
   Forgetting that payday is coming!

And earth's clusters of grapes have been growing—
   Seducing and being seduced:
We are reaping what we have been sowing—
   The chickens have come home to roost!

Are we seeing the last dying ember
   Of a nation too smug and too clever?
Perhaps, and, my friend, please remember:
   God won't keep His anger forever!
   —*Marial E. Beck*

Answers

Answers are not questions, but that is all I find.
Every face holds an identity—Why is mine unknown?
   The pain you see is hidden without one other—
      She can feel the memories.
   Yet, our time is lost never to be found.
Her decisions, once made, cannot be reversed.
    My crying was not hers to hear.
The silent echo of a stranger's love
Leaves a hollow chamber in my heart—
    That only she can know.
She holds the answers in her life,
And she carries my secret with her.
   Some day I will have the answers—
    The keys to unlock my dreams.
     Some day I will find her.
   I will finally know my mother!
   —*Michele E. Hoff*

Models

You see their faces on magazines, and they can be found in
every store; their clothes are half off, and what's left
on is always tore. Men like to look at them, and boys hang
them on their walls; to them they are nothing more than
beautiful, brainless, dolls! Their faces are painted up, and
their bodies are all lean; everyone knows they can be
deceptive, and at times even quite mean. On their finger is a
ring, and on their arm there is a gorgeous man; you can look
them up and down, there is not a single part of them that is
not tan. They are every man's fantasy wife, and every little
girl's dream; their lives are all perfect, at least that is the
way they seem. What is wrong with our world today, why do we
have such unrealistic goals; that in order to be perfect, we
have to starve our body and souls? The message that is being
sent, to me is all too clear; if you do not meet this image,
then you will have no man to call you dear. To me this message
is sick, it's concept is really bad; that if we do not measure
up, then our lives will be awfully sad! We should be stressing
a positive self-image, and that you are your own boss; if guys
cannot accept this, then just chalk it up as their loss!
   —*Sherry Towns*

In The Shadow Of The King

Everybody is always walking in the shadow of the king.
Everybody is always singing the songs Elvis used to sing.

Elvis has fans all around the world people that adore him in
every way.
From women to men, and little boys and girls, too many to say.

When Elvis sang the people cried, he melted our hearts.
And the funny thing is he never really tried.
His records just blasted the top of the Billboard charts.

There's no one who could make people as happy as he could.
And if you can't see Elvis the way I do!
You should.

Elvis is a very special soul, with a voice no one can replace.
   A memory to behold.
No one knows why he left us this empty place.
And no one really knows why he left us in this empty place.
And no one really knows for sure where he's gone.
Whether he's alive or pasted on, where he may be all a mystery.

Everybody will always walk in the shadow of the king.
Until he returns with a new song to sing,
Our hearts will always miss him, if he never returns.
The fire he has built in our hearts will always burn.

Elvis will live forever in the hearts of his fans.
And millions will walk in the shadow of this man.
   —*Patricia Montgomery*

Sonnet to Friendship

Since time began, and 'til its very end,
Ev'ry bard, writer, artist of this earth,
Has tried to capture, express and defend
The meaning of true friendship and its worth.

It has been likened to a summer's day,
To ev'ry species of flora and fawn,
To flights of birds, to imposing arrays
Of gems, to fleeting precious moments gone.

True friendships to eternity belong,
(Infinity we can not finite make,)
In this life they are born, nurtured along,
But do not cease with the last breath we take.

Friendships' bonds are stronger than those of blood,
For they are unions of souls made by God.
   —*Margaret M. Ochwat*

Someone

Heavy gloom engulfs the earth
Eyes become filled with tears from
lack of mirth
Can gloom and tears be washed away
by someone?
Starving children, so alone
Living a squalor and unknown
Can someone please bring an end to the
violence?
The color of our skin may cause strife
But it's not the most important thing
in life
Can someone please teach us to live in
peace so that gloom, tears and death
will forever cease?
Yes, that someone is the almighty God, Jehovah.
   —*Nancy J. Ader*

Heavenly Mysteries

Far away in a distant space,
Exist a mystical, magical place,
Where life begins and ends with almighty grace,

Mystery encompass this beautiful paradise.
Where streets of gold, and seas of glass like crystal ice,

Rainbows encircle his throne appearing like emeralds in the sky,
Sparkling like diamonds to encase the most amazing high.

Melodious tunes emerge from those who found the keys,
To all of life's real mysteries,

Clouds flow gracefully by and no one seems to see,
Or appear to be interested in this great mystery,

All answers to the universe remain on a scroll,
Never opened, but by the Lamb who was sacrificed as foretold.

Too late my world for you to flee,
The path you are on will be your destiny.
—*Yvonne Watkins*

There Once Existed Innocence...

...but that too soon disappeared.
Eye blinked once, and then there was no more to blink.
The fallacy of life is but no truth,
   and of all a lie; a coveted, damning lie.
I once knew of innocence, was even a part of it;
IT...was a part of me.
   But I...was lead astray to lead a lie.
Before long, innocence and I, we both gave way.
ohh how I beg for a reprieve! receiving none.
All that is left now...is blame, confusion and falsity.

 My life is a lie,
 The world my liar,
 My family its co-conspirators,
 My friends, as naive as I was.

Before long. Before long.

There once existed innocence,
       and I too shall soon disappear as well...
— *Rachael M. Lee*

Who? What? Indians?

Rippling waters, streaming by
Eyes enjoying, adoring,
Lands bought with rumors and lies!
Never did I see these things of old,
Stories of braves, tepees, and chiefs,
Handed down by the Grandfathers and I've been told.
Differences, ways, misunderstood.
Moved to reservations, hungry and cold-
Why? Of course, for their own good!
Whites couldn't, wouldn't comprehend;
Easier to banish and control,
Than to gain the trust of a friend.
Years have passed with ways the same,
Never asking in order to learn.
Ignorance remains the name of the game.
Educate, listen, in order to learn-
Take time to understand our ways.
For Native Americans, show just concern!
—*E. Renae Boyd*

The Shadow Of Our Eye

Behind the shadow of our eye we wear.
Faces, voices, of a long yesteryear.
You walked into my life, ever after time tape,
Experiences that memory can't escape.

Days file one into another, life transgress,
Joy, pain, form an everlasting bond I confess.
Destiny rules our world, we comply, you're gone, why?
And all hide behind the shadow of my eye.

Baby, baby, now where are you today?
Searching for happiness so far away.
When people ask, I have no answer, sigh,
A tear forms behind the shadow of my eye.

Imperfections, war, the heart explore,
Famine, death, starvation, hurricane, more.
Multitude of episodes, prey, soul and heart tie,
Look it's all behind the shadow of our eye.

In travels a lonely person may stand,
Joy, pain, form a bond, go hand in hand.
Console, listen, no need to ask,
A special story behind the shadow of their eye.
—*May Kock*

Americo

   My heart knows the tale of a thousand tears
Fallen from my eyes in sadness; to become stars in the night
   sky, wishes and dreams -born and reborn;
 The tracks of their journey well kept and remembered.

   The nights fall upon the day like a blanket,
      Enveloping the light within its folds
 My eyes fill slowly with sleep and then darkness

     I speak to you with my thoughts
     And fight back the feeling of tears;
Hoping -no praying that they have forgotten their way

    I would not want for you to see me cry,
   As you lie there in reluctant anticipation...
    With every breath darkness fills your being
   You feel a pain but, cannot know its origin.

  Though I am frightened for you, I am strong; so —
  Know my wish of peace and if you lose your way,
  Follow the tracks of my fallen tears to my heart,
         Feel safe — rejoice
      And sleep a wondrous sleep Americo,
    This wish I do dream for you this night.
—*Nancy Figueiredo*

On Burdick Street

Rows of colored ribbon paths
Flow by streams of satin grass.
A day beneath the gentle skies
Of Burdick Street, we're lost in time.
We lose our troubles for the day
While roaming past the shops' displays
Of fashions, artists, musicians in the park,
Dancers dancing, romantic hearts
Riding in carriages drawn by horses of white
Past fountains flowing in colored lights.
We catch the aromas that the bakery makes sweet,
As lovers stroll down Burdick Street.
—*Paul Cusano*

Nuke Me Now

Pretty birdy in the sky,
Falling down so ever bright.
Fall upon our city homes,
Make the flesh fly off my bones.
Drip and burn until no more,
Blood and guts; there's so much gore.
Put an end to screwed up lives,
Families, children, husbands, wives.
Good-bye to all I never knew,
The sky, now white, was once light blue.
Where is God? I think I know,
Sitting high upon His throne.
Laughing down upon our face,
From up above where He is safe.
Meanwhile I lay upon my back,
My skull half burnt, half partly cracked.
My eyes are gone, my flesh is too.
My body's ash so I can't move.
I never got to hold her close,
Feel her love burn through her clothes.
And so much more that I can't see,
My body's ash along with me.

—*Steven B. Pedigo*

Is This Heaven?

Maybe just a dream
Far from reality,
Somewhere in between.
Blooming like a flower,
A blossom of life.
An unborn child,
You and I growing stronger,
In each others arms is where we belong,
Dreams along with fears,
Things we share and being near.
Love and friendship,
Start of a new day.

—*Rebecca Hobbs Treece*

Mystery, Challenge And Existence

There are some men that would set sail to faraway oceans. As their ship rips through the icy blue waves, these men souls are shaken by a welcome mystery of the sea.

There are also men who desire to climb high mountains. These mountains have challenges unknown to men. These challenges could cost these men their lives. These men will accept these challenges, because they desire to reach the top and say "I did it."

Finally, there are men who desire to invent and create things that have never been seen by man kind. These men want the world to know that they too, for now and forever, have a place in this world.

I am a man that share the same feelings as other men do. In my quest to satisfy these feelings that I have, I choose to sit down and have a conversation with a woman.

—*Roosevelt Tharp*

A Formula

I am the seed of the Future, oh Mother and
Father of the world; love me, as you do all your
bright hopes of tomorrow, for these shall surely
be in my hands. Prepare me with the fertile
understanding of those pitfalls
of which you cannot begin
to guess. Give me humor
but do not humor me.
Invest your faith in me
that I may hold onto it
when I lose faith in myself.
Protect me by showing me that there
is no protection;
for human life is an equation
of problems that may only be solved by human
endeavor. Tend me so I may mold the world
your soul desires, that upon your arising,
your dreams may be shining about you
everywhere. This is the way —

—*Pauline T. Bussell*

Butterfly Garden

Butterflies wisp by as I watch this day,
feasting on nectar from my flower bed.
They're magnificent, in splendid array;
winged rainbows fluttering around my head.
I envy their simplicity as they
never have any moments they must dread.
They float, then they land on the floral quay,
with no remorse in the lives they have led.
To be fortunate not to know the grief
when the wait for early death is at hand.
I wish I could practice my own belief
in life - That is, always take a brave stand.
Dance for me, now, butterflies of delight,
'til this gun I hold halts my pain tonight.

—*Wilson L. Buchert III*

I

I have Jesus in my soul...it's a love that can't grow old.
Feel Him, need Him every day...He sees me laugh, and he hears
me pray. He's the rock on which I stand...Holy One sent down
to man. He forgave me of all sin...Loved me, woo'd me, drew me in!

I deserve to go to Hell...And He knows this very well.
Yet the blood of Christ for me...Saved my soul and set me free
I have Jesus in my soul...A light that gives an inner glow.
I have life eternally...won't you come and walk with me?

Jesus is the living God...He walked upon this hallowed sod.
He loves me with unending Grace...and there's no one can take
His place. He's my Savior, God and King...Let those Hallejuahs
ring! Won't you come and learn with me...About our God and
  His love for thee?

Mary Magdalene was His friend...She went to the cave and looked
within. The Angel said, "He is not here"...And Mary's heart was
filled with fear. He rose up on that very day...And talked with
Mary along the way.

Thomas said I will believe...When the nail prints in His hands
I see. Jesus stretched His hands way out...And Thomas then
became devout. I am but a grain of sand...in the Great Master's
plan. Yet He reaches out to me...And I'll follow Him to eternity.

—*Wanda J. Olender*

A Child's Touch

Ever feel lonely, or oh so blue.
Feeling as a plague has fallen,
but only finding you.
A tiny little smile, a child's small kiss.
Just a child's gentle touch will make callous
heart melt, cold eyes start to mist.
Young and beautiful so full of God given grace
little arms reaching out towards you,
for your embrace.
For if your ever down of feeling blue
look at their innocent eyes, and find a child's
touch reaching up to you.
 —*Paul E. King*

The Miracle Of Midland

Jessica the brave and small,
fell into a well twenty two feet tall,
The mother shocked when she fell,
into that deep, dark, unknown well,
People of Midland came by in a hurry,
The rescue workers were in a furry,
of not knowing how to get her out,
The mother ran towards the well and gave a loud shout,
"Juicy" as she was called,
with the vibration of the truck only made her fall
lower and lower,
To a point where the girl could no longer be heard,
not even a mumble or a single word,
The teamwork of Midland grew stronger and stronger,
as Jesse remained trapped in the well,
hours went by, and so did the days,
till the final moment of rescue came,
The "Miracle of Midland" would never be forgotten,
Nor would the brave town that stuck together,
ever the same.
 —*Ruth Olsak*

Legend Of Man

I am legend, seek not me
Find yourself all in all
Alone you will never be
Enchanted with reality.

Go the way man must go
Seek the truth at heavens gate
Keep your loved ones and always show
Life is a gift that will forever grow.

Light the world with its song
Find the lies that man has told
For there it will not be long
The truth is wonderful to behold.

The dreams of millions before him cry
To please the wonder of the eye
And walk again in beauties sight
A world that one day will shine bright.

Leave alone what is not yours
Fine your eyes, but never send
The one who lies or will never bend
For I am — legend.
 —*Lisa C. Bays*

The Vestal's Song

With grace he slid his hand down her slender neck,
Fine white fingers pale against mahogany shine.
She glistened with the sweat from his brow,
As he held her to his heart, listening.
The smoothness of curves flowed beneath his hands,
as he lifted her close to his soul,
enraptured by her beauty
and amazed by her innocence:
   she had never been touched before.

He wiped the sweat from her body
And gazed at her, wanting to hear her sing.
only he could make her sing, and he again
lifted her body to his,
clutching her powdered neck as he closed his eyes.
slowly he raised the other hand and breathed in
   her soft, sweet scent
Before at last she would be played:

There was silence
as the young man lifted his bow,
and brought forth music from his new violin,
for the first time.
 —*Lisa Armstrong*

Golden Arrows

Create an arrow golden with tomorrow's
Fire and brimstone
Carefully insert a message from this era
Stating no target's unanswered;

Tomorrow's child will answer
In their turn forward
Marching toward the baton arrow
Golden messages;

This our slated arrow
Targets no one man alone
Protection and survival
Is our humane message;

Hold this our golden arrow
Stand it high as our flag flying
Until the winds no longer
Guide her;

She will outlive the fire and brimstone
This our message clarified
Let no one enemy stand
To unleash her for she will rain upon them;
 —*Mary J. Goodman Armour*

My Father

 I wish I knew him sooner,
For I had so much fun with dad,
 That every time I was with him,
It made me really glad,
 My dad would take me fishing,
Or hiking along a trail,
 My dad would throw some balls with me,
Or make a kite that sailed,
 He never gave me that old excuse,
I've got a headache son,
 For he always had the time for me
So we'd have lots of fun,
 I only wish that everyone,
Could have a dad like mine,
 Then maybe they'd be happier,
And have fun all the time.
 —*Steven E. Patton*

Untitled

Slow pattern of rain drops,
First hits the front windows.
And the clouds can't hold on,
any longer—

Light breaks through the gray,
and shines the raindrops.
Until they glow with inner light.
Within, without.

Rain draws small boys outside.
Into the drip and splatter of small shower.
Let them run and play in an open day-
Free and carefree.

Who made the rain to rain and the clouds.
To open on us here waiting for planting time?
Who made the seeds? Why will they grow?
We saw, they sprout.

He who spoke, creator of all, made the rain.
The Lord and giver of life gives seeds their life
To sprout and green, flourish and flower.
Remember us, O, Lord.

—*Margaret M. Barber*

My Mother

When my mother died
First I missed her face,
Her little dippy nose,
Her brown eyes,
The back of her neck,
Her feet that looked like mine,
Her laugh,
Then I felt lost
Because I missed her strength.
What would I do?
Now it was up to me
To carry on. So much to do
Could I? Would I?
I surprised myself at my own strength.
Without her I was stronger.
She left me her fighting spirit.
Through me she could live on
Not the same but forever.

—*Mary Sams*

I Do

From the depths of my soul
Flow these feelings of love rushing out,
to express themselves to you?
As they surge through my being I know that these feelings
of love, for you are true!
As they enter my heart, it skips several beats!
Then it pounds fast, to rush them on their way.
When they come into my mind, they send me spinning back
into time,
With sweet memories, of you loving me?
I can think of a million things that I long to say,
to let you know, how much I care, for you?
But, as I look into your eyes, with tears flowing down from mine.
I sweetly whisper these words to you.
I love you...I love you...I do!

—*Ray Light*

Jane

Oh, Jane, greatest of daughters,
Flower of your mother's bosom,
Star of your father's eye.
Your mother has left us,
So many, many years ago.
And I must take that trip very soon.
What then, my little blossom?
Will you be old enough to care for yourself?
Will God weigh lightly on you?
Farewell my little girl,
For it will be a long, long time.
So, I will say to you,
My dear and lovely daughter,
The last pain of my life,
Will be parting from you.
But, your mother awaits me,
Long shrouded in death,
And I will take to her your love.
With my last parting breath:
Farewell, my Jane. Farewell, my daughter dear.

—*Lynn Allen Clemons*

My Little Fallen Star

I was packed and ready
for a long journey,
a lifetime with you.
To your destiny you returned
before my arms could hold you.
No volume of tears can fill my empty arms, now.
You are gone
and I am changed forever.
You danced on my heart
showing me joy and hope through your light.
You are gone
  so soon
  so quietly,
my little fallen star.

—*Loretta K. Koch*

Happy Valentine's Day To My Husband

Since Valentine's Day is upon us,
For a moment, will you reminisce,
Returning to one, fifty-two years ago,
When we loved and lived a "life of bliss,"
And we were ignorant of the future we'd face,
Or, how the "winds of life" would blow?

I loved you then as I do now,
But now much less selfishly,
'Cause, these days, to your wishes,
I WANT to bow!

You KNOW how I feel
'Cause over the years, I always felt free to say
That I cherish you more with each passing day!
I shall not ask, because I feel and know YOUR feelings
Which are evidenced by your smile, the twinkle in your eye
Accompanied by that familiar "glow."

This is another year and another Valentine,
And again I thank G-d that you are still here
to be mine!

—*Louise G. Zoble*

Christmas Reckoning

May love abound this Christmas season
For certainly love should be the reason
Two thousand years ago this night
In a manger soft and sweet
Lay the wonder, the beauty, the light
A Bethlehem in awe and a Christ child meet
You announce-oh Bethlehem-a king of kings
Rising as a nation that sends the song of praise on angels' wings
To farthest reaches of time and space
Every where that there is love
That Bethlehem resided within the human race
Our souls are innocent stables of a dove
And Jesus calls us forth
As humans on a humble heavenly course!
—*Kenneth A. Phillips*

Tattoo Annie

Crescent moon, stars, planets — with colors alive
For extra energies — a lightning bolt inside
She has rainbows in the stars
She has come alive —

With the flick of their bic — they pass another one around —
She smiles — laughs to hear them say, "Are you getting sick,
  do you feel like you're going to faint? Does it hurt, at
  all Annie?"

Her friends are there to see if she is brave —
With a reply to them she says, "Pain is all in your mind,
  it's what you make of it.
"Tattoo Annie needs one on her fanny!"
Anyway that's what the guys say.

Instead hers are on the inside of her ankle, on her upper hip
Both with Crescent moon, stars, planets, with lightning bolts
  inside
Rainbows in the Stars —
She is alive —
—*Lois Sitchenkov*

A Mother's Wish

  May you find peace and happiness in your life,
For fame and fortune does not breed empathy, love,
  or a genuineness of spirit,
The pain one inflicts on another,
  Ultimately comes back in kind,
What we give is what we get,
  Life will take you down many long, dusty roads,
Some up and some down,
  May you learn and grow,
Strive to have the courage to ask for forgiveness
  of past transgressions,
May money and power,
  Not be your guiding light,
May you somehow come to know what's right,
  Instead of wandering blindly in the night.
My wish at best,
  Is that you learn to love,
Without qualifications or conditions,
  But to love, with all your heart, and I pray we will never
part.
—*Meredith Diane Moll*

Just One Night

I slept peacefully in his arms
  for he fulfilled my greatest dreams.
The love we made was strong
  yet ever so gentle.
He eased my mind
  but made it more so complicated.
I lost self respect
  though I do not regret a minute.
If asked to relive it,
  I would hesitate
  but, more than likely,
  I would in a heartbeat.
I want to regain the passion
  and to fulfill my dreams.
Even if it is for
  Just one night.
—*M. Elizabeth*

Thanksgiving

I thank you, God, for his love,
For his care and for his presence.
I thank you, God, for his eyes.
His hazel eyes, fountains of light
And the essence of life.
I thank you, God, for his hair,
Blond and silky like caressing sun:
For his loving, gentle mouth
Made for love and blessings.
I thank you, God, for his words and smiles,
For the way he looks at me,
The great and glorious sun
Warming the fragile and lonely star.
I thank you, God, the most, because
By giving me these royal presents:
His love and himself, all only for me,
You inspire me to know
What heaven must be
Just by his being with me.
—*Laura Aram*

Our World

God, Forgive us for hurtin' our world,
For in it, the many pollutants we've hurled!
You gave it to us, so clean and pure,
How sorry we are, for certain and sure.!

Help us to repent, from our bad mistakes,
To clean it up, for comin' generations sakes,
To take care of this treasure, you've blessed us with,
That all livin' creatures, become not just a myth.!

You've made us all stewards, of this world today,
Help us to respect it always, I pray,
To work together, to restore it whole,
To repair our damage, as our common goal.!

With Your help we can do it, and still stand tall,
Fully forgiven, for our colossal fall,
And live in a world, that's lovely and clean,
That's blessed by you, as it should be seen.!
—*Shirley Sebastian*

O Blessed Savior, Precious Lord, You Died For Me

It was for me that Jesus went to Calvary.
For it was I for whom my Savior died, you see.
Yes it was I who nailed Him to that tree, O Lord!
Yes it was I who set in place that crown of thorn.

There on the cross He took my life of sin.
There on the cross my life begins again.
The doubts, the fears, the sins of all the years, are gone!
O Blessed Savior, Precious Lord, You died for me.
O Blessed Jesus, Precious Lord, You died for me.

Yes it was I who pierced His hands and side, that day!
But it was I for whom my Savior died and prayed.
I know that I can't fully understand, Oh no!
Just why it had to be the way He planned, and so
For sinful me, His Righteousness God Sees!
O Blessed Savior, Precious Lord, You died for me.
O Blessed Jesus, Precious Lord, You died for me.

The doubts, the fears, the sins of all the years, are gone!
O Blessed Savior, Precious Lord, You died for me.
O Blessed Jesus, Precious Lord, You died for me.
—*Ray Sansom*

January Rose

Turnout the lights, until tomorrow
For it's been another long and lonely winter's day,
without you.
Now I eye you lying in bed beside of me
And I wish I could hold you close and tight,
in my arms.

But it's too late you're fast asleep and I can't hold on
Maybe one day you'll awaken and still remember me.

Turn away your eyes until tomorrow
For it's been another long and lonely winter's day
without you.
Maybe tomorrow will bring you back to me, I don't know
I just wish I could be with you now, in your heart
So I could wipe away the pain.

But it's too late you're so far away and I can't hold on
Maybe one day you'll return and still remember me.

But you see, I'm like a January Rose in winter time
People say my way of living is so insane
But I can't say good-bye
To you in winter time.
—*Timothy Scott Clapp*

Thanksgiving

For golden dawn, and golden fields of grain;
For lilting bird-song, and the kiss of rain;
For mountains' height, for gentle rolling plain,
We give You thanks today!

For rosy glow, of sun at close of day;
For children's joyous laughter as they play;
For food, for flow'rs, for new-mown fields of hay,
We give you thanks today!

For freedom's dream that lives on through the years;
For love of friends and neighbor, family dear;
For those who worship You now gathered here,
We give You thanks today!

For One Who came that day—so long ago,
To set us free, to lead us here, to show
Your love for us—Your saving grace to know—
We give You thanks today!
—*Margaret R. Thayer*

When My Heart Cries Out

When in the night, your heart cries out
for more than just superficial human needs,
who do you cry for?

Do you cry for someone
from decades ago?
Invariably you do; as do I.

When the pain and loneliness
become too much,
who do you long for?

Do you long for a past love?
Of course, and so do I.

You and I do not
love each other.
We are in love with someone
we cannot touch.

For now, you will satisfy my needs.
Until the next time,
My heart cries out.
—*Valerie A. Maples*

Poets

Poets are dreamers as is necessary.
For no other way could it be.
Life's promises are rarely fulfilled.
Expectations through reality stilled.

And thus the poet will bring back the dead tree,
With words of love make it alive and healthy.
And although one must awaken to see,
The poet will never abandon that tree.

When dreams can calm the shattered,
For moments its all that mattered,
For the trouble they find to stay.
The Poet will push and push it away.

Look about for all who want and need,
Life seemingly not knowing what to feed.
The poet to the troubled will try to depart
Soothing reasons to an aching heart.

Painters can create it one time,
The poet will rainbow it would rhyme.

In a world that cries out for love
Poets have it already from above.
Oh Lord, no doctor, no preacher make of me,
Eternity's poet would I be.
—*Theresa Brouard*

A Poet's Crime

Someday I'll be sentenced for a crime I've committed
For something that I've never intended
What that may be I'm not really sure
But I know there will not be any cure
I will be like a contagious disease
They'll lock me in a jail without any keys
Then no one will ever again care
They will all whisper behind me and stare
No it will not get any better
I'll have to write Myself a love letter
My crime, I think, will be my ink
And my pen the only link
The verdict, they'll say, is your life
They'll cut my heart out with a dagger knife
Put it on display for the world to see
The heart of a poet is something to see
—*Linda Lee Ervin*

On The Way To The Bus Stop

Who would blame the summer birds
For staying on till spring,
The sun has poured a morning
That makes January sing.

The honey liquor of his light
Has drenched the eastern plains.
It washes every window
And seeps into the drains.

This summer brew that fills my eyes
Makes me stagger like a fool.
It's washed the windows of my soul
And left it shining like a jewel.
—*Thomas Motika*

Crown Jewels

Autumn—crown jewels of the seasons, so precious to hold
   for such a short while;
It stimulates, thrills us for so many reasons as we snatch
   every jewel for our memory file.

Fog patches, grain ripened, geese flying, corn standing,
   the smell of honey in the hives of bees;
Spider webs sparkling with round diamond dewdrops....
   Bluejays scavenging hazelnut trees.

The season's phantom bridge gently transporting spent
   spirits away from a busy summer—
We fall under its spell entranced by its jewels, marching
   on into winter to a magical drummer.

When Jack Frost comes with his lacy white net spread over
   everything—fern, flower, tree;
We gaze in wonder at this wintry painting by a Master's
   brush: so priceless—yet free!

Sometimes life snares us and Autumn's enchantment slips
   through our fingers unnoticed, unseen;
Still, the beauty was there tho' we were indifferent:
   Crown jewels waiting for winter's Snow Queen.
   —*Rhoda Hamilton*

He's Coming

He's coming, are you ready?
For the coming of the Lord?
We've prepared so very long, for Jesus to take us home.
He's been speaking through his prophets,
are you ready for Jesus to come and talk to you?

Jesus is coming to the righteous ones.
He's been waiting and watching to see who wants to go.
Repent my brothers and my sisters,
and ask him to forgive.
Jesus is coming, yes coming to take us home.

Do you doubt he has a reason, for all that we endure?
But there's a reason for everything,
keep Faith and you'll be sure.
He's our Father, brother, he's our keeper and our soul.
Are you ready for Jesus to come and take us home.

Jesus is coming to the righteous ones.
He's been waiting and watching to see who wants to go.
Repent my brothers and my sister,
and ask him to forgive.
Jesus is coming, yes coming to take us home.
   —*Robin L. Tobin-Lopez*

Untitled

Words losing meaning expressions so tortured
   For the pain in my heart that can still
   Stifle my being and betray the beauty
   That can be portrayed by my soul

Yet I find solace in the knowledge that I have
   growth within — for nurturing wisdom is strength itself

Time, we do know — does not stand still and, when at one time;
   time was a constant challenge
   an eternity of unwarranted abuse and varied
      forms of imprisonment
   time has become a friend — something to cherish
For the time lost at the hands of others is
   so very hard to make up or re-capture

So-now my challenge is to live every moment
   Ever so carefully and not to allow
   Myself to dwell/to sink or drown
      in the past sorrows and
      woundings I have known
And still unfortunately can haunt to my
very core in constant following at my heels.
   —*Martha Munoz-Knowles*

Quiet Wind

The wind is quiet, resting
For the work which lies ahead
The sky is silent, waiting
A cloud floats softly on its bed

Now, twisting, raging, mad
The wind tears through the trees
Only another mad thing
Can see the things the wind now sees

A roof is thrown, like something
Discarded in pure disdain
The wind now turns and runs away
Fleeing before the winter rain

Soon the rampaging storm has passed
And peace reigns once more within
Deep silence closes over all
The wind now quiet once again
   —*Patricia P. Garate*

Precious Friends

Time had no significance in the beginning
      for they were as one
Keeping there friendship fresh and strong
They were able to overcome all obstacles.
      Reaching out to one another
         They felt all the pain
         Yet able to help the other.
   Their friendship unequaled by any other
         was misunderstand by others.
   Nothing in this world is as precious
to them as time spent together with one another.
         Now they wait for a time
         When the sun won't set
         But continues to shine.
            For in that day
         they'll be together forever
            in a place called
               Eternity.
   —*Teresa L. Moore*

Self Hatred

Black Brothers and Sisters. What are we killing each other for? To even a score. No longer number one minority. Done lost our racial seniority.

Don't we know this is our kingdom? Don't we want our freedom. Killing each other is criminal. Is the message we're receiving subliminal.

We're our own worst enemy and yet we're the epitome. This land is our birthright, so why is it ourselves that we fight. The abuse of alcohol and drugs makes us woozy and some of us gun each other down with an uzi. Shattered to pieces and becoming an endangered species. Think? Yes! We're becoming extinct. There's know forgiveness for a race who can't do business.

Some of our youth is uncouth and that's the truth. Black youngsters drive fast cars and think they're movie stars. If they get killed in this movie, they will come back in the next. Is this a hex? Drive by killings, some are all too willing.

In the beginning there was darkness and then there was light. Let us love one another and call off the fight.

—*Sam Phillips*

Untitled

WHY do we keep saying we cannot see God?

When we see a top spin we are seeing the
   force that stands it erect.

  When we see leaves fly we are seeing the wind.

    When we see a pin drop we are seeing gravity.

      When we see the earth and the sea,
        the birds and the trees,
          the mountains and the sunset,
            the Milky Way and the molecule,
              the Universe and the infinite
                products of life-force therein
we are seeing God.

How can the invisible be more visible?

—*Robert E. Fulton Jr*

Just Let Them Go

Sometimes our friends have to go, but they don't leave us forever. They are always with us whether we know it or not. The funerals are sad and the burials are sad. You'll miss them dearly when they are gone. And you will remember all the great times you and your friend had. Of course you will wish they were still with you and able to run and play. You might see visions of your friends, but they will not be there. They will be in your hearts, and they will be with you when a special event in your life comes. They never will forget you. But since they are very faraway you won't be able to write back and forth to each other and let each other know how you are doing or what is going on in heaven or how it is in a town. So just let them go, and don't forget they will always be with you.

—*Michelle Christine Rasmussen*

Forget Me Not

Forget me not when the dew is on the grass!
Forget me not for time shall surely pass!
Forget me not when the moon is full!
Forget me not for it shall remind me of you!
Forget me not when the flowers bloom in the spring!
Forget me not for I shall think of you and begin to sing!
Forget me not when this day has come to an end!
Forget me not your loving friend!
Forget me not when your alone and feeling blue!
Forget me not for I'll still be loving you!
Forget me not for the time of farewell is at hand!
Forget me not for this you must understand!

As both time and love have no end!
So are my thoughts of you time and time again!
The moment draws closer where my eyes shall never meet yours
   again.
Where only the memories of you and me in the past
Will I be able to walk with, hand in hand!
So I must now say farewell though my heart fights it so!
Farewell my friend, from someone who loves you so!
Farewell! Forget me not ———

—*Philip W. Briggs*

Beholding My Wonder Dream

Pillowing tops of the clouds, as the sky they crowned
Forgotten rocks behind waterfalls, how ageless they are
With children I walked where rainbows touch the ground
Endless horizon of oceans and blazing streaks of falling stars

Many and sundry wonders I beheld as I traveled
Some with mine eye, most in the secrets of my mind
Yet, a single treasure has but left my heart raveled
So very rare and bold, surely alone of its kind

Breathless I'm left, seduced by the very sight
Drunken by your smell, overcome by the awe
Possession I hoped, as I wanton stood in your light
Selfish bliss I thought, if others see not as I saw

Behind my eyes you appear, in a never ending dream
Such beauty immeasurable, ever sparks pleasure untold
Captive in your spell, to have you always I scheme
Not able my thoughts to halt, no wonder I'd rather behold.

—*For Wifey—by Larry M. Spangler*

Born Free

To be born again—is to be free.
Free as the moon above, with the sun on the horizon.
Free as the garden of Eden.
Free as the land we see.
Free as the air we breathe.
Free as the wind that blows.
Free as the ocean that flows.

To be born again - is to be free.
Free as a dove that flies above.
Free as a bird that whistles and makes love,
Free as a man who has a plan.
Free as man who has a helping hand.
Free as one who seeks - before he speaks.

So let it be, so let it be -
That there is a garden of Eden.
Free to see,
Free to believe.
Yes, free to see,
Free to believe!

—*Ray Allan James*

"I" Ordered "My" Groceries!

"I" ordered "my" groceries at 12 noon. The long list is not free! Then I waited, and waited until it was delivered to me! For delivery the cost is a one-ninety eight. Then while I'm waiting....I hope it won't be very late, some of them I have food coupons that pay! The rest must be cash! Folk's all paid "make my day!" Gladly to have it. Sure to arrive, even if it gets to be long after "five!"

For some may be..disabled—such as I! Be "N-E-V-E-R" discouraged! But still willing to try! Many things will go happening all our day long. Give a shout! or a whistle! or sing a happy song! It will help the ones near and dear to you. Watching how you do with jobs: Quite a few! Putting groceries here and there and some on a shelf. God's helping you always taking care of your self!

At 3:30 P.M. My groceries most certainly have arrived! They look so good! Will keep me healthy and much alive! Thankful! For delivery service!..For a small - pay! A watchful eye seeing if the packaging for sure all got here today, satisfied thoughts were in faces that looked on. Made glad hearts in the folks when they all have gone. Surety that hunger never be the cause of my miseries; live alone, yes 85, and "I" ordered "my" groceries!

—*Nina I. White-Allen*

Kula Morning

Granddaughters with glowing faces,
Freshly-watered pink blossoms
On frilly white nightie stalks.
Warm, moist, soap-smell baby-skin envelopes me
With early-morning bear hugs,
Just-washed hair wet against my face.
"Mmmmm, your hair smells good. What did you use?"
"Vidal Sassoon. Granny, will you
Brush my hair? And braid it?
I brought rubber hands for pony tail."
Grandpa, teasing, "Your granny had plenty of practice
Braiding the horses' manes."
I smile as my fingers tame the curls.
The horses weren't glorious blondes
Like these sweet Kula maidens.

—*Mary Leineweber*

Sinspiration

In your wandering gaze through satin ribbons of grey smoke from a burning cigarette so apparent is your heightened grief (that inspires the world to wildly spin on its axis and catch the sun) the secrets of mortality so
safe between your blood red lips, embracing those

Who love (so nakedly profound) under bright lights, knowing no forgiveness and you ask: is it worse to be unjust or merciless? Yet a bouche ouverte you eagerly drink les vins de vie with increasing perplexity, a bras ouverts you encompass the passion of late nights with worthless rewards (finding all that had been lost) under velvet curtains of dreams

Lover of all and friend to none, ma chere ami de cour, you eagerly laugh and cry at whim with bare ivory shoulders heaving (and sparkling eyes that do everything) to light the candle of sensual obliqueness

Remembering who you are and who you once were you shed the past as a snake sheds old skin which withers at once in the scorching sun, devoid of regrets; you talk of that which is the true love of your life, la grande monde, as you turn the world on with a bat of your eyelash, bringing the world heatedly weeping to its knees with desire

—*Shawna A. Hamel*

The Old, Old, Man

He never really seemed to clear the "cobwebs" from his head -
And somehow, all that clutter matched the contents of his shed.
He often saved old nuts and bolts and miles and miles of string,
All moldering like the thoughts he stored of every silly thing.
Ask him about the time of day, he couldn't keep it straight;
But yet, he knew - just what had been in eighteen eighty-eight.(1888)
I like to think I'll never be a carbon of his ways,
And yet, I find I store stuff up, 'cause "wasting never pays;"
And some days when "I go to get" and then forget just "what,"
I know I'm heading for the time my memory's door is shut.
If he had paused to think things through
He would not have seemed so silly-nilly;
And then, I ask, and then repeat, and ramble willy-willy;
But yet, he had a "dignity" that only "age" can give -
A "glowing charm" to all who love, whatever life they live.
As years go by, I eye the pile of stuff I call my own.
I only hope I'll have the "grace" this old, old, man has shown.

—*Ruth A. Black*

Country Girl

Ellie Mae was just a plain country girl. Who never strayed from home. She lived with her Ma and Pa in an old shack high in the hills. Where the wild flowers bloomed, and the birds sang in the spring. She yearned for the big city life. Where she could start a new life. One summer day she left her county home and journeyed to the big city. Here she thought all her dreams would come true. She worked at Pappy's Bar, and met her first city sticker. He promised her richer and diamonds. And she knew she fell in love with the wrong guy. She got her diamonds and richer, by being a hooker. And soon she was unhappy and ashamed of her life. She yearned for her county home in the hills knowing in her heart she could not return. Sick and broken hearted, she knew she would soon die. One sunny day in the spring, Ellie Mae came back to the hills. To be buried in pine box high on the hill.

—*Mel Glass*

Ocean Upon My Beach

Dedicated to Knox Bennett, whose sweet love brings forth poetry from my heart.

Your love is like the ocean's surge
Gentle at times, yet strong and deep
Like waves upon the sand, it comes
And leaves me thirsting, for it's repeat.

Your kisses - like breakers, crashing upon the rocks
Send vibrations through the depths of me
Your strong arms, so soothing and warm
Gently lull me into a contented peace.

When it is late and you must go
A part of me goes with you, each time
Like the tide takes sand from the shore
So, you capture parts of this heart of mine.

When you're near, there's a look in your eyes- so blue
That glistens, like sunlight on an azure sea
It comes and warms the empty cavern, in my heart
And a surge of joy, washes over me.

Your waves bring life, into this unfulfilled body
You sculpt a woman, from my bits of sand
And with your gentle loving and your caring
I know I'm safe, warm, and loved in your hands.

—*Sandy Ballenger*

I See The Gentle Hand Of The Masters Painters Work

The old brick farmhouse stands framed against the hillside.
From the branch of the cottonwood tree, a young child swings.
Apple blossoms and lilacs mix their fragrances,
and the air smells of spring.
I see the gentle hand of the master painter's work.

A creek winds through the green pasture,
trickling over the rocks in peaceful serenity.
Near the waters edge, sits a young boy and his dog.
Violets and buttercups grow freely by his feet.
I see the gentle hand as the master painters work.

A sudden shower fills the air, Leaving sparkling dew on the lawn green.
A rainbow appears arched across the heavens.
Mother and children stand in awe, as the old farmhouse takes on a glow.
I see the gentle hand of the master painters work.

A country church stands in the mist of the trees.
Church bells ringing through the spring air.
Children bouncing up stone steps.
Each thanking God as they bow their heads in prayer.
I see the gentle hand as the master painters work.
Peacefulness creeps within me, your love surrounds me now.
It's time to thank my God, for the many gifts of life.
I see the gentle hand as the master painters work.

—*Margaret Ann Seipel*

Reflections In A Tarn

Free of blossoms, the cherry tree hibernates
From the cold winter chill
My soul lays before her all but forgotten
Like dried flowers on the window sill.

The white wind recalls the summer beauty before her eyes
Wondering how much of her memory breaths truths fragrance
She is hesitant, wondering if her mirror ever lies.

Crystalline tears of the Kami rain upon the earth
Not understanding why his new found friend
Has not come to say goodbye.

In the shadows the tiger sleeps - wounds bound in cotton
No longer on the prowl his strengths forgotten.

Stoic armies of sand, forbidden to climb back up through the hourglass
Know that through dreams they will try.

Through the mist the tiger will awaken, his strengths realized
His spirit no longer tame
The Kami laughs aloud - his friend had never left
They are one and the same.

The white wind tosses aside her mirror knowing it's she who has the power and fills the air with the fragrance of the budding cherry blossom flower.

—*Michael E. Morrison*

Her Garden

From her pain a garden grew
filled with flowers; yellow, blue.

And from her tears a pond appeared
with lilypads and reflections mirrored.

The birds would sing and touch the sky
From bud to bud danced butterflies

In this garden we saw love,
and if she's watching from above,
it amazes me, we never knew,
that behind her eyes her dark pain grew.

—*Stacey Richards*

Creativity

Where does all creation start?
From the head or from the heart?
Like Athena, sprung full-blown
From her Pater Zeus' dome?

Or is it a happy chance,
Like a mystic circumstance,
Whirling all one's thoughts around?
Fertile seed on arid ground.
Paradise in embryo,
Milton's vision rising slow;
Dante in the grips of Hell,
Where the evil spirits dwell,
Found at last through starry space
Beatrice and Heaven's grace.

Times will come and times will go.
Inspiration you would know?
Recognize the silver thread
That led Theseus from the dead.

—*Mary Frances Langford*

Neopallium

The mysteries of life burn deep
from the jagged volcanic protrusions
to towering pinnacles surrounding vast domains
man is on earth but a moment in time.

Strange beasts once roamed these domains
Neanderthals sat deep within dark caves,
Fire, recently discovered by these dwellers
brings visions of a roast turning slowly...

What strange thoughts are these?
Raw meat is what we get to please.
What? an interloper comes upon my land!
Attempting to take the feast for which I plan.

This dweller of the cave rushes to a stand,
forgets his thoughts, grabs his club
and races forth to slay the interloper
who chanced upon his land.

Such thoughts still linger deep in our cranium
within the fibers of the Neopallium.
We too slay interlopers who come upon our land
if only by chance they pass within our span.

—*Morris Eldon Ward*

My Japanese Wife

A silk clad Kimono Doll; like Celadon
From the land of Nippon.
Beautifully Oriental — An Artful Creation.

Like the flavor of Cherry Blossom Tea
So different
So delicate is She.

Creating harmony — blending two into one
As fruit from flowers come
Our minds and bodies thus become
Inseparably One
Two cultures joined in one.

Polite and petite - so pretty and nice
With the perfume of scented incense
This is my lovely Japanese wife.

—*Wendell E. Hauenstein*

Old Saint Nick

Wheezing in the winter mist
Gagging at the smell
Of old socks and of older feet
Not walking quite so well

Staggering under a sack of toys
Stumbling here and there
Grumbling as he pulls his beard
Red face and thinning hair

Blue nose and bloodshot eyes that run
Reindeer that snort and bite
A sleigh that's crammed to overflow
Chimney's fit way to tight

He's seen it all and done it all
What a merry life it's been
Tis a pity that after all this time
Someday it has to end

But Father Time has his way with all
The tock becomes a tick
And no one is immune to it
Not even old Saint Nick…

—*G. Larry Butler*

He Died For You And Me

Christ my Lord and Saviour, loved humanity,
Gave His life upon the cross from sin to set me free.
Suffered pain and agony, He did it willingly,
He died for you, He died for me.

Was betrayed by Judas, whom he dearly loved,
For it was the will of God his Father up above,
He should make the sacrifice, upon the rugged cross,
He paid the price he paid the cost.

As He hung upon the cross, they mockingly did say,
He claimed he could save others Himself He cannot save,
They heard him softly whisper, these words to God above,
Forgive them Lord, thy will be done.

Early on the third day, they went to the tomb,
Found the stone was rolled away, and only clothes of grey,
Were found where they had laid Him, that sad and tragic day,
Where is my Lord, they heard them say.

The radiant angel, ask whom do you seek,
We seek our Lord and Master the words they did repeat,
But why seek ye the living among those who are dead,
He is risen, He is risen.

—*Raymond Bower*

Ant Lion

Find a sandy place that's dry;
Get on your knees and you may spy
A sandy trap that looks like a pit,
Built by the lion hiding in it.

The pit is round with sides that slope;
When ants get caught there's little hope,
For when they try to struggle out,
The lion tosses sand about.

Into the pit the ant then falls,
Grabbed by the lion's needle jaws;
Too late…the ant can't get away,
Lunch for lion is ant that day.

—*May H. Davis*

It Is So Easy To See For Yourself, And So Right and Beautiful

Just think-once upon a time, you were a small baby boy or a girl. How did you get to this world?

"God" made this world, and every person on earth was chosen as "His miracle," and to know "Him" to love "Him" and to serve "Him," in this world, and to be happy with "Him" forever in the next. Everyone should look around to see every creature in the Universe, tiny to largest. How they know so well to care for their babies, and all of the foods "He" arranged for all human beings and every type of animal. We have, "One Supreme Being," watching over every one of us, waiting for us to be happy with "Him" forever. "He will be beside you, when you take your last breath." "Jesus Christ, Son of God" has suffered and died for us on the cross. "He" wants everyone to be saved. "He" waits for us to ask "Him" to help us. Try it. "He never lets you down, but be sure to thank "Him."

I only write the truth—believe me—"He" has showered so much of me, and people I helped. I am happy to be "His" helper, and tell of "His" miracles, until I am happy with "Him" forever in the next.

—*Virginia D. Waters*

Me

Place your lips on mine, so I may feel life.
Give me the energy that will re-life my being, so
that I may see the break of dawn.
Your love, your touch, the hope that I shall see yet another day.
Do we dare to believe in happiness? that we have
but all the joys of life.
Running—Running from all that we fear.
Not knowing that it is me whom I have feared.
So I shall close they eyes, and see me.
What have I hidden from?
Not the soils that I may place my feet and walk
towards life; thy life that I shall see through my heart.
Thy one that has yet to exist.
It shall take but one breath, a vision of trust, a
sense of reality of what I have feared.
Give me, but insight of love and value of honesty.
Guide me towards thy life I have earned.
Teach me to walk to a new beginning, to know and
understand Me!

—*Virginia Aragon*

The Lesson

A brilliant sunbeam snaked through the leaves
  Giving second thoughts to a lesson to heed.
A man is not a man when he can't get what he please;
  Falls to his knees, and just concedes.
  But a man is a man when he clearly sees
No battle is won, when the coward flees.

  Fate did not promise a decade of ease.
    One must fight, one must seize
    All the beauty, in life he sees.
  In days of lemons, squeeze back the tears.
    Make of that day a lemon-freeze

God has blessed the man, who can truly see
  There is beauty enough for you and me.
  We've only to stand, and counted be.
    I am a man, and so is he.

—*Lillian E. Lampkins*

A Mother Has Many Voices

The first voice of a Mother cries out in pain
Giving birth to her baby, a joyous refrain.
A mothers sweet voice, singing to her baby,
A mothers voice saying, No! No! not maybe.

Then a happier voice, with laughter at play
And a softer voice, teaching her child to pray.
A hopeful voice, to school the first day,
A coaxing voice, getting her child to stay.

A disappointed voice, when things go wrong,
A firm voice, when trying to stay strong.
A scary voice, in times of trouble,
With a soothing voice, when trouble is double.

A mothers voice scolding, sounding so mean,
Is the hardest voice used, to guide a teen.
A doubtful voice, asking what she did wrong,
A knowing voice, life's not always a song.

A mothers voice of encouragement, to do ones best,
Yet a voice of acceptance, none the less.
A voice so untiring giving the word,
A mothers voice, whatever tone—is heard.

—*Rose M. Kavanaugh*

Little Things

Little stars shining in the night,
Giving to all your twinkling light,
Knowing that you are always there
Reflects the Father's constant care.

Little flowers nodding in the breeze,
While leaves of green flutter on the trees,
Sharing your beauty for all to see
Reflects God's loving care of you and me.

Little birds singing in trees and sky,
Spreading notes of cheer while flying by,
Endowed and fed for your songs of love
By a watchful Father who reigns above.

Little new lambs romping here and there,
Seeming to have no worry or care,
Growing to be like the sheep of the fold
The Good Shepherd spoke of in days of old.

Little Godlike embryos are each of us,
With divine potential to develop, thus
Obeying, serving, enduring, sharing,
Reflecting God's glory, love, and caring!

—*Virginia A. Terribilini*

To Write

I sit in my chair and hold my pen,
Go over my thoughts from beginning to end.
I go through a list of words I know
And try to rhyme them as I go.
Seems nothing I think of, has beauty or meaning,
The poems I write are more like dreaming.
Still, there is a heartfelt meaning when a poet writes.
Write with feeling, sad, gay or bright,
A poem with some sadness can show beauty too.
Though your heart aches there is a smile for you.
Words can put joy or tears in your voice,
Write them in rhyme, your heart will rejoice.

—*Lucille L. Webster*

As A Whisper

As a whisper in the wind, as a whisper,
God calls His kin. Listening to the enchanting wind
They gather their lot where they have been.

To overcome sin is His domain, for righteousness
will always remain. Awaiting at each listening ear,
is a message to those who care.

So harken to the whistling wind, to the
message to overcome sin, and rejoice
in a message to those who care. He
gathers His lot as a whisper beyond the wind.
as a whisper in the wind, as a whisper God calls his kin.

—*Ruth Goldfarb*

The Way Home

Suffer in gladness, pray in might;
   God in His goodness, will show you the light.
Toil in His vineyard, walk his path,
   Be ever on guard, and free from His wrath.
Worship in love, lend a hand,
   And God up above, will bless our land.
Flee from sin, search for His will,
   As you begin, He will help you over the hill.
When the valley nears, another hill in sight,
   Go the way He steers, and you will find the light.

—*Luther H. Oliver*

Our Marriage

Our marriage is beautiful, filled with love—
God sent you from heaven above—
I can never tell how deep is my love;
You complete me, my dear, make me whole.

I never knew just how sweet love could be.
Till I met you, and you said you loved me.
Your kisses are precious, so thrilling, you see.
You're all the lover I'll ever need.

When we said "I do," and said we'd be true
It seemed like a dream, too good to be real.
I meant every word of our marriage vows,
They reflected the way we both truly feel.

—*Laverne Talley*

Headlines From The Next World News

    Observations of...
      God's cherished planet...
        Of joy and life...
          At the end of
      The 21st century

    Transmitted by...
The Celestial Society of The Heavens

Insanity inundates the blue planet... earth
A vortex of evil envelops it's girth

Cosmic clouds of immorality obscure the air...
Polluted by disease and corruption everywhere

Creatures born with godly spirits are the cost
Annihilated by entities who are virtually lost

Warning; if decent and moral they'll step on you
Danger... honor and merit they'll trudge on too

If you're loving and kind they'll stampede in a herd
...Depraved souls that don't believe in God's word!

—*Linda L. Wells*

The Sunset

The splendor of the sunset by the ocean is
  God's manifestation of his majestic
  beauty of this world.
Radiating golden sun rays reaching for the
  pink and white clouds wandering above in
  the blue of the sky.
A creating magnificent crown
To glorify the world.
The reflection from the sunset gives the sky
  aglow and the ocean glittering with gold.
The white sails passing by the sunset like the
  fairy tale.
And all is still and peaceful and so beautiful
  paying homage to descending sun.
And only the light breeze is caressing the
  waves of the ocean,
As they are endlessly rushing to the shore.
    —*Nonna Prohorenko*

Beautiful Castle Of Dreams

On a lonely tanker sailing far across the sea
goes my one and only - far away from me
And in my room so dreary the thought of him remains
As the cold rain is falling upon the window pane

I breathe a silent prayer
in vision of him it seems
Then I close my eyes to visit
the most Beautiful Castle of Dreams

For I always find him waiting there
with true heart and open arms
and when he whispers Love to me
Romance and happiness alarms.

Yes, he is my dream man
the arrow through my heart
and even this great distance
couldn't keep our love apart.

I know you're sad, my Darling, but just look above
God will give us freedom, happiness and love
Then we'll stroll together as the moonlight softly gleams
And know love forever in the Beautiful Castle of Dreams
    —*Margaret Nell Archuleta*

Speaking of Love

God breathes life into a child,
Granting mind and body and soul.
He molds and shapes and heals all pain
As the child's years unfold.
With a Mother and Father, the child is blessed.
Such a pure, unconditional love.
Taking lessons of heart; giving only their best,
They teach values and pray it's enough.
As years fade past, the child grows
Finding love under starlit skies,
With wedding bells, the exchange of vows
And radiant, joyous eyes.
Love is laughter, hopes and tears.
Love is grace which understands.
It's walking on stones to rest on a cloud,
Holding moonlight in your hands.
And with all the violent rages we face,
All the fearsome and murderous tides,
It's much easier to cope in this frightening world
Knowing somewhere, love still abides.
    —*Sherry Lyn Smith*

Magical Dreams

A twinkle in your eye, magic in the air;
Great expectations in the future we bare.
You can wish upon a star and make it come true;
With the high hopes that luck brings to you.
Tread on the heels of your dreams that escort you to the light;
Leaving you in a phantasm, bringing you to new heights.
Soaring like a bird, angels in the sky;
All the lonely nightmares just seem to pass you by.
Set down your goals and push them to your cloud;
Slowly you will accomplish them and of yourself be so proud.
But do not yearn for something that can't be done;
Cause it's like reaching for a star knowing you'll never get one.
If by chance you stumble upon one of your dreams;
A helping hand will be there to finish it as a team.
But one thing you must promise is to never give in;
Because winners never quit and quitters never win.
So strive to be all and grab your special star;
cause with your dreams your destined to go far.
    —*Michele Michalski*

Mighty Mississippi — Mighty God

The beautiful Mississippi flowed within its banks of verdant green. Nestled here and there were farmlands, cities, cozy cottages cuddled in its banks were seen! Leafy trees, brilliant flowers, singing birds: Beauty without end, with fields of growing grains. Within those tiny little cottages were families and friends! So beautiful, so peaceful, gliding through the Mighty Mississippi waters in a home made raft, upon a quiet sunny day! Then suddenly the rain drops started — Then came the great, mighty flood of 1993! Swollen waters, crescendos of roaring waves, currents strong and deadly came rushing by with great and mighty power—With great and mighty power everything, everything in its way - the power to destroy! Oh, mortal man, where is thy strength, to quell the mighty flood? Stop in your tracks, turn about in your ways acknowledge there is a great and mighty God! Reach out your hand, oh mortal man. He will save you, He will care for you, He will restore within your soul — a will to live! For He is the master of the storm, only He can calm the mighty flood!
    —*Rose B. Stevens*

Nature The Healer

The gnarled savagery of rage
Grips my breast with saber claws,
Injecting my veins with a venomous obsession for revenge.
I burn with a lust for aggression I knew not lurked in my soul.
Hatred and fury fuse imagined horrors into anticipated reality.
A tidal wave of repressed indignations sweeps me into battle.
The violent forces boil within me;
My body mechanically responds to their call to arms.
Nerves steely, muscles taut, every cell readies to attack.
I burst forth form the darkness into a sprinkling of sunshine.
A tapestry of flowers spreads before me in its full spring glory.
A gentle breeze kisses the sweat off my brow.
A scent of honeysuckle, jasmine and rose swirls intoxicatingly.
A monarch tickles my cheek; a ladybug lands on my thumb.
A chorus of chirp, tweet, hum and buzz resounds into a symphony.
Mesmerized, every sense engaged, I accept Nature's invitation.
The grass beneath me soothes, comforts, sweetens, relieves.
The poisonous passions ebb away, drowning in a nearby brook.
I marvel at Nature the Conductor, the Artist, the Perfumer — the Healer.
    —*Lidia Wasowicz Pringle*

Responsible Or Not

From baby to girl to female teen
Growing up fast, maturity lags hell of a thing
Potential woman: full of affection, filled with
intent but no direction

Laying here, going there and everywhere
Been doing it so long don't seem to care
Burning sensation on fire inside, enslaved
by desire, done murdered your pride

Getting good to you, this is what you say
Think about your future, look beyond just today
Where are you headed, have you
considered this
Thank you for giving thought; you're
Innocent; Case dismissed
—*Walter Searcy, Jr.*

When Labor Takes A Holiday

Factory wheels grind to a halt,
Guard dogs settle down in their den.
Moms are allowed to take a break,
Students and teachers sleep in.

Men do not report to work,
Time clocks rest for a while,
The President takes a short retreat,
And fashion models put away their styles.

The postman refuses to make his rounds,
The repairman goes away,
Leaving the TV and washing machines,
To work on another day.

The policemen, firemen and doctors,
Still have to move about.
Because there are still some things
We just can't do without.

The barbecue grills are all fired up,
As workers rest and play,
Taking time out to enjoy themselves,
When labor takes a holiday.
—*Marean J. Price*

The Old House

Lonely the house sits
Guarded by trees,
Knowing what once was
Brings sweet memories.
A silver-haired lady,
The queen of the home,
Watched as her children
Played, grew, and then roam'd.
The master who loved her,
Shared laughter and tears,
Has lain in his grave now
Many long years.
Older she grew, steps slow and eyes dim,
Praying each day that she soon would join him.
Quietly sleep came, the sleep of the blest.
There by his side they laid her to rest.

Still lonely the house sits
Guarded by trees,
Holding forever those sweet memories.
—*Laura Shelton Thurmond*

Grand Canyon

Like massive Sphynxes, dozens in a row
Guarding the gate of eons, each embewed
With its own riddle, carved in deep refrain
With stoic posture, glancing every way
Like watchmen at the entrance of Eternity.

Such multiplicity, adorned in garb of red,
Or, —if such chastity were none too clad,—
Bedecked with greenery and forest plaid
Where graves of rivers, carved in deep array
Through thousands crags astound the greatest buff.

Mid the majestic form they wear their crowns,
Plateau upon plateau, where canyons meet
In frozen majesty, God' legacy in stone
Ennobled sculpture plays the shadow game
For an abortive age and wayward race.

So stands for many unknown years
The silent wonder of this mark of time,
Oblivious to the passing of dimensions.
The distance, faint in angel dust still lauds
The undenial Majesty of God!
—*Peter H. Katz*

An Image

I peered into my mirror
Guess what I saw
A very happy face
Full of smiles
Smiling back at me.

My night had been a restless one
Dreaming of years long passed
When life was simple and quiet.
When families were as one
When love ruled among us all.

Those years of yesterday have slipped away
Their memories will always remain.
My mirror fails to let me know
The years of treasures I hold Dear
Will give me joy and peace.

I peered into my mirror
T'was time to say goodnight
A happy face still met me
Praying to God
For a peaceful and quiet night.
—*Zelda James*

July

Stay, September, two more months
For Sweet July is here.
I touch my lips to her bounteous fruit
Hold her sun-heat near.

To lie with her for thirty-one days
And silent star-lit nights
My fingers in her grasses long
And breathless in her sights.

Stay, September, eight more weeks
July has come of age.
I would bathe in warmth's fertility
My wife of thirty-one days.
—*K. Arthur McGauhey*

War

The missiles scream of their doom to come,
gunfire on the run.
People falling in their tracks, all along
the blood stained ground.
A mothers silent cry of grief as the child
she hold dies.
Another child's plea for peace goes unheard
in a world of endless torment.
The cry of agony lingers from a soldier as
the seconds of life ebb away.
Families pray that their children won't die,
as enemy planes circle the sky.
Spending money for others misery,
while civilians sit back and watch.
Is that what life is all about?
When will it end?
What is our future?
War... is it worth it?
—Missy Kuster

Before The Fall

Green gold of August
hangs hot in the air still
a knowing of crispness

Late season showers
model clouds in blues and blacks
edged with silent iridescent fireworks
and distant mountain lightening flashes

In the lay of rainlight glow
with fresh wet smell of earth
and grass and pine tree bark
children play kickball in the shiny street
and run the last of their merry mighty races
chasing summer
—Stephani Pfau

To Joe

The love I have for you is strong
Happiness for us, not short but long
Eternal life and glory be
Love to the end and cherish thee
My thoughts of you will always be
Among your heart and into eternity
Help we'll give to each one through
Ever lasting, wonderful, times with you
God made us for each other's love
Even in the life above
Romance, kisses, courting too
is all I want along with you.
—Thelma Davis

Love Your Fellowman

In all walks of life, love your fellowman
Hard work is road to success—how it began
Be a self-made guy, smile and try—try
Perseverance overcomes obstacles—we can't deny
When you give a helping hand—strike up the band—
Try to smile—do with a will—that's how it began—
Blessings may come and go—may overflow—
Positive thinking seems to remain—just so
Best contend, life is coming around the bend
Rainbows are up there in the sky—transcend.
—Mary Lou Darnielle

Home

Everyday, life passes by a frail testimony of autumn's harvest. She stands with outdated features and bares no resemblance to her youthful composure. Her owner has proclaimed
her happy; a wondrous collection of timeless moments stored in broken fixtures and scratched surfaces. There is a neatness that bespeaks a comfortable but worn interior. Stairs that squeak
and hinges that wail as if moaning from all the lively moments of times before, are members along the straits of time that characterize what will always be home to the children that were born and raised under her roof.

As the wind blows about storm doors that rattle in the breeze, there is no sense of abandonment. The children increased
while she decreased. Her sacrifice is one that will never be forgotten. Even though there be shiny places with well-kept spaces, there is only one place that will be called home — that frail testimony of autumn's harvest.
—Youri Brun

Focus

It has been said that the fanatic
has a void in his attic,
But it isn't he who goes off in every direction,
never to see anything to perfection.
Many lives have been dissipated in the end
by those who spread their effort too thin.

It is better to do one thing and do it well
than to try to do everything and miserably fail.
With precision of aim and intensity of concentration,
one can confront any situation.
A diffused beam gives a poor quality of light,
But a surgical laser can restore one's sight.
—Robert F. Hunter

Astral Gaze

The winter sky like pewter yesterday
Has been transformed as if by magic into smoke
That coalesces while I watch amorphous figures
Grow rotund

They gaze in dustbins and grow plump
On ashen residue denied the naked eye

Bison they become and woolly mammoths
Manticores and centaurs next
In metamorphosis and myth
Phantoms of Erebus and the river Styx
Mocking death in grotesque gestures
Hosting riddles for the sphinx

Fattened beasts primed for slaughter
Stomping hooves in astral dance
Butchered stormclouds bleed by edict
Blanched in grief and bleached by hand

Demeter's nocturnes, Demeter's dirges,
Demeter's frenzy palls the land
Lending weather to the legend
  Of a sacrificial lamb.
—P. Marguerite Forcier

Am I Gone Yet?

Am I gone yet? Have I breathed my last breath?
Has my life been set strait? Is the next to come death?
What all has happened? Why am I here?
I am surrounded by darkness and the sense of fear.
There are so many voices, voices all around.
My mind is now pounding because of the sound.
Too many voices, can't hear them all.
Afraid to look down because I might fall.
But there is one voice, it seems to be crying.
The feel of such sorrow while I am hear dying.
A cold wind blows through me as I turn from the dawn.
Now I am leaving, I know that I'm gone...

—S. Brynildsen

November Night

The last ruby-rose hue of sunset
Has slowly faded from view,
   Replaced by the gentle dusk
     Of this brisk autumn-wintery night.

The shimmering, glistening stars appear
It seems turned on one by one.
   Sparkling ever so brightly
     With their blue white glow billions
       of miles away.

The moon so full
And bright as morning sun,
   Lighting everything in its cool white glow
     In splendor-like magic here below.

Jupiter glows so bright on this perfect
   crystal night.
A night of surprise as the earth's shadow slips
   Ever so stealthy over this great white ball,
     In an awe inspiring lunar eclipse.

A cool gray mist of fog
Shrouds everything in ghostly array.
   While the moon slowly creeps from behind
     its dark shadow,
   To finish its awesome journey through
     this November night.

—Mary L. Eaton

Upon Seeing Jean For The First In Twelve Years

She pads into the room barefoot,
having just thrown on a long skirt and baggy sweatshirt,
her unassuming laughter floats upon the afternoon air like
Bijan perfume.

I am mesmerized by her still slender, ballerina movements,
long dark hair tied back, a close-lipped smile
crossing her fawn-like face, as she cautiously hugs me.

Slouching down in a papasan chair,
she sits cross-legged, momentarily at a loss for words,
amidst her oak furniture, earthtone art and potted plants.

I stare in awkward silence at this woman of thirty-five years,
my eyes settling upon the silver Makah necklace
resting gently between her petite breasts.

We slowly warm to each other over a cup of spiced tea.
"Twelve years since I've seen you last." is all she
can think to say, raising a proud chin and shaking her head.

—Steve K. Bertrand

My Son

  My son, a treasure of gold. He is the bundle of joy.
He brightens up the day.
  My son, growing big and strong brings sunshine that
keeps glowing each and every day.
  My son, special smile, warm the hearts of those he
touches.
  My son, is special in many ways. The friendly smile
is his way of saying I love you.
  My son, Damon, filled with love is a special friend.
He is cherished forever!

—Lynette Harper

He Alone

He can take away our problems
He can make our problems small
He can take away our cares
  so we have no cares at all

He can smooth the way when it is rough
He can make our pathway straight
He can bring happiness when we are sad
He never comes too late

Let us look to him for guidance
Let us believe he understands
If we reach out just to touch him
He will turn, and hold our hand

—Leontine Capdeville-Smith

Always Hope

Our good Lord is merciful, gentle and kind
He died for us sinners, so ease your mind
Go to Him with everything, He's always there
Waiting with open arms, your inner soul to share.

Look at the Crucifix, be good as He did that for you
Or prepare to burn in hell, for all the bad you do
But His cross brought us hope, so take a closer look
At all the holy bleeding wounds, for you and I He took.

Welts over all His body, with whips they beat
Nails pounded through both, His hands and His feet
His shoulder bone laid bare, from the weight of His cross
Out of love for all, so not one soul be a loss.

On his head a crown of thorns, each bled with pain
Precious Blood to redeem our sins, eternal life to gain
Hanging hours on his cross, until He took His final breath
For each and everyone of us, He loved us unto death.

I look at that crucifix, Lord I love you so
I'm sorry and confess my sins, feeling very low
Then He showers me with Graces, to make a better me
Lord I never want to hurt You, I pray on bended knee.

—Mary Ann Harlan

Jesus Shall Reign

He came with open arms today, oh listen to what
  He had to say,
"Come follow Me and spread My word,"
For this is what they all have heard!
I am the light, "Come follow Me,"
Go to those on bended knee.
Open the eyes of the blind, for then they too
  soon will find.
That I have come to bring them home,
To My Father's golden throne!
I was sent from the One above, to do His work
  of the Little Dove.
So do what I have asked of you,
For I am "Jesus," I'll see you through.
Keep Me close in your heart, there I'll never
  let you part!
  —Nancy Marie Kelling

God's Precious Gift

God has given us many gifts
He has given the gift of life to all and He has
given the things that are important to live that life.

Now at one time or another, God takes away
all these gifts He has given us, but each time
He takes anything away, He leaves something in its place.

He gives the sun in the daytime, then gently
replaces the daylight with dusk and you
barely notice dusk has gone because He has replaced it with night.

He softens the darkness of night with a million
stars and adds a moon large and shining.

When the moon and stars fade away they are
replaced by the dawn and dawn quietly steps
aside to let the new day take its place.

We don't miss all these things because God
has promised that everything will return in its
own time and place, and they do.
And so it is with life.

He gives us life, then we give birth to a child
And when we are called home, He has given us
something to leave behind, to soften the sorrow, to
have courage to carry on, and to give and receive love and
most of all, to have hope.

Like the circle of the day each life on earth must
complete the circle and when all the circles are unbroken
we will be together again in His kingdom.
This will be God's most precious gift.
  —Yvonne Dwight Jerdon

God

  God is in control of my life
He helps me with my daily fights
  God lends me a helping hand,
He is the one that understands
  God knows my daily fears,
He knows my nightly tears,
  God is in control of my life,
I love the Lord
  He helped me through closed doors,
The Lord helps me with my inner fights
  He helps me turn things out right
God is in control of my life.
  —Virginia Morris

My Perfect Love

My perfect love is sweet and huggable as a cuddly teddy bear.
He is beautiful on the outside but his real beauty glows within
And radiates the special goodness of his kind heart.
His soft hissable lips melt into mine and take my breath away.
He is crowned with greatness and touched by precious love.
I see him as a brilliant diamond that shines in a starry sky.
I love him with my whole being and my heart, soul, mind and
Body adore him. I shall love him forever.
  —Renee Fishbough

A Dog Named Bud

This beautiful black dog is very shiny and clean.
He is only a puppy, but he does some things that seem mean.
There are lots of things that he likes to do.
But his favorite thing is to have something to chew.
It doesn't matter if it costs little or much,
He just puts it in his mouth and loves the touch.
His tastes seem to vary from soft to steel.
Many nice things end up making his meal.
We love him so, but we had to make a change.
Now he is on a line, so we can keep him in range.
Maybe he will forgive us and not think of us as mud.
He is just our loving pet, a dog named "Bud."
  —Louise Williams

Why Not Put Christ In Your Christmas?

Why not put Christ in your Christmas
He is the joy that doth inspire
He is the star of all salvation
He is the spirit to live by.

O, come ye! O, come ye! Welcome the Christ child to stay
We can make this Christmas a holy and blessed day
Let us sing of the newborn king
Let His birth the world proclaim
The Christ child has come to eternally reign.

Christ is in my Christmas
No greater gift could I desire
So, why not put christ in your Christmas
And let the world go passing by?

Christ is in my Christmas
Peace, joy and comfort I derive
How could I face this Christmas
If in Christ I didn't abide?

If Christ isn't in your Christmas
Open up and let Him in.
Happiness and holiness to all fellow men.
  —Louise Dent Smith

From The Ashes

       The Eagle,
    From the ashes of a lost love,
    Arises, surveying his terrain,
    Screams a challenge to the skies.
     From the death of a love,
    Comes the dream of a new life.
He shakes the ashes from his talons.
       His wings take him
       Into the winds of life.
He rises, flying through the night,
    Screaming "I will survive!"

       I am the eagle.
  —Kiko Raya

The Unspoken

She crept softly, ye soundly, over his breast —
  He laid beneath the cold floor.
Conceiving of his thoughts, she cried —
    "To weep a silent tear inside
    of the rhapsody he feels not!"

The windows quivered,
  The walls yelled in blasphemy!
    The floor amongst him took his pride!
There he laid, with not an answer
  of the loneliness she felt inside.

The night passed, nae a reckoning, I wonder—
  He laid still upon the floor.
Perceiving of his pain, she wept —
    "Where am I? Can I feel not within
    a simply pity sigh?"

Rain clouds gathered,
  Trees fell ten abound them!
    A storm raged of fear in solemn sky!
There he laid, her hands fell upon him
  to find no soul inside.
    —B. Lee Morreale

The Golfer

The golfer stood poised with a bend at both knees
He looked at his ball it was high on a tee
He bent his left arm and smiled like a cat
But the thing that he did was hit the ball fat
How red was his face when he stepped from the box
He pulled out a towel and looked like a fox
Then over the course his ball he gave flight
A hook to the left and a slice to the right
The sandtraps and water it took from his game
His score was so high he was surely ashamed
He got through eighteen with thorough disgust
Broke all of his clubs and left in a huff
He vowed never again this game would he play
With a new set of clubs he was back the next day.
    —Peggy T. Cooper

Seek Him...

I sought the Lord, and afterward I knew
    He moved my soul to seek Him,
        seeking me;
It was not I that found, O Saviour true,
    No, I was found of Thee.
    Thou didst reach forth Thy hand
        and mine enfold;
    I walked and sank not on the
        storm-vexed sea,
    Twas not so much that I on Thee
        took hold,
    As Thou dear Lord, on me.
    I find, I walk, I love, but,
        the whole
    Of love is but my answer, Lord
        to Thee;
    For Thou wert long before-hand
        with my soul,
        Always Thou lovest me.
    —Mollie J. Persons

"17" "Vietnam"

He had the guts to fight and die,
He paid the price, what did he buy?
He brought you life by giving his,
Who gives a damn what a soldier gives.

You watch your T.V. from your easy chair,
But you don't know what it's like out there.
You burn the kids for marching at dawn,
To plant their flags on the White House lawn.

You knock our ways but have your fun,
And then teach us to use a gun.
There's nothing else you can do,
Yet I'm supposed to die for you.

I'll hate you till the day I die,
You made me hear my buddy cry.
I saw his arm a blood shred,
I heard them say "This One's Dead."
    —P.F.C. Michael R. Mulcahy

Sarah Girl

"This ones for you, Sarah Girl"
he said as he quietly kissed the
delicate lips, which made him reflect
on his love for her.
Quickly,
he looked her over.
Then
slowly,
slowly.
The face he rested upon.
Chin, he saw, was strong.
Eyes, he saw, were, large, inquiring.
Lips... he saw, were full, longing, loving.
    ... And he knew
    then, he could never
    leave his Sarah Girl.
    —Shannon McDaniel

When I Met Death

I met death on my walk through the park one day
He showed to me His ugly face and would not go away
He stared at me until I blacked out and saw a dark hole
Little did I know in that quick moment He had stolen my soul
He showed me a defenseless old lady and quickly disappeared
And left me in complete confusion which I very much feared
I pushed the little old lady and grabbed her purse and ran
It all happened too quickly to realize I was a different man
Each day the temptation I tried to fight grew worse
I wondered about Death and how He left me with a curse
I did things I never thought I was capable of doing
I was desperate to change while my soul I tried renewing
Death made me hide and even take into my own hands life
As I tried to fight off the curse He gave me in a bitter strife
The day I met Him had lost everything including my pride
Now there is nothing I can do for a big part of me has died
My soul is lost forever never to return again
And the pride of who I used to be will never be mended again
The men in blue have taken me away to pay for what I've done
And the day of Death's execution has finally come...
    —Marie-Catheline Jean-Francois

Memorial To A Dog

Once I had a good little dog -
He was the best little dog in town-
This little dog was a smart little dog -
He was the smartest dog around.
He spoke to me with a waggey tail.
He spoke with his eyes so brown -
He spoke to me in so many ways -
And sometimes he was a clown
Sometimes he may have been a problem.
But never ever was he bad.
I tell you now - and this I vow -
He was the best friend I ever had.
Now this little doggie is no more -
His gone where the good doggies go.
Oh! I'll never forget this dear little dog
Because I loved him so.
—*Ruth Stone*

Where Smiling Ends

When he was a little boy
He went to Sunday school
Where they taught him that he should
Obey the Golden Rule.

Time and time again they'd say
"Now listen boy, don't fight,
Fighting is for weaker boys
Who don't know wrong from right."

He was good, so very good,
He learned his lessons well,
But they didn't hesitate
To ship him off to hell.

Off he went to war, this boy
Who called all men his friends,
Off he went to Vietnam,
The place where smiling ends.

Later on they heard he died,
He died on bloody hill.
In his hand he clutched a note!
"Forgive me, I can't kill."
—*Maude Ginn*

Passionate Feelings

See the tear drops freckle the face of love.
Hear the cravings from beyond the heart into the well of
  wanting...the yearning to be in your arms forever.
Touch the pool of liquid that purifies the lasting
  love that we share.
Listen closely to the wonders your heart creates and
  the magic that makes them come to life.
Feel the unending warmth that we hold to warm
  our undying hearts.
Smell the potion that bonds our hearts as one.
And taste the fresh new beginning that love holds
  for the two of us together.
—*Lisa Shioji*

Echoes From Eternity

Seeing beauty I've seen before,
Hearing songs with notes and rhythms
That lift my spirit to seek more
Of the presence of other worlds,
An echo from eternity.

Traveling to places never
Known to me, seeing new faces,
Hearing words spoken I've never
Heard, yet know I've been here before,
An echo from eternity.

Looking at artists' creations,
Reading the words an author writes,
I sometimes feel their creations
Are birthed by a presence in me.
An echo from eternity.

Feeling joys and sorrows of all
Time, before, time now, times to come,
I will live hoping for the call
To stay always with the presence;
Echoing from eternity.
—*Patricia Frauchiger*

Careless Whispers

   I sit here by the phone, waiting for it to ring. My heart aches and then I hear it, and my heart begins to sing. False alarm, my heart hurts deeper and then,
   Finally you call me. Careless whispers are spoken and soon we begin to fight.
   Careless of my feelings, my hopes, my dreams. Careless whispers with no thought. Your words fly by me, most of them painful. Careless whispers spoken from despair
   Whispers from far and near, whispers that will soon disappear. The words I hear now are confusing and I don't know
I feel it happening, I feel you drifting away from me, my life.
   Careless whispers spoken in the night, whispers spoken from fright. I sit here clinched tight, wondering what's in sight. My whispers are starting to be careless.
   Careless whispers in the night. Careless thoughts that have no meaning, I feel my mind leaving. Careless whispers are all I have left, the whispers I hear late at night.
   The whispers that relieve my fright
      Careless whispers in the night.
—*Lisa Riner*

Remembering Richelle

You were here for just such a little while, you filled our hearts with love and joy, which will never fade away. Everywhere we look you'll be there. Each morning I'll see you coming through the door with your little P.J's and blond curly hair that crowned your beautiful face. A little hug and a sweet little kiss and you'd be ready to play. You were so precious and ever so bright, you laughed a lot and wrinkled your little nose, you enjoyed the grass as it tickled your toes you had the most beautiful eyes as blue as the blue blue sea. Your will was strong but your love was warm. Each morning as I hear the meadow lark sing. I'll see relax in your little swing as you watched the kids across the street or saw a kitten passing by. You could find and hold the smallest pebble in your hand. You picked the peddles from the flowers as you watched the robin close by. Neither the wind or rain, can blow or wash away the touch of little hand and when your birth day comes around I'll remember as it was the some as mine and now you are an angel in heaven. We loved you so much for you were so very special.
—*Ruth Mettler*

Homelessness

She reached out to grasp the darkness
Held it to her breast
The night was long the wind so cold
She tried to get some rest
In the huddled slumber
Came the reoccurring dream
Of warmer places and food to waste
And having all you need
But then when she awakes
Reality turns to the nightmare
And all life has to offer
Is faith and hope and prayer
The cardboard castle that she shares
Might be humble but it's home
She may be a stranger
But she's not alone
So many people living
You've got to wonder how
No one seems to care what happens
Is just what we allow
—Paul Markworth

Help Me Lord

Help me Dear Lord,
Help me today.
Help me Dear Lord,
As I kneel down to pray.
Help me Dear Lord,
Find the right words to say.
I need you Dear Lord, please,
Help me today.
Help me, help the little children with no food to eat.
And the precious homeless with no shoes on their feet.
Help the troubled veterans who can't forget the war.
Help the alcoholic person who gets into the car.
Help the unwed mother who don't know where to turn,
Help the many illiterate who find it hard to learn.
Help the loving families who are losing all they have.
Help the ones in depression who are lonely, helpless and sad.
Then help the others of us Father, who cannot find our way.
Help us all, Father, please help us today. Help us to help each other,
As we search for the right words to say.
And after all of this Father, if we don't first succeed,
May we fall down on our bending knees.
—Marva Stewart-Pittman

Two Seeds (A Wedding Poem)

Two seeds blown by the wind,
Helpless they did glide.
Over hill and river bend,
With nature as their guide.

The breezes stopped,
A pause was due.
By fate they dropped,
Together and grew.

Now they're trees that live or die;
Two stems of life, that upward bend.
If they grow more deep than high;
They will not need, the fate of wind.
—Michael P. Holden

Granny

this story's of my granny in the deep hills of Taney,
her eyes, black and snappy,
her frail body bent with time. born to a mother left alone with babes
her young husband blue sleeping with the gray near memphis,
baldknobbers, bushwackers, death, hunger, friends and foe,
feuds long forgotten, ballads, music, a strong faith
tales of kinfolk in tennessee, virginia, carolina and kentuck
with ease, her mounting a horse, holding a gun, brewing herbs,
making a quilt, delivering a newborn, planting flowers by a cabin door
i remember corn shuck ticking on a cabin floor,
hugs and contentment, while the fire burned low
then my dark eyes weeping as she's carried to her final rest
still listening to the wind in the trees over her bed
now I am grandma, singing an old ballad, playing my mountain dulcimer
   in the city
to beautiful grandchildren carrying family names into the future
and the one that plays the dulcimer with me granny...
oh, granny you should see her smile —
and she has snappy, black eyes...
—grandma rice

My Mother's Prayer

Walking into mother's hospital room one day,
Her eyes were closed as I heard her pray.
Please God, help me to bear this pain!
I ask this in Jesus precious name.
I will bear this pain as long as I can,
But please dear Jesus, hold on to my hand!
Lord, I'm so weary and my heart is breakin,
I feel so alone, so helpless and forsaken!
If you're still with me, show me in some way!
And the clear voice of a priest asked, would you like to pray?
Mother, began to cry uncontrollably,
Crying, thank you dear Jesus for showing me!
While looking at her face I had no doubt,
This was the Miracle she had told us about.
Mother would thank Jesus, over and over again,
Because, he did stop her excruciating pain.
We were given a chance to express our love,
And on Saturday at 8:45 on June 2, 1990, God called her above!
—Nino Colo

Their Chores Are Done

Lightning flash and pouring rain,
   Her face pressed against the window pane
Watching for his shadow in the foreboding darkness,
   It's choring time and she awaits his safe return again.

Their days would end when the hens were fed,
   The cows brought home to the milking shed,
The wood and kindling carried in,
   The children fed and tucked in bed.

When the chores were done at close of day,
   The fire burned low as they spoke of ways
To plant or till or rake the hay
   Or improve the farm to make it pay.

The years have passed, she sits alone
   And thinks of the happy years, now gone,
When together they worked the soil and reaped the grain,
   But he has gone home now, his chores are done.

She looks ahead with eagerness, when
   Together they'll roam the hills of heaven
And, at last, be glad to know
   Their chores are done and they are safely home.
—Norma Bobbitt

In The Memory Of Ma Ma Shug

In the slight dark night God took her away.
Her family cried as she slowly died.
They did not need to see her in pain any longer,
but it was hard to let her go.
She was the closest thing to an angel the earth will ever see.
She was so kind and found good in everyone.
In every life she touched she will always be remembered.
I knew this lady well she was my grandmother.
Her memory will live on forever.
I know she is in heaven walking hand in hand with God and Jesus
She may not be alive on this earth but she is in my heart.
I know she is watching over me in heaven.

—*Kathryn Densie McCoy*

Across The Years

Across the years she could recall,
Her friends at Parksite were best of all,

In the stillness of the night,
She awoke in light, my desk oh what a sight.

She saw her hands were spread apart,
Knowing soon she's have to start

A heart that gives a great glow,
That everyone around her is sure to know.

It showed a look upon her face,
That everyone here could trace.

She enjoyed her work, hurrying about, now all the
Memories can be sorted out.

—*Linda Jett*

Her Rag Dolls

Long years ago she used to leave
Her rag dolls on the stair,
A flighty child with willful ways
And energy to spare.

So brief was her concentration
When whimsy led her on;
What fate might befall her rag dolls
Was for the moment gone.

Time passed swiftly and she married
A very special boy.
Two children came to bless the home
And fill their lives with joy.

But some old habits do die hard,
And marriage lost its glow;
Other interests caught her fancy
And it was time to go.

With fickle heart she turned her back
Upon her children fair;
She left them much like her rag dolls
Abandoned on the stair.

—*Ruth Warner*

A Friend

The piercing steel blue eyes now dim
Her well kept tresses no longer trim
The once ample frame, firm and agile
No sits inert, extremely fragile

The mobile chair, its frail captive holds
As the safety bar she weakly rolls
Her trembling hands force it round and round
But nowhere can an escape be found

She tries hard to speak but there's just a cry
While the pleading blue eyes question why
That locked safety bar will not release
She tries again but there is no peace

Her independence stripped page by page
The ragged edges broken through age
I know the book must soon be discarded
And she and I forever parted

This portrait etched upon my heart
Gave me solace from the very start
For I knew that she could never mend
And realized death would be her friend!

—*Linda B. Grube*

So Little Time

Here's to yesterday, here's to a love that could not be.
Here's to yesterday, here's to a dream you stole from me.
Here's to yesterday, here's to the memories you left behind.
Always to haunt me, always to taunt me, never to forget you once were mine.

So many things to do, and so little time,
I was in love with you, someone changed your mind.
Night after night, I dream of what might have been.
And in my heart I know, we will never meet again
They say the whole world's a stage, each one must act his part.
I was the fool that day and you were the rising star.
The show is over now, the curtain must come down.
I still can hear the applause for the one who broke my heart
The years have come and gone, the stage has disappeared
But through it all, I still love you, dear.
Living in the past, I still remember my line,
So many things to do and I've so little time.
So many things to do, I've so little time.

—*Mary Albo*

The Golden Eagle

   A great golden eagle soars about as if
He's a feathered king. Mounting supreme
upon the winds, high above the tallest mountain,
he swoops and views a small quagmire in
the lowlands as he takes his tour,
just seeming to be carried by the wind; he
rides upon the rays of the sun and unfolds his
massive wings in majestic aeronautics, actually
riding upon an updraft.
   He wearies not in his strange, effortless
sort of flight-the sun and the winds are his
friends.
   Effortlessly, he glides through the air,
displaying the ease with which his flight is executed.
   He owns the territory in which his flight
and wing spread covers.
   Only his silhouette is displayed against
the lights of heaven and the sun.

—*Sue J. Brownen*

The Prince Of Peace

Do you know the Prince of Peace, my friend,
He's the one who's true to you to the end,
He's the one who loves you as you are,
To him, you're a bright and shining star.

Your light will shine so others can see,
You have the peace that's meant to be,
That peace will spread throughout the world,
When everyone gives Jesus a whirl.

Love God with all that's in you, friend.
Love and help your neighbor throughout the land,
If we all join together in this mighty endeavor,
We will enjoy God's peace forever!

—*Priscilla Anne Meek*

Plastic Heart

It doesn't matter if you don't write, I'll keep my tears hidden in my plastic heart. That way, my pain doesn't show. No one cares to know the lonely days I go through. When I don't even hear from you, time goes by so slow. Thinking of you makes the teardrops flow, I wipe them away so gracefully and pray you will write me some day.

"It doesn't matter," I tell myself. You will write me some day when you are all alone. Maybe then I'll be gone. You can't hear me or see my smile. Maybe then you will just cry. Then you can say I'll write you another day. But then it will be too late.

Someday you will be all alone, waiting for a letter, or standing by the phone to get a call from someone you love, or hear someone say, "I love you, dear. Did you get my letter today?" It will mean the world to you just to know that someone cares.

"Hello!" "good-bye," "Merry Christmas," "Happy New Year," "I hope you liked you, Valentine." "Easter was a beautiful day." oh well, "Happy Birthday!" "I love you!"

—*Marie Roberts*

Look Up

Look up! Can't you see the sky is burning?
Hide inside your homes, the tide is turning.
Flames are rising higher over the horizon,
Whence they came the winds have turned a shade of crimson.
Then began the acid rain on a cloudless afternoon,
When ascends great havoc from the exorbitant typhoon.

Look up, look up, the sky is falling!
Nights filled with a desperate calling
For help, as the vehement furor raged on,
While the earth quakes beneath the approaching dawn.
Paths are cleared in the iron steeds' and avians' wake,
Closing in to a place and promise we must forsake.

Look up, look up, look up, the sky is crying!
Faces stained with tears and blood of the dying.
It's within our reach to end this senseless misery,
Just let the anger pass and we shall claim victory.
Look into the heavens, you will see a comet from afar
Flashing by, for one moment we will shine brighter than a star.

There is a madness slowly poisoning out our sanity.
Had we somehow in his confusion lost our humanity?

—*Kou Lee*

The Facade

The fake valiant monster, huge, white and clean
Hides it's greed and decay under the facade of caring
It holds the old and helpless, employs the young and middle-aged
Has been's and never will be's
Spitefully and hatefully, they do what they must
To earn a pitiful pay check
Plaster on a smile when somebody from the outside
Penetrates the pale blue openings
Day after day they curse
As they pretend to nurse and feed, happily
The disintegrating half dead, unmoving and unable
While the all-powerful sit in an outside office
To feed the facade of gentle harmony
With one hand to hold and one hand to steal
Uncaring and unashamed
Every month the money is drained
Like blood from a dead body, they smile
Behind closed doors, gloriously
Counting their stolen blood money
And justify it in the name of caring.

—*Sandi Browning*

I Need You

I love a rushing, tearing wind, snatching my soul and sweeping high, Screaming with glee, and bending low; putting on a madman's show, I love a roaring, splitting sky, dense and dark, Shrieking with its wounds of light, protesting to its last echo...
I love a bold, rebellious sea, of heaving, swelling, fluid glass, Rising — like a loosened fiend, a frothing, frenzied, foaming fiend, sea-scorn foaming on its sheen, spitting its scorn at the stars, Rising and groaning; escaping from itself
Rising — from its pounding, painful passion.

I love these things of awful urge, of fearless, daring animation that "will" to move and live, and break their mighty drive against the passive, inert things, the quiet, calm accepting things, the beds of land, the still, gray rock, the strong and soundless things, giving boundaries to their force. I've wondered why I need you... Now I know, for you are the silent strength, you are the calmly accepting, you are the strong and the straight, limiting life's frenzy, I need you — I need you, forever to be, firm and knowing, a boundary for me, while I madly swirl and curl, breaking my agony of force, and finding peace — against you.

—*H. Nevada Anderson*

The Old Man

The old man sat rocking in his old rocking chair
His fingers were gnarled silver shown in his hair
He chewed and he spat then he offered this prayer
Dear God forgive me for what I have done
While drinking my whiskey, my beer, and my rum.
I've known many women, dated a few,
Took them out dancing, spent my money, its true.
Committed adultery, many a sin.
Now angels fear treading where this old man has been
Dear God forgive me for what I have done
While drinking my whiskey, my beer, and my rum.
Then the old man sat rocking in his old rocking chair
He gazed at his families picture with a long fixed stare.
He turned to the table, took up his gun, saying;
Dear God forgive me for what I have done
While drinking my whiskey, my beer, and my rum.

—*Wanda Warrenburg*

Spirit Of Mine

I ride the roads of my mentors teachings.
His balding ashen scalp,
Crystal, poignant, stare
How he cried, laughed, and died without a sound.

The man of heated stone,
Tender, giving, hearty.
Leather, wrinkled mass of intense, emotional soul.
Powerful disdain for the criminal.
Loyal devotion to right.
Polished, command of his kingdom at hand.

Not tragedy,
Evil, vindictive jealousy,
inner heartache,
Outward indifference,
Nor crazed anger for the irreverent,
Raised his external visage to dismay.

How he walked the avenues beaming distinct respect.
Confidence of the sainted knight.
Stride of unmistakable, identifiable, Joseph.
Beacon of laser-like precision.
in a world surrounding him in ebony.
This, the man, my mentor, my friend.

—*Michael Byrne*

Bryan Boy

He comes smiling for my embrace
His brown eyes sparkle on his face,
Handsome lad has nice blonde hair
With skin so smooth, also fair.

We are two birds of a feather
Watching "Barney" on T. V. together,
Singing our songs keeping in tune
Musical career could happen soon.

If your Vacuum Sweeper is seen
There will be buzzing, room gets clean,
A neat little guy, very handy too
Will even clear the table for you.

"Bryan Daniel" turned five this year
Started to Kindergarten without fear,
Loves to ride in big yellow bus
Told me that the driver sure does fuss.

This happy boy is thrilled with school
Will grow up fast being no man's fool,
Yes, "My love to you, dear Grandson"
I feel lucky when another day is won.

—*Rosaline G. Sheets*

Reflections

My small son dips a magic bubble wand into a secret sudsy formula.
His cheeks puff out, full to rounded capacity with hurricane force.
He purses pouting lips and paradoxically produces the merest breath
   of air.
I laugh as his barely whispered "Oh" gives birth to the perfect
   soapy confection.
Springing free, the fragile globe dances past its delighted creator.
A capricious summer air bares it upward, out of our reach.
Where, against the canvas of sun and sky, the flirtatious orb
revolves leisurely, impudently displaying its lazily swirling spectrum.
At last, forced to obey some law of nature, it returns to rest at
   our feet.
Earthbound, nestling perilously amongst some tall spikes of grass,
we are both surprised.
In its last shimmering moment,
mirrored in its translucent core
are our startled reflections.

—*Martha Kay Robinson*

At Life's Rim

Who in this life ascends to fame
His fate is in the end the same.
And he cannot escape that date:
His body cracks: that is his fate.
And if his life spells charity
He still will not find clemency.
Life's High Court will not hesitate:
His body cracks: that is his fate.
Who wantonly their assets spilled,
the loveless, even those who killed
No sterner verdict hits their hate
Their bodies crack: that is their fate.
And yet we live in such a way
As if forever we could stay
Until the hard catastrophe
of sickness, age, war makes us see
That there is no enduring state.
The body cracks: that is the fate.
So do I change my mental frame?
Not ever. I remain the same.

—*Norbert Joachim Kreidl*

Little Boy Gone

His room is filled with memories of long gone by days
His Hopes, his Dreams are still here in a way
If I close my eyes and open my ears
I see him here amongst laughter and tears
Now it's Little Boy Gone for many a year

His smiling face lit up the place
He was a joy to have around
His helping hands were always ready
He kept my life on an even ground

His books are on the shelves
His trophies on the wall
Gathering dust, longing for little hands to touch
Just like he left them so long ago

His Hopes were high
His Dreams were many
He was going to travel the world
And help those who didn't have any

He's gone now.....
I sit here among all the memories
And Miss Him...Oh so much
My little boy gone..........
—*Roma Hogue*

Time Tics...

When the past became present,
His love remained the same,
When hard times arrive, they overcame
He has waited many years
For a love that is so true—
Love so true, and love that is not certain
Is tested through time
Two people fall in love, But time brings them apart
To meet again is the chance of time
But to find your love will be the test of time.
Two lovers meet again
But this time stronger and wiser
This time things are different
Because this love is genuine
Nothing will stop them now
And the puzzle is put in place
The last two pieces were found
And put in place within time
For he and she are together
And stood that test of time.
—*Yvette Leigh Emery*

My Love Of A Foreign Shore

There's a gentle man that shines above
His name is Andy, my English love
His eyes are blue and gentle as the summer sky
He's my greatest love, my special guy.
His scented letters make my heart beat as summer thunder
The love sent within, leaves my heart, nothing to wonder
For he has vowed his love for ever more
Lord, how I wish, he were standing at my door.
My nights are so lonely, just filled with desire
For my English love, still lives on the distant shore,
Amidst English Heather and country briar.
This my nightly prayer I say with love
To be instilled in his heart, by God above..
Sweetheart, as the lonely roads you do roam
Please remember, you shall never be alone
For my voice shall be the whisper in the trees
My kiss upon your face, the soft summer breeze
My eyes shall be the sparkle of the morning dew
Dearest one, in spirit, I shall always be with you.
—*Mary Anne DeLongchamps*

The Indian

He crept slowly, surrounded by the desert brush
His shadow covering the rocks.

Head bent low, against the rail of the wind.

Eyes, black and rimmed with red; weathered brown skin
crinkled as the heat of the sun bore down upon his body.

Weary, oh, so very weary
the memories of long days gone by,
Filled with laughter and songs of pride.

Longing, whispering dreams faded by time.

The families, the children, the elders of wisdom,
the fleetness of foot crushing into the winter's snow.

A people, certain of their future, unashamed of their past.
Reverie, now his only repast.
—*Linda Allmaras*

DIVERSITY

DIVERSITY wears many hats, none of which he owns. Because
his taste is so eclectic, he shops at the local thrift store.
His wardrobe is as varied as the rainbow and fortunately
never goes out of style. By the way, he is still searching
for just the right pair of shoes...

DIVERSITY is well travelled. She has lived in major capitals
of the world as well as in remote regions of various lands.
And although she takes journeys frequently, she never has use
for a map. She can converse in a number of languages and can
understand many more. Her talents are myriad: artist, teacher,
salesperson, fund raiser, poet and prophet.

DIVERSITY has an ample mouth, huge ears and wide eyes. His
smile is warm and laugh contagious. Give him a moment and he
can learn any song, master any dance. Often it appears that
he is nowhere in sight, when in fact he is right under you nose.
Best of all, his long inviting arms are always ready for a hug.

DIVERSITY hangs at the airport and discusses philosophy with the
flower vendors. People watching is her favorite pastime. She
loves to go on long walks and take in all the sights and
smells of her environment. Her family is far-reaching. While she
has had many lovers, she still treasures Camaraderie most of all.

DIVERSITY is simple yet complex. Because he cares for no one in
particular, he is interested in everyone in general.

—Robert H. Levin

Faded Hopes

A faded photograph of black and white
holds the image of girl in a bathing suit
wading in the water to have some fun,
a smile on her face and spirit in her eyes.

Carefree and slim, was that really you?
Does memory recall what your hopes were then?
Promises made and castles dreamed
With a man you believed would be a friend.

Years passed you by and children born
dreams turned to dust and hope care-worn.
weaponed words bruise as much as body blows
a spirit crushed may go alone.

But I have seen and lesson learned
can not forget and must grow strong
Life and Love WILL give me more
as your life ends, mine has begun.

—Patricia Cole Stauffer

There Is A Distant Thunder

There are earthquakes in divers places
Homeless people by the score
Babies aborted by the Millions
Starvation, death, and war.
When we look at our world around us
There is destruction on every hand.
Not just in the place we live,
But also in foreign land.
And yet we know who holds our future,
We know what lies in store
The answer's in the Bible,
In Matthew Twenty-Four!
So when things seem the darkest,
Look towards the sky
This surely is the season,
Our Redemption draweth nigh!

—Wanda L. DeWolf

The Other Side

(In loving memory of my husband Harold Fannin 1909-1988)
Honey, I'm so sorry
I made you cry
Honey, I didn't know
That you would die
I hope and pray each day
That you are safe somewhere
Please wait for me honey
till I can join you there
Honey, I'll come to you
As soon as I can
When the light shines through
And I touch your hand
I weep for you
And days gone by
Honey help me
To the other side.

—Keotah M. Fannin

The United States Holocaust Memorial Museum

This somber museum is a worthy legacy,
Honoring the millions whose precious lives were snuffed out
To indulge selfish whims of an evil government.
Within its walls are reminders of a dire nightmare:
Grim photographs showing mass graves and piles of corpses,
Gas chambers, starving victims resembling skeletons;
Here, too, stands a cattle car — transportation to death.
At this time we ask how all of this could have happened,
Innocent people dying while the world was silent.
This was the darkest period in world history,
Demonstrating man's vile inhumanity to man.
How can we now ease humanity's guilty conscience?
All of the honorable nations on this good earth
Must agree to establish a new moral order
Outlawing cruelty, prejudice, hate and injustice.
These ethical principles demand strict enforcement,
Designed to protect everyone in every nation,
So that there will never be another holocaust.
Man has a right to live in peace, enjoying blessings
Granted him by a most benevolent creator.

—M. Elisabeth Steiner

Plea To A Dying Nation

Once strong and proud, dwelling in the light,
hope in the eyes of the innocent.

Misdirected by greed, and a love for the fight,
clouds in the eyes of the innocent

Were you so blind, that you couldn't see,
fear in the eyes of the innocent.

You told us how to think, you told us what to say,
believe in all your leaders, its the american way.

But your dreams have all turned sour, time is running late,
time to pay the piper, time to meet your fate.

Once strong and proud, dwelling in the light,
tears in the eyes of the innocent.

Misdirected by greed, and a love for the fight,
you've blinded the eyes of the innocent.

   So, here we are, mere slaves to our leaders delusions
Do they not know the dangers of the stage from whence
their vanity hath sprung?

   Only when the crimes and death of war touch their own
do these fools we loosely all our leaders realize the
consequence of their folly and face the task of reaping
the poison fruits of their own mistaking!

—Sean T. Stoliker

Whispers Of Autumn

Twilight falls upon this muggy August day.
Hot breaths from the West bring no comfort.
The air is heavy, stifling butterflies
   from their magnificence.

I wait for rain to wash away this
   stagnation from my life.
But it will not come.

Even night brings no cool to cover me,
No hopes to soar my tired old soul.

Fireflies sprinkle against the dusk of warm
Pastels; they are frivolous like my boyish
Dreams, fluttering too high for me to catch.

My aging heart flows anguish knowing that
   they taunt me.

I have seen too many summers—
I wish no more this strife,
   these troubling days of life,

I wait for cooling pastures, for the gentle
   hands of peace, for the sweet, sweet
Whispers of Autumn.
   —*William T. Smith*

Bide A While

Bide a while, take time to see
   how beautiful this world can be
Wait just a moment, don't hurry by
   look! there's a rainbow high in the sky
Listen! above the sound of the automobiles
   there's laughter of children at play in the fields
Bide a while and try to see
   wild geese in perfect symmetry
Look over there a glance away
   there's a baby smile being sent your way
while sunlight filters through the trees
   playing with the falling leaves
Bide a while, let's pause to remember
   how sweet a love can be
keep love alive just a moment more
   and bide a while with me
   —*Monica Lee*

Heavenly Days

Goodness gracious, mercy me,
How can it ever be?
Summers gone and I don't know where.
There is a chill of frost now in the air.
Summer's bright flowers are ragged and dead.
Bright colored leaves now cover their bed.
Drifting leaves now crunch beneath my feet,
While cool nippy breezes caress my cheek.
Wild geese leave for their southern home
Honey bees work desperately to fill their comb.
Goldenrod by the fence rows nod,
Milkweed spills the silky cotton from their pod.
Apple trees bend low with their bounteous crop.
Smoke curls lazily from a chimney top.
Heaven must be filled with days like these.
When even the angels take their ease.
   —*Viola M. Wurl*

In Perspective

Have you ever realized or seen...
how evenly God has divided the rivers of each land,
although the coastlines are different?
Have you ever realized or seen...
How evenly man has built the highways crossing each land,
although his languages are many?
As the jet flies through rain clouds the sun disappears.
Yet I know, the sun still exists above the clouds,
even though I cannot see the sun thus obscured.
Man, too, should realize and see..
that in life, in spite of clouds of adversity,
God still exists in His heaven.
As the jet flies seven miles above the earth,
Time becomes as infinitesimal as
the landmarks of the earth, as seen from on high.
But, as soon as the jet lands, do you know why
the people begin to bicker because the train or bus is late?
In Perspective, everything revolves around man's, not God's time!
   —*Marlene Martens*

Human Kind

How infinitesimal the understanding,
how false the conception,
of the scope of a universal love.
How very little we really care about our fellow man.
Each and every one of us lives out a narrow existence
walled-in and confined by rituals, creeds, and prejudice;
and so very, very proud of our own accomplishments.

We do not care to touch with tender love
the wretched, ragged, cringing soul;
who, robbed from birth of a right to compete
and to stand among his fellow men,
must seek only the crumbs that are allowed to fall
from the rich man's table.
Instead, we take from him, by means both fair and foul,
the very crumbs of his existence.
Then, we turn our proud backs with scorn
because he lacks our intelligence.
We censure and blame him for striking back
and deny him the right to be discontent.
   —*Lavinia Hunton Palmer*

Without You Here

The wind whispers your name in my ear,
   How lonely I am without you here.

You wonder through my dreams at night,
   I feel you near but your not in sight.

I'm not complete without you here,
   My body aches to have you near.

I feel you through me, I see your face,
   But without you here it's just empty space.

Without you here, I can't take it much longer,
   But somehow it makes my love grow stronger.

I can feel your soft lips pressed against mine,
   But without you here it's all in my mind.

I look at the stars and think of you,
   I wonder if somewhere your looking at them too.

I close my eyes, and rise to the sky,
   To the star that caught my tear filled eye.

I hoped to maybe meet you there,
   A special place that we could share.

I know that soon you'll dry my tears,
   But until then I'll be "without you here."
   —*Melissa A. Crissman Hecker*

My Best Friend

Husband of my later years,
How lucky I am to have you
   as my constant companion,
     my friend.
Your steadfastness makes me feel secure.
You're always there, at my beck and call
To assuage my fears and take away
   my emptiness.
Dear friend, true friend,
So loyal and constant,
The best friend in all the world,
How glad I am that you are always there for me.
All I have to do is look by my side.
   —*Priscilla Culverwell*

The Road Of Life

The road of life traveled by many.
How many stones does one toss them away?
Does one walk around?
The road of life to have, to hold
How many hearts are broken?
Time marches on.
Some are left behind, clinging to old ways.
The road of life
Live and learn
Love is more then a flame of passion.
The road of life
There are sacrifices to be made.
What will tomorrow bring?
Rain or shine?
Who will stand the test of time?
The road of life
Laughter and tears
   —*C. Marie Davis*

Our Love

Mere words could ever quite express
How much you mean to me,
It would take a lifetime to tell you
And part of eternity.
The rhapsody of a sunrise,
The melody of the rain,
The symphony of a star-lit night
Are the sounds of Love's refrain.

True love is all we ever need
To dry our tears and ease our fears,
Sweet caresses heal the pains
Of hurts we suffer through the years.

Our love will last forever
Through the stormy skies and fair..
The music will reverberate...
When we climb the golden stair!....
   —*Lucille Beiersdorfer*

Winter's Tale

Snowflakes, one by one, fall silently
grow deeper
heavy with the weight
of many
Snowbound
my frozen heart
chilled by little
deceits, one by one, pile silently
encompass
isolate
   —*Margarita Isabelle*

Adieu

I often wonder at nature's call
How seasons bid us farewell.
Birth of spring, warm summer breezes
The awakening of winter
as it mourns the death of fall.

Settling frozen flakes of snow
Hay fields, naked forest,
Flowered meadows, remaining still
ceasing to grow.
Autumn leaves, scarlet and gold.
No longer caress, as northern winds
make their presence known.
Nature's loves part, drifting to
their peaceful resting places,
remaining with memories of life
shared. A love that had been sown.

Grey skies sail forth, sheltering
winter clouds, now shun summers
rainbow crowned band.
With a tear and a sigh, I wonder,
How can this seasonal adieu seem
so sad? Yet, so beautifully grand.
   —*Richard A. Johnson*

Lifespan

In the eons of Ages
how small stands man;
in the arch of Time,
how brief his lifespan!

In the blink of an eye
civilizations
develop and die
in endless procession.

When life and death begin
their primordial dance,
and as we live and die
we become the children of tomorrow
and the fathers of yesterday
and in a chosen few
eternity becomes a gleam
in an artist's eye

for after we are gone
something remains behind,
if only a poet's dream!
   —*W. P. Tillinghast*

The Puppet

I think if I made a puppet
How very sad I would be
If when I pulled the action strings
It would never work for me
Made in my own image
With expertise and care
Yet doing things without me
As if I wasn't there
And just suppose it would respond
To the neighbor who lived next door
But never do a single thing
It'd been created for
Suppose it fell in evil hands
That pulled its strings astray
Suppose it nailed me to a cross
And turned and walked away
   —*Sylva Beaureggard*

If Only For A Little While

The sweet embrace of hempen bonds
   hug your body tight.
  One would upon beholding you
   wonder about your plight.
   Sealed lips so silken soft
   Utter such wondrous sounds.
  a sigh, a moan, a whimper.
You're so pleasing when you're bound.
  Gentle caresses bathe your form.
   Light kisses on your cheek.
   I am your eternal lover.
   Your pleasure's all I seek.
    Beautiful Hetaera
   The stars, upon you, smile.
   I wish only to possess you
   if only for a little while.
    —Mike Ursu

If Jesse James Were Alive Today (He'd Be A Lawyer)

Lawyers and corruption, the words go hand in hand,
Hypocrisy and jurisdiction, are the bywords of this land.

Shylocks with flintlocks, still, even better a forty-four,
Bust the trust or shill a will, what's theirs is yours no more.

Take the money and run, son, no need to practice law,
The client is the 'dumb' one, and therein lies the flaw.

You've got to truly wonder, how lawyers sleep at night,
After tearing all asunder, what just men would make right.

What is this of Justice? Dunce! That's just a word, you see,
It's never put in practice once, not for you and not for me.

It is not that I would so displace, those souls who practice law,
Their methods and their dire disgrace, are what sticks within my craw.

Should one day shine upon me, when the legal blessings flow,
From the horn of good and plenty, there will be one thing yet to know.

If a lawyer treats me rightly, and isn't on the take,
Would you pinch me oh so lightly, that this dreamer might awake?
   —Steven Price Turner

The Sun of the Seventh Heaven

Words cannot express, the way I feel towards you.
I always do my best, to show you the way, that you can be loved.
My heart pitter-patters, when you hold me.
Where nothing else matters, but two souls, that sing merrily.
Three words longing, to be breathed.
Given the life beginning, joined as one, that is you and I.
Skies that are blue, the sun that shines.
All that we can do, to bask in the light, that warms our hearts.
Yet here we stand, just you and I.
Travelling the land, as spirits that are free, and everlasting.
In my dreams of tomorrow, the sun hath shined.
Forever gone sorrow, 'tis you are mine, that makes all my dogs smile.
Thee warms thine eyes, 'tis the sight to behold.
No other can surmise, the joy I perceive, that keeps me drawn to you.
What I would do, to capture the essence
The aura of you, which is my glory,
that holds the seventh heaven.
   —Melodie Weir

Black Pearl

There's a saying there's plenty of fish in the sea.
I always wonder how many were 4 me

Going through life throwing fish back in2 the sea.
I tried an oyster to see if their love would be

Cracking the oyster and eating the meat.
I found a black pearl loving and sweet

2 the pearl's beauty nothing could compare.
She was new 2 life with, mine we would share

I've found a jewel so precious and rare.
A heart of gold full of love and care

I cannot say this jewel belongs 2 me.
I hope our lives will enter twine and will be spent as we
   —Kenneth Frazier

The Long Wait

I have a white rose in my hair,
I am dressed in a gown of blue.
I have lighted my candles - everywhere
For, I am keeping my long, date with you.

We were young, the world was young,
Was ever a night so sweet?
Each precious hour - like pearls was strung
To be trampled by fate's braying feet.

I can still hear you whisper, "I love you;
In my arms you will always stay."
But the Gods looked down - with a covetous frown
And the death angel - took you away!

How quickly now - the time goes by
Soon now - with your lips on this rose;
We shall walk up our last path together
And the gates of forever - will close.
   —Sue Russell Slack

...My Only One

Woman, you are my true inspiration;
I am lost without you by my side
  and I love you from the bottom of my heart;
  can we forget the past and have a new start?
You are the apple of my eye,
You are the only one that I truly desire,
And I don't need any other woman but you
  because you are my only one.
My love, forgive me for the foolish thing I've done;
I know that I can act like a child inside this man,
I can admit that I did wrong
  and I am sorry for the foolish thing I've done.
I honestly feel that I lost you forever,
I can not go on without you,
Not now or ever
  because you are my only truly one.
Honey, from the bottom of your heart please forgive me
  because you are the only one that I truly adore;
  you are the only one that I pictured in my mind,
  you are the only one that I talk about,
  and you are the only one that I daydream to.
Darling.. I honestly love you,
  I truly need you,
  and I am forever yours.
   —Mark A. Schroettner

The Keeper

I am my brothers keeper.
I am the protector of my soul
   and yours.
I am the sister who keeps the
   little brothers and sisters in line.
I am the daughter who honors
   and cares for all mothers and
   fathers.
I am your friend, who will be there
   right by your side.
I am your companion who knows
   you better than anyone.
I am the keeper; the protector; I
   am the guardian.
I am His obedient servant who
   loves and cares for you.
I am the keeper of my conscience.
I am the keeper; keeper of my soul.
   —*Tanasha Waters*

I Am Thine Earth

I am the white and shining rock, the grass that grows, the tree;
I am the river running clear, come cleanse thyself in me;
Come rest upon my silken face, my shade will comfort thee.

I am the mountain tall and proud, the wide and rolling sea;
I am the prairie reaching out, far as the eye can see;
Come stand upon my tallest peak and let thy soul roam free.

I am the animals that walk, the birds that fly so free;
I am the fishes sleek and trim, the clouds that shadow me;
I am all things within my sphere; come be a part of me.

As thou hast been placed here on Earth for reasons we suspect
May have to do with all the future, thou art the elect
To save my surface, all that grows, so be thou circumspect.

I know that thou hast special needs to fill thine own require,
As other species in my fold, perhaps 'gainst thy desire,
So thou must balance carefully the quencher and fire.

I am the rock, the soil, the sand, the tall and golden tree;
I am the river running clear, come cleanse thyself in me;
Come rest within my tender arms, thy love will comfort me.
   —*Wesley W. Rees*

Haircut

I searched for the candystripe among the time-worn buildings.
I arrived at the window and peered in—
Four chairs were aligned in succession,
Each identical with arm rests
In which you could see your reflection.
Hair wisps beneath them degrade the tiled floor.
A broom stands in the corner,
As if trying to hide from the abuse.
Weapons adorn the counters—combs, scissors, razors
That point toward heaven.
It's Saturday. Bills to pay.
The interview is in two days;
I have a suit, complete with a stiff-collared shirt
And itchy skirt: the haircut will complete my attire.
I tensely sit in the hard chair
And watch as the red straw falls to the floor,
Like hot rain dropping from a dark sky.
The reflection in the mirror is startling:
Everything is different. Now I can see the world
As if I opened my eyes for the first time.
   —*Sarah Ehrick*

Love Never Lived

You lied when you said, "I Love You!"
I believed you with all my heart.
Then I let myself love you too—
But I knew better from the start!
It was all too good to be true!
I knew it could not be real—
But your actions were right on que!
I could not know you were too cold to feel!
You learned well from others before me.
Words read were put to good use!
Why was I too blind to see
That you thrive on mental abuse?
You've moved on to your next victim.
To keep your ego growing.
One day the tables on you will turn—
From you, sorrow will be glowing!
   —*Myra Hulse*

If Ever

With all I know about the way that I feel, there's nothing
I can do until I have you in my arms.
   If ever there is sunshine, it shows upon your face,
   If ever there are stars at night, they twinkle in
   Your eyes.
If ever there was warmth, Id feel it from your smile.
If ever there is happiness I'll find it in your arms
   The times are changing, at times my heart is
   Aching. I can close my eyes and see your face
   And my feelings go astray.
Have you ever wanted? Have you ever needed, the touch
From someone not around? I try to hide these feelings
Down inside, but every time I see you they all end up unwound.
   If ever love is lost and found,
   If ever I should chance to meet,
   If ever though may never come,
   But all the while I wonder
   If ever.
   —*Teresa Smith*

Letting Go Of The Past

I have emotionally changed from within myself.
I can let myself be shattered by the sad times with hidden tears.
Or I can grow emotionally strong.
Or stay weak through out the coming years.
Or I can let go of those deep inner fears.

In order for that to happen I must let go of the past.
That time is now long gone.
I must now find in my life where I belong.
But I won't rush the future of my life so fast.
I will hold on to the good memories so my happiness will
   always last.

I have fond a new meaning in my life.
I know how I feel
and know what I'm living for.
As for never more
I won't look back, I'm going towards the future because that's
   what now is real.

I have gained some wisdom
In a special kind of way
from each passing day.
The pat of my life emotionally will no longer keep me in fear.
Because I have left go and know the happiness of my life will
   soon be very near.
   —*Lois Lynda Kobs*

Hi! Lord

Hi! Lord it's nice to know who you are,
I can talk to you in church, in the pastures even in my car.
  No matter where, I go you are there,
I can tell you all my thoughts, because you listen and you care.
  You're really a neat friend, you're always by my side,
When I'm happy, when I'm sad, or had pain and really cried.
  You know Lord, you're not only my friend, but I call you
    father too,
I can trust you, and feel your love, Lord you always know
    what to do.
  At times, I think I'm so alone, with no one around me to care,
Then I look at your picture, hanging on my wall, and remember
    so much that you've shared.
  You died on the cross just to set me free.
  You carried me at times, when I really couldn't walk,
Lord, now it's my turn to tell and to talk.
  To tell so many people, how you love them so much,
By talking, and loving and even by touch.
  To bring in your light Lord, to those who feel low,
So they can say Hi! Lord and they to will know.
  —*Mary Sue Estepp*

Quiet Moments

It's very quiet in early morning not a sound is heard.
I can think and plan, create designs or write a word.
I read newspapers, take in nourishments.
I collect my thoughts and think of my accomplishments.

It's a perfect time to put it all together.
There isn't a rush.
There's no hassle
Confusion a hush.
I revitalize to start the day.

I love being alone sometimes
it gives me strength to plan ahead
It helps sort out that possible dread
like living it out in mimes.

It helps me plan out what is next
what to do or not to say,
time to contemplate "do it this way"
  —*Marda Rowe*

And I Love Him So

And I love him so, whenever I see his face,
I cannot help myself for remembering his embrace.
The nights feel cold
But I have to be bold.
Every time he goes away,
I feel I cannot take another day.
And I love him so, I feel I can never let him go.
I remember him and I,
And when I used to cry,
Not knowing if he cared
Or just, he was too scared.
Having love him, only in my heart,
Not ever finding out if there would be a start.
Just by having him as a friend,
I feel my love for him will never end.
And I love you so, if there was only a way I could let him know
  —*Stacey Emiro*

What's Wrong

What's wrong with me
I can't find a reason for this pain
I feel so depressed and hurt
But I can't find the cause of my rain
Do I need help
Or do I find it on my own
I know I have the best of friends
But I feel so all alone
Do I always have problems
Tell me this is a phase I undergo
Please help me find a solution
And let my happiness show
Let me be me
Something that is good
Stop thinking that "I can't"
And start thinking that "I could"
I don't know what is wrong with me
I feel so lifeless and dead
I need to find a reason
For this pain in my heart and head
  —*Marylou Tuazon*

Creation

This day so emblazoned with summer's last duty,
I can't get enough of its splendor — its beauty,
So quietly magnificent, so perfectly pretty,
A time to remember this day in this city,
How perfectly splendid, how quiet supreme!
The slant of the sunshine what a day to dream,
To dream of hours so perfectly spent,
To dream of loves so perfectly meant
I dream of the times I spent with you, loves!
So precious, so silent — compared to the doves,
I wonder, quite justly, what God has in mind,
For all of us weary, poor souls left behind,
With days like today I love to just write,
And think of the people so dear in my sight,
With beauty all round me — a song in my heart,
Our God did His splendorous, beautiful part.
  —*Marjorie Kindell-Watts*

Hiding

This is a day of hiding
I can't go out
can't go anywhere
I need to hide
to stay secluded here with my pain
so I hide and I write
to prove that I'm here
I hide and read others' pain
to validate my own
I hide and I sleep
to make it go away
there are too many people
too many out there
who are tired of hearing about my pain
who are too uncomfortable with my pain
who don't understand the depths of my pain
and I can't keep it to myself today
I can't pretend it isn't there
and since I can't hide the pain
I will hide me
  —*Patty Worrells*

I Could Not Ask For Tomorrow When Today Is So Hard To Bear

Lord, if I fell on my knees to offer a small prayer,
I could not ask for tomorrow when today is so hard to bear.

There is much my heart holds, the weight of everything in life is there,
Lord I know I question who, what, when, why and where.

I won't ask for tomorrow when today is so hard to bear,
If I pray for you to take me, my life you would surely spare.

Rejecting me, until you decide my time, if it is not near,
Lord lift those burdens from my shoulders and everything I fear!

Because my heart is aching, so heavy and filled here,
Lord, I trust you, yet I sometimes doubt when problems and troubles appear.

Keep me as you have because you know my heart is true and sincere
my heart for many days has been filled with many a tear.

Lord, I know you and only you care
But Lord I won't ask for tomorrow when today is so hard to bear.

There are so many needs I have, yet, my heart is pure
But of my life I am not sure.

Lord, when everything is made right and I can see where
I have to go, what I have to do and what I have with others to share,

Lord I will give hope, love and devotion to all who care,
And maybe look ahead for tomorrow, indeed, I do dare.

Ease my heart, please, and let me not despair,
Allow me tomorrow even though I know today is so hard to bear!
—*Marilyn Merry*

Thoughts

When I awoke this morning and begin to meditate,
I could see the crack in Heavens gate.

The silhouette of my Saviors out stretched hands,
ready to accept me when I entered in.

As my thoughts began to unfold, I suddenly felt
the world so cold, why did I feel so drawn and old.

A radiance from my Savior there, made me forget my
every care, and feel the warmness in the air.

As I cried there on my pillow and bed, I remembered
the many things He had said, and his love for me as he led.

My talking and witnessing to others, I couldn't claim,
But I had only myself to blame, and I felt the pain.

My foolish pride had stood in the way, to ask for something
from Him to say, as I went about my busy day.

He said, He will lead the way, if only you will stop
and pray, each and every day.

He helped me to finish my daily chores in plenty of time,
so I could study the lessons line by line.

Since I am alone, I can carry his word in my heart,
and talk with him and pray with each thing that I start.

I do, pray and thank Him each morning, that, I can arise,
with the new day dawning.

He has answered so many Prayers for me over the years.
I think, He understands my fears.
He helps me write what I have to say to others that conveys
my heart more than to talk farther.
—*Lorene Kossey*

Awaiting Friend

When peace comes knocking at my door
I dare not let her in
she stares in wonder exposing her heart
enveloping me with her eyes
but I am afraid
for she came 'round once before
and was suddenly taken away...

I used to long for the day
she would return once more
anxiously awaiting her arrival
but now, it's been too long
and I am used to being alone

Still I am drawn to her
warmth and tenderness
perhaps it is time
to follow her lead
and expose myself once again.
—*Monique Neault*

River Of Tears

Have you ever known anyone to cry a "River of Tears?"
I do, cause I have, over the years.

I'd often look up into the Heaven's so blue
And wish, dear "Lord," I was up there with you.

My burdens here on earth would all be over.
And I'd be happy as could be
Cause there would be no more
"River of Tears," cried from me.
—*Loretta Rine Marschner*

Blue Moon-ology

When I lie awake and can't sleep a night
I don't drink warm milk or try to read a good book.
I look out of the windows at the sky to see the stars go by
The freshness of the nights air is a breeze, but I still look.

I watch the moon as it shines down on my window so big and bright
I look up to see if there's something inside of the moon.
It looks like a face or an animal that's capturing my sight
I get out of my bed to get a good look to see something soon,

The closer I get to the window, the moon moves further away
The face in the moon is smiling and the animal is starring at me.
I tried to think of something worthwhile about the moon to say
Like once in a blue moon or is it really a blue moon that I see?

The moon didn't look so blue and I am calling it blue
I can see why it is called a full moon or a half one.
An explanation about why it's called blue, I wished I knew
Because the blue moon at night with its full glow leaves me stun.
—*Ruby J. St. Jules*

Knocking On Heaven's Door

"Hey, man. What you in for?"
"I don't know. Like you, I'm here at this door."
"You know some people say it's the end of the road.
They say that's it. There ain't no more."
"Huge, big, and gold. This must be our day."
"Nice trumpet. What can you play?"
"Thanks. Everything. I played pretty well in high school."
"Would you play a tune? Wow. Man, that was cool."
"I also played football and ran track."
"Me? I hung out with friends. We were a pack."
"Memories. What we wanted to be and places we wanted to see."
"Dreams. We were young, wild, and free."
"Well, do you think you're ready? Ready to go?"
"I guess. Knocking on Heaven's door with all my heart to show."
"My name is King. What's your name?"
"John. Pleasure just the same."
"Hey, John. Semper Fi. This ain't the end."
"You are going!? Will I see you again?"
"Yeah. All you got to do is knock. Goodbye good friend.
See you again on the other side."
—*Lisa Simhiser*

Hurt

Trying hard to deny your mistake
I don't want to be a fake
You tricked me so good
I didn't know you could
You hurt me and everyone else
Not to mention yourself
You say you don't want to lose me
But what good is that
When you go and abuse me
The mental abuse you put me through
Leading me to believe I was the only one
Boy, that was dumb!!!
Maybe I was
You'll have to prove it
I have doubts—Just because
—*Kelly E. Johnson*

Dreams

Once, long ago, when I was young,
  I dreamed about a life of fun;
Or travelling the earth both far and near,
  Of never having a thing to fear.

I dreamed of riding a great black steed
  With clothes of ebon to fit my need;
Of jumping fences wild and free.
  Oh yes, that would certainly be me.

I dreamed of growing old with grace,
  Of having an ever-smiling face;
Of gliding down a marble stair
  My hand extended to greet guests there.

But I am old, with aches and pains,
  Lucky to navigate the lanes
With aid of cane and unsteady gait;
  Oh yes, that is how I am of late.

So when you are young, dream all your dreams,
  No matter how far-fetched it seems,
For old age is not always blessed,
  And filled with joy and happiness.
—*Sally H. Christensen*

Taking Care of My Cats and Dog Blues

Empty catfood cans and messy litter pans,
I encounter every single day.
There's endless feeding, grooming, and cleaning,
But for me, there's no other way!
I take my dog for a daily run,
While I lag tiredly behind.
Afterwards, as she's resting peacefully,
I'm desperately trying to unwind!
I can't seem to find time to primp,
Nor get enough beauty rest.
It's twenty-four hours a day servitude,
For my year-round guests.
I can relate to Noah on the ark,
Only without the divine heavenly calling.
Imagine the time he spent caring for his animals?
So, I diligently do what others find appalling!
—*Patricia DePuy*

Devil's Daughter

I am a lonely heart's dagger
I evolved from the light, to cause the dark.
The state of Euphoria I bring first
Only depresses you to crush your soul.
The humans, they are the perfect hosts.
I use them- for I am parasite.
I suck their life's blood from them
And still they beg me for my liquid Hell.
I'll call to you in your darkest hour.
I stretch out my sharp talons: Pray upon your fears.
I'll show you my holy power.
Get a hold of your life
To take my one night stand.
Yesterday, Today, Tomorrow—Forever.
You think you are in control
With ever moment control is mine.
I'll leave you retching on the floor.
I'm just another Devil's child.
Together we will start a new religion:
Alcoholism.
—*Samantha J. Black*

Whispers Of Hope

Walking on whispers of hope,
I face glass ceilings and transparent floors.
Do I ignore, his off-colored joke?
Should I let pass the fun he pokes, straight at me,
and what I stand for? A woman!

Competing on a stage already marked;
No place for me to start;
saying my lines and then quickly moving off the stage;
Out of the way and never late;
I still can't find my mark on life's stage.

Cast in a play that already has its lead actor.
I can only know my trade and follow the director.
Understudy to lesser skilled; paying my dues still;

But wait, it is now 17 years of practicing my trade
and I still have no chance for a lead part.
A foul concept lurks in men's hearts;

Not so fast this time!
Glass ceilings and transparent floors
shatter when opposed by strong minds.

No longer will I walk on whispers of hope.
My spirit refuses to be sequestered or condemned.
I have my own life scheme.
My journey is to follow my own dreams.
—Zione Walsh

Seduced By A Spider

Tangled in your web, your voice is a soft caress
I fear what I feel
Your eyes pull me in
I feel like I'm the only one that exists
All I can think of is a kiss, your lips touching mine
Moving to the Rhythm
The web's silk threads captures me
Body and soul
I run my hands through your hair
You trail kisses down my throat
A fire is fed, the hunger within grows
I want you to smile down on me
I feel a danger in you but
Yet a protection that leads me
To ask for the safety of your embrace
You say you need me
You spin your magic
I can't pull away
I'm being seduced by a spider
But there is not a word utter against it
—Magda Tumi Portela

Fairytale Vs. Reality

A far away place that I own
I go there sometimes when I want to be alone
Where the sun in my sky will never die
And even the saddest of angels never cry
Where all my hopes and dreams come true
And every single thought I have revolves around you
Where the stars shine so bright that it burns me inside
And then I wake up and all this has died
Where is this place that I need to go to?
And where is your face when I'm searching for you?
In just a second my fairytale has changed
And I'm back to reality and eternal pain
But for those few moments that I thought all was well
I shall capture in my heart and in my book of fairytales
And I'll look back sometimes just so I can see
There was no love shared in our reality.
—Sandee Hargesheimer

Unrest

The restlessness within me puts terrific force in sway
I feel a strange emotion that invades my heart today.

I'd like to swim the ocean just to reach the other side,
And sift my body through the sand together with the tide.

I'd like to clasp the sighing wind and never set it free.
Until it whispers gently "Won't you fly away with me?"

I'd like to view the breaking dawn and watch the sun come up,
And drink my fill of daylight spilling over from it's cup.

I'd like to walk an alien road—one I have never seen,
And find a flower I could kiss upon a velvet green.

I'd like to feel the living breath of nature's wondrous birth,
If just to prove She's worthy of inheriting the earth.

Then, when moonlight floods the land and nightfall brings release
Perhaps my spirit would relax and once again find peace.
—Wanda O. Trzcinski

The Walls Are Closing In

The walls are closing in around me!
I feel so crushed with emotion, I'm too blind to see!
Crying out loud — "what will be in store for me!"
Everyday, I go through such pain-staking agony.

Lord, please give me patience — my nerves are so tense
The bills are piled high — everything nowadays is such an expense
All I have in my wallet is twenty-five cents
My life is a mystery — it keeps me in suspense.

My head is throbbing, I can't endure this agony anymore!
Shedding some tears, I cried — "I no longer want to be poor!
I feel so depressed, everywhere I go I find a closed door
My body is so weak, everything seems like such a heavy chore.

I will continue to pray for strength and contentment with my Lord,
And my future will be brighter — His gift of love will be my reward.
—Shirley R. Westgate

Living For Love

Once upon a time; a long, long time ago...
I fell into depression, and became my greatest foe.

My heart became heavy; my days became long...
I just laid there at night; wondering what I did wrong.

I somehow felt cheated; knowing not what I'd missed...
I felt it was time that I cease to exist!

My spirits had died; but no one was grieving...
I found myself giving; but never receiving.

As I dickered with death; life's paths became narrowed...
God beckoned me back; by showing me, "Harold!"

When I flirted with him; he just called me a tease...
So I flirted some more; and then I said, "Please?"

We were strangers at first; yet we both knew...
Our story book romance was to good to be true.

I just picture his smile; in my mind's eye...
And I tingle all over; and let out a sigh.

Sharing our lives; giving all that we can...
Together we'll grow, as we walk hand in hand.

Now that I've found someone else who
can give...

My spirit's reborn and I'm eager
to live!!
—Lisa M. Neveil

The Dimming Lantern Out At Sea

Oh love of mine and still so dear to my heart,
I felt that forever mine you'd be, but life
changed your course, and steered your vessel
away from me, when foreign love entered
your drying sea...the one I could no longer fill.

Divided between two worlds, you chose to
draw away from mine, when the siren's dark
eyes slowly drew you in, and entangled
you became in the nets of her beckoning beauty,
where made your restless being still.

Now when midnight ocean waves come crashing in
and pound upon the seashores of my mind,
thoughts of you will remind me that once upon a
time the warmth and glow of your lantern's
light was solely mine, and on me only cast.

Now when by the bay window I stand
looking out into the evening's mist awaiting your
return, your lantern's light will be faintly seen,
making me remember that you're no longer mine, but
to foreign love that you belong, and I to the past.

—*Rafaela Wintham Barker*

Thoughts Of Love

Today while sitting alone among shrubbery and the trees.
I found myself thinking of our future and of how we used to be.

But most of all I thought of us and the future ahead
And while I thought I saw visions of us together and in our
   bed.

I thought of our love and how it has grown.
I thought of our love and the strength it has shown.
I thought of warm caresses and nights we held each other
   so tight.
I thought of our kisses so warm, so moist all through the
   night.
I thought of our love-making and bodies entwined with each
   other.
I thought of our love shared as we lay exhausted knowing
   there could never be another.

Than I had no reason to think for what I know is true.
He has given us the most precious gift ever
   your love for me and my love for you.

—*Paul W. Streeter*

The Gaze

Sleeping there within the chair,
I gazed into your face so dear.
Has it been that many years,
Since I rocked and held you near.

If only time could be a friend,
To live those moments once again.
But time does not a friend make,
It never gives, but only takes.

And in a twinkling of time—
Those little arms that once were mine,
Were eager to find their own way,
Though it seems like only yesterday.

Now these loving memories are a part,
Of the treasures locked within my heart.
Each day I'll hold in cherished trust,
For God has given me so much!

—*Ruth V. Mullen*

Wind

   A gentle breeze against your skin
      I give you quiet peace within.
   Caressing, and gentle to the touch,
   Cooling, soothing, pleasure I give, much.

   Rolling crost the prairie on grass of gold,
   The beauty therein is yours to have and hold.
Leaves of the trees, swaying, dancing to my tune.
      Here am I, but naught, so soon.

      Restless, at times, I become,
   Bending, twisting, yes ruthless, some.
   Reaching, pushing, even tearing apart,
   Sometimes your soul, sometimes your heart.

   The twain are one, the wind, the same.
      One to love, one to tame.
      Love one? Hate the other?
      One is. Therein is the other.

   I am as nothing, until you, I touch.
   Feelings, above all others, much.
      No beginning, no end.
         I am, the wind.

—*J. D. Santee*

I've Got Scars On My Heart

I've got scars on my heart, but no tears in my eyes,
   I guess, my friends, You are wondering why.
      I've been loved, I've been hurt, I've misunderstood.
      But all of my life, I've tried to be good.
I've been told that I was loved, and watched it turn
   Into hate, but this I did not know until it was too late.
      So, my friends, you can see, this is the reason why,
      I've got scars on my heart but no tears in my eyes.

—*Lucille Lindsey Wood*

Sometimes...But then I think of only Sue

Sometimes I think that life has passed me by and I just want to
cry.
I hang my head and give a sigh and wonder why oh why.
But, Then I think of only sue and now I am not so blue.
I think about he long brown hair, and how I wish I was there.
I think about her hazel eyes of blue and how I know I love my
Sue.
I think about the day we will meet and how my heart will skip a
beat.
I think about the day I will make her mine and we will be
together
all the time.
I think the stars up above and how I know I am in love.

—*Michael Paul Randall*

My Destiny's Soul

Hello, My heart's desire:
I believe in you
For these feelings must be true
Because, I am so in love with you!
My faith in you will never go astray
Tick...Tick...Tick...Please do not delay
My dream will come true this winter's holiday
Because, God has written our devotion in our special milky way...

—*Renee J. Daigle*

Bottled Up Inside

Bottled up inside is all the pain and frustrations I have.
Bottled up inside is all the love I have, but cannot show.
Bottled up inside is not the hatred I have for people. For that is what I show.
Bottled up inside is all the life I have and once knew
Bottled up inside is all the love that people have given me, but yet I cannot return.
Bottled up inside is not the hatred I have for people. For that is what I show.
Bottled up inside are my true feelings.
—*Tina Pasternak*

You

You asked me…why
I have never written a poem about you…
It's because you have never broken my heart
You have stayed by my side
And believed in me right from the start.

You could have left for many reasons
I've hurt you many times
But through it all
Through our ever changing seasons
I have seen your love shine.

I am glad I have you
I don't think I have ever said…
Just how much I need you
And how much I really care
And how glad I am
That you are still there…

You are my wife
My lover and my friend
My kindred spirit
A part of my life
Until God says "the end"…
—*Owen B. Oakes*

Father's Day Promise

To you, Dad, on this Father's Day,
I have several things that I want to say.

Mom gave you a gift in 1954;
I was the daughter you'd been hoping for.

You made sure that I got the best of care.
When I've needed you, you've always been there.

You've always been open, and honest, with me.
You gave me good advice; though, I refused to agree.

I know I've let you down, time and time again;
I'm ashamed of what a disappointment I've been.

I really do love you; more than you'll ever know;
And, from this day forth, it's really going to show.

I promise, you'll be so proud of me;
I'll finally be the daughter you've wanted me to be.

HAPPY FATHER'S DAY!!!
—*Karen D. Breckner*

My Love For You

It seems to me you've gone and let me down,
I haven't seen you around for a day or so;
Is it true that you have gone and left this town,
Tell me darling, why did you have to go;

It seems you could not stand my past disgrace
So you've gone and broke the vows that you once made;
Another one is now taking my place,
In time my love for you, will slowly fade;

Know my love for you is true and real,
In my heart I thought that you would make it through;
The love beats from my heart, you no longer feel,
There's no other that I care for more than you.
—*Margarito Villanueva*

Inside Of Jesus

I lost my heart somewhere inside of Jesus
I hear a silent voice echo, beloved believe in me
Secret whispers of love flow from Heaven
I stand near the sky in my mind to know the Holy one
Somewhere inside of Jesus you'll find a special heart
Inside of Jesus there you'll find love

The peace of Jesus calms the world and touches my very heart
The thoughts of Jesus echo and shake the mountains
Listening to a drifting breeze from heaven I hear Jesus lovely voice
The heart of Jesus matches the heart of God

Life they say is a journey through the movements of time
For the earth is like a stage open to the Heavens like showtime
And loneliness is ever active but your not alone
So the stage is set and the curtain of night is open
Therefore stand, don't be afraid, love is alive
Somewhere inside of Jesus there you'll find love, there you'll find God.
—*Ariana Towne*

Peace By The Sea

Meditating by the beach,
I hear the music of the sea,
Imagination playing around,
Peace here is what I found.
Look out to the horizon!
Ships are floating on air,
Never before have I seen such a sight,
The sky is full of colors so bright.
My mind is seeking, my eyes just stare,
The water is clear of colors so rare,
A layer of blue, a layer of green,
A layer of both in between.
If you want to sort things out in your mind,
Go to the sea, it's there you will find,
You may not have found the answers you seek,
But at least you'll have found peace by the sea.
—*Margie Diottaviano*

Ode To Nimbie — The Nimble One

I really love my little car
I now know where my tenders are.
Though you may consider her a "heap"
My gas bill is so very cheap.
And if at times her voice sounds shrill
She's merely laboring up the hill.
But when she's cornering on a curve
You must admit, she curves with verve!
Virginia Prest

Towering Over

The glum, stormy summer day;
I heard the pitter patter as it came down.
A burst of lightning broke through the clouds.
And it started me as it flashed, crashed,
and lit up the sky.
Hanging over like a shadow sitting still,
It starts and stops as it may.

I need help from a friend.
Confusion shouldn't fill my mind.
Not myself, I see the dark towering clouds,
Hoping someone will be ready to lend a hand.
—*Stephanie Jagge*

Physics Blue

I was there on the day that the well ran dry,
  I heard the pump sucking & I saw my daddy cry.
Three days later he plowed up the corn;
  he shot the old Jersey & burned down the barn.
He called Ma & the kids all to his side,
  he hitched up the wagon & said, "Let's ride."
Well he never looked back at that crooked old fence,
  and, Friend, it's been the highway, ever since.

Pa caught the fever & it never broke,
  he died on that wagon with the busted spoke.
Ma never had too much to say,
  the look in her eye was too far away.
My sister worked in a house where the blue lights were dim,
  my brother shot dice until someone shot him.
And, me, I just kinda did what I could—
  I did a little bad & I did some good.

Just seems a little strange that it all came down
from a pump sucking air from a hole in the ground.
—*Mark R. Sheldon*

The Door

I sat in a chair and watched my dad as he stood by the door
I held his hand as he walked through the door
I waited to meet my baby son not knowing he stood by the door
When they brought him to me he had already walked through the door
I went to see my sister when she stood by the door
Friends gathered around and said Sharon get away from the door
But with a cold blank stare she too walked through the door
Then came the night when I stood by the door
As I laid in bed I saw my friends wonder if I would walk
  through the door
But during the night I heard a voice say don't you dare walk
  through the door
My life has really changed since I stood by the door
Because I want to be ready when I walk through the door
And you don't really know when you stand by the door
What things will be like when you walk through the door
—*Ronald O'Donnell*

A Tribute To Mom

Mother, so special to me
I love you always, no matter what may be.
Over all these years, you always cared,
And took away my deepest, darkest fears.
You bring so much cheer, to each and
every day, how I wish to have you and
your laughter always near.
It's always give and never take.
You bear the burden of all for all our sake.
—*Suken Shah*

As A Patient Two

They're staffing my case
I hope they will see
I examined my feelings
To see what was Me.

Aware of my losses, of music and health
I still have assets upon which I can dwell.
Empathy, concern, and regard for others
Still flow from my soul as a wife and mother.

I can tangibly nurture plants, write poetry with ease
Swim in the pool, take time to laugh like a fool.
Assert myself, not denying my needs
And not have to spend each moment doing good deeds.

It's important to remember my appearance and looks
Regardless of the extra time arthritis demands.
I have my needs, my hopes, and ambitions
My activities and friends I plan to expand.
—*Kathleen Dwyer Duych*

A Glowing Luminosity

Don't complicate matters for me
I just want to live my life peacefully
Longing to find some tranquility
Amid this frenetic human sea
I choose not to be tossed and churned
About in these hurried human waters
But work at clothing myself with a Pacific countenance
Which envelopes me entirely
And that will be transmitted for the benefit of others
Accept my invitation to experience tranquility alongside of me
And feel the warmth of a glowing luminosity
Reflecting off a calm human being
—*Teresa Castillon*

That Man

I'd known that man all my life
I knew his children and his wife
That man was a handsome man with style and grace
He was witty and charming anytime anyplace
That man was very special how special I never knew
But when they shot and killed that man that's when I got my
clue the love I had for him was pure, untouched and never
mentioned no strings attached, no heartaches, no pressure
and no tension I'll love that man forever, but did he ever know it?
You see that man was my father, but I waited to late to show it
(I love you……Lisa)
—*Terri L. Autin*

Without Her

Without her, I just can't do without her, no matter how
I pretend, my ways and actions, show the sadness,
My heart's in, no matter how I try, her face is like a
Mirror, in the sky, I see her everywhere, without her,
I just can't do without her, there's no use pretending,
I don't care, cause life a reality, it's not a fairy
tale, though I can go on pretending, but soon my
heart, will surely tell, without her, I just can't do
Without her, so when I find her, I'm going to beg
her please, please, come back to me, cause I love
her so, before I was blind, but now I see,
without her, I just can't do without her.
—*Matthew Wrigley*

Christmas Memories

My heart goes to God at christmas.
  I know it always will
For as a child, I had no permanent home
  Only God to hold my hand.

God warmed my face with a smile
  I needed not a toy
For He filled my heart with joy
  On that yuletide morn.

I knew He died to save my soul from hell.
  This was the only present I needed
I knew there was a smile upon His face
  Oh! What a joyous christmas day.

I hear the merry christmas sounds.
  They echo through the air
None of them is as sweet as
  the whisper in my ear.

My heart goes to God at christmas.
  I know it always will
For I learned young in life
  My home was with Him up there.

    —*Louise Pressley*

I Know

Dedicated to my grandchildren, with love.
I know that one day, everyone will be free.
I know innately, this great day I will see.
I know beatings will then end, for those who did pray.
I know children will never be taken away.

Prison will close; God's images tortured no more.
Discrimination will end; so decreed by law.
The world will be one; all now sisters and brothers.
Unseen faces saved from execution by others.

All doors around the world will be opened wide.
And everyone will so proudly walk inside.
Faces now aglow because the world does care.
Everyone's fingers stretch to reach, touch and share.

I know that there, but for the grace of God go I.
I know I am alive because others have died.
I know my turn is now to share, care and give.
I know I must reach out so others can live!

    —*Muriel Yakir Pickard*

My Little Girl

Hey Little Girl
I know you're in there
I know you need to be loved
I'll try to get you that love
But it's dangerous you know
You've been there before
And I just know that you don't forget it
I just don't want you to get hurt again
And little girls can only be free
So I know you have to be free
Even though you are vulnerable
Yes, you might get hurt again
—remember that, it's very important
Compared to the thrill and joy of love
  that you will feel
The hurt will be little
I'm trying to accept all this for you
So hang in there
We'll do it.

    —*Robin Ritchey*

Untitled

You tell me I am getting old I tell you that's not so the house
I live in, In warm out and that course I know I been in use a
long long time. It's weathered many gale, I'm really not
surprised you think its some, what frail the color changing on
the roof the windows getting dim. The foundation not so steady
as once it used to be. A few short years can make me old I
feel I'm in my prime. Eternity lies just a real life of joy
and peace I'm going to live, forever there life will go on it's
grand you to tell me I am getting old? You just done
understand the dwelling in my little house is young and, bright
and gay just starting on a life to last through eternal day.
You only see the outside which is what most folks see you. Tell
me I am, getting old? You have mixed my house with me.

    —*Pearlie R. Sullivan*

The Answer It's Yes

She asked him if he loved her, and he replied,
"I love you as the fish love the sea,
and the birds love the sky.
Like the sun loves dawn,
And the stars love the black night.
I live deep in your soul,
And survive on your light.
You ask me if I love you,
And the answer is yes."
His words settled over her as soft
As morning dew,
How beautiful to hear the simple words,
"I love you."

    —*Laurel Charette*

Bubby

Bubby,
I love you very much.
I feel like we have something in common.
You have been hurt by your wives.
Like I've been hurt by my one and only husband.
You lost everything you love and dreamed for so did I.
Bubby,
I love you with all my heart.
You make me happy you also make Dee happy too.
You are a good daddy.
I'm glad she has someone to love like you
Bubby,
We love you

    —*Lisa Ann Wade Johnson*

From One Small Seed

The last red tomato of the year
I pick it from its thick green branch
Where long it hung,
A feast of beauty to my eye and soul.
Now it sits, still red and ripe,
Waiting. Does it know my delight?
I planted one small seed and watched it
Grow until now.
Do I bite into that luscious red
And never see it again?
Or do I bite and know
How many ways I've been fed?

    —*Marcia L. Nesset*

One Special, Perfect, Loving Little Girl

Sabrina Richelle Grayson (June 22, 1982-November 5, 1982)
I love you very much, Bree! Marra

Dear Lord, please keep my sister safe.
The beautiful baby, that went to heaven that day!
The date: November 5, 1982,
At the time I thought I was fine and wouldn't be blue!
She was only here for such a short time,
Only 5 months old, what a painful crime!
Over the years, the pain it grew,
And that's when I realized the damage pain can do!
Then it finally hit me, I have no little sister,
To fight with, to love, and to tuck in at night,
To someone who was six, it didn't seem quite right!
All I could do was ask why?
Why my sister, and not someone else?
The only person I thought of was myself!
Y'see, she's no longer in pain. She's happy, and she's gay!
And I know deep within my heart.
That she'd want me to feel the same way!
—T. Michelle Grayson

Dear Dustin

He brought much joy into our lives
   I loved him like he was mine
He was eight and a half but a full grown man
   He had more friends than any group of people could have
People that knew him, loved him, people that didn't, loved him too
   His time on earth was very well spent
He'll be in my mind from now until death
   I'll love him forever whether he's here or not
But he's in a better place sitting right beside the Lord
   Looking down upon us, wondering where he has gone
The Lord will take him and explain it all
   Tell him how much we cried and how much we rejoiced
We were sad that he was gone but happy where he had gone
   We must now say goodbye to our beloved little friend
We love you forever and forever, Amen.
—Ricky Dacus

TRULUV-THRULUV

"When I was 4 & 20, I heard a young girl say
I luvu, luvu, luvu!! Allways, allnight, allday!!"

When I was 5 & 20, I heard her say again
"I'll luvu in the springerfall!! I'll luvu anywhen!!

Well!!! Yonder hies 2morrow, 2day is hardly flee!
& here alone we sorrow!! Eterenmity and me!

So now I'm 26, & U can break my bones
With stoneserstix But nothing this atones:

Womans is as womans does!!! Alas, alack, alas!
& so less I'm than me because, alas, alack, a lass!

& if I live another year, I swear by hellerheaven
Or what U choose that I will be 27!

& through the years that herewards bob,
   I'm nodoubts forced my st&!!
But oh! 4 a breast's like-nothing-else throb!!!
   & the touch of a vanished h&!!!!
—B. Dziengielewski

Untitled

My heart is bursting—
I must see you again,
For I am lost and so empty inside
And all that I'm feeling (I cannot deny)
Had started when you left
without saying good-bye,
Without giving me a chance to show you
I can make you happy as I have been.
Please don't turn away; don't
ignore what we had and what
there could be.
For you may find that you too miss,
Those quiet moments; those nights of bliss!
Time goes on and with it takes,
My shattered heart, "for love's sweet sake!"
—Kathleen T. Cox

I Felt Very Humble

As I sat on a stump to eat my lunch,
I noticed ants at my feet.
They scurried in and out of holes
Looking for something to eat.

As I dropped the bread crumbs,
The ants carried them away.
They dragged them deep into the holes
To save for another day.

Then I thought about God's plan.
How He'd made them so very small,
And gave them the knowledge to survive
In grass so green, and tall.

At that very moment,
As I looked up to the sky,
I felt, I too was very small
Compared to God on high.

So I thanked the Good Lord
For the beauty He had wrought,
And I felt very humble
As I sat there and thought.
—Marjory E. Arends

Hurlyburly Chit

When submissively overcome with an exciting vagary
I prankishly spritz my jackleg dog on the nose
With an inviting garden hose and then guffaw
Truly jaunty, she is a chipper hurlyburly chit
Restively hunkers with turbidity when I blow my kazoo
Filled with levity-lickety split she turns a somersault
Actuating a nonpareil, a total debacle if she wakes the cat
But is entertaining divertissement to quiet my spirits
Pathetically interpenetrates my soul when she foozles
Gauche, but bathetically comforts when she licks my face
Vamoosed lugubriously to the solitude of her doghouse
After she crassly masticated Dad's paper, shoes and tie
She thought she had a delicious nosh, so nutritious
Her frivolous mischief making levitates my melancholy mood
She is a puerile freebooter, she's an ebullient jackanapes
My hilarious ramshackle pet jumps on my keister
Everything is hunky-dory when she is osculating
Or divagating timidly along the quiescent billabong
Her fordone unwieldiness is confusing but comforting
My hurly-burly chit is my boon companion in merriment.
—Leathia R. Siewert

My Seasons

When I was a girl,
  I presumed all persons innocent.
No evil existed, goodness abounded,
  in a child's mind.
When I was a young woman doubts drifted aboard.
Clouds shadowed my pure existence,
  an explosion of emotions.
When I was a grown woman reality shattered my world,
  maturity picturing an unkind portrait,
When I was in my halfway years, I assumed nothing.
  Life and dreams altered by circumstance.
Begin again, this time perception differing,
  and so shall the drums beat.
In my senior years,
  bestows new hope and new priorities.
Mere acceptance the sweetest music from the heavens,
  seasons of wisdom.
    —*Karen Posey Todd*

The Song Of The Sea

I have to know the song of the waves, again,
I remember ... what a large repertoire it makes,
And as I stand and listen to the murmur of the sea,
My face is splashed once more with its soothing coldness.

The sea has a calm face now, the way I like it best.
Its whisper seems to caress me,
And the peace of the universe,
Seems to be captured down there.

I like the way the waves splash against the rocky shore.
It makes a graceful curve and
Glassy smoothness in the air,
Before it tumbles to its destination.

The sea shimmers in the sunshine as though
A million stars are dancing across the ripples on the waves.
While the fringe of the dreamy surf looks like a lace trimming,
The wave's rustle is like a lullaby.
    —*Lilia G. Salvador*

The Progress Of Time

Yesterday, nestled in my arms,
I rocked the baby to sleep.
Today, we celebrate sixteen.
How could so many sunrises have set?
Memories of new teeth, old teeth,
  inches and injuries, are crystalline.
But time has given me a young adult
  before I am ready.
Even with the belief, 'give them the means to fly',
I thought I would have more tomorrows.
Yet the same joy received from the two year old,
  is constant at sixteen.
And I know when the door closes,
the love will remain -
cradled in memory and the grown man.
Happy Birthday, Son.
    —*Lynn S. Moore*

Alone In A Meadow

A flower, a beautiful flower in a million
I see you and your beauty surpasses the rest
Your home, a meadow, in the bright sun
You shine and radiate a brilliance
That captives and leaves me in a trance
You are definitely a beautiful flower, the best.

You aren't like the others, your color,
It contrasts, but lets your beauty flow
Are you the only one or are there more?
Right now, you are the only one to me
The only one that shows such exquisite beauty
You have a special allure that I see and know

A flower, a beautiful flower in a million
Why are you different from the rest? Why?
Is it to be carefree and to stun?
I see your beauty as you and I meet
Oh yes! Your nectar is quite sweet
But what do I know? I'm just a butterfly.
    —*Ryan T. Greene*

Today, Tomorrow, Forever

Everyone's gone and a special silence reigns.
  I sense a calm assurance of perfect peace;
I feel and envision tranquility all around,
  With a tremendous beauty that embraces me.

Maybe I can go there just for a wandering minute.
  To escape those particles of my life;
That crowd the mind and disturb a sinful heart,
  Only to forget about my hurtful past.

Come with me to a quiet meadow where a gentle stream rests.
  And the sun smiles, casting a shadow of hope;
Let us dance among the wildflowers so totally free,
  As our spirits soar amidst the fresh wind.

Stay with me as the afternoon scents linger about,
  Welcoming our weary souls in perfect harmony;
Where the sun flows through linking our calm spirits,
  As the night awaits, rain begins to slowly fall.

Oh the soft, wet, slippery sprinkles of an evening rain,
  Gently tapping against our shameless bodies;
Reminding us of a new dawn in the midst of our trials,
  Today, tomorrow, and forever.
    —*Patricia Anne Weisker*

Trapped

In every crack and crevice of your body,
  I soak into you like rain.
    Falling onto
    and
   then evaporating
   into the midst
  of your very being.
  I become lost
  in your soul.
  Feeling my way around,
I am engulfed more and more,
    finding
   solitude
  and no
   peace
    of
    mind.
    —*Michelle A. Morgan*

Karen's Song

Karen, you ask, why I write my verse
I sometimes feel I live a curse
To be a Kipling or even Robert Frost
I write my verse when bewildered or lost
I write this for you because I see the same
You are tired of the madness and the silly game
When you arrive, you are ever so silent
Asking yourself will the madness ever relent
I see you question I see it in your eyes
I can see you asking behind your disguise
You're only wish is to walk on the beach
You think this dream is out of your reach
To feel the sea breeze in your hair
I see you yell 'it isn't fair!'
To endure this hell, no fault of your own
How long will this trip last through the twilight zone?
Stay the sweet person you are
And perhaps the end isn't that far
—*Rik McGuire*

Oneness

A squirrel sits chittering in leaves overhead,
I stand, senses sun-fused, to hear what is said,
Inner self merges with bee, bird, and breeze
In mystical oneness with rocks, earth and trees.

"We are one," chitters squirrel,
"We are one," drones the bee,

Birds on high voice the cry
"We are one, can't you see?"

Life's pulse is soul's pulse
Livening all things,
Whirling gases and atoms
From these we all spring.

No matter if squirrel,
No matter if bee,
Reality often is not what we see.
Illusion, instead, is the name of the game,
And underneath all we are one and the same.
—*Vesta M. Neale*

Late Autumn

Between the branches of the aspen,
  I trail the timid ballerinas
    gaining confidence in the virgin blue
      as they pirouette in the wind
        spotlit by the sun.

Whirlwinds of time tug at my heart.
I want to be a part of their ballet
  though in my golden years
    I dance with only shadowed
      dreams of youth.

The bonfire's crackling twigs
  consume the fallen leaves raked in,
    their ashen specters
      hurled above the flames
        to whirl forever in Elysium.
—*Sunny Rivera-Reyes*

Seventeen

The first time I met bandleader Vince I was seventeen.
I stopped in this private club to pick up Darlene.
That night I had on my old Sylvania clothes.
Vince came by and thumbed his nose.
Then Darlene and I devised this scheme,
to get back in this night club,
We had to be keen.
Now here I am almost naked in the back of his car,
He said, "how old are you chick"? I said, "24 almost 25"
"How old you?" I then forget and say, "That's as old as
  my dad 35."
"I mean my dad was one time that old" Don't you think?
Then he started to grin, and he said come here,
and it didn't make any difference in our years.
That's when the policeman came by with his light.
I'll never forget this embarrassing sight.
He said, hey Vince, I didn't know it was you.
Parked here outside the place called the Red Shoe.
Vince said, "Hey Mac, stop by the garden for lunch."
Policeman said, "next time Vince, it could cost you a bunch.
Holy Coc-ca! I thought back then,
Even I knew that was the local mob and gangster den.
Now I look down upon his grave,
He told the truth, I lied that day. 1921-1986
That's why I wrote Marciano promises to keep!
As he didn't know the word defeat!
—*Marjorie Henderson*

The One Day

I burn your flag—I spit on it
I tear it apart—I mock it
Your symbols mean nothing to me
only your realities
For every starving American Child—
I burn your Flag
For every Native American living on wastelands and
Budweiser—
I burn your Flag
For every Black American who has been enslaved or hung—
I burn your Flag
My list could go on and we both know that,
but keep this in mind you
Richwhitebluebloodsuburbanurbanmoralisticpatrioticscumbag
millions have died for, and because of—your Flag
For now I am just acting in symbols
Be prepared for the one day
when symbolism
no longer quenches my fires....
—*William D. Schempp (Rhino)*

Forever Young

As the phrase "Forever Young" echoes in my mind,
I think about what's been done and what's been left behind.
We've lived our life as children, full of innocence,
Never thinking about love, or of our lives, years from hence.

Now we face the future about to graduate,
And we look about us seeking for our fate.
We fondly bid farewell to friends and those cared,
To those whom we bid well and those whom with we shared.

We face the phantoms of our youth, those shades which
  scared and teased us,
We turn toward another truth, one that tries to seize us.
And as life draws to a close beginning to be done,
I wish I were among those who are Forever Young.
—*Ron Jenkins*

Love Song

I heard the most beautiful song on the radio today
I think I've ever heard.
I can't quite recall the name,
But I think they called it "love."
Yes, "love"— a strange little word,
It must be foreign.
I enjoyed it so much,
It was so happy and free and young!
But it was short.
The song ended,
The announcer's voice came back-
I was so disappointed.
But I was busy anyway,
You know, I don't have all day
To stand around listening to a silly song...
And besides, maybe I'll hear it again someday.
—J. Lynanne Page

Jeremy

I sit in silence, thinking of him,
I think of how things have been.
I tingle and almost start to cry,
Tears of joy fill my eyes.
All the happiness I have had,
The way he makes me feel when I am sad.
When he says, "I love you!" it feels so good,
More than anything ever could.
So I write this for him this day,
And there is only one thing I have to say,
"I love you!" from deep in my heart,
And I know deep down we will never part.
—Katina Selby

Grand Passion

I was so naive when they talked of love
I thought I understood what they meant
For I had cared about men before
And though I could share my life
Yet I always ran, searching for more

Then I finally met him
And understood the grand passion
I felt as if I were struck by lightning
My feelings rushed so strong and swift

Just being near him thrilled me
Hearing his voice made my heart race
Looking in his eyes made me weak
And I yearned always to touch him

But we were doomed from the start
He belonged to another
And said he had too much to lose
By leaving her now

How could I possibly care for another
When he embodies all that any man
Could conceivably be?
—Katherine Ann Fox

Daffodils

An iron fist within a velvet glove
Is how I thought of the old saying.
And these, lined up on my front walk,
Battered down, but only one betraying
The steel that held the rest.
—Peter Ritchie

Love Hurts

When you said good-bye
I thought the world would end.
The reason I stood by—
You said it would never end.

Our love had gotten so deep
With all the times we shared.
I thought our love was for keeps.
But with love, forever isn't a word.

I'll make it through somehow
Even though it will take time.
I just need my space now
I guess that's why love hurts.
—Shelly Boldman

Remembering The Night

The clouds in the sky,
I thought they would never go away,
  Then suddenly the sun began to shine
and warm feeling filled my soul.
  Now let the rain come down,
let the rivers freeze,
  Nothing can ever take away
the night that made me whole.
  My skies are blue
and the sun shines bright
  within my heart
I have such delight
  So when the clouds roll in,
I'll just send them by
  I'll bring out the sun
That warms my soul
  And remember the night
That made me whole.
—Diana Driscoll

The Fleeting Days Of Youth

As the sun climbs high on a summer's day,
I try to recall the secret smell of childhood,
The smell of dew on the barefoot grass,
The smell of adventure through a sea of time.

As the sun hangs bright in the noontime sky,
Memories vibrate redolent and green,
Recalling the fragrance of those limitless days,
When all was new and tomorrows never came.

As the sun slips into its rapid descent,
The elusive memories begin to fade,
Taking with them the smells of promise and time,
Leaving cold winter frost on the now dying grass.

As the sun sets deep in the reticent past,
The aroma is bitter and musty with age,
Hard, brittle passage has robbed me my time,
And I no longer remember the fleeting days of youth.
—Marti L. Wheat

Y

Thus saith the Lord:
"I
Created
You
To
Love
Myself,"
Turtle: "Pay attention to me I am
    not walking I am running."
—Shrell Lott

From Caterpillar To Butterfly

Once I was a caterpillar, then a butterfly!!!
I use to crawl around a lot! Now I like to fly!
I crawled around as best I could, to get to where I went;
"Slow as Xmas" they would say, but it was time well spent!
I'd stop along a flower leaf, and warm up in the sun;
Or visit Mr. Worm awhile, and that's when we'd have fun!
We'd race up trees and flower stems, to see who won the race.
With all my legs and fuzzy belly, I had time to waste!
Soon the day came, it was time for my nap!
When I'd wrap myself up and weave me a cap!
Warm and safe, I slept a long time; the day I awoke,
I was feeling just fine! Little did I know when I lay down to
nap, that I would grow and grow right out of my cap!!!
I wiggled and I stretched till I set myself free;
And you'll never guess what happened to me!?!?
I looked nothing the same, and had wings of all colors!
Even antennas or something or other!?! It really didn't matter
What all these parts were, cause now I could fly to the ends
of the earth! I saw Mr. Worm and I told him goodbye!
That once I was a caterpillar, but now a butterfly!!!
—*Pamela Elaine Tharp*

The Great Physician

When I was a little tot
I very much feared the dark.
When my mother knew my fear
"Don't forget the great physician is near."

When we had a thunder shower,
I had the same feeling.
Fear of lightning, thunder too.
If the great physician only knew.

Then I went to High school.
"There'll be a test tomorrow."
Again I felt the chills of fear,
And then I knew "The Great Physician" is here.

And on and on it went,
Dark, showers, tests, and storms.
Go back to the same physician.
He'll give a remedy for the condition.
—*Lee Gorham*

Here I Come, Ready Or Not

I want to be born...
I want to be born...
I want to have a mommy
I need you, too, daddy.

Remember now, you are not alone.
I will be there, but not shown.
I can hear your every word...
Everything you say will be heard.

Please don't get mad or even shout.
I feel bad...what's it all about?
I get your vibrations, you know.
So, don't make me quiver and shake so.

I love you both, you know that.
Please take it easy, just like your cat.
Be calm, be cool; forget your spat.
Or I'll end up a horrid little brat.

I'll cry..and whine when you dine...
I'll wake you up any old time.
I'm sure that's not what you will like.
So, Mommy, Daddy, make me a good little tyke.

Here I come, ready or not.
—*Nora Evelyn Wold*

Life

I was there and I wanted to go.
I wanted to live my life focusing on the high points;
Not the low.
I turned my head to the glass door;
Eyes focused steadfast looking past the glass for something more.
Dreams that were once vivid;
Perished with a terror so real and livid.
I wanted more out of life;
The end of misery and strife.
I turned to the glass door once more;
And I saw other's dreams soar.
As I strained to see;
The world continued on in front of me.
My vision of the world was impaired;
I could not see past the glare.
Fear focused my eyes upon the glass that made me see;
It was my hope that revived my dreams inside of me.
—*Laurie Downey*

To Someone So Very Special To Me: My Mother

This day is very special to all of us.
I wanted to take this time out to read you this
In front of God and everyone. I am reading this on a
Happy occasion.
Mom, I wanted to Thank you for everything
you have done and helped me...
You were there to share a laugh, a cry, and even a
Shoulder.
You was there through thick and thin.
I want it to always be that way.
I love you so very much. You are the best mother.
Anyone could have, we've been through a lot together.
You were there to pick my chin up off the floor when I
Was almost walking on it.
Roses are red
Sugar is Sweet,
Without you where would I be today?
Most of all you were there to walk me down that isle today.
We each have our own memories, we like many of the same things.
We have a relationship you are not only my mother, you
Are my best friend. My mother is very special to me in
A very special way.
She always will be my best friend in the world that I
Can trust and talk to.
She has even fixed my heart when it was broken hoping
And praying it would never be broken again.
I love you mom, thank you for everything you have
Done for Tim and I.
We love you...Please never forget and if you do I
Will gladly remind you.
Love always, your baby Robin. April 15, 1989.
—*Robin Miller*

Independent Child

I was born of hot Indian and Spanish blood.
I was born when ten other hungry kids were already there.
I was born at home — home; poor, home; partera,
home-sweet-home.
I was born between the two-faced Gemini and the roaring Leo.
I was born crying, kicking, wanting, fighting.
I was born because of love-because they cared.
I was born because I'm them.
—*Yolanda Hernandez*

Anniversary

His
I was about to see the world before you stepped
Into the picture, weaving chains of mortgages and babies.
I sought escape more times than once, tripping over
Responsibility within reach of freedom, a frigate brought to bay.
Now I scarcely step off my own land as the days
Stretch fore and aft into a tranquil pattern.
You smile across the room, grandchildren at your feet,
And in your gaze I find reflections of
The memories that bind us to each other;
The warm contentment of our love.

Hers
Sometimes I want a hug so badly I could cry!
It's not an easy thing to cope with—living.
I used to think it might be; I was wrong.
Even if we've been arguing and resentment lingers,
I need you to stand with me against the cold.
This double harness has sometimes been a heavy one,
Each pulling in his own direction. But when I'm
Weary and the day winds down, I still desire
Your arms around me. After all these years
Your shoulder seems the right place for my head.

—Sylvia Owens

The Reply
Time; such a small thing to ask of me, truly!
I, who have squandered whole years at a fling —
I, who have scattered days, months, all unduly,
— Counterfeit coins in a counterfeit spring.

Time; when you ask it thus makes it a treasure;
Come, shall I give you long years or a day?
Tell me, dear one, by what rule shall I measure?
I shall be glad to give moments away!

Time; it has lengths from minute to eternal;
Take what you choose, while the thought's at the prime!
Here — to be granting a wish seems supernal —
Take all my over-abundance of time!

—LaVonne Houlton

Distance and Time
Day by day, month by month,
I wonder how you feel.
You used to say you loved me,
but I know its no longer real.
It's been so long since I saw you last,
that my memories have become a part of the past.
I know now I should have acted upon
my feelings, before you moved far away.
But I couldn't express how I felt,
I just didn't know what to say.
I shouldn't have let myself love you so much,
because you're so far away from my touch.
Maybe in a distant time,
we'll meet again some way.
But as for now, I'll go on thinking,
of what might have been from day to day.

—Keri Weber

In The Sunset Of My Life
In the sunset of my life,
I wonder if all the heartaches and the strife,
The triumphs and the fears,
The accolades and the jeers,
The laughter and the tears,
Was it worth it all those years?
In the sunset of my life,
I think of all the ones I loved,
Some are still here, and others up above,
That I caressed and some of them I left,
In the glory of my youth,
Was it all false or all the truth?
The boyfriends that passed by - the man I married,
And the ones that made me cry,
Yet, gave me love that made me sigh.
The loves that said, "Forever yours"
Were they true, or did they lie?
Nevermind — we just pass by —
And if we have to pay the price,
When its bad or when it's nice.
Never mind — it will suffice — in the sunset of my life.

—Rosemary Chandler

Life Cycles
I wonder, Daddy, if you know how much you mean to me,
I wonder, Mommy, if you know how glad I'll always be,
That in his love God gave me you to teach me how to live,
You gave me more than you can know, you taught me how to give.

From you I found the strength of love that never ever ends,
I learned to cope with what life gives, you often helped me mend.
Your words were those that brought me hope when things weren't
    going right,
Come thick or thin—or come what may—your love was like a light.

As I approached the time in life to spread my wings and fly,
I did so with the certainty that you'd be standing by,
To urge me on when times were tough and teach me how to stand,
Or pick me up when there was need to lend a helping hand.

Now as I look upon the man whom God has given me,
Or think of our own precious girls and all that they can be,
My heart is filled with love and praise to two who shaped my life,
And molded me to help me be their mommy and his wife.

—Melinda Sue Lenderink

Before You Go
Before you go
I would like you to know
That my feelings for you are very important
No amount of time can ever change them

I knew from that first enchanting moment
That I would be putty in your hands
And you would remold my heart from the ashes

You would guide my every step
Making the dark places seem brighter
Putting new lace on the ragged and torn curtain

My heart would see a new sunrise
Shining like a beacon through the night
Keeping me from hitting the jagged rocks of loneliness

For you have deeply touched my heart
And I became a changed man
When first I beheld your heavenly glow

I just wanted you to know before you go
That my love will flow
Until time stands still

—T. E. Johnson

I Am Thankful

So many things I'm thankful for,
I wouldn't dare to say I'm poor.
For health and strength I am so glad,
And for a wonderful Mother and Dad.

For friends and loved ones very dear,
For beautiful seasons every year.
For food and raiment and my home,
And a wonderful country to call my own.

For freedom of speech and freedom of press,
I'm truly glad that I live in the U.S.
We have freedom of worship and a nice church,
Doctors and nurses and people who work.

For institutions and education,
And all of God's great creation.
For the Sabbath Day when we can rest,
I feel that I am greatly blessed.

For the blessings in this nation,
I will show my appreciation.
I want my life to be a blessing,
For all the good things I'm possessing.
—*Lois W. Kinder*

If Only You

I'd like to fall in love today, no matter what the wise men say. I'd like to fly and scale the heights, and show my love some brand new sights. I'd like to be a brand new me, with a dear sweet love that's young and free. I'd like to fall in love again, if only you would let it begin. I'd like to breathe some fresh new air, and give and share and love and care. I'd like to soar o'er mountain tops, then ski on Aspen's snowy drops. I'd like to stroll a sandy shore, then dance in love across a floor. I'd like to fall in love again, if only you would let it begin. I'd like to have a brand new start, and give away my wishful heart. I'd like to hear a song that's new, then sing it with a love that's true. I'd like to sail the seven seas, with only you for me to please. I'd like to fall in love again, if only you would let it begin. I'd like to play just like a clown, then drive a 'vette with top turned down. I'd like to be the gleam in your eye, while giving love another try. I'd like to shop, like on a spree, then wine and dine, just you and me. I'd like to be in love again, if only you would let it begin.
—*Mike Murphy*

Picture Painting

If I was an artist
I'd pain the sky blue
with ragged fingers
stretched across the hue!
Billowy clouds their outlines change,
from mountains and valleys to lowly terrains.
Some are lazy, taking a nap,
others floating not caring a rap.
A silver giant in the sky,
an airplane floating by
arrows a line overhead,
a measureless distant unsped.
Across the realms the breezes blow
unchecked by activities below.
Lovely tree tops freshly green
swaying gently as they gleam
beneath the bursting radiance
of the sun's rays so glorious.
—*Lydia W. Dornbush*

Ha Ha Ho Ho Hee Hee

If going out on a limb wasn't so precarious,
I'd say this country we live in is rather hilarious!

I laugh so hard I get a stomach ache,
Thinking of the trip I'm about to make.

So come travel with me.
I'm sure you'll agree.

You can visit this land from sea to sea,
Laughing in the state of Tennessee hee hee.

You can yak it up in Yakima, as you know,
Then go East, giggling, to Idaho ho ho.

You can go from the state of Texas to Alaska,
Passing through Omaha ha ha in the state of Nebraska.

If you go to Nevada very often.
You know you can laugh in the town of Laughlin.

You can be oh so jolly in Joliet,
Oh har-de-har in Hartford, Connecticut.

You can be merry in Marietta, Ohio or GA,
Having so much fun you might want to stay.

50 States of Hysteria, it seems, do exist.
Making laughing and giggling hard to resist.
—*Margaret Stowell*

Wondering When

I wish I could tell him exactly how I feel
I'd scream it from the rooftops with lots of zeal
We've been friends forever, or so it seems
But, when he raises his brows, that certain look he gives,
   sends me flying on moonbeams.

It's a spark
And I feel it even when we're apart
Its odd how we both tiptoe around each other
When neither truly wants another
Both too shy to speak first
But, if I don't I'll just burst
Our questionable fate lends excitement to the romance
Perhaps the answer lies in each sideways glance
When the truth is declared, a risk for one,
Will surely be a day my smile will shine brighter than the sun.
—*Lisa Martin*

Total Indifference

When I said it was fun, you got upset.
If I'd said it was special then you'd regret,
having done what we did, because you'd be scared.
What would you do if I said I cared?

I know I should stop, but I don't want to try.
If you have to ask it's not worth saying why.
Are you really dumb, or playing the fool.
Too shy to show feelings, so you play it cool.

Could you show an interest in what I've got?
Or will you say you're happy, when I know you're not.
You run hot and cold, you're sugar and spice.
Sometimes you're naughty and sometimes you're nice.

They say that in ignorance there is bliss.
And since that is true, I know I'll miss,
the strong embracing of your arms,
and warmth and loving of your charms.
—*Linda Lee*

His Symbol

I wonder do you know
if diligent we grow
Speedy recovery of life
relieving me of strife

Sojourn love to return
Seeking rhythm — a heart can burn
Spacious sky and cautious wind
Baking sunshine — soothing skin

Grief be gone and love be found
Amazing grace how sweet the sound
Intentions good and actions seen,
Find the difference in between!

Once upon this planet earth
Baby Jesus planned his birth
His life was lived, loving God's law
and offered eternal life to all.

So let it be commercial free
With some added creativity
Violence gone—no troubled way
let night pass to enter day.

—Timotheus Dumsha

Oh, Whoopee

I can always tell what he's got in mind,
If his kiss is nice—or the other kind.

There's the flat, dry peck that asks "When's supper?"

There's the kind that make my heart go flutter,
And the kind that smack of peanut butter.

While some are a sham and others grand slam,
Most pecks are just a nuisance wham-bam.

But his whoopee kiss says he's in the mood,
For his usual quickie interlude.

As he sends me a message with dogged eyes,
That after umpteen years lends no surprise.

His fingers say, "hurry with those dishes,"
Then plants him a kiss, wet as a fish's.

I try to pretend a whale scooped me up,
Or he's some poor beast, and I'm his sup.

There's a store-wide sale — the crowds getting rough,
Or I'm running a heat and not up to snuff.

I feign a pain, and if that ain't enough,
I sweetly say, "Hey, kiss off with that stuff!"

—Sybil Riead

Whole Truth

Dedicated to Shirley Baldwin...
If I were deaf,
I would not hear words harshly;
will you listen with an open heart?
If I were mute,
I would not talk of hatred;
will you speak with arms open wide?
If I were blind,
I would not see inequalities;
will you look for the truth of actions?
If I were dumb,
I would not know vanities;
will you teach with purity?
Even if I were without touch,
I should little understand
when you give gracious love.

—Loyal T. Joner, Jr.

Russian Roulette Of Love

Here I am playing Russian Roulette of love
If I win, I'll be flying through the skies above
If I lose, my heart crashes to the ground
But it's worth the pain, when true love is found
Here I am playing Russian Roulette of love again
Will I lose, or will I win
I find myself wondering what the hell is she going to say
Will she hold me close, or tell me to go away
The right words can be hard to find
Like the cylinder of a pistol, they go spinning through your mind
There's no rules to Russian Roulette of love
And when you win, you feel like you could fly like a dove
With your heart at stake
You give, and you take
Words are like the bullets in a forty-five
Will the love die, or will it stay alive
Only God knows, when it comes to playing Russian Roulette of love
It's all up to the man above
When I lose, I break down and cry
But I can always come back and give it another try

—Peter P. Perry

Don't Hurry Love

Love at first sight is a fairy tale for most!
If luck is with you, it happens only once!
To deny that feeling would be a hoax—
But to pretend it's real is just as much as a farce.
My wheel of fortune stopped there years ago!
It was the most enchanting time of my life!
Together we harvested a field of gold—
Unfortunately we chose not to let that stream flow.
Years have passed—Memories remain!
The curtain has been pulled on that stage!
Certainly my life will never be the same—
But at the same time, there is no feeling of rage.
Today you walked into my theater!
You found that your fairy tale has come true!
But for me that script was written long before—
Love can not step forward right on cue.
To pressure me would surely be a misprint!
To love me and to show me just might be an asset!
Don't read the last line in the middle of the play—
Don't portray a part that you're sure to regret.

—Myra L. Hulse

The Deep Side Of A Woman

There was a stepping stone in her life and she was not quite sure
If she could handle the pressures or the many ways to endure.
So she would go to a place alone and seek what she could find,
Knowing in her heart and soul she then could have peace of mind.
She'd glance at the trees and see the dim shadows of the skyline
And assure herself again that the joys of life could intertwine.
So then she would settle herself and return to her quiet home,
Being satisfied with life again just knowing she could roam.
Tranquility brings a smile to her face and frowns always let her down.
She'd crossed bridges and endeavors to say a man can't make her
   a clown.
She gives what she wants and he takes only the easy side of her today.
She remembers the hurt and the pain and tries not to let love
   get in her way.
So if you pass her way please see the stepping stones that are
   in place,
For if you mistake her for a fool she'll gracefully put you in
   a memory and erase.
In the autumn of her life she only means to be kind and treated
   the same.
She's one of a kind with charm and wit, all she asks is that
   you don't play a game.

—Marvine V. Valine

Why Diet??

I just can't imagine why I need to diet.
If they have size 20, I simply go buy it.
Things don't look too bad with a jacket or vest,
It just shows that I have been overly blessed.

But then there is Summer when others wear shorts,
I put on a pair and hear snickers and snorts.
In a swimming suit I look like Eva Gabor,
If you add a few layers and then add some more.

At parties the gowns really show off your figure.
Getting into one takes all my vim and my vigor.
I put on my girdle and can't sit or bend,
Or it rolls halfway down and it pinches my skin.

For some reason I get out of breath fairly easy
And sometimes my tummy feels achy and queazy.
Others say I look nice, why shouldn't I but it?
Knowing all this, why should I need to diet?
—Rita Reynolds

The Highway Of Life

The highway of life can really get long,
if you don't pull over to relax and have fun.
Struggling uphill, finally reaching the top—
Then down you go, where do you stop?
Around a curve, to a dead end,
turn around start over again.

Start over again there's a fork in the road,
how do I know which way to go? I
turned to the left, but that wasn't right,
I went back the other way finally seeing
some light. I took a turn down Memory
Lane, but all I saw was sorrow and pain.

I pulled in a reststop—thought about today—
Nothing seemed right, what can I say? I
turned to the future—what do I see?
Something out there good for me!
—Rose Zacchiroli Smith

Aunt Ellie — "Auntie Mame"

An "Auntie Mame" comes only once in one's life,
If you're fortunate indeed.
Our Aunt Ellie was our "Auntie Mame"
and came when we were most in need.

For Richard he was a very small boy
thinking about Christmas trees, lights and toys.
  She made his dreams come true.

To Michelle she was a model of fashion and poise,
wise, yet funny and full of life's joys.
  She taught her how to live.

For Nora and Aaron she was laughter and fun.
A day with Aunt Ellie was never a dull one.
  She showed them an exciting new world.

To her own dear family she was all things
Preparing them for whatever life brings.
She taught them to love, to think, and to care-
to live a full life always eager to share.
Ellie gave them a sense of how to survive
knowing in this world or the next one's always alive.

So we know Aunt Ellie's presence is always nearby
and we whisper a soft prayer to our "Auntie Mame"
  no goodbyes!!!
—Michelle Sydow

Ready?

Taste me! Take of my meat.
I'll nourish you well. You'll find
no diet can be as sweet,
as salubrious and as kind.

Expand and grow on me
as a flower unfolds on rain.
Your energy, your harmony,
your zeal I promise to regain.

Take of me all your days. I have a lot to offer you.
In many forms — in many ways,
I am complete and ever new.

Take warning! Don't spice me. You'll find me harsh
and grievous. I have my seasons in me — balanced,
healthy, delicious.

Don't gulp me! I won't endure, nor add to me —
you'll take from me all that is right and pure,
precious, good and heavenly.

Curious yet to know my name? Are you ready and hungry
for me? I'm life! You'll see my claim. Just look
around. You can't miss me.
—Monica Harris

Invitation To Dream

This kind of atmosphere creates romantic dreams;
I'm i-ma-gin-ing you inviting me to ren-dez-vous,
Under this great, big blan-ket of blue
Quiet, blue sky.

The desert speaks in a whis-per.
. . . As if to say, "Be my guest."
Just as the Sun is slipping lower, and lower
Then out of sight in the West
Bringing night, so th' desert can rest. . .

'Til dawn
Chas-es the stars. . .
Turning the sky pink, and then blue. . .
And then I think, a-gain, of you.
—K. L. Whitcomb

The Joy Of Living

  I'm living - I'm doing all the things I never thought I'd do
 I'm living - Oh it's such fun to do the things you always wanted to
   I waited - I thought tomorrow was the day I would begin
   Ill fated - I was afraid to start I thought I'd never win.

    But once you try it you won't deny it
    Life grows thrilling despite its chores.

   Your every leaning takes on new meaning
   And don't forget it the world is yours.

           I know

  I'm living - I'm never bored or feel I want to run away
  And I enjoy each day - I'm never sad and offer glad
           THANKSGIVING
—Sylvia Stang

Echoes Of Goodbye

Blinded by darkness
I'm lost in a world of grief.
Sorrow, like slivers of glass
pierce my soul.
   Will I forever be lost.

   Shadows whispers are calling
urging me down their destructive path
cold fingers of death are reaching out.
   So easy to end the pain, so easy.

   In haunting echoes I hear her call
my name. Giving me the strength to
face this world on my own.
   In my heart, she will always
be forever free, forever young.
     —*LaNae M. Roe*

Crepuscule

So light recruits us
Imparts line and form
Movement of the soul shapes
Music in the dark
Peace in the enfolding air
of night, intensifying
Silence through all
The slumbering mind

Dusk when tempos rest for a while
And again, and again, the strings
   Repeat
Nothing is donned, nothing covers the mind's
   Bareness
Except for the bed and chair, the bare
   bookshelves
Under the mottled ceiling, near the fire
Floating between songs of morning
The sound of human voices echoes
Till the deep internal sound arises
And we stare amazement at the sky
    —*W. R. Elton*

The Poet

I am a voice in the wind
in a gathering of many others
Where I paint life and feelings
between the pages of kindred minds.
I am a poet, I am a dreamer
I teach, I learn, I am a song — a singer
I say what I say in a natural way
Because I am a child of wonder.
Natures words have much to be heard. . .
If you listen you can hear the sea
If you look you can see with me
Newer yet deeper horizons
Together we can fly
You and I
Giving wings to the breeze
In temporal sprees
And see for yourself how the poet sees...
   Through Poets' Eyes. . .
    The Poet.
    —*Leslie K. Walton*

The Leather Man

Deep in the woods in the blizzard's blow, the old man huddled
   in a cave.
When it was clear and cold, he built a fire, on
some very flat rocks, some heat to save.
   Then he spread some pine boughs to rest his bones,
   And slept on the warmth of the heated stones.
   There were tears on his cheeks and he let out some moans,
   And the wind in the trees whined plaintive tones.
It was the nineteenth century when he began to roam, for thirty
years he live in the weather.
He walked three hundred and sixty miles a year, in a sixty
   pound suit of patched leather.
   In France his factory had begun to fail,
   And so it was he began to sail,
   To America where he would walk a trail,
   For his Charlotte had left him to no avail.
So he begged for his meals speaking not a word, for he didn't
   speak English at all it is said,
He would never set foot inside a home, but took all his meals
on the back step instead.
   The Yankee ladies knew the day he would come,
   And fixed a small table, and never a crumb,
   Would be left after ten cups of coffee and rum,
   And a loaf, and crackers and meat pie for the bum.
He was Jules Bourglay and he died one night, the lip and chin
   cancer grew worse through the years.
Thus began the legend of the old leather man, and the wind
   wailed for days, and the clouds shed their tears.
    —*Lucy Hadsell Curtis*

The Ace Of Hearts

A king, a queen, and a jack of diamond's greed,
in a society made of gold,
Seemingly always take more than they need
more than their hands can hold.

A king, a queen, and a jack of spades
in a third world made of dirt
watch slowly as their future fades —
next generation hurt.

A king, a queen, and a jack of clubs
filled with compassion and good wishing
now check the deck of 52 cards —
the ace of hearts is missing.

Without the ace, no love is left
kindness and generosity lack.
Together we can make the change
with a king, a queen, and a jack.
    —*Sherri Dennard*

In Dreams

In dreams we were married upon the North Star,
In dreams we flew high and very far.
We went bouncing through the Milky Way's heart
Which cruelly tore us apart.
In dreams we jumped over the moon
As if we had raced through high noon.
We rode the endless boundaries of space
Without whatsoever a trace.
Without dreams what rule could we bend
When love foresees its end?
As we sail along life's streams,
Where would be without dreams?
    —*Sharon E. Walker*

Intrepitude

I am intrepid, but weary and forlorn.
In a world where I don't belong.
On a different path, where the journey's
  been extremely lonely and long.

In touch, yet misconnecting, with many lost souls.
Destined to the karma set forth by their collective woes.

Oh, what a sad state, when you know life could be so different.
Rich and full of substance, in positive proliferation,
  and making magnificent creations.
Displaying mighty powers of love and fulfillment, moving
  in freedom, with no limitations and infinite possibilities.
Abounding in ultimate prosperity.

Oh, what a sorrow, that some are not yet free and can not see
  life's limitless possibilities.

So in a world where you don't belong, you must be fearless,
  brave, and move right along.

Yes, I am intrepid, but weary and forlorn.
For I live in a world that is yet to be born.
—Rosalyn M. King

We Are The Hunters Of The Mind...

In Secret Places cast on High,
In Caverns deep or distant sky...
We seek Elusive Truth to find,
For We are the Hunters of the Mind...

The Truth We seek to set us Free,
The Truth that Finally lets us See...
The Things that Are and still must Be,
The Truth that only We can see...

For we do know or seek to know,
That place beyond we cannot go...
The Final goal at last to be,
Complete as One, the Truth to see...

And then to Share with those we love,
The Lessons learned here and above...
The Simple Truth at Last to Find,
Is Love, the Hunter of the Mind...
—F. Roger Greenawalt

Memories Of Tomorrow

Tomorrow's memories live today,
In everything we do or say.
Life's confused and altered states,
I can easily appreciate.
Because, tomorrow I'll look back on today,
And say, "Thank God I made it through yesterday."
Bearing life's heartaches and its sorrows,
I live for today and long for tomorrow.
Taking things one day at a time,
Peace and eternal sanctity will one day be mine.
Pursued by an inevitable fate,
I think life is just great.
And when I'm at death's door,
And can live life no more,
I'll look back on my life gone by,
And give another life a try.
—Nicole Austin

The Tone Of Things

Why do we have, so great a lack,
In cutting each other, a bit of slack,
Let's show some care, instead of flack,
Be we red or white, or yellow or black.

When day is done, and we've been fed,
Let's review our deeds, before going to bed,
Were we real nice, in the life we led,
Be we white or yellow, or black or red.

Or did we choose, to argue and fight,
To make things worse, instead of alright,
Then couldn't we use, better insight,
Be we yellow or black, or red or white.

So why can't we, like the other fellow,
'Cause color means nothing, once we mellow,
Or when we're scared, with knees like Jell-O,
Be we black or red, or white or yellow.

It makes no difference, where we've grown,
Or that we dwell, o'er many a zone,
For aren't we all, made of skin and bone,
So why such fuss, about the outer tone.
—Darby O'Toole

Wayward Winds

Lonely, I stand as on and on
In every direction the great plains run
With naught but the rustle of futile grass
As wayward winds of the prairies pass.

You barren knoll with clean white sand
Once was a buffalo wallow and stand,
And below is a basin of salt and lime
Where a lake was lost to the hands of time.

Oh, what has become of the lowing herds
And the endless songs of the prairie birds?
I fear 'tis the end of the great domain
Our forefathers fought to conquer and tame.

They could not go, but they dared not stay,
And my heart is sad as I turn away -
Away from the land where grasses sigh,
And darkness covers the lonely sky.
—Paul E. Garrett

Regret

Leaping from cliffs of forgiveness
in haste to accept all blame.
The battle begins to erase the sins
his deep sea eyes had spoken.

Completely insane,
She arose to claim
The shame of her silent Eden.

Waiting for infant loss to pass
Until ashes at last,
explode into tacet truth.

Pride had stolen what was not given.
Affection disguised his evil intention,
and greed sat tall at her table.

Stunted growth, stifled spouse.
Wings of her gasping soul unfolded.
Freedoms window remained to be opened.
—Linda M. Snyder

Angeline

She sits alone quietly at the start of each dawn
In her small weathered house with the oversized lawn,
And begins every morning and the tasks at hand
With cream in her coffee and toast with jam;

Then out the back door she goes with her cane
To work in her garden before it should rain,
And gathers zucchini and plums from the ground
So others may have them when they come around;

Taken to lunch by someone who calls
Gives her such pleasure in the visit and all,
Then off to her nest as her eyes get tired
She knits and crochets until time to retire;

A rosary and Bible in her bedroom she keeps
While reading a book until finally she sleeps;
Angeline is "Grandma" to a very large clan
Our love she holds dearly in the palms of her hands.
—*Nancy M. Miller*

Grandma's Bag

I wish I had grandma's bag.
In it was all the goodies she ever had.
Whenever I asked her for some.
She gave me my favorite chewing gum
and it would make me glad.

There was always something in a box.
This time it was some colored rocks.
She knew I like to play with jax.
Whoever wins got all the snacks.

To grandma it was just a game.
But for me it was always the same.
So next time she visits me
I would clearly see.
It looked like an old carpet rag.
But to me it was grandma's bag.
—*Rosemarie Price*

this, God's Holy House

   The word of God insoluble,
in its undiluted form,
   Means peace and comfort for the faithful
of our church — Immanuel.
   A Sunday school, a day school,
the holy sacraments too,
   Such are the many blessings
which are afforded you.
   Couples are united,
and many are baptized,
   No hungry soul is turned away
from this God's holy house,
   For we count among our blessings
all who come and seek
   The truth of God for nourishment,
for spirits — both strong — and weak.
—*Miles L. Protzmann*

My Father

My old, nice friend, never replaceable,
In my mind alive all the time,
In my heart always a shrine
Built in love to be imperishable.
Of your white hair I can't say
Oh father, how firmly was I lead!
But my hands on your bold head
I'll ever remember, in joy, your day.
Old days really vanished away,
Old days ideally in me for ever;
You will never be forgotten, never
Oh father, you are never faraway.
If remembrances could be allowed,
If at your feet I could take refuge,
Your blessings would still be huge
On my head once again poured.
—*Thomas Benros*

Pure Water Days In Chippewa Falls, Wis.

Pure Water Days
In our town
Has a queen
Ballots cast
At supermarkets,
A parade
With blond jaycettes
Marching in precision
To drum beats.

The mayor rides a convertible.

We celebrate water
Cruising on granite
Ninety feet below earth's skin
Guarded by gravel
Old as glaciers.
Mysterious fluid H2O
Flowing inviolate
Deep in earth, deep in time
Festival drink of life.
—*Lois Austin*

The Gypsies

 The village was quiet when they came into town.
In painted wagons, beads and bright colored gown.
Peddling their wares with tambourines and guitars.
   Hoping to be seen out under the stars.

The gypsies were down by the creek last night.
   Laughing and dancing near the fire.
Chubby little children with beads so bright.
   Red green and blue and colors gold.
   Grandmothers who never seem to grow old.

   King of the gypsies strutting about.
His muscles and white pearly teeth on parade.
   For all to see there was no doubt,
   he was the leader of this charade.

I would like to go where the gypsies play.
Along streams and paths of a life that's free.
   I cannot live another way,
   For another person I cannot be.

The village was quiet as they stole out of town.
   Moving out in their wagons bright.
   Even though I stayed — my heart went along —
   To another town, another night.
—*Roulede Bradbury*

The Dirty Old Man

A dirty old man,
in ragged clothes.
where he comes from,
nobody knows.
He stood on the corner
of the small town square.
Passing out candy to the children there.
They'd hold out their hand,
and run on by.
Never a thank you, or even goodbye.
Why do you do it,
I ask with a sigh.
For the children he said,
then he started to cry.
He bowed his head, and walked away.
I hadn't seem him
since that day.
Where he's gone,
nobody knows.
The dirty old man, in ragged clothes.
—*Virginia Wynne Tucker*

Love In Plea

I rescind and weep regret of despise and exasperation. Weep in refusal of forgiveness. In sorrow of missed caress I lay tears in the path of dialogue. Eyes in shut I pretend he loved and I loved. In clutch of hands I yearn touch, yet shiver in thoughts of the extension.

Why, I plead, did I not forgive
Why, I scream, did I not concede.

Heart of grieve absolve me, lessen the misery. To the beginning return me, endow my soul with compassion. Replace upon our impudent lips words not of detest. The vow better or worse I broke. The vow worse he invoked.

I weep and mar with eyes of swell as he riles with pulse in throat. We love but can not phrase. We crave touch but fear deception.

I recluse to eliminate reason.
He ingests and remains the same.
—*J. M. Bennett Hammerberg*

Dark Age

Seated graciously on imposing thrones, cloaked in royal robes of pretentiousness, we surround ourselves with prophets tailoring their messages to our stately attire, striking our brass scepters of arrogance to marbled floors when rankled by unadulterated truth.

We do well to sentence our false prophets to the dungeon, but manage only the outer court where they frolic among lilies among lilies growing along paths bathed in beams of the daystar, ruining in the process the integrity of them both, effecting the abhorrent birth of truth watered down.

Then, clutching this monstrosity as a mother her lifeless child, we carry the impossible burden, charlatans hobbling along on crutches searching out earth's revered mystics, baffling these miracle workers stoically slumped under their own burdens of the knowledge of unnecessary suffering.
—*Pam Warford*

Shadows Of War

A black rain falls from the sky
In sheets, like a shroud of Death,
And a dark dust of smoke rises high,
The smell of decay choking breath.
Children, terror-stricken and lost,
Naked to their parents' actions—
They pay the ultimate cost
Caught between bloody factions.
Blacks and whites struggling, killing,
Jews and Muslims fighting, too,
And all claiming they'll win, God willing,
In their religious fanatical coup.
All this I saw in dream, maybe more,
A portent, a prophesy, a shadow of war.
—*C. Shawn Smith*

Why I Love You

I love you for your patience
  In simple little things
Like when I lose some papers,
  And the extra work it brings.
I love your gentle teasing,
  The twinkle in your eye
When you have got the best of me
  No matter how I try.

I love you for your faith in me
  When I am feeling low,
The way you whisper, "it's all right,
  Don't let it get you so."
I think I've loved you most of all,
  As down the years we came,
Because, through good times and through bad,
  Your love was just the same.
—*Peggy Opal Snyder*

The Perfect Day

I sit in awe and amazement of the beauty I have seen,
  in skies and clouds and mountains, full of life and color supreme.
The sun on high brings butter-flies and birds from out their nest.
The flowers beam from sunlight's gleam; it's beauty at its best.
A silver lining from the clouds glimmers in the morning dew,
  rolls over snow capped mountain tops, through the skies of blue.
the earth gives birth to new green grass, as spring breaks into the air;
  and I lie in repose 'neath the shade of a tree, and I gaze at
    its blossoms fair.
The mid-day breeze floats through the air and to my heart it brings,
  the song of love and freedom that only birds do sing.
All this I feel, I see, I love, my thoughts are far away.
In far off lands in skies above that lead to heaven's highway.
As I look to yonder horizon wherein lies a reddish orange fire;
  I find my heart with gladness and filled with all its desire.
The sun begins to fade away as it streaks across the sky;
  the clouds turn to a purple gray as they go rolling by.
Though now the day has faded and evening dusk is nigh;
  The sound of crickets calling, the flash of the fire fly,
the glow of the moon above me, the gleam of the stars on high;
  the fragrance of flowers that lingers, brings me dreams of this
    day gone by.
—*Lawrence Spirio*

The Void

How can I say how much I loved you
In this modern world that won't seem trite?
We joked and laughed about it often
Because life together was all so right.
How can I tell how much I miss you
Morning, noon and night-time too?
You're gone but your love is all about me,
Upstairs, down-strairs are memories of every hue.
I always knew we'd have to part;
Over fifty years you held my heart.
You took a lot of me with you;
But dear God, you left me with a lot of you.
Wife and family, grand-kids too,
Try hard to cope with thoughts of you.
There is a void that will not fill
With memories of you that do not fade.
God grant life always stays that way.

—*Louise Butts Hendrix*

Hand In Hand We've Walked Together

Hand in hand we've walked together:
in this world that's full of woe,
But soon we'll go to meet our Saviour,
from this life we all must go.
Hand in hand we'll meet our Saviour
who has filled all our dreams.
Hand in hand we'll walk together:
where the light of Jesus beams.
During our years we've had some heartaches
sometimes sadness filled our hearts,
But most of all we've seen some pleasures
That only Jesus could impart.
A lifetime of love filled with laughter,
we take a glimpse now through the years,
And marvel at how God has helped us
and our children that are so very dear.

—*Sadie Knight Foltin*

I Remember

I remember, I remember, when our children numbered nine
In those work-filled days, so long ago.
I remember those large meals when we sat down to dine,
I can hear their pleading voices yet,
As each, crowding next to Daddy's usual chair
Would often proudly say, "that's where I want to sit."
Then I would hear a squabble starting here and there
With happy, twinkling eyes, father often said,
"I'll cut a hole in the middle of the table,
Then right through the center, you'll see your Daddy's head;
To sit close to me, you'll all be equally able."
I remember our feeling of pride and joy
as we sat at the table about to say "Grace"
Then gazing at each girl and boy,
We thanked God for each little face.

—*Ruby Farnham Skaggs*

Bloody Gold

I see the blood run from your ears
I smash in your face, I suck up your tears.
Just a mere mortal who worshipped his gold
Now it is mine to behold.
I will throw your corpse in a sewage creek
And I will watch the wounds in your body as they seep
Seep forth the blood that kept you whole.
Now which is more precious —that or gold?

—*Steven L. Craig*

Revelation

Then ancient brick housed justice close
In Victorian courthouse on the square.
Lean, curved windows searched our souls,
Dispensing justice stern but fair.

Brave stately marches always fell
Across the green and sun-sweet grass
Where sat the bandstand-sparkling white
Holding magic in her glass.

Across the way the opera house
Stood proudly centered-tall and wide.
The passageway at night would swell
With village folk much filled with pride.

Each country house was wrapped in bloom.
Each store front, office, school and square
Was scrubbed and polished, mowed and trimmed,
Each segment perfect-always fair

Now three score later I've come home.
Church bells are still; the village wan.
I'd thought to see it as it was,
But we'd both changed. Where had we gone?

—*Lois Ijams Hartman*

Guts And Trust

In banking, war and kindergarten;
inclusive of an age quite spartan;
in racing, science, even love,
no, not the one that makes you huff and puff,
you got to trust what's not within your reach
and forge ahead on grounds none can yet teach.

There are no facts, only beliefs!
That also goes for somber briefs,
no, not the ones that itch,
but those that bite worse than a bitch.
Likewise, it applies to holy books,
the devil's burning hooks,
twelve puppets in a box
stamping the conviction for an ambitious fox.

Go with what you truly feel
and life will come together like an unwinding reel.
Speaking philosophically,
that's the meat of our destiny;
and so it seems to me....

—*E. Karl Isbrecht*

Women's Liberation

There are millions of us sitting, lying
Independisizing, sometimes fantasizing
Metamorphasizing
In our cubicles, apartments, in our
Condos, houses, mobile homes and farms
There's not a man out there that's
Worth a damn
'Cause men ain't men no more
We trampled them with liberation
Beat their egos to the floor
They got lost in ideology
In women's new theology
We destroyed their old mythology
Left them nude before our ranks
And then we laughed
Now they don't know what to do
And we sit home alone
And no one really knows who
Should be calling who

—*Kimber Lee Peluso*

Winter Splendor In The Canyon

Breezes wafting through frozen granite walls whisper in indignation;
Leaves still clinging to icy branches tremble in agitation;

Water, low within its banks, gurgles with slushy glee;
Against boulders now uncovered for all to see;

Trails covered in downy white with only animal tracks showing;
Wend a lonely ribbon through stately pines to heights where a brisk wind is blowing!

Suddenly - twilight spreads its violet glow over glistening, glittering ice and snow;
Adding a breathless quality to the entire panoramic show!

They all are crying, "Come! see us! in our icy winter pageantry!
Summer is not the only season that canyons bask in a vision of reverential beauty!"
—*Virginia R. Ashworth*

Twice Betrayed

Amid old baby clothes and pictures wrapped
inside a christening gown, a gleam of light
and metal caught her eye. She reached and touched
the speck of hope and found deliverance there.
Resigned, her eyes held tears of grief, she had
no other choice. She walked in silence through
the rooms and peered around each door, afraid,
until she saw him asleep. He felt no guilt,
no tortured dreams. She stared, remembered how
he crushed her innocence — forever changed her life.
She aimed, caressed her savior held within
her grasp; her rage exploded from her hand.
Reluctant realization dawned — the seeds
he'd sown inside her soul would never die.
—*Kaye Durbin*

Voices

The core of my soul echoes ... voices trapped within my interior...
Summoning me from long ago... biddings I'd stifled — feeling inferior...
to love... to thrive... to feel... again pulsating life to long...
I cry... still - and why?... What have I new to respond?
He beckons to lead me... spirit's pining to go....
Heart races, adrenalin paces from his touch which I barely know...
Will he seek the depths of my heart through soulful windows
when he kisses me?
Will he desire to caress my face before my breast?
Does he care and know how to draw out the truth of me?
Enfold me in his arms, soldier harms, and expand our spirits
into nurtured rest?
Will he embellish me with answers for all the questions I fear to ask?
Talk with me through long white nights - and starve, as I do,
to unveil the shroud of masks?
Composure... eyes brightening... glistening... pensive... a kiss?...
... my throat a swell...
To my earlobe ... lips .... breath quickening ... a whisper...
"I surrender ... God, in fear — I beg you... treat me well."
—*Michelle D. Morris*

Night

Night is most serene
In the hours before dawn.
All the world lies still and watchful
Like a curious dog.
The velvet night sky,
Soft as seawater-smoothed glass,
Reveals its diamond-studded belly;
And flickering points of fire
That hover close to the tips of grass
Reflect in this black bowl of night.
—*Martha Glowacki*

Summer Interlude

In early morning drowsy flowers awakened with a sun
into a full bloom; fragrant tapestry carpeted the valley.
That morning the air was electric. I heard thunder
booming flashing a storm.
Suddenly a ghost-like vapor flooded my senses.
I envisioned a shower of diamonds on branches as the sun
appeared through the mist.
Without a warning, a fawn bounced past me as I stood
awestruck on a soft pillow of moss.
That morning I balanced the price of pleasure against being
late for work.
I welcome that pleasure with childish delight.
A compelling urge guided me to a faster pace as I walked to
my destination. I thought to myself,
What a splurge it was: a grandeur of view as I heard a
whippoorwill sing with a wind.
—*Vera Hruska*

Drifting

I feel as if I'm drowning,
into a sea of sadness.
Drifting far, far away into a blackness no one else can see.

No one to save me, from the currents that pull me down.
no happiness, no laughter,
Just memories and tears.

Help me! Help me!
Is anyone there?
No one can hear me, no one is there.
Drifting far, far away into a blackness no one else can see.

The sand feels like ice.
no one to melt it, or to keep me warm.
Wanting to cry, the tears won't know.

The wind is blowing hard,
no one to block it's cold.
Wanting to scream, no sound comes out.

I don't like this feeling,
won't someone stop me from,
Drifting far, far away into a blackness no one else can see.
—*Kiley Johnston*

The Writer

What makes a writer? Is it the ability to step out of reality, into a world of clouded mist separating what's real and what's not? Into the world, of a writer, you will see a clouded beach, the sun trying to pierce through the thick clouds, holding the sun like a pair of strong hands, goodness in its grasp. On this beach, you will come across a child sitting on the cliffs, overlooking a purple, velvet sea: a sea of anger, a sea of lust, a sea of emotions, black in deeper depths. This child, bare foot, curls of gold streaming down her back, she will sing to you and play her song. The songs are the songs of youth, that sparkle in her eyes, the color of the sea, the child the hope, the life in her eyes. Her brilliance is alive and yet, she is still a child, and she starts to cry, the sound of the waves upon the rocks deafen you, and you can't hear her. The trembling child in your arms, becomes the sand carried away on the wind, and nothing is left behind. And you come to learn, that this child is the writer. Forever trapped in her world, of fantasy afraid to leave it behind and come into reality, and leave behind the child, still she sits and trembles, even in your arms, you cannot hold her. There is a child beyond everyone's eyes.
—*Melissa Williams*

Summers Past

Come, walk with me this winter day
Into hours of summers past;
Where the sunlight trips through daisies
As they dance in knee deep grass.

In the dark of a gray skied morning,
Let's bring back a gentle brook
Flowing quietly through green pastures
Toward a grassy, shadowed nook.

Come, sit with me in cool, sweet shade
And remember sun drenched days;
When soft, gentle breezes touched us
Magically; in childhood's ways.
—*Lola Neff Merritt*

Kaaterskill Junction

Virtual reality without helmet technological,
Is a game the mind plays humanoid biological,
As overlays of boyhood summer days
Cold winter nights become, and rails converge
To junctions; the Kaaterskill is one, where
Coal cinders dance again across the spiked ties
To twirl their tarry partners, creosote balm
Arise, binary sensed, — into the moonlit skies.

Bowlegged, rollicking, unicorn switcher;
Tenor clanking in a heavy heat;
Trestle thumping on skinny spleens;
Pattern stenciling a meandering creek.
Ahead to the switch; a sidle to the siding.

Headlighted Gargantua piercing the icy night,
Windy wailing down double rails
Hammered 'round mountain passes;
Boxy followers drag chained in irons,
Caterpillaring into helical wisps
Of white cheesecloth, — rallentando.
Ahoy! pal switcher; it's Kaaterskill Junction.
—*Richard A. Marten*

Sharing And Caring

Living in a Senior Complex in one big group
Is a sharing, Caring lifestyle...that is a truth.
Most of us have been here quite a long while.
Each time we meet, we see a warm friendly smile.
All have had heartaches, many have had strife;
But we are happy and make the best of life.

Whatever our outlook or nature, no one minds;
Because everyone is helpful, up-lifting and kind.
When there is a need, there is help without end.
We give help freely because we are friend to friend.
We give friendship that is worthy and receive the same.
The "true and caring" heart is worth much more than fame.

We have good days filled with living and laughter;
And the happiness of each day lasts long after.
We share in activities until the day is done.
Our style of living is good for everyone.
We live each day in helping and sharing;
With every day filled with True Christian Caring.
—*Ruby Byrd*

Behind The Door

Behind the door you wonder of all the thing that goes on
is it a door with pain of fear and sorrow of there being
know tomorrow. Is it a door of happiness, of family
laughter, and full of love. Is it a door of children
with no food to eat, or heat to keep them warm. Is it
a door with a girl having a baby, when she just a babe
herself. Is it a door where rape and murders have
stained the walls and floors. Is it a door you are
behind, and just can't make your self to open and step
out. Is it a door in your mind, that makes you stop
filling love, caring or living and just shut it so
you don't have to think know more. Is it a door you
are not with fear or shame or hope for a better
tomorrow, with peace on earth and love for your
brother and sister of every race, this is my door to
love as God love us not to fear more wars or famines
but love for all man kind, just love for all man kind.
—*Patricia Gail Bowser West*

Recovery

A love untimely lost
is life's unreasonable cost.

The loss of one's own health
is a loss of untold wealth.

When your closest friend dies,
a fountain of tears fills your eyes.

Is life only about misery and pain,
always loss and never gain?

How can one discover
a way to recover?

The answer is there before one can see;
It is from deep within you that you learn to be free.

It's like a well of clean water
or a fresh bar of soap.

It's a newness, a bubbling,
a spring filled with hope.

Hope is a tonic, a remedy,
a smile on your face.

Hope is security and comfort.
It is a light in a very dark place.
—*Vera A. Peirsol*

The Friendly Robin

The robin's breast of orange and rust,
  is puffed for us to observe as we must.
Chick eggs are of a soft blue hue,
  their tender care offers life anew.

They are friendly in becoming close to us,
  even becoming a pet in their trust.
My father had awhile a pet robin,
  which sent his heart just a 'throbbin.

He would sit in his lawn chair and smile,
  the bird would come after awhile.
He would stretch out his hand to feed it,
  the robin would move close as to heed it.

His relationship lasted quite some time,
  between man and robin which borders the sublime.
Daddy has long since gone, and I expect the robin too,
  but with a song in it's heart I'm sure still true.
—*Norma Torrence*

Our Hope/Our god

Eternal life and all that's grand
Is what O'man will have.
When God's love is in his head,
His heart and hand.
Yeshua, O'Yeshua,
King of Kings, Lord of Lords.
Our Messiah and soon coming King.
Crucified, the Lamb of God, O', Israel,
Inscribed—King of the Jews.
What Love...He died for you.
   —*Karen McCulley*

The Alcoholic

Although most of society loathes gross insobriety,
It affords me the greatest of pleasure;
And if I talk too loud in the midst of a crowd,
I'm enjoying myself beyond measure!

Many things I'll explain...again and again,
For Redundance is my middle name;
With each swallow of liquor, my tongue becomes thicker,
But it keeps babbling on just the same.

So, come, drink it up...fill the glass, fill the cup,
Let's drink till we're feeling no pain...
Let's mumble our fears into unhearing ears,
And then do it all over again.

Let's talk of our dreams...all our grandiose schemes,
War and peace, politics and much more;
We will get along fine, till your views clash with mine,
Then, old buddy, I'll show you the door.

So, come, drink it up...fill the glass, fill the cup,
Let's drink, though tomorrow we're crying;
Let's stumble around and act like a clown...
Let's drink, though tomorrow we're dying.
   —*Muriel McMaster*

Warrior's Edge

No return is not the point of edge
It could very well be the bottom of the valley
Beginning the long climb up the far slopes
Not worrying about what came before
For some neither precipice nor valleys exist.

With a relaxed watchfulness that never falters,
Seemingly infinite endurance and detail
Reveling in the danger and exhaustion
Only then can one realize themselves
As this had they been born for
They are under no illusions of their importance
The heavy sense of responsibility toward others.

Requiring stability, a coldly intellectual appraisal of
married to the infinite compassion for the follies of man
where fear, selfishness and self pity have no place
ignoring the synthetic clap — trap of sentimentalists
Propagandizing politicians and purveyors.
Instead of simple basic emotions, the positive ones
of love and grief, can carry one across the final frontier.
   —*Wayne F. Schneider*

Forever Eternity

Love is something which lasts forever
It does not always come at a time which is clever
It is nestled in one's heart for always eternal
Happy or sad, it pops its kernel
Love's promise is kept by a secret vow
Destiny ends in marriage whose news is always ready to sow
This vow is taken in and not to be broken
It is something always kept like a charm or a token
If one sees far and wide, love is everywhere and all around
It is not always shown and sometimes hard to be found
But in everyone it is there
Sometimes it makes one's heart just tear
One day love will take on all
It is never blockaded by a stone, brick, or wall
Along the path, there will be bumps and maybe a bend
Love forever and eternal will always be there to attend.
   —*Monique Amy Roy*

A Sense Of Purpose

I like the praise you heaped on me,
It gladdened my heart to some extent,
But when I look deeper to see
To buy or not to buy is the intent.

I have a wealth of poetry books
All costly and paid by me in cash;
They exceed all others in thought and looks.
I keep them safe in a basement cache.

My shelves will not hold another big one.
My brother and I completed one goal:
To write poems and publish when done;
It became our very own aureole.

My thoughts are not as yet your pleasantry,
But we were lucky to do and enjoy
"Provocative thoughts and pleasures in poetry;"
Our town provided a good publisher to employ.

I am lucky to do what I do
With a sense of purpose to enjoy my activities
So that others may benefit — or at least a few;
My space for storage has reached its declivities.
   —*Regina Conrath*

A Friend

What is a Friend? I'll tell you.
It is a person with whom you dare to be yourself.
Your soul can go naked with him.
He seems to ask you to put on nothing, only to be what you really are.
When you are with him, you do not have to be on your guard.
You can say what you think, so long as it is genuinely you.
He understands those contradictions in your nature that
cause others to misjudge you.
With him you breathe freely—you can avow your little
vanities and envies and absurdities and in opening
them up to him, they are dissolved on the white ocean of his loyalty.
He understands—You can weep with him, laugh with him,
pray with him—through and underneath it all he sees, knows and
   loves you.
A Friend, I repeat, is one with whom you Dare To Be Yourself.
   —*Viviane Klein*

Windows Of The Soul

The eyes are the windows of one's soul-
  it is a true, old fashioned belief.
At times they show sweet tenderness -
  and others, the agony of grief.
Beauty, happiness and enduring love
  shine equally from old and young,
Trust, friendship, compassion and pity,
  awe, reverence and praises unsung.
It matters not the color of your eyes,
  your soul is mirrored there;
You may travel far and wide
  and pretend you do not care,
But when you reach your destination
  your soul is with you there.
So allow not hate, anger nor vengeance
  find its way into your heart
For your eyes and soul are one
  and will never be apart.
    —Margaret Beryldine Madrill

Untitled

It has been many days and many years; a lifetime in the heart
It is difficult trying to grow up together while the world tries to
  pull us apart
But the nights have never been dark enough and the winters were
  never too cold
And unlike flowers and fairy tales, friendships never grow old
So hold my hand and dance again when the voices will not speak,
When the hands will not reach out and touch, when your crystal
  eyes are weak
Don't fall into the corner, don't be the one to run
Look for the moon if you are lost and you can't find the sun
You have a sacred beauty, a simple fountain of hope,
An innocence untouched by age, a fragile way to cope
In happiness and misery we spoke to Father Time
He knew not of the paths we'd choose or the mountains we would
  climb
Still we made our sacrifice and based our vows on trust,
Unaware of the turns that we would take or the times we would
  adjust;
The precious moments we would have to show our honesty,
To reach deep down inside ourselves and share the sympathy
Yes, we made our sacrifice, we found a place to go
A church for tears and laughter where passions overflow
A room where life can't find us, I will meet you there, my friend
To remember our lifetime in the heart until we touch the end…
    —Molly Sharpley

Thought

They say, Thought is born of failure.
It is not!
Nor does success seduce this Thought!
Nor is Thought born from objects seen,
Thought grows from somewhere in between,
The spoken word, the lifted brow.
A Summer Breeze can tell me how,
That Thought is born of little things,
A snatch of song, a flash of wings.
The cooing of a mating Dove
An unshed tear,
Remembered love.
Little things, all tucked away,
Give birth to Thought,
Some future day.
    —Ruth S. Ozanich

My Prayer For Peace

My prayer for peace does not end in Amen,
It is not one read in church
Or said before laying a loved one to rest,
It is a prayer for all to live by

In my prayer for peace,
I ask you to open your arms
Live with and by others
In peace and harmony

I ask you to become one
With everyone around you
Please forget race and color
Get to know them for who they are inside.

Be gentle and kind to those in need
Give yourself,
Receive love and companionship
And a feeling of hope, that this
world is better because of you
    —Sheri Theys

Time

What a splendored gift is time.
  It is part of every aspect of life.
Time provides the womb for joy and anticipation.
  It provides the blanket for sorrow and pain.

It was through time that all great
  discoveries were made.
And through time man has solved myriad mysteries.
  Time is the workbench of serendipity.

Time is the common ingredient to every human plan.
  It is the moment of surprise, victory and defeat.
Time is the dimension of mathematical construct
  and it is the symbol of all finitude.

Time is both the limited and the limiting.
  It controls us as well as lets us go.
Time comes to us in snatches and in bundles,
  but it slips through our fingers like sand.

No one has seen the face of the Almighty,
  but sometimes I wonder, just wonder,
if God isn't in someway like time?
  Necessary, creative and always there, just there.
    —Karn W. Griffen

A Strange World

Our Language is strange to say the least.
It is seldom understood by man, women, or beast.
Shoes and wagons have tongues but never talk.
A table has legs but no feet with which to walk.
A boat has ribs to make its shape right.
It has no eyes, but goes to sea day and night.
You can see a saddle in a mountain or a barn.
A person can crochet or tell their yarn.
Now everyone knows that a kid is a baby goat.
So why have so many books for kids been wrote?
Chairs have bottoms arms, legs and backs.
Trains can blow whistles and also jump tracks.
I know that some batteries are found to be dead.
And an engine can have a hole in its head.
If a driver's not careful he can sure kill his car.
And many a cook has put a cap on a jar.
Needles have eyes but still they are blind.
But computers with viruses, that blows my mind.
    —Margaret Anderson

To My Sweetheart

You have a rose named for you;
It is soft and beautiful like your heart,
The source of your warmth and your love.
You shared your heart with me,
That I might share mine and with you be a part.

You have a carnation which is me,
Enduring and complimentary
And made more beautiful by thee.

You have baby's breath,
Pure, soft, and white.
You are delicate and enduring,
And ever young in my sight.

You have sprigs of green,
Fresh in winter and in spring.
You are alive in the spirit of God,
Vibrant, fulfilling, the reason for my dreams.

And we are tied together
With a bow of white.
Our love is bound in promise,
And pure in God's sight.
—*Bob Graham*

The Light Of The Tunnel

The light shines at dawn, within the walls of the tunnel.
  It marks a beginning, a new beginning,
    That has never appeared before.
The light strongly shines, and captures the release of beauty,
  Which is perfectly formed in every way.

As the light moves swiftly, through the walls of the tunnel,
  It reaches a surface so tender and pure...
    And as its beams may flicker every once in a while,
The light never gives way to the wind and rain,
  Or the trampling and abuse which may come its way.

And now, I see the light hold its own,
  The surface, a little marred with patches of rust here and there,
    but through all the bruises,
There's still room for beauty with the light's powerful glow.

And so, as the light continues to shine through the tunnel,
  I can see Serenity, Joy, Peace, Rest and Love,
    Which is the reward of travel from beginning to end.
Yes! What beautiful Creation which only God can bring into view,
  it's the tunnel of life.... God gave it to you!
—*Ophelia Young Wigfall*

Numb

When you run your hands over my legs
it sends electricity down my body and
makes my toes tingle from within, as
your hand moves across my body,
my chest heats up like the hot sun.
My heart begins to boil with passion
when your hands caress over my breast.
I start to shiver with emotions, my head
begins spinning out of control and my body
sweats with desires of love.
Juices begin flowing from my body like
water falls with your every touch.
When your lips meet with mine and we are
intertwined together as one flower of passion,
my body becomes numb with emotion and
I become lost in time.
—*Linda J. Glenn*

Soul Food

What feeds the soul?
It must be a language without words,
for the soul cannot speak.
What feeds the soul?
It must be a sound not heard by ear,
for the soul cannot hear.
What feeds the soul?
It must be a vision not seen,
for the soul cannot see.
And yet the soul lives and must be fed.

The soul is fed by all of these—
language, sound, vision—and yet by none.
It is that deep communication
from one soul to another
which gives life and receives life
on a level far beyond consciousness.
It is real, it is ethereal,
it exists, it is a vapor,
it is sought and found in ways known
only to the soul.
—*Kathryn B. Hull*

Peace On Earth

For peace on earth to really be;
It must begin with you and me;
And God must be first in our heart;
For then this peace we will impart.

Look kindly at your fellow man;
Be ready with a helping hand;
For people all around the earth;
Are loved by God ever since birth.

You'll find some good in everyone;
Around the world from sun to sun;
And if you cannot see this good;
Perhaps you look not where you should.

We're not to judge our fellow man;
Though many people think they can;
It's hard to let the judging go;
To "God", who's really in the know.

So now, my friend, I send you this;
My peaceful poem, with just one wish;
Think Good thoughts as you read these lines;
We need this peace, within our times.
—*Shirley Faig*

Lenell's Last Stand

She always had a sweet smile.
It was never one that was fake.
She suffered from lots of discomforts.
Everything seem to ache.

Time was running out for her.
And with the help of God she knew.
She could hear his voice calling.
But she still felt blue.

The final days drew closer.
She even started feeling great.
"Oh God, don't tell me it's too late."
He had already opened Heavens' gate.

Her late mother's face appeared.
Lenell reached out in defeat.
"But what about Jackie and Paula?"
"In heaven is where you'll meet."
—*Paula Marie Angelle*

Little Things I Can't Forget

When I was just a little child,
   it never crossed my care-free mind.
To value warmth or food and shelter,
   or loving parents who were kind.

But looking back across the years,
   with appreciation and sometimes real regret.
I find some special times and people,
   in life, that I simply can't forget.

A helping hand when some just offered,
   or a friendly smile when I felt blue.
Someone who just stood by and listened,
   and still could say "I believe in you."

The one whose 'decent treatment' stood alone,
   when all the world would criticize.
Or a person who truly thought,
   that I was nice, and beautiful and wise.

A trusted friend that I could lean on,
   someone who'd hold me when I cry.
These are God's many blessings,
   that money simply can not buy.
     —*Telva D. Bolkcom*

The Snow Leopard Waits

All day the wind blew from the south
It scattered the now turning leaves abroad
Ragged clouds scudded across the sky
Now thin enough to let the sun shine through in all of its glory
Then they would pile up dark and ominous hiding its rays
On and on they sped hurrying to meet the oncoming front
Rain and wind was in the offing
And snow was predicted for the north and west
There was no doubt that winter was on the way
Like the snow leopard it is waiting to spring
Sometimes life is like an oncoming storm
Peace and quiet can turn like the leaves and blow away
Cold winds of doubt can wreck havoc
Hopes and dreams can be crushed like flower petals
And the snow leopard waits
     —*Marie Taylor Baldwin*

Family Week

In May we have a "family week."
It sets a special tone for home,
But it should not be just a streak
Of time from which we all may roam.

This week should set a special pattern
For homes to follow every week
So every member comes to learn
The better things of life to seek.

We learn to love, cooperate,
And share desires of other folk,
And each, our time to regulate
To play a game or share a joke.

As family week is one of joy,
So let us plan that every week
Will help each one of us to see
That every person is unique.

Family is a learning place
Where all develop better lives,
And in our living find a space
where friend and God can truly thrive.
     —*L. G. D. Wertz*

Song For A Violin

It was a strange day — it started with a song.
It was a grand day when nothing could go wrong.
The sun was shining, but still the wind blew strong.
It was a strange, strange day.

I was a strange day, I watched the brown leaves fall.
It was a warm day, beside the garden wall.
I saw a vision of you standing tall.
It was an odd, strange day.

I felt a sharp pain of haunting deja vu
For out of time there, a crimson rose now grew.
The wind was sighing a song I thought I knew.
It was a weird, strange day.

It was a strange day, the blossom was the same
The one you gave me in the July rain.
The words you whispered came to my ear again.
It was a queer, strange day.

It was a strange day, the scarlet petals bled
Amid the leaves there, now so brown and dead.
The tears I wept then, I must now leave unshed,
On that strange, strange day.
     —*Stella M. Reed*

A Bad Morning...

Today I really hurt, dear God
It will not go away

The tears just flowed from a broken heart
That was renewed today

Oh, memories are so bitter sweet
I tuck them deep within

I hold them back from all who care
As if it were a sin

I hold and hold until one day
You reach so deep inside

And tell me Sherry, it's time to grieve
Let go and step aside

I'll hold you as your body shakes
And mend your broken heart

I'll lift your spirits high, again
You knew that from the start

So comfort me, my Father and help me know the One
Who better can understand
The lost of an only son....
     —*Sherry Arch*

A Few More Minutes

Oh dear mother, if there is anything that I would like best,
It would be a few more minutes to talk to you, so you could rest.
I'd tell you everything was going to be just fine,
But I guess you know that by now, your with your Creator divine.

I'm sure do miss you here on earth,
You've been a good mother, ever since my birth.
I tried my best to take care of you,
And I'll love you always, my whole life through.
I'll always remember to be glad for this day, that God has made,
Because this day for another, you can not trade.
     —*Karen Elswick*

Long Lost Dad

To the dad I never got to know
It's almost to late to let your feelings show.

I grew up without you all through the years.
You missed my laughter and all my tears.

When I needed a dad you were never there.
I always thought you really didn't care.

You were never there to pick me up when I fell.
Or congratulate me when I would excel.

I am 19 now and still don't know you.
But maybe someday we can start brand new.
—*Shauna Sterling*

One Lovely Leaf

One lovely leaf hangs on that tree
   Its color is bright red
Unless you knew that winter came
   You'd think the tree is dead.

Early last fall the children picked
   Some leaves to press in books
But this one leaf escaped their hands
   How pretty that leaf looks.

As winter winds began to blow
   The other leaves fell off
I raked them up into a pile
   But this one stayed aloft.

As I look out upon that tree
   And see that crimson leaf
Hang all alone day after day
   My heart is filled with grief.

And yet, it's beauty is so bold
   That I can't help but feel,
It's loneliness upon that tree
   Gives it its great appeal.
—*Walter F. Schedler*

Prayer

   Prayer is conversation, a time of talking with the Lord.
     It's heart communication that has its own reward.
  Some feel it's a necessity just when things are going bad,
or that it's only what they need to do when they're feeling sad.
   We're to pray continually, that's what the Bible says to do,
   to be in constant contact with a friend who's always true.
    Take the time to chat awhile about the smaller things;
take the time to praise him, you'll be surprised at the peace it brings.
    Thank him for the answers that you are going to see,
     even though there will be times that you don't agree.
  God knows what he's doing, and it's always for our best,
although we may not see it, and it puts our trusting to a test.
   He is our Heavenly Father, our brother, our best friend,
and talking to him always, brings a closeness, a heartfelt blend.
  He will be your lifeline everyday your whole life through;
   take the time, give him a chance, he will your heart renew.
—*LaDean McGonigle*

Garden Of My Heart

I have a garden you cannot see:
It's in my heart inside of me.
It's filled with friendships sweet and dear
With those I love both far and near.

Some are family, some are friends;
My love for them just never ends;
And each, my precious jewel treasure,
Has value with no way to measure.

My plants, adorned with jewel flowers,
Give joyful love for many hours;
Yet, now I see there in the center
There's One much brighter and more tender.

It is the One who died for me—
Who paid my debt at Calvary.
His name is Jesus: He is mine,
And also yours, oh see Him shine!

For Jesus, in the center space,
Makes all the garden a special place,
As every other jewel flower
Depends for brightness on HIS power.
—*Rowena Stenis*

The Cry Of The Children

A woman has the right to choose
"It's my body," they say
Others stand by,
but I hear the cry
of the children

So small and helpless
she cries out,
as her flesh is burned from her body
Her mother says she's
an "Inconvenience"

Others gather together,
in tears,
We pray for her freedom,
Her right to life
We know she is precious.

And so the battle continues
Some fighting for life
Some for death
Or as they say "the right to choose"
Can't they hear the cry of the children?
—*Laura Moore*

In Search of Color

One trembling gold leafed aspen stood at the top apart
its while trunk with blackened gashes scarred
initials carved above my reach within a heart
reminders of survival: beauty enhanced, not marred.

Awed, I was rewarded for traveling all that way
in search of color on an autumn day.
It clarified my aversion to facade;
my reticence to call the giant jigsaw puzzle "God."
—*Lynn Fisher*

The National Library of Poetry - Outstanding Poets of 1994

To Joy, Our Australian Terrier

A robin hopped over her grave today,
It's red breast glistening in the sun,
As if to say "Come on, let's play!"
"We have some time, the rest of day."
For Joy, her playing days are done.

Our faithful friend, so loved by all,
'Til yesterday, was filled with life,
Ever ready, at beck and call
To fetch a stick or capture a ball.
But epileptic seizures ended her strife.

Her brave, little heart tried hard to beat
As convulsions racked her wee, red frame.
Her eyes, so glazed, with stiffened feet
She valiantly tried to rise to meet
Death's battle. But stronger than life it came.

So now our canine friend is gone
Down paths all living things must tread.
But we shall meet again anon
Where darkness hides; eternal dawn
Shines brightly on God's living dead.

—*Phyllis Brackett Bradley*

The Sea And I

The sea enjoys a rippled satin day,
   its surface calm, with every gentle swell
grasping at sunlight's rays, then sending off
   an iridescent glow of sequins for
   a mermaid's evening gown.
I too enjoy this rippled satin day
   of sun-warmed idleness that fills the heart
with loving thoughts and smile-flecked memories.

But we can change, this placid sea and I,
whipped by wild gales of nature and of fate.

The sea can be a monster, savage in
   its unmatched fury shocking to behold.
And so can I!...in anguish and despair,
   racked by old hurts, futility and pain.
   (How we can roar, this mighty sea and I!)
Storms rip themselves apart, and when they do
   the water and the spirit tranquilize.

Then come new days of satin, smooth and sleek,
   with frothy surf that races to the shore
and breaks in lacy patterns on the sand.

—*Madalyn Maloney*

Double Agenda

    They were twins planning many wins
    Jay and Ray who? Many soon knew two.
    Both played forward: defending and shooting
    Passing and faking, running and jumping.
    Both six foot eleven, coach was in heaven;
    Fans loved to watch guards cut the notch.
    The guards were both six foot four
    Really could score for two twins more.
    Their names were Red and Fred;
    Both red hair they did wear.
    The center at seven-two
    Lou had eyes of blue
    And his hook really cooked
    As the bench smiled and looked.
— *Can you now see the state winners cup?*

The Final Flight

I took a flight today in God's beautiful sky above;
It's the one place I always found joy, the one thing I truly loved.

I felt so close to God as I soared among the clouds;
In my heart, there was never any fears or doubt.

I had no way of knowing, when I climbed aboard my plane;
That this would be my final flight, and I would never soar
   among the clouds again.

I had no way of knowing what was in the Master's plans;
But I always knew as a pilot;
My fate was always in His hands.

He took me to heights that I had never known;
He showed me sights....that merely standing here on earth....
I could never have been shown.

He often took me as close to His kingdom,
as any living being could be;
But there was never any thought that perhaps,
He was preparing a place for me.

I took my final flight here on earth today;
But as my plane descended;
God opened the way....to a new flight path.

He navigated my plane toward his brilliant light,
And opened wide the gates for my final solo flight.

—*Linda Cooper Batchelor*

Shadows

    Though a silent thing, a shadow is real,
      It's visible, it moves, but it cannot feel.
      A shadow is semi-darkness after a sunset.
    Shadows of things to remember, lest we forget.
      A shadow is the end results of one's condition,
    A shadow is the work of God, a miracle on exhibition.
    To rejoice and be glad beyond a shadow of a doubt,
    Is God's spirit upon us, which encompasses us about.
  When we walk through the valley of the shadow of death,
We are adhering to God's withdrawal of life's final breath.
      Perchance we enter the shadow of death by day,
    We hear the comforting words of God, "I am the way."
      Perchance we enter the shadow of death by night,
      We shall not fear, for God is our guiding light.
Fervently believing that God is the shadow upon each hand,
It behooves each and everyone of us to obey His Will and
          Command.
—*M. Evelyn Lee*

Imperial Royalty

    The Eagle has a royalty that we all admire
    Its wide spread wings fly into the sky so blue
  The world is hers and the sun reflects eyes of fire
    She settles on a nest with her chicklets two.

    On high she can see the smallest move below
  And quietly soars to grasp with talons of steel
    Then back to the nest her babies to show
      The prize she caught for them to feed.

  Now would that I can set my eyes to heights unknown
    And make the most of this life yet before me
    Just grasp my opportunities as they are shown
  And keep my eyes open, the good people to see.

    Then may my soul fly as the Eagle does soar
      My mansion to find as the Eagle her nest
      On earth my gains remembered ever more
And I shall hear God say "Well done, you did your best".

—*Lulu Fessler*

Rasta Man

Rasta Man — Sing your song
  Jamaican bad boy.
  One of a kind.
  Hair — flowing, falling like a lion's mane — wild and untamed — I want to touch it — feel it.

Rasta Man — Sing your song
  Drop-dead good looks.
  Your eyes — the twin mirrors to your soul — I want to gaze deep into them — get lost in them.
  Your smile — lights up your whole being — makes me want to smile.
  Your voice - rich, warm, exciting, delightful — I want to listen to it — move to it — let it move me.

Rasta Man — Sing your song
  Look at you.
  Your wicked moves.
  Wicked moves and sensuous rhythm.

Rasta Man — Sing your song
  Beautiful, beautiful Rasta Man
  Sing your song — for me.
    —*Naoma S. Elliott*

Covenant

God, His Son . . . a life He gave.
Jesus. . . obedient to the grave.
His blood an atonement . . . a lost world to preserve.
His children . . . God they'll freely serve.

Sin, the destroyer. . . deceit, Satan's tool.
Separation from God, a truth-starved fool.
A burning hell . . .
Their solitary cell.

Satan's plan . . . rob, kill and destroy.
His tricks on you to hurt God will employ.
Jesus has done all.
Will you answer His call?

Health, peace, and victory He'll give.
But, Satan your life he will sieve.

Satan, the blood of Jesus is against you!
God's children, Spirit lead standing true.
We're armed for battle,
Yelling victory at your death's rattle!

    —*Katie Figueroa*

Childhood Fantasy

    The clowns in diffuse category, with painted faces
Join with trapeze artists and leotard ladies in pink laces,
    While jungle elephant, lion and tiger paces.
  The band marches to music and the miniature car races.

    Popcorn, peanuts, and drinks to quench a thirst;
  Cotton candy, flags on a stick, and balloons to burst,
Can be bought, while the strong man lifts weights with a thrust.
Add suspense to the cycleman on a rope who begins to lurch.

French Poodles bounce through rings of fire excitedly,
Music, laughter, fun and glee bring to the crowd-filled tent
    A childhood fantasy.
    Wish it were me, wish it were me!

    —*Peggy T. Nelson*

I Love Christmas

I love the sounds of Christmas, they really fill my heart with joy,
I love to see the looks on the children's faces as they tear the wrapping paper and look at each and every toy.

I love the way the house smells with the cookies and the pies baking in the oven,
They don't last long around here, but each one was made by hand for that extra touch of loving.

I love to drag out all of the ornaments and decorate the house and the tree,
Almost every ornament and decoration we have, has a very special meaning to me.

I love to put up the manger with baby Jesus, Mary, Joseph and the three wise men,
I love gazing at it and rearranging it over and over again.

I really wish that Christmas came more than just once a year,
It seems to be the only time of year that everyone is happy, friendly, sweet and dear.

    —*Lucy DeFoor*

Disconnected

The aura of blue, red, yellow.
Jumbled words. Something is wrong!
No one has the aura of a rainbow!
Mumbled sentences.
Oh! I see!
Reckless movements, stumbling feet,
body gyrations. Oops!
I just heard morality falling.
And, then, you cry;
"What's wrong with me!"

Ah, my dear!
It's insanity.

    —*Marie Bessette-Clifford*

Little Brother

Little brother your very special, even though we're far apart.
Just as special as these thoughts, which are coming from my heart.
These feelings here written, hard for me to say.
The words don't seem to come out right, So I write them down this way.
Looking back on memories, I see good times that you and I've shared.
I also, often see hard times, when you showed me how much you cared.
From you I've learned, expressing myself doesn't make me less of a man.
Now I thank little brother, for taking the time to care for and understand.

    —*William L. Woodel, Jr.*

Untitled

As I lie in bed and turn out the light,
It is a time to think about the deep, dark Night.
Who lurks out there? Who goes inside
Who sits there calmly in the pale moonlight?
The world was so full, so big, so vast.
Then one person turned, and the world collapsed.
Now the world is full of crime and sin.
This is a situation where you just can't win.

    —*Mindy Levine*

Friend of Mine

I longed for a friend and found one
Just beyond the bend in the road
Life's cares seemed endless, I could not bear the load
Till at last I came to the bend in the road
And there awaited me a ray of hope in a new found friend.
Life seems more worth living as each day I now embrace
The cares of yesterday I can no longer trace.
For where there was sadness, I now find gladness
Because of a friendly face
So if you find your days no longer worth living
Or your time is not worth giving
Search, keep searching for life's road to bend
And maybe you too will find a friend.
—*Vicki Brown*

Remember Your Dreams

Life can be interesting, when you've been through the mill,
Just keep looking ahead, you're not over the hill.
Your future can be bright, if you'll remember your dreams,
You can still achieve them, no matter how difficult it seems.
The past is a history, no one can change,
But the future is a vision, only you can arrange.
The past hurts and mistakes, were a lesson to learn,
Just end that chapter of your life, and to a new page turn.
By learning from the past, gives you a fresh new start,
A bright new world, in which to take part.
Just set new goals, in the direction you choose,
Get on with you life, don't be afraid to lose.
Your new found energy, will bring you to life,
And somehow ends, a lot of past strife.
The lessons you've learned, will increase your strength,
And now you can travel, to most any length.
Be sure to have pride, in all that you now are,
And realize your new chance, to reach for your star.
It may not be as difficult, as it so often seems,
Just always, always, remember your dreams!
—*Richard K. Todd*

Never Say Goodbye

You can tear my Heart strings in two,
Just like all others always do.
You can make me sad enough to cry,
But never say goodbye.

You can laugh and sing and be gay,
Dance the night right into day,
Look into another's eyes and sigh,
But don't ever say goodbye.

Take back your gifts, if you like,
Tear up the photo you kissed each night.
Give a smile when friends ask why,
But, don't ever say goodbye.

Try to forget - as you may -
You will remember me someday.
It might take until you die,
But even then, don't say goodbye!
—*Ruth V. Mackey*

My Testimony

God called to me one morning
   Just like he called my name,
I knew in just a moment
   That I'd never be the same.

So with tears of sorrow
   I asked my Jesus in,
He came so very gently
   And forgave me of my sins.

He tries to teach me through his word
   And I'm learning quite a lot,
How to help that lonely person
   That needs my help today...

My faith is growing stronger
   As I live just day by day,
For I trust my blessed saviour
   To guide me on my way.
—*Nellie K. Dantoni*

Dawn—Temptress Of The Realm

I look to the horizon to greet your promise and savor the
   kiss that needs no voice to be understood. In your
   wonderment, I am breathlessly held sweet captive.
Your fingers gently stroke and taunt, while you elusively
   merge shy violets, blushing roses, and garlands of
   delicate forget-me-not's upon your canvas where
   silver sequins once shimmered amongst reigning
   stardust within its canopy of ebony-velvet nightshade.
You entice with teasing slowness, seductive caresses, and
   tantalize with fluid grace. Your wonderful tumbling
   emotions sweep jubilence to lavish new heights each
   new and glorious day.
You bless each new beginning with endless delight. In
   loving fury mixed with the deepest bond of affection,
   you shake your shafts of golden saffron dust, then
   bathe in lushly-golden glorious rapture.
I watch you recover a semblance of tranquility with a
   delicate conscience that leaves a gentle peace and
   warmth. You have brightened my world from darkness
   today, and, I thank you.
—*Karen Wilson*

The Open Hands Of The Clock

I envision a woodflame glowing off and on
kissing the water with neon rings
empty evergreen room stands in silence
there flies no sparrow to sing.
Solitude crouches like an aging king
on a crumbling throne of times regret
while people beg undeserved forgiveness
for things not happened yet.
Strange how rooms seem darker now
in the absence of eternal love
somehow I found the broken olive branch
but I could not find the dove.
Still I stumble through this stagnation
just another passing hour
and I witness the sky authorities
fall crippled from their towers.
Sealed in a world, I hold the key
yet I see not the lock
my only solution is to weep and reach
for the open hands of the clock.
—*Shawn Overman*

When I Started Loving You

I'll never understand what made you treat me this way. All I know is how I feel, how I really thought this was real. At first I was so sure blinded by love and how much you cared. Everything was perfect then it just didn't feel the same. I started loving you and you started pushing me away. I just can't stay away from you The feelings I have are true. I know you've been hurt before But I'm not that same girl. You told me that I was different, that you never wanted to hurt me. And if you ever started to, you would just walk away Is that why you're pushing me away? There's a part of you that I still don't know, I feel as if there was something I wasn't told. All I want to know is the truth Is it because you don't care? I just want to know why, When I started loving you, you started pushing me away.

—Leslie Martin

Road's Ends

Would you my friend, know a secret
   know the true path of the way?
Then you must probe deeply the night soil of living
For its found only in stench and decay!

You must seek in the haunts of the hype
And in the clime of the concubine
Find the dark outbacks to nowhere
To roads end.

Roads end not a village nor township erected at cost
Roads end is the terminal junction for
   Hoards of the hopelessly lost.

Here a wild, whirling wind is playing
Amidst card board castles of the cast away
Your search now ends. The saving begins
Rescue visit one of these lost souls and
From out that swirling wind, a slender hand
will present you with a golden key

You will no longer be
   Just another common clod
For you have become one
   Within the heart
Of that one and only God

—B. H. Mullins

Dad
(In Memory of Charles F. Massey)

As my dad lived in this world struggling for every moment of life,
   knowing his time was drawing near — he never feared the day of
   departure.
I'm trying to think of the things this loss
   has brought me, such as the emptiness inside,
   and the tears that fill my eyes as I think of the days of the past;
   wondering if maybe I should have done that extra little task.
As I sit here with tears in my eyes crying not for the place he
   has gone,
but for the bed he has left empty, and for the selfishness I feel
   because I wish he hadn't gone.
I know in my heart his breathing is so free, for the easy breaths
   he takes are so much easier than mine.
These thoughts I've put together explain a little of what I feel
I'll try to understand the emptiness inside,
   until one day we sit and talk again.
Your memory will last me a lifetime.

—Robert H. Massey

Peace

In a world of trouble and bitterness
   Lay the dreams of yesterday.
When times were happier
   and so full of life.

In a place of peace and stillness
   Lie the hopes for a better tomorrow.
     When I turn around I see,
       All the days go by.
         I see sadness and sorrow
           Looking at me.

When I doubt my feelings
   and I begin to leave my home.
     I turn once again
       to see that peace and stillness
         lie just beyond
           the door to tomorrow.

—Melissa L. Stevens

The Awakening

Throughout the year, as we learn of peace we grow inside
Learning more and more of which we now must abide.
This is something we live with each day
Not knowing how, we do it in our own way.
Because we don't understand, and now wish to know more
We go right to the heart of it, even the core.
Awakened, we become as we soon will show
Now it is time to say what we know.
Peace is something that can't be measured
Only to learn by experience, it is to be treasured.
The greatest peace comes from with in the heart
Because now you understand and will always make it apart.
Wartime brings hard times to men and yet they learn love
   of country and always show respect.
Learning how to cope is tricky but you'll soon be able to
   deal with it wisely.

—Karen Gilley

Denial

Self-righteousness ravages my better judgement;
Leaves me standing
Alone, helpless, frightened;
Hoping the pieces fall into place
Like they usually do;
But instead,
They further shatter
Into the tattered remnants
Of the times I once knew;
So I cling
To the person I once was;
Afraid of what I may see
If I take a glimpse in the fragmented mirror
Of who I've become.

—Misty McNutt

Dimension Of Love

Let my eyes drink in the beauty of your body
Let my lips taste the longing of your heart
Let my skin sense the sweetness of your passion
Let my body know the depth of your ecstacy
Let my soul soakin the glow of your desires
In this way I may capture the dimensions of your love.

—Robert L. Cole

Lively Adversary of Night

Wraithlike, changing shape of moving clouds
Let slip, like golden pebbles, sparks of light
Among the ferny edging of the night
Into a void that drew the dark like shrouds.
No movement, sound, nor sign of strife
Appeared to break the lone and silent scene
Of darksome space with atmosphere serene.
From earth to sky, from sky to earth, no life.
Then breath of God to man was breathed and lo!
The void took form and liveliness and light
were everywhere displayed, creation bloomed.
Man's mind, like stars that set the dark aglow
Made night as active as the day, and bright.
When man began, the lonely space was doomed.
—*Mattie Belle Barber*

Love Me, Love Me Not

People who have pets
Let them stray, an wonder
If no homes are found
The poor pets, sentenced to death!
They did not ask, to be born
The love they once knew
   No longer exists.
They are prisoners, waiting... waiting...
For their number to be called
The love they once knew
Is not theirs to keep
   Situations like these
   Break my heart
   Blinded by tears
   People are heartless
   Animal lovers ache
   It's a shame
   They did not care
For the pet, they once had
Is no longer there!!
—*Sarah B. Haines*

Untitled

Dance little Angel-dance for me
Let your spirit free
With all the glory you're feeling tonight,
You'll dance beautifully...

Such graceful steps you are taking
you are my very pride
It's been so long, I've almost forgotten
this dance I've much denied

My foolish angel, you've been tricked
Yet never given the chance
To realize that, there was no music
the whole while you danced

Please don't cry, or give up hope
And maybe someday
When you dance again, there will be music
Don't throw your dance away
—*Michele Len Harrington*

His Shadow,

Here stands this tree in the mist of morrowing
light his shadow across the land of God as it
reaches far beyond the souls of man a long the
land of God till know more can it be seening.
—*Mary La Belle*

Unnamed Me

Deep within the recesses of my mind
   Lies a land without a name.
Here dwells a black cloud that consumes
   The traveler to her regions.
What she has held in control for many,
   Many years is called Pain!
She will not let you touch nor care for her.
   Why? No trust - at all - of any!!!
Hurt so deep and continuous with fear of more!
   One day I went to visit with her.
   The outcome was depressing and defeating,
   For, of course, she does not trust me.
I hold the keys to every other room; I walk among
   The halls as a welcome guest.
   But not there.
Consumed with the need to hold dear all the pain
   And rage, she will not relent!
   Yet I seek to help and hold more dear
   This one—this unnamed me!
—*Michaele K. McMurphy*

Life As A Leaf

Sailing in stream above rock and crag below,
Life as a leaf upon unchartered water,
Floating gently and innocently downward,
Skimming fine line between sky and undertow.

Dodging deep, murky valleys and white peaking crests,
The leaf guides itself through strong and stormy currents
Bobbing, gulping for air at climactic moments
Trying to find a peaceful shore upon to rest.

Wind, wave and rain may often beset its course
But leaves, unlike human kind, have no true choice.
Once more the fallen leaf floats surely downward,
Its path destined, chartered, and again restored.
—*Lisbeth A. Cleveland*

Life

In memory of Audra Brown
Life is something we take for granted,
But life's just a seed God planted,
Always thinking we'll be here tomorrow,
Which can easily be uprooted and given sorrow.

Life is full of memories, both good and bad,
We need to appreciate the things we have,
Tell the people we love just that,
Because one day, we may not be able to call them back.

Enjoy life now, while we have it,
Because life isn't something to take for granted.
—*Tiffanney Noelle Schiewe*

Lord Of Strangers

Stone flakes melding, moribund,
liquid sphere conceived,
disembodied souls rejoicing,
to the human parity skein.

Splashing colors conscious,
transformed to dungeons pale,
faces fading, vacuums wrenching,
a red bubble about to implode.

Fingers hanging carpet bones,
to snare another crab-like form,
born the silhouette, no longer torn,
chanting, Lord of Strangers.
—*Reg DeGooyer*

In Marrakech (Morocco)

In Marrakech, unmindful of a changing world
   Life still is coloured as the Ancient Scribes
Marked down — where mixed flags unfurled
   In this market town for Desert Tribes.

Burnoused Arabs who stealthily glide by
   Bronzed Tauregs and Senegalese more dark of face
Than nightfall — in this ancient "Place to Die"
   Name of this restless seething marketplace.

Moorish Mosques with acorn tops — not far
   From Minarets. Gardens lined in glossy tile
Where Roses and Hybiscus bloom behind gates, that bar
   Homeless men with vagrant souls, a while.

Mystery, Intrigue — where a History of Terror hid
   Slaves cemented in the walls alive, in Tears.
As in the day of the Caliph el Raschid -
   The same — unchanged in full a thousand years.

Days of Arabian Nights — when life was cheap
   By values measured of today. For who can know
The Value of each persecuted Slave? Now we weep
   That man, unlearned and cruel, would cause such woe.

    —*Marian F. Gagne*

Buzz Puzzle [To Bee Or Not To Bee]

I was perfectly content to be a Bee.
Life was so carefully carefree for me!
I'd flit from flower to blossom and come spring
Inside each bloom I'd play possum and from
Each relaxed flower steal the precious honey
The sun has nourished so cunningly for me to flee with.

I was happy, yes indeed, until man deserted jam
And desired all my precious honey to make money.
If I had only been wise and known the honeycomb
Into which I carried my sweets to hide away inside
The tiny cells which take much time to make

Were reasonably faked but given a new name.
Man deceived me for I had brought the honey man sought
And deposited it in his private vault. It's my own fault!
If I become the Queen's slave I dig my own grave,
But if a human commands my fate lies in his hands.
Now two things puzzle me:
If man owns bee and therefore owns honey: is that a monopoly?
Or if man just 'combs bee but lets bee fly free
To bring back honey: is that democracy?

    —*Lilian L. Baker*

Hurricane

The hurricane sweeps in from the sea
Like a shipful of pirates,
Unleashed from their vessel
Across the water and upon the land.
Howling and bellowing, they push and shove
With a mighty heave-ho;
And what they cannot knock about
They slash with heavy swords,
Slicing branches, roofs, posts and wires,
Plundering peace and safety from many a home.
And when their frenzy at last is spent,
They turn to gaze with bloodshot eyes
Upon the rubble in their wake;
Then lay down their swords and die.

    —*Laura Morris*

Poetic Moments In Time

One must purify their emotions and perceptions. To experience life's poetic moment of creations and conceptions.

As the mystery of life's magical moment unfolds in quiet solitude. Listen to your answers from the heart, in endless gratitude. Know thyself and strike that inner chord with a positive and glowing attitude.

Time moving forward with perfect precision and good intention. Is the staff of the universe with immaculate direction. On which all else rests, in eternal redemption.

The only real element in the universe is time, which marks one's progression. But time is the constant, the reality of life's continuous work of perfection. And with the passages of time, reflecting in the colors of the rainbow. Eternal vibrations, forever recorded in a precious, ever evolving window.

There is no teacher like the experience of life and its manifestation. Experiencing the body in sensation, temptation, and eventual deterioration. For the human body gives up its youth in time, for the spirit's continuation. Lessons learned are carried, into another transition and dimension.

And so my fellow humans of this planetary existence of space and the sublime. Listen to your inner voice and its own perfect chime. May your journey of the eternal here and now, be in universal prime. And reflect life's poetic moments in time.

    —*Robert W. Osenkarski*

A Friend Forgotten

The trees blow with cold, bitter wind;
Like a friend who has forgotten,
What special times of joy you've had.
The sun doesn't seem to shine at all;
Like a friend who no longer,
Smiles when your around.
The grass has turned brown;
Like a friend who turns their back
In your time of need.
The sky turns a deep, dark gray;
Like a friend who treats you,
With no respect as an equal.
The flowers do not bloom;
Like a friend who tells you nothing,
Of their hopes, and dreams.
The world continues to spin;
Like a friend who should be forgotten.

    —*Sharon R. Euscher*

Alone In The Dark

Surrounded by memories cold and gray
listening to my heart as it ticks away
silence exists but only outside
the echoing of my tear drops are impossible to hide

Closing my eyes, trying to push away the pain
but this aching inside is such a strain
it's pulling me down, I can feel myself fall
into a storm of emotions where fear bonds all

Rapped up tight still struggling to be free
tossing, turning, screaming "Let go of me!"
trapped in a world that's falling apart
I find myself sitting... ALONE IN THE DARK

    —*Vicky-Lyn Ashby*

Half-Breed

Destined to travel on the spine of my mother
like a tight rope walker balancing for her life,
I exist.

A watered down version of those who
grace my minds eye.

Intentionally diluted
for loves sake, for patriotism - fear.

Neither tan nor fair,
this thin face of pottery and porcelain
protects each acquaintance from my loneliness,
their shame.

Inexcusably proud
of a tree whose roots betrayed me.

A stranger,
to the world that created
this stranger
to us all.
—*Michelle King Mainridge*

Dance Of Love

Shimmering white of marble towers....
Like fishes on dark waters playing...
The Taj Mahal in full moon's light swaying...
On the currents of Jumna river's powers
Shadowy ghostly forms dance the dance
Of love's remembered love unending....
Rhythms of silvery waves gently bending....
This pale monument not so by chance....
To the earthly flow that only rivers know...
The bright moon 'round as a `bhindi' bound
To the forehead of the night soon gone....
Adorns this bewitching sight so........
While the frail ghosts of Mumtaz and Shah Jahan...
It is said, rise again and dance till the dawn....
—*Tobi J. Kumar*

A Fool's Gold

Diamonds are hard and pretty, as they glitter
Like people, who sometimes become bitter
Some will be nice and loan
Others are ice cold like a piece of stone.

Searching through life, you sometimes feel cold
Thinking you found someone, you put it into the fold
Until you hear rumors, that have become bold
Then you know, you just found a fool's gold.

An oyster makes a pearl of black or white
Never realizing, it stands for tears or fright
Garnets are ruby red, like blood that flows
Emeralds are green, when the sun makes it glow.

Me, I'm like the amber, yellow and warm
Knowing I must face a many of storms
I can be warm or cold, as I have been told
So don't ever look at me and think, I'm a fool's gold.
—*Nicole M. Aldrich*

Self-Reliance

What once was sacred now seems to be taken for granted—
Like the Bible which people ignore is actually very enchanted.

Faith, hope, and love are very dear to us—
But some people hold back and don't release enough trust.

The only sacred place left which I can find—
Is the integrity stored within my mind.

Although people can ruin some very kind ideas (it has been said)—
The human race can't demolish the purity within my head.

I will always know my thoughts are right—
And I will defend my ideas with an awesome fight.

So people can quarrel and yell and complain—
But I have my integrity to keep me sane!!!
—*Stacy Crocker*

Vortex

A cluster of stars orbit in this vast universe
Like the rings of saturn they circle my heart

I am in a daze of clouds, like the nebulous
nothing but cosmic dust

In this huge galaxy, you are the brightest
star in the heavens. The planet of love Venus

You have shuttled you way into my heart, and
I am accelerating into weightlessness, about
to supernova

Neptune, Uranus, Pluto and Mars
Ascending upward into the stars

To you, I am the milky way, not one but billions
of stars gazing upon you, wishing to embrace
you and become one with the universe
—*Phyllis Desmet*

The Master's Touch
Dedicated to John Frederick Norton
Little boy, so sweet and small, at peace within your bed
with sleepy, dreamy images dancing in your head.

You care not of tomorrow's plight, for today you are content,
with no remorse, no regrets for how your time was spent.

It won't be long you'll lie awake, attentive late at night
with plans to make, problems to solve, debating what is right.

So for a while, enjoy your sleep, free from stress and worry
you'll be grown up soon enough, dear child, so you don't have
  to hurry.

Let your pillow and your blanket bring you comfort a while longer
'till you become a little older, until you are much stronger.

When you become a man, perhaps a Dad, then you may know
what a truly precious gift it is to watch a small child grow.

You brought such magic to our lives, words cannot express,
Your being here has brought us so much more than happiness.

The miracle of creation was brought to life in you
The master's touch imprinted there, so faithful and so true.

Lord, help us love and guide him as he goes along life's way,
the little child, the growing boy, the man he'll be one day.
—*Linda Seiberling Norton*

Untitled

A friend is what I thought you'd be.
Little did I know how to faced you could be.
Talk to me, see what's wrong,
Everyone will know before too long.
Behind my back you always talk.
Anything I do you always mock.
I try not to listen;
I close my eyes and start wishin.
That I wasn't me, that I would cease.
Just for a moment I could have some peace.
  But why should I change?
    There's nothing wrong or strange.
      One thing my wish will never lack,
Is don't be a friend to me and talk behind my back.
    —*Shannon Marshall*

Untitled

With each breath we take
Little do we realize, we breathe the air of our ancestors,
History flows on each breath.
A history of ourselves, our life!
The very life of our universe.
As we plod along in our separate, but connected worlds.
Unaware of the very air that we breathe?
Came from a source far greater than we could perceive.
Neglect and thoughtlessness are the payment we make...
For all the beauty and grandeur that surrounds!
WAKE UP! People! WAKE UP!
For it we cannot take care of our planet and universe
How can we expect to unfold in our own spiritual universe.
Thank about it! Its an awesome responsibility
Remember just think about the very air that we breathe?
And appreciate its eternal source!
    —*Margaret McKell-Jeffers*

Drinking And Driving

No one to talk to, you feel so alone
Longing for a friend, longing to go home
You meant no harm, by what was done
You were just trying to be free, just trying to have some fun
Something always goes wrong, when you try to have fun
This time the price is high, after what you've done

You went too far this time, a little bit over your head
Now because of your carelessness, an innocent victim is dead
Drinking and driving doesn't mix, you've heard it a billion times
Why did you do it anyway, you were dumb to even think you could
  drive
The person that died was young, a three year old little boy
He had a lot of plans made ahead, now he can experience no more joy

You've heard it a million times, and again you're gonna hear it from
  me
Drinking and driving is dumb, is killing someone the only way you
  can see
Nothing can make up for what you did, you can't bring that boy's
  life back
Nothing you do matters anymore, your conscience is under attack
Think about what you've done, if you really care
Now you've learned your lesson, drinking and driving again, you
  won't dare

I'll tell you now and again and again,
I'll tell you a million times
Until you know I mean it when I say, "Don't drink and drive"
    —*Lakshmi Ramnanan*

Your World

I wonder if you notice I sit and
look at you
It isn't because I'm nosey
It's just the pleasant view.

I wonder if you realize
How much the world you own
From just the love and tenderness
That you have daily show,

I hope one day my basket
Will over-low like yours
And God will let me know
I have someone that cares.

It's such a pleasant thing to sit and
watch and view
Of happiness in bloom
And a love you know is true

Forgive me for intruding
for I am sure you will not mind
If I took a little of your world
And called it a little of mine.
    —*Pearl Bragg Krantz*

Be Happy

Paint a rainbow around your heart,
  look for a pot of gold;
the little leprechauns will help you—
  they're clever and oh, so bold.

Be on the happy side of life,
  sing and dance a jig;
gather a basket of green shamrocks
  or chase a playful pig,

for the infinite joys of love and friendship
  that we spread along the way
come back to us (like the luck-o-the Irish)
  on each St. Patrick's Day.
    —*Vivian Way Bonine*

A Prophecy

Throughout the ages comes the cry
Look up, oh youth, your eyes lift high.
The dream comes first and then unfolds,
In skillful hands real beauty holds.
Look up and scan with keener vision
A "bird's-eye" view, with no division
Of brotherhood of all the living,
Of tolerance, of nations giving.
" 'Tis just a dream," I hear you say,
"Too good for truth; a childish way
Of wishing for the moon above,
Of trusting in the power of love."
But dreams precede their consummation,
And ideals sweep throughout creation
Till slowly gathering strength through years
They gradually banish all our fears.
And then, at length, the dream comes true,
Complete and shining, ever new.
It proves the cry's intrinsic worth,
The power to bring a dream to earth.
    —*Nella Hollaway Cole*

The Wall

I wandered down the road of life
Looking ahead as far as the eye could see
Until I came to a screeching halt
Face first into an enormous wall.

As I searched from high to low, side to side,
I tried to climb over, tunnel under or go around
Forever searching for a way to circumvent it,
But regardless of my attempts, it was to no avail.

I can no longer see as far as I once could.
I can no longer plan ahead for the trials.
I am still trying to get around the wall,
But I do not yet know quite how.

I once knew what I wanted out of life,
But now I am not quite so sure.
The wall has made me recall my experiences
That have thrown me into turmoil.

Now I wander around aimlessly
Just trying to get around that wall.
If I ever get through it,
Will it have been worth the effort?
—*Raistlin Ardais*

Suspense

The little bird in the nest
  Looking at his mother,
With pitiful eyes he pleads with her
  To let him stay in the safety of her wings.

She wants him to fly...
  Will he make it?
  Will he fly way up high to the sky?
  or
  Will he fall down to the ground?
  Will his mother rescue him if he falls?

His mother fears that he will
  Fly away forever.
But she lets him go
  way up high
In the beautiful blue sky
In hope of his return.
—*Tasha Sasseville*

Sea Shells

All my life I've found such pleasure,
Looking for sea shells to collect and treasure.
As a small child running along the beach,
Looking for just one more, within my reach.

Then carefully washing and wrapping them up
In whatever I had, a pail or a cup.
I'd bring them home with every intention
Of keeping them forever, each and every one.

In reality of course, this never could be,
I had far far too many... even I could see.
I shared with my children this new game to play
Reliving my childhood as I showed them the way.

To search and find, these gifts so rare
Entrusted by God to our loving care.
My enjoyment continues, as my grandchildren delight
In discovering and gathering every shell in sight.

As I walk the beach now, in my golden years,
Still collecting, reflecting; my eyes fill with tears
As I ponder the power of something so small
To capture my heart as I respond to its call!
—*Madelyn G. Stone*

I Owe So Much

I owe so much, I can never repay,
Lord, grant me just another day,
Help me teach others, who have not learned to live,
How wondrous life can be, when we start to give.
Doing to others, what Gods love has shown,
Making his powerful presence become known.

I owe so much, because each of you care,
Surrounding me with love and always being there.
Grant me the patience and wisdom to be strong,
When others lives, start turning suddenly wrong.
I'll take the time to listen, or just to be near,
Everyone needs to feel precious, special, and dear.

I owe so much, I never can say,
Your caring touches me in many ways.
Notes of cheer, a sunny smile,
Make me feel my life's worthwhile.

I owe so much, because you give your love,
That care and concern, is sent from above.
Gods gentle presence is somehow shown,
In the compassionate people I have known.
Lord, grant me just another day,
To share the love that's come my way.
—*Mary J. Brooks*

My Life

It just amazes me just how my life still sucks
Lost all my credit due to lack of big bucks
Lost my true love and caught the "Blues Deluxe"
Yeh, my life sucks!

How can everyone I meet be a flake?
I've had much more than I can take
I never seem to get a break
Yeh, my life sucks!

My dog and I are still best friends
My back's still hurtin', but it still bends
I need a lender that really lends
Yeh, my life sucks!

Got lint in my pockets instead of spare change
I might have a token or two to exchange
Financial security would make me feel strange
Yeh, my life sucks!

So, suck on life, suck on this
You can have all your talk of eternal bliss
When I bend over you know what to kiss
Yeh, my life sucks!
—*Natalie L. Goens*

A Maiden's Prayer

In truth, yet a maiden
Lost within the realms of a lover's prayer.
Intelligence I found there were none
To justify the untimely calling.

Such fruits of beauty love bore
Tempting the boundaries of my voracious soul.

How cruel the arms of fated bliss
Placing his destiny to linger upon
The terrace of my imprisonment.
How cold the heart of time.

Should have the Gods blessed my humbleness
And allowed the wine of love to flow.

Might I have in reality the love
I've surrendered only in my dreams.
—*Roberta A. Barrera*

Midnight Shadows

Like the midnight shadows on the wall...,
   love fades fast, with the morning light.
Leaving behind only decaying memories of..., a vacant
   life.

Like the midnight shadows on the wall...,
   love ceases with the morning light.
Leaving behind only unsettled memories of something...,
   something..., that was never really right.
Leaving behind memories of two....,

   ...me
      ...and you.
   —S. Hamilton-Nelson

Love, Stage Two

Love, in the rhythm of nature,
Love, in synchrony with the cosmos,
Love, in keeping with ageless traditions.

Love, when the years grow older.
When the spirit grows stronger,
When the sun shines warmer,

Love, when peace and sweetness come again,
And the storms of life subside.

Love, in the twilight hours,
To share mystical visions
Of eternities beyond our realm.

Love, in the hushed silence,
When eternity tempts the spirit
With the music of other worlds.

Love, reaching for immortality
With the creator of the universe.

The creator of love,
The creator of light and shade,
And the resurrection of life and love.
   —Ruth Johnsson Hegyeli

The Key

Patience is the Key that unlocks the door to Love,
Love is the Balance of Life .... Harmony of the Soul,
The Soul is the Spirit which joins a Man and Wife.
Each a half of the other ..... Together forever Lovers,
Lovers who find each other through coincidence of Fate -
   Not actively searching.
For to Seek is not to Discover,
   To Look is not to Find,
      To Hunt is to go Hungry, in the valleys of the Mind.
For to find that special someone to Journey with through life,
   You don't need to seek, look, or hunt,
   But trust in the Guiding Hand of God to bring you two
      together,
      Thereby making each half a whole.
For Patience is the Key that unlocks the door to Love.
   —P. J. Minchak

Let Me Pause Awhile

Life is too short, so pause awhile take "timeout"
"Love" is what life is all about.
Give a hug, hello to a friend
Remember, in the game of life, we cannot always win.
Pause to wipe a tear
Kiss someone and tell them they are "dear."
See the beautiful, blue tide and sunset so fine
Look at the rainbow colors, so "sublime."
Kiss a loved one and spread joy
Give a homeless child a cuddly toy.
Pat a baby's head
Help the homeless to be fed.
Pause to pet a fluffy cat
Take time out to see your child up to bat.
Lick a strawberry cone
Make sure that the lonely "Are not alone."
Sprinkle drops of love day after day.
Have nothing but a kind word to say.
Your life will than be just a little better,
Set apart from all the rest"
For when at last, you reach those "Heavenly " Golden
Gates, surely you'll be "Blessed;" so pause awhile!
   —Mary E. Lamie

Computerizing

Add to your life—love, patience, kindness,
Loyalty, ambition, persistence and religion.
Multiply these by one hundred.
Divide among all your friends.
Subtract all anxiety, greed, mistrust, disloyalty,
Religious indifference and selfishness.
As you add, subtract, multiply and divide,
Suddenly you have a good feeling inside.
You reverse yourself and make amends,
It becomes easy to make new friends.
With these new changes, you have revised,
And you no longer need to computerize!
   —Teresa Chapa Alamia

Secret Thoughts

My inner self has been invaded by a fail stench of hatred.
Lurking about in my soul is the jagged mouth of unforgiving.
My smiles begin to diminish as my heart suddenly freeze into
   that of the dead.
Shivers suddenly ripple throughout my feeble body.
My soul becomes cruel and vengeful.
My mouth waters for the taste of human flesh.
Long gone is the happiness which was once mine.
My dreams are filled with premonitions of my long-awaited passing.
No longer do I fear the grasp of death.
We've become acquainted through others.
Wretched are those who peer down upon my existence and frown.
My sleep shall be eternal.
   —Pattie Simpkins

After A Rain

Up and to the west
It's nearly all blue
The east is full of purple and gray
Down here it's mostly green
In the field below the hill
Quails are feeding
The sun is fading
On a late August evening
After a rain
   —Robert J. Bowden

To My Country

America, magnificent are your prairies,
majestic are your rivers, enchanted
men and women, land of liberty and
opportunity.
America, your children will die for you,
you are an inspiration.
American, your music, candor and vibration
touches everyone around the world.
America, you are the beautiful, full of
energies, visions and love.
America, we are in debt to you, from every
part you may suffer, we your children will
make sure, that the healing process will take
its course.
America, like unselfish course, you give
to everyone, assures that you are
bountiful in every aspect of life.
America, we owe to your part of our lives,
citizens of this great country let us give
America part of our life...

—Ramon Rogulta

Sunset

As the sun sets behind the horizon
Making a wonderful painting in the sky
It reminds me of the feeling of love
That I see radiating from your eyes

A sunset is a wonder of nature
Pure beauty through and through
But it will never compare to the beauty
That is so evident in you

The sunset puts and end to the day
And gives you hope for tomorrow
With the light and love guiding your way
You shall never feel any sorrow

As darkness falls over the land
And the day is now done
Never again shall I fear the dark
As long as you and I are one...

...One beneath the setting sun.

—Ken Gipe

My Dream Of Thee

To watch afar the beauty...
Making small talk
And admiring you at the same time
Only I'm thinking how lovely you are
Only a rose could compare itself
With thee beauty of you
Wishing I could steak your heart away
And send it my way
For only then I can say
I'm not dreaming my feelings away
Why you're more radiant;
    more lovely than a morning in June
You should hear such words
Every hour of the day.

—Ruben Perez

Man's Destiny

Perhaps what I believed is, also, your apothegm:
Man was created to glorify God's kingdom.

Why grieve for the ones who died in wars and accidents;
Those murdered by communists and by fierce events;
Good ones who died with diseases and by starvation;
Thus, God took for his kingdom his saints from nations.

But one should grieve, Oh! God, for the millions like me.
Who fail to perform good deeds required by Thee.
Without Thou mercy and forgiveness of our sins,
and for lacking good works, we'll not be allowed in.
Sinners will be seeking things they are loving
When this earth will burn as if in an oven.
It will be cleansed of all sins and will condescend,
Before into eternity it will ascend.

Perhaps earth will become a new comet in space,
And sail by a host of stars as if in a race
To form a tail of ice with water from the seas
Which many beings living on other planets might see.

—Ruth A. Howe

The Power Of Poetry For Our Time

"Truth shines brighter, clad in verse." — Alexander Pope
Mankind's dream of peace on earth!
What price must be, its heavenly worth?!
For every man and woman and child, today,
The long — sought hope, to find the way!
Such present thoughts, for us all, divine,
With eternal truths, in majesty shine.
Radiating power of poetry — for our time!
As in every immortal age, and clime.
The Old Testament, as our foundation,
The New Testament — our consecration!
Living faith, for future glories, forefathers ever near,
In life's thorns and roses, year after year.
For freedom, country, mankind, the power of poetry, to revere!
With the "still small voice" of God, for us all, to hear,
Through open eyes, and willing hearts, in all, we hold so dear.
United and free, we must all, belong,
One by one, and all, in throng,
For victory of immortal right, over mortal wrong!
For our time — the power of poetry's inspirational song!!

—Richard A. Senser

Sonnet To A Fighter

Each and every man has his hurts,
Many because something dear deserts
Him, leaving an emptiness in heart,
Making spirit and soul to part
From his mind, leaving a broken man
Struggling blindly onward as he can.
This is story of one without the will
To try, though beaten, to reclimb the long hill.
But there are in the world many men who
Would, though thrown back by the worst of luck,
Lift up their heads and chests and then suck
In new air, fresh to see the thing through.
And they climb new heights passing old on the way,
Making new scholars and leaders of today.

—Tom Bonneville

Upon A Mountain Is A Treasure

Upon a mountain is a treasure lost centuries ago.
Many men have fought wars: many leaders and Nations
have passed away.
Sleeping Beauty is so young
as I wrap her body with cloth as my slowly
falling tears fall upon her cheek.
Upon a mountain is a treasure.
Sleeping Beauty is so young.
As a light rain begins to fall
Sleeping for centuries.
—*Stephen J. McCarthy*

Promises, Promises

George Bush, our President, has been through the test,
   many of our citizens feel unrest!
A Great First Lady, "Barbara" is. She has been through it all,
   a delightful person, she stands tall!
Governor Clinton, in his nomination speech,
   promised to all a far out reach!
A "Magic Wand", he must have or perhaps a great deal
   of "Healing Salve!"
His plans, all changes for the better,
   those degraded will no longer fretter!
Most important to him, The American Home,
   with the young content, no desire to unduly roam!
For a proper and better future, he admonished, work hard,
   for too long, our youth have been in the discard!
Parents should work with and for them, not condemn!
With God's help, we will get through, that's up to me and you,
   he said, "don't delay, hustle,
   We've got a job to do!"
—*Letitia M. Elston*

Crystal Tears

Through the many cycles of my life
Many times met with strife
Accompanied by a valley of tears
Wondering how many more years

Endless physical and emotional pain
Are my thoughts and tears all in vain
Gazing up to him
Will he answer my every whim

At last the dense fog lifts
The morning suns rays
gleamed with brilliance
Seeing all with a surge of joy

Focusing on a garden of
exquisite beauty
Crystal tears descending
upon a rainbow of colors
Discovering life's magnificent
beauty
For what my savior has
bestowed upon me
—*Martha Bolduc*

80 Years Of Valentines

I had a sweetheart, many, many years ago and almost as
many years ago we were wed. And so 'twas spring and love
was everywhere.

Then came a long and dreamy summer.
A fall laced with golden dreams and drifting leaves.

The cold of winter and lovely white snow fell so soft and
white. Some of the love we had was taken from us then
and the soft white snow fell on a mound so small.

As longer years and summer, fall and winter came and snow
fell down so soft and white — the bed clothes carried by
angel arms to keep our loved ones warm and dreams and
Valentines, not all on the one day.

The love is the same until the longest year and the
longest love of all my life lay sleeping by our first,
and still the snow was drifting down soft and white to
cover both. Angel arms are busy covering so nicely white
bed clothes to keep our loves warm and hide our broken
hearts, till they can heal a bit.

Happy Valentine Dear Hearts All
—*Mary E. Wiser*

The Quiet Storm

A sea of emotions
Masquerading as a stream
The saying is true
All is not what it seems
The winds and rain are unleashed
All alone when there is no witness
Floods abound in the eye
Of the quiet storm
—*Laura A. Gutteridge*

Beneath Our Feet

Here, deep within the bowels of this
massive land beneath our feet, it is
where endless undiscovered passages
branch out like rambling river tributaries.

It is below, where colorful stalactites hang
from the ceilings, layer upon layer, slowly
forming, millennium after millennium, through
ice ages, droughts, dinosaurs, wars, first man
and other inhabitants who have come and gone.

Drip, drip, drip, oblivious of time.
Here, endless glass-like glimmering, chrystal
formations hang above in awesome, majestic
splendor, untouched by the hands of man,
spreading across massive cave ceilings.

Stalagmites protrude from cave floors,
unmolested by the winds of evolutionary change;
slowly growing towards cathedral heights by
the constant percolantint calcareous water.
Drip, drip, drip!

Somewhere above, we stand upon this thin crust,
Earth, oblivious of this magnificent world beneath
our feet, and perhaps, that too, is good!
—*Thomassine Ringo Keels*

Wings Over America

Somewhere in America fair,
Men are working, wings to prepare,
There is steel we must mold
It is with the torch of liberty we hold,
We need wings over America.

We are working side by side you and I,
There is a land that cannot die,
We must work long, fast and hard,
Our land from foes we will guard—
There must be wings over America.

We think of those before us who fought
Not forgetting it was with a price our land was bought,
One can never Rule the world
Over our land "Old Glory" will unfurl,
There must be wings over America.

We love our land because of the things
  For which it stands,
For ages it has been an open door to Foreign lands,
It has given freedom to heavy hearts and empty hands.
There must be wings over America.

Today there is struggle and strife,
Foes would enter and take life,
From foreign lands to our land war clouds drift,
We shall work long and swift, mighty wings to lift.
There will be wings over America!
—*Margaret E. D. Bryson*

The Mighty Niagara Falls

What a gift you are to our great land!
Mighty Niagara, so royal, so grand!
Your roaring, thundering falls, now centuries old,
Embraced by Canada's natural fold.
With old Horseshoe Bend; historical sight —
Where challenging men have been crushed by your might.

I played at your sources when I was but four;
On "Three Sisters' Island," I gazed at your shores.
Overwhelmed by your power; your beauty so grand,
I soon ran for the safety of my Daddy's hand.

Heavenly angels greet each newborn day
Combing your tresses, preparing your way,
So that whatever the weather, majestical sprays
May flow with the mist, or onto bright rays.

Whether draped over with ice, or the heaviest of snows,
Your beauty improves; your magnificence grows.
When darkness falls upon your daylight show,
Man-made lights enveil you, row by row.

Oh, mighty Niagara, how royal and grand,
What a gift you have been to this wonderful land!
—*Margaret G. Wainerdi*

Autumnfest

Splashes of crimson and gold
mingle underfoot with brown earth tones
upon mother nature's carpet.
Cloudless azure blue sky
frames this breathtaking moment—
An Indian Summer day in October.
The pungent aroma of burning leaves,
plumes of white smoke ascending heavenward.
Feast of toasted marshmallows and apple cider
at the close of a funtastic Autumn day.
—*Shirley Anne Gorman, R.A.*

What Jesus Did For Me?

Mommy and Daddy were fighting and the children overheard.
Mom said Dad was crazy and he always misunderstood!
Then Momma started crying and Dad walked out the door.
Momma took her ring off and threw it on the floor!

Now little Billy was upstairs listening, behind his bedroom door.
While baby sister was sobbing and crying on the floor!

Then Billy thought about Sunday School and what the teacher
said, how Jesus could do anything, so he knelt down by his bed.
He said "Jesus, if you're listening, I have a prayer for you.
It's something very special that only you can do.
Please make my Mom stop crying and tell my Daddy to come home!
'Cause they really love each other and shouldn't be alone.
Just tell them that you love them, as much as Sissy and I do;
And help us be a family, the way we used to do.
So Jesus, if you answer, I'll know my prayer you heard.
And when I go to Sunday School I'll listen to your word!
And when they talk about that lame man, and 'bout that man
who couldn't see, I'll tell them all what happened,
and what you did for me!"
—*Pat Nichols*

Daniel Understood...

Time, being heart-beat of reality, is not defined. Yet, fluid moments are! Time-past — its fast advancing boundary, defiant, mocking — cries out from afar: "Is what you were / what you still are, today?" Sudden remembrance (time-warped) thrusts us back, the now transmuting into yesterday. This, Daniel understood, as did Shadrach, Meshach, and Abednego. Time-present is that highway-to-tomorrow where churning wheels track continuity. Though heavy-laden, who fears joy or sorrow, finds burdens triple-locked... Is Math the key? "Mene, Tekel, Peres..." Upharsin! See? "Number, weigh, divide..." till Eternity! Once, as abstractions, math-symbols soon fused conceptions of Wise Men, ideas they used to make sure Logic would remain - confused! Those graphs of space/time Science has diffused contrast with that PI-Code "Daniel" held dear. Three-keyed-encoding was what countered fear! "Shut up the words, and seal the book," makes clear that math-symbols, as "words," shall re-appear.
—*Phebe Alden Tisdale*

August Moon

I sit and gaze at quivering white ghost patches of grass, moon-kissed on this dark palate of unknown phantom past. No sound of life nor touch of air disturbs the scene, that engulfs my being and lays open wide this stage to see. In the dim, a kiwi bird, off center, whispers of shiny eyes aglow, and remembered voices of little nothing things and faded rainbows. Then strutting forth it twirls, in front of bended knee, a gaily painted umbrella of oriental theme. And on and on the camera clicks, as it performs each varied trick. Oh, what black magic does it spin, to imprint it on every film. Look here! I stand high upon a rock and sip my tea and lean against this rail by sea. And capture yet my eating off your plate and snuggling close for son to snap and see. Now temple shrine, the sandy beach, the park, the cafe, the fishing village be, a paradox parade, when what was real was shorn of truth and made a mockery. An orchestra of stars blink back, in disbelieving silver chorus. Heaven dressed in satin black, lends solace to a mind's hiatus. Gossamer curtains close, as clouds embrace night's glistening orb. A shooting star streaks through infinity, showering diamond dust as it goes. I make a wish, this mirage could never be, mute cries leap from my soul. Tho' in the hue of moonlight lace, I've looked and seen it so.
—*Nancy Yousif*

1994

A toast to the New Year, may it be
More rewarding to the world then 1993.
May the sun always shine a little each day...
And the rains come and go occasionally lets say.
Not the constant downpours we suffered last year.
With rivers flooding destroying all we hold dear.
Lets leave out the fires that devastated the west.
No one needs fires, so practice safety its best.
Practice kindness and good deeds all year...
Don't litter our forests or hi-ways with pop-cans or beer.
Also with sadness there's something we can't overlook..
Napta is still a terrible danger, so don't close the book.
They are promising better medical care for us all...
Let's hope it is so and that life is a ball.
Do away with wars and hunger and fear...
Pray for peace to remain all through the year.
So a toast to the new year I say one time more.
Hope this year is the best ever, this is 1994.
—*Karen A. Pierson*

The Human Race

   The human race is supposed to be from the top
Most branch of creation's tree.
   So why have they never, that is to date,
Learned to get along on this ship of state?
   The deer keep grazing and are satisfied to
Live their lives on grass, and they thrive.
   The lion though called fierce and strong, only
Kills when hungry, or to feed his young.
   The fish in the sea go swimming by, and never
Think to conquer the sky.
   The monkey has never started a fight to
Conquer the world for only his tribe:
   And the long nosed monkey has never frowned
On the ones whose nose can hardly be found.
   So why if the human race is so smart have
They never observed that life is so short, and
   The most important thing to do is to make life
Happy for others too?
   For a world where everyone looked alike to
Mo one would be sure just who was his wife.
—*Mildred Friend Rogers Thomas*

La "Clave De Sol" Del Silencio

Symphony finale,
Mourning dew drops glisten, crystalline,
Sand rains down, there you lie, not yet a legend
Clutching a rare bouquet,
Grasping fading glimpses, fragile sunlight,
and memories, like a slide-show,
of those whom you've entertained-
Fluidly flowing, heartfelt passion,
Entwined furious chord progressions,
Cast reflections, arpeggiations,
Stained the souls of sacred transcriptions.
Disquieting, this dissonance,
Dearly beloved, harvesting of sorrows,
Stifle breath, shuddering echoes of pain,
Now you play a part in God's karmic fashion.
Your invitation to frolic in the afterlife,
With this.....you must.....Transcend.
For you will be remembered for the spirit
of your melody, your tenacious rhythms,
and the wickedness of your intensity.
Forever we sleep with the end concerto.
—*Michael Capuano*

Count On Me

From my eyes I see a visions beam,
   Movements in motion, the complements of a dream,
A creation prosed that's begun to become,
   Albeit beauty in my eyes sight as number one.

From life of the heart as number two,
   This writer's gift of an art to you,

These hands and back are three and four,
   Useful as a worker, able to do more,

Nose and lips number as five and six,
   Through smell and taste senses reel,
     An inner sensation that memories deserve to steal.

As for number seven these are my given ears,
   For is heard the learned lessons of the years.

And number eight has a past that's late,
   A who guest is best is a kicker's trait.

Nine is free so do share with me,
   An imagination of to be and or not to be.

Ten friend are feet on which I depend,
   My feats direction is towards wonders mystery of comprehend.
—*J. R. Pence*

Death Of A Lifetime

I can see our near future
Much too close to bear
Hand in hand, side by side,
And you sleeping there.

Traveling far in the distance
Years have come and they've gone
Nostalgia hits hard,
And my memory is long

When your time passes
Your fragile bones sleep
Once again by your side,
Our friendship will keep.

Now you catch my attention
Not a tear in your eye
Yet you're comforting me
As I try not to cry.

Later on in my lifetime, you've long since flown above,
Those flowers, this cold day, your spirit, our love.
—*Melinda Cooper*

The Seal Has Been Rent

   The darkest hour is upon this land
Murder and abominations are a way of life.
Sexual perversions, Sodom relived a man with a man
For why would a man lie with a man as with a wife?
   In the black horror of Coat Hanger Alley
One and a half million babies are slaughtered a year
We bow our knee to Moloch in the land of the free
Silent pleas unheard, a fire consumes a baby's tear
   "Alas, O great city, what has become of you?"
Remember the fathers of old, the great ones you've forgotten
Remember the King, the very one your sins slew!
Can you? Or is you heart infected with sin and rotten?
   Return to the Lord! America Repent!
We can not deny, the seal has been rent.
—*Stephen Fortune*

My Everything
A tribute to Martha Frances Fuller Middleton
My brave heroine never claimed to have leaped a tall building:
  she merely gave me the courage to do and "to be."

My knight is shining armor can never boast of dragon slaying;
  I slew my own with the aid of her long-nurtured inner key.

My glorious genie, about magic, knows not a thing,
  yet miraculously she transformed all my dreams into reality.

My beacon never failed to shine her love, warming everything;
  she, with her rich rays, guided our way—taught us to see.

No, my precious idol did not bring forth the new born king;
  she gave birth to my sister, my brother, and to me.
    —Rosalind Middleton

My Winning Entry
A poem! A winning poem! This must be good!
My brow is furled, my stomach in knots
What can I say? Oh no, I think not!
The thoughts won't flow, my heart skips a beat
Can anything be worth this much heat?
I've thought and thought and thought some more
Why does all my paper wind up on the floor?
Nothing is good enough; It must be more
My choices are sorry, unable to compete
My heart is heavy; maybe I should eat
The time is short, the deadline nears
And still, I can hear, ringing in my ears
Our grand prize winner of this contest is—
My name of course, no, it can't be yours!
This contest I've won! Oh no, those can't be tears!
The words that I've written all through the years
Have helped to console me when spirits were low
I must say I love it, this feeling of power
The urge to create is my finest hour
To win or lose matters little, my flower.
    —Mercedes V. Lockhart

A Ball Game To Remember
It seemed a long time ago
My Dad said "Come on let's go."
We went to a baseball game,
It was at the Lake Front Stadium

In the rowdy crowd a din began and grew
Into a hullabaloo of booo's
A man walked up to bat,
And to the wild crowd tipped his cap.

To him the first pitch was a called strike.
The crowd roared their delight!
The batter pointed to the right of second base;
then the next pitch
He hit it to the place he had picked!

The ball went passed the cinder track; off the fence the
rebound. The player raced to second base safe and sound.

The next player safely hit and drove him in with it;
As he rounded third base he doffed his cap as he scored
The crowd all stood up and cheered and roared!
Now I tell you the truth;
That man was Babe Ruth!
    —Kenneth Bickley

My Friend
I have been away from you my friend,
my empty page, my lonely pen,
that together fill manuscripts of me.

I missed those late hours where
in lucid pace I've enforced to hug you
and let you disclose myself to me.

And still I hear the train rumble in the distance;
I hear it now, and tell you of it.

And still the eerie silence fills
with my fidgety fetish,
the tranquility and settling furniture around,
and the scratch of your voice
on this flat, white leaf.

As you stay in my grip, docile,
you seize my thoughts;
you've been my memory, my companion,
once again…
    —Simona C. Mardale

Overlooked
I lay in the grass last eve, as the sun slowly sank out of my vision. My eyelids dropped with the power of an eagle swooping downward upon its helpless prey. I found myself encased in a sphere of unheard cries. I drifted over everything I had come to know and love: my friends and family. I tried to scream, but instead choked on my own rush of anxiety. This fear was impenetrable; my screaming and thrashing was unbeknown to the distracted world existing beneath me. The speed of the sphere rapidly increased, flying faster than any speed known to man. My life quickly faded behind me and I plunged into the darkest depths of my subconscious. I was awakened as the first drops of dew settled around me.
    —Stacie C. Kidd

This Child Of Ours
You've never seen this child of ours
My face, your eyes; My hair, your smile
You've missed so much of his little boy life
First steps, first words, first soccer game

He needs very little from you
An hour now and then
A hug, a smile, a word of praise
It would mean a lot coming from you

I love him so fiercely and you would too
Had you been there to see him grow
He's almost a man but it's not too late
He'll forgive you, he always has

You don't know this child of ours
Nevertheless, he loves you still
He needs you still
This child of ours.
    —Suzan Smith Gilbert

Dying Earth
Magical, mystical, moon and stars.
Mother earth is very far.
Planet protector, Lord above
Cries tears of sadness from a dove.
Woe is me how silly humans must be.
Thoughtless, heartless cruel and mean.
Cherish the earth or I will fear.
We will all just disappear.
    —Michelle Christine Robinson

Fishin'

Twas the year 1992,
My grandpa and me we started something new.
A lake we did build,
So big, round and deep,
So we could go a fishin
We thought this would be neat.
Now believe me this was no piece of cake,
It was hard work to make!
Work, work, bulldozers chug,
Backhoes a diggin, they cut such a rug.
A symphony of beauty, their rhythm precise.
My oh my this will be nice.
My brothers Jon and Andy,
My cousins Emily, Colin, Spencer too:
Will have such fun in the years
Through and through.
My grandpa says Tom,
This was hard work
But by golly we have ourselves
A nice little nook.
—*Shirley M. Albertson*

Mariah Lynn

My life is over for just a little while,
My heart must heal before I can smile.
The tears must flow until they're all gone,
Cleansing the ache with their sad song.

Like a soft cloud drifting by,
Her time so short, I wonder why?
The joy she brought, so soon to end.
My time with her only God's to lend.

Her smile was like a precious jewel.
Her fight for life, so hard, so cruel.
Her laughter like a tinkling bell,
With eyes so loving, so sweet her smell.

No pitter patter of tiny feet in flight.
No baby to croon to in the night.
No soft sweet baby for me to enfold.
My empty arms have nothing to hold.

Next to my heart she will always sleep.
My love for her so vast and deep.
There are answers, and I think I know……
He took her, because He loved her so.
—*Karen K. Wendland*

Pray For Peace

Pray for Peace, a motto said,
My heart was strangely stirred.
I had not thought to pray for peace
this peace of God's own Word.
Peace! That all the world may know
The blessings of His love.
Peace! 'Til every living creature breathes
The air of Heaven above.
Now when I kneeling pause,
I pray that God will bless—
Our strife-torn world, with His own blend
Of peace and happiness!
—*Kathleen C. Dempsey*

A Step In Time

Every night I lay me down, in this empty room.
My heartbeat is the only sound. I'm staring at the moon.
Love use to be so plentiful.
Tears were always few.
I wish that you would come back now.
And make my dreams come true.
I wonder through the days of life, destination last.
I understand my foolish pride; realize the cost.
I need a genie in a lamp
To grant a wish for me.
I need to turn the tables back,
And change some history.
You're married now and live your life with some other man.
I'm still alone inside myself, trying to understand.
We use to be so happy girl.
Somehow it all went wrong.
Now all that's left are memories,
And some feeble song.
—*Thomas R. Cummins*

Art Imitates Life

My son and I went for a walk today, Little did I realize how my life would change, when I heard my little one say "Daddy look at that man over there, asking for some food," I hesitate and look over, as an older, well dressed woman, becomes abusive and rude she yells at the man, "Why you are nothing but a bum and a slob, why don't you stop bothering us hard working folks, and find yourself a job?" I felt sick to my stomach, as I watched a once strong and proud man weep, I thought, my God does she believe he prefers the street, as a place to sleep? My son and I walked over, as I intervened on his behalf, as the woman retreated, the man and I, shared a nervous laugh he then shuddered and coughed, as his clothing was worn and wet, as we began to talk, I noticed the patches on his Army field jacket, and realized that this homeless man, was a Vietnam vet his name was Art he told me, "I served in Vietnam from '66 to '68," so I asked him how our government could leave our vets to suffer such a fate, and how he could love a country that taught him how to hate? "If I could put my feelings into words, we would be here over an hour, my firm belief in God and fellow man, provides me my daily power." So this would be the day my crusade, for the homeless vet would start, they day my son and I, entered into the life of Art.
—*Sean J. Brennan*

Heart Over Mind

My mind is thinking hate, my heart is feeling love;
  My love for you is stronger than what I'm thinking of.

My mind has caused my hands to misbehave;
  The pain you've felt could put you in the grave.

It hurts my heart to know that my mind thinks that way;
  But my heart just gets stronger with your love every day.

You sing a little song, when you think no one is near;
  You say "don't hurt me any more", but darling, I can hear.

Actions speak louder than words, my dear;
  So my heart is acting to control this fear.

My heart has since told my hands to rest;
  And has shown you now, that you are the best.

Love conquers all, I learn, as heart over mind;
  Gives me the strength to put our troubles behind.

Mind over matter doesn't matter any more;
  It's heart over mind, what I'm living for.
—*Lloyd J. Adams*

A Note To My Newborn Son

I'll always remember, the day you were born.
My nerves were shattered, and my emotions worn.
For you took your sweet time, once mom's water broke.
Two days of feeling helpless, I neared the end of my rope.

But finally, your arrival! There is nothing which compares!
You will understand, should you have the fortune to be there.
For words can't describe, the miracle that day.
To have a beautiful son like you, for what more could I pray?

Your every feature, was perfect to a tee.
I was truly amazed, how much you looked like me!
Your hands were so tiny, your eyes so big and blue.
The Lord truly blessed us, the day he delivered you!

When I held you in my arms, something swelled up deep inside.
My emotions overwhelmed me, and I started to cry.
For a bond was forged, which will carry my whole life through.
A bond between a father and a son; a bond between me and you!

Tyler: I will not disappoint you; and teach you what I know.
I will nurture, love, and care for you; and be there as you grow.
And hopefully, I will instill in you, the love instilled in me.
And may you always realize, my love for you, will forever be!
—Michael O'Neill

Without You!

Without you, my day's seem so empty;
my nights are lonely and oh so cold. Without you!
We shared a special love whether near
or far; the highway is long and it exists
at my door, now I'm here waiting; this time
I'm waiting without you!... Without you, my
night's are to long, without you I can't sing a happy
song. I miss your smile and that special
gentle touch, I'm just not the same; without you!
You are the star of my show; forever you
will be, no matter what lights you're in you'll
always shine for me!... Now, without you
everything seems wrong; without you, all
I hear are the sad songs!... Do you miss
me too? As you used to do? Or maybe
you've changed? For I have too!
I'm just not the same...
Without you!
—Lois Jean Celani

My Own

In some sort clime where roses blow
My own, my own love waits, I know,
With tender eyes and yearning heart,
And though our paths are far apart,
We closer draw when day is done,
Each to our own, for we are one.

And when I join him evermore
We two shall stand on that bright shore,
And recognize, and know that we
Are destined for eternity
To travel where the stars are born,
And planets glow in pearly morn.

Yes, somewhere on life's changing sea
There is one who's meant for me,
Whose love is changeless—and although
I have not seen his face, I know
That I am his and he is mine
Through all eternity and time.
—Ruth M. Hawkins

Mortal Thoughts

I fear dying, so I fear living, so the story goes.
My parents are weakening with age,
a brother-in-law dies over the course of a year
and we are left stranded.

I feel how the Harbor Whales must feel
beaching themselves
having lost the way.

And I, turning, see the stars,
wondering, not so much on their chemistry
but their dance.

How they play in that ocean
once dreamed a vacuum
and in my dreaming
touch their depths.
—Kevin C. Krycka

My Precious Mother And My Dad

I know you left this life for Heaven
My Precious Mother and My Dad
I want to thank you for the memories
They are the greatest gift I've ever had.

In the little church where we worshipped
When Sunday came we were so glad
We sang the songs of Heaven's glory
With my precious mother and my dad.

Our house was filled with love and sunshine
We didn't know life would become so sad
I'll always have my greatest memories
Of my precious mother and my dad.

I still miss my life in Kentucky
And the riches that we always had
I know you're both happy up in Heaven
My precious mother and my dad.
—Thelma J. Burnham

My Shoes

My shoes go walking, walking, walking.
My shoes go walking over hill, over dale.
down the country side and through the city
streets, as well.
My shoes go running, running, running.
My shoes go running, everywhere; around the track.
along the road, down the highway, on a certain
day-running; for people, in a "special" way.
My shoes go jogging, jogging, jogging.
My shoes go jogging, here and there, until;
they reach the village square. My shoes
go jogging through the park. They jog and jog
into the dark.
My shoes go marching, marching, marching.
My shoes go marching with the band tonite.
Left — right, left — right, my; shoes are shining
very bright.
My shoes go dancing, dancing, dancing.
My shoes go dancing over the ball rooms floor.
Heel - toe, step, step, step, heel - toe, step, step, step,
My, dancing shoes are full of pep.
—Maurice C. Yepsen

My Sons

My sons growing in a world of anger.
My sons don't be angry at the world, be understanding
because you're born with a heart of gold
Be not conformed to the things of this world.
For then you shall be angry.
Rebel against the laws of God, then you shall be
conformed to the world.
For the world loves its own.
Oh young black men, growing in pain, and striking
in anger.
Don't let the world turn your heart, for the world
only loves its own.
To be young, gifted, and black it is the fact.
Be proud to be black.
Don't strike back in anger, strike back with
understanding and love.
Because destruction is from within.
   —*Sheila H. Anthony*

Loss

Pain intense as never before
My soul immersed in a tearful sea
No man did I value more

I walked the hospital corridor
Wished I could run from the eyes of veracity
Pain intense as never before

The beat of my heart began to soar
As I neared the moment I wanted to flee
No man did I value more

I entered the room with a skeptic's furor
To ease the hurt of the doctor's decree
Pain intense as never before

I spread the curtains that hid death's decor
Rustled his shoulder confirming that he...
No man did I value more

Perhaps in time I'll reach a rapport
Loss tends to mimic the sting of a bee
Pain intense as never before
No man did I value more
   —*Robert L. Beason*

Life's Participant

My soul longs for the fight,
My soul longs for the fray.
I will not sit idly by
While the world whiles away.

Let me be bloody and battle worn
Or at least badly bruised,
Not sitting on the sidelines
Without my best efforts being used.

I want to win fair.
Let me follow the rules and let the rules reign,
And let my opponent give nothing less
Than would my victory stain.

The mistakes I will savor,
The success I will treasure,
But please let me try;
For I will not be one of those
Who goes through life on tiptoes
And then silently dies.
   —*Ray Johnson*

The Midnight Hour

In the midnight hour I heard the trumpet sound
My soul was awakened and I was heaven bound
The angels escorted me all the way home
I was not afraid for I was not alone
It is true, the story that's told
The gates are pearl and the streets were gold
But above all that I wanted to see
The Lord Jesus Christ, my savior and me
So I walked up to him and sat in his lap
With a gleam in my eye I was just happy about that
Rejoicing and singing as I got down
I saw some old buddies and they showed me around
The sights I saw were unbelievable to my eyes
And that my friend I'll just leave as a surprise
Then reminded by this thought; A dream it
May be now but soon it will be home.
   —*Sheila G. Huddleston*

Lonely Nights

Last night as I knelt at your lonely grave,
   My tears of anguish flowed;
   I had to ask the reason why
   My dear love had to go,
Now, memories of days gone by,
   Are all I've left of you —
No longer arms to hold me tight
   To comfort when I'm blue.

The nights are lonely and so long
   Without you by my side.
   No one to talk with anymore
   No one to help and guide,
Yet, I must look beyond the grave,
   The quiet, silent grave,
For you would want me to be strong
   And try to be so brave.

Somehow, I know we'll meet again,
   Nevermore to be apart.
It will be sweet to hear you say,
   "I love you, my dear heart."
   —*Mildred E. Olson*

Jesus And Me

My life without Jesus, was shattered and worn
My time was nothing, but now I'm reborn
He took the sad, right out of my heart
With Him in my life, I've got a new start

He takes the problems, and crosses I bare
Upon His shoulders, and for me He'll care
He turned my life around, until it was right
Now I go to Him eagerly, I don't struggle and fight

He guides every footstep, and road that I take
I pray very earnestly, in decisions I make
Now my life is happier, new meaning is there
And I feel his presence, no matter where
   —*Rose Larimore*

Emptiness

I aired my frustration, my deepest hurts, my pains,
  my unfulfilled dreams, my brokenness and bitterness
I sat staring at the floor—
  Empty.
    I was so empty.
The tears had almost stopped
  I had crumbled. This was the end.
I was empty,
  hollow, lacking, shallow...
Now what?
What was I to do?
With nothing left to hide I slowly
  so very slowly
raised my head and met his gaze eye to eye
A flame was aglow in his eyes
  I knew—
Even without hearing him softly say,
  "I love you."
    —*Mary Jane Perry*

The Archway To Glory

Beyond the veil of penetration,
Mystic forces living there
Sing of loveliness and splendor
In that world beyond compare.
Deeds performed through love's compassion
Are stones which make our mansions strong—
So build them in with polished splendor—
Build your future with a song.
Mansions built with stones of kindness
On the streets of purest gold
Are studded with the rarest diamonds
Waiting for the young and old.
Time is fleeting-check your conscience,
Clarion Calls ring strong and true.
The Archway to the path of Glory
Beckons all to pass right through.
    —*Pearl H. Counts*

Cabal Of Nature

Yon orchard, its trees devoid of all fruit;
Naked in winter, barren to the root,
Shakes-off the death slumber when the goddess of spring
Crosses the equinox, her garlands to fling.

Whippoorwills, quietened in the wintry season,
Bring forth their songs for momentous reason...
As fluttering by, I see, but for a minute,
A beautiful monarch, with a spirit trapped in it.

Ego demands that body and soul be one identity,
But the one must cease, while the other has non-entity;
That which gave the cell its life
Was neither father, mother, husband nor wife.

This earthly shell is occupied for awhile by a spirit,
Who, like the hermit-crab, never quite fits in it,
And since there are no paternal bonds to protect it,
The shell, in natural decay, eventually rejects it.

Then, whether it goes or stays, death cannot tell,
For, there is no news from graves where cadavers dwell....
Nor yet a man ascended from calamitous dust,
Who, having no soul, his words we could trust.
    —*D. Jack Sorrells*

Written In Heart And Blood Forever

Ever since my eyes gazed on the priceless beauty of your nature,
My thoughts have experienced the picturesque colors of autumn;
the glistening purity of winter; the heated passions of summer;
and the aromatic fragrances of spring!

I have wished to be with you for a life-time
and endlessly dreamed to be your everything.
I love to be the one that brings you tears of joy
and to be the one that calls you forever, my precious love!

I desire to place the world's blue skies at your feet,
the stars, each at your soft and fair hands,
a rainbow to shine above your head, as heaven's gift
and for me to love you, as he does His created land!

My mind stores memorabilia of everything you do
and all the wonderful and loving things you are.
In moments when your ever-loving presence is far from me
my defiant heart reminds me, we are never apart!

My heart is the pen, I write with each delightful beat
My blood, the ink I compose each cherished words
My body, the lover's scroll that says:
"Given by God, and written forever in heart and blood by me."
    —*Ruben D. Garcia*

Tomorrow Lives

Wild as the untamed wind and gentle as a lullaby,
Near as the end of today and far away as forever.
Tomorrow - wrapt in gleaming folds of hope
And tied with shining ribbons of faith,
A "Do not open" gift of love, from God.
And yet that Faith might catch a glimpse,
And Hope may hear a wisp of song;
Love would touch the unborn heart,
And feel its throbbing pulse and know it lives.
Yes, love will shout from every house top,
With all the power Heaven gives.
Oh world grown old, there's new life coming...
Reach out to hold it - Tomorrow Lives!
    —*Nina Rupright*

Indian's Lost Hope

Solitary figure with moccasined feet
Lightly slips from rock to rock, darting from shadow to shadow;
Finally, he springs upon the summit of the highest rock and
  stands, a proud, insolent figure.
His valley stretches before him, bathed in the golden light of
  the dying sun.
Once lush, green, verdant;
It lies in its death throes now.
Bare trees, half stripped, feebly waving their weeping boughs.
Rough grass underfoot
No longer moist sod —
But now brambles and thistles o'errun the land where his
  ancestors once trod.
Through tear filled eyes he can see
What was, what is, and
What will be.
He can see his and thousands of others' dreams dying with the
  setting sun...
Suddenly in the distance he hears
A deer's scream as it falls;
And, in discordance with the wail, the triumphant shouts of
  the white man
Who have felled yet another "trophy," caring not of the
  consequences to the land.
And the Indian stands, watching the moon rise
With the fears, lost hopes, and tears of his generation in his eyes...
    —*Paula White*

A Happening Is Happening

In these days you can hear,
Negativeness causing people fear

Don't worry don't fret
This negative is humans past regrets

Negative cannot be demised
As long as it can stay disguise

The negative mask has been torn away
And the truth is coming into play

The negative is no long disguise
Its cloak has been demised

Now we know its true disguise
and its deceitful lies

With this knowledge we can save the day
by coming together in a positive way

Positive consciousness is coming into play
Life consciousness unfolding into new divine way

The false concepts is fading away
leaving space for a brand new day

Life consciousness unfolding
new realities are been molded

Earth families will united again
Families of the world will become friends.

The world will be happy and mentally free
True knowledge will break the chain of slavery

A positive happening is happening in the space
A positive happening created from the positive human faith.
—Marva A. Flowers

Winter Twilight

Snow is silently falling all around
   Never, ever making a sound.
   Beautiful flakes so perfectly made
   Covering every hill and glade
   Like a fairy waving her magic wand
Touched by a stroke of the Master's hand.
The wind is whistling through the trees
   Standing open in the wintry breeze.
Smoke curls from chimneys, wafted in the air
   Upon the land, so bleak and bare.
   Lights begin to glimmer in houses afar
      As the twinkle of many stars.
      The silvery moon is shining down
      O'er the quiet and peaceful town.
      And now, another day is done
   Arise, anew to greet the morning sun.
—Nancy Reneau Banks

The Best Friend I Could Ever Have

   He is more precious than gold,
   More valuable than something old.
      He is something in my life
      That could never be replaced.
         He was there when no one
            Else could care.
He is one man who I love very dearly.
   If it was my last day on earth,
   I'd want to spend it with him.
      For he is the best friend
         I could ever have.
For Lucas Lopez
—Nicole Daniels

Secret Life

My name is anonymous. I hide in the shadows of the night. Pleading to be noticed, hungry for the light. My life is a secret, wearing its disguise. No one meets my sadness, no one hears my cries. I feel like the forsaken one, living all alone. Crawling to desolate corners, fearing the unknown. But there must be others like me, afraid to show themselves.... Hiding their true feelings, stashing them on shelves. We are the chosen ones, running in life's race. Wanting to be winners, but settling for second place. Trying to speak up, give us courage, we pray. Our chance comes and goes, well, perhaps another day.
—Natalie Lorenzo

Prayer

Prayer is needed by each weary one
No Battle in life can ever be won
If we strive to walk, alone, by self
You need the necessary Spiritual help

Come to God with an obedient heart
You need to dwell in presence taking part
Giving Him a quiet moment to live
In His Blessed presence, so He can give
You His Strength, the Peace that endures
Keeping you in His Love firm and secure

O' 'tis sweet to come in blessed assurance
That He gives attitudes of passive endurance
O' Father, your love o'ercomes all fears
And dries the penitent sorry tears
We walk afresh in glowing adoration
Conquering in victory over tribulation

No stone that is hurled by our enemy foe
Can bruise or harm, if we onward go
Living with Faith in God's Power and Grace
For dwelling in prayer, we meet face to face.
—Susan Essler

No Choice

Your born into this world.
No choice
God gives you a disease at two
No choice
You grow up too soon
No choice
Your abused physically, mentally and emotionally
No choice
You cry at night so no one can see your tears
No choice
All of a sudden your all grown up
No choice
Missing the childhood memories you never had.
No choice
One night your all fed up with all the hassle
You overdosed on your medication
finally.......... your choice.
—Robin Jaszewski

Satin's Finale

"Oh no!" I said, it couldn't be, A.J. must, must be able to see!
No! He can't see, for when it gets dark,
AJ settles in and doesn't care to bark.
Off to the vet, this has to be wrong! Pra? Pra?
No, not in my dogs.
Crushed by the news, I thought I could take it;
but, when I saw Satin, no longer could I fake it.
I held her and cried, and asked her why?
Satin, she snuggled, her words very clear:
"It's OK, don't cry, do not fear.
Now, is the time for those who don't care;
for you see, Mom, things, now will be fair.
For this is the end—of a trip through time—
so much has been learned, nothing's been lost—
it's been fun, it's been pain, it's been laughter and tears,
but, now, it's the end of all of those years.
It's time to retire, the time is now right,
I did what I did for those who lost sight."
Satin's true to her heritage, she's a true Lion Dog!
Strangers beware! For her title of "Champion" is just a small part,
of this dear little dog, who's so close to my heart.
—*Sharon K. Paynter*

A Parent's Prayer

No longer a babe, Lord, in my arms.
No longer a toddler, full of charms.
No longer a child, I take to school.
No longer is my mind, my son's tool!

I, no longer, say which path to choose,
For he's outgrown me—with his shoes!

My heart still breaks, when he feels pain,
I'm overjoyed, still, by his gain,
My blood still flows within his veins—
I must be having "growing pains"!

I know it's best, he leave the nest,
Put independence to its test!
So, guide him, Lord, o'er troubled ground,
Just keep his new-found freedom sound,
And let him know I'm still around!

O! Keep him safe—I know you will!
You know, dear Lord, I love him still—
And, furthermore, I always will!

He's away from home; now, my begotten,
But, wherever he goes—he's not forgotten!
—*Verle Elizabeth Davis*

Widow-Widower's Lament

  Tears, idle tears
No longer trickle from my eyes
  As the lonely days become years
They're a thing apart of my broken heart.

  'Tis easy to say
Let them stay away
  Let us get on to a more glorious day.
  The dye is cast, the memories past.

But now —
  Whom do I have,
To share laughter and love,
  To give me a kiss, or maybe a hug?

And where do I find
  Another person divine
To share new adventures
  That tickle my mind?
—*Miriam Giles*

The Parade

Do you see them coming? I asked my youngest son.
No ma, but can't you hear the music? They will be in sight soon.
Yes I hear the music, but not the music of today.
It seems but yesterday when my son so tall and straight stepped
blithely to the music as he marched away, with a twinkle in his eye.
Oh, yes I here the music thou dim my eyes with tears.
All I can see is my son lying dead at the bottom of the sea.
He marched so bravely away to fight for the honor of his
  country, he said.
His war was over quickly his ship was destroyed before it reached
  its destination.
They say he fought so bravely his ship was sinking, but he stayed at
his post and manned his gun to bring down his country's enemies.
They award him posthumously with a ribbon and a speech
To me it seems so useless war after war to end the quarrels of
a nation, this should never be.
If friend and foe would seek the guidance of the
Master mind this would stand never be.
Mothers would not stand with tears in their eyes and a faded ribbon
in their hand and their sons at the bottom of the seven seas.
—*Mabelle Agnes Williams*

The Hunt

      The morning started very cold
      No matter, these hunters were bold
And as we stepped into the first field of the day
      The cold wind bit at our exposed places
      Quickly numbing our hands and faces
      But this was soon forgotten
Once the first birds burst forth from their hiding places
      The birds were many and our shots the same
      But the kills were few and far between
      Yet this didn't seem to matter
      And as the day came to its end
      All agreed the day well spent
      Each learning more about each other
A day of sharing others thoughts and laughter
      A day remembered long after
—*Terry Lee Greger*

Let's Set Sail And Live For His Tomorrow

Come — let's set sail and live for His tomorrow
No matter what the future holds in store
Our Lord is there with hope for us to borrow
For a short time here on earth and evermore

Let's make plans and trust in His tomorrow
With prayerful days we need not have a chore
He'll be there to set our hopes come pain or sorrow
To help the stirred up burdens we implore

Help not forget how He loved us dearly
He's our father, savior guardian and friend
Redeemed all from the sins we made severely
No greater love can match or comprehend

Let's praise him now and trust in His tomorrow
He'll save us from the pit of deep despair
Is the refuge for the strength we need to borrow
And shelters every soul with loving care

So let's set sail and live for your tomorrow
No matter what the future holds in store
You're the refuge for the strength we need to borrow
For the short time here on earth and evermore
—*Phyllis Gutho*

Our Swan Song

Come on kids get on your Harleys — we're going to Grandma's home
No more "over the river and through the woods" as in that famous old poem.

Grandma and grandpa will join you; On Grandpa's bike we'll go.
We'll pray to God for a sunny day — we don't want any snow.

Over hills and vales and end up in a beautiful garden, when our work down here is through
"Don't spend your money on flowers. Just one rose will do."

Rejoice, rejoice, again I say rejoice! Grandma and grandpa are heaven bound.
Let a joyous noise resound!

So long for now kids; this is not goodbye...
When the rapture comes we'll all be with Jesus in the sky.

Love mom and grandma,
—Ruth E. Bettenhausen

Follow Our Leader

Only God knows what is to be, not us mortals.
No, not even we can know what is in store.
What will be our future or has gone before.
If it is meant to be so then God will decide. We have not that right.
We can only follow his instructions as they come to his sight.
We must trust in his judgement and know right from wrong.
And live our lives as each day goes along.

—Shelby Jean Aldridge

Time Squared

I had for a summer's eve stroll—
No one with whom to share my soul,
But I had the shadow of memory
Curbing urges of infidelity.

And I think I had the pulse of her:
I had the echo of love whisper,
I had a chance to turn back time's dial
to your baring eyes and loveshine smile.

I had this fellowship out away.
I walked 'til crossing the yesterday.
I turned now renewed and coming back,
I saw no shadow deep night was black.

'Pon the asphalt my clocking feet
recalled here today down the street,
Through four dimensions, if you might,
at when o'clock on a summer's night.

—W. Scott Phoenix

A Waiter's World

Constant frustrations and interruptions galore,
noisy intrusions make our days once more.
Sweaty palms and brows with onion smells before,
Accompany melted chocolate ice cream
Dripping all over the floor.
Tips all to scarce and pennies too many,
No wonder why on pay day, we haven't any.
Only rarely accompanied by a, "Hi",
Too many are anxious to say goodbye.
Why is this the way restaurant business is,
No one knows for certain gee wis, gee wis.

—Nancy Lynne Shanta

Baseball, Football, And Basketball

Baseball is a contest of skills;
No other game gives one such thrills.
Football is played by giants, goofballs, nitwits, and nuts,
While basketball is for freaks and guys without guts.
A baseball player must know how to catch, throw, and hit the ball,
While a football player can either kick, throw, tackle, or stall,
A basketball player bounces the ball like a girl;
If he can't make a slam dunk, he has to pass or swirl.
In days of yore, a football player could do it all;
Now he either runs, passes, kicks, or catches the ball.
In the days of the two-handed dribble and the cage,
Basketball was played by those who didn't show their rage.
A baseball pitcher must have control and stuff on the ball,
While all the other guys must be able to do it all.
A football player has ten other pals to help him score;
In basketball, four other players help him shoot from the floor. But in baseball, a batter is all alone.
Nine opponents try to get him out at home.

—Willard R. Carson Jr.

Little Meteor

Shoot down from the sky, fall from your glowing grace,
No path you follow, glide on.
Never stop for an unwanted break,
Complete darkness surrounds you, eternal grace follows you.
Your beam of light twinkles, like the stars of the night,
Please little glow come to me, please little trail guide me,
Please little meteor fly tonight.
Expect not a band to play, do not ask what will not be,
Let your light trail tonight, do not hide from our weary sight,
Shine through until the day.
Forever you will live in our minds,
Glowing in our hearts,
Speeding through our souls in flight,
We see you, we welcome you,
We won't turn our backs on you,
for we are not blind.
Look up to you in time of need,
we seek you for our greed,
A few lost souls looking for your light,
To take us away,
To lead us in the night.

—William Bonen

World Suicide

Walking down the street
No shoes on their feet
Just lying in the gutter is a lonely young man
With a paper sack
Just cant take it back

See the little children with no place to call home
No mommy or daddy
They feel so alone
There must be something we can do
Its up to me and you

Watching T. V. nothing ever good on
The news is so depressing
The whole world is going wrong
Are we going to war
What is it for?

Looking from the window on the 23rd floor
Looks as though he's jumping
Couldn't take it any more
Got no where to run
Gonna fire a gun

—Robert Firth

Dear Lord

Dear Lord,
No silver nor gold have I it's true
to give you a gift from me to you.
I've thought and prayed about it,
Still, oh, what can I give
That would please You?
I can give you my eyes,
   through which I see.
My hands, to do Your work, for Thee.
My ears, to hear, what must be done.
My feet, to carry me, one by one.
My heart to feel compassion
   for another's pain;
My tongue, to ease away that strain.
I cannot give You much, you see
But all that I have, please take
   Dear Lord, I give You me.
     —*Scandariato*

My Calf Ride

'Twas a hat day in mid July
Not a cloud in all the sky,
My sis and I were sent that day
To fetch the cows a mile away.
The red clay road was like concrete,
'Twas very hot on our bare feet,
Our heifers were very tame but each lacked a flowing mane
We thought we'd ride one just the same,
We each got on without much care
Their backs were slicker than our mare's
My weight slowed down my Calf until I thought
I'd spur her on without a doubt.
By giggling in her flanks I found
My idea was not so sound,
Up went her tail, away she sped
And then she stopped - away I fled
And landed down upon my head.
Then I saw stars of the colored kind
To ride a calf, I've changed my mind.
     —*Lois Perry*

Brain Storm

Let no one ravage broken wind-torn spirits
not graceful nor defining what to be
grasp instead an open conscience; fearless
strong and supple, yet deep like amber leaves

Void meanings can never conjure up such greatness
Wind deep enough in heart will only sigh
Quenching soulful dehydrated faces
Let no one understand the reason why

Flawless assurance is not a guarantee
walls of steel occupy complete control
only gentle ears guide the sailing sea
peaceful calmness; stories left untold

Barren speech is but a mere illusion
Lost innocent not prone to acquiesce
Absolute existence is confusion
It leaves not cause to reason, but regret

Longing sight desires exclusive beauty
Chants of freedom within are not confined
Intense anticipation quarrels rudely
in destructive desolation of the mind
     —*Kimberly Stanley*

Be Careful What You Speak

We speak out in judgment of someone,
not knowing fully, if wrong was done.
We judge at times, on things we've heard.
We judge at times, on another's word.
Some say they have witnessed this and that.
We judge not fully, what we know as fact.
We oft times on how we feel,
and how things seem, although unreal.
We judge others from our points of views,
sometimes unworthy of wearing one's shoes.
We base our judgements on things of the past,
and build our decisions on the unmasked.
We pursue the unfounded, the foolish, the flaws,
we spread it about, while the injured just falls.
Idle talk comes presently without much delay.
But how long will it take to destroy the decay?
Once rumors surface it will be hard to undeclare.
Meanwhile, the injured remain in utter despair.
DON'T MAKE CONVERSATION on what you presume.
Think what you SAY before lowering the boom!
   We can all be so cruel and unkind,
adding insult to injury, in rumors we find.
So JUDGE NOT another, but for him just pray.
YOU MAY BE STANDING, in the same spot one day.
     —*Margaret E. Tucker*

The Old Coal Miner

Winding up the mountain, a caravan of grief
Now at the top they carry the casket to the grave.
Then a young country preacher, with a Bible in his hands,
Preached old time religion to those who gathered 'round.
They sang songs from their childhood,
That would make a grown-up cry,
They sang for the old coal miner, "In the Sweet by and by."
High on a mountain with his place in the sun,
An old coal miner at the age of ninety-one
Was buried today, in a family cemetery
Where two sons and a wife,
Lie waiting for their Maker until the end of time.
He worked hard in the mountains, mining coal most of his life
Trying to make a living for nine kids and a wife
The old house is gone now, it's crumbled away
But the creek still flows through the valley
And cedars grow tall in the hills
The sun still sets over the mountains
And the hollows are peaceful and still
Till the sweet by and by.
     —*Lora M. Penn*

Too Late

We entered through the wrong door as
Now I'm unable to suffocate myself
Tear the law's myth of our license
Put asunder, wrench, tear to excommunicate
My eyes from the sight of you
My ears from the noise of you

I squeeze my false facade
To crumble, rumble in the dust of your denial
Of me and what you wished I be

See it written on the judge's tablet
You can no longer carve me to yourself

Too late you looked me in my true eye
Standing by my dirtied white Toyota,
Virginal under your destructive ash
A Palm Sunday on my innocent forehead
Not once worshipped for my own image.
     —*Teresa Sendra-Anagnost*

The Last Cowboy

He rides alone, of all there were
  now only one
beneath the rising of the moon, the
  setting of the sun.

Hands gnarled and lined, face
  weathered and worn
this is the only job he can do, the
  one for which he was born.

His partner, his pal, on whom he depends
  is now carrying him to the very end.

He recalls when the last foreman tried
  to get him to change his course
with pride he remembers, "Boss, there
  ain't nothing I'll do without my horse!"

Now, heads bowed, they stand alone, the world
  they knew, the West, is gone.

He remembers the good times, the pain, the joy
  he fondly pats his Pal, as the eyes glaze over
The last cowboy.
    —*Robert A. Bowen*

In Memory Of Grandmother

  Grandmother you were number one in our life.
Now, the Lord's will has been
done and cannot be undone. What am I to do
without you? Life goes on.
  You were the pilar of our family. From
you I learned to take one thing at a time.
But without you I feel lonely, lost and cannot
live happily. Though I will try to do so,
for the well being of our family.
  Grandmother Isabel, you were a perfect
example. You were a loving wife, mother, grandmother,
great grandmother and great great grandmother.
I am unable to fill your shoes. The road is
too narrow and difficult to travel.
  We miss your frequent telephone calls
and words saying, "Children I am back home
come on over so we can sing and joke." Our
telephone will no longer ring, but your love
and sweet memories are treasured in our hearts.
  Grandmother Isabel, thanks to you, my son
and I now have a home. No longer will we
be rolling stones.
    —*Maria Guadalupe Saenz*

Christian Heritage

Christian Heritage, is without price,
Nurtured by example and good advise,
Faithful prayers that live in one's memory,
Help to anchor the soul, allowing the lord
  our life to control.
The wisdom of man, was not involved,
In how God forgives our sin,
You will need to know the Savior,
  to enter in.
Generation to generation,
As long as it is day,
Lean upon the Savior,
For there is no other way.
    —*Leo Foltz*

Weltanschauung

The lightning lives within the flower.
O, refulgent white arc of sensuality,
Of electric stamen and pistil, tremulous

Amperes of petal, why dwell
In our vision apart—power and delicacy,
Impulse and longing, separated
by mere causal propriety?

Rather, be uncaused, unwarranted,
unvindicated, as you trail the long dynamo
of your tiny root in numbed earth
toward radiant forkings that weld
all jealous sensations as one.
    —*Milton C. Lundstrom*

Revealing Dimensions

  Tears trickling into lurking ponds!
Oasis hilltops—as far as an eye can see;
  Unleashing changing chameleons of
    Rippling maple umbrellas.
    Barren, tugging deaths,
    Reminiscent of tinted
    Artistic struggles.
  Powerful green velvet berets—
  Contrasting bushy, fawn palettes;
  Manipulating life and sandy—
    Layered-surprises;
  Tilled red, soft inlet fields
Fenced with camouflaged earth.
    —*Martanne Louthan*

Adrift

Sail away, sail away, sail away with me
O'er life's turbulent, and gentle sea
Past forested and flowered lands,
And barren windblown desert sands
To tall rugged cliffs of ancient stone
Where maple colored hills stand alone
And snow capped mountains touch the sky

Sail away, sail away, sail away, you and I
We will dream our sweet passionate dreams
And plan our gaudy little schemes
In laughter and tears we will sing out
Of the game of life and what love is about
Until entwined we reach eternities door
And sail the sea of earth 'nevermore'

Sail away, sail away, sail away
    —*L. June Yates*

True Friendship

I believe the real key to friendship is the searching
of a common ground between two people, that they may build trust.
And upon trust develops admiration, respect and love for their
common fellow and with in love's boundaries there is always an ear
to listen, an eye to see, a shoulder to cry on, and an out
stretched hand with a voice saying I believe in you—
Like you my friend, have always believed in me.
I love you my friend.
    —*Yvonne Daniels*

O Word Of God!

O word of God! O word of God!
It will bless you, every nation;
It gives you inspiration.
Let all the people trust His care
Then you with wisdom can prepare.
You'll change from sword to garden tool,
Then you with good thoughts will rule.
The beautiful you will behold,
You will be led right to the fold!

O, come at once all nations!
Receive fruit from your devotions!
There will be no war, as there was before.
With God as your expression,
You will show pure perfection.
That the Bible can teach you, it is clear;
You know God is listening and will always hear.

—*Allison Doeden Boldra*

Beautiful Child

There's this cloud that's been hanging around, seems to me like
it's been trying to get me down! But your smile my beautiful
child, keeps the sun warm within the even though I can't see.
Your innocent laughter is what I'm after: It fills my ears and
my mind, with memories of younger times. The joy you find in
living every day, makes my heart burst with vibrant love in
every way! Your silly little questions that you often ask,
remind me of a child that I knew in the past. When you wake me
deep in the night, when something unknown has given you a
terrible fright! My beautiful child you hold me oh so tight!
Your small body trembles, and your eyes are filled with tears
they seem to wash away, all the grown-up years. I sense the
fear you feel my little one, and I wish at that moment to share
with you, the warmth of the sun! Your smile my beautiful
child, and your silly little ways are what keep me going, on
the cloudiest days! Your smile keeps the sun warm within me
even though I can't see. So please remember my little one as
you grow every day, that you fill me with the warmth of the sun
in every way!

—*Aggie v. St. James*

Soft Light

A lone candle sits on the cherry wood of my mantle,
Its flame weaving back and forth, jumping up and down.
Dancing to the rhythm of the room,
A room once active with much life.

A flash of yesterday enters my soul
To a time when candles would illuminate my being,
Igniting and blazing the love and passion,
That I had for the one who is now but a shadow.

So primitive is the gift of fire; with the dawn of man it came,
Bringing warmth and light, showing direction
To cave dwellers who travelled the hills of the past,
This gift handed on, from one to another.

I stare at its amber and soft yellow glow,
And long for the excitement and anticipation it brought,
Which I have hidden in the deepest recesses of my soul.
But every now and then, the fire will lick at my heart.

How quickly the light can arouse the warmth within me,
Sending quivers of passion through the essence of my being.
I need to share these primeval emotions,
But reality comes rushing through. The candle dies.

—*Dolores Sloat*

The Rose Garden

The rose is more than just a flower.....
Its fragrance and beauty last for hours.
God placed each petal in it's perfect place,
Old fashioned ladies wore them with lace.

Each rose is different, yet magnificent to see
Like a bird that sings in the willow tree.
If I had a rose garden with a pretty rock path,
In the center I would like a charming bird bath.

My garden would have many bright colors,
I would give a red rose to the young lovers.
Each bush would have tender care so true,
And the first one invited to my garden would be you.

—*Gloria Lee Miller*

Listen, Here The Angels Whisper

Here, we are among people with such qualities
It's hard to find the one that most fits you
You are far more than the average person
Because of your deeds

You can hear angels whispering about you
You can almost see the heavens smile as they call your name
And as you hear them whispering
As though a gentle breeze sweeping through the clouds
The sun bursts through gleaming
As though it was smiling upon hearing your name.

O' if you could hear then whisper about you

—*James A. Wiggins, Jr.*

This Tree

This tree is of need to cultivate
Its many strong, directed branches;
Each having a limb to mate
Needs firm ground in life, not chances.

This trees life depends on more than nature
It needs nourishment, pruning, and light,
Thus growing stronger against failure
Giving its branches an equal fight.

This tree needs no chemicals in its seed
Planted firmly in Holy ground...
Upon the soil of truth it feeds,
Nourishing strong branches - heaven bound.

This tree violently scarred through the ages
Having many battles fought and won,
Standing strong through trying stages
Its many branches protected by the Son.

This tree is of great importance
Nature need clearly see,
Without it life has no substance
For this is the Family tree!

—*Creaestia B. Hall*

Sisters

Glad I have a sister
   Just like you.
Ever if we need someone
   Each other we can turn to.
No matter how it all turns out
   Sometimes we know just what to do,
Even with the good and bad
   We always made it through
Although the miles have been long and far
   I hope you always knew
That I'm glad to have a sister
   Just like you!

—*Connie L. Huffman*

The Window

I am looking out the window trying to see,
   It's raining so hard, the street, a river will be.
I see the Paradise Theater, stars in the sky,
   How active the balcony, the boys sure do try.

The Bronx Zoo, animals galore,
   How I loved the giraffe, the monkeys and more.
A peanut for me and one for the bear,
   The elephant and the hippopotamus also will share.

I see the schoolyard, handball against the wall,
   Then an eggcream and halavah at the nearest mall.
The Park Plaza Theater Saturday morn,
   Eleven cartoons and no porn.

The clouds are moving, the sky looks like a sea of blue,
   The sun is shining, everything looks new.
I am looking out the window trying to see,
   It will be a new day for you and me.
   —*Donald R. Siegel*

The Bridge

I'm building a bridge, you somehow gave me the plan,
   It's right in the book I hold in my heart;
   Each page that I read, helps me understand,
      To build on love, and not on hate;
   I'm building a bridge, across the divide,
   I'm building on love, and not on hate;
You somehow gave me the plan I'm following through,
   I'll make it somehow, but how about you?
   Some people I know, can not understand,
   How I can go on, loving you this way,
   It's hard to explain the way that I feel;
   But I'll not complain for you are real.
     I'm building a bridge
     across the divide,
     I'm building on love,
      And not on hate;
     You somehow gave me the plan,
      I'm following through,
      I'll make it somehow,
      But how about you?
   —*Crissy Anderson*

Oh Father

Oh Father, where can you be?
I've searched all of my life.
Oh Father please come back,
you forgotten, you have kids and a wife.
Oh Father, you were always there to make me feel alive.
You ought to know through the good times.
We had that you don't have to hide.
Oh Father, you have no idea how much influence
you had when you were here.
You were always there to lend a hand and
you always had a free ear.
Oh Father, why won't you come home?
There's love can't you see.
Oh Father, please come back
so we can again be a family.
   —*Danielle N. Nicholas*

Believe

There's so much within me that needs to be known.
It swells up within me, it squeezes my soul.
So full of words that need to be said.
I just can't see how I can believe.
Believe in the words that need to be free.
   —*Alejandra Barbosa*

What Humanity Needs

When I'm sad, discouraged and blue,
Jehovah is the one I pray to.
He gave humanity his beloved son.
With blessed tears in his eyes
His hope was for, humanity to survive.
His blessed tears fall upon the earth.
Knowing the world has little hope.
This world is filled with sorrow and pain.
No hope for a better future
Only emptiness remains.
Poverty and hunger rules the world.
Violence overflows this relentless world.
The blood and cries of victims cover the streets.
Hatred and greed fills the deep.
Only brings anger and despair.
No hope for the future, for humanity doesn't care.
My hope is for the world to hear my pleased,
And join me in a prayer on bended knees.

We must ask God to supply our needs,
For peace is what humanity needs.
   —*Elaine Cotton*

Transfiguration

With
   Jesus's appearance,
still
   she is following me,
and
   she would follow me
       perhaps
          forever,
through
   the repeated hallways of a labyrinth
towards
   horrendous dead ends.
   Diane, Jesus, Lion…
   —*Gorgin Arzemanian*

Sweet Hour Of Bliss

The lights of heaven
Jewels … bright gems sparkling
On black velvet cloth
While my soul ponders tomorrow.

And the hole … the tiny hole in
The wall so thick
Brings roaring water
And rushing wind.

I sing inside me for I
Know they exclaim the quenching of my thirst
They speak at last
Of freedom's song.

And from the tower bell it too rings
Now comes my rest
O, sweet hour of bliss
Eternal night of peace.
   —*Gary T. Muse*

Upside Down World

Would you like to hear the story about upside down world?
It's where you carry your horse instead of the horse caring you
And the grass is above you while blue sky is below you.
It's where you walk on the ceiling, and look up to see the
floor, where you wear your boots on your head, and your hats
on your feet. It's where the fish are in the sky, and the
birds are in the sea. Where dogs howl at the sun and sleep in
the moon beams. Have you ever heard of upside down world?
Have you? Have you? Have you?
   —*Brandie L. Vohwinkle*

New York Subway Train

Come along and take a ride, On a New York Subway train
Join the throng to push inside, of the New York Subway train

With a clang clang clang, and a bang bang bang, the trains come roaring in
And, above all this din there's pandemonium

Above all these noises, you can hear these voices
Let me in, let me out, what's it all about they shout
And more noises and voices
"Get off my lap, mister," — Can't you squeeze me in sister
"Stop your pushing mister," — I'm only musing you up, sister!

There's a mumble and a rumble, in this vast subway jungle
With no one caring, and everyone daring, all are raring to go

Tempers are flaring it's unbearing the action is not slow
Yes, see the turnstile jumpers, and rowdy crowd bumpers
And a cop at every stop, with a gun to make you drop
Glimpse the pimps, and the dips and the pips

Yes, you may be bold and brash, when your dash toward the train
But, then, it's happened again and again, A crash, and you are maimed

And if you are stuck in the door of a moving train you go insane!
You are no more and it's good bye to the N.Y. Subway Train
—Isidore Elfand

School Journals

As if treasures might fall from pages like blossoms pressed,
Journals open carefully.
There, a personal world rests between bars of blue.
A hidden part set free
Life changes when pen meets paper.
Waking from hibernation,
The ideas reach out,
Navigate the blood,
Flow down arms,
Into hands,
Out through pens, and
Onto empty pages.
Taking a life of their own;
Emerging Athenas full grown.
Chased
From dreams and
Spaces of mind.
Netted butterflies
Caught
Between valued pages.
—Jacquelyn Hinton

The Anniversary

I sit here
- Just another night, another date -
-Another passing in time -

I do so especially to
Separate myself from you
The void a barren heaviness in my chest
Making me long for your touch even more
For the feel of your lips as they dance with mine
We'd have a delicious time...

I find myself gazing out my window
Hoping you will parade through that door
Take me in your arms
- and hold me -
Make passionate love to me
Till we can't anymore...

I long for your touch
But would welcome the Sandman's
So this wouldn't hurt so much...
—Heidi Beach

The stillness was loud with no grooms for a bride!

He was quick to battle and his musket!
Just as fleet was his adversary - not one you forget!
With sabres, swords and horse-drawn canon;
They fought in mountains, valleys and canyon.
Through snows and fierce winds that bode ill.
As death lay down its hand until all was still.
Again he was quick to war with his rifle!
His adversary did not relent or try to stifle.
The terrain was reborn and patiently awaited.
Bombs burst, cannonades defiled and men hated!
A large hand raised its scythe and swept all aside!
The stillness was loud with no grooms for a bride!
Death closed over this familiar scene;
Shrouded in black-morbid and obscene.
He was quick to his sabre to rattle!
Zealous for power and others to fight his battle!
Died and reborn with many names and faces.
Battles raged and ravaged with no traces.
A large hand raised its scythe and swept all aside!
The stillness was loud with no grooms for a bride!
—Bill Bundzak, Sr.

Little Me

Together you walk hand in hand,
just as God has planned.

Soon it's no longer just the two of you,
but someone that will be a part of you.

I'll be a little like mom, and a little like dad —
but I'm all me; I'm sure you're glad.

I'm just a little child,
who will start off meek and mild.

Tiny fingers, tiny toes,
don't worry, mom, I'll grow.

At first you won't feel like a mother, I bet.
But believe me, I haven't started yet.

A screech during the night,
will jump you up with a fright.

Teach me right from wrong,
so my faith is always strong.

I'm one of God's collection,
He designed me to perfection.

I was created with love,
Blessed by Our Lord above.
—Alison Hamilton

Just Because

Just because you said "No!" to me,
Just because the wind and rain do meet,
Just because of the noise children make,
Just because nerves and sinew break,
Just because.

Just because I said, "I love you!"
Just because the movies are not true,
Just because a rose is a devious hypocrite,
Just because our lives are taboo,
Just because.

Just because love is splendid,
Just because you are missed so much,
Just because you do so much for me,
Just because you care,
"This is why I chose the other woman!"
Just, just, just because.
—Christopher A. Stevens

Lost Youth

Speak to me o'er rolling hills!
   Just like you ached to before;
When I was a wee tyke-
   and you came knocking at my door,
You, with your shadowy trees,
   teased me with an enchanting chorus,
Until I came out, skipped in your breeze.

Hold me, I command of you!
   Wrap your green blanket around me;
Embrace me o'er majestic land,
   like no other be,
Crave me, you old fool,
   Haunt me with your wind's shrill,
Until I have nothing to will.

Tempt me, I say to you!
   You deluded earth;
My hair almost gray,
   Isn't life but a span?
But ah! What throbs in my memory
   still may.
      —*Donna Sledd*

Is It Too Much To Ask?

Is it too much to ask to have someone to count on to be there
just to hold on to and to show that they care? Is it too much
to ask to have someone show some concern and compassion when
you are down in the dumps and just need a friend to lean on?
Is it too much to ask to have someone to share all the special
moments in time without feeling as though you are committing
some major crime? Is it too much to ask to have someone who
wants to be there and have fun, to play and laugh, spend
quality time with their beautiful daughter and or son? Is it
too much to ask to have someone who takes the time out to show
you what the words love and family are all about? Is it really
too much to ask? Is it...why? That is the question I ask each
day that goes by. Why do so many people let so many things get
in the way of what could be a beautiful and special day? It
doesn't take much time and energy to make a child smile and
that little thing you took the time to do creates a happy
memory that lasts a long, long while. Time is a funny thing,
it keeps on passing, it never stops. One day you will look
back and see that you have missed out on a lot. Don't turn
away because we all need you so much, each and every day!
      —*Debra A. Swearingen*

Sighs From The Seashore

Not so long ago, it was sheer ecstacy
Just to lie by the edge of the gurgling sea.
To escape the mighty steam roller's assault
On my gentle body, with black tar and asphalt.
To escape the never-ending tyrannous reign
Of the ever-speeding truck, tractor and train.

But now, I'm afraid, it's not safe even here,
For I have to stomach the stench, my dear,
Of horrific, blackened death drifting ashore
In the wake of gigantic oil spills, I abhor!

Man, have mercy, a million barrels of oil spills
Torments, tortures and ruthlessly kills
Our flora, our fauna our fabulous fish
Which you have the gall to serve up on a dish!

Back and forth, whether she's high or low,
With gushes she weeps, to and fro.
Her tears I absorb, quickly and quietly,
So no one playing by the sea, may see.
      —*Jameela Alter*

My Love...

There are but two stars up above
Just to remind me of your love;
The mighty breeze, the welcome mist,
Reminds me of the last we kissed.

To count the masses, you count by two,
This brings to mind my love of you;
But don't give up hope, please don't despair,
For soon I'll be with you there.

Soon my love I will be home,
But home to whom? And what? And where?

When these are answered, Oh, my sweet,
Then, perhaps, we shall meet.
      —*Dennis A. Wolfe*

Bluebird Of Tomorrow

Remember to keep smiling when the bluebird lets you down
Keep in mind we all must have our share of ups and downs.

Even though your heart will ache when laden down with sorrow
Don't forget the sun will rise to start a new tomorrow.

The teardrops that fall from your face in all these saddened
   hours
We hope will be as dewdrops that will kiss tomorrow flowers.

So if the song the bluebird sings today is one of sadness
Remember God will lift you up and fill your heart with
   gladness.

Don't forget you are His child and He will see you through
And He is not alone you know because I love you too.
      —*Brenda McDoniel*

Grandma

Quilts pieced together from different patches of cloth,
kept me warm and cozy many nights.
Sewn together with loving finger tips, never store bought.
Baring pieces of material from an old dress my mom had once
   worn.
Feeling safe and secure as an infant new born.
A hug and kiss each and every night expressing emotions of
love, before she cut out the lights.
Grandma has been laid to rest. God you have taken from me
the woman who has guided me from wrong to right.
Please take care of her.
She's the best, and when she comes your way down that tunnel
of light, don't forget when they lay me to rest, to keep the
light burning bright.
      —*Carolyn Dooley*

The Fatal Stairway

Deep digression from
   kindness, sinking slowly
      into a slimy pit, cold and
         dark and feeling useless. Why
           are we even here? Frosted feelings,
         shattered pieces, remnants of a
        bitter time and place. Heartless
       motions with resurrected hatred
      showing nothing but dirt and grime.
     Then comes the last and final step.
    Falling down, no, falling backward
until depression does you in.
      —*Chad E. Wright*

To Kiss The Sky

Feel the tender touch of a rainbow
Kiss a fallen star
Taste the moonlight upon your silken lips
Hear the comet speak its wonders
As its tail sails you off to distant lands
You can see the magic of the night
And live its wonders on your winged flight
Let the pegasus lift you away
As the horn of a unicorn spins a web of beauty
Drape your body with the splendors of dawn
As I bathe you with the dew of a mid summer psalm

to Carrie
—*Jonathan Michael Kish*

River Of My Dreams

    I sit alone watching the full moon
kiss you with the light of a million stars

    Your waters hunt about the marsh
    for the mother sea in which to mingle

    Your colors vanish in the lights that
creep along the banks between sundown and darkness

    Your night-song calls to me from everywhere
      it appeals to my sense and soul
        my will to love

You are the poem and romance of my life
    your song kissed my heart
    your waters passed into my blood
      and I whisper
    SAVANNAH you are my fantasy
      My dream

—*Edward Huguenin*

Grandson's Walk

The first grandchild is always eagerly awaited, not quite knowing what in this world they're fated; brought into the world as Grandparents ponder, just why their Grandson is way over yonder. As time slips by as it surely will, Grandson runs 'round the house - never still. While Mom and Grandma stir pots over cooking; Pawpaw is in the floor playing bear with Grandson - while no one is looking. The farm is the place to take the little boy; riding a real horse instead of a toy. Being bucked off the first time is certainly shocking; afraid but astride again as Pawpaw is mocking. The tractor was always a wonderful ride; we kids got to stand next to the wheel on the side, speeding down dirt roads as fast as we dare... We didn't know better 'cause Pawpaw was there... He showed us the past as we watched and we wondered, as he worked with the engines that pumped as they thundered. The history he taught us was not from books stored away; we got to see what real life was like with him every day. The first grandchild is always eagerly awaited, not quite knowing what they're fated; brought into the world as Grandparents ponder, just why their Grandson is way over yonder.

—*Greg Matheny*

Just Inside The Gate

When I think of all the souls that Jesus came to free, my heart leaps with joy that He loves even me.

In heaven in the by and by, where there are joys unknown, I don't expect a golden crown, I don't expect a throne.

If God would only grant for me just a tiny space. There are times I feel I don't deserve even that much grace.

My heart is filled with joy, oh that would be just great, to think that I might rate just a tiny place just inside the gate.

—*Diane Gallegos*

Time

Long before fire even knew it was hot, and ice was not yet cold
Knowledge was brewing in seeping poise, for life was about to unfold.
Long before there was rhythm and rhyme and nothing was close in sight,
The sun not yet a spot in the sky to change the day from night.

Before raw energy exploded to dust and plans had yet to be laid.
Seeing was still a distant truth beneath a foggy shade.
Wind as still as silent reflection and sound could not be heard,
Seconds lasted a million years as whispers longed for words.

When light was as is darkness and no man walked the earth,
Tightness and space were one and the same and value had no worth.
The wisdom at hand so unclear of fact, for answers would come with age,
The rain as dry as desert sand, as clam threw fits of abandoned rage.

Time can't be bought, will never sell out, yet only time will tell.
Time's held all the answers to the secrets it's hidden so well.
Time will come and time will go and has always led the way.
Time with its constant flow has been around for ever and a day.

Fruitless in our searching for another's soul to mend.
Lost in a sea of reality from beginning until all things end.
Time is what it's all about,
Is there still time when time runs out???

—*Greg Harris*

Bob:

Early fall of '90 you were put on a high "state of alert",
    Kuwait was being invaded and its people being hurt.
You waited your orders and then they came -
    For you to go to the "land of sand" and Saddam Hussein.
It was on a Sunday you called just to say -
    "The time has come - I'm on my way".
Tears rolled down my cheeks - I cried for a spell
    When Will proudly said "O.K. Bob - go give 'em hell.
We watched and we listened to see you win
    The war - more each night - on the TV news channel CNN.
We called Jill each day to see if she was alright.
    Knowing all along she was - 'cause she heard your voice almost every night.
We wrote a few letters and sent a few snacks,
    To you while on your mission in far off Iraq.
Then President Bush ordered all firing be ceased.
    Some of the resolutions were complied with and P.O.W.'s released.
We knew then your mission complete,
    You'd soon be home driving the "Charger" down Nantucket St.

—*Charline G. Womack*

The Wrong Answer

Tears streak down my haggard face
I've never felt so out of control.
Holding a loaded gun to my head
Ready to end it once and for all.

Crouched in a dark, secluded corner
I feel my throat turn suddenly dry.
My heart pounds faster with every beat
Too miserable to live; too young to die.

A shudder streaks through me and I turn cold
As I await my eerie fate...
I've pulled the trigger and it's all over.
I want to go back, but now it's too late.

—*Amber Ruth Austin Lewis*

God's Nature

At a cabin on top of a mountain that over looks Gods beautiful land. The trees are so tall and full of leaves and green as green can be. Through leaves of the trees that's over looks Gods hills, the sky shines it beauty. The dew on the leaves makes me think of Gods tears of joy. As I sat on the porch of the cabin I look under the tall trees there is only one tiny red rose between two logs, it makes me think of Christ on the cross between the two men that was crucified. Out from the rose there's a small tree that a fence is surrounding it as if God has his protection around it from harm, as he does his children. On each side of the drive way there are two hedges that are the guards that protects us. The thunder in the heavens lets us know that God is all around, the winds blowing the trees lets us hear his voice whispering. "Don't be afraid my child". The rain drops on the tin roof are like soldiers marching into battle for Christ. The water that runs off the edge of the roof is like the blood that will be shed on the battlefield for his name sake. And as the lighting strikes like a sword so shall his words on that day.

—*Earnestine Parsley*

Untitled

An imaginary ship of pink glow
landed in hush forest of sherwood green..
Creatures came forth
on a thought
seldom spoken...
Showing a book
of written verse
sealed never opened.

"Open it", they whispered
and I did.

Ink tears mixed
with red blood
published by lost souls
with a dedication...

"For you my love
from this world
exiled forever"

Crying alone in a dream
I dreamed
together
never.

—*Aurelia Cleo A. Battle*

Traveling Symbolism

The conductor calls out "Harper's Ferry! Note this historical landmark. John Brown made his final statement here..." Intonations implore that all ears hear the same thing. The place. The person. The absence of a middle name. A message to the world. But this is not a concrete tongue called "Pennsylvania Turn Pike". No predictable rubber humming rhapsody to hypnotize. This is the Amtrak Express, and at this quiet point there is no hurry. The cold steel rails slowly curve, curling past the once bloodied bluffs where the river's throat swelled, satisfying its deep inner longings heard above human syllables, syntax, or phemerisms. This river may have burped at John Brown's going down. It may have rippled in applause. What was his middle name? Did he cry in pain for his beloved, gag as hot lead dug into his vein puffed chest? Did he hear the final conductor call, "all aboard!"? Or whistle through his half-slit throat to catch a wayward Ferryboat? Silver snake tails wheel us past one hundred ghost. Witness, too, the appetites of new waters called rivers tomorrow's historical markers.

—*Aaron Anthony Vessup*

A Phoenix From The Ashes

The tranquil peace of days gone by,
  lay dormant as the clear blue sky..
'Tis deeds of pity though she dread,
  which all too often fall her head.
Into the dark deep abyss she flows,
  where painful memories cease to slow.
With thoughts of laughter, pain and woe,
  to cloud her mind each day she goes.
Down the narrow focused trails,
  speeding, grasping fears bestowed.

'Tis knowing life's trials, though not a few,
  of times gone by she bid adieu.
Again she climbs, the plan thought through,
  directing her path to start anew.
A time will pass, she'll arise and sing,
  the days have come, I feel no sting.
Like a Phoenix from the ashes, she'll spread her wings,
  and soar to heights still yet unknown.
Knowing with grace, she will have shown,
  across her abyss she will have flown.

—*Diane H. Moulton*

The Sands Of Time

The Sands of Time slip through my hands. Falling, falling,
  leaving me, forsaking me. Timing my life like an hourglass.
  They are gone. They have vanished. They have left me all
  alone.
My only company is the dirt around my coffin and the voice of
  the priest, "The Lord is my shepherd I shall not want..."
The shell that held my soul hostage is now beneath mounds of
  earth. And I am free. Now from heaven I watch my sons and
  daughters pick up where I left off.
My grandchild, now aged from time, cups her hand, chanting the
  words I once knew. "The Sands of Time slip through my hands
  Falling, falling..."
Sometime later, her grandchild will gather the Sands of Time
  into her hands-the ones that I used to hold. She will watch
  them slide away into the hands of another child - an unborn
  child the one that needs them the most.
Then, she will sadly retire, leaving her family to pick up the
  pieces.
And she will join me in heaven to give glory to Him, to watch
  her and God's creations, and to forget the Sands of Time.

—*Christy Evans*

Nothing To Live For......

When the rain hits the ground,
Leaving no sound,
The earth seems to rumble,
And my thoughts tremble,
Is there really nothing to live for?
Or is there nothing that I really want more?
Then a key to my own heart,
For this will never bring me apart,
From the person I love or really myself,
But what do I really want in life?
Is it something that is going to pierce my heart like a knife?
Or is it something that can keep me pure as a dove?
Maybe there is something to live for or maybe it's love,
And when the sound of the rain hits the ground.
Deep inside we know it's been found,
We will all know that there is something to live for...

—*Bunnary Sou*

Sweet Lips

Sweet lips bites his lower one
leaving puddles of crimson blood on linoleum,
yelling, "No man has ever loved you
the way I do,
but woman, you're insane."
Doors slam.

Tick tock
I threw the clock in the garbage can.
Don't wanna know
how many hours have gone by
since that door shut
and the silence crept in.

Sweet lips, candy-coated,
Why couldn't you be everything—you,
telling me next stop Kenya, then Nepal;
yet always landing me down in Disappointment
where I wake up
from farfetched dreams of paradises
we'll never see.

—Debra Machida

Kid Gavilan

The Hawk that soars above us
left his footprints on the summit
at the top of the world.

If shadows could talk
they would of told him
that the pendulum that swings to the east
will eventually swing to the west
and the scales of life will balance.

The money, the women, the cars
the good times
and even the parasites
are gone forever.

His dignity
undefeated

will last until
the final bell is sounded
and his graceful decent
to the earth
is through.

—F. Daniel Somrack

Passionate Ebony At Lone Mountain

I am warm and white from loss of you.
Let me hold your hesitant black hands!
    Songs of honey and cream
    Burst of serious laugher
Your ebony eyes are moist and full,
    I look away ashamed
    Knowing the closeness we share
Is only as deep as the touch of your soft skin.

    Obsequious songs of social unrest
    Strangle strange times of moral conquest
    Never a moment's love
    So shackled by taboo
    While callous subservient glance
Obscures your desperate smile and its chance.

    Let me hold your trembling black hands.
    I weep for growing into you.
    To surge beyond the color line
    Moralities ancient choir
    Can never douse the lust and fire
    Of a love so fine.

—Christopher R. Jennings

Eagle's Prayer

Oh great spirit allow my wings to open.
Let me spread them and learn to fly.
Please don't let me fall.
    Oh great spirit allow me speed and courage.
Guide me to the sky and watch me glide to the sea.
May the waters part for me and allow me to enter them.
    Oh great spirit allow me grace in my flying.
Let me be free and be beautiful.
May I never lose my way and go with me always so that I may
find peace.
    Oh great spirit allow me wisdom.
The wisdom to find just what I am looking for.
And offer me the strength to continue in hardship.
Amen

—Angela Baltes

Hope

The words scribbled on the boarded up store front
Let the Sun Shine In!
Carefully, cautiously stepping my way along through the squalor.
It was repeated again and again
Let the Sun Shine In!

Determined and boldly was the ghostly hand that writ,
Let the Sun Shine In!
Our souls are soothed, warmed, lighted and cheered by the sun.
Let the Sun Shine In!
Brightening the somber cold pale remnants of life.

Let us wade through odors
that make our senses wilt.
Oh, yes the hope is here,
The hope is here.
Let the Sun Shine In!

—Florence A. Navolio

Thoughts On Top Of Another

Time passes quickly
life carries on indefinitely
like our thoughts
And everything revolves in circular motion

changes
rearrange our lives consistently
as ideas filter into memories
that linger in our minds like the sound of wind chimes
It's hard to keep up sometimes

—Denise Harpham

Life's Vision

Life challenges the young and the old
Life develops one to the right or to the left
Does life offer enough?
Or does life bring disappointments?

Without encouragement, life fails us
Without support, life fails us
What vision, therefore, does one see?

Without vision, one loses sight
Without vision, one loses hope
Are we so frail that we allow life to destroy us?
Are we so weak that life disappoints us?

Life is good!
Life is joyous!
With life challenges, it can bring—
    a shine of a new vision
    a strong force
    a new you.

—Donna Crawford

Why

Why do we have spectacular sunrises to start the day?
    Life is full of surprises.
      Yes, that's God's way
    Why do birds sing, winds blow,
    Bells ring and roosters crow?
    Why are some people so wealthy,
    while others have so little.
    Why are some people so healthy
   while others grow weak and brittle.
   Why do trees dance in the breeze and
    kites hang in the sky with ease.
  Why all the beautiful colors of flowers
in bloom or why sun beams float in a room.
    Why do some die so very young
   while others old and sick live so long.
  Why do raindrops make music on a roof?
It is all to give us proof that God has a plan for
  each of us. He is the one we have to trust,
    for there is no guessing,
  we should thank God for each blessing.

—*Gladys White*

I Will Win

I said life, you can't hurt me anymore.
Life said, that's what you think,
There's plenty more in store.
Each day there's more sorrow and pain,
Falling down on me like doomsday rain.
Just when I think I'm on my way up and out,
Guess again, fool, I hear life shout.
I have more troubles and woe in store for you,
To turn your life upside down, and make you blue.
Ah life, one day I'll thwart you and your evil ways,
And I'll find happiness in all of my days.
For I know great strength lies within,
And I will fight you life, and win.

—*Geraldine C. Dobry*

Janus

Life with her, remembered,
Life without her, tomorrow's question,
His gnarled fingers re-chisled
"Eternally Yours," into the granite slab.
December winds, aged as he, scourged his leathery face.
Turtling his snow-cropped head into frayed collar,
He counted cadence to a siren's wail, a grim reminder
Of the ride to the hospital with
His sweetheart, his wife, his bride, his sweetheart.
Memories reinforced the oneness of fifty years,
Loyalty, devotion, passion and compassion,
Her smiles and tender scoldings over trivia
Her guilt of fallow womb, no blame for his sterility,
As the reason for an empty cradle.
Years, silent as a panther's paws marauded their lives
Eroding her parchment face, shadowing the lavender peignoir,
His last gift to her.
Unable to share the requiem, he tottered homeward.
Tomorrow, he'd replace linens, hand-monogrammed "ours"
With a bath towel, labeled "his."

—*Alma J. Barnes*

Yielded

Lord see through my eyes what is pleasing to you.
Lord speak through my mouth words pure and true.
Lord hear through my ears what you want me to know.
Lord walk with my feet wherever I go.
Enlighten my mind with visions from above
And fill my heart with peace and love.
Lord work with my hands 'til there's nothing to do
For I'll forever be totally yielded to you.

—*Dorothy Conner*

Glory

As gentle as the breeze that blows across the channel
lifting the gulls into flight out to sea,
you have softly come upon the wastelands of my life,
and uplifted me.

As serenely as the music of the masters that echoes
off the mountains which surround the Alpine lakes,
you have drifted across the expanse of my consciousness,
reverberating off that thing called me.

As softly as the aged man kisses his granddaughter's
cheek, stooping over with effort and grace,
you have touched my being with kindness, caring, and concern.

As majestic is the sunrise in the mists of dawn that
signals the advent of day,
Your smiles, your glow, have illuminated the darkness
in my life, in this being called me.

And as awesome is the liftoff of the giant rocket that
reaches for the stars.
you have created an explosion of deep love for you in
that person called me.

—*Gary R. Joachim*

Untitled

The boy lies awake in a strange place
Light struggling in
Dark pushing out, way out
Change is taking place inside him
Dropping acid in this cold dark place
Something supernatural is about to happen
The other side is near
He is alone in this desolate wilderness
Emptiness in soul, poverty in spirit
   the time has come
Confusion
Disillusion
Hypocrisy
   the time has come
He hears a rhythmic drumming now
Steady throbbing hypnotic rhythm
He enters a soft hazy glow near the roof's edge
The point of no return
   the time has come
He begins to hear the music...

—*James Woomer*

The Stranger

You disappear and reappear every now and then;
Like a shadow of darkness.
I've never really gotten to know you;
Never really taken the time to try.
You're a mystery to all that know you;
To all that try.
You come and go as you please.
Nobody seems to have the right keys to open you up.
You keep to yourself, never trusting anyone.
People may try to get to know you, but not succeed.
What do you hide in your head and heart?
What does it take to open you up?
What are you hiding? What are your fears?
Why don't you open up and be a Stranger no more?

—*Debra A. Morris*

Pyramid Of Peace

Peace is inner tranquility of the mind,
Like a trinket box simply silver-lined.
Peace comes so softly, like a moccasined toe,
Without primitively alerting the foe.
Leaving lurid traces in a wilderness maze,
Puffing smoke signals by a campfire blaze.
Peace is a covenant of a person's heart,
Beyond earthly splendor — light miles apart.
Utterly abstemious is a start
To get the thorny hate out of one's heart.
Peace is the murmur of a tranquil creek,
Or is compassion for the sick and weak.
Peace is the halo of a baby's smile,
Or the gentle tones of a large base viol.
Peace can be revealed in a poetry book,
Or on a wooden bench in a shady nook.
Peace is instilled by the symphonic, mute, strains
In Johann Strauss waltzes, pulsing one's veins.
Peace may be attained via various ways,
But God has the format, so Him we should praise!!!

—*Alberta N. Williams*

Moment In A Net

Completeness envelopes and caresses me
Like a warm blanket.
My body, heart and mind are one
In tune with the symphony of the universe.

Should I some future day
Lose this delicious time
A vivid memory will succor me
In hours of my dissonance.

—*Eve Holloway*

The End

There's a feeling in my head
Like everything is dead
Life doesn't begin it ends
Never really having friends
Don't understand is why they stare
Lord knows they don't care
When I dream it's in red
Inside of me is already dead
Death creeps up behind my ear
Making me hear things I fear
Icy fingers snatch my life from me
Crumbling to my knee's, could this be
Screams I hear cut me like a knife
Praying to the Lord, first time in my life
Hearing his voice makes me cry
Feeling safe I accept I must die
Peaceful feelings rise into my heart
This is the beginning with the end I shall part

—*Jon Garrett Kelly*

A Day In Slumber

The stock market has crashed
like no room in the inn.
A bankrupt nation, can anybody win?
Beggars poor a-knocking at the door.
Bread-lines form and there's no end in sight.
Millions lost by millions not wrong or right.
A day in slumber. No help to make ends meet.
War on every side, give a grain of wheat.
Banks and piggy banks shiver and shake.
Milk in a baby's bottle is our only goal.
Signs of picket for a nickel or some dough.
A day in slumber, they come all in a row.

—*Diane Ayala*

Silent Secrets

Silent words that hold no meaning drift within my mind,
like tattered clothes worn once to often,
their purpose is left behind.

To talk to you seems useless,
It just isn't worth the tears.
I find it's safer to ache quietly,
than expose to you my fears.

And as I sit in the silence
that has come to know me well,
I share with it my secrets that it will never tell.

So now I hold you close in memories,
though you lay upon my bed,
and I mourn for the man I married,
the man who was my friend.

—*Ann M. Tremblay*

Crystal Hall

A picture of a hallway,
Lit with all its crystal chandeliers,
And windows to let the sunlight in;
Memories of the past,
Come flooding through my mind.
I remembering the two friends I met,
And one old friendship renewed;
A tear comes to my eyes of parting;
But, as long as I have the picture,
The hall of memories will always be there;
In my heart and in my mind.
The crystal hall from some other time,
To remind me of friendships and memories;
Thus, the crystal hall is also,
The hallway of memories.

—*Elsa L. Chase*

With Pain

Granite-hard for me to write these words.
Little I know of you...
Only that we love the same man.

Days and years I called him mine.
Moving next door, you soon found need of him
   To start the mower
   To coax the squirrel from the chimney
   To bring a candle to a storm-blackened house...
   No matter that my lights were out.

With pain I grope
Through dizzying days of change.
Always have I known
A break would come,
Properly,
For mother and son.

—*Joann W. McMaster*

Underground World

Thirty homeless people sleeping by the el...
Living their lives to the fullest on our earth
which is their hell ... Thinking that no one
loves them, wondering, "Does anyone care?"
... Being put down and laughed at by hard
words and cold stares ... It's time we do
something about this, it's about time we face
the facts ... Because someday we may be on
the streets and become members of the pack
   So let's join hearts and hands and voices
and cry out to God above ... To ask him for
strength and courage to give these people our
love.

—*Joan McMullin*

Father's Day

It was just a late Sunday morning pickup baseball game;
Little Leaguers jostled in our front yard.
I watched from my upstairs bedroom window.

My brother hit a hard liner—
Ryan, the neighborhood dreamer, missed the hit
and danced into the street after the ball.

My screams could not make Ryan dance faster,
could not stop the bullet-jeep.
I could only run to his side.

As I knelt by his fetal-drawn body,
I saw his chest move up and down, up and down.
I sprinted to Ryan's house.

"Mr. McCarthy, there's been an accident—
Ryan was hit by a car.
But he'll be all right—he's breathing!"

Ryan's breathing stopped late that afternoon
in the hospital, with his father,
on that brilliantly blue June Sunday.
—*Dianna P. Schmitz*

Tribute To A Martyr

Born alone,
Live alone,
Most certainly will die alone.

Involved in so many lives, yet,
A part of none.
Mine is the last house of the Zodiac,
I live in a kingdom of shadows and darkness.

Loneliness is a thin blanket providing little warmth
Against life's icy bitterness.
When I finally do reach out to partake in life's gusto
I'm told the parade was yesterday!

I'm a prisoner!
Locked within the stout walls of my mind.
My nourishment, my repast, has the bloody flavor
Of pure Masochism!

Perhaps one day
I will face the harsh reality that my destiny, in this life
Is not to enjoy .... but to endure,
In the comfortless solitude of my emptiness!
—*Fred Kurtz*

"Alone?"

Though there is a singleness about alone, alone is not
    loneliness;
It is akin to solitude, but in no form is it
    sentenced solitary.
Alone is not a state, or condition, but opportunity to
    explore a selfness;
To search one's needs and wants and wishes to the
    point of clarity.

Alone is a virtue. When wisely turned to meet an
    internal need
It is tool to clear the soul of confusion, the
    heart of a burden.
Alone is a time to build on that eternal want, and
    plant a seed.
From which grows life, personalized, ready to share
    with someone!
—*George E. McCullough*

Living Memories

So long as the window of memory is unshaded - so
long as the door will open for the passage of memory-
so long as the mind is clear, so long will the past be there.
Only when the mind is destroyed, by whatever means,
will the past be dead.
Only then will the Past be Passed.
There is tragedy as well as beauty with those memories.
The unshaded window and the open door must allow
the ugly and bitter, as well as the lovely and
beautiful to pass through.
Time, fortunately, heals most wounds and allows
the sweet, the lovely and the beautiful to triumph.
—*Harry Morris*

Middle-age

Look at me,
Look at me,
Look at me,
Bourgeois, fat, middle-age.
With scars: tonsillectomy, thyroidectomy, mastectomy, bilateral.
With scars: appendectomy, salpingectomy, hysterectomy.
With scars: oophorectomy, prostatectomy, cholecystectomy.
With scars: hemorrhoidectomy, laparotomy, switcheroo-ectomy.
I'm a wreck to me!
Bourgeois, fat, middle-age.
—*Edwynne G. Bradshaw*

Day's Gone By

What happened to the love you felt
Look at what life has dealt
You were everything in my eyes
You were the dream that ended in lies
All I ever asked for was a friend
But you used my love in your game of pretend
And here we are talking about day's gone by
I want to believe in those words you cry
Your eyes have nothing else to hide
Just a million tears of the years that passed us by
There is no need for us to pretend
No need for you to play my friend
When I needed you to stay
You were the one to run away
How could I explain what I feel inside
You took all I had for a ride
I can still hear the laughter of many years
But all I hear now is empty words filled with fear
My tears were all I had
You should have been there to be my Dad
—*Florika Zgrda*

Remember Me

Look across the fields of wheat, swaying in the breeze,
Look back and see,
And remember me.

Look at the sky, the sea, the clouds,
The blue, the green, the grey,
All into one young pair of eyes
That are so old.

Look away and think of not what is lost,
But of who was found.

Look inside to see who you are,
And where you will go.

Look across once more and see, by the fields of wheat,
By the skies of blue, by the seas of green, by the clouds of grey,
The color of my hair and of my eyes,

Look back and see,
And remember me.
—*Cory Jean Watters*

Receive

The day will come when spirits are low —
Look up and say,
"This is what I have to show!"

   A smile for a stranger
   A card I can send
   One more hug
   As I part from a friend

See diamonds or crystals
Fall from the rain.
Past the mountains
Is a smoother terrain.
Make each day one where a chance can't go by —
To give or receive a cheerful "hi".
Happily spirits will rise
As we create warmth and joy
In one another's lives.
   —*Iris Torres*

Dances With Sharks

He prowls the sea night and day
   Looking for some unwary prey.
They come in all sizes and shapes
   Looking as though they're full of hate.
They destroy their food with fury and might
   Crushing its bones bite by bite.
Men catch and destroy them and then boast about their triumph,
But in reality, that's one less fish in the sea to enjoy by you and
   me.
They must use their hunting weapons to find food, you know
   Just as we use the arrow and bow.
Their teeth are like swords that rip through flesh.
   for they always dine on their meals fresh.
They swim gracefully displaying their elegant side
   But to you and me they are killers, and deserve to die.
We scream in terror when we see them near the beach
   Hurrying to get out of the water and out of reach.
Their reputation is overrated
   And they are far outdated.
Let's let them live in peace
   Before their lives have evaporated.
   —*Jared English*

Silenced

  Sweet and silent laughter quickly sang me to sleep.
    Lost I felt within the depths of white wind.
      Soon I dreamed, I dreamed of magic.
        The power was in my hands.
  The wind I sent was free, it lashed into your mind.
Left your how I had hoped…gone, but you were still here.
    I try to wake but soon I find that, I am here.
        But I can fly.
       I take flight and run.
      But your memory chases me away.
And so I fly 'cause I want to and I dream 'cause I don't.
    I look at something beautiful, as I fall.
        And I want to fly.
     I fly to the heavens and my life.
      I fly to the emptiness and the light.
       But I flew to close and I burnt myself.
        I am falling.
       I am screaming.
      Am I dying?
     But I am silenced.
   —*Cassandra Knight*

It Could Have Been Me

It could have been me, sitting over there
Lost in a world of pity and despair
It could have been me, standing in the street
Begging for money and a bite to eat
It could have been me, walking the highway
Selling my body to a couple of strangers today
It could have been me, buying some drugs
Trying to make up for all the lost hugs
It could have been me, sticking a needle into my arm
Blocking out all the memories of yesterday's harm
It could have been me, coming so close
Of becoming another casualty from an overdose
It could have been me, in a mental ward
With my mind completely gone, locked behind bars
It could have been me, committing genocide
Not even thinking twice about the precious innocent lives
That's why I'm never to forget where I came from
I always thank God for what he has done
Because I finally realize without a doubt
That without Jesus, it could have been me, with no way out
   —*Cantrice L. Montgomery*

Midnight Storm

At midnight, fierce winds began to blow
Loudly shrieking as they banged the doors,
Rattled the window, and shook our farmhouse
Causing echoes, to resound on every floor.

Thunder made a booming entrance;
Shafts of lightning went on display.
Our lights flickered-then went out,
Slowly came on again-then off to stay.

Rain fell in splashing torrents on the windows
As violent explosions of thunder rolled overhead.
Lightning split the sky with jagged bolts of light
While I shook with fear, in my cozy bed.

The rain, the thunderous noises-lightning flashes,
Sounds entered the house with a frightening clarity.
Nearby, pines moaned as winds lifted their swaying boughs
And the howling winds gained in severity.

All night long the storm raged about the farmhouse
Reverberating and quaking-thunder shaking the ground
Followed by lightning's brilliant flashes.
What a rough stormy night-all pierced with sound!
   —*Alby A. Velek*

Welcome

Barriers broken, chains unloosed!
Love in its grandeur, with willingness flies to its roost.
Seeing all things through its all loving eyes.
and freeing the Spirit in human disguise.

Love conquers all, overpowers is more clear.
Its strength is in caring and patience to bear
the waiting, the watching, the pain as we test
our humankind frailties - not loving, not blest.

Yet Love's there for the fullness of spirit to claim
when asked - Ah, the waiting, the long waiting game.
It will be, and is, and was far before.
yet now - is the time to open the door.

Yes - open the door, that's all that it takes to welcome the
Spirit as slowly we wake to the world as it is -
Love's perfection in phase,
all movement and stillness wrapped up in a gaze
of loving and living, of spirit and flesh -
Yes, clearly perfection
God's love at its best!
   —*Jolene Larson-Gardner*

Love Is. . .

Love is something a women feels for a man.
Love is something a man feels for a woman.
Love is something when a man and women are joined as one.
When they become husband and wife.
Love is something a husband and wife share for their children.
Love is something a brother and a sister share.
Love is something when a parent becomes a grandparent.
Love is family.
Love is special for a friend.
Love is something a small child has for their favorite toy.
Love is a way of sending your loved ones a special greeting from afar.
Love is for lovers on a hot summer night.
Love is for telling someone you love them.
Love is for Jesus, because he was the one who died for all of our sins.
Love is never having to say I'm sorry.
Love is to share from me to you.
—*Beth A. Chiatello*

Hydra

How many heads has the Hydra?
How many heads want to devour innocent victims?
Innocent victims in Bosnia, Israel, South Africa....
Innocent victims in hundreds of places
Innocent victims in hatred,
Innocent victims of racial persecution all over the world.
When will mankind have cut off the hundred heads of the Hydra?
When will mankind have the humanity to kill the Hydra for ever?
When will all men be human?
—*Egon Strauss*

Untitled

When I think about you
It makes me smile,
And it reminds me of how lucky I am.
Don't go red when I tell you
How special you are to me.
And don't feel flattered
When I tell you how much I love you,
Because it isn't hard falling for someone like you.
Someone who is caring, loving, and thoughtful.
So baby, you have no worries tonight,
Because I only have eyes for you
And my heart only loves that heart of yours.
And if you ever see any doubt in my eyes,
Just remember you must be dreaming
Because nothing is going to change
the way I feel for you.
—*Kelsey Duncan*

In Due Season

The wind is churning the pile of leaves
Left swept underneath the dripping eaves
While dancing drops of winter rain
Start a lively ballet of spatters again
Spouting up dust in the restless mound
Then seeping quietly in the thirsty ground.

The leaves lie laden in damp despair
Absorbing the sun from the rain drenched air
And thoughts of new leaves green from the rain
Say winter will go and spring come again.
—*Doris Barton*

Slaves

There in the land of ever green.
There is the land of the rich.
They get their riches from slaves.
He stands wiping off the sweat from his forehead,
While his master sits under the tent watching his slaves
Working, his pleasure is in the money he will receive from the
hard work of his slaves.

All he thinks of is the freedom he wish to have and the friends
he lost from the beatings they had. The master would give a
command to his guards to beat slaves if they don't work hard,
Money comes from hard work the master would say to his slaves.

They work wearing nothing on their feet and hands, their feet
cracked, their rough like a diamond nearly finished on a
diamond cutters table.
As he would escape he would be hunted with dogs and guns,
there would be a reward for his capture to the one who caught him.
The life of a slave is the same as a life of a prisoner of war.
—*Gladwin Dijoe*

Untitled

The sparkling of the snow,
the burning of the candles.
The bright lights of the tree,
the shining of the wrappers on the presents,
and the dying of the carolers
as they go home for the rest of Christmas.

It is now the day of Christmas,
the crunched up parts of snow,
which were left behind from the carolers.
The melted wax of candles, sitting on the sill.
and the ripped up wrappers from the presents,
are lying under the still beautiful Christmas tree.
—*Julie Ladik*

Looking Glass

    Twilight comes much, too fast
When you're going through the looking glass
    Darkness falls against, the wall
  Like the shadow falling, far too tall

    Emptiness consumes the masses
    Lonely stares from hollow glasses
  With no warm heart behind those eyes
  They don't know why, love they despise

   Cheer heart now go, with no return
   A pot prepare, a crucible to burn
    Dare we step beyond the door
Beyond the looking glass, if there be a floor
—*A. Melinda New*

Marriage Of Sincerity

Let sincerity talk frankly
lest his story will never be told:
Once in the human Kingdom
he went out in search of a wife:
he cooed to Frank in her frank-chair,
but he thought:
why must I let her take my hand in marriage?
He hissed and walked by.
Later she saw insincerity sit at the end of the road;
her beauty shot out radiance of joy.
He stopped and thought out loud:
"She would make a good match,
must I marry from my own kind?"
Sincerity took insincerity as wife.
When they were asleep,
insincerity unmasked of her beauty
and her ugliness choked sincerity to death.
—*Barine Sanah Ngaage*

Slowly falling, cascading down,
It falls into a puddle on the ground
Its silence and beauty quenches all
   natures thirst,
Never leaving on anything, some kind
   of curse.
To be held so preciously,
But used so carelessly.
It often makes one wonder why
   when we have something
   we abuse it,
But only when it becomes scarce,
   do we treasure it.
   —*Sara K. Davis*

Couples With Love

There is this thing called love,
   It flows throughout the air,
Hoping to find the loving couple
   To love each other and care.
Hoping that they last a while,
   To hope and follow through,
To find the day of marriage,
   The truth between me and you.
Our lives will be filled with laughter,
   Feeling, truth, and respect,
To have the feeling of love,
   In life, it is the best.
It's a feeling you can't live without,
   A feeling of happiness and joy,
Shared between a loving couple,
   A blessed girl and boy.
   —*Michelle Stickle*

Faith Is Personal

Faith is personal and real
It grows big like a mountain
When things go wrong
And your feelings are bruised
It descends upon you instantly
Like an overpowering giant
Spreading its wings about you
Surrounding you, reassuring, serene.

Taste of it and tell someone
It's contagious, it's accessible
As close to you as a prayer
Use it for a small request
Believe and watch it grow
The one who gives you faith
Also gives you hope
What a powerful combination
To enhance your spiritual growth.
   —*Suzy Cox*

Hands of Time

My mother used to say, "Look at my hand
It's hard to understand
That it's mine
So wrinkled and old"
I didn't want to look—but I'd say
It looked fine
And I shrugged the thought away
The years have passed, and now and then
The thought kept coming back again
Today I looked at my own hand
And I did understand—
I saw my mother's hand.
   —*Lorraine Feuer*

It is A Puzzlement

It is a pronoun,
It has no sex,
It has no case,
It has no person — It is.

You is a pronoun,
You has no sex,
You has no case,
You has person — You are.

I is a pronoun,
I has no sex,
I has case,
I has person — I am.

You and I are we.
We is a pronoun,
We has no sex,
We has case,
We has person — We are.

But We is plural
and We have sex!
   —*L. P. Corbett*

Enclosed Insanity

First —
   It hides in darkness
   Looking for the light.
Intelligence-but with no thought.
   Second —
   Dominating its desires.
Success-but with no achievement.
   Finally —
   Welcomed-it came.
All is now unretainable.
   Now —
Actions-but with no movements.
   —*Pam Dworzynski*

Untitled

If it comes natural
   It is good,
If it comes in time
   It is fair,
If it comes at all
   be glad,

If you force it
   It will hurt,
If you clock it
   It will vanish
If you tell it
   It will be stolen

Trust it
It will be wise

Forsake it
It will die
   Listen to it you will hear
So,
Run with it and you
   will never fear.
   —*Starr Page*

Trepihany Fundamaximus

Within my heart there is a tree -
   it knows me not
   it knows very little
At times it doesn't move at all
   when times are cold
   when times are dry
But summer brings the knowledge back
   to reach for water
   earth
   and light
The light it found has helped my eyes
   my eyes have learned much in it
They search for earth and water too
   they helped me build a garden
The garden's brought me even more
   more than beauty
   more than fruit
My gardens brought me other trees
   we stand together
   against the wind
   —*Raymond Recco*

The Vast And Vast Blue Sea

The vast and vast blue sea!
It makes our heart wide and bright
The sea in the evening sun light.
Fills our heart with rosy glorious light.
The sea in the starry night
Gives wonderful starry present
Into the heart of each of us.
The sea knows everything.
   —*Rae Asazuma*

Hi Daddy

"Hi Daddy" is a tender phrase
It means so much to me
The kids all said "Hi Daddy"
As they climbed upon my knee

It was "Daddy, will you tuck me in?"
As they tripped off to bed
It was Daddy who fixed all their toys
And kept the family fed

But soon the kids grew older
I then was known as Dad
It lost a little tenderness
That Daddy always had

When teenage years had rolled around
I then was known as Pop
I felt the kids were being cruel
This nonsense had to stop

But years have passed by rapidly
And Pop I'll always be
And that tender phrase "Hi Daddy"
Is a loving memory
   —*P. LaRue Teaney*

Death And Darkness Toll The Hour

Death and darkness toll the hour,
It shall have you in its power,
It takes humans every hour,
It creeps upon the midnight tower,
It makes many many scream,
It makes you puff into steam,
Death becomes you one dark hour.
   —*Robyn Dollins*

Love Is A Meadowlark

Love is a meadowlark.
It sings of itself
With sweet insistence.

Love is beside me.
It takes my hand
And leads me to the sun.

Could you tell me
Of your joy
That bounces off my soul
Like springtime rain?

We all leave some day,
So why not love
While we have a chance?

Love is a meadowlark
Singing in the field.
Love is a song without end.
—*Spencer Knox Kendig*

The Ladder Of My Ages

When I was one, I walked a mile.
It stretched so far and wide.
When I was ten, I raced the wind.
It was one fantastic ride.
When I was twenty, I drank the sea.
I grew with every drop.
When I was fifty, I climbed the Alps.
Then I rested at the top.
When I was eighty, I walked again.
Only this time with some grace.
For I spent the rest of my ages,
Breathing heavens space.
—*Lonnie L. Veitch*

Music Without Words

I love music without words
It's soothing and pleasing
To the mind
Like the soft breeze
On a summers' eve
Raindrops on silvery blades
of grass
Rays of sunlight dancing
on the lake
—*Sonia Moodie*

Alone

A perfect night... for emptiness.
It's strange how two people
can lie next to one another
yet be so far apart.
Another time, another night —
perhaps.
But can you really forget
or even understand?
We both know as an evening it failed.
Just one night lost,
but it always seems to hurt more
when it's someone you love.
—*William Borovsky*

Angel of Mercy, Angel of Love

Angel of mercy, Angel of love
Jehovah God, our Father
Showed us His love.

Angel of mercy, Angel of love
Baby Jesus in a manger
The shepherds told of.

Angel of mercy, Angel of love
Holy Spirit descended
Down like a dove.

Angel of mercy, Angel of love
Jesus, our Saviour, on the cross
Shed His own blood.

Angel of mercy, Angel of love
The King of Kings, Lord of all
We'll shout from Above!
—*Sue A. Schrowang*

Choices

In the time of peace and quiet
Jesus speaks unto my soul.
As I often pause to seek Him;
how He longs to make me whole.

Oh, please take the time to know Him
for His peace is beyond compare.
Yes, the joy of really knowing
that He keeps us in His care.

So, my friend, you choose each day
the path that you will walk.
It's by these choices that we know Him
while others they just talk the talk.

It's so very important then,
these many choices that we make.
We will choose to walk with Him,
or we will choose to be a fake.

There is no peace or rest in falsehood
and so my weary friend,
Won't you trust in God today and
He will see you safely to life's end.
—*Roy Bowen*

Autumn And The Apple Tree

The apple tree had leaves up to its top
    Just awhile ago.
  But winter winds have passed
This way, the leave were kissed
    by snow
    No cover now
   Beneath the bough
To rest within its shade
  No sign of green among
   The grassy blade
   The sun has taken
  Leave of earth to
    wait the birth
     of spring!
—*Mary Ann Davis*

Fruits For Your Labors

"Hope's"
"Joy's"
"Love's"
"Peace's"
"Laugh's"
"Patient's"
—*Mary Walters*

Love Re-Threading

Eyes —
  Kaleidoscopic windows
  (shimmering incantations
  of Pretense and Folly)
  Vivify us, one to another,
But shade
  our inward suns.

Would we shatter
the polychromatic panes,
shatter the eclipsing smiles
and arachnoid desires.

Still.
  Your latticing voice
  baffles the hollowed darkness
  re-geometrizes the enwebbing glass—
  star-stunning mosaics flower—

  My soul and yours:
  A prismatic bower.
—*Richard D. Lucero*

Attitudes

Treacherous stares from afar
keen looks from the corner of the eye.
Spitballs tossed.
Sneaky chatter.
Hands to mouth.
Naughty boys
and girls
huddled like a football team.
Facial expressions
bodily gestures
implicit plots that conclude
you definitely have it.
—*Sandra R. Kiser*

Grandparents

Grandparents are made from a special
kind of mold, they have away about
them, that can not be told;
wisdom and love, they've gotten
through the years, is making wrongs
to right, and shedding lots of tears;
mommy and daddy say they love us,
I think that is sweet, I guess that
is why they meet our special needs.
Grandpa's deep voice is gruff like a
bear, but deep down inside, he's
only a teddy bear. Grandma's tender
touch, when I've got a cold, I'd
rather have grandparents than a
pot of gold!
—*Martha Jean Kennedy*

Seeking Love

High above the endless sky,
Lies my heart alone and blue.

So high above to keep it safe and warm,
So hence it would not be harmed.

But now I take a glance at you.
And can not stop loving you.

Now my only wish I do conceal,
Is if you would come and glance at me.

With your stare, if I do acquire,
I'd wish you'd seek some love for me...
—*Vanessa Cortez*

Love's Embrace

You were once but a notion
known only in obscurity
now, you are my reality
and as to my immortal soul
the promise of love eternal

With willful resolve
you stole back my heart
from the pain that
so cruelly enslaved it
enfold me and let me surrender to
your mellifluous renderings of love
and with every heartbeat
bring to light what
only the lonely have known

Though it be oft times mortal
and ever elusive
there remains no better place
than the comfort and warmth
of love's embrace
—*Laura L. Abbott*

Divination

Beyond the horizon
Lake Superior escapes the shore
stealing power from the wind
to rush here with solutions
locked in foam and sound.

The Crone of the Lake
casts her bones of wood
in lots upon the shore
crooning our future in the
hiss of the curl
moaning our sorrows
in the backwash.

Bones of past fore-tellings
litter the shore and dunes
symbols locked in solitude.
Tales heard on the wind
only by the sawgrass
staying the dunes.
—*Patricia E. Thurston*

Love's Spark

Comes another one fine day
Late my eyes open to the sun
They sparkle like its rays
The new day has begun

Like the lucky old sun
There's a spark in my heart
It seems to only see shadows
On the days we're apart

This closeness that we share
Has built a bridge to cross
We meet in the middle
And love shows its gloss

Be mine, walk beside me
Put in mine, your hand
Stroll with me to paradise
Let love sail, through this land

Take in all of the sunshine
That towers way up above
And carry inside its glitter
You know your in love
—*Monte R. Shockley*

Glow Worm

Sun of amber, fury with fire,
leaves a glow-worm full of desire.
As far as the sun can reach,
it can't strike the night.

Man can demand
and man can fight.
Man can kill
for what he thinks right.

We can revolt for change
and blow up buildings,
but isn't it strange

Those who don't know
themselves well
spend a life turning
earth into Hell.
—*Lewis I. Chace*

Who's To Blame

The words you told me as a child
Left heartache and great pain.
You said I'm just a stupid kid
And I'm the one to blame.

I won't amount to anything
I'll always be the same.
I believed in what you said
And now I hang my head in shame.

I lack faith in all I do;
This, forever, will remain.
And the guilt I carry with me
Tells me I'm the one to blame.

I wanted with my heart and soul
To join in every game.
I was convinced I'd never win;
Nor would I feel the fame.

I dream to hold my head erect;
That, once, I may stand proud.
I whisper, NOT, this question;
I ask, who's to blame?, out loud!
—*Lisa Schultz*

My Prayer For Today

No matter what comes my way today,
Let me find a reason to smile.
No matter how rough and rocky the way.
Let me go that extra mile.

Give me the will to do my best
To lighten someone's load.
And help me hold my tongue Dear Lord,
Don't let me tease or goad.

Help me to be a loyal true friend
To someone who's in need.
And stop me quick if I should start
A cruel or thoughtless deed.

Let me be a good example
To my children and their friends.
Let me be remembered fondly,
If today my life should end.

Let me stand and look around me
At the closing of today.
And be thankful for your bounty
In these things for which I pray
—*Margaret Cook*

An Unborn Child's Prayer

Please, please,
   Let me live,
If only you could see,
   I'm a Human too,
   God created me.
Don't take my life,
   my breath,
but take the time to see,
That I'm here for a reason,
   God created me.
He fashioned me together
   To be uniquely me.
So please don't take my life,
But let me live like thee.
—*Tracy L. Carver*

Within The Heart

With in the times that we separate
Let us not drift apart.
Only a strong love like ours could
Remain with in the heart.
And upon the time of return when it's
Down to you and me.
Look deeper within the heart for
there is where you'll always be.
—*Michael Lane*

Intrigue

Come let us dance together
Let your warmth lay upon my skin
Doubt not the joy in my eyes
As I look upon you each morning

Stay with me now for the day is short
And I can't see the flowers in the dark

The birds stop singing,
   the doe closes her eyes
Though the stars are intriguing
   I long for the light of your heart
—*Michele McCabe*

Is Life A Voyager In The Universe?

If human is not immortal,
Life is a flash on the pan.
If human is not imperfect,
Climbing the Everest becomes a pinnacle.
If human is impure,
Life is an endless struggle.
If life is a navigation full of danger,
Any joy is a climax.
Only if human is imperfect,
Then life is a voyager in the universe.
—*Yung-Feng Chang*

Three Japanese Poems Of Life

   Slow down be quiet
Life's meaning is all around
   In stillness is God

   Broken dreams today
Faith, hope, and love, united
   May future bring peace

   Teaching one to love
So on each and every day
   Showing constant love
—*William Durbin*

Try To Live It...

How will we all bear up to
life over a long period of time-

Maybe with its successful
trials and sorrows-

Maybe the secret is to try to
live only from a day to day, from
a moment to moment-

Do not worry about tomorrow,
for tomorrow will take care of
if its own-

We can have a piece of mind
and strength for every need, if
we live piece meal, from hour to
hour-

So try not to torment ourselves
needlessly, when trying to live
tomorrow today...

—*Lena Gander*

Untitled

Dreams gone,
like a shattered mirror
never to reflect an image again

Time lost,
like a stolen rainbow
never to cast its beauty again

Feelings change,
like the dead awakening
never to see darkness again

Today is now history,
no longer a burden
left to be reviewed later
looked at as a sad past

Thoughts created,
like the imagery in a book
used to amuse the reader

My heart is broken,
like an abandoned toy after Christmas
never to be held again after
that wonderful day

—*Misty Buchanan*

Father's Love

The child that I am trying to raise,
Like any other child,
Has a sweet tooth for praise.

That I listen & hear what he has to say
  may well be the high point
  of his busy day.

But praise without effort is a
  lie being told,
And not making him listen an
  action so cold.

For he needs my input, my
  nagging, my wile...

To develop someday, to a
  man-child with style.

—*Tim Coogan*

The Orchestra

The drums pulse
like blood flowing
through the body.

The strings ring
like a screeching woman in pain

The horns pound,
like an angry husband
pounding, pounding.

The flutes sing
like a ray of hope
drowned out by the sound of harmony.

The orchestra rushes,
moves onward; it's a race.
Pounding.
A silence.
A pause.
Off again, with more fury.
pounding, pounding,
pounding, pounding.
Silence, this time forever.

—*Sarah Reinecke*

Coming Home Pt. One

  Leaves trickling down
    like snow
As I walk through the countryside
    again

  When did leaves ever
Leave such an impression on me
    So vivid
  That I had to pause

  And bask in a beauty
  I almost forgot existed
Yesterday I would have missed it
  But today I just had to visit

To find something that was taken away
  Emotions inside I thought ridden
  Actually they were hidden
Forbidden until I saw leaves falling along
    The countryside
    Trickling like snow

—*Obiama Iwuoma*

Love....

    Love is unique
  like the sound of waves
    But all seem to seek,
    the good looking babes
    No one ever dares
      to look within
    we only seem to care
  about the beauty and the sin,
    They break your heart
      that's all they do
  then leave you all the pain
    you actually thought
      they loved you
    But they are all the same
    then the day we met
    I have came to see
      that not everyone
        is alike
    Some feel the heart
      with glee...

—*Summer Jones*

Ghosts

Impatient souls
lingering at eternity's end

A watchful eye,
searching for yesterday
and finding a pool of blood

Day's last light is gone
as quickly as is a wisp
of smoke from an incense burner

An old man sits,
inhaling the
sweet, juicy fatness
of a suckling pig

New York, and
the lights are on
but nobody's home

Life goes on.
  Period.

—*Valerie A. Brinson*

Spring Night

Light cloud, nocturnal, proud,
Lite as concealed lamp, tonight,
Moon softly concealed, as shroud,
Attempting to glimmer so bright,

Earth stars, captured in glance,
Around world seen just here,
Gaping, abounding, light as dance,
Wondrous picture of night so dear,

Moment captured forever in humility,
This becomes absolute picture,
Shedding thought of any futility,
Seeing heavens makes one sure.

—*Thomas N. Cranston*

The Lake

Little boy's swim and swim,
little girl's swim and swim, father's
fishing for supper, mother's clean and
clean, fish for supper father's say,
mother's cook and cook, after supper
children go to bed and mother's and
father's talk and talk.

—*Titan Crawford*

Pastels

  I envy those who live their
    lives in pastels
  Who find peace in sandstone
    and azure blue
    Whose worlds remain
    unspoiled and clean
Untouched by the vivid splashes
    that spot the canvas
      I exist in

—*Stacia Giunta*

Untitled

When night come
Loneliness say, I can't see
I am afraid!
Who? Can you be.

I lay in the still-ness of the night
hoping and praying
hurry! hurry! hurry daylight.
For when light comes
loneliness vanish out of sight,
and my fear is set free.

For darkness in prison me
being afraid of darkness you see
is like slow death over powering me,
But day comes you see and set me
my loneliness free.

So, I guess known you can agree
darkness and me don't see.

—*Lorriane Murray*

Untitled

Lonely night,
lonely place,
tears falling
from my eyes,
with no one to see
but the lonely moon.
Aye, lonely me.

—*Sendic Veluz*

Poor Kitty

Kitty was sitting up in a tree,
Longing for some company.
She sat and sat, but no one came;
I thought it was a doggone shame
Kitty sang a lullaby
To the moon up in the sky.
Neighbors heard the midnight blues,
So showered her with clocks and shoes.
One boot kissed her on the face,
Robbing her of time and space.
Kitty now has gone to rest,
And daisies grow upon her chest.

—*Mary Barbara Kozul Blazic*

Ode To A Mama Robin

Well there, Mrs. Robin,
Look at how we've grown!
The season is turning
and another has flown.

We are scattered 'round the country
one is down the hall,
But reach down inside your heart
We aren't far at all.

You have done a great job
just look at us now
The world sees us shining
and they know just how.

How that you brought us up
to be faithful and wise,
We love you Mama Robin
You are the star in our eyes.

—*Lisa McUmber*

"Agony Of Honesty"

Whirlwind sacred fires
"Lord, where are You?"
So deep the desire
   so blood-shot the heart:
      Passion and death!
"To whom shall I go?"
How holy and absurd!
Here - there,
No-where - all-where.
Agony of honesty.

—*Malia Wong*

Lost And Found

Lost in thought
   lost in feeling
Cerebral wandering.

   A solitary realm
      Alone.
      Within.

Lost in thought. Again.

   Discovery
Deeply hidden. Essential.

      Sanctuary.
      Oneself.

   Found.

—*Sean Patrick Mckenna*

Love Is the Devil

Love is unfair
Love is deadly
like a gun that takes a life
Without even a fight
It takes everything from you
It's out of control
There's nothing you can do

Love is like suicide
Stripping you of everything
including your pride
leaving you with nothing
almost taking your life

Love is the devil
he puts that gun in your hand
tells your mind to pull the trigger
to take you to the neverland
you try to scream and yell
Try to get him out of your head
But your on the road to hell
You loved therefore your soul… is already
dead

—*Stacia Rolston*

Untitled

On the wings of wind and time
lulled by seasons lullaby.
A life,
a line.
That bends, curves,
twists, turns
and ends up where it deserves.
Death comes to all
in either violence or serenity.
But either way, fate is fate
and we all have a destiny.

—*Melisa Spencer*

Reverie

Amidst the darkness of the night,
lying down so restlessly beside
a mysterious, melancholic love.

Bewitched, yet bewildered,
wanting to kiss, however barred
by deep, inexplicable thoughts.

Eyes wide open, visualizing
two souls in love united in harmony;
but … the night was devoid of warmth
and passion my aching heart desires.
Suddenly entrapped in a sullen mood,
sensitized by the truth clandestinely
kept within the realms of a mystic
nook … a witness to silent tears.

A misty reverie of an illusioned
romantic, boundless love that
failed to keep its vows -

Marred by the universal perils
of this sinful, ruthless world that
captured our union's sanctity.

—*Yolanda Laurel Merdegia*

The Words Of God

God of heaven and of earth,
Made the skies and gave me birth.
Years have gone and years have past,
And God's love still does last.

God of wisdom and of love,
Once talked to me, while He was above.
God used no words and sang no song,
Yet, spoke to me loud and long.

God of beauty and of joy,
Used nature to talk to me, His boy.
His words were stars and little flowers,
God spoke His awesome powers.

God of wonders and of mysteries,
That day, brought me to my knees,
I saw that almighty God does show
That from everywhere His graces flow.

—*Percy Mamikunian*

Season Of Change

There's the snowman,
made with care.
Carrot nose, such cold toes!
Sunny skies shine upon the fair.
Snow no more, grass is green.

Shooting star across the sky,
way so high, so hard to see.
Maybe I can hitch a ride?
Up above the clouds that storm,
I feel the glow that is so warm.

I know all things must change,
but why so hard, so fast, so cruel?
I will take the time to ride my star,
to slow things down, that is my rule.
I will let the seasons change.
Welcome sun and stormy rage.
Until my star grows dim,
I will appreciate all within.

—*Nancy Seruya*

The National Library of Poetry - Outstanding Poets of 1994

Choices

Choices
   Make choices
      Making choices.
  Choose!
Take responsibility
Take power
   Empowered!
Control
   Controlling
      Controlled!
Don't choose.
   No choice.
     Not responsible.
  Powerless
  Trapped
  Victim
  Caught!

You choose!
—*Mary Till*

Knowledge

As I journeyed through my mind today
   many things discovered.
In deep abyss, emotional turmoil,
   hypocrisy uncovered.

   Idiosyncrasy of the mind
  cause innuendoes of the heart.
   Fear of acknowledgement
     tearing me apart.
—*Melissa K. Folse*

Purple

I love purple and so do you
maybe black can go with it to, if
only it would go with blue maybe
it would look like you.
—*Quintin Natale Fields*

Heaven

You often dream what heaven
maybe like, look like;
above the clouds; there must
be a wonderful sight.

At night the stars touch;
You often wonder; what they
are spelling out for us.

At day break; you can see
The light watching over us;
Heaven is far; but not
out of reach.

Someday, when you look
up in the sky; at the
sunlight
we may all see that wonderful
place; known as
Heaven.

—*Lora Albright*

Lonely

   Their muddled cheers
  meet shouts of anger
and cries of encouragement.
   Together they drift
  through the sweaty air
  and my distant ears.

   They huddle around
  and place their hands
one on top of the other.
  All of them belong,
bound by goals of victory
and friendship unknown to me.

   Till just one
turns to the sideline
and gives me a genuine smile.
   I smile back,
surprised how his simple gesture
pulls me closer to the game.
—*Sheri Watson*

Resting In God

Here, this exhausted body
Melts into the comfort
Of pillows and blankets
Alone with You
And I am blessed
With the warmth
Of Your eternal love.
Here, all things
Confirm the thought
That You are my Provider.
In Your great omnipotence
You have answered every prayer;
And so the indecisions
Of this mind
I place completely
In Your care —
Taking all peaceful slumber.
—*Wanda Lee Porter*

A Friend Gone

In my mind there lives a
memory that time just can't
erase.

It is of many, many friends
with tears streaming down their
faces.

I watched them for a
moment then I knew; so I
turned and walked away.

That was sometime ago, but
I still recall the day.

Now I finally understand,
why God took him away.
—*Tonya Richie*

......As The Barn Crumbles

A chord is struck in my mind
It's hard, harsh, and pitiless
Like the sun settles in the West
By the same degree I am disarmed
This paralytic affection
Idyllic though it was
Has dismembered me
—*Steve Nwaeze*

What Have We Become?

   What have we become?
  Men with clenched fists,
   Instead of open arms?

   Are we capable of love,
   or does hatred reign?

   What have we become?
Children with fear in their hearts,
   and blood on their hands?

Is compassion a thing of the past?
   gone and forgotten?

   What have we become?
   People with weapons,
  Instead of pens and voices?

  If violence is our solution,
   What have we become?
—*Tracy Carr*

Lawn Mower

Giant, earth-bound,
Metal bumblebee,
Gorging on green grass
And on an occasional...
Green water hose!
—*La Retha Adams*

The Impact

Glass shatters!
Metal crunches!
The force of the impact!
Then, a quietness.
Strange, I don't feel anything.
What's happened to me?
I don't feel any pain,
But I can see the blood.
My body is crushed
In the twisted, smoking wreckage.
This isn't what I wanted.
I don't want to die.
Please, just let me feel something....
Anything.... anything at all.
Even pain is better than this.
I don't want to die, but I'm slipping away...
I can feel it.
Then peace settles over me...
Like a cloud of dust.
I'm home free now.
—*Nancy Raley*

The Brown Jacket

When we were young, long ago
Michael bought a brown jacket.
And when he tried it on for me,
a handsomer man I will never see,
I told him so.

When twenty years we were wed,
he put it on again. I said,
you have not changed at all my dear,
you are so young and debonair.
I meant it.

Today I take it from the rack
cover it with tears and hang it back.
How I miss him
—*Thelma M. Lasko*

Beyond

A destined passion,
mixed with pure satisfaction...
A burning desire,
for an exclusive fire...
A drop of misery,
for extreme luxury...
A touch of pain,
for a stainless fate...
A glance of rejection,
for absolute perfection...
A kiss of coldness,
Farther than protection...
But for the unforgiven,
It's beyond damnation...
Fore it's eternal liberation...
Fore years of lamentation...

—*Lissette Almanzar*

Depressed

Rain drops falling on the ground.
Mixed with tears, it's a sad, sad sound.

Trying to find my little space.
In what we call the human race.

For I have not accomplished anything.
Only thing I have is an intense pain.

For when I die who will mourn my death
To bad that will be my last deep breath

—*Sabrina Boyce*

To Those Who Have A Dream

I am in love with the dream
   more so than reality.
And to know the reality is
   to break my heart,
Yet the dream remains only a dream
   and my heart remains intact.
But if the dream were to become reality
   my heart would also become a reality
Broken into pieces unrepairable
Because the dream knew reality.

—*Tahira Haseebullah*

Poetry: A Potpourri

Poems rhyme
'Most all the time;
But sometimes don't.
With clear insight,
They can delight;
But often won't.
Poets ponder philosophy,
And frolic in frivolity.
In haste, they may abbreviate.
At ease, they may expatiate.
People and pets,
Antiques and jets,
Landscapes and seascapes,
Scarcely a subject ever escapes
The poet's perspicacious ken,
And the peregrination of his/her pen.
To say it all in summary:
With candor or with subtlety,
With levity or sobriety,
Poems specialize in VARIETY!

—*Teresita A. Ryan*

As Time Passes By:

As time passes by
My ears hear a cry
Of a life that is lost
Where emotions get tossed
A love which was near
Has left in a tear
Where the fun had once been
There's now sadness within
Where a laughter was found
Now memories abound
So share now the time
It ends like a crime
Death breaks a close tie
As time passes by.

—*Toby L. Timberlake*

Too Seldom

Today
   My heart
Has reason to smile
   For a while
      Anyway
   In the slow lane
   Too seldom
Surrounded by solitude
And the simplicities
      That
   Too often
   Go unnoticed

—*Martin Morgan*

Rodney King: Reactions

   Microwave
my heart until it explodes
   like an egg.

   Black eye peas
dancing in the wired dimensions.

Bushy tail headless leaders
   arranged urgent flight.

   Oh my god
those colored folks are
   mad as hell tonight.

—*Shirley R. Berry*

Without You

As each day passes
My love for you grows stronger
Without you the night grows longer
Only to fear we'll soon be strangers

As each day passes
Your smile makes no escape
My heart makes no mistake
A touch from you is all it takes

As each day passes
Dreams never lasting
Love songs forever passing
Rainy days forever lasting

—*Steve Snyder*

Bennie

Dreams are life, days like song.
My love for you, I waited so long.
Adored treasures, so far away.
Fantasy dreams, from yesterday.

Locked away, forever it seems.
Starlite nights, sun beams.
Caring emotions, hidden inside.
Love for you, tried to hide.

Miracles happen, dreams come true.
This I know, for me and you.

Real awakening.
Daylight sounds.
Knowing you're mine.
The love I've found.

—*Lois B. Buchanan*

Hands Down

I wish I could coordinate
My powers to perambulate
With a metacarpal gait.
The cultivation of this inclination
Might well effect emaciation
Of my cobbler's large vendation.

—*William L. Walker, Jr.*

Life

   Society
   My prison

   My color
   My downfall

   My sex
   My destruction

   My dreams
   Never reality

   My hopes
   Always fears

   My neighborhood
   My sorrow

   A way out
   Always walled

What do you call this?

   Life.

—*Tiffany Pleshette Jones*

Wildflower

I'm no hot house plant.
My seeds were not dropped in some
rarefied air, nor were they placed
gently in rich, black soil, nourished
by soft spring rains and warm summer sun.

No - my seeds fell on frozen ground.
They felt the icy fingers of winter
and there was no escape from the
heavy boot that crushed them into
the hardened soil - somehow they
flourished - unnoticed.

In the spring look for us. We're
found along every country road
every garden path. Our colors are
many, pink, yellow, blue, gold.
We add beauty to God's world.
He calls us His wildflowers.

—*Margaret Gaffney*

The Edge In Sight

I'm on the inside looking out,
my sight is taken away by doubt.
How do I drain these empty dreams,
while I'm falling apart at the seams.

   Wish you could take it away,
   this silence,
   if not I cannot stay,
   I will cleanse... my life.

I have taken it all since youth,
just now that self destruction induced.
All the promise I'd ever shown,
is now muffled to this hollow groan.

   Wish you would take it away,
   this violence,
   if not I will not stay,
   I'm past tense... goodbye.

Once I lay in that fatal womb,
already their well constructed tomb.
Stare as their blows had struck me well,
now resulting in that empty shell.

—*Nathanael J. Spann*

Inner Beauty

   Don't judge me by my appearance
     My treasures are held within
       Behold what you might find
       And discover what I may send
Absorb my knowledge and hold my beauty
     To create a ring of gold
     Pleased to quench your desire
   To discover what my mind beholds

—*Shaunda M. Betts*

The Horizon

Far away on the horizon
nearing twilight time,
I can see the edge of darkness
begin its long and lazy climb.
Reaching to the heavens this
mysterious gloomy shade
will slowly veil the world and
all the things that God has made.

—*Mary E. Lytton*

At Juvenile Detention

Children on the wayward road,
needing a tender touch
with a firm hand.
Who will give it to them?
The attorney?
Who listens, questions, sympathizes
for 30 minutes?
The Judge?
Who questions for 30 minutes,
then imposes sentence?

Is it a Badge of Courage
to be
part of the crowd?
Is it courage
to pay for mistakes
you've made?
How deep are the emotions?
Who is repentant?
See the mother's cry.

—*Ruby Vernon Stull*

Untitled

She is silent
Nervous thoughts
Wandering eyes
random placement of her hands
toying with hair

She is frightened
No niche to fit
Where does she go?
I don't know
I don't know

She is unknowing
the world has no rank
no segregation
no qualifications

The world is me
The world is we
She has no world

—*Reginald Rodriguez*

Revolutions

Changes always come around
New beginnings
Coming full circle
Revolving through time

Repeating the rhythm
Of birth and death
In and through all things
Of substance and idea

Circles of repetition
Acting on life
As well as inert
Adding conscience to dirt

—*Steve Krucker*

God's Perfect Child

  I know she was a perfect child,
No blemish on her could ere be found.
Her sea green eyes, her golden hair,
As bright as sunshine, a child so fair.
  So full of life, so full of love.
    God gave her to me-from above
    I had her for a little while.
  It made my life to see her smile.
  She was so funny, full of glee.
T'was everything she meant to me.
I prayed each day she would be safe.
As she wandered from place to place.
  A perfect child, so close to me,
  But she was God's not mine you see.
He took her back and gave her wings.
With angels above and Him she sings.
  He opened up His heavenly door.
  God's perfect child-forevermore.

—*Marie E. Grant*

Impressions At Vicksbury

Blue skies, still, blue and serene,
No echoes of bugle nor cannon.
Ghosts lie silent and sleeping
Their fears and tears in times keeping
Forgotten the blood, sweat, and fear.
Of what lay ahead, but wasn't clear-
Stones stand where one fell
The message not much to tell
The lad of nineteen, far from home
To end a very short life, a life unknown.

—*Louise Carroll*

Splash Of Color

There was a little spaceship,
No larger than my hand.
On vivid wings of scarlet
I watched it safely land.

I climbed up the mountain;
Went down the other side.
I searched in every crevice,
Where someone small might hide.

My eyes swept the winding valley
Where twisting paths wound.
I listened intensely for
Some whispered sound.

I called, "come out, little one;
Teach me of your ways,"
I quickly turned about and met
His searching gaze.

I couldn't understand him,
But right where we stood,
We clasp our hands in friendship;
And sealed the bond of brotherhood.

—*Tilda S. Akers*

Subpoenaed

I revel in the thought that I am
No longer immortal
Taken for granted, all these years
Especially in the younger days
Tormented by nothing but the sun
Disappearing into the horizon
And the distant ring of the
Black horseshoe chiming through
Autumn air, summoning
The end of play, another
Caustic yet reassuring reminder
Of moments yet to come and the
Subsequent sleep that gives
Reason for waking.

—*William Santos*

Peace

Peace is what we all need,
no matter who we are.
To love one another,
Whether it is near or far.

Peace is a small word,
But it means a lot.
To all of us whatever,
It has brought.

Peace can be beautiful,
If we all get along.
It makes us all happy,
It makes the world strong.

Peace is what we are,
All looking for.
We don't want to
Be in a war.

Peace is all we
Are asking for.
It doesn't matter if,
We are rich or poor.

—*Margaret L. Rodkey*

The Satin Bed

Just knowing you are forever gone
no more on earth to be
has left a space of emptiness
that hovers roundabout me

My cherished mother the sweetest face
a child could ever see
just closed her eyes with one last smile
then died so quietly

I stood beside "the satin bed"
where she lay in final rest
kissed her cheek for one last time
then placed a rose upon her breast

She looked so regal lying there
like a queen, she lay in state
a vision of tranquility
even death could not erase

Tired and weary for life was long
earthly trials here are past
"God" in his infinite mercy and love
gently took her home at last.
—*Wanda E. Pellonini*

Go Through Life

No where to run
No where to hide
About to go crazy
But still I'm alive
Looking both ways
From left to right
Getting my way through
This most beautiful life
It's just like a maze
So find your way through
And once you make it out
Something wonderful
Will be waiting for you!
—*Sally A. Lane*

Guidance At The Light

Sleep softly, whisper not a word,
Not a sound shall escape, not a breath will seep.
Close thy eyes, those that will never open,
In a dream you shall wake, cloudiness you will see.
Open arms will greet you, in heaven you will be.
For dear child I will be near with the open arms you seek.
—*Teresa Sanderson*

Mood

To think of blues and lovely things
  of heather maybe?
To feel the sun as day begins.

To feel the shade of big old trees
  a soft breeze may be?
It's not only what one sees —

To smell the flowers of perfume
  roses maybe?
It's hard to tell, I just assume.

To hear the fast small bustling flutter
  birds flying maybe?
I could be wrong - it does not matter
—*Mary Van Kuyk*

Never Alone Will Two

Two ships passing in the night
    Not knowing
    Not showing
    Any sound or sight

  Waves crashing
  Heaven's gods clashing
  Fiery white bolts
  Of lightning light

One will find safe haven
But never alone will two
One or both stranded in
  Mournful destiny's rue

Two ships passing in the night
    Not knowing
    Not showing
    It's True
—*Mark A. MacLaughlin*

Wanting To Move On

We went our separate ways
Not my choice to make
I see you now and again
It all seems so fake.

One minute things were fine
The next you shut me out
I still don't understand
What was it all about.

I think I've done quite well
Some nights I feel the hurt
Most nights I think about it
Knowing it could've worked.

I'll never know if you regret it
I'd like to think you do
We had something so special
And now it's through.
—*S. Lewis*

My Mom

Truly my Mom is quite a gal;
Not only a friend but also a pal.
She listens to me when I'm feeling blue;
And she always smiles and lets
  her love through.
In all the world there never will be.
As great a Mom as God gave me.
—*Rachel A. Wallace*

To A White Birch

Hail! to thee O tree of majesty,
Of beauty unsurpassed in all
of arboretum.
Of stately, spiraling branches
looking up to heaven in quest
of answers to all being.

In spring and summer fully
Clothed you are nature's
perfection.
In autumn purest gold adorns
your stately form
In winter bereft all
attire you are still queen of trees
Regal without a crown.
—*Lois M. Riegler*

The Mind Of Poetry

There sings the beauty
of a farther knowledge
There howls the screams
of raw reality

That all of whom create,
as such
and know beneath
of what I speak,
are too, blessed-
of the vision you hold;
And tortured-
of the realities you see.

You inhabit this mind,
You are the poet
... gilden of wisdom,
unaware
of the mind's atrocity.
—*Laura Joy Lustig*

Incoming - Ongoing

At night he still fights battles
    of a now forgotten war.
    He's yesterdays hero,
      not needed anymore.

  Memories that haunt him
    and give him no nights peace.
  He drinks the beer and whiskey
    and prays for a release.

  His family has left him;
    his friends there are but few.
  Not too many can stand by him
  with the pain he's put them through.

  Why did he survive the death
    so many had to face?
  Only to find he's allowed his life
    to fall in such disgrace.

What happened to the proud young boy
    who too soon became a man?
Whose life has never progressed far,
  since the day he left Viet Nam.
—*Sharon H. Hendricks*

Memories Of Woolton Woods

I lay on the hill and hear the drone,
of an aeroplane returning home,
the sun is warm upon my face,
I hear children laughing, having a race.
The grass I lay on smells so sweet,
a bee is buzzing round my feet.
My mother's voice is calling me,
to picnic on sandwiches and tea.
I wish that I could go back then,
when I was just a child of ten.
—*Veronica Joyce Moore*

Firenze

There is a thin line
  of blue haze
  laying on the city.

Ancient Gods would simply
  thread it to a spool
  and wind it up.
—*Luce*

A Friend in Jesus

When the angels pull the curtain
of day and pin them with a star
just remember you have a friend
in Jesus where ever you are.

—*Lela Thurman*

Untitled

Do you know the origin
Of my disease
Can you feel the pain
That makes me drop to my knees
Not a pain so physical
But one so damn real
Can you understand
The way I always feel
Look into my eyes
Tell me what do you see
Do you see the pain
Do you see the real me
I bet you only see
The shallow outer shell
Can you get inside
To my self-inflicted hell
If I were to confide in you
Could you comprehend
Is your mind open enough
To catch the message I'd send

—*Randy K. Stracuzzi*

Bright Or Dark Windows

The eyes are the windows
of the soul: what do
I see through your eyes?
Abiding love on the look
that deceives me.
That look that makes my heart
to pant - my lips to yearn
my eyes to reveal that you are
my hearts desire.
I cannot hide it but can you?
I can't ever deny it but can you?
My eyes are the windows of
my soul, they reflect your own.
Your heart and soul are they
bright or dark windows?
The candles of life and love
often go out, the tragedy is
when one goes before the other.

—*Mary N. Dees*

Thinking

I've been thinking now and then,
Of the time my life began,
  Long ago,
Of the good years that have passed,
And which one will be the last
  That I'll know.

And if I should live so long,
That there's not one note of song,
  In my heart,
Then I hope, without a sigh,
I will smile, and say goodbye,
  And depart.

—*Wilma V. Deyo*

Always On My Mind

Thinking of you just because...
Of the ways you always help me
And the way you're always there
For the little things you do and say
That let me know you care;
For the intimate moments we shared
And the way you held me tight
For the times you took care of me
And made everything alright;
For the times you make me happy
When I am feeling low and blue
For the times you've comforted me
Make me love you the way I do.
These are some of the reasons
I think of you as much as I do.
They are all little reminders
Of how much I really love you.

—*Tina M. Rapczak*

A Farewell Salute

Evoking fond memories
Of your happier times,
This verse reminiscent
To you I present
For all those years when you
Did understand me:
I should not forget —
And so I haven't.

As venture you into
Your retirement years,
Just "bon voyage!", Bob,
Seems not enough. So,
May you "now, voyager,
Sail thou forth to
Seek and find" life's
Most marvelous glow!

—*Peter Brown*

Daddy

Father, I miss you
Oh, can't you see
That while you're gone
Something happens to me.

I cannot explain it
Though you know it to be true
It only happens
When I'm not with you.

Oh, daddy, you should see me now
I know you will find
I have found someone new
And very, very kind.

I still love you
Though you're not around
But your love for me
Was never, ever found.

—*Victoria H. East*

Love Says It All

Love is joy and I have joy today.
Joy is the key to love and love
is the key to life, life is the
key to hope and hope is the
key to love, love is the key to
every door, to keep us together
and happy. That's why love says
it all.

—*Tykari Blackmon*

Good Memory Recall Room

  We had them here for a while;
Oh! How great it is to love a child.
  But time moves on,
And too soon they are gone.

  We do have something to possess -
Their sweet memories to redness
  Found in pictures of each child,
When we visit for awhile.

  We cannot go back in time
Not even to seek a pleasing rhyme;
  But our vision of them is there
For we can see them everywhere.

—*Marshall W. Abernathy*

Love Is Here

Love is here,
Oh just look around you,
And listen to what it's saying

Love is here
It's in every town too,
but not in every man

Dreams, they will never come true
Without that glow of love from you.
For as long as love can do
Then you'll have a chance - want you?

Love is here
Such joy, such power
It's how the world began

Love is here just like a flower
Hold on to heaven's hand

Hold your head up towards the sky
Don't let love just pass you by
Soon, someday we all must die
Until then, give love (life) a try.
...Love is life

—*Willie T. Edmonds*

Rest

In a quiet moment
on a quiet day
Only the clock
was ticking
And this heart
of mine was beating
And I though
of days gone by
Friend I lost
who could not stay
So I tap my fingers
on the desk
And think of those
that are now at rest.

—*Ned Wells*

Nature Prevails

No famous face casts a glow
on frozen snow
No glamour exceeds green hills
and tinkling rills
No greatness lingers near
probation
No finish won by any nation
Time is not found out
Form cannot replace the heart.

—*McNeill Thomas*

You Are My Reason To Live

The floor you walk
on I praise and,
The bed you sleep on
I cherish and,
The kiss you gave me
I will never lose.
For you are my life.
No one can give me what
you have, a reason to live.
You are my inspiration,
You are my life.
Do I not only love being,
your wife.
I love being your lover, and,
your best friend.
You are my life,
You are my reason to live.
I could not of made it with out you,
for you are my friend.

—Stefanie Miller

Rainfall And Tears

Rain falls -
On rooftops, trees, plants and flowers.
Rain falls -
Refreshing, cooling, cleansing.

Tears fall from broken spirits -
Are they equal to the tears of heaven?

Certainly -
Washing away sadness and grief,
They are humanity's rainfall.
But please Lord - make them brief.

—Raymond J. Winieski

Alone

I said I was sorry
Once before
But you did not listen
You did not care about me
So now I walk alone
Miles away
And am lost without you
Did you forgive me?
I do not know
For I do not see you
Anymore.
From that day on
I could not resist
The feeling
Of running away.

—Lauren Melso

A Poet

Poetry the way I see it,
or should I say,
the way I sometimes vision myself.

A poet's mind, wisdom in thought
yet not always understood.
A poet's soul, a silver lining
yet not always recognized.
A poet's heart, full of wealth
knowledge of love and pain.
A poet's body, content
to live life day by day.
A poet's pocket, empty of coins
yet the hope still remains.

—Lana Tremblay

Jehovah Dreams

A thought came unto him;
  One of spectacular possibilities.
Where shall this great undertaking
  begin?
He possessed no books or pictures.
Young was he in his knowledge, but
  old was he in his wisdom.
He knew the truths that would be
  laid forth, but what of the
  substance? Where shall it be
  born?
And within his holy words did the
  answer come to be,
  "A grain. A grain shall be my
  my guide; for whomever shall
  know my light, shall know
  my dream."

—R. G. Rickey

Nothing

There is nothing,
Only darkness,
There is nothing,
Only fear,
Not knowing what'll happen,
I'm scared when you're not near.
I feel empty,
Something's missing,
When you're gone,
And we're not kissing.
When I'm empty, when you're gone,
I try to figure out what went wrong,
So confused, as alone,
Won't you please just come home.
But then again who wants or needs you?
All you do is fight and fuss!
In response to loving words,
You just shout and pout and cuss!
Let me go, set me free
Won't you please let me be!

—Liza Fam

Country Side

Country side
Open fields filled with pride;
Empty sky open wide;
Smell of spring,
Lonely road heads far from home,
Old American cars under the stars
A bird flying that I can see,
This place is a part of me.
The day closes, night approaches
Under the oak tree which I sleep,
The full moon contemplates over me.

—Melissa Marie Galiga

What Is A Poet?

Is it someone who repeat a lot
Or changes a thing for their own
liking. What is a poet? A good
speaker or a good writer or is a
poet one who feel all???

—Min Whitelove

Shadows

I'm a shadow hear me cry
or my tears will soon die
faded memories faded plights
that's the shadows in my life.

—Khela Long

There's A Side Of Me

There's a side of me no one sees
or really knows of.

A side that thinks of wild, thoughtful,
intellectual stuff.

I guess I'm afraid of this side, afraid
of being an intellect.

Or maybe I like this side of
me best, I try not to project.

This side likes romantic films, making
love on the beach.

But then I see the side I am,
and it's so far out of reach...

Maybe someday I can grow into,
and be this side of me.

But until then I have to
keep it hidden, no one must ever see...

—Shelley Childs

Moments Beyond

Beyond the shackles of my soul,
  or the chains that bind my mind,
There still are moments in my life
  that no one could match in kind

Beyond the splintered spirit,
  or the body lean and frail,
There still are moments in the world
  that set my life asail

Beyond the fragments of my heart,
  or the loneliness beyond compare,
There still are moments in my life
  that I am proud to wear

Beyond the disappearing passion,
  or belief in myself or man,
There still are moments in my life
  that let me know 'I can'

Beyond the mundane, futile feelings,
  with just one flick of my magic wand,
I am able to enjoy my life. . .
  and forever keep going beyond!

—Margo Braer

Margaret

I can't draw, I can't paint
  or write
I need talent to still fear
  in the night
No longer do I try - I think
  I'm too old.
Then I visit Margaret and
  I'm told
She can't write — her hands tremble
She can't paint and can't remember
I sign her cards, I wash her teeth
  and then go home
I'm so talented.

—Suzanne Christian

To A Physician

A scientist, the conductor of the orchestra,
the leader of the flock.
May wisdom and guidance be companions.
May the Lord be the shepherd.

May the music be of fine precision,
to be read as well as heard.
May the conductor be blessed,
for his task is not as easy as it seems.

—*Sally Hollen*

All My Love Goes To....

All my love goes to my best friend
Our love will never end
She is my heart
She is the start of happiness
She has the kindness of nobody else
But it is bad,
That she hardly ever things of herself.
She is as beautiful as a rainbow
She is so cool yo!
She is like no other,
Did you know
That she is my mother.

—*Nicole Fulmino*

"He Died For Me & He Died For You"

When we think of all the
pain that rips us apart,
Just remember that Jesus Christ
is in our heart.

for Jesus is there to take care
of you,
and add life to a world of blue,

No matter what the hardship or
great the loss,
Just leave your pain at the
foot of the cross

When you think of all the
pain and suffering Jesus went through,
   Just remember he died for
me and he died for you.

—*Todd Anthony*

Untitled

Empathy for the creator
passion for the poison that
creates the seance.

Your beauty is such a surprise
It anticipates me and moves
me miles.
Your love is my life
- the water that sustains me
- the poison that kills thee.
Experience this vision quest
Ride on virgin senses.
Tingling with anticipation.

I once saw the first time
the Earth was born.
I understand the greatest
Art-piece in progress
A masterpiece in the making.
(Sometimes images are wars of illusion)

—*Michael Christian Rudar*

Close To You

A sweaty razor
Penetrates your defense
On a languid Monday mourning:
The obscure eroticism
Of the lemming blood
Diving into the basin
Stroking impressionism
Upon the flecked formica.

The first stroke fondles
Your erect skin;
Goosepimples, ecstatically shiver
Under the whipping soft caress
Of the lascivious hand
Behind your voyeur's eyes.

—*J. Dylan Beals*

Racial Harmony

Racial harmony is caring for
   people different from you
Racial harmony is loving for
   different kinds of colors too.
Racial harmony is beautiful
   that's why God created me
   and you.
So be in harmony with all
   different colors that's my
   message to you.

—*Luz Michelle Guerra*

Untitled

Pick offs provide outs
Pick offs prevent steals
Pivot creates surprises,
Jump gives pop on the throw,
Pivot-Jump-Surprise

—*Noah Wilson*

Tolerance

If I am black
Please don't stand back

If I am brown
Please let me hang around

Because I am not white
That doesn't make me not right

If I make a mistake
Please forgive me for my sake

I try to do my best
Just like the rest

Just give me a chance
Despite my happen-stance

Judge me by my character
And not by my caricature

—*Nicholas J. Kayganich*

Rain

Pennies from heaven.
Rain is good for the grass,
   the lawns
and good for the gardens
vegetable or flower.
Rain brings the flowers up.

—*Robert Ewing*

Happiness

Home is where the heart is,
Poets have always told us so.
It's where our hearts are happy.
And contentment rules our souls.

Happiness isn't lovely mansions
Or palaces in Spain.
It can be a small apartment
With dusty window panes.
Happiness we carry with us.
It cannot be bought or sold.
It comes with years of caring
For another, young or old.

So, if you search for happiness,
It's not found in silver or gold.
Help some needy person,
It's sure to heal your soul.

Happiness lies within us.
Loving others is the seed that grows.
Giving and loving and caring,
Bring happiness to two souls.

—*Mary Parks*

Dissolving Revolving

Poverty, war, poverty-score.
Preordained, foreordained-re-ciprocal
unto Rain-drops on-
she roof-top-falling-falling-
into everlasting-dream-through-
she clouds-from-Africa-to-
Russia and Kingdoms far-
away pain remains to stay -
Disconling, revolving, in
our-lives-through-out-
the day. Cry's that stain
the brain, frowns on-the
Somilian face by year-to-
year we live to see -
the disgrace. Poverty -
war and conflict

—*Lamar K. Mallery*

Old Secrets

Leaves fly over the porch
Pushed lightly by the wind
It whistles through the floor
Whispering stories of old friends

The wood is still strong
On this old porch
The night is cool
The wood no longer scorched

Because this house
Is very old
It holds the stories
of love untold

It knows of babies
Born beneath its roof
The love that was shared
the living proof

And though these secrets
May never be told
You can feel them
Deep in your own soul

—*Shay Crocker*

Ashes To Ashes

The wind blows softly around me,
Pushing, ruffling, sniffing but
Doesn't recognize me as the
Woman it passed many years ago.

I have aged and mellowed.
I am ripe and fragrant,
Rejecting subterfuge and lies,
Refusing pettiness and deceit.

Aware that my life is better.
Travelling light, I jettison
Anything that is not desperately
Needed for the time.

My body has a thousand wrinkles,
All of them channels and valleys of
Thoughts, images, sorrows and laughter
I have allowed to come through my skin.

I have come to grips with life.
Realizing finally that our sadnesses,
Joys and everything in between
Are what makes us who we are.

—*Lita Trent Dorman*

The Dawn Of Reality

Not long before where answers were,
Questions run throughout my mind.
Dissatisfactions' embers stir,
Contentment lost, I cannot find.
Illusionary visions cleared,
from dewy eyed naivete.
Where reality, desperately feared,
was gently touched by truth today.
A tempting suggestion,
a turmoil within.
A well thought out question,
the way to begin.
What was once so uncluttered,
will be again.
With windows unshuttered
the light can come in.
The forever night ending,
a new dawn is breaking.
A life of pretending,
from slumber, awakening.

—*Linda Romano-Colepaugh*

Eastward Breeze

The eastward breeze blows
  quickly through the trees
And gently but firmly
  awakens all it sees
Alone in the green, green valley
  a young woman her lover awaits
The night comes, ever silently,
  and she wonders about the fates
Granting her a love so true
  yet she wonders if he feels it too
"I only have one question, dear,
  do you love me, as I love you?"

Waiting for him here all alone
  there is so much she finally sees
And she is quietly awakened
  by the eastward breeze.

—*Nancy D. Simpson*

Worm Massacre

Soft crashing
rain and slimy-slink
drown human ears with
springtime pleasure.

Seeping from drenched dirt homes
attacking the shining
asphalt desert.

Smiling away their hearty
lives in the instant
of suffocation.

Squished by the
sole of
thoughtless human
supremacy.

Squirmers have
ten hearts.
Humans one.

—*Susan Sarvis*

Under The Lion's Paw

Shade drawn as one empty raincoat
Against weeping waves of heat;
Crawling, suffer not simply we
The acid past of our day of days
Pressed onward, steamed,
Set vast the sails for keeps.
Under the sun
Without raunch and breakfast,
To paw, teeming frets and nails,
Immune behind a grill of irony
Unknown beneath a consuming
  roar.

—*SC Seatter*

Untitled

Ever growing older
Reaching towards the heavens
Weathering life's storms
Battling life's wars
Still standing after it's over
We grow stronger through it all
That is what life is.

—*Lori Schneider*

Another Day

Dawn, the sky is fire all aglow
Reddish orange-purple and blue
Birds flying across the horizon low
The grass glistens with sparkling dew

A cool breeze caresses the skin
Aromas of nature impress the nose
The leaves of autumn slowly bend
The pleasures of life surely grows

Say sky, sun, and breeze if you can
Oh the joy, no illusions or dismay
Completeness of nature is at hand
The cycle of life for another day

Greeted by the lights of early morn
The value of life passes my way
Uneasiness within no longer scorn
Thankfulness abound for another day

—*Lawrence R. Boswell*

Untitled

Sun immense and red
Reflecting on the Gulf's calm
Spreads silent shadows.

—*Sally G. Cook*

The Leaf And The Rose

A cloudless day with sunny sky
Reminds me of the day gone by,
When hand in hand we strolled the park
And felt like children on a lark.

A five star leaf fell to the ground,
You picked it up and turned around
And placed it in my hand to see,
I held it very tenderly.

I brought it home and placed it right
Inside a book and closed it tight,
For if our love was not to be,
I'd have a cherished memory.

Today I looked inside and saw
The golden leaf without a flaw,
And gently, so the book would close,
Beside it, I had placed a rose.

—*Mary Teska*

The Statue In The Park

Warm summer moonlight
  rests on her cold marble breasts
    flaming ancient love.

Soft rain at daybreak
  drips from trees and tranquil tears
    fill her hollow eyes.

—*Sunny Rivera-Reyes*

Autumn's Fantasy

The breeze is gentle and kind
Rich colors from yellow to wine
  Enjoy me.
May there be a reflection of me
  in your wardrobe

On canvass paint me, then my beauty
  will not be lost.
In your song, sing about me
  There, sentiment is felt.

In your sleep, dream of me
That on waking, your thoughts
  are refreshed...
  Time is fleeting,
  I am only here for
  a little while.
So with tenderness,
  Embrace me.

—*Mattie H. Thompson*

Life Reigns

I once had a sister -
she once had me

Through her eyes, I saw
through mine, saw she

Life took away -
what life gave to me

I once had a sister -
She once had me

—*Rhonda R. Bennett*

Brothers Killing Brothers

Brothers killing brothers
Right and left
Each day there's another
Unfortunate death
Brothers killing brothers
With each passing time
There would never be another
Another of their kind
Brothers killing brothers
With no concern at heart
Not even considering
The other being apart
Brothers killing brothers
With no shame or guilt
Just taking lives of others
Not thinking of the lives they built
Hoping to win
We kill one another
When will we put an end
To brothers killing brothers
—*Shakira Jones*

Forsaken Freedom

I have seen my freedom dying
Right before my very eyes
I've heard politician's lying
While the homeless baby cries

And wandering the gang filled streets
The youth that make tomorrow
Gather where the drug lords meet
Despite their mother's sorrow

And nothing just one soul can do
To make it all be better
No remedies like cold or flu
Or putting on a sweater

We have to find a better way
Before it is too late
To stop this social mind decay
That turns love into hate

One thing we should remember
As we stand to face the night
Our freedom's burning embers
Are worth just one more fight
—*Renee Rowley Breedlove*

Heart To Heart

Lord, I feel so alone when I can't hear,
Rise up, my child, Jesus said,
Receive my word, and be fed,
Listen to your heart instead.

Listen to your heart, dear child,
Jesus, your Savior, on you has smiled,
On the cross your name has been filed
Thus, by Satan be not beguiled.

Lord, speak to my heart, I need Thee so,
More of Thee I long to know;
Jesus speaks in cadence low and clear,
"I am the way, and I am near."
—*Minnie Herman*

The Mighty River

See her scream and dance near the
river.
It rushes so violently,
filled with eternal passion,
see that in her eyes.
She is I, wanting to joint the river.
Desire to dive.
Yet stopped, by gentle hand.
He pulls me close as I fall
in arms of heaven,
down to the earth.
Laughter echoes on the banks,
hear the mighty river.
—*Tisha Anne Caruso*

My Child

Little girl with flying feet
Running swiftly down life's street
If your progress I could stay
Keep you happy here at play
Oh I wonder, would you be
Content to always stay with me
Would your active restless mind
Always ample solace find
In a mother grown old and gray
Or yearn for youths joy
At a too late day
—*Mary E. Moreland*

1972

A midnight walk down the country road
   ruts made deep by the jeep
   horses hoofs and people's feet
     and I place one foot
     in front of the other
     walking, not disturbing
   the sleeping deer or the colts
     nursing from the mares
   all of nature is in balance
     as I stop and sit
   in a horse trough to watch
     the moon become full
   and scorpius chase his tail
     not looking back I rise
     and walk further down
   the country road, waiting
for tomorrow and the beginning
   of the Summer Solstice
as all of nature is in balance.
—*Mark Walters*

Untitled

  Be mine, mine I say.
  Say is mine. Do you say?
Let go of my thinks they say
    can you believe?!
  Be mine mine I say -
  Do this if you are mine
    say say-
      let me go
      be mine
        or
    Die doing so.
    e say e say.
—*Maria Daigle*

Forlorned

Forlorned, the body turned away
Saddened by the city worker's
Destroying his meager belongings
Hollow cheeks
Below his sunken eyes
His stomach rumbled
With hunger pains
The body shivered
As the night winds blew
He shoved his hands into his pockets
Heading in an unknown direction
He walked for hours in the cold
Suddenly like an omen from heaven
He saw the church on the corner
As he trodded up the steps
Leading to its opened doors
His hopes surmounted
As his bare feet touched its wooden floors
Times can only get better
He had been told, many times before.
—*Norma E. White*

Moon Rise

Behind the towering
   sandstone cliff
   rises an ashen moon
Massaging the landscape
   while I doze

Moon shadows
   blanket me with swirling
   sand and grit
The desert floor absorbs
   my weariness

Ears listening
   for the heartbeat
   of earth and time
As a sandy pillow comforts
   my heaviness

Fatigue, abraded by dust,
   erupts past soaring
   canyon walls
Adding polish
   to the moon
—*Linda Van Wagenen*

Wicked In The Garden

Something wicked
Scarlet darkness
The dark camellias
Waxen
Dark grass, and burly boxwood
Something wicked
Crepe myrtles kissing
Hollyhock so tender
Dark and moving shadows
Slick and serpent blackness
A figure in the darkness
His eyes they blaze like forge
Soul a depthless Quagmire
Something surely wicked
Can't you feel the darkness growing
Slowly tis' your blood to flowing
He is all around you
Here's the heart of Hell
Here in his perdition
Here the garden swells
—*Richard J. Mann*

Me And The National Deficit

So many things aren't working,
seems we're in a terrible spot.
So many things take millions
   and billions of dollars
     we haven't got.
   Somebody do something,
     do it quick!
   Balance the budget,
     cut programs.
   Which? Take your pick,
     just don't touch
     the one I guard
     with my voting stick.
Solve the problem otherwise,
don't ask me to economize.
   Things could change
   with an economic plan, sir,
     just don't count on me
     to be part of the answer.
       —*Velma Cozzutto*

Reflections

All is very quiet here peaceful and serene
Another day has ended time now to dream
To dream of children far away brings
sadness to the heart
To dream of parents so long gone who
loved us from the start
Ah life what is your message
Are we here for naught
The passing time will have the answer
To all the questions sought
       —*Loretta De Rosso*

Miss Daisy

When Miss Daisy gets her pay
she goes to the horse races
every week-end in May
She bets all her money
on "Johnny eats hay"
One day her horse will win
and she will buy a diamond or two
or a big yellow hat to wear to the zoo
Today is Sunday and Church has begun
but you won't find her there
she's having too much fun
betting on a horse that's #1
       —*Lorelie Nedevick*

Missing You

Although it's been a while
Since I last made you smile
You must believe it's true
That I truly care for you
Although it's been sometime
Since we last shared love
I thank my stars above
For someone as true as you
You came into my life
Without hesitation
We got to know each other
through crazy communication
I wouldn't doubt
as sure as I can be
That you I can't live without.
       —*Phyllis R. Ware*

Lost Ophelia

Ophelia was a good daughter.
She lost her lover.
I weep for her.

Lovely maid Ophelia,
Dreaming through the misty waters,
Singing your little song
To the drooping branches
That reach out
To drown you
In your singing.
I weep for you.

I lost an Ophelia once,
Only daughter, began in love
But never finished.
Somewhere do you wander
In the mists of time?
Singing and making flower wreaths
And floating down the stream.
I weep for you.
       —*Norma Aletha Adams*

His Prize

I want to write the perfect poem,
she said one day to me,
It has to be a special poem
for all the world to see.

It has to cheer the weary,
and it has to dry sad eyes,
It just can't be any poem,
This poem must take the prize.

She sat down so pensively,
and with her pen in hand,
She knew the words would come to her,
they'd be at her command.

Her hand moved with inspiration,
feeling guidance from above,
"The only perfect poems, dear child,
are in my Book of Love.

As a poet I will guide you,
With words divine and true,
Perfection cannot be obtained,
but I will walk with you."
       —*Ruth A. Patrick*

21201

I didn't think I'd like her
She was the least attractive
   in the neighborhood
Neat inside and dependable
   but outside
Not looking the way she should.

Coming home to her on cold days
Was a joy to behold
This was what I could expect
Even when she was getting old.

Finally, she was left with others
And suffered horrible abuse
Trying to repair the damage
Just seemed of little use.

Now she has a new owner
Is he treating her just fine?
I really worry about her-
This house that I called mine.
       —*Roellen Stoerr*

Exile

Tears
shed and shed
not even a single death
what a miserable life
in exile
if
blood spilled
perhaps many men killed
but
they're definitely worth while.
       —*Thanh Nguyen (Houston, TX)*

The Star of Bethlehem

The star of Bethlehem
   shining above
Leading men so wise
   to Eternal Love;
And those of long ago
   heard a voice from within
Saying, follow the Star
   to One, born free of sin.

This Star guiding all
   who follow their lead
Find the Way to their
   own Eternal Love seed.
Jesus is born this day
   in the hearts of all mankind.
And we, too, find the Star
   searching the heavens of our mind.
       —*Paul D. Gray*

Best Friends

Best friends
Shouldn't copy your trends
They should be
true to you

They should try to understand
What you're going through
They should never steal
A guy from you
They should be nice to you

They should try
to stick with you
no matter what you say or do
they should be honest
with you

They should trust you
no matter what you do
or what they're going through
       —*Rani Goldsborough*

Fun In The Sun

Lying in the sun
   Sipping rum
Oh boy! am I having fun.

Crowded beaches
   Sandy feet
Beach ball dodgers
   Lots of laughters
Oh beautiful island in the sun
   Sipping of rum
Oh boy, am I having fun
       —*Suhailah Beyah*

U.S. Applebyrm

Uriah Sam Applebyrm ran a mile,
   showered down,
   ate some bran,
   went to town.

Uriah Sam had a date,
   strings, white wine, cherry flambe',
   bussed her adieu,
   then puffed some hay.

Went to church on Sunday morn,
   croaked out a chorus,
   canned a prayer,
   cocked an eye at Boris.

U.S. Applebyrm clocked in next day,
   straight into the bowels of belly-el,
   now he jogs in molten pitch
   and gnashes his teeth like hell.
—*Richard Hoover*

Some Tomorrow

Slowly, the housing called my body
   sighed deeply and ceased to be.
That which was me, transformed
   into a free floating entity.
The galaxies are my stepping stones.

I use the moon as a ball
   to play jacks with the stars,
I swirl with the vapors of the universe,
   like once on earth.

On clear nights you have only
   to look up to feel me,
I'm all around you - can't you see?
   like once on earth,
I enter you each time you breath,
   now I am forever.
—*Rosemary T. Robinson*

Imagine That...

We have been friends
since I was eight;
They were my comfort
and even my fate;

When reality was tough
They were my only escape;
A world of my own,
then things started to take shape;

I needed them in the morning
When I first wake;
I needed them in the evening
because I started to shake;

They warmed and soothed me
like I knew they would;
No more pain no more worry
even though I knew, that I should;

I would have been sixteen
If understanding hadn't lack;
Your friends are your worst enemy
Imagine that...
—*Liza Desir*

Dead Art

Tumbled stones dead spider webs
skeleton bones surround our heads
it has many faces
some of tin
Crunched and bent with its mangled grin
wrapped around a lamp post
embracing brick walls
Guts that kiss pavement
after a fatal fall
journey bound for sites unseen
slapped from reality or a movie reel
dream
A spine embraces cement as its maker
as brains flow down a sewer drain
still knowing of its own taker
—*Michael Recco*

Wild Things

Did you know that a lizard
sleeps with its head up!

It's neat how a Giant
Sequoia starts from a little
seed to a big tree!

It's neat how pretty birds chirp!

It's really neat how your body
works inside!

I wonder how God makes
Blue Bonnets!
It's neat how the ducks at
the pond don't run away when
I feed them!
It's nice how life is!
—*Marie Nicole Fjordholm*

Harmonized Bliss

From first ray of light, til twilights
   slumber dreams.

My world is enriched through Gods
   blessed gifts.

Each moment filled with harmonized
   bliss, each hour kept in memory.

Each season stored in victory of
   wondrous love embracing me.

As gentle hands guide me from
   this mortal land.

My seasons shall be victories, as
   shall my moments kept in memory.

Simple faith, and answered prayers
   give me proof of eternal care.

Being a child of God, I am born
   again in everlasting life.

And More Harmonized Bliss.
—*Pamela Sears Mitchell*

Space Placed at Center's Edge

A signature signed
small on the line space
small character tall.
As the hours glass sand sifts
life as a gift God
character tall.

The thoughts of Lola
—*Lola Hansell*

Sweet Song

So sweet the morning song.
So bright the light within.
This is how the melody
Of each day will begin.

Let the words flow.
Be swept from shore to shore.
Let the music carry you
Until you're sad no more.

Find the peace that's offered.
Find the eternal friend.
Don't let trouble overcome you.
Don't let the music end.

Take hold the tie that binds.
Let your sorrow go.
Place your feet on firm ground,
And let the music grow.
—*Lucy Barnett*

Dream

My dream day, the animals
so gay, will dance about their
merrily way.
   The sky is clear, I rain
a tender tear. So happy, so bright,
no darkness, no fear.
   Sunlight glares down on
me, flowers bloom under
an old twisted tree.
   The breeze is soft, a
herd of deer prances by. The
red birds nest, and the
eagles fly.
   Pure crystal water
rushes down a stream. I
wish it would last...
....But it's only a dream.
—*Natasha Curtis*

At Seventy-two

Wisdom comes with age they say,
   So I should know more and more
But as the years go by I find
   The less I know for sure.

I envy some who firmly state
   Their opinion as final word,
But some of the things I used to know
   I now find quite absurd.

I suppose I'll sit in my rocking chair
   If I live to be a hundred and four
Still wondering about so many things
   With questions and questions galore.
—*Marian T. Johnson*

Thoughts

The wind that blow's
So sweet through the leaves
Whispers, thou art with us.
The flowers that bloom.
Their order is like spring
They are always with us.
The sun that shines,
Smiles on us showing us the
ways of life.
And then the moon comes
Out at night to tell us,
God is right.
—*Lee Searcey*

For That Is The Way

We fall to rise
So it is said
So do not terry
Get out of your bed

The failure of yesterday
Is experience for today
So don't let despair
Lead you astray

You fail today
So you can succeed tomorrow
But only if you don't give in
To heart break and sorrow

A loss, a win, is
One in the same
One step after another
To finish the game

Listen to what I say
We fall to rise
For that is the way
—*Wanda Simpson*

Deception

Deception
So sweet,
So dangerous,
So tantalizing,
Delightful.

How long will it last?

Dreaming,
Scheming,
Laughing.

Does it have to end?

Deception.

Deception,
A circle
Which symbolizes
The gold wedding band
Around my finger.
—*Sonja Ann Keserica*

Motives

You wish to be impressive
So to others you are good.
Goodness is my sole intent
no motives understood.

These actions find the same result
each person well refined.
Both modes of kindness seem sincere
but goodness is goodness defined.

Affairs can be so falsely judged
in acts which meet one goal.
For truth lies in one's character
Where motives reveal the soul.
—*Patricia Ann Buckelew*

Unanswered Prayers

Ungranted prayers - they haunt us
  So we pray in utter fear
In hopes that He is listening
  With an eager open ear.
It seems that we do call on God
  In our selfish time of need
We expect Him to be listening
  To what we pray and plead
You must share with Him every day
  Of every give year
If you want Him to cleanse your soul
  And every shedded tear.
Though prayers they go unanswered
  In times of deep despair
It's because we don't have faith
  And know He's always there.
—*Rhonda S. Bailey*

Soldier Of Stone

You bravely marched to battle
Soldier of stone
But one in a herd of cattle
Yet all alone

And as the wounded lay around you
You heard them not
Nor did you hear the sound to retreat
Nor the bullets that you bought

Now your remains lay in a field
A million miles from home
Where bullets soon will fly no more
And grazing sheep will roam

But your loved ones had already lost you
Now they pray without a grave
Never to know the hell you suffered
the courage you displayed.
—*Raymond Maxwell*

Shelter

Let my soul find shelter elsewhere,
Some place where it needn't hide
Behind this mask of a body
Behind this facade of a mind.

Let my soul find shelter elsewhere,
Where all possible dreams come true
Where my body language isn't
Interpreted as orange or as blue

Let my soul find shelter elsewhere,
Amidst the future or the past
The present leaves it empty
Or more simply, leaves it aghast.

Let my soul find shelter elsewhere,
It's weary of this plane
A shelter where I can explore
Other probabilities without feeling insane.

Let my soul find shelter elsewhere,
With no more need to roam
It longs for its true companions
It longs for the quiet of its home.
—*Tracy Causey-Jeffery*

One And Only Heart

I need a heart to call my own
  Someone loyal and true
Someone who will stand by me
  Cheer me when I'm blue.

Give me strength to see life through
  With a smile and a hug
Believe in me and all I do
  Though outsiders may pull and tug.

I've tried in vein to find that heart
  That to me alone belongs
My life is passing quickly
  Soon I will be gone

When my maker I do see
  He'll take me in his arms
"Dear child for all your life
  This heart was yours to take
I waited and hoped
  It was your decision to make
Now we are together, never to part
Aren't you glad to finally find, that one and
only heart?"
—*Wendy Moritz*

Paradox

We were looking for a hero;
  Someone who could win the fight.
Finally, he came to us,
  and filled our hearts with light.

He taught us much
  For we were eager to learn.
We followed where he led
  and watched the pages turn.

Yet we sent him to his death
  For we lacked the vision.
We saved and damned ourselves
  With one swift decision.

We've spent many years in sorrow
  and pure regret.
Teaching others to remember
  While we tried to forget.

Our past was dark,
  But the future's still grim
'Cause after two thousand years,
  We're still shouting, "Crucify Him!"
—*Shaunathon Davids*

Memory

You are gone
  So far away
It seems you were
  here the other day
    Some knew you barely
And some knew you well
  A lot hurt right now
And a lot you can't tell
  You taught us a lot
About the person inside
  You showed us the person
With nothing to hide
Even though your face
  Never will we see
In each of our hearts
  Is your memory
—*Sharon Slade*

A Love That Never Goes Cold

We seem not to let each other go
Something strong holds us together
Love in each of us
Love that seems to last forever

Even though your not around
You end up in my dreams
My heart you make pound
My mind you make scream

I'm dead without you
I seem to be lost
You are the road to truth
I will have you at all cost

Some say it's not to be
What do they know
As sure as the sun rises in the east
So does our love grow

Your beauty overwhelms my eyes
Your spirit invades my soul
Your love for me a surprise
A love that never goes cold
—*Xavier Ovalle*

The Blues

The blues came knocking at my door
I tried to tell them, "I don't live here anymore"
But they just kept knocking at my door

We're just the blues, we won't stay long
We promise we won't do anything wrong
We'll stay awhile and then we'll be gone

So I opened the door and let them in
Okay, I said I guess you win
So slowly but surely those blues came in

When they entered my problems seemed to multiply
All I did was sit and cry
Everything's so awful, I don't know why

The blues decided to hang around all day
Wherever I went they got in my way
Didn't know what they wanted, they wouldn't say

As I sat in despair and looked at the hour
And seemed to wallow in my sorrow
I decided they could stay but they must go tomorrow
—*Ruth Nagy*

I Try To Remember

As my hands shake and my headaches,
    I try to remember
When my lips speak of tales,
    I try to remember
My legs stagger no where,
    I try to remember
My eyes are red, did they see the truth?
    I try to remember
My ears hear nothing,
    I try to remember
My heart is heavy, did I say those words?
    I try to remember
As I look at the bottle I cannot remember
Please, take my hand and cradle my head,
    And please God help REMEMBER.
—*Madelyn Brown*

True Friend

I cast a faint smile and lowered my eyes
I turned to walk away but to my surprise
I heard a soft, "hello," so I turned around
My eyes are no longer looking at the ground
We both reached out with a lonely hand to lend
Standing face to face we feel we have found a "true friend"

Hand in hand down the path our faces aglow
First we quicken our step then we go slow
Giggling girls looking for something to do
My friend kicks a pebble so I kick one too
We promise our friendship to the very end
Hand in hand we know we have found a "true friend"

To school, to parties we are together every day
Not once do we think of looking far away
Into the future into our life
When someday each of us will become a wife
With children of our own to care for and tend
And pray in their life they will find a "true friend"
—*Marylee Buerkle*

Awareness

I look at the tree. The brain brings the word, I remember...
I used to see a tree just like this as a girl in school. Now
the heart starts pounding, there is pain and anguish; The tree
no more there; there is only thought, and this feeling fear.
If I see the tree, and no word is there; no thought, and no
image recalling the past. Then I am all there; no pain and no
sorrow appear. But who is aware? Just the tree; no one. Can
I look today at that one who hurt me last week; and just see
his face, and do not remember the hurt? Then I look anew. His
face, and the tree are just there. Then I am aware, I can
really see. But I well remember the hurt of the past; and
looking at him note only my hurt; and although nearby, he is no
longer there; there is only anger, and pain. And who is this
one in front of the mirror? The sum of all memories from all
yesterdays. And that looks at life, the birds and the
prairies; and sees only images of long, long gone days. Could
I ever look at that which is here, and when thought arises,
just observe the thought: Watch how subtly rises, bringing
sorrow and fear, and see that this image is a shadow, a ghost..
And if I persist in watching the image each time it appears.
—*Olga Diner*

Memories

As I sit and watch the sun drift out of view,
I usually cry, and think of you,
I'm not embarrassed to show I cared,
About the friendship that we shared.
You were the best friend I've ever had,
A friend who helped,
Through good times, and bad.
You are a special friend,
We share a friendship I know will never end,
Because, although we've been pulled apart,
We both have a special place in each other's heart.
—*Liliana Mary Cabrera*

The Baseball Gardener

Yes dear, wait a minute, I'll do the outside work,
I want to watch our pitcher first, throw one past this "jerk."
Why does my wife's poor memory seem to remember better
All those jobs for me to do when there's a double-header?
No "ifs", "ands" or "buts", once she's made her decision
It doesn't matter a bit that the game's on television.
If only she would realize that knocking off the Cubs
Might be more important than trimming those darn shrubs.
Some day I may surprise her, she won't know what to think;
I'll pitch right in but won't tell her the TV's on the blink.
—*Robert E. Brazell, Ph.D.*

Grandma Can You Hear Me?

Tuesday night, ICU.
I.V.s beeping. Monitors alarming.
I love you Gram.
"I love you too."
Wednesday morning, stroke.
I love you Gram.
Silence.
I love you Gram, can you hear me?
The rise and fall of your chest tells me you can.
Monday afternoon, the call.
I love you Gram, can you hear me?
Your absolute breathlessness leaves me uncertain.
Raw pain, tears, rage.
Please come back to me.
An impossibility.
You are on the other side of the night sky,
A lifetime away - my lifetime away.
I love you Gram.
Can you hear me?

—*Margie Boyle*

Tenderness, Love And Devotion

I want to be your only one
I want to feel what your feeling
When you fall down I want to be
there with my hand held out helping you.
I want tenderness, love, and devotion.
I want to caress and stroke your tights gently
I want to give you a warm peck on the cheek
To let you know I care.
I want to walk right beside you, never
Behind you because I cannot compliment your beauty
I want to wake up in your arms with a
Safe and secure feeling
I want tenderness, love, and devotion
I want you to never feel you owe me anything
I want to love loving you
I want tenderness, love, and devotion...

—*Lynette Roberts*

But The Best Thing Of All

As I walked outside on a nice spring day
I was awakened by the sound of birds
Chirping and bees buzzing by.
Everything in sight was full of bloom:
The flowers, trees, and warm grass at my feet.
As I looked up into the sky
The sun's hot rays felt warm on my skin
But the best thing of all are the butterflies
They look so pretty as they fly around
   through the air,
so gracefully, without making a sound.

—*Michelle Weber*

As I Continue To Dream

As I lie here
I wish you were near
I can't believe you're gone
As I continue to dream on...

I wonder if our feelings are the same
An I hope we never forget each others name
You are the best thing that's ever happened to me
As I continue to dream free...

I hope our love for one another never dies
Similar to that a bird never forgetting how he flies
An in our hearts we will always be together
As I continue to dream forever...

—*Richie John Eggers*

To An Unknown Friend

I rode on his strong shoulders into the surf.
   I was no more than eight or nine.
   He carried me lightly into unbounded euphoria.

From my perch, I could see the coastline reaching to
   forever. My chest expanded with excitement.
   A high adventure - unspoken friendship -
      laughing without words.

I cried when we were back in the family car,
   ready to leave Daytona.
      Deep, uncontrolled tears for a companion
         whose name is lost to me now.

My father told me to be quiet.
   I choked back pain and tried to breathe
      and pretend that I was OK.
         But part of me had gone away with him.

I was alone. As alone as I could ever remember.

And then I cried once more.
   This time, quiet inner tears for a friend
      that I would never see again.

—*Terry Emerson Ward*

Baby Cries

I was the shadow, the shape of darkness in her heart.
I was the bad memory that she never forgot.
It was so long ago, and I painfully heard her sigh,
so today I visited my mother.

It was the beginning of November
the beginning of my life years ago.
The days passed on and in her womb,
I began to grow.

She didn't understand I suppose, that I now had a heart.
I had feelings by now and fingers, hands, and toes.
My brain developed and I could make a fist.
I felt so grand, for I began to expand.

When all in one day
It was taken away.
The wonderful feeling I had.
I felt such pain, and I began to slowly shrivel away.

My angel came and took me home,
to where I now lay
looking upon this person who is called
my mother, my murderer, who took my joy away.

—*Michele Cabana*

My Brother

My brother is a total dork,
I wish I could stab him with a fork.
He always starts to whine,
He'll have to learn to pay the fine.
He is a total brat you see,
'Cause he's always trying to hit me.
We disagree in every way,
We fight and argue every day.
He steals the remote control from me,
When I'm trying to watch T.V.
He is an ugly, dirty rat,
I'd like to hit him with a baseball bat.
My brother is a royal pain,
He locks me outside when it's pouring rain.
If he's not bothering me,
He's stuffing his face and watching T.V.

—*Nicki Moore*

Indifferences

"You engender indifference"
   I was told that once…

"You belabor the obvious"
   I was told that once…

"You make psychological judgments you're not qualified to make"
   I was told that once…

"I love you"
   I was told that once…

But the world is different now
and, we don't live in that reality anymore.
and, although you may
   or may not be pre-eminent in my thoughts,
   allow me the leeway to move on!

No fantasies recycled
No memories revisited
It all pre-dates current affairs
The end justifies the means, so let's not "press-to-test!"

That was then!
This is now!
   —*Sylvia Elaine Jones*

I Hate The Word Tiny

  I loathe the people who call me tiny,
  I wish that I could kick their hiny.
    My mother tells me not to care.
      But being called tiny,
     Is something I cannot bear.
If the people who call me that are rolling
      with laughter
   They are the ones that I am after.
   I don't think that it's very funny,
After all, they don't get paid any money.
     I am not tiny.
     Why can't they see?
I just wish they knew what it's like to be
      me.
   —*Thanh Giang*

The Garden Of Flowers

I am a girl who loves flowers
I wonder if I can have my own lovely garden
I hear the rain hitting on the purple feather hyacinths
I see the colorful roses, tulips, and daffodils
I want them to grow tall, strong, and healthy
I am a girl who loves flowers

I pretend I am walking through a field of yellow daisies
I feel the soft petals brushing against my skin
I touch the slippery, wet sunrays after it rains
I worry when the beautiful pink buttercups die
I cry when people destroy red and white marilyns
I am a girl who loves flowers

I understand why people use flowers for decorating
I say let the wild flowers grow!
I dream of the magnificent red firecrackers when I go to sleep
I try to water the blue grape hyacinths regularly
I hope I can have my own exquisite greenhouse
I am a girl who loves flowers
   —*Sojah Hurt*

One Girl's Dream

I am a girl who likes football
I wonder if the officials will ever let a girl play for the
  Redskins
I hear the wind whistling through my bright red helmet
I see the ball in the hands of the opposing team
I want to tackle the front line
I am a girl who likes football
I pretend I am quarterback and do nothing but make touchdowns
I feel the impact of the Steelers' quarterback
I touch the ball with my foot as I make the punt
I worry that I will break my arm
I cry out to the Steelers, "You lost!"
I am a girl who likes football
I understand how women are afraid to play football
I try to change the minds of women who don't like football
I dream that I will play in the Superbowl
I am a girl who likes football
   —*Tedeidra Zickefoose*

In Memory Of Alvin Lock

As I set and watch my life inspirer,
I wonder what has happened to our cowboy;
The one whose strong hands helped us saddle up the horses,
Time seems to go by so fast.

Even tho we see them once a year - it seems a lifetime.
To watch a loved one age, fills me with sorrow - it don't seem
fair - no doubt he's lived a great life,
But life should go on forever.

To watch his lady busy in the kitchen is touching to everyone's
eyes. She shows of her love all minutes of the day.
We will take care of her when in need
And will have the right touch to handle her with.

My thoughts grow deep, as I watch them together,
And I pray I will be just as they.
My dear Uncle, you give a gift as no one I have ever known.
You encourage me, and help me understand.

My love for you is strong,
And will grow deeper ever day
May God be with you-
Always.
   —*Susan Welch*

I Am Her Granddaughter

I am her granddaughter.
I wonder what she's thinking,
I hear her mumble words that have no meaning.
I see her in my heart from when I was little,
I want so much for her to get better.
I am her granddaughter.

I pretend at times that she is okay.
I feel her love.
I touch her hand.
I worry what will happen to her.
I am her granddaughter.

I understand that she has Alzheimer's disease.
I say I love her.
I dream of the day that she will understand,
I try to let her know by holding her hand.
I hope and pray that God is with her.
I am her granddaughter.

Dedicated to my Grandmother, Lucy Russell.
   —*Peggy Golis Sayad*

Desert Storm

I walk along, the desert's hot and dry.
I wonder who's been here before and why?
How many battles have been fought here, too
And ask how many soldiers yet must die?

In swirling sands the leaders give commands,
And soldiers fight with bloody hands.
They're told to jump, but not how high
While plodding on to save their lands.

Why do men have to fight anew?
Have they no other work to do?
I fear I never will know why.
Someone must stop this — WHY NOT YOU?
—*Marie Regina Van Doren*

The Lovers

If I was asked how to make love last
I would say "search your heart and your deep dark past"
For it lies in you - and in you alone
so come to truth with yourself
And you will unlock the unknown
Reach out for true love with all of your might
never give up - 'til the end of the fight
For if there need be true love
Then so shall it be
For when you find your true love
you will have found me
—*Michael French*

I'd Like And I'd Hate

I'd like to remember the things we shared
I'd like to think that you really cared
I'd like to remember that nice strong kiss
I'd hate to remember that I got dissed!

I'd like to remember the things we did
I'd like to know why you acted like such a kid
I'd like to think you didn't want anything but sex
I'd hate to think you now tell people I'm your ex!

I'd like to cherish every memory
I'd like to be with you for eternity
I'd like to know where I stand
I'd hate to see you holding another girls hand!

I'd like you to touch me all over
I'd like to have a wish on a 4-leaf clover
I'd like to tell you that you are fine
I'd hate to say that you ain't mine!

I'd like to have a new beginning
I'd like to see my whole world spinning
I'd like to hear "A new relationship we will begin,"
I'd hate to hear you say "Never again!"
—*Michelle Eramian*

When I'm Wrong

You'd think, I'd stuck a dagger, in the middle of your heart.
 I'd need to say I'm sorry, and I would if I was smart.
  Things get kinda crazy, when battle lines are drawn.
   And it's hard to say I'm sorry, when I'm wrong.

We can be, down right vicious, in the middle of a fight.
Every now and then, it seems, the flames of hate burn bright.
Soon before you know it, words are said that don't belong.
 But, it's hard to say I'm sorry, when I'm wrong.

You'd think, I'd shot an arrow, through the center of your soul.
 I wish I could explain to you, just why I lose control.
There's, two sides to every story, and my love for you is strong.
 But, it's hard to say I'm sorry, when I'm wrong.
—*Thomas K. Porter*

Loving Hearts

What a bare world this would be
 if each day we failed to see
  a lovely flower-green grass- a tree.

Our Heavenly Father knew our need,
 and so - He started with a seed
  that's nourished through His loving care
   whose final beauty all can share.

But so much more He cares for us
 He wants to see us grow
  to develop full potential
   with an inner beauty glow.

And so He planted loving hearts
 around us - everywhere
  to nourish us - through sharing
   of their tender, loving care.
—*Lillian Lins Ulsh*

What Would Christ Say?

What would Christ say,
 if he walked the earth today?
Would he turn and walk away,
 or would he destroy it that very day?
Would he be pleased
 with the way you treat your mother,
 or would he cry at the way we treat each other?
What would he say about the way we sin?
Would he reach out his hand,
 or would he raise them up and
 say just let it all come to an end?
Would he hang his head in shame,
 and say no one knows my name?
What would he say, if he walked the earth today?
—*Thelma Jean Bryant*

Time

Oh time, where do you go, so quickly?

Why don't you linger or stand still!

Time doesn't wait for anyone
If I stand still time goes on
I must keep up with time; else time will slip by.

Time is oh so precious
If I take advantage of time, it will bring me many things
But, yet, if I linger knowing time does not, I will waste
precious time.

Time is not an object that can be felt
Neither is it a ruler that can be measured, but many
accomplishments can be reached in time.

Time past, time present, and time in the future
These three parts of time let us know that every moment that
has been or ever will be, is time.

Oh time, keep on going, do not linger
For if you did, we would not value time.
—*Martha McAfee*

Kieran

How I wish to hold you tight,
In my arms throughout the night.
To lay my head upon your chest,
Would ensure a goodnight's rest.
For never farther than a fingertip away,
Is where I always want to stay.
To be kept safe and secure in your love,
Is as precious to me as a Morning's Dove.
Our love together will forever be,
Especially when two become three.
—*Pamela Johnson*

A Near Encounter

Round a curve there stalked a Griffin, just a youngster, not as
if in his adulthood, he was yet a fearsome beast from ancient
        and long-hidden lore.
Toward him crawled a feathered Dragon, young as he, large as a
  wagon, proudly noble, brazen, strong, and fierce right to her
  very core. In canyon bleak and snout to beak, they met upon
     the rocky floor. Met and stared and nothing more.

Now, dear reader, please remember, it was in a past December
That these creatures with their kin, vowed ages of unending war
Both youngsters knew their families' strife must be upheld,
        should it cost life,
Or at least they'd send the foe a-running for a distant shore.
Each would prevail and could not fail to discharge this scared
    chore. So each prepared a mighty roar.

As if one beast, they voiced their cry, so loud was it that
        they did fly
Quite far away, each promising to ne'er return to stroll upon
     that canyon floor.
Into that canyon they would venture, claimed the children,
        "Nevermore!"
—*Susan Helton*

For My Love

Even though he is only a few miles away
If our hands do not interlock I feel astray.
His smile, his laugh, his tone of voice
Make all my worries seem rejoiced.
I know one day we will have to part
But right now it is only the start.
Because of all the trust we have built
Never will one of us experience guilt.
All his feelings he will never hide
In me he always can confide.
Ways to help he tries to find
When many troubles cross my mind.
Something mysterious brought us together
Like a child and its most valuable treasure.
I'd be willing to pay the most expensive price
To be with this man for the rest of my life.
But times will change over the years
And he'll be the man for whom I shed my tears.
So maybe it sounds a great big old myth,
But this is the man who I am in love with.
—*Nisha Gonsalves*

The Original

   In my basket, I bare fruit,
 If someone eats from it becomes loot,
  should someone paint it must change,
 For no two descriptions are the same.

   In my basket, contents past ripe,
 Slowly becoming a most hideous sight,
  Not to mention the odor from where,
 A different vision of fruit does appear.

   Inevitably, all things will change,
When it's impossible to identify the remains,
  Only those who before were to see,
Could attempt to describe the original to me.
—*Vincent D. Ince*

Pregnancy

She went down town to see,
If there was a pregnancy,
The harsh reality, of deciding what will be,
Comes crashing down around me.

She holds me close and leans to me for strength,
Asking for nothing more than my confidence,
Believing in me, she follows my lead,
My decision, of never my baby to see.

The pain won't subside in me,
Of those dark days now history,
Of what my child might now be,
But was a victim of my insanity.

I can't change what now was,
But I keep wondering how it might have been,
If I hadn't been young and weak,
I might now be holding my son, next to my cheek
Sharing a love which now seems incomplete

Love, I can't ask for forgiveness, for I can't forgive myself,
I just try to live with the doubt and work it out,
Though I'll never be the same within or without.
—*Randolph V. Schmotzer*

Mentor

I often wonder who I would be
If you had not given of yourself to me.
Potential was dwelling in dreams in the dark
But it found its life with your special spark.

When anyone gives to me acclaim,
You are the mentor that I will name.
And I will be working all of my days
Until that sweet debt can be repaid.

My fondest hope
Is that proud you will be
When you look on the person
That I grew to be.
—*Terri W. Jerkins*

Think Twice

You will change your life
If you hit that pipe
Never in your life have you seen such power
It will keep you up for hours and hours
You think you slick gett-n dem kicks
But it ain't kool
Being a fool
Think twice or you just might end up on ice

Eyes glisten
But something's missen
Disturbed and hurt
Lying in dirt
Body in lock
On a mental ward in a state of shock

His name is coke
This ain't no joke
Listen up folks
He'll take you for a high ride
Then give you the low dive
Think twice or you just might end up on ice
—*Virginia Lee James*

Earthenware Urn

Gathered from the four corners, usher sands that stir.
I'll form myself into an earthenware urn.
Inside lit with a molten glow.
So I feel what the earth must know.
Now I'm not easily broken, hardened by fire.
  Sunbaked countenance, with futile desire. (This makes even laughter smile).

Literally, land of my birth.
I've been kneaded from pure earth.

Can I enclose the spark from the Thunderbird's gaze?
It supplies the heart that lusters my glaze.

I cry, (it resounds to grounds' root).
  "Liberty fields once formed me, now their use is underfoot."

I'm kept, captured a sad vessel.
  Reflecting setting sun light.
My land is an offering, not a sacrifice of sight.

Anticipate your fire, it brings re-birth O'Phoenix.
I cry your name, too late. My world has been crushed,
I return to dust from whence I came.

Alas earthenware run, when will we ever learn?
—*P.J. Miller*

I'll Love You For Forever

I'll love you through the laughter.
I'll love you through the tears.
I'll forgive you when there's anger
and comfort when there's fear.
I'll be your shoulder to cry on,
and give advice when its due.
I'll trust you when I have my doubts,
and hope you'll tell the truth.
I'll promise you tomorrow, if that's what you wish.
I'll share your every hope and dream
and let you know you're missed.
I'll think of you on sleepless nights,
and long to feel you near.
I'll sit next to you and hold you close
and whisper in your ear.
I'll love you for forever, every week, and everyday.
I'll love you through those little misunderstandings,
and I'll love you in every way.

—*Robin Elizabeth Knisley*

Dreamer

If this is a dream then don't let it end
I'm happy this way just picturing you
Could you really be as perfect as this image in my mind?
No one else can see you the way I do.
So I've never talked to you
But we've exchanged a million words in my mind
More than that
Because I've memorized each line, each touch
Every movement of your lips on mine
And I've grown used to the thrill
of being close to you
Sliding my fingers through your hair
And savoring the feel of your arms wrapped about me
But I'm dreaming, dreaming, dreaming
Still once in a while I catch your glance
Surely you must see these dreams in my eyes
If dreams are made to become real; to be true
Then my own dream tonight is only of you.

—*Rosie Valentino*

"Mommie Dearest"

I thank you Mom for choosing me to come and live with you.
I'm just about the sweetest thing, but I want your attention!

You see, I'm very small and I know more than most.
I'll tell you when it's time to start a brand new day if you'll give me your attention.

I don't want you to work so hard, don't cook without my permission.
Just sit down, Mom, and hold me tight, brush my hair, wash my clothes, tickle my toes, and rub my nose so I can go to sleep.

When I awake, I've planned a trip for only you and me - to Mamaw's house we'll go,
For I'm her pride and joy. Pappa Dodd, he loves me too, but I have got him fooled.
I'm only his Great Big Dollar Bill.

I'm ready now to go home, now, to live with you and dad on Millionaire Street, there to make our life complete,
Where faith, joy, peace and love abide,
our life will be so sweet.
—*Zelma Sumerel*

My Husband, My Love

A thoughtful look, the loving touch
I'm privileged to received each day

And when I'm sad, who is there to make me smile,
He'll find a way.

A voice so kind and comforting,
There are none to compare.

Support when I need it, is there a chance
That he walks on air?

The days may come and go, I know
But I won't soon forget

The richness I've experienced
Being married to my Ed.
—*Linda Brady*

Untitled

Can somebody help me?
I'm sitting here in a world full of people yet I still alone. Can this be possible? I have so many people that give me companionship, but I feel they're not enough. Is it that I'm jaded and all I need to do is be satisfied with what I have? I'm always leaping and shooting for the stars, but my feet never actually leave the ground. Is what I want sitting here in my face? Do I even know what I want? I think the only thing that I want is love, not just the word love, not someone just saying it to me, but someone feeling if for me as I feel it for them. Am I alone in a world were I have so much that amounts to so little?
—*Michele Millard*

Prejudice

What is prejudice? Prejudice is denial, immaturity, guilt and negativity. It describes one as looking at the color of one's skin and judging on that, and that alone. Prejudice is fear. Fear of not knowing. Not knowing right from wrong. Good from bad. No one should be judged on the color of one's skin, but by things much deeper. By attitude, by intelligence, and personality. Prejudice is not an image. Prejudice is a reality. Prejudice will never die, it's here to stay. It is up to us, to change that.

—*Renee Teresa Robles*

A Veteran Reminiscing

Yes, I am a veteran
I'm that little scalawag
Who climbed the fences - jumped over hedges
Swung on the gate - teased the dog
Scared the cat and annoyed the neighbors
Constantly whistling "Olde Black Joe"

Yes, I'm that little so and so
Who tossed daily paper up on porch
Just missing a plate glass window
Causing many folks to scratch their heads
And rub their chins murmuring
If only I could lay my hands on that little so and so

Today I'm proud to be that veteran
While on brow of a hill
Looking out over the horizon
At my feet lay my buddies
Row upon row
Who in their youth and their dreams
And Love of Life - gave for you
Gave for you - gave for me
  Their lives
  —*Mary Agnes Moran*

Untitled

To the heavens minds will soar, past mountains through impenetrable walls. They will, they will take stride. Unstoppable as they go, untouchable their pride. Cannons can sound not stopping this flow. To the heavens the minds will go.

People understand their lives this day and age but are lost to their purpose. For each is given a place to find but stray from the path that leads their way. The unlucky few find it someday.

Their lives are so clear and they see that of others but the world is so cold and minds are so cluttered. Can we change our path through the clouds or do we hit the walls and cry aloud.

I tell you mine is all too clear. Yours my dear friends, well look beyond your fears. For I am here to tell you, your mind will prevail. If your heart lets it follow its winding trail.

Remember this because it is true. Follow your heart, follow your mind, follow your path, follow through. To the heavens minds will sour, past mountains, through impenetrable walls to the heavens minds will go.
  —*Ronnie Boals*

A Forest Rain

A dark rain falls
in a forest glen.
Trees blow
as lightning brightens the sky.
The light flashes again,
but the black blanket covers
the sky, once again.
Like tear drops from heaven,
the rain continues to fall.
The dark clouds lower and the rain thickens.
Just as this fury climbs to its peak,
a great rush of light fills the air,
a great sphere of glory stops in midair,
it shines brighter than King Midas's gold.
Then the cold rush turns to warmth,
like a loving hold on it all.
Then a stream of color crosses the sky
with a glow of happiness,
to add to the glow of light already smiling
across the sky.
  —*Melissa Koch*

Premonition

A man no more than fifty-five, casually dressed
  in California's best,
Disturbed my view today.
He lived here but a month or two, with a bride
  of twenty-two.
I waved, I smiled, as he passed by.
My gaze was open, his was ominous.
I recoiled in fear that eyes so blue,
  could never drown my tears.
Besides, he never before was impolite.

The sightless evening came and lulled me asleep.
My dreams abridged, by a knock on my door.

She stood before me like a waif,
  wrapped in grief and sorrow.
"Pete is dead" she said to me.
A widow now, to cry with pain.
Life is brief, grief is deep, her eyes said to me.
  —*Millicent Sen*

Glory of the East

Minarets and Pagodas of the East
In domes of gold the people feast
They feast with hearts so light and gay
Yet in those temples the people pray.

Beautiful mosques with their big round domes
Beautiful buildings and castles and homes
Golden temples of the Orient
On the worship of Idols some people are bent.

Pillars, columns and pyramids will never, never die
For their beauty will give ideas to the modern man's eye.
  —*Phyllis S. Freedman*

Just Believe

I believe...
  in fairy tales and love stories.
I believe...
  in honesty, truth and friendship.
I believe...
  in picnics in the park.
I believe...
  in walks along the beach.
I also believe...
  there is someone for everyone.
I believe...
  in time, for time holds the future.
I believe...
  it takes time to find the right prince.

It may not be tomorrow,
  it may not be next week.
It may even take a month or more,
  but believe in it, it's worth waiting for.
So keep your chin up, live for tomorrow.
  but most important of all, just believe.
  —*Pam Swenson*

Angels

In the mist of Angels: A small child in a hospital bed is healing.
In the mist of Angels: A teenage girl is alone with no one to care.
In the mist of Angels: A young mother is crying for her child is
  gone.
In the mist of Angels: An old lady is wondering who she is.
In the mist of Angels: A small child, a teenage girl, a young
mother and an old lady are laid to rest to never suffer again.
In the mist of Angels: My mother walked into heaven to live
with God who loved and took care of her, as she walked her path
  of life.
  —*Shirley Gillum*

Untitled

Uncle Funky Bar Malone carries greasy chicken bones
In leather sacks hangin' close besides his wallet.
Likes to share them all around with lonely dogs down on the
    ground,
Canine picnic's what he'd probably call it.

He's got followers you see,
Hangers on and two or three cats show
Sunday evenings for community affairs.

Over chicken bones the town comes quiet,
Funky Bar averts a riot,
Dogs and cats reign serene
On the civil civic side,
Gaily submarining on grease jowled contentment,
Chicken calories spent on raising Monday's sun.

—*J. Nelson*

Landscape #1

Behind the heather there was a bee's hive,
in moldering boards, through which dripped
a stream of honey once carried by diligent wings.
Under the sun and into buzzing silence
I heard their thoughts, quietly sailing on the landscape.
I bid them hello with a smile when they returned, tired
from a field, somewhere, far from here, absorbed by fatigue.
Among the flowers one stopped, weary.
Sitting between the clover it told a sleepy story
with a hoarse voice.
There was a place for me, lulled to sleep near a sweet
stream, into whose hands my head escaped into thickening worlds
vanished beyond the hill,
disappearing in an increasing croak of garrulous frogs,
escaping into darkness with stormy responses of animal desires,
which tore the quiet dream hammered by a blacksmith's arm,
like an old cart's axle, like a hoop perfect in form,
boasting on art along traveled villages,
the quiet rumble measured.

—*Marek Nej*

My Town Is Made Of Concrete

My town is made of concrete and it's not just in the street. In my town, concrete begins and ends where both horizons meet. My town is made of concrete, the school, the churches, and the store, all are made of concrete, there is concrete galore. Go to the concrete hospital when you become ill, on your way out stop by the concrete office to pay your bill.

Every house is also made of concrete, the walls, ceiling, and the floor; just step out your door and you will see the concrete, there is much, much more. Walk down the concrete sidewalk past the concrete town hall. Mail a letter at the concrete post office which is in the concrete mall. Park your car in the concrete garage or fill it up at the concrete gas station. It is safe to say in this town there will never be a concrete ration.

Walk up the concrete stairs into the concrete bank where you put your money. If you think about it, there is so much concrete it's really kind of funny. Trains speed over the concrete bridge along the track; here in Morgan Park concrete we do not lack.

There is a concrete police station and concrete fire department as well, although in Morgan Park you will never hear a fire bell. You see, the fire-fighters soon did learn, concrete simply will not burn.

You would think that Morgan Park being made entirely of concrete would have concrete weather, and we do. It snows concrete every night; stop by some time and you will see it too. If you don't believe my town is made of concrete, you think it just can't, I would suggest that you talk to the workers at the nearby concrete plant.

—*Mike L. Flaherty*

Your Pain — God's Gain

The beauty of the Lord is seen
In persons who've been tested and tried.
And have realized that to God they must cling,
    For adversity happens so that He'll be
        glorified.
    Their hearts become soft and tender.
They've learned to see life differently.
    God, the Great Character Builder,
    Has taught them the principles
    They need to live Victoriously.
The Holy Bible becomes their guide.
The Old Testament becomes alive.
For answers, explanations, and insights
    Have come through this at night.

    With Jesus as their friend,
    They've got great joy within,
    Inner peace and great fortitude,
But most importantly a new attitude!

—*Marilyne St. Louis*

Dance Of The Atoms

Finally escaping the storm waves of mind,
in pure nudity stripped of thought activity,
ego and desire
can we serenely dive to the depth of being
where, in the fountain of life, we are honored
to witness the miracle dance of the atoms.

Infinitesimal atoms...myriads...
their swirling energies ever alert.
Each atom—a thinking and feeling entity—
though placed in pattern, is free in its individuality.
At the slightest signal from another,
they harmonize with the whole—
like improvising musicians.

Dancing in light, joy and majesty...
they emanate ecstasy.

—*Margaret Bowen Deitz*

Reflections Of The Fire

Thoughts spin through my head,
in quiet reflections before the dawn,
of things that have been and could be,
of lives that have lived but now are gone.
In silent solitude I sit with my shadow,
with muffled resistance I watch my life pass.
Through the fields of my childhood my mind races,
Till it meets with the blackness of my passing youth.
Sometimes, on the edge of remembrance I'll linger,
just long enough to catch a smile or feel the sun.
Never knowing if tomorrow will bring sadness or elation,
it's the battlefields of my mind where no wars are won.
If by some divine grace I awake on the morrow,
to find the stopwatch of the day has begun again.
I will remember the night that I sat by the fire,
and sifted through the ashes of my memories and thoughts,
and I will live my life not so much by the words that are
spoken, but by the action I take when they are spoken to me.

—*Shawn F. Graham*

Contemporary Lexicon

  The Dumbest words of which I know
   In the chatter of the day,
  Is for one to interrupt his thoughts
  With just two words and say, "You know."

  He knows at once that you don't know
   Of all that's to be said,
  But still he interrupts himself
  And you are being led with; "You know".

Exasperating? yes it is, you wonder what comes next,
  Just what the hell he's saying
And you're completely vexed with; "You know."

It's not that he is asking if you really truly know,
  Just what conclusion he will reach,
And then go on and blow with; "You know."

It cannot be a guessing game, or think you're just a jerk,
  Perhaps he thinks you're stupid
Or have a mental quirk, with: "You know."

I'll tell you what should temper it, and really make it pay,
  Just interrupt with — "Yes, I know",
   And slowly walk away.

 —*B. B. Hutchinson*

A Peak At The Real Me

I empty my burdens and brighten scarlet skies.

And see the tears I have shed silently,
in the darkness of my fear

Anger strikes me weak from the hammering of the
lustful hands that I forbid to touch my feelings

I grow leery of my defensiveness that frame my loveable
self that desires to be loved and touched gently

I look into your eyes and become yours
melting into your warm embrace

As I peak at the real me

I manifest the emptiness of my soul
And yearn to have it filled with your love

My heart is lonely and my mind's eye trembles scared
 yet drawn, Again and Again

  To peak at the real me
 —*Stephen Crutchfield*

Angel With A Broken Wing

She strolls down the long, shaded hollow
In the fields, she lives with the flowers
In need to fly, high in the sky
But lost all her powers
All dressed in white with golden hair
Ready to take flight on a road to anywhere
Upon the highest hill carrying her load
Hoping for another rainbow
so she can take the colorful road
Wondering where it will lead
She waits in pain while her lonely heart bleeds
Making so many plans
Her dreaming never ends
And it will take time for her broken wing to mend
A curse has her hanging by a string
No stairway to get home
An angel with a broken wing
Left on earth to roam.

 —*Stephanie Johnston*

The Paths of Yesterday

Yesterday is lost forever
In the forever memories of what might have been
The what ifs and the why nots
Will never be answered now
Let it go
The paths we take
The directions we head
As if traveling in total darkness
Only to be surprised
Tomorrow
What might have been
If only
Yesterday
Would the other path have been brighter
Would the joy have been more
Would the love have been stronger
If only
We will never know
Let it go
 —*Linda Gomez*

Nightfall

Nightfall has taken over another day, as lighting-bugs dance
in the glow of our headlights along the highway, all the while,
our eighteen wheels keep on turning, we slowly approach
another town, with quiet looking streets and dogs roaming
around, surrounded in the darkness comes all my thoughts,
staring out the window at the silhouettes of the tree tops,
I watch as the lights of the houses appear, and silently
wonder what everyone's doing in there, with the hum of the
engines beneath our feet, I look out at the town, are they all
fast asleep?, we are so far from the place we call home, all
the while our eighteen wheels keep on turning as we continue
to roam, the bill-board signs fill my mind, I'm still reading
them through the rear view mirror as we leave them far behind,
Wishing for a truck stop with an open space, as we persist on
our run at this governed pace, as yet another town slowly
disappears, all the while our eighteen wheels are shifting
gears, into the night, into the quiet night, and I glance at
the man I love driving our truck, all the while our eighteen
wheels keep on turning.

 —*Susan Mary Twarog, Higgins*

Untitled

Walk with me,
in the land of the frozen spirits,
where the mighty oak is frozen and lonely,
the wind will rattle your soul,
as it does the few brittle skeletons,
still clinging to that frozen tree.
 The spirits talk,
they whine and moan in the vicious violence
that howls through the frozen land,
when spring comes,
the spirits of the forest will be released,
in billowing, breathtaking shades of green,
the land will be free,
free from the biting wind that blows by me.

 —*Thomas P. Chapman*

Untitled

There was a little fellow, all so black and white
Innocence and sweetness were all his very might
We nourished, we cared for him, as if our little boy
And he in turn grabbed hold our hearts and gave us simple joy
Our home was his domain, and he loved to browse about
But a certain something in our cat said Lord, I must get out
Days went by, we searched and watched, kept running to the door
And then we knew in our aching hearts we'd see our cat no more
An emptiness prevails now, all through the day and night
For that little fellow's gone who was so black and white

 —*Natalie Buzil*

The Hollywood Sunset Machine

O brother, can you spare me a glimpse of the world,
In the light of the video screen,
Where the dreams of the people are superbly unfurled,
On the Hollywood Sunset machine.

Where Jackie and Lucy and Aunt Bea still reign,
With Alda and Dansen and Sheen.
And Snoopy is following Spock's missing brain,
On the Hollywood Sunset machine.

The children all learn from the Big Bird and Ernie,
And their elders from Roger and Gene.
News and the arts are discovered in turn,
On the Hollywood Sunset machine.

Arrangements are made and debuts are played
In the contest for Almighty Green.
Commercialized, cable-ized, advertised trade,
On the Hollywood Sunsent machine.

O brother, can you spare me a glimpse of the world,
In the light of the video screen,
Where the dreams of the people are superbly unfurled,
On the Hollywood Sunsent machine.

—Robert M. Wallace

Being There

Where are you when your babies cry
  in the middle of the night?
When thunder roars and lightning strikes,
  making such a fright?
Huddling for a hug; or just needing to be near;
Spilling out their little hearts,
  to someone who will hear.
Where are you when these fleeting things are met -
  with each 'Kid day'?
-when laughter pierces the quiet air
  with impulsive play;
-capturing a moment, to praise a deed
  or comforting a doubt;
-chasing butterflies and lightning bugs; roly polies in ajar-
Finding the big dipper, or answering a-why;
Where are you, Mom/Dad - My child?
A tear or shrug cannot undo or mend-
Where will we be, when days are gone-
Who will be left to tend?

—Mona Gonzalez

Today

Today all the knots have been tied
in the proverbial rope. I've depleted all
the reserves from my fountain of hope.

I've a need to expel all the poison within.
I've journeyed inside and had a talk with a friend.

Today, I sent out a summons, for spiritual fortitude.
I'm exhausted and need a higher court to change my attitude.

The light I bask in, says open your spirit,
for that's where I live.
Reach out your hands, through you I give.

Today, trust in me, I am the way.
The force, that guides you, through many.
Today, today, and today...

—Luthenia Gould

Daytime Soap Opera

She tells me this woman and man
in the serial we watch,
grope for each other day after day:

They eat, talk, kiss and fade in
to her sitting on his lap.

Truly,
the script needs some well-meaning neighbor
to advise the handsome, young man,
"Go back to work
before it's too late."

I personally would caution
the beautiful, boring ingenue,
"Wash your dishes,
and more than that, get a life!"

The issue is not really illusion,
but 'Daytime Digest.'

—Marilyn Hochheiser

Overwhelmed By The Darkness

The beauty of the day surrenders to the majesty of the night.
In the stillness of a darkened room my soul has time to rest.
I cry in the empty room. Oh Lord, how much longer can I last.
The quiet walls return the echo of my plea. Now even they cry
  for me.
The strength of the day has flown from my body just as the joy
  has fled my heart.
The humid air is broken by the fresh cool breeze of the
  approaching storm.
I hear the gentle rain as it embraces my window.
I silently start to pray. Oh God, My God. I've stood another
  day.
From where the strength came and went I know not whence.
How will I stand again. The days have weakened my heart.
The tears stream from my defeated face.
I feel a warmth that causes my body to glow.
The radiant love of my Father has changed the ebb and flow.
The power of His love has given me back my hope.
The quiet reassuring voice of the Most High has a word for me
  tonight. "The strength of today is the hope for tomorrow"

—Ron Levi

The Lady Of The Sea

  On a boat out to sea, sails a lady like me.....

Her dreams of adventure and beautiful cascades while bathing
in the sun and daring escapades. Sailing the islands,
her sails full of wind, with a broken heart that would never
mend.

  On a boat out to sea, sails a lady like me......

A handsome rich gentleman in her life once appeared, gave
promises of grandeur and passions that seared. Her love flowed
freely, her heart given completely. But alas, his love
could not be acquired, for his riches it was believed she
admired. His family, of high social standing, a poor
girl he would not be banding.

  On a boat out to sea, sails a lady like me......

From port to port, over oceans and seas, for her true loves
heart she still grieves. Alone with the wind, the dawn of a
new day, her riches are boundless as she sails away.

  On a boat out to sea, sails a lady like me.......

—Linda Wesley

Michael Jordan

Michael Jordan you're one of a kind, and we know you're hurting
In your heart, and mind, but Jesus Christ son of God above, will
Heal your pain, by blessing you with the gift of your fathers
Spiritual love, and like your father, you are captivating, most
Definitely stimulating, not to mention vigorating, and when you
Are performing your magnificent game of basketball, you never
Let your audience down with a fall, because you're always on time
With the right shot in mind, so son, always remember, you're one
Wonderfully bless young man, for Jesus Christ son of God, bless
Your parents with you born in their nest, which express, that
Your parents with you born in their nest, which express, that
You're apart of each parent's best.
                        Who could ask for anything more?
                        God Bless You!!
                        Michael Jordan
    —*LaVerne D. Nixon*

Willow

Oh! Weeping willow,
   In your long tresses that hang to the ground,
Reminds me of a love lost and never found.
   Oh! Weeping willow, as the wind blows you sway,
I listen for whispers, to here what you say.

You tell me, "man can save face,
   Then try to help the human race.
The way they are going is a shame,
   And have only themselves to blame."

Oh! Weeping willow,
   Let me borrow your Salicin, to ease my pain.
Then maybe,
   I won't feel so drained.

Sometimes life can get so tough,
   And things can get really rough.
Oh! Weeping willow, as time goes on,
   I hope we can learn to sing a song.
To get along with one another; to love our sisters and
   brothers.
    —*Patricia Purdy*

Word Play (II)

"As you wish!" I said; yet wished myself to be
In your wish, as you, in mine,
Are mover prime and, yet, not moved to magic
   (Our birthright, we two, we too, we to be...)
For in this darkest hour of night,
   (The day, without you, is as dark)
The Incubi and Succubi come by-the-bye,
And buy, with fearsome currency,
That P(eace,iece) of mind(ful,less) Dreamscence, Dream Screen
Play in which I once played all parts....
The audience of one, for which this was rehearsed
   (On, endlessly, and yawn, sometime,)
Is, all too jury-like, not in:
The curtain cannot rise, the lights not struck, and
Cue-less, the actors, too, two (now,) to
   (For the audience plays as well
   In this theatrical mirror)
Wait, wonder, prepare, despair, repair,
In anxious anticipation of the performance
Of their lives, too, two, to ————— ?
    —*Max Middleton*

Beautiful Child Of Mine

You once were a part of me.
Inside my womb you grew
You grew to be a precious child
One day, that great day -
You were born.
Your eyes were as blue as the crystal sea
Your cheeks became rose -
When you smiled with me.
Your mother, you knew I was.
You cuddled with me
As if to share a time of love.
You yawned and snuggled
Close to my heart ...
Secretly telling me. - we will never part.
That was the moment of true light
That was the moment God made you right.
In God's eyes you are beautiful ...
In my eyes you are -
My world, my heart
Beautiful child of mine, I love you always.
    —*Ralna Lynae Rowan*

Hypatia, A True Story

It is written that she was very beautiful; born in 370 and most
   intelligent in science
she was the last to work in that library so full of knowledge,
our planet's promise for advance
a mathematician, astronomer, physicist, neoplatonic philosopher,
a rebel in her time, when men owned women, she chose freedom.
Her name in history is whispered softly in the hall corner;
even today in the age of information, equality, and wisdom,
for her story embarrasses faith in our civilization, our religion
   and vision.
A time when the Ptolemys built the greatest city of learning and
   creating,
Rarely has a state promoted so much evolution of human
   understanding;
Sophocles, Aeschylus and Euripides, all published in this book
   capital of mind
where Euclid wrote his geometry, later rediscovered by Kepler,
   Newton, and Einstein
where citizens of the globe came to live, trade, learn and invent
   the word cosmopolitan
for the Cosmos was discovered here and here became known to
man and then forgotten for one thousand years of Dark Ages, lost
   from Alexandria,
city for the elite, where many suitors wooed her, this lady called
   Hypatia;
close friend to the Roman governor, well connected, a symbol of
   freedom,
but to the rising mob, the Christians, she was a mere wealthy
   pagan
the fanatical mob of parishioners shredded her with abalone shells;
   she was Cyril's enemy.
The library, most of its memory, died with her and the city built
   by slavery.
    —*Mark Biskeborn*

Intimacy

Intimacy comes in all shapes and sizes,
Intimacy comes in all disguises,
Intimacy is listening to the Robin sing,
Intimacy is waiting for the phone to ring,
Intimacy is a kind word, a dream or two,
Intimacy can cheer you up when you're blue,
Intimacy can take you and make you a star,
Intimacy a wonder, a closeness from afar,
Intimacy is love, is trust in you and me,
Intimacy is wishing to be free.
    —*Shirley Yan*

David Stone Sheffield

Double diamond, double daring, darling David, legs churning, intent on the horizon, you drove your big wheel with abandon, a tiny world explorer, who, in your wide-ranging voyages, transported your parents to a state of worried pride. When sides were chosen, you were first-drafted, quick and fast, you transformed a soccer field into a Land of Opportunity and claimed it for your team. Above the curve of your triple-treat smile (shy, amused and secret), and behind the windows of your eyes, your thoughts flickered tantalizingly, but usually remained unspoken, and, ultimately, your own. Careful of others and careless of self, you skied mountains and waters, picked, rolled, passed and took it to the hoop. Racing time, you were first to break the tape. When earth could no longer contain your venturesome spirit, you carved a bright trail to some new place where there are flesh slopes to test and challenges to meet. Out of our sight, you remain in our hearts, deft and graceful, so at ease in your body, your luminous memory serves as a brilliant beacon for those who will follow when you lead.

—*Trish Cole*

A Flower Blooms

A seed is planted and starts to grow,
Into a world that consists of chaos
To whom things are unknown.
It's fertilized with religion and watered
With a loving care.
A whisper in the wind to let me know
God is there.
As a harsh winter approaches, it snows
Sin and thunderstorms temptation.
Still, a flower grows past every thorn of speculation.
Spring appears and everything is anew.
A flower is blooming, a warm soft rose,
Also some things I still do not know,
But with wisdom of others and the
guidance from God,
Just as a flower,
I shall continue to blossom and grow.

—*LaTonya Simmons*

The End?

Where will I go when life is gone
Into the blue or out beyond
Or deep within the changing earth
To silently wait for my rebirth

Or will I just relive again
The same sweet life that I did then
Who knows I may just roam this land
Trying to touch a friendly hand

Or lurk in shadows eerie and black
To send cold shivers up mortal backs
Perhaps I'll return as a siamese cat
With a knowing look when humans chat

I hate to think that when we've died
And there's nothing left of our human hide
But ashes and insignificant dust
That that's the final end of us

—*Patricia A. Ashforth*

Untitled

A hawk descends through my vision, through my eyes,
into the paths of my direction,
swooping me up on its wings where my soul lies.
It flies dangerously close and dangerously low
into the valleys of perception,
and out of the duality of confusion.
I am a Sinbad, a pirate, roving the sea of skies in search of logic.
I will steal it and hide it
under my overcoat of feathers.
I will return it to man, through the hawk,
through the sky,
through my soul which lies naked on the wings of fear,
exposed to the rays of the sun and wings of morrow.
We, who drift on the trade winds of life,
can only touch the tranquility of man's destiny
before we eat the seeds of our inevitable demise
and fade into the sun which is our home.

—*Muriel Wolfson*

Un-Union

I took the war to paper 'cause I couldn't stand the noise:
   inward, propaganda; outward, calm and poise.
I think the change of venue was a strategy of self.
I didn't give permission,
I don't think I agreed.
I moved the thing to paper so my ownness could secede.

—*Pamela R. Burkland*

The Art Of Living

The art of living, so hard to learn.
Is filled with many a twist and turn;
Lessons lost, never to be learned,
Passions empty, emotions burned.
Guilt and shame bring doubts unfounded;
My sails are empty and my craft grounded.
Learning to share, care and trust,
Basics yes, but for all a must!
With the basics you then can find love,
Granted and guided as if from above.
Understanding, tenderness and deep emotion,
With trust and loyalty comes devotion.
The art of living, a skill divine,
With determination may come to all in time.

—*E. "Shadow" Maddox R.A.*

Morning-Mourning Time

Birds chattering in the wind
Is it already daybreak again?
The safety and insanity of night has
left me and mourning time returns.

Why is morning so hard without you
Oh yes! Our breakfast calls, our morning talks
Now a blur of mourning tears as the
Months roll by and fade to a year.

Gone-Dead-Away-Forever-Never-
Your form-your presence! Present but
Not in the usual way.
So I awaken to face another day.

—*PhiloMena Mudd*

Shakespeare's Cottage

To see it from the outside, Shakespeare's home
is like its pictures, neat and primly built.
But go inside! Our first reaction is
surprise to see how low the ceilings are.
A six foot man would have to watch his head
lest he might bang against the portals there.

Their rooms are small, as though they huddle close
together from some fear of parting soon.
The floor is laid with wooden puncheons that
in places squeak. Though ancient flooring, this
still holds the hordes of visitors who come
to see the bard's first home. The open hearths
are big, as well they might be when you think
their fires were used for warmth and cooked as well.

This place is proud. Though men were not as tall
in stature then, here lived a mighty man.
—*Mildred Fielder*

The Unknown

    The fears I face in my dreams
    Is much more than a cold stone scream
    They are the pictures of life and death
    That lead me onward to an unknowing path
    Frightened of what I'll see and not
    But relieved to see the pleasures I've got
    Try to achieve all that is right
Without betraying in the middle of the night
    For I am human that's plain to see
    Still frightened of what's become of me
    My fear is great of the unknown
    And what He has yet to me be shown
    Clutching at life and the love for tomorrow
    And hoping I'll see her never in sorrow
    I think so hard that this is impossibly real
But it must be, for I have a soul and it can feel
So I'll watch my life blow past like a breeze
    Until I can see my fate in the trees
    And on that day then I will know
What is yet to be seen and called The Unknown
—*Michelle E. Rogers*

Winter Song

Oh, one of the noteworthy songs, I have heard
Is the clear winter call, of the crimson redbird
High in a tree, the first month of the year
It's a pretty, pretty, pretty, and a cheer, cheer, cheer

It's a beautiful song, from high in a tree
Trumpeting happiness, for you and for me
He bugles his clarion call, far and near
On ice covered branches, he sings without fear

He's plainly intent, on declaring one thing
Bursting forth boldly, the coming of spring
Hoping his concert, will bring it along
He gladdens our hearts, with cheer in his song

With snow on the ground, and ice in the trees
No attention is paid, to either of these
Yes, one of the praise worthy hymns, I have heard
Is the clear winter call, of a flaming red bird
—*Ruth Hall*

Under The Spell Of A Leprechaun

Under the spell of Leprechauns in their green,
is the only way they are able to be seen.

In the mist of Erin they dance and they sing so bold.
While the song's of the Celts are told.

Clovers unfold, with a touch of a kiss, and
gently they become four leaves in the mist.

As Leprechauns paint an aurora of hues in the sky,
in the sun rise of morning it will catch your eye.

A rainbow of hues, on which you can wish,
dreams and schemes for Leprechauns have told you,
at the end of a rainbow is your pot of gold.

And if you stand under its hue you'll love the view.
For the Leprechauns wish will come true.

And the pot of gold will be for you,
if you believe the Leprechauns tale,
then it is there for all to avail.
—*Roxanne Mosher*

Soft Mad Children

Is there a place for me here?
Is there a place for my words?
Where can a faithful heart turn?
Where are the dreamers?
As I reflect now, on those days of doubt
I see faded photos of a lost generation of an age
I can't envision of an age
I don't recall
Is there a place for us?
For our words?
—*Stacy D. Sells*

Sweet Woodruff Reeve

What is this heavenly white point?
Is this my fortune star, or is this my anoint?
Oh, can this be a holiday.
A shorebird or just a snipe - at bay.

Her affection has filled my cup.
All that sweetness has ruffed me up.

What does this provost dove have to woo this mist.
Can potent bravery solar charm this fair
Fragrant perennial kiss.

How can this whist partner migrate from capitol to perch?
Perhaps this is not a shorebird.
But a pigeon, a pheasant or a grouse.
Something in a birch.

Has the sight failed the solar?
Where is the pathway into the grove?
No! This wood, has she to rove.

Be this the primrose path and is she.
What at bath? Is this the reeve?
Oh look a lovely bird of paradise
No! It is the sweet fair perennial kiss mist.
—*Sonny Trost*

Poem

Although these word's are not much of a poem
It is all I could muster from deep in my bones.

Phrases may match words may rhyme
Yet it's a simple thought spinning round my mind.

But still I conspired to put it on paper
For some contemplation sooner or later.
—*Robert J. Delahanty*

Hand In Hand

The time of day I love the best,
Is when the sun has gone to rest,
When the moon is coming up real bright,
And a strange bird calls into the night.
The sound of a wolf in the distance is heard,
Again there comes the cry of a bird,
As a blanket of peace settles over the land,
We walk together hand in hand.
We walk beside a little stream.
In which the tiny pebbles gleam.
We then sit down upon a rock.
Where we can have a quiet talk.
You ask me then if I love you.
Although of course you know I do.
And then with hearts that are aglow.
Hand in hand back home we go.

—*Twila Weisenberger*

My Sister

She's seventy today, that's no big deal
It all depends on how you feel.

Her step is light, her mind is bright,
She still can give you a darn good fight

Her fingers move nimbly as she knits,
Sometimes, really, the sweater fits.

She challenges drivers on the road,
As she proceeds in a reckless mode.

Her shopping sprees are most historic
As through the malls she will frolic

Her husband attends to her every whim,
Where did she get a guy like him?

Her children are the joy of her life,
Some more joy, some more strife.

But when needed, she always there,
To acknowledge this is only fair.

The number of grandkids increased to eight
With the arrival of "Kiss me Kate".

She's seventy today, that's no big deal
It all depends on how you feel.

—*Rose Mellie*

Tonight I Feel Forgotten

Whenever we spend time together
It always feels so right.
We laugh, we tease each other, we open our hearts!
We never yell or fight.

But it's now so rare that we're together
And for weeks I've been feeling rotten.
I've called, I've written, with no reply.
And frankly, tonight I feel forgotten.

My head advises "This too shall pass, it always does",
As it mentally prepares for "No Reply".
But for my poor heart tonight's been rough, very rough.
To say it's not, is a lie.

Your phone message, "I'll call you tomorrow" revived my heart,
But that was twenty nine long days and nights ago.
Are you OK? I have no way of knowing,
But if you miss me, it sure doesn't show.

Each time I see you I fall in love,
So on August 18th my heart was hoppin'.
But it's now September 16th, and I'm again way out of touch,
And so, tonight I feel forgotten...

—*Robert Berardi*

A Quiet Vacation

If there is an answer in this crazy world of ours, where might it be? The city has lights and bars, skyscrapers and sports arenas, yet where in the city can I relax and think— of the ocean, a sea of blue expanding far, into the listless horizon, yet how can I concentrate with such monotony in plain view— of a desert with its warm breeze and cool shade, yet how can I comprehend with no human life around me, as I dream of the plains, and smell the fresh vegetables, yes the plains are a land of freedom, yet what obstacle must I overcome, to walk along the flat terrain— so as I sit here on nature's doorstep, I decide to breathe the air and hear the animals, while feeling the breeze of the rolling hills, I notice two lights in the distance, the first reassures me, the second relaxes me, so maybe there is an answer in this crazy world of ours, perhaps you should just see the elk, or smell a rosebud, drive a sports car, or wish upon a star, but in the hills you can realize variety, just let the answer come to you, as the rest of the world passes by, like a newly formed butterfly, peace, love, happiness, thank you. And one more thing, I suggest you decide.

—*Michael Alan Scott*

Remembering Dad

There is an empty chair in the circle of my heart;
  It belonged to my Dad, but God set him apart.
In mansions of Glory, in heaven so bright,
  I know he is singing in endless delight,
With the light of Glory on his face
  He is singing now God's Amazing grace.

Each time through the years when we gathered there,
  We worshipped the Lord in song and in prayer.
"Throw out the life line across the dark wave,
  There is a brother whom someone should save;"
"How firm a foundation" we sang at his pace
  Then lifted our voices in "Amazing Grace."

I wish there was room to write all the songs;
  To tell of Christ's love to whom he belonged;
To repeat all the scriptures he read to us there;
  To show us God's love and infinite care.
With the circle complete, as around him we face
  Hallelujah! We'll sing "His amazing grace."

—*Wilma Jones*

Untitled

Yes it's been a long hard road.
It could of been easy, it could of been sold.
How sad it is not to want to grow old.
This time is given to us for free, although
all through life we have to pay, our maps we
make from day to day.
Some are unfortunate and may not get lead,
while some souls are starving and not get fed.
There are many questions that have yet to be asked.
To reveal the answers, uncover the mask.
We do the footwork and the unknown does the rest.
He passes out the problems, we do the test.
Failing the course, we then learn the lesson.
Experiencing the pain, fighting back the aggression.
Yes, I have witnessed the evil, and deep in my heart
have felt the good.
One day I'll meet the creator.
One night I'll walk within the man in the hood.

—*Sheri Tucker*

Night Shades

Hark! What in yonder woodpile lies?,
It dares not move; it does not cry.
   Could it be a watersnake?; crawled in there
from yonder lake;
   Or perhaps a startled loon, seeking refuge
from the moon.
   Me thinks! It is a little fawn seeking shelter
until dawn.
   A closer look reveals to me, a mooncast
shadow from a tree.
   —*Paul H. Schwan*

A New Star In Heaven

She was a frail little girl, and she suffered so
It eased her pain when God called her. We had to let her go.
Tho, she wasn't with us long - The years just numbered three
   We know for now and forever she will be pain free.

There must be toys in heaven, and other children too
And with new life she'll play, just like the others do
The agony is over, of waiting for that fateful call
For now she is in Heaven with the greatest Healer of all

These are times that try the soul, of us here on earth
For we loved Samantha and cared for her since her birth,
   We must not feel cheated tho, as we shed our tears
   Because of the hugs and kisses of the past three years

   Whenever she is thought of, Samantha isn't too far
Because, if we look to the Heavens we'll find a brand new star
Behind this window of Heaven is this child with good health,
And tho she is with God now, He gave us more than any wealth
   —*Robert H. Watkins*

Past

The cool refreshment soothed my throat
it filled a need in me so deep.
It entered me and worked its miracle
and penetrated me to my innermost keep.

You cradled it with your flawless hands
you let it run down your face.
You held it above me, poured it softly
as we were lost in the pleasure of inner space.

We rejoiced in what we shared
joined with fleshy bonds.
Experienced all that was new, together
we swam in the sensual, lush ponds.

The forest held new treasures for us,
we searched and touched and left all bare.
So consumed with the experimentation
and went beyond what we shouldn't dare.

We continued moving, traveling
from green, plentiful trees
ferns, the copious lush of the forest and came
to a place where there was no peace.
   —*L. Renee*

Farewell Fear

All alone when fear is around,
it stalks me then hunts me down
an evil prince, a deadly villain,
it has come here on a mission
I feel as though this is the end
but wait, laying quietly is my best friend
a strong warrior clothed in black
always ready and on the attack
he protects me from all evilness
my favorite dog "Guinness."
   —*Michael Savage*

Love

Love is a beautiful thing,
It fills you up with happiness,
You feel like you're flying and spreading
your wings.
Love makes you feel great,
It can happen any month like June, December,
or May.
It can happen any minute of any given day.
You can't think of anything else, except
the one you love.
To you, they're special, wonderful, funny,
and perfect in every way.
You hear songs on the radio and think
about him or her.
Whenever you hear their name, your heart fills
with joy and begins to flutter.
Sometimes it's hard to explain what your mouth
cannot utter, but love is a beautiful thing.
   —*Shannon Andrews*

The Promise of Better Times

The land laid parched and dry.
It had not seen water for quite sometime.
But the hint of rains to come echoed in the distance.
Once more the ground would swell with moisture
Brought by the laden clouds.
It would be soaked up by the barren soil.
Again the ground would become green and fertile
With renewed strength and hope that the water would remain
Leaving the land afresh with abundant life
And the promise of better times.

But the hint of rains to come,
Once more, is one of false hope.
And so, for yet another year the plains will remain desolate
Without the much needed water essential
To foster new life, and hope.
Allowing no chance to know what might have developed.
Growing and exploring all the possibilities existence can bring
Thus, like in the past, life will remain obscure and unattainable.
And the promise of better times, like the land,
Will remain empty and unfulfilled.
   —*Linda Rubio*

Lois

Such a warm - yet unfamiliar feeling,
It happened from the start;

This gentle-yet powerful yearning,
Steadily pulling at my heart...

These strange - yet comfortable sensations
That are churning from within;

Are signs of much deeper feelings
Than from just being friends...

Also, these feelings seem to be growing
with each passing day;

And I've been longing for your tenderness
Every moment since I've been away.

So I've come to realize,
In these few days apart;

These yearning and comfortable feelings,
Must have been "Love" from the start...
   —*Scott*

About A Parting

You ask me how I feel about losing him
It is like standing over a perilous cliff
Staring into the depths, seeing nothing but feeling
darkness seizing air from my lungs
sensing underfoot
the division of land and nothingness
in my mind
the blood in my head pounding thunderous
sweat bleeding from my face mingled with
burning tears from the wells of my eyes

The water evaporates, leaving me with words forming
from cracked lips dry as desert

I love you
is sucked from my lips into nothing
I scream, my love and pain unheard
My love, I only want to touch you one more time.

—*Mary A. Reavis*

Divine Love

What is the most precious commodity that can be ours?
It is our speck of that same Divine Love that powers
planets, moons, and stars.
Without it we are poor regardless of how much material
success has been achieved in our name.
The richness it imparts to our lives is much superior
to great, wealth and fame.
This super, magnetic, power is guaranteed to heal
everything that is wrong.
Keeping it forever alive in our hearts helps us to
always sing a happy song.
Being filled with this highest form of love will
enable us to be open and receptive to everyone's needs.
No longer will we be selfishly focusing all attention
on ourself because it will be others we want to please.

—*Marion Cureton*

This Thing Called Life

The wait is over and the egg cracks open
It is the beginning of new life and old work
Mother feeds her young without knife or fork
And father stands guard, a proud old stork

The time is spring and before long summer
Up close the change seems ever so slight
But in reflection it is a powerful might
This thing called life and one's first flight

Nature calls and refuses to be ignored
The first try may look like a mistake
The falls are many and all the bones ache
But the will is strong and does not break

Parents look on with growing expectation
Their guidance proceeded by words of criticism
Because each sees life through a different prism
And many times appear the only victim

Despite their rebellion many lessons are learned
Like the prodigal son they cease to sponger
The young soon mature and the gap is no longer
For with each other's love the bond grows stronger

—*Melanie Winters*

Heartland

I peered into the window of my child's heart;
it is there he sometimes goes. A quiet place,
his refuge from a world that doesn't always play fair.
A place he slips into and out of silently-where others cannot
   invade.
Scattered about are his favorite things:
his teddy bear, a ball, his bicycle.
They are all reminders that this heartland is his very own.
In his heart he is free. He expresses who he is and
how he feels, and it is always okay.
He scribbles messages on the walls of his heart.
He draws happy faces and sad faces, friendly ones and mad ones.
He knows them well. They are all him at one time or another.
Sometimes, he runs carefree and happy
through golden meadows filling the air with laughter;
his aches and cares tossed away like old, forgotten toys.
Other times, he nestles in a corner seeking security and
   reassurance,
snuggling his raggedy blanket, clinging to it tightly
as if it holds all his hopes and dreams in its threads.
Today he saw me peeking in at him.
He looked out at me and smiled, then he invited me in.

—*Sharon Warren Coberly*

True Love Is Forever

True love is like a fan revolving.
It must keep on turning to be alive
If it stops it will surely die.
True love is something forever.

The love we shared was such True Love.
A few bad times crept in to tempt us,
But happiness was never far away,
Because True Love is a thing forever.

The love we shared was a quite love.
For us to show the way we really felt,
Thrills and excitement were never needed,
Because True Love has a voice of its own.

Even though he's no longer at my side,
I still love him just as much as ever.
For me he'll always be here with me,
Because True Love can never be denied.

Once again some day we'll be together,
Hand in hand to stroll the fields of clover.
Never more shall we be apart because,
True Love is something forever.

—*Marie Davis*

Time

Time is such a priceless thing,
   It passes us so swiftly by,
This is our moment to live and do,
   For some of us, perchance, to die.

But while we live, let's fill it full
   Of worthy things and true,
Of words that count and deeds that bless,
   To lift another's hope anew.

And when that bright tomorrow comes
   For which we all have prayed,
We'll look into the face of God
   Alone, perhaps, but not afraid.

—*Velma Kienel*

Inertia/City Dweller

I sat and I heard what seemed like a pounding thunder;
It roared; It clapped; It rapped; It moved over and under.
"Maybe," I uttered. "It's a passing storm or a rare sonic boom ."
"What a noise!" I thought. As it moved through the room.

Alone in my space, as it moved through the house.
So, I crept to my window to peep-out, tippy-toeing quiet as mouse.
Although, the sun was bright; the sky was clear.
I heard the rapping of thunder coming. It was very near.

The clock in my house struck twelve o'clock
Tick-Tock, Tick-Tock
Along strolled a Brother, on his shoulder was a loud rapping boom box.
—*Rae McBride*

Family:

Why do you argue, cuss and fight
It seems to happen almost every night
Have you ever took the time to discuss
That we are tired of Satan leading us
Family look at me
Don't you see it's time to be free
People don't you see the enemy is so vile
Just take out one minute to smile
Our children are not very amused
Look on their faces they are totally confused
Mom and Dad stop flirting
Don't you see your children are hurting
It must not be a fable
We never sit at the table
Are someone going to ever say
Can we hold hands and pray
—*Roy Chambers*

Three Key's

Arise my son from your place of rest, though the day is young, it soon will pass, reach for the top, your goal to excel, climb to new height's never yet held.

For desire and ambition are simply the key's to open vast treasures of secrets and dreams. Let faith be your strength yield not unto doubt, for great ideas are born, from within ones self.

The strength of a person as measured by time, is not physical strength, but power of mind. For the power of knowledge, put in motion by deed, is the greatest weapon the world has yet seen. So seek after knowledge, for then you shall see, you will hold in your hand the master key.

Knowledge, desire and ambition indeed, are all that is needed for one to succeed. The door to success, though closed it may be, will surly be opened by these Three Key's.
—*Michael Dawson*

Preservation - Luke 17:33

A rose will bloom forth from the broken ground
Its petals embrace life without a sound
The aroma will not linger from its earthen bed
The sweetest scent comes after the flower's crushed and dead
From the brokenness of man came another tender shoot
Some only saw the surface, very few the root
A man of sorrow, acquainted with pain
He was crushed as petals, under the strain
From the weight of the world He bore it all
That we may live and know our call
Like a rose, crushed and dead
So he may reign in us instead
—*Monica Kittleson*

Separate Pieces

Who is or what is
  it that keeps me
from myself -

that keeps me out of
   c o n n e c t i o n s ?

Who claims and proclaims
  my unworthiness!

I cuddle in the arms of the angel;

Crying out of separateness
     severed, scattered, dispersed among the cosmos!

Will those particles come
together? What is this
frantic force which

  Spins the winds of divisions?

My anger burns an
  empty spot.
Coals of longing are left.

Alone - Because

I am not with MYSELF

Devastated on the brink of possibilities.
—*Penny Schricker*

The Ghosts Of The Sea

The ghosts of the sunken ships remember the fog,
It was like the danger of a wild, mad dog.

Hidden in the darkness it came into the night,
Everyone aboard the sailing ship became affright.

They lost their way in that thick cloud as they felt the rhythm of the waves,
They could hear the water as it crashed against the shore and caves.

Before the sailors knew it they were in the sea among the rolling, foaming crests,
The deep sea was calling them as the waves broke across their breasts.

The high seas had taken another ship as it lay battered among the rocks, moving slowly with the tide,
Softly they could hear the whispering of the fog as it spoke to the ocean wide.

The ghosts of the sea beckon as the ocean becomes a sheet of glass,
The fog has lifted and the ghosts of the deep invite the ships who would dare pass.
—*Ronald K. Dawson*

Expression Of Love

How do I express my love?
It's so pure, it's like a Dove.
The only way I know, is to write instead of show.
The love for my father so handsome and strong
The love for my mother, how could I go wrong.
All the years I was there, they showed nothing but care.
Through all the hard times, we heard the music chimes.
God gave me to you because only he knew
That I needed tough love so I could battle and shove
My life has been hard and I've also been barred
from taking the easy way out.
Thank you my father, thank you my mother
For wiping my tears along with my fears.
—*Martha Brocho*

A Blade Of Grass Grows In Berlin

A blade of grass grows in Berlin.
It was watered by tears and blood and fertilized with
The frustration and helplessness of a living city.
"Stop - Freedom ends here" ordered one hundred miles of
   concrete.
Courage

A green field flourishes in Berlin on once-barren land.
Runners creep across east-west lines where tanks stood firm.
Fresh growth melds the divided city into one field,
One plot of unification.
Freedom

A tree grows in Berlin in no-man's land.
The Wall is gone; the Iron Curtain destroyed.
Oh roots of peace grow deep; Oh limbs stretch toward Heaven
And leaves, touch the land of God.
Peace

A blade of grass grows in Berlin.
   —*Lana Robertson Hayes*

Sadness

Sadness is in everyone's heart
It will make you weak
Sadness takes part of your soul
It is part of your life
Sadness can turn to joy
But joy can turn to sadness
If you lost someone or something
Sadness will be there in a second
As long as there is happiness
There is sadness
Sadness makes you hurt, cry and feel empty
For sadness is loneliness
no one can replace
When there is happy feelings
There are sad feelings
And when there is sad feelings
Something or someone can
Brighten your day
   —*N. Eldred*

After The Womb

My mothers love has made a darkened stop,
It will not give what is want or need.
A deep want for feeling, to find I know not were.
I look to find my gift to share,
I look to find offering and know it never there.
The clues have been dropped over many many years.
I pay no mind, I reason her behavior.
I stop to worry, could this be wrong?
Finding only pain, anger, confusion in my life,
To her a life, that is gone.
Only she holds the key, should the lock be picked?
To try for her love and live once again.
I could wait longer for the key in her heart,
I need her gift of freedom, will it
come to my door? My heart beats sadly,
All I want is her love. For now I sit and wait,
I hope for Mom with nothing close to hate.
For I also hold a key, it is to my open door,
To this I tell you I love you and forgive you even more.
I love you Mom…I will wait…
   —*Tina Burrus*

The Special Living Doll

Katie Doll is her name - K. D. for short,
It would be meaningful to describe her,
The special living doll on mother earth.

She has blonde-curly hair and big blue eyes,
She stands two feet and seven inches tall,
And she weighs practically within her size.

Katie Doll has clothes like an ordinary girl wears,
Short, T-shirts, caps and sun glasses for summer,
Skirts, blouses and long dresses for winter.

Katie Doll is charming and exceptionally lovable,
She is tender, gracious and extremely beautiful,
She has a magnetic personality that attracts a human soul.

Katie Doll has the family's uppermost support,
To place her name on the honor roll list,
For the special living doll on mother earth.
   —*Philip Muldez*

Changing Winds

The wind blows in my direction.
It's a gentle wind not a gusty wind.
When it's peaceful, the wind whistles;
When it's angry the wind becomes turbulent,
Like the thunder and lightning from a rainstorm.
The wind has inner strength like the human soul.
The fortitude to grow like from a tiny baby to an adult,
or to blossom like the flowers do in Spring.
There is a winter wind that is like the Almighty
and scares the gallant and bravest type of people.
The Summer doesn't have much of a strong wind.
It's rather calm with a touch of a breeze.
The Summer's almost over and the fall will take its place with
the colorful leaves falling to the ground without making a
single sound.
I love the fall. It's a beginning for adventure.
Just grab a light jacket and walk along the scenic view of the
country, and enjoy life's little treasures.
And soon the wind will start howling
and then we know Winter is here with a vengeance.
   —*Susan Simon*

Prejudice

It's a black thing
It's a white thing
It's a human thing to me
and I don't understand why people don't leave it alone
It is a thing that is not of any importance.
There are a lot of things that the world should think about
not the stupid things as Prejudice.
If everyone in the world minded their own business,
we would not have this problem.
There a lot of things that people do that you dislike,
but why linger on it???
Just let it be and forget about it. . .
The world has become a place of hatred, violence, and of no
Love whatsoever. .

Why has it become a place like that? ? ?
In the beginning it was okay,
but now look at it. . .
Go on and do the things that are wrong if you like,
but don't bring me into it. . .
Sincerely, unhappy…
   —*Stephanie Ijames*

Happiness

Happiness is something wonderful.
It's all over the place.
A rose in bloom with beautiful red color.
The policeman on the corner tooting his whistle,
Tipping his hat to me as I cross the street.
A doorman saying good morning to me with a big
　smile on his face.
The chocolate on a child's face as his tongue tries
　to lick it off.
Happiness is the newspaper man asking me, "where
　have you been, stranger?"

So you see, it doesn't take much for me to find
　happiness.
All I have to do is look all around me.
Up at the sky with the birds flying above,
The trees swaying in the breeze,
The sweet aromas coming from the bakery shop.

But most of all, you see happiness is something
I don't have to buy, for it's waiting there for me.
　—Rosette Mines

An Ode To A Mango

It was sitting there
Its awesome presence and luscious covering captivated my entire
　being
Its bulged skin depicted the unending nectar to be sucked from
　its fruit
I stared at it
My eyes began to roll
My mouth began to dribble like a leaky faucet
drip.. drip.. drip
I took it up
Slowly...
I placed it under my nose
I inhaled its delicate aroma
It was intoxicating
Its skin felt smooth
I could taste it
My teeth wanted to sink into its beauty
And my mouth wanted to bring its taste to life.
　—Lorna Grant

Untitled

I see a light shining far away.
Its glimmer gives hope of a better today.
The darkness holds my prayers
And like the sun, they too, will rise again at
the start of the day.

Angry children fight on the streets.
With their guns and their gangs their future looks bleak.
But they are us ... a side we don't see.
They hold our future and they put it at our feet.

There's more than the nightly news or the papers can do.
It's up to each of us to help pull this world through.
By reaching out to a troubled soul
We can make today grow into a better tomorrow.

It won't be easy ... the pain will be great.
But if our heart is true then we know what we must do.
So reach out to someone in pain. Show them that you care.
We have a better world to prepare.
　—Tirana Blok

Dionysian

The sun rises and sets day after day-
Its light beaming with brightness and reason.
Like a photograph it seems, and seeks,
to stop time.

Clouds sometimes beckon the horizon-
Airy and moving they flow, provoking our deepest emotions.
Like a musical composition they can be
associated with many different arrangements:
Rain; Lightning; Thunder;
in a Dionysian atmosphere.

The sun, with its light and reason,
is the symbol of our present-day culture
in which man comprehends the earth from afar.

The clouds, with their moving depths,
are characteristic of tribal times —
Times when women ran into the darkness,
unencumbered by domesticity and reason,
searching for their god, Dionysus.
　—Lisa Heffernan

A Mother's Wish

It's not the fancy gifts you give to me at certain times.
It's not the colorful cards you buy with pretty words and
　rhymes
It's not a big show of affection or acts of love pretended
It's not of promises made and promises rescinded.
I'll tell you what it's all about, it's simple and it's free
It's a pat on the back, a little hug and a wink especially
　for me.
It's now, you're special, Mom you look pretty
Or something silly like that
But oh it's all those little things that make my heart pit-pat.
If I had but this one wish to make my dream come true.
It wouldn't be on expensive gift
Just a quiet mother I love you.
　—Marilyn H. Welch

It's So Hard

There comes a day that we all must cry;
it's the day we say good-bye. You try to
hold back all your tears, but you can't
because the love you shared through
the years. It hurt so bad to lose the one
you had come to love so much; because
her spirit had a golden touch.
Nevertheless you can rest your tears;
because an angel of God has appeared.
She now can put her soul to rest; for
we all know that God knows what's best.
Although we know we'll never see her
face, deep in our heart we know she's
going to a better place.
　—Roy Bogan, III

Got The Cyrus Virus

Well I got the cyrus virus
It told it on the Rido
Just sit and listening at him
and they ant nothing to take for
it cause it ant like the flu
I even went and seen him in Dalton, Georgia,
and Knoxville and it just keeps getting worse
and worse every day,
well it's just hard to get rid of it
　—Star Elaine Mambur

Listen

To speak is easy, to listen is not
It's what we must learn to move from this spot
To listen to words or the wind or a song
Can shorten the way that we fear is too long
By listening we learn most of what's known
It's let us progress, it's how we have grown
What we've attained, the seeds that we've sown
Are from what we've heard, not we on our own
The tools of the present, come from the past
We've listened and learned how they can last
How can we learn what others are feeling
Listen and learn their words are revealing
In order that speech be a means for sharing
With what we teach we must be caring
To show that we care we must be attuned
That the tree of this knowledge be carefully pruned
It has often been said that knowledge is power
To listen's the water than makes its seed flower
Listen and learn so that we might gain
By what we have learned, what we've attained

—*Matthew DiMinno*

My Dad

When trying to make a decision, I throw in the dice.
It's you, my darling Father, I come to for advice.
When life seems to become unfair, tears fall from my eyes.
It's your compassion, Dad, that separates truth from all those lies.
And if someone asks, "Who is that lad?"
My heart swells and I reply, "Why, that's my Dad!"
When money continues to rule this world, sometimes I fall in the ditches.
It's with you, my loving Father, I know of true riches.
When God's forests come rumbling down, the world seems so small.
It's your knowledge and achievements, Dad, rebuilding structures tall.
And if someone asks, "Who is that lad?"
My pride sweeps and I reply, "Why, that's my Dad!"
When other men have dropped their seed, and forgot their sons and daughters wept,
It is through your goodness and unselfishness, Dad, our bond is stronger kept.
When the day comes when fate may pull us apart,
It's you, my sweet Father, who will be forever in my heart.
And if an angel asks, "Who is that lad?"
My prayers will shout, "Why it's my Dad!"

—*Patricia Sommers Barnett*

Columbia River Communion

I've been acquainted with the river.
I've felt its presence, wet and deep.
In empathy I've visited
The fishes where they sleep.

Sliding only a foot below
The deck on which I stroll,
The voice of the river calls me
From the swells that, endless, roll.

The river's knowledge of the past;
Its prescience of time to come,
And the power of its continuum
Commands me, "Come, come home!"

I back away with trembling breath
And steady my eager tread
Determined to resist the river's pull,
And to savor life instead.

The moment is gone and I turn away,
But with ecstasy aquiver
Knowing I have been, in a mystic way,
Acquainted with the river.

—*Mary B. Hurley*

Lost Love

Although you and I had to part,
   I've never gotten you out of my heart.
I think of times we used to share,
   how nice it felt to have you there.
And when I sleep it always seems,
   memories of you are in my dreams.
I miss you more than you'll ever know.
   my love for you burns deep in my soul.
Because you see I love you still,
   and as long as I live I always will...

—*William C. Woodson*

In A Corner Of My Mind

In a corner of my mind,
   I've tried to block the memory,
To protect me from the pain.
   Pretend I never knew you,
And never heard your name.
   But the walls I built aren't strong enough,
And though I fight my tears in vain,
   The feelings still come creeping through,
And the hurt is still the same.
   I wish that I could forget you,
Or make you disappear.
   I thought I could trust you,
But somehow I was wrong.
   How you could do this is beyond me.
The pain may go away,
   And the tears may pause.
But the painful memories will exist forever
   In a corner of my mind.

—*Tabitha Rice*

It's Easter Time Again

Hooray, Hooray, it's Easter once more,
Jesus has risen and opened the door,
For spring to warm us and greet us
And light the way;
The darkness of winter has passed away.

It's Easter time with renewed hope and love,
The blessings have come from Heaven above.
Again and again, every year we awake
To new life and a chance
To renounce all our hate.

So cherish these luscious days of Spring,
With robins and flowers and everything.
The sunshine, the clouds,
The gentle rain, that bless us all
Over and over again.

—*Mary Lucci*

A Poem

Why, is a poem called a poem. Is it meant to rhyme, form a jingle or create a song, but to me a poem is words of love and thought ..... a thing of beauty to be sought.

—*Tommie Lee Watkins*

The Flower

Rain drops fall to the ground
Later to from a stream
Suddenly a flower grew not knowing
Where it came from or how it came
It is the most beautiful thing you've ever seen
The only thing more beautiful is you

—*Mark Saleeby*

Joy Of My Life

Early one fall before the morning sun, a new
Joy entered my life. So tiny, so warm, so full
of life. The agony and pain was well worth it.
You are so unlike any other. You make my day,
when it has been dark and gray. You are the love
of my life. Your big brown eyes are the mirrors
of the world, for in them you I see all that could
be and I see me. Many a day I stand and watch you
and shed a tear. A tear of pain and a tear of joy.
I wonder what life holds in store for you.

Will you be happy? My motto to you my son,
"Stand tall and never fall. Be a man, the very best
that you can." As I enter the fall of my life and
you enter the early spring of your life, I wish you
all the very best that life has to offer. You are the
Joy of my life, My son.

—*Sam H. Hughes*

Who Will Step Forward?

How far have we come
Just a few more steps it may seem
Then who will step forward
And say we have reached the dream
How far must we go
Just a few more years it may seem
Then who will declare we have reached the dream
Equality, dignity, self-esteem and pride
Who will analyze the dream before it's put aside
How long will it last
How far must it go
What man or woman will step forward and say
I know!

—*Wendell S. Hawkins*

Happy Little Christmas Tree

I'm a happy little Christmas tree
just come and take a look at me
In the summer I'm bright and green
In the winter I'm snowy white
But I'm the prettiest of all at Christmas
Just you wait and see.
When I'll be red, green and blue and maybe silver too.
At Christmas that's me.
Yes, I'm a happy little Christmas tree
At Christmas I'll have a front row seat
to see Santa Claus
And he'll be dressed in his Christmas best
With a big bag of toys. And all the kids are full of joy
Now you see why I'm a happy little Christmas tree.
Then I see under my decorated feet all the presents
Wrapped so neat. Waiting for the kids to get a treat.
There's Mom and Dad with their faces lit up like mine.
Waiting for the kids to have a good time.
Now you can see why I'm a happy little Christmas tree.

—*Robert C. Allen*

It Hurts

It hurts to be mad
It hurts to be sad
But it really hurts when you're not there
Or when you don't say you care
It hurts when you break my heart
It hurts when we are apart
It hurts to know you may not come back
It hurts to think it might be a fact
It really hurts when you don't say I love you

—*Mary Livesay*

Loves Sweet Reality

Come walk with me my darling. You'll be amazed by what you'll
   find.
Just take my hand and open your heart to the wonders of my mind.
Come explore these precious feelings and the love I have to give.
Come see this joyous world in which your love gave me to live.
The beauty and the wonder. Vast elation you've made known,
Are in my mind for you to see. Just ask and you'll be shown.
The peace that has engulfed me since you surrounded me with
   love,
Is not for words for most know not the peace I do speak of.
That tranquil easy feeling when true love has been found.
Given pure and naturally from the heart without a sound.
So experience all these feelings whose depths with you I share.
Come fly with me into the clouds and walk with me on air.
And as we soar up through the clouds setting our love free,
Our two make one, this dreams becomes love's sweet reality.

—*Severn*

Untitled

Is love just another four letter word? Something people say
just to hurt others. Because as soon as you use it you let
down your guard and soon the pain comes, the pain of which this
word brings? What is love? To some people it's just a word,
something they say because they think it's the right thing to
do, but is love something that you can just think up, or is it
an emotion, something that you feel. People mistake thoughts
and feelings it's easy to do they both come from inside ones
inner self, but one is down low in your heart and isn't always
easy to get to. Love is something someone gives to someone
else to show how much they care. Love is a special gift that
is given to you, but like a drug people abuse it, think they
can casually use it, take it in stride, but sooner or later
someone gets hooked and they are all caught up in something
they don't understand. Love is a two way street but for some
people this street ends up in nothing more than a dead end.
Love to me is getting to know someone while they get to know
you. Sharing feelings with someone and not being embarrassed
to have them. To respect one another. To care for one
another.

—*Sara Arreola*

Sweet Surprises

Dainty white lace curtains; pastel pink from wall to wall,
Just waiting for a baby girl, so precious and so small.
I anticipate the moment I can hold her in my arms
And brag as all good parents do about her many charms.

Later when she's toddling, as mothers do with girls,
I'll dress her up with pearls and lace and fix her hair in curls.
Someday we'll share our secrets as we snuggle up in bed
And watch a scary movie while we paint our toenails red.

We'll shop until we drop—I'll buy her everything in sight!
We'll be the best of friends and we will never, ever fight.
When she's older we'll put makeup on, my grown-up girl and I.
And I'll have all the answers every time she asks me why.

I feel it in my heart that she will soon be on her way.
The doctor says that he suspects it might be any day.
And then I'll have the one thing that will make my dreams come
   true,
A darling daughter all my own, so beautiful and new.

I check the nursery one last time and close the door real slow.
Then I wake my husband gently, telling him it's time to go.
The baby's born, and I confess I never felt such joy
When I became the mother of a bouncing baby boy.

—*Linda J. Knaus*

Retirement Is Bliss

In the office I sat, day after day
  Keeping books, there was no other way.
Some day, old enough I would be,
  To retire and come home, you see.

We flew to Jamaica, what a beautiful scene!
  Ninety degrees weather in January, I mean.
Mini vacations are what we have now,
  New places, new friends and how!

No, I wasn't anxious to get old.
  I'm younger than 10 years ago.
Magazines - time to read all of mine.
  Many books I've read every line.

Ceramics, doll making, crafts of all kinds.
  Time for volunteer works I find.
Take grand-children to the beach for fun.
  They all like games (even if I've won).

New and old recipes and times to bake.
  No alarm clocks startle me awake.
Aquatic exercises begin at 10:00,
  Bored? This I don't intend.
    —*Mary Barnes*

Drugs

Drugs is one of the problems that plagues our society today;
Killing, maiming and robbing us of our safety in every way.

Whether it be on the streets or behind a closed door;
Drugs are causing grief and pain and much, much more.

There are some things that Drugs can cause you to do;
Like being cruel, irresponsible and dishonest too;

Drugs cause greed and violence in nearly every community;
Clearing a path a devastation at any given opportunity.

Adults and children alike are innocent victims of crime;
No one utters a word, fearing it may be them the next time.

Dealers use our children for cover-up, profits and greed;
Destroying the minds of our future and planting a bad seed.

Deformities present at birth occurs from Drugs effects;
The ending result is death or children becoming rejects.

Drugs give you the illusion that your totally in control;
Deceiving you into destroying your mind, body and soul.

So stop, look and see what Drugs are causing around you;
Drugs are surely the last thing you'll ever want to do.

Get your education, reach your goals, leave behind the rest;
Say No To Drugs and your on your way to achieving your best.
  —*Stephanie S. Wallace*

Clowns

Clowns are supposed to make you laugh, but not cry,
Laughter is good as gold, tears are dross,
Behind a clown's make-up, there can be pathos,
Pagliacci hid behind his make-up, a broken heart.

Cupid's arrow had pierced too deep,
He did nothing but sing, and once off stage, did weep,
Sunshine and rain mixed together,
Can produce a rainbow,
With streams of light in tow,
So it follows suit, that life is made up of ups and downs,
One day wearing a frown,
The next a crown, a halo of happiness.
  —*Sylvia Ashley*

Giving New Love A Chance

Caring, sharing, trusting is...
Laborious, frustrating, perplexing ...
Difficult to do
When love has hurt so much
Leaving the heart ...
Barren, unyielding, fruitless
Love's defeats leaves a doubting,
Questioning state of mind
Too cynical, skeptical to try again
That's when one needs to give new love a chance

New love is a refreshing breath of air
Scented like the smell of grass cut on a sunny day
Aromatically rich as a rose
New love, a perfumed bouquet of spring flowers
The essence bringing one's heart alive
Deeply breathing in the fragrant joys

Sweet and pure is the fruit of a bountiful new love ...
  Abundant in its caring ...plentiful in its sharing ...
    Natural, fertile and rich flavored like vintage wine
  —*Terri L. Johnson*

His Game's Name Was Love

One warm February day in Richmond, VA, beside his mother was
laid to rest, a quietly gentle prince of humble birth.
Whose color denied him playing tennis on most public courts
of clay or dirt. His close knit family prioritized academics
first, then pursued his dream, wielding a racquet across planet
Earth. Championships at Forest Hills and Wimbledon, broke
barriers, setting the pace. Sharing personally in South Africa's
struggle, helped bring justice to his race. Took our three young
children to see him practice on the Davis Cup Team. Years later,
as symphony receptions, guest of honor, autographed my napkin
with his name. Heart problems, in his life's prime, caused great
concern, noting from competition, his exceptional courage taught
many youths to learn. To play life's game rules on the court,
rather than breaking them and landing in court. Life's greatest
challenge, he wasn't able to back, when media headlined his
illness, medical science has yet to defeat. His grace, strength and
dignity helped erase much stigma, giving hope for the AIDS cause.
Funeral celebrations of his life was interjected with loud applause.
Wife, Jeannie, and daughter, camera, should be proud of loving
tributes.
  —*Laura Crowder*

City Of Angels

I live in the City of Angels,
Land where only demons survive.
Home of the fallen angels.
Where innocence comes when it's willing to die.
I'd begun to give into temptations,
My will to survive, gave into the fight.
My virtues devoured by wicked sensations,
Of being who kept me away from the light.
Then on mystical day, out of the blue.
Fate decided to bring me to you.
Presenting me with wings anew,
You made me feel your love was true.
Now your gone, I'm here alone,
I fight to keep away my fear,
And evil deeds of which I'm prone.
Oh how I wish that you were here,
With me, in the City of Angels.
  —*Nicole Rhea Hansen*

Free Your Mind...

Free your mind,
Learn how to be color blind.
Don't judge people by the way they look,
Just like you don't judge the cover of a book.
Don't think the kid on the back
Seat can't read and write, just because he's black.
Don't be afraid to say hello
To the new girl in your class, just because her skin is yellow.
Don't think the boy named Pablo
Is naive and less ambitious, just because he's from down below.
Don't assume that all whites are snotty
And that they have no respect for minority.
C'mon, you know we're all human beings,
let's not hurt each other's feelings.
Instead, let's accept one another,
And join our hands in unity together.
—*Maria Ailen Borromeo-Dolatre*

Missing Feather

This is the way, walking by myself
   learning to love
Smiling, head up and arms back
   The pain wasn't too heavy til I met
You, experienced liar with a graceful sway
   My, I, rebellious heart drown in tears of your say.
Tripping over my mindless soul,
   What is see-through?
Music, laughter and claps of approval
   While into the passage, my flowers bud blossom,
Reformational soul and spirit as my feet ferment
Walking along with the sunlight,
   blind by the dark trees as you watch
the sadness aroma swifts by me.
     I'm walking by myself learning to love;
    You for what, I sing softly with the birds,
   While flying away from the prey. Turn around
and looked, learned and love as I save my day.
—*Stephanie Woodall Jawaid*

The Storm

Proud men and women were sent to the storm,
Leaving behind their families and babies unborn.
I had my doubts and I had my fears,
Praying each night as my eyes filled with tears.

Fighting for our country scared as can be,
Wondering if another day they will ever see.
Barely getting their rest and losing sleep,
Praying to God their soul he will keep.

Yellow ribbons displayed and flags flying high,
Mourning families cried as they said their final goodbye.
I never thought this country would be in a war,
Don't our leaders give a care anymore.

Watching the evening news for the latest,
Bush & Hussein competing to be the greatest.
Lives being lost over oil prices,
I wish they had the heart to end this crisis.

Prisoners of war want to be set free,
Hoping that the two leaders would soon agree.
Brave soldiers fighting in a country far away,
Asking God for world peace is what I pray.
—*Yolanda Joiner*

Human Spirit

The rain washes over my face
leaving not a trace of tears
scars from the fears of years passed by
and yet... I still want to try

To begin again and again
a true survivor from the wars
of circumstances and lies
and yet ... I still want to try

I feel an ocean of beauty within me
to come forth upon this planet earth
a new beginning - a rebirth
from all the evil and the cries
and yet ... I still want to try

If you ever get lonely, need a true friend
if the road seems too weary, and you cannot bend
call to me - I will come
and listen to your sorrows
of the days gone by
and yet... I know
you will still want to try
—*Nancy E. Keeler*

The Loss

Death steals away the ones you love,
Leaving you to face life on your own.
You temporarily stop believing in God up above,
And no one calls you on the phone.
You walk around for a while in a daze,
And your friends are there now to help you again
You're feeling better in so many ways,
Even though it still hurts every now and then.
Eventually the hurt and anger become a dull ache,
And you've put your memories away in your heart on a shelf.
   You've learned that life is never a piece of cake,
and the strength to get through this . . .
lies within yourself.
—*Sharon L. Torres*

A Prayer For Life

If I am to drown,
let it be in the North Sea
where the water's cold can numb
me past caring for the world.

If I am to die by fire,
let it be while rescuing a stranger's child
from that crackling anger.

If I am to be a traffic fatality,
let me swerve to avoid a deer
scrambling across an unnatural path
we have cut across her land.

If I am to be claimed by AIDS,
let me be counted among the many
while taking no one with me,
and let my obituary not mince words.

If my heart stops short,
let someone else see with my eyes,
let me help even at the end.

But if I am to live
let it be with you.
—*P. Dean Pearson*

Black Unity

Let B stand for B eauteous, not for B ullets
Let L stand for L earning, not for L ooting
Let A stand for A chieving, not for A rson
Let C stand for C ultivate, not for C rack
Let K stand for K indness, not for K illing

Let U stand for U pright, not for U ptight
Let N stand for N otable, not for N otoriety
Let I stand for I nsight, not for I ndifference
Let T stand for T hrifty, not for T houghtless
Yes Y ou be all Y ou can, develop Y ourselves.
—*Yvonne Pamela Shepherd-Marshall*

Silent Night

Silent night, how sweet the sound, that saved a wretch like me Let there be peace on Earth, and let it begin with me. Hallowing cries from youths mislead. Misleading. James, 4 and 10. Hiding his face, hiding his soul, and mounting the steps to number 411. And silenced from the roar of media, and shut away for correction. A trigger's flash, a stray thought...mislead. Dust blown tears echo from the belly of abysses unseen. Mislearned. Mary, 12 years. Raking her mother's purse for one more moment of rainbow-drenched spirals...strobe stars...and choruses of pretty lights. Laying on this satin pillow, her eyes wide with greedy expectation. As her mother lowers the enameled handles over her still form. Mislearned. Carrie, age 13, and not yet a woman; again enters the sheets which envelope her pain. everyday challenges becoming a war, thanks to the solution she found. Seeping depression...sanity ajar...Screams capsulated in her tears as he again forces himself upon her. Muted. Misloved. Peace on Earth! Goodwill toward men... One thousand, nine hundred and ninety-three years have yielded. How long? How long until another, Silent Night?
—*Susan Hassell*

Oh, Israel, Promised Land Of The Bible

Oh, Israel, promised land of the Bible,
Let us cultivate your deserts
Into blooming orchards and fertile fields.
Let us build foundations for the future
On the history of the past
With a firm grasp on the present.
Let your land be a land of peace
And sanctuary for all people.
Let us live in the warmth of the sun
That extends into our hearts.
May the land of milk and honey of the Bible
Again give forth the sweet fruits of loving labor
And dream for peace.
But if we must fight for our cherished land,
Give us the strength to preserve the laws of the Torah
And remember that while the land rests with the people,
Our hearts belong to God.
—*Shirley Cheifetz Silverburg*

Going Crazy

     Going crazy, want to come?
      Let's leave reality behind
       Let's take our thoughts
    And burn them beyond recognition
Let's take our sorrows to the extreme
And shelter our souls from the rest of the world
   Let's take everything we've ever learned
    And disregard it from our heads
     Let's create a paradise of passion
      To ignite the flames of hell
      That live inside our hearts
     Going crazy, want to come?
      Just turn on your t.v. set
—*Mark Rosier*

Rockport Memories

The morning call of a raucous crow
Lets me know it's time to be up, on the go,
As with Orff-like pattern and precision
It announces town-wide a personal decision
To enjoy a God-given day in Rockport.

Then the Town Clock follows with its message
In tones round and resonant, announcing the hour
Reminding all: "Make the most of this day!"
It's a special spot, this beautiful place...
Whether off to work or just to play, in Rockport.

If the beach calls, waves lapping beige damp sand,
Add footprints with terns, gulls and town pigeons
That land, sociably sharing the beach
But always just out of reach, on a balmy day
Left from summer's display, in Rockport

From a pond on the hill, beachward running,
A fresh-water rill travels down over rocks,
Its sparkling flow all birds welcome and know
As they happily drink near the ocean's brink
On a bright end-of-summer day in Rockport.
—*K. Helena R. Laramee*

Every Day Is s Piece of Gold!

Every day is a piece of gold.
Letters lining up to enter my brain.
News waits me to read.
Politicians, sociologists, naturalist, artists face me
on T.V., newspapers, and books.
What do I lack?
My God!
You do love me in our color world.

Every day is a piece of gold.
Birds wait me to sing in chorus.
Trees have contest with me, oh, who grow up faster?
Flowers smile to me, oh, who win more appreciations?
on air, ground, and hearts.
What do I need?
My God!
You do love me in our cold world.

Every day is a piece of gold.
I put it in a furnace, to build pure human faces.
—*Millie Lee*

Reminiscence

At the ripe old age of eighty-seven
Life has not all been hell
Nor has it all been heaven
With the fine young son to take my place
And a beautiful grandson to join the race
A loving wife, who is a fine cook
Who, at any time reads me like a book
I think of the young man who liked to play
Chasing the girls night and day
Now I walk down the street with cane in hand
And wish I were back where it all began
I see pretty girls with their skirts in the wind
Gosh, it would be great to be only Eighty again.

If we could see the same girls 30 years hence
With added weight that make the scales wince
With blue and grey hair and a wrinkle or two
Ask them their age, they lie about that, too
With too much red on cheek and lips
Their skirts no longer fly in the wind
'Cause it can't get 'em over their hips.
—*Les Ferguson*

Upon Waking

When a shard from death
pierces the shield
of anesthesia,
anguish mutilates
the tapestry of being
and spills its life
in a blood-stained crawl
into the journey of return
into the lap of existence.
—*Alice P. Smith*

Run On Sentence

When, alas by blight diffused,
Weary muse laid pen to rest,
She tossed and turned till early morn
Suffered light, at last, confess

How, pen is fed, when nectar bled
Feeds flowers, and, trees, and, bees,
As honey stored pours golden words
That rime, in time, might hum and please

Still, if sentence runs beyond her ken,
Will beauty thus, again, be torn,
Or breasted rose by time sore pressed
Know grief beyond invasive thorns?
—*Marie C. Andrea*

Haunted

Where are love's flames,
Where is the fire
Of burning lust
And wild desire?
I must accept
The dry cold dust
Of death's pyre—
Riches of joy
And piles of pleasure,
Amor's white pearls
And passion's treasure
Are lost forever—
But their shadows
Never leave me,
They haunt my heart,
Pulling it apart
With the rough strings
Of memory.
—*Magda Herzberger*

Night

Night's beauty is a fast winged humming bird
That never hovers long, but flies from me
Into the distance, grey as memory,
Whose short flight ends when morning's song is heard.
But yet a bird whose silver-coated throat
Pours forth exquisite music from the heart,
Exceeding virtuoso's frenzied dart
With a medley of tunes or single artless note.
A bird whose subtle coloring, soft and grey,
Fades quietly into dark surrounding ground
As beauty in the morning newly found
Fades into lengthened shadows of the day.
   Such beauty is too delicate and rare
   To stand the day's unknowing graceless stare.
—*Lydia Ann Kapell*

God's Plan

The sun is burning our souls.
With blistering heat that hums with insects
Still we swing the scythes with precision and grace
Time is like a shadow that hounds our trail.

Any delay could cost an acre.
Hands as rough as stone beat back the loss, the heat, the insects
The harvest is bountiful, and the winter just an afterthought

But God has a plan and we don't always understand.
Old man river is thundering down our doors.
Old man river is raping our fields.
Old man river is a mighty image.

Last year he fed our crops and this year he's taking them away.
The rain keeps coming, drenching us in our own private hell.
Yet we toss the sand bags with determination and love for our homes.

And hands as rough as stone gently brush away tears of sorrow.
There won't be any harvest this year, and the winter is foremost in
   our minds.

But God has got a plan, and yes, we don't always understand
But it's God's plan and this helps us to stand.
Because old man river ain't bigger than God.
—*Margaret Taylor*

The Souls Of Our Youth

Tides slip away,
leaving the souls restless.

Grasping at nothing;
looking towards white.
Everything gone,
walking in black.

Kisses of red
turn the white to pink,
and black is blacker
as the souls wander on.

Meaningless is this life.
Worthless is this tear.
Careless are the seas,
washing the souls colorless.

A sea of red,
on the shore of white.

Black are we;
as we wander in the night.
—*Rebecca Baumgarner*

Survivor

like a cactus   bearing untold riches
of moist softness   beyond its
gates of desert armored,   skin,
my modern love stands silent
in this desert, so aware of its own peril,
and the cruel world, and the   hard earth.
soft as any nectar, wet, clean.
capable of pleasure or pain
searing sun   or winter night.
survivor.
—*Susan D. Tausch*

Checking False Labor At Two A.M.

The sadness no one takes for love
at the beginning

I pass on.

Flash/light flits
across the building
the little dog
washed
by icy waters.

Whatever it is
waits with us in the dark.

At the fourth corner
sniffing along baselines
rooting
nosing around
a buried nest
a stone.

What we can't find isn't anywhere.
I listen for it

I hear breathing
and can't stop.
—D. P. Dresbach

Sonnet To My Son

Today my soul near died a thousand deaths
Of strangulation, and each time it came
Alive again it gasped anew for breaths
Of pure and unpolluted air to shame
The shabbiness of weakness at a time
When strength of mind and heart were vital to
The mission God placed in my hands. The chime
Played by my heart upon my soul was too
Discordant to be music. Life was out
Of tune, its harmony upset by chords
Of strife and tribulation. Then the bout
Was won; for peace, with night, dispersed the swords.
   My child is once my heart, again my soul.
   Not one without the two can make me whole.
—Ruth G. Boyer

The Branch That Carried A Dove

With your hands, unformed,
Reach my face and cry.
I will hold your time
In a shape and form.

With your eyes, opaque,
Search my soul and cry.
In a forsaken corner of time
Is light, bathing and dry.

With a name, yet unknown,
Call a smile to my face.
I have lost the immense
Joy that I once had.

But do smile and simper
And tenderly, hug your self.
I have memories of the future
And a few laughs from the past.

And then, in a night so dark
That a bat lost its branch,
Go away. To the boys of barren chests
Give the smile I once had.
—Vahe A. Kazandjian, Ph.D.

The Immortal Artist

The easel stands desolate in the corner of the room,
Paints and brushes that once created images lie Idle.
The Portraits stare down from the walls;
As though they too know that life is drained
From the Source that once created them.
Stillness Prevails, but haunting tunes linger
with sweet memories of times gone by,
When vibrations beckoned, and telepathy of minds entwined
In thoughts of beauty, color, grace and love.
Inspiration sought no bounds, it soared to heights of greatness.
One being all devoted to one cause, that of love.
Happiness is lost, it faded with the loss of life,
But having knowledge of what will be
Brings rapture to the soul, and hopes of Immortality.
—V. Ursula Galley

Ruins

Splintered paddles, bolts and dowels
Rivets soaked in sodden planks
Keel and rudder poke from mounds of sand

Tide comes in, it creaks the timber
To rhythms of his ravaged bones
As tremors uncontrolled
Quiver with each ripple of the sea

He sits amid the remnants of his boat
With rheumy eyes observes the flotsam
Of a wrecked and shattered craft
Sits there in the sun's warmth

Surrounded by the ruins
Of a seaworthy dream
That once was home.
—Shirley Brezenoff

Promise To My Lover

In the middle of the night
silence, night and me,
we are one entity.
We have no shadow.

In the middle of the night,
I remember, long time ago
I made a promise to my
lover, that I will write one
hundred and five poems
about our love, so fast I wrote
only one about our separation.

In the middle of the night
I realize that silence, night
and me, we don't know
how I will keep the promise
to my lover.
—Sait Mohan Das

Misunderstanding

My sanctuary of darkness,
I've fallen again.
Don't deny me my chance.
Stop this insanity.
The light breaks the silence.
Stop the noise,
it is too loud,
it blinds my hearing.
Save me this once.
Don't walk away now;
Finish what you've started.
—Neela Graham

Requiem Mass

In the darkness of a winter night
the city was asleep
laying like a crescent
below my window.
I seem to remember
the lonely sounds
of a Requiem Mass.

In the brightness of a summer day
the city was alive
moving like a symphony
all around me.
I clearly remember
the forceful vision
of a Requiem Mass.
—*Lynda Lambert*

I Wonder

From whom, gracious, did you get
The nice color of your hair
That makes you look so attractive
Every time it waves into the air?

From where, beloved, did you get
Your delightfully beautiful eyes?
From someone of the glittering star swarms
That adorn the gorgeous, spacious skies?

From where, charming, did you get
The brilliance of the pearls divine
That shine behind your tempting lips
Whenever you gracefully smile?

Who, darling, the sculptor was
That sculptured you body so well?
Was it Bartholdi, Crawford, Cellini,
Phidias, Michelangelo, or Raphael?
—*Victor M. Navarro*

Broadway

Broadway, bright river of light, its mystery
Of dark alleys and closed stage doors, well concealed
Backwaters of an actors' world revealed
To a curious child, who saw school history
In costume, a parade of pointless swords;
The silken ladies and the steel-clad lords
Might go to beaneries to eat oyster stew
When the greasepaint was washed off. And yet she knew
That the descending curtain always fell
At the perfect moment when all things went well
Near midnight. At that witching hour it seemed
That life might yet become what Broadway dreamed!
—*Mary F. Lindsley*

Chalkboard

The world is but a chalkboard
And we are just pieces of chalk
We are packaged
We are used
We are broken
Then we are erased
—*Nicole Marie Larsen*

Smoke Rings

Smoke rings are just like
The good things in my life —
   once, there is a perfect one
   beautifully fragile, round, i's wispy white continuity
   constant while the smoke flows and fluctuates
      within its circular frame.
I hold my breath, hypnotized,
   so as not to disturb its perfection,
   wanting to touch it, but not daring to,
   in full knowledge of the destruction
      that simple act would bring.
But it dissipates anyway, and becomes
   distorted
   and is lost in the other air in my room
And disappears.
—*Lynn C. Lewis*

The Best Watermelon

The best watermelon
we ever ate
was chilled in the icy water
of the Trinity River.
We wiped the sweat
from our foreheads
and watched with saucer eyes
as the crystal water
splashed over the emerald rind
chilling to the core.
Papa pitched pennies
in a shallow place
while Laurie and Lee squealed
to find gold in the river.
He cracked the melon open
on a rock
and handed us a dripping hunk.
The juice ran down his hairy arms.
We spit the seeds at each other
laughing.
—*Kerri L. House*

On Reading What Comes Into My Head

With my eyes wide open
I read what comes into my head:
To define a world where any tree
Can be a cross or ladder,
Any need a silent prayer
Screaming to be heard,
And where nothing equals love.

The rhetoric of my mind
Defines the world without,
Designs my world within.
On its streets I read
The "don't walk" signals
Of my failing dreams.

I'll reach for a winning dream,
Read the language in my head,
Until the scissors of death
Clip my cognitive threads
And I'm unraveled.
—*Joan L. Gordon*

Ode To A Lightpole: Our Urban Metal Sentinel
(An Anti-Graffiti Poem)

Oh, Lightpole, so stately and tall,
Looked up to for guidance by one and all,
We can find our paths with your light.
You safeguard our way, in the darkness of night.

Oh, Lightpole, how with dirt did you get so smeared?
For you, obviously, some citizens had no fear!
They marred your grace with scribblings in black,
Knowing you could not answer back.
Upon you they stuck paper messages of housing and jobs,
Not caring that from you, your grace and dignity they robbed.

Oh, Lightpole, we will try to keep you clean,
So that your beautiful shapes can be seen.
We'll restore your function to give us light,
And not demean you into an urban blight.

—*Rosalind Pinto*

Untitled

The moon searches over a sullen sky,
Looking for clouds to rest on and sigh.
Dreaming of lost loves - of mouchlens so fair,
Or of finding a prince who would really care
The water ripples in moonlight or gloom.
And the moon frames a halo around a lone loon.
the night shivers with fear at his eerie cry.
And loneliness fills the land and the sky.
Soon the darkness will pale,
Night doffs her clock and prepares to leave
Her work is done.
There is a still before the oncoming sun
Stirs the dormant sky awake
As he prepares to span the heavens on his daily run

—*Rose Harkins*

The Little Mouse

Through a crack in the wall, out came a mouse,
   looking for some cheese.
  No one was home, in the big old house,
   So the mouse did what he pleased.

  Into the kitchen, he did scurry,
   To see what he could find.
He knew that he would have to hurry,
   'Cause he didn't have much time.

On the counter, there sat a cake,
   Oh, it looked so yummy.
He gathered up the crumbs to take,
   And filled his little tummy.

The door did slam, the family is back,
   But don't be filled with sorrow.
The mouse ran back, into the crack,
   And will be back tomorrow!

—*Rosemary Ingram*

The Reality Of Things

Peeling off the layers of self deception,
Looking for the truth about myself.
Fighting off the waves of accusation,
And oppositions of those who would oppose.
Digging through all this verbiage,
Looking for the truth; about God, about,
The reality of things.

—*Robert A. O'Brien*

Sea Travelers

As I was sitting on the sandy shore,
Looking out across the sea,
Wondering if the ships I saw,
Were looking back at me,
I wondered if the people there
Were happy and content,
Or were they just pretending,
Was it really what they meant?
And I wondered if their travels,
Would take them to distant shores,
To London Town, or Singapore, or even Zanzibar.
I wondered what it'd be like,
To just sit and talk awhile,
About where they went and what they saw,
Or just to see them smile,
And when they'd remember back again,
At all the things they did,
I bet that they'd be ready,
To travel the seas again.

—*Nora Wright*

No Pain

Alone in my room tears in my eyes.
Looking out the window at the pretty blue skies.
Thinking to myself why always me?
Wondering why, I'm as sad as can be.
But of course there is no pain.
No not for me.
Crying away with no were to go.
Alone in my world with no sense to show.
Don't understand why my family argues, and fights
But of course there is no pain, for me tonight.
No not for me.
Don't know why it had to be I.
I get so sad I start to cry.
Don't want to go, but I must say bye.
Now I must go no tears to show.
With no pain, no pain for me.

—*Tandinika Smith*

Lest We Forget

From the moment of your anxiously awaited birth
Love and favors have been lavished on you.
To your mother and daddy you were the dearest thing on earth.
To brothers and sisters you were extra special too.

Life is so wonderful it is not our desire to forfeit one day.
YOU are YOU - because mother and daddy passed life your way.
You owe them lots of love they were always there for you.
Are your payments up to date or are you overdue?

Your life could have been rough - for all around you to see.
Had mother and daddy not met your needs and lovingly bounced
   you on their knee.
They met your needs because they loved you - their precious child.
Your smiles and laughs pleased them so - your tears drove them
   wild.

It matters not how old we are or where on the road of life we
   might be.
If its happiness you are seeking - then love is the key.
Besides mother and daddy, and brothers and sisters, many others
   will bring love into your life.
I thank God for my precious children and a wonderful loving wife.

Go to a cemetery and notice all the beautiful flowers you see.
All trying to say, "I love you" to someone that used to be.
Let us show our love while the precious gift of life is ours.
Don't wait too late and have to say it with beautiful flowers.

—*Leon Griffith*

First Love Sign

It came a time in life; where the present became the past
Love came and went as a reality, and you wondered if the world
would last. You began living one day at a time. Not looking
ahead nor looking behind. But you were always wondering.
With just one thing on thy mind... Love, love, love, love, love
For it had hit you for the first time.
You were excited, but you were scared. It took you awhile to
see the first sign. Because the signs are not all the same.
For it can be a kiss or a stare; As that love grows stronger,
That sign will always be there.
One morning you might awake and your relationship is gone.
But the love never stops, your memories will always be there
of what you've done. Sure it will hurt for a long time; and
there'll be times it hurts more;
But that's only because you're thinking...thinking of all the
times before. There's no need to look ahead
Because with an attitude like that your love will soon be dead!
—*Sara Bartels*

Love

How do you tell it apart.
Love has to come from the heart.

Just when you think you've found a new start
Love can tear you apart.

One person can come and one can go.
But the time it takes to learn love no one will know.

It just happens in day or night
Love can come from hindsight

But learning love is the biggest test of all
Whether in the spring, summer, winter, or fall

When you find someone you love take care
If you do, their love will always be there

If everyone loves one another
There will be peace, happiness to our sister and brother.
Love what's your meaning.
—*William Robert Davis*

My Wife

Here's this woman in my life,
  Love her so she's my wife.
Anything I need she's always there,
  No other love to compare.
When I'm sick she'll understand.
  Treats me like a baby, I'm a man.
Have a problem that I can't solve.
  Never one bad enough, she can't resolve.
She's always with me, body, soul and mind.
  Never says no, never declines.
Explores my questions, and tells me what's right.
  Always there to hold me tight.
I've never been this close before.
  To this woman that I adore.
Love this lady love her so,
  Hope to God, she never let's me go.
Can't say enough about this girl.
  All I got, all I got in the world.
—*Leslie G. Kimble*

The Greatest Is Love

Love that is self-sacrificing - Love that is so dear.
Love that bears all things; it cast out fear.

Love covers transgressions - forgiveness and hopes for the best.
Never keep account of injury — endures the most severe test.

Love rejoices with truth and never fails —
It is long-suffering when trying situations prevail.

Love is an expression of caring and sharing for those in need.
Never expecting or looking for returns for unselfish deeds.

Love looks for opportunities to uplift troubled hearts and minds.

To brighten and bring smiles to those unhappy faces because
this wonderful emotion of love is so compassionate and kind.
—*Sandra L. Hollinger*

Love And Sex And Marriage

Sex and love were not equated
Love was special sex x-rated.

Love and marriage would someday arrive
Sex was happenstance it satisfied a drive.

But if sex and love are not equated
Then sex and marriage might be overrated

Now, love and sex and marriage were never the same for me
I should bring them altogether but I'm having some difficulty.

To bring all three into harmony is more than just a yearning
If they're to work including me I must change my early learning
—*Sol Tannebaum*

Caught By Surprise

I loved a man so much...before...
Loved and trusted him with all my life
One day...he just got up and took his love away..
I often ask myself, is it something I did?
I often pray to God he'd show me and not keep it hid

The pain so often stays...
The memory of it all will never go away...

Some time has passed now...
The pain has lessened...
A little stronger I'm sure sometimes insecure...

"Know that I love you"
"Believe in me"...
"Know that I'll always be here for you"...
Are familiar quoted words

Laid my heart out on the line...
Caught by surprise another time.
—*Whittonia M. Hobson*

Each Of Us

Each of us with our secret gifts,
Magic potions, lovely notions,
Wanting to be shared. Waiting to be aired.
Each of us a half, a whole,
A mind, a soul, a heart and yet
A part of a better, richer more
Looking for the door, the key, the you, the me.
I'd always dreamed and never seen
Always tried and never been.
Always thought but never knew.
Until at last, I discovered that the gift I
always sought was you.
—*Renee A. Goggans*

Alone

How does it feel to be alone? When nobody
loves you, when nobody cares. You find yourself
just being nobody to talk to, nobody to stare.
No one to say hi or goodbye. No one to tell you
they care. Some will say I care but down inside
they don't care. At those times everyday you
wish you had a person your own age down by your
side. When you look no one is there. At those
times you wonder why. Why was I born? Then you
say why no one knows you're alive. Why live no
one to do it for. But then I guess that's the
way I was to be, I was born alone, so - I'll stay
alone, be alone, play alone, talk alone. Someone
would say why you're alone you would say because
the word alone is more than a word. The word
alone describe my life.
  That's what it feels to be alone!
—*Lissette Padilla*

Freedom

Look at that bright light in my eyes
Ma'am it is pretty
Ain't it freedom?

It's love in a gentle bit,
Not master throwing his whip
Ain't it freedom?

Running through streams, meadow and mottons
Not in the hot fields picking cotton
Ain't it freedom?

Moses is coming soon tonight then everything
gonna be alright

The star from the north is going to take
us home
With God help we'll never be alone
  That Freedom!
—*Natalie R. Arnold*

Thoughts

  You are what you think you are:
    Maybe a bum, maybe a star

  You are what you think you are:
    For thoughts are living things
  Thoughts can bury you deep in the mud,
    Or help you soar with wings

  You are what you think you are:
    For thoughts are living things
  Everything you see, is a thought:
    Manifest, with the luggage it brings

  You are what you think you are:
    So think your own success
  Born to go far, you may shine like a star
  If your thought life won't settle for less

    Cultivate your thought life well:
      For thoughts are like your garden
    Weeds will come, and weeds will grow,
    And choke at your heart till it hardens

Thoughts seek expression so there lies the lesson:
  Think of the luggage they bring
—*Michael P. Garnes*

The Flagpole

During early school years, it shadowed and drew me like a
magnet, until one day, urged on by two taunting high school
companions, I shed shoes and socks to begin the assault on a
benign enemy. The first few feet are easy.

With height, caution increases and speed slips away.
Past twenty feet, toes touch toes on narrowing widths.
Perspiring hands use trousers as towels.
Wind velocity increases sway with the next pole length.
Would the pole drop me like the young sapling years ago?
I hesitate; the pole wavers, yet seems to imprint
"Proceed cautiously" on my clammy hands.
Adversary becomes friend, steadying me, urging me upward.

Finally, triumph! Suspended in mid air, I caress the cold cap.
The exposed view past trees and rooftops turns fearsome
as I glance down at gaping mouths and unforgiving cement.
A few quick breaths, an inner calm; a moment to savor.
A rapid descent blisters hands and feet to a burning red.
Friends stand in awe as my eyes and heart salute
that fragile friend—
Etched forever in warm memories of steel.
—*Wesley A. Edwards*

Blackwater Refuge, Maryland

Magenta skyline lays the day to rest.
Majestic heron steps his stately way.
Heraldic eagle swoops across his bay.
Busy muskrat paddles to his nest.
This is their refuge: here the weariest
Worldly creature comes to feed and stay,
Footloose and fed, a month, a week, a day.
Refuge—a vital need most manifest.

Those who enjoy such respite in their flight
And happily rebuild their strength anew,
Regardless of their species, size or hue
(And this of course is every creature's right)
I'd sorely envy, save that I delight
In one sweet, joyous, lasting refuge — you.
—*E. Donald Davis*

Strictly Confidential

What could I give that would
  make his eyes shine

This dear little, sweet little
  son of mine?

So we visited Santa Claus today
And he whispered his hopes in the age old way.

"What did you ask from Santa, dear?
You talked so low that I couldn't hear.

Then with a wise little nod
  of his wise little head

And a wise little smile
"You'll see"! he said.
—*Rachel L. Sykora*

Love

Love is what brings two people together, to
love one another, care for one another, and to
be with one another. It is a wishing well, to
wish that you can spend your time and love
with someone who you care for very much. It
can bring tears to your eyes, sorrow to your
heart, and it can bring thoughts to your
mind. So love is a precious thing to two
people who care and love one another.
—*Susan A. Stephens*

Emotional Scars

So many feelings more than one thought, spinning round my head making dizzy my heart. My feelings and thoughts of love for you have run true, spinning round and round, but feelings and thoughts of hate are there too spinning round and round. Triumph to the one who wins your heart, God knows I've tried. Once I believed I had it, but you tore it from my hands. You cut me with cruel and desperate words and left me bleeding of pain alone. Emotional scars run deep. You told me once your heart was mine forever, but I guess to you our forever ended yesterday. You told me give up now and let things alone, we weren't destined to be together and we were never carved in stone. Emotional scars run deep. Love and hate spinning round and round is what I feel for you, spinning round my teary soul crying love and hate because of you. Need I say? Emotional scars run deep.

—*Story Earlene Tylor Hofstetter*

Memories, Memories

Memories, memories, what great joys they hold,
Making room for the new yet keeping the old.
With this precious gift, God did bless,
All mankind, so that we might possess,
The power to keep forever in our mind,
All the love and happiness in life we find.
It keeps the "old, so young and alive,
Remembering when they were twenty five."
Imagine not remembering the childhood you knew,
All your hopes, all your dreams, that came true.
Or not remembering the happiest day of your life,
Or the love of your parents, children, husband or wife,
Their faces, their smiles, and their tears,
Their everyday courage, their everyday fears.
Or the love of friends that you have known,
All their kindness, the love they've shown.
Memories grow and grow, they have no end,
They are truly "man's greatest friend,"
For without them all of life's joy and sorrow,
Would be lost and today "be just like tomorrow."

—*Philomena Notaro*

Alaskan Old Town Road

Skating at the Lily pond, was so much fun,
many games were won... Walking to windmill hill,
along the way red fireweed, bloomed in early may...
Passing the harbor, with many boats painted with
colors, of bright coats... Reaching a place called,
the willow tree many friends, there I would see...
The sky so pure and crystal clean many people have
not seen... Following the road, to old woodriver
a chill in the air, gave me a shiver... Across the
tundra, I could see the town around the bend, as I
look down... Spruce trees are grown and so fair
wild salmon berries, scent the air... A ptarmigan
bird, gently flies above my head giving me a message
as if he said this land is full of beauty from above
given to us, with so much love...

—*Linda Nicholson, Forrester*

Forever In My Mind

Oh, how the years pass,
  may happy memories -
  forever last.

Hold on to those feelings wherever you are,
  let it help you reach that shining star.

The happy moments we share in time,
  will remain forever in my mind.

—*Sherrie B. Barkhurst*

"A Memorial Day Salute"

When I saw this old flag cast aside I thought of how
many men had died, and the hardships the living still
had to bear to keep this old flag flying high in the air.
  A flag so pretty should never fall, but instead put in
a place of Honor on your wall.
  And when your eyes gaze upon the Old Stars and Stripes
just keep in mind how everything is so precise.
  Each star reminds me of the soldiers in my platoon.
All covered down and dressed right too.
  So let me reveal to you some of my innermost thoughts.
I see four squads of stars with twelve men to each.
  I can call their names right off to you, there's Kermer,
De Gregory and Sgt. Paul he was the best soldier of us all.
  They are all stars in heaven this very day, for didn't
they give their lives that we might stay.
  Just as that man died on a hill called Calvary.
  They say as you grow older your mind does regress,
your body dies, and your soul goes to eternal rest.
  This may worry some, but not me in the least. For I know
I'm going to join my buddies and make my squad complete.

—*Ray O'Neil Sr.*

Environmentalists' Song

Dead deer in the back of my truck
Maybe next season I'll kill me a duck
No respect for nature or land
I feel manly with a gun in my hand
Pass the beer, chauvinists delight
there to rape the forest at night
An owl's call foretells death is near
Head hunters do not hear
The earth is crying her last few tears
Bulldozers mow down its mist of years
Majestic mountains crumble in shame
Oh mighty dollar they call your name
Powerful seas sludge with black
Exotic birds that won't be back
Trophy hunters gather round
Search for truth it can be found
Mans mentality is all but lost
But in the end, who will pay the final cost?

—*Cheyenne Autumn*

Time

Time continues to fly by, what does it really
mean anyway?

From stop watch's to sundials, we all go
About our way with a confused smile.

Since the beginning we have all wanted to
try and measure this - time. Fitting everything
into this frame we have given ourselves.

From minutes, to seconds, to eons. We carry
On in hopes of experiencing, growing to our
full potential, and gaining knowledge.

Live now, in the moment. Look at the past
for memories, the future for dreams. God for
the highest - after all, we still have time

—*Stacie Moniz*

The Painter

On the soiled walls of use and tear, of white splattered
memories; moved his hands that adorned the song color of a
brand new melody. And ever so silently she stood, softly
trembling at the fancy of his touch; of the same polish and
vigilance he used, that intrigued her such. They conversed as
he dared not turn to behold her face, and she never prompted him
to do so, while the words coursed with ease and conveyed a
fragment of the untamed and unknown. A smile formed in the way
he spoke and forced its way down the ladder to her, and needfully
she embraced what they held, but proceeded to laugh at what they
were. How she loved this painter of ambiguous talents, of his
hands and of her heart, and longed to be the walls of white
that stood unyielding to keep them apart. It was as if they
too were alive and required him more than she and so maintained
to mock her with ripples of imperfections that he would surely see.
And as she turned to conclude her pain, the ladder creaked on
each step down, and he was there in front of her, hearing her
breathe, savoring its sound. "My lady I seem to have completed
here and shall be parting soon; for once more I paint the colors
of the heart, yet the solemn secluded colors of the moon."
—Tiffany Jobe

Untitled

From the time we met
Memories of you and me I will never forget
You'd put me down and act real cool
But still I go back to you like a fool
You stayed out with your friends and partied all night
While I sat at home and knew it wasn't right
I still sit here thinking of you while you're out
hitting the booze I would call you on the phone
But someone there would say, Delbert is not home
We'd make love and things would be alright
then days later we'd be in a fight I gave things up
so we could be together but things still don't seem to
get any better I really loved you Delbert, so very much
But there were things you couldn't give up
I listen to the radio and think of you
But when our song comes on, I get to feeling blue.
You call me stupid, dingy and dumb
When I went on thinking you were no. 1.
I still go on hoping everything will be fine
But I finally realized you were just feeding me a line.
—Sandra Kinser

A L'Ombre

Have you seen humility's ravages lately?
Millions of crushed skulls
Bobbing on postures erect
Fate laconically interjects:
"The diet of pathos is essentially sedative"
"Tragedy's food is excessively masochistic"
What good is your parasol
at the bottom of a rabid cliff?
The invisible avalanche is a jealous patriarch
Why "humble thyself"?
Commit abstract patricide instead
—get a hologram of King Hamlet's Ghost—
Many murders need tending
The threshold of this blood inspires
the totality of everything desired
here we are both victim and God
"be ready to cast off everything"
"prepare to move"
"walk naked beneath the sun"
—(all quotes from the deceased Danish throne)
—Susie Weir

To My Sister

Tis once again Thanksgiving time, and as the day draws near,
Memories revived once more, a favorite time of year.

Remembering our childhood days, and dreams that we once
    shared,
Telling secrets, scratching backs, to show we really cared.

A birthday lunch, a phone call, a letter long past due,
Little things, that mean so much, when they have come from you.

Through all the smiles and laughter, amid sadness and the tears,
You have stood beside me, to banish all my fears.

Your kindness to all you meet, your ever gentle way,
Brings gladness into all their lives, and sunshine to each day.

The miles that separate us will never change the fact,
Of the special bond between us, that will always be intact.

May blue skies surround you, calm waters soothe your soul,
You have a certain quality that has made you truly whole.

The inner strength that you have found, from your faith in God,
Will lead you on to greater paths, no matter where you trod.

And now at this Thanksgiving time, when I sit down to pray,
I'll thank the good Lord above for giving us this day,

And for a sisters precious love, so warm, true, and sincere,
May His blessings shine upon you throughout each coming year.
—Shirley M. Houser

Untitled

A woman standing in her bedroom in front of a full length
mirror with tears in her eyes she unbuttons her blouse
and caresses her left breast, and this what she says: "For
tomorrow a cut of cold steal will take you away from me,
For tomorrow I will not longer be a whole woman.
For I remember the first day you started to form. For I
was only twelve years old, when you first became a part of me.
For from the first day you came, my life started to
change. For my grandmother used to look at me, and say,
you're becoming a little woman. And now tomorrow I'll
once again become a little girl. I also remember the first
time that I made love, you were there. For he caressed
and kissed you just as much as me. Now tomorrow I'll be a
virgin again. I also remember how you fed my hungry
baby with your milk. Now after tomorrow my next baby
will starve. Oh well, I guess this is goodbye, for tomorrow
you will be removed so I will live longer, but also
tomorrow a part of my womanhood will die."
—Ronald Smith

Feelings Come As Fall Sets In

Long ago when you were here
missing you - wishing you near
Leaving things so unclear
makes me think and cry a tear

When you talked that night long ago
you said your heart wanted me so
but mind and heart don't mix you know
'cause it was that night we let each other go

Years have past, now your far away
two lives lived apart, living day to day
why then now, in Fall I may say
the feelings still come, yet in a strange way

Remember those times wherever you are
To cherish the memories so dear to my heart
When the fall comes, I will start
To hold those past memories, 'cause we're forever apart
—Michelle P. Raccosta

Winter Moment

Barren trees are cracks in soft gray skies;
mist dripping from their branches,
the sky is shattered...leaking.

Shivering, sat huddled at the window,
the tracery of trees
plays in my memories.

My eye sees nature's golden child
in sunspots on the ground,
in brightness all around.

Whispering, your softness speaks to me,
becomes your windy smile...
I'll stay with you a while.

Memories have brought you here in sunlight,
while this misty day
I find a different way,

Pondering the patterns in my mind,
to look through magic eyes
at ancient winter skies.

—*Lily Gebhart*

Kismet

Daylight brings the cry of birth
Morning surprised us as the
cold November air tightened round the heart
The chill of winter never thaws.

Sahara fire on the frozen tundra of my brain
Cold moon over Babylon, Great Harlot of our time
surrounded by mushrooms, running like a watercolor
in the rain.

Solitary passerby, reaches out to a
fleeting companion, but she's never there
Long haired madonna in a tincan town
Empty pulchritude, punishable by time.

The night is endless
The gleaming whites of my eyes
a sorry indication of life
There is no need to tell the children so.

—*Nirmal Velayudhan*

My Brother

It's been three years since you died,
Most of my tears have dried.
When you left I was ripped apart,
Now you give me strength for a new start.

You were so young,
Your life had just begun.
No one can change the past,
But I can live each day like it was my last.

I want you to live through me,
Use my eyes to see.
You're gone forever,
But I'll always have my memories to treasure,
All the great times we had,
Who knew it would end so sad.

Do not fret,
You have helped me more than you know,
Having had you in my life made me grow,
Try and try I must,
I'm doing my best for both of us,
I love you my brother,
For you see, Matthew, I will never have another.

—*Tiffany Graves*

The Mortal Enemies Of Peace

If one can not become the tallest tree on top of a high
mountain, then, be contented with just being the tallest shrub
on top of a molehill; for everyone's fate had already been
destined before being born by a mother, for every womb, pocket
and tomb have limits to any prince, king or ruler. So, be
happy and contented of what you are and shall be, without
lament or remorse for having none of ephemeral wealth and
luxury; for what you lack today shall be compensated and
rewarded someday, GOD in His infallible wisdom can not forget
to give anyone a bountiful mercy. The very root causes of a
country's tribulations, misfortunes, distress and miseries, are
the unquenchable greed and pride of "some" local and national
leaders; though they already have abundance in life to bequeath
to their generations, yet they still grab some more wealth
regardless of any means of acquisitions. Everyone's ambitions
may surely reach a CROSSROAD of "TO BE", or "NOT TO BE",
to rise and fight against OPPRESSION, TYRANNY,
IGNORANCE, POVERTY and DYNASTY; for in politics are
rampant GREED, PRIDE, DISHONESTY, BRIBERY and
HYPOCRISY, causing SOCIAL CANCERS and
poor people POORER down to the PIT of INFERNALITY.

—*San M. Luna*

Atmosphere

The moon and the earth coincide.
The pull of gravity, the mountainside.

Tons of weight floating in space.
Light as a feather, lifted by grace.

Clear summer night on top of a hill.
The stars shine bright, flooding the sky, until...

Morning sun rises above, invading night with day.
Lifting the darkness, watching children play.

The leaves fall into the tall green grass.
The seasons of time all come to pass.

The fresh water stream, carving through stone.
Changing through time, the loveliness shown.

Far away places, reaching out.
Beyond the world's realm, shadows of doubt.

Creation is evidence, there is more to the story.
Believing in God, all his glory.

The voice of his command, created by his hand.
Separating light from dark, water and land.

Creating man, beast, heaven and earth, in just six days.
A work of art, a reason to praise.

—*Lori Hollenbeck*

Untitled

Some say America is bad
My childhood was very sad
But I looked to America,
that I could prepared myself for what I
never had.
I haven't had a normal life in beautiful America.
For I had no education record,
To give back to America.
I'm three score and ten
I still don't believe it's too late to win
I pray to the Lord day and night
Before my end come, let me be discovered in the lights
This would be the joy of my whole life.
I'm mother, and have been a wife,
There was no joy day or night.
I thank God for Jesus in my life.

—*Maxine Whitaker*

My Illusive Dream

I drifted off to sleep last night and then I had a dream.
Mr. Right appeared before me with beautiful eyes of green.

He stood by a babbling brook and then he reached for me.
I knew I should resist this man because I am not free.

He stood alone upon a hill, so handsome was he.
Somehow I knew his true desire was really only me.

The longer I stood, the more I stared-how vivid he became.
I knew just then this man was meant to be all mine to claim.

His hair was really dark, his muscles well defined,
This vision of beauty I could never leave behind.

And then he turned and looked at me and smiled a little smile.
His gaze caught mine and time stood still as we stood there for awhile.

He gently pulled me to him; the blood began to flow.
The tenderness between us I could feel from head to toe.

We loved and laughed and loved again as I lay there in his arms.
Feeling his touch I knew to me would never come any harm.

Cool rain drops started falling, I don't know for how long.
But when they stopped I looked around and noticed he was gone.

I woke up then-it was only a dream-my Mr. Right still very illusive.
Suddenly I know the man beside me is Mr. Right-it's very conclusive.
—*Marilyn Schuelke*

Exterior Inverse

Body aching,
muscles stretched to
the point of no return,
legs twisted and forced
in impossible directions,
feet maimed beyond belief,
arms graceful as a blowing scarf
on a summer's night,
sweat dripping down the concaves
of her neck,
her hungry body wants to do more,
has to be more,
her mind is in knowing confusion,
her body in patient waiting of what's to come.
Why does she push? Push herself to her last stem
of stamina,
to her last ounce of strength?
Why does she make herself do everything to her highest limit,
then beyond?
Why can't she give in?
—*Nicole Romano*

Haunting Past

My past haunts me night and day
My dreams call me home to stay.
"No!" I cry "Let me be," I say
I awake to find I have not left
Filled with relief I try to go back to sleep...
But my mind of memories will not keep
For the haunting past of mine is deep
My soul is naked exposed to life,
Living in another's strife.
My dreams of past be oppressed,
Leave me be memories, I pray in silent quest,
Jesus put my thoughts to rest.
Please don't haunt me anymore my past
Remind me not of my fading memories to last
But of my future my life.
 Now in its beginning...
—*Veronica Last*

To You I Pronounce....

Through the endless days, I think of you.
My concentration is lost completely.
Through the darkest nights, I dream of you.
And the love you give so sweetly.

In the desert sand, I thirst for you.
With your oasis, I hope to meet.
In the tundra ice, I freeze for you.
And beg for your thawing heat.

On hot summer days, I play for you.
Waiting patiently to win the game.
On cold winter nights, I cry for you.
And slowly drive myself insane.

In all my experiences, you are wanted.
Everyday of my life to you I'd give.
And if you'd believe me when I speak my heart
You'd notice for only you I live.
—*Susana Gutierrez*

Cold And Distant

I talked with her and disclosed
My deepest feelings.

She wouldn't pay me any
Attention or listen to my revealings.

I told her of my deepest emotions.
She laughed mockingly and said, "Oh, what sadness."

Her words seared my ears and burned a whole in
My heart. I became stricken with madness.

I pleaded with her to love me.
And told her that there could be no other.

She just looked at me frivolously
And said, "Oh brother."

It was then that I decided to give up and
End this quest for love.

And to this day, I still cry out
To the heavens above.

Some times I go and sit with her
In the orchard under the apple boughs.

I talk to her there, but only the trees
Seem to listen, for she is very cold and distant.
—*Michael C. Winkler*

What's In A Name?

Someone mentioned your name today
My eyes clouded over as the sky turned to gray
As if both the sun and I had suddenly lost our way
And like the waves that thunder in the bay
The syllables crashed against my heart in betray
Someone mentioned your name today

Someone mentioned your name today
Outwardly, no emotion did I display
Inwardly, my world collapsed in disarray
And the ache returned like a contrite stray
The sound invoked my soul back to life inveigh
Someone mentioned your name today

Someone mentioned your name today
After a lifetime spent pulling myself out of the fray
One word and I find myself right back amid the game we play
And in reply to them, I didn't know what to say
The conversation ended; they quickly walked away
Someone mentioned your name today
—*Rae M. Zweber*

The Difference

I speak at night,
  My family draws near.
We're illusive and shy,
  You need not fear.
Some things of yours we take to live.
  You took our home,
What did you give?
  These in the pack,
I care for them.
  Is there a difference 'tween wolves and men?
We hate and love,
  Feel joy and shed tears.
We fear hunger,
  You hunger fear.
Our carnivorous ways you can't abide,
  While destroying the helpless,
Just for the hide.
  We live our lives,
Not guilty of sin.
  Is there a difference 'tween wolves and men?
—*Timothy Gause*

Cancer

I've waited for this day to arrive,
My friends all thought it was just a lie.
Well, I couldn't believe it myself, you know;
  But it's here and pretty soon I'll go.
  I think my life has only been,
  A small part and I'm about to begin.
  I ache and the pain's so strong,
  But pretty soon I'll be where I belong.
    All this started so tiny,
  And it just grew, and grew entirely.
  You know... I'm young, very young you see,
    Not a day over twenty-three.
  And they say the young must also go,
So, I wait...The time will come I know.
  "Oh God, I beg and ask to thee;
I know you are to choose the time to be,
  But could you hurry it, just for me?
    The pain gets worse, you see."
    —*E. Isabel Herrera*

Longing Made Manifest

Come to me now my love
My God is jealously alive
Alluring, taking pleasure in my endeavor to achieve
Burning from within, consuming love like a hungry beast
Devouring, feeding, feasting, dancing, singing
Celebrating the love of life
Ever wanting, ever stalking
Prowling the face of the earth
To touch your essence with conception
Joy within desire, the purest of passion
Flourishing toward the completion of evolution
Taste of me, drink of me
Feast upon me for I am what you seek
My soul cries for the light of your touch
The radiance of our union
I partake in the divine flame dance
Aligning the secret chamber of soul to the compounds of
  existence
Be swift my love, time awaits no one
  —*Roxanna Mason*

Dear John

  I understand where your grief is and I realize your pain.
  My great concern in leaving you is to show you what you've
    gained.

  I know you hurt inside and your pain seems great to bear,
Your happiness is soon to come, it's waiting for you somewhere.

  You were lost in happiness you thought would last forever
  You blinked the eye of eternity and suddenly it was over.

  I understand. I've been there too.
  And that's why I made sure that I was there for you.

  Lean on me, depend on me, ask me why.
  And dear sweet friend - never be afraid to cry!
  —*Sarah L. Pinkston*

It Ain't Over.....

My eyes don't see so well
My hands don't work as good;
It takes a little longer to get around,
Sometimes I shake a little more than I should.

I can still make out smiles on faces and feel hugs that I receive
Some of us can still sew, and cut and glue, would you believe?

We play Bingo and Dominoes have dances and sing alongs;
Movies and Popcorn, exercise to make us strong.

Nursing homes are not what they have been thought of
A place to waste away; they are instead you see,
A place to make the most of every day.

It's like a motel you know
With dinning room's and T.V.;
Only with added medical care and entertainment,
People to share my days with me.

It ain't over till it's over
And until that day comes;
You can be sure my time is spent,
With companionship, love, and fun.
  —*Rachelle Vogelsang*

I Am One

The Loneliness of being one; empty
My heart full of love and
My arms ready to embrace.

But there's no one here; alone.

Moments spent wondering if
Time will pass with a void.
Nothing to fulfill me, oh yes;
the parents, the friends, the family...

But where is love?
No children? No love?....ever?

Shout to me love,
My inner soul shall be the recipient of fulfillment
And my heart, the giver of passion.

I will find my being, I will laugh, I will live!

I shall be free to give however I choose.

For I am one.
  —*Robin Kittrell*

And I Proclaim..."How Great You

In my aloneness I walk in the rain...there no one will notice
my tears, the sky is so dark...that it is a reflection of my
soul this very moment, the clouds in hurried motion, like my
thoughts, are without order, going to and fro, like autumn
leaves played by the wind.
And I call on my angels to take all this bundle to you...oh
Lord... for you understand all my fears...you that sees all
my tomorrows...the only one that cares when the unbearable
pain...that overwhelming hurt creeps in and smothers my heart.
Then...I hear...that unspoken voice...that ruffling of angels'
wings deep in my heart...in that perfect moment it seems to be
quoting verses that speak directly to my sadness and are needed
so badly...and full of awe... I wonder...where or when...did
I learn those truths that tenderly are guiding me through the
path...or is it you oh Lord...holding me close to your heart
once again? I know you will make a way once more, but you leave
me free to choose, many times unwisely, to stumble over and
   over...
but as I stand before you...my Saviour dear, with a grateful
heart...I proclaim...how great you are!.
   —*Ligia Zeledon Lloyd*

Ashamed

Enclosed in a secret world all my own
My thoughts are deep and personal; to no one else they're known
The others try to pry beneath my outer shell
But no one will discover my dark burning hell
I crouch in a corner of a room with no door
No windows or air leaking through a single pore
Out pour tears of sadness for I hate myself so
I am my worst enemy; my worst hated foe
My fists punch the walls so many times until my knuckles bleed
My soul leaks of guilt and bitterness for my self-contained greed
My heart screams for love and tenderness for the one that I have
   lost
Curdling of skin and hair standing on end is caused by all that
   have double-crossed
The others; they stare through the bars of my zoo
They snicker; poke fun at me, are so very cruel
I don't try to stop them; I just curl up so small
the few crumbs they throw me I quietly gnaw
My eyes slowly start to shut; Relief is so near
I can now sleep eternally and diminish my fear
I crumble into ashes such as a dry crackling leaf
And the wind forever blows away my never-ending grief
   —*Rachel Worcel*

Untitled

Sitting in my lonely room, thoughts of you begin to bloom.
My thoughts of you flow through my head,
While I lay sleepless in my bed.
Visions of you stay in my mind,
When I think of you time after time.
I lay awake at night, hoping you'll soon be in my sight,
for me to hug you, to love you, and show you I care.
These are my feelings I'd like to share
Your touch is so gentle, your voice is so sweet,
You show me you care when our eyes meet.
When I touch your skin, my feelings, begin to grow
higher and higher it's your love I desire.
The times we shared I keep close to my heart
To remind me you love me while we're apart.
   —*Wendy Roman*

Scanning A Dream

Am I dead or is it a dream
My thoughts run naked through the night
My vision is lightning often touching the ground
My hearing is keen picking up a faint scream
My sense of touch and smell an ambrosia of fright
Death is but a door, time is but a window with pain
End of the day beginning of the night
Flying with silver fire in the sky
To whiten their hair a scream of fright
Mummy dust to age skin and clothes
A human skull and loves first kiss
On a mountain of stone I sat on a throne of bone
Inside four walls of pain
What was will be, what is will be no more
Bed to the light today is merely history
Don't be afraid of what you do not understand
For I am just someone scanning a dream
   —*D. Warner*

Morning Dew

Her morning run gets shorter,
Needing rest, she stops, leans against a tree.
This is quiet time, her time,
The world sleeps, responsibilities still in bed.
Movement in the branches,
There, a robin just above her head.
Its beak filled with breakfast.
Breakfast, she must go now,
Must outrun the sun.
Quiet time goes away,
Like morning dew, erased by the heat of the day.
   —*Mike Epps*

We Saw A Baby Soldier At The Airport...

He had a cheek so soft that if a rose petal brushed it,
neither would have felt the difference.
His neck was so whitely vulnerable that
the moist print of his mother's kiss
could still be seen.

Hi shoulders trembled under the weight of
an oversized khaki trench coat
(they did not, you see, make coats small enough
for his delicate frame).
Looking hardly old enough to be out alone,
his eyes were glazed with his effort to be drunk
his lonely tears barely withheld.

We stopped laughing, stopped celebrating ourselves
stopped to wonder how he could anyone's
enemy when even his girl was a virgin.
   —*Susan Maxson Smith*

Everlasting

We met through that boy of yours,
No one could seem to keep
God gave to me a friend,
More than "just the mother of" he
He, that boy of yours, and I,
We lasted just over three
Three years of time that still left me you.

Thank God you still remain with me,
I care more than time will ever take
Never take this friend I have of you,
I need you longer than he.
   —*Lorraine Lewis*

Power

Never again! No matter how beckoned
Never again will I go second.
I am parched with incurable thirst,
I want to be the one who goes first.

Never again will I follow the crowd
You'll find me up front standing tall and proud.
It's not my style to wait on the side
If I can be the one to preside.

You'll not find me at the back of the stage
I want that spotlight! Is that an outrage?
You need someone to speak, sing or dance?
Call on me! I refuse no chance.

Just stand me near a microphone
And I have Power! (Though you may moan.)
And who is that leading the major parade?
Good grief! It's me, the renegade.

From whence did it come, this confidence
That makes me in love with the audience?
Never again will I quiver with fear.
I'm the best there is. Do you hear? Is that clear?
—Muriel Roth Kulwin

Fleeting Moments

....And so I sat,
Never closing my eyes.
For time is wasted
On those who choose to see the world
Behind nature's sunglasses.

....And so I watched
As shadows cloaked my face.
For time passes too quickly
For wristwatches and clocks
Made by technology's hands.

....And so I listened
As the wind's breath caressed my ears.
For time is gentle;
Creating sounds of wonder
Instead of drumbeats that quake the ground.

And so I dreamed
As time passed by.
For as long as reality remains,
Fantasy awaits occupancy.
—Merrie B. Donehoo

Dreams

Only the dreams that are never dreamed
  Never come true
Only the thoughts that are never said
  Go unsaid
Only the deeds left neglected
  Go undone
Only the "heart" never touched, never loved
  Feels no sorrow.

But the dreams that are dreamed
  are forever remembered
A kind word of love is well
  worth being said
The deed if only to offer a shoulder
  To cry on - is done
And A "heart" that sheds sorrow finds joy
  In knowing - that you're loved.
—Melinda Martin

A Mother's Prayer

May your flame
Never lessen
May springs of peace
Spew forth from your heart
May your bones never weary
And the veins of your wrists and ankles
Like iron bands ever be
May your life be
The salt of remembrance
To those whose lives you touch
And may the laughter of children
Ring joyously in your yard
May that man in your life be a morning, ever renewed
In a love eternally blessed
May his face shine for you always
As surely as day follows night
And may the Lord's life be mirrored in yours
For my child, you are
Deserving of all that's good.
—Mercy John-Ekanem Umoh

Enclosing Bubble

Never seen, never heard,
  never touched,
as if a bubble were enclosing my thoughts.
Never questioned, never noticed,
  never bothered.
As if they weren't even important so
I never spoke, never touched.
Never listened to anything
  but my thoughts.
In this miserable state of life
  never a friend
  but the friend.
That was in my thoughts
  and not even then
did he see, hear, touch, question, notice
or even bother to understand
my enclosed bubble of thoughts.
In this miserable state of life
  I'm left all alone
  with nothing in my heart!
—Tswana Sewell

Climbing The Ladder To Success

Waking up everyday, just to see a brand
  new day, starting fresh, starting clean
  trying not to forget the dream.

Competing against the outer world, stumbling
  over stupid quarrels, being yourself
  everyday is what's going to keep you on
  the runway.

Pausing at a route, is meant for you to pout
  you've got to keep going to continue your
  way about.

To live easy means to die easy, to live for a
  challenge means to create and get a balance.

Waking up, doing what you have to do to make it
  in life, is it a meaning? Yes. Live a life,
  live a good life, live it at the best ability
  of all the strength you've got inside. If this
  process is being done, you will then see the
  meaning of life.

Life is short, so grab what you want, for you will
  see, to succeed is life's creed.
—Latoya Evans

Fate Of Mankind

As I lay awake in a lonely bed, I long to hear a heart beating
next to mine. As I lay twisting away in a tormented mind
Could I ever hope for a future for all of mankind
Can anyone hear our sullen cries
Come back to reality and hear more lies
People are dying and paying in bloodshed
We're embarking on a new age, but yet why are our children like
walking dead gone from their homes and left to die
Where are the empty arms and souls to embrace them?
Is this a cold glimpse of the future where we're just a number
in line; dare we not laugh or be sent away
Where have the sweet flowers gone, even they are now recycled
Is there hope for mankind in the future?
We no longer can be dehumanized as machines take away our jobs
As the inner cities take our youths and turn them into killing
machines, we are slowly destroying ourselves and the earth
Let's stop and become whole again with faith and trust
in the One above us all, our inner worth!
—Laura Collins

A Mother's Prayer

Thank you Jesus, for my son
Next to You, he is the one
To touch my heart, to hug my soul
Oh Dear Lord, never let him go

Hold him in Your loving hand
Help him Lord to become a good man
For he is my love, my life, my joy
My bouncing bundle of baby boy

Oh Dear Father in heaven above
Help others to know, the joy of this love
To see in his eyes all the love that they miss
When he reaches to me for a hug and a kiss

Someday in the future, we'll look back to the past
And know that our lives are gone much to fast
So for now precious Jesus, my prayer will be
That you lead and guide him safely for me
—N. L. N. R.

Food For Our Soul

To survive we must forever partake of our victuals
No matter how much or how little
All of us must consume our delectable
Whether with, or without a table

Many eat to live day to day
While the very fortunate live to masticate
All the treasures of their palate
Their prime rib, lobster, and caesar salad

But, despite whatever exotic, or simple sustenance
It definitely makes no difference
For we must feed our stomach no matter what
To remain alive to continue to do our part

While some struggle daily to breathe
Many sometimes forget to feed
Their heart and soul with their grub
The one and only provision is love

Love is the food for our soul
The only prerequisite for abundant growth
Bringing forth our very own truth
So as to truly see, and appreciate, our meat, drink, and fruit
—Vanessa Hart

Empty Room

There's an empty room in my house tonight,
no more my son will I see.
Oh God, why did he have to die, why couldn't it have been me.
Last night he came home late from school,
so I wouldn't let him play.
I spanked him and made him go to bed without a chance to say,
I stopped off for your birthday present Dad,
I didn't think it would take much time,
It isn't much of a present Dad, for I only had a dime.
he cried himself to sleep last night and when I went to bed,
I saw there were still teardrops, on his new bedspread.
The next day, when I came home from work,
he seen me across the street,
He had completely forgiven me, and to me he ran to meet.
I hollered stop, but out he ran, that big car hit my little
man. I ran up to him and I heard him say,
Forgive me Dad, for yesterday.
Yes, there's an empty room in my house tonight,
No more my son will I see, Oh God, why did he have to die,
Why couldn't it have been me.
—Larry E. Lindgren

Put Love For God And Country Above Those Of 1776

Love for God and Country in 1776 was great that year
No one had any great need of fears
They all laboured in love for their country
With God to back then everybody
They knew with God as their leader He's show them the way

In 1994, put love for God and Country above these of 1776
Put your maker number one on your list
Let love for God and Country be your guide
You will never need to make a tight first
Love will truly lead you on
Let love for God and Country keep you in tone.

Upon your maker, make your call today
Ask God the right step to take get upon your knees and pray
Ask God the right step to take then 1994 will be a great year
In every year, now and everyday.

Everyone, small, large, old, young, short and tall
In 1776, they called upon their maker to lead them on
The love of God and Country was what made them a tone
In love they laboured and served so that freedom will ring
So let's all with joy turn with love sing.
—Mary Matlock

No One Home for Christmas

With no one home for Christmas, should I decorate this year?
(No one here to share the happiness, or demonstrate good cheer.)
Should I get the wreaths and manger out, and trim the Christmas
   tree?
It seems like such a waste of time to do it just for me.

But in this busy hectic life we cannot live apart.
We'll let His good and steadfast love shine through us from the
   heart.
And I must nevermore forget, He said; "All men are brothers,"
And; "Go ye into all the world to bring my love to others".

I'll not forget the Christ Child, who did so much for me.
I'll put candles in the window for everyone to see.
Ah yes! I'm not a hermit living in a world apart,
And I must show to others I keep Christmas in my heart.

And so I'll decorate with care,
In memory of the Babe so fair
And place the wreaths for all to see
My love for Him, who came for me.
—Ruth V. Roushey

Unfulfilled Dreams

He stood apart from all the others
No one wanted him around.
He seemed lost in a sea of fish
just waiting for a shark to devour him.
He didn't give a damn about me.
He even hurt me beyond repair.
I will get rid of my visible bruises,
but I will always have the scars.
His voice alone hit me like a leather belt across the face.
I want to rip his heart out,
like he ripped mine out,
then turn my back on him when he's bleeding,
just like he did to me.
But now when I see him, I weep.
I weep over his cold, dead, rigid body.
Maybe he hurt me but that was all he knew.
Neither of us knew what love stood for.
I make a silent vow over his corpse to never be like him
as hot, salty tears drip on all his unfulfilled dreams.

—*Melissa Arbaugh*

The Disbeliever

If end of time, be upon us, it must be a far, for I have seen,
No signs, coming, of this strange happening, that you, tell me
of. For I hear, no rumble, of clouds, falling away all I see,
is the sun, in the sky, shining, what a beautiful, glorious,
day. If you say, that this be so, why then, would I not know?
Everyone, would know, wouldn't they? Why do I fear if I
disbelieve?

Did, He say, He would come again? Did He really go? Can you
show me, that this will be? For I really want to know. You
say, The Bible, has told us lo, I am with you always, where, is
He today? If this time, be upon us!

What is that rumbling of thunder? I hear up there? And clouds
moving so swiftly, past us, in the air. I see, three angels,
I hear their voices, calling out - the names of those, on
earth, down here.

My God! Thou has forsaken me! As I fall down, humbly on my
knees. Why was I so blind? All this time. Why did I
disbelieve? He is leaving me, He is leaving me, with all the
other, disbelievers down here .....

—*Ruth Rogers*

Whisper In The Night

   The night was calm and dark,
No stars in the heaven to light me,
   I was alone and in reverie,
Couching my lonely heart to sleep.

   The consolation I got,
Is the cold breeze of the night,
   Giving me a little relieve,
Refreshing my broken heart,
   Until it goes to sleep.

   Oh! God how can a person being hurt,
With all the things she has done,
   Is this just a trials in life?
Oh! God it is just too hurting to impart.

   I gave everything to you my God,
Relieve me a little and console my heart,
   If this is a part of my suffering,
I'll accept it, for trials is a
   part of your love.

—*Socorro Ch. V. Trinidad*

Untitled

Blessed be the Lord, my children dry your eyes
Non-believers crucified me, but I did arise
My Father sacrificed me for everyone's sin
All you have to do is let me in
I've built many mansions in heaven for you
This wouldn't have been said if it wasn't true
Sometimes my followers, the battle seems long
But that's how I decipher the weak from the strong
And no matter what hardship, I'll be by your side
For my love goes deep, and my heart is wide
So trust in me and don't find these words odd
I am Jesus Christ, the true Son of God

—*A. Gardner*

Untitled

Life is of the essence, but some perspectives are
not as bright,
Though some people are successful, others have given
up the fight.
They may wish upon stars but to no avail, and the
moon may light their way,
Only to find they are heading in the wrong direction,
with nothing more to say.
The sun creates radiant clouds, only to see that
there are shadows inside,
And as the mist clears from the window, there are
less people in whom to confide.

—*Sharon Neumann*

I Saw Death

I saw death today.
Not in the sight of one who had succumbed.
Not in the specter of events that would cause it.
Not in the written words that would describe it.
Not on a stage or screen as authors would portray it.
Nor in picture images that would preserve it for eternity.
It was revealed in the middle of a routine ordinary day.
Quietly and quickly and then it went away.
Yet, I am left forever in its sway.
I saw it in the eyes of a tormented young soul.
One filled with demons for which there was no control.
In a murderous rage and I was the victim.
I could not rely upon his mercy at this stage for he has none.
I must rely on the mighty one in whom I believe.
He alone can grant a reprieve from my swiftly meeting my
final destiny.
I saw death today and briefly felt its sting.
But I did not die.

—*Lita Duke Holmes*

Flower Daughter

   We sowed our seed carefully.
Nursing roots in fertile ground,
We worshiped each petal of the blossom we found.

   We flaunted our flower proudly.
We sought possession, not to borrow,
Because she belonged to us today and tomorrow.

   We lived her life fully.
When our bloom suffered, crying teardrops of rain,
We wept along with her to soften the pain.

   Winter wind slaps our faces, commands without mercy:
"Leave your garden, shut the door!
Your flower is full grown now — she needs you no more!"

—*Louise Bronoski*

Pictures In A Still Mind

The profound silence of the still mind. . .
Not like the blowing of the wind,
But more like the wind that you can't see,
A silence of the eyes.

Picture:

The naked branches of winter
Shaking with snow,
And no sound accompanies the wind
That blows them. . .
The dark trees with their
Scrawny fingers stretched out
In the air,
Tracing arcs and circles
Over the almost frozen lake. . .

Picture:
The bald hill,
Across whose green grasses
The edged wind blows.
The low clouds
Brush the plain's horizon.

—*Robert M. Baker*

Hate The Battle's Won

Another day you curse.
Not satisfied with what others do,
People can only give their best and the rest is up to you,
So, do not be angry when your day isn't going right,
But, let it serve as a reminder there is no darkness
found in light,
You can't expect others to live and walk in your shadow,
Each person has a mind and heart of their own.
Life is a series of choices.
But, the ones who are strengthened know they don't walk alone.
The race isn't always to the swift,
But to those who continue to run,
When we're living for the thrill of victory
Instead of mere survival hate the battle's won.

—*Terry Lowery*

China Dolls

    Women are fragile
  not to be tousled and tossed about.
   We are the ornaments of life
    while we are hollowed out
    left empty with solid facades

   Much the same as china dolls

    Placed atop mantels
  we become ornaments of beauty, of life
  becoming more precious and fragile with age
If you break us we're yours so we fear your touch

   You adorn us in gold and jewels
If we keep quiet and don't tell your secrets

   Much like a shattered china doll
    reassembly is difficult
   We gaze helplessly, hopelessly
  as we long to be given life again

You many posses us but the price is high
  The price is our lives and souls so look
    but make your touch gentle
Once reassembled your touch is what we fear the most

—*Lucy Fritz*

O Christmas Tree

O Christmas Tree, O Christmas Tree, you're such a fire hazard.
O Christmas Tree, O Christmas Tree, you're such a fire hazard.
Your bulbs are loose, your wires are bare,
Your needles dry, fall everywhere.
O Christmas Tree, O Christmas Tree, you're such a fire hazard.

O Christmas Tree, O Christmas Tree, when can I take you down?
O Christmas Tree, O Christmas Tree, when can I take you down?
You take up all my living space,
I'd like you in the fireplace.
O Christmas Tree, O Christmas Tree, when can I take you down?

O Christmas Tree, O Christmas Tree, another year is ending.
O Christmas Tree, O Christmas Tree, another year is ending.
Though your lights will be in a box,
I'll still find needles in my socks.
O Christmas Tree, O Christmas Tree, another year is ending.

—*William H. Shontz*

Morning Exultation

Let's see what You brought me this morning,
O Magic of Magics!
Gossamer ribbons of spider webs, traced by the dew.
Arachnids of uncounted thousands were summoned to spin them;
then You woke me in time just to harvest the view.

What was it You gave to me yesterday,
Worker of Wonders?
All orange-yellow brilliance is all I remember.
Oh yes! Bittersweet cups opened wide by the frost
of September.
And I feasted my eyes; then I knew
that the Giver was You.

What gift will You proffer tomorrow,
O Dispeller of Dis'ease?
What gift to bedazzle, discover,
to play with, or simply to shine?
For the world's still all Yours
As You make it all, gradually, mine.

—*Shirley M. Steinman*

The Old Sailor's Last Voyage

Shimmering, silken wings of water dance their way across the ocean to an appointed destiny with the beach. Conducted by the hands of God, they rise and fall as if orchestrated to a melody from heaven. The old sailor stands statue-like on the shore, staring out, his eyes reflecting visions of days long past.
His heart aches as he remembers bold, adventurous days aboard the mighty sailing ships. Deep inside his nautical soul, he longs to stand watching the sun rise and set on the ocean from the deck of a peaceful ship, its luminescence splashing across the water. Bewildered, the old man closes his eyes blinking in disbelief. The ship had magically appeared through clouds of golden mist, a young sailor standing at her helm...the old sailor knew he was not alone. Turning, he looked upon his youthful
   image.
He no longer felt the icy sting from the wind around him. The young sailor reached out his arms beckoning the old man to him. Together, hands clasped, their footprints on the sand disappeared. Only the young sailor remained, his commanding figure now stood alone upon the majestic ship as it drifted out from the shore. On a course mapped out and navigated by the Creator of all seas, the sailor turned the ship's wheel toward eternity.

—*Melinda Miller*

Dolphin's Song

I have watched dolphins move swift and graceful through deepest
   oceans.
Their bodies tracing delicate curves beneath waves of dark
Indigos and blues.
As I saw them move, together alongside my ship, I smiled:
To think that the one leaping was the souls echo of the one
   swimming.
Reaching to leap above the liquid horizon, again and again.
In playful mastery of motion without effort, almost silent.
Complete in the rhythm of air, water, and time.
   —*Richard Clay Smothers*

The Resurrection

Waiting impatiently for the resurrection
   Of a dear friend
   Of a lost life
   Of a last hope

In an unending dress rehearsal
   For what life could be
   For what life should be

Going through the motions in a meaningless existence
   Through a twisted and distorted maze
   Totally ignorant of the cost
   To rekindle the spirit

But with full knowledge of the price to be paid
   If myself,

I could
   Never
   Again
   Find.
   —*Roslyn Clear*

The Mirror's Reflection

A piece of glass reflects the tainted past
Of a frightened child who may not last.
A distorted image with secrets to hold,
The child is torn as the story unfolds.

One man beat her, another used her,
Not one loved her, but all abused her.
The faces hazy, the damage clear,
The fear surrounds her, yet she look in the mirror.

Faces of people who truly did care
Not one did she trust for love, to her, was rare.
As she stands at the mirror continuing to peer,
The haziness leaves and a stranger appears.
   —*Laurel Bundy*

Grammy

When I sit and think of memories long past
of a life that I loved which would be gone too fast

I remember sitting feeling such pride
Knowing you loved me as I sat by your side

A dime under my pillow, a surprise by my plate
the tooth fairy, a friend and always my playmate

A grandmothers love, a hug and her smile
The twinkle in her eye, are so important to a child

When I sit and think of memories long past
of a life that I loved which would be gone too fast

I love you and miss you, as I'm sure you can see
but somehow I know you're still watching over me

I love you grammy...
   —*Susan E. Duguay*

Us

US! For most a statement of fact
Of a love that gives; and love given back.
Two loving and giving, dedication and trust
Which must be; if there is to be an US.

US! To me the question which lack
The answer of only your love given back.
For love can live alone if it must,
But it is better with two. Better, with US.

US. Is it possible that my love should find
Love in return or is my love blind.
My happiness can never be a must
But sadness can be lifted only by US.

US. Love is the one force that never dies,
But without an US, love's heart cries
With sorrow and loneliness, an absolute must
Unless replaced by love, replaced by US.

US? Love's true answer to giving and trust
Must be answered with the answer US.
Is there an US? I'm afraid your heart does show
For US there is an answer, the answer is NO.
   —*Michael L. Hofacket*

Spiritual Stairway

To find our own place in the sun, and to help release our minds
of all limiting mental shackles, and bring to birth, the God
that is within. To succeed you must pray, have faith, be
patient, work hard, be honest; if you cannot do all that you
desire, you will have the satisfaction of knowing that you've
done your best. You must put forth energy determination
because it's, not what we have, but what we use, not what we
see, but what we choose.
   These are the things that make or break the sum of human
happiness. The things nearby, not the things afar, not what we
dream, but what we are. These are the things, that make or
break that give the heart its, joy or ache. Not what seems
fair, but what is true, what we dream; but what we do, these
are the things that shine like gems; not as we pray, but as we live.
   These are the things that make for peace. Both now and
after time shall cease:

"I pray as never sure to pray again, and as a
dying man to dying men"
   —*Willie Brown*

Becoming Real

Life is a struggle against the unknown. Buried beneath fears
of being alone. Turning from pain and hiding your will to find
happiness - taking a lifetime to fill. A child will sense
needs and learn to relate to the world in a way so secure in
his fate. Trying to fill those he loves with his soul while
hiding his tears as he acts out his role. Time marches on
passing innocently and a child is hurting but no one can see.
Venting the pain through substitute means. Expressing an anger
that lives through extremes. What does it mean to be without
sadness after years as a prisoner in a world full of madness?
Yearning for love and on one to rely. Searching for truth
through living a lie. How do you open your heart and accept
the love that got caught in the anger you've kept? Being slave
to that anger and the need to be real. Which has led to
perfecting a way not to feel. Be strong as the emptiness
drains confidence. Gearing your strength to fight pain so
intense. Taking that stand can relinquish your role and head
you toward peace with your mind and your soul. Deep in our
hearts we all hold the key to live out our destiny confidently.
Believe in your love, accept with care. For patience will show
you that loved ones are there.
   —*Lisa A. Stancati*

Lily Of The Fields

A wreath of daisies resting on her sunlit head
   of flowing golden tresses.
Emerald eyes and lips of red
   upon her nature blesses.
With purple heather as her heady scented bed
   she is beauty beyond compare.
No one remotely aware
   of the silent tears she has shed
   among the dew stained grass of dawn.
Many long to touch her face of alabaster fair.
   None seek to stir her soul
Nor merge her heart within their own.
   She cries out for love yet finds it not.
Reaching for understanding - emptiness returns.
They call her lily of the fields
   She roams a sea of wildflowers and swaying grass.
With wind dancing in her hair
   among the fields she stands alone, still as though glass.
She stands alone among the flower spotted fields
   the fairest of the garden.
     —Sheri Marie Boyd

Writer's Pledge

Come, let us seek the light, the truer light
of literature, the inner light of life -
quelling the darkness of ungodly night,
setting aside all struggle, stress and strife
conquering hate through love, declaring war
on war, creating grace from ugliness.
We do not wrong but right; we do not mar
But make; we writers do not curse but bless:
For we building ever-new empires
of wisdom, where revenge is folly, where
forgiveness is law, where deceased desires
are born delights, and where our only care
is the discovery of our destiny
in our awareness of divinity.
     —R. M. Challa

Who Am I

"Who am I" is the hue and cry
Of multitudes questioning before they die
You must know yourself as well as you can
Else you'll ne'er understand any other man (woman)

If you allow others to run your life
In a vain attempt to escape any strife
In that freedom from hassle, you must pay a price
By foregoing the pie and settling for a slice.

Those that talk behind another's back
Have a life as exciting as a burlap sack
If they can influence in untold ways
Maybe it's time to self appraise.

No one can hurt you without your consent
To really know that, you must pay the rent
There might come a time to show that world your face
And lead yourself to your proper place.

The choice is yours, you must decide
If it's important to find out what's inside
And answer the question "Who am I?"
Then proceed to the next one - "Why?"
     —Maurice Levy

Life

When time has healed the wounded sole
of one that has been so strong
Will another's eyes gaze upon
the one I loved for oh so long
So just live on in gentle love
and gather strength from up above
Remember times of long ago
when weeks were long and slow
But as you age and years go by,
like shadows on winter's snow
Don't look back on life with pain
remember the sunshine not the rain
so live your life with love and care
For you know I will be waiting, for you,
Up there.
     —Tim W. Green

Sin

I feast on the bones, in the shade
Of the grave, in the eve
By the light of the moon;
The pale moon, white like the bones which I chew;
And tear at the gristle of each sinew.
I gorge on the bones, and feast
On the meat, aah what a treat
So sweet to eat the flesh that hangs on the bones.
Oh how I love the crack, and the snap, and the sound
Of each tendon that pops, as I pull
The fleshy curtain from its skeletal rod,
To peer in the window of each man's soul.
And snack on his flesh as I go.
What pleasure I find when nothing is there
Though this is common to find
For something I rare. The darker the soul
The fuller the feast, and best is the man
Who lives like a beast, for his flesh is so tender form
Indulgent behavior and his heart is unseasoned
By salt of the saviour.
     —Michael Schellman

Painting The Music

As you listen to the beautiful sounds
Of the music that is heard
A picture is forming in your mind
Just waiting to be transferred

You may not have the artistic talent
To make the picture look great
But all one needs is to look at your eyes
And they know you don't have to illustrate

Your face shows all the expression
Of how wonderful your pictures look
The music is your paintbrush
And minutes was all it took

They won't find your pictures in a gallery
Nor will they find them on the wall
But to the lucky one who reads you well
Will see the greatest masterpieces of all
     —Randy Woody

Lovers

Love beckons with silent longing eyes.
Offers with warm lingering hands.
Voices with yearn aching lips.
Entices with shy trembling smiles.
Returns with close craving arms.
Surrenders with passion suffering bodies.
     —Sammie Edmondson

The Hand on the Sand
(Omaha Beach, Normandy, France - 1944)
A Tribute to an Unknown Soldier on the 50th Anniversary of the Normandy Invasion of June 1944

Wet from the sea I stepped ashore
And moved over the sandy beach,

My eyes looked down and there I saw
A hand from the sand upward reach.

A man had walked this way before
On Omaha beach he had died,

His palm was all I saw that day
Proclaiming to all he had tried.

"Carry on" his plea in silence
Summoned us passing from the sea,

I paused a moment, then moved on
Wondering who this man might be.

Upon this sand so many died
To gain a foothold on this land.

But on Normandy's shore that day
Etched on my mind was this one hand.

Two score and ten have passed away
That hand in mind does still remain,

I pray this death was not in vain
A gift for peace to one day reign.

—*Lynn A. White*

Compensation For Date With The Devil

    Lingering
Like the acrid stench
  of whiskey on your breath.

    Last night's touch

Sandpaper-fingers brushing,
  scouring, course against the grain.

Your bulbous lips
  Suckling, like those of hungry babes
    clutching at their mothers' empty pitchers.

      Wiry bristles
  trace the aura of your sardonic grin—
    I shut my eyes to slip away,

    But

    The sable gargoyle
    dances in my head.

—*Sabrina Profili*

Webster's Reversal

When we are young we are confused.
Often we are suicidal.
As we grow up we do not know which way to go.
Sometimes we pick the wrong road and people get hurt.
We are hated by people we do not know.
We are discriminated against constantly.
There is little protection for us under the law.
If we are lucky enough to find love, we can't marry.
Some of us are beaten — fatally.
When we die, nobody cares.
Isn't it funny that once upon a time being gay meant that you were happy.

—*Michael E. Coleman*

Senseless But Endless

Where do all the young men go?
Off to war on orders to destroy some other's hated foe.
Why do these young soldiers go?
To kill a distant someone for reasons they do not know.

To remote places these soldiers go with rifles held high,
Battling for a moment; only to fall, struggling to rise.
Bullets sent from an unknown someone, whining through the air,
Striking down all these young soldiers in an unknown somewhere.

Blood drains from their young bodies to stain the far away ground.
Their foreheads crease in a bewildered, eternal frown.

The world does not care to know their names.
They died playing someone else's game.
Where do we place the discomfort of blame?
We, ourselves, avoid any sense of shame.

Though we share in their anonymous deaths,
We seldom look to our own souls in quest.
We pass our guilt to any and all the rest.

—*R. W. Reynolds*

Where Is Glynis?

"Where's Glynis?" You asked.
Oh she just went inside. Herself.
She had a few things she needed to do,
   To clean up, to clear up
    And try to undo.

Is she returning? I suppose
When she's through learning
About she, her and most of all me.
But don't worry
I
Am here to answer anything you may need.
Is she alright? Sure.
She's just fine.

She had to go inside. Herself.
To reorganize, reshape, redecorate her fate.
Lie around and recline in the mysteries of her mind.

Where Glynis?
Oh she just went inside. Herself.

—*G. A. Freeman*

Intrigue

Oh the happiness of the moment
Oh the thrill of the fight
Oh the excitement that rushes through you
Telling you the time is right
Oh the joy of victory. The days after
are so sweet will excite you, will amaze
you, will intrigue you, endlessly.

When you know that you have made good
After you have toiled so hard.
On a project for your public.
It took you so long to start. It
amazes you it intrigues you. Knowing
you have come so far.

Now you're all done and the verdicts
in and now you're a shinning star.
Shinning so bright in your public eyes
And intrigued is what you are.

—*Mabel Edith Briscoe*

Rain Child

Rain child, I linger in your undying splendor,
oh Venus, for you walk the humbling earth in garb
of crescent moons.
   Deliver me from the angry eye that is the sun
where vultures soar in silhouette in the desert of my
blighted hope.
   I hold reverence for you such with piety through
nuances of electric scenarios in which we might indulge.
   Tears of divinity cascade from the blue empyrean
and through this haze of falling water you smile.
   Pigeons abound at your feet like tiny soldiers marching
into battle as we who fear seek shelter in the bowels
of our twisted creations.
   For you Rain child are the Phoenix rising from the
pyre of man's defeat.
   —*Matthew Aaron Gorman*

Mom

I dream't of you, last night.
Oh' what a beautiful sight
You stood on a long bridge made of stone
I 'could tell by your eyes, you were not alone
As you were smiling down on me
There were two small children clinging
Their arms around your knees
Pink, blue, yellow colors were in the sky
And clear blue water, I watched flow by
If I could have a dream come true
It would be the one I had of you
Oh' how happy you seemed to be
No more, sadness, sickness or misery
Joyful and happiness were the
Expression on your face. I know it
Must be heaven, oh' what a beautiful place
   —*Sharon Weaver Keller*

Buried Down Deep

Chemicals, cans, bottles and diapers,
Old rubber tires and windshield wipers,
Possessions we purchased but just couldn't keep,
So it came upon us to hide them down deep.
Our neighbors have cancers and no one has answers.
So could it be the toxic waste
That somehow was just misplaced?
Is it in our water or the food that we eat?
That was raised upon the soil of what we buried down deep?
   —*Shelley Halzel*

Tiny Little Stranger

He came to us one Saturday morn,
On agonizing wings of pain.
His coming filled our hearts with joy!
Like glorious sunshine after rain!!

A tiny little stranger sent to us,
From God to care for and to adore;
We all loved him so very much,
But God must have loved him more!!

On angel wings he silently departed,
Leaving heartbreak and tears to beguile;
He's gone, but he'll ne'er be forgotten,
Though he stayed for such a little while!!
   —*Pauline A. Turner*

Keeper Of The Lighthouse

While sailing on a stormy sea,
On a dark and lonely night,
A sailor searched most desperately
For a guiding lighthouse light.

He searched until he thought
He could not search anymore,
When at last he finally saw
The light shining from the shore.

The light's warmth was an invitation
As the sailor opened all of the ship's sails.
His heart was pounding in his chest
As he fought the tempestuous gales.

When, at last, he reached the lighthouse,
His heart was filled with a joyous song,
For the Keeper of the Lighthouse
Had kept the light shining strong.

The gracious sailor soon realized
The Keeper was from heaven above.
The light that shone so brilliantly
Was God's undying love.
   —*Lynda S. Mitchell*

Fleeting Beauty

Huge spheres of fragrant beauty
On a long slender stem — each one,
Standing erect and majestic,
With pride, they bask in the sun.
Raindrops descend in a torrent;
Destruction and sadness abound;
Stems broken-and blossoms all muddy,
In humility - my peonies lie flat on the ground.
   —*Lylah Casper*

The Judgment

With her hour glass figure, and her diamond mink coat,
On a scale of one to ten, she is a ten.

Watching her dine at the dinner table,
She uses each fork for just the right use, and she of course,
Has a napkin in her lap.

She is oh so polite, and laughs, just so.
The others at the table, linger on her every word.

Her hair is long and straight, not a strand out of place,
And she wears no make-up, having a naturally beautiful face.

Her nails are perfect,
Which of coarse, means she is kept.
Can you image having to sit next to her, and bare this.
Let me tell you, it is awful.

As if all that isn't enough, she now, just has to get up and
Take a stroll, or something.

I have a headache, my heart is in my lap,
Just maybe, if I'm lucky, she'll fall down.

As she slides back her chair from the table, her escort hurries
to help. I am, I am, I am ashamed, for she only has one leg.

I judged and convicted her without even a second thought.
I hope my judge isn't, me.
   —*Tewonia L. Bradley*

Desert Monsoon

Cotton-candy clouds slide flat-bottomed
on glass supported by hilltops
flickering out like light bulbs

A dustdevil lifts her thin wide skirt
and flees
squinting out the sun
Color seeps back up plants
bleached by the glare

The skeletal trees bow to the wind
bushes giggle and the saguaros join in
with their song of whistles
The clouds grumble under their own weight
and the glass cracks
parting the heavy heat
and filling the air with the smell of dirt

Lightning throws broken chalk
growling across the blackboard sky
—*Larry Samson*

My Hand

An x-rayed jellybean sitting lifeless
on my finger,
A wrinkled old lady that does nothing but linger,
Worms slipping and sliding all over the place,
Lasagna still in its microwavable case,
A mass of string all tied in knots,
Whirlpools swishing in pans in pots,
Fields of tall green grass that reaches forever....

Rolling hills that really roll if you flick the lever,
And last but not least a bucket or prunes, that reach all over
my knuckly dunes.
—*Lindsay Eve Ellis*

The Wait

The days roll by as the minutes we see
On the face of the clock seem an eternity
To hold on to the faith, the trust, the memory
Of the one the promise was made 'cause of fate
Makes it easy to deal with the pain of the wait

Though some days are tougher than others to get through
As the loneliness sets in when we're thinking of two
We gather much strength in our words so true
That we smile again and can stand up straight
And without any doubts we believe in the wait

The wait itself we'll happily endure
As its meaning is a symbol of all that is pure
In our hearts as we both are so positively sure
That in our lives this union could never come too late
And that adds value to the price of the wait

There's none more respected, none better the name
Than we who have withstood and have victory to claim
In this battle of loneliness, we understand it's no game
'Cause there's none more beautiful, there's none more great
Than the Sunshine I love, completing the wait
—*Larry Dean Powell*

Falling Leaves

I watched a maple after a sudden freeze.
One after another the falling leaves
   Raced each other to the earth.
The breeze that set them free
   Also seemed to blow through me
To prepare my soul for a spring re-birth.
—*Rosella Virginia Wood*

Anastasia

I always wondered why I saw the lady
   on the grassy rise,
her dress wind pressed against her thighs.

The breeze blowing her hair around
With only a glow for a crown.

But the crown that she knew was in
   her heart,
Life to her had become an art.

And on this windy stretch of ground
In the breeze, her vibrations found...

Carried her thoughts up to the sky,
What is this world will live or die.

To her aloneness she now succumbs
as closer her years come.

The pictures in her mind made clear
as decisions from a far come near.
—*Nancy B. Lovell*

A Friend

A friend is someone special to me,
   One I often like to see.

A friend is someone who brightens my day,
   Even when it's cloudy and gray.

A friend is someone I enjoy talking to,
   About the things we like to do.

A friend is always there when I call,
   Winter, summer, spring, or fall.

A friend is someone who truly cares,
Gives of their time and always shares.

A friend is what I've found in you,
   I'm glad you are my friend so true.
—*Sharon B. Word*

Faces

In two different faces does happiness shine,
One questions the future, one reflects on past time.

One vision young, full of wonder, full of fun,
Growing, unstoppable, like the fires of the sun.

The other image careworn, scars of past years,
One who's felt pain, smelled the fresh scent of tears.

Two common threads weave these two souls together,
Joy and freedom like an eagle, no storm they can't weather.

They're content just to be, to live, never quit,
Like silence, like winter, on your days it does sit.

In two different faces does happiness shine,
Silent as night, yet priceless as time.
—*Sarah E. Ungerer*

Autum's Dance

I saw what could have been a picture today
Of a little boy who was out in play
with his arms raised high in sheer delight
"Look at me momma!"
as he spun round and round to dance with the
leaves before they hit the ground.

Leaves of yellow, brown and gold
swirled about him in their dance of flight
and nature and the child become as one
then the wind dies down and their dance is done.
—*Nancy R. Torres*

Trust

The same, the same, peacock politicians cannot tame
One self-respecting dame
And homeless children roam the streets
Without a parent's claim.
The same, the same, phony prophets all overuse His name
Boat loads of Chinese immigrants are lost at sea
And any mutilated Bosnian could be you or me.
The same, the same, though nameless terror lurks everywhere
The sun and the stars are still there
The birds in the sky still fly high
That baby pilot whale's been cured
And soon will be let out to sea
To be free, even as you and, hopefully, me.

—*Solomon Pogarsky*

God's Salvation Plan

Jesus made His earthly journey,
One which He did not have to make;
But through His love and compassion,
He took the journey for man's sake.

All men were sinners lost and doomed,
But God 'fore knew the ways of man
And loving as only He could,
He provided salvation's plan.

Jesus willingly stepped from Glory
Knowing the price He had to pay,
Dying the death—the sinners' due;
This He knew was the only way.

The cold, dark tomb could not hold Him;
No power could thwart God's redemptive plan.
He arose the Supreme Victor,
Jesus Christ the Saviour of man.

Saviour of all who trust in Him,
Believing He's God's sinless Son,
Who paid our sin debt on the cross
And for us the victory won.

—*Rudolph Townsend*

To A Cinder Cone

The last time we were together there was no bridge between us,
Only a footpath leading to the top of a wind-swept cinder cone
    mountain,
Where violence of weather twists Union Pines and the Hopi
    mesas
Stacked up the horizon all the way to Colorado

We huddled together on the Lee Slope whispering
I had found vocabulary made quiet to describe my feelings,
You seemed stiff and bound-up tightly in your muffler and
    mittens,
So we turned away from each other and found fossils within the
    Limestone.

Together we carried our heavy silence back down the trail,
Each with our separate load, a fossil in each pocket
And a catch in our throats where the tears were frozen,
The artifacts of our hearts buried like treasures unremembered.

—*Lori Goldberg*

Questions

Oh, how it hurts to know that you no longer care
    Or —— did you ever?
So many years since we were wed and now you say you must be
    free, free of me?
What happened to a marriage so happy? Or so I thought ——
    But was it ever?
I just don't know, I just don't know
    Now will I ever!

—*Marie A. Van Wagner*

To Be Perchance A Randolph Or A Lee

To be born in the South for us was meant to be.

Not hardly ever are we considered provincial, but
    only Southern, or not at all.

Possibly because of the way we pronounce Atlanta,
    Georgia, Carter, garbage, house and oil.

If only we could say, "nuclear."

As to manners we are thoroughly schooled and
    unselfconscious.

Our heavy silver-plate tureens are instantaneously
    transformed into luscious candied yams, and

Gentlemen stand before ladies at table as well as
    in the parlor, where in Richmond and Baltimore
    the word rolls mellifluously off proper lips.

If only hats would come back all the way (preferably
    grey), so that we could tip and doff.

If only the General had been younger, smarter,
    victorious...or had known when to quit.

Much of this one-hundred and twenty five years ago.

But the good times there cannot be forgotten,
    nor should we ever look away...

—*William Buchanan*

Esoteric Thought

Running to see who the winner will be
    only to find
    it's not me.
So I'm pedaling my new bike
    faster than the wind
    then I fall.
Swimming underwater racing the sea nymphs
    only to breathe better
    no more air.
Quiet inside around is not a sound
    but a faint beating heart beating
    and running water barely running.
So to become all these wonderful things
    that I thought would make me immortal
    would be foolish
    for I am not.

—*Sara Hiller*

Transformation

A miracle: That sometimes life simply opens up —
Opens to me like a flower shimmers and glows,
And as little daily things come, it shows
Me richness all around, without measure.

I know these late, lovely days of summer
Are but a last, exuberant bloom before dreary
Days of winter come, and then I'm weary
And hemmed in by the world's demands.

But this season, it's different, and my heart
Seems to have expanded in the golden days,
So that I see beauty in a thousand ways;
My soul filled with the wonder of joy.

I received a message, one day beside a waterfall,
Words from a Spirit, clothed in a mantle of peace,
And that happening has given me release
From the doubts and pain of "before."

"When the heart is ready, the learning will come"
Echoes the teaching someone gave to me;
I only know it is wonderful to be free
And to trust in all the tomorrows.

—*Rosalind Caryl*

My Flight

If I could soar with wings as the mighty eagle
or even the smallest sparrow

I would climb to heights that can only be imagined

I would touch the clouds with my finger tips and
catch the raindrops on my tongue

I would look down on the highest mountains and behold
their majesty and also on the valley to marvel in its beauty

I would drift across the deepest sea and across the deserts sand

I would look down upon my family, loved ones and friends and
blow them a kiss from the brightest star just to say I love you

I would whisper the deepest feelings in my heart, to be taken
by the wind and be scattered about to those who love me, to
those who care

I would say I'm sorry to those I've disappointed or hurt, and
let my tears fall from heaven to ask their forgiveness

Reaching heights that could not be spoken in word, I would
climb higher and higher until I would be in His presence.
—*Theresa Shepherd*

A Choir Director's Lament

Oh why do people say "yes" and then don't.
Or faithfully say that "I will" and then won't.
And never a word or a sign do they give
That the promises made always leak like a sieve.

When we practice at eight, it is style to be late.
They sing a few notes and then leave for a date.
So the few that are faithful still plug right along
On the louds and the softs 'till they make it a song.

It's fun and it's work and discouraging too
To enroll so many that end up so few.
But somehow we manage by means to aspire
And bring in on Sunday a pretty good choir.

Of this we are sure, that the sun will arise.
The clouds will disperse to show the blue skies.
And Gabriel's trumpet will sound the last call,
There will only be seats for the few—not the all.
—*Sidney R. Sonnichsen*

Seeking Restful Sleep

Just think of things that never were,
Or gold and frankincense and myrrh,
Or things that baa and coo and purr,
Or beds as soft as rabbit fur.

Or think of sultry ladies fair,
With black or red or flaxen hair.
Their realm's a place you'd like to share.
They gently take you in their care.

If sleep eludes you, think of how
Your life got from past tense to now,
Or how to milk or how to plow,
Or why cows moo and cats meow.

Relax your mind by thoughts of things
Like pirate ships or poet kings,
Or lovely girls with angel's wings,
Who say they'll be your underlings.

Then contemplate the ways of Zen,
Or why the sun darkens your skin,
Or all the things that might have been,
If men were gods and gods were men.
—*Richard Danner*

Ordinary Men

Once these men were heroes marching proudly in review;
ordinary men doing what the ordinary do.

Left behind their country and familial love they knew;
ordinary men doing what the ordinary do.

Faced uncertainty, horror, wrenching sorrow, terror too;
ordinary men doing what the ordinary do.

Youthful innocence lost to the wretchedness in view;
ordinary men doing what the ordinary do.

Home at last, they found who was and wasn't true;
ordinary men doing what the ordinary do.

Sleepless nights, haunting memories, nocturnal tears like dew;
ordinary men doing what the ordinary do.

Many nights have passed now, men's numbers dwindling to a few;
ordinary men doing what the ordinary do.

Old men, old memories, old comrades who;
as ordinary men, did what the extraordinary do.
—*Mike Morton*

Do Unto Others

The adage I heard in a whisper once was to consider someone
  other than me. This secret broke in verse it spoke
for my actions would be the key. I dispatch invitation to this
  grand orchestration and I'd like it to start with me.
I'll make tender effort to be kind to those in which I share
  the planet, Earth. I'll yield to others feelings for I
may not get a second chance, to restore, my own self-worth. A
  gesture of kindness can bring full-circle round, those
with doubts, that harbor fear. Still, we can't know the cross
  that one man bears if his shoes we do not wear.
Assess your actions, are they to model, to this you do believe?
  Therefore, you've done unto others as you've seen fit
as well as you would like to receive.
—*Maria Christine Fritz*

Home In Miami

Preface: In years to come, we will remember
our home in Miami, circa 1993.

Our homes have become our prisons,
It's just like being in jail.
Our inept system has failed us.
We feel like we're held, without bail,
Outside bullets are flying,
Our air is full of lead,
Be just a little unlucky,
In a moment — you could be dead,
Steel bars cover our windows,
Six sturdy locks on the door,
You become afraid of your shadow,
For outside, there rages a war,
Our leaders wring their hands,
They are helpless,
Our spirits, once high.
Will soon break,
How much more, must we suffer?
How much more, can we take?
—*Larry London*

Untitled

I guess your concrete fashions are fading out,
or at least I tried to notice that in your eyes.

Don't become, just be.
—*Rui Miguel Saramago*

January

January—stark, lonely, flash-back scenes of holiday festivities;
outdoor landscapes of greys, whites, ice blues and dark greens;
finding and dreaming of self and past loves

A time for beef stews, homemade yeasty breads, crusty chicken
pies, thick vegetable soups, apple cobblers, hot chocolate with
marshmallows and lightly salted buttery popcorn

Glowing warmth from the fireplace allowing the fire within to
rest and the mind uncluttered for crossword puzzles, painting
in pastels, sketching pictures to while away your time in many
poses

Reading a classic or a book enjoyed as a child, planning and
designing the garden for spring planting from delicate Baby's
Breath to peach-colored roses

All the while music surrounds you from the jazz of Kenton to
the lilt of Chopin—and best of all—a billowing quilt envelops
you from eve 'til morn

Remember—don't venture out 'till you're dressed in layers from
head to toe with those hard-working, story-telling hands
snuggled in fleece-lined gloves

—Lorraine E. Lant

An Ode To The Forest

Majestic wonders tower into the heavens; arms
outspread: Protecting territory and inhabitants
from the glaring fireball above them.

Moss carpeted, soft and green, I lay; dreamily
Peering upward into the blue and cloud free sky.

Blotches of sunlight creep through their swaying
Arms, tickling; warming; chilling my presence.

Onward through dancing shadows; alone - but not lonely

Sound everywhere: Some echoing in the distance; and
The compelling flow of water makes its way through the riverbed

A whisper; a quiet roar: Flowing; rushing; falling

A plunge into the pond: A swim

Rejuvenating falls shower my near nakedness:
Numbing cold; then soothing warmth

A rest on the rocks; and then returning

Satisfaction: Finally finding the time to
make this trip; a few hours; a day; memories
to last a lifetime!!!

Next time, I'll share it with someone!
Want to come along?

—Ronald Antone

My Life Without Love

As a child I grew up asking myself one question
over and over. Does anyone love me?
I often sat by the window watching the children play
Hoping and praying I would get a chance to go outside today.
Oh...another day goes by and again
I don't get a chance to play outside.
I would just sit by the window staring at the sky
Asking myself with a sigh...does anyone love me.
Trying to convince myself without disbelief
The stay in this foster home would be brief.
But another day goes by, no mom, no dad
They said they would be back I guess again they lied.
The question I keep repeating must really be
I don't understand why nobody loves me.
Now at whatever age I may be
I realize if nobody else cares
I love me...

—Patricia L. Rice-Diggs

Lost Love

Once upon a summer's day, as the clouds turned a dulling gray,
Over many a suffering months of care, the end was slowly coming
near, as I watched, my heart felt sad, of the times we could
not have. Sweet memories of him, soft whispers in my ear, all
the things I held so dear.
The future without him, my biggest fear, is slowly becoming all
too clear— nothing left; only a tear.

Some years ago when our love began, laughing and gently holding
his hand, on that dreamy fun-filled night, the stars were
shining extremely bright, I was staring at him—it was love at
first sight. Over many a years his heart he would send, all
of his love to me in the end.
Thinking of what it could've been, knowing that I'll never see
him again—it was almost the end.

Looking back it seemed so fine, walking along his hand in
mine, but now he's gone, there's nothing to say, in the world
he cannot stay. The smile on his face, the twinkle in his eye,
why oh Lord does he have to die? My tears fell on the bed
where he lay, hoping for a miracle that day in May, while I
cried, I began to pray—as the memories fade away.

—Tammy Henderson

Another Day

The sun rises another day
Parents are at work, kids at play
While along side my bed I pray
Can I make it another day?

Another day of hatred and crime
While so many lives ran out of time
Another day and night of food, beer,
T.V. and fright, another day another fight.

Another day of poverty, or will it
come to be, another phone call, or
Refusal for peace, another country
goes to war, rich get richer, poor stay poor.

Another day of wishing for a blind man eyes
Only left to hear the world cries
Never to see suffering of the young or old,
treated so badly and sometimes even cold, or
even unjust, yet there is nothing being done.

Another day as night seems to fall
I finally made it through it all
Will I miss anything, if I don't wake at all.

—Taneka D. Beckman

Birth Of A Season

Clouds in rambling silence float,
   Pastures grazed by beef and goat.
Oak trees stretch in languished green,
   Flowers waving to be seen.
Screen doors open for cool breeze pleasure,
   Carriages transport newborn treasures.
Gardens sprouting lettuce and beets,
   Barbecues rotate succulent treats.
Swimming pools filled with mountain water,
   Tractors plow under last years fodder.
Cherry trees bloom, or are they peach?
   Newly-weds stroll on moonlit beach.
Toddlers with bruises from sidewalk falls,
   Violets for one we love most of all.
Mailman exchanges his longs for his shorts,
   Lawyers seek settlements instead of courts.
Bees and mosquitos appear from nowhere,
   Bicyclists in helmets fixing a spare.
Awnings are hung to shield from the sun,
   Cold winter has vanished, spring has come.

—Mary Moline

Gods Dream

Peace - A distant dream it seems
Peace - A rippling stream
Peace - A battle field silent
Peace - Only God can grant it
Peace - Not all men seek it
Peace - Mans greed won't get it
Peace - Women and children seek it
Peace - God wants it
Peace - The humble spirit prays for it
Peace - God is waiting for all men to ask for it
Peace - Free for the taking for God is ever living
Peace - Guns and money can't buy it
Peace - Won't be granted to unchanged spirits
Peace - Given by the man from Galilee
Peace - The wish of God living
Peace - Is love driven from God in heaven
—*Sidney Lee Phelps Sr.*

Untitled

Whatever happened to our beautiful earth?
People are too worried about what the land's worth.
Just make lots of money, and get much richer.
If the land gets cut then we'll just stitch her.
Where's all the animals who used to graze and roam?
I don't know, I guess we just sort of took their home.
Just better yourself, who cares about the rest.
But look what we've created, oh what a mess.
It's time for the world to open its eyes.
Face reality and forget all the lies.
Were will we be in another ten years?
That's the problem, nobody really cares.
—*Tammy Wroble*

Street Action

The action in the street is getting very fast
People just stare and refuse to blink
Could it be their living in the past
Or maybe search for the missing link

They leave their hearts at the door
To put on a protective face
which will frown when it sees the poor
And smile when it sees a pretty face

If all those eyes could look into the skies
they would see we're made of the same material
and not a high paid player in a daytime serial
So lets stop this high speed pace
Or else we'll end up like the rest of the human race
—*William Duke Davis*

A Way Of Life

I watched him today, all tattered and torn, while he was at play, it was just early morn.
He tugged at his trousers, that kept slipping away, they were just a bit large, the knees they did fray.
Tin cans went in this bag, bottles in that, he gathered them up, while ignoring the rat's.
He spied me watching, then gave me a grin, said "how ya doin' lady, got any tin?"
"Well no," I replied, "not with me," I said, "Oh well," he then smiled, "we can do without bread."
I thought for a moment, then realized, with pain, from these bottles and cans, he had so much to gain.
For what he does, he does not for play, he searches and gathers, to eat once a day.
—*Lori E. Collins*

The Day We Met

Do you remember the day we met?
Personally it's a day I'll never forget,
We acted as if we'd always be together,
But somehow I knew it wouldn't last forever.

I often times wonder, how it could be;
How such a special love could happen to me?
During the times we spent as one
I prayed that day would never come.

That day when I would say good-bye,
My heart would ache and just ask why?
That last day came and went by
And you were strong and didn't cry.

This poem isn't meant to make you shed tears
Or fill your loving heart with fears,
It's just to let you know
Away from your love I will never go.
I'll always love you with all my heart
I won't let anything tear us apart,
Before you know; I'll be home
And never again will I leave you alone!
—*Steven J. Flores*

When I Need You

The jukebox sat silent in the corner,
Play some American music you said,
The jukebox played a happy tune of trombones,
blues, an instrumental song.
Let's dance - dance to the music,
You can not dance to that you said
I reached for you and you took my hands
And your arms encircled my waist
Swirling to the music, dancing, gliding like on air,
And, the jukebox played on...
My eyes met yours, yours hazel, mine brown,
The music filled the air and we swirled on a small dance floor,
Swirling to the music, oblivious to others,
The music filling our ears. Happy in each other's arms
Our hearts and thoughts were one. The music played on
You swirled me once more and our hearts met
And I will remember the dance and the
music you and I danced to and you and I became soul partners
   forever
When I need you all I have to do is close my eyes
and you and I are dancing...
—*Sandra Kay Temple*

Three Men And A Stove

   Three men sat round a pot-belly stove
Playing checkers and reminiscing about times long ago.
   In younger days, each man was brave and strong
Now their advice and wisdom is never wrong.
   Each wear Fedoras low on their brow
Their style and grace make their grandchildren proud.
   If you listen and do not rush
You will hear stories that make the whole room hush.
   Adventure and courage and all that is right
Three wise old men tell their tales tonight.
—*Vicki Ledesma*

Winging It

An airline passenger out for a fling,
Peers across the aisle and observes -
"Why you folks still have your wing!"
And thereby set atingle a tangle of nerves!
—*Leonard Pigott*

Don't Go

Please don't go
Please don't go for I want you to stay.
You have taught me so much from life to death.
You have even taught me that I should pray.
You have showed me that I need not walk alone,
and should never be afraid.
For you said I would never be alone even when I betrayed.
For if you do go, I don't know what I
would do without you helping me along the way.
Please don't go I beg
Please don't go I want you to stay...
—*Nikki L. Price*

Untitled

On a cold wintry night in a land far away
Poor Joseph and Mary had nowhere to stay,
At the Inn they were turned away from the door,
So in a stable so lowly our Saviour she bore...

On the hillside the shepherds were watching their sheep,
While roundabout villagers all were asleep..
When up in the sky came a wondrous sight,
It gave off a glow and lit up the night...

So fearful were they, they fell to the ground
While the Glory of God shone all around...
An angel appeared and told of the birth
Of the One who was sent to bring hope to the Earth.

The Star guided their steps to where the Babe lay
In peaceful slumber in a manger of hay.
They knelt to give Honor and show Him their love;
They knew He was sent from the Father above.

They brought to Him gifts of silver and gold,
And things of great value I have been told...
So what can I bring when the Manger I see?
Since I have no riches I'll just bring Him .... Me.
—*Ollis L. Beach*

Origins

Somewhere in the depths of the soul
pops a tiny spark, formless as the fire
that fuels it. The spark then flashes forth
burning a swath through the aging images
of the hemispheres, right and left,
to let the one picture shine brightest
among the multitude of paling shadows
engulfing the creator and the creature,
in addition to itself.

Now the ball picks up momentum
in an everlasting spin where
nothing matters. The flames spread
every which way, cleansing all they touch,
imploding in self-sustaining fragments
of utter illumination. There is no return
from the blinding blaze in whose wake
lies the artifact in its fresh-minted glory,
like an old truth retold.
—*I. S. Madugula*

Melanie Faith

Today we met sweet Melanie Faith—
Our baby great-granddaughter, so precious and dear
As I held her close, she stole my heart.
Her big blue eyes, so bright and clear,
Spoke lovingly to me—we'll never really be apart.
I pray to God to keep her healthy and strong
Our first great-grandchild—in our hearts she'll always belong.
—*Sarah L. Greer*

A Portrait

If I were an artist or a poet
Possessing their great gifts
To capture the candor and contours of life,
I'd paint the prose
Or write the ode
That speaks of splendor of sea and sky.

My pallet and brush would
Dab only the hues of love
And of beauty.
In rhyme, there'd be no time
But the enchanting ecstasy of eternity.

Though we pass but briefly
Through this puzzling plan,
We see what we wish to see,
Hear what we wish to hear;
And when our visit is ending,
The pastels fading,
Will we be ready to
Become a part of that grandeur
Of which we paint and write?
—*Philip W. Rothman*

Soulfully Pretending

I'm very good at pretending
Pretending that you're here
But "yet" in actuality
Your love has never been near.

I'm very good at forgiving...
Forgiving all that is done
While I was afraid of losing your love!
I found you had none.

I do not blame you
For what could not be.
I only wish for your happiness
Although it's not with me.

"Dear God" let him help me
Help me to descend
Descend from being her lover,
To just being a friend.

I'm good at pretending we're as happy as can be!
But by pretending, I found reality!!...
The only person in love, you see
The only person in love, was me.
—*Nate Rutledge*

Pride

Pride is not something you're able to give
Pride is a feeling that shows as you live.
Through words and actions you're able to show
What you hold close and what you let go.
Pride is a word that makes you stick out
Standards you have that others won't doubt
Values you set a long time ago...
That help you decide what's a yes or a no.
   Pride lets you hold your head up high
You take life at a steady course.
You go the extra mile, and you don't do it by force
You're willing and ready, you try not to fall
You give all you've got or you try not at all!
You seek the right path on the journey you walk
You smile at put downs and petty talk.
You hold your hand out to help another.
Yes, if you've got pride, your like no other.
—*Mandy Mosley*

The Truth

Slavery, instituted in the Black race. Being sold like property, such a disgrace. Serving, cooking, and cleaning for the white man. Not only that, also cultivating the land.

The white man who stood tall and proud to own a Black slave. Whipping and punishing them if they didn't behave. How disappointed the white man must be, when the Black slave suddenly became free.

Yes, freedom! How sweet the sound. No more of being pushed around. Freedom didn't come overnight. It was a long hard struggle, and a difficult fight.

Although slavery isn't in existence any longer. Everyday racism and prejudice is getting stronger. Since Blacks didn't ask to come to America anyway. It's time to realize that blacks and whites are here to stay.

In order to make our lives better. The black race must join together. Let's show each other that we care. Get rid of the attitudes and beware of the negative feelings of the white man. There's no way that he can understand the problems and hatred that we've been through. He's just on the outside looking in, not having a clue.
—*Zabrina Miranda Grisby*

Runaway

I find my self thinking about it a lot,
Question is what will happen if I get caught.
It seems so easy to just get up and run,
I just need the courage and it will all be done
I've tried everything else and I still feel blue,
In my head this seems to be the best thing to do.
I've wanted to do it for quite some time now,
But I just really wasn't sure how.
Eventually I'll get rid of these feelings someday,
But for now I just want to runaway.
—*Mindi McCallum*

Steps Of Quiet

Quiet steps of patience, when there was never time.
Quiet steps of kindness, so very hard to find.
Quiet steps of whispers, when shouting reigned supreme.
Quiet steps of gentleness, today so rarely seen.
Quiet steps of lend an ear to what we had to tell.
Quiet steps of give advice.
Quiet steps of wish us well.

Quiet steps we hear no more, your gentleness is gone.
In each of us in some small way, your memory lives on.

So quickly Mike you left us.
You were taken from our midst.

We weren't ready...
You had to go...
If only we had had more time...
If only...
To tell you
How we loved your
Quiet steps
—*Patricia J. Dugan*

World Tears

I can see a mountain peak and the sun with its rays bursting out the last sparks of warmth for the night. I can feel a cool breeze as it passes. Echoes of animals call me. I can hear children's laughter as they are called in from the night air. Memories are keeping me alive. It hurts to see the oceans, the air, and the land cry. I am the world, treated with hate, but loved because you live with me and on me...
—*Lisa Blacksmith*

The Quilting Room

My grandma Maime stitched her
quilting pieces for hours on end.
In a room reserved for ladies only,
sewing, gossiping and mending.

The movement of needles, back and forth;
stopping only briefly to stretch
her aging hands, racked with pain.

As I watched the orchestration of
skillfully crafting works of art
in the company of family and friends,
creating priceless things to pass down
again and again, I knew I would never know the
camaraderie of working side by side,
at the quilting table, chatting all day long;
keeping time with the rhythm, like a favorite song.
—*Pamela Kaufman*

Do You See What I See?

In a world of unforgiving people with unreconcilable differences
Racist views, sexist choices, discriminating voices,

Unreasonable arguments, unsatisfying lives, abortioned girls
who will never be wives, men who cheat and lie,
women who listen and buy, all that is told to them.

Animal testing, helpless deer people digesting, blind men
who don't want to see, if for he one day you could be.

Singing voices in a mind that turn into screams. It's
a trap, I wish I had a map, to life that is. It isn't easy.

Do you think I'm a feminist? I gave this ending a nice
little twist.

After reading this should you be crying? No. You should start
Helping the dying. This world that is.
—*Shalan Marie Restum*

What I Dream...

A forest of pure crystal glints with the paint of a
   rainbow sunset.
The mimicking images of the friendly star beckon
   saying, "Come, dance."
I join it, and am pulled into a world of nothing but color.
I then spent all night dancing with the darkness,
   and the mysterious secrets that it held.
Then, once again, the befriending star came to play
   and with it the dawn of a colorful new world.
"Stay," the colors said, "We have so many things to share."
And with that, I left the heavens and joined the
   rainbow of crystal forests and misting mountain
   streams.
—*Suzanne C. Myers*

The Education

What is education? It is knowledge
Road to better things in life
It needs discipline and sacrifice
That we do not like to feel or see
It will determine what you are going to be
The time it short when we are young
It quickly passes us by, we can't be weak
We got to be strong, challenge in life is
Nothing new to be prepared will get you through
Lets keep on learning all we can
And have some fund now and then
When we receive our degree we will be traveling
First class in deed
—*Rudy Slomiany*

Biographies of Poets

ABRAHAM, DOROTHYE B.
[Pen.]Bks only "Je Suis Moi"; [hon.]Golden Poet 1991, Mayor's Commission of Women 1st Literary Award 1992; [oth. writ.]1992 1st endeavor children's literature, ie "Easter Egg Pony"; [pers.]Of German, Irish and French descent, writing has always been a valued par of my life. Having shared years of civic, church school activities with family and friends, I live part time in a small Florida town and continue to create paintings and pottery, another field of art I enjoy. Having written for years for trade journal, I was encouraged by close friends to try a more public endeavor. My writings are mystical, yet humorous and profound. With anticipation like birth, it would be good to read more of my works. They are though provoking and well versed.

ACEVEDO, CHRISTINA
[Pen.] Tina Acevedo; [b.] December 8, 1937, San Juan, TX; [p.] Estefano A. Yanez (a.), Daniel E. Yanez (D.); [m.] May 4, 1958; [ch.] Tina Marie, Noe, Jr, grandchildren - Ryan, Noe Robert; [ed.] High School Graduate, "Writers Institute Graduate, one yr Liberty University (student); [occ.] Student, poetry writer; [memb.] American Poetry Newspaper (Institute), World of Poetry; [hon.] Golden, Silver, Who's Who of Poetry; [pers.] I write out of the empathy of my heart and my Dad's poetic gem.

ADAMS, CATHERINE
[b.] October 8, 1957, Peekskill, NY; [p.] Mr. and Mrs. James P. Miller; [m.] Paul S. Revis (fiance'), May 15, 1994; [ed.] Graduated from Walter Panas High School, 1975. Presently attending Dutchess Community College; [occ.] Operator NY Telephone Company; [hon.] 1993 Editor's Choice Award, National Library of Poetry for "Letting Go Isn't Easy"; [oth. writ.] "Letting Go Isn't Easy", "The Winds of Change", and "Miles of Time", are poems of mine that have been published; [pers.] "Miles of Time" is dedicated to all of the angels who were lost to muscular dystrophy especially my brother, Jimmy. I pray that someday soon they won't ever have to "walk alone" ever again, only then can we share the "Miles of Time" together; [a.] Putnam Valley, NY

ADAMS, ELLEN CARLSTROM
[b.] July 19, 1924, Iberia, Missouri USA; [p.] Walter Dickerson and Marcia Gardner Dickerson; [m.] Dewey Carl Carlstrom - Married 5/18/45 - Divorced, Edwin John Adams, Jr. - Married 1/30/76 - Deceased; [ch.] Dewey Kent, Paul and Richard Carlstrom; [ed.] Roosevelt High School, Mound City Business College; [occ.] Travel Consultant; [memb.] Gasconade County Historical Society, PETA-People for the Ethical Treatment of Animals; [hon.] None in recent years only a college scholarship when I was young; [oth. writ.] Many other poems and a children's book as yet unpublished; [pers.] I am a lover of people and of animals and of preserving our heritage - old things - old ways, old building. I believe the written word is mightier than the spoken and try to live my life by the Golden Rule; [a.] Owersville, MO

ADAMS, LLOYD J.
[b.]July 21, 1940, L'Anse, Michigan; [p.]Oliver J. Adams and Ellen C. (Seelye) Adams; [m.]single; [ed.]L'Anse High School Grad.; [occ.]Fieldman, County Tax, Equalization Dep't.; [memb.]American Legion, Baraga County Eagles #2287; [hon.]Award of Merit Certificates and Golden Poet Certificates, 1990-1991, from World of Poetry; [oth. writ.]Several other poems, some published locally, and all have "rhyme with reason."; [pers.]As a picture can be worth a thousand words, so can a word be worth a thousand pictures, and with freedom of speech, our words can be limitless; [a.]L'Anse, MI 49946

AEPLI, MEGAN
[Pen.]Holly Williamson Christopher; [b.]July 3, 1978, Pittsburgh, PA; [p.]Robert Goodrich, Deborah Goodrich; [ed.]Linsly School; [oth. writ.]Poems published in local newspapers and school publications; [pers.]I am influenced by the events and people around me. Whether they be joyful or sorrowful, they are the reason for which I write.; [a.] Zanesville, OH 43701.

ALAMIA, TERESA
[Pen.] Teresa Chapa Alamia; [b.] October 15, 1918, Edinburg, TX; [p.] Miguel Chapa, Adelina Vela; [m.] Jose R. Alamia, April 18, 1942; [ch.] Leticia, Gracie, Addie; [ed.] BA degree in Education from Pan Am University in Edinburg, TX; [occ.] 26 yrs elem school teacher (now retired); [memb.] Jr Service League, President of Catholic Mother's Club. Vice Pres of Pan American Roundtable; [hon.] Published several children's books. Write poetry and one was published in the congressional record. Names of books "Mr & Mrs Migrant", "Eeny Meany Miny Mo"; [oth. writ.] Member of Valley By Liners - a writing group (non profit) for preservation of history. We have published 4 books. Names of books are "Gift of the Rio", "Roots by the 33027 River", "Rio Grande Round-Up", "100 Women of the Rio Grand Valley"; [a.] Edinburg, TX 78539

ALBO, MARY
[b.]December 13, 1908, Brooklyn; [p.]Virginia Mazzeo and Antonio Mazzeo; [m.]Antonio Albo, April 1, 1950 (deceased); [ed.]Girls Com'l. High School, Brooklyn; [a.] New York, NY 10011

ALBRACHT, MARK
[b.]December 14, 1973, North Platte, NE; [p.]Jim Albracht and Ann Albracht; [ed.]Grand Island Senior High. Currently a freshman at the University of nebraska-Kearney; [occ.]Bank Sorter Operator; [oth. writ.]A vast array of unfinished and/or unpublished works ranging from haikus to screenplays; [a.] Grand Island, NE 68801.

ALBRECHT, BRIAN
[b.] July 15, 1966, Fargo, ND; [p.] Frank and Florence Albrecht; [ed.] I am currently a sophomore working towards my Ph.D in Industrial Organizational Psych at NDSU; [pers.] I am fascinated with and enjoy writing about human behavior; [a.] Fargo, ND 58102

ALBURY, MARK
[b.] July 20, 1953, Coral Gables, FL; [p.] Cecil and Anne; [m.] Ellen, March 7, 1991; [ch.] Mark II; [ed.] Some; [occ.] Firefighter/Paramedic; [oth. writ.] Wind of Power; [pers.] My religion is truth; [a.] Mirama, FL

ALLWORTH, JACK C.
[b.]January 15, 1921, Windsor, Ontario Canada; [m.]Yuko N. Allworth, October 4, 1978; [ed.]U. of Alberta B.SC, Charleton U. B.A., UC Santa Barbara M.E.D., U.S. Int'l University Ph.D.; [occ.]Retired; [memb.]Sierra Club; [oth. writ.]Feature articles in university paper. Contributions to several periodicals and books; [pers.]Writing poetry is a great source of peace and harmony; [a.] Campbell, CA 95008-4564

ALSTON, STEVEN GREGORY
[b.] March 13, 1944, Jamestown, NY; [p.] Leondras and Inez Alston; [ed.] State University of New York at Buffalo, Buffalo, NY; [occ.] Employed by Burnham Service Corp, Forest Park; [oth. writ.] Several poems published in World of Poetry anthologies; [pers.] The striving toward a goal is the most vital aspect of living; [a.] Atlanta, GA 30301

ALVES, JACQUELINE M.
[Pen.] Jackie Della Monica; [b.] November 27, 1941, Lived in Bedford, Mass 11-yrs - Danbury, CT 35 yrs - North Carolina since 1988; [p.] Mary V. O'Sullivan Alves (deceased) 1986, Joseph J. Alves - 85 yrs young; [ed.] Holy Family Elementary School, New Bedford, Mass; Danbury High School, Danbury, Conn; American Institute of Banking Courses; Personal Computer Course Work; [occ.] Interior Designer and Author; Vice President of Administration - Sea - Tec Co, Salisbury, NC; [memb.] Society of Plastics Engineers, Tutor - Laubach Literacy Action; Board of Directors, Salisbury NC Historical Society; [hon.] Two Honorable Mention Awards of Merit - World of Poetry 1990 and 1991, Editors Choice Award - National Library of Poetry, 1993; [oth. writ.] "Tree of Life", published in a Break in the Clouds - National Library of Poetry, 1993, "French Country Inn" published in the Wisconsin Door County Advocate Newspaper July 1991; [pers.] Reading and writing poetry is like a stroll on a warm and sunny beach. It conjures life's memories and refreshers my senses; [a.] Salisbury, NC 28146

ANBE, KATHLEEN B.
[b.]June 5, 1947, Syracuse, NY; [p.]Grace Sarah Faucher and William Dwyer; [m.]Harold A. Anbe, July 6, 1985; [ch.]Two by another marriage, they're residing in Alaska; [ed.]High School; [occ.]44 yrs. Nurses Aide in hospital, Sales Clerk in clothing store; [memb.]The Church of Jesus Christ of Later Day Saints; [oth. writ.]One poem, semi finalist in the 1992, North American Open Poetry Contest, On A Threshold Of A Dream, Vol. III is the anthology book of poems. Other poems as yet unpublished; [pers.]I hope to touch peoples lives through my writing for the betterment of mankind, especially the youth of today as well as for tomorrow.; [a.] Lahaina, Maui, HI 96761

ANCHELO, GERTRUDE L.
[b.]July 2, 1966, New York; [p.]Louise Anchelo and Gerald I. Anchelo; [ed.]Stuyvesant H.S., Queens College, Queensborough Community College; [occ.]Student; [memb.]Junior Arista at Beard Junior High School 1981; [hon.]NY State Regents Scholarship; 3rd Science Grant, American Institute of Science and TEchnology; The Benjamin S. Chancy Citation of Honor (In recognition of an abiding love for and interest in music); Concours National de Francais Certificate de Merite (1979 and 1980) Golden Poet 1990-1991, Contest Winner Honorable mention, Stuyvesant High School Scholarship Award Bronze Certificate; [oth. writ.]Orderliness and Splender, A Young Socialist's Guide to Intelligence, Behind Locked Doors, (an Espionage Novel) various poems and short stories.; [pers.]There is great orderliness and splen-

dor in nature and tradition. We ought to celebrate the Sequoia, and all the life with which we share the planet; [a.] Flushing, NY 11354

ANDERSEN, DOROTHY REDNOUR
[b.]March 17, 1923, Gorham, Illinois; [p.]John Rednour and Laura Sickler Rednour; [m.]Byron C. Andersen, December 27, 1941; [ch.]Scott Andersen, Gary Andersen, Debra Andrews; [ed.]Gorham Grade and Gorham Community High School; [occ.]Wife and Mother; [memb.]Grace Baptist Church, PTA, Local Community Associations, etc.; [hon.]Golden Poet Award (World of Poetry 1989-90-91); [oth. writ.]Book of Poetry "Poems for Fun, Thought and Pastime" June 1965, Short Stories For Children; [pers.]Poetry like flowers, is created for consolment and enjoyment. Poetry is a word picture of the minds thoughts and soul's feelings; [a.] Mason, OH 45040

ANDERSON, BARBARA ANN
[b.] Chicago, IL; [p.] Aaron & Sadie Moore (Deceased); [m.] (Husband) Cecil Anderson, March 29, 1958; [ch.] Clayton, Donald, Barbara Jean, Angela, Michael, Rodney; [ed.] Elementary & High School; [occ.] Writer; [hon.] Received several honorable mentions for poetry; [oth. writ.] Several point of view letters published in news papers, also an article. Many children's craft articles published in Ebony Jr magazine. Poem published (AIM magazine); [pers.] Children have always been an influence in my life, because of my love toward them I have always found myself writing about them. My dad was my motivation.

ANDERSON, FLORENCE
[b.] August 16, 1917, Fulton County, Georgia; [p.] Looney Vivian Mixon Anderson and Clarence Frederick Anderson; [m.] Single; [ed.] Girls High, Atlanta, GA; Scarritt College for Christian Workers & several other undergraduate schools; B.S., Lambuth College, Jackson, TN; MS in Psychiatric Social Work, Univ. of Chicago; [occ.] Psychiatric social worker mostly with adolescents and private duty nursing with older patients; [memb.] National Association of Social Workers; Rico United Methodist Church; [oth. writ.] Edited newsletters for several small organizations including the atlanta Dialogue Center, Inc.; [pers.] Enjoyed and collected poetry since midteens but could never write it no matter how hard I tried. After I was 71 years old, on the sam day that I had a miracle healing of my right eye which had been damaged by several strokes, I wrote my first poem. Since then many more have come mostly about close friends and religious topics; [a.] Fairburn, GA 30212

ANDERSON, MARGARET
[b.]March 30, 1926, Cannon City, Colorado; [p.]Edith and Willie Canterbury; [m.]Royal lee Anderson, January 28, 1946; [ch.]Edith Arlene Drake, Royal Lee Anderson II; [ed.]High School; [occ.]Housewife and Rancher when younger; [memb.]Church, Former Home Extension Club President; [hon.]Local Papers and State Extension Club 3rd Place Author Award, "Golden Poetry Award "Honorable Mention Award of Merit Certificate" By Worlds of Poetry; [oth. writ.]Mr. Chips and the Haunted House (children's book), "The Bronkbuster", "Family Ties", "Canterburys Tale", Rocky Mountain Spring", "Life's Artist", "Cowboy Poetry", "Box Social", and too many too list; [pers.]Our world will continue to be in chaos until the value and purpose of life is taught in our homes, schools and portrayed on TV and in our music and movies instead of violence; [a.] Canon City, Colorado 81212

ANGELLE, PAULA MARIE
[b.] August 16, 1963, Lafayette, LA; [p.] Joseph Clifton Angelle, Lenell Mary Brown Angelle; [ed.] Opelousas High, T.H. Harris Vocational Technical School; [occ.] Computer Specialist; [memb.] Conoco Volunteer Club; [oth. writ.] "The Test", "Why is This", "This Lady", "Getting Together"; [pers.] "Make the best of the time that you share with your parents because just as they are here today, they may be gone tomorrow; [a.] Houston, TX 77042

ANGYAL, CHERYL LYNN
[b.]December 22, 1972, Washington, D.C.; [p.]Joyce and Stephen Angyal; [ed.]Graduated from Largo Senior High School; Currently pursuing Associate of Arts degree at Prince George's Community College; [memb.]United States Achievement Academy for Band 1988.; [hon.]Chosen to participate in the All Maryland Ceremonial Marching Band in 1990.; [oth. writ.]Other poems I have written, one poem "Friendship Is A Prized Possession" published.; [pers.]Always keep the Lord in your heart for he will strengthen and comfort you!; [a.] Upper Marlboro, MD 20772.

ARCHULETA, MARGARET NELL
[Pen.] Mickety; [b.] February 14, 1930, Olney, IL; [p.] Charles Washington Smith and Lilly M. Holmes; [m.] Jose Maria Archuleta, February 28, 1952; [ch.] Three, Two boys, one girl and 11 Grandones; [ed.] High School; [occ.] Nurse Retired; [memb.] ASCAP, Song Writers Guild, World Poets; [oth. writ.] Songs, lyrics, poems; [pers.] I have been writing since age 6; [a.] Concord, CA 94519

ARMSTRONG, HAZEL
[Pen.]Hazel Lee Armstrong; [b.]August 27, 1907, Arkansas; [p.]Mable and Frank Lee; [m.]Harry Shaw Armstrong, December 23, 1928; [ch.]Two, John Norman and Yvonne Virginia; [ed.]High School and Business Course; [occ.]Teacher's Aide and Arkansas Power & Light Co.; [memb.]At present time only Poets Round Table of Arkansas, Presbyterian Church; [hon.]To numerous to mention. By many organizations and recognition by Mayor's etc. Through these eighty six years.; [oth. writ.]Book of Proverbs Transposed into R, Children's Favorite Stories Transposed into R. and publications for news papers. Poet by Columns for newspapers.; [a.] Stuttgart, Arkansas 72160.

ARRANTS, GARY
[b.]July 4, 1959, South Arizona; [p.]Bill and Jean Arrants; [ed.]Farragut High School, Two years at Tennessee Tech.; [occ.]Electrical Sales; [memb.]Knoxville Arts Counsel A.H.B.A., Order of the Sleepless Knights; [pers.]While some people strive to make a statement with their poems, I just want mine to rhyme; [a.] Lenoir City, TN 37771

ARZADON, BIBIANO B.
[b.] Baboc, Ilocos Norte, Philippines; [p.] Bibiano A. Arzado, R, Felicisima B. Arzado; [m.] Niceforz Rubio Arzadon, November 13, 1957; [ch.] Judith, James, Sylvia, Sigmund and Eunice; Grandson - Jaysen; [ed.] MS Kansas State Univ; Cert in Statistics - Int Statistical Educational Centry, Calcutta, India; Bachelor of Bus Adm - Univ of the East, Manila, Phil; [occ.] United Nations Principal Officer (Ret); Adjunct Professor; International Business Executive; [memb.] Delta Omega Delta; 32 (degr) Scottis Rite Valley of Houston, Orient of Texas; Phil-American Chamber of Commerce; [hon.] Colombo Fellow; Fellow of the International Statistical Education Centre; Golden Poet Award - World of Poetry '92; Cert of Achievement - USDA '57; Honorary Citizen of the State of Washington '85; [oth. writ.] Transcendence (poem); Technical Papers and Documents (used as studies and background documents for UN Conferences, etc). Published articles in marketing. Essays; [pers.] " The success of a man if measured by the number of times he resurrects from his falls"; [a.] Houston, TX 77083

AUMAN, CINDY
[b.] June 16, 1959, Detroit, Michigan; [ch.] Sara, John Auman; [oth. writ.] Recently published in A Break In The Clouds and soon to be released Tears of Fire published through the National Library of Poetry.

AUSTIN, NICOLE
[Pen.]Nicky; [b.]January 22, 1974, Georgetown, Guyana; [p.]Aileen Austin (mother) and Derrick Austin (father); [ed.]Boro Hall Academy, Queens College; [hon.]Golden Poet Award, Listed in "Who's Who Among American High School Students; [oth. writ.]Poem published in "The Great American Poetry Anthology." Lyrics published by several record companies and various awards of merit.; [pers.]I think that poetry is the best way of expressing the self that early philosophers longed to find. Poetry is a mirror to the self, soul and mind. It always has a heart; [a.] 190 East 42nd Street, Brooklyn, NY 11203.

AXTON, FLORENCE G.
[b.]March 6, 1915, Saguache, CO; [p.]Agnes and Earl Golthelf (Deceased); [m.]F. Tracy Axton, January 7, 1939; [ch.]Gordon T. Axton; [ed.]Sequache CO, Elementary School, Saquache County High School, College Ferry Hall, Lake Forest P.H.D., History; [occ.]Interior Design, Homemaker; [memb.]Carson Brierly Dance Librarian, University Historian; [hon.]Five Awards American Cancer Cystic Fibrosis Assoc, Woman's Club of Denver; [oth. writ.]Over 17 original poems published. Golden Poetry Awards. over 15 original Gourmet Recipes Published, Article Clean Air and Water; [pers.]A poet has a gift of poetic thought, imagination and creation. An innate eloquence, a expression endowed with a bit of the unknown; [a.] Denver, Colorado 80209.

AZEVEDO, FRANCESCA ARAGON
[b.] February 9, 1921, San Francisco, CA; [p.] Frank Aragon and Josephine Navarro Aregon; [m.] Joseph V. Azevedo, June 5, 1938; [ch.] Daughter, Margaret J. Azevedo, teacher of spanish language in high school; [ed.] I went to high school and Grammar school and 9 yrs to college for creative writing classes, 5 yrs. art, painting, sang in choir (Napa Valley Choral Society); [memb.] Native Daughter of Golden Forest, BA, PC, Poets, In a Coolbrith Circle, Past Presidents, twice of NDGW, Chr. of Civic Americanism, Participation and 40 yr. chairperson of 8th graders ND., History, Calif. Speech Contest for N. Valley Schools, Napa V. Art Assoc., History and Landmark, NDGW; [hon.] Five Golden Poetry Awards from World of Poetry. "Best Flag" charge given in the state. Calif. for NDGW. Napa Valley Laureate Poet of 1979,

554

Trophy won many 1st 2nd, 3rd prizes from In a Coolbrith, World of Poetry, Poets of Amer. Poetry Assoc. and Sparrowgrass; [oth. writ.] My poetry, printed in over 125 books and magazines since 1972, 3rd prize, short stories an books; such as Sparrowgrass and Pegasus: 6 times) Amer. Poetry Assoc., World of Poetry, Solano College, Napa College, "Bay Area" College Poetry Press. "Enclave", Who's Who", "Harvest" Best Poets and World of poetry Gold Book; [pers.] My voice is the well of my poetry. Thoughts rise to quench tho heart. Images begin to come about. My heart feeds my mind and I communicate with a deep poem. I relate with; [a.] Napa, California 94558

BABB, DENICE JANE
[Pen.] Penelopy; [b.] March 29, 1952, Price Hill, Cincinnati, OH; [p.] James Berling and Alice Schnieders Berling; [m.] Sir Kevin Dane Babb, July 5, 1992; [ch.] Jonathan Neal Berling, James Justin Berling, and my lovely daughter Cherish Penelope; [ed.] St Williams School, Seton High School and Pasadena College; [memb.] Hope Chapel of Kihei, Maui, Hawaii; [hon.] Won third price in a poetry contest by the National Library of Poetry. I also received the honors to be one of the top 2% selected for this book, Outstanding Poets of 1994; [pers.] In this book my poem is in highest regare to my incredible son, James Justin Berling, who is the "Finest Epitaph". With his father gone he has left his image inscribed on my son's face and physique. Justin is a paragon even in the way he carries himself with grace dignified; a monument, personified of his father's eminence and captivating charm. Yet, something goes much deeper in my son's sky-blue eyes, the color God illuminates of serenity and peace. Justin, when life's trials, the storms that come in dark and gloomy, remember, the sky is always blue. Your heavenly father has everything under control. Trust His care in the same way you trust Him to hold the blue sky in place. Your His sweet-smelling "Goldenrod" and He will never leave you. Justin, remember too, I will always love you very, very, very much, Momma; [a.] Kihei, Maui, HI

BALDYS, SISTER MARY MARCY
[b.] March 23, 1915, Calumet City, IL (at age of 4 became a resident of Medford, WI); [p.] deceased; Our family consisted of seven children, three boys and four girls. At present, only my sister Sophia Kleparski, in Spencer, WI, and Jenny Iburg in San Jose, CA are living. I was initiated into the Felician Sisters Community in 1933. I taught black students in Ensley, AL for six years during the segregation period. In 1961, I set up a library for the American Embassy school in 1961 - 63, for the purposes of accreditation with the Southern Association of America. I completed my elementary school in Medford, WI, and the secondary school, at Good Counsel High, in Chicago, and Rosary College, in River Forest, IL. After returning from my mission in Ensley, AL, I was asked to chair Chicago's 14th District Education System for the Archdiocese of Chicago. In 1982, I was granted a certificate in Clinical Pastoral Education by the Catholic Bishops conference for the National Association of Catholic Chaplains. All in all, I taught 32 years in the elementary schools, 10 years in high schools, four years at the college level and was a librarian for 31 years. I also served as a pastoral minister for 12 years; [a.] Chicago, IL 60659

BANGE, LARRY H.
[b.] March 24, 1950, Gettysburg, PA; [ch.]Rachael Rae; [memb.]Int'l. Society of Poets; [oth. writ.]Numerous published poems, working on articles and novel for publication; [pers.]Through substantial travel and time spent in many places, my perspective of life permeates in the living of love of mankind. Understanding others is understanding oneself first; [a.] Abbottstown, PA 17301

BANKS, NANCY L.
[Pen.] Nancy Reneau Banks; [b.] June 19, 1912, Pontotoc, Mississippi; [p.] John A. Reneau and Nannie Bolton Reneau; [m.] Milo Banks (deceased); [ch.] Nancy J. Banks, Robert E. Banks, Judity A. Rhodes; [ed.] Beloit High School Graduate, Beloit, Wisconsin, Class of 1931; [occ.] Homemaker; [memb.] Quayle United Methodist Church, Quayle United Methodist Women; [hon.] Grandchildren: Anthony C. Scott, Carla L. Banks, Darrell B. Banks; Great Grandchildren: Tandon L. Scott, Courtney Scott; [oth. writ.] Poem published in "On The Threshold of a Dream, Vol. III; [pers.] My writings are mostly on family, countryside and the love of God; [a.] Oklahoma City, OK 73120

BARBER, MATTIE BELLE FIREBAUGH
[b.]Palestine, Texas; [m.]J. L. Barber (deceased); [ch.]Son, Fred and two granddaughters; [ed.]Huntsville Teachers College, Midwestern University and Palestine, TVC College; [memb.]Instituted Palestine Poetry Society; [hon.]Awards in National and State contest; [oth. writ.]Published in twelve national anthologies and has received several awards in National and State contests, and is in the local anthology; [pers.]Hobbies are reading (biography and history) and writing poetry some of which is in New Dimensions and Living Lyrics. Some time is devoted to family, friends, and church.

BARE, DEBRA SUE
[b.]August 20, 1954, Gallipolis, Ohio; [p.]Dale (deceased and Millie Burnette; [m.]Eddie R. Bare, October 25, 1974; [ch.]Jonathan Aaron and Jennifer Louise; [ed.]1972 graduate of Gallia Academy High School in Gallipolis, Ohio; [occ.]Homemaker; [memb.]First Missionary Church of Lima, Ohio; [hon.]Outstanding Poet 1994, Golden Poet 1990 and 1991; 3 Honorable Mentions 1990; [oth. writ.]"Whisper God," "Love's Shadow," "Heart Talk," "Ma's Old Book," and "In His Eyes', are a few.; [pers.]I pray that my life will always "Whisper God" and that "Shadows of God's love" may surround all who read my poetry.; [a.] Lima, Ohio 45804.

BARKER-WINTHAM, RAFAELA
[b.]October 22, 1947, Los Angeles, CA; [p.]Amanda G. Wintham and Humberto P. Wintham; [m.]Henry H. Barker, October 26, 1968; [ch.]Albert H. Barker & Hank R. Barker; [ed.]Our Lady of Loretto High/Chaffey Junior College; [occ.]Free Lance Computer Word Processor - Bilingual Interpreter; [memb.]Audubon Society, Sierra Club; [hon.]Honorable Mention World of Poetry Two times; [oth. writ.]Poems published in poets of the Golden West Anthology for World of Poetry; [pers.]To my three main constants in life who are: God-never leaves me, Myself-I never leave myself, Death-Death will never leave me; [a.] Riverside, CA 92509

BARNES, DONNA MARGUERITE STROUGH
[b.] October 12, 1910, Kalkaska, MI; [p.] Herman Strough, Ruby Mila Wagar Strough; [m.] Robert Henry Theodore Barnes, September 3, 1943; [ed.] Muskegon High and Junior College, University of Michigan, Ann Arbor, B.A., Columbia University, New York City, M.A.; [occ.] Teacher and Civil Service Veterans Administration Ins; [memb.] Tampa Civic Association Students Art Club - AARP and National Association of Retired Federal Employees; [hon.] Theta Sigma Phi, Honorary Journalism Society; [oth. writ.] Books published "Under Tropic Stars", "Manhattan Moods", "Songs of the Sand Dunes, also several poems in "World of Poetry"; [pers.] I love nature and animals and do what I can to help them and the environment; [a.] Tampa, FL

BARTOW, BARBARA J.
[b.]June 26, 1950, Buffalo, NY; [p.]Nicholas and Lillian Bojack; [m.]Michael H. Bartow, December 2, 1986; [ch.]Edward Bartow, Barbara Simmons, Grandchildren Andrea and Diamond; [ed.]Jr. College, Air University USAF, Non-Fiction writing, journalism; [occ.]Poet, Disabled Veteran Viet Nam Era; [memb.]International Society of Poets, Disabled American Veterans, American Biographical Ins., Int'l Bio Centre; [hon.]Who's Who Registry, World of Poetry, Golden Poet 91, 92, Honorable Mention 92; [oth. writ.]Poetry, local newspaper article; [pers.]Disabled is a frame of mind created by these lacking in words.; [a.] Channahon, IL 60410.

BATCHELOR, LINDA COOPER
[b.] September 1, 1949, S.C.; [p.] Fannie L. Cooper (deceased), Enoch Cooper, Sr. (deceased); [m.] William Batchelor; [ch.] Casey L.; [ed.] Easter High, Sumter, SC, South Carolina State College (2 1/2 yrs), Orangeburg, South Carolina; [occ.] Maintenance Administration C&P Telephone Company of MD; [oth. writ.] Fragile Flower, Toss Reality To The Wind, My Friend, Hollow of a Man, Don't Cry For Me: Please Be Glad, The Open Window; [pers.] I strive for total inner peace, to find good in the most tragic situation, to draw strength from adversity to prepare for the next challenge life will offer. I have always been encouraged by my sister Rita K. Outen to continue to write; [a.] Waldorf, MD 20601

BATEMAN, KNIAL R.
[b.] April 9, 1916, Sparta, MO; [p.] Andrew J. Bateman; [m.] Ida Bell (Walker) Bateman, August 7, 1963; [ch.] Donna Kay Rothermel, Debi Ann Murphy; [ed.] High School, ICS correspondence Radio Telephony LUTC Life Underwriter Training Course at SMS Springfield, MO, US Army Radio School; [occ.] Retired Life Underwriter - 37 yrs; [memb.] Chruch of Christ, AM&FM Free Masons. Charter Lifetime Member International Society of Poets; [hon.] Army-Purple Heart. Many Insurance Awards. Poetry - Golden Poet 1988, 1989, 1990, 1991. Grand Prize winner Poet Laureat Fall 1990 Iliad Press Literary Awards. Other lesser awards from Iliad Press; [oth. writ.] Daughter, Harmony, Drifting With Time, Because I Love You, Ozark Hills, Remember, Soldier's Mother, The Children,

Falling In Love With A Dream. Arden Valley, Ode To A Friend, Hillbilly Girl, Father, Mother, Letter to Santa, Grandpa met the Devil; [pers.] I write for the pleasure of attempting to create word paintings and minds of readers. I feel fortunate to have grown up in the beautiful Ozark Hills at a time when the world moved at a slower pace; [a.] Springfield, MO 65803

BAUCHSPIES, DEE MADDUX
[b.]April 5, 1938, Miami, Florida; [p.]John Willard Maddux and Margrette Vetterl Maddux; [m.]Frank Thomas Bauchspies, September 28, 1957; [ch.]Kathryne Lee, 1958, Susan Lynn, 1959, Thomas Maddux, 1966. Grandchildren, Michele and Mark Mason, James and John Ballow; [ed.]Red Bank High School, NJ, Some College at Douglass College, NJ; [occ.]Homemaker, Composer, Writer, Poet, Painter; [memb.]Champion Forest Baptist Church, TX, Poets Northwest, TX; [hon.]Golden Poet 1991, Medal of Merit, Awarded by former President Bush, June 1990; [oth. writ.]Christian Testimony "The Sign of The Cross" published by Women's Aglow Magazine, World of Poetry published "Left Behind and Wounded at Gettysburg"; [pers.]If you can even remember what started the rift please give the gift...of forgiveness; [a.] Spring, Texas 77379

BAYS, LISA C.
[Pen.] Lisa C. Bays; [b.] November 17, 1957, Houston, TX; [p.] Donald B. Bays and Joanna S. Bays; [m.] Single; [ed.] Western Heights High, Wildlife/Forestry and Animal Science, Basic Computer Program; [occ.] MIS dept, Carpenter Paper Co, Okla City, OK; [memb.] Planetary Society; [hon.] Golden Poet 1991 & 1992; [oth. writ.] 4 poems published with the World of Poetry; [pers.] Most of my poetry comes to me through dreams or the beauty of God's creations that I see everyday. Most of my poetry has wonderful stories behind them; [a.] Oklahoma, City, OK

BEACHAM, GLORIA MERCEDES
[b.]January 2, 1926 (Capricorn), White Plains, NY; [p.]Winifred Jones (89 years young and Jack Jones (deceased) Brother Ed Jones; [m.]William (Bill) Beacham, April 20, 1947; [ch.]Diane, Linda, Gloria Vera, Precious Godchild - Eileen Swart; [ed.]St. mary Gate of Heaven, Ozone Park, NY, bishop McDonnel MHS Brooklyn; [occ.]One year Pace Inst. Housewife, couch potato, dreamer poet; [memb.]free spirit; [hon.]Two Golden Poet Cert., 6 Certificates of Honor from World of Poetry for poems entered in contests, 3 poems published 1992 World of Poetry Anthology; [oth. writ.]Many poems, 3rd daughter compiling them for my book to be "The TearJerker Poet" inspiration "Pagliacci"; [pers.]My Epithet, Here lie the remains of poor old me who drowned in my own philosophy. I went not alone, before my last breath I analyzed all things to death; [a.] NY 11701

BEAN, HELEN E.
[b.]October 19, 1921, Mercer Co. PA; [p.]Gilbert and Jessie Dick; [m.]Robert I. Bean, 1943; [ch.]Kenneth R., Cheryl L., Robert (deceased) Sandra L., Larry H.; [ed.]High School Graduate (Rocky Grove School) Franklin, PA; [occ.]Retired Bookkeeper, Franklin, PA; [memb.]First Ave., Baptist Church, Tucson Mall Walkers Club, Jacobs Club, S.C. Card Club; [hon.]Seven Golden Poet Awards, Ten Merit Certificates, Honorable Mention (World of Poetry); [oth. writ.]Poems in school paper. Poem in "The Clover Collection of Verse" Vol. ll. Also a poem in "Who's Who in Poetry" by World of Poetry; [pers.]In my poems I try to convey God's love, natures beauty. He has created, just for us and the need for him in our every day life.; [a.] Tucson, AZ 85705

BEASON, ROBERT L.
[b.]December 10, 1941, Ozone Park, NY; [p.]Vivian and William; [ed.]College, Hofstra University; [occ.]Mailman; [pers.]I never realized how strong the bond was with my father until he had to leave.; [a.] Mass. Pk., NY 11762

BECKERDITE, CAMI
[b.]June 19, 1967, Livermore, California; [p.]Carl and Karen Beckerdite; [ed.]Granada High, Solano College; [occ.]Customer Service, Home Depot; [hon.]Editors Choice Award for 1993, National Library of Poetry; [oth. writ.]Had my first poem published in the Anthology "A Break In The Clouds" published by The National Library of Poetry.; [pers.]It is my goal to touch and inspire as many young people as I can so that they too can achieve all that they put their mind to.; [a.] Marietta, Georgia 30067

BELLO, JERIDEAN
[b.] Cho, IL; [p.] Dewitt and Nerissa Potts; [m.] Najib Bello, June 30, 1973; [ch.] Nereasa, Jemila, Najib Jr; [ed.] BS Psychology from Loyola Univ and Extended Business Courses at Chgo St U and Chgo City College; [occ.] Early retiree from IBM Corp now entrepreneur - Admin Svc Business for Small Businesses; [memb.] Several Church Auxiliaries; [hon.] Numerous honors and awards for commentaries and speeches at schools, musicals and public affairs; [oth. writ.] Manuscript entitled, 'To God Be The Glory' and numerous other poems for special occasions as well as for special people; [pers.] Through my poetic expressions and writings to God be the glory; [a.] Chgo, IL 60664

BELTON, CHARLIE M.
[b.] May 9, 1953, Fairfield County, SC; [p.] The Late Charlie L. Benton and Mary Jane Benton (Living); [ed.] Attended public school Fairfield County, Carroll Engineering Boston, MA old Dominion Univ Nor, VA; [occ.] Welder, Merchant Marine; [memb.] VFW #4264, Masonic Lodge #33, V.S. Merchant Marine; [hon.] Several Army and Navy Awards; [oth. writ.] A Drunk Dream Called Reality, In Passing, Paradise, From the Heart, Had A Dad, The Merchant Marine, Persian Excursion 1990; [pers.] Life: like a mirror, a true reflection of what we really are; [a.] Winnsboro, SC 29180

BENNETT, DAROLD LEROY
[Pen.]Darry Bennett; [b.]January 9, 1943, Bremerton, Kitsap County, Washington; [p.]Darold E. Bennett, Father & Alice L. Reardon (Bennett) Mager; [m.]Eileen NMI Bennett, November 24, 1981; [ch.]Lionel D. Bennett, Timothy E. Bennett, Kevin L. Bennett, Donald Gruntowicz, Daniel Gruntowica; [ed.]Billings Senior High School, Billings, MT; Bachelor of Science Degree, Cum Laude, Criminal Justice/Psychology, College of Great Falls, MT; [occ.]Military Retiree, Seeking a job in investigations, criminal/industrial; [memb.]Delta Lodge No. 128, A.F. and A.M. (Masons); [hon.]Miscellaneous military awards and decorations, none in writing; [oth. writ.]Poems: Great Falls; The Capital of Western Art; My Philosophy Professor; The Lewis and Clark Interpretive Center; [pers.]Great poetry must make a philosophical statement, right or wrong, of the beliefs and values a person holds to be true!; [a.] Great Falls, MT 59405-3923.

BENROS, THOMAS
[b.]December, 29, 1928, Cape Verde Islands; [p.]Emilio Firmino Benros and Rosa Ferreira Lima Benros; [m.]Marie Filomena Pinto Benros, December 10, 1956; [ch.]Ricardo Jorge, Filomena Marie Dulcidia and Gardenia Benros; [ed.]Master's of Education by Rhode Island College, Master Social & Political Science by University of Lisbon Portugal; [occ.]Several Social Clubs; [hon.]Several Awards from World of Poetry; [oth. writ.]Several articles published in magazines and newspaper on social, political and educational subjects; [pers.]Life is easy depending on the way you face it; [a.] Pawtucket, RI 02860.

BERGERON, CYRILLA
[b.]October 31, 1945, Framingham, Massachusetts; [p.]George and Virginia Etzel; [m.]Ronald E. Bergeron, August 7, 1991; [ch.]Geoffrey and Michael Willis; [ed.]B.S. Gorham State College (USM), M.S. Eastern Ct. State College (ECSU); [occ.]Grade 8 Teacher, H.W. Porter School, Columbia, CT; [memb.]Columbia Teachers Assoc., Connecticut Education Association, National Education Association; [hon.]Who's Who in American Education, 1989-90, 1992-93, 1994-95 Editions; [oth. writ.]Poems - "Toward Universal Love", "Passing On", "Promise"; [pers.]677 Gilead Street, Hebron, Connecticut 06248.

BERGMAN JR, GEORGE F.
[b.] March 30, 1944, Oceanside, CA; [p.] George F. Bergman, Sr, Ruth Hazel Hines Bergman; [ch.] Michelle Louise Bergmann; [ed.] Rochester Institute of Technology; Univ of Rochester; [occ.] Projectionist, freelance writer; [memb.] Second Spiritual Science Church of Rochester, Churchville Lodge #667 F and AM; [oth. writ.] Poems published in anthologies, technical documentation; [pers.] I believe it is through the images created in my poems that I can best express the beauty I see in nature and affirm the unity of al life and brotherhood of all humanity; [a.] Rochester, NY

BERRY, EILEEN
[b.] January 27, 1931, Warrington, England; [p.] Stuart and Elizabeth Haskew; [m.] William, January 3, 1953; [ch.] Brian David, Anne Claire, Peggy Dianne and Scott Martin; [ed.] English School System including High School; [occ.] Retired Elementary School Librarian; [memb.] Pera, Women of the Moose, Rocky Mountain Story Teller's Guild, National Author's Registry; [hon.] Various; [oth. writ.] Several poems published in newspapers, Poet's Voice Magazine, and several anthologies. Wrote school song for where I worked. Have had words set to music - country

western songs; [pers.] In my poetry I cover just about all human emotions or feelings. I am affected by everything and everybody!; [a.] Loveland, CO 80538

BETTENHAUSEN, RUTH E.
[b.] April 28, 1917, Blue Island, IL; [p.] William W. Wood, Florence G. Brewer Wood; [m.] Russel W. Bettenhausen, May 21, 1938; [ch.] Helen, Russel Jr., Roscoe, Claudette, Benjamin, Larry; [ed.] Graduate of Joliet Township High School Class of '37; [occ.] Homemaker; [memb.] Cross Roads Community Church, Cross Roads Community Senior Omega Club Olympia Field Hospital and Medical Center VIP Club, and International Society of Poets; [hon.] Golden Poet Award, '88, '89, '90 and '91. Certificate of Merit Awarded by the International Society of Poets, '93. Several newspaper articles written about myself and my poetry. Poems often read aloud to the Cross Road Congregation by our Pastor; [oth. writ.] Poems published in the VIP Club Newsletter, lines quoted from various poems published in local newspapers and my church's Sunday bulletin; [pers.] My talent is God-sent. I write for my own pleasure and for the joy and blessings my poems seem to give to others; [a.] Orland Park, IL 60462

BIGGER, EMORY M.
[b.] June 12, 1951, Washington, DC; [p.] Earl Edwards (deceased), Agnes M. Edwards; [ed.] Howard University; [occ.] Computer Programmer Analyst; [memb.] National Trust for Historic Preservation; National Audubon Society; National Geographic Society; [hon.] Who's Who in the East 1989-1990 and 1993-1994; Golden Poet Award 1987 (World of Poetry); [oth. writ.] Contributed poems to anthologies. Working on first book of poetry; [pers.] The objective of my writings is to instill thought in mankind. Too much ignorance is spoken by people proclaiming to be intelligent; [a.] Silver Spring, MD 20910

BILLISON JR., JAMES G.
[Pen.]James Gilbert Edward Billson (not often used); [b.]December 4, 1932, Willoughby, Ohio; [p.]James G. and Anna R. Billson; [ed.]Willoughby Union High School '50. Some college. Private music study.; [occ.] Ret. Postman, Organist '45 yrs., have worked in stained glass, fine art paintings, Landscape, portrait, enamel; [memb.]N.A.L.C., American Guild of Organists, Willoughby Hist. Soc., C & E Re. Hist. Soc., Genega Co.; [oth. writ.]I have been writing poems since I was sixteen. I never had any published until one appeared in "A Book In The Clouds." Some I have set to music. These have been sung (The Carols) in church.; [pers.]Poetry, music, and art all go together. I prefer to use a set meter and/or rhyme seldom using blank verse. Vowel quantity and harmony are often used instead of strict rhyme, and the ear is that of music. Inspiration can come from anything; [a.] Willoughby, Ohio 44094-7952

BISHOP, DOUG
[b.]July 17, 1944, Seattle, WA; [p.]Evelyn Bishop, father (deceased); [m.]Jane Bishop, December 19, 1987; [ch.]Tiffany Anne; [ed.]Irene S. Reed High, Eastern Wyoming College; [occ.]Author; [memb.]St. Paul's Catholic Church, Nampa, Idaho; [hon.]USA, NG NCO Leadership school, Commandant's List; [oth. writ.]Several poems published in anthologies. Preferred Poets Anthology, Publisher's Choice, 1989, American Poetry Association, book Smiles...and other things, pub. 1993, Carlton Press; [pers.]I like to write about the human condition in most instances. I greatly admire the works of Emily Dickerson and Robert Frost; [a.] Nampa, Idaho 83651

BLACK, JOY LOCKHART
[Pen.] B. J. Hart; [b.] June 13, 1943, Baton Rouge, LA; [p.] Quinton and Jewel Lockhart; [m.] Jay Black, June 30, 1963; [ch.] Lynne Black-Wall, Greta J. Black, Jara Black-Miller; [ed.] Humphrey, High School, U of A at Montecello, Phillips Community College; [occ.] House-wife/office worker for husbands flying and farming business; [memb.] American Cancer Society Arkansas Agricultural Aviation Association, National Poetry Society; [hon.] Won cross stitch state level/Merit Award International Society of Poets/Chosen to attend Milton Berle's 85th Birthday Lifetime Achievement Awards banquet at L.A. Poetry Festival 1993; [oth. writ.] Chosen for 1994 IPS Outstanding Poets of 1994 book of poetry. Had poems in Ag Air Update and International Pilots Mag, Poetry in On The Threshold of a Dream - 1992 and National Library of Poetry weekly calendar for 1993. Poetry in The Coming of Dawn - 1993; [pers.] I enjoy poetry and most of all I enjoy the writing of novels that I have yet to have published, since I have no literary agent to date. I love writing special poems for my children and grandchildren and hope to one day be Poet Lauret of my town and county; [a.] Humphrey, AR 72073

BLACKBURN, JOHN H.
[Pen.]Johnny; [b.]January 23, 1949, Preslonsburg, KY; [p.]Elbert, Jr., and Anna Mae; [m.]Lenora Sue Blackburn, November 7, 1988; [ch.]Three stepsons, Richard Allen, James Patrick, Timothy Lee; [ed.]Prestansburg High School, Photography Course at Pittsburgh Comm. Coll.; [occ.]Transporter of Hazardous Materials; [memb.]new Bethal Frevill Baptist Church; [hon.]Honorable Discharge/Army (Sgt./2nd. Inf. Div./Korea); [oth. writ.]Songs for churches; poems for local newspapers; two poems published by this library of poetry; The Journey and A Heavenly Ride.; [pers.]I'm looking forward to the hereafter. If sinner people would just take that "first-step"...my how easy and enjoyable step No. 2 would be! (God Bless This Nation); [a.] Blue River, KY 41607.

BLAKE, EVELYN K.
[Pen.]Evelyn Kimball Blake; [b.]July 10, 1912, Lancaster, NJ; [p.]J. Wendall Kimball and Susan Johnson Kimball; [m.]George Ernest Blake, September 12, 1937; [ch.]Susan Blake Chamberlain, Katherine Kimball Blake; [ed.]Lancaster Academy and Concord Business College; [occ.]Homemaker; [memb.]New England Writers/Vermont Poet's Awards, published in Who's Who in Poetry by National Society of Published Poets.; [oth. writ.]Poems read at Daughters of the american Revolution meetings, printed on Church programs, published in and out of state contests, published in Touchstone, a publication of P.S.N.H., town paper and the N.H. Manchester Union, read at funerals.; [pers.]A painter sees- a poet feels; [a.] Lancaster, New Hampshire 03584.

BLASH DR., HOSEZELL
[b.]December 12, 1939, Twiggs County; [p.]Roosevelt and Mattie Blash; [m.]Rosa Shines Blash, May 30, 1967; [ch.]Kimberly, Rajyumar DeShawn and Kendra; [ed.]Albany State College, B.S. in Science/Math; MED, Georgia Southwestern; DEd Nova Univ., Florida.; [occ.]Elementary School Principal; [memb.]TAE, GAE, NAE, Phi Beta Sigma, United States Advisory Board; [hon.]Golden Poet Award 1988, 1989, Silver Poet Award 1990, Awards for Merit for many poems; [oth. writ.]"The Optimist and Pessimist" (Kansas and Georgia Poets). "A New Baby" (Great American Anthology World of Poetry."; [pers.]I try to bring out the weak and strong points of people in my writing; [a.] Jeffersonville, GA 31044.

BLOCK, CHERYL J.
[b.] July 27, 1957, Charleston, SC; [p.] Dr. William and Miriam Block; [ed.] Currently working on a PH.D. in Spanish Literature at UNC Chapel HiU.; [occ.] Teaching Assistant Department of Romance Language; [memb.] Philological Association of the Carolinas, Phi Sigma Iota; [hon.] International Society of Poets, nominated 1991. Nominated to International Writer and Artist Association 1993. Indeed in the biographical reference, fall 1993, 2000 Notable American Women (American Biographical Institute); [oth. writ.] Poems published in journals and anthologies in the U.S., Venezuela and Belgium; [pers.] I hope that my writing is loyal to those who hare shared their thoughts with me, and I thank those people for sharing their experiences; [a.] Carrboro, NC 27510

BOBO, ARLIE U.
[b.]April 5, 1909, Fayette, AL USA; [p.]Ira Bobo, Catherine E. Bobo; [m.]Lucile E. Shroeder, May 1, 1936; [ch.]L. Douglas, Suzanne, Richard K.; [ed.]Junior College; [occ.]Minister; [memb.]North Alabama Methodist, Master Mason; [oth. writ.]Several poems published in local papers; [a.] Alexander City, AL

BOGOWITZ, CHERYL
[b.] January 5, 1952, San Diego, Ca; [p.] Ray Bagowitz and Gloria Bogowitz; [ed.] Poway High, San Diego State University; [occ.] Research Scientist, specializing in immunobiology; [memb.] Charter Member of the International Society of Poets, Homer Honor Society for Poets; [hon.] SDSU Graduate with honors and distinction, Golden Poet 1991, Award of Merit for "Lover's Eternal" Honorable Mention 1991; [oth. writ.] Selected poems in "Our World's Favorite Poems, Who's Who in Poetry; [pers.] I find poetry writing a mental catharsis, enabling me to come to grips with daily emotions, thoughts and/or experiences. I thank the Trinity for everything; [a.] San Diego, CA 92122

BOKA, CHRIS
[b.]September 5, 1968, St. Louis, MO; [p.]John and Mary Boka, Living in St. Louis; [ed.]Graduated from Parkway West High 1986. Graduated from Drury College 1990; [occ.]Baker for Marriott Corp.; [a.] St. Louis, MO 63117

BOLDUC, MARTHA M.
[b.]September 7, 1941, West Stewartstown, NH; [p.]Mr. and Mrs. Royal Boldve; [ch.]Angela A. Umbro 22 yrs., Dino V. Umbro 19 yrs.; [ed.]High School, Beautician Personal Psychology I; [occ.]Beautician; [hon.]Two Golden Poet, 1 Ruby, 5 Merit Certificate Awards; [oth. writ.]Rendezvous With A Dream, Love Me Forever/ My Son, I Saw You Today, Grandpa, I Remember So Well; [pers.]Hold Close Your Silent Wishes. For dreams really do come true.

BONEN, WILLIAM R.
[b.]September 28, 1971, Galion, Ohio; [p.]John W. Bonen and Doris I. Bloomfield; [ch.]Emily Kay Stockmaster; [ed.]High School, U.S. Military Training; [occ.]U.S. Air Force Security Police; [hon.]Southwest AISIA Campaign Medal, National Defense; [pers.]The greatest success is never seen by the world, only the heart knows this as a true great accomplishment; [a.] Bucyrus, Ohio 44820

BONNEVILLE, A. THOMAS
[Pen.]Tom Bonneville, Will Kane (Prose); [b.]June 27, 1921, Portsmouth, VA; [p.]W.H. and Johnnie Gray Bonneville; [m.]Helen Mary, June 5, 1949; [ch.]Dorothy Gray, Mary Helen, Eva Tomlin, Bonnie Lee; [ed.]Woodrow Wilson High, Univ. of Alabama, Univ. of Hawaii; [occ.]Retired from marketing; [memb.]Orlando Advertising Federation, C of C; [hon.]Silver Medal 1963, Adv. Fed. of America, many awards in advertising (locally, state and national); [oth. writ.]Poems and Prose since 9. Have attempted publishing other than newspaper column and features in 1947-47 which was my job; [pers.]Do unto others as you would have them do unto you.; [a.] Orlando, FL 32812

BOROK, ARON
[b.]September 17, 1973, Chicago, IL; [p.]Bev Sandler and Jack Borok; [ed.]Fremont High (Sunnyvale, CA) Northwestern University; [occ.]Student and Humanist; [memb.]Science Outreach Program in Education; [oth. writ.]One other poem, Essay "Just a Little bit of Cheeseburger"; [pers.]Start with the children, then in 30 or 40 years everything should be fine.; [a.] Evanston, IL 60201

BOSTON, SUSANNE IVEY
[b.] May 1, Aguadilla, Puerto Rico; [p.] Harvey W. and Sandra M. Ivey; [m.] Roddy Gregg Boston, May 9, 1992; [ch.] John Harvey and Caitlyn Elizabeth; [ed.] Pre-Med, International for Deaf; [memb.] LDS; [oth. writ.] Ribbons and Lace published numerous other poems; [pers.] The poem is in memory of my nephew Nathan Bridges Callahan (Peterson) who died as a result of a gunshot wound on November 15, 1992. Nathan we love you, April 19, 1979 - November 15, 1992.

BOURREE, FELIX
I am of both American Indian and French decent, having served with the USAF in the Korean and Viet-Nam wars. I am now retired from service with a 100% disability and serving in my third term with the Disabled American Veterans as Legislation Officer. My wife Leola and I have six children, sixteen grandchildren and three great grandchildren. While trying to keep the veterans up to date on the latest veterans legislation, I work with genealogy digging up the past is as much fun as keeping up with current events. I have received about ten awards from veteran organizations for work I have done with the veterans. Plus I have three awards of merit three honorable mentions and a editors choice award for my poems. In June of last year my home town of Gulfport, MS presented me with a proclamation naming June 16 as poet Felix Bourree day, for the poems that have been published in the newspaper. Starting this year I will be doing my best to help take poetry into the future by serving on the International Society of Poets Lifetime Member Advisory Panel, and I have written a book called "What's Next" published by Vantage Press of NY. I wrote this poem in honor of a close friend Carl D. "Smity" Smith who served on the submarine Flying Fish the most decorated ship in world war two. He lost his last fight to cancer; [a.] Gulfport, MS 39501

BOYD, GEORGE A.
[b.]July 5, 1950, Los Angeles, California; [ed.]B.A. Psychology UCLA (1982) Certified Alcohol Drug Counseling UCLA Extension (1987); [occ.]Counselor, Meditation Teacher, Metaphysician; [hon.]Who's Who in Poetry 1992, Who's Who Among Young American Professionals 1988.; [oth. writ.]Night of Dates, Destiny Unfolds, Meditation for Recovery and The Discourses of Swemi Prem Deyal Mudrashrem Publishing. Drug and Sex, The Rosen Publishing Group. Poetry published in various anthologies, magazines and newspapers.; [pers.] My poetry has been influenced by the Sufi and Hindu poets who made the ineffable speak, the invisible visible, the silence audible and revealed the hidden sacred mysteries.; [a.] Venice, CA 90294

BRANDT, EDWARD REIMER
[b.]November 17, 1931, Satanta, Kansas; [p.]Abraham V. Brandt and Anna, Nee Raimer; [m.]Marie Schmidtke, October 24, 1953; [ch.]Rosemarie, Eileen (Winckler), Douglas, Bruce; [ed.]PH.D in Political Science, University of Minnesota, Pre-College Education in Canada; [occ.]Disabled professor and part-time Genealogist; [memb.]League of Minnesota Poets, Mississippi Valley Poets & Writers Association, Minneapolis Poetry Club, CA. 25 Genealogical Societies; [hon.]Graduated Summa Cum Laude & Phi Beta Kappa, 1976 Award for Outstanding services in cleaning up Minnesota indoor environment, over 50 poetry prizes and honorable mentions; [oth. writ.]Editor, Minneapolis Muse (Anthology); Author, "A Butterfly's Dozen" (Book of Sonnets); Dozens of articles and books on genealogy and government; [pers.]I appreciate intricacy of form, similar to gothic cathedrals. I think poetry should be intelligible to a broad spectrum of poetry lovers.; [a.] Minneapolis, MN 55414-3101

BREAULT BR., SC., EDWARD C.
[Pen.]Brother Fidelis; [b.]December 10, 1929, Pawtucket, Rhode Island; [p.]Edward A. Breault & Rita E. Beauregard; [occ.]Executive Secretary; [memb.]Brother of the Sacred Heart, Worldwide teaching order.; [hon.]Eight "Golden Poet" Awards from World of Poetry, and many other prizes and honorable mentions; [oth. writ.]Poems appear in 14 other anthologies and in the Order's publications; [pers.]I specialize in religious poetry and "thought poems."; [a.] Pascoag, RI 02859.

BREES, FINLEY
[b.]July 28, 1917, Volin, So. Dak.; [p.]John L. and Edith (deceased); [m.]Bernie Brees, May 29, 1949; [ch.]Joan, Jean, Janet, John, James, Jeff; [ed.]Grad. Mechanical Arts H.S. 1936; [occ.]B.N.R.R, Retired 1980; [memb.]55 Club, Mens Club, Relaxed Rail Retirees; [hon.]Dale Carnegie Publ. Spkg.; [oth. writ.]More than 100 letters to editors; [pers.]I will be happy to live to 80 yrs. of age; [a.] Paul, MN 55106

BRELAND-DAVIS, BARBARA
[b.] July 12, 1940, Brooklyn, NY; [p.] Charles and Bessie Wise (both deceased); [ch.] Anthony Breland (deceased), Joy D. Powell; [ed.] Kingsboro Comm College, Prospect Heights High School; [pers.] I thank the National Library of Poetry. Also, taking this time to dedicate my poem to my children, my beloved son, Anthony Dwayne Ireland, bus driver for New York City transit (who is now deceased), daughter Joy R. Powell, whom I love dearly; [a.] Brooklyn, NY

BRENNAN, SEAN JOSEPH WILLIAM
[b.] October 3, 1962, New London, CT; [p.] Terry W. Brennan, Claire F. (O'Keefe) Brennan; [m.] Milka S. (Carrion) Brennan; [m.] August 13 & 14, 1982; [ch.] Sean Joseph Brennan Jr, Brian Jonathan Brennan; [ed.] Harbor Elementary, New London High, US Army Military Police School, Mohegan Community College; [occ.] Machinist - Tool Grinder; [memb.] International Association of Machinists and Aerospace Workers Local Lodge #1871 Groton, CT; [hon.] 1993 - A Break in the Clouds editor's choice award for Happy St. Patrick's Day; [oth. writ.] Happy St. Patrick's Day published in The National Library of Poetry's A Break in the Clouds, various other publishable hopefuls and personal writings to family members; [pers.] To try and convey a positive message in everything; [a.] Waterford, CT 06385

BRENON, HELEN M.
[ed.] Art Institute of Pittsburgh, Barnes Foundation, Philadelphia, Otis, Parsons School of Design; [occ.] Commercial Artist, Fashion Illustrator and Designer Instructor; [memb.] Otis-Parsons School of Design in Los Angeles; [oth. writ.] Many others for my personal expressions and my feelings about life. Would like to write lyrics to songs; [pers.] I have been influenced greatly by the two Indian poets Kahlil Gibron and Rabindrinath Tagore. I think life and people are beautiful; [a.] Phoenix, AZ 85024

BRESNAHAN, KELLY
[b.] September 4, 1976, Park Ridge, IL; [p.] Donna and Jonas Macivlis and Gerard Bresnahan; [ed.] Attending Mother Theodore Guerin High School currently as a senior in the class of 1994; [occ.] Student, an aspiring writer; [memb.] The Pacific Whale Foundation; [hon.] High School honor roll, a Who's Who Among American High School Student's Student; [oth. writ.] A Friend For Life published in Wind in the Night Sky, no other works have been published; [pers.] In order for this world to be at peace, people have to first realize that there is only one race, the human race created equally in God's image; [a.] Chicago, IL 60634

BRETON, LISA
[b.]March 8, 1971, Bridgeport, CT; [p.]Real and Gale Breton; [ed.]High School diploma from Central Catholic H.S. in Norwalk, CT. Pursuing a Bachelor's Degree in English writing and English literature.; [occ.]Bank teller for Norwalk Savings Society and freelance journalist; [memb.]National Writer's Union, World of Poetry; [hon.]Golden Poet 1991, Published in "World's best Poets of 1991" and the "Fairfield Review"; [oth. writ.]I have written newspaper articles and I have a book in the process of being written along with several children's stories.; [pers.]I hope to open the eyes of all people to world peace. I also hope to show everyone the importance of keeping our environment clean so all can enjoy the Earth.; [a.] Wilton, CT 06897

BREWER, DORIS E.
[Pen.]Doris Hartsell Brewer; [b.]April 14, 1935, Stanley County, NC; [ch.]Brothers and Sisters Nancy Hartsell, Max Elmore, Carol Hopkins, Marian Hartsell, Michael, Sherron and Francis Marion; [ed.]High School, Norwood, NC; [occ.]Retired Restaurant Mgn., started writing poetry 1991.; [memb.]The Poetry Society of VA, Poetry Academy, International Society of Poets; [hon.]Won several awards with World of Poetry, golden poets award 1991-1992, Editor's Choice Award the National Library of Poetry 1993.; [oth. writ.]Published in Anthologies by The National Library of Poetry. Sparrowgrass forum and Contemporary poets of America and Britain, First book of verse to be published soon.; [pers.]Even in imperfections beauty can be found. I believe Poetry is a reflection from the soul.; [a.] Chesapeake, VA 23323.

BRIGGS, PHILLIP W.
[b.]January 5, 1950, Eustis, FL; [p.]William Franklin and Sylvia Alice Briggs; [m.]Divorced; [ch.]Phillip Andrew and David Franklin Briggs; [ed.]Associate of Applied Science in Electronics Technology; [occ.]Maintenance Technician; [memb.]World of Poetry and International Society of Poets; [hon.]Golden Poet Award 1989, ALPHA BETA KAPPA; [oth. writ.]Great Poems of the Wester World Vo. II., World Treasury of Golden Poems; [pers.]Love is like a white rose, it blossoms and grows the more it's nurtured each day. Then for some unknown reason? That white rose that was once so beautiful is now gone and faded away.; [a.] San Antonio, TX 78245.

BRILLANTE, ANN
[b.] March 17, 1981, St Raphael's Hospital, New Haven, CT; [p.] Margaret F. Brillante and John M. Brillante; [ed.] Pond Hill Elementary School, Dag Hammarskjold Middle School; [memb.] Citizenship Committee, softball, chorus, band; [hon.] Softball Trophies, Student of the Month certificate, DARE, certificates, honor roll; [oth. writ.] Poem in "Where Dreams Begin" Poem in the Record Journal Newspaper; [a.] Wallingford, CT 06492

BROCK, MARTHA
[b.]May 23, 1930, Syracuse, NY; [m.]Clarence Lee Brock, Jr., December 27, 1960; [ch.]Byron, Katherine, Heather, Beth; [ed.]Masters in Education; [occ.]Retired Teacher; [memb.]MI Science Teachers Association, MI Math Teachers Association, Michigan Reading Association, MI Science and Technology; [hon.]Quest Award 1992, ISP Award 1992, World of Poetry 1990; [oth. writ.]Several poems published in area newspaper; published in school newspaper; World of Poetry Anthology; Distinguished Poets of America; [pers.]I try to view things through others eyes and experiences particularly my students, and granddaughters.; [a.] Marysville, MI 48040.

BROOK, CAROL A.
[b.] July 3, 1946, Bismark, ND; [p.] John Gregoryk, Mary Gregoryk; [ch.] Lisa Ann; [ed.] Wilton High School; [occ.] Executive Secretary; [oth. writ.] Sparrow Grass Poetry, Poetic Voices of America, Wind in the Night Sky, The National Library of Poetry, Halcyon, Mile High Poetry, Editor's Choice Award; [pers.] Upon seeing myself from within, not without gives me the balance in my life I have never known before; [a.] Mesa, AZ 85202

BROWN, ALICE S.
[b.]May 9, 1911, Lewis County; [p.]James K. Sessions & Etta Franz Sessions; [m.]Leslie C. Brown, December 12, 1936 (deceased); [ch.]Leonard L. Brown, Syracuse, NY; [ed.]High School; [occ.]Retired; [oth. writ.]Poems published in local and out of town papers; [pers.]May this meandering world grab the wheel of life and return to the real values of Christianity, family and love.; [a.] Boonville, NY 13309

BROWN, BARBARA ANN
[b.] August 15, 1926, Washington, D.C.; [ed.] B.S. Ed. in Maryland Univ.; [occ.] Teacher, RE Sales and various clerk and office jobs; [hon.] Many from World of Poetry; [oth. writ.] A small poetry book I published myself locally in FL in 1960 called "To Wish Upon A Star"; [pers.] Asked to read one of my gold poems at World of Poetry's last convention. But, I couldn't attend. I thought that was a neat invitation. The gift of poetry that I possess, is a gift from Heaven above. And when I write, I'm truly blessed, by the one who understands; [a.] Berlin, MD 21811

BROWN, DOROTHY I.
[b.] April 24, 1929, Freewater, Oregon; [p.] Albert Monroe and Lucille A. Wehr; [m.] William C. Brown; [ch.] Kenneth L. & Diane L. Showalter, William C. Brown, Jr.; [ed.] Lake Stevens High - E.C.C. G.E.D., Everett C.C. for Nutrition Therapy for Asst Dietitian; [occ.] Retired from Providence Hospital Everett, WA 17 yrs total 30 in dietary; [memb.] Peal Center for Christian Living God Sam Life time memb A.I.B.C. of So. Dak. Salvation Army; [hon.] School Penmanship and Arts; Den Mother B.S.A. Girl Scout Leader Poetry Nat'l, International and Editor's Choice; [oth. writ.] I've always written my own verses for personal cards. WA to WA published in CA Easter dedication Hand in Hand, By the Sea: Surf, Nov Morning-KY Christmas Past, in GA Creative Arts Forum; [pers.] I feel it is a gift of God, to be able to write, and I am thankful to Him, to express many feelings on paper. I believe to live each day as it is your last you will be a better person; [a.] Mill Creek, WA 98012

BROWN JR., DENNIS W.
[Pen.]Denny Brown; [b.]May 23, 1964, Newport News, VA; [p.]Dennis and Kathy Brown; [ed.]Denbigh High, Automotive Training Institute; [occ.]Landscaper, Williamsburg Country Club; [hon.]Distinguished Tank Crewman, Golden Poet, World of Poetry 91 & 92; [oth. writ.]An Angels Tear, A Thousand Rivers, Crying, Time Is Like A Dream, Our World, A Thousand Rivers I'm Hoping To Make Into A Song."; [pers.]I would like to save the endangered animals, so I hope by my poems some one out there understands how I feel. I would also like to thank my sister Tiffany. Her love for wolves is why I wrote our world.; [a.] Newport News, VA 23602.

BROWNEN, SUE J.
[b.]February 13, 1945, Oklahoma City, Oklahoma; [p.]Harvey and Lorene Brownen; [occ.]Writer; [memb.]International Society Poets, World of Poetry, Southern Poetry Society; [hon.]To many to mention; [oth. writ.]"News" papers and letters and many poetry anthologies; [pers.]Criticize not anyone unless you have worn their shoes and walked in their path.; [a.] Oklahoma City, OK

BROZAITIS, HELENE
[b.]August 27, 1901, Kenduskeag, Maine; [p.]Edith Waite, Austin David Coleon; [m.]Lloyd Snyder, 1929 and Dias Brozaitis 1944; [ch.]Son, Lloyd Snyder; [ed.]High School and Business Course; [hon.]Golden Poet's Award 1990, Eddie Lou Cole; [oth. writ.]Book of short stories published in 1984 from NY State. "The Legacy."

BRUN, YOURI
[Pen.] T.L. Travis; [b.] May 15, 1964, Cap Haitian, Haiti; [p.] Marcelin and Huguette Brun; [ed.] Varied and Simple Long Island City High School, Medgar Evers College; [occ.] Life and all it's experiences; [oth. writ.] Nakia De'Lente (not yet published), Window to the Gods and Journey Through Midnight (both not yet published); [pers.] I'm always five minutes away from fame; [a.] Queens, NY 11428

BRYNILDSEN, SCOTT
[Pen.] William Rymic; [b.] September 12, 1977, Hospital; [p.] Katherine McKenna and Ben Brynildsen; [ed.] Sophmore, currently; [occ.] Student of the Elements, Arts, and Life; [memb.] Bunkergroup, Drama Club, Coffee Club; [hon.] Honorary notice for outstanding poetry and a lot of other awards; [oth. writ.] Seeking Love, Under the Umbrella, Just For a While, I Love You, X-mas Poem and Confessions; [pers.] I'd like to dedicate this to my brother, Ian. No matter how far away you are, you'll always be right here. I love you, how about some coffee; [a.] Marysville, WA 98270

BUCHWITZ, JACOB R.
[b.]October 23, 1915, Martin, ND; [p.]Deceased; [m.]Deceased, February 3, 1992; [ch.]none; [ed.]7th grade, country school, born on the farm in ND; [occ.]Farming, Rodeo, Landscaping; [memb.]C.C.C., V.F.W., Battle of the Bulge in WWII; [hon.]1993 Editor's Choice Award from National Library of Poetry; [oth. writ.]Two short stories, one long one, dust in North Dakota, they are not published, my poems can be sung;

[pers.]Riding the freight train looking for work at age 21, no crops, dust was blowing; [a.] Harvey, ND 58341

BUERKERT, EDWARD V.
[b.]January 6, 1920, Brooklyn, NY; [p.]Carl and Catherine Buerkert; [m.]Marie C. Buerkert, May 3, 1947; [ch.]Edward J. Buerkert; [ed.]Erasmus High School, Rockland Community College; [occ.]Certified Painter, Retired.; [memb.]Hernando Symphony Orch. Violinist, Hope Alliance Church, AAA, AARP, DAV.; [oth. writ.]Poems, Christian Publications, Christmas stories, Suncoast News, Pasco County; [pers.]The touchstone of writing is joy and satisfaction in it. Though mentally exerting, a tonic to the spirit, sharing thoughts can be an inspiration to others; [pers.]Spring Hill, FL 34608-4440.

BUFFALO, JUDITH K.
[Pen.]Hinu Buffalo; [b.]Wisconsin Rapids, Wis.; [ch.]Amity Sage and Osage Buffalo, Sheyenne Buffalo Ball and J. Thomas Buffalo Ball; [memb.]Winnebago Tribal Affiliation [hon.]Editor's Award in 1993 from the National Library of Poetry; [oth. writ.]Several poems published in other anthologies: An American Heritage, Labyrinth Magazine, Jeopardy Magazine and the Poetry Motel and Broadside Series; [pers.]I write what my eyes see, what my ears hear, and why my heart remembers. Through those I construct in poetic form a dream or a reality toward peace.; [a.] Bellingham, Washington.

BUFFUM, SR., CARROLL R.
[Pen.] Buff The Simple Man; [b.] July 28, 1936, Arlington, VT; [p.] Cecil & Christie Buffum; [m.] Nancy Buffum, March 23, 1957; [ch.] Carroll Buffum, Jr.; [ed.] 10 yrs; [occ.] Retired from GE; [memb.] League of Vermont Writers, Buffum Family Association, N.R.A., Middletown Springs Alumni and International Society of Poets; [hon.] Silver Tray, GE plaque, first prize ribbon for driftwood sculpture and my book of poems, The International Poet of Merit Award, $50 cash award and Editor's Choice Award; [oth. writ.] Numerous poems and news articles published in local newspapers and grit magazine. Poetry in one local book and six nationally, my book of poems in print, working on second book (Good Old Country) poems; [pers.] I strive to write about nature, The Good Old Days, Togetherness, Vermont Poetry. I have been greatly influenced by the Raven by Edgar A. Poe, The Old Swimming Hole by James W. Riley; [a.] North Clarendon, VT 05759

BULL, DEBORAH LEE
[b.] April 19, 1958, Lansing, MI; [p.] Arlene and Eugene Prentler; [m.] Stephen K. Bull, March 26, 1983; [ch.] Tabitha Lynn; [ed.] Did not complete high school, but while there, my mother made me take typing. Which helps greatly for my writing; [occ.] Mother, writer and housewife!!!; [memb.] Onondaga Fire Department Auxilary; [hon.] In 1993 Poet of Merit Award Plaque from International Society of Poets; [oth. writ.] Have first poem published in the book "A Break in the Clouds". Second book called "Poetic Voices of America". I write many poems about the "Onondaga Fire Department"; [pers.] I like to write about things that have happened in my life, no matter how sad they may be. I also like to write about things that happen in and around the community in which I live; [a.] Mason, MI 48854

BULLOCK, JENNIFER
[b.]November 9, 1978, Ontario, Oregon; [p.]Patricia Bullock; [ed.]Attending Christie School, High School; [oth. writ.]"Is there a Place", and many other unpublished songs and poems; [pers.]Take your dreams and fly. I would like to say that I love everyone who has inspired me and thank you. I love you Clint Bryant; [a.] Marylhurst, Oregon 97036

BUMPHUS, ANITA LOUISE
[Pen.] Nita Sister; [b.] February 1, 1954, General Hospital, Marion County; [p.] Willa Belle Allen and Henry Lee Allen (stepfather), Roy Curtis Offeh (father); [m.] William George Bumphus Sr., June 9, 1979; [ch.] Cleresa O'Guin, LeVeda Reneee Wilson, Natysha Kinne Offeh, James Welch, William Bumphus Jr., Angel Renee Bumphuss, Grandchildren Cher Rebecca and Stacy Renee; [ed.] 9th Grade; [occ.] Housewife, Evangelist, Assistant Director of Jesus Inside Prison; [memb.] Faith Center Church; [hon.] Services for ministering to men, women, boys and girls i prison in twelve States, thirty-some prisons; [oth. writ.] Personal book "Nobody to Somebody in Jesus. Other poems Mr. Big Stuff, Hey Ms It, My Grandbaby Cher, etc., publications in newspaper articles. Poem published in 1993 Wind in the Night Sky; [pers.] I delight in leading people from darkness to light which is to Jesus Christ "Jesus is the way"; [a.] Indpls., IN 46208

BURGER, SISTER BERTILLA
Sister Bertilla Burger, 86, of the Monastery Immaculate Conception in Ferdinand, Indiana, died Wednesday, February 23, at 11 a.m. in the monastery infirmary. Born Elenora, the second child of Peter and Rose (Mehringer) Burger, on September 3, 1907, in Jasper, Indiana, Sister Bertilla entered the Sisters of St. Benedict in 1927 from St. Joseph Parish in Jasper, Indiana. She professed her first vows in 1929 and her final vows in 1932. Sister Bertilla celebrated 60 years of religious profession in 1989. Sister Bertilla is survived by a sister, Rita (Burger) Schultz of Dayton, Ohio, a brother, Alphonse Burger of Jasper, Indiana, and nieces and nephews. Sister Bertilla was preceded in death by three brothers, Bernard Burger, Linus Burger, and Herbert Burger, and three sisters, Sister Imelda Burger, Clara Mehringer, and Ardella Burger. Sister Bertilla received a bachelor of fine arts degree from Notre Dame in 1951, and a master of arts from Indiana State Teachers College (now Indiana State University) in 1960. She served as a teacher over a 52 year time span in numerous towns in southern Indiana including Haubstadt, Vincennes, Troy, Schnellville, St. Anthony, Tell City, Floyds Knobs, Fulda, Montgomery, and Mariah Hill. Sister Bertilla also served as an instructor at St. Benedict College; Vincennes University, Jasper Center; and Marian Heights Academy. After retiring from her teaching career in 1981, Sister Bertilla worked in the monastery vestment department through 1993. Through her life, Sister Bertilla had a love of the art and would apply this love in various forms, including poetry and the art of making stained glass.

BURKHOLDER, ANNE R.
[b.] April 14, 1948, Lebanon, PA; [p.] Peter Strickler (deceased), Beatrice Stohler Strickler; [m.] John F. Burkholder, Jr, September 11, 1971; [ed.] Eastern Lebanon County High, Harcum Jr College, McCann School of Business. The Institute of Children's Literature; [occ.] Postmaster replacement; [memb.] Society of Children's Book Writers, International Society of Poets. Christian Writers Guild. Board of Directors and Advisory Committee member of ISP; [hon.] Merit Certificates for four poems. World of Poetry Award - Golden Poet 1991 trophy for poem. Poem put to music on Impressions. Three commemorative wall plaques; [oth. writ.] Poems published in several anthologies. Currently writing a novel for teenagers, and have written short stories for children; [pers.] "Self is the conception of conventional ethics and idealism, embodying the wisdom of the soul."; [a.] Newmanstown, PA 17073

BURMAN, DOROTHY KRUEGER
[Pen.]Maude Elyria Auchencloss; [b.]August 27, 1920, Somonauk, Illinois; [p.]The Rev. George W. Krueger, D.D. and Elizabeth Mutschmann Krueger; [m.]Roy B. Burman, November 17, 1942 (deceased); [ch.]Craig, Claire, and Anne; [ed.]Clinton High, Scovill Schools, and Wartburg College; [oth. writ.]Poems also published by Sparrowgrass Poetry Forum and Great Lakes Poetry; [a.] Chicago, Illinois 60640-1007

BURROWS, ELIZABETH MACDONALD
International Lecturer, Author, Emissary for World Peace, Personal: Born January 30, 1930; Descendent of Lord MacDonald of the Isles, Scotland and Marquis de Lafayette, France. [ed.] Self-taught through specialized studies including many years of research and interpretation of ancient Christian manuscripsts and origins, transformational psychology and alternative medicine; Intensive study under the tutelate of Professor Edmond Bordeaux-Szekekly, former Professor of Philosophy and Experimental Psychology at the Univ of Cluj: Trained in Elocution and Public Speaking since 1934. Career: Credit Manager, Home Utilities 1958, Montgomery Ward 1961; Oregon District Plant Clerical Training Supervisor over two states, West Coast Telephone, 1963, President and Director of Christian Church of Universal Peace and Christian College of Universal Peace, 1973 to present; President, Archives International, Publishing and Production, 1973 to present. [memb.] James Tyuler Kent Inst of Homeopathy, Seattle (Vice Pres), The Cousteau Society, International Order of Chivalry, Planetary Society, and International Platform Association; Author of Pathway of the Immortal, Harp of Destiny, Maya Sangh, Crystal Planet, Odyssey of the Apocalypse, and commentary for The Gospel of Peace of Jesus Christ According to John. Covenant at Sinai (in process). Poetry: Selected Poets of the New Era, Distinguished Poets of America, The American Poetry Anthology, and featured by Cader Publishing and Sparrowgrass Poetry. Twice semi-finalist in Poetry at International Platform Assoc. Subject of Feature Articles in over 200 Newspapers International; Appeared on over 600 Radio and Television Shows across the United States. Honors and Awards: Youngest

Grange Installation Officer in the United State, 1944; Designer of the First Known Course in Telephony for Women, 1963: Semi-finalist in Public Speaking, International Platform Assoc, 1991. Listed in: Who's Who in the World, Who's Who in America, Who's Who in Education, Who's Who in Religion, Who's Who in the World, Who's Who in America, Who's Who in Education, Who's Who in Religion, Who's Who in the West, Who's Who in American Women, International Who's Who of Intellectuals, and Directory of Distinguished Americans; [a.] Seattle, WA 98133

BUTLER JR, CHARLES LEO
[Pen.] Charles L. Butler, Jr.; [b.] February 9, 1946, Augusta, GA; [p.] Charles L. Butler Sr. and Julia Collier Butler; [ed.] Lucy C. Laney High School, Paine College 3 yrs; [occ.] President Booking Agency (King Kong Productions); [memb.] International Society of Poets; [hon.] Dr. Martin Luther King Jr; Brotherhood Award 1981; [oth. writ.] For Block the Dutch Blues Magazine 1983-87 coveyed blues in Fla - poems in several anthologies by Eddie Lou Cole; [pers.] Don't let adversity stop you. Without experiences of all types. You have no reason to write; [a.] Augusta, GA

BUTTS, DONNA
[Pen.] Manny Roe; [b.] February 6, 1952, harper County, Kansas; [p.] Helen and Perry Moore; [m.] Wayne Butts, December 24, 1970; [ch.] Linn, Christopher, Joseph, Cassandra and Gavin; [ed.] Anthony High School, Cartoonist Exchange, Student of Physics, Psychology, Astronomy and Religion; [occ.] Writer/Homemaker; [memb.] National American Female Executives, National Rifle Association, PTO, North Shore Animal League, Smithsonian Institute, Georgia State Troopers Lodge, #2; [hon.] Republican Task Force, Gold, Platinum Outstanding Poet 1987-1993, Notable American Woman 93, VFW Merit Award, National League of Female Executives 1992, International Notable Women 1993; [oth. writ.] Nine poems published and two books to date, with a third in progress; [pers.] I strive to always be open minded and innovative in all aspects of life. Always learning and growing, I seek life's ultimate experience; [a.] Washington, Georgia 30673

BYERLY, CHARLOTTE J.
[b.] March 4, 1940, Reading, PA; [p.] Emory A. Reed and Clara A. Reed; [m.] Deceased; [ch.] Deanna, Danelle, Eric, Edward; [occ.] Own and Manage a gift shop with FAX & copy service and Desktop Publishing.; [memb.] Grace Community Church assistant organist; [hon.] Received award from the Nat'l. Library of Poetry; [oth. writ.] Have had other poems published in other Anthologies. Also have had 2 songs published.; [pers.] My poetry is inspired by God love for mankind, the beauty in nature, the love of my family and the love of my beloved Kermit who was killed in an Auto Accident 6/8/92.; [a.] Herndon, PA.

BYRNE, MICHAEL
[b.] June 18, 1964, Roscoe, PA; [p.] Linda L. Wolford and John G. Elosh Way; [ed.] Monessen High School, Community College of Allegheny County; [occ.] Freelance Writer;

[memb.] International Society of Poets; [hon.] Co-editor after Image Magazine, Editor's Choice Award from NLP.; [oth. writ.] Several poems for the Children's Magazine Poem Train. Numerous Poems and Short Stories for After Image Magazine; [pers.] All people have a gift in life. Music is to share pure emotion in the form of poetry. My gift of prose is the one thing I truly cherish. I hope it will give to all who read it, pure, untainted passion.; [a.] Pittsburgh, PA

CALHOUN, PATRICIA NELL
[Pen.] Pat Calhoun (Pat C); [b.] July 8, 1929, Amarillo, TX; [p.] C.A. "Doc" and Margaret Washburn; [m.] Melvin Ray Calhoun, September 16, 1950; [ch.] Cathleen "Cathy" Immelleen Calhoun and Terence Ray "Terry" Calhoun; [ed.] A graduate of St Mary's Academy, attended the Musical Arts Conservatory; [occ.] Retired from telephone sales work. Am now a part-time associate of T.J. Maxx Co; [memb.] Belong to the Epsilon Sigma Alpha Sorority. A member of the St Mary's Rosary and Altar Society; [hon.] Have been published in the Now Magazine. In the Sparrowgrass; [oth. writ.] Book and several books of the World of Poetry and honorary membership in the National Library of Poetry; [pers.] I always try to leave the reader with an uplifting thought or a relaxed feeling; [a.] Amarillo, TX 79109

CAMPBELL, CHARLES ANDREW
[b.] Monday, October 18, 1948; [b.] Dallas, TX; [p.] Barney Jackson Campbell (Deceased) and Mary Louise Campbell; [ch.] none (true love waits); [ed.] R. L. Turner High, Carrollton, Texas-1967, Oklahoma Christian College, B.S., Bible, 1973, Draughons Jr. College, Montgomery, AL 1988, Associate of Science Degree in Computer Information Systems; [occ.] Unemployed, Goodwill 1974-1988 let go on August 8, 1980 due to Fair Labor Standards Act; [memb.] Visionary Guild, Sponsored by State Art Council and Office of Consumer and Ex-Patient Relations; Member Webb Chapel Church of Christ, 1959-1969, Cloverdale Church of Christ, 1973-1993, Carriage Hills Church of Christ, 1993; [hon.] Dean's List - Draughons Jr. College, Dean's List, Oklahoma Christian College, Golden Poet's Award, Certificate of Merit, World of Poetry; [oth. writ.] Bulletin Article in former Cloverdale Church of Christ Cloverleaf Bulletin, poem in teenage christian magazine, poem in former Christian College of the Southwest 1970 Ilion Year Book. Poem in college newspaper, poem in Singles Odyssey; [pers.] I enjoy expressing my feelings through poetry. Some of my poetry is inspired by other writings and some is distilled from things I see and hear, and become a part of my poetry. I hope my poetry will be a source of enjoyment and help other people when I leave this world indeed.; [a.] Montgomery, AL 36111

CAMPBELL, VIRGINIA H.
[b.] June 3, 1980, Oklahoma City, OK; [p.] James Robert Hopper and Emily Hess Hopper; [m.] The Rev. Canon Walter Erlin, June 3, 1950; [ch.] Walter Erlin III, James Andrew, Mary Catherine, Anne, Charlotte Patricia, nine grandchildren; [ed.] BM in Piano Performance Cum Laude, Okla. City University, M.M. in Piano Performance, Okla. City University Cum Laude; [occ.] Concert Pianist, teacher, Composer, Artist, Poet; [memb.] Ladies Music Club, EAI, Gamma Phi Beta, Beta Sigma Omicron; [hon.] Who's Who in Universities 1985, Blue Ribbons in Art

Shows, Chairman Composer Programs for Ladies Music Club, many concerts given in Europe, Mexico and US; [oth. writ.] Many poems published in newspaper, My Mother's Antique Dolls Nambed Bump; [pers.] I strive for beauty, truth, honesty in my writing. I am inspired by romantic poets; [a.] Okla. City, OK 73120

CAPUANO, MICHAEL
[Pen.] Gypsy Daydreamer; [b.] April 5, 1973, Chicago, IL; [p.] Richard and Deanna Capuano (brother) Matthew Capuano; [m.] Laura Kay Capuano (married: May 18, 1993); [ed.] Psychological/Parapsychological, World Theologies and Cultures, Ancient Martial Arts, Telekinesis, Cosmic Dualities; [occ.] Bakery Manager (Aspiring Musician); [memb.] Greenpeace, AMFAR, Global Relief; [hon.] Editor's Choice Award (1993), The National Library of Poetry; [oth. writ.] Compilation of "song lyrics" all intended for publication with the "Gypsy Daydreamer" project, hopefully due for recording latter 1994; [pers.] This particular writing was written in dedication to one of my greatest influences. Christopher Michael Oliva, guitarist for Savatage. The poem was inspired by his tragic death, October 17, 1993; [a.] Largo, FL 34641

CARANI, DOROTHY M.
[Pen.] Angie "D"; [b.] April 6, 1927, Pittsburgh, PA; [p.] Mr. John Spencer Meyers and Dorothy Frost Coffman (both deceased); [m.] May 15, 1949; [ch.] Melanie, Denis, Dorothy, Jr. and Lois (M.D.); [ed.] Blair High, Takoma Park, MD; [occ.] Author, Poet, Lyricist; [memb.] NAR, CMA, S.O.C.A. (Songwriter's Club of America) The "100" Club (Chapel Recording - 12 Free Recordings a yr.); [hon.] Won Silver Jubilee Album Award, (92) "I am here" (Hollywood Song Jubilee) inclusion in "Who's Who in U.S. Writers, Editors, and Poets, U.S. and Canada (90) inclusion in "Best and Most Commercial Lyrics (92) and Best of Unknown Song Writers - LP Cassette -93, NAR-Nat.'l. Authors Registry, CMA Country Music of America; [oth. writ.] Non Fiction Book, presently with publisher, inclusion in, Sparrow Grass, Illiad, Amherst Society, American Poetry, Danae, Poetry Press; [pers.] "If we fail to strike the match that ignites our fire never will we know the intensity of its hear, nor will we ever bask in its warmth"; [a.] College Park, MD 20740.

CARBONE, MARY GRACE
[b.] July 2, 1914, Poughkeepsie, NY; [p.] Carmine Bocchino, Concetta Barletta Bocchino; [m.] Frank Carbone (deceased), October 18, 1936; [ch.] (2) Anne Carbone Killmer, Edward Angelo Carbone; [ed.] completed 1 yr high school went to work on my 14th birthday, went 3 yrs 1/2 day continuation school 14 to 17 yrs okd; [occ.] Sewing machine operation did - most of my dresses, coats, etc, several most of my sisters clothes; [memb.] Children of Mary, etc Catholic Church; [hon.] Honored student in my 1st yr high school, Golden Award - poem made for my deceased husband - a tribute to: Frank Carbone and His name (World of Poetry); [oth. writ.] Loved to write poems or sayings - To Jesus - "Our hold, Our God", etc; [pers.] I love to be good to people - do nice things whenever possible - love to be with and care for children; [a.] Pleasant Valley, NY 12569

CARLSON, MAJORIE ANN MCKUNE

[b.]February 4, 1935, Seattle, WA; [p.]Frank McKune (deceased), Alice Mildred Day McKune (deceased); [ch.]Steven Robert, Laura Jane, Timothy Nathaniel, Matthew Douglas (deceased); [ed.]Abraham Lincoln High School, San Francisco, CA; [hon.]Editor's Choice Award, The National Library of Poetry 1993, Honorable Mention, Quill Books 1993; [oth. writ.]Flight of Peace in Wind In The Night Sky, Where Were You In The Desert Sun, The National Library of Poetry, If You Ever in All My Tomorrows, Vol. III, Dust Off Your Dreams in Dusting Off Dreams, Quill Books; [pers.]I always try to write from the heart. I believe it's the purest form of expressing honest feelings; [a.] Santa Clara, CA 95051-4623

CARPENTER, ALEXANDRA C.
[b.]August 22, 1974, Encino, CA; [p.] Raymond and Susan Carpenter; [ed.] Rosarian Academy; Palm Beach Atlantic College; [occ.] Accountant pursuing B.S. in Management, M.B.A., and C.P.A.; [memb.] Palm Beach Literary Society, International Society of Palm Beach; [hon.] B.A. in Accounting, Summa cum Laude, from Palm Beach Atlantic College, May 1, 1993; Valedictorian of graduating class; received the following awards: 1993 Top Honor Graduate, Most Outstanding B.A. Graduate, 1993 Rinker School of Business Accounting Award, and 1993 Foreign Language Department Award (for German); featured in Who's Who Among Students in American Universities and Colleges, National Dean's List, editorial-interview in The Florida Catholic, editorial in the current (College Alumni Magazine), and The National Debutante Register; President's List; Early Admission to Palm Beach Atlantic College MBA program; presented at the 1990 Palm Beach Debutante Cotillion and Holiday Ball and the 1991 National Debutante Cotillion and Thanksgiving Ball in Washington, D.C.; [oth. writ.] Several poems and short articles published in the college newspaper, The Rudder; poem "The Drizzle" in A View from the Edge and poem "Dark Passages" in Distinguished Poets of America, both published by the National Library of Poetry; [pers.] "Giving up a dream is easy, but it makes your next dream harder to reach...Hold firm to your dreams,...a dream is the one thing no one can take from you."--Kimmer Ringwald; [a.] Palm Beach, FL

CARR, JAMES S.
[Pen.] "Jimmie"; [b.] January 6, 1933, Indianapolis, IN; [p.] Charlene Humphrey (Mom - deceased), James Ruben Carr (Father - deceased); [m.] Wilma Murtis Carr (divorced), January 10, 1953; [ed.] Public school #26 Crispus Attucks High School graduated June 1 1951, Indiana Vocational College May 19, 1978, Military (NCO) Academy C122 1971; [occ.] Air Frame Repair School, SSG US Army (Retired); [memb.] Ind Lodge #104 (IBPOEoW), Trinity Lodge #18 F&AM; [hon.] Associates Degree: May 19, 1978, Architectural Drafting, 10 poetry awards of merit, plus 4 published poems; [oth. writ.] (Poems included in); "Selected Works of Our World's Best Poets", "Whispers in the Wind"; [pers.] "I try to depict meaningful visions of life put them to prose"; [a.] Indianapolis, IN 46208

CARR, SUSAN E. T.
[Pen.]Elizabeth Carr; [b.]July 2, 1913, Lunenburg County, Virginia; [p.]The late Thomas and Martha Ann Rainey Tisdale; [ed.]Sixth Grade, New Grove Elementary School of Lunenburg County; [occ.]Domestic Worker; [pers.]I've always loved poems of rhythm and rhyme. I began writing rhymes in my mid teens, endeavored to have several published but without satisfactory results; [a.] Richmond, VA 23224.

CARTER, ALICE D.
[Pen.] A.C. Hummer; [b.] June 9, 1959, Washington, D.C.; [m.] Kevin Forrest Carter, October 24, 1981; [ch.] Matthew-9, Cameron-6; [occ.] Registered Nurse; [memb.] Professional Engineers of N.C. Women's Auxilliary, Good Shepherd Lutheran Church; [hon.] Nidan (2nd degree black belt), Ishinjuku style, American Okinawan Karate & self defense instructor; [oth. writ.] Poetry previously published by National Library of Poetry, locally published poetry and short stories; [pers.] Reach out for that high warrior within the woman's lodge embrace her and be free -- Lynn Andrews; [a.] Raleigh, NC

CARTER, EDWIN T.
[Pen.]Sometimes, "RED" Carter; [b.]February 4, 1926, Portland, Maine; [p.]William T. Carter and Verda M. Turner; [m.]Betty Lou Pierce Lewis, June 17, 1950; [ch.]Marvin, Dennis, Ruth, Adopted Jamie, Brandilyn; [ed.]Portland High School, University of Maine 1 yr., American Institute of Business, Des Moines, IA; [occ.]United States Air Force, Retired; [memb.]Seventh Day Adventist Church; [oth. writ.]Many poems, some published in newspapers, books and high school and college journals; [pers.]I have been writing and reciting poetry for over sixty years and enjoy it very much.; [a.] Moore, OK 73160-1871.

CARTER, GERTRUDE JACKSON
[b.] July 15, 1948, Winston-Salem, NC; [p.] Willie and Louise Jackson; [m.] Smith Carter, Sr, April 25, 1964; [ch.] Michael, Kim, Kenneth Smith Jr, Steven and Matthew; [ed.] Atkins High, Winston-Salem State Univ, Forsyth Technical Community College; [occ.] Director, Dancers Unlimited Dance Troupe; [memb.] NC State Notary Public, Executive Board of Dancers Unlimited Mars Hill Baptist Church Sunday School Committee; [hon.] Kelly Assisted Living Services article in the W-S Journal on daily living and needs of the elderly; [oth. writ.] Thank you Dear Jesus, Welcome Sweet Spring Time, A Man Called Jesus; [pers.] In writing I strive to reflect on the good and positive aspects of life; [a.] Winston-Salem, NC 27105

CARTER, STEPHENIE L.
[b.] October 22, 1971, Ft. Bragg, NC; [p.] Gary and Sandra Carter; [ch.] Nicole LeAnn Carter; [ed.] Associate Degree in Electronics; [occ.] USAF; [oth. writ.] Night Song, Wind in the Night Sky; [a.] Gallatin, Missouri 64670

CASAS, WALTER DE LAS
[b.] February 3, 1947, Havana, Cuba; [p.] Mario de las Casas, Aracelia Vivo; [m.] single; [ed.] BA Iona College, MA Hunter College, Doctorial student Graduate Center of City University of NY; [occ.] High school teacher; [memb.] American Association of Teachers of Spanish and Portuguese, Circulo De Cultura Panamericano; [hon.] Americanism Medal from American Legion (San Post 1110 A.L.) for essay on Americanism as a high school senior; [oth. writ.] (english verse) Tributes, (Spanish verse) La Ninez Que Dilata Libido; [a.] Brooklyn, NY 11218

CASSNER, CARL
[b.]May 14, 1950, Detroit, Michigan; [p.]Mr. & Mrs. Alvin B. Cassner; [ed.]Lees Junior College, Jackson, KY, Associate in Arts; [occ.]Writer; [hon.]Golden Poet Honorable Mentions 83, 84, 85 World of Poetry, Sacramento, CA; [oth. writ.]The Chrysanthemum, Give Me Love, 'Tis The Season; [pers.]One must have a basis upon which to build. Study the classics; [a.] Hillsboro, Ohio 45133.

CASTILLON, TERESA
[b.] July 27, 1944, Maywood, CA; [p.] Edward S. Valencia, Manuela Valencia; [m.] Manny Castillon, November 7, 1964; [ch.] Mona Lara, Conrad Christopher Castillon; [ed.] Arroyo High School; [occ.] Data Processing; [hon.] Poem published in "A Break in the Clouds"; [oth. writ.] Poems and children's short stories - not yet published; [pers.] I'm greatly affected by the people and situations that surround me. In my writing I try to capture the feelings of what I observe. I'm thankful for life's every creation and for the gift of a mind capable of putting down on paper the thoughts and feelings often submerged in humans; [a.] Rosemead, CA

CHAINANI, SONESH
[b.] April 22, 1977, Miami, FL; [p.] Suresh and Sheila Chainani; [ed.] Currently enrolled in 11th grade at Ransom-Everglades High School; [memb.] Drama Club, 2-Club, Student government, peer counseling; [hon.] Three-Star Thespian, 1st place in Florida State Poet's Contest, 1st place in Sinclair Community College writing contest, 1st Honorable Mention in Poets of the Vineyard Contest, 3rd place in Distinguished Poets of America contest; [oth. writ.] Poems in America on my mind, For Poets only, '93, Best Poems of the '90's, Poems of the Vineyard Anthology, '92", Distinguished Poets of America, of Diamonds and Rust, Vol II and Creative Kids Magazine, '92; [pers.] Poetry is my own personal statement on life and reflects my feelings, emotions and thoughts on many subjects; [a.] Key Biscayne, FL 33149

CHAMBLISS (Ed.D), CHARLOTTE J.
[b.] East Feliciana Pariott, LA; [p.] Henry and Daisy A Green Jackson; [m.] Robert F. Chambliss; [ed.] Gram School, High School, New Orleans Public Schools - BANOUN, NO; graduate school - Mills College, DAKME school art; [occ.] Teacher - retired; [memb.] Beth Eden Baptist Church, Oakland, CA, Zeta Phi Beta Sorority, Nat'l Council of Negro Women, Charter member - Nat'l Museum of Women, International Society of Poets; [hon.] World Who's Who of Women - 1980, Cambridge, Congressional Award Outstanding Contribution to Community, State, Nation, 1987, Golden Poet Award, World of Poetry 1989, 1990, 1991, 1992; [oth. writ.] Books of poetry, The Inner Me In An Outer World, 1976, Now Let Pray; Novel: Deep South When, poetry and short and short, short stories play: Equasion X, song: forgive us, we pray (sacred); [pers.] Prayer and perseverance are two strongest cogs in my wheel of life; [a.] Oakland, CA 94610

CHANDLER, ROSEMARY BERTRAND
[Pen.] Rosemary Chandler; [b.] March 8, 1921, Buffalo, NY; [p.] Anna O'Donnell and George Bertrand; [m.] Robert Chandler, August 24, 1946, Diane Robin and Douglas Michael; [ed.] Central High Syracuse NY, Theodore Irving Studio for Theatre, NY; [occ.] Actress, writer, director, poet, artist,

homemaker; [memb.] Southern California Motion Picture Council, SCMPC Serendipidy Players; [hon.] SCMPC, Bronze Halo, Entertainment Industry Silver, Golden Poet World of Poetry Awards; [oth. writ.] Biography "Hollywood or Bust" and over 200 poems. "Winter Lass" children's book of verse. Play "Double Surprise," screenplay, The Last Indian and The Last Cowboy; [pers.] I would like to express the best of life to enrich others in my poetry or writings and bring joy to others and family; [a.] N. Hollywood, CA 91607

CHANG, DIANA M. P.
[b.]March 21, 1937, China; [p.]Boa Chen (father) Lueng-Yee Wong (mother); [m.]deceased; [ch.]one daughter; [ed.]B.A. degree, majored in English at Taiwan, and teaching credential in the U.S.A.; [occ.]A substitute teacher of San Francisco Unified School District; [hon.]Art showed in Taiwan and in the U.S.A. Poems were published in the anthologies in 1992 and 1993. received Editor's Choice Award in 1993 from the National Library of Poetry; [oth. writ.]"An Animal Named Year" and some stories in Chinese.; [pers.]Fantasy is the blossom. Organization of a thought is the bud. Expression in writing is the fruit.; [a.] S.F., CA 94126

CHASE, ELSA L.
[b.] April 2, 1949, Camden, NJ; [p.] Ervin and Marcella Chase; [ed.] High School graduate; Drafting Technical School; on the job training program for drafting; [occ.] Machine operator now; was draftsman (3 yrs); sales, cashier (17 years); [memb.] International Society of Poets; [hon.] Ruby Poet (ISP); [oth. writ.] "Invisible Tears", "Sam" - Break in the Clouds, "Blake" Coming of Dawn; "A Monument of Innocense" - Peace Poem for UNICEF, "Jim" and "Mother" - Our World's Favorite Poems; "A Death of a Friend" - ISP Convention (8-13-93); [pers.] Always loved nature; believes that the "Dance of Lights" is in everything alive and animated; inspired by a verse read to me by my mother when I was 3. "Look around you with an open heart and mind and you will find all the answers. To all the questions, stop, look, and listen. Nature will tell us what we need to know; [a.] Camden, New Jersey 08105

CHAUSSEE', SANDI
[b.]March 25, 1940, Waukesha, Wisconsin; [p.]Lloyd and Loretta Tiffany; [m.]Tim Chaussee', December 3, 1960; [ch.]Timothy Lloyd, Jody Ray and Danielle; [ed.]Ladysmith High School, Holyoke Hospital School of Nursing; [occ.]Homemaker II (Human Services Worker) Calumet Co. Dept. Human Services; [memb.]Zion Lutheran Church; [hon.]1990 Golden Poet Award, World of Poetry; [oth. writ.]Poems published in "New American Poetry Anthology", The Golden Treasury of Great Poems," "Poetic Voices of America, and "The Wisconsin Poets Calendar" 1993; [pers.]I work with folks from all walks of life and have great concern for those who are less fortunate. I have a great love of animals and nature. Some of this is reflected in my writing. Family is very important to me.; [a.] New Holstein, WI 53061.

CHILCOTT, CHARLES T.
[b.] February 20, 1952, Lafayette, Inc.; [p.] Robert M. and Mary F. Chilcott; [m.] Betty Jo, June 30, 1987; [ch.] Jeffrey, Cory, Jeremy; [ed.] College, Home Study; [occ.] Meat Personnell, Kroger Co.; [hon.] Editor's Choice Poetry 1993; [oth. writ.] "Ode To Man" published in "Wind In The Night Sky" several newspaper articles, local; [pers.] Poetry and all writings should be used as educational tools for our young ones for it is they who shall learn from what we do; [a.] Kokomo, Ind. 46901-1843

CHINCHILLO, JEAN G.
[Pen.] Jeanie Bell / Granny Jean; [b.] Boston; [p.] Roy and Sarah Bell; [m.] Tory (deceased - March 9, 1993), June 25, 1939; [ch.] Janet Siemasko, Joyce Griffin; [ed.] Boston Univ, and Malden Business School, Revere High; [occ.] Writer and homemaker; [memb.] First Congregational Church - Revere and Cancer Society Member; [hon.] Golden Poet - 1991, Editor's Choice Award, National Library of Poetry - 1993; [oth. writ.] Book, The Caterpillar and other poems for children; [pers.] Poems published in the Revere Journal Newspaper.

CHOUDHURY, ALPANA
[b.] September 3, 1981, New York City; [p.] Mom, Neeruj Choudhury, Dad, Aswini Kumar Choudhury; [ed.] The Melrose School; [occ.] Student; [memb.] "The Journal"; [pers.] I like to express my feelings in my poems; [a.] Carmel, NY 10512

CHRISTIAN, BOBBIE J.
[b.]April 10, 1946, Tremont, Mississippi; [p.]Alvin A. Powell and Hazel B. Upton Powell; [m.]C. L. Christian Jr., January 20, 1979; [ch.]none; [ed.]Tremont Grad. and Jr. High G.E.D 1976; I.C.S. 1984 Forrest and Wild Life; [occ.]Housewife; [memb.]Humane Society, U.S. Greenpeace; [hon.]Several Golden Poet Awards over the years, poem published in Poetic Voices of America; [oth. writ.]A few news paper articles in Itwanba Co. Times, Fulton, Miss., Pahatka Daily News, Palatka, FL; [pers.]To live in Harmony with all living things for each has its place and reason for being on earth; [a.] Palatka, FL 32177.

CHRISTOFIC, JIM
[b.]February 3, 1947, Altoona, PA; [p.]Andrew C. Christofic (deceased) and Betty M. Hershberger Christofic; [m.]Divorced; [ch.]Two Daughters, Shirley Ann and Lori Lynn, Five grandchildren; [ed.]Huntington Area High School, Oregon School of Real Estate, Retail Bakers Institute of Manhattan KA; [occ.]Bakery Technician; [hon.]Golden Poet Award, Two Silver Poet Awards and Bronze Poet Award; [oth. writ.]Vermic - published, 120 poems currently being completed for illustration and book; [pers.]Most of my work comes from within my self as they tend to reflect my moods at the time of writing.; [a.] Marietta, PA 17547.

CISCO, MECHEL
[Pen.]Ahzariah; [b.]November 23, 1963; [occ.]Artist; [oth. writ.]Glistening Wings; [a.] Stone Mtn., GA 30083

CLAPP, TIMOTHY SCOTT
[Pen.]Scott Dreamer; [b.]March 15, 1969, Almanac, [p.]Donald Lee Clapp; [ed.]Southeast Guilford H.S.; [occ.]Salesman at Radio Shack in Burlington; [hon.]Two poems published in the National Library of Poetry; [oth. writ.]I'm now working on the second draft of my book entitled "Arch Angel"; [pers.]Though one day I will leave this world. At least I leave behind my mark, in the form of published word.; [a.] Liberty, NC 27298.

CLAUTICE, EDWARD W.
[Pen.] Big Ed (for children's works); [b.] October 13, 1916, Baltimore, MD; [p.] George Joseph Clautice, Janet Harwood Wellmore Cl; [m.] Madelyn Spraker, August 30, 1941; [ch.] Elizabeth F. Stephen F., Christopher G., Michael J. Edward G.; [ed.] Johns Hopkins Univ 1938, BE Boston Univ MBA 1964, US Army Command & General Staff College; [occ.] Army Oronance Officer, 2yrs manufacturing engineer 20 yrs, industrial consultant 5 yrs; [memb.] Yorktowne Tennis, Fitness Club; [hon.] Marquis Who's Who in the East; World of Poetry Who's Who in Poetry; several Military Awards; Athletic Awards for Running, Tennis, Squash, Football, Wrestling, etc; [oth. writ.] "A Little Nonsense"; "A Lotta Nonsense" (books of mostly humorous poetry); "Time Transition in Gov't Personnel Relations"; (Master's Thesis); several technical reports an ballistics and manufacturing; [pers.] Dedication of "A Little Nonsense". This book is humbly dedicated to the great God above Who is His love created us, and in His wisdom gave us a sense of humor; [a.] York, PA 17402

COBOS, EVE
[b.]March 22, 1937, Albuquerque, New Mexico; [p.]Ruben and Rita Cobos; [m.]Mohamed H. Yusuf, December 20, 1981; [ch.]Christopher, Dave, Sean, Lauralee, Claressa, and Jason Salaz; [ed.]BFA in Music; [occ.]Piano Teacher; [memb.]Daughters of the King, Holy Trinity Church, Tops, Music Teachers of Calif., and New Mexico; [hon.]Sigma Alpha Iota, Editor, Thunderbird and Yucca. Music Teacher of the Year, Milpitas, Calif., Who's Who in California; [oth. writ.]Short stories published in the "The Duchess" a magazine of Albuquerque. "Mystery City" published in National Library of Poetry; [pers.]Thank you, god, for leading me along the paths that you have chosen for me.; [a.] Rio Rancho, NM 87124

COHEN, SAMUEL
[Pen.] Sam; [b.] April 21, 1938, Lower Eastside, New York City; [p.] Sadie and Ezra Cohen; [ed.] Public School 205, High School 227; [occ.] Foreman and truck checker at Bradley Imports, Newark, New Jersey; [hon.] Golden Award from the World of Poetry; [oth. writ.] Poem published with National Arts Society. Wrote to President Bush, based on a patriot poem "Give Us Our Flag", President Bush wrote back and thanked me for it. 8/69; [pers.] That all things in life is an art, from the graceful flight of a bird, to the unstill ocean waves, to the way one about life and the beauty of it. But the greatest all is love, for love is the highest art form of all for its own purity; [a.] Brooklyn, KY

COLANGELO, DOROTHEA
[b.]July 12, 1952, New Rochelle, NY; [p.]Josephine Colangelo and Frederick Colangelo (deceased); [ed.]Port Chester High School; [occ.]Clerical for Allstate Ins. Company Claims Dept.; [hon.]Several Golden Poet Awards. Honorable Mentions from World of Poetry; [oth. writ.]Several poems published by Quill Books and World of Poetry.; [pers.]I gather my thoughts from nature and human kind alike, I look to God for answers and deep thoughts; [a.] Port Chester, NY.

COLE, DIANE
[Pen.]Georga, Diana Barnes, Diana, Hartzinger; [b.]June 10, 1958, Kissimgao, FL; [p.]Self created;

[m.]confirmed bachelorette; [ed.]Continuing legal education; [occ.]Legal Investigator; [memb.]NAFE; Public Library; Who's Who; [hon.]Golden Poet, Poet of the Year 1991; 1992 World of Poetry; Who's Who; [oth. writ.]George Soldier, Liberty Legacy; Burrough of Batley Belfry; Old Age Blues, Sonnetts; Haiku; Ad's; Essays; Greeting Cards; [pers.]I may not agree with what you say, but I'll defend to my death your right to say it" - Voltaire; [a.] West Union, IA 52175.

COLE, NELLA H.
[b.] April 9, 1905, Sanantonio, TX; [p.] Bert and Wilma Holloway; [m.] Elton J. Cole (deceased), April 28, 1929; [ch.] Richard, Wilma; [ed.] B.A. Florida State University; [occ.] Retired teacher (high school); [memb.] AAUW; Altrusa International of Tampa; Friday Morning Musicale; First Christian Church (Disciples of Christ); [oth. writ.] Writings in local newspapers; poetry book "It's Never Too Late" published 1991; [pers.] My life, like my poetry, must sing of hope, and cheer of courage, of conquering fear. Be optismistic!; [a.] Tampa, FL 33629

COLEMAN, GREGORY
[b.] January 27, 1966, NY, NY; [p.] Cathy Coleman; [m.] Tracie Coleman, September 25, 1993; [ed.] Magna Dental School, NCA&T St Univ, John Robert Powell Modeling School; [occ.] Dental Tech; [hon.] The Golden Treasury of Great Poems, On the Threshold of a Dream, etc; [oth. writ.] 2 song written: Tomorrow is Your's, Loving you Forever; [pers.] I would like to tell my wife I love her and my family. I love them also. Keep the faith and hope alive and we will all survive; [a.] Richmond, VA 23233

COLLIER, JACK FREDERICK
[b.]June 22, 1930, New Orleans, LA; [p.]John Ashton and Gladys Collier; [m.]Gayle Ard Collier, July 16, 1966; [occ.]Retired; [oth. writ.]Unpublished manuscript (76 pages) Voice's and Verse's from here, there and everywhere, Treasured Poems of America 1993, "A Quiet Conservation With The Universe"; [pers.]We come into this world of everything, usually crying. Way through our live's, can't we learn, to laugh at the thought of leaving; [a.] Mandeville, LA 70448.

COMBS, VE'LVA' MARIA
[b.] December 13, 1984, USA; [p.] Lily Combs Do'Villa, Betty and Tommie Calderon; [m.] Godmother and Godfather; [ch.] (Sib) Raquel Washington big sister; [ed.] Third grade, Echo Loder Elementary, Reno, Nevada; [occ.] Full-time student, poet; I help mommy clean house; [memb.] Immaculate Heart of Mary Church, Phoenix, AZ, Boys and Girls Club, Cloverdale, CA; [hon.] Received honor roll, June 11, 1991 from Bessie Carmichael School, San Francisco, CA. When I attended kindergarten there, Super Scientist Award, March 18, 1992 from Jefferson Schools Science Fair, Cloverdale, CA received kindergarten diploma from Bessie Carmichael, June 14, 1991; [oth. writ.] Why I Will Not Hate You, published in Wind in the Night Sky-1993 by National Library of Poetry. Poem published in the Cloverdale Reveille, July 28, 1993; [pers.] My poems, are feelings about life experiences. Love: I live in the biggest little city in Reno, NV. Full of hate and discrimination; [a.] Reno, NV 89504

CONNER, CLARA JANE
[Pen.]Sarah Rebecca Ely; [b.]May 4, 1952, Lewis Co; [p.]Otto and Verna Burns; [m.]Kyle Daniel Conner, July 12, 1971; [ch.]Late: Nathan Daniel Conner, present Bethany Necole C.; [ed.]High School Graduate; [occ.]Wal Mart Associate; [memb.]Baugus Church of God, International Society of Poets; [hon.]Golden/Silver Poet World of Poetry; Editor's Choice Award; Library of Congress; Anthology publication- Wind In The Night Sky.; [oth. writ.]Local newspaper editions.; [pers.]Through Praise-n-Poetry, I offer encouragement, and inspiration, compassion and understanding; [a.] Nohenwald, TN 38463.

HEITNER, CONSTANCE
[b.] April 15, 1909, Lima, Peru, S.A. (brought to America at 10 months); [p.] Thomas Stannage, Elizebeth Graham; [m.] Samuel Heitner, May 4, 1909; [ch.] John (English Professor), Elizabeth -Kathleen - Hatha Yoga teacher - Diane - former opera singer; [ed.] High School; [occ.] Housewife - grandmother of 7 and great grandmother of 4; [hon.] Golden Poetry Award from "World of Poetry" in 1989 in Washington - in person for poem "The Capricious Sea"; [oth. writ.] Surrender published in 1984 by American Poetry anthology in Words of Praise American Poetry anthology "The Freedom of Love" New American Poetry anthology 1988, He Watches; [a.] Wantagh, NY 11793

COOK, DAVID
[b.]February 13, 1930, Madison, Wisconsin; [p.]Homer and Vida Cook; [m.]Carolyn, December 9, 1972; [ed.]College B.A. Degree; [occ.]Custodian (General Services) City of LA; [memb.]Rock and Gem Club; [hon.]Poetry Commendation, White Ribbon at the fair for my rock display; [oth. writ.]Personal poems for personal friends consumption, such as nieces weddings, friends pets, etc.; [pers.]I get the inspiration to write poetry while at work writing down what comes to mind; [a.] Sylmar, CA 91342

COOLBAUGH, MARGARET D.
[Pen.]Lois D. Coolbaugh; [b.]February 6, 1917, New Albany, PA; [p.]William and Jessica C. Dunbar; [ed.]High School Graduate; [occ.]Retired; [memb.]Independent Baptist Church; [oth. writ.]"Through the Eyes of A Child", "The Way Things Were", "My Thoughts-Wise and Otherwise", all peroses; [pers.]There is nothing wrong with the world, its the people in it; [a.] Towanda, PA 18848.

COOPER, MELINDA
[b.] November 25, 1975, Granite City, IL; [ed.] Granite City High School; [occ.] Secretarial, odd jobs; [oth. writ.] Several poems and short stories, however I have only submitted one other for publication (that was published with the National Library of Poetry); [pers.] My main goal is to gain understanding of myself as well as others; [a.] Granite City, IL 62040

COPPOLELLA, ANTHONY S.
[b.] December 2, 1947, Easton, PA; [p.] Anthony C. Coppolella, Marlo Lynn Coppolella, Angelica C. Coppolella; [ed.] 1966 Graduate Bangor High School, Bangor, PA in business, Famous Artists School, Westport, CT; [occ.] Textile worker - Beaufab Mills, Stroudsburg, PA; [memb.] United Textile Workers of America Local 600. Our Lady of Mt Carmel Catholic Church and Church Latter Day Saints; [hon.] Penna Newspaper Publishers Association Outstanding Service - Easton Express 1964, 1966 Champion Baseball Team Bangor High School. Southwestern Publishing Co Award 1963 for typing. Team Bowling Trophies, 1968, 1975. (Ordained) Priest, Church Latter Day Saints North Atlantic Industries Champions - Hackettstown, NJ 1985, 1986, 1987. Poem - Statue of Liberty (Our Lovely Lady) Editor's Choice Award top 3%; [oth. writ.] Poem - "Statue of Liberty (Our Lovely Lady)" appeared in News 'n' Views Newspaper Hackettstown, NJ and on cassette "The Sound of Poetry". Poem "World Peace" on cassette "Impressions"; [pers.] "The world is my story and my poems are the words. Love and peace to all".; [a.] Roseto, PA 18013

COTTER, BARBARA G.
[Pen.] Barbara Cotter; [b.] Douglas, AZ; [p.] Gertrude Thornton Maxwell, Glen W. Maxwell; [ch.] Walter Richard, Kevin George; [ed.] Richmond High School, San Francisco St Univ; [occ.] Admin Secretary King Ave Elem School, Yuba City, CA; [memb.] PEO, St Andrew Presbyterian Church; [hon.] PTA of CA Outstanding Service Award, Who I Am Makes a Difference Award; [oth. writ.] Several poems published by World of Poetry and The National Library of Poetry; [pers.] I strive to enhance the lives of loved ones, friends and mankind in my writing. I am greatly influenced by achievements. Celebrations and feelings of those who touch my life; [a.] Penn Valley, CA 95946

COVENEY, CHRISTINA M.
[Pen.]Samantha; [b.]May 31, 1970, Massachuttes; [p.]Patricia and Hamid Barakat; [m.]Paul D. Coveney Sr., June 5, 1988; [ch.]Paul Jr. and John; [occ.]Purchasing Manager, Rentex Inc. in Boston; [pers.]My words will live on long after I'm gone; [a.] So. Boston, MA 02127.

COX, ANNA JANE BLACKBURNE
[Pen.] Jane B. Cox; [b.] September 3, 1919, Chester, PA; [p.] Edward Watson Blackburne, Eva Maria Malany Blackburne, Eva Maria Malany Blackburne; [m.] Townsend Colmore Cox, Jr, September 23, 1944; [ch.] Marcia Blackburne Cox Kuck, Henry Wirz Cox, II; [ed.] Woodbury High School in ND (diploma), Community Art Center-Wallingford, PA, Painting and sculpture; [occ.] Retired; [memb.] Brandywine River Museum, Chaddsford, PA, AARP, The National Library of Poetry; [hon.] Eight Golden Poet Awards, Blue Ribbon -Oil Painting/Sculptor, Blue Ribbon - Volunteer - RM Hospital, Media, PA; [oth. writ.] Several poems published in poetry books; [pers.] The sky is full of wonderment - when seeing the wild geese fly in great formation - to the destination of their will; [a.] Glen Mills, PA 19342

CRAMER, ELEANORE F.
[Pen.] April 4, 1913, Denver, Colorado; [p.] Francis W. Bosco and Adaline Mugrage Bosco; [m.] Morris W. Cramer, August 19, 1933; [ch.] John, Wendell, Linda, Louise, Steven, Edward, Kathleen, Michelle; [ed.] Denver Public Schools, Osmosis; [occ.] Retired; [memb.] Poetry Academy and Poetry Society of Colorado (25 years), The Heritage Foundation; [hon.] Freedoms Foundation, Golden and Silver, World of Poetry Awards, Johnny Appleseed Was My Great 1/2 Uncle; [oth. writ.] Letters to Editor, misc. articles in Denver Post and Rocky Mtn. News; [pers.] I live by the "Golden Rule", I hope I am a "Humanist"; [a.] Denver, Colorado 80209

CRAMPTON, GEORGE W.
[Pen.] Mike Victor; [b.] August 25, 1930, Moline, IL; [p.] Albert M. Crampton and Josephine Von Maur; [m.] Barbara J. Crampton, June 6, 1953; [ch.] Four Children, Six Grandchildren; [ed.] Cornell Univ., B.A., Norwestern Univ., J.D.; [occ.] Lawyer (Ret.); [memb.] Illinois State Bar Ass'n., Waterway Radio and Cruising Club, Search Rescue Charitable Foundation (Dir. 1989); [hon.]Award of Merit, Golden Poet 1991 (World of Poetry; [oth. writ.] "Rhyming Verses, The Boating Life" Nov. 1991; [pers.]If a window of opportunity opens for you, climb through it, no matter what else you're doing at the time; [a.] Bath, NC 27808

CRANE, MADELINE D.
[Pen.]ibid; [b.]August 29, 1915, Newark, NJ; [p.]Marie and Jack Dwyer; [m.]Senter H. Crane, August 22, 1938; [ch.]Col. Kerry J. Crane U.S. Airforce, CDR. Stephen H. Crane, U.S. Naval Flyer; [ed.]Glo. High School; Regis College, AB; Boston University Ed.M; C.A.G.S.; Thro Univer. of Mass. (tutored summers in private school); [occ.]Retired Tch. on Jr. High level after 40 yrs. of teaching; [memb.]MTA of Mass.; R.T.A., 13 yrs in R.S.V.P. Advisory Board for RTR Seniors; Regis College Alumnae; B.U. Alumni Assoc.; R.S.V.P. Organized Quilting; 1st Parish Church Congregational Member; Advisory Board of Manchester, Friends of Library 13 yrs; Archives Researcher for 13 yrs. for Peabody Inst. Library of Danven; [hon.]College Dean's List; Outstanding Sr. Citizens Award for 1992 for Council Work; Outstanding Contribution to RSVP Organ for 1984; French Book Prize, High School Graduation of 1933; [oth. writ.]Short Stories for Boston Post; two children's book. "Jack & Jill of Pirate Cove" and "Jo-Ann's Adventure in Enchanted Forest." N.B. taught novelette writing to 8th graders for 8 yrs. Write a poem monthly for Manchesters, "The Cricket"; [pers.]Influenced by pantheistic poets while in college. "We have not yet fathomed the mysteries of nature; [a.] Manchester-By-The-Sea, Mass., 01944.

CRANFORD, RALPH LOCKEE
[Pen.] R. Locke Cranford; [b.] July 17, 1926, Burke, County, NC; [p.] George Davault Cranford and Oaklona Shuffler Cranford; [m.] Charlotte Travis Cranford, March 29, 1947; [ch.] Walter M. Effie Charlene, Michael L. and Lisa G.; [ed.] Elementary, High School and two years Clevenger College; [occ.] Owner - auto parts wholesale co, poet, author, lyricist; [memb.] Songwriter Club of America, Poets of America, Brittain and Canada, Volunteer Literacy Tutors at CVCC, A Volunteer Social Shrine Worker and a Member of the Lutheran Church; [hon.] Songwriter for Rainbow Records, Certificate of Merit from Chapel Records, Golden Poet Award 1989, 1990, 1991 and 1992. Awards of Merit from various publishers and recording companies; [oth. writ.] Author of over 1200 poems, 34 songs, three books and one "How To Manual", "How to Remanufactor Alternators"; [pers.] From God I receive my strength. Without Him I am nothing. He's my shield in times of trouble; [a.] Newton, NC 28658

CRAWFORD, JOHN K.
[b.] January 31, 1931, Madison, Wisconsin; [p.] Elizabeth Kuenzli Crawford and Howard Dean Crawford (both deceased); [m.] Roberta John Crawford, July 7, 1973; [ed.] Clarkdale, Arizona, Schools, Univ. of Arizona, Univ. of North Carolina; [occ.] City and Regional Planning (Retired); [memb.]Professional, Historical, type societies; [oth. writ.] Thesis, Univ. of Arizona; [pers.] I like writers such as Conan Doyle. Thomas Hardy, Carl Salan, Lewis Mumford, Emily Bronte, and Emily Dickinson. I like their writings and the essences of their lives.; [a.] Tucson, Arizona 85712

CRESON, KEN M.
[b.] July 31, 1952, Hendersonville, NC; [p.] Kenneth and Celestine Creson; [m.] Sharon P. Creson, September 24, 1977; [ed.] J.H. Rose High School; [occ.] Caretaker - security; [hon.] 1991-92 Golden Poet, 1992 Gold Medal of Honor/Poetry; [oth. writ.] Publication in "Whispers in the Wind"; Science Fantasy, Fiction-unpublished; [pers.] Poetry is a gift of the soul that you share with those who do not laugh; [a.] Cedar Bluff, AL 35959

CRIDER, VIOLA M.
[b.] March 16, 1919, Paducah, Kentucky; [p.] Bishop and Mrs. John Clarence Whiteside; [m.] Arnett Crider, August 22, 1937 (widow as of December 22, 1991); [ed.] High School graduate, graduate of Safair Financial School. Attended adult class for spanish and guitar. Worked as a collector and skip tracer for finance companies; [memb.] None. I am a hobbyist that stays busy painting making greeting cards and writing my poetry; [hon.] Ten merit awards for my poetry. Poems published by Heritage Magazine, World of Poetry and Sparrowgrass Poetry Forum, Inc.; [oth. writ.] I have written over two hundred poems, a short story and many songs -- mostly religious; [pers.] God has given me the talent to write poetry that has brought much happiness to my friends and family. Never won a contest nor a monetary prize; [a.] Los Angeles, CA 90018

CRISSMAN, ROBERT CLIFTON
[b.]September 9, 1922, Durham, NC; [m.]Ruth Foltz Grissman, August 30, 1952; [ch.]Anthony Raymond Crissman (Risa) Rise Jan Crissman Harris; [ed.]Oxford NC High School, Appalachian State New University, University of North Carolina, Chapel Hill, NC, Johns Hopkins University, Baltimore, MD; [occ.]Teacher, English and Creative Writing, athletic coach, now retired. Columnist, Journalism--still writing; [hon.]Winner of Newspaper Fund fellowship at UNC, Chapel Hill, Nine Poetry Awards; First Place Award in North Carolina Sports Writing, Daily Newspapers, Shelby Daily Star; [oth. writ.]Novel "Hostage", "Shannon", "The Iron Men of Sewannee"; Poetry, "Day of The Gun", "Elvis and different Drum"; "Akin" of "The Sparks Fly Upward." [pers.]"Akin"; [a.] Jonesville, NC 28642.

CRIST, EVA M.
[b.]September 27, 1960, Johnstown, PA; [p.]John Derna Jr. and Jean Dernar; [m.]Brian M. Crist, September 15, 1990; [ed.]Conemaugh Valley High School, Conemaugh Valley Memorial Hospital School for Laboratory Technology; [occ.]Medical Laboratory Technician, Conemaugh Hospital, Johnstown, PA; [memb.]American Society of Clinical Pathologists, Holy Trinity Byzantine Catholic Church; [hon.]1992 Golden Poet Award, Two Honorable Mention Awards, World of Poetry Contest; [oth. writ.]Several poems published by the National Library of Poetry; [pers.]I enjoy writing about a variety of subjects including my own true-life experiences, current events, and how they affect the world; [a.] Johnstown, PA 15909.

CROTEAU, DAVID
[b.]January 10, 1975, Lowell, Massachusetts; [p.]Dave and Pat Croteau; [ed.]Currently attending Fresno State University; [occ.]Student; [oth. writ.]A Look To End All Looks, A Great Man; [pers.]Thanks to J.D., Sis, and my parents for all the encouragement in my journey; [a.] Pleasanton, CA 94588

CROWDER, SHIRLEY
[b.] September 7, 1942, Memphis, TN; [p.] Mr. Joseph Dortch (deceased), Mrs. Charlie Dortch - mother; [ch.] (3 children) Angela, Gina and Justin Crowder; [ed.] 1 yr college; [occ.] Food Service Worker; [memb.] Member of the Missionary Board of God's Temple of Faith, Church and a member of the Pastor's Aid Committee; [pers.] I pray God's blessings upon the readers of my poems. The purpose of my writing the type of poems that I write, is to encourage people and to teach them how to receive blessings from Godj; [a.] Shirley Crowder

CROWLEY JR., JAMES F.
[Pen.]"Jimbo"; [b.]September 19, 1937, Peabody, Massachusetts; [p.]Mrs. Janet G. Crowley; [m.]Nathalie Ann Elizabeth Crowley, October 6, 1957; [ch.]Nancy Jean Crowley Linda, James Gene Crowley; [ed.]Salem High School, United States Army "Stevedore"; [occ.]Maintenance Supervisor, Salem Hospital, Retired, 100% disabled; [memb.]National Library of Poetry, Editor's Choice Award, American Heart Association, A.A.R.P.; [hon.]Humanitarian Award, Salem Hospital Humanitarian Award, Shughnessy Kaplan (rehab.) Hospital; [oth. writ.]"A Love of Dolphins", "My Son," "My Son The Fisherman," "My Brother Lenny," "My Kitten", "My Bride", "Love is You," "My Little Monkey," "My Grandchildren," "Mother", "Little Sister"; [pers.]As I stumble through this life, help me to create more laughter than tears, dispense more happiness than gloom. Spread more cheer than despair..and in my final moment may I hear you whisper; when you made my people smile, you made me smile; [a.] Salem, Massachusetts 01970.

CUMMINGS, PAT A.
[b.]November 19, 1963, El Paso, TX; [p.]Herman C. Cummings and Felicia Cummings; [ed.]Three years UTEP Diploma and Graduated from Institute of Children's Lit.; [occ.]Freelance; [memb.]SFFA, Society of Poets; [hon.]Silver Poet 1990, Honorable Mention 1989; [oth. writ.]Nicky Meets A Leprechaun, Out to Lunch; [pers.]Poetry comes from the "Heart" whether from pain or from overwhelming joy.; [a.] El Paso, TX 79905.

CUNNINGHAM, CARL M.
[b.]May 20, 1911, Concrete, Washington; [p.]Charles and Georgia Cunningham; [m.]Jane E. Cunningham, Retired School Teacher, October 11, 1937; [ch.]Four; [ed.]Hanover College, Wash. State University, U of Washington; [occ.]Retired inspector with the Bureau of Alcohol, Tobacco and Firearms. Much of my poetry, short stories and novels relate to data within my daily experience.; [hon.] World of Poetry Award in San Francisco, CA; [oth. writ.]Short Stories and Novels Poems in reviews, Story in Stories; [pers.]Friend of Carl Sandburg while living in Chicago. Am presently a friend of his daughter, Helga Sanburg.; [a.] Raymond, WA 98577-9803.

CUNNINGHAM, CATHY BORDAYO
[Pen.]Smiley-Hollywood-Sunshine; [b.]May 29, 1964, Electra, TX; [p.]Ramiro and Dolores Loredo; [m.]David Wayne Cunningham, January 14, 1989; [ch.]Billy 8yrs, Savanna 5yrs., David 3 yrs.,; [ed.]12th Lansing Eastern High; [occ.]Health and Beauty Aid Coordinator; [memb.]St. Michaels Church; [hon.]Graduated from Lansing Police Explorers Academy, Editor's Choice Award, National Library of Poetry. Have also written for Vantage Press; [pers.]Needing to Know, National Library of Poetry, Love One Forever, Vantage Press Inc.; [pers.]Taking my life's experiences and putting them in writing have opened my eyes to a better tomorrow.; [a.] Southfield, Michigan 48076.

CUPIDO, IRENE
[b.] May 21, 1928, New Kensington, PA; [p.] William J. Gravatt (poet and artist), October 19, 1976; [ed.] 1) Pennsylvania College for Women, 2) Opera Training, 3) Univ of Pittsburgh; [occ.] Joint-Proprietor of a used book stor; [memb.] International Society of Poets, Southern Poetry Assoc, National Library of Poetry; [hon.] Awards from World of Poetry, Southern Poetry Assoc, National Library of Poetry; [oth. writ.] Presently completing a book length poem: "The Captive" (about a canine friend) and a collection entitled "Puckety Creek Anthology", about our townspeople; [pers.] I believe the truth of the Talmud which states: "He who can protest and does not, is an accomplice in the act". I believe most people are highly motivated to do absolutely nothing; [a.] New Kensington, PA 15068

CURRAN, JAMES P.
[b.] August 7, 1914, Woonsocket, R.I.; [p.] Patrick J. and Nora Curran; [m.] Yvette Curran (dec), June 24, 1939; [ch.] James Jr., Maureen, Kerry Nancy; [ed.] Woonsocket High School; [occ.] Retired Deputy Clerk R.I. State Supreme Court; [memb.] I belong to the greatest organizations in the world…my family! If there is one outstanding facet to my personality, it is "great love of family"; [hon.] Editor's Choice Award for Outstanding Achievement in Poetry, presented by The National Library of Poetry; [oth. writ.] I have amassed a portfolio of poetry that I have been working at for over 20 years. My poem "To Our Mother" was recently published in "A Break in the Clouds", a poetry anthology produced by the National Library; [pers.] I am a firm believer in the quotation, "To thine own self be true". I strive to reflect my true feelings in all of my writings and I always dedicate my work to my beloved wife, Yvette, and my wonderful children; [a.] Woonsocket, R.I. 02895

CURTIS, CATHERINE GENIVIEVE
[b.]July 17, 1917, Portland, Oregon; [p.]Earl L. Sweek and Drucilla Anne Sweek; [m.]Gilbert R. Curtis, February 13, 1936 (deceased); [ch.]Carolyn E. Giles, Robert L. Curtis; [ed.]Lewis & Clark High School, Spokane, WA, Los Angeles College of Chiropractic…Glendale, CA. Sierra States University..L.A., CA Bernadean University, Las Vegas, NV; [occ.]Retired; [memb.]None; [hon.]L.P.N., DC, ND, Th.D, Associate in Physiotherapy, Basic Science Certificate, AZ; [oth. writ.]Several poems published in a local newspaper, write a newsletter on religion in prophecy…correlating current events with Bible Prophecy.; [pers.]I write about personal things in the lives of people….Personal universal loves, memories and irritations… Things which occur in people's lives…to let them know that nothing has overtaken them except such as is common to man."; [a.] Bangor, CA 95914

CUSTODIO, ULDARIO P.
[Pen.] Dario; [b.] October 14, 1904, Lezo, Aklan, Philippines; [p.] Santiago and Ursula Prado Custodia; [m.] Anisis T. Custodio, August 25, 1934; [ch.] Edgar, Edsel, Sherwin, Winston and Evelyn; [ed.] High School graduate - 1928 Kalibo Institute Normal School Graduate - 1938, Baguio Vacation Normal College, Third Year BSE Iloilo City Colleges - 1952; [occ.] Retired Philippine public school teacher with 40 years teaching experience, 1968; [memb.] Philippine Public School Teachers Assoc, President, Aklan Teacher Association - Lezo, Aklan, President, Young Builders Assoc - Lezo, Aklan, President, Elite Club; [hon.] First Prize Winner - Poetry Contest in local dialect, December 30, 1931 Rizal Day Celebration, Editor's Choice Award - National Library of Poetry Contest 1989 - Washington, DC; Six Consecutive Semi Finalist in poetry contest - National Library of Poetry - Washington, DC; Poet of Merit - 1990 - International Society of Poets, Washington, DC; Cassette Album - Poem for Peace - Ideals of Peace ISP 1991 - Washington, DC; Outstanding Poet of 1994 - National Library of Poetry; Lifetime Member to the International Society of Poets - Washington, DC; Editor's Choice Award - NLP 1994; [oth. writ.] Unpublished poems and essays; [pers.] Great heritage of mankind is the landmark of achievement in the footprints of the pen in poetry and prose where words of wisdom will remain enduring to hold a challenge to exalt life free from despondency and misery. I deplore lawlessness, idleness, and dishonesty which cause that great distress in life.

DANIELS, YVONNE
[b.]June 15, 1962, Waukegan, IL; [p.]Janet Mathews, Reynold L. Daniels; [ed.] Mayflower High School, Draughus Business School; [occ.] Customer Service Representative for Contact Lens Laboratory; [hon.] 2 Silver Poet Awards, 2 Golden Poet Awards; [oth. writ.] Poems published in magazines and local poetry guild; [pers.] The key to a successful relationship is not finding one anothers faults - but learning to live with them; [a.] Mayflower, AR

DAVID, KENNETH
[b.]August 20, 1929, Arkansas City, Kansas; [m.]Divorced; [oth. writ.]Poem: "One Fine Day" appearing in "Wind in the Night Sky."

DAVIDSON, GENEVA HOOD
[b.]March 20, 1946, Scoh Co., Virginia (Home); [p.]Jay and Lottie Hood; [m.]Divorced; [ch.]Crystal Davidson Edens; [ed.]12th grade High School Graduate; [occ.]Disabled; [hon.]Merit Awards; [oth. writ.]The Dogwood, Spring, Helen Steiner Rice, The Sky; [a.] Duffield, VA 24244.

DAVIDSON, KELLY
[b.] February 13, 1977, Pomona, CA; [p.] Clyde and Maureen, (brother-Ben); [ed.] Prescott High School; [memb.] The Nature Conservancy, World Wildlife Fund, and other organizations; [hon.] Editor's Choice Award in "On the Threshold of a Dream"; [oth. writ.] Several poems published through the National Library of Poetry and many more finished and unpublished stories; [pers.] To write is to look at the world through the eyes of a glistening star above; [a.] Prescott, AZ 86301

DAVIGNON, JUNE
[b.]June 19, 1924, North Troy, VT; [p.]Beth and Gerald Pottengill; [m.]Francis Davignon, June 16, 1945; [ch.]Seven, 5 sons, 2 daughters, 11 grandchildren, 4 great grandchildren; [ed.]High School 12 years; [occ.]Live on Working Dairy Farm in Town of Brownington; [memb.]International Society of Poets; [hon.]The International Poet of Merit Award 1992, Editor's Choice Award 1993, Sound of Poetry 1992, 1993; [oth. writ.]Local Newspaper Article, Other Anthology's, The Sound of Poetry Album 92, 93; [pers.]Some of my poems express my feelings of everyday life, that I can not express in any other way and even amaze myself at times to see the results, my written words bring, to my poems and others; [a.] Orleans, VT 05860-9222.

DAVIS, JACK
[m.] Tiz Davis; [ed.] Philadelphia College of Art; [occ.] Painter, previously San Francisco Ad Agency Art Director and Designer; [hon.] 1st Prize (Poster), Advertising Assoc of the West Creative Competition, Western Exhibition of Advertising and Editorial Art, 1st and 2nd prizes in 1st two annual N. Vancouver Arts Council Painting competitions, 1st award World Federalists of Canada Creative Peacemaking Competition (poetry); [pers.] My paintings are in the Canada Council National Art Bank Collection, the City of Vancouver Art Collection and in a number of public art gallery, corporate and many private collections. In poetry, I often used humor to express my ideas. I've long been a peace and human rights activist in the US and Canada. I used my amateur talents as a composer and performer of melodies and song lyrics and my professional ones as both painter and designer to help promote the causes of world peace and equality of all peoples; [a.] Kelowna, BC

DAVIS, LORRAINE
[Pen.]L. J. Davis; [b.]September 22, 1942, Lansing, MI; [p.]Russell and Evelyn Jessup; [m.]Robert, August 8, 1964; [ch.]Heather Aileen, John Paul; [ed.]Hoh High School, Alma College, CMU, MSU; [occ.]Instructor, Sussex County Community College, Newton, NJ; [memb.]Academy of American Poets; [hon.]Who's Who in Writers, Editors and Poets (1991-93), Golden Poet 1992, World of Poetry; [oth. writ.]Poems have appeared in "The Journal of Poetry Therapy and "Hob Nob"; [pers.]For me, poetry is a kind of therapy in which thoughts, feelings and images get clarified and crystallized. Sometimes the metaphors come unexpectedly or are original intent gives way to a quite different perspective; [a.] Sparta, ND 07871

DAVIS, MAY H.
[b.]Winnipeg, Canada; [m.]Pierce W. Davis; [ch.]James Winston Davis; [ed.]U. Of Mich. B.A. Social Work; Wash., Teacher's Cert., 1959; [occ.]Children's caseworker until married and later Drama and English Instructor until retired; [hon.]World of Poetry, Golden Poet Award, 1990; [oth. writ.]Do You See What I See? A collection of verse for children, 1975. No Ordinary Clam Book, A Cook Book, 1983; [pers.] I like to focus on the minute oddities of nature, to arouse the curiosity and wonder of a child in his surroundings; to encourage his questioning and imagining; [a.] Suquamish, WA 98392.

DAVIS, NENITA T.
[b.]October 13, 1954, Zumarraga, Samar, Philippines; [p.]Carlos Amor Tamayo and Engracia Cgo Tamayo; [m.]Everett James Davis, October 26, 1972; [ch.]James Michael, Katherine and Joseph; [ed.]Samar National High Samar College, Palomar College University of Maryland; [occ.]Owns papering full service beauty salon; [memb.]Cosmetology Association, Fleet Reserve Ladies Auxiliary, Sacred Heart Parish Counsel; [hon.]Notable Achievement Award in Education (DODDS), Golden Voice Award (Folk Music) First Place Winner University of Maryland "Extemporaneous Speech Tournament 1985", Golden Poet 1992, Golden Poet 1991 World of Poetry; [oth. writ.]Several poems published in DODDS "Sun Magazine", The Bounters, local newsletters, World of Poetry Great Poems of Our Time; [pers.]Luck are those who have their loved ones, and those who have no idea what loneliness does to a man.; [a.] Orange Pk., FL 32073

DAVIS, THELMA
[b.] January 21, 1928, Cincinnati, OH; [p.] Elmer and Philomena Heger; [m.] Joseph L. Davis, Jr, June 7, 1947; [ch.] Connie Werling, Dan David and Cindy Polk; [ed.] Mason High School (1945), Mason, OH (The War was going on so we all became Rosie the rivetor.); [occ.] Secretary/bookkeeper; [memb.] Order of the Eastern Star; [hon.] Several art and poetry awards in school; yearbook editorial staff; [oth. writ.] A poem published in "A Break in the Clouds". Several poems written for family and friends; [pers.] I write for a special occasion for the enjoyment and the satisfaction I obtain from the closeness and love to others; [a.] Emory, TX 75440

DAVIS, VERLE ELIZABETH
[b.]October 19, 1934, Mukdew, Manchuria, China; [p.]Otis G. and Julia Erich (Medical Missionaries); [m.]Lloyd T. Davis, June 20, 1981; [ch.]Paul, Kurt, Stacey, Kathy, Karen, Carol; [ed.]AA Degree, Nursing Shasta College; [occ.]Disabled R.N.; [memb.]S.D.A. Church; [hon.]KCPM Chan. 24 TV 1987, "North Valley hero of the Week Award for "Just Say "No"! Poem. Graduated, Shasta College with Honors 1971.; [oth. writ.]Published "The Goldsmith", "Together," "Just Say No!", "Beside Still Waters," "Someone Cares." Writing a book, not yet finished; [pers.]I enjoy writing substance abuse poetry for youth suitable for programs. I also write heartfelt inspirational poetry; [a.] Redding, CA 96001.

DAY, ROBERT E.
[Pen.]Bob Day; [b.]September 1, 1919, Lynn, Mass.; [ch.]Robert J., Laurraine, Janice, Verna and Sharynn; [ed.]Graduate of Cogswell Memorial High School, Henniker, NH; [occ.]Civil Service Retiree, Former USAAF Pilot; [memb.]World of Poetry (Formerly) International Society of Poets, Poetry Academy; [hon.]Second prize in Big Winner Contest, World of Poetry in 1992, Several Lesser Awards in Poetry; [oth. writ.]Two Sci-Fi Novels, 9 variety puzzle books, numerous poems; [pers.]Teach your children to walk with Christ and they will never walk alone; [a.] St. Augustine, FL 32095.

DE ARMOND, TIFFANY
[b.] October 5, 1980, San Jose, CA; [ed.] Valley Christian School; [memb.] Bethel Church; [memb.] Bethel Church; [hon.] Excellence in ASCI, many other musical awards, President's (Honor Society) Physical Fitness, 3 sport letterman; [oth. writ.] One other poem published in "Where Dreams Begin"; [pers.] Bible: Philippians 4:13; I can do all things through Christ, who strengthens me. Colossians, 3:17; Whatever you do, whether in word or deed, do it all in the name of Jesus, giving thanks to God, through him; [a.] San Jose, CA 95123

DE CICCO, JOSEPH
[b.] May 16, 1929, Brooklyn, NY; [p.] Emilio and Josephine De Cicco; [ch.] Joseph A., Lawrence N., Marcus T.; [ed.] G. Westinghouse VHS, NYC Community College, St Univ of NY; [occ.] Contract Administration Servie (Industrial Specialist); [memb.] Light of the World Music Ministry; Veterans of Foreign Wars; [hon.] Editor's Choice Award, National Library of Poetry; Federal Government Awards; [oth. writ.] Poems published in local church bulletin; poems published in Dpro Newsletters; [pers.] It is better - much better to have knowledge and wisdom than to have gold and silver; [a.] Littleton, CO 80123

DE STEFANO JR, JOHN J.
[b.] August 30, 1936, Norwich, CT; [p.] John J. De Stefano, Sr, Rose Dolores De Stefano; [m.] Elizabeth Ann De Stefano, July 4, 1957; [ch.] John III, Jeffrey, Gerald, Donna; [ed.] Norwich Free Academy, Williamtic State College Univ of CT; [occ.] Principal, Samuel Huntington School; [hon.] Dean's List; [oth. writ.] Over one hundred unpublished poems; [pers.] My poetry deals with all aspects of life; [a.] Canterbury, CT 06331

DEIGNAN, CAROL ANN
[b.] April 26, 1957, Bronx, NY; [p.] Elaine and Lawrence Deignan; [ch.] Erin, Timmothy and Amy; [ed.] Morris Knolls High School; [occ.] Administrative Assistant in Environmental Department of Porzio, Bromberg and Newman, P.C., Morristown, NJ; [oth. writ.] I have had other poems published in the Pike City Courier; [pers.] I am grateful for the gift of being able to express my inner most thoughts through my poetry; [a.] Milford, PA

DELANEY, FRANCIS E.
[b.]October 20, 1936, Chicago; [p.]Martin R. Delaney and Mary E. Delaney; [occ.]Plumber #130; [memb.]ASCAP, SGA Songwriter's Guild of America Country Music Society of America; [hon.]Several Poetry Awards; [oth. writ.]Blinky the Blue Nosed Snow Deer, Song Book for Children 1971, Other songs "I'm Chicago (all me tagg 93 Country Music in My Heart 81, Quiet American 1968, many other songs; [pers.]To Maureen T. Murray 1940-1993: "When we were something 20, love blossomed in our lives though our 30's and our 40's the roses bloomed again and again when we were something 50, they withered and died. Now, I'm on the road again, looking for that love (rose) again."; [a.] Chi-Ridge, IL 60415.

DENTON, RUBY IDA
[b.]February 6, 1932, Gilmer, Texas; [p.]Marshall Bivins and Amie Bivins; [m.]Marvin R. Denton, February 22, 1950 (Deceased); [ch.]Janell, Beverly, Antonio, Rita, Tommie Sue, Carolyn; [ed.]MLS, 1982, BYU Provo, UT, M.A., 1974, French, English, B.A., 1973, English/French, ETSU, Commerce, TX.; [occ.]Archivist, LDS Church Historical Dept., SLC, UT; [memb.]SAA, SSA, CIMA; [hon.]Pi Delta Phi, French Honor Society, Sigma Tau Delta; [oth. writ.]Sonnet To A Lantern Bearer Marvin, We Hardly Knew Ye; [pers.]Don't worry about the road not taken. Do your best with the road you're on while there. Sometimes the only way out is through.; [a.] Salt Lake City, UT 84115.

DEPAOLO, DONNA
[b.]June 24, 1939, Portland, Maine; [p.]Helen King & Murdock Day; [m.]Divorced; [ch.]Thomas M. DePaolo; [ed.]Portland High School Several Courses at University of Maine; [occ.]Stenle Tech, Brighton Medical Center; [memb.]St. John, The Evangelist Catholic Church, Italian Heritage Center; [oth. writ.]Poems published in Where Dreams Began, Wind In The Night Sky, In The Desert Sun, Celebrations; [pers.]To express oneself on paper which ordinarily would not be verbalized, is in itself a wonderful kind of therapy.; [a.] South Portland, Maine 04106.

DEPORTER, JEANNE
[b.]August 31, 1933, Moline, IL; [p.]FLI and Mary Meersman; [m.]Don DePorter, September 12, 1953; [ch.]Diane,, Dan, Debbie, Doreen, Donna, David; [ed.]Alleman High School; [occ.]Accounts Payable Clerk for Eagle Country Markets; [oth. writ.]I use my poems for special people for Birthday's Anniversaries or on the death of a loved one.; [pers.]I'm a country girl that values my husband, children and now grandchildren and the good earth the Lord has given us.; [a.] Milar, IL 61264.

DEPUY, PATRICIA G.
[b.] December 9, 1949, Richlands, VA; [p.] Clarence Gillespie (deceased) and Ruth Gillespie; [m.] Divorced; [ed.] Sword's Creek Ele., Richlands High School, some college (SUCC); [occ.] Housewife; [memb.]McGlothlins, Chapel Freewill Baptist Church, PETA; [oth. writ.] Poems published in local newspapers; [pers.] I write about the pure love between human beings and animals, God-given love; [a.] Cedar Bluff, VA 24609

DERRINGER, JUANITA
[b.] May 24, 1921, Dayton, Ohio; [p.] Chester M. Greer and E. Gertrude Greer; [m.] Lawson G. Derringer, March 17, 1945; [ch.] George Derringer and Jeffrey Derringer; [ed.] Grade school was Jackson and High School was Roosevelt, completed 12 years; [occ.] Homemaker; [memb.] Active membership in Church Women United and Reorganized Church of Jesus Christ; [hon.] Invitations to Poetry Conventions to read my poems. "The Giant Apathy" in 1990. Creations Secret in 1991; [oth. writ.] Daily Bread contributions offered as daily thoughts. "A Little Child Shall Lead Them and "A Reminder the Rainbow" and other thoughts of spiritual value; [pers.] Psalm 121 and Psalm 139 inspire me in today's world. Also my "down to earth life on the farm!; [a.] Dayton, Ohio 45426

DESMET, PHYLLIS
[Pen.] Ester Brooks; [b.] August 19, 1940, Newburyport, MA; [p.] Colburn Estabrooks and Flossie Simpson; [m.] Emile D. Desmet, October 7, 1967; [ch.] Doreen Desmet and Dawn Desmet; [ed.] Kelly Grammar, Newburyport High; [occ.] Retired AT&T 30 years; [memb.] AFL-CIO; [hon.] Golden Poet Award 1990. Numerous suggestion awards, AT&T, 10 years perfect attendance 1981-1991; [oth. writ.] The Past, Enchanted, I Want To Be Your Lover, Desire, Life; [pers.] How can there be preju-

dice against a race when there's only one, The Human Race.; [a.] Methuen, MA 01844

DESPAIN, RACHEL
[b.] June 28, 1979, San Diego, CA; [p.] Lawrence and Dorthy De Spain; [ed.] High school freshman; [memb.] High school color guard, distict choir '90-'91; [oth. writ.] Love?, Alone, Game Keeper, Behind those eyes; [pers.] I write in my sparetime and when I want to get my feelings out. Most of my poems are about love or lonliness; [a.] Herndon, VA

DEVRIES, CECILIA
[Pen.] DeDe DeVries; [b.] July 21, 1913, Grandrapids, Mich.; [p.] Leo O'Connor and Nellie Testin O'Connor; [m.] Peter W. DeVries; [ch.] Judy Hansen, Sue Miller, stepdaughter Donna Devries; [ed.] High School Diploma, Amateur drama work from age 15 to age 32. I loved it.; [occ.] Retired; [memb.] Elks Lodge, Country Club meadows Golf Club Florida; [hon.] Two from World of Poetry, On The Sea Of Life and To My Love. Also according to the letter I received from Milton Berle, I was to be awarded by him at the banquet in San Francisco, The New Poet of 1992 Award, it was accepted for me, I could not go. I never received the award from him, tho I asked him for it.; [oth. writ.] To many poems and lyrics to count. I have kept them all. Thru the years I sent 6 more to World of Poetry. "Steadfast" "Meditation" "Love Came By" in 1992; [pers.] I have been writing poetry since I was 15 yrs. old. I love the way it lets me express my feelings and emotions. It fulfills me.; [a.] Plant City, FL 33565

DEWOLF, WANDA L.
[b.] September 24, 1939, Chicota, TX, Lamar County; [p.] Charles Perry Hale and Jewel Fay Grant Hale; [m.] Gary Leland DeWolf, September 29, 1977; [ch.] Donna Hayles Elliott, Karen Hayles Goins; [ed.] High School, bible Study, Life's Experiences, Wife, Mother, and Grandmother.; [occ.] Radio Evangelist and Bible Teacher; [memb.] 700 Club, NRA and National Jugglers Association of America; [hon.] Humanitarian Award 1993 with certificates of Recognition from the City of Glendora, County of Los Angeles and The State Legislature of California; [oth. writ.] One poem published in "Our World's Most Beloved Poetry." By World of Poetry publications. Several articles in the opinions section of local papers; [pers.] I strive to reflect the spirit of God in my life, in my work, and in my service to my fellowman. I have been greatly influenced by my loving, romantic, and upright husband, who is my inspiration.; [a.] Glendora, CA 91740.

DIAL, ELNORIST E.
[b.] December 2, 1922, Greenwood, SC; [p.] Roosevelt and Evelyn Evans; [m.] Deceased; [ed.] Graduated from Brennor High School, S.C., S.C. State College, Orangeburg S.C.; [occ.] Clerical for the city of NY; [memb.] Democratic Club; [hon.] World of Poetry Award 1988 and Golden Poet Award 1990 and 1991.; [oth. writ.] Two songs have been written and recorded: There's a Dime, 1992 and That Passion, 1984; [pers.] There is nothing that beats trying, trying, trying; [a.] New York, NY

DIAS, SCOTT
[Pen.] Jon M. Dark; [b.] May 13, 1963, Dorchester, MA; [p.] Matthew W. Dias and Sis Dias; [occ.] Happy Bear Auto Repair; [hon.] Editor's Choice Award for Dear Sweat Death I Come Calling; [oth. writ.] Dear Sweet Death I Come Calling, Fall Has Come, Missing You, Season's of Our Lives, I'll Be Home, Looking Glass, Hope, Lost Love, never Was, Friends For Life; [pers.] When in doubt close your eyes and open your heart then you will see things much clearer; [a.] Bridgewater, MA 02324

DICKERSON, JANIS
[b.] July 7, 1933, Philadelphia, PA; [ed.] Master's Degree in Ed. Antioch University Philadelphia; [occ.] Teacher Pre-Kindergarten, Head Start Program; [memb.] National Asso. for the Education of Young Children, Board of Directors of Delaware Valley Asso. for Ed. of Young Children; [hon.] Honoree; Phila. Women in Ed., Women's Way Banquet 1988, Legion of Honor Award, Chapel of Four Chaplains, Temple University Phila, PA 1988; [oth. writ.] Poems published in Antioch University "Imprints" magazine Ed. articles including poems for children in DVAEVC conference journal 1990-1993, poem printed in "Where Dreams Begin" National Library of Poetry; [pers.] My goal is to present writings that bring to light the University of human thought, feelings and aspirations; [a.] Philadelphia, PA.

DILLON, ELLA M.
[b.] February 20, 1933, Wenatchee, Washington; [p.] L. H. (Red) & Rose E. Bush; [m.] Gerald E. Dillon, June 25, 1960; [ch.] James Douglas McFall, 2 G-Chdn. Matt and Taisha McFall; [ed.] High School; [occ.] Night Auditor/Office Mgr./Publisher/Editor; [memb.] Eastmont Baptist Church National Authors Registry International Society of Poets; [hon.] Golden Poet 1991 & 92, ISP 1992 & 93 ISP Semi Finalist 1993, Centennial Poet 1992, Who's Who 1992-93; [oth. writ.] One book "A Night Auditor Tells All," Poems for Centennial Concert 1992, Cover poems for Portrals Magazine (my own creation) Edit and publish Portals; [pers.] All that I ever accomplished I owe to my Mother, I hope she knows. I would be very proud to follow in her humble footsteps; [a.] Wenatchee, WA 98807-2163.

DINGWALL JR., JAMES ALBERT
[Pen.] J. A. Dingwall, Jr. (J.D.); [b.] April 10, 1946, Monrovia, Lberia, WA; [p.] Dr. James A. Dingwall Sr. and Mrs. Maggie Louise Dingwall; [m.] Lonnie Mae Dingwall, August 25, 1971; [ch.] none; [ed.] Graduate Monrovia College (1967), Bryman College, SF, CA (1978) and Hargest College of Printing, Houston, TX (1988); [occ.] Printer G'Boro News and Record also Mailer; [memb.] Quality Team (Greensboro News and Record) Greensboro, NC, World Trade (International Trade); [hon.] Award of Merit Certificate from World of Poetry (1987, 88, 89), Silver Poet Award; [oth. writ.] Song Lyrics to Rainbow Records, And Chapel Recording Company; [pers.] To turn today's experience and realities into poetry and song; [a.] Greensboro, NC 27401.

DIOTTAVIANO, MARGARET
[Pen.] Margaret Samothrakis; [b.] June 4, 1955, Poughkeepsie, NY; [p.] Margaret and John Diottaviano (both deceased); [m.] Joel Medina, separated (from Nick S.); [ch.] Zeke Samothrakis (April 15, 1976); [ed.] Early Childhood Development, Dutchess Community College; [occ.] Teacher (ECH), homemaker, poet and photographer; [memb.] St. Jude Children Research Hospital, Salesion Missionary, United Way/Paralyzed Veterans Assn; [hon.] World of Poetry - A Gift from God. Love is Growing. Reach Within Yourself. Honorable mention and Golden Poet also to appear on television with John Campbell and Eddie Cole. A Child's Dream - NL of Poets - Our World's Favorite Poems - Who's Who in Poetry and Sound of Poetry - Published; [oth. writ.] "Mother May You Rest In Peace", Poughkeepsie Journal. Many poems aired on WCZX F.M. radio station in Poughkeepsie; [pers.] I have been writting poetry for 20 years. I have over 60 poems that relate to life, nature, religion, politics and love relationships. My motto is "Learn to Live and Live to Love"; [a.] Poughkeepsie, NY 12603

DIVARIS, APOSTOLOS
[b.] December 2, 1946, Athens Greece; [m.] Tina Hornes, october 7, 1972; [ch.] Andreas, Terri (sons); [oth. writ.] A monograph on the supplemental feeding of honeybees in periods of death, Sparta, Greece 1973. Over 150 poems, written between 1967 and 1971, typewritten and circulated privately; [pers.] Being a painter as much as a poet, I have a very simple rule by which I decide if something is Art or not. Poetry as well as painting should have rhythm and evoke some sort of feelings to the reader/viewers; [a.] Livermore, CA 94550

DIXON, ELLA SMITH
[b.] April 15, 1945, Epps, LA; [p.] Mr. and Mrs. Sandy Smith, Sr.; [ch.] Bill Stewart, Jr. and Robyn Selena Stewart; [ed.] Carroll High, BMI Business College, Northeast Louisiana University; [occ.] Volunteer for Monroe Police Department; [memb.] Disabled American Veterans; [hon.] Received seven awards from World of Poetry; Inducted with the International Poets, 1993 in August; [oth. writ.] Book, "God's Word Is Our Only Foundation."; [pers.] God's beautiful gift of life is the inspiration of my writing.; [a.] Monroe, LA 71203

DMITRIEV, ANDREI L.
[b.] June 11, 1957, Moscow, USSR; [p.] Leonid Dmitriev and Lidia Dmitriev; [m.] Natalia Balandina, August 18, 1993; [ed.] Moscow Special School #69, Philological Faculty of Moscow State University, Graduate School of Academy of Pedagogical Sciences of the USSR; [occ.] Instructor of Russian Language and Literature at Lafayette College, PA; [oth. writ.] Five articles on Anna Akhmatova's Poetry in the Institute of Social Sciences and magazines Russian Language at School, poems in the anthologies of The National Library of Poetry "Wind In The Night Sky" and "In the Desert Sun"; [pers.] "And they twain shall be one flesh: so then they are no more twain, but one flesh." "Herein is our love made perfect, that we may have goodness in the day of judgement..." "Beloved, I wish above all things that thou mayest prosper and be in health..."; [a.] Easton, PA 18042.

DOLE, JANET B.
[b.] September 11, 1906, Somerville, Massachusetts; [p.] John Eugene Finn, may Shears Finn; [m.] William L. Dole, 1930, (1906-1969); [ch.] Barbara Ann, Richard Stuart, and Linda B.; [ed.] Framingham State Teacher's College 1927; [occ.] Artist; [memb.] Friends of Mark Twain Memorial, Ruth Wyllis Chapter of DAR, College Club of hartford, W.Htfd. Women's Club, Immanuel Congregational Church, W.Htfd. Art League and Retired Persons Grps. Blue ribbons for paintings - Am. Federation of Women's Clubs in Connecticut, Art shows in the Htfd., CT, area.; [oth.

writ.]Book of children's poems (unpublished), poem on Christmas in Africa published in The West hartford news; [pers.]Friends are flowers in the garden of life; [a.] West Hartford, CT 06107.

DOMAN, JOSEPH I.
[Pen.]Willy B. Dare and Neuar; [b.]March 12, 1949, Philadelphia, PA; [p.]Isaac and Mary Doman; [m.]Elizabeth, December 9, 1969; [ch.]Joseph Jr., Sunny Christine, Laurain Mary; [ed.]I have a General Education Diploma (GED) from high school; [occ.]Heavy Equipment Operator; [hon.]1989, 1990, 1991 Golden Poet Awards, 1990 Who's Who in Poetry; [pers.]Poetry has been an outlet of hidden fears and emotions for me.; [a.] West Berlin, NJ 08091

DONAHUE, MARILYN D.
[b.]May 17, 1961, Houston, TX; [p.]Viola Mitchell and Robert Mitchell; [m.]Terence Donahue, May 14, 1983; [ch.]ASHA Denay Donahue; [ed.]Phyllis Wheatley High School, Jarvis Christian College, University of Houston; [occ.]Medical Secretary; [memb.]Member of Greenville Ave., Church of Christ, National Honor Society; [hon.]Valedictorian of High School Class; [oth. writ.]Poems published through National Library of Poetry, currently working on a book entitled "Poetry To Stir The Soul."; [pers.]Through my poetry I wish to share the goodness of God's love with others.; [a.] Irving, TX 75062.

DORLAND, JESSE
[b.]April 20, 1983, Ontario, Oregon; [p.] Bobbi and Tom Junier; [ed.] 5th grade student at Horizon Elementary; [memb.] Asst Managing Editor of School Side News; [hon.] Published in "A Break in the Clouds", semi-finalist in National Poetry Contest and two time winner of "Young Author's Contest". Five years on Honor Roll; [oth. writ.] "A Golden Place" (published). Local publications include several poems and short stories; [pers.] Roald Dahl has been a big influence for me. I try to use my sense of humor in my stories but my poetry is more serious; [a.] Jerome, ID 83338

DORSANEO, JOHN
[Pen.] Karl Oleksak, JC Dorsan; [b.] May 6, 1947, New York City; [p.] Mario D'Orsaneo and Clair Oleksak; [memb.] Animal Rights Organizations, People for the Ethical Treatment of Animals; [oth. writ.] Manuscript tentatively titled "Victims of the Vortex"; [pers.] Mankind defines itself by the attitude and treatment of it's animal population; [a.] Phx., AZ 85016

DOTSON, JANE ADELINE
[b.] April 10, 1939; [p.] Mr. and Mrs. Travis HOuston Powell; [ch.] Four, Kermit E. Dunwood, Kenneth E. Dunwood, Kimberly E. Dunwood, Keith E. Dunwood; [ed.] High School; [occ.] Poet, writer, novelist; [oth. writ.] Six novels, twenty six short stories, poetry, marriage vows, special request from friends and neighbors; [pers.] Thoughts that are created in the boundaries of my mind can not be kept there. Uncaptured by the pen they are able to fly away like the birds of summer.

DOUGHERTY, MARGARET
[b.] August 2, 1907, Castro County, TX; [p.] Ira and Annie Ricketts; [m.] Archie Dougherty, August 16, 1928; [ch.] LeNelda, David, Ruth, Noel, Wylie, Allynda, Neil, Bill, Jane; [ed.] High school, Hereford, TX, College, Canyon, TX, school of hard knocks; [occ.] Teacher, homemaker, historian, family, school-bus driver; [memb.] Gateway Christian Church, Cloud Extension Club, Encanto Garden Club; [hon.] Horticulturist and Herbalist of 1991-92, New Mexico Garden Clubs. Pioneer Woman of the Year Extension Club 1991-92, Mother of the Year Church; [oth. writ.] Church Programs Family History, "Wings and Roots", many programs on wheat weaving, all aspects of organic gardening, flower arranging, wild flowers and wheat weaving; [pers.] I have lived in the most fantastic era of history. Remembering trips in a covered wagon home steading with my parents - to men orbiting the earth and walking on the moon. I believe God is still in control; [a.] Clovis, NM 88101

DREW, DOROTHY
[b.]January 28, 1919, New Bedford, Mass.; [p.]Harry Drew and Constance Drew; [m.]Deceased; [ch.]Eleven, Sandra, Cheryl, Dale, Bruce, Brian, Gary, Dianne, Gaye, Jeff, Ronald, Richard; [ed.]College and High School; [occ.]Painter, Author, and Poet; [hon.]Children's Book Published, 5 Merit Awards for Poetry, 3 Golden Poet Awards, 1 Silver Poet Award; [oth. writ.]Children's Book Short Story for Fate Magazine; [pers.]Where there is beauty, truth, love and wisdom, there you will find the mind of God.

DRUMMOND, LAVENA MAY
[b.]June 23, 1931, Arcola, Missouri; [p.]John Hastings, Beatrice Hastings; [m.]Jack Wilbur Drummond, July 15, 1949; [ch.]Jacque LaVerna, James Lester; [ed.]Bronaugh High School, Fort Scott, Jr. College, Pittsburgh State Teachers College; [occ.]Teacher, Executive Sec., Rancher; [memb.]Eastern Star Outlook Club; [hon.]Eleven Honorable Mentions. Two Golden Poets Awards; [oth. writ.]"Pegasus Aloft", "Music Room", "Black Letter", "Whom To Love", "Peace and Love", "Oil Rigg", and "Tidal Wave."; [pers.]I write for my own pleasure about the things that I know and the things that I see that inspire me to prose; [a.] Severy, Kansas 67137.

DUEST, CAROLYN P.
[b.]October 11, 1943, Portland, ME; [p.]Ernest Valente and Mabel Valente (both Deceased); [ch.]James Allen, Tracey Ann; [ed.]Cathedral High School; [occ.]Self-employed, also do part-time data entry work for direct mail of scarborough, ME; [hon.]Award of Merit Certificate 1988, Golden Poet Award 1989, Silver Poet Award 1990, All from World of Poetry, Sacramento, CA; [oth. writ.]Several poems published in local newspapers, as well as two poems published in World Treasury of Great Poems, World of Poetry Press; [pers.]Whatever the subject, I try to write what I feel, and find it easier to express my thoughts in writing, rather than to verbalize them; [a.] Portland, ME 04103.

DUKE, OSCAR M.
[b.]February 3, 1927, El Paso, Texas; [p.]Charles and Beatrice Duke (deceased); [m.]Gloria M. Duke, November 18, 1950 (deceased); [ch.]O. Kevin, Karen Clarisse, Brian K. Duke; [ed.]AA Degree, Social Studies; [occ.]As an ordained Catholic Permanent Deacon of the Los Angeles Archdiocesses, ministering the Homebound and hospitalized in my present vocation.; [memb.]Santa Clara Eucharistic Minister; [hon.]Speech: Dramatic Sty;e; [pers.]A spiritual life is vital. It builds an inner terrace in the soul for the Spirit to visit and reinforce one's mission.; [a.] Oxnard, CA 93030.

DUKE REV. JR., JAMES H.
[b.] January 8, 1934, Murphysboro, IL; [p.] James H. Duke, Sr. (deceased) Mabel N. Lively (Duke) (Haney); [m.] Pauline Jane (Stark) Duke, December 2, 1956; [ch.] Cynthia Jane (Duke) Reichrath and Stephn Edward Duke; [ed.] Attended SIUC, SBL Seminary, Member Elm St. Bapt. Church and Deacon, Direcotr of special ministeries; [occ.] Pastored nine churches, now retired, disability soc. sec.; [memb.] Was a church planter for one of the nine memberships from 1-350 in some churches; [hon.] Volunteer of year for Beverly Enterprises; Bronze Plaque for 20 years service in a men's clothing store; [oth. writ.] For 12 years I published a 6-page newsletter (legal size paper). In it was poems and articles I'd written. Jail Newsletter (Jail Talk), that contained writings of the inmates; [pers.] Thought out writing leads one to thoughtful reading. Reading and writing foul language ruins your own character; [a.] Murphysboro, IL 62966

DULTZ, GREGORY M.
[b.]December 8, 1946, Glendale, CA; [p.]Marvin Dultz and Josephine Dultz; [m.]Maruka Dultz, August 12, 1984; [ch.]Shane, Travis, Shannon, Beau, Arrow, Gabby; [ed.]2 yrs. USC; [occ.]Transportation Coordinator for Studios; [memb.]Local #399 Studio Teamsters; [hon.]2nd Place, Nation World's Fair Seattle, Photography Combat Photo, Viet Nam, Published Nation. Geographic September 1968; [oth. writ.]Four screen plays, 20 songs, 300 poems; [pers.]God's gift to man is his talent, man's gift to God is what he does with it.; [a.] Agoura, CA 91301.

DUNCAN, CHRISTINE
[Pen.] Khrys Duncan; [b.] January 12, 1975, Hosptital Room (Vallejo); [ed.] High School - so far; [occ.] Proof Operator for Bank of America; [oth. writ.] Several poems published in high school literary magazine. Poem published in "Where Dreams Begin"; [pers.] Before I sink into the big sleep I want to hear, I want to hear the scream of the butterfly". - Jim Morrison; [a.] Vallejo, CA 94591

DUNDAS, DAVID
[Pen.] David Dundas; [b.] December 20, 1968, London, England; [p.] Lucile and Herbert Dundas; [m.] Single; [ed.] SCS Business School -Essex County, and Kean College in New Jersey; [occ.] Loss Prevention; [hon.] Honorable mention - World Anthology of Poets; [oth. writ.] Thinking of you, Jealousy, Rage, Shadow; [pers.] It's not the pen that writes on paper, its the mind that takes it on; [a.] East Orange, NJ 07017

DUNLOP, LOIS JEAN
[Pen.] Lois Jean Celani; [b.] April 18, 1956, North Kingstown, RI; [p.] Rocco L. Celani, Jean C. McKinley; [ch.] Michael James -son (January 17, 1972), Mary Anthony - son (June 19, 1974, Barry Alan - son; [occ.] Homemaker, singer, songwriter, poet; [memb.] V.F.W. Ladies Aux; [hon.] Poem published in the anthology "A Break in the Clouds" title "The Poet" it won Editor's Choice award, 2

poems published in the anthology "The Coming of Dawn" both are listings with the National Library of Poetry. I'm honored to be recognized as one of Americas most outstanding poets of 1994; [oth. writ.] 2 songs copywritten 1988 Library of Congress entitled "Hundreds and Thousands of Men" and "When he goes back on the Road" A poem titled "My Dad Came Home" other various poems - lyrics - local newspapers have run some of my poems; [pers.] A true poet does more than rearrange words to rhyme - as not all poem's do! They feel deeply all of life's emotions and share them with eternity!; [a.] Danvers, MA 01923

DUNNAM, DEE
[pers.] A native Texan who loves the land, the wonders of nature, and the color green; [a.] Graham, TX

DURANT, BEA BON
[b.] October 10, 1923, Corbin, KY; [p.] Thomas and Susan Lockard; [m.] Don Bon Durant; [ch.] Three Daughters: Elizabeth, Patricia, Teresa; [ed.] High School, College; [occ.] Retired Buyer and Manager; [hon.] English, Math; [oth. writ.] Many poems, Life of the Singing Lockard Sisters; [a.] Columbus, OH 43204

DURRETT, CATHY
[b.] February 13, 1958, Seattle, WA; [p.] Fred and Onibe Carpenter; [ch.] Kenneth and Jason Durrett; [ed.] Eureka Adult School, HROP Certificate of ACMA California Medical Assistants; [occ.] Cashier; [memb.] I'm a member of the Moose; [hon.] Editor's Choice Award from the National Library of Poetry 1993; [oth. writ.] I have put alot of my poetry in a paper called (works in progress) and I have one in (womens work); [pers.] I know every one has a dream, mine is to publish my poetry book. Don't ever give up on a dream because someday it could become a reality!; [a.] Olympia, WA 98502

DUYCK, KATHLEEN DWYER
[b.]July 21, 1933, Portland Oregon; [p.]Anthony Jos. Dwyer and Edna Hayes Dwyer; [m.]Robert Duyck, February 3, 1962; [ch.]Mary Katherine Boeyen, Anthony Joseph, Robert Patrick; [ed.]St. Mary's Academy H.S., Oregon State, B.S. Home Economics Univ. of Washington, M.S.W., Social work; [occ.]Retired Adoption Worker and Symphony Cellist, Homemaker; [memb.]AZ, Cello Society, Scottsdale Cultural Council, Phx. Symphony Guild, St. Theresis, International Soc. of Poets; [hon.]Cello Scholarship in H.S.; Exemplary Rating on Master's Comprehensive; Euterpe (or Music honorary); Principal Cellist in H.S.; OSU; Phoenix College, Scottsdale Symphony; [oth. writ.]Master's Thesis on Vocational Rehab. Poetry used at banquets, anniversaries, and in grace notes and the trumpeter, local newsletters; [pers.]My Home Ec., Social Work, and Musical training have contributed to my poetry; focus on the home; sensitivity to others; meter, credence, and flow of musical line; [a.] Phoenix, AZ 85018.

EARLS, DEBRINA JOYCE PEEK
[Pen.] Debrina Peek; [b.] September 10, 1956, Sacramento, CA; [p.] Forrest Calvin and Marian, Catherine Peek; [m.] Michael Jeffery Earls, September 3, 1991; [ed.] Lincoln High School, Lincoln, CA, honors graduate, Sierra College Dean's List - Rocklin, CA/Acctng Major/ Dance Minor; [occ.] Accountant for Calif Youth Authority; [memb.] World of Poetry, National Library of Poetry, International Society of Poets; [hon.] Life Member Calif Scholarship Federation, Bank of America Scholarship in Foreign Language - Spanish, head songleader San Francisco 49'er cheerleader - 1971-72, several poems published by World of Poetry. Golden Poet Awards 1989, 1990, 1991 Who's Who in Poetry 1990, Outstanding Poet 1993; [oth. writ.] I am working on a gothic romance (historical) and a children's book series. Lots of poetry already written and published; [pers.] I tend to be a romantic and an idealist. Maybe someone will read one of my works and be inspired to bring a little peace, love, and God back into the world; [a.] Sacramento, CA 95838

EATHERTON, ANDREA L.
[Pen.] Andrea Lee; [b.] September 29, 1974, Westminster, Colorado; [p.] Debi Eatherton and Mark Eatherton; [ed.] Overland High School, University of Northern Colorado; [occ.] Student; [hon.] Dean's List 1992-93; [oth. writ.] 1st place in Teen Magazine poetry contest; Break in the Clouds, Euterpe; and several high school literary magazines; [pers.] "With me poetry has not been a purpose, but a passion" - Edgar Allen Poe. Writing has always been an integral part of my life. However, with the inspiration of Mark Moe and Geneva Corace, plus a little friendly competition with my best friend Michelle Cantwell, I have discovered the true poet inside; [a.] Aurora, CO 80014

EATON, BETTY MAE
[b.]July 8, 1935, Indianapolis, Indiana; [p.]Dorothy L. Burgard and John W. Fishback; [m.]Charles H. Eaton Jr., November 1977; [ch.]Three, Cindy, Mark and Penny; [ed.]Tenth grade, Tech High School; [occ.]Housewife and Cashier, Mother, Grandmother and Daughter; [memb.]O.E.S. #485 Beech Grove, Ind.; [hon.]Several honor awards for poetry. Published in Library of Congress; [oth. writ.]I write for people who can not express their feelings and want to.; [pers.]I write from experience and from my deep inner thoughts and common sense. I write to be funny, happy and sad. A good release of self; [a.] Indianapolis, Indiana 46219.

EBERSOLE, H. H.
[b.] September 25, 1920, Cleveland, Ohio; [m.] Ann L., December 10, 1949; [ed.] B.S. in Business Administration, Miami University, Oxford, Ohio 1942; [occ.] Retired 1976 as a Vice-President Finance and Comptroller which included 27 years of residence in five foreign countries; [hon.] Numerous retirement volunteer activites in Clearwater and Pinellas County including Board of Directors of Hospice Care, Project Self Sufficiency and Neighborly Senior Services; 1986 GTE Community Enrichment Award for Clearwater; [pers.] Retirement has brought the rewards of experience. To volunteer keeps the lights on in these later years; [a.] Clearwater, FL

EDWARDS, GINNY A.
[b.]July 31, 1976, Ft. Lauderdale, FL; [p.]Dr. and Mrs. E.K. Edwards, Jr.; [ed.]Senior in High School, Cardinal Gibbons High School; [hon.]Certificate of Appreciation from the Grand Lodge of free and excepted mason's, state of Florida, Editor's Choice Award, National Library of Poetry; [oth. writ.]Two other poems previously published by N.L. of P., many publications in Knights Templar Journal; [pers.]Place all hope in yourself because tomorrow is selfish and today blames you for what you didn't do; [a.] Lighthouse Pt., FL 33064.

EHLERS, FLORENCE RAUSH
[Pen.]Flora June (prof. actress); [b.]March 20, 1925, Brooklyn, NY; [p.]Deceased; [ch.]Four, Allen R. Ehlers, Phillis (Chris) Ehlers-Hardie, Donna L. Ehlers, Anita E. Torres; [ed.]A.A., Thtre Arts, B.S. Health Science, other drama, psychology, voice-song writing; [occ.]Actress, (retired) Psychiatric Technician; [memb.]Writing Club, drama club, A.F.T.R.A., The Drama Guild; [hon.]Many for poetry, nominated Woman of the Year 1993 from Amen Biographical Assoc., plaques as chorus founder, honors-International Biog. Assoc., nominated Best Actress, S. California; [oth. writ.]24 song musical play (full production style) Autumn Promise. Others published and unpublished (too long). Nat'l. Poetry Assoc., the Poetry Center, Amherst Society, The National Library of Poetry, News Reporter; [pers.]Compilation of my poetry would be under the heading (title), It Matters, so as not to lose comprehension that nature, that each individual put imprints upon another of same or different species.; [a.] Seal Beach, CA 90740

EHRICK, SARAH JULIA
[b.]December 2, 1969, Toledo, Ohio; [p.]Michael Ehrick and Carol Long; [ed.]BBA, University of Cincinnati, DeVilbiss High School; [occ.]Account; [hon.]World of Poetry's Award of Merit Certificate 1990, Golden Poet Award 1991; [oth. writ.]"You And Me" On The Threshold of a Dream, Vol. III; [pers.]If you believe in yourself, others will take your lead; [a.] Cincinnati, Ohio 45225.

EISCHEN, DON
[b.] fresno, ca; [p.] Emily and Joe Eischen; [m.] Jennie Capriola, February 1947; [ch.] Donna-Marie Eischen, Emily Kamansky; [ed.] CSU, Fresno, CA, BA Degree; Columbia Univ, NY, MA Degree; Stanford Univ, CA, Post Master's Degree; [occ.] High school teacher of english, emeritus, McLane High School, Fresno, CA 1952-1991. Poet in Santa Cruz, CA; Antiques and Collectibles Licensed Dealer; Site Manager, on-call for food and nutrition services, Capitola, CA; [memb.] Life Member International Society of Poets; Life Member National Council Teachers of English; Calif Assoc of Teachers of English; Romance Writers of America; [hon.] Editors Choice Award for Outstanding Achievement in Poetry, March 1993; Honorable Mention Selection for 1 to 10 poems selected for cassette, "Sound of Poetry" 2/93; Outstanding Teacher of English, McLane High School, Fresno, CA and for Fresno Unified School Districk, Fresno, CA; Vice President Al Gore sent a letter of commendation for "Little Flower of the Grassland-I" emphasizing the poem's environmental message; [oth. writ.] "Little Flower of the Grassland -I", published in Where Dreams Begin, 3/93; 12 poems in Treasured Poems of America, fall 1993; Sequel to "Little Flower of the Grassland-I (and) II" will be in the magazine The Hungry Poet; [pers.] I write about the trends of society, past present, future; and my poems point to a theatic reality which reflects nature and humans. I have to some degree been influenced by poets: William Blake Shakespeare, Emily Dickinson, my mother, and my sophomore english teacher, Kathleen McMurtry; [a.] Capitola, CA 95010

EISENHOFFER, ANGELA MARIE
[b.] December 28, 1977, St Louis, MO; [p.] George and Marie Eisenhoffer; [ed.] Winston Churchill High School; [occ.] Student; [memb.] Alamo Area Potbelly Pig Association, National Junior Honors Society, 4-H; [hon.] Presidential Academic Fitness Award; [oth. writ.] Beach Beauty; [a.] San Antonio, TX

ELIAS, AMY
[b.] November 28, 1978, Wilkes-Barre, PA; [p.] Joseph and Mary Susan Elias; [ed.] 9th grade-James M. Coughlin High; [occ.] Student; [memb.] Band, Orchestra, Chorus, Karate, Hockey, Soccer, Softball, Rainbows, Science, Olympiad, National Honor Society; [hon.] All-American National Champion, PA State Champion in Karate; [oth. writ.] Poem published in Windows on the World Vol II; [a.] Wilkes-Barr, PA

ELLIOTT, BRUCE F.
[Pen.]Bruce Elliott; [b.]July 2, 1909, Fort Collins, Colorado; [p.]Thad and Lulu Elliott; [m.]Evangeline Elliott, September 20, 1935; [ch.]Three, Phyllis, Roger and Kenneth; [ed.]B.S. Degree in Forestry, Colorado State University; [occ.]Retired; [memb.]Rotary Club, Masonic Lodge, Society of American Forest, Methodist Church etc.; [hon.]Several public service awards, 37 yrs. employment with U.S. Forest Service. G.T.O Fraternity; [oth. writ.]Several poems; [pers.]I write mostly for pleasure usually it is for some event. I try to bring out humor; [a.] Van Buren, MO 63945.

ELLIOTT, JUNE ALLEGRA
[Pen.]Lehuna Nani Na Lani; [b.]June 15, 1920, Los Angeles, CA; [p.]Raymond Morgan Elliott and Margaret Cate Elliott (deceased); [ed.]Graduate of UCLA and Claremont Graduate School (California); [occ.]Retired Secretary (secondary schools and community college, and Arthritis Foundation); [memb.]PEO and Orange County Chapter American Guild of Organists; [hon.]Golden Poet Award (1990-1991-1992) from World of Poetry; [oth. writ.]Several poems published in Maui News Vacationer Magazine Supplements; other anthologies; Aloha Magazine of the Pacific; Miscellaneous brochures for Pan Am and United Airlines travel tours to Hawaii; [pers.]In order to express my inner most feelings about my environment including people, places and things, I enjoy writing poetry!; [a.] Seal Beach, CA 90740.

ELSTON, LETITIA M.
[b.] March 2, 1903, Cool County, Pennsylvania; [p.] Charles Martin Avery and Jennie Garfield Jones Avery; [m.] Merle B. Elston (Deceased) April 8, 1922; [ch.] Kenneth Merle Elston, robert Blair Elston, Sherrill Elston Holley; [ed.] Grammar School; [occ.] Home Executive; [memb.] World of Poetry, National Library of Poetry; [hon.] Six Golden Poet, Honorable Mention Awards, Special Mention Awards, Listed, Who's Who In Poetry Years 89 and 91, poems published in local and church paper also in six anthologies; [pers.] Live and let live it is human to give, divine to forgive; [a.] Port Jervis, NY 12771

ELSWICK, KAREN
[b.] June 15, 1943, Warren, OH; [p.] Ruby and Glenn Whittaker; [m.] Millard E. Elswick, December 25, 1960; [ch.] Glenda Adms Tami, Ayers Kevin Elswick; [ed.] Mineral Ridge; [occ.] Prototype Harness maker at Packard Electric; [hon.] The last 3 years, I had been taking care of my mother. It was a great honor for me to do so. Going on 7th grandchildren; [oth. writ.] World Treasury of Great Poems - Times, Our World's Favorite gold and silver poems - I thank God alone your still with us great poems of our time. Words; [pers.] Yesterday has many memories and tomorrow has many dreams and hopes, but especially use your todays because they are well what you build on; [a.] Niles, OH 44446

ERRECA, EVELYN
[b.]June 29, 1931, Oklahoma, Haskel; [p.]Mr. and Mrs. Luther Black, (1749 Cypress Way, Merced, CA); [m.]Leon Erreca, September 1, 1951; [ch.]Patricia, Danny, David, John; [ed.]12th Grade Graduate, One year Jr. College, Diploma from Children's Literature; [occ.]Retired; [memb.]Attended The Institute of Children's Literature; [hon.]Award of Merit Certificate, Golden Poet Award; [oth. writ.]Short Stories for children and teenagers thru "The Institute of Children's Literature." Poems published in newspaper; [pers.]The poem I'm sending in was written on my sisters 40th birthday. She was 2 1/2 when I got married; [a.] Los Benos, CA 93635.

ERVIN, LINDA LEE
[b.]September 19, 1964, Paducah, KY; [hon.]Editor's Choice Award for poem "Dear Granny", 93; Accomplishment of Merit Award for poem "Ode To The Ocean,"93; [oth. writ.]I have many poems yet to be published; [pers.]My poetry expresses some of my deepest thoughts and feelings. I try to make people think and feel things they otherwise wouldn't; [a.] Boaz, KY 42027.

ESCALANTE, ESPERANZA H.
[b.]January 29, 1900, Gubat, Sorsodon, Philippines; [p.]Cipriano Munogholaso and Julia Fiqueraz; [m.]Esteban Encinas Escelante, April 3, 1929; [ed.]Edmundo, Esteban, Jr., Patricia, Libertad, Jose, Jaime, Aqaton, II, Antonio; [ed.]Passed Junior Teacher Civil Service 1917 Exam; [occ.]Grade VII English Teacher, Philippine Public Schools; [memb.]Philippine Public Schools Teachers Assn., Catholic Women's League, Nat. Federation of rural Improvement, and Women's Clubs; [hon.]Plaque for Outstanding President Provincial (State), Federations of Women's Clubs, Plaque from Gov. Frivaldo as Civic Worker; [oth. writ.]Christmas, Philippines People Power of 1986, Kites at War, Festivals in Summer. The first 2 poems were published in Selected Works of Our Worlds Best Poets World of Poetry, CA. USA. The last 2 poems, Nat'l. Library of Poetry, Owings, Mills, MD; [pers.]Love, Prayers, Live. Live and Let Live; [a.] Crisfield, Maryland 21817

ESTEPP, MARY SUE
[b.]May 23, 1953, Tampa, Florida; [p.]Mr. and Mrs. John A. Scott; [m.]Charles Alan Estepp, May 24, 1971; [ch.]April Lee Avila, Charles Alan Estepp Jr.; [ed.]H.B. Plant High School; [occ.]Housewife and Poet Grandmother, Priscilla and Anthony Avila; [memb.;Golden Poet For 1992, Golden Poet For 1993, Charter Member Of The American Poetry Society; [hon.]Golden Poet Twice, Five Awards of Merit, Honorable Mention; [oth. writ.]Local newspaper articles, letter sent to me from Milton Berle.; [pers.]I have always's wanted to write about the thing's that mean so much to me. The beauty that God created for all of us too see. It is his beauty, that has inspired my writings.; [a.] Zephyrhills, FL 33541.

EUSCHER, SHARON R.
[b.]March 28, 1973, Dover, Delaware; [p.]Ronald and Pauline Euscher; [ed.]Junior Year at Wesley College Dover, Delaware, major Elementary Education; [occ.]Student; [memb.]International Society of Poets, Blood Bank of Delaware, YMCA of Delaware Democratic Party, and Future Educators of America; [hon.]Honorable Mention in Great Poems of Our Time, outstanding, sportsmanship, Bob Sheeler Sportsmanship Award, and NCO Wives Honorary Scholarship.; [oth. writ.]Published in Great Poems of Our Time, and several poems published in various newspapers and magazines.; [pers.]I've always enjoyed writing, poetry since I was a child. I was truly inspired in high school by my creative writing teacher who told me to write from my heart. I strive to reflect true inner feelings of myself and mankind; [a.] Camden, DE 19934.

EVERLETH, JEFFREY
[b.]March 14, 1962, Plattsburg, NY; [p.]Woodrow and Thelma Everleth; [m.]Jennifer Everleth, May 22, 1982; [ch.]none; [ed.]Graduated from Schuylerville Central School; [occ.]Personal Fitness Trainer; [hon.]Editor's Choice Award from The National Library of Poetry; [oth. writ.]The Success of My Kite, Snow Crystals, She Stands Alone, Love is Such a Little Word, Morning Sun; [pers.]My poetry is derived from my own life experiences, memories and feelings. For anyone who read my poems may you find the happiness that the simple things in life bring.; [a.] Saratoga Springs, NY 12866.

FASSLER, EDITH B.
[Pen.]J. E. Ardeane; [b.] April 4, 1904, Sterling, Illinois; [p.]John Woessner and Caroline Bort Woessner; [m.]John A. Fassler, January 4, 1933; [ch.]John A., Edward W., Elizabeth K.; [ed.]Limited, about 2 years High School; [occ.]Retired Homemaker and Farmer wife; [memb.]Messiah Lutheran Church, IPBW Business Women's Club; [hon.]Honors from International Society of Poets, Quill Books, Clover Collection; [oth. writ.]A book of poems, self-published, "Leaves of our Prairies"; [pers.]Having lived on a farm all my life, I write about what I have experienced and know best.

FENNELL, JONATHAN E.
[b.] June 24, 1948, Kittanning, PA; [p.] Donald M. (deceased) and Rella F. Fennel; [ch.] Eric Grant Fennell; [ed.] Indiana Area Senior High School, Indiana Univ. of Pennsylvania (BS), Southern Illinois University (MBA); [occ.] Supervisor Systems Development Delmarva Power and Light Co. Wilmington, DE; [hon.] Gamma Rho Tau, Beta Gamma Sigma; [oth. writ.] Other poems published by The National Library of Poetry; [pers.] I write on a variety of subjects, most of which are personal experience, interpretation of other's experiences and fantasy.; [a.] Newark, DE 19711

FINAU, LOUISE M.
[b.]November 2, 1930, San Francisco; [p.]Louis and Mary Stelling; [m.]Keliti Lose Finau, February 20, 1971; [ch.]Lois, Bruce, Kathleen and Michael; [ed.]Geo. Washington High School, Los Angeles City College; [occ.]Medical Secty./transcriptionist. High school English teacher.; [memb.]World Vision, Church of Jesus Christ of Latter Day Saints.; [hon.]American Legion of Honor Award; [oth.

571

writ.]"Toki-A Tongan Trilogy" (A historical novel) "Poems for Young Dancers" (Book of Prose and Poetry) "Deborah" a play.; [pers.]Straight, strong words of truth I seek. nothing vague, nothing weak. Symbols forceful, simple and true. Giving classic clarity her homage due.; [a.] San Francisco, CA 94117.

FINLEYSON, ELLEN
[Pen.]Marty; [b.]June 27, 1936, Moscow, TN; [p.](Foster) Late-Hugh H. Hansell, Mrs. Gwendolyn Hansell (Rossville, TN); [m.]Late-J.E. Alexander, Jr (March 29, 1957), Clayt N. Finleyson (October 3, 1975); [ch.]5 children, Darlene A., Sonja, Stanford, Donna Moore, Patty Thompson, J.E. Alexander, III; [ed.]Collierville High School - Collierville, TN, De Shazgo College of Music - Memphis, TN; [occ.]Housewife, mother and grandmother, babysitter or Nana to grandchildren; [memb.]Veterans of Foreign War #5066, Collierville, TN and First Baptist Church; [hon.]The Institute of Children's Literature, April 30, 1990 (diploma); [oth. writ.]Listed in "Our World's Most Treasured Poems" on page 151, "My Little Friend" also "On The Threshold of a Dream" Volume III page 260, "Something Has to Give" page 541, "Wind In The Night Sky" - "My Memory"; [a.] Collierville, TN 38017

FINN, DICK
[b.] April 30, 1948, Minneapolis, MN; [p.] Luella and Lorney Finn; [ed.] Three years of college; [occ.] Poet and mathematician; [memb.] NAMI, RCAMI, US Air and Space Smithsonian; [hon.] Blue Ribbon for tapestry art show in high school; [oth. writ.] Wrote a poem for the AMI of Minnesota newspaper for Dec '88 / Jan '89 - wrote a poem for the National Library of Poetry published in a book in 1992; [pers.] I try to see some good in everyone. I love beautiful witty women, good music, art, and good times; [a.] St. Paul, MN 55116

FISHER, LYNN
[Pen.] Arm Chair Philosopher with Ants in her Pants; [b.] March 15, 1937, Houston, TX; [p.] Julius M. Gordon, Carey Kurth Gordon; [m.] Widowed 1980 - Ray Fisher; [ch.] Laurie Lynn Lee, Jeanne Jones Jamail and Sharon Gayle Jones; [ed.] Gulf Park College, Texas A&M, U of Colorado, U of Houston; [hon.] Editor's Choice Wind in the Night Sky; [oth. writ.] 2 books - printed not published, Reticence Resilience and Reciprocity, Resisting, Marketing 301, published in Wind in the Night Sky (Out to Pasture); [a.] Lufkin, TX 75901

FLOWERS DR., MARVA
[ed.] Mscd. D.TH D.D.; [hon.] Best New Poet of 1988, 1989 America Poet Anthology Award, International Poet Award, Poet of Merit Award, Leader in America Innovation award, Who's Who America Inventors Award, Patent Holder, USA, Patent DES 318293 Pyramid Pen; Korea, Patent 108550 Psisonic Pen; [oth. writ.] Best new poet for 1988, 1989, Publishere Choice America Poetry Anthology. Leadership in America Innovation, 1991 Edition; [pers.] Each in there own time will reach God Conscious in there mind.

FOLK-LEWIS, FRANKIE
[b.]March 10, 1945, Cleveland, Mississippi; [p.]Albert and Nellie Clasper Lewis; [m.]George H. Folk Jr., November 24, 1970; [ch.]Ricky and Byron Folk; [ed.]Castlemont High, Oakland California College, Millersville State, Millersville, PA; [occ.]Group supervisor for the handicapped, Lancaster, PA; [memb.]Boys and Girls Club, Lancaster, PA 17602; [hon.]Rec. and awarded for volunteer in drug and alcohol counseling, Lancaster, PA.; [oth. writ.]Has written several books. Short stories has three poems published in Prairie Dog Press and Local newspaper, new era.; [pers.]I strive very hard to express the goodness and feelings of all mankind, I started writing at a very young age (8).; [a.] Lancaster, PA 17602.

FORD, COLLEEN ANN
[b.]June 28, 1971, Waterbury, CT; [p.]Lawrence J. Ford and Janet M. Ford; [ed.]Holy Cross High School, University of Connecticut; [hon.]Golden Poet Award; [oth. writ.]Publication in selected works of our World's Best Poets; [pers.]Though what dusk might have sought him, he shall remember not his passage is long gone and his worth is no more. Take life into your grasps and do with it what you may.; [a.] Waterbury, CT 06708.

FOUNTAIN, EDWIN B.
[b.] March 11, 1930, Manassas, GA; [p.] David T. and Laura P. Fountain; [m.] Single; [ed.]B.F.A., B.R.E., Th.B., M.R.E., M.L.S., D.D., These from Univ. of GA., Univ. of KY, Lexington Baptist College; [occ.] Retired Librarian and actor, still an active Baptist Minister; [memb.] Beta Phi Mu, A Fellow of Univ. of KY. Assoc. of Christian Librarians and several others.; [oth. writ.] "Scriptural Index to B.H. Carroll's Interpretation of the English bible. Scriptural Index to J.P. Simmons Baptist Doctrine, The Librarian as Educator and other articles, Poems published elsewhere, indexes of Religious Collections, 46 articles in religious publications and professional publications. Three plays produced off Broadway in New York City; [pers.] Poetry should sing not hobble along. I admire Sidney Lamier and Irene Edit Sitwell; [a.] Garfield, GA 30425

FOUTZ, AGNES ADELE
[b.] December 24, 1915, Thatcher Hollow, CO; [p.] "Doc" and Mamie Woodruff; [m.] Virgil "Bud" Foutz, August 21, 1935; [ch.]; Adele "Buddy" Gary Stepson Doug and Jack, Nephew Kenny; [ed.] High School; [occ.] In the 70's outreach worker Office of Navajo Economic Opportunity; [memb.] Presbyterian Church; [hon.] I have been writing poetry for 65 years; [oth. writ.] Home of the Navajo in A Break In The Clouds, Nat'l. Library of Poetry; [pers.] I strive to make my poems warm the heart and whisper love; [a.] Farmington, NM 87401

FRANCIS, PATRICE
[b.]April 3, 1976, New Orleans, Louisiana; [p.]Ken and Maryann Francis; [ed.]Texas City High School, just starting my senior year.; [memb.]Youth in Government, St. Mary's Youth Group and Retreat team; [hon.]Head of our drill team stingarettes, various dance honors, graduating with English Honors; [oth. writ.]Several poems about various topics, one poem published in Selected Works of Our World's Best Poets; [pers.]I haven't been influenced by any early poets, and I don't have a philosophy about why or how I write; it's what I do to say what needs to be said.; [a.] Texas City, Texas.

FRANSE, JEAN LUCILLE
[Pen.]Jean Franse; [b.]January 24, 1952, Duncan, Oklahoma; [p.]Robert Sydney McDonald and mary Lee Hooper; [ed.]B.S. English/History, M.A. English, PhD Educational Administration; [occ.]Teacher; [hon.]Phi Delta Kappa Delta Kappa Gamma; [oth. writ.]Poems published by World of Poetry, Articles published in "Amarillo Daily News" Amarillo, TX; [pers.]"Once I gave what I can't keep for that which I can't lose" (lines from one of my poems); [a.] Farewell, TX 79325.

FRAUCHIGER, PAT
[b.]March 26, 1925, Spokane, WA; [p.]John L. and Ruth Brophy; [m.]Erwin F. Frauchiger, August 30, 1947; [ch.]Linda Ann and Karen Lee; [ed.]Through 3rd year of college; [occ.]Retired Insurance Underwriter; [memb.]Local YWCA formerly in Spokane Poets Assoc., CAA; [hon.]WA State Poetry 3rd Place First, Second and Third place local writing groups; [oth. writ.]Animal stories in national magazine. Biographical story in local magazine; [pers.]Started writing when I was 63 yrs. old, after my husband died, as a healing experience and now have to continue through my sight is waning; [a.] Spokane, WA 99205.

FRAZIER JR., KENNETH CORNELL
[b.] November 13, 1970, Phila, PA; [p.] Louise Inez Carey, Kenneth Cornell Frazier; [m.] Valerie, October 26, 1993; [ch.] Casandra, Natasha and the one one the way; [ed.] West Philadelphia High School; [occ.] Chemical Operations Specialist US Army; [oth. writ.] "As One" in a previous book in 1993; [pers.] I would like 2 thank the one who inspired this poem. I'll never 4 get U; [a.] Evans Mills, NY

FREDERICK, CAROL F.
[Pen.]Carol Frederick; [b.]July 24, 1938, Greeley, Nebraska; [p.]Father, Lester R. Bengel (Mother) Celestia G. Widmeyer; [m.]June 28, 1957; [ch.]Douglas Frederick, Janelle Frederick, Nancy Frederick Niebergall; [ed.]1955 High School (part time work program) at Grand Island, Nebraska; [occ.]Accountant; [hon.]For Poetry: National Library of Poetry; Cadence Publishing; Creative Arts Sciences.; [pers.]"While physically, handicapped and legally blind. I write these verses to my mind. Then they're transferred onto paper which is indeed a different caper. Any talent I may possess is truly God given as I have studied neither poetry nor creative writing. I've had MS since age 15 and lost vision in 1990.; [a.] Gig Harbor, WA 98329.

FREES, MARGARET M.
[b.]April 21, 1911, Parkside, Camden, NJ; [p.]Robert J. Donaldson and Mary M Donaldson; [m.]George S. Frees, September 14, 1940; [ch.]Joan M. Boyd and George J. Frees; [ed.]Camden Catholic High School; [occ.]Homemaker Apt. Hse. (18 yrs.) owner, buying and selling horses; [memb.]A.A.R.P., Missionary Oblates of Mary Immaculate, Nat'l. Shrine of Our Lady of the Snows Belleveill, IL; [hon.]Won Golden Poet Award, 1991 World Of Poetry and numerous honers in newspapers and first prizes; [oth. writ.]I long to be a seagull and wing the ocean blue. To leave all earthly cares behind. To be along with you, my God. I love God's beautiful creation.; [a.] Cape May, NJ 08210.

FREMGEN, DARLENE
[Pen.] d miner; [b.] July 19, 1958, Schenectady, NY; [p.] Jacob (Scott) and Diane Miner, Foster parents; [ed.] Greencastle, Antrim High School, Green Castle,

PA, Clerical Office Procedures Certificate, Shippensburg University, PA 1985; [occ.] Crane Assembly Clerk, Grove Worldwide, Shady Grove, PA: Manager Phil Carbaugh; [memb.] Since 1992 "Super Cities Walker" for Multiple Sclerosis; [hon.] First publication in 1993 National Library of Poetry, Owings Mills, MD, Wind In The Night Sky, 2nd publication in 1994, Nat'l. Library of Poetry, In The Desert Sun Anthology; [pers.] Many thanks to Donna McGinnis, former Business English Instructor at Shippensburg University, PA, for a literary critique of my manuscript; [a.] Chambersburg, PA 17201

FRICK, DUMAS F.
[hon.]International Pen Award, (The International Society of Poets), Editor's Choice Award (The National Library of Peotry), Award of Merit Certificate (World of Poetry); [oth. writ.]"Silent Majesty," "Poet's Quill, "Solitude," Air Force One," "Father," "The Message," "Time For Tears."; [pers.]Refer to myself as a "Renaissance Man." Combat veteran of World War II. Ex-teacher (engineering drafting), composer (have written songs, including music and lyrics), music to "Poetry In Motion" used as entertainment by "American Literary Press," author of three short stories and "The Adventures of Phineous," play the violin (performed in several symphony orchestras) poet (several poems published), lover of nature. Philosophy is to contribute to humanity so that I may validate my existence. Feel that as long as my poems are read, I will be with you in spirit. Desire to leave a happy legacy.; [a.] Philadelphia, PA.

FRIEZE, CLARA L.
[b.]November 8, 1909, Dallas, TX; [p.]Mother Josepha Vilbig, Father Adolph Peter Lenzen; [p.]Homer Henne Frieze, November 12, 1928, Dec'd; [ch.]none; [ed.]9 years: Studied art and language at the Art School, Artist Colony - San Antonio, TX. Graduated from Southern Methodist University in 1948 with a Bachelor of Arts Degree in World Literature and Language. Completed Master of Arts in World Literature in three years from SMU while fully employed and teaching night courses at Crozier Tech High School; [occ.]37 years as a Fashion Designer; [memb.]Charter member of "The Fashion Group"; [hon.]Numerous First Prize Awards for Women's Fashions at the annual State Fair of Texas competition; [pers.]"Education is the stepping stone of life."; [a.] Dallas, TX 75225-1634.

FRISCH, PETER R.
[b.]February 17, 1944, Budapest, Hungary; [p.]Gizella Blau, Michael Eichler (Deceased), Joseph Frisch; [m.]Paula R. Frisch, June 16, 1968; [ch.]Meredity Dawn, Adam Neil; [ed.]Erasmus Hall High School, Fairleigh Dickinson University, Monmouth College; [occ.]Sales and Leasing Consultant; [memb.]Monroe Township Jewish Center and Men's Club; [hon.]Presidential Sports Award for Racquetball, Honorable Mentions for many of my poems; [oth. writ.]Several poems published in local newspapers, magazines and anthology book; [pers.]Poetry is my passion, and it serves as a specific purpose and vehicle, in which I can escape, to allow me to make the world a better place to live; [a.] Monroe Township, NJ 08884.

FRY, DARLENE
[b.] July 6, 1975, Latrobe, PA; [p.] Robert and Doreen Fry; [ed.] Attending the Pennsylvania State University; [occ.] Student; [memb.] Latrobe First Church of God, 4-H, Member of Penn State University Honors Scholar Program.; [hon.] Nation 4-H Congress, National 4-H Conference, National Science Scholar, 1989-93 Who's Who Among American High School Students, High School Valedictorian; [oth. writ.] Two essays published in the PA Arabian Horse Association's, "Oasis Magazine". Poem published in The National Library of Poetry's "A Break In The Clouds", and in the Famous Poets Society Anthology; [pers.] I feel poetry creates a link between our hidden desires and the reality of the world; [a.] Latrobe, PA 15650

FULLER, DELORIS A.
[b.] January 10, Shreveport, LA; [p.] Mrs. Ruth Fuller of Shreveport, LA; [ed.] Northwood High, Draughton Norton Business College, Southern University, Grambling College; [occ.] Computer Proctor, at Linear Middle School, Shreveport, LA; [oth. writ.] Several poems published by The National Library of Poetry. I wish to publish a full book in the near future. I'm also an artist; [a.] Shreveport, Louisiana 71107

FULMER, DELORES I.
[b.]July 7, 1934, Pennsylvania; [p.]Clarence Bobberts, Stella Burns; [m.]Paul H. Fulmer, September 26, 1950; [ch.]Paulette, Linda, Paul Sr., Larry, Diane, Joh, Frank; [ed.]Computer Literacy and word processing, GED, C.E.F. Teachers Training Program, Kittanning High School; [occ.]Homemaker, Child Care; [memb.]Summit, Church; [oth. writ.]God's Word Pittsburgh, PA, Local Radio, Mother local newspaper; [pers.]This poem was written for my granddaughter Jennifer Fulmer who was born with C.P. The words comfort her. All children seem to like it by inserting their name; [a.] Butler, PA 76001.

GADE, BETH
[Pen.] Beth Gade; [b.] May 6, 1959, Denver, CO; [p.] Ray J. and Helen P. Hawkins; [ed.] AGS - Pueblo Community College; [occ.] Contract Manager in the Glass Industry; [memb.] Vocational Advisory Council, General Contractors Assn; [hon.] Dean's List; [oth. writ.] "Reflections" published in 1977, "The Luckiest Donkey", a children's play and various other poems in recent anthologies; [pers.] When a reader experiences the same emotion as the words read portray, then I have done my job; [a.] Pueblo, CO 81001

GAGNE', MARIAN F.
[b.]March 30, 1920, Hermann, Missouri; [p.]John A. Stortz, Father Meta L. Fricke-Stortz, Mother; [m.]E.N. Olsen 1938-1956 and E. R. Gagne' 1956-1974; [ch.]Jane and Edward Olsen and Gina Gagne'; [ed.]Graduated from L.A. Washington H.S., Studied Business Law and Real Estate Principles, Bellevue, WA (2 yrs.); [occ.]Presently retired, once in Real Estate, Electronics and Cosmetology; [memb.]N.R.A., National Association of Chiefs of Police, Crime Task Force, Life Member Republican Presidential Task Force; [hon.]Freedom Fighter Award N.IC, Golden Poet Award 1991, also 1992 Congressional Certificate of Merit 1992; [oth. writ.]"The Godfather" published in American Poetry Anthology 1984, "From My Childhood" and "Byzantium" World of Poetry 1992, "At Paul Lass Wells Piano Bar" National Library of Poetry. "Of Time and Space" 1993 NLP.; [pers.]From my early years when I first learned to read I have loved poetry. It is a kind of magic that can turn back time or even carry us into the future; [a.] Palo Alto, California 94306-3849.

GAGNON, CHRISTIE
[Pen.] Quills; [b.] May 6, 1977, Manchester, New Hampshire; [p.] Roland and Jocelyne Gagnon; [ed.] Colonial High; [occ.] Student; [memb.] National Beta Club, Pres. National French Honor Society, Junior Class Cabinet, Girl Scouts of America Colonial Academic Honors Program; [hon.] Girl Scouts Silver Award, Outstanding French Student, Outstanding Art Student, Honor Roll; [oth. writ.] Poems published in Distinguished Poets of America, and In a Different Light, and many others not yet published; [a.] Orlando, FL 32825

GALLAHAN, EYDI
[b.]July 2, 1948, Clarksville, TN; [m.]Henry M. Gallahan, August 3, 1990; [ch.]Erica, Edward, Echelle, and Roger Rookstool; [occ.]Director of Marketing with Distribution Concepts, Entrepreneur, Full time wife and mother; [memb.]International Woman's Writing guild, American Red Cross, International Society of Poets, ADA member; [hon.]"Editor's Choice Award" from National Library of Poetry, "Special Breed of Woman" Award from 5th Special Forces, Guest appearances on several television stations and several newspaper articles, book signing at Bookland Bookstore, recognition from Parchment Press, The Stockroom, Can's Books.; [oth. writ.]It's Just Me, Erica!, poetry book, published 1992. Several poems published in local newspapers. Also published in local newspapers. Also publication in A Break In The Clouds and Whispers In The Wind.; [pers.]There is an emptiness that I was challenged to fulfill. Poetry is the medicine I choose to fulfill it with.; [a.] Oak Drove, KY 42262.

GANGE, CLARA M.
[b.]December 6, 1928, Jamestown, NY; [p.]Hazel and John Patton; [m.]Dennis Gange, February 22, 1964; [ch.]none; [ed.]High School 2 years of college; [occ.]now housewife, but worked as Price and Figure Clerk and served in U.S.M.C. Marine's, [memb.]American Legion, VFW, Eagles; [hon.]Americanism Award honored by President's Reagan and Bus for my program. Also, a medal from American Legion.; [oth. writ.]Hi Dad, Stars and Stripes Forever, Silence Is Beauty, Award of Honor; [pers.]Dedicated to my Nation and the Flag which represents her and may she always be there flying high for all to see and hope that my work for her will not be forgotten! God Bless; [a.] Bremerton, Washington.

GARATE, PATRICIA P.
[Pen.]Pat Garate, Grandma Pat; [b.]March 8, 1930, Klamath Fall, Oregon; [p.]Delbert D. McKee, Gertrue M. Seyferth McKee; [m.]Roy R. Garate, February 28, 1958; [ch.]Aaron; Delberta; Fredrica; Kit; Margene; Cindy; Glen; Jackie; [ed.]Modoc High, Alturas, CA; Lassen College, Susanville, CA; Various correspondence courses: Cartooning; Bookkeeping; Auto Mechanics (self preservation); [occ.]Truck driver for 17 years; have been Motel Maid; Waitress; ranch hand; wife; mother; [memb.]LDS Church; National Library of Poetry; World of Poetry (now defunct); International Society of Poets; American; Sparrowgrass; Watermark Press; American Poetry Assn.; Western Folklife Center; Sparrowgrass; Wa-

termark Press; Mile-Hi; Golden Poet Award (several years). Won trip to Sweden with high school Essay Contest.; [oth. writ.]Children's stories for 31 grandchildren, 3 gr. grand children. Cowboy Poetry; Article for Colliers and Saturday Evening Post (many years ago). Poems published in Trucker's, USA Golden Treasury of Great Poems and more.; [pers.]Raised on a ranch, I was influenced by cowboys and westerns. Mom was a romantic, as are all cowboys and their wives.; [a.] Beowawe (pronounced Bee-o-wa-wee. It is an Indian word for "Bare Behind"), Nevada 89821.

GARCIA, RUBEN D.
[b.] September 17, 1945, Panama City, Panama; [p.] Berzalia Rodriguez and Ceferino Garcia; [m.] Carmen I. Garcia, September 25, 1992; [ch.] Stephanie N. Garcia and Jennifer M. Garcia; [ed.] Masters Degree; [occ.] Chief Training Division Professor, Methodist College; [memb.] American Personnel and Guidance Association, National Board for Certified Counselors; [hon.] Outstanding Poetry Award by the National Library of Poetry 1993; [oth. writ.] Currently writing two novels "God's Chosen Ones" (under edition) "A Grand and Divine Commandment" (writing) "Quiet Moments" and "Thoughts for Unforgetable Moments" copulation of poems to publish some day; [pers.] A humble writer of human emotions. I'll pass away on noticed. But my thoughts of fragile passions will endure until times end. Man to realize, he's still God's greatest creations; [a.] Fayetteville, NC 28306

GARDNER, JOANNA G.
[b.]September 4, 1935, Washington, D.C.; [p.]Rozelle and William Beitelo; [m.]Robert D. Gardner, July 8, 1970; [ch.]Colleen, Iris and Lola Irene; [ed.]High School Saint Euphrasia, Georgetown University; [occ.]Was a Registered Nurse; [memb.]V.A. Association for Hosp. Vets. and paralyzed vets.; [hon.]Poetry and Penmanship, The Star of Loyalty, Award from Paralyzed Vets.; [oth.writ.]Poems published in World of Poetry Book, also in newspaper.; [pers.]I strive to put on paper, what sometimes I cannot say what my heart really feels. On paper it is very genuine and sincere; [a.] Fort Worth, TX 76124.

GATCHELL, FELICITY
[b.] May 30, 1943, Herne-Bay, Kent England; [p.] George and Joan Allen; [m.] Paul Robert Gatchell, June 1973; [ch.] Valerie Joan, David George; [ed.] Nurses Training, Radcliffe Infirmary, Oxford England; [occ.] R.N; [oth. writ.] Many letters and poems written to leaders of the world and locally; [pers.] As a volunteer RN with the American Red Cross disaster team, and often out on assignment, I write poems as a way of unwinding from the high stress level so often faced with; [a.] Birmingham, AL 35226

GAYLE, NANCY ANN NELSON
[Pen.]N. Nelson Gayle; [b.]November 25, 1938; [p.]Mr. and Mrs. W.T. "Dub" Nelson; [m.]Judge James Ray Gayle, III, May 26, 1963; [ch.]Shannon Lea Gayle Sebesta, James Ray Gayle, IV; [occ.]Artist; [hon.]Art (Oil Paintings) Ribbon Competitions, President Reagan was given a large painting (lifesize of three horse heads which was hung in the White House, later taken to his presidential library (1983). Golden & Silver Poet Certificates, Award of Merit; [pers.]Painting is the music of my soul...the poetry becomes the lyrics. The execution of each is paramount. The art must stir my emotions, and it must please me. If it so effects another, my existence is justified; [a.] Angleton, TX 77515.

GEFFNER, HOWARD K.
[b.] May 24, 1959; [p.] Elita and Joseph Geffer; [occ.] Executive Director for People with Disabilities.

GELBACH, MARTHA HARVEY
[Pen.]February 21, 1913, Hagerstown, MD; [p.]George Gelbach and Carolyne Racker (Knode) Gelbach Schlagel; [ed.]Student, Columbia U. 1943-45, U. ILL, Chgo., 1945-46, B.S., Seton Hall U., 1950; [occ.]Reporter Herald-Mall Pub. Co., Hagerstown, MD, 1929-33, rep. genealogist Flagstone of Chester, N.J., 1933-83; Sr. Pres.; [memb.]Children of the Am. Revolution, Ledgewood, N.J. 1950; author, genealogist, poet, Brigade Hill Pub., Flemington, NJ, 1983-89, author, genealogist Penwell. Quincy PA., 1989, Author, Prayers of the Anwell Valley, 1987; [hon.]American Poetry Anthology 1989. Best New Poets of 1989, Echoes of the Valley, 1992. Contbr. articles to newspapers. Recipient Meritorious Svc. award Fed. Security Adminstrn., Washington, 1946. Eastern USA News Reporting award NJ, DAR. 1977, Spl. Collections award Raritan Valley Community Coll., 1990 Prayers Hist. Moments award New Brunswick Presbyn. Award. 1990, named Poet of Yr. Am. Poetry Assn., 1989. Mem. NRA, DAR (registrar 1937, NJ Heritage Commn. award 1976) Am. Inst. Parliamentarians, Genealogical Soc., N.J., Hunterdon County Hist. Soc., Nat. Soc., U.S. Daus of 1812 (registered 1936, regent 1980-83), Nat. Soc. Children Am. Revolution (Sr. Pres 1983-88), International Soc. Poets. Republican, Episcopalian Clubs; Spring Brook, Chester Gun. Avocations: horticulture, mountain schs. of Appalachia, bible study.; [pers.]Today is the future. Begin by praising the Lord with gladness, courageously research life's handbook, the Bible to understand the journey. Cheerfully obey the laws of God and man. Give, serve, and do freely with might, heart, mind, and spirit. (Well done my servant.)

GHUPTA-WILLIAMS, NYOKA BEVERLY
[b.] November 27, 1960, Oakland, CA; [p.] Jessie James Williams and Augusta Audry Austin-Williams. I am one of three sisters: James Etter Williams-Hunter, Theresa Smith and Donna Smith-Marion. I have two nieces Danica Dorraine Hunter - 18 yrs and Ariana Terez Tillman - 4 yrs . I raised a baby girl, Faith Branch as my very own from three days old to 8 yrs old. I desire all my new friends to know I don't at present or will I ever take this honor lightly. I'm deeply greatful and indeed honored that you would acknowledge any correspondence or poems from me. Until Now, the only wonderful and gratifying thing I've accomplished is living itself being an ADD child with learning disabilities that were not addressed in my childhood and now being an ADD adult dealing with a chemical imbalance of the brain not to mention ten years as a test study for a rare skin disorder at University of California Medical Center San Francisco, CA. I have had my share of challenges in life. Until now I have never felt the feeling of such grandure and achievement, thanks to God, the International Society of Poets and three wonderful sensitive teachers I had in 1992. I've been able to experience a large portion of happiness in this life others have talked about. I want to say a special thank you to Jim Turner my self esteem and English teacher for his faith in me. He open a door and avenue in my life I thought would be closed to me forever my horizons are broaden and I'm a better person because of it. I hope this experience will be a positive encouragement for so many other invisible people that have learning disabilities; [a.] Oakland, CA

GIBBENS, RUBY
[b.] October 12, 1923, N.C.; [p.] Eleanor, Benjamin; [m.] deceased (Dec, 1952); [ch.] two; [ed.] High School, Hair Dresser; [occ.] Hair Dresser; [memb.] Life Study Fellowship; [hon.] Typewriting, general housekeeping; [oth. writ.] My autobiography; [pers.] Of my grief, I do not need publicity; [a.] Brooklyn, NY

GILCRIST, PENNY JANUARA OLIVER
[b.] November 10, 1962, Front Royal, VA; [p.] Virginia Marie Matthews-Oliver and Adeleno Franklin Oliver, Sr; [ch.] Takesha Cheri Gilcrist, Keith William Gilcrist, Jr and Jared Tylor C.-Gilcrist; [ed.] William Penn High aka Harrisburg High, Harrisburg, PA; [occ.] Customer Service, Sales Correspondent for AMP Incorporated, HBG, PA; [memb.] Lingo Memorial COGIC and sing with the Mass Choir in HBG, PA also American Heart Association; [hon.] 1st honors in Harrisburg High; [oth. writ.] Several poems published by World of Poetry and received Golden Award throphys and certificates and several Silver Awards. A copy of my poem publish in Logistically Speaking a newspaper for AMP inc; [pers.] I strive to reflect the goodness of mankind in my writing. I have been greatly influenced by God, Friends, Family and early romantic poets whom touched my heart greatly. Most of my poems are based on feelings and true stories; [a.] Harrisburg, PA 17110

GILLEY, KAREN S.
[Pen.]Gilligan's Island; [b.]April 22, 1949, Cook County, Chicago; [p.]Joan Amy Pearson Gilley and Philip F. M. Gilley, Jr.; [ed.]Have had 12 yrs. of school including 2 yrs. Jr. College where I was a Teachers Aide.; [occ.]Part-Time Dishwasher and Poet on my way to a teaching job.; [memb.]I belong to the NAR and a Diabetes Association along with Central Friends of Retarded; [hon.]I've received honorable mention an International Poet of Merit, etc.; [oth. writ.]I've got 4 books that I plan on doing over the winter. Two are poetry, one is on the Restaurant life and rewrite my auto-biography as well as send into magazine.; [pers.]Never be afraid to follow your heart. If you like doing something like poetry pursue it, but never give up or make the wrong decision.; [a.] Leominster, Mass.

GILMORE, MABEL D.
[b.]October 12, 1909, Hundred, WV; [p.]Harry B. Mayne and Aliberta Rose Mayne; [m.]Delbert E. Gilmore (deceased 1975) March 31, 1989; [ch.]Adopted Daughter - Chloe Ann Jester; [ed.]Elementary and High School, Hundred, WV, graduated 1927; West Virginia University, Morgantown, WV, AB, 1931; Geo. Peabody College for Teachers, Nashville, TN, MA, 1938; Post Graduate Work: West Virginia University; Morris Harvey College and mason School of Fine Arts and Music (now Charleston University, Charleston, WV); [occ.]Taught in secondary education schools for 36 years until retirement from Magnolia High School, New Martinsville, WV; [memb.]County, state and

national teacher's organizations; Phi Epsilon Phi (honorary botany); Delta Kappa Gamma and Alpha Delta Kappa (international honoraries for women educators); West Virginia Garden Club, Inc. (held committee chairmanships); Trillium Garden Club (local); Wheeling Garden Center, Inc., Wheeling, WV; Friends of Library and Order of Eastern Star, New Martinsville, WV; West virginia Writers, Inc., (state office); First Christian Church (Disciples of Christ) (offices).; [hon.]West Virginia Biology Teacher of the Year 1973; several awards in poetry and garden club contests.; [oth. writ.]Poetic Potpourri (a volume of original poems) 1983; theme poem from this volume, Poetic Potpourri and Master Artist in Poetic Voices of America (1987, 1988); In Due Time and Just as Predicted in 1989 and 1990 editions of Treasured Poems of America; Always, With Love (dedicated to my husband who died in 1975) in Great American Poetry Anthology (1988); [pers.]Writing and reading my originals and conducting workshops in therapeutic as well as genuine joy; [a.] New martinsville, WV 26155.

GINGRICH, MARIE E.
[b.]October 2, 1916, Portland, Oregon; [p.]George and Bessie Comontos; [p.]Harold R. Gingrich, July 18, 1943; [ch.]Jeanne Carol, Linda Kay, Joyce Beth, Beth Lee; [ed.]Elementary, and High School; [occ.]Homemaker; [memb.]United Methodist Church, United Methodist Women, Helpmates Volunteer, Titonka Women's Club; [hon.]Golden Poet Award; [oth. writ.]Several Poems published, shower programs (for Brides to be); [pers.]I believe in being appreciative of my family and friends and using my poetry to express my feelings in these matters. Edgar Guest and Shakespeare are my particular favorites; [a.] Titonka, Iowa 50480.

GLASS, MEL
[b.]July 9, 1923, Youngstown, OH; [p.]Mr. & Mrs. James Flint; [ed.]High School, College; [occ.]Writer; [hon.]Seven Awards, New Voices American Poetry; [oth. writ.]Wrote Filler for magazine, article for weekly paper, lyrics for record for Nashville; [pers.]I like to write about real people; [a.] Struthers, Ohio 44471.

GLINBIZZI, JACALYN
[b.]February 26, 1970, Passaic, NJ; [p.]Albert and Barbara Glinbizzi; [m.]Anton Konrad, June 6, 1993; [ed.]Butler High School, Montclair State College, BA in Psychology; [occ.]Full-time student presently seeking masters in Psychology; [memb.]Volunteer on a Crisis Hotline; [hon.]Honorable mention in high school poetry contests, Dean's List; [oth. writ.]Poems published by The National Library of Poetry's, A Question of Balance and Distinguished Poets of America; [pers.]Special thanks to my former high school teacher, Danilie Howe, and to my husband, Anton Knorad, who forever serve as sources of inspiration in my life; [a.] Hawthorne, NJ 07506

GOENS, NATALIE L.
[b.] August 8, 1959, Santa Ana, CA; [p.] Richard Morton Pierce and Harriet Mable Hayden; [ch.] Serena Lynn Heck and Justin Douglas Goens; [ed.] Hayward High School, Orange Coast College, Professional Escrow Training (cert. course), Hairmasters Beauty College; [occ.] Certified Reflexologist and Pedicure Specialist; [memb.] National Honor Society, DAR; [hon.] Editor's Choice Award for my poem "Love Is" published by the National Library of Poetry "A Break In The Clouds"; [oth. writ.] Various poems and song lyrics over the years and had my first publication through the National Library of Poetry "A Break In The Clouds" entitled "Love Is"; [pers.] I like to make people laugh and knowing how many people are in the same depressed economical situation as me, I hope my poem brings some laughter into their lives when they read my poem. Then I will feel I am a successful poet; [a.] Riverside, CA 92506

GOLDSTEIN, MITCHELL
[Pen.]Raistlin Ardais; [b.]November, 1971, New Haven, CT; [ed.]Hamden High School, Boston University, B.A. Cum Laude, University of Richmond Law School; [memb.]Society for Creative Anachronism; [hon.]Cum Laude, Dean's list, Omicron Delta Epsilon; [oth. writ.]Several articles in school papers; Emotionless, USA in Our World's Most Treasured Poems; several unpublished poems; [pers.]The greatest risk in life is not taking a risk at all, the worst part of it is you'll always lose. My poetry reflects upon that risk in my lie. It provides the greatest inspiration.; [a.] Hamden, CT 06514.

GOODHUE, JEAN W.
[b.]June 3, 1927, Cedar Creek Township, N. Dak.; [p.]Frederick and Alma Marie Schaar; [m.]Norman E. Goodhue, February 25, 1945; [ch.]Adrian Leigh Goodhue, Terrill Norrine Goodhue Fuhrman-Likes, Lynne M. Goodhue Gilge Continuous, a source of amazement and delight; [occ.]Living as a "Child of God"; [memb.]Church, clubs, etc.; [hon.]Golden Poet's Award, Award for Poetic Achievement, Division Queen in T.O.P.S. Inc., Designer to Artist for Book "Prairie Tails." [oth. writ.]Old West of Dakota, Threats of Indian Raids, 1986, Lure Of The West, Mail Order Brides, Murder On Cedar Creek, Death Of Hash, Knife Cowboy, Typical Homesteader, The Medica and Christmas Didn't Come.; [pers.]"In Her Heart" is dedicated with love to Eddie and Fern Koppinger who lost their beloved daughter.

GORMAN, SHIRLEY ANNE, R.A.
[b.] March 9, 1940, Cave Springs, Missouri; [p.] Herbert Gorman and Frances Lucille (Grant) Gorman; [ed.] Central High School 1958, Mid-America Business College 1973; [occ.] Registered Author/Poet Volunteer Teacher (music and writing); [memb.] Missouri Mental Health Consumer Network, American Bell Association Int. Inc., National Authors Registry; [hon.] Accomplishment of Merit, two Honorable Mention, Editor's Choice Award, Award of Merit, President's Award for Literary Excellence; [oth. writ.] Children's book entitled "Fairy Kittens" and "Tammy's Adventures." Numerous poems, essays and short stories. 100 poems, one essay, and four short stories have been published; [pers.] A born-again Christian, my writings reflect my faith in Jesus Christ. I just recently became a member of the International Society of Authors and Artists. Sing in my church choir.; [a.] Springfield, Missouri 65803

GRACE, RUTH C.
[b.]June 26, 1916, Philadelphia; [p.]IDA and Thomas Calhoun, one sister: Louise C. Harris (all deceased); [m.]Thomas Bayard Grace, Jr., April 15, 1939; [ch.]One Daughter, Ruth L. LeSage, Grandchildren: David, William, Catherine, LeSage; [ed.]B.S. M.ED, Education Specialist from Wayne State University, Detroit M.; [occ.]Retired Teacher, Bible Teacher, Speaker, WRiter; [memb.]Methodist Church, 700 Club, MARSP, NEA-R, AARP, Support Center for Law and Justice, Humane Societies Bible Societies, Peale Center for Christian Living; [hon.]Merit and Golden Poet Awards from World of Poetry. Plaque and invitation for World of Poetry's 1992 ED. of Who's Who In Poetry, Also in Best Poems of the 90's By National Library of Poetry. Also in coming Outstanding Poets of 1994 by invitation of National Library of Poetry; [oth. writ.]Booklet "Ponderings" a (42 original, inspiration poems) several poems in local papers and church bulletin, many anthologies including American Poetry, World of Poetry and National Library of Poetry, also magazine articles.; [pers.]I believe the chief end of man is to glorify God and enjoy him forever. My poems reflect my personal faith and my desire to inspire and reach.; [a.] Alpena, MI 49707-3807.

GRADY, CHARLES E.
[b.] March 13, 1939, Englewood, TN; [p.] Gilbert Grady and Lora Phillips Grady; [m.] Widowed; [ch.] Delaine, Connie, Carolyn, Joni, Annette, Patricia; [ed.] Southern States Academy, Southern College [occ.] Disabled; [hon.] "I have just started to release my writings for publication"; [oth. writ.] "Glory" Our World's Favorite Poems, "The 23rd Lamentation", "Angelheart", "Twice", "King Of The Sand", Etc.; [pers.] "The grain of truth in every paranoid thought if left in place may someday become a pearl of wisdom"; [a.] Cleveland, TN 37323

GRAMOLINI, DENTE
[b.]January 28, 1924, Brighton, MA; [p.]Erminia and Julius Gramolini (deceased); [ed.]High School Graduate; [occ.]Draftsman, Architectural Struct. Steel, Conc. & Civil; [hon.]Editors Choice Award for Outstanding Achievement in Poetry by the National Library of Poetry; [pers.]Composing and writing poetry is a way of giving and is also intellectually, emotionally and spiritually, rewarding; [a.] Billerica, MA 01822

GRANDCHAMP, JULIANN M.
[Pen.]Jeanne-Marie Gautier; [b.]Manhattan Island, NYC, NY; [p.]Deceased; [m.]September 14, 1932 (Deceased); [ch.]Julie G. Neal and Robert Jean Grandchamp; [ed.]B.A. MS-Education, Studied at Sorbonne, Paris, France; [occ.]Teacher, Published Writer; [memb.]National League of American Pen Women, Clearwater FL, branch; [hon.]Many for Poetry and Young Adult Novels; [oth. writ.]Columnist for Times of Ti, Ticonderoga, NY; [pers.]Education-the impetus to knowledge; [a.] St. Petersburg, FL

GRAVES, JACQUELINE C.
[b.]March 27, 1948, Washington, D.C.; [p.]Charles W. Finne; [m.]Divorced; [ch.]Kimberly Bynum, Levi Graves Jr.; [ed.]Springarn Senior High University of the District of Columbia; [occ.]Day Car Teacher; [memb.]Hughes Memorial Methodist Church; [hon.]Dean's List Departmental Honors Award in Education Technology; [oth. writ.]Award of Merit from Creative Enterprises, Certificate of Poetic Achievements, and have been published in several books of poetry.; [pers.]May the pen dictate from my heart, which my tongue fails to utter.; [a.] Washington, D.C. 20019.

GRAYSON, TAMARRA MICHELLE
[Pen.] T. Michelle Grayson; [b.] March 13, 1976, San Bernardino, CA; [p.] Jerome, and Linda Grayson;

[m.] single; [ed.] Senior in High School, Home Schooling, Newport/Pacific High School; [occ.] Singer/Songwriter; [memb.] Various collectable companies; [hon.] Editors Choice Award from the National Library of Poetry 1993; [oth. writ.] "A Million More" in Wing In the Night Sky, "When Tears Fill Up Your Eyes in In The Desert Sun, unpublished poems and 100's of songs, and stories; [pers.] Poets use their talents to let their feelings out! That's what I did with this poem. The pain I felt when my sister died will be with me always. But I'm stronger now.

GREEN, FORDYCE FRANK
[Pen.]Fordyce Green; [b.]June 28, 1922, Genesee, PA; [p.]Erville Green and Anna Green; [m.]Helen Green, January 7, 1979; [ed.]High School; [occ.]Farming; [memb.]Grange; [hon.]Award of Merit Certificate My Best Friend. Those Good Old Day's. The Shuttle Challenger Tragedy, Golden Poet 1990, 1991, 1992; [oth. writ.]When we come to the end of the road. God gave his only son. Singers and Song's They Sing. Rose's; [pers.]I mention "My dear saviors name in most of my poem's I write. For "Jesus Christ is the one that made me see the light.; [a.] Genesee, PA.

GREENBERG, AUDREY B.
[Pen.] Audrey Bickart; [b.] September 30, 1906, New Orleans, LA; [p.] Phillip Rosenberg and Florence; [m.] Myron H. Bickart, September 17, 1925; [ch.] Deonne Claire; [ed.] Henry Wallen, Alexandria, LA, Cooper-Union Univ. NY; [occ.] Artist; [memb.] American Cancer Soc. Red Cross, Ect.; [hon.] Newspapers, poetry 15 awards, Honorable Mention; [oth. writ.] "Good Morning With A Smith" My PuP, Golden Poet Award 91-92, Mardi Gras, etc. now is the time; [pers.] The love of family and to try to make each day a happy once.

GREENBERG, SANDRA
[Pen.]S. J. Monroe; [b.]December, 12, 1943, Queens, NY; [p.]Frances and Francis Larmon (No Kidding); [m.]Harold Greenberg, October 29, 1985; [ch.]Roy Jr., Stephen Paul and Brooke-Ellen; [ed.]University of Rochester Graduate of 83; [occ.]Certified Nurses Asst. and Entrepreneur; [memb.]Poets Society and Scrabble, Club and Poets of America; [hon.]Outstanding Poet 1992, Dean's List 1979 thru 1983; [oth. writ.]Two pieces published in college paper 1980; [pers.]To reflect god's Love is my greatest desire to serve him with my eyes, arms and body is my life's work and pleasure; [a.] Pittsford, NY 14534.

GREGER, TERRY LEE
[Pen.]Langenkama or Tleeco; [b.]August 4, 1947, Bassett, Nebraska; [p.]Frank and Kay Greger; [ch.]Four beautiful daughters, Tracey Lynn, Lisa Jo, Kathleen Marge, Ginger Leigh; [occ.]A livestock consultant; [memb.]D.A.R.E. Sponsor, N.R.A. Charter member, Master of Chi Ta; [hon.]Golden Poet 88-92, Who's Who in Poetry 90, 91, 92; [oth. writ.]Love feud, True Love, Her Decision Alone, Death, Mary, Cocaine Run, I'm a Lover, God and Eve, Easter, Thanksgiving, Christmas; [pers.]Those who look for opportunity rather than wait for opportunity fine more success in their lives; [a.] Central City, NE 68826.

GREGERSON, JENNIFER
[Pen.] Evilyn; [b.]June 3, 1978, Seattle, Washington; [p.] William Gregerson and Jill Gregerson; [ed.] Olympic View Junior High, Kamiak High School; [occ.] Student; [memb.] Honor Society, natural Helpers, Kamiak High School Swim Team and Track Team; [hon.] Ruth Frack Poetry and Prose Awards, 1st place in District Spelling Bee, yearbook editor for junior high, honored for community service; [oth. writ.] A new short story (Dot) published with young authors one novel and several short stories and poems, one poem published "The World Turns On"; [pers.] I only write what I'm felling at the time; [a.] Mukilteo, WA 98275

GREGORY, EVELYN B.
[Pen.]Sugar; [b.]August 8, 1954, Battle Creek, Michigan; [p.]Ina Rose Simmons; [m.]Timothy Bay Gregory Sr., August 12, 1989; [ch.]Robert, Nicole, Timothy, Tramaine, Grand kids, Marcell, Robert Jr., Davontay, Ravontay; [ed.]9th GED, College (12 credit hours); [occ.]Senior Aide - Headstart Preschoolers; [oth. writ.]Publication in the National Library, I Have a Dream; [a.] Parkway Dr. W.

GRIBBLE, MARY
[b.]November 10, 1928; [m.]Donald Gribble,, February 14, 1970; [ed.]Incarnate Word College, Draugh's Business College; [occ.]Secretary Office Bldg. Mgr., Appraiser for S & L, Real Estate Broker; [hon.]1990 Publisher's Choice Watermark, Poet Laureate, Iliad Press, 1992 Golden Poet (3) World of Poetry, Sound of Poetry Recognition, National Library of Poetry, (2), Hon. Mention, Iliad Press, 1993 National Author's Registry and Cader Publishing, President's Award for Literary Excellence in ongoing Poet of the Year Contest, (2), Hon. Mention Longfellow Contest, Cadet Publishing, Ltd. As of 7/93 Writer's Digest Annual Contest, in the 100 finalist, Hon. Men. Gunvor Skogsholm, Chapbook.; [oth. writ.]Thirty-five poems published in anthologies, since 1990); [pers.]I believe poetry does its humble bit in the battle against our country's decline in patience and gentleness, manners and humaneness.; [a.] San Marino, CA 91108.

GRINKLEY, ETHEL MAE KELLY
[Pen.] Heartlight; [b.] July 23, 1952, Darlington, SC; [p.] The Late Richard & Annie Mae Kelly; [m.] (Deceased) Steve Grinkley; [ch.] Joey Kareem Grinkley and Stephen Isaiah Grinkley; [ed.] B.A. English J.C., Smith Univ., Charlotte NC, M.ED Education (Guidance) Francis Marion University, St. John's High School; [occ.] Parent Activities Coordinator, Darlington Co., Schools; [memb.] Phi Delta Kappan, NAACP, Pee Dee, IRA, NCTICIP, Zeta Phi Beta, Sorority, Friendship Baptist Church; [hon.] Who's Who Among Students in American Universities and College; Outstanding Young Woman in America; [oth. writ.] Published in Windows on the World; Distinguished Poets of America; The Best Poems of the 90's. Treasured Poems of America Summer 1994 Ed.; [pers.] Poetry reflect the beauty and sadness of life. My poetry expresses what I have experienced and what those around me have experienced. It is also an expression of my relationship with God; [a.] Darlington, SC 29532

GRUETTER, DANA
[b.]January 5, 1972, Chattanooga, Tennessee; [p.]Frank and Dianne Gruetter; [m.](Fiance) Danny Daugherty, May 14, 1994; [ed.]Tennessee Wesleyan College; [occ.]Customer Service Representative; [memb.]National Dean's List; [hon.]Dean's List; [oth. writ.]Poetic Voices of America, Where Dreams Begin; [pers.]Poetry is an art form that is easily misunderstood; [a.] Chattanooga, Tennessee 37407

GUADAGNINO, ANTHONY MICHAEL
[b.]August 15, 1971, New Jersey; [p.]Michael & Annette Guadagnino; [ed.]B.A., English, holding a concentration in Creative Writing, Montclair State College (9/89-5/93); [memb.]Phi Alpha Delta, Law Fraternity; [oth. writ.]Publications in school newspapers and Our World's Most Treasured Poems 1991.; [pers.]Transform your worst situation to benefit your future. I speak from experience.

GUENTHER, EDRIS L.
[b.] September 12, 1907, Texmo, OK; [p.] Kenneth and Laura Wilson; [m.] Paul Guenther, December 23, 1929; [ch.] Arno and Carole Guenther; [ed.] 1 yr college and business college; [occ.] HW; [memb.] World of Poetry, Artist Assn; [hon.] 4 awards - 1 World of Poetry - Washington, D.C., 1 - New York, NY, 1 San Francisco, CA; [oth. writ.] Poems - "Gods More", "Thoughts", "Mama", "To Papa", "Pansies", "Pepe", Sunflowers", "Love Your Life", "A Dream", "Universal Brother", Just Wondering", "Oh, Katie"; [pers.] I strive to write something of value - to be helpful in a meto physical sense; [a.] Port Hueneme, CA 93041

GUIRAL, SHIELA
[Pen.]Shiel; [b.]January 24, 1924, Lahore (Pre-Partition); [p.]Mr. Hukam Chand Bhasin and Mrs. Kartar Devi Bhasin; [m.]I. K. Guiral, May 26, 1945; [ch.]Naresh (son), and Vishal (son); [ed.]M.A. (Econ.) Dip. Journalism, Dip. Montessori; [occ.]Writer, Social Worker, Educationalist; [memb.]Pen Author's Guild, Lakhika Sangh (Women Writer's) and various educational organizations; [hon.]D. LTT. Academy of Art & Culture 1992, Nirala Award (Hindi Poetry) 1989, Golden Poet Award 1989, Mahila Shrimoni Award 1990, Outstanding Woman 1990.; [oth. writ.]Five poetry books Hindi. Two in English 2 in Puntari, One in English and one in Hindi (poetry). Many books to children, adults and writings in newspapers and journals; [pers.]Work is highest form of devotion and nothing can be more fruitful than self-expression; [a.] New Delhi, India 110065.

GUMAN, PAULINE TATIANA MIZOK
[b.] February 15, 1934, Jermyn, PA; [p.] Anna Chup Mizok, Michael Mizok, Sr [m.] Joseph Guman, Jr April 8, 1953; [ch.] Joseph III, Paul J. Judy Guman McCabe; [ed.] Jermyn High School Class of 1952; [occ.] Homemaker - sewing machine operator; [memb.] Mid-Valley Sr Activity Club, Over Fifty Club of Jessup, PA, AARP, WIBC; [hon.] 4 grandchildren: Brandon & Justin Guman and James and Jonathan McCabe; [oth. writ.] Lost Treasure, All This and a Meal, Too!, Blizzard of 1993; [pers.] Live life to the fullest. Choose whatever you enjoy. Enjoy whatever you choose. Life is a one way ticket, so make sure you pick it. Whatever you choose - you will never lose; [a.] Olyphant, PA 18447

HABIB M.D., EMAMI*
[Pen.]Habib-Lover; [b.]Tehran, Iran, Columbus Day, 1921; [ed.]University of Tehran Medical School, 1948, Professor Emeritus in geriatrics, Paris University Medical School, 1956; [occ.]Physician, retired, poet, professional lover; [memb.]Fellow, International Academy of Geriatrics, New York Academy of

Sciences, Lifetime, permanent member of American Medical Association; [hon.]Two golden statues of triumph for two poems, in each statue a plaque reads, "In recognition of the best poetry ever said in English!"; [oth. writ.]Poetry: Trigger Happy Ray-Gun, satiric for sending messages, American Poetry Anthology, Beautiful Ann, poetically romantic, American Poetry Anthology, Fall-Winter 1984, The Savior Is Coming, a genuine translation from Hafiz, Women Make Us Paradise, translation from Arabic, A Word About Iran-gate, political; [pers.]It is absolutely unfair to ignore my origin! In plain English, it takes a lot of guts to learn a language far from mother's tongue. It takes even more if you master that language to the point to say poetry in that tongue. But I have been even more! So much that two thousand poets of Orlando, Florida unanimously voted for me as the best poet in English Language? Can you bust? Then express yourself properly; [a.] Brooklyn, NY 11230

HADDAD, ADELE
[b.]November 18, 1928, Portage, Pennsylvania; [p.]Edward Haddad, Jamele Haddad; [m.]unmarried; [ed.]Portage High School, Pennsylvania Academy of Fine Arts, George Washington University, Grenoble Uni.; [occ.]Art teacher High School, Translator of Arabic in Federal Agency; [memb.]Poetry and Art Class Readings, Theology Discussions, Story Telling, Ten O'Clock Scholars; [hon.]I have awards, but I do not know where they are placed.; [oth. writ.]Poems in anthology for Senior essays and pen and ink illustrations for the McClendon Senior Center newsletter every month; [pers.]For years my main interest has been for universal peace, extending cultural programs among all racial groups and friendship with all nations of the world.; [a.] Washington, D.C. 20037.

HADBAVNY, BARBARA
[Pen.] "Barb"; [b.] December 8, 1960, Pittsburgh; [p.] Rosemary and Charles Coughenour; [m.] Robert Hadbavny, December 8, 1990; [ch.] Jason Allen Klacik, Michael Anthony Klacik; [ed.] Life!; [occ.] Primerica Financial Service; [hon.] Award of Merit, Love of my family; [pers.] My life and my family are my inspiration, without them none of this would be possible. Love to them all; [a.] Irwin, PA 15642

HAETELE, MARK
[Pen.] Mark H. Ferris; [b.] Modesto, CA; [p.] Jimmie D. and Joyce C. Haetele; [ed.] Two years at Consumers River College; [occ.] Student; [hon.] Dean's List; [pers.] The thing that have been, it is that which shall be, there is no new thing under the sun.; [a.] West Sacramento, CA 95691

HAHNE, JANET S.
[b.]June 9, 1943, Jersey City, New Jersey; [p.]George E. Holford and Evelyn E. Silkowitz; [m.]George W. Hahne, September 28, 1963; [ch.]George E., Susan E. Hahne and Melissa A. Kirk; [ed.]Weehawken High School; [occ.]Vice-President Communications Company; [memb.]St. Mary's Rosary-Altar Society; [oth. writ.]Poem for Melissa; [pers.]I write a poem for each of my daughters on their wedding day. It was my hope that they would read them and realize how much they mean to me.; [a.] Middleton, NJ 07748.

HALL, BERTHA
[Pen.] Bert; [b.] June 22, 1949, Shreveport, LA; [p.] Mr. & Mrs. L.B. and Annie Scott; [m.] Divorced; [ch.] Darien Dewayne, James Jr. and Angela Trevette Hall; [ed.] Linear High, Southern University, Vo-Tech, and Blalock's Professional Beauty College; [occ.] Instructor of Cosmetology owner and operator extra-ordinaire, Hair Boutique and Angele's Fashion Gallery; [memb.] Lake Bethlehem Baptist Church Choir, Shreveport Chamber of Commerce; [hon.] Poem written in the Shreveport Times and Sun local newspaper. Poem in National Library of Poetry, Dean list National Honor Society, Miss Physic and Blalocks Beauty Queen. Also won bowling championship - 1986; [oth. writ.] I Am Glad We Met My Special Friend, Unknown Friend, A Man Sent From God, What Manner of Love Can This Be, and I Am A Lost Piece of Puzzle; [pers.] Special thanks to Mr. Ken Wasmer for his encouragement. I dedicate this poem to Mrs. Delia Hamilton for 40 years plus in her music ministry at Lake Bethlehem Baptist Church and of all thank God, in a mighty way; [a.] Shreveport, LA

HALL, FLORINE HUGHES
[b.] August 6, 1928, Hanover County, VA; [p.] Alcidee and Nannie W. Hughes; [m.] Melvin R. Hall, Jr, December 31, 1951; [ch.] Cynthia and Mel, III, and Naneaster F. Hall. Grandchildren: Mel IV, Mark and Megan hall; [ed.] VUU A.B. Social Sciences, VSU - MEd. Early Childhood Education; [occ.] Living a Christian Life - blessing all mankind; [memb.] Retired Teachers Association Head-start Policy Council; [hon.] Recipient of an Early Childhood Education Fellowship and devoted (22) twenty two years in the classroom in this area. Prior to this, I worked as a child welfare worker, with children considered to be pre-delinquent. Prior to this I worked with the aged, blind and dependent children as a welfare worker; [oth. writ.] An Ode To Dads; [pers.] My poems are dedicated to the family -- all mankind. To me, they capture the vision which God has given President Clinton to bless America and all mankind; [a.] Ashland, VA 23005

HALL, JULIE
[Pen.]Julie Jarrett Hall; [b.]September 2, 1952, Elwood, Indiana; [p.]Lindell and Phyllis jarrett; [m.]Thomas F. Hall, Jr., April 6, 1974; [ch.]Amy Elizabeth, Ashley Evangelien and Linsay Lee; [ed.]Madison Grant H.S., Milligan College, East Tenn. State University; [occ.]Homemaker devoted to family, song writing and poetry; [oth. writ.]Recording of original music in album titled "Women of the Word", published poem, "They Came To Me."; [pers.]I particularly enjoy the poetry of Henry Wadsworth Longfellow and the writings of John Muir, Naturalist. The messages of my songs and poems are what I want people to remember of me after I am gone.

HAMEL, SHAWNA A.
[b.]December 19, 1972, Dearborn, MI; [p.]Dennis and Patricia Hamel; [ed.]Presently a Junior at Wayne State University in Detroit; majoring in English and German; minor in French; [occ.]Arts and entertainment Writer for "The South End" newspaper in Detroit; [memb.]Member of PETA (People for the Ethical Treatment of Animals), Children International, Downriver Tap Dance Club; [hon.]Golden Poet Award 1987, Silver Poet Award 1990, Editor's Choice Award 1993; [oth. writ.]Several poems published in National Library of Poetry anthologies and numerous book, music, theatre, move and art exhibit reviews in The South End, as well as interviews with artist and performers; [pers.]Never sell yourself short. If you've got talent, you'll make it to the top. To all those who've believed in me: Mom and Dad, Jill, Barb, Laura, Beth and Joanne. Inner et toujours, and fare ye well; [a.] Southgate, MI 48195

HAMILTON, KARLEEN
[Pen.] Karleen Hamilton-Lankford; [b.] May 18, 1956, Brawley, CA; [p.] Waymon and Maggie Hamilton; [ch.]Jonathon and Madesa Lankford; [ed.] Calipatria High School, Rio Hondo College; [occ.] Sr. Security Officer, J. Paul Getty Museum; [hon.] Golden Poet Award 1991 - Merit Awards; [oth. writ.] World Best Poets 1991 - Who's Who in Poetry - 1992.

HAMILTON, SCOTT T.
[Pen.]T.F.W,; [b.] October 19, 1971, Las Vegas, Nevada; [p.] William Harold Hamilton and Becky Jo Lamb; [m.] Single; [ch.] none; [ed.] East Bay High, Hillsborough Community College; [occ.] Cook, Longhorn Steakhouse; [oth. writ.] Several poems published in various medias; [pers.] The second that you change your way of life for someone other than yourself, is the second that you die and that someone begins living twice; [a.] Tampa, FL 33613

HAMPTON, CHARLES ROBERT
[b.]February 5, 1949, Lebanon Jct. KY; [p.]Herbert and Mary Hampton; [m.]Belinda Lyon Hampton, September 25, 1970; [ch.]Charles Robert Hampton II; [ed.]Shepherdsville High Sch. Locksmith Degree, various engineering courses; [occ.]Disabled Veteran; [memb.]DAV, 1st Calvary Div. Assoc.; [hon.]Two Bronze Stars with "V" and Oakleaf Cluster Air Medal, Vietnamese and American Army Commendation Medals; [oth. writ.]Published in "A View From Edge" and "Distinguished Poets of America. Have written many poems and copyrighted 48.; [pers.]All of my writings are from experience in Viet Nam and its effects on my life; [a.] Lou, KY 40229

HAMRICK, ALAN
[Pen.]Alan Stewart, Eddie; [b.]April 18, 1969, Haines City, FL; [p.]Carol Bradshaw; [m.]Sandra Hamrick, February 14, 1993; [ch.]Matthew, Kandis, Heather; [ed.]Kathleen High, Hillsborough Comm., Florida Southern, USF.; [occ.]Artist, The Art Palette; [memb.]Lakeland Art Guild; [pers.]Poetry, like art, illustrates the vast imagination of people, demonstrating one of the greatest forms of freedom.; [a.] Lakeland, FL 33809.

HANCOCK, BRANDIE LEIGH
[b.] July 22, 1977, Dayton, TN; [p.] Perry, Zella Hancock; Brothers: Charles, Brian; [ed.] Junior in High School, at Bledsoe County, Pikeville, TN; [memb.] Future Nurses of America; [oth. writ.] Poetry and short stories; [pers.] I have wrote several poems and have got two of them published. I look forward to my future writings; [a.] Pikeville, TN 37367

HARDEN, CONNIE
[Pen.] Connie Wayne; [b.] November 10, 1945, Tallahassee, FL; [p.] Thomas E. White and Mary Virginia Harvey White; [m.] Ronald Wayne Harden; [ed.] Crawfordville High School, Crawfordville, FL; [occ.] UC Examiner I; [memb.] Sopchoppy United Methodist Church; [oth. writ.] Poems in three other anthologies and 2 in church letters; [pers.] If anyone has a talent for writing, please use your God given

talent to the best of your knowledge; [a.] Sophchoppy, FL

HARDING, HELEN D.
[b.] January 17, 1927, Nelson, NE; [p.] Adolph and Lauretta Klawitter; [m.] James "Jim" Harding, April 9, 1943; [ch.] Jimmie Rae, Judith Kay, Roland Raymond; [ed.] Buhl High School/Idaho Ohlone College/ Calif Business College/Twin Falls, ID; [occ.] Retired - before secretary, real estate, personnel; [memb.] Varied but no longer very active; [hon.] Golden Poet Award, Honorable Mention Award (World of Poetry), [oth. writ.] Jonathan and Me, Generations, Creation; [pers.] Life is wonderful - I have been married for 50 yrs. I not only write but have been painting for 3 yrs. I have 3 children - 8 grand children and 4 great grands; [a.] Boise, ID 83709

HARDY, JULIA IRENE
[b.] August 11, 1917, Montrose, IA; [p.] Carl Alfred Peterson, Achsa Leah LaDuke; [m.] Francis W. Hardy, October 12, 1940; [ch.] Judith (Jeudi) Kay Eblin, Bruce William Hardy; [ed.] Keokuk Senior High; Western IL Univ: B.S., Education (June 13, 1965); M.S., Education (June 6, 1970); University of HI; Post Graduate Work in six countries; [occ.] Retired Reading Specialist: Tutor; [memb.] First Lutheran Church, AAL (Aid Association for Lutherans), Bread for the World, Kappa Delta Pi, Beta Sigma Phi, Delta Kappa Gamma, American Legion Auxiliary, Order of the Eastern Star, KCSE Credit Union Board, Congregational Social Ministry, International Reading Assoc, IRSPA (Iowa Retired School Personnal Assoc), and last, but not least, the International Society of Poets and the National Library of Congress; [pers.] I lived by this one throughout my life: "Like the lifting of the FOG, disillusionment, fear, and doubt may be dispelled to reveal already existing realities with blessings abundant." At this point in time, this is my personal statement: "If only by virtue of age -- My walk on earth grows ever shorter -- For I have been given -- My three score and ten. To the East, I look forward -- When I shall see the light of His face -- My aim until then -- Is to witness for Jesus through poetic embrace."; [a.] Keokuk, IA

HARLAN, MARY ANN
[b.] October 13, 1947; [p.] Wallace and Helen Olsasky; [m.] Frank W. Harlan; [ch.] Three, Bruce, Tina and Brandi; [ed.] St. Joseph Academy; [occ.] Mother and Bookkeeper; [oth. writ.] True Peace published in Break In The Clouds; [pers.] With God everything is possible, without Him life is impossible; [a.] Des Moines, Iowa

HARRIS, ANDY
[b.] February 14, 1968; [p.] Morris and Nancy Harris; [ed.] Delmare High, Delaware State University (1987-1991), Bachelor Science Degree in Gen. Ag.; [occ.] Animal Technician at Intervet Inc.; [memb.] YMCA; [oth. writ.] Had a poem in the National Library of Poetry Book Dreams; [pers.] I just write what I feel.; [a.] Delmar, DE 17940

HARRIS, CLAUDE E.
[b.] February 4, 1922, Shattuck, Oklahoma; [p.] Vermon and Edna harris; [m.] Mary Jane, May 19, 1945; [ch.] John R. and Douglass Lee; [ed.] Grade school and high school, Shattuck, creative writing, Wichita State University; [occ.] Consultant; [memb.] BMI New York, NY; [oth. writ.] Lyric writer recorded on several labels, published unknown number of poems in various publication. Owner of Douglas Records and Bellflows Publishing company; [pers.] Writing poetry is my hobby, teaching the scriptures is my love. Began Bible study at age of six. Active in Theocratic Ministry School of Jehovah's Witnesses for past 49 years; [a.] My desire is to gain everlasting life. Jo 17:3 My hope is to live forever in happiness on earth Ps 37:29

HARRIS, MONICA
[b.] May 13, 1935, Seattle, Washington; [m.] Widowed; [ch.] Five and ten grandchildren; [ed.] Aquinas Academy and UPS; [occ.] Interior Designer; [memb.] NWSID; [oth. writ.] A Question of Balance (Nat'l. Lib. of Poetry), Depressions (Iliad Press) A Place In The Sun (Creative Arts) Treasured Poems of America (Sparrowgrass Poetry); [pers.] I am forever seeking and finding the beauty in what at first appearance is the beast; [a.] Mercer Island, WA 98040

HARRISON, CECIL
[b.] January 18, 1921, Malad, Idaho; [p.] Lorenzo and Edith Harrison; [m.] Nola Howell Harrison, June 7, 1941; [ed.] One Semester College, 2 yrs Brooks Institute of Photography; [occ.] Retired; [memb.] American Legion, AARP; [hon.] Editor's Choice Award in "Where Dreams Begin", Two National Awards in Photography; [oth. writ.] "War Is Never Over" to be published in "Utahs Veterans," Oct-Nov Issue 1993, "Snowflakes" to appear in "Tears of Fire" National Library of Poetry; [pers.] Have enjoyed writing poems for 70 yrs. Enjoy taking pictures and combining them with poems, dreamer and romanticist at heart and see beauty wherever I may be; [a.] S.L.C, VT 84111

HARRISON, E. CHARLOTTE
[Pen.] Charlotte Knight Harrison; [b.] July 27, 1913, Chicago, IL; [p.] William Leslie and Cecile Dorothy Knight; [m.] Paul Dean Harrison, March 5, 1938; [ch.] David, Mary Ann and Wm. Henry Harrison; [ed.] Robinson Ill. HS, USC, Ch. Lit. Berkeley, Art Scholarship, McMurray College, Institute of Children's Lit. (Cert.); [occ.] Secretary to Pleasant Valley School Dist. Supt. Ed., Camarillo, CA 10 yrs.; [memb.] National Honor Society, Planetary Society, AARP, Green Peace Habitat for Humanity, Americus Georgia; [hon.] Nat'l. Honor Soc. Golden Poet, Life Membership PTA, SKALD (Royal Viking Line) Congregation Church; [oth. writ.] Short stories, children's stories, "Bouquet" and "Bittersweet Lament" published Easter Cantata (book/music) performed by church choir; [pers.] I believe if we are given talents we should use them and leave something of value; [a.] Camarillo, CA 93010

HARVEY, CHARLES EARL
[b.] August 20, 1940, Oceanside, CA; [p.] Thomas E. Harvey; [m.] Nancy J. Harvey, 1970; [ch.] Jennifer Lynn Michelle Ann; [ed.] Master Degree in Social Work, MSW Wayne State University, Bachelors Degree in Social Work, BSW Cum Laude University, Associates Degree, Liberal Arts, Cum Laude of Detroit; [occ.] Clinical Therapist/Rehabilitation Counselor; [memb.] Certified Social Worker, State of Michigan, National Association of Social Workers NASW, National Rehabilitation Association, National Rehabilitation Administration Association, National Rehabilitation Counseling Association; [hon.] Co-Founder, Phoenix Club University of Detroit, Golden Poet Award 1991 World of Poetry, Volunteer Award, St Joseph Hospital, Third Place Award, Combat Shooting Competition, Councilman of Hazel Park, MI 1988, Police Reserve,, Hazel Park, MI; [oth. writ.] Presently finishing 3 books; ("I have a Rhyme"), ("Don't Cry, My Child Within"), ("Sodom and Gomorrah, Tale of Two Cities"). Over 50 articles in newspapers statewide. Poems published in World of Poetry; [pers.] "Life is the best or the worst of what we give to it. Since I only have one shot at life, I shall give the best I can, care for others the best I can, and thank God for each and every day I wake"; [a.] Shelby Township, MI 48316

HASKINS, JO LOUISE
[b.] June 27, 1915, Lufkin, TX; [p.] Eula and Kenneth Hoskins; [ed.] Attended University of Texas, Stephen F. Austin College, Nacoqdoches, TX; [occ.] Retired; [hon.] Several Golden Poet Awards (World of Poetry), Several Merit Awards (American Poetry Association and National Library of Poetry. Poem on cassette tape (National Library of Poetry; [pers.] Like to write nature poems

HAUSER, BERNICE C.
[b.] November 13, 1895, Marshaltown, Iowa; [p.] John and Mary Rhoades; [m.] Floyd Jay Hauser, September 22, 1921 (Deceased); [ch.] Naomi and Marianne; [ed.] High School; [occ.] Registered Nurse, Retired at age 63; [oth. writ.] Children's stories ages up to 8 or 9.; [a.] Tallahassee, FL 32304.

HAWKINS, SARA GRAHAM
[b.] September 6, 1949, Sanford, NC; [p.] David P. Graham. Jr. & Violette Mizelle Graham; [m.] Thomas G. Hawkins, September 15, 1968; [ed.] First Colonial High School, St. Leo College; [occ.] Office Manager, Accountant, Computer Programmer; [memb.] Treas. First Colonial Bapt. Church; Treas., Delta Nu Chapter of Delta Epsilon Sigma Honor Society; [hon.] National Den's List (multiple years); [oth. writ.] Poems published in local newspaper and several anthologies; [pers.] I believe that poetry should push a button--touch the soul of a reader, and evoke emotion. Even anger is better than apathy; [a.] Norfolk, VA 23503.

HAYES, JAMES ALLEN
[Pen.] Gabby, G.A.B; [b.] August 19, 1937, Nashville, TN; [p.] Allen R. Hayes and Anna E. Hayes; [m.] Rita Lee Hayes, April 18, 1962; [ch.] Lee Allen and Lorre Gail; [ed.] East Nashville High School; [occ.] Captain, Metro Fire Dept.; [memb.] American Legion, International Association of Fire Fighters, Nashville Fire Fighters Association (Local #763); [oth. writ.] Short novel (not published); [pers.] I use writing as a hobby to fantasize and reflect on past experience; [a.] Nashville, TN 37206

HAYNES, EARNEST B.
[b.] June 21, 1957, Calhoun County, South Carolina; [p.] Emma J. Bagley and M. J. Haynes; [ed.] TAFT High School, some college at Bronx community College; [occ.] Clerical Clerk, Goldman Sachs; [hon.] Three Golden Awards for poetry writing; [oth. writ.] I have poems published in various anthologies; [pers.] I would like my poetry to be a window to new existences and ideas that would integrate with others and flourish like a flower. That we can all grow as one and shine like a rainbow; [a.] Bronx, NY 10453

HEINDEL, JENNIFER
[Pen.]Sasha; [b.]February 15, 1973, Perth Amboy, NJ; [p.]Mary Bell Heindel and Lee Heindel; [ed.]Bernards High School; [occ.]Student who is studying for an environmental science agree; [hon.]Editor's Choice award for a poem; [oth. writ.]Poems and articles published in a dormitory newsletter; [a.] Bernardsville, NJ 07924

HEISER, MARIA
[b.] May 2, 1937, Berlin; [ch.] 2 - Andrea, Robert; [ed.] High School, 2 years college, Leipzig; [occ.] Ins Clerk; [memb.] American Life League; [hon.] 1991 Golden Poet in California; [oth. writ.] Local newspaper from 1969-1977, 2 times a month poems, 1975 New Voices in Am Poetry in New York, my own paperback 1977 in spring "About People and Things", stopped writing summer 1977 - Divorced, started again 1989; [pers.] I have to write from the heart and speak to the heart of the reader. I write about people, their pain, their sorrow and their joy. Each poem is a message, if it is written with feelings and meaning then I know I have touched the readers heart, an empty poem is like an empty shell. My own favorite is Longfellow - My german Schiller; [a.] McHenry, IL

HELLER, MARY FRANCES L.
[b.]May 23, 1961, Bethlehem, Pennsylvania; [p.]Catherine A. Frabotta (mother) and Alfred L. Frabotta (father); [ch.]Linsay May Heller, 11 years old; [ed.]Freedom High School, Northampton County Community College, Allentown Business School; [occ.]Accounting Clerk; [memb.]Pennsylvania Federation of Black Powder Shooters; [hon.]Golden Poet Award 1988, Silver Poet Award 1990, Honorable Mention 1988, Magna Cum Laude Graduate; [oth. writ.]I have published about four poems in various anthologies and have had two chosen to be set to music and read by a professional reader; [pers.]My heart is the ruler of my planet and it becomes my "sword in hand" as I write poetry; [a.] Grand Junction, CO 81504

HELTON, SYLVIA
[b.] December 11, 1948, Sanger, CA; [p.] Chalmer and Sylvia I Ferguson; [m.] Harold Helton, February 7, 1988; [ch.] Step- Karen Annette, Anita Gay, Greg Edward, Timothy James; [ed.] Aymesworth Elementary, Roosevelt High, 4 C's College; [occ.] Loving Homemaker; [memb.] Parksdale First Southern Baptist Church, National Rifle Association; [oth. writ.] Several poems, children's short stories; [pers.] It is my hope that in each writing God's love shines through, and helps someone in their daily walk in their Christian Life.; [a.] Fresno, California 93722

HENDERSON, MARJORIE L.
[Pen.] Margie or Maggie; [b.] September 20, 1939, Martinsburg, PA; [p.] Georgia Grace Mowery (Price) and Tom Arnold Noffsker (Henderson); [m.] Luther H. Batts, 1958, divorced 1981; [ch.] Pamela A. Batts and Gary Batts; [ed.] Yuba College, Marysville, CA, Altoona and Roosevelt High School, Honor Student and Dean's List; [occ.] Licensed Nurse; [memb.] Martinsburg, Baptised Church of the Brethern Sacramento, Former member Capital Christian Center, Former Officer Two Cities Kennel (AKG), Club, Yuba City, CA, Wibe Bowling Association; [hon.] Honors list Roosevelt High, Yuba College; [oth. writ.] Published in local newspapers, many Golden Poet Awards, Altoona Shade Tree Commission published Kings Trees and it spread to other States; [pers.] A Non-Conformist. A Free Thinker. A stroke in Childbirth at age of 23 in a U.S. miliary Hospital 1963, still effects my, opinions and poetry. Infarct remains on the left brain. Pro-Choice Activist.

HENDON, WANDA
[b.]March 28, 1928, Oklahoma; [m.]Jesse Hendon, September 1, 1945; [ch.]Carol, Franklin and Betty; [ed.]High School; [occ.]Retired from Beckman Instruments Inc. in Porterville, CA; [hon.]From International Society of Poets this year 1993; [oth. writ.]Several poems; [pers.]I am a Christian and I love to write poetry. I am influenced most by my family, whom I love dearly; [a.] Porterville, CA 93257

HENDRIX, THOMAS BURGESS
[Pen.] Burgess Hendrix; [b.] January 19, 1965, Reno, NV; [p.] John and Georgia Burgess, Marlene and Bob (in-laws); [m.] Mourlyn, August 20, 1988; [ch.] Owner small business, Burgess Tire Repair; [memb.] The Asshold Society of Life Club; [hon.] Editor's Choice Award, 1993, Wind in the Night Sky, International Poet of Merit; [oth. writ.] "Babies of Life", Wind in the Night Sky - 1993; [pers.] To my wife who for her none of this would have ever been possible. She truly believed I had talent. I love you; [a.] San Clemente, CA 92674

HENRY, HELEN
[b.] November 6, 1923, Charlotte, NC; [p.] Monroe Sane, Frances Sane; [m.] Hazel Henry, February 16, 1943; [ch.] Sara Elaine, Rhonda Lynn; [ed.] Lancaster High; [occ.] Retired Nurses Aide; [memb.] First Baptist Church; [pers.] Hobby ancient, modern and biblical history and daily bible reading which helps me in my daily life and in my writings; [a.] Lancaster, SC

HERNANDEZ, GIL
[Pen.]The Born Again Fox; [b.]December 11, 1931, Fabans Texas; [p.]Alfred and Genoveva Hernandez; [m.]Darlene Hernandez (deceased); [ch.]Mark Hernandez (killed age 24), Anthoney, Rhea, Dovana Hernandez; [ed.]Self taught-Sophomore; [occ.]Retired, jockey, patrol judge and film analyst; [memb.]Disciple of Christ Jesus; [hon.]Golden Poet Award 1989; [oth. writ.]Before God I Married Thee; [pers.]When everything is said and done. The things that will count are, the things that you've said and done; [a.] Escalon, CA 95320

HERNANDEZ, TONIE TOMAS
[Pen.] "Cequoya" Tomaz; [b.] January 28, 1947, Los Angeles, CA; [p.] Chester Thomas, Otto Hopkins, Margaret Thomas, Beatrice Burrell; [ch.] Alicia, Edward, Polo, Franklin, Miguel - who I love dearly; [ed.] LA High and LA Valley J.C., San Diego State Univ; [occ.] Counselor Immigracion; [memb.] Save the Children Foundation, Ponce Association, Praise the Lord, Dallas, TX TBN; [oth. writ.] Adios - San Joaquin, The leaves where green, Where I use to play; [pers.] "To God We Prevail". Try to live in peace and harmony; putting prejudice, envy and greed aside; help others in need, trust in God to succeed all trials and tribulations; [a.] Santa Barbara, CA and Reedley, CA

HERNANDEZ, YOLANDA
[Pen.] Polie Hd'z; [b.] July 5, 1952, Laredo, TX; [p.] Fransisco and Margarita Hernandez; [ch.] Juan, Victor Alberto, and Duvina; [ed.] R. and T. Martin High, Laredo Junior College, Texas A & M at Loredo State, Texas A & M International Un; [occ.] Language Arts Teacher; R & T Martin High School; [memb.] NEMA, ASCD, TESOC, TCTE, LSA, mother Cahrin: Altar Society, UIL; [hon.] Dean's List, Teacher of the Month, Dedicated Teacher of the Year; [oth. writ.] I am completing a Chapbook of poems and have two short stories for future publication; [pers.] Writing, to me, is a 3D reflection (desire, determination, and dedication), of ones inner self; it is an expression of live emotions; [a.] Laredo, TX 78044

HERRERA, EUFRACINA ISABEL
[b.] August 20, 1965, Piedras Negras, Coahuila, Mexico; [p.] Maria Perez and Marcos Perez; [m.] Victor C. Herrera, November 10, 1984; [ed.] Reagan High School, Durham Business College; [occ.] Admn. Asst., Dept. of Advertising, University of Texas at Austin; [hon.] Golden Poet 1991; [oth. writ.] Poem published in Great Poems of Our Time, Poem published in Whispers in The Wind; [pers.] Victor... I dedicate this to you. I don't ever want to lose you...; [a.] Austin, TX 78723

HESTER, SARA HELEN JONES
[b.]February 9, 1926, Dublin, Georgia; [p.]Gladys Raffield Jones and David Jefferson Jones; [m.]Thomas Blackshear Hester, June 19, 1941 (Deceased); [ch.]Daryl Thomas hester Born March 25, 1957; Works at Johnson Space Center in Houston, TX; [ed.]Glenwood High School, Glenwood, Georgia, Etc.; [occ.]Scheduling Technician, Georgia Department of Transportation; [memb.]Tifton First Baptist Church, Order of Eastern Star, Garden Gate Garden Club, American Heart Association Board of Directors, Georgia Department of Transportation Engineers Association, Blanche Chapter Past Matrons and Past Patrons Club, OES, District 18 Past Matrons and Past Patrons Club, OES; [hon.]Grand Chaplain Order of Eastern Star 1974-1975; [pers.]Remembering each day that the race is not always to the swift--and that there is more to life than increasing its speed.; [a.] Tifton, Georgia 31794.

HETZEL, ALICE M.
[b.] August 12, 1950, Albuq, NM; [p.] Ella Mae Gray; [ch.] David, Brad, Tisha, Kristie, Dallas, Houston; [pers.] I wrote this poem: Dedicated to Houston: He was in a near drowning accident, He's 5 yrs old; [a.] Wichita, KS 67216

HIBBS, SUSAN ADELE
[Pen.] Crystal Jade; [b.] June 10, 1951, San Francisco, CA; [p.] Nadine Stafford, Harry Hibbs, father died, mother remarried; [m.] Gene Hodge, November 21, 1970/Bill Sweatt, April 22, 1972; [ch.] Jady Hodge, William Sweatt, Steven Sweatt, Misty McAninch; [ed.] Richmond High School, Contra Costa College, Tongue Point Job Corp.; [occ.] Electronics/Housekeeping; [memb.]International Society of Poets; [hon.] Merit Certificate Award Plaque Poem of Hate N Crime, Convention at Hilton in San Francisco; [oth. writ.] Hollywood Artists Record Company for my poem. NCA Record Company of Nashville, TN. Both want to make songs with my poems; [pers.] I wish to fulfill my dreams, to publish my poems and songs. I started when I was 16 yrs. old, was influenced by my Grandpa, who has been dead for years; [a.] Sacramento, CA 95825

8th grade teacher to write. I express my feelings in my poetry and my success; [a.] Kiel, WI 53042

KELLY JR., JAMES WILLIAM
[b.] August 24, 1962, Lansing, MI; [p.] James William Kelly, Sr, Josephine Kelly; [m.] Laura Lee Kelly, November 3, 1990; [ch.] Jamie Leigh, Nicole Re'Anne, Angel Ann, Maria Elizabeth, Amelia Mae; [occ.] Certified Surveyor; [memb.] Human Race; [oth. writ.] Poems: "My Best Friend" published by National Library of Poetry, "A Night With God" published by Quill Books, and "Adieu" published by Sparrowgrass Poetry Forum; [pers.] Make a friend, it'll make your day, but don't let your eyes stand in the way; [a.] Gladwin, MI 48624

KELLY, MAGGIE
[b.]November 27, 1936, Rosario, Argentina; [p.]Axel Kyster and Sabina Pilar Manzano; [m.]December 25, 1960 (Deceased); [ch.]Cecilia Harvey, Valerie Kelly, Denise Boicey; [ed.]University of Cambridge, Literature Courses, Orange Coast College, Business; [occ.]Administration, Court Reporting; [memb.]National Association of Court Reporters, American Society of Notaries; [hon.]Silver Poet 1989, Silver Poet 1990; [oth. writ.]Poems, Happiness, Depressed, Good Morning, One Big Question Mark; [pers.]To quote the words of the great poets, "Life is Real, life is dearest and one crowded hour of glorious life, is worth an age without a name."; [a.]Santa Ana, CA

KELSEY, LAURA K.
[b.] April 17, 1977, Lima, OH; [p.] Ken and Mary Kelsey; [ed.] 11th Grade at Ada High School; [memb.] Varsity Swim Team, Year Book Staff, Choir, Language Club; [hon.] Scholar Athlete, Interclass Competition; [oth. writ.] Several poems published in previous books out by The National Library of Poetry and in boating newsletters. I also like to write short stories; [a.] Ada, OH 45810

KEMP, ALYN E.
[b.] February 28, 1932, Pembroke, Bermuda; [p.] Julian W. Kemp, Nina M. L. Kemp; [m.] Elmina Clarrisa (deceased), June 7, 1952; [ch.] Keith Aly, David William, Elmina Elizabeth, Julian Beardsley; [ed.] Educated in Bermuda School System attained equivalent "Grade 12"; [occ.] Sales; [memb.] First Baptist Church of Goodrich Michigan; [hon.] 1990 Golden Poet Award from world of Poetry; [oth. writ.] Several poems published - planning booklet of my poems and working on book titled "The Rask"; [pers.] Started writing words for my Xmas and birthday cards. Evolved to my personal feelings and life happiness - having what I feel; [a.] Goodrich, MI

KEMP, MARJORIE EASTER
[b.]April 16, 1922, Rochester, New York; [p.]Howard H. Kemp and Ruth Brown Kemp; [ed.]Bachelor Music Degree, U of Miami, Coral Gables, Florida; [occ.]Professional Cellist; [memb.]Sigma Alpha Iota, DAR, Downtown Presbyterian Church; [hon.]Sword of Honor, Sigma Alpha Iota (for 18 years as a certified volunteer Braillist.); [oth. writ.]Ten poetry books; [pers.]Born on Easter Sunday, 1922, Avid Oil Painter. Composer 8 Anthems and miscellaneous other compositions; [a.]Rochester, NY 14619.

KENNEALLY, MARY L.
[b.]May 9, 1918; [p.]Orphan; [m.]John W. Kenneally, September 21, 1943; [ch.]Three children; [ed.]Mt. St. Mary College, Hooksaett, New Hampshire; [occ.]Housewife, Artist, WRiter, Illustrator; [memb.]Lion's Club of the Greater Westbury's, Westbury, L.I. New York; [hon.]About 20 in my lifetime; [oth. writ.]Just had Golden Wedding Anniversary, September 21, 1993; [pers.]Writing is a wonderful way to express yourself and let others know your true thoughts.; [a.]278 Jerome Ave. Carle Place, Long Island, NY 11514.

KEREK, KIM
[Pen.]Kimeo; [b.]October 9, 1965, Baton Rouge, LA; [p.]Jerome P. Kerek Sr., and Cheryl (Lebkinc) Kerek;; [ed.]High School Graduate; [occ.]Dispatcher in family owned business; [memb.]L.A. jaycees, Gonzales, St. Annes Catholic Church, Sorreno LA; [hon.]Golden Poet Award, Merit of Honor Awards, Poet Laurett of Sorreno; [pers.]In front of a crowd I am nothing, but put a pen in my hand and boy am I something!!; [a.]8314 Ruby St., Sorreno, LA 20228.

KERN, RUBY FERN
[b.] October 26, 1920, Ono, PA; [p.] Dittner and Sarah Allison; [m.] Robert L. Kern, May 25, 1940; [ch.] 3 children, 8 grandchildren, 1 great grand child; [ed.] 8th grade; [occ.] Homemaker; [oth. writ.] Poetry for family celebrations, church and community affairs. Poem for Mother's Day in Grit Magazine; [pers.] To take the ordinary and make it a challenge; [a.] Chambersburg, PA 17201

KETCHUM, PIERCE STITH
[b.] June 16, 1933, Champaign, Illinois; [p.] Gertrude S. Ketchum (dec.) and Pierce W. Ketchum (dec.); [ed.] Included 6th grade in Laredo, Texas, where I got good instruction in parts of speech; [memb.] Honorary Charter Member of International Society of Poets in 1973; [hon.] Seven Poetry Awards during 1990-1993 period without a rejection slip; [oth. writ.] Aesthetics and Other poems (self published chapbooklet), 4 poems in Matrix 17 (anthology), 1 poem in Our World's Favorite Poems, estimated 300 unsubmitted poems; [pers.] I have been influenced by the Miami Herald and Sydney Dobell of Victorian England and Mac Gregory of Florida (born India of Armenian descent?; [a.] Urbana, Illinois

KETRING, ANNA BERNICE
[Pen.]Abizinn; [b.]November 29, 1927, Louisville, KY; [m.]August 17, 1953; [ch.]Four; [ed.]Our Lady of the Woods Orphanage, graduated High School 1947; [a.]Dayton, OH 45424

KETRON, BENNIE D.
[b.]July 20, 1959, Ft. Knox, Kentucky; [p.]Bennie and Carol Ketron; [ed.]Ft. Knox High, North Hardin High, Elizabethtown Community College, Western Kentucky University; [occ.]Board Operators and Radio Announcers, Elizabeth Broadcasting Inc. (WIEL-AM 1400); [memb.]ECC Alumni, WKU Alumni; [oth. writ.]Several poems and short stories in Gyres (a college creative writing publication); [a.]Radclif, KY 40160

KHABEER, BERYL ABDULLAH
[b.]January 7, 1952, Cleveland, Ohio; [p.]Doris Thompson and Berry Thompson, SR., [m.]none; [ch.]Faheem H.A. - Khabeer; [ed.]Ohio University 2 yrs., Brandeis University, B.A. Cleveland State University Masters; [occ.]Job Search Specialist; [memb.]American. Philo. Phical. Assoc., African Studies Association; [hon.]Dean's List, Civil Rights Scholarship; [oth. writ.]Poetry published in newsletters in Ohio. Two plays produced at Cleveland Academy Theatre.; [pers.]Aside from person reflection I try to mirror the society and sse the sexism and racism in our American Society; [a.]Cleveland, Ohio 44112.

KHING, JAMES G.
[b.] April 16, 1945, China; [ed.] B.S., Class of 1970, Atlantic Union College, S. Lancaster, Massachusetts; [occ.] Medical Technologist; [oth. writ.] The stories of Angels and of Men. Ivanhoe, the poem; [pers.] God is the greatest. He owns the Earth and He rules the World. He is worthy of the highest praise for his mercy to the rebellious beings on earth; [a.] Banning, CA 92220

KIEFER, ROBERT J.
[Pen.]Bob Kiefer; [b.]December 7, 1936, Cleveland, Ohio; [p.]Paul and Beulah Kiefer; [m.]none; [ch.]Kelly Keifer and Paul Kiefer; [ed.]Monroe High, Ohio State University; [occ.]Mechanical Engineer, Financial Services Marketing; [memb.]American Society of Mechanical Engineers, Vista Grande Baptist Church; [hon.]Tau Beta Pi, Outstanding ROTC Engineering Student, Engineering Honor Award; [oth. writ.]Book of love poems. Bible chapters into verse, including song of Solomon, Rom. 12 I Cor. 13. Modernization of Elizabeth Barett Browning.; [pers.]Work hard, deal honestly and with integrity. Show love, interest and concern for everyone.; [a.]10215 Saunders Dr., San Diego, CA 92151-1313.

KILLEBREW, JOYCE L.
[b.] April 20, 1945, Harlem, NY; [p.] Gertrude Brown Spriggs, Archie Thomas; [m.] Mack, June 27, 1963; [ch.] Richard A. Killebrew; [ed.] Adjunct professor, PG College Teacher of English Francis J.H.S., Federal City College, MAT Trinity College; [occ.] Adjunct Professor, Teacher; [memb.] Washington Teacher's Union, National Council Teachers of English, D.C. Council Teachers of English; [hon.] Who's Who of American Women 15th Ed 1987-1988; [oth. writ.] Shaka Zula - poem entitled Eye; [pers.] Poetry is the music of the world. Through poetry, the reader is exposed to a whole new world of enjoyment; [a.] Oxon Hill, MD 20745

KILLEBREW, STEPHEN C.
[b.] October 18, 1949, Greenville, MS; [p.] Raiford C. Killebrew & Ruth S. Killebrew; [m.] Patricia F. Killebrew, August 5, 1971; [ch.] Christopher A. Killebrew and Jonathan B. Killebrew; [ed.] Greenville High School, MS Delta Community College, Self Study, Certified Electronics Technician, FCC First Class Engineer; [occ.] Biomedical Manager/Supervisor; [memb.] Life Member - ARRL, Member of Mississippi Biomedical Society; [hon.] Golden Poet - 5 times, Who's Who in Poetry, One of the World's Great Living Poets (World of Poetry); [oth. writ.] Computer Programs, a book on building computers; [pers.] I don't believe in the word impossible; [a.] Greenville, MS 38703

KILPACK III, WILLIAM DONALD
[Pen.]W. D. Kilpack III; [b.]November 20, 1970, Salt Lake City, Utah; [p.]William D. and Jan Maureen Kilpack; [m.]Cydnee Leigh; [ch.]Ella-Maereen, Kenny and Nobel; [ed.]Bachelor of Arts (Communication

and Philosophy); [occ.]Manager, Graphic Design/ Typesetting Department, Seagull Printing; [memb.]Christopher Diehl Lodge #19, F&AM; Order of DeMolay; International Association of business Communicators; East and West Literary Foundation; The Planetary Society; The Republican National Commission on the American Agenda; [hon.]Past State Master Councilor, Utah State DeMolay Association; Cum Laude graduate of Westminster College of Salt Lake City; Who's Who Among Students in American Colleges and Universities, 1991-92 Editor, Forum, campus newspaper, National AAU Wrestling Champion; State AAU Boxing Champion; [oth. writ.]Thirty-Three publications credits wit poems and short stories, including; American Collegiate Poetry Anthology; American Poetry Anthology; American Poets of the 1990's; Best Poems of the 90's; Distinguished Poets of america; Ellipsis; Literature & Arts; Envoy Collection; L'esprit; Literary/Art Magazine; On' The Threshold of a Dream; A View From the Edge; Where Words Haven't Spoken; [pers.]There are many things I consider passions. Foremost among them are family, writing, reading and a well rounded symposium. Subjects vary.

KIM, KWI AE
[Pen.] King David; [b.] May 14, 1956, S. Korea, Pusan; [p.]Joe Goan Kim; Woi Taik Kim; [m.] Young Song Kim, June 3, 1982; [ch.] Daniel S. Kim; Susan E. KIm; [ed.] Eui Chun Junior High Isabel Girls High entrance, Eui Lyeo Girl's High School Korea; [occ.] Discount Beauty Supply Owner; [memb.] The Korean Salt and Light, Presbyterian Church in American; [hon.] The National Library of Poetry. 1993 Editor's Choice Award. A poem in Where Dreams Begin, titled "Faithful Breathing"; [pers.] When you're discouraged and lonely, nobody to cheer you up call on "God" read Psalms 23; [a.] Norcross, GA 30093

KINDALL-WATTS, MARJORIE
[b.] November 12, 1922, Rock Run Township, Stephenson; [p.] Ralph and Bernice Kindell; [m.] Lester G. Watts - deceased 6/14/91, June 16, 1945; [ch.] Dennis L. Watts, grand daughter - Kimberly Nicole Watts; [ed.] 1 yr college. I was rated #47 (scholastically) in a class of nearly 1,000 students; [occ.] Homemaker, sales lady for Avon, Fuller Br and Electrolux; [memb.] Member of Bethesda Evangelical Convenant Church, Honorary Charter Membership (Int'l Society of Poets 1993); [hon.] National Honor Society, Golden Poet of the Year for many years; published in many volumes of poetry, including "American Anthology of Midwestern Poetry" 1988, and World of Poetry, many volumes; [oth. writ.] Hundreds of poems have been compared to Shakespeare, Browning, Keats, etc by my Dean in "Creative Writing" at college; [pers.] Began being chosen at age 8 or 9 yrs to recite "I Have a Little Shadow" in front of the PTA - large group! Loved songs and poems very early in my life. Began singing very young!; [a.] Rockford, IL 61114

KINDER, LOIS W.
[b.]Seth, WV; [p.]Dennis C. and Myrtle Cline Wade; [m.]Edward W. Kinder, September 28, 1946; [ed.]Sherman High, Morris Harvey College; [occ.]Retired Elementary School Teacher, Second Gd., Nellis, WV; [memb.]Nellis Wesleyan Church, International Society of Poets, N.R.T.A., Life Member WV Cong. P.T.A.; [hon.]WV Congress of Parents and Teachers, nellis Wesleyan Church for Dedicated Service.; [pers.]My only child and dear husband are deceased; [a.]Nellis, WV 25142.

KINDRED SR., HOWARD R.
[b.]May 18, 1950, Queens, New York; [p.]Lawrence and Florence Kindred; [m.]Kathleen, June 16, 1973; [ch.]Howard R. Kindred Jr.; [ed.]Enrolled in college for associate degree in business; [occ.]Front line supervisor, awaiting a liver transplant; [memb.]International society of poets, The Highlander Club; [hon.]Golden Poet Award for 1989, 90, 91, World of Poetry; [oth. writ.]Great Poems of the Western World Volume #2 for poem Afraid; [pers.]Life is like a chess game; [a.]RD #8, Box 8585M, East Stroudsburg, PA 18301

KING, ALMA JEAN
[b.] April 24, 1944, Cleveland, Ohio; [p.] John and Pearlie Phillips; [ed.] Audubon High, American Career Institute College, Cleveland, Ohio; [occ.] Certified Nursing Assistant, Franklin Plaza Nursing Home, Cleveland, Ohio; [memb.] American Heart Association, Cleveland, Ohio, Hollywood Recording Artists, Hollywood, CA; [p.] Golden Poet 1990, Golden Poet 1991; [oth. writ.] Poem published in World of Poetry Anthology; [pers.] Too all poet's world-wide, may you continue to grow, and flourish, as a bud of a rose. And forever stand tall, in your heart, mind, and soul. And forever reign in the name of love, peace.; [a.] Cleveland, Ohio 44108

KING, CATHERINE BERNICE RODGERS
[Pen.]Catherine B. King; [b.]October 28, 1914, Youngstown, Ohio; [p.]William and Anna Barnes Rodgers (Deceased); [m.]June 23, 1934, Euguene D. King (Deceased); [ch.]Alma Jane McClure and Carol Ruth Justice; [ed.]Beech Grove Ind. High School, Beauty Operator; [occ.]Housewife; [pers.]Written about my grandson who is now 32 yrs. old. I still remember it by heart.

KING, JENNIFER RENEE'
[Pen.] Jennifer; [b.] November 11, 1974, Dayton, OH; [p.] Richard and Deborah Setty; [ed.] Blanchester High and Laurel Oaks CDC - Vocational School; [occ.] Hair Stylists, O'ney's Hair Salon, Kettering, OH; [hon.] Jan 11, '91 - Honorable Mention "He Heard My Prayer"; March 31, '91 - Honorable Mention; "Thanksgiving Prayer"; Golden Poet 1991 "Thanksgiving Prayer" Sept 20, '91; [oth. writ.] One poem published in the Blanchester local newspaper, 1990 and a poem published in selected works of Our World's Best Poets, "He Heard My Prayer" 1992; [pers.] I was most inspired with poetry by my mother. She started me at a very young age, to get me to express my feelings. And I thank her for that; [a.] Beavercreek, OH 45432

KING, PAUL EDWARD
[b.]December 17, 1954, Fostoria, Ohio; [p.]Isabella and Edward King (Deceased); [ch.]Jacob John Edward King, Age 7; [ed.]Fourteen years; [occ.]Heating and Air Conditioning Installer, Bowers Heating, Findlay, OH; [oth. writ.]Sharing, To My Son, Several Poems published in the Findlay Courier; [pers.]We should always try to be here for others and take time to enjoy life. We only get one chance.; [a.]1224 E. Sandusky, Apt. 5B, Fostoria, Ohio 44830, 2728.

KING, RENEE P.
[Pen.] Sadiqa A. Malik; [b.] July 1, 1953, Phila, PA; [p.] Josephine Goins King, Charlie V. King, Jr; Fiance: Basheer Abdul-Malik; Sister: Gail King-Burney; [ch.] (1 niece) Nicole M. Burney; [ed.] 1 yr RN study - Phila, PA - 1971-1972, 1974 Associates in Medical Science - Pierce Jr College Phila, 2 yrs Computer Science Wake Tech Raleigh, NC 1982-1984; [occ.] Entrepreneur, Flea Market Boutique Essential Oils, Custom made jewelry, clothes, incense, antiques, 6 yr artist in residence, Durham; [memb.] Arts Council - Teaching in Durham City County School Systems - Poetic Expressions Residency Grades K-12, NC Poetry Society, Nat'l Federation of Poets; [hon.] Dean's List Pierce Jr College, Golden Poet Awards - World of Poetry, 3 Talent Show Awards in DC; 2 first place, 1 third place, Outstanding Women in America, 1987, Flea Mkt Business Home Business, The Essence of Time Enterprises, 5 yr Poet Residence appearance with Kuaanze Program Sponsored by Chuck Davis/African American Dance Ensemble, 6 year Artist in Residence - Durham Arts Council; [oth. writ.] Published in the Carolinian Newspaper, Raleigh, NC, Our Western World's Most Beautiful Poem, Who's Who in American Poetry, World of Poetry Anthology, first book, The Essence of Time to be published in 1994 - personal poems designed decorated and sold my boutique; [pers.] By the grace and blessings of Allah (God) I Sadiqa, born Renee am a poet who as a servant to our creator am a vehicle through which words from the soul touch the hearts and minds of us all. I am blessed; [a.] Raleigh, NC

KING-MC GOVERN, FAYE LINDA
[Pen.]Faye, Linda King, Danelle, Kaithlin King; [b.]October 9, 1953, Portland, Maine; [p.]Philip MacDavis, Beverly Jean Lewis; [ch.]Ted West, III; [ed.]I hold a Masters Degree in Business. Attended Deering High School, Westbrook College, Southern Maine Vocational Technical Institute and American Institute of Ban King; [occ.]Writer, Retired LPN, and EMT. Presently a student with the Institute of Children's Literature; [hon.]Honorable mentions and a Grand Prize winner from the World of Poetry Contest.; [oth. writ.]Poems published in Great poems of our Time, Family Treasury of Poems, Poems that Will Live Forever. Have written short stories for "Mainly Women".; [pers.]Don't get discouraged with writing. Eventually, all of your hard work will pay off! Just keep trying and always further your education if possible.; [a.]Westbrook, Maine 04092.

KINNE, PEARL MARCELLA
[b.] June 28, 1912, Valley City, ND; [p.] Mary and Henry Mayhew; [m.] Guerney M. Kinne, May 8, 1933; [ch.] Kenneth Leo Kinne, John Douglas Kinne; [ed.] St. Mary's High School, Lansing, MI, B.A. Univ of MO, St. Louis, graduate courses - Univ of IL; [occ.] Business owner, writer, housewife, emergency volunteer; [memb.] Eagle's Aux #851 Owesso, MI, Honorary Assn Blue Max, International Society of Poets; [hon.] Writing certificate -- Univ of MO, Editor's Choice Award -- National Library semifinalist, ISP contest 1993; [oth. writ.] 2 cookbooks -- The Front Page and My Momma. A book of short stories and other short stories and poems. I am a people watcher. Its not to be critical, or discriminate -- just quietly observant. I love excitement, crowds, parades. My many years of working in various jobs and occupations have gained for me a wide worldly experience. On the quiet side I love home, friends, and entertaining; [a.] St. Louis, MO

KINSEY, MONICA
[b.]January 25, 1936, Oskarshamn, Sweden; Phjalmar and Ingrid Svensen, Vastervik, Sweden; [m.]Lawrence E. Kinsey; [ch.]Frank C. and Craig S. Colby, San Francisco, California; [ed.]Vasterviks Gymnasium and Lund University, Sweden Linguist (fluent in five languages); [occ.]Counselor Psycho-Therapist for 17 years. Airline Tour Company Mgr.; [memb.]Freelance Decorator, Sculptor and Writer, Translator of Children's Books; [oth. writ.]"Where the Sky Meets the Sea" a place of healing. "The Christmas Foot" poetry.; [pers.]To live your spiritual best each day, to value and bring out the best in everyone you meet, to greet each day with joy and passion; [a.]North Redington Beach, Florida 33708

KINZIE, ANTHONY ALAN
[Pen.] A. A. Kinzie; [b.] January 19, 1968, Warsaw, Indiana; [p.] Richard E. and Janet S. Kinzie; [ed.] Warsaw Community High, Indiana University College for Gifted and Talented Youth, Indiana U. Purdue U at Ft. Wayne, Indiana State University, University of New Mexico; [occ.] Polyhistory; [memb.] Society for creative Anachronisms, Mensa; [hon.] Department of Honors, Dean's list, Who's Who American High Schools 1985-86, Amigo Scholar, Indiana Outstanding Student in Government, National Honor Society, Presidential Academic Fitness; [oth. writ.] Poetry, fiction and non fiction, philosophical treatises and sayings; [pers.] "Great spirits always encounter violent opposition from mediocre minds." Albert Einstein; [a.] Warsaw, IN 46580

KIRBY, ANNA H.
[b.]May 4, 1943, Mt. Vernon, Kentucky; [p.]Pearl and Goble Hayes; [m.]Furmon Kirby; [ch.]Bonnie, Susan, Darrell and Angie; [ed.]High School; [occ.]Assembler at General Motors Dayton, Ohio; [a.]Lynchburg, Ohio 45142

KIRBY, DOUGLAS
[Pen.] Kirby; [b.] July 20, 1944, Dean, TN; [p.] John and Aldo Kirby; [ed.] T.C. Howe H.S., Lake City Community College; [occ.] Life; [memb.] Homer Honor Society of International Poets; [hon.] Golden Poet 1992, Editor's Choice 1993 National Library of Poetry; [oth. writ.] "Dragon Dreams" (Honorary Mention World of Poetry) "Altered Thoughts" (Wind In The Night Sky The National Library of Poets); [pers.] All you touch, all you see are the visions of life's rhapsody all you think, all you feel could be false, could be real; [a.] San Pedro, CA 90731-0207

KIRBY, MARY PAXTON
[b.] October 27, 1914, Vicksburg, MS; [p.] Frank and Mary Young; [m.] Durward Kirby, June 7, 1941; [ch.] Randall and Dennis Kirby; [ed.] Butler Univ; [occ.] Writer; [memb.] Kappa Alpha Theta, Aftra, DAR, Sherman Historical Society; [hon.] Dean's List, Golden Poet Award, 1988 and 1989, World of Poetry Award of Merit, Honorable Mention 1987 and 1989; [oth. writ.] Poetry Anthology, View From Under the Table, Jingles for the Jangled; [a.] Sanibel, FL 33957

KIRKHOFF, JOHN L.
[b.]July 24, 1923, Indianapolis, Indiana; [p.]Louis Kirkhoff & Ruth Cunningham Kirkhoff; [m.]Jo Ann Kirkhoff; [m.]April 9, 1949; [ch.]Kim Snay and Kay Reinhardt; [ed.]B.A. Butler University, M.A. University of S. California; [occ.]Realtor, Writer;[memb.]San Diego Realty Assoc., Writer's Group, Academy of Am. Poets., So. of Poetry Assoc.; [hon.]Second place poetry, National Assoc. of Aging 1994, Editor's Choice, Nat'l. Library of Poetry (1993); [oth. writ.]"A Corner of Time" (novel) pub in 1992 by Guild Press "Of Time and Flight" Chap Book, Yes Press, the Camp Bowie Run (Chap Book) 1992, the Plowman Publisher; [pers.]I believe poetry should transform through imagery and transcribe the ordinary into the extraordinary.; [a.]18211 Verano Dr., San Diego, CA 92128-1238.

KIRKLAND, KAREN J.
[b.] May 31, 1960, Sharon, PA; [p.] Robert & Lillian Marley; [m.] William O. Kirkland Jr., May 8, 1982; [ch.] Stephanie; [ed.] West Middlesex Jr. Sr. High, currently studying medical transcriptionist; [occ.] Housewife, mother, student; [oth. writ.] Approx. 300 poems and quotations in three book forms all registered in the Library of Congress. A few poems published by poetry press.

KIRKPATRICK, ANNA LEE
[b.] March 4, 1923, Burk Burnett, TX; [p.] Ralph D. and Lena Holman; [m.] Roy G. Kirkpatrick - expired 8-7-93, Jauary 9, 1943; [ch.] David and Dennis Sr Kirkpatrick, Anna Jean Willia; [ed.] Graduate Baylor University Registered Nurse; [occ.] Retired RN; [m.] Baylor University Alumnai, VFW Aux #6796 Dallas, TX, American Poetry Asso; [a.] Dallas, TX

KIRSCHBAUM, PHILLIP
[b.] June 9, 1972, Chicago, IL; [p.] Elaine and Leslie J. Kirschbaum; [ed.] Winkelman Elementary School, Stanley Field Jr HS, Glenbrook North and Glenbrook South HS; [occ.] Student at Northern Illinois University; [memb.] World Wildlife Fund, Congregation Beth Shalom; [hon.] Two Editor's Choice Awards from National Library of Poetry for my poem "Beyond Confusion"; [oth. writ.] Several poems published in anthologies and many, many more that are not yet published; [pers.] The only thing you need to make the world a peaceful place is believing in G-D, studying the Old Testament, and by finding the heart to treat man, beast, and mother Earth with respect, to the best of your ability; [a.] Lake Forest, IL 60045

KITTS, REVA L.
[b.]May 15, 1935, Paintsville, Kentucky; [p.]Blanche and George Charles; [m.]Carl K. Kitts, December 1949; [ch.]Carla, Kevin, Locpaw "God", Jimmy, Edward, Kenneth; [ed.]Eighth grade, six months civil service. Self taught to life from God, Minister Training. Self taught typing; [occ.]Mother first, writer-freelance, wanted to be a minister; [memb.]National Rifle Club, Audubon, Smithsonian. Wildness Society; [hon.]Two years Golden Poet, Honorable Mention and Silver Poet Award; [oth. writ.]I have a book of poetry written for publication, a book called, "The Little Green Christmas Car." Two anthology's with "World of Poetry of California."; [pers.]I believe that God mad all humans, the earth, the stars and the moon. Humanitarian efforts are for woman and children and that love is a supremacy; [a.]P.O. Box 15752, Columbus, Ohio 43215.

KLAHORST, CAROL CONLEY
[b.] January 10, 1942, Somers Point, NJ; [p.] Enoch L. Higbee and Virginia Higbee Dehn; [m.] Bob Klahorst, June 28, 1986; [ch.] Lara Evonne Conley; [ed.] Atlantic City High School, Montclair State College, New School for Social Research Graduate Faculty, National Psychological Assoc. for Psychoanalysis; [occ.] Art and Nursery School Teacher; [hon.] Art work displayed, New Jersey State Museum, Delaware Ar Museum, Weaving Shown in Book: Weaving Without A Loom; [oth. writ.] Poetry published in anthologies: Where Dreams Begin, A Break In The Clouds and unpublished poems; [pers.] The inner nature of God in man has always intrigued me. There is a deep longing in many for conscious unity with our source; [a.] Northfield, NJ

KLATT-SCANLAN, MARGARET M.
[b.] March 28, 1958, Chicago, IL; [p.] Walter C. and Yvonne Klatt; [m.] James J. Scanlan, Jr (10/10/54), October 31, 1989; [ch.] James Walter (8/29/90), Joseph Charles (7/7/92-6/26/93); [ed.] 3 1/2 yrs college finished Northeastern Univ Chicago; [occ.] Housewife/writer; [hon.] Editor's Choice Award, Golden Poet 1991, Golden Poet 1988, Honorable Mention 1991 and 1988; [oth. writ.] Several articles in local papers, 4 poems in 4 different poetry books, articles in local newspapers; [pers.] Live dan often seem like a treacherous minefield. But I have found that if I try to live right the mines won't explode as much. We are put on earth to be happy, to live and explore the wonders surrounding the set backs we experience can only enrich our lives if we try to be positive, greatful and helpful; [a.] Wheeling, IL

KLEIS, EDNA
[b.]EKA; [b.]September 28, 1916, Rapid City, Michigan; [p.]Henry and Dora Van; [m.]Claudis D. Claypoole, 1982; [ch.]Danabeth Holleman, adopted, Opal Chilson, adopted; [ed.]B.S. Secretarial Science, Ferris State Big Rapids, Michigan, MA, Western Kalamazoo, Michigan; [occ.]Teacher, literature, social science; [memb.]Orange Women's Club, PTA, School groups of teachers; [hon.]Two Golden Poet, Creation of Clothes for Salvation Army Dolls, four first, one second; [oth. writ.]A myriad of poems as yet unpublished, children's stories, lots of essays, including character sketches of people I knew; [pers.]God is prominent in most of my poems, essays, stories. He is my love. Nature and natural surroundings inspire me.; [a.]Oceanside, CA 92054

KLOCK, MARTHA RINNIE
[b.] March 7, 1920, Los Angeles, CA; [p.] Ralph Lewis Klock, Ruth Howard Klock; My grandmother - a published writer. I've been writing since 12 yrs old, My mother also a writer; [ed.] Belmont High School Biola College Teachers Training Course - Westmont College 1 yr; [occ.] Retired Missionary, Church Secretary, Writer; [memb.] Pilgrim John Howland Society, Mayflower Society; [hon.] 8 Golden Poet Awards, Six place poetry award plus many awards of merit and honorary poetry awards; [oth. writ.] A Letter Home, Togetherness, God's Little Angels, and Memories of Yesteryear (and Miracles of Today). Many poems published; [pers.] May I never be too busy to shed a broad God's love. For it only flows through me, but 'tis from the father up above; [a.] Ontario, CA

KLOCK, MARTHA RINNIE
[b.]March 7, 1920, Los Angeles, CA; [p.]Ralph Lewis Klock and Ruth Howland Klock; [ed.]Graduate of Belmont High School, Los Angeles, Attended Biolax Westmont College for one year; [occ.]Retired

Missionary Former Vice President of Voice in Wilderness Magazine; [memb.]Mayflower Society, The Pilgrim John Howland Society, Calvary Faith Center of Ontario; [hon.]Eight Golden Poet Awards, Numerous Honorable Mention Awards, One sixth place award; [oth. writ.]A Letter Home, Togetherness, God's Little Angels, Numerous poems in the World of Poetry Books and Church bulletins; [pers.]We know that though lonely, we're never alone for the Lord reminds someone to pray; [a.]1061 E. 4th St. Apt. 1-A, Ontario, CA 91764.

KLOSTER, AMANDA M.
[b.] October 28, 1977 to December 6, 1991; [p.] James and Nicoletta Kloster; [ed.] St. Joseph's School, New Hampton, IA; [hon.] Speech Contests.

KNIGHT, GOODWIN J.
Widow of the former Governor of California, has been an enthusiastic member of the ettie Lee National Advisory Council since 1971. She is very active in many civic groups and clubs as well as various Veterans' Rehabilitation organizations. During WWII she was active in War Bond drives and organizing entertainment for Veterans' hospitals, and was awarded a national citation for these activities. She is a past president of the American Legion and Veterans of Foreign Wars auxiliaries. Mrs. Knight is a former pupil of Ettie Lee's, and remembers her fondly as "my favorite teacher." She brought a report card with all A's given her by Miss Lee to the last National Advisory Council Banquet. She is an accomplished poet, having had many of her poems published, and was awarded a Fellowship in the American Inst of Fine Arts. She was recently honored with a life membership in the International Clover Poetry Association's Society of Literary Designates, in Washington, DC with the title of "Danae." She was commissioned as Honorary Poet Laureate of the State of Delaware. [pers.] The ropes of the past ring the bells of the future. The perfume of a rose is the fragrance of God's Breath; [a.] Los Angeles, CA 90020

KNIGHT, MICHAEL K.
[b.]April 20, 1974, Payson, Utah; [p.]Gary L. Knight and Susan D. Knight; [ed.]Hillcrest High, UTI (Universal Technical Institute); [occ.]HVACR Technician; [memb.]Amvets (American Veterans); [hon.]Alpha Beta Happa Director's List; [pers.]I try to put my heart into everything I write. Straight forward, honest poetry is what I enjoy writing. I am influenced by Robert Frost; [a.]1554 Wagon Wheel Cir., Sandy UT 84093.

KNOX, JUDY A.
[b.] February 20, 1943, Batesville, Arkansas; [p.] James and Viola Hawkins; [m.] Gaylon C. Knox, December 24, 1962; [ch.] Rodney Knox and James Knox; [ed.] Attended Senath High School, Senath, Missouri 12 yrs.; [occ.] Housewife; [memb.] Holly Springs Civic Club, Friends of the Library, American Heart Association, and American Cancer Association; [hon.] Publication in World of Poetry, Sparrow Grass Publishing and Award of Merits from World of Poetry Press, plus golden Poets Award for 1991; [oth. writ.] "Garden of The Mind" and "Sonnet To A Sleepy Child" both published; [pers.] All credit for my work belongs to Christ Jesus. Only through him am I able to write or accomplish anything and serving him is my greatest joy in life; [a.] Holly Springs, Mississippi 38635

KOCH, LISA A.
[b.]August 1, 1962, Perryville, Missouri; [p.]Vincent P. and Janet R. Hermann; [m.]Fred E. Koch; [ch.]Derek Joseph, Jared Michael (deceased), Sarah Maria, and Hanah Maria; [occ.]Homemaker; [memb.]Children's United Research Efforts, Compassionate Friends; [oth. writ.]In Memory of jared Michael Mueller; [pers.]My poetry reflects person and special experiences; [a.]DeSoto, MO

KOCH, SUZANNE M.
[Pen.] Sue Koch; [b.] December 21, 1958, Buffalo, NY; [p.] Lewis McDonald Sr. and Joanne McDonald; [m.] Edsel R. Koch, December 16, 1979; [ch.] Melanie, Amy, Christina and Ryan; [ed.] Depew High School, Parkland College; [occ.] Housewife; [oth. writ.] "Ode To A Man At Sea," "Carry It On" and other poems; [pers.] Life's to short…go for your dreams; [a.] Franklinville, NY 14737

KOONTZ, PEGGY J.
[b.]August 17, 1931, Mason City, IA; [p.]Deceased; [m.]Russell L. Koontz, January 29, 1987; [ch.]David Roemer, Susan Combs, Bruce Roemer; [ed.]Hampton High, Hampton IA, American School, Chgo, IL; [occ.]Manager, and clerk now retired; [memb.]Disabled American Vet. Aux., Farm Bureau, was 4H Leader and also Methodist Church; [hon.]Editor's Choice Award for outstanding Achievement in Poetry; [oth. writ.]Several poems in local newspapers and in the National Library of Poetry; [pers.]Yesterday is past, and tomorrow will not be, so I lie each day for itself and my writings are from past happenings.; [a.]155 W. Middleton Dr., Orleans, IN 47452.

KOTLINSKI, MICHAEL A.
[b.] November 2, 1953, Chicago, IL; [p.] Eugene B. and Lottie V. Kotlinski; [ed.] High School, Glenbrook North Building Const. courses at Lake County College; [occ.] Mailman, Northbrook, IL; [oth. writ.] The Spirit Stak, Unspoken Love, The National Library of Poetry; [pers.] Wishing one day to attain the wisdom of thought to understand the wonders of existence and its infinity; [a.] Gurnee, IL 60031

KOUDELA, DIANE
[b.] December 23, 1952, Star Lake, NY; [p.] Cliff and Faye Pratt, Melbourne, FL; [m.] Keith Koudela, August 15, 1987; [ch.] Steven, Andy, Leslie; [ed.] 12 yrs. plus vocational/nursing 2 yr. community college; [occ.] Domestic engineer, Mother of 2 boys and 1 girl, LPN; [hon.] Editor's Choice Award, Untimely Death; [oth. writ.] Freelance birthdays, anniversary, wedding vows, death for friends and family; [pers.] I usually place myself in their shoes. Love of the Lord and family and friends encourage me to go for the gusto of life; [a.] Margate, FL 33063

KOWALCHYK, MARIA RESTAINO
[b.] October 1, 1925, Marsico Nuovo, Italy; [p.] Raffaele Restaino, Louisa Degregoria Restaino; [m.] Stanislaw Kowalchyk, April 28, 1951 (Brooklyn); [ch.] Diane Louise Kowalchyk, ABDOO; [ed.] 2 schools in Italy, grammar, junior and high, Sea Bright, NJ. My finishing schol TJ night; [occ.] Housewife, poet writer, journalist, community leader; [memb.] Cancer Society, Honorary Member of Police Dept, Thirteen the Smithsonian Ass; [hon.] Badge from Police Dept, Honorable Mention for 1990 and Golden Poet for 1991, Plaque as one of world's great living poets 1992, Who's Who in Poetry, 1993; [oth. writ.] Gun Control, God's Appropriate Place, For the Handicapped, The American Flag Majestic Tree, Mopsy My Dog, Assay for 100 on Statue of Liberty, John Lennon for his movie, about 1000 poems in all; [pers.] I picked all the right people and places as role models read all the right books from Louisa M. Alcott on; [a.] Brooklyn, NY 11204

KRAUS, JAMES G.
[Pen.] Jim Kraus; [b.] Valley Stream, NY; [p.] George and Annette Kraus; [ed.] Air Frame Licensed to repair aircraft, some college study; [occ.] Aviation Student (completing certification) waiter, mechanic; [memb.] Aeronautical Society; [hon.] Some literacy distinction on a college level; [oth. writ.] Numerous other works as yet unpublished except, "Gift Of A Goddess" in Wind In The Night Sky; [pers.] I enjoy writing as an effort to create a feeling in another person. My writing allows me to know the creative side of myself.; [a.] Union City, GA 30291

KREIDL, NORBERT JOACHIM
[b.]July 3, 1904, Vienna, Austria; [p.]Ignaz and Hildegard (nee Krenn) Kreidl; [m.]Melanie (nee Schreiber), September 22, 1934; [ch.]Joachim (John) deceased, Martina Dunn, Tobies; [ed.]PhD, Physics 1929 Vienna; [occ.]Professor retired, consultant (Glass Science) [memb.]Am. Ceramic Society, British and German Glass Technology Societies, Sigma Xi; [hon.]Honor, PhD Alfred, NY, U Jena (Germany), U Vienna and Jepson, Morey Award Am. Cer. Svc. etc.; [oth. writ.]Some poems published by Am. Soc. of Poetry. All other writings in science magazines and books; [pers.]Live your honest differences, but refrain your arguments; [a.]1433 Canyon Rd., Santa Fe, NM 87501.

KRIPALANI, LAKSHMI A.
[b.] August 24, 1920, Hyderabad Sind Pakistan; [p.] (Father) Assudomal Kripalani, (Mother) Hemi A. Advani (maiden); [a.] Upper Montclair, NJ

KRISTENSEN, JACQUELINE
[b.] September 1, 1930, Denver, Colorado; [p.] Charlie and Alice Towne; [m.] Andrew Kristensen, August 15, 1948; [ch.] Kathryn, Kenneth, Daniel and Ronald; [ed.] College of Marin; [occ.] Small Business Owner; [memb.] Marin Christian Life Church, Women's Aglow International; [hon.] 1992 National Library of Poetry; [oth. writ.] Many spiritual poems; [pers.] God is the source of my peace and joy; [a.] San Rafael, GA 94903

KROMER, DELLA HARRISON
[b.] April 10, 1925, Whitewater, Kansas; [p.] Mable Miller Harrison and Raymond Harrison; [m.] Kermit Kromer, June 17, 1965, Newton, KS; [ch.] Nona Joelene Alderfer and Loreda Dianne Horutz; [ed.] Newton and Valley Center Kansas; [occ.] Cake Decoration Teacher; [memb.] Polk Township Ladies Auxiliary Volunteer Fire Co.; [hon.] Cake Decorating, Crafts at West End Fair; [oth. writ.] Autumn, My Great Granddaughter also Time and You and Me, Big Sister, My Sister Evelyn who passed away. Published in local newspaper; [pers.] I get the most enjoyment out of life from our family we have 2 daughters, 5 grandchildren, one step grandchild, one great granddaughter and one grand child on the way. We are very proud.; [a.] Kunkletown, PA 18038

KRONER, LUCILLE M.
[b.]August 8, Rolla, MO; [p.]Theodore W. Kroner and Virginia Wilson Kroner; [ed.]Santa Monica City College and U.C.L.A.; [occ.]Retired, prior contract administrator; [memb.]First Christian Church of Santa Monica, Elder Choir Member, Santa Monica Lyric Chorus; [hon.]Approximately 100 Poetry Awards; 2 first awards, 8 Golden Poet Awards, 3 Poet of Merit Awards, 3 Editor of Choice Awards, Etc.; [oth. writ.]First Christian Church Bulletin and many anthologies; [pers.]Let us all circle our wagons in protection of world peace.; [a.]Los Angeles, CA 90066.

KRUGER, BETTY LOU
[b.] August 4, 1940, Metropolis, IL; [p.] August Henry (Gussie H.) Bremer and Lillian Clara (Wilkins) Bremer; [m.] LaVerne D. Kruger, November 23, 1962; [ch.] Kendrick Lew Kruger; [ed.] High School Graduate, Adult classes, computer literacy, DOS Windows, WordPerfect 5.0 and 5.1, Graphic Arts, Oil Painting; [occ.] Housewife; [hon.] Third place in my first oil painting show with my first oil painting; [oth. writ.] Poems "Age Before Beauty" "Memories" both published by Nat'l. Library of Poetry. In process of typing autobiography. Small poems for personal use; [pers.] Don't wait for a "second chance" to fulfill your dreams or do the things you want to do in life. Do them now! You may not get that "second chance."; [a.] Metropolis, IL 62960

KRUGER, NANCY LEE
[b.] March 21, 1957, Berlin, New Hampshire; [p.] Leo H. Kruger, Ph.D. and Anne L. Kruger, Ph.D.; [ed.] I graduated from South Brunswick Regional High School in 1976; [occ.] Choral Soprano; [memb.] Presbyterian Church, USA; [hon.] South Brunswick High School Chorus Award, Church Service Awards 1990-1993; [oth. writ.] Eivel Qurial, To Make A Perfect Pizza Pie; [pers.] People should not be thrown away; [a.] Asbury, NJ 08802

KRUPER, MILLY
[b.]October 31, 1946, Lassa, Nigeri, W. Africa; [p.]John and Mildred Grimley; [m.]Philip Kruper, 1969; [ch.]Stefanie Anne and Allison Elizabeth; [ed.]Jr. College- Montgomery Co., Commun. Nursing School, Bradywine School of Nursing; [occ.]Registered Nurse, Neonatal Intensive Care; [oth. writ.]Poetry in magazines and an anthology book. Unpublished children's stories and science fiction books; [pers.]The mind is a garden wherein imagination grows. I write the colors of my imagination; [a.]Phoenixville, PA 19460.

KUEHNLE, MINNIE B.
[b.] January 13, 1907, Sullivan, MO; [p.] Benjamin Joseph and Louisa Hummel Spindler; [m.] Willy Kuehnle, November 24, 1927 (deceased); [ch.] Constance Louise, 1934 (deceased), Shiela May 1935, Willy Benfred 1948; [ed.] Eighth grade; business college; [occ.] Worked with my husband for 25 years in an electrical contracting business; now retired; [memb.] Merrillville (IN) First Assembly of God; AARP; National Republican Committee; had been in art league; sponsored Girl Scout Troop; [hon.] Won 1st and 4th prizes and numerous Merit Awards for Poetry; [oth. writ.] I've published three books of poetry, had poems in local newspapers; [pers.] "To keep learning, keep growing in knowledge; keep faith in God; keep busy."; [a.] Hobart, IN 46343

KUEMMEL, ELLEN MARIE
[b.]March 13, 1950, Mt. Clemens, Michigan; [p.]Sabatine and Dorothy Pedicone; [m.]Baron Kuemme, June 16, 1990; [ch.]Johnna, Sarah, Elisha, Katherine and Louis; [ed.]GED and Technical College 104 Credits, presently enrolled in College Parallel; [occ.]Clerk Typist for VA Hospital; [memb.]Federal Women's Program; [hon.]Outstanding Employee Award for 1993; [oth. writ.]Babbling of the Soul, New Friendship and newsletter article for the Veterans Hospital Highlights Newspaper; [pers.]I strive to treat all people with the same compassion and respect I would like to receive.; [a.]P.O. Box 88, 4643 Selje Rd., Morrisonville, WI 53571

KUHN, GRAYCE E.
[Pen.] Beth Artman; [b.] May 17, 1906, Dunlap, IL; [p.] Charles and Margaret Missen; [m.] John C. Kuhn, February 10, 1937 (deceased); [ch.] William L. Cutler, Janet C. Kuhn; [ed.] Dunlap High School, IL Normal Univ (Normal, IL), Bradley Univ (Peoria, IL), Mid State College of Commerce (Peoria, IL); [occ.] Retired School Teacher and Realty Salesperson, taught school in a 1 room country school for 24 yrs; [memb.] NRTA of Retired Teachers, Rebekah Lodge, royal Neighbor of America, 74 yr member of Grange, State and Nat'l 7th Degree Member, 1st Christian Church (Henry, IL); [hon.] From American Assoc of Best Poets of 1989, from Nat'l Library of Poetry 1992, helped write a set of 4 books of American Guide, writer 1st class; was Grand Marshall of Dunlap Days i 1990 (Dunlap, IL); [oth. writ.] Short stories to IL Sr. Citizen Voice, Welcome Home, Modern Maturity, books - Kathy and Corn Husk Doll, Round the Bend of the Road, song - Gobble, Gobble, Gobble, have had 2 books published; [pers.] I write for the enjoyment of others. Many can relate to my stories. I have enjoyed 87 yrs of life. I spend my winters in Florida and California, have for 28 winters. I have 3 great grandchildren; [a.] Henry, IL

KUKES, LOUISE M.
[b.]September 18, 1913, Fresno, California; [p.]Vincenzo, Giazia M. Pepe; [m.]Divorced, George Kukes, Sr., September 29, 1938; [ch.]George D. and Richard V. Kukes; [ed.]AB-Commerce Fresno State College; [occ.]Stenographer; [oth. writ.]Lyrics for songs, same broadcast on T.V. various cities in U.S; [pers.]Stay close to God; [a.]Fresno, California 93705.

KULA, EDWARD J.
[b.]October 13, 1958, Waukegan, Illinois; [p.]Darlene and Richard Kula; [ed.]Bachelor of Arts, 1980 Western Illinois University, 1985 Elementary Education Concordin College; [occ.]ESL Instructor, Dallas, SER part-time ESL Instructor, Richland College; [hon.]Golden Poet Awards, World of Poetry 1987, 1988, 1989 and 1990; [oth. writ.]To Be A Teacher, Land of the Kaisers and The Legacy of JFK; [pers.]Poetry is my vehicle to express my thoughts and feelings about the world past and present; [a.]Dallas, TX 75252

KULLBERG, RHEA REBECCA
[Pen.]God's Chosen Servant; [b.]September 28, 1914, Middletown, Indiana; [p.]Cecil J. & Hallie Ghall Saunders, Cecil, direct descendant of Queen Victoria of England, Blood King David Jews; [m.]Andrew G. Kullberg, March 10, 1936; [ch.]Seven, I hope some of them get to heaven with me; [ed.]High school, and business college. Bible studied diligently for 52 years.; [occ.]Housewife, Mother, Bible Student and SAGE Teacher; [memb.]I belong to God and am a member of the Saints who will inherit eternal life!; [hon.]I want the God of Heaven to say "Welcome home sweetheart, I love you, as I enter eternal life!; [oth. writ.]Autobiography, Rebecca Love's God, unpublished.; [pers.]God chose me to be his servant. I am a prophetess. I hope to please God and get a happy eternal life.; [a.]920 W. Bonanza Rd. #424, Las Vegas, NV 89106.

KUMAR, TOBI J.
[ed.] BA Kent St Univ, Art Students League of NY, New York Inst of Photography; [occ.] Photographer, artist; [memb.] Ellis Island Foundation, NY NY 1988, Democratic Party - USA; [hon.] Golden Poet Awards 1989, 1990, 1991 from World of Poetry in Sacramento, CA; [oth. writ.] Haiku published by the Asia Society, NY, NY; [pers.] "To be, is to be the value of a bound variable"; [a.] New York NY

KURTZ, JEANNE E.
[b.] March 12, 1933, Providence, RI; [p.] (Mother) Theresa Barrows - maiden, (Father) Vincent D'Alessio, (Stepfather) John Cain; [m.] widow; [ch.] Carole Kelsall, Elizabeth Bell, Lloyd Kurtz,III; [ed.] East Providence High Jr High, RI Cope Cod Community College - Courses - english, comp, phyc, writing; [occ.] semi-retired; [memb.] Volunteer Muscular Distrophy, handicapped. Honorary Charter Member of International Society of Poets; [hon.] Golden Award for Poetry. Ruby Poet Award for poetry; [oth. writ.] Poems published in the New York Poetry Foundation anthology, and Images Reaching Out; [pers.] My poetry reflects of myself, and the feelings of others. Always hoping for peace and harmony among people; [a.] W. Yarmouth, MA 02673

LANCASTER, CRAIG
[b.] February 3, 1955, Hot Springs, SD; [occ.] Musician, Log Home Builder; [hon.] Golden Poet Award for '89, '90 and '91; Who's Who In Poetry 1990; [oth. writ.] Poetry compilation titled, Thoughts of Thor; Children's short story titled, Mithra the Grasshopper; various poems published in an area periodical; [pers.] I wrote the poem, lightning, while working at a US Forest Service lookout tower in the Black Hills of SD. The powerful thunderstorms and breath-taking scenery of the region inspired many poem that summer; [a.] Custer, SD

LANEY, NINA
[b.] April 7, 1933, Pisqah, AL; [p.] Albert Gilbert, Ludy Hall Gilbert; [m.] Orbie Laney, June 12, 1950; [ch.] Sharon, Vicki ; [ed.] GED; [occ.] Housewife; [m.] New Hope Church; [oth. writ.] My Mother, Heaven's Beauty, Lonely Road, The Cross, Little Children; [pers.] Thanks for your letter. I never dreamed any one would want to read my poems beside myself. You are the only one that has ever seen or read my poems; [a.] Henagar, AL 35978

LANGDON JR., ROBERT M.
[p.]Robert and Lillian Langdon; [m.]Evelyn, January 21, 1972; [ch.]Robert Langdon III; [ed.]11th Grade; [occ.]Window Display Man; [hon.]Golden Poet Award 1988, 1989, 1990, 1991; [oth. writ.]Christmas Cheer, Summer Fun, Heart Break of Drug's, Four-Seasons; [a.] Island Park, NY 11558.

LARUE, RUTH N.
[b.]October 24, 1923, Bloomsbury, NJ; [p.]Wm. Smith and Eliz. Harrison Ditmars; [m.]October, 3, 1945 (Divorced); [ch.]Linda, Betty Jo and Jack; [ed.]eighth grade; [occ.]Retired; [hon.]From the National Library of Poetry; [oth. writ.]Only one published in "Where Dreams Begin"; [pers.]I never thought of myself as being a poet, but my diary seems to be in poetry form. I can express my feelings much better that way; [a.] Galeton, PA 16922

LATORRE, FRANK
[Pen.] Raven Cobbs; [b.] January 24, 1967, Schenectady, NY; [p.] Louis and Maria Latorre; [m.] Holly, June 1, 1991; [ed.] Linton High School, H.V.C.C.; [occ.] Entrepreneur, Poet; [oth. writ.] The Silent Voice; [a.] Waterford, NY 12188

LAU, ARNOLD J.
[b.] April 27, 1923, Newark, NJ; [p.] Edward Lau, Ethel Arrants Lau; [m.] Mary Louise Lau, September 6, 1952; [ch.] Nancy Lau Prescott, John Andrew Lau; [ed.] BS Education; 3 yrs graduate study; Federal Executive Institue; Graduate Brookings Institution Program; [occ.] Retired US Secret Service Asst Director; [memb.] International Assn Chiefs of Police, Kiwanis; [hon.] US Treasury Meritorious Award Medal; Who's Who in Gov't; Outstanding College Alumnus Award; [oth. writ.] One poem published by the National Library of Poetry - "Gloria"; [a.] Chapel Hill, NC 27514

LAYMAN, DONALD G.
[b.] October 26, 1956, Morton, Washington; [p.] Don Layman; [ed.] Liberty High School, Southwest Baptist University; [occ.] Private Accountant for Layman Lumber; [pers.] Poetry is liquid emotion; [a.] Birch Tree, MO 65438

LE, XUAN-NHUAN
[Pen.]Thanh-Thanh (poems), Kieu-Ngog (short stories), Nguyet-Cam (dramas), Nguoi Tho (critiques), Tu Ngong (satires), etc; [b.]January 2, 1930, Hue, Vietnam; [occ.]Former war correspondent, broadcast director, psy-war lecturer, English teacher, former Security and Intelligence Director, Central Vietnam; [memb.]Leader of the Xay-Dung (Construction) literary group, which has published lots of poems of many fellow poets and of mine and was depicted as one among the main branches of the Vietnamese Cultural Tree diagram exhibited at a pre-1975 National Cultural Festival in Saigon, the capital of the former Republic of Vietnam.; [oth. writ.]Already published: (Poems:) Anh Troi Mai, Anh Troi Mai New Edition, Kiem Xuan Thu, Tuan Trang Mat, Voi Thuong-De, Nhac Ngay Xanh, La Thu Roi, (Poetical Drama:) Quan Ben Song; (Selected Short Stories and Poems:) Nua Gat Moi I, II, and III, Nang Moi. Currently printed: (Various Poems and Short Stories:) in Phu-Nu Dien-Dan (Women's Forum), Van-Nghe Tien-Phong (Vanguard Literature and Arts), The-Gioi Moi (New World), the well known Vietnamese magazines in the States and abroad. Going to be published: "Ve Vung Chien-Tuyen (Back To The Front Line) Revelation of the Untold Causes of the US-Backed Republic of Vietnam's Fall) and Con Ac-Mong (The Nightmare) (Poems written during 13 years imprisoned by the communist); [pers.]I worship and strive to reflect the True, the Good, and the Beautiful in my writings as well as in my life, regardless of potentially suffered disfavor and even harm; [a.] Fairfield, CA 94533, USA.

LEACH, JOYCE
[Pen.]Joyce Scroggs Leach; [b.]June 6, 1933, Spearman, Texas; [p.]Oakes Ames Scroggs and Opal Faus Scroggs; [m.]Albert Hamilton Leach, August 25, 1950; [ch.]Alar Hamilton Leach, Arnold Wade Leach, Chester Glenn Leach; [ed.]Spearman Public Schools, Spearman High School; [occ.]Housewife; [hon.]Golden Poet Award 1991, Who's Who in Poetry 1992; [oth. writ.]Children's stories; [pers.]If I would have had the means, I think I would have been an artist. But since I didn't have the paints and canvas I just printed pictures with words.; [a.] Dumas, TX 79029

LEE, MARY EVELYN
[Pen.]M. Evelyn Lee; [b.]July 2, 1928, Bastrop, Texas; [p.]Deceased; [m.]Lawrence E. Lee, December 16, 1967; [ch.]one step-daughter; [ed.]Graduated from High School, B.S. Degree, Tillotson College-Austin, TX. Masters Degree, University of Alaska; [occ.]Retired Teacher; [memb.]Mt. Zion Bapt. Church, Heroines of Jericho, Life member of Delta Sigma Theta Sorority, [hon.]I have received certificates from my church, my sorority and several awards from the now defunct World of Poetry; [oth. writ.]I was on the eve of getting my poems in order to be published by, "World of Poetry" when they filed bankruptcy.; [pers.]I shall permit nothing, or no one to encourage me to dethrone Christ our Lord and Savior, who is our Eternal God.; [a.] Kirkland, Washington 98033.

LEFCOURT, STAN
[memb.]President of the Brentwood Homeowners' Association, Brentwood Area Chamber of Commerce, Founder and President of PACT (Police and Community Together); [pers.]1990 Brentwood Citizen of the Year, received the Poet Laureate award at the World of Poetry's eighth annual convention held in San Francisco. Poem "Color Me Equal". Mr. Lefcourts' role in several community organizations illustrates his belief that everyone should give something back to the community in which he lives. He will be spending more time writing and perhaps publishing a collection of works he calls "Poetry and People, By a Reluctant Poet.

LEHAN, HEIDI ANN
[b.] July 28, 1971, Annapolis, MD; [p.] John Lehan, Sr., Phyllis Lehan; [m.] Unmarried; [ed.] Northern High, current undergraduate student; [occ.] Prince George's County Government Employee for Circuit Court system; [oth. writ.] "A Better World" published in a 1991 anthology; [pers.] Throughout my lifetime, writing has often served as the best form of sublimation. I hope that it may serve others, as well; [a.] Oxon Hill, MD 20745

LEHMANN, HELEN JETTA
[Pen.] Helen Tate Lehmann; [b.] December 10, 1934, Anson, TX; [p.] Cinnie Louise Robbins Tate, James Calvin Tate; [m.] Divorced, June 27, 1959; [ch.] Frederick Arthur Lehmann, Jr (BA, BS), Marie Louise Lehmann (BA, MSBM); [ed.] Milton High School, AA degree, Pensacola Junior College, BSW degree, Univ of West Florida; [occ.] Developmental Services Support Coordinator, The Avalon Center, Inc; [memb.] Saint Rose of Lima Catholic Church; [hon.] President's List; Outstanding Achievement Awards; Editor's Choice Poetry Awards; [oth. writ.] Poems published in six national anthologies: "Broken Vows", "What I Like", "Solitude", "In My Garden", "Saturday Appointment", "Always Among Us"; [pers.] I began writing poetry two years ago while reading an anthology of Emily Dickinson's poetry; [a.] Milton, FL 32570

LEITZ, JANICE E.
[b.] November 1, 1939, Rockford, IL; [p.] Joseph H. Lyford (deceased) and Marian E. Lyford; [m.] Douglas D. Leitz; [ch.] Daniel R. Sarver, Garry A. Sarver; [ed.] East Rockford High Coe College; [occ.] Live-in aid for elderly; [memb.] Faith Baptist Church, Guildord Gleaners; [hon.] Winnebago County Dairy Princess 1958, Outstanding 4-H Clothing Project in Winnebago County 1955; [oth. writ.] "Your Sweet Way", and many nonpublished writings; [pers.] Most of my poetry is inspired by my relationship with my Lord and Savior Jesus Christ. I give Him all the praise; [a.] Loves Park, IL 61111

LENDERINK, MELINDA SUE
[b.] November 8, 1961, Meeker, CO; [p.] Kenneth and Jane Mannel; [m.] Greogry Karl Lenderink, December 26, 1988; [ch.] Amie Sue and Erin Jane; [ed.] Grand Rapids School of the Bible and Music; Kansas City Business College; [memb.] Larimer County Four-Wheel Drive Club; [oth. writ.] Poem published in The National Library of Poetry's Anthology, Where Dreams Begin; [pers.] The further I walk in life, the more I realize how greatly my parents have affected my life. Thank you Dad and Mom!; [a.] Olathe, KS 66062

LEONARD, JANET
[b.] November 6, 1955, Hot Springs, SD; [p.] Robert and Nancy Leonard; [ed.] Degrees in Law Enforcement, Legal Receptionist and Fashion Merchandizing; [occ.] Security Officer; [oth. writ.] Published several times by the National Library of Poetry and the Western Poetry Assn; [pers.] I should not be all that I am today if not for parents who kept me interest in life. And Mr. William Hensleigh my Eng Lit Teacher for always saying; [a.] Spokane, WA 99021

LEPORE, ANASTASIA D.
[b.]February 27, 1975, Hartford, Connecticut; [p.]John and Carol Lepore; [ed.]Graduate, Mercy High School, Middletown, CT., currently a freshman at University of New Hampshire; [occ.]Student; [memb.]National Honor Society, Who's Who Among American High School Students; [hon.]English Department Award, mercy High School, Presidential Award for extraordinary effort to achieve academic excellence, The Connecticut Association of Schools Award, Editor's Choice Award for Poetry (National Library of Poetry) 1993.; [oth. writ.]"Toy-Soldier", Watermark Press, The Other Side of the Mirror and The Best Poems of the 90's "Painted", Distinguished Poets of America, The National Library of Poetry; [a.] Old Saybrook, Connecticut.

LEPORE, CHRISTY ELIZABETH ANNE
[b.]November 29, 1976, New Rochelle, NY; [p.]Stephen and Elaine LePore; [ed.]New Rochelle H.S.; [occ.]Student - Hopeful to be a future author; [memb.]PETA (People for the Ethnic Treatment of Animals); [hon.]A publishers choice award from the National Library of Poetry, been published in "Where Dreams Begin and in school newspapers; [oth. writ.]I write personal poems and stories and keep them in a place for myself and nobody else to read; [pers.]"I

profess not talking, only this: Let each man do his best," Shaks. Henry IV "Great things thro' greatest hazards are achieved and then they shine." Beaumont and Fletcher: loyal subject; [a.] New Rochele, NY 10804

LESSER, DENA BETH
[b.] October 30, 1954, Los Angeles, CA; [p.] Al and Carol Lesser, Stepmother: Martha Lesser; God chidren: Travis Allen Davis, Katelyn Blair Davis; [ed.] UCLA and Antioch College; [occ.] Director of regional marketing for a major cosmetic corporation in the beauty industry, Haute Couture Fashion Consultant for an exclusive company in Beverly Hills. Make-up artist, actress, dancer, poet, screenwriter, astrologer; [memb.] Screen Actors Guild, American Federation of Television and Radio Artists, Actors Equity Association; [hon.] Outstanding Achievement in the American Poetry Associations, Editor's Choice contest on 10/21/88 for the poem 'Legacy (The Gold Band on the Third Finger of My Left Hand)', the National Library of Poetry Editor's Choice Award for the poem 'Clear Water' in 1993; [oth. writ.] Medical research articles on children's leukemia in the nurses file at the City of Hope Children's Hospital in 1966, a screenplay entitled 'The Camel Pusher' registered at the writer's Guild of America West in 1979, 42 poems published in 15 different anthology volumes from 1986-1993; [pers.] Words alone are not enough. Action is the stronger voice; [a.] Beverly Hills, CA

LEVIN, DORAYNE M.
[b.] Butterworth, Transkei, South Africa; [ch.] one son; [ed.] B.S. in Nursing; [oth. writ.] Poems and a novel; [pers.] As an aspiring poet she writes poetry as an expression of what she hears and sees around her; [a.] Texas

LEVINE, ABE L.
[Pen.]Abe (Al) Levine; [b.]November 9, 1915, Denver, Colorado; [p.]Herman and Yetta Levine; [m.]Mollie Katz Levine, September 1, 1940; [ch.]Barry A., Gary L. and Linda J.; [ed.]High School and Criminal Investigation.; [occ.]Retired Police Detective and District Attorney Investigator; with Denver Police from 1941-1966; D.A.'s Office in Denver 1966-1973; [memb.]American Society of Composers, Authors & Publishers, New York, NY; National Law Enforcement Officers Memorial, Washington, D.C.; [hon.]Several commendations from Police Department, Mayor of Denver, American Legion, Denver Post Newspaper, Hall of Fame for Outstanding Police Work.; [oth. writ.]Seven published songs: "Don't Say You're A Dream", "The Man Behind The Badge", "Keep The Faith" "I Love To Eat Chili in Chile", Member of ASCAP since 1953; "God Is Everywhere."; [pers.]Love is The Name of The Game.; [a.] Denver, Colorado, 80224-2933.

LEVINE, ADINA
[b.] July 11, Bronx, NY; [p.] Jerry Levine, Syma Levine; [ed.] HANC Elementary School, HANC High School; [hon.] Received the all-around student award in 6th grade; [oth. writ.] Published a poem in Anthology of Poetry by Young Americans; [pers.] I like to write all different kinds of poetry: serious poems, funny poems, poems that rhyme, poems that don't rhyme, and factual poems. I hope to be discoverdd someday; [a.] West Hempstead, NY 11552

LEVINE, MINDY
[b.] July 27, Boston, MA; [p.] Dr. Jerry Levine, Mrs. Syma Levine; [ed.] Hebrew Academy of Nassau County; [memb.] Emunah Women of America; [oth. writ.] Poem published in Antholody of Poems of Young Americans; [a.] West Hempstead, NY 11552

LEWIS, DEANNA LAVOY
[Pen.]Deanna LaVoy; [b.]May 7, 1943, Glens Falls, NY; [p.]Winifred and Robert LaVoy; [m.]none; [ch.]son; [ed.]High School one year college; [occ.]Electronic assembler; [memb.]International Society of Poets; [hon.]Editor's Choice Award National Library of Poetry 1993; [oth. writ.]Poems published Stellar, Strife of Life, Sailplane of the Sky, Guitar Strummer.; [pers.]The more I seek and find myself, the more I understand my fellow peers, with each year my life won't seer.; [a.] Houston, TX 77055-6907.

LEWIS, MARJORIE WINCHELL
[Pen.]Marjorie W. Lewis; [b.]September 29, 1913, Philadelphia, PA; [p.]Elsie Zieber Stearly and Samuel Dickson Winchel; [m.]May 23, 1942, Don E. Lewis; [ch.]Son, Dickson Winchell Lewis; and three grandchildren.; [ed.]Upper Darby High School, Class of 1930, Palmer Business College, 1932.; [occ.]Secretary until 1948, then a switch to feature writing and reporting; [memb.]Past Pres. of Phila Writers' Club; American Red Cross and Political and community activities; [hon.]Class Salutatorian at Palmer; Presidential Award as Red Cross Instructor; PA Voter Hall of Fame for 54 years of consecutive voting.; [oth. writ.]All facets of news for the former Upper Darby News; part-time police reporting for the old Philadelphia Bulletin. Poems appearing in several anthologies; [pers.]Moving to Havertown in 1957 led again to 7 years secretarial work as Parish Secy, followed by 13 in the Vice-President of U of P. Retirement in 1975, travels with Don, re-lit the poetry spark and now gone full circle. To all poets I say go for it.; [a.] Havertown, PA 19083-1117.

LEYLAND, DOLORES
[b.] June 22, 1938, McKeesport, PA; [p.] Stanley Borkowski, Stella Borkowski; [m.] Robert Leyland, April 18, 1955; [ch.] Deborah, Kathleen, Robert, Cheryl; [ed.] St Peter HS, McKeesport, PA, MAVTC, Bradenton, FL; [occ.] Licensed Practical Nurse - Manatee Memorial Hospital; [memb.] St Joseph RC Women's Guild, Licensed Practical Nurses Assoc of FL; [pers.] By attaining life's short term goals, life's long term goals will come; [a.] Bradenton, FL

LIA, LINDA S.
[Pen.] Linda Lia; [b.] October 26, 1949, Kenosha, WI; [p.] Angelo and Sonia Innocenti - Conforti; [m.] Ronald F. Lia (deceased May 7, 1988), November 10, 1973; [ch.] (1 son) Anthony M. Lia; [ed.] Gateway College Interior Design and Business Degree - Kenosha, WI; [occ.] Kenosha Unified School District - Special Education; [memb.] Friends of Italian Culture and Deaf Club of Kenosha; [hon.] Golden Poet for 1991 - World of Poetry; [oth. writ.] "The Empty Chair" Golden Poet for 1991 - World of Poetry - Sacramento, CA; [pers.] I believe that self expression leads to growth, and only expands ones awareness. Those who express themselves - unfold health, beauty and human potential; [a.] Kenosha, WI

LIDDELL-DONALD, ODIES
[b.]January 23, 1939, Grenada, Mississippi; [p.]Ruthe O'Neal; [m.]David Donald, April 25, 1981; [ch.]Lesa, Linda, Lorice, Leslie; [ed.]Engerwood High, Triton College, Pierce College; [occ.]Practical Nurse, American Lake V.A.; [memb.]Shiloh Baptist Church, Tacoma, WA; [hon.]Five Merit Awards, Golden Poet Award, Outstanding Achievement Award; [oth. writ.]Poetry published in Pierce County Herald, Tacoma, WA, Maywood, Harald, Maywood IL; [pers.]Live each day to its' fullness and praise, tomorrow may never come for you, life can be what you want of it, do right by life just maybe life will do right by you; [a.] Tacoma, WA 98404

LIKES, JAMIE
[b.] February 21, 1971, Stillwater, MN; [p.] Vinton and Nancy Likes; [ed.] I attend school at National Education Center, Brown Inst for my degree in Radio/Television Broadcasting; [memb.] I am a lifetime member of the International Society of Poets; [hon.] A couple of awards that I received are: The International Poet of Merit Award and the Editor's Choice Award; [oth. writ.] I have written a collection of many upoublished poems. Hovever, I was just recently published in an anthology; [pers.] In writing the poems that I have written, I am hoping that someday they will be turned into songs, because my lifelone dream is to become a successful country music songwriter; [a.] Stillwater, MN 55082

LIPSCOMB, WILMA V. SINES
[Pen.]Wilda Lips; [b.]May 25, 1931, Swallow Falls, MD; [p.]Raymond and Mary Sines; [m.]Guy F. Lipscomb, May 26, 1947; [ch.]Bob, Ron, Gay, Tim Rick and Guy Guy; [ed.]About 13 yrs. in school, make dolls, quilts. Finished H.S. in 84 with my last 2 sons. Took extra courses.; [occ.]Wife, Mother, Meat Clerk Retired and love to care for my elders; [memb.]Baptist Church, Authors Reg. Doll Club; [hon.]The first poem I ever sent in was in top ten. It was Procrastinate? That was a long time past. Been writing since I was 13. Five Golden Poet Awards, 15 Merit Award, many Honorable Mentions; [oth. writ.]Book published, Steps Through the Garden of Life.; [pers.]Always do to others as you would have them do to you. It all comes back.; [a.] Prudenville, MI 48651.

LISOVICH, JOHN V.
[b.] April 8, 1921, Rillton, PA; [p.] Charles Lisovich and Catherine Kolanko Lisovich; [ed.] Bachelor of Science in Chemistry - St. Vincent College Latrobe, PA; [occ.] Chemist (Analytical); [memb.] American Legion and Veterans of Foreign Wars; [oth. writ.] Poem: "Love and the Whippoorwill", Song: "Come Home Today"; [a.] Charleroi, PA 15022

LOBERG, VIRGINIA
[b.] April 6, 1932, St. Louis, MO; [p.] Allie and Oscar Aubuchon; [ch.] Lyman Jr., Randy, Kathy, Shawn, Michael, Aaron and Scott; [occ.] Line Worker; [pers.] I like a poem easy to memorize; [a.] Perryville, MO 63775

LONG, DONNA M.
[b.] October 3, 1935, Beloit, WI; [m.] William J. Long; [ch.] 7 children; [oth. writ.] National Library of Poetry "1993", Great Poems of Our Times; [pers.] I try to obey the golden rule - Do unto others as you would have them do unto you! The Lord greatly influences my poetry; [a.] Delavan, WI

LONG, FRANCES R.
[b.]April 7, 1928, Sanger, CA; [p.]Pete and Millie Gumber; [m.]Frank Lee Long, August 5, 1950; [ch.]Mark and Marshall; [ed.]Sanger Union High School; [occ.]Housewife, rancher and Basset, Hound breeder; [memb.]Chamber of Commerce, Native Daughters of the Golden West, Golden Chain, Council, Rebekahs, Selective Service; [hon.]Brd. Member; [oth. writ.]Several local newspaper have published a few other poems. Another publishing firm has published two of my writings; [pers.]I strive to paint a picture with words in the minds eye; [a.] Mariposa, CA 95338

LONG, FRED N.
[b.] December 14, 1938, Wilkes-Barre, PA; [p.] Amzie and Eunice Long; [m.] Martha, September 17, 1960; [ch.] Eunice Ann, Jennifer, Cynthia; [ed.] GAR High School, Wilkes-Barr, PA; [occ.] Lab Technician Marisol, Inc, Middlesex, NJ; [hon.] Editor's Choice Award from the National Library of Poetry; [oth. writ.] 1 poem published in Arcadia Poetry Anthology (1993). Also 1 poem published in National Library of Poetry, Wind in the Night Sky. Two poems a month published in our church letter mail out monthly Middlesex Presbyterian Church; [pers.] I like to write about my years growing up, also humor, love and religion; [a.] Middlesex, NJ 08846

LONG, JAMES B.
[b.]July 26, 1936, West Deer Twp. PA; [p.]Anthony Long and Marie Sullivan; [ed.]High School Diploma, ABT Certificate, Journalism Certificate, some college credits; [occ.]Custodian; [pers.]Nature is my favorite theme in poetry. Walks in woods and reading inspire my poems. I am a romantic at heart, an aesthetic!; [a.] Jeannette, PA 15644.

LOPEZ, ROBIN L. TOBIN
[Pen.]Robin Tobin; [b.]July 30, 1962, Sterling, Kansas; [p.]Mike and Carol Tobin; [m.]Louis W. Lopez, June 21, 1985; [ch.]Jamie Lynn and Melissa Marie; [ed.]High School Graduate 25th in class of 252 at Tahlequah High, Oklahoma, College NEOSU, Tahlequah, OK, Completed Writer's Digest School (A+); [memb.]P.T.A. (VP) running for school board. Rainbow Counselor Incest Survivors; [hon.]4 yrs. Vocal Scholarship, Most Talented Girl Class of 1980, numerous World of Poetry, Library of Poetry, etc. Recognized by home town.; [oth. writ.]"Two Poetry Books" available to public. Three novelettes, 100+ songs, free-lance articles for local paper. Publicity chairman for P.T.A.; [pers.]I believe everyone can write. Just put your inner most thoughts on paper. Always, Always, remember, God gave you the will and talent; [a.] Oregon, IL 61061.

LORING, CHERYL MARI LAKEY
[b.] August 29, 1950, Chelsea, MA; [p.] Jan and Keith Lakey; [m.] Paul W. Loring, June 9, 1974; [ed.] First Year College; [occ.] Writer; S National Library of Poetry; [hon.] Award of Merit, Life in a Grave, That's How it all came to be; A Home Away From Home, Who's Who in 1990, Some Day What is Love, Golden Poet 1986-1992; [oth. writ.] Working on a book - Life in a Grave, ready to go to publisher; [pers.] I am in a wheel chair and working with handicapped; [a.] Newton Centre, MA 02159

LOTT, SHRELL TURTLE
[Pen.]Turtle; [p.]Edward Lott Jr., Clementine F. Lott, Brother, Stanley J. Lott; [m.]Jesus Christ (Isaiah 54:5) When Shrell was born again; [pers.]Shrell refuses to use any words that refer to self (me, my and I) because I died, and I gave my life to Christ. Shrell is inspired by Jesus Christ, Shrell's technique is derived from the Bible. Shrell tends to focus on the realities of life, preferably the short coming of man. Shrell's endeavor is to spread the wisdom and simplicity of Jesus The Christ; [a.] Lafayette, LA 70509-0284

LOVELL, DONNA MARIE
[b.]November 6, 1951, Springfield, Vermont; [p.]Walter and Patricia Lovell; [ed.]High School, Minne Chaug Technical Assistant to Walter Carl Lovell Inventor (Who's Who In The World); [occ.]Poet, song writer, verse writer for card Co's., graphic artist; [memb.]Minister, American Fellowship Church; [hon.]Golden Poet 1991, Silver Poet 1990; [oth. writ.]Lyrics for "It's My Country." Presidents Reagan's Campaign, Our Worlds Favorite Gold and Silver Poems, Love; Miracles Writer's Pen; Poems published in local newspaper and the Union Leader "To Be President"; [pers.]Love, Like a thread woven into life's tapestry is intertwined with truth and compassion for all who dwell on earth.; [a.] Wilbraham, Massachusetts.

LOWREY, JULI M.
[b.] August 15, 1963, New Britian, CT; [m.] Paul H. Lowrey, April 4, 1992; [ch.] Kiter (our 3 year old persian); [occ.] self-employed; [oth. writ.] Poem published in a book called "A Break In The Clouds" 1993; [pers.] I'm exotic, exststic! Did somebody say Fate? All my love to my husband; [a.] Charlestown, NH 03603

LOZANO, VIRGINIA M.
[Pen.]Kina Velasquez; [b.]July 28, 1929, Sacramento, CA; [p.]Juan and Herlina Macias; [ch.]Irene McLaughlin, Steve Lozano and Charles Lozano; [oth. writ.]Summer's Love and My Gift Poems; [a.] Sacramento, CA 95828

LUCAS, GRAFTON EWART
[b.] July 1, 1929, Brooklyn, NY; [p.] Mr. and Mrs. Edward Lucas (deceased); [m.] Single; [ed.] B.A. Degree, NY University, 1977 M.A. Degree Major, Liberal Arts. Also hold Certificate of Religion 1980; [occ.] Pharmacy Technician, East Orange, Medical Center, U.S. Gov't.; [memb.] Choir, Schubert Music Society Tenor, St. Philip's Episcopal Church, Brooklyn, NY; [hon.] A plaque from the Home for the Aged in Brooklyn, NY 1964; [oth. writ.] Golden Poet Award 1989, World of Poetry. My first poem written when I graduated from Textile High School, NYC (1947); [pers.] I write from the depths of my heart; "cast away hatred, seek freedom from the self, love alone is true liberation"; [a.] Brooklyn, NY 11207

LUCAS, MARY ROBERTA
[b.] May 12, 1939, Santa Ana, CA; [p.] Mary A. Cunningham Jacobson, Edwin Carl Jacobson; [m.] Donald E. Lucas, Sr, November 17, 1962; [ch.] Mary Beth, Kim Dawnel, Linda Kay, Dawn Marie, Donald E. Lucas, Jr; [ed.] Lin Benton Community Liberal Art Degree College; [occ.] Sign Language instructor, CNA - Home Care Network; [memb.] Bowling League; [pers.] This is not only a honor for me but for my friends, teachers, family and deaf people all over the US. Because I am deaf, I hope this achievement motivates other deaf people to love the art of poetry and writing as I do; [a.] Springfield, OR 97478

LUCEY, THOMAS A.
[oth. writ.]The Living Debate, Wind In The Night Sky 1993, Contemplating The Quest, In The Desert Sun, View From the Other Side, (unpublished, under pen name), After the Fall (in process of development under pen name). The latter two are children's stories; [a.] Memphis, TN 38117

LUDOLFF, CONNIE
[b.]April 12, 1925, Pittsburgh, PA; [p.]John and Stella Gronau (deceased); [m.]Frederick Ludolff, August 18, 1956; [ch.]Three, Fred Jr. (Buzz) Carole (dec. 7/93) Melanie Williams; [ed.]H.S. Graduate, New Kensington High; [occ.]Fishing Camp Owner and Ferry Owner, Retired 7/92; [memb.]Faith U.M. Church Orlando, FL, Royal Neighbors of America, American Legion; [hon.]Three poems published in important poets and authors 1947 under Bernadette Wisniewski, Golden Poet Award, Who's Who in Poetry; [oth. writ.]Monthly poem in church letter, several publ. in Palatka Daily News, Golden Poet Award for The Greatest Gift; [pers.]Ludolff, Connie, nine grandchildren, 12 great grandchildren. I try to show in my poetry thanks to God for all his gifts especially the gift of salvation; [a.] Christmas, FL 32709

LYNCH, GEORGE
[b.] October 14, 1912, Asheville, NC; [p.] Dr. J. M. and Anne Duff Lynch; [m.] Alice Wilson Lynch, February 23, 1943; [ed.] Asheville Schools, Riverside Military academy, 1 yr. UNC-Chapel Hill, Asheville-Biltmore Junior College, (Now UNCA), Blanton's business College; [occ.] Eng'g. draftsman, substitute teacher, handyman, organic gardener, gospel songwriter; [memb.] American Nutrition Consultant's Association, Elkwood Methodist Men & Elkwood United Methodist Church Choir, Asheville Garden Club; [hon.] Honor Roll, Riverside Military academy, Certificate of Appreciation, Walk for Mankind, Mug winner, MUG Poetry Contest, "God's Golden Rest", World of Poetry; Effective Teaching Training Certificate, N.C. Department of Public Instruction; [oth. writ.] Gospel songs, and cookbook, as yet unpublished, many published shortcuts for auto work in national & Canadian Auto Journals; [pers.] I am an Army survivor of WWII and a believer in hard work, yet I strive to always mention God and mercy in my writings, because it was only God that let me survive alive without being shot in the back through WWII. And I have been greatly influenced by the bible, John fox, Jr., writer, and Robert Frost, poet; [a.] Asheville, NC 28804

MACK, HELEN
[b.] April 10, 1944, Ridgeville, SC; [p.] Mr. and Mrs. Samuel Husser (deceased); [m.] divorced; [ch.] Antoinette, Andre, Anthony Mack and Samone Smith granddaughter; [ed.] B.A. in Liberal Arts, College of New Rochelle Bronx, NY; [occ.] Outreach worker, Douglas Leon Senior Center; [memb.] Planning Board #1, Community Advisory Bd., National Council of Negro Women; [hon.] The National Lib. of Poetry, Dean List, Borough President's Award, Social Services; [oth. writ.] Community Advisory Board Newspaper, The National Library of Poetry, 1993; [pers.] I would like to dedicate this poem to my best friend Ruby Pierce for her inspiration; [a.] Bronx, NY 10455

MACKEY, RUTH VIRGINIA
[b.]June 4, 1919, Willoughby, Ohio; [p.]Byron Lamos and Mary Couhig Lamog; [m.]W. Oliver Mackey, September 24, 1955; [ch.]Bonnie Brown, Patricia Peck, Margaret Starr, Elizabeth Stitzel; [ed.]High School Grad, Several Management Courses; [occ.]Inspection Floor Supervisor; [memb.]VFW, Ladies Auxiliary International Society of Poets; [hon.]Golden Poet Award, 1991 Certificate of Merit, for poem The Painter in 1991; [oth. writ.]Over 50 poems, On Days Like These, and The Painter, are published and Never Say Goodby as published as a song; [pers.]Ruth passed away January 1, 1993, so I would like to say she was a loving and gentle person with the soul of an angel and the heart of a poet, (submitted by Husband, W. Oliver Mackety; [a.] Painesville, Ohio 44077

MACKLIN, LINDA T.
[b.]September 14, 1957, Ft. Dix, NJ; [m.]Richard A. Macklin, December 20, 1975; [ed.]Mayfield Central School; [memb.]Mayfield Central School; [memb.]International Society of Poets; [hon.]Editor's Choice Award, 1990 & 1993 from The National Library of Poetry, Editor's Preference Award from Creative Arts and Science. Listed in Who's Who in Writers, Editors, and Poets put out by December Press; [oth. writ.]Several poems included in Anthology's put out by Sparrowgrass, National Library of Poetry, and other smaller collections.; [pers.]I am inspired by nature, and I try to reflect goodness and positive thinking. I find inspiration in music also, particularly songs from the Moody Blues; [a.] Mayfield, NY 12117.

MACY, BETTY
[b.]January 30, 1941, Blue Mound, Kansas; [p.]Herbert & Goldie DeMott; [m.]Jimmy C. Macy, April 12, 1963; [ch.]Brett Alan Macy and Jerry Leon Macy, four grandchildren; [ed.]Newspaper Institute of America Blue Mound High; [occ.]Betty Macy & Co. (crafts & the Arts) Potwin, KS; [hon.]Golden Poet Award 1989, Silver Poet Award 1990, Who's Who in Poetry 1990 (all from World of Poetry); [oth. writ.]Published recording of song entitled "Up To My Neck In Heartaches" A poem in book titled "Magic of the Muse"; [pers.]Most of my writings are inspired by moments of impressionable memories.; [a.] Potwin, KS 67123-0223.

MACY, BONNIE L.
[b.] July 12, 1943, Dayton, Ohio; [p.] Chester and Miriam Lipps; [m.] Divorced; [ch.] Daveda, Wade, Mary and Kimberly; [ed.] Graduated from Lewisburg High; [hon.] Editor's Choice Award for Outstanding Achievement in Poetry; [oth. writ.] Several other poems have been published. The Calorie Saver, The Great Release, An Easter Dream, and the Flirtation in memory of Mom; [pers.] Be patient, be kind, believe in yourself and God and together those mountains in you life will be no more; [a.] Lewisburg, Ohio 45338

MADRILL, MARGARET B.
[b.]April 10, 1922, Las Animas, CO; [p.]Etta mae and Thomas Wesley Pritchard (deceased); [m.]Albert Madrill, March 25, 1940; [ch.]Greg and Gary Madrill, Sheila Pontaleo and Rhonda Hoback; [ed.]Graduate of Central High School, Pueblo in 1939, in top 10 graduates; [occ.]Supervisor of personal property taxes, Pueblo County Treasurer-Retired; [memb.]American Business Women's Assoc.; [hon.]Speaking before 3,000 members at National Convention in Detroit, Michigan, American Business Women's Assoc.; [oth. writ.]Poetry, 3 in Books of Poetry, several others published by newspapers; [pers.]Live by the Golden Rule and Ten Commandments to receive life's richest rewards; [a.] Pueblo Colorado 81005-2707.

MAHALKO, ANN
[Pen.] Wandering Pen; [b.] July 24, 1913, McAdoo, PA; [p.] Rev Gregory Gleboff Anna Gleboff; [m.] John (Deceased), October 3, 1934; [ch.] Gerald Mahalko; [ed.] Penn Twp High School Teacher's Training Stanley, WI; [occ.] Teacher, private secretary; [memb.] Sterling Estates Senior Club; [hon.] High School Class Valedictorian, World of Poetry 1992 Gold Medal of Honor; [ed.] Write quatrains monthly for our monthly park paper and a page titled, "From the Wandering Pen of Ann Mahalko"; [pers.] Poetry has always been a joy in my life so I wanted to see if I could master it; [a.] Justice, IL 60458

MAILHOT, JOHN MICHAEL
[b.]September 17, 1964, Connecticut; [p.]Ernestine Mailhot and Raymond Mailhot; [ed.]Electronics Diploma 1982, Harvard H. Ellis Tech, Animal Science Diploma, 1992 I.C.S. of Pennsylvania, Certified Bartender 1993, Johnson and Wales University; [pers.]The World would be a much better place to live if more of us would smile and also forgive you should abide by the ultimate statement that's not new of "Do unto others as you would have them do unto you!" Everything starts with the individual! I wish everyone finds love and the happiness that we all deserve to have!; [a.] Dauville, CT 06241.

MAINE, ANGELINE
[b.]June 1, 1919, Phoenixville, PA; [p.]Charles and Charlotte Maine; [m.]Single; [ed.]Graduated Phoenixville High School 1937; [occ.]Retired, Phila. Nat'l. Bank, at one time Librarian, Freedoms Foundation; [memb.]First Methodist Church, AARP, United Church Women, SAAC (Senior Adult Activity Center) Meals on Wheels Volunteer; [hon.]Editor' Choice Award Nat'l. Library of Poetry; [oth. writ.]Sold several, many published in company magazine where I worked. Several published in local papers.; [pers.]Poems come easily. I can write one about almost anything. Live to write my own verses in greeting cards and sympathy cards. Get many compliments on these.; [a.] Phoenixville, PA 19400-3570.

MAISH, JEAN
[b.]February 23, 1937, Elwood, IN 46036; [p.]Deceased; [m.]Junior Lee Maish, June 30, 1956; [ch.]Deborah, Letitia, Lisa, Tracey, Mary, Doreenna; [ed.]11 1/2 - I went to St. Joseph's School, Delphi, IN. Finished in Wendel-Wilkie High School in Elwood, IA; [occ.]Housewife; [memb.]Excel Fitness, Rosary Society, St. Joseph's Church, Teacher of C.C.D., Bible Study, County Line Dancing; [hon.]Bowling, Poetry, Pageant (2nd. place); most miles in "Meals on Wheels"); [oth. writ.]Poetry in newspapers Elwood Call Leader, Sunday Visitor. The National Library of Poetry; [pers.]I base most of my poetry on life experiences from childhood to my present age. Hopefully, my children will enjoy them.; [a.] Elwood, IN 46036.

MAKSAD M.D., ALI K.
[b.]August 14, 1930, Beirut, Lebanon; [m.]Ann Knowles-Maksad, January 1, 1990; [ed.]M.D. American University of Beirut, Post-Doctoral Training, Columbia University, NY; [occ.]Retiring Heart Surgeon, Music Composer, poetry; [memb.]Member of Poets of the Palm Beaches, Florida State Poets Association, International Society of Poetry, American College of Surgeons, American College of Cardiology and several other medical societies; [hon.]Golden Cedar Medal (by the President of Lebanon) for pioneering Heart Surgery in that country; Silver Medal for pioneering Coronary By-Pass Surgery; [oth. writ.]Several medical articles in National and International Journals; several poems in (English, Arabic and French) published in several magazines and papers; a book on Meditation; [pers.]I strive to find the truth about human nature, so that we could shift mankind, from the good to the better and therefore, live a healthier more beautiful, and more productive life.; [a.] Boca Raton, FL.

MALLUM, BULAH
[b.]December 20, 1909, Mapleton, Iowa; [p.]Joe Golden, Nellie Dale; [m.]January 29; [ch.]Two girls, Elaine, Marilyn and Loran, Floyd, all educated. Loran. Very Best, Floyd Electrician, Very Best, Marilyn a Nurse, Best, Our Savior Lutheran of Lutheran's all. Loran passed away, bad diabetic; [hon.]Yes, I have been all the way, Honored.; [oth. writ.]I have been a patient of Illness (50 years), Iowa City University Hospital. I am very thankful they have been with me all the way.; [pers.]Diabetic, I feel good. Sorry, I have no money. Love to write poetry; [a.] Dr.'s want me here, Good Samaritan Nursing Home.

MALONEY, MADALYN
[Pen.]Eleanor George; [b.]April 14, 1915, Stroudsburg, PA; [p.]George and Edith Hanna (both deceased); [m.]Homan J. Maloney, deceased, November 1941; [ch.]H. James, Maura, Elizabeth and a deceased son, George Timothy; [ed.]Stroudsburg High School, class of 1932, and additional training in voice and media communication; [occ.]Nine years as social editor of The Pocono, Record: fifteen years as daily columnist, radio commentator and public relations director for a department store; [oth. writ.]Daily newspaper column, "Looking Around with Eleanor George", daily column "The Wychkoff Shopper", poems in Array magazine, London's Daily Mail, Sign, the Salesian collection, "Poems of Inspiration", the National Library of Poetry's "A Break In The Clouds", the Pocono Record, and the Monterey, CA, winter quarterly; [pers.]At seventy-seven, my one desire is to leave something of myself in beautiful thoughts and words that my grandchildren will know what, and who, I was. If this is all I can leave them, I want at least to give them a sense of pride and lasting faith in God's eternal goodness; [a.] East Stroudsburg, PA

MALOY, EDWARD J.
[b.] November 14, 1917, Conyers Rock Oaleco; [p.] Tommie Lee Maloy, Delia Maloy; [m.] Melda Maloy, December 16, 1989; [ch.] 4 children previous marriage, first wife deceased; [ed.] high school; [occ.] Grocery Store Manager; [memb.] I belong to Campbell Stone Poetry Club; [hon.] National Library of Poetry Editor's Choice Award; [oth. writ.] Many other writing; [pers.] I have been retired 4 years and spend a lot of my time writing; [a.] Atlanta, GA

MANNING, DR. EMMA JOAN
[Pen.] Joan Manning; [b.] Atlanta, GA; [p.] Emma Kate and Mack H. Thomas (deceased); [m.] Willie James Manning; [ch.] Zario Laurenz Manning; [ed.] David T. Howard High, Morris Brown College, Atlanta Univ, Univ of Oklahoma; [occ.] College Professor; [memb.] Georgia State Poetry Society, Int'l Society of Poets; [hon.] Editor's Choice Award, published in Distinguished Poets of America; [oth. writ.] Golden Years, The Fateful Two Have Impressions, What is a Rose, Portrait of Zario; [pers.] I write to portray beauty and to cheer and inspire mankind; [a.] Decatur, GA

MANNING, JEAN
[b.] April 11, 1937, Hamilton, TX; [p.] W.O. Manning, Hazel O'Bannon Manning; [ed.] Hamilton High School, BA Texas University and Master's of Health Education - U.C.L.A.; [occ.] Health Educator and Head Start Program Specialist; [memb.] National Breast Cancer Coalition, Arthritis Foundation, National Assn for Female Executives; [hon.] Beta Beta Beta, Alpha Mu Alpha, Dean's List; [oth. writ.] Poems and short stories published in San Francisco literary publications, such as poetry, USA; [pers.] I write to express my personal feelings. Favorite poets: Emily Dickinson and Mayo Angelou; [a.] San Francisco, CA 94114

MARGOLIN, ABRAHAM E.
[Pen.] Abe; [b.] April 18, 1963, Miami Beach, FL; [p.] Alan Margolin and Phyllis K. Margolin; [ed.] Cortez High School, Phoenix, Arizona; [occ.] Steel Fabrication Technician; [hon.] Editor's Choice Award from The National Library of Poetry; [oth. writ.] Poems published in tow anthology's by The National Library of Poetry and several others not yet published; [pers.] God bless the world and everybody who lives in it! Special thanks to my friends in Morgan Hill and San Jose; [a.] Morgan Hill, CA 95038

MARIE, HALIA
[b.] May 5, 1975, Daly City; [ed.] High School Aragon, College of San Mateo; [hon.] Editor's Choice Award, National Library of Poetry; [oth. writ.] Fake Sounds published in where dreams begin; [pers.] The only things worth searching for are within; [a.] San Mateo, CA 94403.

MARKOWSKI, BENEDICT STEPHEN
[b.] March 5, 1932, Hamtramck, MI; [p.] Lawrence J. Markowski and Gladys nee Jaskowiak Markowski; [ed.] B.A., Central Michigan University, Jan. 1954; M.A. in L.S., George Peabody College For Teachers, 1958; post-grad. at Wayne State U., University of Warsaw, 1962-63, dual scholarship; [occ.] Ethno, Archivist for European Materials, Burton Historical Collection, Detroit Public Library, Smithsonian Institute, Detroit Institute of Art, Friends of Detroit Public Library, Friends of Polish Art (collector of Polonica; art, rare books, textiles and memorabilia); [hon.] National Honor Society 1967; 1977 Annual Alumni Award, Central Michigan University. Elected to the Central Detroit Bd. of Education, 1973-75 and simultaneously served as Chairman of Region 6. Submitted my plan against court mandated busing. Many of its elements were incorporated into the final Master Plan. While attending college, from 1949-1953, each year I was recognized as "poet laureate" by the English Dept., at the annual convocations; [oth. writ.] Carissima, A Lyric Drama, Detroit, The Poet's mark, 1980; Promethea (a bio-drama of Mme. curie), unpublished, 1967; Kopernik, the Great Humanist, Detroit, Endurance Press, c1973; Centian Versus Gibraltar; Collected Poems (to be published by my press, The Poet's mark. Also many magazine articles.; [pers.] I espouse "Romantic Futurism." I believe that all great creativity stems from some powerful emotion. Most of my poetry describes the creative process, aspects of all art, my philosophy of art and life, its wonders and the verities: love, beauty and death. I believe we must insist on the best audible language for poetry, which should be profound, sublime, noble and utilize various metaphors, both lyric and dramatic, as well as distinctive. Poetry is a profound and uncommon language. We must try to recover its former merits for the future. I employ free verse in my poetry; I have invented the Free Sonnet, a 14-line construction, where in the first half (6-8 lines), I make my statement or query, and in the second half I offer my answer or philosophy. The Poet's mark is my personal press, established in 1980 to publish my poetry.; [a.] Detroit, MI 48203.

MARSHALL, PETER
[Pen.] Pet Marsh; [b.] April 28, 1954, Rep. of Trinidad Tobago W.I.; [p.] Cynthia Marshall and Francis Marshall; [m.] Luzerne Marshall, June 3, 1989; [ch.] Joseph P. Marshall, Trevor Jonathan Marshall, Katrena Marshall; [ed.] R.C. Boys School T.W.I., Eccles Welding and Engineering, Albert Merrill Computer School, Pointfotuna Vocational School, Central High St. Croix; [occ.] PC Operator/Data Entry/Stock & Bonds Clerk; [memb.] World of Poetry, R.C. Boys track team; [hon.] Golden Poet for three years (World of Poetry) Computer Awards (Albert Merrill); [oth. writ.] Several poems published by World of Poetry in various anthologies; [pers.] In my poetry I strive to warm the heart of those around me to make them laugh or cry. But mostly to see life through my eyes; [a.] Bronx, NY 10452

MARTENS, MARLENE
[b.] June 14, 1936, Hoboken, New Jersey; [p.] Wilhelm and Kathe Heinemann; [m.] Hans H. Martens, June 1, 1958; [ch.] Peter John (May 6, 1960), Edward Gene, November 27, 1965; [ed.] Richmond Hill High School, Bus C of NY; [occ.] Housewife, secretary; [memb.] Busy Bees HC, Poetry Society of VA, Cartersville Garden Club, Friends of Library, St John's Lutheran Church of Farmville, VA; [hon.] Golden Poet Award for 1985, 1986, 1987, 1988, 1991 in World of Poetry - CA, 1993 Anthology of Poetry Society of VA; [oth. writ.] Best Poets of 20th Century, WPUP NY 1974, Poets Celebrate America, JM Press, Bicentennial NY 1976; [pers.] To share, To share my thoughts, To bare my soul, To be unafraid, To bear witness, that is my goal; [a.] Cumberland, VA

MARTENS, PAT KENNEY
[b.] Wash, DC; [m.] Maj Helmer J. Martens, USAF; [ch.] Karol L. Newton, grandchildren: Brandon L. and Kristy L. Newton; [ed.] Business College, D.C.; Assoc of Arts Degree (honors) American River College, Sacramento; Retired from Federal service 22 years. Certified Graphoanalyst, IGAS, Chicago. Honor assignments with Dept of State: 1946 - Council of Foreign Ministers (NYC); China White Paper, Marshall Plan, Wash, D.C.; American Mission, Athens, Greece (1948); UNESCO Conference, Paris, France, 1949. Air Force Awards (1963-1973: Outstanding and Sustained Superior Performances. Articles published in national magazines: Color Psychology, Doodles, Handwriting Analysis, True Experiences, Short Story, Poetry. Member: California Writers Club; The Cottage Tappers of Sacramento. Recent activities: Actress, Mystery Suspense Theater; TV Show-Tap Dancing Grandmothers; TV Show: "Senior Dating Game". Received Poet of Merit Award from the Int'l Society of Poets, DC. Poem published on tapes and calendar. Poem in 1993 edition On the Threshold of a Dream; [pers.] To love life is to live it; [a.] Carmichael, CA

MARTI, JO ANN
[b.] December 18, 1947, Ancon, Canal Zone; [p.] Ann and Ted Marti; [m.] Divorced; [ch.] Theodore and Johnathan; [ed.] Canal Zone College, Athens College, Sogetsu School in Tokyo Japan; [occ.] Professional Organist, Sense of Ikebana; [memb.] Teacher's Assoc. of Ikebana, Organ Guild, National Library of Poetry; [hon.] Golden Poet 2 times, Sense of Ikebana Sogetsu. My poems published in several books and college newsletters, songwriter of 12 songs, one on a record Come, Follow Me; [oth. writ.] Sixteen poems copyrighted, eight poems published in 8 books, editor of Navy Newsletter in 1976; [pers.] I try to express my feelings of my experience of divorce hoping to help others identify and heal with me; [a.] Orlando, FL 32839

MARTIN, CARROLL M.
[b.] October 23, 1937, Carey, ID; [p.] Marjory M. Kelly; [ch.] Gary, Gregory, Douglas, Sharon, Debbie, and Bob; [ed.] Sunnyside High, Yakima Valley Bus College; [occ.] Administrative Officer; [memb.] Organization of Professional Employes of the Department of Agriculture; [ed.] Poem published in Our World's Favorite Poems, 1993; [a.] Gainesville, FL 32608

MARTIN, IRMA JEAN
[b.] March 14, 1947, Woodstock, VA; [p.] Forrest Cullers and Catherine Cullers; [m.] Floyd John martin, December 22, 1984; [ch.] Chad David Plauger and Shelia Ann Plauger; [hon.] Awards of Merit Cert. Rank Honorable Mention for two poems. Golden poet certificate for 1990 and 1991 from World of Poetry. Waterfall published by World of Poetry Anthology, John Campbell, Editor and Publisher; [oth. writ.] Waterfall, Time, Oceans of Beauty and others.; [a.] Stephens Chg., VA 22655.

MASKEL, HAZEL
[b.] May 7, 1916, Georgetown, IL; [p.] Fredrick and Mary Ruth Morrison; [m.] Boyd N. Maskel, February 11, 1937 (deceased); [ch.] Arthur, Daryl, James, George, Fredrick; [ed.] Georgetown High; [occ.] Homemaker; [memb.] United Methodist Church, Homemakers Extension, church choir, church women society (V.P.), Georgetown Historical Society; [hon.] Who's Who in World of Poetry, published several anthologies; [oth. writ.] Poems published in local newspaper, IHEA Newsletter, Local HEA Newsletter, Local CRIS Newsletter; [pers.] It takes a lifetime to build a reputation. It can be torn down overnight; [a.] 102, Georgetown, IL 61846

MASTERSON, JANE
[b.] September 30, 1922, Lexington, KY; [p.] William Henry and Evelyn Green Masterson; [ed.] 1 yr U of Kentucky, Cosmotologist; [occ.] Cosmotologist - manager, KORI, U of KY; [memb.] Life Member

DAV (Disabled American Veterans), American Legion Eagles; [hon.] American Legion Certificate of Appreciation - Disabled American Veterans Citation of Honor - Disabled American Veterans Chapter #96, Outstanding Contribution as Commander Ch #96 (1985-1991) - WWII Victory Medal; [oth. writ.] Other poems and some articles for newspapers; [pers.] Life and let live in honor, truth, integrity. I fight for the underdog, against the greedy among us. Tell it like it was and is; [a.] Morro Bay, CA 93442

MATHEWS PH.D, VIVIAN
[b.]November 24, 1911, Waterloo, WI; [p.]Amanda Hints-Vocalist and Charles Archie- Architect, Memorial Arts Corp; [m.]Dr. Willis Mathews, February 20, 1942; [ch.]Willis-Artist, creative jewelry, Moris-Teacher, Charles-Engineer; [ed.]U of Wis. B.A. B.S. MA Ph.D; [occ.]Professor, University of Chattanooga; U of Wisconsin, Wayne State U.; [memb.]Sigma Psi Graduate Honorary Sigma Delta zpsilon, Woman Graduate Honorary, Lakeside Pallette Club, Eastern Star; [hon.]Oil Paintings, Hand Quilts, Published Amanda Archie Cookbook, Piano Recitals, Published Genealogy "Archie's Clan"; [oth. writ.]Histology and Developmental History of Grotestis of Lymnea, Stagnalis, Amanda Archie Cook Book, Genealogy Archie Clan; [pers.]Be on the level with mother and the world will be square with you.; [a.] St. Clari Shores, MI 48081.

MATIC IV, TOMAS ESTOLLOSO
[b.]May 16, 1978, Quezon City, Philippines; [p.]Thomas Q. Matie III and Delfa S. Estelloso; [ed.]Second year (9th grade) high school, University of Philippines, Quezon City, Philippines; [occ.]Studying; [occ.]Studying; [memb.]Artist's Club, Modeler's Society (Model planes, boats, dioramas); [hon.]First Honorable Mention, World of Poetry, California. First Prize, painting contest, College of Fine Arts, University of the Philippines, Quezon City, Philippines with a $1,000.00 prize, Recipient of DeJoya Award for Most Talented Artist (Painting) 3 consecutive years, 1991, 1992, 1993; [oth. writ.]Poems written: destiny, Iron clads, Jutland, The Day They Stopped The War. This Land is Ours, The Ghost of the Abandoned Guard House, Manila, Civil War Battles, Bunker Hill, Race of Adversity, Margaret; [pers.]Poetry is the finest and enduring expression of emotions. With its rhyme and rhythm, the wisdom of the ages are expressed in words. When these words are rendered to music, they become the language of the human soul.; [a.] Duarte, CA 91010-1935.

MATTHES, GRACE
[Pen.]Joan Zeep; [b.]February 12, 1937, Chicago, IL; [p.]Jacob & Roseina Strauch; [m.]Waldemar Matthes, April 12, 1958, separated 1974; [ch.]Nora 60, John 62, Heidi 64, Michael 65 (deceased), Kevin 67, Bruce 71, four grandsons, two granddaughters. [ed.]Loretto Academy, DePaul University; [occ.]Was Copywriter and Layout Artist, various firms, Asst. PR Director, Chicago's Museum of Science and Industry; Copywriter, Easter Seal Foundation, Colo. Wrote Resumes, taught art, California; [memb.]PAL (Poway Artist League).; [hon.]World of Poetry Golden Poet, 1987, 88, 89, 90; [oth. writ.]"Elegy to the Eucalyptus Tree", World Poetry Anthology, 1987, "The Flag that is America", Great Poems of Today, 1987, "Moon Exposure", new American Poetry Anthology, 1988, "Wave Avenue", "Confession of an Ingrate". "A Question for Baby", "Sonnet About Aunt Grace and Uncle Charlie", Love's Greatest Treasurers, 1988, "The Silent Debt", World Treasury of Great Poems, 1989, "Requiem for Rhett", "The Brass Ring", Best New Poets of 1988, "Profile of a Daytime Moon", "March Blizzard", "Book Hugger", "Soul City", Love's Greatest Treasures, Vol. II, 1989, "Stranger than Fiction", "Some Things Ain't", "The Search", "Let's Shake on it", Publisher's Choice: Selected Poets of the New Era, 1989, "In the Twilight of a Storm", Best Poets of 1989.; and unpublished poems, authored 100 limericks 40 satires, 30 sonnets and 300 assorted free verse, blank verse, traditional and irreverent poems--most, either too short or too long for present day prerequisites.; [pers.]I know I was born in the wrong century and therefore have affinity with dinosaurs. Look for triple meanings in my work.; [a.] Poway, CA 92064.

MATTHEWS, CINDY J.
[b.] March 3, 1969, Hospital; [p.] Robert and Janet Matthews; [ed.] I graduated in Valpariso High School in '88; [occ.] I work as a diswasher at Valparaiso Univ; [hon.] I received an Academic Achievement Award for having the highest grade in the class. I also received an Editor's Choice Award for my poem; [pers.] I really enjoy writting my poetry a lot, inspired by my feelings and surroundings; [a.] Valparaiso, IN 46383

MATULA, JEAN ANDERSON
[Pen.] Jean Anderson; [b.] February 27th, Staten Island, NY; [p.] William Anderson, Albertina Anderson; [m.] Theodore Matula, D.F.C., P.H., June 30, 1956; [ch.] Francis, Christopher, Jean Elisabeth; [ed.] New Dorp High School, Hunter College, Wagner College; [occ.] Teacher; [memb.] Guardian Angels Church Choir, King Charles the Martyr, A.A. U.W., Zeta Tau Alpha Alumnae, Civil Service Board Chair, Smithsonian, Friends of the Everglades, former Camp Fire Girl; [hon.] High School Artist, Dean's List, Life Certificate Teacher (NJ) Grades 1-8; [oth. writ.] Columnist and reporter for "The Staten Island Advance," Poem "Lament for Old Florida", 1982 edition 20th Century's Greatest Poems and newsletters for the Staten Island Club of Hunter College and the Gifted Class of Lantana (Fla.) Elementary School; [pers.] Writing poetry is a luxury I wish I could indulge more often. I guess my philosophy is the same as anyone's who lives with a disabled son and husband, my spouse was forced to retire...just keep going day by day, and pray; [a.] Lantana, FL 33462

MAXSON, DARREL C.
[b.]March 1, 1908, Sanger, CA; [p.]Isaac and Lucile Maxson; [m.]Vera May, May 12, 1935; [ch.]Charles Daniel, Sarah Margaret; [ed.]1/2 yr. college; [occ.]Retired from Pan Am World Airways, Supvr. Supply; [hon.]Elder, First Christian Church, Disciples of Christ; [oth. writ.]Poetry in local newspapers, developed, used and copyrighted "A Basic Supply Manual", Copy in U.S. Library Short Stories for Family History; [a.] Pleasanton, CA 94566-3205

MAXWELL, KATHERINE GANT (PH.d)
[b.] November 27, 1931, El Paso, TX; [p.] Leslie and Lillian Gant; [m.] Fowden G. Maxwell, Ph.D; [m.] July 14, 1955; [ch.] Steve Maxwell, Ph.D; Rebecca Harvey, DDS and Randy Maxwell; [ed.] B.S. Abilene Christian University in 1955; MS from Mississippi State University in 1972; Ph.D from Mississippi State University in 1974; [occ.] School Psychologist and Poet; [memb.] National League of American Pen Women; Society of Children's Book Writers and Illustrators; International Society of Poets; [hon.] Poem "Voices of Nature a semi-finalist in the International Society of Poets Convention in 1992; Book Buck and Mike Strike It Rich won 1st place in the State of Texas Convention of the National League of American Pen Women; [oth. writ.] 23 of my poems are published in different national poetry anthologies; 2 books Buck and Mike Strike It Rich and What Makes Bosses Tick; [pers.] I strive to reflect the value of a positive attitude in my writings; [a.] College Station, TX 77842

MC AFEE, HELEN M.
[b.]November 9, 1920, Princeton, Missouri; [p.]Cliff George and Cinda Ellen George; [m.]William J. McAfee, July 13, 1985; [ch.]Sharon L. Burden; [ed.]High School; [occ.]Retired; [memb.]Open Door Baptist Church; [hon.]Golden Poet Award 1989, World Treasury of Great Poems 1989, Award of Merit 1989, Who's Who in Poetry (1990) Golden Poet Award 1991; [oth. writ.]All during my school days I wrote many poems. My first poem written in Grammar school, was published in the St. Louis, MO, Gazette. I was in 7th grade and was very happy.; [pers.]I write most of my poems from my own experiences. It is my desire to uplift and bless others and somehow the written word can lift us to higher ground.; [a.] Lee's Summit, MO 64063.

MC BRYDE, JOHN M.
[b.] February 25, 1962, Holdenville, OK; [p.] Mr & Mrs Matthew G. Mc Bryde, October 2, 1987; [ch.] Lisa Pearce, James Pearce, Grandson - J.R. Pearce; [ed.] High School Diploma, Motorcycle Technician Degree; [occ.] Motorcycle Mechanic; [memb.] Harley Owners Group, American Motorcycle Association; [hon.] Golden Poet Award 1989, 1990; [oth. writ.] Publications with National Library of Poetry and World of Poetry; [pers.] I believe every person is given a gift, no matter how large or small, to share with the world. An unused gift is a wasted gift, and a wasted gift is soon lost. I pray that my poems give strength, to those who read them, to bring out and share with the world the gift they have been given; [a.] Parker, AZ 85344

MC COMBS, MARY DIANNE
[b.] October 19, 1957, Cabarrus Memorial Hospital; [p.] Arlen Dale McCombs, Frances Ollene McCombs, Stepmother - Doris Elaine McCombs; [m.] soon to be engaged to marry Ronald Keith Marlin, March 26, 1994; [ed.] Graduated AL Brown High School 1976. Art Inst Corres Course, English Literature Corres; [occ.] K&W Cafeteria dining room attendant; [memb.] Science Club, Art Club, secretary. Pep Club, Facci Club, Church choir, Swimming and Jogging Club, Neighborhood Club (sponsor); [hon.] Art Certificate, English Certificate, Ceramic Certificate, 5 yr perfect attendance, Jr and Sr High Swimming Award, YMCA, Writing Certificate, Merit Award (outstanding lyric writing) for selective writers - Jeff Roberts Company, Member of the International Society of Poets; [oth. writ.] "Lift Up Thy Hearts" In a Question of Balance, Arcadia Poetry Anthology. And in America Poetry Assoc - Voices of America, "Special" - same poem - Am Poetry Assn, American Poetry round up published a song for Jeff Roberts company, Lift us thy Hearts; [pers.] I've been told I was gifted and creative

and talented through my writings and paintings. Drawing since I was so high; [a.] Kannapolis, NC

MC GONIGAL, CLAIRE
[b.] June 28, Torresdale, Phila, PA; [p.] Frederick and Catherine Jane; [m.] Charles, November 26, Thanksgiving Morn; [ch.] Biological - Andrea and Terry; Adopted children - Timothy and Angie; [ed.] Private Elementary School, Public High School, Two years of college, eight years of French, five years of Spanish; [occ.] Secretary; [memb.] Sierra Club Wilderness Society, Audubon Society, Nature Conservancy, World Wildlife Fund, Defenders of Wildlife; [hon.] Golden Poet Award 1989, Certificate of Poetic Achievement 1990; [oth. writ.] One poem published in "Great Poems of the Western World". One poem published in "World Treasury of Golden Poems". Severn poems published in "American Poetry Anthology, 1990"; [pers.] Laugh at life, and good things will happen to you; [a.] Culver City, CA

MC CROSKEY, DOROTHY M.
[b.] November 14, 1930, Iowa City, Iowa; [p.] Herbert and Freda Creighton; [m.] George D. McCroskey, July 18, 1963; [ch.] Allen Moon, Vickie Wade, Yolanda Pendley, Randy Moon, Diana Strange, Brian M.; [occ.] Homemaker Artist in Acrylic; [hon.] Scouting 26 active years Silver/Fawa/Good Shepherd; [pers.] My writings are inspired by my love for children, family God and my art work. Flowing together on canvas or in a poem; [a.] Maryville, TN 37804.

MC CULLEY, KAREN
[b.] Lincoln, NE; [p.] (the late)

MC CULLEY, KAREN
[b.] Lincoln, NE; [p.] (the late) Albert Oldenburg, Moreen Pomajzl; [ed.] Lincoln High, Moorpark College; [occ.] Personal Services; [memb.] Calvary Bible Church; [oth. writ.] Wonderin (published 1992, On the Threshold of a Dream, Volume III); [pers.] To listen to the voice of God and to become like Yeshua is the only thing in the world worth caring for. Remembering John 3:16 "For God so loved the world that He gave His only begotten son, that whosoever believeth in Him should not perish, but have everlasting life"; [a.] Encinitas, CA

MC CULLOUGH, BETH
[b.] January 5, 1965, Findlay, OH; [p.] Dennis Lemons, Linda Bowdoin; [m.] Shane McCullough, May 7, 1988; [ch.] Colten Alan; [ed.] McComb High; some courses at Owens Tech; graduated from a Dale Carnegie Course; [occ.] Production Control Analyst; [oth. writ.] 2 poems published in books - received honorable mention for both; [a.] McComb, OH

MC CULLOUGH, EMMA MELINDA
[b.] April 26, 1966, Marietta, Ohio; [p.] Julia F. McCullough and S. Kenneth McCullough; [ed.] B.A. Marietta College; [occ.] Flight Attendant, American Airlines; [hon.] Valedictorian, Cum Laude, Recipient of "Young Woman of Distinction", Dean's List, Who's Who Award Students in America's Colleges and Universities; [oth. writ.] Yellow Ribbon published in NLP "Great Poems of Our Time; [pers.] I would like for my work to be seen not only with one's eyes, but with one's heart and mind as well; [a.] Pennsboro, WV 26415

MC DANIEL, SHANNON
[Pen.] Summer Chances, Pmal; [b.] October 21, 1079, Cleveland, OH; [p.] Barb and Dave Evans; Brother: Shaun McDaniel, Sister: Holly Jean Evans; [ed.] All grades to 8th currently attending Hillside Jr High, Seven Hills, OH; [memb.] Quilting Guild of England, National Ring of Tatters, SCORE Committee; [hon.] My poem was published last year in "In The Desert Sun", got 6th place in CCCG contest; [oth. writ.] Article published in the Plain Dealer too, and 2nd place in my spelling bee, "Sarah Girl", other small paragraphs and speeches; [pers.] (To Grandpa, passed away May 4, 1993, this one's for you, Love Shannon). I want to thank my mom for paying for my books! And Aimee, for being my friend (and my roomie for DC!) I would like to say thanks to grandpa, he knows why. And to Shaan and Holly and Dad and Jeff and Grandma; [a.] Parma, OH

MC FADDEN, H. J.
[b.] January 27, 1898, Georgetown, Ohio; [ed.] High School graduated 1916. Attended Wittenberg College; [occ.] World War One, General Motors Frigidaire Division and The Servel Corp. Opened own company in 1952 "The Apex Products Co."; [hon.] Fourth poem written won a trophy at a convention of poets in 1991. It is titled "Home"; [oth. writ.] Poem, Reflections on 92 Years, published in A View From The Edge; [pers.] Wrote first poem on 92nd birthday. Book "A View from the Edge" placed in The Congressional Library 1992.

MC GONIGLE, LADEAN
[b.] August 23, 1940, Thedford, Nebraska; [p.] Keith and Barbara Blauvelt; [m.] Dale McGonigle, August 29, 1959; [ch.] Vonna, Miles, Karma and 3 grandchildren; [ed.] Thomas County High School; [occ.] Retired Farm Construction Boss, Presently a Bookkeeper; [memb.] Friend Christian Assembly (Sunday School Superintendent); [oth. writ.] Two poems published in books and many poems in area newspapers; [pers.] I want my poems to be thought provoking and to always be uplifting to those who read them; [a.] Beaver Crossing, NE 68313

MC GREGOR, JENNIFER
[b.] January 29, 1977, Mayfield, KY; [p.] Terri Anne and Ronald Patrick McGregor; [ed.] School, Sophomore 10th grade; [occ.] Student; [oth. writ.] Bitterness poem, unpublished poems and stories; [pers.] In my life I live by a quote which I read on a plaque once. It goes: "The gift of life is God's gift to you, what you make of yourself is your gift to God."

MC GUIRE, RIK
[Pen.] Druid; [b.] November 17, 1951, Port Washington, NY; [p.] Josephine and Robert McGuire; [m.] June 25, 1977 (Divorced); [ch.] Justin 13 yrs. old, Sarah 11 yrs. old; [ed.] B.A. Sociology, SUNY at New Paltz, Computer Learning Center; [occ.] Former Computer Programmer, Now Disabled; [memb.] International Society of Poetry, National head Injury Foundation, Sons of Italy; [hon.] International Poet of Merit 1993, Golden Poet 1992; [oth. writ.] Worlds Favorite Poems, Medius, Plum Island Paper; [pers.] I write from and about the other side of life and also most importantly to ease my pain; [a.] Newburyport, MA 01950

MC KEE, JANE CLARK
[b.] November 14, 1948, La Mesa, California; [p.] Hal W. and Marilyn J. Clark; [m.] Howard L. McKee, June 28, 1985; [ch.] Neil L. McKee, Rosemary McKee-Ellsworth, Colin H. McKee; [ed.] Caletico Union High School, San Diego State University; [occ.] Owner, McKee Fur and Feather, Grooming and training for pets; [memb.] American Grooming Shop Association, Hookbill Hobbyist of Southern California; [oth. writ.] Many of my poems have been commissioned as gifts for personal occasions, such as birthdays and anniversaries. Published in the 1992 Edition of Who's Who In Poetry" compiled by World of Poetry; [pers.] My poetic talent is God's gift. I hope to thank Him by using it to his glory; [a.] San Diego, CA 92111

MC KIBBIN, MICHAEL G.
[b.] August 30, 1973, Arnot-Ogden, Elmira; [p.] Nancy Ann Wood; [p.] Grandparents: Wilma McKibbin, Dick McKibbin; [ed.] Horseheads High School; [occ.] Buser at Red Lobster; [memb.] Club Nautilus and Columbia House; [hon.] Golden Poet Award and Editor's Choice Award, Visions & Voices 1989!; [oth. writ.] The Unification, The Wonders of Life, published by the National Library of Poetry unpublished What Is Poetry, What Is True Love, Her Magical Touch and many more...; [pers.] If your father knew you existed, but he did not want anything to do with you. Most likely he does not love you. So he is not worth your time!; [a.] Horseheads, NY 14845.

MC KINNON, AIMEE
[b.] Charles McKinnon, Sr., October 31, 1932; [ch.] Roger mcKinnon and Dr. Charles M. Kinnon (Physicist); [ed.] Graduate, Ventura College, Ventura, CA; [occ.] Retired; [hon.] Golden Poet Award, 1988, Golden Poet Award, 1990, Silver Poet Award, 1991; [oth. writ.] The Reaching Tree (Poems); [pers.] Like him whose name was changed to Paul, like him, desire, pray and seek, in his same words, with heart made me, lord, what will, thous have me do? Then need what he will say to you; [a.] Corona Del Mar, CA 92625

MC LAIN, ALYSIA
[b.] January 12, 1979, Richmond, VA; [p.] Dennis G. Mc Lain, Aleta M. Mc Lain; [ed.] Currently in the ninth grade at Moon Area High School; [oth. writ.] "Flying Unicorn" in Treasured Poems of America Fall 1991; "Hand of Life" On the Threshold of a Dream Vol III; [pers.] My writing mainly relates to the theme of life or mankind. I also describe my writing as simple, overal; [a.] Moon Twp, PA 15108

MC MULLEN, JAMES
[Pen.] James A. McMullen; [b.] July 6, 1923, Lawrence, Massachusetts; [p.] Agnes and Arthur McMullen; [memb.] Gladys J. McMullen, September 11, 1948, James Jr., Sandra, Charlene (seven grandchildren, Cammie, Jason, Walter, Dancy, Matt, Ryan, Chacy; [ed.] Lawrence High School, Massachusetts College of Pharmacy, Wilson School of Applied Science (Medical Lab); [occ.] Manager, food distribution; [hon.] Golden Poet Award, World of Poetry 1989; [oth. writ.] Several poems in local newspaper, eight poems published in our World's Favorite Poems; [pers.] All my poetry is dedicated to my beloved wife Gladys; [a.] Carson City, NV 89706

MC MURRY, GLORIA PATRICIA
[Pen.] by glory; [b.] December 16, 1937, Chicago, IL (Brideport); [p.] Carleton Amos Sawyer and Maxine

Ruth Boone Sawyer; [m.] William Curtis McMurry, June 4, 1955; [ch.] Gloria Patricia, William Curtis, Terrance Michael and Pamela Jo; [ed.] Healy Elementary, Holden High, Jones Commercial and Elgin High; [occ.] Wife, mother, grandmother, freelance writer, designer, pattern tooling; [memb.] Christ's Family since childhood, arm chair philosophy, Baptist church, Republican party, Assn with the National Library of Poetry; [hon.] Golden Poet in 1990, 1991, 1992; Editor's Choice award 1993, Who's Who in Poetry, 1990 and many certificates of award and 12 publishings; [oth. writ.] Poems of life's stages of consequence, and of simple pleasures. Also working on children's stories, several poems published by World of Poetry and the National Library of Poetry; [pers.] To inspire, the celebration of worth has put into words, joy, pain, the hectic and the Quiet Solitude. That will embrace, each one of us. In our journey, of present, "called life"; [a.] Zeeland, MI

MC NIVEN, SARAH
[b.]January 15, 1915, Burlington, Wyoming 82411; [p.]James Robert and Nellie Elizabeth McNiven; [m.]Divorced, I use my maiden name, August 14, 1942; [ch.]Charles mcNiven Humphreys and Scott McNiven Humphreys; [ed.]University of Wyoming, Washington State College, Pullman, Washington and Washington University, St. Louis, MO; [occ.]Music teacher with a B.S. Degree; [memb.]Member of the Church of Jesus Christ of Latter Day Saints all my life; [hon.]My two Sons, Charles and Scott; [oth. writ.]Thousands of poems shared with family and friends, especially those living with cancer etc. from day to day; [pers.]God is real. He answers our prayers. Life is eternal. Each day is a new day of our eternal lives. Jesus is the Christ.; [a.] Berkely, California 94709.

MC QUILKIN, RANDY E.
[b.]May 8, 1958, West Point, NY; [p.]Earnest mcQuilkin and Mary McQuilkin; [m.]Wendy McQuilkin, June 4, 1988; [ed.]Bethel High, Western Ct. State College, 2 yrs.; [occ.]I work for Kimberly Clark Corporation; [memb.]International Society of Poets, Lifetime Member Advisory Panel; [hon.]Golden Poet Trophy for 1992, Honorable Mention, World of Poetry 1991; [oth. writ.]Lyrics, Melody and read vocals for the Album Poetry/Dark Waters with co-songwriter and producer Jerry Boutot. Copies may be ordered thru my address; [pers.]I use my poetry to explore my thoughts feelings and spirituality. Hopefully it will enlighten and or entertain others; [a.] New Millford, CT 06776

MC VEY, JUDY KAY
[Pen.] Southern Star; [b.] October 13, 1957, Oneida, TN; [p.] Bronson G. Brown (deceased) and Loma Jean (Duncan) Brown; [m.] Kenneth Andrew McVey, Jr., August 29, 1976; [ch.] Jason Howard Fike 17, Jeremy Eugene Fike 15, Juston Lee Fike 13, by first husband; [ed.] Churubusco High School; [occ.] Over-the-road truck driver with husband. A team for US XPress, Tunnel Hill, GA; [memb.] Bedford 1st Church of the Nazarene, Bedford, IN; [hon.] Editor's Choice Award 1993, by National Library of Poetry; [oth. writ.] Several poems published in different anthologies; [pers.] I only write what I feel. Each poem contains a part of me or my life; [a.] Allardt, TN 38504

MEIER, ANNEGRET
[Pen.] Annegret; [b.] June 20, 1951, Wustrow, Germany; [p.] Marie-Luise, Alexander Richert; [m.] Karl-Heinz Meier, February 3, 1970; [ch.] Olaf, Olivia-Patricia; [ed.] Realschule, Germany apprenticeship medical assistant; [occ.] Homemaker/Artist; [hon.] Praises by family and friends; [oth. writ.] Many poems, one book, not published, written in german; [pers.] I always loved to write, and I like to put the facts of life into poems that makes it easier to deal with today's hard times of living; [a.] Bloomfield Hills, MI 48304

MELGAR, KIRA E.
[Pen.] Kira E.; [b.] July 19, 1968, South Lake Tahoe, CA; [p.] (late) Alonso and Angela Melgar; [ed.] Associated Travel School, Miami, FL; [occ.] Travel Agent, Missoula, MT; [memb.] American Heart Association, Big Brothers and Sisters, March of Dimes; [hon.] 1986 - 87 U.S. Achievement Academy (book) track - 1985-87; [oth. writ.] Several poems published in birth town newspapers, 1992 National Library of Poetry and in school; [pers.] I believe in communication and how it reflects the person speaking, therefore in my writing I hide nothing in what I believe in, which is life; [a.] Missoula, MT

MELLO, DONNA LEE
[b.] April 21, 1947, Hanford, CA; [p.] Clarence and Dolores (Toste) Fagundes; [m.] Michael Ernie Mello, November 27, 1965. Date of divorce July 27, 1989; [ch.] Michael, Frank and Tiffany Mello; [ed.] Fresno State Univ of Calif; [occ.] E.S.L. Hanford Adult School; Instructional Aide; [memb.] International Society of Poets; [oth. writ.] A-Binder-Full; [pers.] Dedicated to Michael Ernie Mello; [a.] Hanford, CA

MEMOLI, CHRISTINA RUSSO
[b.]January 4, 1956, Newark, NJ; [p.]Michael and Mildred Russo; [m.]Divorced; [ed.]College A.A.S. and Union College Degree of Science, Roselle Park High School; [occ.]Respiratory Therapist, currently disabled; [memb.]Ostomy Society, head Injury Society, Trio Transplant organization; [hon.]Awards for Poetry; [oth. writ.]Several other poetry published in three World of Poetry books; [a.] Roselle Park, New Jersey

MERCORELLI, ANTHONY
[b.]September 7, 1924, NYC; [p.]Nicola and Theresa Mercorelli; [m.]Anna Marie Mazza, September 7, 1947; [ch.]Mary Theresa and Nicholas; [occ.]Meat Cutter for Arthur Stern Meat Co., Retired; [memb.]World of Poetry, National Library of Poetry, Amherst Society, Cedar Publishing, The Poetry Forum, Sparrowgrass Poetry; [hon.]Nine Honorable Mentions, Five Golden Awards, 1 Poet Laureate; [oth. writ.]Prayer for peace. The Prayer, The Old School, The Subway People. The Master Anna Marie, Rejoice, Hero's of the Stark, Week Summer Ends, A Word of Love, Gift of Life; [a.] New York, NY 10467.

MERRITT, JOAN KENNEDY
[Pen.] Jessica Rawlings/Snow; [b.] February 6, 1944, Holyoke, MA; [p.] James and Eileen Kennedy, Brother - James Kennedy, Sister - Eileen Hartling; [m.] Sgt James C. Merritt, February 18, 1967; [ch.] none; [ed.] 12 grade - commercial course graduated, graduated 1966, Licensed practical nurse, 1st Class Dean Vocational (former Holyoke Trade 1965-1966), graduated IBM; [occ.] LPN (Charge Nurse), disabled - Hodgekins Disease (Cancer 90% - 5 yrs cured 1993); [memb.] DAV Auxillary; "Holyoke Women Club" Veteran's Chairman 14th District Veteran's Federation of Mass Chairman Women's Club; [hon.] 3 Academy Awards, Golden Poet 1989-1993, Golden Medal of Honor, all from World of Poetry Hall of Fame. One of World's great living poets whose poetry has been for inclusion in the World of Poetry's landmark anthology "Poems That Will Life Forever", protected in pegasus time capsul to be opened October 1, 2091; [oth. writ.] Published 1989-1990-1991-1992-1993, Love You - Love Me Forever, "My Special Guy", "Bione Soldier", "Policemen in the Highway", received Gold Medal of Honor; [pers.] I have always loved helping people. It really feels good to be able to express my thoughts to all through my Poetry; [a.] Holyoke, MA

MERRITT, JOSEPHINE CARR
[b.]October 5, 1934; [hon.]For poems written in World of Poetry contests, 1989 and 1990; [oth. writ.]Numerous poems and songs, etc.

MERRY, MARILYN
[b.]July 28, 1946, St. Louis, Missouri; [p.]Elnora and Roscoe Hoover; [ch.]Meana and Jason Ward; [ed.]Attending College, Marywood College, Scranton, PA; [occ.]Cartographer; [memb.]NAACP, Coalition of Labor Union Women, National Council of Negro Woman American Federation of Government Employees; [oth. writ.]Books, Treasurers, "Courageous" papers, sexual harassment, another dimension; [pers.]My goal is to help someone and give as much as I can to my community, country and humanity; [a.] Capitol Heights, MD 20743

MERRYWEATHER, JOYCE JOHNSON
[b.] October 18, 1920, Utah; [m.] Clarence B. Johnson (deceased), now married to Max B. Merryweather since June 2, 1990; [ch.] Rosalie J. Smith, Glade Raymond Johnson, Janell, J. Lawrence, Jeffrey J. Johnson, and Julie Ann J. Ferguson; I am retired now. Education was Provo H. School, and Brigham Young Univ - majored in Business and Social Work. I belong to the Lions Club, BYU Emeritis Club, LDS Church, DAVA - NARF, Utah State Legislator delegate, Utah County Legislative Council, Orem Women's Club and Senior Citizens. I was a semifinalist at the International Society of Poets contest both times I have attended and will be getting a Lifetime Membership award to the ISP and I will be appointed to the ISP Advisory Panel. I have written stories, plays and poetry all my life for friends, church, and all organizations that I have belonged to. I am finally getting ready to publish a book mostly for family and friends. I believe in the brotherhood of man and service to mankind. Service to my church, country, and family. I have spent many hours of service to the disabled veterans organization. I write articles about veterans as my husband still has shrapnel from WW2. I have 25 grandchildren and 7 great-grandchildren; [a.] Orem, UT

MESSERALL, IRENE G.
[b.]July 31, 1927, Cochranton, PA; [p.]Elmer Wayne Messerall, Martinette Frances Messerall; [ed.]Peabody High School, Pittsburgh, PA; [occ.]42 year career with major oil company: Pittsburgh, PA, Houston, TX and Orlando, FL; [memb.]Various Humane Societies FL; [hon.]Amateur photography; [oth.

writ.]Author/Editor, company newsletters and newsletter; [pers.]I believe writing to be the manifestation of the soul's best and purest thoughts. My life has been profoundly blessed, many thoughts inspired, by the awesome beauty and wonder of the world of Nature. My writings are simply a rephrasing of those thoughts and ideas; [a.] Lehigh Acres, FL 33936

MEVERDEN, ANNA M.
[Pen.] Anna Marie Meverden; [b.] October 8, 1936, Jacksonville, OH; [p.] Roy Mullins (deceased), Erna M. Bond; [m.] Nick Meverden (deceased), December 15, 1983; [ch.] Matthew R. Chini, Leslie Ann Engelmeier, (4 grandchildren); [ed.] High School, self improvement courses; [occ.] Hotel/Motel management; [oth. writ.] Two other poems published by NLP; [pers.] I wrote the first poem before my husband died and it was published by NLP which gave me confidence to continue. I felt that I was too old to start anew, but I guess not; [a.] Fairfield, CA 94533

MEYER, MARIE ZEISLER
[b.] November 10, 1909, Marion, Ohio; [p.] Glen Barnhart Zeisler and John Zeisler; [m.] David Alfred Meyer, May 17, 1933; [ch.] David A. Meyer Jr., Frank J. Meyer and Betty Meyer Perkins; [ed.] Graduate Grant Hospital School of Nursing; [occ.] Volunteer, Church civic and community activities; [memb.] Tennessee Federation of Women's Club (past president), Lunch Forum, Presbyterian Church, past president Women of the church; [hon.] Cranbury New Jersey Tribute of Honor 1993 by General Federation of Women's Clubs, Tennessee Colonel from Governor Buford Ellington, Keys to City of Memphis and Shelby County; [oth. writ.] Editor General Federation of Womens Clubs International News Bulletin, poem published scouting magazine, many poems for special club, church and local groups; [pers.] Give me confidence, Lord, that I may say and do the things You would have me do; [a.] Cordova, TN 38018

MEYERS, EDITH F.
[b.] Danbury, CT, August 21, 1949 (raised in the New England environment in the 1950's and 1960's; [p.] Edith and Leonard Meyers; [ed.] Fairfield Univ, CT and Antioch School of Law, Washington, DC; [memb.] The Academy of American Poets, The International Society of Poets, and The Author's Registry; The award winning poet author is noted for her vivid depictions. Noteworthy poems include "The Backwoods of Connecticut". The poem received "The Editor's Choice Award" from the National Library of Poetry in Owings Mills, MD in 1989; "Slow Dancin' in Candlelight" in "Distinguished Poets of America 1993" by Watermark Press, also received the "Editor's Choice Award" from the National Library of Poetry in 1993. Other poems include "One Town Away", "Irish Shamrocks, Yellow Stars", "Chameleon Lover". She is currently in the process of shooting video poetry for broadcast via public television; [pers.] Ms. Meyers is of mixed ancestry. Mother Irish, Father Jewish. One can sense the mix and blend of cultures reflected in her work, yet she knows what its like to be different. In this regard, she is the k.d. land of the poetry world.

MIDDLETON, DOLORES P.
[Pen.]D.P. Campion; [ed.]Hunter College H.S., NYC; B.A., Nazareth College of Rochester; M.A., University of Rochester; [occ.]English Instructor; [hon.]Cum Laude, Kappa Gamma Pi; [oth. writ.]Poems published in World of Poetry Press Anthology and New Voices in American Poetry; [pers.]I follow Keats' philosophy of poetry: that it is "a Refuge as well as a Passion; [a.] Rochester, NY 14625.

MIETH, CHRIS MICHAEL
[b.] August 10, 1975; Bellville, TX; [p.] Lawrence J. and Dorothy Jozwaik Mieth, Grandparents: Wanda A. Jozwiak and the late Mke J. Jozwiak, Mary Mieth and the late Edwin Mieth; [ed.] 1993 Graduate - Katy High School; [occ.] Part-time Medical Office Assistant Aide; [memb.] Katy American Little League, St Bartholomew Catholic Church Altar Server, St Bartholomew Catholic Church Jr and Sr Youth Groups, Student Council, KISD Art Club, KISD Sr Executive Committee, Health Occupation Students of America, STAAND (Smart Tigers Against Alcohol 'n Drugs); [hon.] West Oaks Mall Teen Board, West Oaks Mall Teen Board Advisory Council, "St John Berchman Award" for being the outstanding altar server of the year; [pers.] My love for "Baseball - America's Favorite Sport" greatly influenced my writing the poem found in this anthology and also "Wind in the Night Sky"; [a.] Katy, TX 77450

MILLER, BECKIE A.
[b.] August 14, 1954, Biloxi, Mississippi; [p.] Linus and Deloris Herrman; [m.] Don, November 24, 1972; [ch.] Brian and Christie; [ed.] High School; [occ.] Childcare; [memb.] President, Parents of Murdered Children, ACJC Juvenile Crime Task Force; [hon.] Salvation Class of 1972, Honor Society; [oth. writ.] Several poems, articles published in Republic and Gazette Newspaper, several short verse contests in magazines and papers. Currently writing book; [pers.] Life and love inspire my writings including the pain of having my 18 year old son robbed and murdered in 1991. "The answer to all is the love we impart; [a.] Phoenix, Arizona

MILLER, CHARLES W.
[b.]November 29, 1909, Lancaster County, PA; [p.]Jacob Z. and Ella E. Miller; [m.]Mary Laverta Miller, October 30, 1932; [ch.]Three sons living: Donald Mills, age 60; Kenneth W. Miller, age 56; Gerald Miller, age 54; [ed.]Completed Elementary School; graduated from Academic Course, 4 yrs. High School; permanent diploma after 24 yrs., Millersville State University; [occ.]Retired insurance agency owner; in earlier life taught elementary school 13 yrs.; [memb.]Previously local Lions Club for 15 yrs.; Methodist Men's Club Aldergate United Methodist Church; also Casualty Agents of York County, PA and Life Underwriters of York County, PA; [hon.]Prefer to avoid this area. Had about 4 award on previous poems. Poem entered for contest and your publication titled "Lovely Minnesota"; [oth. writ.]I've written an article for Insurance Magazines, another for a church 100th Anniversary booklet. Should mention that I've written 74 poems, most of them in past 3 years.; [pers.]As stated in one of my poems, Dealing With Aging: Live everyday without dying before real death; and breathe positive fresh air with each new breath." Try to keep moving on.; [a.] York, PA 17402-2617.

MILLER, CLAUDETTE
[b.]April 8, 1944, Richlands, VA; [m.]David Miller, April 27, 1970; [ch.]Virginia Christine, Cathy Louise, Jimmy Darrell, Jeannie Ann and James Jason; [ed.]Garden High School in Oakwood, VA; [occ.]Housewife and mother; [memb.]Parent to Parent, Special Olympics, and Angel Acres; [oth. writ.]Yardsale, Runaway, Angel Acres, Day of Boom, Monsters, My Special Boy, You Know You're Getting Old, When! Going For The Gold; [pers.]I am a designer and director of Angel Acres a non profit organization for families with handicapped children. Our youngest son "Jamie" has Down's Syndrome. He is 8 yrs. old. We strive to work with families with disabilities of all types.; [a.] Okeechobee, FL 34974.

MILLER, HERBERT
[b.] February 25, 1913, Chicago, IL; [p.] Harry and Rose Miller; [m.] Sylvia K. Miller, January 4, 1942; [ed.] Harrison High Crane Jr College; [occ.] Foreman, Main Post Office Chicago, IL (Retired); [memb.] World Changers (Help Native Indians), Jewis War Vets, American Legion, Vets Foreign Wars, Cousins Club; [hon.] For post office suggestion, Poet Laureate of Synagog, have prize rose garden; [oth. writ.] Copywrited 3 poetry books, Editor Post Monthly Bulletin J W V, Write poems for synagogue; [pers.] Sponsor American Indian boy, help nephews and nieces. My poems aim to uplift all people with truth and love. Good food, homes and job training is need for all; [a.] Chicago, IL 60645

MILLER, JUNIOR L.
[Pen.]Jr. Miller; [b.]April 8, 1937, Kalona, IA; [p.]Lewis Miller and Fannie Miller; [m.]Ruby Ellen Miller, September 18, 1958; [ch.]Merle Dean, Morris Dale, Gloria Lorrane, Gary Lynn; [ed.]Middleburg School; [occ.]Bus Driver; [memb.]PV. Mennoite Church; [hon.]Safe Driving Awards; [a.] Phoenix, AZ 85029

MILLER, MARY LEAH BLAKE
[b.]October 29, 1907, Nashville, Tennessee; [p.]Vachel Weldon Blake (father) and Cecil Bailey Blake (mother); [m.]Walter Gunn Miller, April 21, 1925; [ch.]3 sons, Walter Blake, Weldon, Joseph Bailey--all deceased; daughter Ann Miller Curtis; [ed.]B.A. Degree, S.W., Texas State Teacher's College, San Marcos, TX; Two years graduate work--Peabody College, Nashville, TN; [occ.]Teacher; [memb.]Honor Society, Univ., TX, Texas Classroom Teacher's Assoc., Texas Teachers Assoc.; [hon.]Valedictorian High School, Honor Society--University of Texas President Texas Classroom Teachers Assoc.; [oth. writ.] Bible studies for use in teaching study groups in home. poems--published in church periodical.; [pers.]The greatest reward that I may hope to receive from my writing is the knowledge that those who read it may find their own lives enriched and their hopes and dreams heightened by what I have written.; [a.] San Antonio, TX 78201.

MILLER, NANCY M.
[b.] February 2, 1955, Kalispell, Montana; [p.] Pauline Nuzum, Johnny Miller; [ed.] Kentridge High, Green River Community College; [occ.] Procedures Anayst, Boeing Commercial Airplane Co; [memb.] Lewis and Clark Bowling Association, Federal Way Women's Softball Association, Boeing Pre-Management, Homework Club; [hon.] Dean's List (1974-1975) Federal Way Women's Softball Association "Allstar" (1978-1980). Boeing Fabrication Division "Employee of the Year" (1988), Golden Poet (1989). Homework Club Tutor (1991, 1992, 1993); [oth. writ.] Poems published in "World of Poetry Anthology", "World

Treasury of Great Poems" and World Treasury of Golden Poems"; [pers.] I strive to reflect the best of my abilities in all my endeavors. This poem is dedicated to my grandmother, Mrs. A. Frese, October 10, 1993'; [a.] Sumner, WA 98390

MIRANDA, JILL
[b.] April 13, 1979, Birmingham, AL; [p.] Donna Miranda, John Miranda (deceased; [ed.] WA Berry High School; [occ.] Student; [memb.] Berry High School "Pride of the Mountain" Band, Christian Club, Youth Choir. Riverchase United Meth Church; [hon.] 1st place - Ala Power Co Art Show, 2nd Place - Bluff Park Art Show; [a.] Hoover, AL 35244

MITCHELL, CHARLOTTE R.
[b.]March 10, 1943, Jeffersonville, OH; [p.]Charles L. Montgomery and B. Marie Rose Montgomery; [ch.]James Doyle Mitchell, Dennis Charles Mitchell, Bethany Rose Mitchell; [ed.]Chillicothe High School, Ohio University, Chillicothe; [occ.]Licensed Property and Casualty Insurance Agent, Office Manager; [memb.]Kerouac Society, League of Saint Dymphna, Board of Contributors for Chillico, The Gazette Volunteers for Literacy, and tutor for A.B.L.E. Program; [oth. writ.]Poetry published in 1990 American Poetry Anthology and The Best Poems of the 90's. Columns published several times a year in Chillicothe Gazette; [pers.]Although my poetry is as informal as my lifestyle, I enjoy identifying a different perspective in ordinary happenings. For me the best things in life are love, laughter, learning, and looking for beauty; [a.] Chillicothe, OH 45601-1006.

MIZUTA, IWAO
[b.]March 21, 1915, Honolulu, Hawaii; [p.]Iwakichi and Tamino Mizuta; [m.]Tamayo Mihara, 1943; [ch.]none; [ed.]B.A., University of Hawaii, 1938; M.S., Education, University of Pennsylvania 1947; M.P.H. University of California, Berkeley 1952; [occ.]English, social studies teacher (retired) Kailua High School, Kailua, Hawaii; [memb.]Hawaii Writer's Club, National Education Association, Hawaii Education Association; [hon.]Gold Medal of Honor, 1993, 4 Golden Poet Awards 1985-1988, 10 Awards of Merit; [oth. writ.]Poems published in World of Poetry Contest Anthologies, New Voices in American Poetry, 32nd Annual Mid South Poetry Festival Collection Memphis; [pers.]Basic poetic theme is change. I write poetry, chiefly influenced by English and American Lyric Poets; [a.] Kailua, Hawaii 96734.

MOBUS, SCOTT WARREN
[b.] May 31, 1968, Springfield, VT; [p.] David Morus and Carol Mobus; [ed.] Pima Medical Institute, Seattle Massage School; [occ.] Massage Therapist; [hon.] Editor's Choice Award for Outstanding Achievement in Poetry, presented by The National Library of Poetry; [a.] Seattle, Wash. 98109

MONTGOMERY, PATRICIA ANN
[Pen.] Trish Montgomery; [b.] February 16, 1965, Menard, TX; [p.] Wanda Ann Hanaway; [m.] Gary Montgomery Jr., October 12, 1991; [ch.] Ryan and Tyler; [occ.] Homemaker; [memb.] none; [hon.] Won Honorable Mention, Golden Poet Awards in the World of Poetry; [oth. writ.] I had a poem published in a book called Great Poems of the Western World in 1990. I also had some published in local newspapers; [pers.] I would like to dedicate this poem to the memory of Elvis; [a.] Dale, IN 47523

MOORE, EARLINE
[b.]November 2, 1924, Shamrock (Wheeler Country) Texas; [p.]Earl and Virgie Conner; [m.]B. F. Moore, my dear for 53 yrs., August 17, 1940; [ch.]Benny Earl Moore, Larry L. Moore, Patricia Gail (Moore) Brown; [ed.]I have a very limited education "formal". The talent I have has truly been given me by the my Lord; [occ.]Homemaker; [memb.]I belong to the Eleventh Street Baptist Church and Choir Singing Group "The Hallelijsa Squares"; [hon.]Along with this Gospel group. I have received a certificate of honor, for our singing in nursing homes for the aged. Honors for poetry published in American poetry anthology in 1990; [oth. writ.]A few gospel songs and a few tributes to friends in our local newspaper.; [pers.]I have always been able to better express my thoughts and feelings by writing them down. However; I didn't begin to write songs and poems until my mid to late thirties. My subjects are family, friends and spiritual things.; [a.] Shamrock, TX 79079.

MOORE, FRANCES JO.
[b.]March, 18, 1972, Connerville, IN; [p.]Sallie Jo and John Caldwell; [m.]Aaron Moore, June 30, 1992; [ch.]Jerry Moore; [ed.]Graduate High School, Take a home study program in hotel restaurant management; [occ.]Mother; [hon.]Editor Choice Award from The National Library of Poetry; [oth. writ.]I've had two other poems published "Dreams of Life" and "For Love"; [pers.]No what has happened to me in my life, I've always been able to get through it by writing; [a.] Cambridge City, IN 47323-0092

MOORE, LAURA A.
[b.]November 17, 1972, Morenci, Michigan; [p.]Lowell and Louise Witrick; [m.]Brad Moore, June 8, 1991; [ch.]Brandon Richard; [ed.]Hilltop High, Four Country Vocational School; [occ.]Press Operator at Winzeler Stamping; [oth. writ.]Several poems; some are included in other anthologies; [pers.]Never say "I Can't; just try, you might surprise yourself; [a.] Pioneer, Ohio 43554.

MOORE, LAVERNE
[Pen.] Vern; [b.] November 7, 1918, Gibson, TN; [p.] Allen Monroe Pillow, Lillie D. Pillow; [m.] James Henry Moore, February 19, 1943; [ch.] 1 son; [ed.] High school, some college, Raughon Business College, Cosmetology College; [memb.] Membership of First Baptist - 51 yrs; [hon.] Awards - Memphis Arts.

MOORE, TERESA L.
[b.] January 30, 1970, Winston-Salem, NC; [p.] Mary D. Moore and Wesley E. Moore; [ed.] ASS in Business Administration; [occ.] Manager at Bojangles Famous Chicken-n-Biscuits; [memb.] Jesse Duplantis Ministries, First Assembly of God; [a.] Winston-Salem, NC 27106

MORENO, ROBERT MICHAEL
[b.] June 9, 1950, Brooklyn, NY; [p.] Vincent James Moreno, Anna Frances Moreno; [m.] Single; [ed.] Valley Stream Central High, State Univ of New York at Delhi, Board of Cooperative Education Services, Molley College - (Two Certifications but no degree); [occ.] Unemployed ex-mental case - innocent ex-convict - lifelong self taught student; [memb.]: The Roman Catholic Church, The Right to Life Party; [hon.] Golden Poet Award, Two Honorable Mentions from World of Poetry Publications, and Two Varsity Letters; Writings; Asylum In The Sky - 1993, His Hope Prayer (inspired) - 1981, Litany of a Stray Dog - 1982, The Lord's Tear and Terror (Afflicted Teardrop) - 1983, Secret Dialogues In a Public Institution (a Play) - 1993, Joseph - 1993, Baptist Beatrice - 1993, Michael - 1993, Mac C. - 1993, Withershins (The March of Contrition) - 1993, Ode to Saint Dymphna - 1993, Ongoing Story - 1993; Personal note: Whether you are Person, Family, Religion, Country, Planet, or Universe - you speck of dust can not run from the True God - His Terror or the Horrors of the other. Jesus I trust in Thee. Sorrowful and Immaculate Sweet-Heart of Mary be My Salvation; [a.] Freeport, NY 11520

MORGAN, MICHELLE-ANNE
[Pen.] L. Michaela Morgan; [b.] January 3, 1969, LICH Brooklyn, NY; [p.] John Columbus and Claudette A. Evans; [ch.] Niece: Krissy - age 5, nephews; Pooh - age 3, June - age 9 mos; [ed.] Currently attending Medgar Evers College - Cuny Liberal Arts AA (Humanities); [occ.] Full time student and tutor (Teacher's Assistant) of english; [memb.] New York Zoological Society, Museum of Natural History, Adafi; [hon.] Editor's Choice Award; [oth. writ.] Expressly for TW, It's Love That Makes a Woman, No Name, Natural High, Mis-Story, Teacher (For Professor Dorothy Hopkins), Trapped, various letters to editors and essays; [pers.] Special thanks and blessings to my Mother, Cynthia, Marc, Stacey, African Voices, Dorothy Hopkins (love ya!) Dr. Keith Gilyard and my Writing Crew. "It takes a whole village to educate a child" --Nigerian saying; [a.] Brooklyn, NY

MORREALE, BONNY L.
[Pen.]Bonny Lee, B. Lee Morreale; [b.]March 30, 1956, Pasadena, CA; [p.]Ben Fortner, Shirley Fortner, (step-father) Robert H. Beal; [m.]Dean L. Morreale, January 7, 1973; [ch.]Four sons, Darrell, Anthony, Brandon, Christopher; [ed.]Royal Oak High School, Covina, CA; Trend Business College, Olympia, WA; [occ.]Writer, mother, housewife; [memb.]International Society of Poets 1992-93 nominated; Instated in the Library of Congress; [hon.]Golden Poet Award and Honorable Mention both by World of Poetry Publishers; [oth. writ.]"Grandma's Many Seasons" in New American Poetry Anthology by World of Poetry Publishers, 1988, "Timbered" in On The Threshold of a Dream by The National Library of Poetry, 1992.; [pers.]It is my pleasure to be chosen for publication in this book. I hope the opportunities never cease for me as an author. This one is dedicated to those who gave me the opportunities, and to my husband for encouragement; [a.] Ogden, UT 84401

MORRIS, LAURA
[b.]February 26, 1948, Santa Monica, CA; [p.]Maurice Rosenberg and Frieda Shiner Rosenberg; [ch.]Samantha, Leah M.; [ed.]B.S. in Elementary Education, University of Montana; [occ.]Teacher; [memb.]Music Teachers National Association, International Reading Association; [hon.]Who's Who in American Education; [oth. writ.]Three poems accepted for publication by The National Library of Poetry; [a.] Baker, Montana 59313.

MORRIS, MICHELLE D.
[b.] June 25, 1962, North Western US; [p.] J. Alan and Carol R. Hochstrasser; [m.] divorced; [ch.] Elisabeth (age 12); [ed.] Certified NetWare Engineer - scheduled completion 1994, Accounting and Busi-

ness Law Majors - 1983; [occ.] MD Morris and Assoc Pres/Public Relations Consultant, Journalist/High Tech Industry - 1993/current Inteq. Corp. Finance and Tax Planning/Ltd Partner, PR Director - 1993/current; [memb.] International Biographical Assoc, Cambridge England, Fellow by nomination - 1993/current, National Assoc of Female Executives, Honorary Membership by Nomination - 1992/current, International Society of Poets - Honorary Charter Membership - 1992/current, Gem State Writer's Guild, Vice President Elect - 1990/1991, Gem State Writer's Guild, Publicity Director - 1989; [hon.] Who's Who of Intellectuals - 1994, Who's Who of Contemporary Achievement - 1994, Nominated Woman of the Year - (Selection Pending) -1993, The World Who's Who of Women - 1993, 2,000 American Women - 1993, Woman's Inner Circle of Achievement Award - 1993, Who's Who in Poetry - 1992/1993, World Poetry Society, Golden Poet Award - 1992, International Society of Poets, Outstanding Achievement - 1992, Various awards through Gem State Writer's Guild - 1988/1991; [oth. writ.] Selected Works of the World's Greatest Poets, "Longings" - 1992, Selected Works of the World's Greatest Poets, "Spirit of Light" - 1992, Various works published through the Gem State Writer's Guild - 1988/1991. Ms Morris has and continues to author articles for anumber of industry trade magazines and newspapers, including: Electronic Engineering Times, InfoSecurity News, Physicians and Computers, Government Technology, LAN Times, NetWare Solutions, NetWare Connections, NetWorld Today, Houston Chronical, Modern Office Technology, PC Today, PC Novice, and From Nine to Five; [pers.] The mastery of poetic communication breathes new life and expression to the soul. Enrichments such as articulating the complexity of an emotion, the intrinsic nuances of individualism and portals of awe rendered with watercolor inflections of ambience; [a.] Hillsboro, OR

MORROW, LINDA L.
[Pen.] Yada Yee; [b.] January 1, 1963, Willow Creek, California; [p.] Donald and Betty M. Morrow; [ch.] Naomi Renee Stockson; [ed.] Hayfork High; [memb.] Nor-el-muk Tribal Council Members Board of Director for Trinity Rural Indian Health Project; [oth. writ.] The Wapfti poem published 1992. Poetry book finished and ready for publication. Working on novel; [pers.] Inspired by everyday life occurrences and reflect them in to writings. The Big ol Bass Dedicated to my father and his Big ol Bass that hangs on his wall; [a.] Hayfork, CO 96041

MORTIMER, PHYLLIS
[b.] July 16, 1933, Roane County, WV; [p.] Rev. Herbert Clark Moore (deceased) Dorothy Moore; [m.] Monroe C. Mortimer, April 2, 1955; [ch.] Allen Monroe, William Eugene, Teresa Ann; [ed.] Walton High, H & R Block Seminars; [occ.] Income Tax Preparer; [hon.] Valedictorian, National Honor Society; [oth. writ.] Three poems published in anthologies, one poem published in Milam Regional medical Center newsletter, several Golden Poet Awards, two Silver Poet Awards and several Honorable Mention Award of Merit certificates; [pers.] My father believed there is good in everyone and I strive to reflect this belief in my life and in my writing. I enjoy sharing my poetry with our church congregation.; [a.] Rockdale, TX 76567-9502.

MORTON, CHARLES W.
[b.] August 6, 1916, Knoxville, TN; [p.] William P. Morton and Jennie Morton; [m.] Norma Morton, January 19, 1946; [ch.] Nancy Ann Vest; [ed.] B.A. University of Tennessee, MBA Indiana University; [occ.] Lt. Col. USAF (Ret) and retired Industrial Development Coordinator; [memb.] Military Order of Wars, and Veterans of Foreign Wars; [hon.] World of Poetry, Golden Poet Award 1991, Numerous Military Awards; [oth. writ.] A paper presented at a National SAVE conference in Library of Congress and two poems in Library of Congress; [pers.] Poetry through ear appeal is more communicative than conventional verbage or writings. Ear appeal improves retention as President Lincoln's famous words "Four score and seven years ago"; [a.] San Bernardino, CA 92404

MORTONSON, JEAN SUTTON
[b.] June 26, 1963, Moline, IL; [p.] Vere and Ruth Sutton; [m.] Steven Mortonson, September 14, 1985; [ch.] Todd Steven; [ed.] Alleman High School, Rock Island, IL (writing certificate from the Institute of Children's Literature.; [occ.] Redding Ridge, CT, Homemaker; [memb.] American Diabetes Assn.; [oth. writ.] The song "A Seed of Hope.", written for PACT, child abuse foundation. "You" included in National Library of Poetry's "Wind In The Night Sky" publication. One hundred plus, poems.; [pers.] "While flowers offer beauty, their lives are shortly lived, but words and deeds of love are lasting gifts to give."; [a.] Sterling, IL 61081.

MOSHER, JEAN W.
[b.] December 23, 1940, Milford, MA; [p.] Susan Harris Mosher Patten, Carroll L. Mosher; [ed.] Newton High School, New England Deaconess Hospital School of Nursing; [occ.] Registered Nurse; [memb.] Affiliated with the First Parish of Westwood, United Church, MA Mental Health Nurses Assoc, Holliston Writer's Group; [oth. writ.] Church monthly newsletters, "CFIDS, An Owners Manual" 2nd Edition, self-published, internationally marketed; The National Library of Poetry - "A Break In The Clouds", and to be published in the spring of 1994 through the National Library of Poetry, "Tears of Fire."; [pers.] My poetry reflects my journey in life. I strive to enhance awareness and personal growth to create beauty, like the gardenia. I have been greatly influenced by seeing life through the eyes of nature and my nursing experiences; [a.] Norwood, MA 02062

MOSTELLER, JR., HERMAN J.
[Pen.] "Me"; [b.] December 15, 1953, Riverside, NJ; [p.] Herman J. Mosteller, Sr, Caroline V. Mosteller; [m.] Kathleen L. Mosteller, April 7, 19??; [ch.] Tara Lynn - 19, Scott Joseph - 16, Alyssa Ann - 14; [ed.] Engineer of Electronic Technology; [occ.] Technical Supervisor Public Service Electric & Gas; [memb.] International Society of Poets; [hon.] 1991 & 1992 Golden Poet Award, World of Poetry; [oth. writ.] Currently writing a book of poetry titled "Thoughts By Me"; [pers.] In a world of so many trials and hardships if my poetry helps but one person no greater reward could I receive; [a.] Riverside, NJ 08075

MOULDER, BARBARA NOTESTINE
[b.] Kansas City, MO; [p.] George D. Notestine; Alberta Stinson Notestine; [m.] Jack Dudley Moulder; [ch.] Gregg, Gloria, Daniel and Elisabeth; [hon.] Publication in Anthology of High School Poetry; 2 Honorable Mentions: World of Poetry, Outstanding Achievement, Who's Who, 1990, Golden Poet, 1989 & 90 Outstanding Poets of 1994 National Library of Poetry; [oth. writ.] Songs, short stories, devotionals observations; [pers.] What began as a means of comfort and pleasure to myself has grown into a ministry to others and a praise to the Lord Jesus Christ whom I serve; [a.] Forest, VA 24551

MUJA, KATHLEEN A.
[b.] June 24, 1965, Denver, CO; [p.] Thomas R. and Bridget C. Cramer; [ch.] Thomas C. Muja; [ed.] BSBA General Business; [occ.] Labor and Employment Specialist; [memb.] Network Colorado! Denver Jaycees, Denver Museum of Natural History; [hon.] Outstanding August Jaycee 1993, Woman of the Year 1992 - ABI; [oth. writ.] Several poems published by National Library of Poetry and one by Pacific Rim Publications. News articles for organizational newsletters; [pers.] Life is an adventure and the more creative the solutions to problems are the easier it is to be happy; [a.] Denver, CO 80210

MULHERN, BRIAN
[b.] January 12, 1953, Astoria, NY; [p.] Patrick and Jean Mulhern; [m.] Single; [ed.] St. Anthony's H.S., Iona College; [occ.] Landscape Construction, Arborist; [memb.] New York Pinewoods Folk Music Club; [hon.] Honorable mention free poetry contest World of Poetry 1992, Golden Poet - World of Poetry 1992. Honorable mention Babylon Council of the Arts songwriters contest 1992; [oth. writ.] Red Sky Serenade, songs and poetry; Idyll Hours song book, original songs, Five tunes original songs; [pers.] All honor and glory to God and His muses; [a.] Centerport, NY

MULLINS, B. H.
[Pen.] Axton Flane; [b.] May 10, 1918, J'ville, TX; [p.] Hughe and Georgia Mullins; [m.] E.L. Mullins, July 11, 1944; [ch.] Billy, Johnny and Faye Ann; [ed.] 3rd year UNM; [occ.] Retired USAF Capt.; [memb.] 32 Degree Scottish Rite, york Rite, El Sariba Shrine DKE; [oth. writ.] Poems published, postmasters of America, Clover Club; [pers.] Forever imprinted on my soul are the works of Lawrence Hope; [a.] Phoenix, AZ 85024-1704.

MULVANY, ELISABETH
[b.] August 5, 1977, San Diego, CA; [p.] David and Clara Mulvany; [ed.] Rancho Bernardo High School, Sophomore, current student; [memb.] Band, Drama Club, Girls Softball; [hon.] Honors Comp./Lit.; [a.] San Diego, CA.

MURLEY, BEULINDA S.
[b.] Amburgy, KY; [p.] Mr. & Mrs. Bob Murley; [m.] unmarried; [ch.] no children; [ed.] School in Oak Ridge, TN; [occ.] Factory, unemployed now; [memb.] Central Heights Church of God; [oth. writ.] Poetry written: Poetry for song lyrics written; Paid for them set to music; Others: I've written; [pers.] Hope to achieve occupation with waitings; [a.] Columbus, IN

MURPHY, JACQUI E.
[Pen.] Jem; [b.] September 5, 1937, Baimbridge, NY; [p.] Charles H. Carnall, Bertha A. Carnall; [m.] Bobby Murphy, August 24, 1959; [ch.] Bobby Ellis, Shon Patrick, David Porter; [ed.] Cooley High, Univ of Detroit, former model; [occ.] Business Woman - self employed; [memb.] F.O.E., Poetry Academy,

Evangelical Echos; [hon.] Three Golden Poet Awards, Academy Medallion presented by Milton Berle - July 3, 1993; [oth. writ.] Aphorisms, Childrens stories, poems published by Quill books for the past five years and other publishers; [pers.] My inspiration for poetry derived from a musician - songwriter of the early 50's, Billy Ward. Any success I may have achieved, since then, I owe to God; [a.] Wyandotte, MI

MURPHY, JAY P.
[Pen.]Jay Thing; [b.]August 31, 1957, Washington, D.C.; [p.]Barbara E. Gurch, Harry T. Murphy; [m.]Janice M. Murphy, October 7, 1991; [ed.]Northwestern H.S.; [occ.]Branch Administrative Assistant, Citizens Bank of Maryland; [oth. writ.]"Underground Albums': "The Slap Of Baby On Pavement", "The Last Hurrah", "Arrowhead", "Stranger Who Was Passing" (Song Compilations).; [pers.]I am concerned with transcending darkness and "evil" by confronting it in my artwork which serves as my primary form of psycho-therapy and spirituality; [a.] Landover Hills, MD 20784.

MURREY, JEAN
[Pen.] J. Murrey; [m.]A.L. Murrey, July 24, 1944 (50 years in 1994!); [ch.]Mikal Murrey; [occ.]Retired, 33 years service.; [memb.]Who's Who In Poetry 1990; [hon.]Honorable Mention, Golden Poet 89, "Old Glory" (published) World Treasury of Golden Poems and 90 Silver Poet (published) 93. "Poems That Will Live Forever," "Little Lad", dedicated to my six year old grandson Morgan Mikal Murrey in 1985.; [oth. writ.]Many poems; also appeared on "Song Writer's Corner" (for 2 songs copyr. by J.M.) on cable T.V. Program (Eastfield College). "Oh Heavenly Peace," 5/5/92. "Santa And The New Born King", for a Xmas Program, Dec. 8, 1992, songs written by J. Murrey; [pers.]Dedicated to my nine year old granddaughter in 1986; Michelle Mekel Murray.; [a.] Dallas, TX 75218.

MUSSER, JEAN W.
[b.]Akron, Ohio; [p.]Harvey and Lucile Musser (deceased); [m.]1963, divorced 1979; [ch.]Matthew C. Batie; [ed.]B.A. Smith College, M.A. Case Western Reserve Univ., M.Ed. University of Puget Sound; [occ.]Counselor, writer; [memb.]American Counselor Assoc., Old St. Peter's Church, Tacoma, WA; [hon.]Fellowship from the National Endowment for Humanities, 1973, First prize in poetry, playwriting, novel writing from the Pacific Northwest Writers Conference (1961, 1969, 1977); [oth. writ.]Art criticism for The Seattle Times and American Craft plays, currently working on a novel; [pers.]Writing is the quiet journey into illumination and the understanding of experience. Poetry quickens the senses and sharpens our perceptions; [a.] Tacoma, WA 98406

MUSTAIN, JOYCE GRYMES
[b.]February 4, 1937, Houston, TX; [p.]John W. Grymes, Jeanne P. Grymes; [m.]Don E. Mustain, January 31, 1964; [ch.]Shawn D. Mustain, Shannon E. Mustain; [ed.]Jefferson Davis High School, Texas Women's University; [occ.]Housewife; [hon.]Alpha Beta Alpha, Alpha Beta Chi, Golden Poet Award; [oth. writ.]Poem published by "World of Poetry" Editor; [pers.]Poetry is the window of the soul, and therefore, my hope is that every person can see a little of himself in my writings.; [a.] Crosby, TX 77532.

NASON, DONALD CHARLES
[Pen.] Don Nason; [b.] June 30, 1946, Rochester, NH; [p.] Charles and Ruby Nason (both deceased); [m.] Judy Ann Nason, June 26, 1965; [ch.] Sandra, Charles II, Edward; [ed.]Temple Union High School, Ariz; Clackamas Comm College, Oregon; Cal Baptist College, Cal; [occ.] Entrepreneur - DCUN Enterprises; [memb.] International Networking Assoc; [oth. writ.] Poem for Whispers in the Wind; [pers.] I believe in glorifying God, living life to the fullest, and that helping others is the greatest reward; [a.] El Sobrante, CA

NELSON, DUANE S.
[Pen.]D.S. Nelson; [b.]January 16, 1937, Charleroi, PA; [p.]Vernon B. and Martha F. Nelson; [m.]Kay Nelson, September 16, 1958; [ch.]Duane S. II, Lynne R., and Eric J.; [ed.]Charleroi High School, California University, Waynesburg College; [occ.]Tavern Owner; [memb.]Presbyterian Church; [hon.]International Art School Graduate; [oth. writ.]Published: "Sweet Bird of Youth" and numerous unpublished poetry; [pers.]I live, I dream, for as long as I live, may I always dream.; [a.] Belle Vernon, PA 15012.

NIBARGER, IRENE
[b.] August 14, 1919, Manitoba, Canada; [p.] Wm John Dunbar, Mildred; [m.] Ted A. Nibanger, October 30, 1947; [ch.] Kimberly Ted (Kim), Corey John, 5 grandchildren; [oth. writ.] Poetry and short stories in newspapers magazines since 12 yrs old, earlier in Canada, later years in the states; [pers.] Always written for the sheer joy of it. Last few years much written through inspiration from the spirit of God - Testimony to His caring; [a.]Oak Harbor, WA 98277

NICHOLAS, CONNIE
[Pen.] Stupio; [b.] December 5, 1917, NYC; [p.] Wonderful; [m.] none - thank God; [ch.] 4 wonderful girls; [ed.] B.S. Stanford; [occ.] Writer; [hon.] National Library of Poetry; [pers.] Life is wonderful; [a.] Downey, CA

NICHOLSON, BRENDA
[Pen.]Lenore; [b.]June 15, 1973, Seattle, WA; [p.]Ken and Dollie Nicholson; [ed.]Federal Way High School, Highline Community College; [occ.]Student; [a.] Kent, WA.

NIELSEN, SHIRLEY
[b.]November 21, 1936, Greenville, Michigan; [p.]Elmer harris (deceased) and Helen Harris; [m.]Rexford Nielsen, March 27, 1954; [ch.]Virginia Wise, Bary Nielsen and Mark Nielsen (Deceased); [ed.]High School 1976, Jordan College 16 credits; [occ.]Homemaker, Volunteer at Chamber of Commerce, Cedar Springs; [memb.]Royal Neighbors of America; [hon.]Editor's Choice Award, Honor Pins for Newspaper Delivery (Grand Rapids Herald now defunct); [oth. writ.]Away and With The Wind, too many poems and articles, too numerous to mention, but never published.; [pers.]No one is ever too old to get an education. Never give up on anything, do your best, set goals. If at first you don't succeed, try and try again.; [a.] Cedar Springs, MI 49319.

NORTH, BARRY W.
[b.] February 1, 1945, New Orleans, LA; [p.] Albert G. North, SR and Rosemary D. North; [m.] Marilyn Perrer, April 15, 1973; [ed.] Jesuit High School; Loyola Univ; Tulane Univ; [occ.] Refrigeration Mechanic, St Charles School Board; Luling, LA; [oth. writ.] Poem published in anthology "Great Poems of our Time"; [pers.] Omnia Vincet Amor; Love conquers all; [a.] Boutte, LA

NORVILLE, NANCY JO
[b.] February 9, 1963, Lander Wyoming; [p.] Leland and Betty Morris; [m.] Wes Norville; [m.] October 5, 1985; [ch.] Randy Michael, Angela, Dayle, and Melinda Elizabeth; [ed.] Seeley-Swan High, Prairie Bible Institute; [occ.] Homemaker/mother; [memb.] National Rifle Association, Fundamental Baptist Church; [oth. writ.] "Mother" in Wind in the Night Sky; [a.] Seeley, Lake, MT

NUCKOLS, PEGGY L.
[Pen.]Lois Palms; [b.]February 16, 1946, Charleston, SC; [p.]David and Marie Nuckols; [ed.]BS in Psychology and Economics; [occ.]Telephone Operator; [pers.]Grow all you can, when you can, while you can.; [a.] Jacksonville, FL 32211.

OAKES, OWEN B.
[b.]may 3, 1960, Bangor, ME; [p.]Lawrence and Ethel Oakes; [m.]Nancy A. Oakes, June 22, 1985; [ch.]Kristen Marie; [occ.]Salesmen; [hon.]Editor's Choice Award, National Library of Poetry; [oth. writ.]Poem published-A Break In The Clouds, 1993, many unpublished poems; [a.] Levant, ME 04456

OBUCH, JUDITH A.
[b.] February 11, 1941, Belleville, Illinois; [p.] Donald R. and Edna Santel Bingheim (both deceased); [m.] Msgt. James D. Obuch Sr. (Ret), June 4, 1960; [ch.] Sharon Obuch Peacock, James Dale, Jr., Lynn Obuch Speaks, Donald Denver; [ed.] Eight years parachial and graduated Belleville Township H.S.; [occ.] Homemaker, community and Wive's Club Volunteer; [memb.] Local Groups, International Society of Poets; [hon.] Certificates of Appreciation, etc., Editor's Choice Award from The National Library of Poetry; [oth. writ.] Poems, all subjects. One short story for a contest. Wrote poems for the Wive's Club Newsletter, and for family members; [pers.] My writing is a gift from God and comes naturally. I am totally encouraged by so many! My philosophy is to give the readers a picture and make them want to see more! Sign all you write; [a.] Schertz, Texas 78154

O'KELLY JR., ANDERSON D.
[b.]Pittsburgh, PA; [m.]Evelyn (Clemons) O'Kelly; october 20, 1989; [ch.]Caleb Anderson, Marc Anderson; [memb.]Pastor: Christ Ministries; [hon.]Certificate of Induction in Homer Society; [pers.]I write with compassion, passion and affection, with Love for God and all creation, I interpret people's thought in writing.; [a.] Morgan, PA 15064.

OLIVERA, JAMES A.
[b.]September 13, 1955, Hempstead, NY; [p.]Anthony and Stella Olivera; [m.]Single Parent; [ed.]Mera Arizona High Graduate, Graduate of St. Johns, NY; [occ.]Amway, Sales Representative; [memb.]Fort Meade Cheer Club and Laurel Theater Group. Glen Burnie Baptist Church, World Vision; [hon.]Best New Play, South Florida, Summer Struck, "Absurdity We Parr" 1991. Also, Best Actor in South Florida Production of "All My Sons" played Cevore Peever; [oth. writ.]Have had short poems published in various organizations around the U.S. Wrote a few

local plays in South Florida and sad lyrics to D.C. Band; [pers.]I believe poetry is a secret passage to happiness and beauty, I also suspect the lines we pen are wish fulfillment and honesty shadow; [a.] Fort George Meade, MD 20755

OLSON, JEANETTE
[b.]May 29, 1939, Cando, ND; [p.]Arthur and Ethel Haugen; [m.]Arvid Olson, July 29, 1967; [ch.]Lesli Olson; [ed.]Bachelor of Science in Elementary Education; [oth. writ.]Amazing Man published in "On The Threshold of a Dream." Vol. III and numerous other poems, spiritual and non spiritual.; [pers.]My purpose is writing poetry is to put forth truths that appear in the Bible as a comfort to my readers and as a catalyst to get them interested in turning to God's Word; [a.] Devils Lake, ND 58301.

OSENKARSKI, ROBERT W.
[Pen.] Robert Senkar; [ed.] Assoc in Arts Degree, Mesa Community College, Bachelor of Science Degree, Arizona State Univ; [pers.] And so my fellow humans of this planetary existence of space and the sublime....Listen to your inner voice and its own perfect chime....May your journey of the eternal here and now, be in universal prime....And reflect life's, poetic moments in time....; [a.] Peru, IL

OSTROM, HELEN M.
[b.] February 19, 1919, Davenport, Iowa; [p.] Earl and Eva Mackenzie; [m.] Richard Gail Hult Ostrom (deceased), September 18, 1938; [ch.] Eddy R. Ostrom; [ed.] High School Graduate; [occ.] Retired, U.S. Government Selective Service System; [oth. writ.] Many published poems to numerous to mention; [pers.] Poetry often reflects the inner self. Each poem written leaves an indelible stamp as to the mind of the poet. The reader catches a glimpse of the poet's soul; [a.] Mojave, CA 93501

OTTO, ELEANOR
[b.]Rochester, NY; [m.]Gerald Frederick Otto, author of 50 textbooks on science, artist exhibited in Maine and NYC; [ch.]Eva-Lee, daughter, art teacher (father's early training), grandchildren, Noah and Freedom (college grads.); [ed.]Univ. of Rochester (with Gerald) BA; graduate studies pol. science Columbia Univ.; Juilliard School of Music, Manhattan School, Music, City College, Educ.; Opera Ballet workshops, priv. voice. Poet, author, teacher, singer, actress (PRIZZI's honor, crocodile dundee, LA BOHEME (Metropol. Opera, Lincoln Center.); [memb.]Past Nat'l. Pres. Composers, Authors & Artists; Amer. Guild Mus. Artists; Screen Actors Guild; Shelley Soc.; NY Poetry Forum Nat'l. Assoc. of Female Executives, ASCAP; [hon.]Cultural Doctorate Laureate Int'l. Laurel Crown; poetry Chmn. CAAA Symposium. 1993 NY Univ.; Translations to Foreign Lang.; plaques, trophies, diplomas, presided banquets. Exhibited my painting Red, White and Blue IVY at CAA Exhibit and 2 banks in Manhattan. (dedicated to U.S. Space Program); [oth. writ.]Numerous anthologies 3 books published poetry; 2 published plays (one off Bdwy.) articles in CAA Mag. (one on Georgia O'Keefe) Two brochures-long poems on U.S. Space projects: 1969 Riverside Pr. Moon Ring Christmas 1968) Read these in public APOLLO (Eagle on the Moon); [pers.]Deeply involved in cultural arts; humanistic and social philosophy; promoter of advanced social legislature (Nat'l. Council on Arts; Nat'l. Health, Women's Rights, vs Child abuse, child labor, sweatshops, etc.); [a.] New York, NY

OVERTON, JANE T.
[b.]August 12, 1935, Jonesboro, Arkansas; [p.]Lewis Earl and Alma Nichols Taylor; [m.]Lt. Col. (Pet.) James W. Overton, November 3, 1953; [ch.]Daniel Earl, Rebecca L. Bostian, James W. II; [ed.]EE Bass Senior High School; [occ.]Writer/Homemaker; [memb.]Mississippi State Poetry Society; [hon.]1990-Miss. Poetry Society Presidents Award, 1990-93-Hon. Mentions various poetry contest, 1993-Miss. Poetry Society, North Branch, 3rd Place, Spring Contest; [oth. writ.]Book of Poetry, pub, 1984, "The Potter's Clay" other poems included in several anthologies. Agent pegasus International, currently articulating novel to publisher; [pers.]Life is the stuff good books are made of. If you don't go for it, what good are the words; [a.] Holyoke, MA 01046

OWNBEY, JENNA V.
[b.]January 1, 1919, Lipscomb, Texas; [p.]William Henry and Lena (Hill) Stephenson (both deceased); [m.]Robert James Ownbey, November 10, 1941; [ch.]Nancy Ownbey Archer, Dr. Jimmie S. Ownbey, Robbie Faye Ownbey Butts, Dr., James L. Ownbey, William D. Ownbey, Donna Ownbey, Jane Ownbey (18 grands and 2 great grandchildren); [ed.]MA additional work in Psychology and Journalism, teachers cert.; [occ.]Mother, office mgr., Librarian, legal secretary, court reporter, book publisher, comm. artist, journalist, author; [memb.]DAR, Col Dames XVII Cent, United Dau Confederacy, CAU Amer. Colonist, Jamestowne Soc, Past Matron Order Eastern Star, certified as programmer; [hon.]Numerous; [oth. writ.]Cloud-Moods, Star-Moods, Cloud-Moods (poetry), Fate's Brew (fic.), In Memory and Honor of My Parents Lena Hill Stephenson and Wm. Henry Stephenson (gen), Hist. of Postal Serv. In Early Tex Panhandle (hist), My Miller Lines (gen), Chaplain for 3 of my heritage groups; [pers.]I feel that God has given me a special talent and I am obligated to pray, entertain and serve God for and with the talent he gave me.; [a.] Amarillo, TX 79106

OXLEY, ANNE T.
[Pen.]A.T. Oxley; [b.]November 20, 1921, Aitken, Minn.; [p.]Felix Cormier and Nelida Carmier; [m.]Wayne Emerson Oxley, September 20, 1942; [ch.]Jamie, Gary, Errol, Karen, Gina, Julie, Shawn; [ed.]Cathedral High School, Villa St. Scholastic; [occ.]Housewife, Artist Writer; [memb.]SE Colo. Art Guild, Dawbers, Brush and Palette, "30" club; [hon.]Two Best Of Show, many in art, novel in progress, poems published in magazine and anthologies; [oth. writ.]Children's stories, short stories, novel; [pers.]Writing and painting are my great escape; [a.] Lamar, CO 81052

PAGE, J. LYNANNE
[b.] July 3, 1974, Marion, IL; [p.] Dexter and Earlyon Page; [ed.] College Sophomore at present; [occ.] Student; [hon.] IL State Scholar, President's List; [a.] Johnston City, IL

PAGE, MARTHA C.
[b.]September 27, 1926, Centerville, TN; [p.]Jim and Lillie Bradley Harrington; [m.]C. G. Page, April 13, 1946; [ch.]Judy Page Fenner, Larry, David, Kenny, Kimberly Page Loker; [ed.]Watkins Institute, Principal English and the command of words, English Language Institute of America.; [occ.]Retired, Personnel Manager, Corroon and Black of Nashville, Inc.; [memb.]The International Society of Poets, Fairfield Church of Christ; [oth. writ.]Things I am Thankful For, pub. by The Nashville Banner, Walking Together, pub. Wind in the Night Sky, The National Library of Poetry, Christmas in May, pub. by Mountain Trails; [pers.]Growing up in a family of twelve children, in a three room log home, I learned love, honor, and obedience, and best of all to share. I have tried to instill these ideals in our own five children; [a.] Centerville, TN 37033.

PAINO, CYNTHIA
[b.] October 7, 1964, NYC; [m.] October 31, 1987; [ch.] Awaiting birth of first child due May 28, 1994; [ed.] AAS; [occ.] Registered Nurse; [oth. writ.] Many unpublished poems; [a.] Otisvile, NY

PAINTON, CLYDE W.
[b.] August 29, 1902, Orion Oklahoma; [p.] Wm. Henry and Anna (Poe) Painton Pioneers in Oklahoma; [m.] Mary Inez McMurtrey and Lillian Aldrich; [m.] May 20, 1928 (deceased) 5/24/54; [ch.] Loreta Glee, Anna Lee Inez, Marion Haskill, Kermit Clyde; [ed.] Northwest Teachers College Alva, Oklahoma and Oklahoma Baptist University, Shawnee, Oklahoma; [occ.] Teacher and Gospel Minister, Former Supt. of Associational Missions; [memb.] First Baptist Church, Republican Presidential Task Force; [hon.] Various awards and certificates; [oth. writ.] Poems and articles in various publications, published volume of poems "Jewels at Twilight", Newsletter for 20 years, many poems for years; [pers.] I personally believe the divine creation of mankind and the universe as well as all nature. It is my purpose in life and my writings to portray something of the beauty of nature, the love for people and the one who made it all.; [a.] Poplar Bluff, Missouri

PALOMBI, RAE LYNN
[Pen.] Mourning Knite; [b.] March 1, 1979, Pasedena, CA; [p.] Barbara Jean and Attilio John Palombi III; [m.] Single (Of Course); [ed.] Hanford High, Benjamin Franklin Academy; [oth. writ.] None other then the one's published by The National Library of Poetry and those not yet published; [pers.] In most of my writings I endeavor to mirror the world around us whether it is through love, hatred, war or beauty; [a.] W. Richland, WA 99352

PARDALLIS, VASILIKI ALEXIS
[Pen.] Vicki A. Pardallis; [b.] December 12, 1970, Athens, Greence; [p.] Mr. Alexis John Pardallis and Dr. Maria Papanicolaou-Pardallis; [ed.] American Community Schools of Athens, Greece (ACS) and Boston University; [occ.] Graduate student at Boston University; [hon.] British Literature Award in 1987, Dean's List, Honorary Mention in Poetry in 1993; [oth. writ.] Poems published in other anthologies and literary magazines. I have also written for "The Oddysean" "Vocis" "The Daily Free Press"; [pers.] I thank that the things that inspires me the most to write is my country, Greece, with go its rich history and culture and its endless beauty and life; [a.] Athens, Greece

PARKER, JO LEA
[b.] August 25, 1944, Scotia, CA; [p.] James Houck (dec) and Alyce Houck Booth; [m.] Darrell Parker, June 22, 1968; [ch.] Joy Alissa Parker; [ed.] Placer

High School, Sacramento State College, Moore's Business School; [occ.] Homemaker and secretary for our janitor business; [hon.] Eta Sigma Phi medal; various poetry awards; [oth. writ.] Thirteen of my poems have been published; [pers.] Writing runs in my family. My mother is also a poet and my nephew, Michael Payne, is a scriptwriter. I want to write poems that are understandable, entertaining and inspirational; [a.] Shingle Springs, CA

PATENAUDE, CAROLYN ANN
[b.] April 27, 1975, Taunton, MA; [p.] Joanne Patenaude; [ed.] Taunton High School, Newbury College; [occ.] Sales Clerk; [hon.] Cheerleading Stunt Award Trophy, being published in On The Threshold of a Dream; [oth. writ.] "Happiness" published in On The Threshold of a Dream; [pers.] Writing poetry has helped me deal with certain emotions and feelings. This poem was influenced by my boyfriend, Robert; [a.] Taunton, MA

PATENAUDE, JENNIFER JEANNE
[Pen.]JenniferJeanne; [b.]December 25, 1977 (Christmas), Wonnsacket Hospital, Rhode Island; [p.]Jeannie Theresa Patenaude and Daniel Alfred Patenaude; [ch.]Siblings - Joshua Daniel Patenaude and Tracy Lea Patenaude; [ed.]Currently a junior at North Smithfield Junior/Senior High School; [memb.]Confirmation Candidate and Parishioner at Holly Family Church; [hon.]Presidential Academy Fitness Award (6th Grade), poems among top 3 percent in "A Break In The Clouds" National Library of Poetry; [oth. writ.]"A Dream" published in A Break In The Clouds and Quest For A DReam. I have written almost 300 poems, but have made few attempts to publish any; [pers.]My poems make people smile, I think that's why I enjoy writing them. If writing poems will make people happy, than I thank God for my talent.; [a.] North Smithfield, Rhode Island 02896.

PATRONELLA, ROSE MARIE
[b.] December 19, 1938, Humble, TX; [p.] Helen Josephine Bila Patronella, Clarence Clinton Patronella; [m.] Wilson E. Shafer, Jr., April 2, 1961 Houston, TX; [ch.] Judith Marie Shafer, Russel Edward Shafer; [ed.] Minors in Spanish, English, Theology, Philosophy, Math, Chemistry, Physics; Texas Certification for Elementary Education from Dominican College (Elementary Life Provisional); Texas Certification for SP. ED. (LLD Life Provisional) from Houston Baptist University; working on Masters of Supervision at U.S.T.; [occ.] Special Education Resource Teacher, Executive Director/ Owner of Humble Private Academy, a private school w/3 areas: 1) Unit School: grades Pre-K-12; 2) Tutorial School: all grades, subjects, levels; 3) Alternative school: Preparation for GED, workplace literacy, adult literacy ASCD, Kiwanis, Texas Literacy Council, TFT; [memb.] Prof and Assn Membe: T.S.T.A., A.T.A. Aldine, Texas, T.S.T.A., H.T.A. Houston, Texas, Houston Federation of Teachers, National Honor Society, Quill and Scroll, Thespian Society; Pol. Aff.: Independent; Rel: Catholic; Civ and Pol. Act.: Kingwood Sherwood Trails Crime Watch 1982, Boy Scouts Den Mother 1970-72, Girl Scouts Assistant Troop Leader 1969-72, Taught C.C.D. Sunday School 1969-72, Board Member on Sherwood Trails Community Association, ASCD, Kiwanis, Texas Literacy Council, TFT; [hon.] 1973-75 Won a $3,000 Social Studies Grant, enabling two Sixth Grades to learn more about other nationalities, $1,500 Grant from Burkitt Foundation, $500 Grant from BFI Industries, and $3,000 Grant from Exxon, Most Notable Women in Texas 1982, Most Notable Women in Texas 1984; [oth. writ.] Article published by Texas Outlook (for teachers); [pers.] I feel every person can and should be able to develop their own capabilities to their fullest potential-whether it is in poetry, education, their job or in life. We should never be satisfied with who and what we are. Changes occur daily. Yesterday's reached goal is today's bottom rung on the lader. Poetry is only one avenue, for me, to feel achievement, success and pride in myself; [a.] Humble, TX

PATTERSON, EVA D.
[b.] May 5, 1910, Preston, ID; [m.] Married; [ed.] 2 yrs college, 1 yr trade school, 29 yrs food service; [hon.] Poems published by National Society of Poetry; [pers.] I embrace yoga philosophy; [a.] Glenns Ferry, ID

PATTESON, GOLDIE ETHEL
[b.] March 13, 1918, Marshall, IL; [p.] Silas S. Chambers, Lucy E. Chambers; [m.] Charles Elizabeth, Audrey Elaine, Sharon Eloise; [ed.] Jackson Elementary, Hiem Beauty School; [occ.] Beautician, Meals on Wheels, Housewife and Mother; [memb.] Presbyterian Church, OES #314 Hobart, IN - AARP, SOAR, Church Women United; [hon.] Presbyterian Life Membership in Women's Association, Ruth Circle Leader USA; [oth. writ.] Church paper - Lenton Book, anthology's - "Passages" Illiad Press, "Poetic Voices of America", Sparrowgrass Poetry Forum, "On the Threshold of a Dream" by National Library of Poetry; [pers.] Inspired by mother, grandmother, great uncle, church school teacher, and husband. Poems inspired by my love for my savior and my God who is my eternal help and hope of the world; [a.] Hobart, IN

PATTON, ANAH
[b.] June 27, 1910, Huntington, WV; [p.] Arnold Lakin, Cosby Marie Booth, [m.] Herbert Patton, July 15, 1939; [ch.] none; [ed.] 8 yrs elementary, 4 yrs high school; [occ.] Retired Trade Journalist, 25 yrs freelance; [memb.] Soc (Environmental) Committee, East Liverpool, OH; [hon.] Golden Poet Award 1991 from World of Poetry; [oth. writ.] Ideals Publishing Co, Shamie Publications, Gillum Book Co, Nationwide Trade News Service, St Anthony Mess Aneer, Baby Talk, Catholic Journal and others; [pers.] Writers are born not made. I am a self taught writer you must love to write to succeed; [a.] East Liverpool, OH

PAUL, JEAN C.
[b.] May 9, 1922, Mineola LI, NY; [p.] Theodore Schmidt and Charlotta Schmidt; [m.] Frank C. Paul, July 15, 1943 (deceased); [ch.] Harvey Martin Paul and Steven Frank Paul; [ed.] Four yrs. high school, Associate Degree Adelphi Univ. Garden City, NY; [occ.] Retired Hospital Ward Clerk; [memb.] St. Alfreds Episcopal Church PH, Aux. of the Reserve Officers Assoc. in USA, Volunteer Mease Hospital, Safety Harbour, FL; [hon.] Given Award for 100 hrs. as hospital volunteer. Soprano soloist with many choirs and choral groups while living in NY; [oth. writ.] Other poems not published; [pers.] I write religious poetry. My faith has brought me through many tragedies in my life. Without it I could not have survived; [a.] Palm Harbor, FL 34683

PAULSEN, JESSIE
[b.] April 30, 1952, Blackfoot, Idaho; [p.] Ralph and Gladys Carrier, Step-Father Walter Westerness Arco, Idaho; [m.] Terry Lief Paulsen, September 23, 1972; [ch.] Butte High, Arco, Idaho; [occ.] Mother, Wife, Grandmother, Poet; [hon.] Golden Poet Award 1991, 1992 Award of Merit 1990, 1991. Honorary Charter member International Society of Poets 1993; [oth. writ.] Poetry has been published in various books and magazines from 1976; [pers.] Henry Wadsworth Longfellow has been my inspiration from childhood days. My Mother would read "The Songs of Hiawatha" to me. At age 12 I became intrigued with the poetry of Edgar Allen Poe; [a.] Cottonwood, CA 96022

PAVLIC, JULIA
[Pen.]Jewel Bartins; [b.]December 15, 1913, Noblestown, PA; [p.]Leo Bartins and Amelia Kaczor Bartins; [m.]Stanley Pavlic, August 20, 1935; [ch.]Georgia Lee and David Pavlic; [ed.]High School, Summer Course in Poetry at Pitt University; [occ.]Homemaker; [memb.]St. Joan of Arc Church U.M.W.A. of America; [hon.]Editor's Choice Award. The National Library of Poetry 1993; [oth. writ.]"Distant Thunder" published in "A Break In The Clouds" 1993; [pers.]I strive t write of the beauty of the world. Flowers, people, animals and the bright side of life; [a.] Library, PA 15129

PAYNTER, SHARON K.
[Pen.] Satin; [b.] June 5, 1942, Philadelphia, PA; [p.] John R. Baskerville and Victoria F. Baskerville; [m.] Thomas A. Paynter; [m.] April 10, 1986; [ch.] Charles, Sharon, Victoria and James, Jr.; [ed.] Associate in Applied Science; [occ.] Administrative Assistant; [memb.] Marlton Lakes Civic Association, Burlington County Kennel Club, Tibetan Spaniel Club of America; [hon.] Camden County College, Permanent President's List, Legal Award; [oth. writ.] "A Gift For Susan", "Shame On You, Susan", "Storm Warning", and "Satin's Finale"--All have been published by the National Library of Poetry; [pers.] My Tibetan Spaniels have been my inspiration for writing, especially, my girl, satin.; [a.] Atco, NJ 08004

PAZ-LIGORRIA, ELIZABETH
[Pen.] Mariabelem; [b.] December 9, 1947, Guatemala City, Central America; [p.] Marta Ligorria, Antonio Paz y Paz; [ch.] Otto, Hedthel and Nelly; [ed.] Drama Education (Masters) Major in Theater, Univ of San Carlos, Associates Degree in Communication Salt Lake Community College (Utah); English, Orange Coast College, CA - diploma; [occ.] Multicultural Affairs Assistant, Hispanic Association Student Coordinator; Notably, has recently been nominated to become a Consul for Guatemala, and if appointed, will maintain a Consulate in Salt Lake City; [memb.] Camara Evatemaltera de Periodismo, Guatemala, International Order of Merit, International Biographical Centre, Cambridge England; [hon.] Has received many honors: Best Critic of Art (1973); Best Actress (1983) in Guatemala; included in the Dictionary of International Biography (1993); awarded International Woman of the Year (1993); selected for International Order of Merit (1993) by the International Biographical Centre in Cambridge, England; and denominated Most Admired Woman of the Decade (1993) by American Biographical Institute, Inc. of North Carolina; [oth. writ.] "Songs to Life", "To be Read by Alexander", "Epistles to Elizabeth",

"Furtively I Come", "Absence of God", "My General, the Boots are Reading". More poems published in Guatemala, France, Chile and California; [pers.] I have learned that in life no one can go alone. One always needs someone to love and to take care of. If you have no one to talk with or cry on his shoulder, be patient. One of these days he would over come to give you contentment and profound love which would transform you into a beautiful little flower. Oct 14-93, 5:35pm; [a.] Salt Lake City, UT

PEACHER, RUBY TIPPIT
[b.] August 5, 1917, Indian Mound, TN; [p.] Bernice Seay Tippit and William Augustus Tippit; [m.] Joseph William Peacher, June 13, 1936 (deceased); [ch.] Teddy Joe, Terry Gene, William K., Wanda Fay and Artie Peacher; [ed.] B.S. Degree, Austin Peay University, Clarksville; [occ.] Retired Teacher, Stewart Co., TN, Indian Mound and North Stewart; [memb.] United Methodist Church, President of UMW, Secretary of SCRTA Stewart Co. Historical Society; [hon.] Dean's List, Invitation to Eta Rho Chapter of Kappa Delta Phi, Indian Mound Certificate of Appreciation as a teacher, Golden Poet Awards and Award of Merit for Poetry; [oth. writ.] Poetry published Poems of the Great South, Let Freedom Ring, Poems of Great America, Windows of the Soul, Poetic Voices of America, and others. Rainbows and Roses, 4 genealogies; [pers.] Rainbows and Roses is about memories of my childhood. I also helped in writing Stewart County Heritage and other books by Stewart County Historical Society. I look for beauty and goodness in this world; [a.] Indian Mount, TN 37079.

PEASE, PAUL ANDREW
[b.] May 11, 1951, Berkley, California; [p.] Paul Chester Pease and Josephine Sherman Pease (both deceased); [m.] I am single; [ed.] Nevada Union High School, Sierra Junior College, IPT School of Electronics; [occ.] Electronic Technician, TV, Stereo, VCR, Vintage Sets Repair; [memb.] none; [hon.] Merit Awards and Golden Poet Awards from World of Poetry, Sacramento, CA; [oth. writ.] Several poems published by World of Poetry, several editorial's published by G.V Union. Recorded audio tape of poems and editorials written and recited by me.; [pers.] My poems I write not only speak out as a poem but also a message including my latest poem when we are not forgiven.; [a.] Grass Valley, CA.

PEDIGO, STEVEN B.
[Pen.] Stilletto; [b.] August 24, 1924, Riverside; [p.] Harold and Paula Pedigo; [m.] Still looking, still waiting; [ch.] not yet; [ed.] Survived 9 years of catholic school. 4 years at Ramona and 1 1/2 years at RCC; [occ.] Knife dealer, Pizza Hut driver; [memb.] A member of the I.P.P.A and a proud member of Pathway Christian Church; [hon.] Creative Writing Award at Ramona in senior year; [oth. writ.] Broken Vows, Twister, Sequel to Jabberwocky, once a family, in my cell, Plead of the Greedy, Demons, Demons, everywhere. Mostly I enjoy negative things; [pers.] Many individuals in this world live in a dream and all they need is a cold hard slap in the face to awaken them to reality; [a.] Riverside, CA

PEIRSOL, VERA A.
[occ.] Small Business Accountant and future author; [memb.] National Society of Public Accountants; Oregon Assoc of Independent Accountants; [oth. writ.] My Sweet "P", Our Worlds Most Reasured Poems; [pers.] I enjoy creating poetry for the pleasure of others; [a.] Portland, OR

PELUSO, KIMBER LEE
[b.] February 6, 1960, Easton, PA; [p.] Micki Butch Peluso; [m.] Robert Sharib, January 2, 1991; [ch.] Ian (10), Jesse (7), Benjamin (2); [ed.] High school - Loyalsock High School, Williamsport, PA; [occ.] Homemaker, financial services rep for my own business; [memb.] National Library of Poetry, American Poetry Association; [hon.] Honorable mention for "The Dragon's Children"; [oth. writ.] I have several poems published in newspapers, magazines and anthologies. I write songs, poems and am almost finished with the first novel in a Fantasy Trilogy. I sew quilts, paint and sing as well as play a 12 string to accompany myself; [pers.] There's no shame in getting knocked down by life. The only shame is in not getting up; [a.] Staten Island, NY

PENG, LING FAN
[b.] Suzhou, China, Guo Yan Peng and Xian Min Xu; [ed.] MD in China, MS in University of North TX; [occ.] Research Associate John's Hopkins Medical Institute Pediatrics Cardiology; [hon.] Who's Who Among Students in American Universities and Colleges; [oth. writ.] Poems published in "Wind in the Night Sky" (1993), American Poetry Annual (1991), and American Collegiate Poets (1987). Several articles published in Milwaukee Journal and daily scientific papers are not included; [pers.] Simplicity is the sublime of all the arts. Time is the image of eternity. History should be honest and correct, but history is written by the winner and it is always unfair to it's victim; [a.] Baltimore, MD

PERDOMO, ORESTE FLAVIO
[b.] June 22, 1919, San Diego del Valle, Cuba; [p.] Enrique F. Perdomo and Maria E. Navales; [m.] Zoila Esther, August 3, 1957; [ch.] Oreste Flavio and George Louis; [ed.] Ph.d and Lic. in Juris in Italy, Juris Dr in Havana, Cuba and Master in Art in Spanish at Mount St. Mary's, LA, CA; [occ.] LACC Spanish and Italian Profession; [memb.] Cuban American Teacher Assoc., The Cuban American National Foundation Pres. Rep. Party Task Force; [hon.] Cert. in Poet. Achievement, American Poetic Assoc. Literary Contest Enrique Jose Varona, Tampa, FL; [oth. writ.] Italian Grammar, Italian Course (3 books) Poems in Newspapers. Poems in Anthologies in English and in Spanish; [pers.] Life is a complete fantasy. Family is the most wonderful and innovating reality. Love is the music of the hearts; [a.] Hollywood, CA 90038

PEREZ, RUBEN
[b.] July 5, 1961, Elgin, IL; [p.] Fidencio Perez and Guadalupe Perez; [occ.] Sales Clerk, Marshalls of Elgin #282; [pers.] All my poetry comes from true feelings and events of my life.

PERRY, SR., CLAY
[Pen.] Clay Perry; [b.] July 18, 1912, Simpson County, KY; [p.] Lester Perry, Addie Perry; [m.] Wilma Fritz Perry, June 25, 1933; [ch.] Edward C. Perry Jr, Ruth Ann Garverick; [ed.] Graduated Mt. Zion High School 1931; [occ.] Retired from General Electric Company; [memb.] Member of Gospel Baptist Church, Member of Galion Hospital Auxiliary; [hon.] Chosen Crawford County's Healthiest Boy -- 1 free week at the Ohio State Fair. Played on High School Champion Basketball team. Won honors and awards in Track meets; [oth. writ.] I sold my first song lyric in 1936 to Asher Sizemore of the Grand Old Opera in Nashville, TN. In 1970 my poem, "I Live In Faith", was set to music and copyrighted, and sung in many churches and also by the Gospel Singing Spicer Family; [pers.] My poems and songs are mostly religious. I thank my Heavenly Father for this wonderful gift, and also the National Library of Poetry for making a dream come true; [a.] Galion, OH

PETER, BONNIE S.
[Pen.] Bonnie Simmons Peter; [b.] May 22, 1944, Pontiac, Michigan; [p.] Oleva and Harold F. Simmons; [ch.] Angela Marie and Douglas Albert; [ed.] Tell City High; [occ.] Author, Songwriter, Poet; [hon.] Eight Golden Poet Awards from World of Poetry and 33 Awards of Merits from Publishing companies throughout the U.S. Competitor Great American Screen Test and Extra in "A League of it's own"; [oth. writ.] Included in the Presidential Collection in the white House, Washington, D.C. and Public Libraries. Non Fiction Book Blue Scarlett, 42 poems published in poetry anthology books. Fiction short story "Magnificent Trifles"; published and recorded song words for 12 songs "Wherever You Are Come To Me and Yahweh Yahshua Is My Name" were aired on Magic Key Video Show in Hollywood, CA, Cable, T.V.; [pers.] In my writings of spiritual ecstacy I wish to reach the stars, especially Elizabeth Taylor and may we meet in my next book to be published "White Lily"; [a.] Tell City, Indiana 47586

PETERS, PATTY
[b.] April 10, 1974, Phoenix, AZ; [p.] Jerry Joe and Sherry Peters; [ed.] Graduate, Amanda Clearcreek H.S. Freshman at Ohio Dominican College; [occ.] College Student; [memb.] Ohio Dominican College Student Council, Ohio Dominican College Mascot Cheerleader, Campus Ministry, Admissions Volunteer; [hon.] Heart H. Award, Citizenship Washington Focus, American Soya Festival Scholarship Winner, Pickaway Co. 4-H Scholarship Winner, FFA Chapter Star Farmer; [oth. writ.] Poem "Flying High" in A Break In The Clouds, invited to write devotional's for Guidesposts Co., Daily guideposts, 1995 Edition. Numerous prize winning articles throughout school year; [pers.] I am the voice for all the unwanted and homeless in our world. I have been there and there is hope; [a.] Amanda, Ohio 43102

PETO, JENNY
[Pen.] JJ Peto; [b.] July 1, 1974, Sharon, PA; [p.] Richard and Adamarie Peto; [ed.] Graduated from Brookfield High School 1992, Sophmore at Youngstown State University; [occ.] Student; [hon.] National Honors Society in High School; [oth. writ.] Several poems published in different anthologies. One entitled "Starless Skies", published in a local book called Youngstown Poetry; [pers.] Keep hold of your dreams and never give up on reaching them; [a.] Masury, Ohio 44438

PETRALI, JOHN
[b.] July 20, 1909; Italy; [p.] deceased; [m.] Yolanda, July 25, 1931; [ch.] (2) John and Marie; [ed.] 12th grade (taking continuing education courses); [occ.] Aircraft and automotive technician (now retired); [memb.] Breda Buck Masonic Lodge NY, Advisory Committee Member of United Westland, Founder of Citrus County Property Owners Assoc - FL; [hon.] Who's Who in Poetry, FL State Golden Poet Award

1989, Florida State Silver Poet Award (4 yrs); [oth. writ.] Published book of poetry "The Good and Sad Days" - Vantage Press, NY (Collection of 50 poems) my own writings; [pers.] Mankind, once united, will unlock triumphs over all illness, all fear, all insecurity, all hatred and all inequity; [a.] Inverness, FL 34451

PFAU, STEPHANI
[b.] 1942, Brooklyn, NY; [p.] Nee Katzenstein; [m.] James Lee Pfan; [ch.] Danny (both beloveds passed on); [ed.] B.U.S. with distinction W.N.M. (ALB.NM) in comparative Lit and Art; [occ.] Retired; [memb.] A.R.C./Center for Marine Conservation/N.M. Art League; [hon.] Certificate of Merit for Advocacy San Diego Assn for the Retarded/NM Designer Craftsmen - Juried Display - Multimedia/NM for IL Art Museum Santa Fe, NM - Juried Display - Multimedia; [oth. writ.] Published '93 National Library of Poetry (Editor's Choice Award) unpublished short stories, travel journals, poetry; [pers.] Influences: kindness, respect and appreciation as power; nature; Mahalo (Hawaiian - The giver and receiver are one). I portray visual moments and insights; [a.] Albuquerque, NM

PHILLIPS JR., HUGH
[Pen.] Sam; [b.] July 2, 1931, Batesville, Arkansas; [p.] Hugh Phillips, Sr. and Hattie Hudson Phillips; [ch.] Susan and Stephen, twins; David and Debora, Jonathan; [ed.] Graduated, Newport High School, Newport, Ark., May 1949. Aviation Cadet Class 55-D, Retired a Command Pilot at the rank of Major. Many schools throughout my career.; [occ.] Retired Air Force Pilot and early retirement!; [memb.] American Poetry Society; [hon.] Honorable Mention, The National Author's REgistry, Iliad Press, Editor's Preference Award-Creative Arts and Sciences, Ent.; [oth. writ.] "Life" published in "A Break in the Clouds" by The National Library of Poetry. Published in "Poetic Visions" Live works third place for "Decisions"; [pers.] I attribute the pleasure I realize from poetic expression to all experiences throughout life. Poetic expression seeks me!; [a.] Denver, CO 80204-2846.

PHILLIPS, KENNETH ANTHONY
[b.] May 27, 1956, Norwalk, Ohio; [p.] Andrew and Emma Phillips; [ed.] Willard High School; [occ.] Utility Worker at Huron County Landfill; [memb.] Member of Rod and Gun Club in Monroville, Ohio; [hon.] Several Golden Poet Awards and Honorable Mentions from World of Poetry; [oth. writ.] Poems, Seasons of Promise, Valentine, Duel, Artistry of Passion, Truants of Time (short stories), A Clock Maker's Dream, A Debtor's Gain; [pers.] Through the following of movement, there is a separation into individual experiences we call real; [a.] Willard, Ohio 44890

PHILLIPS, SAM
[b.] December 16, 1943, Lake Providence, Louisiana; [p.] Nathan and Dora Phillips; [ch.] Tina Marie and Lavelle Arnette; [occ.] naval Aircraft Painter; [hon.] Three Honorable Mentions, Three Golden Poet Awards; [oth. writ.] "Minister of Wealth", "Vision of the Homeless", "No Mo' Sharkin", "Hocus Pocus"; [pers.] No one is as smart as they say that they are and no one is as stupid as you wish them to be; [a.] Oakland, CA 94603

PICKARD, MURIEL YAKIR
[b.] May 29, 1929, NY; [p.] Ida and Morris Seidman; [m.] Ed Pickard, June 19, 1948; [ch.] Three sons, six grandchildren; [ed.] George Washington High School, NY graduated with honors; [occ.] Formerly, Office administration and accounting. Currently, part-time student, crafter and school volunteer; [memb.] The International Society of Poets, Community Affiliations; [hon.] 3 Golden Poet Awards from The World of Poetry, 1990-1992, Editor's Choice Award from the National Library of Poetry 1993; [oth. writ.] Published in three anthologies: World of Poetry anthology, Our World's Most Treasured Poems and through the National Library of Poetry, Whispers in the Wind; [pers.] I believe in the Art of Communication. This is accomplished through my poetry, photography and meaningful relationships with family and friends. I am grateful to have the opportunity to be published. In this manner, I hope to be an inspiration to my grandchildren; to instill in them a love of the written word and thereby leave my legacy of love through communication; [a.] Hollywood, FL

PICKRELL (III), FRED A.
[Pen.] Pick; [b.] December 11, 1948, Birmingham, AL; [p.] Fred (Jr) and Hazel Y. Pickrell; [ed.] High school, two years college; [occ.] Disabled; [hon.] Who's Who Awards, Golden Poet Award; [oth. writ.] Too many to list; [pers.] My life has been a tornado, hail has left a mark with a pen or quill in my hand and a thought in my mind, there's no getting close to the fact, Pick's one of a kind; [a.] Tuscalooga, AL

PIERSON, KAREN A.
[b.] January 25, 1940, Maquon, Illinois; [p.] Mr. and Mrs. Charles F. Little, two sisters marlene and Diane; [m.] Jackie Lee Pierson, January 7, 1962 (deceased); [ch.] Debra Jo and Tammie Sue; Grandchildren, Keary Wignall, Aaron Welin; [ed.] Graduated Galesburg Sr. High, Carl Sandburg College, computer, data base, blueprints; [occ.] Admirals Office 1958-1960, Dick Blick Office, Admiral Assembler 1973-1994...still working admirals; [memb.] Methodist Church, Admiral Local Lodge 2063 IAM & AW, American Legion Auxiliary; [hon.] 1988 Golden Poet Award 1991 Golden Poet Award, 1991 Golden Poet, 1992 Golden Poet Award, 1990 Silver Award. Various Awards of Merit and honorable mentions. Won Editor's Choice Award by National Library of Poetry; [oth. writ.] Have attempted few articles for papers and magazines.; [pers.] My poems are mostly taken from life around me and thoughts I have. A great way to relax and express my ideas on things around me; [a.] Galesburg, IL 61401

PIKE, ALICE M.
[b.] May 30, 1933, Erie, PA; [p.] Raymond and Goldie Wiswell; [m.] Arthur W. Pike, October 18, 1952; [ch.] Arthur Ray, Kenneth David, Christine Linda, Cindy Lu; [ed.] 12th Grade, Academy High School; [occ.] Telephone Receptionist, now retired; [memb.] Holiday Village Ladies, Aux. St. Johns R.C. Church Aux., G.S. of A Senior Centers; [hon.] Blue Ribbons, Red Ribbons, White Ribbons, Medals for things other than poetry, 1 trophy.; [oth. writ.] Poems and short stories published in newspapers and magazines. Working on a manuscript of poems at present. Children's Inst. of Lit.; [pers.] I write for the enjoyment. I am fascinated how the words just come to me so I put them down on paper.; [a.] Erie PA.

PIPER, JO
[b.] April 5, 1929, Lake City, IA; [p.] Wilber E. Chase and Ella Chase; [m.] Charles M. Piper, April 23, 1951; [ch.] Steven, Kevin, Alan; [ed.] Lake City High, University of Northern Iowa, BA Degree; [occ.] Widow, retired from teaching english; [memb.] Church of Christ, UNI Honor Societies, PHI TAU PHI Sorority (UNI); [hon.] Iowa Teachers First, Torch and Tassel, poem published in "Break In The Clouds"; [oth. writ.] Several with "Feelings" Magazine; "Reminisce" Magazine, poem for Larimer Co. Alzheimers Newsletters; [pers.] Writing was a wonderful therapy to bring out of clinical depression. Prayer and love mean much to me; writing gives me constant hope; [a.] Loveland, CO 80538

PLANTE, DAVID PAUL
[b.] February 18, 1957, Lew., ME; [p.] Paul Plante and Mary Moseley; [m.] Brenda, October 4, 1986; [ch.] Brad "Michael", Markie "Elise"; [pers.] Empires are built upon foundations of Dreams: Empires crumble and dreams fade away; [a.] Lewiston, ME

POIRIER, JOYCE A.
[Pen.] NYMKIM; [b.] October 9, 1938, Peabory, MA; [p.] Joseph E and Florence E. (Langan) Poirier; [ed.] Salem, MA High Class of '56, College of St Elizabeth, Convent Station, NJ - BA English Fairfield University, Fairfield, CT - MA English; [occ.] High School English teacher, Beverly, MA; [memb.] National Council Teachers of English, Massachusetts Council Teachers of English, National Education Association, Massachusetts Teachers Assn; Beverly Teachers Assn, The International Society of Poets; [hon.] Ledger (news) Person of the Year (1991), Nominee - Massachusetts Teacher of the Year (1991), Honary inductee, Gamma Chapter of National Honor Society (1991), Who's Who Among American Teachers (1992); [oth. writ.] "Last Respects" published in Wind in the Night Sky (1993, "Suspended Animation" published in Contemporary Poets of America and Britain (1994) "Fledgling" in The Coming of Dawn (1994). 2 copyrighted collections of poetry: Revelations I, and Christalized. Another 70 poems to be copyrighted, and several "In Process"; [pers.] My poetry continues to inspire my own growth. My wish is that it will support others in their process as well. I thank Christine Bavard for directing me to this previously untapped inner resource; [a.] Danvers, MA 01923

PORTER, EDITH MARINIAK
[b.] May 19, 1921, Petersburg, VA; [p.] Michael W. Mariniak; [m.] Franklin Glen Porter, March 14, 1946; [ch.] 2 adopted song, George Alexander & Richard Haywood Porter; [ed.] Petersburg High School, Spotswood Business College; [occ.] Secretary retired. Personal Finance Company; [memb.] Seniority Club, Chippenham Hospital Ettrick-Matoaca Rescue Squad, Lifetime member 11 years active duty, New Life Baptist Church; [hon.] Cardiac Tech Ettrick-Matoaca Rescue Squad. A Merit Citation for outstanding Rescue and handling of 14 yr old boy hit by auto (Chesterfield County Police); [oth. writ.] Personalized poems written for friends of Immanuel Baptist Church and New Life Church; [pers.] My poems either have a moral or I try to glorify my God. Since I was fifteen, I have always had a desire to write that which God directs me to say; [a.] Petersburg, VA 23803

PORTER, MICHAEL LEROY
[b.]November 23, 1947, Newport News, VA; [p.]Doretha B. Porter and Leroy Porter; [ed.]Hunington High School (Honor) Diploma, Virginia State Univ. B.A. (Honors), M.A. Atlanta Univ., Ph.D, History, Emory Univ.; [occ.]Writer, Consultant; [memb.]International Academy of Poets, Elite International, International Council of Advisors (Chairman); [hon.]Outstanding Achievement in Poetry 1990; Outstanding Black 1990; U.S. Congressional Medal of Freedom 1993; [oth. writ.]Black Atlanta; An Interdisciplinary Study of Blacks in Atlanta, GA 1890-1930 (1974), Read Between The Lines (1985); Who's Who in Poetry 1990; Distinguished Poets of America 1993.; [pers.]When one is born the brain is a blank sheet. Any perception made by that brain may be an indelible influence; [a.] Hampton, VA 23669-3814.

POUCH, JOHN MALCOLM
[Pen.]J. Malcolm; [b.]April 30, 1943, Winchester, KY; [p.]Mary Pauline Collier and Clarence Alfred Pouch; [m.]Valerie Jean Lowe, December 29, 1979; [ch.]Brandi, Makeyla, Corrina, Durenda, Keara, Michael and Scott; [ed.]Completed 9th grade, then moved out of house and took a job; [occ.]District Manager for Retail Distributor; [hon.]Silver 1989 and Gold Poet 1987 Awards.; [oth. writ.]Four Volumes of Poetry 1959 to Present; Seasons of Myself; A Frame of Mine; Things A Pen Remembers; Words and Fools; [pers.]I've lived my life in Toil and Pain, but wouldn't change a single thing!; [a.] Detroit, MI 48219.

POWELL, WILLIAM J.
[Pen.]Billy Powell; [b.]August 25, 1960, East Liverpool, Ohio; [m.]Wilma J. Powell, June 6, 1980; [ch.]Jason T. Powell; [ed.]Center are High School; [oth. writ.]I have over 111 writings that are unpublished that I possess, and that I may hand down to those who will receive of them, when time permits this to be so.; [pers.]As water and air, is to our Bodies; Words in Graceful Poem, bring life and refreshing fulfillment to the Soul. To express your inner thoughts unto others is to offer that in which is pure and incorruptible. For what else binds mankind to each other?; [a.] Aliquippa, PA 15001.

POWERS, RAE KAE
[b.]March 31, 1917, Dayton, OH; [p.]Lewis R. and Gertrude M. Suman; [m.]Bill Powers December 23, 1939 (deceased November 19, 1992); [ch.]Keith A. and Theresa L. Powers (Mrs. Al Finlay); [ed.]Fairview High School Graduate, Miami Jacobs Business College, Graduate 1939; [occ.]Write music for piano and the lyrics (self taught); [memb.]WPCA (CA Widowed Persons), Keyboard Teachers Association, International, Inc., NY; [hon.]Song with Lyrics "I Had A Dream" 1989; [oth. writ.]some poetry; [pers.]Want to feel alive and free? Just let your heart sing a melody. The land, the sea, the sky and we all play a part in this harmony. For you to feel alive and free, just let your heart sing a melody!; 1460 Gary Way, Carmichael, CA 95608-5910

PRESSLEY, LOUISE
[Pen.]Louise Pressley; [b.]August 2, 1937, Haywood County, NC; [p.]William V. Reece, Retta Lee Reece; [m.] Frank D. Pressley; [ch.] Ricky Frank, Diane Louise; [ed.] Waynesville High; [occ.] Textile worker, housewife and (retired textile worker of 35 yrs) babysitter now; [memb.] Cruso United Methodist Church, American Heart Association, Friend of Library Association, National Arbor Day Foundation; [hon.] Several Golden Poet Awards from World of Poetry and Several Certificates of Honorable mention; [oth. writ.] Poem published in Waynesville Mountaineer (local newspaper) 2 poems displayed in Pastor's study at church and local rest home for the patients; [pers.] I strive to reflect the love of God for mankind and the beauty of the earth and all that is in it. God is love, hope and peace. I have been greatly influenced by the pain and loneliness and hurt that is in our world today; [a.] Canton, NC 28716

PRINGLE, LIDIA WASOWICZ
[b.] April 3, 1951, Krakow, Poland; [p.] Janina, Kazimierz Wasowicz; [m.] Douglas Hall Pringle, November 13, 1982; [ch.] Alexandra Judith, 7, Christina Janine 3; [ed.] St. Mary of the Wasatch High School, B.A. in Communications, with Honors, University of Utah, Stanford University; [occ.] Science writer for United Press International; [memb.] Women in Communications, Phi Beta Kappa, Sigma Delta Chi, Smithsonian Institution, Mortar Board; [hon.] Rotary Club Scholarship, Russel S. Marriott Scholarship, Honors at Entrance Scholars Chip, Minute Woman Scholarship, Maude May Babcock Scholarship, Sherwood Music School Scholarship, Outstanding California Journalist Award, Award for Outstanding Coverage of Mt. St. Helens Volcano, Award for Outstanding coverage of Drug Abuse in Marin County, First place in news reporting from Peninsula Press Club, two first place awards for Best News Series, 1st place Sigma Delta Chi Award, 1st place Lincoln Steffens Award for Outstanding Investigative Reporting, Award for Outstanding Investigative Reporting, on California Prisons, Pulitzer Prize nominee twice, finalist Livington Award, Winner of Professional Journalism Fellowship to Stanford University by the National Endowment for the Humanities; [oth. writ.] Poem Happy Anniversary Darling, published in Wind In The Night Sky; more than 800 articles on a wide variety of subjects published in newspapers, magazines and other publications around the world; [pers.] Begin each day with a prayer of thanks; realize each second is irretrievable and use it accordingly; [a.] San Rafael, CA 94901

PROBASCO, JOHN MUNCK
[b.] October 2, 1919, South Amboy, NJ; [p.] John Weyland Probasco and Anna Mattilda Probasco, Nee Munck; [m.] Katherine Claire Probasco, nee Rivior, April 29, 1946; [ch.] Shirley Lorraine Clark, John Douglas Probasco, David John Probasco, Kenneth Wayne Probasco, Patricia Claire Towles, Kathy Joyce Probasco; [ed.] Bridgeton High School 1937, West Point Prep. School 1939, Life Underwriters Training School 1959, Sec.'t Exchange 1976; [occ.] Shipping and Receiving Clerk; [memb.] VFW, NRA, AM-Legion; [hon.] Met. Life Wis. Co., six Times President's Club; [oth. writ.] Over 300 poems written, I published Our World's Most Beautiful Poems", one in "American Poetry Annual", Front Page, "Bridgeton Evening News, Memorial Day, Guest On" "Off The Cuff," Radio Station WWNJ; [pers.] I was night supervisor, Owens Illinois Glass Co, Shipping Dept. Field Engineer, Chas. A. Fuller Co., Brakeman on Pennsylvania Railroad, Mail Sorter, U.S. Postal Svs., Agency Mgr. Met. Life Ins. Co. and Cashier at Sands Casino in Atlantic City, NJ; [a.] Bridgeton, NJ 08302

PROBSDORFER, ANDREA M.
[b.]May 25, 1947, Sewickley, PA; [p.]Andrew and Josephine Probsdorfer; [ed.]BS in Education, University of Akron, Masters of Science in Education, Duguesne University; [occ.]Third Grade Teacher, Big Knob School, Freedom Area Schools; [memb.]Delta Kappa Gamma Society International Chapter President, Leotta Hawthorne Reading Council, FAEA Representative, Zion's Lutheran Church Council, Music, Worship Committee, Church Soloist; [oth. writ.]Several poems published in World of Poetry, school publications; [pers.]My poetry is a pastel window through which I reflect my feelings of soften warmth and enriched thought which to share with all who read it; [a.] Ambridge, PA 15003

PROTZMANN, MILES L.
[b.] July 24, 1927, Milwaukee, WI; [p.] Herbert and Judith Protzmann; [m.] Luclla Protzmann; [m.] May 14, 1949, Linda Berth and Jill Gigante; [ed.] Custer High School, Univ of WI - Milwaukee; [occ.] Retired Teacher, Vieau and Engleburg Elem - Milwaukee; [memb.] St John's Lutheran Church of West Bend, Phi Alpha Theta for conspicuous attainments and scholarship in the field of history; [oth. writ.] Poem - "The Unknown Child" published in A Break in the Clouds and written as a tribute to the many 10, 11, and 12 year old, as well as adult crossing guards and all others who may have been instrumental in the saving of a child's life; [pers.] I write in order to contribute something to an occasion and because I enjoy doing it; [a.] West Bend, WI

PRUITT, ANN
[b.] September 2, 1944, Tennessee; [p.] Norman and Estelle Pruitt; [ch.] Jeff, Mingo, Norman, Doug, Charmeleta and Carmeleta; [ed.] Hancock High; [hon.] Editor's Award; [oth. writ.] Local newspaper, books, cards; [pers.] I have been greatly influenced by life around me so I strive to see the real side of mankind; [a.] Sneedville, TN

PURUSHOTTAMDAS, PATEL B.
[Pen.]Das; [b.] July 1, 1929, Uttersanda Gusarat India; [p.] Father, Bhailalbhai Govindghai; Mother, Divaliben Bhailalbhai; [m.] Ansuya Allas Hansa Patel, May 11, 1947; [ch.] Kiran, Kaushik, Deepak and Kamlesh; [ed.] Matriculation Examination Passed in 1947; [occ.] Retired Businessman; [memb.] Founder of The Lared Records Department Class III Government Servants Association, Gujarat State India 1956; [hon.] Obtained little amount of cash prizes from leading magazines in India. Editor's Choice Award from The National Library of Poetry for Outstanding Achievement in Poetry; [oth. writ.] Several social and religious articles, narratives, essays, numerous poems, biography of my 3 1/2 year old grandson Kunjal., etc. published in leading newspapers literacy magazines in India. Documentary film script entitled "Riddhi-Siddhi" on land reforms for Gwarat State Government India. Little Knowledge of English Language. Poems: "Word and Blood" selecting for its sound published in the National Library of Poetry anthology. Also., "Light", "Islame" and "Witness", accepted for publication by the National Library of Poetry..in their forthcoming anthologies. I'm grateful to the earth and sky of America where my pen is welcomed and where I take air presently. I've dedicated my pen for mankind; [pers.] But my grandson Anish has been my inspiration for writing poems in English Language. artistic manuscript in my own

hand writings in 247 pages, entitled "child", a collection of 58 poems in Gwarati and English with 94 pictures and one social novel "When Got Blower..In Ash" scheduled to be published during my visit to India; [a.] Harrisburg, PA 17109

PUTTA, JANE H.
[b.] June 17, 1936, Nova Scotia, Canada; [p.] Dan and Janie Bigney (father deceased, mother living in N.S.); [m.] Stan Putta, July 19, 1955 (from Szechoslavakia); [ch.] Two, Darlene and Dan, one grandchild, Kimberly, another on way; [ed.] High School, Classes at Riverside City College and Certificate in Commercial Design from University of CA, Riverside; [occ.] Retired from Kaiser Foundations Hospital (25 yrs. service as Adm. Secretary); [hon.] Editor's Choice Award from National Library of Poetry 1st and Honorary Mention Awards for Oil Paintings; [oth. writ.] Local publication's and one publication with Quill Books in All My Tomorrows, song "Nostalgia" not published. Many poems not yet published; [pers.] Live and let live!; [a.] Riverside

QUALLY, DEAN LOWELL
[b.]May 31, 1930, Alexandria, MN; [p.]Ferdinand and Myrtle Qually; [m.]Betty 9/30/51; Donna 7/13/91; both deceased; [ch.]Lowell Qually, Eric Qually, Elaine Fass; [ed.]Mt. Vernon High School; Flushing High School; Queen's College, NY; [occ.]Painter of Fine Arts; Poet; Writer; Composer; [memb.]Metropolitan Art Museum; Montclair Art Museum; American Legion; First Ev. Lutheran Choir; [hon.]Flushing High Honor Roll; Arista; navy Good Conduct Medal; Overseas Occupational Medal (Korean War); Editor's Choice Award 1993 from the National Library of Poetry; [oth. writ.]Short stories for the Flushing High School "Folio"; Poems published in "A Break in the Clouds."; [pers.]My paintings, poems, writings and music reveal my search for creative human emotions.; [a.] Bloomfield, NJ 07003-3866.

RADZANOWSKI, DARLENE
[b.]December 8, 1956, Pittsburgh, PA; [p.]Jack Thomas Talak and R. M. Geraldine Talak (white); [m.]Edward J. Radzanowski, May 17, 1986; [ch.]Edward, Daniel, Cassandra, Lee; [ed.]Carrick High School; [occ.]Housewife; [memb.]Bon Air Civic Assoc.; [oth. writ.]Gardenia; My Brother; My Son; both poems published in National Library of Poetry; [pers.]I find that writing poems help me to express my feelings and my personal beliefs.; [a.] Pittsburgh, PA 15210.

RAETHER, ARNOLD L.
[Pen.]Arnie, Arn; [b.]May 23, 1954, Eau WI; [p.]Lawrence and Doris Raether; [ch.]Alisha Susan Raether 19 yrs. old Minneapolis, MN, Amanda Lynn Raether 16 yrs. old Eau Claire, WI; [occ.]Hardware Buyer and Sales Assistant, Busy Bee Hardware (Santa Monica, CA); [memb.]Pilgrim Lutheran Church; [hon.]Editor's Choice Award, 1993 National Library of Poetry; [oth. writ.]Red Eye He Was Quite The Boy, The National Library of Poetry Wind in the Night Sky; What Dad and Mom Meant To Us All, National Library of Poetry, The Coming of Dawn; Dells Mill Augusta, WI, In The Desert Sun; [pers.]Many thanks to April J. McKay for teaching me to lead the turns on the slow beat and for making my life a two step worth dancing. In my book you'll always be the best. Thanks to Dennis and Diamonds in Santa Monica for a dance floor to spend our time.; [a.] Santa Monica, CA 90405.

RAGOLTA, RAMON
[Pen.] Ray; [b.] June 28, 1943, Guantanamo, Cuba; [p.] Ramon Ragolta, Melga Marta de La Caridad Ragolta; [m.] Delia L. Ragolta, June 3, 1963; [ch.] Odalys, Oneida, Ramon Osmary; [ed.] High School Buanta - NAMo Secondary, Eletro Mechanical, Electronic; [occ.] Tech TV Electronic and Computers; [memb.] Church of Jesus Christ of Latter Day Saints; [oth. writ.] Several poems to my wife, family and friends. Article to newspaper, work related support group; [pers.] My life in these wonderful land has been fulfilled and I like to express to others this happiness; [a.] Tampa, FL

RAGSDALE, DANIEL E.
[b.]August 16, 1972, Huntingdon, TN; [p.]Bonnie D. Hicks (stepfather), Nancy Hicks (mother); [ed.]Gorman Christian School; [memb.]Mt. Carmel Congregational Methodist Church, Big Sandy, TN; [hon.]Editor's Choice Award, National Library of Poetry; [oth. writ.]Reflections of Life, Sparrowgrass Poetry Forum; Many Colors; The Unlucky Spider; The Cross, National Library of Poetry; [pers.]I would like to thank my Lord and Savior Jesus Christ, my family, and outlay, my Boa Constrictor, who consistently inspire me; [a.] Camder, TN 38320.

RAMNANAN, LAKSHMI
[Pen.]Lakshmi; [b.]September 24, 1976, Trinidad; [p.]Angad J. Ramnanan and Leela Ramnanan; [ed.]Plantation High School; [oth. writ.]That Special Someone; [pers.]Believe in yourself and anything is possible; [a.] Plantation, FL 33317.

RANDALL, LEONA W.
[Pen.]Lea Dora Boudar; [b.]May 14, 1928, Mobile, Alabama; [p.]Booker T. Washington and Alice B. Washington; [m.]William A. Randall Sr., June 1, 1950 (Deceased); [ch.]Adolph C. Randall, Alice A. Flanders, William A. Randall Jr.; [ed.]Xavier Preparatory High, Xavier University of New Orleans; [occ.]Retired Elementary School Teacher (Joseph A. Hardin Elementary School); [memb.]Louisiana Retired Teachers Association, Louisiana State Museum, St. David Catholic Church Choir, American Cancer Society; [oth. writ.]Poems, "Lay Down Your Pillow", published in National Poetry Association, Los Angeles, California; [pers.]We as poets, weave America's dreams, by extending dimensions of her literary works at home and abroad. America's dreams are also cultivated and harvested with love, respect and devotion in the poetic fields of this great nation.; [a.] New Orleans, Louisiana 70117.

RANDALL, MICHAEL PAUL
[Pen.]Myhee; [b.]March 14, 1952, Sidney, Ohio; [p.]Paul G. Randall and Pauline Randall; [m.]Divorced; [ch.]Emily Ann Randall, Micah Allen Randall; [ed.]High School; [occ.]Poisher; [oth. writ.]Oh Here Is Me; Sometimes; Oh How Long For Someone; [pers.]Pen name is Myhee (Mike) I've been writing for two years now because of my Daughter Emily who said go ahead dad and do it and so I did, Thanks Emily and thanks to my pen pal Sue Prigione in Conn. who encouraged me to write too. Thanks Sue, for everything; [a.] Jackson Center, Ohio 45334.

RASMUSSEN II, ELMER A.
[Pen.] Bud; [b.] February 13, 1922, Racine, Wis.; [p.] Elmer A. Rasmussen I and Gwendolyn L. Newman; [ch.] seven children, twelve grandchildren, seven great grandchildren; [ed.] BSME, Marquette University of Milwaukee, Wis., MBA, University of Wisconsin, Racina Wis.; [occ.] Retired Mechanical Eng. and Entrepreneur; [memb.] American Legion Post #303, A.A.A.S., A.S.T.M.E., A.M.E., N.A.P.E., S.A.E. and N.R.A.; [hon.] Phi Beta Kappa, Golden Poet Award 1989 and 1991, Silver Poet Award 1988 and 1990, "Hall of Fame" for living poets 1992, San Diego Honor Blood Donor (38 Gals) to date.; [oth. writ.] Currently In Progress, Three Poetry Books completely of my own writings and a separate manuscript of Philosophy on Communication of Nature and Human Beings; [pers.] My person inspiration is derived from my relationship with my Mermaid named Holly. "Material things will never satisfy love, life or happiness." But, "togetherness will."; [a.] Santee, CA.

RAY SR., KIRK M.
[Pen.]The True Dreamer; [b.]August 7, 1957, Birmingham, AL; [p.]Alice F. Ray and Olan M. Ray; [m.]Jo Annette, June 1991; [ch.]Bobby 17, Cassie 15, Dejuna 13, Teresa 12, Kirk Jr. 10, Mary 9, Candice 7, Ashley 5, Kirsty 4; [ed.]Woodlawn High School and Electronics Training. Most importantly...The Dreamer is a student of life! Ever watching, ever listening, ever learning; [occ.]Management; Injection Molding or Retail Sales; Volunteer in the fight against sexual abuse; [memb.]Christianity; The Philadelphia era of God's Church; International Society of Poets; Guest speaker at survivor groups and vigils.; [hon.]Poet of Merit Award from International Society of Poets. Honored by God with a gift. That truly helps survivors; [oth. writ.]Other poems now published by the N.L.P. in The Coming of Dawn and A Break in The Clouds. Work written for and dedicated to survivor groups, mental health centers, Fultondale Elem. School, Emily Court, D.H.R., Family and Child Services, etc.; [pers.]Stop child sexual abuse! Place the same where it belongs..On the abuser! Make them pay a high price for these crimes! The children never forget! Their sentence is Life without probation or parole. Christ loved the children!; [a.] Fultondale, AL 35068.

RAYA, FRANK
[Pen.]Kiko Raya; [b.]May 30, 1935, Hutchinson, Kansas; [p.]Francisco and Luz Raya; [m.]Rachel Raya, July 20, 1957; [ch.]Cynthia, Annette, Rachel Anthony, Gregory, Christopher; [ed.]Hutchinson High School, Hutchinson Jr. College, Salt City Business College; [occ.]Restaurant Owner; [memb.]Our Lady of Guedelupe Church; [hon.]Poem published in Wind In The Night Sky; [pers.]In our creator's drawing we are but a brush stroke on his canvas, insignificant in isolation, essential for completion; [a.] Hutchinson, Kansas.

READ, M. MARGARET
[b.] May 31, 1936, Indiana; [ch.] Jennifer P. Read, Laurie A. Read; [ed.] B.S. Western Michigan Univ, M.S. Univ of Wisconsin, Adv grad, study - Wisconsin, Northeastern Univ; [occ.] Speech/Language Pathologist; [memb.] American Speech-Language-Hearing Association, Mass Speech-Language-Hearing Assoc, Nat'l Org for Women; [hon.] Who's Who of American Women, Honors - Massachusetts Speech-

Language-Hearing Assoc, other; [oth. writ.] Chapters in: 1) New Thoughts on Old Age Springer Publishing Co, 1964; 2) Physical Activity and Child Develop, Mosby Publisher, 1980; [a.] Newton, MN

REED, DEBORAH
[b.]April 7, 1952, Lakeport, California; [p.]Maxine and Eugene Ford; [m.]Divorced; [ch.]Sirre "Jay", Sean Michael; [ed.]Kelseyville High School, presently attending Mendocino College to become a Psychiatric Tech.; [occ.]Medical/Clerical Assistant; [oth. writ.]A poem in a Montana newspaper, a poem in Wind In The Night Sky, The National Library of Poetry; [pers.]All my poems have been inspired by my ex-husband, who taught me to see, love, and respect all the beautiful things in nature and not take them for granted; [a.] Kelseyville, CA 95451.

REED, DOROTHY M.
[b.]September 13, 1944, Bottineau, ND; [p.]Clarence and Thelma Thompson; [m.]Harold A. Reed, June 22, 1964; [ch.]Emma E. Howard, Grandson Matthew A. Howard; [ed.]A.A. Degree; [occ.]Housewife; [hon.]Golden Poet 1991, World of Poetry, Sacramento, CA; [oth. writ.]I have other poems in books published by Quill Books, Harlinger, TX; [pers.]I give all credit to my Lord Jesus Christ; [a.] Pensacola, FL 32526.

REED, GARNET INEZ
[b.] December 17, 1922, Wilkinsburg, PA; [p.] Adam and Inez Bartlett Fornof; [m.] Rev. Dr. Walter Duff Reed, June 23, 1944; [ch.] Walter D. Reed, Deana Louise Reed; [ed.] Wilkinsburg High, Univ Pittsburgh School of Nursing, Wooster College Bible Study, St. Mary's College - St. Andrews University - Scotland; [occ.] RN - Bible Teacher - Day Care Founder; [memb.] Historic Franklin Presbyterian Church - Elder, Christian Women's Club; [hon.] Assoc Retarded Citizens Palm Beach Cnty; Achievement Award of Business and Professional Women - Lake Worth, FL; [oth. writ.] Newsletter Editor - N.E. FL Presbyterial; Poems in local papers; Articles - Norwalk Press - Norwalk, OH; Articles and Feature Editor - Listener Magazine - Palm Beach County, FL; [pers.] My compulsion to write comes from God to share His love; [a.] Hendersonville, TN

REIFF, KATHRYN L.
[b.]October 25, 1928, Elkhart, Ind.; [p.]Charles E. Kelley and Grace L. (Kaufman) Kelley; [m.]Maurice E. Reiff, September 1, 1946 (deceased 3/9/88); [ch.]Maureen Kay Mauzy, Michael Ray Reiff; [ed.]Attended grade school in Chicago, IL and Warsaw High School in Warsaw, IN; [occ.]Housewife; [memb.]Dutchtown Brethren Church, Auxiliary of Gideons International, Auxiliary of Kosciusko Community Hospital, CLIO Literary Club; [hon.]Eight Golden Poet Awards, numerous poetry Award of Merit's and Outstanding Achievement in Poetry; [oth. writ.]Book of poetry, To God Be The Glory. Book, Surviving The Wound of Grief and several writings in local paper's. Also, several books of poem's by poet's.; [pers.]If from my word's a blessing you win, then thank the Lord they came from him.; [a.] Warsaw, Indiana 46580.

JEANNE ALBERS
[b.]July 11, 1944, Cleveland, Ohio; [p.]Janet Louis Albers and Lawrence Frederick Albers; [m.]John Davis Rennell, November 30, 1991; [ch.]not yet; [ed.]St. Augustine Academy, Lakewood, Ohio; Marymount College, Tannytown, NY; University of London, London, England; [occ.]Writer, General Manager; [pers.]I feel uncomfortable touting myself. My mother always taught me, if it's good and worth repeating, someone else will say it for you.; [a.] Santa Monica, CA 90405.

REYES, BENITO F.
[b.]March 21, 1914, Manila Philippines; [p.]Antera Fernandez and Areadio Reyes; [m.]Dominga L. Reyes, November 12, 1937; [ch.]Siddharta, Thor-Alcyone, Alcor-Mizar, Amita, Nourhalma, Adita, Noemi; [ed.]Ph.B Summa Cum Laude Philosophy, University of The Philippines, 1937, M.A. Far Eastern University, Manila, Philippines, 1949, Ph.D., Great China Academy 1971, Ph.D. International College, Los Angeles, CA USA 1983, LL.D Kyung Hee University, Seoul, Korea 1972, Litt. D. John Dewey University Consortium New York, NY, USA 1981, D.H.D. Institute of Human Development 1981; [occ.]Educator, President of World University of America; [memb.]Phi Gamma Mu; [hon.]Summa cum laude, First Filipino Government of India scholar to the University of Calcutta and first Filipino scholar to study yoga at Sivananda's Rishikesh in the Himalayas, 1949, Voted Most Outstanding Student of the university of the Philippines in Manila 1936, Voted Most Outstanding Professor, Far Eastern University, Manila, 1965-66, Recipient of Papal Medal of Honor from Pope Paul VI, 1970. Poet Laureate of the Philippines in 1969; [oth. writ.]Meditation Cybernetics of Consciousness, World Peace Through Education, Dialogues With God, Conscious Dying, Scientific Evidence of the Existence of the Soul; [pers.]I am a child of God; [a.] Santa Paula, CA 93060

RHEA, DOROTHY SEIBER
[b.]July 25, 1932, Clinton, TN; [p.] Owen Seiber and Ola Seiber; [m.] Carlos J. Rhea, Jr (deceased), June 17, 1951; [ch.] Charles, Wilma, Rebecca, Laura, David - raised Angela and Lorinda my grandchildren; [ed.] Grad Clinton High, Clinton, TN; [occ.] Homemaker; [memb.] Baptist Church; [hon.] World of Poetry - 3 poems; [oth. writ.] Published Poetry in High School. Won Jesse Stewart Award in 1951 and other books; [pers.] I strive to do God's will and give Him the glory in my poetry and my songs; [a.] Tampa, FL 33612

RICHARDS SR., HENRI L.
[b.] May 28, 1938, Muskegon, Michigan; [p.] Frank C. and Helen G. Richards; [m.] Janet K. (Tobin), December 25, 1964; [ch.] Michelle M. September 9, 1965 and Henri Jr. December 18, 1967; [ed.] Completed 8th grade plus G.E.D.; [occ.] Deliver Motor Homes all over U.S. and Canada; [memb.] Nappanee, Amateur Radio Club, Charter Member Nappanee Optimist Club A.R.R.L; [hon.] 2nd place talent contest at work, reading five of my favorite poems; [oth. writ.] Nappanee Advance News "Whispers In The Wind" has my poem "Special Place"; [pers.] I am working on my own book, love to write on Amtrak when returning from trip out west; [a.] Nappanee, Indiana 46550

RICKER, DENISE
[b.]September 12, 1969, Philadelphia, PA; [p.]Barbara and Russell Ricker; [ch.]Nicholas Andrew Richer; [ed.]John W. Hallahan High School, Associate Degree in Nursing, Community College of Philadelphia (CCP); [occ.]Oncology Nurse at Temple U. Hospital, Phila., PA; [memb.]Pennsylvania Nursing Assoc.; [hon.]Golden Poet Award for 1989 from World of Poetry. Second place in poetry contest at Community College of Philadelphia in 1992; [oth. writ.]Comparisons, published by World of Poetry, in Great Poems Of The Western World. Silent Moment, published by The National Library of Poetry. Several poems in CCP's Library Magazine.; [pers.]I can only hope that whoever may stumble upon my writings can feel my words and somehow touch their world and grow.; [a.] Philadelphia, PA.

RICKETT, MARY JUDITH
[Pen.] Judy Rickett; [b.] January 2, 1941, Hillsboro, IL; [p.] Robert Finley, Irene (Grant) Finley; [m.] John Sidney Rickett, July 4, 1989; [ch.] Lisa, Tony, Melissa, Mechelle, Payne-Daniel, Judith, Jamie, Ken, Jasmine Rickett, stepchildren: Darena, Deanna, J.R. Rickett; [ed.] Graduated Noko Mis High School, CNA training, real estate school; [occ.] Home Engineer; [memb.] Eagles Club, United Methodist Church, International Society of Poets; [hon.] Golden Poet 1991, invited for inclusion in Who's Who in Poetry 1992, The International Poet of Merit Award 1993; [oth. writ.] Poem published in "Our World's Most Treasured Poems" 1991. Poem published in local paper; [pers.] I write about the things in life that have had the deepest meaning for me. Love sees us thru all things; [a.] Vandalia, IL

RIEAD, SYBIL C.
[Pen.]Clare Ivers; [b.]July 13, 1933, San Francisco, CA; [p.]John and Gwenith Hargens; [m.]Harry D. Riead, December 7, 1972; [ch.]Eric Heuschele; [ed.]San Jose State University, Univ. of California at Davis, San Diego State University; [occ.]Writer, Poet, Water-Color Professional Artist; [hon.]Art Awards through out California, miscellaneous poetry awards; [oth. writ.]Poetry, Romance Novel; [pers.]I enjoy the creativity of writing; [a.] San Diego, CA 92128.

RIGGS, DARIS
[b.]February 28, 1942, Christian County, KY; [p.]Virgil Mannahan and Della Garrett Mannahan; [m.]Divorced; [ch.]James Allen Riggs, Theresa Darlene Novak, Timberly Deane; [ed.]King Grammer, Kelly High, Daly College, Moraine Vally College; [occ.]Nurse, Nurse-Power Agency; [memb.]AARP, International Church of God; [hon.]Golden Poet Awards 1988, 1989, 1990, 1991, poems published in local neighborhood papers and nursing homes publications; [oth. writ.]Children's stories, Lady Bug June; Darcey and the Silver Fox; Darcey and Buzzards; Bluff; Darcey in the Land of Wishes; [pers.]My personal philosophy is: To know God and yourself is the greatest accomplishment you can attain. To know love and honor is the greatest reward; [a.] Chgo, IL 60638.

RILEY, VERA B.
[b.] January 6, 1929, SC; [m.] The Rev. Mr. Clyde L. Riley; [ch.] Sandra Riley Romig, Pamela Riley Cates; [ed.] M.Ed., Ed Sp. Degree, C.P. Education (clinical pastoral ed.); [occ.] Minister's wife, retired teacher, counselor; [memb.] NEA, SCEA, RCEA, IPA, Prime Times, AARP, USC Concert Series, USC Alumni; [oth. writ.] Poem included in anthology for Wives of Ministers, Religions and Educational periodicals. Poems included in Who's Who in Poetry,

609

Vol. III, Great Poems of the Western World, Vol. II and World Treasury of Great Poems, Vol. II; [pers.] Remembering is an integral part of experiencing; therefore meaningful moments are significant; [a.] Blythewood, SC

ROBINSON, PAULETTE
[b.] December 6, 1951, Duluth, MN; [p.] James Lorntson, Donna Yang; [m.] Randall Robinson, August 1, 1993; [ch.] Joel Baumert, Jeremy Robinson, Kimberly Baumert, Scott Robinson; [ed.] B.A. Religious Studies - U of Hawaii, M.A. Asiah Religion - U of Hawaii, M.A. Non-profit Administration - U of San Francisco; [occ.] Executive Director/Educator; [memb.] Belmont Chamber of Commerce Board; [hon.] Phi Beta Kappa, graduated with distinction (U.H.), 1993-94 Who's Who Registry for Global Business Leaders, 1993-94 Who's Who in U.S. Finance and Industry; [oth. writ.] "Whispers of Asia" collection of poetry exhibited at Antioch Univ Santa Barbara and Los Angeles; [pers.] My writing comes from the emotional impact the world makes on me. I am particularly touched by the people around me and how we embrace life together; [a.] San Jose, CA

ROBINSON, STEVEN RICHARD
[b.] December 8, 1952, Chicago, IL; [p.] Bernadine, (father unknown); [ed.] 3 yrs college; [occ.] Security Officer; [hon.] Poet of Merit, American Poet's Association; [pers.] "When all is said and done, it was and always shall be all about love"; [a.] Chicago, IL

ROCKEY, BILLIE
[b.] May 27, 1933, Lincoln, Nebraska; [p.] Faye and Frank Murrey; [m.] Lonnie Rockey, December 22, 1956; [ch.] Garth Rockey, Kevin Rockey, Arlan Rockey (all married); [ed.] High School; [occ.] Sharing retirement with my husband; [memb.] Independent Order Foresters; [hon.] IOF Awards for Outstanding work with Child Abuse Work; [oth. writ.] I write children's stories and I am an artist and musician. Four poems published in World of Poetry Press and some private publications; [pers.] I write about things I feel and people I know, always looking for the good and the happiness; [a.] Grants Pass, OR 97527.

RODGERS, IDA MAE
[b.] August 25, 1908, Marion County, Ohio; [p.] Elmer and May Osborn; [m.] Carl Rodgers, January 28, 1928; [ch.] George Carl, Robert William; [ed.] Ashley High, Valedictorian of Class; [occ.] Matron in High School, Teacher of Sunday School Children; [memb.] United Methodist Church; [hon.] Awarded a week at the sesquicentennial in Philadelphia 1926; and a certificate and gold coin as winner of state essay contest 1927; [oth. writ.] Poems published in church bulletin and monthly news letters. Winner of a county wide essay and a state wide essay; [pers.] I've tried in all my writings to express hope, and encouragement to others, and to acknowledge Christ's claim on my life; [a.] Medina, Ohio 44256.

ROE, LANAE M.
[b.] November 2, 1972, Tware, California; [p.] Peggy and John Barger; [m.] David H. Roe Jr., September 12, 1992; [ed.] Kingman High School; [occ.] Pilot car driver; [oth. writ.] David...A Break In The Clouds; [a.] Kingman, AZ 86401.

ROESEN, NANCY J.
[b.] February 6, 1932, Lancaster, PA; [p.] John and Ethel Kirchner; [m.] Richard A. Roesen, July 7, 1951; [ch.] Jacquette, Ninette, Stanton, Vanessa, Rebecca, 14 grandchildren, 1 great-grandson; [ed.] 12 yrs; [occ.] Shipping supervisor, Susquehana Glass Co; [oth. writ.] New American Poetry anthology, Great American Poetry anthology, Poetic Voices of America, World of Poetry anthology; [pers.] For me writing is a great relaxing time, which I do mostly in our cabin the the mountains; [a.] Columbia, PA

ROGERS, ALICE
[b.] September 21, 1921, East Jordan, Mich.; [p.] Flora and Allison Pinney; [m.] Leland Rogers, September 10, 1944; [ch.] 3 girls and 6 boys; [ed.] Bachelor of Arts; [occ.] Retired Teacher; [memb.] R.L.D.S., Church, Y.W.C.A. Worked in Conservation; [pers.] I feel we should leave the world a little nicer than we found it. The world is beautiful so let's not spoil it; [a.] Ph. AZ 85033

ROGERS, DREW PRESCOTT
[b.] December, 29, 1971, Camden, NJ; [p.] Paul David Rogers, Charlene M. Outt; [ed.] Grad Millville High, also grad Navy Nuclear Field MM 'A' school and power school; [oth. writ.] Published "A Cold Day in Heaven" in Our World's Favorite Poems; [pers.] I write straight from my heart, and I hold nothing back. Hate is hate, love is love. Everyone knows what strange emotions linger inside themselves, I put them on paper...atleast I try; [a.] Millville, PA

ROGERS JR., JOHNNY
[b.] May 19, 1946, Florence, South Carolina; [p.] Johnny Rogers, SR. and Katie Elizabeth Price Rogers; [ed.] A.A. Business Administration, 1971, Brevard Community College (Cocon, FL); B.S. Bus. Admin 1978 Francis Marion College (Florence, SC); [occ.] Registered Respiratory Therapist, Duke University Med., Center, Durham, NC; [memb.] I.S.P. Honorary Charter Membership, Active Member American Association for Respiratory Care and National Board of Respiratory Care and International Society of Poets.; [hon.] World of Poetry Golden Poet 1990-91-92. Honorable Mention 1990-91. I.S.P. Editor's Choice Award 1993; Ruby Poet 1992-93; [oth. writ.] Thirteen poems, World of Poetry Anthology 1991; 12 poems, Selected Work of our World's Best Poets, 1992; 1 poem, That Will Live Forever, 1992; 13 poems, Our World's Favorite Poems, currently being published; 1 poem, Distinguished Poet's of America, 1993; 1 poem, Whispers In The Wind, currently being published both by The National Library of Poetry, Duke University Medical Center, Cultural Services Dept., currently, Chap Book and possible publication; 1 poem, Write USA Poem Contest; [pers.] I strive to reflect humanity, nature, and lyrics for song poems, both good and bad on a wide variety of subjects; [a.] Durham, NC 27705.

ROGOW, MELINDA ROSELLINNI
[b.] March 29, 1953, Oxnard, California; [p.] John and Mary Gresham; [m.] Barry M. Rogow, February 14, 1992; [ch.] Melanie Kloian, Daliah Rogow, Hayley Rogow; [ed.] Pensacola Christian College; [occ.] Promoter of Consumer Shows, Special Events/Cream of the Crop Show Production (co-owner). Also owner Professional Imaging; [memb.] NASE; [hon.] Certificate of Merit for Achievement in Voice; [oth. writ.] Poems published in Windows On The World and The Best Poems Of The 90's, short stories and inspirational articles, instructional work books on selling techniques and methods, and power solutions, creative selling; [pers.] I humbly thank God for the ability to reach within the human spirit. For the sensitivity to listen to the heart. To possess the desire of expression. May he grant to all of humanity the serenity to accept the things we cannot change, the courage to change the things we can and the wisdom to know the difference.; [a.] La., West Hills, CAlifornia 91307.

ROLANDO, ADRIANNA M.
[Pen.] Maria Duran; [b.] August 8, 1962, Cleveland, Ohio; [p.] John Rolando and Rita Rolando; [ed.] Parma High, Cuyahoga Community College, Dyke College, Bachelor Science, Paralegal; [occ.] Paralegal; [memb.] A.C.I.M., Poetry Academy, National Association for Female Executives, Royal Doulton Collectors Club; [hon.] Baseball, Three Golden Poet Award, Lab Assistant Service Award; [oth. writ.] Garden of Beauty, Vision Unknown, Dreams of Success. Not published. Won Golden Poet Award; [pers.] Follow your dreams for you are the best that is yet to come. My writings are influenced by my heart, soul and mind is the inter beauty of a creative poem; [a.] Seven Hills, Ohio 44131

ROLLE, FLORENCE
[b.] December 14, 1993, Erie, PA; [p.] Joseph/Genevive Zalenski; [m.] Walter Rolle, December 31, 1982; [ch.] Laurence Herwald, stepchildren: Diane and Mark Rolle; [ed.] High school graduate; [occ.] Housewife; [memb.] International Society of Poets; [hon.] Achievement Award - ISP, Gold/Silver Awards - World of Poetry, ("Hole-in-one" golfing - HA!); [pers.] Poetry, to me, is a release, a very private solution and understanding of events, whether good or bad, happy or sad, that I have met and have yet to meet; [a.] Aquebogue, NY

ROSENBERG, LOUISE DODD
[b.] November 24, 1917, Chicago, IL; [p.] T. Leo Dodd, Harris Monroe Ridenhower (III); [m.] Dr. Charles J. Rosenberg, August 1, 1940; [ch.] Rebecca Mary Thake, Stephen C. Rosenberg, David J. H. Rosenberg; [ed.] HS, college, SIU 4 yrs; [occ.] Elementary teacher - retired; [memb.] James Smithson Society, IRT - Life member; NWL - Life member, AARP; GFWC; WIBC; OES; Prim Bap Church; [hon.] WOP: 2 Cert of Merit OES Rose Award, 1993; 1st place Poetry Award GFWC (1957); [oth. writ.] Contributed to Ill sesquicentennial publication; several short poems printed in Teachers magazines; monthly cont. to local newspaper; Our World's Favorite P. current; [pers.] Enjoy the range of free verse and the control of the sonnet form. I read. I write. I am. Therefore, Carpe Diem; [a.] Norris City, IL

ROTHGEB, CHARMIN
[b.] September 25, 1975, Columbia City, IN; [p.] Byron Rothgeb and Karen Rothgeb; [ed.] Still in High School (Columbia City High School) will graduate in spring 1994.; [occ.] High School Student; [oth. writ.] Many unpublished poems and stories; [pers.] Be yourself when you write. No one can be liked by everyone.; [a.] Columbia City, IN 46725.

ROTON, JOHN L.
[b.] February 15, 1928, Jacksonville, FL; [p.] Ruth Marie and Joseph L. Roton; [m.] Virginia R. Roton, December 13, 1952; [ch.] John Larue and George Cecil; [ed.] Educated in Jacksonville Schools;

[occ.]Journeyman Electrician; [memb.]Member of North Jacksonville Baptist Church; [hon.]Honorable Mention (1989) for Outstanding Achievement in Poetry 1990, Golden Poet Award, World of Poetry (1989); [oth. writ.]Who's Who in Poetry, Vol. III, Page 263, World of Poetry Anthology page 155; [pers.]A family with God is a family's might; [a.] Jacksonville, FL 32218

ROUCH, CONNIE
[Pen.] Connie; [b.] May 20, 1947, Troy, Ohio; [p.] Mr. and Mrs. robert L. Reineke; [m.] Fiance-Glen Bridenbaugh, engaged to be married; [ch.] Laurie Rouch; [ed.] Tipp City High School, Victor Comptometer School, Keypunch Operator and Computer Operator; [occ.] Retired from General Motors; [memb.] Tipp City Catholic Church; [hon.] Poem published, Selected Works of Our Worlds Best Poets, The future I write to bring happiness to other human beings.; [oth. writ.] I help children write for their school paper and also for their church paper; [pers.] To live each day to its fullest and not to let one day pass me by for life is a very precious gift. Given to each and everyone of us. I stand for truth and honesty we must all stand as one and strive to make this a better world the way God intended for it to be; [a.] Tipp City, Ohio 45371

ROURKE SR., FRANKLIN J.
[b.]April 15, 1945, Albany, NY; [p.]Wanda Young and John Rourke; [m.]Divorced; [ch.]John F., Sherri L., Franklin Jr.; [ed.]Bishop Burk High School; [occ.]Die Tech; [memb.]American Legion, Arrow Club, Honorary Member New York State Sheriffs Assn.; [hon.]Editor's Choice Award; [oth. writ.]The Sin To Ours, published in Where Dreams Begin; [pers.]I believe if we take more pride in our own lives and trust in the father it would be a much better world; [a.] Gloversville, NY 12078.

ROWE, MARDA
[b.]April 3, 1940, Woodland, CA; [p.]John O. and Lillian Wood Rowe; [m.]James Henry, July 17, 1993; [ch.]Five between us, Scott, John, Kathy; Stepchildren-Mike, Michelle; [ed.]Salano Community College, AA in Interior Design, Continuing at Yuta College Woodland in Fine Arts/Computer Aid Design; [occ.]Housewife/Poet/Receptionist (when working); [memb.]Dixon Community Church, Dixon Chamber of Commerce; [hon.]Honor Society College, many 4-H awards as a child; [oth. writ.]Poems published in various anthologies, especially proud of "I've Been There" published in Compassionate Friends.; [pers.]My poetry reflects life and it's happenings within my family or close friends. Sometimes it's happy thoughts, but I tend to write more during trying times; [a.] Dixon, CA 95620.

ROY, EVA M.
[b.]October 31, 1932, Owosso, Michigan; [p.]Frank A. Austin and Viola V. (Sanders) Austin; [m.]Gordon D. Roy, June 27, 1959; [ch.]Rian A. Roy and Lisa S. Roy; [ed.]High School Graduated 1951 with honors in writings; [occ.]Housewife, Poet and traveler; [memb.]International Society of Poets; The National Library of Poetry; [hon.]Eight Golden Poet Awards; Thirty-Five Awards of Merits; Twenty-four published poems; [oth. writ.]Published in local newspapers, school and church newsletters, and greeting cards.; [pers.]Poetry has been a big part of my adult life. Reading and reciting it back in school, brought the seeds to full growth in later life.; [a.] Lakeview, MI 48850.

ROY, MONIQUE AMY
[b.]November 20, 1975, Cape Town, South Africa; [p.]Michael Roy and Nicole Roy; [ed.]J. J. Pearce High School; [memb.]BBYO, United States Tennis Association; [hon.]Who's Who Among American High School Students for 2 years running; Editor's Choice Award; [oth. writ.]Several poems published in books of National Library of Poetry; [pers.]Everything around me influences me and my words are the words of nature and the well-being of others.; [a.] Dallas, TX 75248.

RUBIN, BEN
[b.]February 7, 1903, Russia; [p.]Deceased; [m.]Fay Rubin, March 15, 1958, second wife; [ch.]Two by first wife; [ed.]Grammar School, one year high school with the Green Thumb.

RUBINSTEIN, HOPE
[b.]April 12, 1955, Washington, D.C.; [p.]Joy and Philip Rubinstein; [m.]Michael Piechowski, September 6, 1990; [ed.]Two & one-half years of college; [occ.]Nursing Employment Agency Administrator; [hon.]Three Honorable Mention for poetry; [pers.]I'm a Hebrew christian and proud of my faith. How I feel is reflected in a lot of my poetry.; [a.] Silver Spring, MD 20906

RUCKDESCHEL, HUGH W.
[Pen.]The T. I. Poet; [b.]July 28, 1932, St. Petersburg, Florida; [p.]Edith Marion Beattie Ruckdeschel and John Frances Ruckdeschel; [m.]Divorced; [ch.]Michael Wesley, Martin Victor, Teresa Jo, Tammi Lynn; [ed.]High School G.E.D, 4 yrs. U.S. Army (Infantry); [occ.]Electrician, Retired Disability; [memb.]Disabled American Veterans, Military Order of Purple Heart, American Legion, Korean War Veterans Assoc.; [oth. writ.]None to mention. Submitted poems to the Island Reporter newspaper, Treasure Island, FL; [pers.]I've written poems just for friends. Too many, I have thrown away. Do I write for publications? Well that depends on just what I have to say; [a.] Treasure Island, Florida 33706.

RUGGLES, JUNE DAKAN
[Pen.] Dale L. Wilson; [b.] June 4, 1947, Summer, IA; [p.] Evelyn and Dale Wilson; [m.] Derwood Ruggles; [ch.] Theresa, Kathleen, Becky, James, Christopher, David, Ken; [ed.] Major - English writing, Black Hawk College, Moline, IL; [occ.] Merchandiser; [hon.] Editor's Choice Award 1993 by the National Library of Poetry; [oth. writ.] Short story, news articles and several poems; [pers.] I feel rhyming words mean nothing if the thoughts they create do not come from the soul or reach out and touch a soul; [a.] Aledo, IL

RUHLAND, CHARLES
[b.]October 24, 1944, Camden, NJ; [p.]Earl Howard and Eleanor Ruhland; Mary & Frank Calabria; [m.]Marie Calabria Ruhland; [ch.]Jeffrey Ruhland, Louis Berenato; [ed.]Woodrow Wilson, 1962; [occ.]Cowboy; [pers.]Chuck was diagnosed with a brain tumor in May 92 and wrote this poem after his surgery in June. Chuck was a man with a big heart and loved life and all people. I am glad I got to know and love him for a short while. Chuck died August 7, 1992. He will be missed. His Wife: Maria; [a.] Waterford, NJ.

RULE, EVE DARRINGTON
[b.]Honey Creek, Iowa; [p.]Christena and George Darrington; [m.]Wayne Brewster Rule, July 27, 1936; [ed.]B.A. Degree University of Iowa; [occ.]Teacher Metallurgical Laboratory Technician, Artist; [hon.]Finkbine Scholar, Golden Awards for Poetry, International Society of Poets Grand Prize Award 1992; [oth. writ.]Gathered Leaves, Even Songs and Three Short Stories for Children; [pers.]Poetry is for all who do not regard the world as their own, but as a gift from a Benevolent hand and compassionate spirit, it is for those who see and honor, cherish and preserve beauty in all forms, for those who regenerate their spirit with vibrations from the universe on high and see themselves only as a floating leaf on a surging stream bound for the great unknown; [a.] Holland, PA 18966

RUSH, BETTY M.
[b.]May 21, 1931, Nebraska; [p.]Rose and Claud Mann; [m.]Clyde E. Rush, September 27, 1989; [ch.]Ross Dunkle, Karen Story and four step sons, 12 grandchildren; [ed.]High School; [occ.]Nursed for 25 years, then a Day Care Director for 9 years; [memb.]Eastern Star, Press Women's Aux. Baptist Church, Publication Anthology Where Dreams Begin 93; [hon.]Have been selected as one of Outstanding Poets of 1994; [oth. writ.]Have written over 100 poems, mostly sent to family and friends. Mainly Christian poems; [pers.]My poems are mainly influenced by Christ, friends, family, things around me, my philosophy is love yourself and others and all things will love in return.; [a.] Alta Loma, CA 91737.

RUSSELL LVN, LPT, WILLIAM JOHN
[b.]1933, Chicago, Illinois; [ed.]St. Martin's College, Lacey, Washington, B.A., Psychology, 1982; [occ.]Quality Improvement Coordinator Mendocino County Mental Health, Ukiah, California; [memb.]Deputy Gov. American Biographical Institute; [hon.]Editor's Choice Award, National Library of Poetry, 1988 and 1989, third place award for poetry 1992, Creative Arts and Science Enterprises Editors' Preference Award of Excellence, 1991 & 1992; Marquis Who's Who in the West, 1989-1990, World of Poetry, Who's Who In Poetry, 1990, Listed in The National Author's Registry, Cader Publishing, Ltd., as well as receiving an Award of Merit for the works: "The Sound of Time" and "California Mental Health is Going Down"; [oth. writ.]Poems in print: Alternative Press, Poetry Forum, Poetic Page, Poetry, Today and Verses, Chapbook: California Mental Health Is Going Down, 1991, Book: The Sound Of Time, 35 pages, January 1992, Book: Medical Terminology by the Mnemonic System, to name only a few; [pers.]Verse, then, is a way for man to speak of the realities for which no concrete referent exists. A way to capture a quality about something that words alone can seldom declare; [a.] Ukiah, CA 95482

SABBATIS, AMY
[b.]June 6, 1977; [p.]Mr. and Mrs. Johns (My loving parents); [ed.]Lakewood High School, Junior; [occ.]Grum-Bellies (pizza place); [oth. writ.]My Grandpa Has Cancer in Wind in the Night Sky.; [pers.]I'm influenced by my "everyday happenings in my life. Also, I give thanks to all who have stood behind me!; [a.] Lakewood, OH 44107.

SABER, CHARLES
[b.] January 20, 1922, Poland; [p.] Dina and Joseph;

[m.] Rose, November 3, 1945 (deceased 4/4/92); [ch.] Gary Lawrence, Edda Gail, Bruce Jeffrey, Elyse Paulette; [occ.] Retired Seaman Merchant, Poet; [memb.] East Coast Academy of Poets, Presenter of Broward Community College, International Society of Poets, World of Poetry; [hon.] World of Poetry third place international prize, Who's Who in Poetry published in New American Poetry Anthology; [oth. writ.] Portrait of a Stallion, Hippies, Last Prayer, Song of the Ghetto, Success, The Gambler, Ecology, Ballard of Vietnam, Tragedy of Aid's, Eulogy at Sea, The Toast, Allah's Will, Elusive Sleep, Love Lost, The Greatest Gift, Israel, Vagrant Son, Dreamer, Holocaust, Star Wars, Willow Brook, Lessons; [pers.] Poetry is the crown jewel of literature and I believe poetry is a window to the heart, the mind and the soul of the poet. Exposing there frailties and inhibitions and deepest emotions; [a.] Margate, FL 33068

SAENZ, MARIA GUADALUPE
[Pen.] Lupita Saenz; [b.] November 14, 1947, Rio Grande City, TX; [p.] Encarnacion Sr. and Francisa L. Saenz; [ch.] Jorge Santiago Zarate; [ed.] Rio Grande City High School and Pan American Univ; [occ.] Accountant, Physical Education Assistant, disabled; [memb.] Woodmen of the World, Rio Grande City High School Band; Mennonite Brethern Church; [hon.] Woodmen of the World (Plaque in Recognition), National Honor Society, Perfect Attendance, Honor Roll; [oth. writ.] Several poems published in local newspapers - Rio Grande Herald and Town Crier, poem entitled Christmas in book, A Break in the Clouds; [pers.] This poem is in memory of my grandmother Isabel Saenz, who encouraged me to write. I also strive to touch others with my writing which comes from my heart; [a.] Garciasville, TX

SAFKO, DARREL ROBERT
[b.]May 11, 1948, Cleveland, Ohio; [p.]Donald R. and Helen A. Safko; [m.]Rosalie F. Safko, October 6, 1972; [ch.]Michael William, Anthony vincent, Donna Roschelle, Darrel John; [ed.]Maple Hts. High, John Carroll University; [memb.]Loyal Order of the Moose, Masons, and Ashtabula County Writer's Guild; [hon.]Moose Legionnaire of the Year 1992, Moose Legion of Honor 19993, World of Poetry Award of Merit 1990, Golden Poet Award 1991 and 1992, Honorable Mention Ashtabula County Writer's Guild 1993, selected by National Library of Poetry for publication in "Outstanding Poets of 1994"; [oth. writ.]Poems published in 1993 National Library of Poetry's "Our Worlds Favorite Poems, Who's Who In Poetry" and Sparrowgrass Poetry Forum's "Treasured Poems of America" Fall 1993; [pers.]Be kind to all God's creatures for man alone can dream and accomplish and thus should bear the responsibility; [a.], Conneaut, Ohio 44030

SAGERS, IDA
[b.]August 4, 1915, Austria; [p.]Philip Dubowy and Eva Stein; [m.]Herbert C., December 25, 1941 (deceased 1950); [ch.]Diana M. Sagers and Paul E. Sagers; [ed.]B.A. San Francisco State Univ. Gen. Sfc. Teaching 1958, Teaching Credential 1959, two years toward M.A. 1962-1964; [occ.]Retired Teacher; [memb.]CRTA, AARP Jr., College Honor Society, Graduate Magna Cum Laude, SFSV, Unitarian Univ. Church; [hon.]Alpha Gamma Sigma Calif, Jr. College Honor Scholarship, Soc. Life Member, ETA Chapter, 2nd highest scholastic average in H.S. Grad. Class (98.6%) Won Gold Medal upon graduation. Also medal from French Consulate in NYC, 3 yrs. Golden Poet for California 1989, 90, 91; [oth. writ.]None, except two letters to the editor of the S.M. Times to plead for recover program for addiction. It got results in my county, San Mateo; [pers.]Einstein "The more we discover about the physical universe the more we must stand in awe and reverence before the power beyond it which must forever remain a mystery."

SAHR, NANCY J.
[b.]August 19, 1944, Blue Farth, MN; [p.]Ron and Marion Hanson; [m.]Elwood R. Sahr, August 26, 1961; [ch.]Carrie, Cristy, Craig, Curt; [ed.]High School, A.L.T.C.; [occ.] Presently Housewife; [memb.]DECA, S.B.E. Welca; [hon.]Dean's List; [oth. writ.]Newspapers, Western Poetry Association, National Library of Poetry; [pers.]My poems are my true feeligs and are based on life itself. I just love to create; [a.] Bricelyn, MN 56014.

SANCHEZ, MARILYN
[b.] June 12, 1944, McAlester, OK; [p.] Mother-pen name - L.W. Loree, King-moon-Williamson - great-granddaughter of poetress - Lida Stanley Moon; [ch.] Angelic-Sanchez (15), Terry-Jones (12); [ed.] GED Co Officer, still in college for my BA in Correctional Law; [occ.] C.O. in correction; [memb.] The Lords Church; [hon.] Poems published, Golden Poet 1991; [oth. writ.] Explanation of III, Ex - I of Keats - Nightingale - Ex II of Melville's Billy Bad - Ex of Coleridge, Tis Midnight - VIII, Cold Winters Night and Life and Death; [pers.] If I can make simple with understanding a poem or writing so all can love to read and be whole to digest with complete understanding of one's work. Arad map into the writers ode soul; [a.] McAlester, OK

SANDIFER, JIMMY RANDLE
[b.]September 22, 1961, Quincy, LA; [p.]Curtis and Helen Sandifer; [memb.]B.M.I. Music; [oth. writ.]Songs; [pers.]To be published is to be forever. Thank you National Library of Poetry; [a.] Antioch, TN 37011.

SANTEE, J.D.
[oth. writ.]Two books 1996 "Originals", "One Man's Opinion" 1992; [a.] Clovis, NM 88101

SANTIAGO, GABRIEL B.
[b.] September 17, 1965, Houston, TX; [p.] Matilda and Vincent; [m.] Single; [ed.] Our Lady of Mt Carmel High; [occ.] Antique Sales; [hon.] Golden Poet Award; [oth. writ.] Welcome Defeat, (Our World's Favorite Poems), Where God Prevails, (Whispers in the Wind); [pers.] Love God, love other's, love yourself, and simply try; [a.] Houston, TX

SANTONE, JOHN MICHAEL
[b.]November 1, 1971, Waterbury, Connecticut; [p.]Linda Hitchcock and Michael D. Santone, Jr.; [ed.]B.A. in Philosophy from central CT State Univ., working on MA at the University of Notre Dame; [occ.]Student; [hon.]Dean's List; [oth. writ.]Poem published in "A Break In the Clouds", and a letter published in a book in russia entitled Americans Write to Mikal Gorbachev.; [pers.]Savor not the day or the hour, but rather the people that make that day or hour come alive. For this life of our's is short, and we must appreciate our loved ones while we have them.; [a.] Waterbury, CT 06708.

SASS, CHERYL BILDERBACK
[b.] September 30, 1945, Boston, Mass; [p.] Francis W. Bilderback and Gladys L. Ead (8 brothers and 3 sisters); [m.] James R. Sass, December 3, 1971; [ch.] Four stepchildren, Watt, Cliff, Addie Jackie, one mine, two ours Jennie, Julie, eight step grandchildren, Trevor, Corey, Casey, Russle, Jennie, Andy, Katie, Thomas, one grandchild on the way; [ed.] Graduated from high school 1964; [occ.] Homemaker, mother, grandma, whatever part time job I can find; [hon.] Six Merit Awards, World of Poetry; One Presidents Award for Literacy Excellence; Golden Poet of the Year Award 1989-1992; Who's Who in Poetry Honor 1990; [oth. writ.] Several poems published; [pers.] Treat people with respect no matter who they are, and they'll do the same for you. Always carry a spare smile, you may need it some day. the one I like the most is: Enjoy everything no matter how small, life's too short not to, besides there may be no tomorrow; [a.] St. Paul, Minnesota

SAUNDERS, MADGE ELISE
[b.]August 25, 1913, Scottsburg, Indiana; [p.]Johnnie & Lottie Keigh; [m.]Etson P. Saunders (Deceased) February 10, 1935; [ch.]Paula Ann, Steven Eric, John Alfred, Pamela Jean; [ed.]High School and Business College; [occ.]Retired Secretary; [memb.]Volunteer Pink Lady at Coshocton, Co. Memorial Hospital; [oth. writ.]Weekly column for the Free Enterprizer Paper Locally owned in Coshocton, Ohio. Poem published in The Tribune Newspaper; [pers.]"If I die tomorrow I will be happy that I lived today."; [a.] Coshocton, Ohio 43812.

SAVUKOSKI, SINIKKA
[b.]March 2, 1979, Boston, Massachusetts; [p.]Joana and Sauli Savukoski; [ed.]Freshman in High School; [occ.]Student; [memb.]National Junior Honor Society, Messiah Lutheran Church; [oth. writ.]Poem published in a question of balance.; [a.] Fitchburg, MA.

SAWTELLE, ELIZABETH HALDANE
[b.]August 25, 1932, Errol, New Hampshire; [p.]Rev. Dr. and Mrs. Robert Haldane (Inez Elwell Haldane); [m.]Robert J. Sawtelle, April 10, 1954; [ch.]David, Kenneth, Janis, Scott, and five grandchildren; [ed.]Madison High School, Husson College in Bangor Maine; [occ.]Secretary I (Sr. Secretary) Guidance Office Westbrook Jr. High School; [memb.]International Society of Poets, National Honor Society, Maine Educational Secretaries, Cumberland County Secretaries, National Teachers, MEA, WEA; [hon.]Several, Editors Preference Awards (Creative Arts & Science) Music Award Husson College (1952 Words to the Husson Song) Letters from President Reagan 1984 and First Lady Barbara Bush (1991) in response to poems sent them; [oth. writ.]Magic Moments, A Boy of 3, Image In The Mirror, Why This? Inner Reflections, To Follow In His Steps (All winning recognition) plus many others. Many published in local papers-one in Marriage Encounter June 1977.; [pers.]Through the gift of writing I hope to bring happiness and love to my fellowman. I am humble and grateful that God has given me this way to express myself.; [a.] Westbrook, Maine 04092.

SAWYER, BRENDA J.
[b.] May 4, 1962, Ventura, CA; [p.] Stanly and Betty Sawyer; [ch.] Kellie Marie Richards (2), Robert James Sawyer (deceased) 1988; [ed.] Graduated from

Buena High School 1980, Completed Truck Driver School, Ventura College; [occ.] Driver; [hon.] 1991 Golden Poet Award honorable mention, 1992 Golden Poet Award honorable mention, honorable discharge from US Army National Guard; [oth. writ.] What ever happen to world peace, a drug free life, it's the cool and only way, hardcore and Kellie Marie have been published by the National Library of Poetry; [pers.] Being able to write poetry is a gift from God, I'm very thankful. It's my one and only way to tell people how I feel and release my feelings of all kind, it's my serinity in life; [a.] Ventura, CA 93004

SCANLAN, HILLARY
[b.]August 17, 1970, Northampton, MA; [p.]Jack Scanlan and Judith Scanlan; [ed.]Northampton High, Leeds Elementary, West Field State College; [occ.]Student; [oth. writ.]First poem ever entered into a contest; [pers.]I try to reflect the simple and unforseen pleasures life has to offer. I am influenced by my family friends, people and everyday life; [a.] Northampton, MA.

SCANLON-ROCHE, JEAN M.
[Pen.]Jean M. Roche; [b.]December 30, 1911, Mass.; [a.] Westfield, MA 01085.

SCHEMPP, WILLIAM D.
[Pen.] Wm D. Schempp; [b.] May 2, 1960, Brooklyn, NY; [p.] Doris B. Schempp, Alfred W. Schempp; [ed.] Masters of Fine Arts; Television Production, 1986, Brooklyn College of the City University of NY; [occ.] Television Director/Producer; [memb.] A.I.V.F. Assoc of Independent Video and Filmmakers; [hon.] NATAS Grant/Award 1986; [pers.] "It is a sad and beautiful world..."; [a.] Central Islip, NY

SCHIRMACHER, STANLEY L.
[Pen.]Joe Dryland; [b.]September 21, 1908, Beaver Dam, Wisconsin; [p.]Charles W. and Martha Mittelstadt; [m.]Ruth Arlene, August 24, 1935; [ch.]Jimmy Ruth Vaughan; [ed.]B.D. WI 1926, M.A. 1951; [occ.]Carpenter (26-29) Retired teacher (39 1/2 yrs); [memb.]Who's Who in Photography, Who's Who in the West, Who's Who in Hereditary Societies, Who's Who in American Education, International Freelance Photographers Organization #27467, International Biography's, England; [hon.]Freedom Foundation at Valley Forge Teachers Medal, 1945 Navy "E" Living History Hall of Fame, Writer "Slide Rule in a Nutshell" [oth. writ.]Founder: "Sons of Sherman's, March to the Sea. Founder: "Civil War Shack" (Veterans records sources). Shop articles in "School Shop" and "Industrial Arts and Vocational Education Mags.; [pers.]Originator of "It's in the Bible" cartoons in "Power" of Scripture Press; [a.] Tempe, AZ 85281

SCHNEIDER, WAYNE FRANKLIN
[Pen.]Wayne Schneider; [b.]June 23, 1942, Ft. Sam Houston, San Antonio, TX; [p.]Questionable, Military Brat; [m.]None at this time; [ed.]Schertz, Cibolo High, Many Community College Courses, Business and Self-Improvement Studies, Practical OJT, U.S. Navy Schools, Courses, Training Over A Wide Array of Subjects and Occupations; [occ.]Management and Planning, Principal Owner, Partner, Director, D.B.A., Redi-Bilt Corp.; [memb.]Business & Community Self-Help Related Projects; [hon.]Have been subject of many, but prefer informal, electing the sudleness of increased income and achieving goals sought, both private or public avoiding possible undesirable acquaintances or conflict of interest situations; [oth. writ.]Numerous, that touch on a studied common sense approach view, opinion related to understanding or in self-help directions; [pers.]An honest, active, hard working life is a bitch, but a hell'va lot of fun-ny and very rewarding when handled properly; [a.] Butner, NC 27509

SCHULT, CHRIS DOWDALL
[b.] April 27, 1916, Humphrey, NE; [p.] Catherine and Louis Hittner; [m.] Charles H. Schult, November 27, 1976; [ch.] (4 sons) - Daniel, Michael, James, Richard Dowdall; [ed.] St. Francis High School, Humphrey, NE, Northwestern Univ, Illinois - English Major; [occ.] Artist, W.C. Ptg, sculptor in clay and alabaster; [memb.] AZ Watercolor Assoc (juried member), National Pen Women Assoc; [hon.] Numerous prizes and awards - for watercolor ptg and Golden Poet Awards - 1989, 1990, 1991 - World of Poetry competition. Published in "World Treasury of Golden Poems", "Our World's Favorite Poems", "World Treasury of Great Poems", "Whispers in the Wind" - National Library of Poetry; [oth. writ.] Writing a book "Quality of Greatness" all about Father Wegner, Director of Boystown 1948-1973 (25 yrs) succeeding Fr Flanagan upon Flanagan's death; [pers.] I try to reflect the joy of the spirit in creative pursuit, and the great gifts from God within all of us; [a.] Sedona, AZ

SCHULTZ, SUSAN EVANS
[Pen.]Aleia (Ahliah) Vlentaer; [b.]Los Angeles; [ed.]College and study courses, but I consider myself a learner and explorer; [occ.]Ambassador (II. Cor. 5:20); [memb.]The International Society of Poets, Founding Member of The Challenger Center, The Planetary Society; [hon.]Golden Poet Award for 1990 and 1991, Honor Roll; [oth. writ.]Articles for local publications, autobiographical material for radio, other poetry for publication, currently completing a novel; [pers.]Hopefully my poem, Endangered Species, will engender some thought provoking questions: Who are these people who are endangered? Are they extraterrestrials or are they humans; [a.] La Mirada, CA 90638

SCOTT, ESTHER
[Pen.] Essie; [b.] December 7, 1957, Washington, PA; [p.] Esther Scott and Joseph Miller; [m.] Single; [ch.] Alexi Scott and Jared Loren Scott; [ed.] Charters, Houston High 1975. Two years of College: Major Psychology; [occ.] Daycare Operator; [memb.] The Mayan Order First Church of God, Houston, PA; [hon.] National Poetry Society, California University Poetry Society, Publisher of the "People of Color" Magazine; [oth. writ.] God Is Like Coke...He's The Real Thing; What Makes A Man Be A Man; Deception; [pers.] Fear is nothing but a negative belief. If you spend most of your life in fear, you're staying underground too long before coming up to soak in some sun. The sun is for everyone.; [a.] Canonsburg, PA 15317

SEE, MILLARD M.
[Pen.]Lee Monroe; [b.]September 12, 1934, Frankfort, Indiana; [p.]Leon R. and Ruby M. See; [m.]Janice L., August 25, 1962; [ch.]Kenni, Sherel, Janessa, Millard II; [ed.]Senior High; [occ.]Retired Railroad Cond. Presently supervisor of security; [memb.]Moose life member P.T.A Life Member; [hon.]Poetry and Essay Awards, Political and Religious Awards; [oth. writ.]Short stories, news articles, poems published locally, political speeches, religious sermons; [pers.]Look to your fellowman for inspiration. It's every where, find it, write about it, then live it. You'll be better for it.; [a.] Frankfort, IN 46041.

SEEBER, JULIE JENNINGS
[b.]May 2, 1923, Jellico, TN; [p.]Ruth and Tom Jennings; [m.]Lynn Seeber, December 28, 1946; [ed.]B.A. Univ. of Tennessee; [occ.]Amateur archaeologist and photographer, ranch foreman; [memb.]various poetry groups; [hon.]Blue Ribbons and editor award and inclusion in national publishing; [pers.]Do not take from our fragile sphere, rather, leave it better and more peaceful and beautiful.; [a.] Louisville, TN 37777.

SEELY, DARLA MAE
[b.]April 9, 1967, Downey, Idaho; [p.]Henry A. Jensen and Saramae P. Jensen; [m.]Gil Seeley, October 10, 1992; West Side High School, Ricks College, Certified Careers Institute; [hon.]Outstanding Speller as a Freshman in High School. Received a Golden Poet Award in The World of Poetry contest. Received National Library of Poetry Contest in July 1993; [oth. writ.]Have written 47 unpublished poems. Had the poem A Friend published in the Other Side of the Mirror.; [pers.]I love to write poems, and I appreciate the art of good poetry; [a.] Ogden, VT 84404.

SEELY, DOROTHEA SAUL
[b.] July 2, 1914, Newark, NJ; [p.] Michael Saul, Newark, NJ; [m.] Earle J. Seely, August 11, 1935; [ch.] One son, Earle Saul Seely; [ed.] High School, Newark, NJ; [occ.] Poelese Newspaper Reporter, Legal Secretary, Salesperson, Tailoring Business; [memb.] Secretary of Firemans Auxiliary, P.T.A., Church Choir, etc.; [hon.] Twenty Awards, eight Certificates, nine Golden Poets from World of Poetry; [oth. writ.] Letter to the Editor, two Church Histories in New Jersey; poems and more poems. Church histories in Historic Society Philadelphia, Presbyterian Reformed; [pers.] I derive a great deal of satisfaction in sharing my literary endeavors with friends in this beautiful country, plus pen friends in Germany, etc.; [a.] Sparta, NJ 07871

SEIDLER, THOMAS
[b.] December 25, 1909, Brooklyn, NY; [p.] Deceased; [m.] February 28, 1938 (Deceased); [ch.] none; [ed.] High School; [occ.] Retired; [memb.] Fleet Reserve Association Auxiliary of Mease Hosp., American Legion, V.F.W., Military of Cooties 40/8, DAV; [hon.] Three Purple Hears, I was wounded three times, 10,00 hours at Aux. for Mease Hospital in Dunedin, FL; [oth. writ.] Poems and songs and prayers; [pers.] I retired from the Navy after 20 years as a Lt. Commander, then I put in nine years in the Marines where I was wounded three times, two President Cirtaions, Philippines and one from the U.S.; [a.] Clearwater, FL 34621

SELLS, JOYCE GREEN
[Pen.]Rebecca Steward Chandler; [b.]January 7, 1946, Pensacola, FL; [p.]Ellen Chandler and Elbert Paul Green, Jr.; [m.]Haskell Lee Sells, II, February 7, 1976; [ch.]Sherry, Leigh, Kimberly, Jimmy; working on B.A. in Health Care Psychology - Graceland College; [occ.]Registered Nurse, Salesperson; [memb.]Cash award for poem "Summer Son" at the

International Society of Poets convention, Washington, D.C. 1991; [hon.]Poet of Merit Award, American Poetry Assn., Poet of Merit Award, International Society of Poetry, Who's Who of American Woman, Who's Who of Emerging Leaders in America, Who's Who in the South and Southeast; [oth. writ.]What's Gonna Happen to the Brothers and the Sisters/ a book on discrimination and race relations. Numerous poems published by the National Library of Poetry, The American Poetry Assn., NY Society of Poets; [pers.]Poetry for me is cheap therapy; [a.] Raleigh, NC 27612.

SENN, PAMELA J.
[b.]April 23, 1954, Choteau, Montana; [m.]Calvin W. Senn, September 27, 1975; [ed.]Fontana High School; [occ.]Manager, Fast Food; [memb.]International Society of Peots; [pers.]I love writing poetry. It lets me express my feelings for not what only I see with my eyes, but with my Soul; [a.] Redding, CA 96003-3969.

SETTY, DEBORAH BURGETT
[Pen.] Deborah Lynn Burgett; [b.] November 23, 1954, Dayton, OH; [p.] Gentry Burgett, Ethel Burgett; [m.] Richard Roland Setty, July 3, 1979; [ch.] Jennifer King, Angela and Kimberly Setty; [ed.] Stivers High School, Beavercreek High School, Cin Metropolitan College, Miami Jacobs Jr College; [occ.] Retail accounting payable clerk; [memb.] Eagles; [hon.] Awards: 1 Silver Poet Award, 3 Golden Poet Awards, 1 Special Mention Award, 4 Honorable Mention Awards and 1 Honor Award; [oth. writ.] I have two poems published in the American Poetry anthology for 1984 and 1987. One poem published in the World Treasury of Golden Poems; [pers.] I have been influenced by John Keats; and other poets, plus music, love songs. Poetry is a way I express my emotions to other people; [a.] Blanchester, OH

SEVANDAL, MARCIANA ASIS
[Pen.] Mars Sagun or Marian Ambil; [b.] March 9, 1912, Catarman, Samar, Philippines; [p.] Father: Ambrosio Ambil Asis (deceased) Mother: Dominga De Los Reyes Sagun (deceased); [m.] Simeon Enriquez Sevandal, November 30, 1935 (deceased); [ch.] I have seven children all living with families; [ed.] Bachelor of Science in Elemntary Education (BSEED) with Elementary Teacher's Certificate (ETC); 26 Units in Master of Arts (No thesis); [occ.] Retired Public Schools District Supv.; [memb.] Civic and Religious Organizations, particularly the PPSTA, the CWL and the Society for the Propagation of Faith; [hon.] First Honors in the grades High School Valedictorian; College Honors. Poetry Awards in World of Poetry and in Who's Who; [oth. writ.] Playlets: World Brotherhood; Royalty In My Native Land; Christmas and other pageants; Newsletter; Wodrad; Creations; Declamations and Essays; [pers.] To waste time is to wast life for time is the stuff life is made of. Do not put all your eggs in one basket. If you drop the basket, you lose all the eggs.; [a.] San Francisco, CA 94170

SFORRA, CHRISTY J.
[b.]July 6, 1973, Poughkeepsie, New York; [p.]William and Joyce Sforra; [m.]Boyfriend, Jeff Wcariello; [ed.]Arlington High School; [occ.]Day Care Assistant; [memb.]Active volunteer fire fighter for hopewell hose co. #1 in the town of East Fishkill; [oth. writ.]Poem published in "On the threshold of a dream" called My Last Goodbye; [pers.]This poem is dedicated to Jeff Wcariello, who made such a difference in my life, you will always remain deep in my heart. I love you.; [a.] Hopewell Junction, NY 12533.

SHANNON, JOYCE ANN
[Pen.]Joyce A. Shannon; [b.]February 6, 1935, St. Louis, MO; [p.]Noble A. Ceaser Bass and Joseph L. Bass; [m.]Leon Shannon Sr., August 8, 1985; [ch.]Kathy Washington, James Washington III, Patty Glenn, Audrey Chaney; [ed.]St. Alphonsus Rock High, Forest Park Community College; [occ.]Homemaker; [memb.]SLPC, St. Louis Poetry Center; [hon.]Outstanding Family Member Award for Reading at Public School; [oth. writ.]Rainbows Edge, Sunnyside Up, From My Heart, Tender Touches; [pers.]When you love someone, you love them as they are; [a.] St. Louis, MO 63115-3212

SHANNON-CARETTI, EMELINE
[p.]Mr. and Mrs. John Caretti; [m.]Harold D. Shannon (Deceased); [ch.]John H. Shannon a Broadcast Engineer; [occ.]Retired, Former Prothonotary and Clerk of Courts of Armstrong County; [pers.]My poem is dedicated to my beloved son, John H. Shannon.; [a.] Kittamming, PA.

SHEAHAN, PATRICK B.
[b.] September 23, 1943, Saginaw, MI; [m.] Gloria Lee Sheahan, April 5, 1986; [ch.] Heather Erin Sheahan; [occ.] Nurse; [oth. writ.] Why Is It, published in Our World's Most Treasured Poetry; [pers.] I have enjoyed writing poetry most of my life, my wife is my inspiration for writing. I have no other poetry published; [a.] Huntsville, AR 72740

SHEARER, GLADYS
[b.]march 21, 1911, Portland, OR; [p.]Wm., Cuthil and Ira Gwinn; [m.]Gerald Shearer, August 16, 1959; [ch.]none; [ed.]High School, various specialized commercial classes; [occ.]Private Secretary (now retired); [memb.]First Christian Church; [hon.]none; [oth. writ.]none; [pers.]Do you best each day; [a.] Portland, OR 97202.

SHELDON, MARK R.
[b.]April 11, 1951, San Antonio, TX; [p.]Joseph L. Sheldon Jr., and Mildred M. Sheldon; [m.]Dietra R. Sheldon, June 18, 1990; [ch.]Reece J. & Mariah F. Sheldon (7 & 9) Stephen L. & Ryan J. Stolle (13 & 11); [ed.]Jusuit High School/Shreveport, LA/1969.; [occ.]Soldier/Harmonica Player/Unpublished Poet; [memb.]Vietnam Veterans of America; [hon.]Much honor, no awards; [oth. writ.]Vegas Nam, Piedres Negras Lannslide, Jim Morrison's Purple Heart Club Band, Last Rodeo & Many more unpublished works; [pers.]Thanks to Carl Sandberg, Richard Broughtigan, Robert Hunter, Robert Zimmermann (Bob Dylan). The Grateful Dead. May we find the peace, and keep it with us. To my wife, I love you.; [a.] Homedale, ID 83628.

SHELTON, THOMAS A.
[Pen.] Austin Thomas; [b.] July 5, 1923, Fort Pierce, FL; [p.] Tom and Bertie Shelton; [m.] LaVerne, June 2, 1951; [ch.] Tom, Tobi, Betty Ann; [ed.] AB Duke, BS Foreign Service, Georgetown; JD American University; [occ.] Realtor, Retired USAF, (memb) Masons, Rotary, Chamber of Commerce; [hon.] Airforce Commendation Medal, Defense Meritorious Service Medal; [oth. writ.] Poetry for World of Poetry; [pers.] Poetry is everywhere you look. All you have to do is tune in; [a.] Fairborn, OH 45324

SHERWOOD, PATRICIA E.
[b.]October 27, 1915, Vancouver, BC; [p.]Mary Anne and Henry Cross; [m.]Jay Robert Sherwood, April 6, 1944; [ch.]Three sons, J. Robert, Kenneth, David, 6 grandchildren, 3 great-grandchildren; [ed.]College; [occ.]Retired Executive Secretary; [memb.]Grace Episcopal Church, World Peace Organization; [hon.]Oratorical World Peace, Won World Poetry Contest; [oth. writ.]Several poems, music. Written music to accompany poetry I intend to publish as Anthology of verse; [pers.]I strive to reflect the beauty of God's universe. His love for us and the brotherhood of man

SHOWELL, JR., GREGORY LEVAUNT
[Pen.]Gregory L. Showell II; [b.]September 22, 1968, Wilkesburre, PA; [p.]Gregory L. Showell, Sr., and Patricia Whatley Showell; [ed.]B.A. English Arts, Hampton University, Hampton, Virginia; [occ.]Entrepreneur/writer; [memb.]Calliope Literary Society, Providence Missionary Baptist Church; [hon.]Mr. Calliope 1989; [oth. writ.]Several poems and short stories published in University newspaper and the Saracen University Publication; [pers.]Life is a God given gift given to all men. So I hope to uplift and unite all of mankind with my writings as my gift back to God; [a.] Atlanta, GA 30306.

SHUTT, ALICE MAY
[b.]September 20, 1943, Chicago, IL; [p.]Fred Raymond and Nora May (Lynn) Shutt; [ed.]Graduated Garrett High School (May 1962) and Tabernacle Baptist Bible Institute; [occ.]File Clerk, Baptist Medical Center, Cola, SC.; [memb.](In the Past) American Poetry Assoc., World Poetry Assoc., (Presently) National Library of Poetry; [hon.]Golden Poet for 1989, 1990 and 1991 (World of Poetry) Four Honorable Mentions (World of Poetry), Editor's Choice Award for 1992, The National Library of Poetry; [oth. writ.]Twenty three other poems published in American Poetry Assoc., and World of Poetry Assoc. and The National Library of Poetry.; [pers.]I write as I am inspired of the Lord. I believe this is a gift from My Lord and I intend to use it for his honor and glory.; [a.] Lexington, SC 29072.

SHUTTLEWORTH, WILLIAM
[b.]May 6, 1937, Phila, PA; [p.]William and Irene Shuttleworth; [ed.]Murrell Dobbins Voc. Tech. High; Cheyney State Teachers College, Cheyney, PA (1 yr.); Phila. College of Bible (1 yr.); [occ.]Furniture finishing and repairs (34 yrs.); [memb.]Art league of Jacksonville 1985-91; American Rescue Workers Mission Ministry 1962-72; [hon.]Industrial Arts Award 1955; Ordained Minister 1967; Hon. Mention in Art Show at Jacksonville Fair 1991; [oth. writ.]Poems: Columbus and You, Winds of Andrew 92, Pearl by the Sea and many others. Pamphlets: Not by Race but by Grace, Bible Reading in School, etc.; [pers.]Another poet's statement that has impacted my life greatly is, "only one life "Twill soon be past. Only what's done for Christ will last."; [a.] Jacksonville, FL 32207.

SIBREL, KATHERINE KLINE
[Pen.]Posterity; [b.]January 2, 1905, St. Paul, Minn.; [p.]A.J. (Andrew) Kline and Christine Tolmie Kline

(both deceased); [m.]Lester M. Sibrel (Deceased); [ed.]Kindergarten at 2 1/2, U. of Minn, 2 yrs. College Medicine, 1 yr. college of music (piano major), the College Pharmacy Sr. Class; [occ.]Retired, Dad's Pharmacy, Sears 10 years, newspapers 20 years; [memb.]Alpha Chapter Chaparral Poets, Calif. Press Women and National Press; [hon.]Won Hon. Award and 2nd place Cal. Chaparral, 2nd place Calif. Press Women Statewide Contest; [oth. writ.]Published 1st ed. Minneapolis Skylines, Voice of America NYC book, award 1992, World of Poetry, My book of poems "My Heart Speaks, published 1991; [pers.]I've written poems, stories, etc., since I learned to write. I still write regularly for 2 (sometimes 4) newspapers, plus articles, stories. Working on 2 books now, to sell. Writing music are lifetime pleasures.

SIERRA, GISELLE
[b.]Cuba; [m.]December 4, 1980 and June 6, 1981; [ed.]Montclair State, New Jersey Institute of Technology (NJIT); [occ.]Teacher/ Student; [memb.]A.S.J.A. (The American Society of Journalists and Authors); [hon.]Nat'l. Library of Poetry Editor's Choice, Distinguished Poets of America, Outstanding Poets of 1994; [oth. writ.]Cochran's Corner, Another Place in Time (Watermark Press), Of Diamonds and Rust (N.L.P.) Visions (Iliad Press), Sunrise Sunset (The Poetry Corner); [pers.]For what shall a person profit if (s)he gain the world and lose her/his soul?; [a.] Jersey City, NJ 07307.

SIMON, FLOYD A.
[b.] July 21, 1928, Youngstown, OH; [p.] Floyd and Christine Simon - deceased; [m.] Leona Simon, December 15, 1991; [ed.] 11th grade, South Wph Ygst OH; [occ.] Retired - Teamster Truck Drive; [memb.] Elks; [memb.] United Seniors Assoc NRA; [hon.] Golden Poet Award; [oth. writ.] "O God", "An American Soldier's Prayer", "Two Hrs Till Daybreak"; [pers.] I try to capture the feelings of men and women who died in the past; [a.] Battle Ground, WA 98604

SIMPSON, DON M.
[b.]December 16, 1970, Inglewood, California; [p.]Don Sr., and Carol Simpson; [m.]Single; [ed.]Hillsboro High, Portland State University; [occ.]Warehouse Manager; [memb.]International Society of Poets, Willamette Writers; [hon.]First Place O.S.A.A. Young Writers Comp. 1988.; [oth. writ.]Several published and unpublished poems and short stories; [pers.]Yankees baseball, neoclassical guitar and stacks of blank paper are the fuel for my soul; [a.] Aloha, Oregon 97006-2404.

SKAGGS, RUBY
[Pen.]Ruby Farnham Skaggs; [b.]January 16, 1912, Commercial Pt., Ohio; [p.]Pearl N. Farnham (Father) Sarah Alice Green (Mother); [m.]William P. Skaggs, November 21, 1935; [ch.]Sons, David, Keigh, Kenneth, Wayne; Daughters, Elaine, Maxine, Nancy, Joy; [ed.]Elementary through Soph. High School; [occ.]Homemaker and helpmate in sales work with my husbands business; [memb.]Quill Books, Top Records, National Library of Poetry; [hon.]The International Poet of Merit Award by National Library of Poetry 1992, Editor's Choice Award by the National Library of Poetry 93; [oth. writ.]Poems in two Anthologies "Listen to Your Heart" and "All My Tomorrows" published by Quill Books 92 and 93; Poems in Anthologies "On The Threshold of a Dream"

and "Wind in the Night Sky"; [pers.]I have precious memories of hearing my mother read her poems. She wrote them. That talent was passed on to me and God nurtured it. I Praise Him.

SKERENCAK, ELIZABETH
[Pen.]Elizabeth Marilyn; [b.]June 28, 1951, Bridgeport, CT; [p.]Evelyn Gizub Skerencak & Paul Skerencak; [ed.]Harding High School, Emmays Bible School (General Teaching Certificate); [occ.]Data Computer Operator; [hon.]Eight World of Poetry Press Golden Poet Awards; [pers.]I strive to give honor, praise and glory to God who gave me my talent; [a.] Bridgeport, CT 06610.

SMALLS, BYTHFORD C.
[b.] February 10, 1955, Cong Beach Memorial Hospital; [p.] McKinley and Leatha; [m.] Kathy Sparks Wendi, May 7, 1977; [ch.] Lici and Ryan Smalls; [ed.] Long Beach High, B.O.C.E.C. Electronics, Miami-Dade University, Guest Lib-Art; [occ.] Computer Manifest Operator, Lighting Systems Engineer; [memb.] B.S. of a Leader in Troop 152 and 289 Long Beach, P.M.R. Pro-Musician Referral; [hon.] World of Poetry; [oth. writ.] Lonley, Universal Man Tri-Ter (Rainbow); [pers.] Writing poetry is like a pillar of fire within a sphere of darkness with only the soft touch of thought tickling the inner edges of that sphere. The outer edges of the sphere you see the sea with dancing paints of fire remembrance of you and me!; [a.] Long Beach, NY 11561

SMITH, BETTY
[b.] September 21, 1931, Chicago, IL; [p.] Alfred and Marcella Thimmes; [m.] Harold Smith, November 17, 1951; [ch.] Terry Smith (son); [ed.] 3 1/2 yrs Washburn High; [occ.] Homemaker; [hon.] Golden Poet Award 4 times, from World of Poetry, 2 honorable mentions from same; [oth. writ.] Wrote a few poems for hospice center news letter. Also had a few poems published in World of Poetry; [pers.] I try to have a lot of my poetry reflect what I can hear between the lines, from deep inside others. To maybe bring a smile or if need be a tear. A lot of my poetry has been with the cancer patient in mend; [a.] W. Valley City, UT 84120

SMITH, BRENDA C.
[b.]January 19, 1944, Phila, PA; [p.]William H. Carter and Edythe M. Carter; [m.]Henry Smith Jr., October 13, 1970 (Deceased Nov. 90); [ch.]Sharisse Smith Freeman, Grandson Tyler D. Freeman; [ed.]Overbrook High, Philadelphia, PA; [occ.]Assignment Administrator, Pacific Bell for 31 years; [hon.]Golden Poet, Silver Poet, World of Poetry 1990 and 1991. International Society of Poets Merit Award and Induction into ISP 1992; [oth. writ.]World of Poetry Anthology 1990, National Library Poetry, Best Poets of 90's, 1992 and 1992 calendar and tape vip newsletter monthly entry. Poems for various church functions, special occasions birthdays, weddings and anniversaries; [pers.]I believe poetry to be love notes from God.

SMITH, CAROL MAE
[b.] March 2, 1939, Newport, Washington; [p.] Walter J. Smith and Helen J. Smith Ice; [m.] Single; [ch.] Connie Jo Rice, Ronald Christian, Karen Mc Kenna; [ed.] High School Graduate, Salem Academy, Salem, Oregon; [occ.] Professional Singer, Poet, Sales and Marketing; [memb.] Mayflower Society

(Application in Process) Church Affiliation; [hon.] High School Drama Society, Leading Roles; [oth. writ.] Songs and poems, some in process of being published; [pers.] I wish to acknowledge my Lord and creator; the one who gives me constant inspiration for my writing. I was greatly influenced toward creative poetic writing by my great uncle, Edwin Waldron, an Architect. He was a member of the American Poetry Society and had many published works; [a.] Rancho Santa Fe, CA 92067

SMITH, CHARLOTTE LINES
[b.]August 13, 1908, Pembroke, Bermuda; [p.]Dighby H. Lines, Susan Lines; [m.]Frank Smith, June 2, 1932; [ch.]Seven, 15 grandchildren, 8 great-grandchildren; [ed.]Bermuda High School, R.N. Degree, Canada; [occ.]Retired; [oth. writ.]Poems as a child published in local paper; [pers.]To take each day as it comes and to do the best I can with it; [a.] California 95160

SMITH, DEDRA J.
[b.] October 3, 1969, Newport Beach, CA; [p.] Dana Smith, Diane Smith; [ed.] Newport Harbor HS, University California at Santa Barbara; [occ.] Still studying - student; [memb.] Astronomical Unit Club, American Cancer Society intern; [hon.] Outstanding student Award, Leadership Scholarship; [oth. writ.] Won honorable mention - published in a Poetry Anthology, several poems written not yet published; [pers.] My poetry is influenced by experiences and hardships I've encountered. I seek to depict a happy medium in the world, found without myself and through my friends and family; [a.] Costa Mesa, CA 92626

SMITH, INA
[b.]August 17, 1932, Dandridge, Tennessee; [p.]Trula Ridings and Lloyd Matthews; [ch.]Gail, Julia, Phillip, John, George, Kenneth, Debbie, and Dean Smith; [ed.]8th grade; [occ.]Salesperson at The Monster Fireworks Market; [memb.]Memphis Songwriters, The National Library of Poetry; [hon.]Editor's Choice Award for "No Last Goodbye's" Poetry first for song "One of These Days" 1993, 3rd for "More or Less" 1992, Contract for "The Whispering Pines" (co-writer Larry Davanport of Memphis Songwriters; [oth. writ.]One book published "Uninvited Memories" Rivercross Publisher NY; [pers.]My greatest accomplishments are getting through a marriage to a husband who rambled and gambled, and rearing my seven children, the youngest of whom is now in college. My greatest honor is to have the love of my friends and family; [a.] Dandridge, TN 37725.

SMITH, LOUISE DENT
[b.] Reynolds, Georgia; [p.] Earl and Lula Dent; [m.] Herman Smith (deceased), November 24, 1945; [ed.] Reynolds High, Reynolds, GA, Freshman yr Ft Valley State College, Ft Valley, GA, Lewis Business Col, Detroit, MI; [occ.] Retired Library Book Professor, Detroit Board of Ed Detroit, MI; [memb.] Mt Cavary Miss Bpt Chr, MARSP and AARP; [hon.] Golden Poet 1991 poem "Earth's Day 1991 hon award 1991 final tribute to D.D. Eusenhower" World of Poetry, Who's Who 1992; [oth. writ.] Green Thumbs Green Acres, Threshold of a Dream VIII 1993; Editor Choice Award "In Concert", Wind in the Night Sky, N. L., The Mirrow Self published book of poems; [pers.] Let all your thoughts be good ones. They are your future deeds.

SMITH, TERESA
[b.]May 10, 1966, Denton, Texas; [p.]James and Teresa Thompson and Calvin Bland; [m.]Raymond Smith, August 1986; [ch.]Raymond and jenny; [ed.]North Mesquite High School; [occ.]Housewife; [oth. writ.]Poem published in "A Break in the Clouds" 1993; [pers.]This poem is dedicated to the many events and to the many people who have participated in my life. Each and everyone has brought trial and tribulation, happiness and joy, but special thanks go out to "Sunshine", for he has helped me realize that if you look above and beyond, all is not lost, not even the chance for love.; [a.] Portland, OR 97231.

SMOOT, JANETTE S.
[b.]Yulee, Florida; [ed.]Morris Brown College and received B.S. degree from Edward Waters College, Graduate work in education ad psychology at Temple University; [occ.]Social Worker, Senior Psychiatric Technician, Self Esteem Group Leader at Belmont Center for Comprehensive Treatment; [hon.]Psychiatric Technician of the Year Award in May 1990, Golden Poet Award 1990-91, The International Poet of Merit Award; [oth. writ.]Poem, Underneath My Feet.

SNIDER, HAROLD R.
[b.]May 1, 1915, Helmsburg, Indiana; [p.]Rutherford & Bessie Snider; [m.]Wilma G. Snider, 1946; [ch.]Harold Lee Snider; [ed.]Grade school, two years high school, and 5 years Army as enlisted man. Army Officer WWII; [occ.]Carpenter, Builder, and several other trades; [memb.]Morgantown Baptist Church, and Masonic Lodge 358 Morgantown; [hon.]South West Pacific Medal, and Phllipine Liberation Medal; [oth. writ.]Many poems; [a.] Morgantown, Indiana 46160

SNOW JR., RICHARD ALVIN
[b.] July 5, 1956, Savannah, Georgia; [p.] Mr. Richard A. Snow Sr. and Mrs. Betty Jean Snow; [ed.] California State University, Sacramento, Sacramento City College, Riverside City College, Focus Automation, Skadrom College of Business; [occ.] Student; [hon.] Participated in Model United Nations of the Far West for two years 80, 81. A 1991 golden Poet as well as award of Merit Certificates a 1981 AA/EOPS Student Intern. Received Honorable Mention in High School Art Contest; [oth. writ.] "Quiet Time" published in World of Poetry Press," "The Encounter" published in "The Coming of Dawn" by The National Library of Poetry; [pers.] I am striving for unity with a minimum of impunity. thanks to family and friends for their support and a shoutout to the Carribean for their inspiration; [a.] San Bernardino, CA 92411

SNYDER, BERTHA
[b.] September 24, 1911, Yucon, OK; [p.] William F. Peck, Florence Willmann Peck; [m.] Gilbert R. Snyder, June 30, 1935; [ch.] Vea Lynne Snyder, Sue Anne Wickens; [ed.] Hannibal La Grange College, Mac Murray College, Jacksonville, Rockford College, Rockford, IL; [occ.] Retired Teacher; [memb.] Central Christian Church; [pers.] I was a wife, teacher, mother, homemaker until my husband died and my daughter becme adults. Since then I have swung back to my first love, poetry; [a.] Winston-Salem, NC 27104

SON, ANNE
[b.]April 21, 1911, Boston, MA; [p.]Anthony J. & Michalina Son; [ed.]Hyde Park High 1928 Cum Laude, Scholarship to Boston Teachers College, Warren Beauty Academy, Credits from Boston University, Harvard College, Senia Russafoff Academy of the Dance, Diploma in Ballet and Choreography; [occ.]Beautician, Charles of the Ritz, Ritz Carlton, Boston, REal Estate Broker; [memb.]Plymouth Garden Club, Plymouth Woman's Club, Plymouth Guild, Inc. for the Arts, (Charter Member) Polish Society of Cape Cod & the islands; [hon.]One of the six seniors in the South Shore Area-1991, "Great Lady" at the Claflin Health Fair, Awards from Plymouth Council on Aging from 1979 to present for volunteer work, Plymouth Garden Club Poster Contest; [oth. writ.]20 poems, several published in local newspapers and club award newsletters; [pers.]I try to share and reflect my talents as an inspiration to mankind. I try not to let a single day go by without making someone "less sad".; [a.] Plymouth, MA 02360.

SOROKA, CYNTHIA
[b.]September 28, 1967, NY; [p.]George and Diane Soroka; [ed.]1985-1987 Bergen Community College as Broadcasting, 1987-1989 Suny New Paltz, B.A. Communications; [occ.]President of Ariel Starr Productions, Ltd., V. Pres. Expressions Photography, Inc. and V. Pres. Flash Blasters, Inc.; [memb.]United We Stand America; [hon.]Outstanding Achievement in Poetry. The Editor's Choice Award by the National Library of Poetry; [oth. writ.]The Dark Chronicles Vol. 1 to be published this year.; [pers.]If you want something go for it!; [a.] Closter, NJ 07624.

SOUZA, ARVETTA M.
[b.] December 31, 1935, Burlington, CO; [p.] Roy A. Walters, Elizabeth Andrews Walters; [m.] Manuel Souza, April 11, 1959; [ch.] Seven; [ed.] East Denver High, Parks Business School, random, ongoing study in science and spirituality; [occ.] Bookkeeper, Homemaker and community volunteer (peace education); [memb.] Spiritearth, Nat'l Poets Soc, Noetic Sciences Institute, and local Pastoral Council; [hon.] State Rep Citation for Outstanding Community Service; [oth. writ.] Several poems with publication in NLP's 1993 "Whispers In The Wind" ; [pers.] I strive for greater understanding and wisdom, and to help create a better world for all humanity through education and awareness; [a.] Malden, MA 02148

SOUZA, EILEEN A.
[b.]October 16, 1951, Fall River, MA; [p.]Jean B. LeBlanc and Charlotte (Freshline) LeBlanc; [m.]Joseph F. Souza, February 22, 1969, Divorced 1982; [ch.]David, Mark, Jeremy, Jason, Cheryl, Joseph Souza; [occ.]Housewife, Mother, Grandmother of 7; [memb.]Fall River's Writer's Assoc.; [hon.]World of Poetry, Merit Awards 1988, 89, 90, Golden Poet Awards 1989, 90, 91; Who's Who 1991, 92, The National Library of Poetry 1990, 91, Editor's Choice Award 1990, The Best Poems of the 90's; [oth. writ.]Dear Children; Trail of Toys; Who Is This Image I See; Where There Is Light; Insane; Keeping You Under Lock and Key; As I Believe In You; Get Yourself Straight My Son; Like A Bolt Of Lightning; The Lamp Beneath My Feet; Let It Be; Dead Or Alive; Crashing In On Me; [pers.]Writing for me has been a type of therapy, a way so to speak of getting it off my chest without hurting anyone. Each verse was written with my inner feelings; [a.] Fall River, MA.

SPEIGHTS, HELENJEAN HAYS
[b.] November 24, 1934, Lubbock, TX; [p.] Byron M. Hays, Addie Jane Hancock Hays; [m.] Nathan L. Speights, November 26, 1958; [ch.] Allen Wayne Speights and Darrell Lee Speights; [ed.] Idalou High, Wayland Baptist College, and Texas Technological College, three years of college completed; [occ.] Homemaker, musician, secretary for husband and sons family owned business; [memb.] World of Poetry, Rockwall First Baptist Church, International Society of Poets; [hon.] World of Poetry, 3 Golden Poet Awards, 2 Silver Poet Awards and several honorable mentions; [oth. writ.] Wayland's Literary Magazine; posted on thought for the day at college; was chosen out of several entries to be performed by church choir a stanza that the church picked that I had written; [pers.] I strive to reflect in my writing the beauty of the closness that my parents showed me from the closness of their parents: the beauty in life; the goodness in man and the encouragement for hope and the future; [a.] Royse City, TX 75189

SPENCER, STEPHEN E.
[b.]June 26, 1966, Plymouth, NH; [p.]James C. Spencer and Irene Spencer; [ed.]College Graduate; [occ.]Professor Harvest Christian College in Theology; [memb.]Assembly of God; [hon.]Doctor of Biblical Studies, Calvary Christian College and Seminary, Bachelor of Arts in Theology, Harvest Christian College; [oth. writ.]I Alone Am Left, book published by Soul Winners Press in Warren MS., book Praise by the same publisher; [pers.]This poem I sing a sad song is dedicated to Trisha Dow; [a.] Thomaston, ME 04861

SPIKER, T. D.
[Pen.]R. K. Finch, Kelly Crawford; [b.]November 12, 1970, Martinsburg, WVA; [ed.]Pleasant View Elementary Berkeley Springs High School Shepherd College; [hon.]Dean's List, Who's Who Among American High School Students, 1987-89, The National Dean's List 1989-91, Catherine C. Fix Essay Contes; [oth. writ.]Several poems published in local magazine, essay published in W.VA. Senior High Magazine 1989; [pers.]From the ashes of the most hurtful experiences can blossom the most life-altering revelations as well as the most sorrowful regrets; [a.] Hedgesville, WV 25427

SPINE, DEBORAH R.
[Pen.] Debbie; [b.]November 7, 1953, Roseville, CA; [p.]Charles F. Castell and Eddy L. Castell; [m.]Charles P. Spine Sr, December 15, 1973; [ch.]Charles P. Spine Jr., and Heather L. Spine; [ed.]Currently a student at Palomar College and preparing to enter the Nursing (R.N.) program; [occ.]Waitress; [memb.]New Song Community Church of Lake Elsmore; [hon.]"Editor's Choice" Winner in writing a poem called "My Desire"; [oth. writ.]My poem "My Desire" was published in the 1993 anthology titled "Wind In The Night Sky"; [pers.]I thank my Lord Jesus Christ always for loving me so much, because without the love of God and his abundant grace in my life, I would be so very lost in every sense of the word; [a.] Wildomer, CA 92595.

SPIRES, JOANNE
[b.] October 11, 1976, Alma, Michigan; [p.] Jim and Karen Bradfield; [ed.] Currently a junior at Centaurus High School; [memb.] First Baptist Church Youth Group; [hon.] Editor's Choice Award for poem; [oth.

writ.] Poems in A Question of Balance and Distinguished Poets of America, poem in Lafayette News; [pers.] Poetry is a beautiful thing that everyone should experience. It's a shame not many people do; [a.] Lafayette, IO 80026

SPRUNG, JOHN GEORGE
[b.]March 4, 1913, St. Louis Missouri; [p.]John Nicholar Sprung and Magdalena Tremel; [m.]Loa Ruth Sprung, April 26, 1947; [ch.]John Leon Sprung and Lori Lee Sprung; [ed.]Waller High School, Chicago, B.S. Degree Northwestern University Scholarship, Chicago Art Institute; [occ.]Retired Plastics Engineer; [memb.]Delta Beta Phi Society of Plastic Engineers; [oth. writ.]Tennis is a Racket Tianitus Aural; [pers.]My poems have bilateral symmetry. I call this balanced verse or poetry in stereo. The first syllable of every line rhymes with the last syllable at that line; [a.] San Pedra, CA 90732

ST. JULES, RUBY JEWEL
[b.]July 30, 1942, Wichita Falls, TX; [p.]The late Mr. Cleo and Mrs. Roxie Smith; [ed.]Bachelor of Science in Business Education and Library Science, Masters Degree in Library Science Education; [occ.]Librarian, Adult Services (First Baptist Church Scholarship Committee) Hospitality Committee, First Baptist Church; [memb.]Honorary Charter, membership for outstanding achievement in poetry presented by Intern'l. Society of Poets; [hon.]Golden Poet Award, Who's Who in Poetry and Award of Merit certificate all presented by World of Poetry, City of New york Certificate of Appreciation by Big-Apple Fix-up Home Improvement Award. Certificate of Appreciation by the Hospital Committee of First Baptist Church, Brooklyn, NY, First prize winner in a historical contest sponsored by the Brooklyn Borough President Office, Brooklyn, NY received Special Award from Brooklyn Union Gas Company in recognition of a role in neighborhood revitalization in Brooklyn, NY, Certificate of Appreciation from the Mayor's Office of the City of New York. Employee of the Month, Personnel, One, Miami, Florida; [oth. writ.]Poems published by World of Poetry, Brooklyn Public Library, Newsletter, New York Amsterdam Newspaper; [pers.]I try to relate what I am writing on about things that involve us in our everyday life and surroundings; [a.] Miami, Florida 33127

ST. LOUIS, DOROTHY A.
[b.] September 25, 1931, Lamar, CO; [p.] Edward Maynard, Flora Maynard; [ch.] Dottie, Jackie, Kevin, Karla; [ed.] Visalia High Fresno City College - AA Degree; [occ.] Medical Transcriptionist; [hon.] Graduated with 3.8 GPA, honorable mention on several poems along with a Merit Certificate; [oth. writ.] Several poems and articles published in a hospital newspaper; [pers.] In order to write poetry, I must experience those feelings. I cannot just put words down.

STALLINGS, JAMES WILLIAM
[Pen.]Nicholas the Viking; [b.]September 1, 1909, Williston, SC; [p.]Robert E. Lee Stallings and Ada Black Stallings (dec.); [m.]Alice Gregory Stallings, December 11, 1933; [ch.]Jane, Jerry and Sybil; [ed.]Williston-Elko High School, Furman University; [occ.]Research Chemist; [memb.]American Men of Science, Who's Who in the South and Southeast, Fellow American Institute of Chemists, Chi Beta Phi; [hon.]Army-Navy "E" award. Five U.S. Patents covering developments essential to World War II needs. Descendent of Viking ancestor Nicholas Stallings who came to Charles City, VA on November 5, 1635.; [oth. writ.]Many poems published in area newspapers, guest columnist Augusta Chronicle, poems (and pictures) for personalized exchange of Christmas and New Year's cards with Anwar (el) Sadat.; [pers.]If procrastination is the "thief of time." I am happy that Nicholas didn't miss the boat to Virginia; [a.] Barnwell, SC 29812.

STANSELL, ELLEN ANN
[Pen.]Ellen Ann Green; [b.]January 22, 1937, Liverpool, England; [p.]Thomas Green and Martha Green; [m.]Richard L. Stansell (Expired) April 1, 1951/Divorced; [ch.]Robert, Catherine, David, Donna, Barbara, Richard, Jacqueline; [ed.]Anfield Road, High School, Craven Community College and CCHS California College; [occ.]Respiratory Technician, Medical Assistant CNA; [memb.]President of the USAF, Wives Club, First Assembly of God, Pentecostal Church; [hon.]Dean's List; [oth. writ.]Several poems for schools and churches. Some plays for elementary school; [pers.]I feel my poem writings are a gift from God. I study people and the beauty around me, the happiness and sometime the despair. It gives me joy to put my feelings and context together and to leave something of me when I have gone to be with the Lord.; [a.] Raleigh, NC.

STANTON, BERNARD P.
[Pen.] Bernie; [b.] January 8, 1915, Cambridge, England (Naturalized citizen); [p.] Lord and Lady Percival Stanton of St Petersburg, FL; [m.] Ora Lee Stanton, August 23, 1945; [ch.] David, Carlene, Daniel, Douglas, Delora, Dale; [ed.] ABMA and DD; [occ.] Minister, salesman, Bible teacher, Pastor (retired); [memb.] Open Poetry Assoc (local), World of Poetry (formerly), Christian Poets (church); [hon.] "America's Golden Poet", "Man of Letters" (patriotic assoc); [oth. writ.] "I was there" (biography), Bible and seminary Bible courses. Poet's Corner (Book of Poetry) "America's Golden Poet"; [pers.] Spiritual motivation spells personal success; [a.] St Petersburg, FL 33703

STAPLES JR., PAUL R.
[Pen.] Wildroot; [b.] March 6, 1954, Akron, Ohio; [p.] Paul and Norma; [m.] Margie, March 28, 1975; [ch.] Karen Gayle and Steven Dale; [ed.] High School Harry Doss, Attending Writer's Digest School Ohio, Fiction course; [occ.] Major Appliance G.E. Assembly and Carpentry; [memb.] AFL-CIO, The Smithsonian, NRA, NARF, NPCA, Audubon Society, PFCU, BOJAF; [hon.] Perfect attendance G.E., Three years 89, 92 & 93. Editors Choice Award 1993. The National Library of Poetry; [oth. writ.] Icon, White Rose, One Poet, Mate, and many more to come; [pers.] We are all only imitations of those who came before us. The circumference of each lifetimes point is the image where two worlds intersect by being whole as one; [a.] Cub Run, KY 42729

STENIS, ROWENA
[b.]September 27, 1922, Norman, Oklahoma; [p.]Matthew Irving Smith and Hazeline Emily Ingram Smith; [m.]Tom B. Steinis, September 22, 1943; [ch.]Melody Stenis Phillips, Vaughn Allan Stenis, Bonnie Stenis Walvoord, Wayne David Stenis; [ed.]Austin High (Austin, TX); B. Music, Univ. of Texas (Austin), Master of Education, Texas Tech. Univ.; [occ.]Music Teacher, Mother, Housewife, Orchestra Librarian, Symphony Musician; [memb.]Wednesday Morning Music Club, Great Hills, Baptist Church in orchestra, Austin Civic Orchestra (Played in Lubbock, TX Symphony 38 years) Mu Phi Epsilon (music fraternity), Mu Phi Epsilon (then Music honorary), Phi Kappa Phi (scholastic) National Honor Society; [oth. writ.]Poems in various local and state publications. Article on teaching beginning string (violin, etc.)students, various devotional, poetry volume to be released soon ("Reflections" Carlton Press); [pers.]Faith in God, trust his goodness: "All things work together for good to thee who love the Lord" Living by God's rules, see the good in life and enjoy it fully. It's not circumstances that make our outlook different, but our reaction to them.; [a.] Austin, TX 78731-1419

STEPIEN, GEORGE
[b.]February 11, 1946, Regensburg, Germany; [p.]rose Ulanowski; [ch.]Jason, Ehren, Myriah, Tanrah; [occ.]Cabinetmaker, Singer, Songwriter, Musician; [pers.]I would hope my poetry and the songs I write and sing will bring someone joy and comfort in their lives; [a.] Goshen, CT 06756.

STEWART, BRIAN
[b.]September 3, 1981, St. Paul, MN; [p.]Kirby and Karen Stewart; [ed.]Kindergarten - 5th grade, Kindergarten - 4th grade Sacred Heart St. John's, 5th grade - Trinity Catholic; [hon.]6 yrs. perfect attendance in school. The Editor's Choice Award; [oth. writ.]A poem published in book "Wind In The Night Sky." A poem published in book "Whispers in the Wind." Story written in Pioneer Press Newspaper at age 8.; [pers.]I am 11 yrs. old and I have loved to read since kindergarten. I love to write and plan on continuing to write more.; [a.] St. Paul, MN 55106.

STEWART, GERALDINE
[Pen.]Gerri Stewart; [b.]February 17, 1943, Marks, Mississippi; [p.]Annie Bell and Issac Stewart; [ed.]High School graduate, took music courses, singing and writing courses. Took florist and art courses; [occ.]Nurse Aide; [memb.]AAA Club an one driver, the best driver on the road. No membership of any performing art; [oth. writ.]I'm a songwriter, have written many songs. Gospel, pop, folk, one country song, jazz. They call me the Gospel Jazz Singer; [pers.]I have rent out songs to record company, some wanted to record if I pay them to record it. I've sent out poetry to some publishing co. everyone liked my work; [a.] Farmingdale, NY 11735

STEWART, JAMES
[b.] May 31, 1954, Detroit, MI; [p.] James and Verna Stewart; [ed.] Library Assistant, Detroit Bar Assn Library; [memb.] Jazz Alliance of Michigan, Rebirth, Inc; [oth. writ.] Poem in National Library of Poetry publication "Wind in the Night Sky" Between conscience and objectivity; [pers.] Words that move people move me to write more; [a.] Detroit, MI 48208

STEWART, TAMRA
[b.]January 27, 1959, Charleston, WV; [p.]Jim Johnson & Joyce Johnson; [m.]Scott Stewart, August 15, 1981; [ch.]Shea, Drew & Reed; [ed.]Charleston High, University of Charleston, (Bachelor of Arts); [occ.]Free Lance Artist, Poet, Florist; [memb.]Museum of Fine Arts, Boston, Morris Memorial United Methodist Church, International Soci-

ety of Poets; [hon.]Golden Poet Award for 1990 and 1992; [oth. writ.]Anthology of personal writings in hopes of completing a book someday; [pers.]I want to touch people with my poetry. god and my family have been the biggest influence in my writing; [a.] Charleston, WV 25304,

STOECKEL, JIM L.
[b.]July 9, 1913, Almont, North Dakota; [p.]Rose & Louis Stoeckel; [m.]Dagmar M. Stoeckel, June 28, 1936; [ch.]Mary ann Tipton and James Louis Stoeckel; [ed.]High School and N. Dak. Colleges; [occ.]Retired from Corporate Management and private business; [memb.]Rotary Club, National Mgmnt. Club, Boy Scout Work; [hon.]Editor's Choice Award from National Library of Poetry in 1993 for poem "To A Humming Bird" published in "Where Dreams Begin"; [oth. writ.]Book of "Love Poems to My Wife." Poems and Prose on various subjects. Poems to children and friends.; [pers.]I feel life is what we make it and we reap what we sow. give a helping hand when 'er we can.; [a.] La Crescenta, California 91214-1633.

STOKES, CAROLYN ASHE
[b.]November 18, 1925, Philadelphia, PA; [p.]Charles Malcolm Ashe and Louisa Ashe Shelton; [m.]Joseph H. Stokes, D.D.S., October 29, 1947; [ch.]Michael, Monica, Craig Stokes, Grandchildren, Scott, SY, and Kai Stokes; [ed.]West Phila. NILH, Howard Univ., U.C.B., JFK University, M.A., Consciousness and the arts; [occ.]Hologramatic Planning Consultant; [memb.]Numerous civic and community organizations; [hon.]Various community and poetry awards; [oth. writ.]Poetry; [pers.]Poetry is my outlet for deep emotions which resonate with others following their life's journey; [a.] Orinda, CA 94563

STOKES, DONNA L.
[b.]October 24, 1954, Baltimore, Maryland; [p.]Richards Hallock and Nancy Lee Hallock; [m.]Alan P. Stokes, September 20, 1975; [ch.]none; [ed.]Graduated from Franklin Sr. High School; [occ.]Comprehensive Accounting Serv., Self-employed, Sales and Marketing; [memb.]Executive Women's Network, Pro-Net Int'l, Volunteer for Pets On Wheels; [hon.]1991 Annual Sales Achievement Award, 1990 Hall of Fame Sales Award 1990, Albert E. Jungles Quality Circle Award, various other sales achievement awards; [oth. writ.]published 1993 Library of Poetry; [pers.]Been married for 18 wonderful years and he's my inspiration; [a.] Parkton, MD.

STOLIKER, SEAN TALLON
[b.]October 17, 1966, Winsted CT; [m.]Single; [occ.]Mechanic; [memb.]Rocicrucian order, AMORC; [pers.]Longing for the touch which once was yours, you search, never finding till one day the light returns and purpose claims the stage; [a.] Winstead, CT 06098

STOLZENBURG, ELDON L.
[b.]April 11, 1993, Wapakoneta, Ohio; [p.]Mr. and Mrs. Henry Stolzenburg; [m.]Mary L. Fogt Stolzenburg, June 19, 1947; [ch.]Linda Sue Kramer, Eldon L. Stolzenburg Jr., Robert D. Stolzenburg; [ed.]11 years, 8 grade, 3 high school.; [occ.]Retired Factory Worker; [memb.]Eagles, Nazarene Church; [oth. writ.]Local Paper, Sparrow Grass Publishing, Amherst Society, National Library of Poetry, two is Mississippi and one in Misouri; [a.] Wapakeneta, Ohio 45895.

STOREY, ELVIN
[b.] March 3, 1925, Grattan, Michigan; [p.] Louland and Lila Storey; [m.] Deceased, August 30, 1952; [ch.] Four, Janet Lefevre, Roger, Ron and Terry Storey; [ed.] Belding High School, Grand Rapids Baptist Bible College; [occ.] Retired Clergyman; [memb.] American Legion Post 100, Lifetiem Member, John Birch Society (Honorary Member), American Poetry Society, International Society of Poets; Alumni Association, GR Baptist bible College; [hon.] Golden Poet Award 1992; [oth. writ.] Author of "Trailways to Poetical Thought", Fisherman's Press, Tucson, AZ; [pers.] "Everyone should pub forth their best effort in making this world a better place to live."; [a.] Tucson, AZ 85705

STOTTLE, C. ROBYN LYNN
[b.] October 9, 1969, Virginia, Fairfax; [ed.] Franklin Pierce College, B.A., Institute of Childrens Literature Diploma Newton High School, Sandy Hook CT; [occ.] Photographer, Graphic Designer, Writer; [hon.] Who's Who in Poetry 1990-1992, Our World's Favorite Poems; [oth. writ.] Several poems published in newspapers in CT; [pers.] Beloved, when I gave all diligence to write unto you of the common salvation, it was needful for me to write unto you, and exhort you that ye should earnestly contend for the faith which was once delivered unto the Saints...Jude 3 [a.] Greenville, SC 29615

STREETER, PAUL W.
[b.] September 18, Kansas City, MO; [p.] Paul H. Streeter; [m.] Norma R. Centz; [ch.] (3) Donald V. Streeter, Robert T. Streeter; [ed.] Notre Dame - Liberal Arts; [occ.] Entrepreneur - Supper Club's, restaurant and lounges; [hon.] World of Poetry "Golden Poet" 1991, 1992, 1993; [oth. writ.] Quiet thoughts; [pers.] Have written over 200 poems. All deal with factional surroundings and happenings; [a.] Fort Lauderdale, FL 33304

STROZIER II, GLEN L.
[Pen.]Pete Floyd; [b.]February 16, 1958, jasper, AL; [p.]Glen and Xan Strozier; [oth. writ.]"Poems From The Dead"; [pers.]The first cry comes from the womb, the last cry dies in a tomb; [a.] Childersburg, AL 35044.

STUCK, NORMA P. VON
[Pen.] Nona Perle; [b.] December 30, 1912, Grand Rapids, MI; [p.] Gladys and Norman Hansen; [m.] Harold H. von Stuck, October 11, 1930; [ch.] Rev Myra Lee Sparks, Lt Col Monte L. Stuck, (USAF ret) Cdr Murlowe L. von Stuck (USN ret); [ed.] BA - MA - MFA; [occ.] Retired; [memb.] Walker Bible Church, Life member Central Michigan Lapidary Club, Lamalug (Computer Club); [hon.] Kappa Delta Pi, Phi Kappa Phi, MSU Writer's Award, SWMCCC Awards, Youth Talent Judge, National Exhibitor of Jewelry, Sculpture, Silk Screen Prints and Photography; [oth. writ.] Odd Ditties, The Coals Burn Hot and Zebra, Publisher of a monthly Newsletter, Contributor to radio, various magazines, writer's newsletters, and state papers. Community News Reporter for The Grand Rapids Press and the Grand Rapids Herald; [pers.] It is my aim to notice the world around me in something other than just the ordinary way, and then to put what I see into words for others to enjoy; [a.] Lansing, MI 48906

STUFFLE, GRACE M.
[b.]January 21, 1922, Martin Co., Ind.; [p.]Wilbert and Belma "Bough" Dove; [m.]Calvin Stuffle, January 4, 1941; [ch.]Five Loren, Nancy, Marilyn, Joseph and John; [ed.]High School; [occ.]Retired, I work with the less fortunate citizens; [memb.]Catholic Church; [hon.]Poems pub. in N.T.L of Poetry from other anthologies, Awards of Merit, Golden Poet Awards, Who's Who In Poetry; [pers.]Inspired by early poets my poems are loved by many; [a.] Loogootee, IN

STUTCHMAN, AMANDA
[b.]June 12, 1976, DeKalb; [p.]Brenda and Dale Stutchman; [m.]none; [ch.]none; [ed.]High School, 11th grade, Salem High School; [occ.]none; [memb.]none; [hon.]Editor's Choice Award; [oth. writ.]Thought, Grandparents, Nanny, Dad, Mom, Myself, Love, Parents, Guys, School, Feelings, Friends, My Brother and Ellen; [pers.]Put all you've got into life and you'll get all you put in back. If you want something don't give up till you get it.; [a.] Conyers, GA 30208.

SULLIVAN, CAROLINE M.
[b.]October 28, 1961, Lynn, MA; [p.]Leonard Guarente and Carol Ann Guarente; [m.]Glenn P. Sullivan, October 8, 1988; [ed.]Masconomet High School, B.S. Hotel Restaurant and Travel Administration, University of Massachusetts, Amherst, MA 1984; [occ.]Manufacturing/Quality Assurance Specialist, ESC, Hanscom AFB, Bedford, MA; [memb.]American Management Association; [oth. writ.]"Shels" published in Where Dreams Begin, The National Library of Poetry, 1993 edition.; [pers.]Memories are the poetry of life; [a.] Hudson, NH 03051.

SULLIVAN, PEARLE R.
[b.]October 14, 1905, Taytarsville; [p.]Damond and Bettie Robinson; [m.]Deceased, December 3, 1923; [ch.]Three; [ed.]Finished High School; [occ.]Substitute Rural Mail Carrier; [memb.]Baptist; [hon.]Ten dollars from Blue Bonnet Margarine, a princess telephone and set of luggate with name on it.

SULLIVAN-RUSCH, COLLEEN
[b.] August 25, 1944, Toledo, OH; [p.] Mildred Herbster-Sullivan, Robert Thomas Sullivan; [m.] Douglas Clayton Rusch, August 27, 1964; [ed.] De Vilbiss High School, Univ of Toledo; [occ.] Writer and illustrator of children's stories; [memb.] Toledo Zoological Society, North Toledo Area Corporation, Honorary Member of National Library of Poetry; [hon.] Art and English awards in high school - 1st prize National Bank Art Show (2 yrs) - several Honorable Mention awards in poetry - named "Golden Poet of 1992" by World of Poetry - Editor's Choice Award for 1993 from National Library of Poetry - painting sent to Toledo, Spain in sister city art exchange 1962; [oth. writ.] Several poems published in poetry anthologies, including "Survival" - "True Love" - "Forms" and "Writing Poetry". Articles for the "200-Ed" newspaper; [pers.] The big affairs of the world are only what is big to each person. In life, all is relative to vantage point; [a.] Toledo, OH 43620

SUMMERLIN, CHAPLAIN CAPT. JAMES C.
[b.] October 3, 1956, Homerville, GA; [p.] Dr. Nanjo C. Dube', Ph.D, Mr. James C. Summerlin, Sr.; [m.] Sarah Copeland Summerlin, January 5, 1991; [ch.] Cynthia Ann Summerlin (by previous marriage);

[ed.] High school graduate, seminary graduate, college graduate; [occ.] Chaplain; Christian Clinical Counselor, Certified Youth Leader; [memb.] Nat Chaplains Assoc; American Evangelistic Assoc; Int Society of Poets; Int Assoc of Christian Clinical Counselors; Certified Layspeaker United Methodist Church; [oth. writ.] Poems published in Who's Who in Poetry from World of Poetry, and Treasures of Golden Poems, and in The Coming of Dawn by National Library of Poetry; [pers.] It is truely an honor to be a Lifetime Member of the International Society of Poets, and to serve as a member of the Advisory Panel helping other poets around the world; [a.] Suffolk, VA

SUMMERS, LUCY COOPER
[b.] June 27, 1920, Greenville, MS; [p.] Eugene and Mayne Cooper (deceased); [m.] Don A. Summers (deceased), June 27, 1942; [ch.] Sandra, Barbara, Lucy, Dona, Don Jr., 6 grandchildren; [ed.] New York public schools/BA, NY Hunter College/graduate study Atlanta Univ Sch of Social Work Atlanta, GA; [occ.] Homemaker (with social work and administrative Head Start library back ground, real estate; [memb.] Unitarian Church, Poetry Fellowship of Maine, Midwest Chaporral Fed Poets Nat'l Council of Negro Women, Amistad Affiliates, Corporator Hartford Public Library, North Hartford Senior Center, One Chance, Inc; [oth. writ.] Book, "99 Patches", Carlton Press, New York City, 1969, Golden Quill Anthologies, "On Common Ground" (The Stone Day Foundation 1975, Hartford, CT) an anthology of Hartford Poets/and other works; [pers.] To have peace on earth we must reflect on our daily lives that "God is Love"; [a.] Hartford, CT

SWEENEY, THOMAS J.
[Pen.] Darby O'Toole; [b.] January 21, 1934, Poughkeepsie, NY 12603; [p.] Thomas E. and Rose Hurley Sweeney; [m.] Mary A. (Hellard) Sweeney, July 25, 1959 (deceased); [ch.] Patricia O'Hanlon, Kathleen Chapman, Richard and William Sweeney, plus 4 grandchildren; [ed.] Graduate, Poughkeepsie High School, Class of 1951; [occ.] Retired, Regional Loss Prevention Manager; [memb.] AARP, Knights of Columbus, Former Member, ASIS, Connecticut Narcotic Enforcement Officers Assoc., Nat'l Assoc. of Chief of Police; [hon.] Have been cited for Outstanding Volunteer efforts during past 5 years with the Dutchess County Tourism Promotion Agency and 2 1/2 years with the Hyde Park, NY Chamber of Commerce; [oth. writ.] Sense and Nonsense, Treasured Poems of America, Winter 1991. We Fall For Autumn or In Autumn We Fall, Treasured Poems of America, Fall 1991. Wit-A-Sarcasm, Poetic Voices in America, Spring 1992. Power Plants, A Question of Balance, Fall 1992, received a 1993 National Library of Poetry, Editor's Choice Award. The Flavor Is Dutchess, Dutchess County (NY) 1993-94 Travel Guide; [pers.] Will occasionally be motivated to write a poem of serious note, but generally, writes light hearted poems depicting friends, relatives, acquaintances or situations as if observed thru the eyes of an inexpressible roseal; [a.] Poughkeepsie, NY 12603

SWEETING, BERRY L.
[b.] November 7, 1943, Miami, FL; [p.] James and Vernice; [m.] Dorothy Cook, May 13, 1985; [ed.] 2 yrs. College, Miami-Dade Community College; [occ.] Military; [a.] N. Miami, FL

SYNEK DR., M.
[b.] September 18, 1930, Prague, Czechoslavakia, United States Citizen; [p.] Frantisek and Anna Synek; [ch.] Mary and Thomas Synek; [ed.] M.S. (with distinction), Charles University, Prague, Czechoslovakia; Ph.D., The University of Chicago; [occ.] College Prof.; [memb.] Life Fellow, The American Physical Society; Fellow, A.A.A.S., Amer. Inst. Chemist, Texas Academy Sci., etc.; [hon.] Listed in Who's Who in the World; Who's Who in Science and Engineering (Marquis); Personalities of America (ABI)--International Man of the Year, etc.; [oth. writ.] A number of publications of scientific and general interest.; [pers.]"Free elections in the nuclear age--that is a historical urgency for the survival of humanity on this planet.; [a.] San Antonio, TX 78249

TALBOT, JACK M.
[b.] July 6, 1964, Merrill, WI; [p.] James and Mary; [ed.] B.S. University of WI, OshKosh; [occ.] High school English Teacher OshKosh West High; [memb.] Names project, AIDS, Friends of the Quilt, Phi Kappa Delta, NEA; [hon.] Golden Poet, World of Poetry; [oth. writ.] Poetry "Modes of Immortality, 5 poems featured in "Our World's Most Treasured Poems", plays, Liebestrame, Flowers of Thyme, Short Story "A Reminiscence"; [pers.] I strive to enlighten people about the power and magic of creativity and compassion. I believe in the goodness of humankind; [a.] OshKosh, WI 54901.

TAM, AMY C. KALEIHO'OPI'O
[b.] Macao, China; [p.] C. Amona Chang (f); Sau Wo Loo Chang (m); [m.] Major Edward K. Tam, MPD; [ch.] John Edward and James Kellet, Attorneys, Hawaii, Brenda R. Kailani, Pub Def. Investig., Akido Instr. Portland, Oreg.; [ed.] MacMurray Coll, Ill State Univ., BEd Eng., Post Grad U of Minn., Sch. of Journ., Eng Dept. Chr., UH-MCC, Eng., Journ., Hawn Studies, Lib. Arts. Div. Chr., Accred. Team Hi Schls., Curr. Prog. Develop; [memb.] DKG; HGEA; NCTE Maui Chpt. Hawn Girls Golf, Maui Country Club Ladies Golf; [hon.] DKG, Dow-Jones Fellow 1958; Outstanding Educator of America 1976; Journ.; All American Award in Publications 1956 to 1965; Golf Club Champion, vice Pres.'s Trophy Champion, Hole-In-One.; [oth. writ.] Critical Essays in Maui News, Ka Wai Ola, Moui Press; Sequential Guide for Teaching English Gr. 9 to 12; Creative Drama; Individualized Learning Hawn Studies texts for A-V units; Legendary Beginnings; Origins of a Land; Birth of an Island; An Island Grows; Archaeology in Stone; Polynesian Seafarers; Coming of a People; Mele O Na' Ali'; The Kamehomeha Kings; Lunalilo and the Kalakaua Dynasty, Culture Essays: Au'a 'la-Hold Fast to Heritage; Hi'iaka's Chant Atop Pu'u Onioni, The Pele Family of Gods. Chants of Children; A Song for Na Pua Naupaka; My Word, Hawaii.; [pers.] Poetry celebrates the soul and spirit of man, the uncomplicated order of nature and her universe, the love and grace in heart and hand of God.; [a.] Kahului, HI 96732.

TAMBO, JO
[b.] June 23, 1933, LI, New York; [p.] Joseph and Anna Bastos; [m.] William, December 23, 1956; [ch.] Andrea and Craig; [ed.] Grad. Michigan State University 1956-BA in Speech Pathology Cum Laude; [occ.] Speech Pathologist; [memb.] American Speech, Language and Hearing Assoc., Nat. Educ.; [hon.] Honor Society, various other awards; [oth. writ.] I am new at this, have never before had the courage to publish or even let it be known that I write poetry; [pers.] My writing reflects my "innerself" and expresses my thoughts best. Life is a gift and throughout it we receive much-but like a flower's beauty it must be cherished and cared before it's bloom fadest is missed. Some of us never see the beauty for all the pain that exists. I think we have to work at finding the beauty in human frailties. Writing poetry helps me do this.

TANG, JEAN LACY
[b.] September 23, 1948, Hettinger, ND; [p.] Clayton and Tomina Larson; [m.] Larry Tang, June 30, 1984; [ch.] Erin Lynne Lacy, Aaron, Amy, Adam Tang; [ed.] Master of Arts, Counseling and Guidance, University of ND; [occ.] Counselor, Chemeketa Community College; [hon.] Award of Merit Certificate, Honorable Mention, World of Poetry, 1988; Silver Poet, 1990, World of Poetry; Golden Poet Award, 1988, World of Poetry; [oth. writ.] Poems published in "A Collection of Poems" by the North Dakota, Ohio and California Society of Poets 1976 and in "Our World's Favorite Gold and Silver Poems, 1991; [pers.] The writing and reading of poetry allows one to "gently" move through life and appreciate all that life offers; [a.] Salem, Oregon

TATE, JAN
[b.] September 1, 1930, Texas; [p.] James and Alice Knowles (Deceased); [m.] Divorced; [ch.] Four sons; [ed.] Through Jr. College; [occ.] Retired; [memb.] none presently; [hon.] received award in 1991 from World of Poetry; [oth. writ.] Short prose and children's stories; [pers.] Have had several poems published in Sacramento newspaper in 1960's; [a.] Modesto, CA 95350

TAYLOR, GAIL TAMARA
[Pen.] Tammy Taylor; [b.] February 7, Walpole, Massachusetts; [p.] A.W. and Katherine Blake; [m.] Bill R. Taylor; [m.] October 1987 (2nd); [ch.] Christopher, Heather, Grand-babies, Blaine and Danielle; [ed.] University High, Santa Monica City College; [occ.] Housewife, writer; [hon.] Editor's Choice Award for "Sunday Child" Poem. Past scholarships in two different ballet, dance school's, Boy Scout of Am. Denver Mother Award; [oth. writ.] Poem in "Wind In The Night Sky" Book and one "In The Desert Sun." Children stories, novel and poems not published as yet; [pers.] As said before, I believe in keep trying, you never know what's down the path. This has been proven to me many times over.; [a.] Monrovia, CA 91016.

TAYLOR, JESSIE
[b.] July 4, 1917, Wise County, Bethlem, Texas; [p.] John and Jannie Read; [m.] Clyde Terry Taylor, April 24, 1971; [ch.] two children and three step children; [ed.] High School and some college; [memb.] Baptist Church, Eastern Star, LUTC, Life Under Writers Assn.; [hon.] National Quality Award; [a.] Aledo, TX 76008.

TERREBONNE, ANNE
[b.] March 17, 1932, Isola, MS; [p.] Alpha Cooper and Tommy Patterson (Deceased); [m.] Frank Paul Terrebonne, May 7, 1960; [ch.] none; [ed.] B.S., Mississippi State University, Assoc. Arts Co-Lin College, Certified Medical Technologist; [occ.] Medical Technologist in Hematopathology at Univ. Texas Med. Branch, Galverston, TX;

[memb.]Positive Thinkers Club, Methodist, Democrat, ASMT, ASCP, A.E.S., Alumni Club, AARP, I.S. of Poets; [hon.]Scientific publication, WWIAW, WWIW, Who's Who in South and Southwest, Editor's Choice for 1993, poem: Empathy; [oth. writ.]Non-published Peace Poem 1993, collection of song poetry unpublished; [pers.]I believe poetry can be used to express emotions that can be express emotions that can be expressed no other way. It's strength could again become the literary pulse of the nation; [a.] Hitchcock, TX 77563.

TERRELL, BARBARA J.
[Pen.]Barb Ungeright-Hutcheson; [b.]April 17, 1948, Anderson, Indiana; [p.]Irvin Ungeright and Lewis and Virginia Hutcheson; [m.]Rick D. Terrell, June 11, 1981; [ch.]Daniel Shetterley and Amanda Shetterley; [ed.]Mt. Vernon High School, Fortville; [occ.]Professional Mary-K Beauty Consultant; [memb.]Shepherd Nazarene Church, American Cancer Society; [hon.]Teen Counselor, Indianapolis, Indiana; [oth. writ.]Publication in book of Where Dreams Begin, National Library of Poetry; [pers.]I trust in Jesus, my personal saviour for every decision of my life, that I choose to make by praying first; [a.] Columbus, Ohio 43232.

TERWILLIGER, ELIZABETH
[Pen.]Elizabeth; [b.]October 11, 1923, Putnam, CT; [p.]George and Grace Mildred (Jacques) Slater; [m.]Wesley Terwilliger (Deceased), June 7, 1945; [ch.]Claudia, Donna, Ann, Carol, Linda, Wendy, David and Paul; [ed.]Killingly High School; [occ.]Retired office worker and homemaker; [memb.]South Killingly Church, Highland Grange #113; [oth. writ.]About 70 other poems when I plan to publish. A few have at times been published locally and in poetry books; [pers.]I would like to return love, joy and laughter to the world through my poems.; [a.] Danielson, CT 06239.

TETREAULT, CAROL ANN
[Pen.] Carol-Ann; [b.] May, Providence, RI; [p.] Alba H. Bellows, Jr, Edith Barr Bellows; [ch.] (son) Mark Tetreault, (daughter) Melanie Tetreault; [ed.] Graduate RI School Practical Nursing, attending RI College - BSN - Psychology American Baptist Church of RI Biblical Studies; [occ.] Motherhood, Nurse; [memb.] Concerned Women of America, Cranston Christian Fellowship, Coalition to Preserve Traditional Values; [hon.] American Baptist Church of RI for Leadership; Cranston Public Schools - Commitment to Community Children, World of Poetry - Excellence of Poetry Writing; [oth. writ.] "Peace Rose Yellow", "Thanksgiving Gold", "May Day", "America the Beloved", "Symphony of Summer"; [pers.] The goodness of life has something to offer and a place for everyone. In accepting each other unconditionally, there would be no need for unhealthy competition and greed. Only genuine care and concern for one another; [a.] Cranston, RI

THACKERAY, BETTY FERN
[b.]July 10, 1922, Minneapolis, Minn.; [p.]Both deceased; [m.]Vern E. Thackray, January 2, 1946 (deceased); [ch.]Two--boy/ Daniel, girl/Debra; [ed.]1 yr. at Drake University, Des Moines, Iowa, Business School/Creative Writing; [occ.]Retired Administrative Sec'y, Legal/Medical; [memb.]Idaho Writers League/Cda, Chapter, No. Idaho Christian Writers, Women's AGLOW, Cda. Community Theater, St. Mark's Lutheran-Hayden Lake, Idaho; [hon.]Numerous small ones relating to my writing (beauty contest award in my youth-Ha!); [oth. writ.]Skits, personal essay, currently writing a novel based on husband's manic-depression and how this malady affects family and social and financial life. (Poor Little People); [pers.]My most enjoyable pastime is to engage in conversation relating to meaningful topics with open-minded, intelligent, Christian people. "Judge not, lest ye be judged." [a.] Coeur d'Alen, Idaho 83814.

THAYER, MARGARET R.
[b.] November 3, 1932, Highland, Michigan; [p.] Chester L. Sleep and Lydia M. Sleep; [m.] James E. Thayer, September 12, 1975; [ch.] Valerie, Kathy, Bobbie and five stepchildren (Barbara, Charlotte, Kevin, Dale and Gary) in Australia; [ed.] High School, 1 yr. Post Grad, Radio Operator Trng. (USAF), LPN Trng.; [occ.] Licensed Practical Nurse; [memb.] DAV; [hon.] Several Plaques, Trophies, for writing; [oth. writ.] Number of poems published in books, number of children's stories, several articles; [pers.] I have always had a profound love of nature; I strive to indicate this in my poetry; [a.] Hamburg, Michigan 48139

THEYS, SHERI H.
[b.]September 19, 1977, Raleigh, NC; [p.]Linda and Bobby Mauldin; [ed.]Fuquay Varina High School; [occ.]Subway; [memb.]Key Club; [oth. writ.]Published in "A View From The Edge" and "Distinguished Poets of America"; [pers.]I'd like to thank my parents and my best friend Christy, Especially would like to thank my fiance, Clint Dean. I love you.; [a.] Fuquay, Varina, NC 27526.

THIBODEAU, MARYANN B.
[b.]September 18, 1937, Westbrook, Maine; [p.]Raymond and Arle Bean; [m.]Paul R. Thibodeau Sr., May 30, 1959; [ch.]Paul Jr. (U.S. Army) and Wendi L. (Deceased); [ed.]Clinton High, Grey Business College, Maine; [occ.]Housewife; [hon.]Editor's Choice Award, National Library of Poetry; [oth. writ.]Poem, "Beauty In The Roses" in the National Library of Poetry's "Where Dreams Begin"; [pers.]I like to write what ever I feel at the time of my writings. I have never tried to be published in my "40" some years of writing but finally decided to in Oct. 92.; [a.] Minot, N. Dakota 58701.

THOMAS, ALFRED A
[Pen.] Al Thomas; [b.]April 23, 1942, Birmingham, Alabama; [p.] (one living) mother-Luvenia Thomas; [ed.]High School - G.E.D.; [occ.]Checker on Roadway Express freight dock; [memb.]International Society of Poets; [hon.]Golden Poet, Honorable Mentions, Quality Award for a poem published at work; [oth. writ.]I have over 100 poems typed that I would like to publish in a book. One poem was published in a book. One poem was published in a district newsletter. Two poems in a woman's church news letter; [pers.]I desire to promote love and peace from Goad and as friends and countrymen we share. God is my #1 inspiration; [a.] Norcross, GA 30093.

THOMAS, ERMINIA PIA
[Pen.]Mini; [b.]February 19, 1928, Great, NY; [p.]Marx and Antonina Perugini; [m.]Elisseus John Thomas, November 19, 1955; [ch.]John, Gregory, Gina, Grand daughter Michelle; [ed.]9th grade, 1942/43; [occ.]Pen and Pencil Lab Tester (Eagle Pens and Pencil Co., NYC), United Parcel NY (IBM Key Punch); [hon.]Wife and mother are the greatest; [pers.]Love to write, cook, and exercise best. Love children, Husband, Sis. Noke and Friends, my 2 dogs, 3 children and granddaughter Michelle (new baby). Tanto Tanto, I made it!! Arise O' God, judge the earth, for you shall inherit all nations.; [a.] Carson, California 90745.

THOMAS, JAMES A.
[Pen.]James Arthur; [b.]June 14, 1951, Bryan, TX; [p.]Frank & Geneva Perry; [m.]Margaret Thomas, September 14, 1984; [ch.]Jaime Rose, Jocelyn, Roselyn, Thodecia, Jasmine, Yamonte; [ed.]Prairie View A&M University, Texas Southern University, LaSalle Institute; [occ.]Office of the Texas State Chemist Technician I; [memb.]New Poets, American Artist, Jungians, Smithsonian Institute; [hon.]Golden Poet 1990 and 1992, Who's Who in Poetry 1992, Poet of the Month (Legacy Magazine); [oth. writ.]Anthology of Black Writers in Houston, "Proverbs and Verses", and many other creative writings; [pers.]Love...the bitter sweet truth...in us all.; [a.] Bryan, TX 77801

THOMAS, JANETTE C.
[Pen.] J. Crowder Thomas, Jaycee C. Thomas; [b.] August 12, 1939, Wadesboro, NC; [p.] deceased; [m.] divorced; [ch.] Willette Del Payta, Dana Simore, Ana Arlette, William Isaac, Lena Cecile; [ed.] Graduate Public Schools, Columbus, OH, Ohio Dominican College; [occ.] Health Center Administration (retired); [memb.] Associate Minister, Refuge Baptist Church, Fort Hayes Career Center, Medical Assistant Program Advisory Bd, Columbus Public Schools; Interdenominational Prison Ministry Group; [hon.] Marian English Community Service Award, United Way; Years of Service Awards, DCSC; Years of Service Award, St. Stephens Community House; Volunteer Service Awards, Rosemont Center; Prisons Ministry Awards, Linden Youth Service Award, World of Poetry Awards; [oth. writ.] Several poems published by World Poetry. Many unpublished poems used in obituaries, church papers, personal gifts; [pers.] I strive for a holistic approach to life in my writings as well as my daily living. My writings are an expression of my soul's desire for the good of and the unification of all men to live together in peace; [a.] Columbus, OH

THOMAS, MAXINE
[b.]April 13, 1925, Gunnison, UT; [p.]Parley Kimball and Emily Tanner Jensen; [m.]James LaDell Taylor, May 14, 1944, Presently married to Elmer Thomas; [ch.]Myron, Howard, Ron, Randy and Connie; [ed.]High School; [occ.]Retired, Immediate past Duchesne County Treasurer; [pers.]This poem is dedicated to Howard who is paraplegic. He oversees an 80 acre ranch in Loma, Colorado. He has a wonderful sense of humor, lots of courage and endurance. He lives with his wife and 4 children.; [a.] Duchesne, UT 84021.

THOMPSON, BRENDA GENTRY
[b.]Calhoun, Georgia; [p.]J. R. Gentry and Ruth Gentry Anderson; [ed.]Calhoun High School, Dalton College, A.S. Business Administration, University of TEnnessee, B.S. Business Administration; [memb.]Alpha Honorary Scholastic Society; International Society of Poets; [hon.]Editor's Choice Award

"The Infinite Mile", The National Library of Poetry; [oth. writ.]"The Infinite Mile" National Library of Poetry; "Kindred Souls" Amherst Society; [pers.]Life and nature continually offer us much inspiration and many opportunities to express our creativity. I humbly strive to rise to that challenge.; [a.] Dalton, Georgia.

THOMPSON, ELIZABETH ANNE
[b.] February 25, 1979, Akron, OH; [p.] Lyle M. Thompson (Jr) and Cynthia Crowell Thompson; [ed.] Graduated as Salutatorian from Holderness Central School; [occ.] Student, Plymouth Regional High School, Plymouth, NH; [memb.] International Order of the Rainbow for Girls; [hon.] Various academic and athletic awards, as well as awards in public speaking; [oth. writ.] A poem published in the anthology, "Where Dreams Begin", also through the National Library of Poetry; [pers.] Life is just like a river, while it is most often slow and meanders, other times it forks, providing you with many options on the way, but the whole time, be it dangerous or calm, the river of life remains beautiful, but the beauty lies within. You must find it in yourself to move along with the current to discover what lies around the next bend; [a.] Holderness, NH

THOMPSON, JENNIFER L.
[b.]June 29, 1969, Baton Rouge, LA; [ed.]B.S. in General Management from Louisiana State University, August 1, 1991; [occ.]Library Technician I for the east Baton Rouge parish Library; [oth. writ.]Several poems published in other anthologies; [pers.]A negative outlook will make life either too long or too short. I try to reflect this is my writings.; [a.] Zachary LA 70791.

THOMPSON, MANDALIE
[b.]September 30, 1910, Colgate, Wis; [p.]Frank and Ann Bulgrin (deceased); [m.]L. G. Thompson, December 30, 1944; [ch.]Timothy & Cheryl; [ed.]High School and Business College; [occ.]Steno-Sec.; [oth. writ.]Group of Poems; [a.] Aptos, CA 95001

THORNHILL, ELROY
[b.]November 29, 1925, St. Charles, MO; [p.]Roy Dale Thornhill and Esther Mae Thornhill; [m.]Juanita Thornhill, March 15, 1948; [ch.]Anita, Danny, David, Kathy; [ed.]Life itself, 68 years; [occ.]Farmer, Engineer, Writer; [oth. writ.]Over 100 songs sung in France, Germany, Netherlands, Denmark, England and Australia as well as the USA; [pers.]I strive to write the truth about life for our youth, prisoners, underprivileged and all those who have been denied and unexposed as well as renew memories to our aged.; [a.] Rolla, MO 65401

TIBBS, PAUL J.
[Pen.]Just Me; [b.]December 9, 1953, Cape Girardeau, MO; [p.]Lillian R. Tibbs; [m.]Sherry A. Tibbs; [m.]December 18, 1972; [ch.]James; [ed.]Ash Grove Grade and High School, Ash Grove, MO: [occ.]Human Resources; [oth. writ.]"The Sword & The Beast" published by the National Library of Poetry.; [a.] Lee's Summit, MO 64063.

TIEN, JENNY
[Pen.] Robin, Jin-Jin, and M&M; [b.] April 17, 1979, Malaysia (one of the islands); [p.] Sin Lam (mother) and Michael Tien (Father); [m.] not married; [ed.] Will be attending Falls Church High School in the fall; [occ.] school; [hon.] Presidential Academic Fitness Award; [pers.] Dedicated to all the guys I ever loved; [a.] Falls Church, VA

TIFFANY, BARBARA J.
[Pen.]Barbara Morgan Tiffany; [b.]May 27, 1932, Battle Creek, Michigan; [p.]Paul M. Morgan and Kathryn Abbey Morgan; [m.]Terry A. Tiffany, August 4, 1951; [ch.]Tamara R. Jackson, Lisa K. Jones; [ed.]High School; [occ.]Antique Dealer; [memb.]Humane Society; [hon.]Best Letter Award, local newspaper; [oth. writ.]Local newspaper, published poem Sparrowgrass Poetry Forum, and others, Nat. Library of Poetry.; [pers.]Greatly influenced by the writings of Anne Morrow Lindbergh, "to communicate is the essence of relationship." "It is relationship!"; [a.] Battle Creek, MI 49017.

TILLINGHAST, WILLIAM P.
[b.] February 29, 1916, Mount Vernon, NY; [p.] Harold M. Tillinghast, Dorothy P. Tillinghasty; [m.] Loraine Gregg Tillinghast (dec), December 27, 1941; [ch.] Janet Fitzpatrick, Susan Padin; [ed.] AB Harvard 1940 in English, in US Army Air Force 1942-1946 as weather observer - meteorology; [occ.] Administrative positions in Gannett Newspapers in NY, Personnel Director; [memb.] Retired in 1974; [hon.] Deans List; Golden Poet of the Year for 1989; [oth. writ.] One book of poetry published in 1985, "Recollections" and other poems. Various poems in several newspaper and magazines; [pers.] Am a lover of all the Arts - poetry and music especially. Have many hobbies like meteorology, chess, games of strategy, bird watching. Without the Arts, the world would be a wasteland!; [a.] Pelham, NY

TINIO, ELEANOR CALASARA
[b.]September 5, 1974, Beloit, WI; [p.]Ricardo and Marilu Tinio; [ed.]Davenport North High School, University of Iowa; [hon.]Editor's Choice Award, National Library of Poetry; [oth. writ.]The Doll; Deadly Shadow; [a.] Davenport, Iowa 52806.

TIPPIN, JENNIFER DIANE
[Pen.]Jenny Regnarts; [b.]July 6, 1975, Greencastle, IN; [p.]Larry and Lisa Tippin (Sister, Cristina Tippin); [ed.]North Putnam High School, Indiana University, Purdue University at Indianapolis; [occ.]Journalism Student; [hon.]Presidential Academic Achievement, Academic Honors, High School Government Award, Outstanding Choral Student, National Honor Society Medal; [oth. writ.]Several poems and essay. One short story.; [pers.]I like to write about people, places, and things everyone can relate to reading should please the soul.; [a.] Coatsesvill, IN 46121.

TOLVTVAR, LORELEI LOUISE
[b.]April 12, 1955, San Francisco, California; [p.]Leona and Paul Hedon (stepfather); [m.]Wilhelm C. Tolvtvar, June 15, 1957; [ch.]3, Daniel, Ronald and Liane; [ed.]High School, graduated 1954, 1 yr. Merritt Business School, Oakland, CA. Two or 3 years of recreation art., 2 yrs. college, Art; [occ.]Clerk typist, Treasure Island, CA; [memb.]ABWA Path Finder Chapter, Fremont, CA; Pleasanton Art League, Pleasanton Women's Club, Volunteer Auxiliary; [hon.]A plaque awarded 3rd place 1970 City of San Leadro for a contest (Hawaii theme) numerous other awards in ceramics w/c and oil, 1989 3rd Place in Photography Alameda County Fair, 1991-1992 Best of Show w/c General Federation of Women's Club and numerous awards, 1st 2nd third and Honorable Mention in Christmas Craft, Ceramics etc., Honorable Mention in Poetry and Golden Poet Award Certificate; [oth. writ.]Poetry published, numerous books, from World of Poetry Press published in Who's Who in Poetry Vol. III Printed 1991, "Linens and Lace #1. Also a poem published in World Treasury of Poems "Magic of the Wind" Most recently a poem published in Treasured Poems of America Summer 1993, Sparrowgrass Poetry Forum, Inc., Poem Oh! The Train; [pers.]Someone once said to me; "What is there to see going down the road?" It isn't, there is color, beautiful trees, wild life and much more if you take the time to see.; [a.] Pleasanton, CA 94566.

TOMAINO, JOSEPH R.
[b.] March 7, 1920, Campbell, OH; [p.] Joseph P. Tomaino, Clara Nuzzo Tomaino; [m.] Mary Y. Tomaino, May 8, 1944; [ch.] Kathleen M. Kopala, Joseph Roy Tomaino, John R. Tomaino; [ed.] Westinghouse H.S., U of Pgh, Purdue Univ, Marine Corps, Engrg School; [occ.] Trade School Instructor, Comm. College Instructor, Refrig and Air Cond Repairman; [memb.] Marine Corps League, V.F.W., Amer. Legion, ITAM, DAV, Moose Lodge; [hon.] Purple Heart, Golden Poet for 1991-92 from World Poetry Organization; [oth. writ.] War experiences published in the book "Voices". Songs recorded by Joey Records Co; [pers.] I strive to put my heartfelt feelings into words. Joyce Kilmer poems are my favorite; [a.] Monroeville, PA

TORPILA, FRANK T.
[b.]December 21, 1951, New Jersey; [p.]Frank and Ann; [ed.]yes; [occ.]Artist; [hon.]Poetry and artistic achievements; [oth. writ.]Wolf Tales Red Wrapped Rose; Like Wow LA Fornarina; Eyes For You Wishes; Girl In Window; Wonderin; Prayer; Foul Weather Blues; Blue Ball Blues; Santa..If You Would; Red Wrapped Rose; Blues To Rose; Rose Marie; Star Gazer; Bananas; Wishes; Hard For You; Questions; Turmoil; [pers.]Thanks to Rose Marie Calla for inspiring me.; [a.] Trenton, NJ 08610.

TORRENCE, NORMAN
[Pen.]Norma Torrence (wife); [b.]October 20, 1926 (deceased), South Bend, Indiana; [p.]Howard Hamilton, Edna Hamilton (deceased); [m.]Norma Torrence writing for deceased Norman Torrence, May 25, 1973; [ch.]Kent H. Turner (son), Jeane VanLear, Neblett Montague and Katherine Feldmann (stepdaughters); [ed.]Jefferson High School, Mary Washington College; [occ.]Medical Transcriptionist in medical records, many hospitals (25 years); substitute church organist, teacher piano and organ; [memb.]Elected to be in American Guild of Organists (an honor, did not do this). Active in Hammon Organ Society; [hon.]In Daughters of The King-A National Order in Episcopal Church (an honor); Byliners in Corpus Christi, writer's assoc., Dean's List college, In International Society of Poets and an award by The National Library of Poets. Three certificates of Appreciation for volunteer work done in Retirement Homes. Poem about the Lexington ship docked in Corpus Christi is in their archives.; [oth. writ.]Poems published in our retirement monthly Tid-Bits here; [pers.]I strive to live for God, and his dear son, Jesus, and try to bear witness to this in my life to the best of my ability, as in music and poetry and in my eventful life as I have lived it.; [a.] Corpus Christi, TX 78401.

TOTH, JOANNE
[b.]September 14, 1941, Akron, Ohio; [p.]Michael Angelo Toth and Mary Knost Toth; [ed.]Rootstown High School, Professional Career Development Institute; [occ.]Animal care-giver, Verde Valley Humane Society; [memb.]Verde Valley Humane Society; [oth. writ.]Articles for local newspapers; [pers.]I believe we are all God's children. We need not suffer. Death is not something to be feared. It is a beautiful experience.; [a.] Cottonwood, AZ 86326.

TOWNES, CORRELL LOUNDERMAN
[b.] February 13, 1947, Danville, VA; [p.] Graham Lounderman, Sr, Fannie Lounderman; [m.] Jesse J. Townes, July 14, 1984; [ch.] Nekita Picole, Jesse William IV; [ed.] John M. Langston High, Johnson C. Smith Univ, Univ of N.C., Greensboro; [occ.] Health and Physical Education Teacher - Danville Public Schools, Danville, VA; [memb.] Charister - Shiloh Baptist Church, Senior Choir, Vice Pres - Danville Alumni Chapter, Delta Sigma Theta Inc, member, DEA/VEA/NEA; [hon.] Golden Poet Award/World of Poetry 1989-92, several poems published by World of Poetry; [oth. writ.] Master's Thesis won an award 1976 (only work at the time in physical ed with a dance concentration); [pers.] I write from personal experience and observations of the world we live in. I strive to print out the ability of mankind to rise above hardship to succeed in life; [a.] Danville, VA 24540

TOYER, DAVID K.
[b.]January 2, 1977, Everett Washington; [p.]Richard and Jean Ann Toyer; [ed.]1993-1994 I will be a Junior in High School (Lake Stevens High School); [occ.]Student; [memb.]Basketball 1993, Lake Stevens Junior Athletic Assoc., Ebenezer Lutheran Church, American Field Service (AFS) Been in several plays. I am Santa Claus at Winter Concert each year.; [hon.]Varsity Golf Letter, Page for House of Representatives, Honor Roll; [oth. writ.]Poems: Magical Spring, Prejudice, Friends Are, My First girl; [a.] Snohomish, Washington 98290.

TRAYLOR, HAROLD AUBREY
[b.]May 13, 1912, Repton, Kentucky; [p.]Holbert W. Traylor and Vera Anna Summers Traylor; [m.]Josephine Ida Traylor, June 26, 1959; [ch.]None by this marriage; [ed.]One year college; [occ.]Semi retired, part time employee U.S. Forest Service; [memb.]Southern Baptist Church and The John Birch Society; [hon.]Several awards from U.S. Forestry Service; [oth. writ.]Some one hundred poems and two volumes on family and national heritage; [pers.]I have a deep conviction that our people, our nation, must return to a fundamental belief in God and a return to the Constitutional form of government if we are to survive as a free people. A republic, if you please, not a democracy; [a.] Onyx, CA 93255

TREECE, REBECCA HOBBS
[b.] November 8, 1974, Richmond, VA; [p.] Leonard and Elsie Hobbs; [m.] Scott Treece, April 16, 1993; [ed.] Middlesboro High; [oth. writ.] My first poem written was published in the book Where Dreams Begin, the title was "Little Things"; [pers.] Always believe in yourself. A special thanks to my Senior English teacher Miss Linda Leach for encouraging me to write. And a special thanks for my family's support; [a.] Middlesboro, KY 40965

TRESTER, EVELYN V.
[Pen.] Paige M. Anthony; [b.] October 1, Fairfax, VA; [p.] Leonard and Julia Trester; [ed.] Lake Braddock HS and additional; [occ.] Student; [memb.] First Baptist Church of Springfield, Choirs (private); [hon.] Various honor rolls, Reflections '91, received personal letter; [hon.] From author Piers Anthony; [oth. writ.] Various short stories and poetry. I am currently writing a novel; [pers.] I am aware that the subject of love, romance is quite over used; yet as I am a hopeless romantic, can you blame me? [a.] Burke, VA

TRIMALDI, ANGELA H. CARINI
[b.] February 23, 1963, Brooklyn, NY; [p.] Enrico Carini and Anna Maria Carini; [m.] Robert Michael Trimaldi, September 29, 1991; [ch.] Vincenzo Enrico Trimaldi; [ed.] B.A. Social Sciences Minor, Youth Agency Adm.; [occ.] Communications Consultant; [memb.] Parents Coalition Against Violence on Television N.A.F.E.; [hon.] NYC Public Schools, Chancellor's Roll of Honor, Pace University Dean's List, Kiwanis International; [oth. writ.] Orchids and Daffodils, A Lyrical Bouquet, Selected Works of Our World's Best Poets, Poems and short stories in literary magazines throughout high school; [pers.] In loving memory of my husband, Robert, whose smile and love will forever shine through; [a.] Brooklyn, NY 11214

TROCOLLI, BARBARA ANN TUNGL
[Pen.] Barbara - Ann; [b.] June 1, 1938, Hungary, Europe; [p.] Alex and Barbara Tungly; [m.] John J. Trocolli, November 13, 1985; [ch.] one, Agi; [ed.] Music Conservatory, Business Col., Dr.' Nurs.; [occ.] Composes, Pianist, Teacher, Dancer, Dr.s Nurs.; [memb.] ASCAP, American Society of Composers, Authors and Publishers, NYC, American Assoc. of Doctors Nurses; [hon.] Entertainers Awards in Budapest, Hungary, Golden Poet 1991-1993; [oth. writ.] My Compositions of Music, also my poems. Hungarian folklore stories in several New york City Newspapers, etc...also a special gypsy pianist; [pers.] Nice to be important but more important to be nice; [a.] Las Vegas, NV 89121

TROTINER, SYLVIA ANFANG
[b.]September 1, 1922, NYC, NY; [p.]Charles Anfang and Mary Goldstein Anfang (brothers, Arnold and Marvin); [m.]David Trotiner, December 25, 1947; [ch.]Alan Robert and Mark Harold wed to Laurie Latham, grandchildren: Melissa, Susan, Rose; [ed.]Tilden H.S., Brooklyn College, Hunter College (Night Sessions); [occ.]Secretary, Union Officer, Teacher, Staff of Queens Borough Public Library in NY; [memb.]Hadassah, Bnai Brith, AARP, Retires Assn. ASH; [hon.]Arista Assoc. Editor Yearbook, Choir Laurelton Jewish Center, Secretary QBPL Local 1321 AFSCME; [oth. writ.]Poetry published "Anthology of World Poetry", book "Everything is All Mixed Up". Articles, columns in varied publications. Correspondence with Israel's Prime Minister Menachem Begin; [pers.]The love of writing is reflected in my novel, letters, poetry, songs, short stories, playlets. I seek to convey the emotions and striving of mankind in a diverse world; [a.] Jamaica, NY 11413

TUCKER, JANICE LEE
[b.]October 12, 1937, Huntington, WV (Cabell County); [p.]Harry Lee Grant & Dorothy E. Grant; [m.]divorced; [ch.]Penelope, (twins) Heather & Holly and Craig also 5 grandchildren Meghan, Andrew, Greg, Aaron and Tim; [ed.]Huntington East High, Huntington School of Business, Cabell County Vo-Tech Center, attended Marshall University; [occ.]Secretary, Director of Voc. Ed., Cabell County Vocational Center, Huntington, WV; [memb.]20th Street Baptist Church Decorating Comm., Steele Singles Group, Single Points Group; [hon.]Many awards and 9 publications 1991 Golden Poets Award received in NY City, a cassette album featuring my poem 1992. Honorary Charter Member of International Poets Society For Outstanding Achievement in Poetry 1992, Who's Who in Poetry 1993.; [oth. writ.]Poem written for 20th Street Baptist Church 100 year anniversary and placed in the corner stone. Peace poem written for the United Nations for the Worlds largest poetic work. I have written for many of my friends; [pers.]I write to show the world of peace and love that comes from within and overflows touching those that wish to find the beauty of mankind and striving to make a better world by stirring the souls of man; [a.] Barboursville, WV 25504

TUCKER, VIRGINIA WYNNE
[Pen.]VA-Wyn-Tue; [b.]January 14, 1941, Williamston, NC; [p.]Willie M. Wynne and Mary Louise (Lula) Rawls Wynne; [m.]Charles J. Tucker, May 5, 1963; [ch.]Steven, Jeffrey, Bonnie and 4 grandchildren, Dustin, Chuck, Ashley and J.T.; [occ.]Switchboard Operator, Hancock Bank, Gpt, MS; [oth. writ.]God Walks With Me, published by National Library of Poetry (A Break in the Clouds); [pers.]My writings are from the heart. They seem to become a part of me. I sometimes think they express the emotions of the person within; [a.] Long Beach, MS 39560

TURBYFILL, LORI
[b.]October 5, 1966, Raleigh, NC; [p.]David H. Fuquay, Jr. and Harriet P. Fuquay; [m.]Joseph D. Turbyfill, December 28, 1985; [ed.]Garner Sr., High School, Graduated 1984. Some college courses taken at Wake Tech Community College and Johnston Community College; [occ.]Secretary IV, State of NC; Dorothea Dix Hospital, Raleigh, NC; [memb.]N.C. State Employees Assoc.; [oth. writ.]Poetry published by: Quill Books, "All My Tomorrows", Pacific Rim Publications, "Quest For A Dream", National Library of Poetry "On The Threshold of a Dream" Vol. III. ANIH. Ser., Nat'l. Library of Poetry "Coming of Down;" [pers.]My poetry reflects my personal feelings. My desire is that others will relate as they too have shared such. Jim Morrison's poetic abilities has been an inspiration to me; [a.] Raleigh, NC.

TURNER, JENNY
[b.]April 3, 1980, Pontiac, IL; [p.]Joan and Tom Turner; [ed.]Washington Elementary School; Pontiac Jr. High School; [memb.]Church, Girl Scouts, Jr. High Band, Art Camp; [hon.]Editor's Choice Award, Band Contest Awards, Art Awards, Grade Honors; [oth. writ.]unpublished stories poems and plays; [pers.]My writing is what I feel and from experience my last poems were inspired by a fight and then make-ups with my best friend; [a.] Pontiac, IL 61764.

TURNER, STEVEN PRICE
[Pen.] Jules Longman; [b.] July 9, 1948, Los Angeles, CA; [occ.] Private Investigator, Poet, Short

Stories, Letters; [hon.] Offered Listing, Oxford's Book of Who's Who 1992, 3 time Golden and Silver Poet, 5 Certificates of Merit, twice published; [oth. writ.] Peace Offering, Whenever A Poet Dies, The Rat Up In The Rafter, Sierra, many others; [pers.] Honesty, unity, mercy, activity, neighborly, equality, (humane) words we all need more of; [a.] Crestline, CA

TYLER, FRANCINE M.
[Pen.] Francine Madeleine Tyler; [b.] August 9, 1929, Rochester, NY; [p.] Rebecca Paoseus de Fere, Roland F. de Fere; [m.] July 22, 1950; [ch.] Two boys, two girls; [ed.] Scripps College Claremont, CA; [occ.] Homemaker; [hon.] 1 Golden Poet Award, 1 Honorable Mention; [pers.] I like this definition of a poet: "A poet is one who has a thought, or thoughts, images, words and phrases that take control of him (her) and in order to be himself (herself) again. She writes the poem; [a.] Mah Wah, NJ 07430

TYNER, DORIS WYONA
[b.] November 17, 1939, Hartsville, SC 29550; [p.] Harrison and Marion Tyner; [m.] Divorced; [ch.] James Dale Lewis; [ed.] G.E.D. as of 5/93; [occ.] Unemployed; [memb.] Songwriters Club of America (lifetime member); [hon.] Golden Poet Award (1985-1992), Who's Who in Poetry, two poems put to music (45 rpm and cassette), Lead sheets for first two poems put to music; First Poem was rated #3 on a chart of 30 evaluation chart; First two poems won songwriters award and certificate; All poems ranked honorable mention; 1981 member of the Top Records Songwriters Association; [oth. writ.] Poems published: Dear Lord We Want To Thank You, I'll Love You The Rest Of My Days, My One Desire In Life, My True Feelings, Thank You Lord, God's beautiful Children, A Shining Light For Jesus, Darling, A Christian Life, To Be Your Loving Wife, To George With Love; [pers.] The Lord deserves all the credit He gave me the words to write.; [a.] Hartsville, SC 29550

UNANGST, ELIZABETH B.
[Pen.] Betty Unangst; [b.] July 11, 1918, Edgewater Park Twp. (N.J.); [p.] Mina and Elton Horner both deceased; [m.] Deceased, married 1st 1935, 2nd 1959, 3rd 1977; [ch.] Samuel, William, Elton, Force, Elizabeth Force Salber; 10th grade (8 grammar Beverly, NJ., 2 high school Burlington, NJ); [occ.] Retired; [memb.] Senior Citizens (Riverside) Riverside Moose (279), Delanco Fire House Aux.; [hon.] Honorable Mention from World of Poetry, Golden Poet (1991) World of Poetry; [oth. writ.] Ten other poems to World of Poetry; [pers.] Thank you for remembering me. I am anxious to see at least one of my poems in your book. I have many.; [a.] Riverside, NJ.

UPSHAW, GRAYCE B.
[Pen.] Grayci; [b.] March 28, 1938, Nyack, NY; [p.] Earl S. (Sip), Blackburn, Magaret (Peg) Quill Blackburn; [m.] Bob, (2nd) 1980; [ch.] Kelly Marle, Douglas Wayne, Scott Aneritt, Lloyd Earl, Stepchildren: Robert Jeffrey, Lori Jean; [ed.] Ft Lauderdale High, Boward Community College, Advanced Coronary Care; [occ.] Registered Nurse, also own hardware store; [memb.] Former Instructor EMT, also AHA, active in Merchant's Assn, Condo Assn Board; [hon.] Several awards for poetry; [oth. writ.] 1) Formerly wrote daily column, Women's page for newspaper in Titusville, most notable was 6 part series on AA, 2) Trade Magazines; [pers.] I want the world to know that I was here and that I made a difference. My best friends are in my family - husband, children, and sister. We help one another to achieve, I am most proud of that; [a.] Ft Lauderdale, FL 33324

VADALA III, JOHN E.
[b.] September 8, 1966, Portsmouth, NH; [p.] John E. Vadala, Jr (Jack) and Elizabeth A. Vadala; [m.] Bonnie A. Vadala, June 19, 1993; [ed.] BS in Business Administration - minor Human Relations from New Hampshire College; [occ.] Retail Store Manager for CVS, Inc - a drug retailer; [memb.] 2nd VP NH College Board of Directors, and a member of the Alumni Advisory Committee; [hon.] Graduated Cum Laude in 1990 from NH College; [oth. writ.] I have currently 70-80 other poems and phrase work, of which some earlier work has been published in local newspapers and privately published magazines; [pers.] Poetry is the sculpture of words into art, that captivates both reader and writer, and then sets them free. My inspiration and my mentor - Robert Frost's works and writings; [a.] Newmarket, NH 03857

VALLEJO, JOSIE LEA
[b.] February 13, 1971, Fresno, CA; [p.] Rogelio Vallejo and Marita A. Vallejo; [ch.] Cassandra A. Perez; [ed.] Sanger High, Barclay College; [occ.] Security Officer; [hon.] Golden Poet Awards for 1991 and 1992; [pers.] My poetry is made of pure feelings and emotions in my life, which becomes my poetry written from the heart; [a.] Sanger, CA 93657

VAN DYKE, ELINOR FLOYD
[Pen.] Elinor Van Dyke; [b.] June 6, 1929, Orlando, Florida; [p.] Linton E. Floyd, Jr. and Elinor Melton Floyd; [m.] Joseph H. Van Dyke, June 6, 1949; [ch.] Holly (Mrs. J. A. Cummings), Cliff Van Dyke, Lynn (Mrs. R. L. Johnson), seven grandchildren; [ed.] Fletcher High School, Jax Beach, FL, Wesleyan College (3 years); [occ.] Homemaker, Exec. Family Business until 1979, Retailer, Admin. Asst. Florida, Reagan for President Campaign, Political Party Campaign Manager; [memb.] Nat'l. Society, Daughters of Am. Revolution, Repub. Party of FL, Chrmn., Dist. 4, (Congressional Dist. 4) 1981-86, State Committee 1980-1988, Delegate Rep. Nat'l. Convention 1980-84; [hon.] Florida Eagle of Year 1989, Frequent Guest Speaker, Various service awards, St. John's County, Rep. Women of St. John's, Honorable Mention World of Poetry 1993; [oth. writ.] "Mr. Spats" Children's Series, 1945, Beaches Leader (weekly) Remembrances, History pieces, innumerable speeches, press releases campaign literature, etc., "Star Spangled Anthem", World of Poetry; [pers.] Republican Party Activist, Upholding Constitutional American Values has been my mission for thirty years or more; [a.] Ponte Vedra Beach, FL

VAUGHAN, SARAH DANIEL
[b.] May 3, 1915, Logansport, Louisiana; [p.] Paul Foster Daniel and Roberta Neal Stubbs; [m.] LCDR Joe Brandon Vaughan, April 20, 1946 (deceased); [ch.] Joanne Vaughan, Virginia Vaughan Bollinger; [ed.] Tavares High School (FL), Lagrange College, GA, O'Hara School of Ikebana (Tokyo); [occ.] Retired Homemaker; [memb.] International Society of Poets; [hon.] One Silver Poet Award, Six Golden Poet Awards, Who's Who In Poetry Vol. III; [oth. writ.] "Infinity" published in Science of Mind July 1970, published in fifteen books--other poems; [pers.] I try to do unto others as I would have them do unto me; [a.] Greenbrier, TN 37073

VEGA, ODALIA C.
[b.] November 18, 1970, Dominican Republic; [p.] Marino and Victoria Santos; [m.] Edwin S. Vega (Shuggles), March 18, 1993; [ch.] In memory of our daughter Angelle Claret Vega (1993-1993); [ed.] BMCC, FTC; [occ.] Early Child ed and now I am a homemaker until furtehr notice; [oth. writ.] My 1st poem from last year was dedicated to my husband the oem was published under Where Dreams Begin; [pers.] I dedicate this poetry to the daughter we recently lost. Our daughter Angelle we will never forget loving you. Sleep well in heaven! I thank God that we had a little girl so special. I dedicate this poem to her, and our future children if God's willing. I realized how fortunate I am to have a wonderful husband, I love you my dear husband, always; [a.] Brooklyn, NY

VERDE, JOANNE
[b.] July 24, 1968, Bronx, NY [p.] Anthony F. Verde and Diana M. Verde; Fiance'- Larry Bischofsberger, Jr (hopefully fall'94/spring'95); [ed.] Carmel High; Westchester Community College (AAS-1988), Suny Albany (one year), Dutchess Comm College - still enrolled; [occ.] Development Specialist Putnam Associated Resource Centre Carmel, NY; [memb.] National Audubon Society, Dian Fossey Gorilla Fund; [hon.] Honorable Mention 2-3 years from World of Poetry. Various awards/honors throughout my school years. National Honor Society in high school; [oth. writ.] Poem "Mother Nature" published in a book. My goal is to publish my own book of poems and writings - some day in the near future; [pers.] I try to do the best I can to see the good in everyone. I just live one day at a time until I succeed, and I'll keep following the fire that burns within; [a.] Carmel, NY 10512

VERRILLI, JOSEPH
[b.] May 2, 1952, Bridgeport, CT; [p.] Leonard Verrilli, Lena Verrilli; [m.] Janet Ochs Verrilli, November 21, 1981; [ed.] Graduate of the Kolbe High School Class of 1970; [hon.] An Editor's Choice Award for a poem recently published by the National Library of Poetry; [oth. writ.] 3 poems published by Quill Books, a poem and short story published in Housatonic Community College's Beanfeast Magazine, a poem published in "Behind the Scene with Jennifer Brooks"; [pers.] To write is to relive episodes once forgotten. I have been influenced by the writings of Jack Kerouac, Barry Gifford, Richard Price and Bryan Ferry; [a.] Bridgeport, CT 06604

VILLANUEVA, MARGARITO
[b.] June 10, 1927, Scarbro, W.VA; [p.] Norberto Villanueva (father) and Annette Lewis (mother); [m.] Gullermina Acosta, December 7, 1957; [ch.] Herman A., Mark A., Michael and Annette; [ed.] High school, W.VA, Academic, Armed Forces Institute, (Military Service), Real Estate Graduate, Criminology (Armed Forces) Military Police Corp.; [occ.] Retired; [memb.] Post 7138 VFW, Norwalk, CA; [hon.] Military Service Only; [oth. writ.] My Loved One, published in Wind In The Night Sky (1993). Poetry in "Poetry an American Heritage, Western Poetry Assoc. in Colorado. Country Western Sun Writer; [pers.] 13732 S. Fairfield Ave., Norwalk, CA 90650-3716

VOGLER, ETHEL M.
[b.] March 17, 1932, Mound City, MO; [p.] Tom

Roop, Geneva Roop; [m.] Daniel W. Vogler, February 11, 1961; [ch.] Stephen Wayne, Betty Jo Richard Allen, James Daniel; [ed.] Fairfax RIII High School 3 yrs - High School Diploma from American School; [occ.] Nurses Assistant Community Hospital, Fairfax, Mo; [memb.] Baptist Church; [hon.] Dr. Frist, Humanitarian Award at Community Hospital - 1984, Golden Poet Award from World of Poetry - 1985 through 1989, Silver Poet Award from World of Poetry - 1990; [oth. writ.] 1 poem in each of these books our World's Most Cherished Poems - 1986 - World Poetry Anthology 1987 - Great Poems of Today - 1987 - Poems of Great America - 1989 - Great Poems of the Western World, Vol II 1990; [pers.] Jesus is Lord of all; [a.] Fairfax, MO 64446

VOLSCH, LOUIS L.
[b.]July 13, 19910, Hartford, South Dakota; [p.]Louie and Jessie Volsch; [m.]Ethel Del, July 8, 1930 (Deceased); [ed.]Grade 9; [occ.]Laborer (Retired); [memb.]AAA; [hon.]Award of Merit, World of Poetry 1990, The Governor of South Dakota placed my books in the Capital Library. They are available in all 50 States.; [oth. writ.]The Collected poem and autobiography of Louis L. Volsch. 2nd book, How to Write and Teach Poetry, By Louis L. Volsch...Also, letters, cards, short stories, autobiography; [pers.]Sorry, I am in a foul mood this morning. Forgive Dear Lord and help me through this day. I am weak and ask for help. Please guide me in my words and actions today. I don't want to make a bad mistake. Help me in my judgement of people I have to deal with.; [a.] Sioux Falls, SD 57104-1321.

VOORHEES, RAY NELSON
[Pen.] Same as above and "Ray of Light"; [b.] April 1, 1955, Stuben County, NY; [p.] Rev Joseph Robert Voorhees, Delores Ellen Voorhees; [m.] Single - wanna be!?; [ch.] Eldest son: Joshua Robert Michael Voorhees, Young son: Nicholas Ray Voorhees; [ed.] Stilwell Business Management School, Calvary Grace...Bible Institute. Dean's List; [occ.] Inventor, Artist, Composer, Singer, Songwriter, Story Teller, and Poet; [memb.] Evangel Temple Assembly of God Church and President: Alpha & Omega Society of Business Leaders; [hon.]Several Golden Poet Awards and A Silver Poet Award from World of Poetry. Published since 1985; [oth. writ.] A Silent Prayer, Garden Date, Grandpa Leads the Prayer, Everlasting Love, Beautiful You, Star Trek...The Most Amazing Adventure!, and The Willy Snatcher!; [pers.] The Truth is: All Decent Poetry. All beautiful poetry, all majestic poetry, and all splendifferous poetry, comes from the heart of God; [a.] Jacksonville, Fl 32236

WAGNER, ADELE LYNNE
[Pen.]A. Lynne Wagner; [b.]January 14, 1946, Springfield, MA; [p.]Thomas F. Darrah and Adele Darrah Fahey; [m.]William A. J. Wagner, August 2, 1969; [ch.]William, Karl, Kurt; [ed.]BSN, MSN, CAGS, Ed. University of Massachusetts; [occ.]Professor of Nursing, Family Nurse Practitioner; [memb.]ASPO/Lamaze, International Childbirth Education Association, American Public Heath Assoc., Association of Women's Heath Obstetric and Neonatal Nurses (AWHONN); [hon.]Sigma Theta Tau, Phi Kappa Phi, Sigma Theta Tau, Air Force Educator's Award, Coburn Award for Excellence in Research, University of Mass/Lowell, various excellence in Writing Awards; [oth. writ.]Poem, National Library of Poetry, A Break In The Clouds, 1993, an essay, National League of Nursing Press, Caring as Healing, Renewal Through Hope to be published in 1994; [pers.]Nature provides me with new perspectives as I am challenged by the ebb and tides of life; [a.] Chelmsford, MA 01824

WAGNER, GLEN
[Pen.] Earthman; [b.] January 19, 1949, San Francisco; [p.] Grover Karl Wagner, and Florence Irene Wagner; [m.] Angela Maria Wagner, December 27, 1987; [ch.] Adrianne Frances, Sarah Kay; John Russell; [ed.] Kofa High, Arizona Western College; Blunder Tech; [occ.] Electronics Technician; [memb.] Blockbusters; [hon.] At Phelta Thi, Deans List; [oth. writ.] Many! Equisitly tailored for, and friviolously distributed to the broke and down-trodden taxpayers; [pers.] I am compelled to promote the values of "basic truths", which are the integral foundation of the soul. Amused, shall be those whom recognize in it the Fellowship of Man, and offended shall be those whom cannot see in it. Inspirations: Woody Guthrie -- "My land I'll defend with my life if it be, For my Pastures of Plenty must always be free." Bob Dylan -- "Keep a clean nose. Watch the plainclothes. You don't need a weatherman, To know which way the wind blows."; [a.] Yuma, AZ

WAKEFIELD, LACY ELIZABETH
[Pen.] Lacy Elizabeth Geist; [b.] February 25, 1954, Salem MO; [p.] Floyd Geist and Stella Gabel; [m.] Richard A. Wakefield, July 3, 1993; [ch.] (1 boy) Aaron Michael Geist; [ed.] Graduate from the Salem Sr High School, Salem, Mo; [occ.] Housewife; [memb.] Salem Full Gospel Church Hwy 19 North Salem, MO, Pastor Robert Robinson; [hon.] Editor's Choice Awards for Outstanding Achievement in Poetry; [oth. writ.] When We See The Face of Jesus Our Lord; [pers.] These all have help and inspriration from God and help from my Church family to back me up. I just wish that some soul would be saved when they read these poems; [a.] Salem, MO

WALBORN, IAN
[Pen.] Ian; [b.] January 24, 1970; [b.] Mishawaka, IN; [p.] Ellie Martin; [m.] not married; [ed.] Coral Shores High; [occ.] Asst Manager of Local Cannery; [oth. writ.] I have many other writings only one published. My love for a girl. I just hope I find enough time some day to put a book together; [pers.] I try to put my feelings on paper. Sit sometime with your soul perched on your pen point open your mind release your heart. Then let your soul point you a new universe; [a.] Tavernier, FL

WALDEN, ELAYNE GOCEK
[b.] September 24, 1927, Archer, Florida; [p.] John and Zobia Gocek formally of Poland; [ch.] Lisa M. Walden and Granddaughter Eisa Nicole Murphy; [ed.] Archer High School, Louisville School of Art, Louisville KY; [occ.] Plant Maintenance, Bonsai, Fashion Designer Trades, Name (One of A Kind) Elayne the Fair; [hon.] World of Poetry and American Poetry Association and Kmart Customer Care Award; [oth. writ.] I have over 1,000 poems and songs inspired from God. Hopefully they will be published in book form; [pers.] Each one a sequel to the other. Basically the story of my life. First book "Gods Grace and Memories." Second book "Being with God in Every Thought." Third book "Without A Song, There Would Be No You." Fourth book "Weights That Become Wings In Flight."; [a.] Gainesville, FL 32603

WALDEN, LAUREL J.
[b.] October 12, 1973, Shelby Co, IL; [p.] Joan Walden and the late Hugh Walden, Jr; [ed.] Graduated with honors from Hadley School for the Blind, continuing education Hadley School; [occ.] Studying through Library of Congress for certification as braille proofreader while pursuing career as a pianist/vocalist in easy listening music; [memb.] Supporting member of Illinois Fiddlers' Assn and Friends of Libraries for the Blind and Physically Handicapped; [hon.] Was voted Student of the Year by faculty and staff of Hadley School (10-6-93); [oth. writ.] Assortment of unpublished poetry and songs; [pers.] A special thanks to the instructors at Hadley School, Winnetka, IL, who have encouraged and inspired me in my endeavor; [a.] Shelbyville, IL

WALKER, JAMES
[Pen.] Jimmy; [b.] February 24, 1962, Savannah, GA; [p.] Charlie H. (Deceased) and Sandra K; [m.] Single; [ed.] 12th grade, Richland Northeast High; [occ.] Correctional Officer, S.C. Dept. of Corrections, Frycook CuCo's; [hon.] Two Honorable Mentions, Poetry, Golden Poet 1992, Editor's Choice; [oth. writ.] The Dreams, Picture's in the Sand, both published 170 other's; [pers.] I write my songs/poem's through my heart, with inspirations of love by the special ladies in my life, Jaci W. Jami G., Abi R; [a.] Cola, SC 29223

WALKER, SHARON E.
[Pen.] Charlotte Marie Bronson; [b.] September 2, 1945, McAllen, TX; [p.] Mr. & Mrs. Doyle and Pearl Elliott; [m.] Billy Don Walker, December 23, 1964; [ch.] Tina, Kyle and Jason Walker; [ed.] Mission High School and Durham's Business College; [occ.] Nurses Aide; [memb.] Mission Hospital Auxillary; [hon.] Several honorable mentions through World of Poetry contests; [oth. writ.] Several poems published in anthologies for World of Poetry; [pers.] I have always strived to better myself; life a good life and love all mankind; [a.] Mission, TX

WALLACE, HUGH
[b.]January 5, 1923, Grove, Oklahoma; [p.]George Winston Wallace and Blaine Browning Wallace; [ed.]Aklai Jay Hi, S.E. State, Olkahoma University, ND University (Cadet) no Grad.; [occ.]Retired DOD.

WALLACE, JOHN A.
[Pen.]Jack Wallace; [b.]November 17, 1935, Akron, Ohio; [p.] Dorsey S. Wallace, Emma I. Wallace; [m.]Lorraine W. Wallace, December 29, 1956; [ch.]Patricia, Thomas, Judith; [ed.]High School, ICS and 2 yrs. college; [occ.]Industrial Engineer Tech.; [memb.]Penfield United Methodist Church, United Methodist Men, Penfield Vol Fire Dept.; [oth. writ.]Many poems, some songs and short stories. Wrote outdoor column for local newspaper; [pers.]I believe that the true beauty of poetry is achieved through simplicity; [a.] Penfield, PA 15849

WALSH, ZIONE
[b.] July 4, 1944, New York; [m.] Frank Farnacci; [ed.] BSEE (Electrical Engineer undergrad work in math and physics); [occ.] Owner of Comp Networking (An engineering house and consulting firm); [oth. writ.] "Listening for the Song of Life", 12/93 pub Dorrance Publishing Co; [pers.] The nature of living is to be realized in the act of living itself; [a.] New York, NY 10019

WARD, DOROTHY M.
[Pen.]Dorothy Miller Ward; [b.]May 23, 1925, Hamilton, Illinois; [p.]George and Lulae Miller; Glenn Melton Ward, September 3, 1946; [ch.]Michael Ward, Bill Pierre Ward, Pamela Sullivan, Melody Ward, Glenn Ward II; [ed.]Carthage College-Carthage, Illinois-Humboldt State University, Arcata, CA.; [occ.]Musicologist; [hon.]Golden Poet Award 1988, New American Poetry Anthology, Christ Saw Love, 1991 World Poetry Anthology, Violet Love, 1989 Days of futures Past; [pers.]Poetry should be published to be read and enjoyed, happily representing goodness for the world to see; [a.] Yucaipa, CA 92399.

WARNER, RUTH
[b.] October 6, 1923, Toledo, OH; [p.] David B. Edwards, Sr., Pearl (Beyer) Edwards; [m.] Neal E. Warner, October 27, 1945; [ch.] Craig A. Warner; [ed.] Woodward High School, Stautzenburger Secretarial School; [occ.] Housewife (former secretary); [memb.] Int Soc of Poets, Int Soc of Authors and Artists; [hon.] 1991 Golden Globe Award from World of Poetry, 1992 Golden Globe Trophy from World of Poetry, Four "Award of Merit" certificates from World of Poetry, 1993 International Poet of Merit Award from Int Soc of Poets; [pers.] During times of sadness, stress, or if injustices occur, writing a poem can be great therapy; [a.] Northwood, OH

WARREN, HOPE
[Pen.] Esperanza Vispera Warren; [b.] September 26, 1975, Portsmouth, Virginia; [p.] Kenneth Barry Warren Sr., and Gwyne Ellen Jeter; [ed.] High School diploma working on a doctorage of psychology; [hon.] Honors graduate in High School. Member of N.O.R.S.T.A.R.; [oth. writ.] Life (poem); [pers.] I now realize that no matter how far away I move, the love of my brother Kenny, my mother Gwyne, my Father Ken, and my Grandparents Richard, Phyllis and Virginia will be my guide through life. And is that which I cherish deeply.

WEAVER, JOSEPH A.
[Pen.] Joe Weaver, March 5, 1949; [b.] Punxsutawney, PA; [p.] John S. Weaver, Mary C. (O'Leary) Weaver; [m.] Debra L. Weaver, April 4, 1984; [ch.] Chad - Luke - Jason - Christine - Joseph Jr; [ed.] High School; [occ.] Flooring Retailer, owner - installer; [memb.] NRA, PSAA, Punxsutawney Sportsmans Club, Buck Masters; [oth. writ.] On The Threshold of a Dream, Vol III, over 30 in local newspaper; [pers.] With perseverance anything can be accomplished; [a.] Punxsutawney, PA

WEBB, AUDREY JEAN
[b.] September 26, 1930, Roanoke, Virginia; [p.] James Will Webb (father) and Celia Elizabeth Scyphers (mother); [m.] Divorced; [ch.] none; [ed.] A graduate of Central High in Chattanooga, TN, additional home studies too.; [occ.] Operator, Retired from Southern Bell Telephone Co.; [memb.] Christian Baptist, Past Member of Rasicrusian of A.M.O.R.C., Self Taught Musician of Piano and Guitar, use to sing choir, solo's and duets, etc.; [hon.] Minor and insignificant awards; [oth. writ.] "In God's Plan" and other poem's "Be Still" and "Created In God's Own Image", "Miraculous Transformation", "The Christmas Spirit Headset" "An Operator's Thanksgiving"; [pers.] Life is Short so do good. Show Love and Goodwill and be a peacemaker and forgive all. It starts in our homes. Parent's should teach their children this and live it in their lives so to show children the way. Peace and love in the world starts in the home.

WEBER, KERI KATHLEEN
[b.] June 27, 1977, Seattle, WA; [p.] Patrick and Kathleen Weber; [ed.] Attending Thomas Jefferson High School; [memb.] National Honor Society, French Club, Varsity Soccer for high school, varsity drill team, premier soccer team; [hon.] Scholar Athlete Award, Academic Letter Award; [oth. writ.] One other poem that I have written which was published in "On the Threshold of a Dream" was titled "Shane"; [a.] Auburn, WA 98001

WEBSTER, DEBBIE
[b.] July 4, 1959, Waverly, NY; [p.] Mary and the late Max Camp; [m.] Richard, July 1, 1978; [ch.] Stepchildren - Cynthia, Jimmy, wonderful Boxer dog - AJ; [ed.] Waverly High School, currently attending Corring Community College - Nursing; [oth. writ.] PoemJ "Evening" published in World Treasury of Great Poems; poem "Maxie" published in A break in the Clouds; [pers.] I would like to dedicate this poem to my sister, Paula; [a.] Waverly, NY

WEINACKER JR., CHARLES W.
[b.]February 21, 1948, Mobile, Alabama; [ch.]Two daughters, Michele and Amy; [occ.]The President of Essential Pet Products, Inc., of Alabama, a Wal Mart stores vendor, where Weinacker Licenses Essential Pet to produce exclusively his patented pet toys.; [memb.]The President of the Alabama Inventors Association, A Vietnam Veteran; [oth. writ.]Have written numerous poems about Mobile, New Orleans, Tampa, Atlanta and many more cities. These city poems are printed with sketches of old historic buildings associated with those cities. I enjoy all of the arts but enjoy inventing new products avidly; [pers.]The Poem, "Lady Bay" is a fiction about a historic lighthouse built in the mid 1800's.

WEINER, GLEE LOANN STEVENS
[Pen.]Glee; [b.]February 16, 1930, Long Prairie, MN; [p.]Lyle C. Stevens and Merry DuFrene Stevens; [m.]Arthur T. Weiner, May 13, 1949; [ch.]Cheryl, Dennis, Kenneth, Sharon, Steven; [ed.]Long Prairie High School, Art Instruction Inc.; [occ.]Artist, Doll Maker, Designer, Poet, Author, Song writer, Pianist, Lyricist, O.K. Carousel Horses.; [hon.]Golden Poet Award, Silver Poet Award, Certificate of Merit (Lyrics) and letters from Queen Elizabeth II, George and Barbara Bush, Dave Draveky, Danny Thomas Family and Helen Steiner Rice Foundation's personal recommendation for poetry; [oth. writ.]"Michael": in World Treasury of Great Poems and in World Treasury of Golden Poems. "The Reason": in Down Peaceful Paths. "To Grasp The Rose": in Poetic Voices of America, "The Bars": Chapel Records, "Llewellyns Yellow Rose": by Talent, "The Girld In The Red Velvet Swing": by East Coast Record Productions, also "One of Us": by East Coast Production, "That Old Old Wishin Well": by Country Western Sound City.; [a.] Sauk Centre, N 56378.

WEIR, MELODIE ANN
[b.] November 30, 1968, Elmhurst, IL; [p.] Jack and Jeannie Northcutt; [m.] divorced; [ch.] Robert David Weir (III); [oth. writ.] Two unpublished books, third in the making, Rainbows and Gold, Poetry in Motion. One poem published in One the Threshold of a Dream, Vol III; [pers.] To my parents for pushing me, and supporting me. And my son, Robert, the greatest joy of life; [a.] Richardson, TX

WEISHAAR, MARILYN MCQUEEN
[b.]May 19, 1930, Orange, Texas; [p.]Arthur T. and Florence McQueen; [m.]David Joseph, March 30, 1947; [ch.]David Lee and Ronald Joseph; [ed.]High School, College, Nurses Training; [occ.]Retired; [memb.]St. Mark Lutheran Church (Charter member) Financial Secretary; [hon.]Published in National Library of Poetry's "Wind in the Night Sky" with an Editor's Choice Award.; [oth. writ.]Authored a publication of a book of poetry entitled "Garden of the Mind" various local writings; [pers.]I can't remember a time when I did not love poetry. I believe life is a gift from God, to be lived and enjoyed to the fullest; [a.] Bridge City, TX 77611.

WEISKER, PATRICIA ANNE
[Pen.] PAW; [b.] October 24, 1949, Red Bluff, CA; [p.] Alfred Kaznowski, Betty Kaznowski; [m.] Conrad William Weisker, February 13, 1971; [ch.] Jason Conrad, Jared William, Karl Robert; [ed.] Rio Americano High School, American River College, Cosumnes River College; [occ.] Homemaker/Stewardess on Boat; [memb.] First Baptist Church, Herald, CA SS teacher, Sacramento Reads, SALC; [hon.] Honorable Mention for poem Dec 15, 1991, International Poet of Merit Award 1993; [oth. writ.] Poem published in 1986 and 1993 Herald Day Community Book; [pers.] My poetry is a reflection of the many blessings in my life, including family, friends, and community. I applaude ISP for this opportunity to share my poetry and hope it will be an encouragement to all; [a.] Galt, CA

WELLS, VIRGINIA THOMAS
[b.] December 12, 1937, Massaic County, Near Metropolis, IL; [p.] Pearl M. Thomas and Charles E. Thomas; [m.] James Douglass Wells, June 2, 1979; [ch.] Gini Gay Grace and Tracy Lynn Grace; [ed.] I took writing classes at Paducah Community College, KY; [occ.] Free Lance Writer, formerly Banking and Real Estate; [memb.] P.C.C. Writer's Group, Western KY Writers Association; [oth. writ.] Published writings, short stories, Q.V.C., Very Strange, A Time To Read Poetry, Day

Poetry, Love's Memory, Adonis of LA, Parking Space, Men at War, Lady Clown; [pers.] When I started to write poetry, I write about love. Love was all. Now I see that the road to love and family contains many complexities and hidden elements. Now I am searching the area of human relationships.

WERTH, AMANDA
[Pen.] Nada; [b.] March 19, 1979, Appleton, WI; [p.] Thomas Werth and Theresa Werth; [hon.] I was invited to be a member of the International Society of Poets; [oth. writ.] I had one poem published in the 1993 anthology, Wind In The Night Sky; [pers.] How many minds are wasted in the birth of the ancestroy division, slightly ironic in the sense of forgotten longings placed in the communal mind of the forever young?; [a.] DePere, WI 54115

WHALEN, AMY M.
[b.] June 7, 1968, Point Pleasant, NJ; [p.] Catherine Boehm, Bernard Whalen, Charles Boehm, Karen Whalen; [ed.] BA Old Dominion Univ VA, MA New York Univ, currently working on PhD at NYU in Higher Education Administration; [occ.] Director of Student Activities - College of Saint Elizabeth; [memb.] Assoc of College Unions - International, National Assoc of Foreign Student Advisors, Assoc of Student Judicial, US Sailing Assoc, Barnegat Bay Yacht Racing Assoc and Manasquan River Yacht Club; [pers.] The bigger, the hairier, and the sloppier the dog; the better!; [a.] Manasguan, NJ

WHITAKER, ETHEL R.
[b.]November 15, 1931, Chattanooga, TN; [p.]Alice Morris Whitaker Hughes and Roderick E. Whitaker (Both Deceased); [ch.]Spec. Allison M. Whitaker-Bullard, U.S. Army; [ed.]B.S., M.A. Degrees-Ball State University, Munice, IN. Completed course, Writing Stories For Children and Teenagers from the Institute of Children's Literature, West Redding, CT., 1991.; [occ.]Retired Teacher, Indpls. Public School System; [memb.]Trinity Episcopal Church, Indpls. Alumni Chap. of Delta Sigma Theta Sorority, Nat'l. Assoc. of Female Executives; [hon.]Three Golden Poets, Semi Finalist Award-1993- International Society of Poets; [oth. writ.]Poems published in six World of Poetry publications; The Nat'l. Library of Poetry's In A Different Light. Published a poetry book, Life Can Be Beautiful, and recordings, The Sound of Poetry, The Contemporary Poets Series, Visions, Ethel R. Whitaker.; [pers.]It is hoped that my being born has helped many people find peace, love and joy in this world; [a.] Indpls., IN 46226.

WHITE, ANNA H.
[b.] September 26, 1921, Melrose, MA; [p.] Maud Jacquard (alive at age 96); [m.] Herbert J. White, January 3, 1943; [ch.] James Herbert, Richard Allen, Mary Allen; [ed.] High school graduate, Melrose High School, Class 1940; [occ.] Retired Hostess, Waitress; [memb.] V.F.W. Auxilliary, past secretary C.C.C. Chapter 128, retired Senior Volunteer Program; [hon.] 1988 Senior Volunteer of San Diego County, San Diego, Credit Union Golden Service Award; [oth. writ.] 2 poems published. My poems vary from religious, humor, family (grandchildren, etc) to everyday life, nature; [pers.] Poetry is such a relaxing form of writing for me and my family enjoys my accomplishments. It has also been an inspiration to my grandchildren. Have begun my autobiography; [a.] Thousand Oaks, CA

WHITMORE, KELLY COSTA
[b.] August 19, 1960, Boston, MA; [p.] William and Helen Costa; [m.] Keith Whitmore; [ch.] Drew 5, Brittany 2; [ed.] B.A., Framingham State College, Framingham, MA 01701; [occ.] Mother; freelance writer, computer assistant; [memb.] Mills Republican Town Committee; [hon.] Editor's Choice Award for "Brittany" as published in Wind In The Night Sky; [oth. writ.] Press releases; The book Reminiscences: Millis the First 100 years. Poems about families, published in Allusions, Wind In The Night Sky and A Threshold Of A Dream. Currently writing a poetry book for children; [pers.] Most of my writing expresses my feelings for my family especially my children; [a.] Millis, MA 02054

WHITNEY, DORIS NEWTON
[b.]August 21, 1913, Utica, New York USA; [p.]Lusina Orner Newton, William Clinton Newton; [m.]H. Frederick Whitney, February 12, 1937; [ch.]Kenneth Newton, William Hugh, Frederick Hill Whitney, Rachel Doris Lander; [ed.]Syracuse University, BA 1935; [occ.]Home-Keeping, family tending and volunteering; [memb.]Chi Omega, Eta Pi Upsilon, Phi Beta Kappa, Presbyterian Church (USA), Sebring Area Literacy Council; [oth. writ.]Public Relations articles for various groups and as P.R. staff appointee at Lees College in KY (as volunteer) various poems and stories in newspapers and anthologies; [pers.]Reading and writing have always been my top priority for creative activity. For me, poetry is the ultimate for expressing the whole range of human emotions, even bordering on this divine; [a.] Sebring, Ohio 44672

WIEST (JR), FRANK H.
[Pen.] HAW; [b.] October 23, 1936, Klingerstown, PA; [p.] Frank H. Wiester, Molly Mae (Saltzer) Wiest; [m.] Rosemary E. Wiest, June 2, 1990; [ch.] Frank, Duane, Melissa Jo, Sheila J. Kimberly L.; [ed.] Milton Hershey Trade School, Steelton High School, 1955 graduate; [occ.] Overhead crane operator (retired); [memb.] Loyal Order of oose U.S.S.W. of America 1688; [hon.] Golden Poet 1991, 1990, 1989 - from World of Poetry, Sacramento, CA; [oth. writ.] World Treasury of Golden Poems. Poem's - "People", John Campbell, editor and publisher: "A Man Called Pap" and "Here"; [pers.] I write strictly from feelings, dreams, fantasy and, reality, some music, past experiences; [a.] Steelton, PA

WIGFALL, OPHELIA YOUNG
[Pen.] Felia; [b.] June 18, 1945, Augusta, GA; [p.] Mrs. Maggie M. Young and The Late Ernest Young; [m.] Divorced; [ch.] Phillip Benson Carswell (son); [ed.] B.S. Biology - Paine College - Augusta, GA, graduate studies - USC (Aiken); [occ.] Seamstress and Poet and former school teacher (reading, math); [memb.] Liberty Bapt Church, Voices of Liberty Chorus; [hon.] Honorable Discharge from U.S. Naval Reserve, published poem in Where Dreams Begin, and recorded song, "Why Wait Until Tomorrow" Rainbow Records; [oth. writ.] Several poems and songs; [pers.] My writing brings out my inner most feelings during stressful moments as well as moments of great beauty and joy. I trust my poems will reach the hearts and minds of others as well; [a.] Augusta, GA 30901

WILBUR, ROGER
[b.]July 17, 1936, Alton, IL; [p.]Val and Ralph Wilbur (teacher and chemist, now deceased); [m.]Edith Lindsay Wilbur; [ch.]And grandchildren: Carolynn, Wendy; Jay, Kathleen and Hannah; [ed.]Illinois Wesleyan Univ., B.F.A.; Bowling Green State U., M.A; Doctoral work-Univ. of Denver; [occ.]College professor, Atlanta Metro/ Defry Tech/Saint Leo College; [memb.]National Council of Teachers of English; Speech Association of America; [hon.]Teacher of the year, 1986-87 (Saint Leo College Military Ext. Program); [oth. writ.]Poems published in The New England Sampler, Poetry Today and other magazines. Books published: Being Yourself, The Human Connection, Communicating with People (A Natural Approach), Mindtrembling; The Straightline Society.; [pers.]I believe in the vitality of natural processes and in the validation of uniqueness.; [a.] Ellenwood, Georgia 30049.

WILKINS, KEN
[b.]January 31, 1927, Chicago, Illinois; [m.]Mabel Elizabeth, September 9, 1950; [ch.]Kathleen, Timothy, david; [ed.]BA Wheaton College, MA Cal State, Los Angeles, BD Fuller Theological Seminary; [occ.]Retired Teacher; [memb.]So. Cal. Academy of Sciences, Calif. Writers Club, Gopher Flats Sportsmen Club, Grace Community Church; [hon.]Several Photography Awards; [oth. writ.]Poems published in several anthologies and Ellery Queen Mystery Magazine; [pers.]I attempt to live in the light of Matthew 6:33 in The New Testament; [a.] Northridge, CA 91343.

WILKS, MELODY NICOLE
[b.] April 20, 1976, South Carolina; [p.] Earle and Brenda Wilks; [ed.] Senior at Seneca High School; [memb.] Seneca High Government Club, SHS Key Club, SHS French Club; [hon.] Appear in Who's Who Among American High School students 93-94 edition; [a.] Seneca, SC 29678

WILLBANKS, ARGIE
[b.] February 9, 1919, Theodosia, MO; [p.] Willis and Dora (Pelham) Honeycutt; [m.] Lawrence Willbanks, July 4, 1936; [ch.] daughter, Nina married to Bernis Blair; three grandchildren and five great grandchildren and another great one on the way; [ed.] Seventy-three years of education!; [occ.] Retired Chef; [memb.] Price Place Church; [hon.] Seven Golden Poet Awards, ten Honorable Mentions, Who's Who in Poetry, Golden Poet Award; [oth. writ.] Numerous poems and songs; [pers.] I have a photographic memory. Anyone can ask to hear one and I can sing it. I may sing some of them several times before I ever write them down.; [a.] Pontiac

WILLIAMS, AMY
[b.]September 24, 1971, Canadian, TX; [p.]C.E. and Pat Williams; [ed.]Graduated Electra High

School, College at Liberal, KS and at WTA&M University, Canyon, TX; [occ.]Student majoring in Kinesiology; [memb.]Church of Christ, various poetry clubs and associations; [hon.]Various athletic awards, poetry recognitions; [oth. writ.]Poems published in magazines and books; [pers.]To Rhonda: Thanks for being a good friend but even more, being a great teacher and coach to me. To Doc and Doris who I love greatly.; [a.] Canadian, TX 79014.

WILLIAMS, BEVERLY N.G.
[b.]November 27, 1960, Oakland California; [p.]Jessie James Williams and Augusta Audry Austin Williams; [ch.]Siblings, James Etter Williams, Theresa Smith, Donna Smith-Marion. Also, 2 nieces Danica Hunter and Adrianna Tillman and a child I raised from 3 days old to 8 yrs. old Faith Branch; [ed.]Castlemont High School, Elmhurst Jr., High, Highland Elementary; [occ.]Aesthetician; [memb.]International Society of Poets; [pers.]In my poems, I try to reflect certain events in the past that were sad and unfortunate that follows one to the present. Through time, we learn to release excess baggage and carry on with our lives and plans; [a.] Oakland, California

WILLIAMS, ENID JO.
[b.]February, 6, 1920, Laverne, Oklahoma; [p.]Father, Oliver John Bourgois, Mother, Esther Root Bourgois; [m.]Edward Lynn Williams, August 8, 1936; [ch.]Daughter, Loretta June Smith, Son, Gary Lynn Williams; [ed.]Elementary School, High School, Business College, over 30 yrs. Volunteer Sunday School/Adult Basic Bible Teacher; [occ.]Retired, free-lance writer, preparing past writing into books; [memb.]I.O.O.F/Rebekah Lodge, First United Methodist Church; [hon.]Golden Poet, Two Trophies 1990-1991 from World of Poetry, 7 awards, World of Poetry Charter Member Int'l. Nat'l. Society Poetry, Washington, D.C. Editor's Choice Award, Library of Congress, Washington, D.C. 1993; [oth. writ.]Desert Winds Magazine, Six Newspapers, articles, letters, six children's stories in newspapers, three books poetry, 16 my copyright books, children, poetry, etc.; [pers.]I enjoy people, writing and especially sharing my poetry with others. I love my home and family sewing, gardening, above all writing; [a.] Deming, NM 88030

WILLIAMS, MELISSA
[b.] October 5, 1979, Atlanta, Georgia; [p.] Gray and Elaine Williams; [m.] not married; [ch.] none; [ed.] Five Forks Middle School, R.D. Head Elementary; [hon.] Editor's Choice Award from National Library of Poetry, Outstanding Writer Award, FFMS; [oth. writ.] Shadow Dance, Bright New Road; [pers.] I try to look at both sides of human nature and reflect each in a conflict between, good and evil, in most of my writings; [a.] Snellville, GA 30278

WILLIS, JOLENE
[Pen.]"Jennifer Rose"; [b.]March 15, 1929, Cleburn, Co., AL; [p.]Claudus F. and Audra W. Pritchett (Claudus deceased); [m.]Arthur N. Willis, April 11, 1947; [ch.]Herman Randall, 10/20/49 and Jerry Eugene, 10/26/52; [ed.]High School, Beauty Course. merit Test (90 grade), class will,

wrote and presented; [occ.]15 yrs. beauty work, Dept. of Education 7 yrs.; [memb.]Salem Baptist Church AARP; [oth. writ.]More poems and short stories, articles for paper; [a.] Tifton, Georgia 31794.

WILLMANN, JULIETH
[Pen.]Julie Willmann; [b.]January 17, 1948, Cayman Island, BWI; [p.]Cassie Smith; [m.]Donald Willman, 1974; [ch.]Two; [ed.]High School Graduate; [occ.]Housewife, and gardening, writing poems; [memb.]American Fitness Center, AAA Club. AMA Academy of Medel Aeronautics; [hon.]1983 I won the model of the year. State of Florida and 1992 I won The Golden Award for my poem, The Night; [a.] North, St. Petersburg, FL 33710

WILLS II, JERRY A.
[Pen.]Ariphon, Vesivian; [b.]October 19, 1964, Chambersburg, PA; [p.]Jerry A. Wills, I & Patricia A. Wills; [m.]Chong Hui Wills, July 2, 1985; [ch.]Jerry A. Wills III, Janita K. Wills; [oth. writ.]None published, working on a piece since 1990 entitled "The Diary of the Sacred Rose." I mention this because the "Rose" is an entire philosophy to me and sacred.; [pers.]I have found constant inspiration in the contemplation of the Ancient Chinese Taoist Texts and various other ancient manuscripts from other cultures. The yelds are timelessl; [a.] Chambersburg, PA 17201-8691

WILMOUTH, DAVID M.
[b.] April 9, 1974, Farmville, VA; [p.] Robert and Brenda Wilmouth; [ed.] Randolph-Henry High School, College of William and Mary; [occ.] Student; [memb.] Alpha Lambda Delta and Phi Eta Sigma Honor Societies, Baptist Student Union, Health Careers Club, International Society of Poets; [hon.] High school valedictorian, first place AEL Writing Contest, National Science Scholar, Byrd Scholar, Virginia's 1992 Representative in the Dept of Energy's Supercomputer Honors Program at Lawrence Livermore National Laboratory, Dean's List; [oth. writ.] Paper published on Eric database, poem published in On the Threshold of a Dream; [pers.] You may note from the title of my poem that I'm a football fan; however you may also note from the subject of my poem that it's God and His love that inspire and guide me; [a.] Keysville, VA

WILSON, FLORA BILLINGS
[Pen.] La'Vone Wilson; [b.] August 20, 1943, Jacksonville, FL; [p.] Ezella and Robert Henderson Billings; [m.] Clarence O. Wilson, January 24, 1961; [ch.] Talissa, Susan, Darrell; [ed.] Lakeshore Jr, Sr High; [occ.] Homemaker, quilter; [memb.] Royal Arch Widow American Quilders Society; [hon.] 1998-89 Award of Mreit, 1989 Silver Award, 1988-90-91 Golden Poet Award; [oth. writ.] The Golden Treasury of Great Poems, World of Poetry Anthology; [pers.] Keep in touch with the past, live for today, and keep an eye on the future; [a.] Fort Pierce, FL 34947

WILSON, JEAN LE VAN
[b.] March 29, 1915, Greater New York; [p.] Frank and Lucy Wilson; [m.] K. Norah Peck, 1957; [ed.] 1 yr college; [oth. writ.] "Broken Hearted" received a silver rating in a poet contest about 4 yrs ago; [pers.] I'm quite sure that my out work of gardening at a very young age started my poetic life; [a.] Blaine, WA

WILSON, JR, ESAW
[b.] February 18, 1928, Jackson, MS; [p.] Esaw and Jessie Mae Wilson; [m.] Ida B. Wilson, May 30, 1953; [ch.] Valerie, Edgar, Kenneth Wilson; [ed.] Elementary Sith Robinson High Ganier High, 2 yrs Tougaloo College; [occ.] Air condition refrigeration and appliance tech; [oth. writ.] The Wedding, copyright - 1992 by World of Poetry Press p.g. 49; [a.] Crystal Springs, MS 39059

WIRKOWSKI, BARBARA ANN J.
[b.] February 28, 1946, Pittsburgh, PA; [p.] Mr and Mrs Walter Wirkowski; [ed.] Continuing High School; [occ.] Mason Shoe Dealer and songwriter; [memb.] St Vincent De Paul; [hon.] Hall of Fame from World of Poetry. Golden Poets Awards, Merit Certificate from World of Poetry, poems published by American Poetry Association; [oth. writ.] PMQ Poetry Assn, made #10 award in songwriting from NCA Record Co - A Fool in Love; [pers.] To love and to be loved is the most precious thing in life. It is the diamond of the soul; [a.] Pittsburgh, PA 15201

WITHEE, BEVERLY
[b.] December 26, 1967, St. Thomas, Virgin Islands; [p.] David Frederick Withee, Sr., and Pamela Brackett Withee; [ed.] Oliver Perry Walker Senior High School, University of New Orleans, Delgado Community College; [occ.] Rehabilitation Technician; [memb.] International Society of Poets, Symphony Chorus of New Orleans, Bible Study Fellowship International; [hon.] Golden Poet 1993, Editor's Choice Award 1993; [oth. writ.] Published poems in the National Anthology "Whispers in the Wind"; [pers.] My writing reflects specific life experiences, which have strengthened my character. I hope that my works will inspire future poets; [a.] Harry, Louisiana 70058

WITHEE, DONALD F.
[b.]August 29, 1922, Westfield, MA; [p.](deceased); [m.]Blanche R. Withee, July 5, 1948; [ch.]Robert H. and Donna R. Jacobs (4 grandchildren and 4 great grandchildren); [ed.]W.S. High School; Northeastern University (BBA); [occ.]Retired (volunteer for Radio Reading Service live-broadcast reading to the Blind and Print-handicpped. English Tutor at STCC, Springfield, MA; [hon.]Golden Poet with World of Poetry (1985 through 1992); [oth. writ.]Haiku published in Point Judith Light; Eight Golden Poet Awards for Poetry in World of Poetry Anthologies; [a.] W. Springfield, MA 01089.

WITTENBACK, MARY BETH
[Pen.] M. Elizabeth; [b.] August 5, 1971, Laurel County, KY; [p.] Joyce H. and Jacob E. Wittenback; [ed.] Graduated Laurel Co High 1989, attended Eastern KY Univ 1989-90, currently attending Sue Bennett College; [occ.] Administrative Assistant to the Dean of Student at Sue Bennett College; [oth. writ.] Several poems and articles published in high school newspaper. Other publications for the National Library of Poetry; [pers.] Live for today and live for yourself. Do not live to please others. Please yourself. The opinion

of yourself is more important than anyone else's opinions!; [a.] London, KY 40741

WOLBECK, ALISON M.
[Pen.]Alison Marie; [b.]January 5, 1975, Thief River Falls, MN; [p.]John Wolbeck and Sue Wolbeck; [ed.]Graduate of Lincoln Senior High School; [occ.]Amoco Co. Employee; [memb.]Lincoln High Wind Ensemble and Northland Community Band; [hon.]National Library of Poetry Editor's Award and Who's Who Among American High School Students; [oth. writ.]Poem published in "A Break In The Clouds", published by the National Library of Poetry; [pers.]My poems reflect the way the world is in hopes that people will see this and strive to make changes; [a.] Thief River Falls, MN 56701

WOOD, LUCILLE L.
[Pen.] Scars on my heart; [b.] February 8, 1934, Sayorsville, KY; [p.] Kelly and Vena Bradley (mother's maiden name, Thomas); [m.] May 4, 1950, deceased; [ch.] Two grown sons, Eldest a Detective, youngest a mechanic; [ed.] Graduated from Columbia Broadcasting School, October 31, 1989; [occ.] Surgical Tec. at VA Medical Center in Indpls.; [memb.] Eagles and FOP Clubs, also Indiana Friends of Bluegrass Music Club; [hon.] Two silver, 2 gold and 3 Merit Awards for my poems from 1988-1991, also 1993; [oth. writ.] I have many poems written. All originals, also all mine, also have put many into songs..on tape only for myself use; [pers.] I write my poems from exp. and feelings. They all have much meaning and feelings in them, even to the people that have heart them.; [a.] Indpls, Ind. 46203

WOODARD, FRANCES PHELPS
[Pen.]Wind Song; [b.]January 18, 1925, Portsmouth, Virginia; [p.]Ernest Linwood Phelps and Edna Rowland Phelps; [m.]Ray O'Neal Woodard, January 29, 1943; [ch.]Brenda Raye Woodard and Ray O'Neal Woodard, Jr.,; [ed.]Woodrow Wilson High School; [occ.]Retired from the Federal Gov't, Norfold Naval Shipyard, Ports., VA., as a Budget Analyst-38 yrs. service; [memb.]International Society of Poets, Charter Member Believers Baptist Ch. Chesapeake, VA. & Teacher of Gleaners SS Class, Tidewater Genealogical Society, Birthright member of the Nansemond Indian Tribal Assoc., Inc. Chesapeake, VA, Member of the Phelps Family Assoc. of America., Charter Member of the National Museum of the American Indian, Smithsonian Ins. Wash. D.C., Member of the Assoc. for the Preservation of Virginia Antiquities.; [hon.]Many outstanding and superior accomplishments by the Federal Government for on job performance. Also, several by the U.S. Treasury Dept. for Work with U.S. Savings Bonds, Golden Poet Award 1991, Golden Poet Award 1989, Listen to the Drum 1990; [oth. writ.]Several poems published in the local newspaper's. Several poems published in the program booklet of the Nansemond Indian Tribe Annual Festival's. Several poems published in books by World of Poetry. My first poem published when I was a child in the fourth grade.; [pers.]I try to give God glory in all my poetry. Anything I undertake to do, I strive to give it my best efforts with God's help. My ability to write poetry is a special gift given to me by him. May his name be praised forever. In the last 10 years I have written around my heritage, as a descendant of the Algonquin Indians of Virginia, Once ruled by Chief Powhatan; [a.] Chowan Dr., Portsmouth, VA 23701.

WOODEL JR., WILLIAM L.
[Pen.]Woody; [b.]May 28, 1963, Cleverfield, PA; [p.]William and Darla; [m.]Schanna Woodel, August 30, 1986; [ch.]Ashley and Alyssa (Twins); [ed.]So. Plfd. High School; [occ.]Sheet Metal Mech.; [hon.]Golden Poet 1991, Golden Poet 1990, Two Honorable Mention, Merit Certificate 1990; [oth. writ.]Four poems published by World of Poetry; [pers.]My writing reflects the love I have for my daughters and other family members, which are feelings I find hard to express.; [a.] So. Plfd., NJ 07088

WOODS, MARY
[b.]November 28, 1959, Columbia, SC; [p.]Grandparents, Ethel M. Muller and The Late Austin Muller (raised by grandparents from birth); [ed.]Swansen High, Rutledge College of Columbia 1981 Graduate; [occ.]Civil Engineering SC DOT; [memb.]The International Society of Poets (An inductee into this organization); [hon.]Editor's Choice Award 1993 by The National Library of Poetry, The International Poet of Merit Award, Special Recognition from The May or Newberry; [oth. writ.]Poems published in five different anthologies: Where Dreams Begin, The Coming of Dawn, 1993, American Poetry Annual, Treasured Dreams of America and Contemporary Poets of America and Britain; [pers.]Life is a precious gift and we should treat it as such; [a.] Newberry, SC 29108

WOODS, VINCENT
[b.] December 26, 1949; [a.] Mobile, Alabama

WRIGHT, CHRISTINE
[Pen.] C.J. Wright; [b.] February 5, 1973, Hammond, [p.] Robert and Shirley Wright; [ed.] Oak Park High, Missouri Western State College; [hon.] Honor Roll, Dean's List; [pers.] My imagination allows me to see the world in many different ways. In my writing, reality and fantasy can be both the same or different like day and night; [a.] Kansas City, MO

WRIGHT, ELDA SCHWARZ
[b.]August 6, 1903, Decorah, Iowa; [p.]Robert Frederick and Sibylla Margretha Schwarz; [m.]Thomas Marvin Wright, Sr., July 26, 1935; [ch.]Thomas Marvin Wright, Jr. of ElCentro and Lake San Marcos, California; [occ.]Retired High School Chemistry, Biology, U.S. History, Political Science and Literature Teacher, Housewife; [oth. writ.]Paper on Photosynthesis and the Correlation of Photosynthesis with other subjects in the Curriculum.; [pers.]"let us live our lives in such a way that all of God's children will know that the world is at peace, because it will show in our lives, in our actions and in our good deeds; [a.] Decorah, Iowa 52101-1318.

WRIGHT, SHIRLEY J.
[Pen.] S. J. Sright; [b.] February 28, Hammond, IN; [p.] Carl and Ilta Cremeens; [m.] Robert F. Wright; [ch.] Christine Jane and Catherine Janle; [ed.] Indiana Univ Northwest, Maples Woods Community College, Missouri Western State College; [occ.] Freelance writer; [hon.] Dean's List, Honor's Program, Merit Scholarship, Honor's Certificates; [pers.] I believe that each person should strive to be the kind of person that we all would dream of being.
I think people need to believe in themselves; [a.] Kansas City, MO

YAN, LI
[b.]August 28, 1954, Beijing, China; [p.]Yao-Wen Wei; [occ.]Artist, Writer, Chinese Poetry Magazine Publisher; [memb.]Chinese Speaking Writers Aboard-New York, Chinese "Star Star" Artist Group; [hon.]First New Poem Prize by the Association of Modern Chinese Literature and Art of North America 1991; [oth. writ.]Several poems published in "The Literary Review 1990," "The Portable Lower East Side 1990," "American Letters and Commentary 1993," "A Break In The Clouds 1993, and many more in chinese newspapers and magazines; [pers.]Poetry is the petroleum in the soil of a human body. Like real petroleum, it is formulated in the body for a very long period of time. Although each individual poet has the ability to explore and dig it up, it is used, just like petroleum, in a variety of ways. People are studying how to use petroleum economically. By the same token, poets are pondering how to use this human petroleum peacefully.; [a.] Flushing, NY.

YATSO, ANITA
[b.] July 30, 1961, Angola, IN; [p.] Patricia and Norman Bidwell; [m.] George Yatso, Jr, February 8, 1986; [ch.] Corey and Amanda; [ed.] Coldwater High School, Coldwater, MI, Nursing Branch Area Career Center, Coldwater, MI, Unif of IL computers, Children's Institute of Literature; [occ.] Office Manager, Kewanee, IL; [memb.] St Mary Catholic Church; [oth. writ.] Poem in Where Dreams Begin; [pers.] I try to write of things that have a great meaning to me. Children are my favorite topics; [a.] Kewanee, IL 61443

YINGER, DORIS N.
[Pen.] Doris Natalie Yinger; [b.] August 9, 1937, York, PA; [p.] The late Chester F. Creager, Edna M. Creager; [m.] Jay P. Yinger, October 13, 1956; [ch.] Lisa Renee, (grandson-K.C.); [ed.] William Penn Sr High - Class of 1955, York Academy of Art, York Art Assoc; [memb.] Fourth United Methodist Church; [hon.] Recognition by York County Society for pen and ink drawing of local church in art contest. Poem published in local newspaper. Poetry contest winner in Western Poetry Society, poem published in book Voices of America ---- The National Library of Poetry, poems published entitled Black Stallion in book A View from the Edge and Intangible Creation in book Distinguished Poets of America; [occ.] Presently a housewife but for a number of years worked as a successful freelance commercial artist; [pers.] I aspire to have a book of poetry published with my own are illustrations. I attempt to express my personal feelings and share them with my readers. I have been influenced and encouraged by my mother to write; [a.] York, PA 17402

YORK, SERGE R.S.
[Pen.] Serge York; [b.] September 25, Oslo, Norway; [p.] Foster Parents from before age of one, Sea Captain Anders Martinius, mother Marianne Jeligne

York; [m.] Lucienne Bouvier; [ch.] None, six dogs and two cats and a very old tortoise which was named Columbus; [ed.] Twelve years in Oslo. Fourteen years classical ballet in America. Under early Russian Masters; [memb.] S.A.G., Actors Equity, withdrawal from all. Also attended U.S.C. I did Best in Drama, Public Speaking, Science; [occ.] Worked in minor positions in the capacity of supply supervisor at C.B.S. Also appeared in the Orson Wells Show; [hon.] Selected to play a leaping role in an all college trope; [oth. writ.] Many other poems, personal bibliographies; [pers.] During my two years at C.B.S Hollywood I was a active ember of the First Presbyterian Church of Hollywood; [a.] Palm Springs, CA 92262

YOUNG, SHAY BANKS
[Pen.] Shay; [b.] September 3, 1944, Columbus, Ohio; [p.] Francis Bernice Harris (Mom) and Charles Sanford (Dad); [m.] Curtis K. young, July 29, 1990; [ch.] Rev. W. Douglass Banks (son) and Michael A. Young (stepson); [ed.] Attended Franklin University and Columbus College, Journalism and Business; [occ.] Public Affairs, Community Specialist; [memb.] Maynard Ave. Baptist Church, Action Alliance of Black Professionals, Several Community Boards of Directors; [hon.] Outstanding Ohioan, Outstanding Young Woman of American, Producer/Host 1/2 hr. Cable TV Show "Generational Harmony", Grant Recipient-Columbus, Foundation, Adelphi University, Educational Study tour of 8 countries Africa; [oth. writ.] Book: Butterflies and Me; Play: Can You Hear The Rain. Numerous poems, news articles published in magazines and local newspapers; [pers.] Creative writing has served as a stimulator for growth from my cocoon state to my personal butterfly state. As a writer I am able to share my philosophy and my God.

YOUSIF, NANCY L.
[b.] January 6, 1938, Detroit, Michigan; [p.] Albert de Manigold and Florence de Manigold; [m.] Dr. Salah Yousif, June 28, 1967; [ch.] Michael, Stephen, Catherine, Mary, Dina and Leila; [ed.] St. Mary Academy (Monroe Michigan), Michigan State University; [occ.] Teacher in Sacramento City School District; [memb.] American Assn. of Univ. Women, National Educational Assn, California Teacher's Assn., New Shanghai Literary Group; [oth. writ.] Poem, published "The Quest."

ZANDER, CHERYL M.
[b.] June 12, 1961, Kaiser, San Francisco, CA; [p.] Walt and Lois Zander; [ed.] Lynwood Elem School, Carden School, Novato High School; [occ.] Teach Art in Dixie Dist in Marin County; [memb.] Marin Puzzle People; [hon.] Marin County Fair, Marin Puzzle People, Dixie School - Pr Dr Lohwasser; [oth. writ.] Articles and Poems for Marin Puzzle People Publications; [pers.] Doing what is in your heart and to know who you are on the inside is all that counts. Thanks for giving me life Mom and Dad; [a.] Novato, CA 94947

ZBORAY, GEORGIANNA W.
[b.] January 25, 1961, Staten Island, NY; [p.] Wanda H. Barbach Zboray and John S. Zboray, Sr; [ch.] 2 daughters: Corkey & Misty (2 cats that are thelight of my life!); [ed.] Graduate - Katharine Gibbs Business School; Graduate - Curtis High School, S.I.; [occ.] Legal Secretary - for partner at Wall Street law firm; [memb.] World of Poetry Society, World Wildlife Fund, National Wildlife Assoc; [hon.] Golden Poet Award, 3 Awards of Merit and Who's Who status (all from World of Poetry Society); [oth. writ.] "A Dream", "The Struggle Within", and "Changes"; [pers.] All of my poetic achievements (publishings) and awards are to be credited to my mother, who is the best friend a person could ever have and who has been supportive of all my endeavors; [a.] Staten Island, NY 10306

ZOBLE, LOUISE G.
[Pen.] "Ell-Gee-Zee"; [b.] October 22, 1920, Bayone, New Jersey; [p.] Mildred and Samuel Witkind (deceased when I was 8 mos. old) legally adopted by maternal grandmother Eva Grodberg, upon parents death; [m.] Charles Zoble, May 19, 1941; [ch.] Edward J. and Judity E. Kisstrin; [ed.] Bayonne H.S. Syracus Univ (1937-41) dual enrollment, Schools of Lit. Arts & Edu.; [occ.] Retired 1982 as French Tearcher at Trenton, NJ High School; [memb.] The Greenwood House, NJ Hosp. and Rehab Center, Educ. Assn., American Heart and American Cancer Assoc., Sloan Kettering Memorial, American Arthritis Assn., Miami Heart Hospital; [hon.] Dean's List 4 yrs, Pi Lamba-da-Theat, National Education Honoraroy Society, National Romance Language Honorary Society; [oth. writ.] An unpublished compilation of well over 200 rhymes (personalized for the Times) primarily geared for family, friens and neighbors who are our "Florida Family." Frequently requested to submit appropriate rhymes for organization "affairs"; [pers.] Family and friendships have been my most cherished treasures; charity returned more to me than I am able to give, my rhymes usually reflect that.

ZUMAULT, VIOLA
[ed.] English Major, Warrensburg State Teachers College; [occ.] Retried, 37 years in Real Estate; [memb.] State President, The National League of American Pen Women, member of International Platform Association; [hon.] Listed in Who's Who in Poetry, Who's Who of American Women, Two Thousand Women of Achievement, plus various poetry societies, countless honors and awards in the United States and European countries. 1993 top winner in National League of American Pen Women's annual contest, winning honors in all 5 categories; [oth. writ.] Over 1000 poems and 2 books of poetry published. Recently completed autobiography, "Watching The Past Go By; [pers.] All awards are donated to charity in the hope that I can make a difference in the lives of others while making my little corner of the world a happier place than I found it.

Index of Poets

Index

NAME

Abaya, Amadeo 169
Abbott, Edward E. 124
Abercrombie, Glenn 301
Abernathy, Jenny 93
Ables, Christina 239
Abraham, Dorothye B. 295
Abshagen, Dorothy 32
Acevedo, Christina Y. 92
Acosta, David G. 61
Acosta, Martha L. 318
Acuna, Toni 327
Adams, Cathy 43, 72
Adams, Cleveland 33
Adams, Ellen Carlstrom 227
Adams, Lloyd J. 457
Addington, Marie 371
Ader, Nancy J. 379
Adkinson, Brooke W. 246
Aepli, Megan Susanne 315
Agnellini, Jeanne S. 243
Ahearn, Barbara F. 63
Akers, Joan 31
Akhtar, Amina 250
Alamia, Teresa Chapa 449
Albertson, Shirley M. 457
Albo, Mary 400
Albracht, Mark 354
Albrecht, Brian 119
Albury, Mark 341
Alderson, James R. 305
Aldrich, Nicole M. 446
Aldridge, Shelby Jean 463
Alexander, Constance Joy 205
Allee, Jo Anne 283
Allen, Florence E. 32
Allen, Harley 191
Allen, Marjorie 375
Allen, Melody Lynn 366
Allen, Miriam Elizabeth 337
Allen, Rayson L. 355
Allmaras, Linda 403
Allworth, Jack C. 47
Almada, Edward P. 202
Alpert, Al P. 46
Alston, Steven G. 364
Altman, Adam 246
Alves, JoAnne 38
Amburgey, Ada 75
Amnah, Goldie L. 287
Amoros, Rosamaria 344
Anastas, Helen 87
Anchelo, Gertrude L. 274
Anders, James R. 247
Andersen, Dorothy Rednour 276
Anderson, Anna Toma 265
Anderson, Barbara Ann 39
Anderson, Dorothy 219
Anderson, Eldora 163
Anderson, Florence 115
Anderson, H. Nevada 401
Anderson, Jackie Land 151
Anderson, Jean 48
Anderson, Margaret 436
Andrea, Marie C. 521
Andree, Debbie 294
Andrews, Marie 338

Andrewski, Becki Lynne 140
Angelle, Paula Marie 437
Angyal, Cheryl 224
Ansari, Annette 161
Anthony, Helen 231
Anthony, Sheila H. 459
Aragon, Virginia 390
Aram, Laura 384
Arch, Sherry 438
Archuleta, Margaret Nell 392
Ardais, Raistlin 448
Arends, Marjory E. 417
Armentrout, Christy 106
Armour, Mary J. Goodman 382
Armstrong, Hazel Lee 13
Arnett, Albert Joseph 67
Arnold, David B. 99
Arnold, Enola 125
Arnold, Eunice 131
Arnold, Loyed L. 350
Aronhalt, Annabelle 42
Arrants, Gary 130
Arzadon, Bibiano B. 49
Asano, Sachiko 374
Ashby, Vicky-Lyn 445
Ashworth, Virginia R. 433
Askew, Ina 102
Atkinson, Charles 238
Atwood, Dorothy R. 35
Auman, Cindy L. 141
Austin, Armittie 345
Austin, Lois 428
Austin, Nicole 427
Autin, Terri L. 415
Axelrad, Harriet L. 223
Axton, Florence G. 86
Ayers, Mildred 320
Azevedo, Francesca Aragon 158
Babb, Denice Jane 150
Bailey, Carol 214
Bailey, Carrol Rowan 301
Bailey, George A. 245
Baker III, William 344
Baker, Eris M. 32
Baker, Jennifer 154
Bakker, Irene 145
Baldao, Annette H. 184
Baldwin, Wynn 354
Baldys, Sister Mary Marcy 376
Ballenger, Sandy 388
Balls, Darlene 181
Balogh, Gloria R.A. 136
Banford, Lucille 367
Bange, Larry H. 348
Banks, Nancy Reneau 461
Baptista, John F. 112
Barber, Margaret M. 383
Barber, Mattie Belle 444
Bare, Debra Sue 292
Barger, Jeanette 258
Barker, Barbara S. 248
Barker, Rafaela Wintham 413
Barlet, Ann Aldrich 280
Barnes, Donna Marguerite 118
Barnes, G. Jujuan 256
Barnhardt, Carolyn 233
Barnum, Billy 118
Baroni, Forrest J. 105
Barrell, Dawn H. 55
Barrera, Roberta A. 448
Barrett, Joseph E. 161
Barrington, Amy 103
Bartholomaus, Brett W. 142
Bartins-Pavlic, Julia 276
Bartolomeo, Grace Ann 25
Bartow, Barbara J. 104

Basford, Rebekah Elizabeth 313
Batchelor, Linda Cooper 440
Batesman, Knial R. 363
Battis, M.L. 431
Bauchspies, Dee Maddux 151
Baumgarner, Rebecca 521
Bave, Emelia L. 95
Bays, Lisa C. 382
Beacham, Gloria Mercedes 180
Bean, Helen E. 168
Beason, Robert L. 459
Beatty, Charles 204
Beaty, Alyssa K. 110
Beaulieu, Nancy 431
Beaureggard, Sylva 406
Becerra, Maritya 260
Becerra, Maritza 260
Beck, Cindy 204
Beck, Marial E. 379
Becker, Bess 284
Becker-Wiech, Cheryl L. 217
Beckerdite, Cami 269
Bedard, Harriet (Shove) 46
Beecher, George 35
Beiersdorfer, Lucille 406
Beland, Charles C. 109
Belikoff-Sherr, Irene 225
Beliveau, Brett A. 287
Belknap, Ginger S. 81
Bello, Jeri 83
Bells, Tina Marie 316
Belton, Charlie M. 4
Benfante, Ignazio 3
Benn, June 110
Bennett, Darold L. 173
Bennett, June 253
Benros, Thomas 428
Benson, Clynis A. 248
Berg, Alice Dommer 159
Berger, Debra K. 246
Bergeron, Cyrilla 16
Bergman Jr., George F. 196
Bernal, David A. 270
Bernardy, Diane Marie 152
Berry, Eileen 290
Berry, Genevieve Paone 213
Berry, June 267
Berry, Maxwell R. 430
Berry, Stephanie D. 368
Bertrand, Steve K. 395
Bessette-Clifford, Marie 441
Bessire Sr., Rodney 325
Beswick, Mildred 352
Bettenhausen, Ruth E. 463
Beymer, Howard 270
Bickart, Audrey 68
Bickford, Joan 265
Bickley, Kenneth 456
Biddle, Beverly A. 118
Biggers, Emory M. 294
Biggs, Candi 197
Biggs, Eleanor 152
Billson Jr., James G. 280
Binion, Forrest A. 154
Bird, Camille 31
Bishop, Douglas L. 159
Bishop, Eva Bass 237
Bishop. Debra Ann 56
Black, Joy 288
Black, Ruth A. 388
Black, Samantha J. 411
Blackburn, John H. 130
Blackwell, Crystal 191
Blair, Jayne 198
Blake, Evelyn Kimball 220
Blake-Miller, Mary Leah 330

Blanco, Ursel 308
Bland, Florence 239
Blasberg, Stacy 317
Blaschak, G.Mark 317
Blash, Hosezell 286
Blatchford, Gladys F. 296
Blazer, Jimmy L. 227
Bliss, Elissa 285
Block, Cheryl 58
Block, Evelyn 202
Blount, Diana M. 87
Bobbitt, Norma 399
Bobo, Arlie U. 75
Bobrow, Betty Lemke 46
Bogowitz, Cheryl 201
Boka, Chris 225
Boland, Susan 308
Boldman, Shelly 420
Bolduc, Martha 451
Bolkcom, Telva D. 438
Bonen, William 463
Bonine, Vivian Way 447
Bonneville, Tom 450
Borok, Aron 282
Borschneck, Gloria M. 5
Bosch, Deborah A. 261
Bosinski, Christine Ann 197
Boston, Susan Ivey 320
Boston, Susanne 359
Bourassa, Jean L. 215
Bourree, Felix 162
Bowden, Robert J. 449
Bowen, David S. 304
Bowen, Robert A. 465
Bower, Raymond 390
Bowman, Dawn 298
Boyd, E. Renae 380
Boyd, George A. 276
Boyer, George H. 190
Boyer, Jonathan 199
Boyer, Ruth G. 522
Boynton, James L. 179
Bradbury, Roulede 428
Brading, Robbie 342
Bradley, Edie 38
Bradley, Phyllis Brackett 440
Brady, Anne V. 235
Braithwaite, Beulah Gill 23
Braman, George 293
Bramhall, Betsy J. 98
Branau, Edward Francis 10
Branch, Bertha L. 18
Brandon, Darrell 76
Brandt, Edward Reimer 18
Brasseau, Juanita Mouton 9
Bratsky, Betty 139
Brauet, Dolores Maria Bolivar 145
Brayman, Elsie 241
Breckner, Karen D. 414
Breedlove, Betty 27
Brees, Finley A. 302
Breland-Davis, Barbara 52
Brennan, Sean J. 457
Brenon, Helen M. 33
Brensike, Gail Ranae 166
Bresnahan, Kelly K. 351
Bressan, Dorlene 5
Breton, Lisa 341
Brewer, Doris Hartsell 193
Brewster, Betty Jeanne Wilhite E. 167
Brezenoff, Shirley 522
Bridgegroom, Roger W. 313
Briggs, Philip W. 387
Brillante, Ann 36
Briner, June 82
Britton, Joseph 242

The National Library of Poetry - Outstanding Poets of 1994

Brock, Martha 357
Brodbeck, John 113
Broekhuizen, Vicki 314
Brogdon, Judy C. 254
Bronco, Anna Maria 73
Brook, Carol A. 75
Brooks, Helen S. 185
Brooks, Mary J. 448
Brouard, Theresa 385
Brown Jr., Dennis W. 185
Brown, Alice S. 201
Brown, Barbara Ann 296
Brown, Debra 128
Brown, Delsie Eaton 203
Brown, Dorothy I. 17
Brown, Fannie C. 168
Brown, Gloria J. 164
Brown, Heather E. 179
Brown, Kathleen Marie 366
Brown, Kenneth W. 351
Brown, Vicki 442
Brownbock, Lloyd F. 348
Brownderville, Colene K. 79
Brownell, Chloris B. 228
Brownen, Sue J. 400
Browning, Peggy B. 371
Browning, Sandi 401
Brownlow, Elizabeth D. 98
Brozaitis, Helene 35
Bruce, Craig 111
Brumbaugh, Helen J. T. 168
Brun, Youri 394
Bruster, Pamela 337
Bryan, Elmer J. 95
Bryant, John 94
Bryant, Melissia 312
Brynildsen, S. 395
Bryson, Margaret E. D. 454
Buchanan, Jacque 220
Buchert III, Wilson L. 381
Buck, Sue 311
Buckwitz, Jacob R. 188
Buekert, Edward V. 302
Buettner, Debi 297
Buffalo, Judith K. 228
Buffum Sr., Carroll R. 156
Bull, Deborah Lee 130
Bullock, George 159
Bullock, Jennifer 134
Bumphus, Anita L. 15
Bunch, Doris J. 167
Burch, Jim 39
Burford, Christopher L. 8
Burger, Bertilla 88
Burgess, Craig E. 234
Burkett, Betty Joan 14
Burkholder, Anne R. 220
Burks-Shiver, Jacqueline 62
Burman, Dorothy Krueger 154
Burnham, Thelma J. 458
Burns, Edna 13
Burris, Margaret Peel 375
Burrows, Elizabeth MacDonald 14
Bussell, Pauline T. 381
Butler Jr., Charles L. 71
Butler, G. Larry 390
Butts, Donna 90
Byerly, Charlotte J. 162
Byers, Winifred 316
Bynum, Barbara K. 24
Byrd, Ruby 434
Byrne, Jacqui 229
Byrne, Michael 402
Cage, Christina 78
Caldwell, Emilie Joan 15
Calhoun, Pat 332

Callihan, Helen Pierce 41
Cameron, Jean 262
Camley, Glenn P. 114
Camp, Joan Therese 202
Campbell Jr., Harley 140
Campbell, C.M. (Red) 268
Campbell, Charles Andrew 298
Campbell, Doris Kuenne 268
Campbell, Melissa 453
Campbell, Virginia 345
Campion, D.P. 29
Campione, Alan B. 29
Canada, Marcus S. 364
Canales, Maria L. 361
Candee, Jean 156
Candiotti, Victor 309
Capdeville-Smith, Leontine 395
Cappas, Humberto 136
Capuano, Connie A. 235
Capuano, Michael 455
Carani, Dorothy M. 100
Carey, Belva 148
Carini, Angela M. 63
Carlson, Alma A. 236
Carlson, Jeannie 151
Carlson, Margo 316
Carlson, Marjorie Ann 354
Carpenter, Alexandra C. 227
Carpenter, Ben 302
Carpenter, Eleanor M. 30
Carr, Adam E. 22
Carr, Barbara A. 232
Carr, James S. 118
Carr, Susan J. 336
Carr-Merritt, Josephine 211
Carraabine, Cynthia 191
Carson Jr., Willard R. 463
Carson, Marilynn 377
Carstens, Patricia L. 320
Carter, Alice D. 161
Carter, Edwin T. 18
Carter, Evelyn 248
Carter, James T. 65
Carter, Stephenie L. 324
Casey, Byron C. 286
Cassidy, Janice B. 96
Cassner, Carl 147
Castillon, Teresa 415
Castro, Angel Malisa 96
Catalan, Kemal 322
Catalano, Susan M. 260
Catalano, Susan M. 260
Cate, Carter P. 202
Cathcart, Heather 74
Cebulak, Brandon A. 15
Celani, Lois Jean 458
Cerka, Cindy 210
Chadwick, Debbie 136
Chamberlain, Joy 285
Chambliss, Charlotte J. 123
Chance, Frances M. 128
Chandler, Ann L. 190
Chandler, Rosemary 422
Chang, Diana M.P. 92
Chapman, Ginger 293
Chapman, Jesse Thaddeus 180
Chappelle, Guen 154
Charette, Laurel 416
Charnani, Sonesh 369
Charping, John 167
Chase, Elsa L. 27
Chasse, Dot 286
Chastain, Alice H. 251
Chaussee, Sandi 340
Chernick, Cheryl 262
Chiesa, Carmen 257

Chilcott, Charles T. 228
Children, Your 210
Childs, Charles R. 63
Childs, Jacqueline L. 140
Chinchillo, Jean Bell G. 26
Chipman, Duane S. 113
Choudhury, Alpana 79
Christensen, Helen 280
Christensen, Sally H. 411
Christian, Bobbie T. 153
Christner, Betty Gentry 243
Christofic, Jim 109
Church, Frances M. 194
Ciavarella, Betty 192
Cipolletti, Dolores 99
Circello, Justine Levasseur 234
Cisco, Mechel 367
Claissie, Stephen G. 373
Clapham, Bonnie (Richmond) 21
Clapp, Timothy Scott 385
Clar, Irma 4
Clark, Bobby 169
Clark, Crystal Grace 237
Clark, Dean A. 172
Clark, Jenny 30
Clark, Nancy Hayes 370
Clark, Valerie S. 328
Clary, James 257
Clautice, Edward W. 282
Claytor, Jeanne 61
Cleary, Barbara Perkins 93
Clements, Frenchie 186
Clemons, Lynn Allen 383
Cleveland, Lisbeth A. 444
Clipner, Bessie G. 65
Clough, Doris 146
Cloyd, Gwendolyn 117
Cobos, Eve 126
Coffey-Tomlin, Vivian 327
Cohen, Margie 338
Cohen, Samuel 352, 368
Colangelo, Dorothea 174
Cole, Anita H. 37
Cole, Diane 119
Cole, Nella Hollaway 447
Cole, Robert L. 443
Coleman, Gregory 191
Coles, Margaret E. 308
Collier, Jack Frederick 157
Collins, Corinne 32
Collins, Cynthia 65
Colo, Nino 399
Combs, Ve'Lva Ma'ria 375
Compson, Hallie C. 274
Conley, Betty Lee 112
Conley-Klahorst, Carol 87
Conner, Clara Jane 162
Conradt, Christine 3
Conrath, Regina 435
Conroy, Joan E. 17
Cook, Andy 261
Cook, Billie 240
Cook, David Glen 129
Cook, Eva 209
Cook, Herbert 240
Cooke, Chantelle 59
Cookson, Christopher 91
Coolbaugh, Margaret D. 331
Coon, Anna Bernice 279
Coon, Edna 152
Cooper, Houstine 189
Cooper, Lou-Peck 348
Cooper, Melinda 455
Cooper, Peggy T. 397
Coppolella, Anthony 218
Corbin, Bette 290

Cordaro, Josephine 191
Corish, Sherry 337
Cornelius, Byron G. 107
Cornish Jr., Arthur Guy 145
Cotter, Barbara 273
Counts, Pearl H. 460
Coveney, Cristina M. 157
Cover, Berniece 187
Cowherd, Zana 360
Cox, Alberta A. 159
Cox, George 227
Cox, Jane B. 209, 269
Cox, Jerry 93
Cox, Kathleen T. 417
Coyle, Ann M. 303
Craig, Steven L. 432
Craig-Clrk, Tracy 343
Cramer, Eleanore Bosco 187
Cramer, Elizabeth Ann 108
Cramer, Georgia S. 148
Crampton, George W. 76
Crane, Madeline D. 346
Cranford, R. Locke 335
Cranford, Ralph L. 335
Craven, Florence M. 90
Craven, Patricia A. 368
Crawford, Grantley 131
Crawford, John K. 11
Crebbin, Donna M. 209
Creson, Ken M. 347
Crider, Viola M. 323
Crisp, Alva McGregor 236
Crispin, Charles 155
Crissman, Robert C. 316
Crist, Clara M. 303
Crist, Eva M. 105
Crites, Dorothy A. 233
Crobaugh, Emma 197
Crocker, Stacy 446
Croft, John J. 289
Crosby, Chris 78
Croteau, David 39
Crouch, Glenn 47
Crouse, Curtis M. 183
Crowder, Shirley 319
Crowley Jr., James F. 175
Cserepy, Joseph F. 134
Culverwell, Priscilla 406
Cummings, Clara Evelyn C. 249
Cummings, Ethel M. 69
Cummings, Pat A. 328
Cummings, Willie Johnson 327
Cummins, Thomas R. 457
Cunningham, Carl 279
Cunningham, Cathy Bordayo 158
Cunningham, Charles L. 253
Cupido, Irene 23
Curran, James P. 275
Curran, Tim 377
Curtis, Cartherine G. 132
Curtis, Kris 348
Curtis, Lucy Hadsell 426
Cusano, Paul 380
Custer, Carolyn Jean 87
Custer, Celestine J. 145
Custodio, Uldario P. 324
Cuyle, Barbara J. 82
Cynan, 182
D'Andrea, Natasha 313
DaVee, Lowell "Ted" 344
Dabiri, Ghazzal 144
Dadonas, David 245
Daigle, Renee J. 413
Dallinger, Carl A. 261
Daly, Doris C. 15
Dame, Edna 176

Daniel, John F. 53
Daniels, Nicole 461
Daniels, Yvonne 465
Dann, Daisy V. 235
Dantoni, Nellie K. 442
Darby, Dorthea 183
Darden, Kathryn E. 370
Darnielle, Mary Lou 394
Das, Sait Mohan 522
Daughtry, Florence 250
Daveler, Angie 12
Davey, Boyd T. 16
David, Kenneth D. 323
David, Priti 349
Davidson, Geneva Hood 93
Davies, Betty 53
Davignon, June 155
Davis II, Floyd E. 235
Davis, C. Marie 406
Davis, Colleen L. 182
Davis, Diane M. 189
Davis, Ernest L. 244
Davis, Jack 175
Davis, Jennifer 30
Davis, Jennifer A. 20
Davis, LJ 102
Davis, May H. 390
Davis, Millie 430
Davis, Nenita T. 339
Davis, Thelma 394
Davis, Verle Elizabeth 462
Day, Bess Eileen 55
Day, Bob 252
Day, Garland Ennis 188
De Cicco, Joseph 101
De Peralta, Ursula 364
DeArmond, Tiffany 376
DeFoor, Lucy 441
DeGooyer, Reg 444
DeLongchamps, Mary Anne 403
DePaolo, Donna 88
DePorter, Jeanne 62
DePuy, Patricia 411
DeRitter, Carole L. 56
DeRosa, Constance Rose 178
DeSpain, Rachel 315
DeVries, Dede 107
DeWolf, Wanda L. 404
Dean, Jessica 109
Deason, James 70
Decker, Lindsay 361
Deignan, Carol Ann 213
Deitz, James Nelson 274
Del Ianziti, A. J. 315
Delaney, Francis E. 171
Delay, Bette 255
Dell, Irene Prater 149
Demps, John 86
Dempsey, Kathleen C. 457
Dennard, Sherri 426
Dennis Sr., William H. 360
Denton, Ruby I. 372
Derringer, Juanita 62
Desmet, Phyllis 446
Destefano Jr., John J. 155
DiBella, Grace L.A. 255
DiTrolio, Elena 103
Dial, Elnorist E. 12
Diamond, Montez Tiana 373
Diaz, V. A. 362
Dick, Clara S. 99
Dickerson, Janis J. 146
Dickson, Dorothy 129
Dillard, Agnes Lys 206
Dillon, Ella M. 61
Dimeska, Ljubinka 312

Dingwall Jr., James A. 83
Diobilda, Angela M. 249
Diottaviano, Margie 414
Divaris, Apostolos 35
Dixon, Ella Smith 298
Dlugosh, Kim 349
Dmitriev, Andrei 180
Dobberpuhl, Holly 86
Dobias, Agnes M. 295
Dodge, J. M. 352
Dodrill, Davan J. 143
Doebbler, Phyllis 313
Dolby, Darell D. 289
Dole, Janet B. 255
Doman, Joseph I. 36
Donahue, Marilyn D. 452
Donchez, Helen 279
Dorgan, Cornelia James 262
Dorland, Jesse 76
Dornbush, Lydia W. 423
Dorsaneo, John 290
Dosier, Angela L. 203
Dotson, Jane Adeline 49
Dougherty, Claire W. 101
Dougherty, Margaret R. 355
Doughty, Nina B. 318
Douglas-McCargo, Catherine F. 228
Dowdy Jr., Harry K. 218
Dowlen, Rubye H. 350
Downey, Laurie 421
Draxton, Delphine 138
Dresbach, D. P. 522
Drew, Dorothy 187
Dreyer, Jennifer L. 236
Driscoll, Diana 420
Drummond, La Vena M. 350
Drummond, Patricia 306
Drummond, Phyllis 332
Drusch, Georgia M. 117
DuBeau, Susan M. Dorie 370
DuEst, Carolyn P. 169
Dube, Kathleen A. 309
Duca, Angelo R. 235
Duckett, Lila W. 357
Duff, Gloria 108
Duitsman, Joyce L. 192
Duke Jr., James H. 61
Duke, Oscar M. 317
Duke, Rosetta J. 332
Dultz, Gregory M. 119
Dumsha, Timotheus 424
Duncan, Christine 205
Duncan, Richard A. 352
Dunn, James G. 135
Dunn, Janice L. 61
Dunnam, Dee 32
Durant, Bea Bon 146
Durbin, Kaye 433
Durrett, Cathy 34
Dutton, Chris 126
Duych, Kathleen Dwyer 415
Dziengielewski, B. 417
Eardley IV, Bill 104
Easterling, Cathy Jones 29
Eatherton, Andrea L. 157
Eaton, Betty Mae 134
Eaton, Mary L. 395
Ebersole, Hal H. 115
Edgell, Ruth 328
Edra Sr., Gerardo C. 153
Edwards, Jerry 11
Edwards, Virginia Anne 323
Eerikainen, Inkeri 5
Egland, Rae 322
Ehlers, Florence Raush 85
Ehrick, Sarah 408

Eicas, Ruth Poorman 360
Eichstaedt, Kristy C. 329
Eischen, Don 46
Eisenhauer, Lynn 369
Eisenhoffer, Angela 72
Elgin, Florena M. 126
Elias, Amy 160
Elias, Debbie 184
Elizabeth, M. 384
Elkins, Alfred 247
Ellickson, Bonnie 16
Elliott, Bruce 275
Elliott, June Allegra 58, 88
Elliott, Naoma S. 441
Elliott, Willa 362
Ellis, Alma L. 291
Ellis, Elaine 217
Ellison, Kathryn M. 341
Ellsworth, Joyce 116
Elston, Letitia M. 451
Elswick, Karen 438
Elton, W.R. 426
Emami, Habib M.D. 94
Embse, Beth Vonder 161
Emery, Yvette Leigh 403
Emiro, Stacey 409
England, Norma M. 306
England, Perry W. 351
Epperley, Jean 195
Erickson, Cathleen 24
Erickson, Doris J. 117
Erreca, Evelyn 11
Ervin, Linda Lee 385
Escalante, Esperanza H. 81
Eskew, Janet 24
Essance, Ann R. 250
Essex, Fred 14
Essler, Susan 461
Estepp, Mary Sue 409
Ethridge, Jeani 149
Euscher, Sharon R. 445
Eutic, Herman 146
Evans, Betty 252
Evans, Jeanette Todd 19
Evans, Joyce 223
Evans, Sali Ford 372
Everett, Dorothy J. 121
Everleth, Jeffrey 176
Ewald, Clara 212
Ewing, Arthur 210
Exume, Aderson 159
Ezell-Gray, Deborah 187
Fahey, Linda Marie 331
Faig, Shirley 437
Fairhurst, Nona 317
Falter, Roberta J. 332
Fangmeier, Julia Strain 60
Fannin, Keotah M. 404
Fanning, Martha J. 312
Farlow, Colleen 89
Farneth, Erica 196
Farrell, Kate 307
Farrow, Alice M. 232
Fassler, Edith 297
Faulkner, Wilfred H. 319
Feder, Caroline 146
Fennell, Jonathan E. 84
Fenstermaker, Betty Brobst 247
Ferrell, Joanne K. 262
Ferrier, June Dawn 96
Ferrill, Amy 219
Fessler, Lulu 440
Fhynn, Julia L. 215
Fiamella, Connie K. 196
Fick-Cox, Dorothy A. 186
Fidelis, 200

Field, Scott 350
Fielding, Aileen 291
Figueiredo, Nancy 380
Figueroa, Brenda Eileen 58
Figueroa, Katie 441
Finau, Louise M. 367
Finch, John Boyd 160
Finger, Arlene 54
Finkbeiner, Hilda V. 232
Finkenbiner, Heather Lynn 10
Finleyson, Ellen Martha 263
Finn, Dick 145
Finn, Mary Ellen 365
Firth, Robert 463
Fischer, Fran 297
Fishbough, Renee 396
Fisher, Lynn 439
Fiskaali, Audrie M. 274
Fitzpatrick, Velma 306
Flanagan, Anna 239
Flanagan, Burnardine 138
Fleischer, Adeline 280
Fleming, Daniel L. 40
Fleshood, Huntger Bridgeford 282
Flett, Florence 199
Flick, Jeannie Ann 189
Flood, Dorothy 72
Flowell, Darlese McCraw 74
Flowers, Marva A. 461
Floyd, Pete 72
Flure, Lucille 376
Flynn, Sue 347
Foellner, Donald M. 116
Folk, Frankie Lewis 114
Foltin, Sadie Knight 432
Foltz, Leo 465
Forcier, P. Marguerite 394
Ford, Colleen 217
Forest, Bob 14
Forland, Amber 149
Formanek, Hedy Wolf 66
Forrester, Annie R. 132
Fortna, Ira 170
Fortune, Roxanne 378
Fortune, Stephen 455
Foster, Andrew J. 135
Foster, Cindy Sue 151
Foster, Virginia 324
Fought, Elsie Nelson 125
Fountain, Edwin B. 142
Foutz, Agnes 10
Fox, Katherine Ann 420
Francis, Patrice 369
Frank, Francie A. 263
Franklin, Jeanne C. 87
Franse, Jean 166
Frantz, Elizabeth L. 210
Frauchiger, Patricia 398
Frazier, Kenneth 407
Frederick, Carol 50
Frees, Margaret M. 317
Fremgen, Darlene 279
Frick, Dumas F. 284
Frick, Emily June 7
Friedlander, Anita 150
Frieze, Clara L. 108
Frisch, Peter R. 452
Fry, Darlene 275
Fry, Harry A. 177
Frye, Elizabeth J. 141
Fuhr, Jean I. 270
Fuller, Deloris A. 266
Fulmer, Delores I. 8
Fulton Jr., Robert E. 387
Furby, William C. 358
Gade, Beth 205

Gagne, Marian F. 445
Gagnon, Christie 173
Gaines, Dorothy E. 140
Gallahan, Eydi 38
Galley, V. Ursula 522
Gane, Sally 329
Gange, Clara M. 286
Garate, Patricia P. 386
Garber, H. L. 309
Garcia, Carmen 255
Garcia, Eleanor D. 47
Garcia, Ruben D. 460
Gardner, Donald D. 141
Gardner, JoAnna G. 34
Garka, Dorothy V. 98
Garner, Jacquelyn C. 132
Garrett Jr., Grover J. 87
Garrett, Charlotte Ladshaw 186
Garrett, Lester E. 342
Garrett, Paul E. 427
Garrison, Therese 369
Gatchell, Felicity J. 78
Gates-Kirk, Helen S. 72
Gayer, Brett S. 134
Gayle, Nancy Nelson 315
Geeting, Catherine 52
Geffner, Howard K. 76
Gehlen, Heidi 245
Geist, Lacy E. 317
Gersbach, Helen 47
Gertz, Estelle 226
Ghupta-Williams, Beverly Nyoka 83
Gibbens, Dianne 294
Gibson, Anne Evans 42
Gilbert, Suzan Smith 456
Giles, Judy 130
Giles, Miriam 462
Gillenwater, Zeddie 306
Gillespie, David D. 185
Gilley, Karen 443
Gilliam, Juanita Creech 161
Gilman, Ruth F. 373
Gilmore, Mabel D. 339
Gilweit, Edwin R. 166
Gingrich, Marie E. 333
Ginn, Maude 398
Giordana, Nadia 366
Gipe, Ken 450
Gjertsen, Britt Meredith 115
Gladman, Diana L. 245
Glass, Mel 388
Glazer, Ian 129
Glenn, Linda J. 437
Glinbizzi, Jacalyn 259
Glowacki, Martha 433
Gobor, Andreas 226
Goens, Natalie L. 448
Goetz, Eldrus 175
Goff, Cathi 175
Goff, Jamie 62
Goldfarb, Ruth 391
Golightly, Helen Trouton 139
Golley Jr., Howard 252
Golliher, Ruby 351
Gompf, Edward D. 244
Gonzales, Diane 249
Gonzales, Maxene 338
Goodhue, Jean W. 200, 215
Goodspeed, Cassie 135
Goodstone, Erica (Ph.D.) 251
Gordon, Brian 245
Gordon, Ellen K. 237
Gordon, Joan L. 523
Gordon, Ray 262
Gordon, Ruby Coggins 353
Gorham, Lee 421

Gorman, Shirley Anne (R.A.) 454
Gosch, Alice 63
Gouti, Sammy 307
Grace, Christine 222
Grace, Ruth C. 325
Grady, Charles E. 125
Graf, Anne Browne 132
Graham, Bob 437
Graham, Doris 217
Graham, Neela 522
Gramolini, Dante 252
Grandchamp, Barbara 273
Grandchamp, Juliann M. 64
Granieri, Celeste Kusnell 111
Grant, Gladys 28
Grassi, Gayle W. 305
Graves, Jacqueline C. 263
Graves, Jacqueline C. 263
Gravseth, Todd A. 452
Grayson, T. Michelle 417
Greaves, Barbara P. C. 203
Green, Elbert P. 90
Green, Ellen Ann 78
Green, Elmer R. 133
Green, Fordyce 218
Greenberg, Sandra J. 328
Greene, Ryan T. 418
Greene, Vivan 362
Greger, Terry Lee 462
Gregersen, Carolyn D. 277
Gregerson, Jennifer 59
Gregg, Cecilia Roseline 279
Gregory, Evelyn "Sugar" 136
Gregory, Lura Nancy 453
Greywolf, Billy 207
Gribble, Mary 361
Griesel, Charlotte I. 47
Griffen, Karn W. 436
Griffeth, Tanya 323
Griffin, Darren 59
Griffin, Lucille 354
Griffin, Richard B. 355
Grimes, Ralph E. 430
Grinkley, Ethel K. 218
Griswold, Jeani 300
Griswold, Portia 331
Grouf, Inez Spradling 25
Groves, Garry 299
Grow, Barbara 281
Grube, Linda B. 400
Gruetter, Dana 158
Guadagnino, Anthony Michael 196
Guardiano, Holly Jeanine 241
Guenther, Edris 192
Guess, Dory 277
Guman, Pauline Tatiana Mizok 375
Gunn, Zack Marvin 353
Guth, Chrissi 200
Gutho, Phyllis 462
Gutteridge, Laura A. 451
Haase, Jeri 178
Hackett, James H. 17
Hadbavny, Barbara 111
Haddad, Adele 203
Hadden, Margaret Sutton 325
Haggerty, Mark W. 357
Hahn, Jewell 45
Hahne, Janet S. 52
Haines, Sarah B. 444
Hale, Jennifer 94
Hall, B. Washburne 340
Hall, Bertha 244
Hall, Connie Ayers 248
Hall, Elizabeth A. 107
Hall, Florine H. 190
Hall, Grace R. W. 151

Hall, Gwen H. 77
Hall, Julie Jarrett 156
Hall, Robert 326
Halliwell, Doris M. 70
Hamel, Shawna A. 388
Hamilton, Rhoda 386
Hamilton-Nelson, S. 449
Hammerberg, J.M. Bennett 429
Hammond, Joan Crawford 92
Hampton, Charles R. 261
Hamric, Ramona E. 359
Hancock, Brandie Leigh 268
Hand, Eleanor J. 276
Handler, Dorothy S. 34
Handsaker, Edith A. 198
Handy, Barbara 128
Hansen, Floyd 40
Hansen, Helen P. 120
Hanson, Julia 68
Haranago, Beatrice 251
Harden, Connie 265
Harding, Charles G. 93
Harding, Helen 111
Hardy, Julia Irene 81
Hargesheimer, Sandee 412
Harlan, Mary Ann 395
Harper, Lynette 395
Harper, Monterey J. 346
Harrington, Michele Len 444
Harris, Andy 66
Harris, Claude E. 79
Harris, Monica 425
Harrison, Cecil 25
Harrison, Charlotte Knight 103
Harrison, Clara 23
Harrison, Valda M. 310
Hart, Doloras J. 48
Hartley, Brenda 184
Hartman, Jessie V. 218
Hartman, Lois Ijams 432
Hartnell-Stobbe, Kate 360
Harvey, Charles E. 37
Hatch, Willye 364
Hauenstein, Wendell E. 389
Haupt, Cecilia G. 234
Hauser, Bernice 194
Haverland-Reynolds, Betty 113
Hawk, Heidi D. 50
Hawkins, Ruth M. 458
Hawkins, Sara Graham 344
Hayes, James Allen 163
Hayes, Jessica T. 114
Haynes, Earnest B. 181
Hayslett, Evelyn Ver Dow 80
Heape, Iva Lou 103
Heaton, Carol 267
Hecker, Melissa A. Crissman 405
Hedrick, Edward 140
Heffley, Hollie 88
Hegyeli, Ruth Johnsson 449
Heikes, Judy 294
Heindel, Jennifer 224
Heiser, Maria 358
Held, Janet M. 174
Heller, Mary Frances L. 326
Hellmers, Frances Wilber 10
Helton, Sylvia 327
Henderson, Marjorie 419
Hendon, Wanda 324
Hendrickson, Dale 239
Hendrix, Louise Butts 432
Hendrix, Sylvia 306
Hendron, Sarah A.E. 376
Henley, Carolyn 269
Henry, Eugene R. 171
Henry, Helen S. 304

Herman, Gary Allen 273
Hermann, Edna May 268
Hern, Bonnie Jean 238
Hernandez, Gil 91
Hernandez, Yolanda 421
Herrera, Eufracina Isabel 67
Herring, Chanie 198
Herrington, Bary Lee 226
Herzberger, Magda 521
Herzog, Julie 136
Hester, Sara J. 335
Heywood, Helen 128
Hickey, Ardelphia 162
Hicks, Ben 252
Hicock, Clarie Waeber 201
Higdon, Grace 30
Higgins, Jinny 49
Hilderbrand, Gilbert L. 60
Hill Jr., Eugene B. 85
Hill, Candace 127
Hill, Clara 58
Hill, Diane 130
Hill, Emma Lee 132
Hill, Eric v. K. 135
Hill, Thomas E. 327
Hilliard, Dawn 62
Hilmer, Jodi Ann 9
Hite, Delmer R. 190
Hite, Eunice H. 23
Hite-Smith, Helen L. 233
Hlavach, Jenn 76
Hobby, Ellen Jane 230
Hockenberry, Gloria 45
Hoey, John J. 260
Hoff, Michele E. 379
Hoffman, Anna Mae 102
Hoffman, E. 157
Hoffman, Freida 90
Hoffman, Lynn M. 320
Hogan, Joseph M. 80
Hogue, Roma 403
Holbrook, Carol A. 156
Holden, Michael P. 399
Holland, Angela 292
Holland, Regina B. 342
Holloway, Dawna Lee 272
Holloway, Vivian L. 358
Holmes, Brother Michael 316
Holmes, Edithe Zeigler 208
Holmes, H. Bud 60
Holmes-Daniel, Jonette 98
Holt, Thelma Lou 431
Homan, Gary M. 223
Hooper, Eulaliah T. 144
Hornacek, Tim 337
Horrocks, Alice L. 40
Horsley, Helen H. 131
Hougham, Duane 214
Houlton, LaVonne 422
House, Kerri L. 523
Houvener, Eloise M. 46
Howard Jr., Donald C. 150
Howard, Christina 109
Howard, Dusti D. 300
Howard, Katrina 355
Howe, Ruth A. 450
Howell, Barbara 167
Howell, Darlene M. 72
Howell, Eileen 38
Howell, Sherry 323
Hruska, Vera 433
Hu, Jane Hwa 56
Huber, Betty 271
Huddleston, Sheila G. 459
Huff, Carla Marie 77
Huffman, James M. 242

Huffstutler III, Dean 80
Hughes, Audra Jerlene 119
Hughes, Christine R. 9
Hughes, Joyce 190
Hughes, Lucille 342
Huie, Joella A. 298
Hukill, Robert M. 307
Hull, Kathryn B. 437
Hulse, Myra 408, 424
Hulsemann, William 347
Hult, Helena 289
Hummel, Eleanor Henry 229
Humphries, Channing 3
Humphries, Jo Leemonda 78
Humphries, Linda K. 371
Hunsinger, Margaret V. 308
Hunt, Dorothy K. Dr. 216
Hunt, Patsie Messinger 348
Hunter, Agnes 170
Hunter, Cheri Lynn 9
Hunter, Iris 88
Hunter, Robert F. 394
Huntington, Daphine 54
Hurn, Della 295
Hutchinson, Lawrence 369
Hutchison, Effie B. 256
Huyck, Betty 91
Hyche, Jerri Dean 298
Hymer, George A. 43
Ihde, Betty Neeb 284
Inman, Edna 197
Irvin, Evelyn Locke 235
Irving, Faith T. 37
Isabelle, Margarita 406
Isbrecht, E. Karl 432
Isenia, Elvanelga C. 123
Ivory, Jewelene 48
Jackson, Brian M. 254
Jackson, Joey 197
Jackson, Susan Taylor 345
Jackson-Carter, Gertrude 110
Jaefer, Barbara 181
Jagge, Stephanie 415
Jaksha, Clifford 117
James, Ray Allen 387
James, Zelda 393
Janson, Daivd C. 119
Janssens, Andre' M. 73
Jarrell Jr., Green 229
Jarrell, Donna L. 242
Jaszewski, Robin 461
Javines, Francisco O. 235
Jean-Francois, Marie-Catheline 397
Jenkins, Cassandra 224
Jenkins, Dorothy E. 282
Jenkins, Dorothy Jean 95
Jenkins, Ron 419
Jennings, Aileen 63
Jennings, Jo Linda 287
Jensen, Gertrude G. 188
Jerdon, Yvonne Dwight 396
Jeske, Billie 281
Jett, Linda 400
Jette, Christine 65
Johnson, Agnes 152
Johnson, Chris 115
Johnson, Constance M. 44
Johnson, Elsie V. 221
Johnson, Elva Nell 95
Johnson, Freddie Mae 148
Johnson, Gladys Taft 144
Johnson, Henrietta LaVerne 299
Johnson, J. J. 60
Johnson, Janet M. 206
Johnson, Jean Stephens 134
Johnson, John O. 303

Johnson, Kelly E. 411
Johnson, Lisa Ann Wade 416
Johnson, Ray 459
Johnson, Richard A. 406
Johnson, T.E. 422
Johnson, William R. 326
Johnston, Kiley 433
Johnstone, Andrew A. 127
Joner Jr., Loyal T. 424
Jones, Annie Gay T. 78
Jones, Bobbie 109
Jones, D. Rosena 71
Jones, Donald 225
Jones, Dorothy Johnson 138
Jones, Elaine 148
Jones, Grace 154
Jones, James M. 198
Jones, Joan M. 153
Jordan, Harold D. 44
Joseph, Dorothy Ludowyk 28
KC, Amanda 104
Kabe, Aino Kohaloo 36
Kachurak, Christine M. 74
Kaems, Charlotte J. 159
Kafaf, Jennifer Lyn 107
Kahanek, Jennifer 303
Kahn, Leslie M. 343
Kaminski, Debra S. 27
Kane, David M. 283
Kantor, Anatole 255
Kapell, Lydia Ann 521
Karaszewski, Douglas Alan 145
Kasian, Dorothy 222
Kathman, Brenda Doe 289
Katz, Judith 233
Katz, Peter H. 393
Kavanaugh, Rose M. 391
Kayson, Annelyn 174
Kazandjian, Vahe A. 522
Keefe, Elizabeth 299
Keels, Thomassine Ringo 451
Keens, Teri 326
Keith, Karoline 372
Kelalis, Barbara Annalisa 301
Kelling, Nancy Marie 396
Kelly, Eileen 86
Kemmerer, Anna B. 259
Kennedy, Isaac Jay 39
Kennedy, Joyce Ann Carter 300
Kenyon, Lauri 430
Khabeer, Beryl 273
Khing, James G. 171
Kidd, Stacie C. 456
Kiefer, Bob 219
Killin, Mamie Lou 365
Killion, Paula L. 347
Kilpatrick, Geraldine E. 293
Kimberley, Eleanor 21
Kindell-Watts, Marjorie 409
Kinder, Lois W. 423
Kindred, Jewel 239
King, Alma Jean 170
King, Floyd W. 90
King, Paul E. 382
King, Rosalyn M. 427
Kingsbury, Lisa 374
Kinte, Kunta 364
Kinzie, A.A. 286
Kirby, Anna 247
Kirby, Serena Ann 331
Kirkland, Charlotte 105
Kittinger, Don C. 206
Klabunde, Florence A. 99
Klavitter, George H. 270
Kleckley, Edgar H. 31
Kleckner, Johnnye L. 278

Klein, Viviane 435
Kleis, Edna 215
Klingbeil, Glennie M. 105
Kniff, Dawn Cahoon 120
Knight, Virginia Carlson 351
Knox, Judy A. 203
Knupp, Lori Souder 346
Koblentz, Bunni 119
Kobs, Lois Lynda 408
Koch, Loretta K. 383
Koch, Sue 334
Kock, May 380
Konobeck, Beverly C. 19
Koontz, Kay 378
Koontz, Peggy J. 356
Korte, Sallie 325
Kossey, Lorene 410
Koster, Della 240
Koudela, Diane 219
Kovach, George D. 71
Kovaleski, Nancy L. 323
Krambeck, Amy D. 172
Krantz, Pearl Bragg 447
Krebs, John C. 28
Kreidl, Norbert Joachim 402
Krikorian, Jim 178
Kristensen, Jacqueline 205
Kromer, Della Harrison 221
Kruckow, Sarah 363
Kruger, Betty Lou Bremer 42
Kruper, Milly 356
Kruttlin, JoAnn 19
Kruttlin, Josie 263
Krycka, Kevin C. 458
Kuhn, Grayce E. 299
Kuhns, Julie 56
Kula, Edward J. 150
Kullberg, Rhea Rebecca 334
Kumar, Tobi J. 446
Kurtz, Curt 147
Kurtz, Jane 253
Kuster, Missy 394
Kwaterski, Caroline C. 115
La Belle, Mary 444
La Bianco, Dolores 180
La Prell, G.W. 165
LaBranche, Gregg 60
LaRocca, John W. 305
LaTorre, Frank 261
LaVoy-Lewis, Deanna 45
Lacy-Tang, Jean 6
Lai, Merle K. 352
Laird, Eric 148
Lakan, Pamela J. 314
Lake Jr., Donald F. 55
Lamb, Auburn J. 264
Lambert, Beth 36
Lambert, Lynda 523
Lamie, Mary E. 449
Lamkin, Rebecca 337
Lampe, Anna M. 278
Lampkins, Lillian E. 390
Lancaster, Craig 138
Landry, Jennifer A. 185
Lane, Jennifer 165
Lane, Mary Jean 364
Lane-Geswien, Mary 363
Lange, Violet D. 360
Langer, Frank A. 32
Langford, Mary Frances 389
Lanier, Naomi 349
Lanier, Sandra Fulton 319
Lansing, Bee 7
Larimore, Rose 459
Larsen, Heather M. 304
Larsen, Nicole Marie 523

Larson, Carol C. 127
Lason, Holly 76
Latif, Abdul 216
Lau, Arnold J. 89
Lau, Harri 301
Lauer, Jon Lee 259
Lawler, Brownie 193
Layden, Joseph 283
Layman Jr., Donald G. 31
Lazzari, Jennifer 263
Le Barron, Shannon 376
LePore, Christy 296
Leach, Betsy H. 149
Leach, Joyce Scroggs 39
Lee, Coralie 102
Lee, Curtis Donald 104
Lee, Doris 8
Lee, Doris M. 101
Lee, Imogene V. 295
Lee, Jim H. 53
Lee, Jimmy 44
Lee, Kou 401
Lee, Linda 423
Lee, M. Evelyn 440
Lee, Monica 405
Lee, Rachael M. 380
Lefcourt, Stanley R. 367
Lehan, Heidi Ann 34
Lehmann, Helen Tate 291
Leineweber, Mary 388
Leitz, Janice E. 51
Lenderink, Melinda Sue 422
Lenn, Airec 196
Leonard, Janet 133
Lepore, Anastacia D. 22
Lesser, Dena Beth 14
Lettsome, Elizabeth Adelaide 13
Leturgey, Gladys L. 212
Levin, Dorayne 192
Levin, Robert H. 404
Levine, Abe 126
Levine, Adina 302
Levine, Jeffrey 82
Levine, Mindy 441
Lewis, Ed 268
Lewis, Kathleen Kay 353
Lewis, Lynn C. 523
Lewis, Sarah 310
Lewis, Walter J. 319
Lia, Linda S. 308
Libby, Doris G. 271
Licastri, Cheryl 284
Lichoski, John 289
Liddell-Donald, Odies 349
Light, Ray 383
Likes, Jamie 137
Limon, Beatrice H. 157
Lindmeier, Judy A. 56
Lindsley, Mary F. 523
Ling, Tany 375
Linsalata, Amy 137
Lipman, Julie Ann Bailey 56
Lipscomb, Wilma 431
Lipson, Jonathan D. 158
Lisovich, John V. 179
Little, Amy 66
Little, Gloria M. 53
Loberg, Virginia 363
Lockhart, Mercedes V. 456
Lockwood, Jean C. 103
Lofton, Eleanor R. 86
Logan, Margaret M. 362
Lombardo, Julia 106
Londgrof, Ellen 277
Loney, Hazel S. 114
Long, Darcy Erin-Marie 105

Long, Donna M. 140
Long, Frances R. 204
Long, Fred N. 216
Long, James B. 195
Lore, James 145
Lorenzo, Natalie 461
Loring, Cheryl Mari Lakey 58
Lott, Shrell 420
Loughney, Edna Van Dyke 28
Louthan, Martanne 465
Lovell, Donna Marie 209
Lowell, Edna Mae 212
Lowery, Juli M. 29
Lozano, Virginia M. 431
Lucas, Amelia 135
Lucas, Gayleen 211
Lucas, Grafton E. 177
Lucey, Thomas A. 373
Ludolff, Connie 270
Ludwiczak-Cadd, Anna 208
Lummus, Barbara 298
Lunceford, Melva J. 363
Lundin, Darrell 144
Lundstrom, Milton C. 465
Lundy, Brian W. 113
Lunsford, Joseph 121
Luporini, Josephine S. 147
Lux, Dorothea Ruth (Urban) 247
Lynch, George 5
Lynch, Mary Agnes 365
Lyon, Beverly 75
Lyons, Beryl A. 155
Lyson, Kasia 318
Mac Donald, M. Bernice 313
Mace, Marilyn 373
Mack, Helen 206
Mackaig, Janet 12
Mackey Jr., Howard H. 241
Mackey, James T. 48
Mackey, Ruth V. 442
Macklin, Linda T. 329
Macy, Betty A. 239
Macy, Bonnie 85
Maden, Tesha M. 366
Madison, Anne Marie 182
Madison, Jacqueline E. 24
Madrill, Margaret Beryldine 436
Mahalko, Ann 34
Mahan, Brandi 73
Maier, Albert M. 40
Mailhot, John Michael 73
Maine, Angeline 143
Mainridge, Michelle King 446
Maish, Jean 227
Majors, Ella 243
Maksad, Ali K. 42
Malleen, Beulah 245
Maloney, Madalyn 440
Maloy, Edward 117
Mangrum, Bonnie B. 267
Manley, Chris 82
Mann, Florence Weber 84
Manning, Jay F. 189
Manning, Jean 258
Manning, Jean 69
Manning, Mandie Lee 373
Manon, Helenmae 240
Manoogian, Joanna 266
Maples, Valerie A. 385
Marble, Juanita 116
Mardale, Simona C. 456
Margolin, Abraham E. 234
Mariano, Carmela 162
Marino, Eugene A. 57
Markowski, Benedict 292
Markworth, Paul 399

Marschner, Loretta Rine 410
Marsh, J. Daniel 182
Marshall, Doris 110
Marshall, Peter 359
Marshall, Shannon 447
Marski, Beverly 63
Marten, Richard A. 434
Martens, Marlene 405
Martens, Pat Kenney 335
Marti, Jo Ann 216
Martin, Ann 181
Martin, Carol A. 194
Martin, Carroll M. 80
Martin, Charles F. 91
Martin, Hattie 143
Martin, Irma Jean 196
Martin, Leslie 443
Martin, Lisa 423
Martin, Ralph E. 342
Marzano, Carin 265
Masi, Nancy 354
Maskel, Hazel 264
Massey, Linda J. 354
Mast, Melissa 348
Masterson, Jane 122
Mates, Annette 272
Mathaller, Dolorine 242
Mathews, Vivian 343
Matic IV, Tomas D. Estolloso 314
Matthes, Grace 4
Matthews, Cindy J. 124
Mauceri, Joseph J. 249
Mauldin, Dorothy (OWG) 54
Maunakea, K. Kamalukukui 312
Mauro, Anne 241
Maxson, Darrel 81
Maxwell, Katherine Gant 338
May, Tanya 329
Mazrolle, Barbara C. 163
McAfee, Helen M. 35
McAnally, Elizabeth Haynes 24
McBryde, John M. 34
McCabe, Christieann 116
McCall, Bunny 194
McCandless, Dolores M. 120
McCane, Candi 82
McCarthy, James J. 122
McCarthy, Stephen J. 451
McCauley, Jacqueline 257
McCliment, Frances Bucaro 236
McClure, Betty Jo Pursell 201
McClure, Jerry L. 25
McCoy, Holly A. 166
McCoy, Kathryn Denise 400
McCoy, Roxie Oxford 310
McCreary, Paul D. 330
McCrory, Beverly Lynn 200
McCroskey, Dorothy 225
McCulley, Karen 435
McCulloh Sr., Charles W. 286
McCulloh, Evelyn Butler 167
McCullough, Beth 208
McCullough, Emma Melinda 22
McDaniel, Glenda 13
McDaniel, Shannon 397
McDaniels, Dorice 70
McDonald, Brennan 294
McDonald, Helen Pearl 121
McDougal, Jennifer 204
McElwain, Judith Kay 9
McFadden, H. J. 108
McFall, Micky 453
McFall, Myrna C. 371
McGauhey, K. Arthur 393
McGhee, Wayne 310
McGill, Esda L. 217

McGlothlin, Berta 202
McGonigal, Claire 3
McGonigle, LaDean 439
McGovern, Fay-Linda (King) 176
McGowan, Luana 336
McGraw, Charlyne 144
McGraw, Rebecca 331
McGregor, Jennifer 43
McGuire, Rik 419
McInnis, Annie 64
McKay, Charlotte 230
McKee, Jane Clark 12
McKee-Abbott, Glenda 44
McKell-Jeffers, Margaret 447
McKelvey, Carl J. 136
McKibben, Joanne 183
McKibbin, Michael G. 356
McKinley, Michael 362
McKinney, Charlotte Borsos 184
McKinnon, Aimee 83
McLain, Alysia 20
McLain, Miriam 337
McLendon, Betty 160
McMaster, Muriel 435
McMorris, Arlene V. 256
McMullen, James A. 22
McMurphy, Michaele K. 444
McMurry, Gloria P. 138
McNeal, Carrol 169
McNutt, Misty 443
McQuilkin, Randy 353
McRee, Giorgetta 94
McTavish, Claire 125
McVey, Judy Kay 233
Mcwatters, Edd David 181
Meade, Ernestine Collins 69
Meadows, Thelma L. 337
Medendorp, April L. 74
Medley-Lopez, Jodi 179
Meears, Joan Doddis 11
Meek, Priscilla Anne 401
Meeker, Don L. 174
Meier, Annegret 265
Meilahn, Nancy 334
Melgar, Kira 374
Mello, Donna Lee 241
Mendoza, Anthony 188
Mentry, Flora J. 22
Mentzer, Sally Jo 453
Menzie, Jane 107
Mercorelli, Anthony 270
Merritt, Gerald O. 255
Merritt, Joan K. 97
Merritt, Lola Neff 434
Merry, Marilyn 410
Merryman, Helen L. 301
Merryweather, Joyce Johnson 286
Merth, Jennifer 253
Meshaw, Gregory 195
Messerall, Irene G. 129
Messner, Mabel J. 355
Metcalf, Diana Richardson 15
Mettler, Ruth 398
Meverden, Ann Marie 168
Meyer, Mark M. 430
Meyerink, Harriet C. 170
Meznarsic, Amy C. 188
Michalski, Michele 392
Michanczyk III, Michael J. 359
Michels, Carmen Bozzone 27
Middleton, Rosalind 456
Mieth, Chris Michael 229
Mihalik, Bianca 166
Milazzo, Carolyn 53, 267
Miller, Beckie A. 161
Miller, Charles W. 281

Miller, Gerald L. 137
Miller, Helen 26
Miller, Herbert 24
Miller, John W. 4
Miller, Junior L. 305
Miller, Kristine Elizabeth 357
Miller, Marjorie M. 312
Miller, Nancy M. 428
Miller, Robin 421
Mills, Jeni 100
Milton, Georgia (Rev.) 11
Minchak, P. J. 449
Mincy, Daniel S. 199
Miniter, Christopher 296
Miranda, Jill 98
Mitchell, Ann 6
Mitchell, Charlotte R. 178
Mitchell, Lynn 320
Mixon, Gladys 147
Mizuta, Iwao 35
Moad, Joy 123
Mobus, Scott W. 365
Moe, Deborah R. 267
Moffet, Mary 330
Moll, Meredith Diane 384
Monaco, Addie 221
Mongtomery, Patricia 379
Monica, Jackie Della 220
Monroe, Jennifer P. J. 74
Montz, Lynne 368
Moody, Eula M. 276
Moody, Kathy 343
Moore, Dorothy 269
Moore, Dorothy 269
Moore, Earline 100
Moore, Frances 51
Moore, Freeman Edward 295
Moore, Gina M. 168
Moore, Laura 439
Moore, Lynn S. 418
Moore, Teresa L. 386
Moran, Charles 135
Moreno, Robert Michael 309
Morgan, Michelle A. 418
Morganna, 84
Morreale, B. Lee 397
Morris, Dorothy 262
Morris, Emeline Pennock 68
Morris, Heather Nicole 120
Morris, Johanna 122
Morris, Laura 445
Morris, Michelle D. 433
Morris, Virginia 396
Morris-Dillon, Dorothy 38
Morrison, Emily 112
Morrison, Michael E. 389
Mortimer, Phyllis 453
Morton, Charles W. 178
Mosher, Jean W. 209
Mosteller Jr., Herman J. 122
Motika, Thomas 386
Moulder, Barbara N. 176
Mouren, Juanda Hurst 89
Moutoux, Ernest E. 227
Mowat, Duedene K. 304
Mowry, Linda S. 319
Moylan, A.M.C. 378
MucHille, Joanne 234
Mueller, Jennifer 137
Muja, Kathleen A. 321
Mulcahy, P.F.C. Michael R. 397
Mulhern, Brian 73
Mullen, Ruth V. 413
Mullins, B. H. 443
Mulvaney, Nikki 349
Munoz-Knowles, Martha 386

Murdock, Edward Nolden 98
Murdza, Lydia 333
Murley, Beulinda S. 280
Murphy, Jacqui E. 133
Murphy, Jay P. 98
Murphy, Mike 423
Murphy, Sarah 345
Murray, Connie 240
Murrey, Jean 19
Mushinsky, Joseph 50
Musloski, Jamie C. 81
Musser, Jean 94
Mustain, Joyce 155
Muth, Heather 143
Myers, Bernice 182
Nada, 115
Namia, M.L. 340
Nason, Don 31
Navarro, Victor M. 523
Neale, Vesta M. 419
Neault, Monique 410
Nebeker, Eileen 213
Neff, Ginny Mae 100
Neidig, Isabel O. 167
Nelson, Annie 44
Nelson, Charles L. 238
Nelson, Clara I. 3
Nelson, Duane S. 193
Nelson, Peggy T. 441
Nesmith, Barbara R. 19
Nesset, Marcia L. 416
Neveil, Lisa M. 412
Newcome, Joel Thomas 254
Nibarger, Irene 190
Nichols, Bessey 71
Nichols, Charlene F. 152
Nichols, Cornelius J. 200
Nichols, Pat 454
Nicholson, Brenda 39
Nickels, Lisa 335
Nielsen, Shirley 374
Niles, June 17
Nissel, Anna Lee 271
Nobles, Addie Belle 165
Nolan, Joan 91
Norris, Sheri Lin 452
North, Barry W. 11
Norton, Edna 176
Norton, Linda Seiberling 446
Norville, Nancy Jo 324
Nuckols, Peggy 378
Nunez, Mariah 307
O'Donnell, Ronald 415
O'Kelly Jr., Anderson D. 257
O'Malley, Donna 95
O'Neill, Michael 458
O'Toole, Darby 427
Oakes, Owen B. 414
Oakleaf, Edna R. 173
Obuch, Judith A. 30
Ochwat, Margaret M. 379
Oehmke, Dorothy S. 304
Oellien, Alyce Marie 245
Olender, Wanda J. 381
Olesen, Don 139
Oliver, Luther H. 391
Olivera, James A. 8
Olsak, Ruth 382
Olson, Christin 96
Olson, Jeanette 261
Olson, Mildred E. 459
Osborn, Chris 54
Osborne, Jean 26
Osenkarski, Robert W. 445
Ostrander, Genevieve 218
Ostrom, Helen M. 13

Ostrowicki, Alice 57
Otis, Faylene 214
Otto, Bill 129
Otto, Eleanor 272
Oum, Channaly 221
Overman, Shawn 442
Overton, Jane Taylor 247
Owen, Norma Jean 452
Owens, Frances 248
Owens, Janice Sherfy 202
Owens, Sylvia 422
Ownbey, Jenna V. 26
Oxley, Anne T. 214
Pacht, Janice 267
Padilla, John Paul 114
Page, J. Lynanne 420
Page, Jack C. 199
Page, Martha C. 321
Paino, Cynthia 35
Painton, Clyde W. 22
Palabasan, Ann Casanova 295
Palermo, Cheryl G. 232
Palmenta, Christina R. 51
Palmer, Lavinia Hunton 405
Palombi, Rae Lynn 315
Papadopoulos, Joanne 101
Pappacoda, Frances M. 228
Parbs, Robert C. 357
Pardallis, Vicki Alexis 333
Parker, David W. 48
Parker, Dortha Mae 259
Parker, Jo Lea 123
Parkinson, Mary Eveleyn 308
Parsons, Beulah Lockhart 281
Parsons, Jean N. 30
Pasternak, Tina 414
Patenaude, Carolyn 221
Patenaude, Jennifer Jeanne 13
Patronella, Rose Marie 346
Patterson, Eva D. 249
Patteson, Goldie E. 96
Patton, Anah 64
Patton, Steven E. 382
Paul, Jean C. 155
Paulsen, Carrie Cross 112
Paulsen, Jessie 9
Pawlowski, Catherine E. 250
Payne, Edith Mae 296
Payne, Erin 219
Paynter, Sharon K. 462
Paz, Elizabeth 131
Peacher, Ruby Tippit 352
Pease, Paul Andrew 375
Peck, Isabel M. 116
Pedersen, L.A. 314
Pedersen, Virginia 312
Pedigo, Steven B. 381
Peek, Debrina 124
Peirso, Vera A. 434
Pelland, Jo 224
Peluso, Kimber Lee 432
Pemberton, Irene C. 74
Pence, J. R. 455
Peng, Ling Fan 306
Penn, Lora M. 464
Penn, Richard 353
Perajica, Diana 79
Perdomo, Oreste Flavio 318
Perez, Gilda M.221
Perez, Renelle 368
Perez, Ruben 450
Perkins, Rodney 321
Perry Sr., Clay 177
Perry, Lois 464
Perry, Mary Jane 460
Perry, Peter P. 424

Persons, Mollie J. 397
Peter, Bonnie Simmons 299
Peters, Jane S. 179
Peters, Patty 358
Peterson, Alpha Arme 145
Peterson, Diane 244
Petes, Karen A. 308
Peto, J.J. 165
Petrali, John 81
Petrovic, Debra 5
Petrut, Dorothea M. 128
Pezzica, Andrew L. 97
Pfau, Stephani 394
Phelps Sr., Sidney Lee 313
Phelps, Francis 60
Phelps, Ila 16
Phillips Jr., Hugh 7
Phillips, Agnes 179
Phillips, Elizabeth 123
Phillips, Julia M. 42
Phillips, Kenneth A. 384
Phillips, Rose Anne 361
Phillips, Sam 387
Phillips, Sarah E. 370
Phoenix, W. Scott 463
Pickard, Muriel Yakir 416
Pickrell, Fred 5
Pierce, Parnell 344
Pierritz, Jane 107
Pierson, Karen A. 455
Pike, Alice 230
Piper, Jo 201
Pitts, Avis 41
Plante, David P. 157
Plytynski-Young, Judith M. 258
Pohlman, Clarence 284
Poirier, Joyce A. 127
Pollestad, Betty Lou 106
Portela, Magda Tumi 412
Porter, Betty Flanagan 266
Porter, Edith Mariniak 292
Porter, Grace E. 205
Porter, Joyce 227
Porter, Michael Leroy 324
Posey, Glory 264
Post, Deborah Mae 181
Powell, Billy J. 182
Powers, Rae Kae 338
Pressley, Louise 416
Prest, Virginia 414
Price, Ina 57
Price, Leslie Dean 430
Price, Marean J. 393
Price, Rosemarie 428
Pringle, Lidia Wasowicz 392
Pritchet, Carolyn Sue 29
Probasco, John 20
Probasco, John Munck 134
Probsdorfer, Andrea M. 101
Prohorenko, Nonna 392
Protzmann, Miles L. 428
Pruczinski, Christina 84
Pruitt, Ann 108
Pugh, Julie 205
Purtee, Clara C. 51
Putnam, Vera E. 330
Putta, Jane H. 153
Pybus, Helen M. 215
Qually, Dean Lowell 69
Quamme, David 256
Rabe, Heidi Lynne 83
Race, Anna 229
Racette, Jenny 110
Radosevich, James A. 230
Radzanowski, Darlene C. 300
Raether, Arnold L. 97

Raeuber, Ethel 206
Ragsdale, Daniel E. 55
Raines, Annie 245
Raines, Annie 287
Rains, Ed 40
Raley, Dilys 278
Ralston, John 211
Ramirez, Jennifer 238
Ramnanan, Lakshmi 447
Ramsey, Amanda 138
Randall, Michael Paul 413
Raquepo, Connie R. 69
Rasmussen, Michelle Christine 387
Raugh, Sally 332
Rauschning, Jean I. 121
Rawls, Lisa 343
Raya, Kiko 396
Raybal, Sharon Ruth McEntire 324
Read, M. Margaret 363
Reap-Williams, Agnes Theresa 185
Recupero, Anna A. 66
Redell, J. Buckland (Professor) 85
Redwine, Diana 83
Reece, Delores Wilson 61
Reed, Deborah L. 128
Reed, Dorothy Marlene 95
Reed, Emma Noon 55
Reed, Garnet 290
Reed, Gladys 293
Reed, June E. 290
Reed, Stella M. 356, 438
Rees, Wesley W. 408
Reiff, Kathryn L. 327
Reilly, Diane E. 106
Remillard, Jennifer 97
Remy, Joyce Kay Williams 305
Rennell, Jeanne Albers 251
Rensel, Anne Marron 282
Repiscak, Chris-Mary 243
Repiscak, Chris-Mary 285
Retkowski, Catherine Dunham 132
Reyes, Benito F. 50
Reynolds, Rita 425
Rhea, Dorothy Seiber 52
Riccardi, Michael 306
Rice, Fred 233
Rice, James Michael 106
Rich, Archie G. 66
Richards Sr., Henri L. 289
Richards, Stacey 389
Richardson, Deval 49
Richardson, Wanda Gibson 356
Richman, Libbie 322
Rickard, Grante 189
Rickards, Catherine 51
Ricker, Denise 153
Rickett, Judy 278
Ridgely, Jeff 243
Riead, Sybil 424
Riepe, Charlotte 143
Rieti, Marilyn A. 336
Riggs, Daris 165
Riley, Carmen 122
Riley, Vera B. 351
Riner, Lisa 398
Ringer, Violet Hiles 369
Ringle, Gloria Anna 297
Ritchey, Robin 416
Ritchie, Alycen 291
Ritchie, Josephine O. 168
Ritchie, Peter 420
Rivera-Reyes, Sunny 419
Robedee, Joy J. 204
Roberson, Alma 158
Roberts, Marie 401
Robertson, Elizabeth 182

The National Library of Poetry - Outstanding Poets of 1994

Robertson, Harry 41
Robertson, Wesley 365
Robinson, Anne 124
Robinson, Beverly G. 16
Robinson, Debbie 133
Robinson, Martha Kay 402
Robinson, Michelle Christine 456
Robinson, Paulette 366
Robo, James E. 230
Rockey, Billie 49
Rodgers, Ida Mae 238
Rodocker, Sarah 366
Roe, LaNae M. 426
Roeser, Nancy J. 363
Rogers Jr., Johnny 84
Rogers, Alice 266
Rogers, Drew 173
Rogers, George W. 207
Rogers, Raymond F. 375
Rogulta, Ramon 450
Rolando, Adrianna 230
Rolland, Fernand 292
Rolle, Florence 174
Rooper, David James 82
Roper, Erma 214
Rosario, Marguerite 339
Rose, Josephine 207
Rosellinni-Rogow, Melinda 319
Rosenberg, Louise Dodd 358
Rothgeb, Charmin 132
Roton, John L. 129
Rouch, Connie 36
Rourke Sr., Franklin J. 278
Rowe, Donna Belle 92
Rowe, Donna Irene 244
Rowe, Marda 409, 474
Rowell, Janice 257
Rowell, Janice E. 177
Rowland, Robert A. 357
Roy, Eva M. 222
Roy, Monique Amy 435
Rozenfeld, Juniya 41
Rubin, Ben 171
Rubinstein, Hope 260
Ruckdeschel, Hugh W. 104
Rudin, Danielle Louis 262
Rudolph, Dee 296
Ruffner, Nina 309
Ruhland, Charles 294
Ruiz, Mitzy A. 359
Rule, Eva Darrington 59
Runyon, Frances 4
Rupright, Nina 460
Rurup, Amber 219
Rush, Betty M. 152
Rush, Carol Frances 142
Rush, Edna 52
Russell, Cynthia 147
Russell, Hazel S. 210
Rutherford, Charlie 57
Ryan, Frances H. 186
Ryan, Guy V. 109
Ryman, Clark 217
SMith, Dorothy V. 250
Sabbatis, Amy 172
Sabella, Marlena 378
Saber, Charles 275
Saenz, Maria Guadalupe 465
Safko, Darrel Robert 162
Sagers, Ida 88
Sahr, Nancy J. 336
Saint Felix, Cynthia 139
Salerno, Josephine 33
Salvador, Lilia G. 418
Sams, Darlene 273
Sams, Mary 383

Sanasarian-Hovasapian, A. O. 23
Sandifer, Jimmy R. 151
Sansbury, Jo 128
Sansom, Ray 385
Santee, J.D. 413
Santell, Carol M. 55
Santens, Charles K. 120
Santiago, Gabriel B. 254
Santone, John M. 257
Sass, Cheryl 237
Sasseville, Tasha 448
Sauer, Heidi R. 171
Saunders, Virginia 328
Sawtelle, Elizabeth Haldane 89
Sawyer, Brenda J. 238
Scandariato, 464
Scarbrough, Jackie 183
Scarpino, Keith 372
Schacknow, Mary 359
Schaffer, Amanda 10
Schaffer, Jamie 18
Schedler, Walter F. 439
Schempp, William D. (Rhino) 419
Schiewe, Tiffanney Noelle 444
Schilling, Alberta 264
Schirmacher, Stanley L. 367
Schneider, Wayne F. 435
Schnikwald, Erik 288
Schofield, Frederick I. 143
Scholze, Frances R. 41
Schonfeld, Arlene D. 304
Schreiber, Dorothy M. 160
Schroeder, Charlotte A. 4
Schroettner, Mark A. 407
Schuck, Casey 62
Schuckmann, Barbara Jo 142
Schuessler, Nancy J. 311
Schuetz, Jaime 247
Schult, Chris Dowdall 20
Schulz, Cornelia 281
Schulz, Jeannette Vollmer 77
Schustereit, Cynthia 287
Schweers, Lucy 377
Schweickert, Carol A. 192
Scott, Helen 129
Scott, Latosha 372
Seal, Aretta Nash 75
Seals, Jane 8
Sebastian, Shirley 384
Sedgwick, Ben 256
See, Millard M. 345
Seeber, Julie 38
Seed, Neysa E. 340
Seely, Darla Mae 216
Seely, Dorothea S. 173
Seidler, Thomas J. 325
Seifert, Stephanie 344
Selby, Katina 420
Sells, Joyce Green 85
Sendra-Anagnost, Teresa 464
Senn, Pamela J. 330
Senser, Richard A. 450
Senter, Alice H. 178
Setty, Deobrah Burgett 154
Sevandal, Marciana A. 361
Seward, Bessie 208
Sewell, Virginia 334
Sforza, Christy 18
Shah, Suken 415
Shannon, Emeline (Caretti) 6
Shannon, Joyce A. 222
Shanta, Nancy Lynne 463
Sharpley, Molly 436
Shaw, Jill Josette 224
Sheahan, Patrick B. 364
Shearer, Gladys 33

Sheets, Julie L. 232
Sheets, Rosaline G. 402
Sheldon, Mark R. 415
Shelley, Dorothy 262
Shelley, Dorothy 262
Sherman, Elden W. 212
Sherwood, Patricia E. 305
Shioji, Lisa 398
Shortt, Carrianne 237
Showen, Jennifer E. 201
Shriver, Mary L. 314
Shumaker, Betty J. 111
Shutt, Alice May 226
Shuttleworth, William 339
Sibrel, Katherine K. 321
Siegel, Beatrice 104
Sierra, Gisella 91
Silverstein, Christine 3
Simao, Albertino 126
Simhiser, Lisa 411
Simmons, Julia D. 68
Simmons, Nina D. 316
Simms, Mattie 356
Simon, Floyd 236
Simpkins, Pattie 449
Simpson, Alex 45
Simpson, Don 191
Simpson, Michelle A. 377
Sims, Kathy 318
Sims, Timothy Gene 307
Sinko, Bridget K. 69
Sitchenkov, Lois 384
Skaggs, Glendola 213
Skaggs, Ruby Farnham 432
Skerencak, Elizabeth 149
Skinner, Paul 431
Slack, Sue Russell 407
Sloan, Elizabeth 183
Sloan, Glenna 6
Smalls, Bythford C. 142
Smith II, Jesse E. 253
Smith, Alexandra 80
Smith, Alice P. 521
Smith, Angelica M. 77
Smith, Betty 244
Smith, Brenda C. 241
Smith, C. Shawn 429
Smith, Charlotte 283
Smith, Dane 242
Smith, Debra J. 297
Smith, Dwight 73
Smith, Elaine E. 92
Smith, Glenn 111
Smith, Harold O. (Ole Shep) 283
Smith, Herbert T. 139
Smith, Hilda 184
Smith, Ina 264
Smith, Jackie 285
Smith, Jacqueline R. 166
Smith, Jeanette L. 90
Smith, Jim 249
Smith, Judith M. 271
Smith, Junerose 125
Smith, Junerose 181
Smith, Kathy 322
Smith, Louise Dent 396
Smith, Rose Zacchiroli 425
Smith, Sherry Lyn 392
Smith, Teresa 408
Smith, William T. 405
Smoot, Janette S. 268
Sneed, Frances 160
Sneer, Snake 186
Snider, Harold R. 77
Snider, Jessica 172
Snow Jr., Richard Alvin 344

Snyder, Bertha 214
Snyder, Linda M. 427
Soler, Dona K. 169
Somers, Gerald A. 29
Son, Anne 86
Soroka, Cynthia 220
Sorrells, D. Jack 460
Souza, Arvetta M. 118
Souza, Eileen A. 45
Spangler, Larry M. 387
Spanier, Stuart L. 354
Sparks, Garret Bradley 206
Speights, Helenjean Hays 141
Spencer, Ada M. 67
Spencer, Stephen E. 361
Spine, Deborah R. 26
Spinetti, Dorothy 79
Spires, Joanna 207
Spirio, Lawrence 429
Spousta, Rob 378
Sprague, Dale J. 142
Sprague-Fuller, Brenda A. 287
Spriggs, Edna M. 302
Sprung, John George 284
Spry, Allen 226
St. Jules, Ruby J. 410
St. Louis, Dorothy A. 33
Stalcup, Jamie 260
Stallings, James Williams 80
Stamper, Alene 281
Stang, Sylvia 425
Stanley, Eulah 156
Stanley, Kimberly 464
Stanton, Bernard 228
Stanton, Martha N. 329
Staples Jr., Paul R. 349
Stark, Iris T. 120
Stark, Madilene 339
Stauffer, Patricia Cole 404
Steele, Floyd George 202
Steele, Jamieson 253
Steiner, M. Elisabeth 404
Stenis, Rowena 439
Stepien, George 290
Sterling, Shauna 439
Sterling-Heyns, Sally 365
Stevens, Debra S. 178
Stevens, Jean 133
Stevens, Jennifer Lynn 277
Stevens, Marilee K. 314
Stevens, Melissa L. 443
Stevens, Rose B. 392
Stewart, Brian 164
Stewart, Crystie 217
Stewart, Ed 194
Stewart, Geraldine 36
Stewart, James 70
Stewart, Marie 318
Stewart, Tamra 313
Stickle, Charles E. 297
Stocker, Harry A. 148
Stockl, Gladys 268
Stoeckel, Jim L. 273
Stokes, Carolyn Ashe 213
Stokes, Donna L. 195
Stoliker, Sean T. 404
Stolzenburg, Eldon L. 139
Stone, Gladys F. 27
Stone, Hassie H. 37
Stone, Madelyn G. 448
Stone, Ruth 398
Stoneking, Jeff 116
Storey, Elvin E. 189
Stout, Tae W. 372
Stowell, Margaret 423
Strange, Carmichael 137

Stratman, Thomas M.K. 311
Strausbaugh, Ingeborg 121
Street, Jessica Marie 133
Streeter, Paul W. 413
Strickland, Etta J. 300
Strothers, Juanita 233
Struble, Donna 288
Stuckey, Annelle 207
Stuffle, Grace 169
Sturgill, Gregory 102
Stutchman, Amanda 278
Sullivan, Caroline M. 269
Sullivan, Joan 131
Sullivan, John W. 16
Sullivan, Pearlie R. 416
Sullivan, Terence P.M.E. 310
Sullivan-Rusch, Colleen 66
Surls, Frances Marie 58
Sutton, Jimmie Nell Bush 121
Sutton-Mortonson, Jean A. 299
Sweet, Ada 11
Sweet, Joyce 209
Sweeting, Berry L. 165
Sydow, Michelle 425
Synder, Peggy Opal 429
Synek, M. 339
Szewczyk, Gerald S. 204
Szili, Ann Marie 117
Szymanski, Petar E. 315
T.F.W., 334
Talbot, Jack M. 203
Talley, Laverne 391
Tallman, Darlene 170
Tam, Amy Kaleiho'opi'o C. 271
Tambo, Jo 8
Tangway, Daniele 112
Tate, Jan 232
Tatom, Mary Arthur 340
Tausch, Susan D. 521
Tavassoli, Alan 220
Taylor, Christine 215
Taylor, Edith 164
Taylor, Eileen M. 211
Taylor, Frances Moss 54
Taylor, Gail E. 3
Taylor, Gail Tamara 237
Taylor, Janette 200
Taylor, Jessie 264
Taylor, Margaret 521
Taylor, Mildred L. 309
Taylor, Robert F. 333
Taylor, Virginia A. 358
Teierle, Dina 149
Terrebonne, Anne 28
Terrell, Barbara L. 146
Terribilini, Virginia A. 391
Terwilliger, Elizaberh 190
Tesh, Ruby Nifong 369
Tetreault, Carol Ann 97
Tetto, Mike 322
Teufel, Dolores E. 127
Thakray, Betty Fern 21
Thanh-Thanh, 332
Tharp, Pamela Elaine 421
Tharp, Roosevelt 381
Thayer, Margaret R. 385
Theberge, Teri L. 311
Theys, Sheri 436
Thibodeau, Maryann B. 343
Thomas, Ada 96
Thomas, Al 266
Thomas, Albertine 171
Thomas, Austin 118
Thomas, Austin 92
Thomas, Cheryl 246
Thomas, Erminia Pia 172

Thomas, Fannie 199
Thomas, James A. 223
Thomas, Janet K. 214
Thomas, Janette C. 194
Thomas, Jeanne 277
Thomas, Mary Anne 345
Thomas, Maxine Taylor 374
Thomas, Mildred Friend Rogers 455
Thomas, Sharline Maria 318
Thomas, William B. 330
Thompson, Angela 12
Thompson, Anna O. 14
Thompson, Brenda Gentry 272
Thompson, Dorris L. 47
Thompson, Durwood T. 70
Thompson, Elizabeth Anne 283
Thompson, Jennifer L. 33
Thompson, John L. 258
Thompson, Joy Nicole 272
Thompson, Mandalie 326
Thornhill, Elroy 71
Thornton, Laurie C. 336
Thrower, Lorene Dunaway 367
Thurmond, Laura Shelton 393
Tibbs, Paul J. 346
Tien, Jenny 188
Tifft, Carol 224
Tillinghast, W.P. 406
Tinio, Eleanor Calasara 25
Tippin, Jennifer Diane 68
Tisdale, Phebe Alden 454
Tiska, Gail O. 175
Titus, Lucie G. 342
Tjomsland, Danielle 131
Tobin, Geraldine T. 20
Tobin-Lopez, Robin L. 386
Todd, Karen Posey 418
Tohill, Alice 252
Tolson, Frances E. 225
Tomanio, Joseph 112
Tomasello, Dawn 64
Tomasic, Mary Ann 321
Tonelli, Eugene F. 85
Toney, Joanna 52
Torpila, Frank T. 6
Torrence, Nancy 340
Torrence, Norma 434
Torres, Anthony 130
Toth, Joanne 147
Toth, Julie 180
Towne, Ariana 414
Townes, Correll L. 43
Towns, Sherry 379
Townsend Jr., Bennie 140
Toyer, David K. 50
Travaglini, Denise Marie 216
Traylor, Harold A. 48
Traylor, Holli Johnston 251
Treaster, Jeanette 258
Treatman, Ethyl 292
Treece, Rebecca Hobbs 381
Trehey, Denis Allen 254
Trejo, Christopher 51
Trent, Emma D.S. 197
Trester, Evelyn V. 12
Treumuth, Marjory A. 311
Trewhitt, Herb 172
Trinidad-Aradanas, Angeles 243
Trittler, Elizabeth Jane 288
Trotiner, Sylvia Anfang 336
Trotter, Juanita Farrow 7
Trowbridge, Alesia 70
Trzcinski, Wanda O. 412
Tuazon, Marylou 409
Tucker, Janice 151
Tucker, Judith I. 164

Tucker, Margaret 377
Tucker, Virginia Wynne 429
Tugend, Joseph 10
Tuominen, Connie 210
Turbyfill, Lori 453
Turdo, Carmelo 293
Turner, Brian 86
Turner, Byron E. 65
Turner, Jenny 103
Turner, John H. 57
Turner, Steven Price 407
Twining, Lillian 356
Tyler, Francine M. 229
Tyner, Doris 92
Ulmer, Joan 205
Unangst, Elizabeth 225
Upchurch, Joyce 100
Upshaw, Grayce B. 180
Urban, Eleanore V. 285
Urbanczyk, Louella 347
Ursu, Mike 407
Utterback, Almeda 160
Vadala III, John E. 260
Valine, Marvine V. 424
Vallejo, Josie Lea 243
Van Bibber, Karl 326
Van Dyke, Elinor 222
Van Horn, Patricia A. 334
VanDenburgh, Esther H. 18
VanRaden, Katie J. 320
Vanderburg, David 265
Vannatter, Laura D. 371
Vanorse Sr., Bert J. 174
Vaughan, Cathy "Cat" Michele 226
Vaughan, Sarah Daniel 362
Vaughn, Bonnie Jean 263
Vaughn, Frank J. 53
Vavra, Leslie L. 317
Vedder, Marilyn Jane 335
Verde, Joanne 6
Verma, Dale Ann S. 124
Verrilli, Joseph 150
Vickery, Elizabeth 77
Victor, Alvera 242
Vidal-Torres, Nora A. 371
Villanueva, Margarito 414
Vincent, Beverly E. 59
Voboril, Daniel Ray 198
Volger, Ethel M. 222
Volkman, Celia 211
Von Bieberstein, Dolores 266
Voyt, Barbara Leigh 202
Wackler, Joe 18
Wagner, Adele Lynne 43
Wagner, Glen 26
Wagner, Joan A. 93
Wainerdi, Margaret G. 454
Wainwright, Linda B. 372
Waite, Linda D. 328
Walborn, Ian 113
Walden, Elayne Gocek 67
Walden, Laurel J. 322
Waldsmith, Annie Ruth 28
Walker, James 52
Walker, Sharon E. 426
Wallace, Alfred Leon 127
Wallace, Geryle 110
Wallace, Hugh 79
Wallace, Jack A. 144
Walsh, Brian J. 84
Walsh, Douglas M. 146
Walsh, James Joseph 17
Walsh, Phillip 440
Walsh, Zione 412
Walter, Doris Brubaker 279
Walter, Hugo 123

Walters, Arthur L. 124
Walters, Gustave 141
Walton, Leslie K. 426
Walush, Elsie 40
Ward, Camella 54
Ward, Dura 67
Ward, Frances 234
Ward, Judith L. 21
Ward, Morris Eldon 389
Warden, Jaime 195
Ware, Christopher 7
Warford, Pam 429
Warmack, Harriet J. 184
Warner, Jamie Lynn 246
Warner, Ruth 400
Warren, Hope 193
Warren, Vickie L. 360
Warrenburg, Wanda 401
Warrick, Mary Ellis 350
Washburn, Constance E. 37
Washburn, Gwen 230
Wassall, Irma 43
Waters, Tanasha 408
Waters, Virginia D. 390
Watkins, B.B. 355
Watkins, Yvonne 380
Waugh, Albert Paul Thomas 255
Wayne, Joseph 164
Weaver, Joseph A. 251
Webb, Audrey Jean 280
Webber, Brent 263
Weber, Keri 422
Webster, Debbie 102
Webster, Lucille L. 391
Weetman, Robert R. 374
Wegner, Helen Rae 237
Wehrmeister, Evelyn M. 25
Weiler, Jennifer D. 44
Weinacker Jr., Charles W. 223
Weiner, Amy 19
Weiner, Glee L. Stevens 100
Weingart, Jerry B. 285
Weir, Melodie 407
Weishaar, Marilyn McQueen 347
Weishoff, Bonnie Lee 101
Weisker, Patricia Anne 418
Welch, Dawn 144
Weller, Jonas James 114
Wells, Hazel H. 59, 77
Wells, Lee 319
Wells, Linda L. 391
Wells, Virginia Thomas 370
Wendland, Karen K. 457
Wentworth, Pearl 341
Wertz, L.G. 438
Wesner, Robert J. 331
West, Doris Pack 97
West, Miriam E. 333
West, Patricia Gail Bowser 434
Westenfelder, Judy A. 185
Westerman, Jean 208
Westgate, Shirley R. 412
Westhuis, Elvin L. 132
Whalen, Amy M. 170
Wharton, John G. 141
Wheat, Marti L. 420
Whitaker, Ethel R. 122
Whitcomb, K. L. 425
White, Anna H. 17
White, Clara Jo 71
White, Eunice C. 236
White, Glenna S. 50
White, Jeff 289
White, Paula 460
White, Sandra M. 366
White-Allen, Nina I. 388

Whitehead, James Madison 193
Whiteman, Edith 277
Whitmore, Kelly Costa 307
Whitney, Doris Newton 213
Wiener, Florence K. 252
Wiest, Frank H. 103
Wigfall, Ophelia Young 437
Wiggs, Catrina 177
Wilbur, Bryan 291
Wilkin, Dawn 279
Wilkins, Ken 359
Wilkinson, Liz 212
Wilks, Melody Nicole 377
Willbanks, Argie 41
Williams, Adelaide 292
Williams, Amy 53
Williams, Barbara 212
Williams, Colleen 64
Williams, David 7
Williams, Enid Jo 68
Williams, Frederick 125
Williams, Joyce J. 163
Williams, Judy 79
Williams, Louise 396
Williams, Lucille G. 311
Williams, Mabelle Agnes 462
Williams, Melissa 433
Williams, Sarah 325
Williams-Sanchez, Toni A. 341
Willmann, Julieth 229
Wills, II, Jerry A. 45
Wilmouth, David M. 46
Wilson, Basil W. 36
Wilson, Cindy 274
Wilson, Dale L. 230
Wilson, Elnora 223
Wilson, Esaw 47
Wilson, Flora Billings 65
Wilson, Jean Le Van 49
Wilson, Karen 442
Wineland, Betty 254
Wink, 183
Winkelman, Doris June 259
Winters, Mildred R. 338
Winthrop, Ashley Falon 198
Wirkowski, Barbara 156
Wiser, Mary E. 451
Wisner, Jean D. 99
Withee, Beverly 108
Withee, Donald F. 193
Wolbeck, Alison M. 302
Wold, Nora Evelyn 421
Wolford, Alyssa 301
Wood, Debbie 75
Wood, Dorothy 234
Wood, Howard W. 274
Wood, Lucille Lindsey 413
Woodard, Dicie Selman 126
Woodard, Frances P. 291
Woodel Jr., William L. 441
Woodruff, Alice Lincoln 137
Woods, Mary 368
Woods, Vincent 430
Workman Jr., Joe E. 230
Worrells, Patty 409
Wright Jr., Floyd T. 257
Wright, Chris 221
Wright, Elda Schwarz 192
Wright, Julienne 158
Wright, Shriley J. 346
Wrigley, Matthew 415
Wurl, Viola M. 405
Yates, D.D. 310
Yates, Janelle 240
Yates, L. June 465
Yatso, Anita 271

Yepsen, Maurice C. 458
Yezuita, Loretta 308
Yinger, Doris Natalie 27
York, Serge 370
Young, Daniel Albert 135
Young, Edith 57
Young, Jean 275
Young, Lois Williams (Ed.D.) 256
Yousif, Nancy 454
Zamorsky, Michael 249
Zander, Cherly 106
Zastera, Jeanne 175
Zboray, Georgianna W. 163
Zebik, Mary Wyant 368
Zelle, Karen S. Burr 333
Zielsdorf, Adolph 207
Ziller, Bonnie 270
Zimmer, Edith Piercy 303
Zimmerman, Melissa 234
Zinn, Abi 272
Zischke, Amie 164
Zoble, Louise G. 383
Zona, Diane 300
Zumault, Viola 316
kelly, bev 64
parsons, dennis 195
rice, grandma 399
von Stuck, Norma P. 452
wilbur, roger 341